WITHDRAWAL

"Communications Standard Dictionary"

Martin H. Weik, D.Sc.
Dynamic Systems, Inc.
McLean, Virginia

VNR VAN NOSTRAND REINHOLD COMPANY
NEW YORK   CINCINNATI   TORONTO   LONDON   MELBOURNE

Copyright © 1983 by Van Nostrand Reinhold Company Inc.

Library of Congress Catalog Card Number: 81-21842
ISBN: 0-442-21933-4

Manufactured in the United States of America

Published by Van Nostrand Reinhold Company Inc.
135 West 50th Street, New York, N.Y. 10020

Van Nostrand Reinhold Publishing
1410 Birchmount Road
Scarborough, Ontario M1P 2E7, Canada

Van Nostrand Reinhold Australia Pty. Ltd.
17 Queen Street
Mitcham, Victoria 3132, Australia

Van Nostrand Reinhold Company Limited
Molly Millars Lane
Wokingham, Berkshire, England

15 14 13 12 11 10 9 8 7 6 5 4 3 2 1

Library of Congress Cataloging in Publication Data

Wiek, Martin H.
  Communications standard dictionary.

  1. Communication – Dictionaries. I. Title.
P87.5.W4   001.5'0321   81-21842
ISBN 0-442-21933-4   AACR2

To my wife, Helen,
for the love and encouragement she has given me during
the preparation of this volume.

Now the whole earth had one language and few words. And the Lord said, "Behold, they are one people, and they have all one language; and this is only the beginning of what they will do; and nothing that they propose to do will now be impossible for them."

Genesis 11:1, 6

In the beginning was the Word, and the Word was with God, and the Word was God.

John 1:1

Preface

Communications* Standard Dictionary is a comprehensive compilation of terms and definitions used in the field of communications.

Communications is defined as the branch of science and technology concerned with the process of representing, transferring, and interpreting the meaning assigned to *data* by and among persons, places, or machines.

Communication is defined as the transfer of *information* between a *source (transmitter, light source)* and a *sink (receiver, photodetector)* over one or more *channels* in accordance with a *protocol,* and in a manner suitable for interpretation or comprehension by the *receiver;* or as a method or means of conveying information of any kind from one person or place to another.

In short, communications is a branch of science and technology, whereas communication pertains to the actual transfer of information. Thus, the word communication should be used as a modifier, as in *communication center, communication deception,* and *communication line,* just as in the field of electronics one speaks of electronic devices and electronic circuits.

Only data is actually transferred by a *communication system,* that is, physically moved. But data is the representation of information. Therefore, it may be said that information is moved by a communication system, with the proviso that the sender and the receiver agree on the meaning assigned to the data. In a properly designed communication system *data integrity* will be preserved. The meaning will not be lost and errors will not be made during *storage* and *transmission.* However, it is the responsibility of the *source user* to enter the proper data and the responsibility of the *destination user* to properly interpret the data.

---

*Italics indicates that the term is defined in this dictionary.

SCOPE

This dictionary covers the terminology used in the following subfields:

Acoustic communications	Microwave communications
Aeronautical communications	Military communications
Air–air communications	Navigation communications
Air–surface communications	Networking
Analog communication sytems	Optical communications
Battlefield surveillance	Optics
Communication devices	Radar
Communication systems	Radio
Communication theory	Radionavigation
Computer engineering	Satellite communications
Computer programming	Signaling
Cybernetics	Signal processing
Data conversion	Space communications
Data processing	Spread spectrum systems
Data transmission	Strategic communications
Digital systems	Switching systems
Display devices	Tactical communications
Documentation	Telecommunications
Electromagnetic theory	Telegraphy
Electronic warfare communications	Telemetering
Fiber optics	Telephony
Facsimile	Television
Information management	Transmission security
Information systems	Video telephony
Information theory	Visual communications
Lightwave communications	Wire communication systems

Coverage is also given to hundreds of subtopics, for example:

Antennas	Gating
Broadcasting	Interactive systems
Checking systems	Interference
Circuits	Jamming
Coding	Layering
Command guidance	Modulation
Computing systems	Multiplexing
Control	Noise
Data base management	Office machines
Data integrity	Polarization
Detection	Reception
Direction finding	Signal distortion
Emanation security	Transmission
Error control	Word processing

SOURCES

The terms defined in this dictionary are those written and spoken by designers, developers, manufacturers, vendors, users, managers, administrators, operators, and maintainers of communication systems and components. They are also the terms used by educators and standards organizations in the field of communications.

The terms were taken primarily from the technical literature. Terms were also taken from oral presentations and discussions. The definitions are based on technical society, international, national, Federal, military, industrial, carrier, and communication system user standards. For those terms for which standardized definitions could not be found, definitions were based on context, common usage, and authoritative sources.

Since definitions contained in standards are usually highly precise, technical, and professional, and often the result of compromise, explanations, examples, illustrations, and cross-references were added. Certain editorial changes were made to provide clarity, logical consistency, and uniformity of format.

ORGANIZATION

Entries are arranged in natural spoken English alphabetical word order. Spaces, hyphens, slashes, and other forms of punctuation are ignored in the sequencing.

Every significant word in a multiple-word entry is also entered in the main listing, with a *See* reference to the multiple-word entry. For example, in the entry for *modulation,* one would find the statement "See *frequency modulation*" following the definition of modulation. Synonyms are also entered in the main listing with a *See* reference to the preferred term. Definitions are always placed with the preferred term in the case of synonyms.

USE

This dictionary is designed to be used in the manner of an encyclopedia. The italicized words in a definition are also defined in the dictionary. The standard defining phrase, explanatory remarks, examples, illustrations, cross-references, and italicized terms enable the reader to obtain a thorough understanding of the concept for which the entry term is really only a label.

This dictionary can serve as a handy basic reference manual. It can readily be used in the preparation of technical articles, oral presentations, contract specifications, and other technical publications; for studying or teaching; or for holding discussions in the field of communications. For example, it meets the professional needs in the field of communications by presenting the meanings given in standards. It satisfies the needs of communication system users for effective interaction with communication systems by providing explanatory remarks in addition to the defining phrase, and it meets the needs of students and teachers by providing examples, illustrations and cross-references to other entries.

MARTIN H. WEIK, D.SC.

Acknowledgments

The author wishes to gratefully acknowledge the technical and editorial assistance given by Mr. Eric Fallick of Van Nostrand Reinhold.

The author also wishes to extend his appreciation to all the members of the staffs of the Defense Communications Agency, the National Communications System, and the Military Communications-Electronics Board, with whom he was directly associated during many years of employment. In particular, appreciation is extended to Miss Janet Brooks and Mrs. Janet Orndorff; Colonels F. R. Van Laethem and James Wheeler; and Messrs. Dennis Bodson, Marshall Cain, Paul Tolovi, and George White.

Appreciation is especially extended to my wife, Helen Harrison Weik, RN, for her assistance in organizing the material for this volume, and her contributions in those areas of communication systems that are related to the human factors in the man–machine interface.

MARTIN H. WEIK, D.SC.

A

A-AND-NOT-B gate. A two-input, *binary*, logic coincidence *circuit* capable of performing the *logic* operations of A AND NOT B. Thus, if A is a statement and B is a statement, the result is true only if A is true and B is false. For the other three combinations of A and B, the result is false. Synonymous with *exclusion gate;* with *A except B gate;* with *AND NOT gate;* with *NOT if-then gate;* with *sine-junction gate;* with *subjunction gate;* and with *negative (A implies B) gate.* See Figure A-1.

```
IN        0      1     B   IN
A
        ┌──────┬──────┐
0       │  0   │  0   │
        │      │      │   0   OUT
1       │  1   │  0   │
        └──────┴──────┘
```

A-1. A table showing the *input* and *output digits* of an **A-AND-NOT-B gate.**

abbe constant. A mathematical expression for determining the correction for *chromatic aberration* of an *optical system.* It is usually expressed as

$$V = (n_d - 1)/(n_f - n_c)$$

when n_d, n_f, and n_c are the *refractive indices* for *light* of the *wavelengths* of the *D* line of sodium and the *E* and *C* lines of hydrogen, respectively. The ratio may also be considered as the *refractivity/dispersion.* Synonymous with *Nu value; Vee value.*

abbreviated address. An *address* that has fewer *characters* than the full address, usually for special *communication* and other services or for certain *users* (subscribers). For example, a four *digit telephone* number for a user calling another user connected to the same *switching exchange,* or a *message addressee's* name and *zip-code* only. Synonymous with *short address.*

abbreviated address calling. *Calling* that enables a *user* to employ an *address* having fewer *characters* than the full address when initiating a *call. Communication network users* may be allowed to designate a given number of *abbreviated address* codes. The allocation of abbreviated address codes to a destination or group of destinations may be changed as required by means of a suitable procedure. See *group abbreviated-address calling*.

abbreviated answer. In *radiotelegraph communications*, a response to a preliminary *call* in which the *call sign* of the calling *station* is omitted. An abbreviated answer is usually used after good communication has been established.

abbreviated title. See *short title*.

abbreviation. See *aeronautical communication system abbreviation*.

aberration. 1. In an *optical system*, any systematic departure from an idealized path of *light rays* forming an *image*, causing the *image* to be imperfect. 2. In *physical optics*, any systematic departure of a *wavefront* from its ideal plane or spherical form. Common aberrations include spherical and *chromatic aberration, coma, distortion* of image, curvature of field, and *astigmatism*. See *chromatic aberration*.

abort. In *data transmission*, a function invoked by a *primary* or *secondary* sending *station* causing the recipient to discard (or ignore) all *bit* sequences transmitted by the sender since the preceding *flag sequence*.

absent user service. A service furnished by a *user* (subscriber, customer) to automatically advise all callers that the *called terminal* is not available.

absolute coordinate. In *display systems*, a coordinate, expressed in *absolute coordinate data*, that identifies an *addressable point* in the *display space* on the *display surface* of a *display device* or in the *image storage space*. It indicates the *displacement* of the given addressable point from the origin of the particular coordinate system in which it lies. Contrast with *relative coordinate*.

absolute coordinate data. In *display systems*, such as computer *interactive CRT display* terminals or *faceplates* on the end of a *coherent bundle* of *optical fibers*, values that specify the actual coordinates in the *display space* on the *display surface* of a *display device* or in the *image storage space*. The absolute coordinate data may, for example, be contained in a computer program, stored in a storage unit (memory or buffer) within a display device, or recorded on a *hard-copy* document, such as a sheet of paper. In a *coherent bundle* of *optical fibers*, the coordinate that specifies the actual physical location in the bundle would constitute absolute coordinate data. Contrast with *relative coordinate data*. Synonymous with *absolute data*.

absolute data. See *absolute coordinate data*.

absolute delay. The interval or the amount of time that a *signal* is delayed. It may be expressed in time units, such as *microseconds*, or as a number of *charac-*

ters, such as *pulse* times, *word* times, major cycles, or minor cycles. Also see *delay equalizer; delay line.*

absolute luminance threshold. The lowest limit of *luminance* necessary for visual perception to occur in a person with normal or average vision.

absolute luminosity curve. The plot of spectral *luminous efficiency* versus *wavelength.*

absolute magnetic permeability. The ratio of the magnetic flux density, B, to the *magnetic field* intensity, H, at a point in a *material medium.* Mathematically $\mu_{abs} = B/H$. Also see *incremental magnetic permeability* and *relative magnetic permeability.*

absolute magnification. The *magnification* produced by a *lens* placed in front of a normal eye at such a distance from the eye that either the rear *focal point* of the lens coincides with the center of *rotation* of the eye or the front focal point of the eye coincides with the second principal point of the lens. The *object* must be located close to the front focal point of the lens. This magnification is numerically equal to the distance of distinct vision divided by the equivalent *focal length* of the lens, with both distances expressed in the same units.

absolute order. In *display systems,* a *display command* that can cause a *display device* to interpret the *data* following the order as *absolute coordinate data* rather than *relative coordinate data.* Contrast with *relative order.* The display command can occur in a *segment,* a *display file,* or a *computer program,* or it may simply be listed in an *instruction* repertory.

absolute potential. A *voltage (potential difference)* between a specified point and ground (zero potential reference level). An electric *circuit* element functions with other circuit elements in accordance with potential differences across its *terminals* and in accordance with relative potential differences (bias) maintained between its terminals and the terminals of the same circuit. However, for the circuit to exist and operate in its environment, the absolute potential may be significant, requiring that the circuit be *insulated* from its environment.

absolute power. The active *power* developed, dissipated, transferred, or used in a *circuit.* Also see *dBr.*

absolute refractive index. See *refractive index.*

absolute signal delay. The time difference between the generation or occurrence of the leading edge or other point of a *signal* waveform at the beginning of a *transmission medium,* such as a *waveguide,* and the arrival or reception of the corresponding point or same edge of the same signal at the end of the transmission medium; i.e., the *transit time* from one place to another for a specified point on a signal waveform.

absolute temperature scale. See *Kelvin temperature scale.*

absolute vector.   In *display systems* that have *display devices* with *display surfaces* such as computer graphic *CRT* screens, *fiberscope faceplates,* or *LED* or *gas panels,* a vector with starting and ending points that are specified by vectors that originate from a designated point, usually from the point designated as the origin.   Contrast with *relative vector.*

absorptance.   See *internal absorptance* and *spectral absorptance.*

absorption.   The transference of some or all of the energy contained in an *electromagnetic wave* to the substance or medium in which it is *propagating* or upon which it is *incident.* Absorbed energy from incident or *transmitted lightwaves* is converted into energy of other forms, usually heat, within the *transmission medium,* with the resultant *attenuation* of the *intensity* of the *light beams.*   See *atomic defect absorption; band edge absorption; bulk material absorption; extramural absorption; fiber absorption; hydroxyl ion absorption; hydroxyl ion overtone absorption; impurity absorption; infrared absorption; intrinsic absorption; selective absorption.*   Also see *Bouger's law.*

absorption coefficient.   The coefficient in the exponent of the absorption equation that expresses *Bouger's law,* namely, $F = F_0 e^{-bx}$, where F is the electromagnetic (light) flux or intensity at the point $x;$ F_0 is the initial value of flux at $x = 0;$ and b is the absorption coefficient.   If an infinitesimally thin layer of absorptive material is considered, making x nearly zero, the absorption coefficient is proportional to the rate of change of flux intensity with respect to distance; i.e., it is proportional to the slope of the absorption curve at that point.   The absorption coefficient is a function of *wavelength.*   See *spectral absorption coefficient.* Also see *absorptivity.*

absorption electronic countermeasure.   In *electronic warfare,* an *electronic countermeasure* involving devices and materials that reduce the *electromagnetic reflectivity* of a target.

absorption index (AI).   1. The ratio of the *electromagnetic radiation absorption constant* to the *refractive index* as given by the relation:

$$AI = K\lambda/4\pi n$$

where K is the *absorption coefficient,* λ is the *wavelength* in vacuum, and n is the *refractive index* of the absorptive material.   2. The functional relationship between the sun's angle (at any latitude and local time) and the *ionospheric absorption.*

absorption loss.   When a wave travels in a *transmission medium,* the loss of energy, experienced by the wave, caused by *intrinsic (material) absorption* and by impurities consisting primarily of metal and OH ions in the transmission medium. Absorption losses may also be caused from atomic defects in the transmission medium.

absorptive modulation.   *Modulation* of a *lightwave* by variation of the *optical absorption* of the *transmission medium* in which the wave is *propagating.*   The optical absorption is usually varied by means of an applied *electric field.* Optical absorption takes place near the edges of the *absorption band.*

absorption peak. In *lightwave transmission media,* the specific wavelength at which a particular impurity absorbs the most *power* — that is, creates maximum *attenuation* of the propagated lightwaves. Absorption by these impurities at other wavelengths is less than the absorption peak. Glass, quartz, silica, and plastics used in optical fibers, slab dielectric waveguides, integrated optical circuits, and similar devices, usually display absorption peaks. Particular impurities that cause absorption peaks are copper, iron, nickel, chromium, manganese, and hydroxyl ions.

absorptivity. The internal *absorptance* per unit thickness of a material medium. Numerically, absorptivity is unity minus the *transmissivity.* Also see *absorption coefficient* and *transmissivity.*

AC. *Alternating current.*

accentuated contrast. In *transmission systems* involving the transmission of *images,* such as *facsimile* or *optical fiber systems,* the *contrast* in a picture or document that is produced when it is required that *elements* with a *luminance* less than a specified value be transmitted as nominal black and that elements with a luminance greater than a specified value be transmitted as nominal white, while all values in between are transmitted at their respective level.

accept. In *data transmission,* the condition assumed by a *primary* or *secondary station* upon accepting a correctly received *frame* for *processing.*

acceptance angle. The maximum angle, measured from the longitudinal axis or centerline of an *optical fiber* to an *incident ray,* within which the incident ray will be accepted for transmission along the fiber, that is, *total internal reflection* of the incident ray occurs. If the acceptance angle for the fiber is exceeded, total internal reflection will not occur and the incident ray will be lost by leakage, scattering, diffusion, or absorption in the cladding. The acceptance angle is dependent upon the *refractive indices* of the two *media* that determine the *critical angle.* For a *cladded fiber* in air, the sine of the acceptance angle is given by the square root of the difference of the squares of the indices of refraction of the fiber *core* and the *cladding.* In mathematical notation, $\sin \theta = (n_0^2 - n_1^2)^{1/2}$ where θ is the *acceptance angle,* n_0 is the *refractive index* of the core, and n_1 is the *refractive index* of the cladding. Synonymous with *acceptance one-half angle* and with *collection angle.* See *maximum acceptance angle; total acceptance angle.*

acceptance angle plotter. A device capable of varying the *incidence angle* of a narrow *beam* that is incident upon a surface (such as the end face of an *optical fiber*) and measuring the intensity of the *transmitted light,* i.e., the light coupled into the fiber for each angular position of the *source* relative to the face of the incident surface (i.e., the *incidence angle*). See Figure A-2.

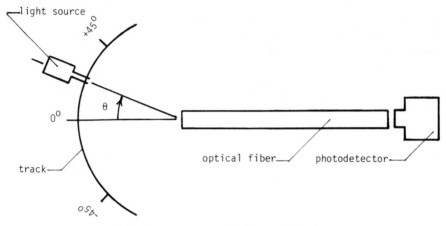

A-2. An **acceptance angle** *plotter* schematic.

acceptance cone.   A *solid angle* whose included apex angle is equal to twice the *acceptance angle*. *Rays* of *light* within the acceptance cone can be *coupled* into the end of an *optical fiber* and still maintain *total internal reflection* for all the rays in the cone. Typically, an acceptance cone is 40°.

acceptance one-half angle.   See *acceptance angle*.

acceptance pattern.   For an *optical fiber* or *fiber bundle,* a curve of total *transmitted power* plotted against the *launch angle*. The total transmitted power or *radiation* intensity is dependent upon the *incident intensity, launch angle* (input or incident angle), the *transmission coefficient* at the fiber interface, and the *illumination* area.

acceptance trials.   Trials or tests carried out by representatives of the eventual *users* of equipment to determine if specified performance characteristics have been met.

accepted.   See *call-accepted signal.*

accepted signal.   See *call-not-accepted signal.*

acceptor.   In an intrinsic semiconducting material (such as germanium or silicon), a *dopant* (such as gallium that has nearly the same electronic bonding structure as the intrinsic material, but with one less *electron* among its valence electrons than that required to complete the intrinsic bonding structural pattern. This pattern leaves a "space" or *"hole"* for one electron for each dopant atom in the structure. The dopant atoms are relatively few and are far apart and hence do not interfere with the electrical *conductivity* of the intrinsic material. An electron from a neighboring intrinsic material atom can fill the hole at the dopant site, leaving a hole from whence it came; thus, the hole can appear to move or wander about, although with less mobility than the electrons that are free and that are excess to *donor* atoms. Also see *donor; hole.*

access. The ability to approach, store, or retrieve data; to communicate with or to make use of any resource (component) in a *computer* or *communication system.* See *closed user group with outgoing access; code division multiple access (CDMA); direct access; dual access; failure access; frequency division multiple access; multiple access; pulse-address multiple access; remote access; satellite access; satellite-switched time-division multiple access (SS-TDMA); serial access; space-division multiple-access (SDMA); spread-spectrum multiple-access (SSMA); time-division multiple access (TDMA).*

access attempt. The process by which one or more users interact with a *telecommunication system* in order to enable initiation of *user information* transfer. An access attempt begins with an issuance of an *access request* by an *access originator.* An access attempt ends either in *access success* or in *access failure.* Also see *access request; called-party camp-on; calling-party camp-on.*

access-barred signal. In a *communication system,* a *signal* sent in the *backward direction* indicating that a *call* will not be *completed* because of a *called* or *calling user* (subscriber, customer) *facility* requirement. This may occur as a result of failure of a *closed user group validation check* or because of an *incoming-calls-barred facility.*

access category. A class to which a *user* (person, program, process, or equipment) of a system may be assigned based on the resources each user is authorized to use.

access code. The preliminary *digits* that a *user* must *dial* or *key* to be connected to a particular outgoing *trunk, channel,* or *line.*

access control. 1. Actions taken to permit or deny use of the components of a *communication system.* 2. The process of limiting *access* to the resources of a *system* to authorized *users.* Synonymous with *controlled access* and with *controlled accessibility.*

access coupler. A unit placed between *optical fiber* ends to enable *signals* to be withdrawn from or entered into an *optical fiber cable* that is passing through the junction, station, or position. For example, a *mixing rod.* Also see *coupler.*

access denial. 1. *Access failure* due either to the issuing of a *system blocking signal* by a *communication system* that does not include provision for *calling-party camp-on.* 2. To exceed the *maximum access time* and nominal *system access time fraction* during an *access attempt.* Synonymous with *system blocking.* Also see *blocking; system blocking signal.*

access-denial probability. The ratio of *access attempts* that result in *access denial* (system blocking) to total *access attempts* counted during a measurement period.

access-denial time. Elapsed time between the start of an *access attempt* and *access failure* due to *access denial* (system blocking). Access denial times are measured only on access attempts that result in access denial.

access digit. In *automatic telephone direct outward dialing,* a *digit* that enables *access* to outside a *local switchboard* or *exchange.* The access digit is *dialed* before the *long distance* number. It is usually dialed before an *area code* number. It is often a 1 or a 9.

access failure. In a *communication system,* an *unsuccessful access* that results in termination of an *access attempt* in any manner other than initiation of *user information transfer* between the intended *source* and destination *(sink)* within the specified maximum *access time.* Access failure can be the result of *access denial* (system blocking), *user blocking,* or *incorrect access.* Also see *access success; blocking; system blocking signal.*

access line. The part of a *circuit* between a *user* and a *switching center.* Also see *data link.* See *dual-use access line; marked-access line; network access line; special grade access line.*

access list. A catalog of *users* (persons, programs, processes, equipment) and the *access categories* to which each is assigned.

access originator. In a *communication system,* the function entity responsible for initiating a particular *access attempt.* An access attempt can be initiated by a *source user,* a *destination user,* or the communication system itself. Also see *disengagement originator.*

access period. The time interval during which *access* rights prevail.

access phase. In a *communication system,* the first phase of an *information transfer transaction* and the phase during which an *access attempt* is made. Also see *disengagement phase; information transfer phase.*

access plan. See *demand-assignment access plan; preassignment access plan.*

access point. In a *telephone system,* a junction point in an *outside plant;* a semi-permanent splice point at a junction between a *branch feeder cable* and *distribution cables;* or a point at which connections may be made for testing or utilization of particular *communication circuits.*

access request. A control *message* issued by an *access originator* for the purpose of initiating an *access attempt.* Also see *access attempt.*

access-rights terminal. See *multiple-access-rights-terminal.*

access success. In a *communication system,* termination of an *access attempt* in such a manner that *user information* can be *transferred* between the intended *source* and destination *(sink)* within the specified maximum *access time.* Also see *access failure.*

access success ratio. The ratio of the number of *access successes* to the total number of *access attempts* counted during a measurement time period. The ratio can be converted to a percentage by multiplying by 100.

access time. 1. In a *communication system,* the elapsed time between the start of an *access attempt* and *access success.* Access time values are measured only on access attempts that result in access success. 2. In a computer, the time interval between the instant at which delivery of *data* is completed, or the time interval between the instant at which data are requested to be stored, and the instant at which *storage* is started. See *maximum access time.*

accommodation. A function of the human eye, whereby the eye's total *refraction* power (accomplished by a neuromuscular feedback system from the fovea of the retina to muscles that cause the lens to thin or thicken) is varied in order for the eye to clearly see *objects* at different distances.

accommodation limits. The distances from an observer to the nearest and farthest points at which an *image* of an object can be clearly focused on the retina of the eye of the observer. Accommodation limits are usually 4 to 5 in. and infinity.

accountability. In *communiciation system security,* the quality or state that enables violations or attempted violations of *system security* to be traced to specific persons who may then be held responsible.

accounting legend. In *communication system security,* a number assigned to items listed on accounting reports. This number is assigned by the producing organization and usually identifies the minimum accounting controls required for the item.

accounting symbol. In a *communication system,* a combination of letters used in *message headings* to identify the organization that is financially responsible for the message.

accumulator. 1. A device containing a *register* that stores a quantity and, when a second quantity is delivered to the device, forms the sum of the quantity standing in the register and the second quantity, and stores the result. 2. A *storage register.* 3. A storage battery.

accuracy. 1. A quality of that which is free of *error.* 2. A qualitative assessment of freedom from *error,* a high assessment corresponding to a small error. 3. A quantitative measure of the magnitude of *error,* preferably expressed as a function of the relative error, a high value of this measure corresponding to a small error. Also see *precision.* See *frequency accuracy; frequency standard accuracy; timing tracking accuracy.*

achromat. A *compound lens* corrected to have the same *focal length* for at least two different *wavelengths* of *light* passing through the lens. Also see *achromatic; achromatic lens.*

achromatic. Free from color or hue. For example, an *optical system* free from *chromatic aberration.* Also see *achromat.*

achromatic lens. A *lens,* consisting of two or more elements or parts, usually made of *crown* and *flint glass,* that has been corrected so that *light* of at least two selected *wavelengths* is *focused* at a single point on the *optical axis.* Also see *achromat.*

ACK. The *acknowledge transmission control character.*

acknowledge (ACK) character. **1.** A *transmission control character* transmitted by a *station* as an affirmative response to the station with which a connection has been set up. **2.** A *transmission control character* transmitted by a *receiver* as an affirmative response to a transmitter. An acknowledge character may also be used as an accuracy *control character.* Also see *negative acknowledge (NAK) character.*

acknowledgement signal. A *signal* generated at the receiving end of a *communication circuit* to confirm the receipt of *signaling digits* from the sending equipment and sent back to the sending equipment. See *circuit-released acknowledgement signal.*

acoustical conduction. The conduction of sound as longitudinal compressional waves in an elastic material medium. Energy exchanges with *phonons* can occur, which affects electrical conductive, magnetic, and quantum electronic properties of the material medium.

acoustic coupler. **1.** Equipment that generates and uses *sound-wave codes* to permit *data transmission* via *telephone lines.* Sound *modulation* of *light sources* can be used as *transducers* between sound wave, *lightwave,* and electrical current transmission devices, such as between *optical fibers* and wires encountered in the *transmission of signals.* **2.** A device that enables *digital data* to be transmitted over *circuits* designed to accept sound waves or *pulses* that have been converted to *modulated electrical currents, radio waves, microwaves,* or *lightwaves* for *transmission.* For example, an acoustic coupler could produce from sound waves electric currents, which could be used to *modulate* the *output* of a *laser* or *LED* for *driving* an *optical fiber.*

acoustic noise. An undesired *disturbance power* or *noise* in the *audio frequency range.*

acoustics.   The branch of science and technology that is concerned with the production, transmission, control, processing, transformation, reception, and effects of sound, particularly as vibration, pressure, or elastic waves and shock phenomena in material media. Also see *phonons.*

acoustic sensor.   See *optical fiber acoustic sensor.*

acoustic wave.   See *sound wave.*

acoustooptic (a–o).   Pertaining to the interaction of *optical* and *acoustic* waves. Also see *acoustooptic effect.*

acoustooptic (a–o) modulator.   A *modulator* that uses the *acoustooptic effect* to *modulate* a *lightwave carrier.*

acoustooptic effect.   The changes in *diffraction gratings* or *phase* patterns produced in a *transmission medium* conducting a *lightwave* when the medium is subjected to a sound (acoustic) wave, due to the *photoelastic* changes that occur. The acoustic waves might be created by a force developed by an impinging sound wave, the *piezoelectric effect,* or *magnetostriction.* The effect can be used to *modulate* a *light* beam in a material since many properties, such as light-conducting velocities, *reflection* and *transmission coefficients* at *interfaces, acceptance angles, critical angles,* and *transmission modes,* are dependent upon the *diffractive* changes that occur. Also see *acoustooptic; photoelastic.*

acoustooptics.   The study and application of the interrelation of *acoustics* and *optics.* Synonymous with *optoacoustics.*

acquisition.   **1.** In *satellite communication systems,* the process of locking *tracking* equipment on a *signal* from a *communication satellite.* **2.** In *radar,* the process of locking a *tracking radar* on a moving object (target).

acquisition radar.   *Radar* used to detect and locate targets to be tracked by the *tracking radar. Scanning* is required of acquisition radar. Acquisition radar maintains continuous surveillance of a sector or area. It obtains position data, such as height, *azimuth,* and direction of moving objects (targets, aircraft) and passes this *data* to the tracking radar. Synonymous with *surveilllance radar.*

acquisition time.   **1.** In a *communication system,* the amount of time required to attain *synchronism.*   **2.**   In *satellite communications,* the time required for locking *tracking* equipment on a *signal* from a communication satellite. See *synchronization acquisition time.*

actinometry.   The science of measurement of *radiant* energy, particularly that of the sun.

action.   In quantum mechanics, the product of the total energy in a stream of *photons* and the time during which the flow occurs. Or, mathematically,

$$A = h \sum_{i=1}^{m} f_i n_i t_i$$

where f_i is the ith *frequency;* n_i is the number of photons of the ith frequency; and t_i is the time duration of the ith frequency, summed over all the frequencies, photons, and time durations of each in a given *light beam* or beam *pulse;* and h is *Planck's constant.* Also see *Planck's constant.* See *tracer action.*

action addressee.   The organization, activity, or person required by the *message originator* to take the action specified in a message. Also see *exempted addressee; information addressee.*

action office.   The office or *action addressee* required to take the action specified in a *message.*

activated chemical vapor deposition process (PACVO).   See *plasma-activated chemical vapor deposition process (PACVD).*

active.   See *mark-active; space-active.*

active atom.   See *radioactive atom.*

active communication satellite.   A *communication satellite* that *transmits* a *signal,* in contrast to a *passive satellite* that only *reflects* a signal. It contains at least one *receiver-amplifier-transmitter* unit that automatically relays *messages* from an *earth station.* It usually receives, regenerates, processes, and retransmits signals between earth stations. Also see *passive communication satellite.*

active connector.   See *optical fiber active connector.*

active detection system.   A *system* that emits *electromagnetic radiation* to determine the existence, location of *source,* nature, and type of received radiation. The system usually consists of *early warning radar, height-finders,* and *acquisition* (surveillance) and *tracking radar.*

active device.   A device containing a source of energy, the *output* of which is a function of present and past input *signals* that *modulate* the output of the energy source. For example, an operational *amplifier,* an *oscillator,* a *transistor,* a *photomultiplier,* a *laser,* a *maser,* or a *photodetector* operating on *photovoltaic* principles (in which case the *light source* is the outside energy source). Contrast with *passive device.*

active electronic countermeasure. In *electronic warfare,* an *electronic countermeasure* that produces detectable *electromagnetic radiation.* This can include *electronic jamming* and *electronic deception.*

active filter. A *filter* that requires *power* to perform its function. Also see *passive filter.*

active homing. Pertaining to a missile-to-target guidance system in which the missile tracks *radiation* that is originated by the missile itself and that is *reflected* by the target. The missile contains the *radar transmitter* and *receiver.* Also see *passive homing; semiactive homing.*

active infrared device. An *infrared (IR)* device that contains a source of IR *radiation.* Active IR devices include sniper scopes, night vision surveillance devices, and IR searchlights. These devices are subject to *jamming* by other IR sources, such as fires, furnaces, and the sun. They are relatively immune to deception-type *electronic countermeasures.* Also see *passive infrared device.*

active laser medium. A material that actually *lases.* For example, crystal, gas, glass, liquid, or semiconductors. Synonymous with *active material; laser medium; lasing medium.*

active material. See *active laser medium.*

active network. A *network* that includes a *power source.* Also see *passive network.*

active optical countermeasure. An *optical countermeasure* that makes use of an *emission* of a *signal* or substance, for example smoke screens, unidirectional aerosol (micron-sized) clouds, high-intensity flares, flashing lights on board aircraft, or techniques that produce illusions or psychological effects by optical means.

active optics. The development and use of *optical* components, the characteristics of which are controlled during their operational use in order to modify the characteristics of an *electromagnetic wave* in the *visible* or near-visible region of the frequency *spectrum.* Such characteristics include the *wavefront* direction, the *polarization modulation,* or the *transmission mode,* intensity, or path. This is in contrast to inactive, rigid, or fixed optics in which the components are not varied, with primary attention being given to measurement and control of wave fronts or rays in real time in order to concentrate radiated energy on a *detector,* target, *waveguide,* or other device. Contrast with *fixed optics.*

active particle. See *radioactive particle.*

active sonar. *Sonar* that relies upon reception of a *sound wave* reflected by an object (target) against which a sound wave was launched. Also see *passive sonar.*

active time. Time spent in the *information transfer phase* within the *user service time interval* of an *information transfer transaction.* A user's active time excludes all the time spent in the *access phase,* the *disengagement phase,* the *idle state,* the exit state, and all time outside the *service time interval.*

active wiretapping. The unauthorized attaching of a device, such as a *telephone, transmitter-receiver,* playback recorder, or *computer terminal,* to a *communication circuit* for the purpose of obtaining *access* to *data* by generating false *messages,* falsifying *control signals,* or altering the messages of *users.*

activity. In *communications,* an organization that performs a *communication service,* function, or operation. See *mean circuit activity; radioactivity; sun-spot activity.*

activity factor. For a *communication channel,* the percentage of time during the *busy hour* that a *signal* is present in the *channel.*

actual transfer rate. The average number of *binary digits, characters,* or *blocks transferred* per unit time between two points whether accepted or not accepted as valid at the receiving point.

A-D. *Analog-digital.*

ADA. A *computer programming common language* designed for diverse applications with capabilities offered by classical languages, such as *PASCAL,* and capabilities found only in specialized languages. It is a modern algorithmic language with the usual control structures and the ability to define *data* types and subprograms. It serves the need of modularity whereby the data types and subprograms can be packaged. The language is the result of a collective effort to design a common language for programming large-scale and real-time defense systems.

adaptation. See *dark adaptation; light adaptation.*

adapter. See *homing adapter; panoramic adapter; right-angle adapter.*

adapter circuit. See *line adapter circuit.*

adaptive channel allocation. A method of *multiplexing* in which the *information* handling *channel capacities* are not predetermined but are assigned on demand.

adaptive predictive coding (APC). A *narrowband analog-to-digital* conversion or *coding* technique employing a one-level or multilevel *sampling system* in which the value of the *signal* at each sample time is adaptively predicted to be a linear function of the past values of the *quantized* signals. APC is related to *linear predictive coding* (LPC) in that both use adaptive predictors. However, APC uses fewer prediction coefficients, thus requiring a higher *information bit rate* than LPC. Also see *linear predictive coding.*

adaptive technique. See *coherent optical adaptive technique.*

added bit. In a *communication system,* a *bit* delivered to the intended *destination user* in addition to intended *user information bits* and *delivered overhead bits.* Synonymous with *extra bit.* Also see *bit-count integrity; character-count integrity; deleted bit.*

added block. Any *block* or other group of *bits* delivered to the intended *destination user* in addition to intended *user information bits* and *delivered overhead bits.* Synonymous with *extra block.* Also see *deleted block.*

added-block probability. The ratio of added *blocks* to total blocks received by a specified *destination user* during a measurement period. Synonymous with *extra block probability.*

adder. A device whose *output* represents the sum of its *inputs,* for example a *logical adder* produces the *logical sum* (sum without carry) and an arithmetic adder produces the arithmetic sum of its inputs. See *binary adder; modulo-two adder; quarter adder.*

additive white Gaussian noise (AWGN). See *white noise.*

add-on security. Additional protective measures, *hardware* or *software,* adopted after a *communication system, computer,* or other *system* has become operational.

address. **1.** In *communication systems,* the *coded* representation of the destination of a *message.* **2.** In *data processing,* a *character* or group of characters that identifies a *register,* a particular part of *storage,* or some other *data source* or *data sink.* **3.** To refer to a device or an item of *data.* **4.** The part of a *selection signal* that indicates the destination of a *call.* **5.** An expression, usually numerical, that identifies a location. See *abbreviated address; call address; codress message address; destination address; message address; postal address; redirection address; satellite address; street address.*

addressability measure. In the *display space* on the *display surface* of a *display device,* the number of *addressable points* within the *display space.* Display surfaces may include the surface of a *faceplate* of a *fiberscope,* the screen of a *CRT,* the surface of an *LED* or *gas panel,* or the surface of a *plotter bed.*

addressable horizontal positions. See *display line.*

addressable point. Any *coordinate position* that can be addressed in the *display space* on the *display surface* of a *display device.* The number of addressable points within a specified display space is a measure of the *addressability* of the display space. Usually, the addressable positions are finite in number and form a discrete rectangular or polar coordinate grid over the display space.

addressable vertical positions. See *display column.*

address calling. See *group abbreviated-address calling.*

address calling facility. See *multiaddress calling facility.*

address code. See *cable address code.*

address designator. A combination of *characters* or pronounceable *words* designated for use in *message headings* to identify an organization, authority, unit, *communication facility,* or other entity; or to assist in the *transmission* and delivery of messages. The four classes of address designators are *call signs, address groups, plain language address designators,* and *routing indicators.* Synonymous with *station designator.*

addressee. The organization, *activity,* or person to whom a *message* is directed by the *message originator.* Addressees are often indicated as *action, information,* or *exempted addressees.* Also see *action addressee; exempted addressee; infortion addressee.*

address field. In *data transmission* and particularly in *high-level data link protocol,* the sequence of *bits* immediately following the opening *flag sequence* of a *frame* identifying the *station* that is transmitting a *response frame* or that is designated to receive a *command frame.*

address field extension. In *data transmission,* an enlargement of the *address field* to include more addressing *information.*

address group. 1. In *radiotelephone communication systems,* the *word* that means that the group that follows is an *address indicating group.* **2.** A *station* or *address designator* usually consisting of a group of four letters assigned to represent organizations, authorities, activities, units, or geographic locations and used primarily for the forward and backward addressing of *messages.* See *collective address group; conjunctive address group; geographic address group.*

address group allocation. The assignment of individual *address groups* to specified elements of an organization, activity, unit, or geographic location.

address indicating group (AIG). A *station* or *address designator,* often used by the military to represent a set of specific and frequently recurring combination of *action* or *information addressees.* The identity of the *message originator* may also be included in the AIG. An address group is assigned to each AIG for use as an address designator. See *international address indicating group; national address indicating group.*

address indicating group allocation. The assignment of *address indicating groups* to specified groups of elements of an organization, activity, or unit, or to a group of geographic locations.

address message. A *message* sent in the *forward direction* containing the *signaling information* required to *route* and connect a *call* to the *called line.* For example, a message containing *address information. Service class information* and additional information relating to *user* and *network* facilities may also be included. An address message may also contain the *calling party* identity or the *calling line* identity. See *multiple-address message.*

address multiple access. See *pulse-address multiple access.*

address part. The portion of a *computer word* that identifies the *storage* location or that identifies the *register* in which the operands are stored or held.

address pattern. See *frame synchronization pattern.*

address separator. The *character* that separates the different *addresses* in a *selection signal.*

address signal. A *signal* containing one element, such as a *decimal digit* or an end-of-number indicator, of the *address* of an *addressee, user, network facility,* or other entity.

add-without-carry gate. See *EXCLUSIVE-OR gate.*

adjacent channel. A *channel* that is contiguous to another channel in the time, *frequency,* or spatial domain. For example in *time division multiplexing,* the channel occupying the *time frame* immediately following the time frame of a given channel, or a channel that uses an *optical fiber* adjacent to the fiber used by another channel in an *optical cable.*

adjacent channel interference. **1.** Extraneous *power* from a *signal* in an *adjacent channel.* **2.** *Interference* in a *receiver* operating at a given *frequency* caused by signals received at the frequency of either or both of the immediately adjacent or neighboring channels of the *frequency spectrum.* The interference can be caused by inability to discriminate (fine tune) because of drifting of either or both of the neighboring frequencies, or by high-powered *transmissions* at either or both of the neighboring frequencies.

adjacent channel selectivity. The degree to which a *receiver* is capable of *discriminating* or differentiating between the *signals* in the desired *channel* and the signals in an adjacent channel.

adjacent domains. In *distributed data processing systems,* two *domains* that are directly connected to each other by a *data link* with no intervening domains.

adjacent nodes. In a *network,* two *nodes* that are directly connected to each other by one or more *data links* with no intervening nodes.

administration. In *telecommunication system control,* a governmental agency responsible for implementation of *telecommunication* standards, regulations, recommendations, practices, and procedures.

administrative network. A *communication network* that is used for the exchange of *messages* of a nonoperational nature, operational messages of a nonurgent nature, messages that contain administrative *information* in contrast to operational information, or messages containing information needed to operate a *communication network.*

administrative security. *Security* implemented as management constraints, operational procedures, *accountability* procedures, and other controls to provide an acceptable level of protection against access, by unauthorized persons or devices, to the *information* in a *computer, communication,* or other *system.*

ADP. *Automatic data processing.*

ADPE. *Automatic data processing equipment.*

ADPS. *Automatic data processing system.*

advantage. See *range advantage.*

advisory station. See *aeronautical advisory station.*

aerial cable. A *communication cable* installed on or suspended from a pole or other overhead structure.

aerial insert. In a buried *cable* run, a raising of the cable followed by an overhead run usually on poles, followed by a return to the ground, in places where it is not possible or practical to bury a cable, such as might be encountered in crossing a deep ditch, a canal, a river, or a subway line. See Figure A-3.

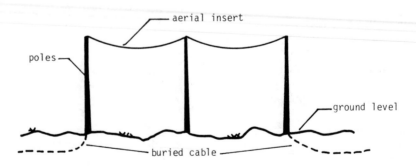

A-3. An **aerial insert** in a buried *cable.*

aerial optical cable. An *optical cable* designed for use in overhead suspension, such as from towers or poles.

aerodrome control service. *Communication activities* and *services* used for the control of operations in an airport or aerodrome.

aeronautical advisory station. An *aeronautical station* used for advisory and civil defense *communications* with private aircraft stations.

aeronautical broadcasting station. **1.** An *aeronautical station* that makes scheduled *broadcasts* of *meteorological information* and notices to airmen. In certain instances, an aeronautical broadcast station may be placed on board a ship or aircraft. **2.** An *aeronautical station* that *broadcasts meteorological information* and notices to airmen.

aeronautical communication system abbreviation. An abbreviation of frequently used *words* and expressions that may be used, when authorized, by operators in the *aeronautical-mobile service* to facilitate copying of voice *transmissions.*

aeronautical emergency frequency. See *international aeronautical emergency frequency.*

aeronautical fixed service. A *radio communication* service between specified fixed locations, intended for the *transmission* of *information* relating to air navigation and the preparation for, and safety of, flight.

aeronautical fixed station. A *station* in the *aeronautical fixed service.*

aeronautical marker beacon station. A *radionavigation land station* in the *aeronautical radionavigation service* that provides a *signal* to designate a small area above the station. In certain instances, an aeronautical marker beacon station may be placed on board a ship or aircraft.

aeronautical mobile service (AMS). A *radio communication mobile service* among *aircraft stations* and *aeronautical stations,* or among aircraft stations, in which *survivalcraft stations* may also participate.

aeronautical multicom land station. An *aeronautical station* operating in the *aeronautical multicom service.*

aeronautical multicom mobile station. A *mobile station operating* in the *aeronautical multicom service.*

aeronautical multicom service. A *mobile service* not open to public *communication* and used to provide communication essential to activities being performed by, or directed from, private aircraft.

aeronautical radio beacon station. A *radionavigation land station* in the aeronautical *radio navigation service.* The *emissions* of the station are intended to enable aircraft or other *mobile service* elements to determine their *bearings* or their direction in relation to the aeronautical radio beacon station.

aeronautical radio navigation service. A *radionavigation service* intended for the benefit of persons engaged in navigation of aircraft to assist them in the performance of their tasks.

aeronautical station. A *land station* in the *aeronautical mobile service* carrying on a *communication service* with *aircraft stations.* In certain instances an aeronautical station may be placed on board a ship. An aeronautical station may be a *guard, secondary,* or *standby station* during the flight of an aircraft. See *primary aeronautical station; secondary aeronautical station.*

aeronautical station master log. A brief record of major or significant events that occur at an *aeronautical station* during a *radio day,* including *station identification,* time of station opening and closing, date, pertinent actions, interruptions, troubles, failures, and supervisors' signatures. Also see *position log.*

aeronautical telecommunication log. A record of the activities of an *aeronautical telecommunication station.*

aeronautical telemetering land station. A *telemetering land station* used in the flight testing of manned or unmanned aircraft, missiles, or major components thereof.

aeronautical telemetering mobile station. A *telemetering mobile station* used in the flight testing of manned or unmanned aircraft, missiles, or major components thereof.

aeronautical utility land station. A *land station* located at airdrome control towers and used for control of ground vehicles and aircraft on the ground at airdromes (airports).

aeronautical utility mobile station. A *mobile station* used for *communication,* at airdromes (airports), with the *aeronautical utility land station,* ground vehicles, and aircraft on the ground. All *transmissions* are usually subject to the control of the airdrome control station and are usually discontinued immediately when so requested by the airdrome control operator.

A-except-B gate. See *A-AND-NOT-B gate.*

AF. *Audio frequency.*

AFRS. *Armed Forces Radio Service.*

AGC. *Automatic gain control.*

agency. See *communication agency; operating agency; telecommunication private operating agency (TPOA).*

aggregate bit rate. See *multiplex aggregate bit rate.*

agile radar. See *frequency agile radar.*

agility. See *frequency agility.*

AI. *Absorption index.*

aid. See *radio landing aid; radionavigation aid; runway approach aid.*

aided tracking. A *system* of *tracking* a target in *azimuth, elevation, range,* or all three variables together, in which a constant rate of motion of the tracking mechanism is maintained.

aids service. See *Meteorological Aids Service.*

aid-to-navigation. See *long-range aid to navigation (LORAN); short-range aid to navigation (SHORAN).*

AIG. *Address indicating group.*

A-IGNORE-B gate. A two-*input binary, logic coincidence circuit* or device whose normal operation can be interrupted by a *control signal* that enables the *gate* to function so as to pass the A input signal and completely disregard the B input signal. The output is therefore the same as the A input signal and completely independent of the B input signal. Synonymous with *ignore gate.* See Figure A-4.

```
IN      0     1    B   IN
A      ┌─────┬─────┐
       │     │     │
0      │  0  │  0  │
       │     │     │  Q   OUT
       ├─────┼─────┤
       │     │     │
1      │  1  │  1  │
       │     │     │
       └─────┴─────┘
```

A-4. A table showing the *input* and *output digits* of an **A-IGNORE-B gate.**

aiming circle. An *aiming symbol* that has a circular shape.

aiming field. The area in the *display space* on the *display surface* of a *display device* covered or bounded by an *aiming symbol.*

aiming symbol. A pattern of *light* used to guide the positioning of a *light-pen* or to indicate the area in the *display space* on the *display surface* of a *display device* within which the presence of a light-pen can be detected at a given time. For example, a circle, square, angle, or pair of brackets of light on a *CRT* screen, fiberscope faceplate, *LED* or *gas panel,* or ink on a plotter bed. Also see *aiming circle* and *aiming field.*

A-implies-B gate. See *B-OR-NOT-A gate.*

air-air communications. *Communication* methods, systems, or equipment used for the *transmission* of *messages* containing *information* about air-air (*aircraft station* to *aircraft station*) operations or facilities; to or from air units in flight; or for the purpose of using, directing, or coordinating air units in flight.

airborne command post. A suitably equipped aircraft used by a commander for the control of units involved in an operation, such as military, rescue, fire fighting, crop dusting, police, evacuation, disaster, or emergency medical operations.

airborne direction-finding recorder. A *direction-finding* recording device that records all *intercepts* so that detailed analysis can be made by processing units to ascertain *signal parameters.* Typical manual systems include the operator's written *logs, audio* and *video magnetic recordings,* and *photography.*

airborne direction-finding unit. A *direction-finding* unit that uses a portion of the *receiver output* to visually *display relative bearings* from an *aircraft station* to another *transmitter.* The *emitter* location is thus determined through computation of a series of *relative bearings* versus aircraft *headings* and through *polarization* of the *received signal.* The polarization of the received signal is determined using specialized *antenna* circuitry.

airborne early warning. Pertaining to *systems,* devices, personnel, and procedures used to *detect* and *signal* the approach of airborne or space vehicles.

airborne early warning net. A *network* of *airborne radar* equipment that provides long-range detection, identification, and relaying of the *radar signals* to *land, aircraft,* or *ship stations.*

airborne intercept radar. In *military communication systems,* a *radar* carried aboard aircraft on an airborne interception mission. Airborne intercept radar equipment is in contrast to ground radar. Ground radar acquires a strike attack force and tracks it so that interceptor aircraft can be guided (vectored) toward it. In most cases an airborne intercept radar performs two separate functions: search *(scan)* and track *(lock-on).* In some of the latest type airborne intercept radar, these functions are combined into one *track-while-scan airborne intercept radar* set. See *track-while-scan airborne intercept radar.*

airborne interception. **1.** Pertaining to the location, identification, and maintenance of contact with airborne objects (targets) such as missiles, aircraft, and other airborne vehicles. **2.** The interception of a mobile object (target) or vehicle by means of an airborne vehicle, such as an aircraft or missile.

airborne radar. See *side-looking airborne radar.*

airborne radar jammer. A *jammer* carried aboard an aircraft and used to *jam* ground, ship, or airborne *radar.*

airborne radar warning system. A *wideband system* capable of *detecting radar signals* in several *frequency bands* and capable of performing an analysis of the threat. It usually is capable of providing *video information* to the aircrew.

airborne radio direction finding. The conduct of airborne *search, intercept, direction finding, range* estimation, and *signal analysis* of *radar* and *communication emitters.*

air-circuit-breaker switchgear. See *low-voltage enclosed air-circuit-breaker switchgear.*

air communications. See *air-air communications; airways/air communications; maritime air communications; surface-to-air communications.*

air control authority. See *maritime air control authority.*

aircraft call sign. Aircraft *signal* letters or identification numbers used as an *international call sign.*

aircraft communication standard plan. A table listing standard *communication equipment* recommended as minimum equipment for long-range maritime patrol aircraft.

aircraft control-warning system. A *system* consisting of observation facilities, including *radar, passive* electronic, visual, or other observation means, control centers, and necessary *communications,* established to control and report the movement of aircraft.

aircraft emergency frequency. An *international aeronautical emergency frequency* for *aircraft stations* and stations concerned with safety and regulation of flight along national or international civil air routes and *maritime mobile service stations* authorized to communicate for safety purposes. An aircraft emergency frequency is 121.5 MHz.

aircraft signature identification. A technique for identifying aircraft by properly analyzing and cataloging the way the compressor and turbine blades of jet engines modulate radar signals. This technique provides a capability of identifying and discriminating between different aircraft, discriminating between decoys and warhead missiles, and discriminating among other moving objects when sufficient signatures of the *modulation* are available. Also see *radar signature.*

aircraft station. 1. A *radio station* or *radar station* located in an aircraft or airspace vehicle. **2.** A *mobile radio* or *radar station* in the *aeronautical mobile service,* located on board an aircraft or air-space vehicle. See Figure A-5.

A-5. Cutting *connector cables* for an **aircraft station.** (Courtesy of Wyle Laboratories Corporate Communications Department.)

air-defense command-control-communication network. All the facilities used to integrate the operations of the *passive detection systems,* the *active detection systems,* and the weapon systems of an air-defense system.

air-defense communications. *Communication* methods, *systems,* or *equipment* used for *transmission* of *messages* containing *information* about military air-defense situations; to or from air-defense units, facilities, or communication activities; or for the purpose of directing, coordinating, or conducting air-defense operations.

air-defense communication system. A *communication system* established among ground, air, and sea units to permit recognition of aircraft by visual, *radar,* or other means, and to transmit the *information* obtained to appropriate units.

air dielectric coaxial cable. A *coaxial cable* with air between the inner and outer *conductors* and with *insulating* spacers at intervals to maintain separation of the conductors. The cable may be used for *transmission lines* from a *transmitter* to an *antenna.*

air-ground communication emergency frequency. A *frequency* to be used during emergencies primarily for contact purposes rather than as a working frequency for handling the emergency situation itself. *Aeronautical communication systems* use 121.5 or 243.0 MHz as emergency frequencies.

air-ground communications. 1. Two-way *communications* between *aircraft stations* and *land stations.* 2. *Communication* methods, *systems,* or *equipment* used for *transmission* of *messages* from air-to-ground and from ground-to-air stations, containing information about air and ground units, or for the purpose of using, directing, or coordinating air and ground units.

air-ground worldwide communication system. A worldwide military *network* of ground agencies and *stations* that provide a two-way *communication link* between aircraft and ground stations for navigation and control, including air route traffic control. The system may also provide support for civil aircraft providing support to military missions, for meeting communication requirements for aircraft flying distinguished visitors, and for other special functions.

air net. See *ship-air net; ship-to-air net.*

air operations communication net. See *maritime tactical air operations communication net.*

air portable. Pertaining to material that is suitable for transport by an aircraft loaded internally or externally, with no more than minor dismantling and reassembling.

air surface detection equipment. 1. A *radiolocation* device employed for air landing surface surveillance to determine the distribution of equipment on airport surfaces. 2. A device for locating the landing surfaces of an airport.

air radio organization. See *maritime air radio organization.*

air reporting net (ARN). See *maritime patrol air reporting net (ARN).*

air-sea rescue frequency. See *scene-of-air-sea rescue frequency.*

air sounding.   Measuring atmospheric phenomena or determining atmospheric conditions usually by means of apparatus carried by balloons or rockets.

air-spaced doublet.   In *optics,* a *compound lens* of two elements or parts with air or empty space between them.

air-supported fiber.   An *optical fiber* that relies on air-filled space between the *core* and the *cladding* to provide a *refractive index* that is less than that of the core in order to insure *total internal reflection* of *lightwaves* in the core.   See Figure A-6.

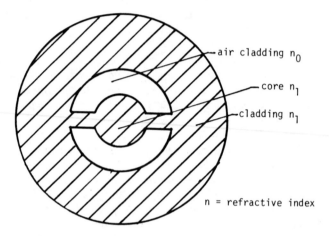

air cladding n_0

core n_1

cladding n_1

n = refractive index

A-6. An **air-supported fiber.**   Since the *numerical aperture* for this case is $(n_1{}^2 - n_0{}^2)^{1/2}$, the *coupling efficiency* can approach 100%.

air surveillance.   The systematic observation of airspace by electronic (*radar* or *radio*), visual, or other means primarily for the purpose of identifying and determining the movements of aircraft and missiles in the airspace under observation.

air telecommunication organization.   See *maritime air telecommunication organization.*

air traffic control communications.   *Communication* activities and equipment used to provide services for the purpose of preventing collisions between aircraft, and between aircraft and obstructions, as well as for expediting and maintaining an orderly flow of air traffic.

airways/air communications.   *Communication* methods, systems, or equipment used for *transmission* of *messages* containing *information* about air routes, terminals, and facilities; for transmission of messages to or from air operation and communication facilities; or for the transmission of messages for the purpose of conducting air-related military operations.

alarm. See *emergency signal alarm.*

alarm center. In a *communication system,* a location that receives local and remote alarms and control signals. It is usually located within a *technical control facility.*

alarmed cable. See *intrusion-resistant communication cable.*

alarm rate. See *constant false alarm rate (CFAR).*

alarm sensor. See *variation monitor.*

alarm signal. 1. A *signal* that draws the attention of a *user* or *operator,* for example, a bell or a blinking light. 2. In *distress and rescue communications,* a *signal* that precedes the *distress call* to operate automatic alerting equipment. In *radio telegraphy,* the alarm signal is normally followed in order by the distress call, an interval of two minutes, the distress call again, and then the distress message. In *radio telephony,* the alarm signal is usually followed in order by the distress call and the *distress message.* In *international radio telegraphic Morse code (CW),* a series of 12 *dashes* is sent in one minute. Each dash is 4 seconds long with a 1 second interval between them. In voice, two *sinusoidal audio-frequency tones,* one of 2200 Hz and the other 1300 Hz are *transmitted* alternately. Each tone is 250 milliseconds long. Also see *distress traffic.* See *ship alarm signal.*

albedo. A measure of the surface *reflective* capability of a body that is not self-radiating. For example, earth albedo is 0.39, moon 0.15, mars 0.15, and venus 0.59. It is similar to the reflection coefficient applied to the body as a whole. For *earth satellites* the term is usually applied to the *infrared* and *visible frequencies.* In connection with *incident light* and heat at the satellite, which comprise not only the energy directly received from the sun but also that from the earth and the moon, the greater the albedo of the satellite itself the less it is heated by solar *rays.*

ALGOL 60. A standard block-structured *computer programming language* used primarily for arithmetic and logical operations and computations. The name is derived from Algorithmic Language 1960.

ALGOL 68. A block-structured extensible *computer programming language* used primarily for numeric and logical operations, *string* handling, and record handling. The name is derived from Algorithmic Language 1968.

algorithm. A set of rules or procedures for the solution of a problem, e.g., a computer program for evaluating π, or e^x given x, usually in a finite number of steps and to a stated precision. See *encryption algorithm.*

aligned bundle. See *coherent bundle.*

alignment. See *frame alignment; level alignment; message alignment; octet alignment.*

alignment connector. See *grooved fiber-alignment connector.*

alignment indicator. See *message alignment indicator.*

alignment signal. See *bunched frame-alignment signal; distributed frame-alignment signal; frame-alignment signal; multiframe alignment signal.*

alignment time. See *out-of-frame alignment time.*

Allen belt. See *Van Allen belt.*

allocation. See *adaptive channel allocation; address group allocation; address indicating group allocation; frequency allocation; indicator allocation.* Also see *authorized frequency; assigned frequency.*

allocation plan. See *call-sign allocation plan.*

allocation plan. See *call-sign allocation plan.*

allotment plan. See *frequency allotment plan.*

alphabet. **1.** An ordered set of all the letters used in a *language,* including letters with diacritical signs where appropriate, but not including punctuation marks. **2.** An ordered set of *symbols* used in a *language.* For example, the 26 letters of the Roman alphabet, the Morse code alphabet, or the 128 ASCII (International Alphabet Number 5) characters. See *data alphabet; digital alphabet; N-unit code alphabet; phonetic alphabet; telegraph alphabet.*

alphabetic character set. A *character set* that contains letters and may contain *control characters, special characters,* and the *space character,* but not *digits.*

alphabetic character subset. A *character* subset that contains letters and may contain *control characters, special characters,* and the *space character,* but not *digits.*

alphabetic code. A *code* according to which data is represented using an *alphabetic character set.*

alphabetic coded character set. A *coded character set* whose character set is an *alphabetic character set.*

alphabetic flag. **1.** A *flag* used on an international basis in *visual communication systems* to represent a letter of the *alphabet.* **2.** In a *visual communication system,* a square flag on which a pattern of *colors* is used to represent a letter of the *alphabet.*

alphabetic string.   A *string* consisting solely of letters from the same *alphabet.*

alphabetic telegraphy.   1. *Telegraphy* applicable to texts, where *coded signals* are used, each signal or group of signals corresponding to a *character* such as a letter, figure, or punctuation mark. **2.** *Telegraphy* in which the received *characters (signals)* are automatically recorded as printed characters. Synonymous with *printing telegraphy.*

alphabetic word.   A *word* consisting solely of letters from the same *alphabet.*

alphabet number.   See *international telegraph alphabet number 1, 2, 3, 4, 5.*

alphabet translation.   See *transliteration.*

alphanumeric.   Pertaining to a *character set* that includes the letters of an *alphabet, numerals,* and other *symbols* such as punctuation marks or mathematical symbols.

alphanumeric character set.   A *character set* that contains both letters and digits and that may contain *control characters, special characters,* and the *space character.*

alphanumeric character subset.   A *character subset* that contains both letters and *digits* and may contain *control characters, special characters,* and the *space character.*

alphanumeric code.   A *code* according to which *data* is represented using both letters and digits, and, possibly, *control characters, special characters,* and the *space character.*

alphanumeric coded character set.   A *coded character set* whose *character set* is an *alphanumeric character set.*

alphanumeric data.   *Data* represented by letters and *digits,* perhaps with *special characters* and the *space character.*

alpha particle.   The nucleus of a helium atom. It consists of two protons and two neutrons, and has a positive electric charge equivalent to two protons.

alternate communication.   See *two-way alternate communication.*

alternate communication net.   A *communication net* used when other nets break-down or fail due to atmospheric conditions, overloading, destruction, saturation, or other reasons.

alternate mark inversion (AMI) coding.   See *bipolar coding.*

alternate mark inversion (AMI) signal.   A *pseudo-ternary signal,* conveying *binary digits,* in which successive *marks* or *spaces* are of alternative polarity (positive and negative) but equal in amplitude and in which spaces or marks are of zero amplitude. Synonymous with *bipolar signal.* Also see *modified alternate mark inversion (AMI) signal; paired-disparity code.*

alternate mark inversion (AMI) violation.   A *mark* or *space signal* that has the same polarity as the previous mark or space signal in the *transmission* of *alternate mark inversion signals.*

alternate routing.   The *routing* of a *call* or *message* over a substitute *route* when a given route is unavailable for immediate use.

alternating binary coding.   See *bipolar coding.*

alternating code.   See *paired-disparity code.*

alternating current (AC).   *Electric current* that is continuously changing in magnitude and that reverses its polarity, usually *sinusoidally.*

alternation gate.   See *OR gate.*

alternative-denial gate.   See *NAND gate.*

alternative frequency.   A *frequency* or a group of frequencies that may be assigned for use on any *channel,* or on a particular channel, at a certain time or for a certain purpose to replace or supplement the frequencies normally used on that channel.

alternative routing.   A process in which substitute routes are used for *transmitting messages* when *circuit* failures occur on operating *transmission paths* or message backlogs occur. Also see *primary route.*

alternative-routing indicator.   *Information* sent in the *forward direction* indicating that a *call* or *message* has been subjected to an *alternative routing.*

altimeter.   See *radio altimeter.*

altimeter station.   A *radionavigation mobile station* in the aeronautical *radionavigation service.*   Its *emissions* are used to determine the altitude above the earth's surface of the aircraft aboard which the altimeter station is located.

altimetry area.   See *radar altimetry area.*

altitude.   See *azimuth-over-altitude.*

altitude-over-azimuth.   Pertaining to an *antenna mount* in which the *azimuth* axis is the *primary axis* fixed to earth, and the altitude (elevation) drive is secondary.

It is used in moderate latitudes for *tracking* drifting equatorial satellites where considerable azimuth movement is required. Synonymous with *elevation-over-azimuth.*

aluminum garnet source.   See *YAG/LED source.*

AM.   *Amplitude modulation.*

amateur service.   A *communication activity* of self-training, *communication,* and technical investigation carried on by amateur radio *operators.* The operators are duly authorized to operate *radio transmitters.* The operators are primarily interested in radio techniques and have a personal rather than pecuniary interest.

ambient noise level.   The level of acoustic *noise* existing in a room or other location, as measured with a sound level meter. It is usually measured in *decibels* above a *reference level* of 0.00002 newton per square meter in SI units, or 0.0002 dyne per square centimeter in centimeter-gram-second (cgs) units. Synonymous with *room noise level.* Also see *noise.*

ambient temperature.   The *temperature* of air or other media surrounding equipment.

AME.   *Amplitude modulation equivalent.*

American (National) Standard Code for Information Interchange.   See *ASCII.*

AMI.   *Alternate mark inversion.*

amphibious communication net.   See *maritime amphibious communication net.*

amplification by stimulated emission of radiation.   See *microwave amplification by stimulated emission of radiation.*

amplifier.   A device that has an *output signal* that is a function of, and greater than, its *input signal.* The *gain* is expressed as a *transfer function* and often in positive *decibels.* If the gain is less than 1, or negative decibels, it is an *attenuation.* See *linear-logarithmic intermediate frequency (IF) amplifier; low-noise amplifier; operational amplifier; parametric amplifier (paramp).*

amplifying message.   A *message* that contains *information* that is in addition to information contained in a previous message.

amplifying prefix.   In *communication net* operation and nomenclature, a prefix or *word* that may be used to modify the basic functional word that describes or names a type of communication net. For example, the words navigation, search, safety, police, broadcast, medical emergency, amateur, or rescue when used to describe a *communication net, land station, ship station, aircraft station,* or other communication entity that is part of a net.

amplifying suffix.   In *communication net* operation and nomenclature, a suffix or *word* that may be used to modify the basic functional word that describes or names a type of communication net.   It follows the basic functional word, for example, the word *relay* or the letters *UHF* following the *call sign* of a *radio station.*

amplifying switch message.   A *message* that contains detailed *information* in addition to that contained in a previously sent *switch message.*

amplitude.   The magnitude or ordinate value of a periodic variation or excursion, for example one half of the peak-to-peak (crest-to-trough) value measured in a direction that is transverse to the direction of *propagation* of a *wave* or measured perpendicular to the time axis of a time-plot of the wave. Amplitude is a measure of intensity, density, or quantity in the *space domain* rather than of *phase* or *frequency* in the *time domain,* though one can speak of the amplitude of a *phase shift* or the amplitude of a *frequency shift.*   See *pulse amplitude; signal amplitude.*

amplitude-amplitude distortion.   See *amplitude distortion.*

amplitude distortion.   **1.** *Distortion* occurring in an *amplifier* or other device when the *output amplitude* is not a linear function of the *input amplitude* under specified conditions.   Amplitude distortion is measured with the *system* operating under steady-state conditions with a *sinusoidal fundamental frequency input signal.*   When other frequencies are present, the term amplitude refers to that of the fundamental frequency only.   It is usually an undesired variation with respect to the magnitude of the fundamental input.   **2.** The part of *nonlinear distortion* that is an undesired variation.   In a *system* intended to be linear it is the departure from constancy of the ratio of the *fundamental frequency* component of the response to the magnitude of a *sinusoidal* excitation.   Synonymous with *amplitude-amplitude distortion.*   See *phase-amplitude distortion.*

amplitude equalizer.   A device capable of changing or modifying *signal* amplitude levels, regardless of the type of *modulation,* of a *circuit* or system to desired values over some specified range (e.g., *frequency* range).

amplitude-frequency distortion.   See *frequency distortion.*

amplitude frequency response.   See *insertion loss versus frequency characteristic.*

amplitude hit.   In a *data transmission channel,* a momentary disturbance caused by a sudden change in the amplitude of a *signal.*   Also see *hit.*

amplitude limiting.   See *video amplitude limiting.*

amplitude modulation (AM).   The *modulation* of the *amplitude* of a *wave* serving as a *carrier,* by another wave serving as the *modulating signal.*   The amplitude excursions of the carrier are made proportional to a *parameter* of the modulating signal that bears the intelligence to be *transmitted.* See *balanced amplitude modulation; pulse-amplitude modulation (PAM).*

amplitude modulation equivalent (AME). See *compatible sideband transmission.*

amplitude quantized control. See *amplitude quantized synchronization.*

amplitude quantized synchronization. In a *signal transmission control system, synchronization* in which the functional relationship between the actual *phase error* and the derived *error signal* includes discontinuities. In practice this implies that the working range of phase errors is divided into a finite number of subranges and that a unique signal is derived for each subrange whenever the error falls within a subrange. Synonymous with *amplitude quantized control.*

amplitude system. See *frequency-and-amplitude (FRENA) system.*

amplitude-versus-frequency distortion. See *frequency distortion.*

AMS. *Aeronautical mobile service.*

analog. Pertaining to the representation of *data* or physical quantities in the form of a continuous *signal.* Usually, the instantaneous *amplitude* is a function of the value of the data or physical quantity being represented. For example, the instantaneous intensity of a *light beam* in an *optical fiber,* used to represent the instanteneous value of the electric wave of an electrocardiogram, is considered to be an analog signal. Contrast with *digital.* Also see *discrete.*

analog adder. See *summer.*

analog compression. See *analog speech interpolation.*

analog computer. A *computer* in which the variables used to represent *data* are continuous rather than *discrete.* For example, *electric currents* and *voltages* that vary continuously from value to value rather than abruptly, discretely, or as a step. The variables are represented by *analog data.* Components of an analog computer are connected together, the *output* of one to the *input* of another. Each component performs a single function, such as *summation,* multiplication, *integration,* or *differentiation.* Accuracy is limited by the *precision* with which the parts are made and the extent to which they will change in value as *temperature,* humidity, pressure, or other factors vary. Analog computers offer a continuous solution to a problem for as long as the inputs are present and the components are properly connected and functioning. Also see *digital computer.*

analog control. See *analog synchronization.*

analog converter. See *digital-to-analog (D-A) converter.*

analog data. *Data* represented by a physical quantity that is considered to be continuously variable and whose magnitude is made directly proportional to the data or to a suitable function of the data. Analog data may be considered as the *information content* of an *analog signal,* or the signal itself. The information content of the analog signal is conveyed by the value of the magnitude of some characteristics of the signal such as the *amplitude, phase,* or *frequency* of a *voltage;* the amplitude or *duration* of a *pulse;* the angular position of a shaft; or the pressure of a fluid.

analog data channel. A one-way *path* for data *signals* that includes a *voice-frequency channel,* an associated *data modulator,* and a *demodulator.*

analog decoding. A process in which one of a set of reconstructed *analog signal* samples is generated from the *digital signal* representing a sample. Also see *analog encoding.*

analog-digital converter. See *analog-to-digital converter.*

analog-digital encoder. See *analog-to-digital encoder.*

analog divider. A device whose *output analog variable* is proportional to the quotient of two *input* analog variables.

analog encoding. A process in which *digital signals* are generated, representing the sample taken of an *analog signal* value at a given instant. Also see *analog computer; uniform encoding.*

analog-intensity modulation. In an *optical modulator,* the variation of the *intensity* of a *light* source in accordance with an intelligence-bearing *signal* or continuous *wave,* with the resulting *envelope* normally being detectable at the other end of a *lightwave transmission medium* or *system.*

analog interpolation. See *analog speech interpolation.*

analog multiplier. A device whose *output analog variable* is proportional to the product of two *input analog variables.* An analog multiplier may also be a device that can perform more than one multiplication at a time, for example, a servo-multiplier.

analog representation. A representation of the value of a variable by a physical quantity that is considered to be continuously variable. The magnitude of the physical quantity is made directly proportional to the variable or to a suitable function of the variable.

analog signal. A continuous *signal* that varies in some direct correlation with an impressed phenomenon, stimulus, or event that bears intelligence. The signal may assume the form of an electric current variation, *light intensity* or *wavelength* variation, *electromagnetic wave amplitude, phase,* or *frequency* variation, mechanical *displacement* variation, or other physical phenomenon that varies continuously. See *quasi-analog signal.*

analog speech interpolation. The utilization of the inactivity periods that always exist in both *transmission* directions of a *telephone* conversation. The interpolation is used in order to increase the efficiency and lower the cost of *long distance links.* *Analog signals* with quiescent periods or long vowels are compressed, for example by *time assignment speech interpolation,* transmitted, and expanded by inverse compression (expansion) at the receiving end. This principle has been used for many years with analog signals and is now being developed for digital speech. When *pulse code modulation (PCM)* is used the process is known as *digital speech interpolation.* Synonymous with *analog interpolation* and with *analog compression.* Also see *digital speech interpolation.*

analog switch. *Switching equipment* designed, designated, or used to connect *circuits* between users for *real-time transmission* of *analog signals.*

analog switching. The interconnecting of *input* and *output terminations* in a *switching matrix* for the purpose of *transferring analog signals* between them.

analog synchronization. A *synchronization control system* in which the relationship between the actual *phase error* among *clocks* and the error signal device is a continuous function over a given range. Synonymous with *analog control.*

analog telephone. A *telephone* whose *output* is a nominally continuous *electrical signal* correlated with the sound pressure variation on its *microphone (transmitter).*

analog-to-digital coder. See *analog-to-digital encoder.*

analog-to-digital (A-D) converter. **1.** A device that *converts* an *input analog signal* to an *output digital signal* with the same *information content.* It accepts an analog signal at its input, operates on this signal, and produces a digital signal containing the essential information that was in the analog signal. **2.** A device that converts *data* from an *analog* representation to a *digital* representation. Synonymous with *analog-digital converter.* Also see *digital-to-analog (D-A) converter.* See Figure A-7.

A-7. **Analog-to-digital converters** and *digital-to-analog converters* designed and packaged for microprocessor compatibility, for commercial and military applications, and for use with low *power* instrumentation. (Courtesy of Beckman Instruments, Inc., Electro-Products Group.)

analog-to-digital (A-D) encoder. A device for *encoding analog signal* samples. Synonymous with *analog-to-digital coder* and with *coder.*

analog transmission. The *transmission* of a continuously variable *signal* as opposed to a discretely variable signal. Physical quantities such as *temperature* are described as *analog* quantities. *Data characters,* such as *binary digits,* are *coded* in *discrete* separate *pulses* or signals levels and hence are referred to as *digital.*

analog variable. A continuously changing phenomenon representing either a mathematical variable in a mathematical function or a physical quantity. For example, the *luminous intensity* of a *lightwave* in an *optical fiber* representing the *temperature* of a body by using the current in a *thermocouple* to *modulate* the *light intensity* produced by a *laser* or *LED* for *transmission* of the lightwave in the fiber.

analysis. See *electromagnetic compatibility (EMC) analysis; Fourier analysis; risk analysis; signal analysis; signature analysis; spectrum analysis; traffic analysis.*

analyzer. See *integrated optical spectrum analyzer; jammer analyzer; light analyzer; multichannel optical analyzer; pulse analyzer; wave analyzer.*

anamorphic. In *optical systems,* pertaining to a configuration of *optical* components, such as *lenses, mirrors,* and *prisms,* that produce different effects on an *image* in different directions or different effects on different parts. For example, the production of different *magnifications* in different directions or the conversion of a point on an *object* to a line on its image.

AND circuit.   See *AND gate.*

AND element.   See *AND gate.*

AND gate.   A device that is capable of performing the logical AND operation — namely, that if *P, Q,* and *R* are statements . . . , then the AND of *P, Q, R* . . . is true if all statements are true, and false if any statement is false. *P* AND *Q* is often represented by *P·Q, P∧Q,* or simply *PQ.* Synonymous with *positive AND gate; intersection gate; conjunction gate; coincidence unit; logic product gate; coincidence gate; AND circuit; AND unit; AND element.* See Figure A-8.

IN A	0	1	B IN
0	0	0	
			Q OUT
1	0	1	

A-8. A table showing the *input* and *output digits* of an **AND gate.**

AND NOT gate.   See *A-AND-NOT-B gate.*

AND unit.   See *AND gate.*

angle.   See *acceptance angle; Brewster angle; convergence angle; critical angle; departure angle; deviation angle; elevation angle; exit angle; horizon angle; launch angle; limiting angle; look angle; maximum acceptance angle; pointing angle; reflection angle; refraction angle; total acceptance angle.*

angle-between-half-power-points.   See *emission beam angle-between-half-power-points.*

angle break lock.   In *radar systems,* a loss of the ability of *tracking radar* to continue tracking an object in *azimuth* or *elevation* rather than *range.*

angle diversity.   In *tropospheric scattering propagation* of *electromagnetic waves,* the difference created by two or more *feeders* that produce multiple *beams* from the same *reflector* at slightly different launch angles.

angle modulation.   *Modulation* in which the *phase angle* of a *sine wave carrier* is varied. *Phase* and *frequency* modulation are particular forms of angle modulation.

angle modulation noise improvement.   An improvement in the *output signal-to-noise ratio* obtained in a *receiver* through the use of *threshold extension demodulators.*

angle of incidence.   See *incidence angle.*

angle tracker.   See *infrared angle tracker.*

angular frequency.   See *angular velocity.*

angular magnification.   The ratio of the apparent size of an *image,* seen through an *optical system,* element, or instrument, to that of the *object* viewed by the unaided eye, when both the object and image are at infinity, which is the case for telescopes, or when both the object and image are considered to be at the distance of distinct vision, which is the case for microscopes. Synonymous with *magnifying power.*

angular misalignment loss.   In an *optical fiber transmission system, signal* power loss at the junction of two fibers that are not butt-joined in a straight line, i.e., when there is an angular displacement between the *optical axes* of the two fibers. The angular misalignment loss is usually expressed in *decibels* (dB). Synonymous with *axial misalignment loss.*

angular resolution.   In *optics* and *display systems,* a measure of the capability of a device to distinguish two points as separate at a given distance, i.e., to distinguish between two *divergent* directions from a given point. The smallest such angle that can distinguish the points as separate is the *limiting resolution angle.*

angular velocity.   The rate of rotation of a rotating body, normally measured in radians per second. The angular velocity, ω, is given by $\omega = 2\pi f$, where f is the *frequency.* When applied to a *wave* the angular velocity is 2π times the number of waves or complete cycles per unit time, each complete cycle of the wave corresponding to one complete rotation. Synonymous with *angular frequency.*

anisochronous.   Pertaining to *transmission* in which the time interval separating any two *significant instants* in sequential *signals* is not necessarily related to the time interval separating any other two significant instants. Also see *heterochronous; homochronous; mesochronous; plesiochronous.*

anisochronous transmission.   A *transmission* process in which there is always an *integral* number of *unit intervals* between any two *significant instants* in the same group. In *data transmission,* this group is a *block* or a character; in *telegraphy* this group is a character. There is not always an integral number of unit intervals between two significant instants located in different groups. Also see *asynchronous transmission.*

anisotropic.   Pertaining to a material with characteristics or *parameters* that are different in different directions. Thus, for example, two identical *light beams* propagating through an anisotropic material in different directions will be affected in different manners. In *lightwave transmission media*, significant parameters are *magnetic permeability, electric permittivity*, and *electric conductivity*.

anode. A collector of negatively charged particles such as negative ions or electrons. It is usually charged positively in order to attract them. Conventional current direction is from the anode to the cathode through the inside of the device, such as a vacuum tube or photomultiplier.

anomalous propagation. The *propagation* of *electromagnetic waves* along paths other than expected or designed paths because of unexpected variations in *transmission media attributes*, thus giving rise to changes in *refractive index, coupling, ducting, velocity of propagation, trapping, transmission mode* changes, and the *reflective, dispersive, diffusive, absorptive*, and *scattering* characteristics of the media.

answer. The *transmission* made by the *called station* in response to the *call* received. See *abbreviated answer; call forwarding don't answer*.

answer-back code. A unique sequence of *characters* identifying a particular *telegraph terminal* or *data station*. See *automatic answer-back code exchange*.

answer-back unit. The part of a *telegraph* or *data terminal installation* that automatically *transmits* its *answer-back code* on receipt of the *who-are-you signal*.

answering. The process of responding to a *calling station* to complete a *connection* between *stations*.

answering facility. See *manual answering facility*.

answering frequency. The *frequency* used to respond to a received *message*. Also see *calling frequency; crossband frequency; working frequency*.

answering net. A *communication net* that is normally associated with *ship-shore communication systems* and that is used for answering *calls* from ships.

answering plug. In *telephone switchboard operations*, the *plug*, of the two associated with any *cord circuit*, that is near to the face of the switchboard and that is normally used for *answering calling signals*.

answering sign. In *semaphore communications*, the *flag position* used as an *answer* to a *call*. If necessary, the answering sign may be preceded by a *call sign* to denote the *station* answering.

antenna. A *transducer* that converts *electrical* energy from a *source* (such as a *transmitter* or *light source*) to *electromagnetic waves* in *free space* or in a *transmission medium*, or from free space or transmission medium to a receiver or *detector*. A transmitting antenna usually carries the *currents* that launch the transmitted waves. A receiving antenna usually carries the currents that are induced by the waves that impinge upon it. A light source and a *photodetector* may be considered as antennae. See *aperiodic antenna; billboard antenna; buoyant antenna; casse-grain antenna; diel-guide feed antenna; dipole antenna; directional antenna; elec-trically-despun antenna; global beam satellite antenna; halfwave dipole antenna; high-gain antenna; Hogg-horn antenna; horn antenna; image antenna; isotropic antenna; jamming antenna; light antenna; log-periodic antenna; lossless halfwave dipole antenna; mechanically-despun antenna; multielement dipole antenna; narrow-beam antenna; notch antenna; omnidirectional antenna; parabolic an-tenna; periodic antenna; periscope antenna; reference antenna; rhombic antenna; slot antenna; telescopic antenna; test antenna; unidirectional antenna; wide-beam antenna; Yagi antenna.* Also see Figure E-1.

antenna aperture. The physical area of the main *reflector* of an *antenna,* which acts as the *radiating* area of the *source* of the *transmitted electromagnetic beam* (such as a *light beam* or a radio beam). The effective area may be less than the physical area due to blockage by intervening parts, such as a subreflector, antenna supports, or *waveguide* feed supports. In front-fed systems, the area is measured in a plane normal to the beam axis. Synonymous with *antenna capture area.*

antenna array. *Antenna* or *light source* elements arranged so that the resulting *electromagnetic radiation pattern* has its *main lobe* such that the *transmitted* waves *propagate* with maximum *power density* in the desired direction. See *broadside antenna array; colinear antenna array.*

antenna blind cone. The volume of space, usually approximately conical with its vertex at the *antenna,* that cannot be *scanned* by the antenna owing to limi-tations of the antenna mount.

antenna blockage. The portion of the *antenna aperture* that is blocked, or shaded, by equipment mounted in front of the antenna, such as *subreflectors* and subreflector supports.

antenna capture area. See *antenna aperture.*

antenna design. The physical, electrical, and *magnetic* characteristics of an *an-tenna,* including its geometrical shape and spatial orientation.

antenna diversity. See *spaced antenna diversity.*

antenna dynamics. The *electrical, magnetic,* and structural characteristics of an *antenna* or *light source* during operating conditions. Such conditions include *cur-rent, voltage, power, impedance, cross section,* efficiency, average power, *power density,* instantaneous power, peak power, *luminous intensity, directive gain, antenna pattern,* shape, size, and orientation.

antenna effective area.   That certain area, expressed in square meters, from which an *antenna* directed towards the source of the *received signal* gathers or absorbs the energy of an *incident electromagnetic wave.* In the case of *parabolic* and *horn-parabolic antennas,* the antenna effective area is about 0.35 to 0.55 of the geometric area of the *antenna aperture.*

antenna feed.   The *conductor, cable,* or *waveguide* that conducts the energy that is to be transmitted from the *transmitter* to the *antenna.*

antenna feed system.   See *monopulse antenna feed system.*

antenna gain.   1. The ratio of the *power* required at the *input* of a *reference antenna* to the power supplied to the input of the given antenna to produce, in a given direction, the same *field* at the same distance. **2.** The maximum *power density* divided by the power density of a *reference isotropic source.* **3.** The ratio of the maximum *radiation intensity* or *power* of an *antenna* to the maximum radiation intensity or power from a *reference antenna* with the same power *output.* **4.** The effectiveness of a *directional antenna* in a particular direction as compared with a *standard dipole antenna.* The gain is usually expressed in *decibels.* Most often it is the ratio of the standard antenna power to the directional antenna power that will produce the same *field strength* in a given direction at the same distance. When not specified otherwise, the figure expressing the *gain* of an antenna refers to the gain in the direction of the *radiation main lobe.* In *communication systems* using *scattering* modes of *propagation,* the full gain of an antenna may not be realizable in practice and the apparent gain may vary with time. Synonymous with *power gain of an antenna.* Also see *directive gain.*

antenna gain-to-noise temperature (G/T).   For *satellite earth station receiving systems,* a figure of merit that equals G/T, where G is the *gain* in *decibels* of the *earth station antenna* at the *receiving frequency* and T is the *equivalent noise temperature* in *kelvins* of the receiving *system.*

antenna height above average terrain.   The average of *antenna* heights above the terrain from two to ten miles from the antenna for the eight directions spaced evenly for each $45°$ of *azimuth* starting with true north. Usually a different antenna height will be determined in each direction from the antenna. The average of these various heights is considered the antenna height above average terrain. In some cases, fewer than eight directions may be used. Also see *smooth earth.*

antenna interference.   The *mutual interference* caused by *electromagnetic coupling* that occurs when two or more *antennas* are located in close proximity.

antenna length.   See *effective antenna length.*

antenna lobe.   A three-dimensional section of the *radiation pattern* of a *directional antenna* bounded by one or two cones of nulls or regions of diminished *field intensity.*

antenna matching.   The process of adjusting *impedance* so that the *input impedance* of an *antenna* equals the *characteristic impedance* of its *transmission line.*

antenna mount.   See *nonorthogonal antenna mount.*

antenna multiplier.   A device applied to an *antenna* that permits the use of several pieces of equipment to be connected to one antenna.   Though the number of antennas is reduced, the *channel frequency* spacing will have to be greater than when a separate antenna is used for each frequency in the channel.

antenna noise temperature.   The *temperature* that a resistor would have to produce a *noise power* per unit *bandwidth* equal to that of the *antenna output* at a specified *frequency.*   The noise temperature of an antenna depends on its *coupling* to all noise *sources* in its environment as well as noise generated within the antenna.   Also see *noise.*

antenna pattern.   See *radiation pattern.*

antenna power gain.   The ratio of the *power* required at the *input* of a *reference antenna* to the power supplied to the input of the given antenna to produce, in a given direction, the same power flow per unit cross-sectional area *(field strength)* at the same distance from the antennas.   The antenna power gain refers to the gain in the direction of the *main lobe* axis.   It is a measure of the extent to which the power or energy of an antenna is concentrated in a given direction, the narrower the beam the greater the concentration and hence the greater the antenna power gain.

antenna reflector.   The portion of a *directional antenna array* that reduces the *field strength* behind the array and increases it in the forward direction.

antenna rotation.   *Antenna* movement that may be accomplished in many different ways such as by mechanical movement of the antenna, by *phasing* from different elements of an array, or by *reflection* methods.   For example, antenna rotation may be accomplished by irregular motion, turning, *beam switching, holding, lobe switching,* searchlighting, or *phase* control.

antenna rotation period.   The time required for one complete revolution or movement cycle of an *antenna.*   The period is usually measured in seconds while the *sweep* rate is usually given in revolutions per minute.

antenna sweep.   The space angle in which a mutating or oscillating *antenna* moves relative to its base or other fixed or moving reference.   For example, in addition to its mutating or oscillating motion, it may be sweeping in a vertical or horizontal direction.   Antenna sweep may be designated as fixed, continuous, or sector.

anticlockwise polarized electromagnetic wave.   See *left-hand polarized electromagnetic wave.*

anticoincidence gate. See *EXCLUSIVE-OR gate.*

anticoincidence unit. See *EXCLUSIVE-OR gate.*

anticyclone. A distribution of atmospheric pressure in which the pressure increases towards a center of high atmospheric pressure. Anticyclonic winds circulate in a clockwise direction in the northern hemisphere and in a counterclockwise direction in the southern hemisphere. Anticyclones give rise to fine, calm weather conditions, although in winter fog is likely to develop. They usually advance at 30 to 50 km per hour, with a diameter of 2500 to 4000 km, and often bring cool, dry weather.

antielectronic jamming. Organizational, tactical, strategic, and technical measures taken to overcome the effects of *electronic jamming.*

antijamming. **1.** Pertaining to the ability of a device or system to withstand *jamming* or *interference* without seriously degrading its performance. **2.** Pertaining to measures that are taken to reduce the effects of attempts to deliberately cause *interference* in a *system.*

antijamming margin. The maximum *jamming-to-signal power, voltage,* or *current* ratio at which a device will still continue to satisfactorily perform its intended function.

antijamming measure. A measure taken to minimize the effect of *jamming* or reduce the effectiveness of jamming efforts.

antinode. A point in a *standing* (stationary) *wave* at which the *amplitude* is a maximum. The standing wave should be identified as a *voltage wave* or a *current wave,* if it is an *electric wave.* Also see *node; standing wave ratio (SWR).*

antireflection coating. A class of single or multilayer *coatings* that are applied to a surface or surfaces of a *substrate* for the purpose of decreasing the *reflectance* of the surface and increasing the *transmission* of the substrate over a specified *wavelength* range.

antisinging device. A device that prevents *singing* (resonant oscillations), usually of an *audio frequency,* in a circuit.

a–o. *Acoustooptic.*

A-OR-NOT-B gate. A two-*input, binary, logic coincidence circuit* or device capable of performing the logic operations of A OR NOT B. Thus, if A is a statement and B is a statement, the result is false only if A is false and B is true. For the other three combinations of A and B the result is true. Synonymous with *B implies A gate,* with *if-B-then-A gate,* with *implication gate,* and with *inclusion gate.* See Figure A-9.

IN A	0	1	B IN
0	1	0	
			Q OUT
1	1	1	

A-9. A table showing the *input* and *output digits* of an **A-OR-NOT-B gate.**

APC. *adaptive predictive coding.*

APD. *Avalanche photodiode.*

APD coupler. *Avalanche photodiode coupler.*

aperiodic antenna. An *antenna* designed to have an approximately constant *input impedance* over a wide range of *frequencies;* for example, a terminated *rhombic antenna* or a wave antenna. Synonymous with *nonresonant antenna.* Also see *periodic antenna.*

aperture **1.** In an *optical system,* an opening or hole that is equal to the diameter of the largest entering *beam* of *light* that can travel completely through the system. The aperture is usually symmetric about the *optical axis* of the system and is usually limited by the *objective.* **2.** That portion of a plane surface near a *unidirectional antenna,* perpendicular to the direction of *propagation* of maximum *radiation intensity,* through which the major part of the radiation passes. See *antenna aperture; facsimile receiver aperture; facsimile transmitter aperture; numerical aperture; output aperture; tone-control aperture.*

aperture distortion. In *facsimile transmission systems,* the effect caused by the finite dimensions of the *scanning spot* at *transmission* and *reception.* Contours of *images* become blurred. Details that are smaller than the scanning spot are suppressed.

aperture ratio. The value of R_a in the equation: $R_a = 2n \sin A,$ where n is the *refractive index* of the *image* space and A is the maximum angular opening of the axial *bundle* of *refracted rays.* The speed (i.e., energy per unit area of images) of an *objective* is proportional to the square of its aperture ratio. When the angular opening is small, when $n = 1,$ and when the *object* distance is great, it is approximately true that $n \sin A = D/2F,$ or that $F/D = F\text{-number} = 1/(2 \sin A) = 1/$ aperture–ratio. Also see *F-number.*

aperture stop. The physical diameter that limits the size of the cone of *radiation* that an *optical system* will accept from an *object* point on the *optical axis* of a lens system. Also see *axial bundle; exit pupil; field stop.*

aperture tagging. In *image restoration,* a method of *wavefront control* in which the distortion of the wavefront of an *electromagnetic wave,* introduced when passing through an *aperture,* is compensated by prior or after-the-fact methods; i.e., trial perturbations are made in the outgoing wavefront, and the resulting variations in *power reflected* from an *object* are analyzed to optimize the *power density* in specific portions of the wavefront.

aperture-to-medium coupling loss. The difference between the theoretical *gain* of a very large *antenna,* as used in beyond-the-horizon *microwave links,* and the gain that can be realized in operation. It is related to the ratio of the *scatter* angle to the antenna *beamwidth.* A very large antenna is several *wavelengths* long or in diameter. This loss can apply to *line of sight (LOS) systems* also.

APL. A *computer programming language* primarily used in a conversational (interactive) mode for mathematical applications with multidimensional arrays. The name is derived from A Programming Language.

aplanatic lens. A *lens* that has been corrected for *spherical aberration,* departure from the *sine condition, coma,* and *color.*

apogee. **1.** The point in an earth orbit where the satellite radius vector from the earth to the satellite is a maximum. **2.** The point at which a missile trajectory or a satellite orbit is farthest from the center of the gravitational field of the controlling body or bodies. Also see *perigee.*

application layer. In *open systems architecture,* the *layer* that is directly accessible to, visible to, and usually explicitly defined by, *users.* It provides all the functions and services needed to execute their *programs, processes,* and *data* exchanges. Also see *layer.*

application network. A *network* of interconnected *data processing equipment,* such as *computers, processors, controllers,* and *terminals,* for the purposes of *processing* and exchanging *user data.* The network may include public or private *communication* facilities provided by private organizations, *common carriers,* or *recognized private* or *public operating administrations* or *agencies (RPOAs).* Synonymous with *computer network* and with *user application network.*

application-oriented language. A *computer programming language* that has capabilities or notation schemes specially suited for solving problems in specific classes of applications, such as *communication,* scientific, business, engineering, design, or *simulation* applications. Synonymous with *problem-oriented language.*

application program. A *computer program* that directly meets the need of a *user,* such as a payroll, inventory control, *data* base, or traffic control program.

applique. *Circuit* components added to an existing *communication system* to provide additional or alternate functions. For example, some *common carrier* *telephone equipment* designed for *manual ringdown* operation can be modified with applique to allow for use between points having *dial* or *key* equipment.

appointment directory. A *telephone directory* in which each *user telephone number* designates the title, appointment, assignment, or function of that user. Personnel changes do not affect updating such as a directory as long as there is no reorganization of the *user group.* Entries are alphabetical by title, appointment, assignment, or function. Also see *fixed directory.*

approach. See *carrier-controlled approach (CCA).*

approach aid. See *radio-approach aid; runway-approach aid.*

approach control service. A *communication system* used to communicate with *aircraft stations* that are approaching an airport.

approved circuit. A *circuit* that has been authorized by responsible authority for the *transmission* of *information.* Approved circuits usually relate only to those *wireline* or *fiber systems* to which *electromagnetic* and physical safeguards have been applied to permit transmission of *unencrypted information.* The circuit includes all the individual *conductors* in the *path.* From a security or privacy standpoint all *radio* circuits are usually considered as nonapproved circuits. Also see *protected optical fiber distribution system; protected wireline distribution system.*

APT. A *computer programming language* used primarily for the numerical control of machine tools. The name is derived from Automatically Programmed Tools.

architecture. The organizational structure of an entity such as a *computer, data processing,* or *communication system.* See *network architecture; open systems architecture.*

area. See *antenna effective area; blind area; broadcast area; controlled area; elemental area; maximum call area; maximum calling area (MCA); radar altimetry area; restricted area.*

area broadcast shift. The changing from listening to *transmissions* intended for one *broadcast area* to listening to transmissions intended for another broadcast area. For example, as a ship or aircraft crosses the boundary between areas, the changing from listening to one *area broadcast station* to listening to another. Shift times, normally 0001 *Greenwich mean time (GMT)* on the date a ship or aircraft is expected to pass into another area, must be strictly observed or the *ship* or *aircraft station* will miss *messages* intended for it. Synonymous with *radio watch shift.*

area broadcast station.   1. A *land station* responsible for *radio broadcasting* to a specific geographical area of the earth. **2.** A *radio station* responsible for *broadcasting* to one of the 12 numbered areas into which the world has been divided for operating the *merchant ship broadcast system.*

area code. A *telephone system* number that is assigned to a grographical area.

area communication organization. The *communication* organization designed to provide communication between *radio*-equipped organizations in a given area, including *ship stations, shore stations,* and *aircraft stations,* particularly maritime patrol aircraft on a mission, ships at sea, and aircraft in flight.

area coverage. See *jammer area coverage.*

area radio station. See *ship broadcast-area radio station.*

arithmetic. See *modulo-n arithmetic.*

Armed Forces Radio Service. (AFRS). A *radio broadcasting* service that is operated by and for the personnel of the armed services in the area covered by the broadcast. For example, the radio service operated by the U.S. Army for U.S. and allied military personnel on duty in overseas areas.

ARN. *Air reporting net.* See *maritime patrol air reporting net (ARN).*

around. See *ring around.*

ARQ. *Automatic recovery quotient. Automatic request-repeat.*

array. See *antenna array; broadside antenna array; colinear antenna array; phased array; solar array.*

arteriovenous oximeter. See *fiber optic arteriovenous oximeter.*

artificial language. A *language* in which the *symbols,* conventions, and rules for its use were explicitly established before its use. Also see *natural language.*

artificial pupil. A diaphragm or other limitation that confines a *beam* of *light* to a smaller cone; e.g., a *pupil* that confines a *beam* of light entering the human eye to a smaller cone than that admitted by the iris of the eye.

artificial transmission line. A four-*terminal electric network (circuit)* that has the *characteristic impedance,* the *transmission time delay, phase shift,* or other *parameter* of a real *transmisison line* and therefore can be used to *simulate* a real transmission line in one or more of these respects.

ASCII (American National Standard Code for Information Interchange). The standard 7-*bit code,* using a *coded character set* consisting of 7-bit *coded characters* (8 bits including a *parity check bit*) used for *information* interchange among *data processing systems, data communication systems,* and associated equipment. The ASCII set consists of *control characters* and *graphic characters* and is properly an *alphabet* rather than a *code.* It is the U.S. implementation of the *International Telegraph Alphabet Number 5.* Also see *code.*

aspect.   See *image aspect.*

aspect ratio.   The ratio of a break, that is, an *aperture,* gap, or opening, to the height or width of a picture, object, or *scanning field.*

assembler.   1. A *computer program* used to *translate* another *computer program* expressed in an *assembly language* into *machine language* for execution by a specific computer.   **2.** A computer program used to prepare a *machine language program,* usually a *symbolic* or higher-level language, for execution by a specific computer.

assembly.   See *cable assembly; multiple-bundle cable assembly; multiple-fiber cable assembly; optical harness assembly.*

assembly-disassembly facility.   See *packet assembly-disassembly (PAD) facility.*

assembly language.   1. A *computer-oriented language* whose *instructions* are usually in a one-to-one correspondence with *machine (computer) language* instructions and that may provide facilities such as the use of *macroinstructions.*   **2.** A *computer programming language* whose statements may be *instructions* or declarations.   The instructions usually have a one-to-one correspondence with *machine language instructions.*   Synonymous with *computer-dependent language.* Also see *computer-oriented language.*

assigned frequency.   The *frequency* at the center of the *bandwidth* assigned to a *station.*   The frequency of the *radio frequency (RF) carrier,* whether *suppressed* or *radiated,* is usually given in parentheses following the assigned frequency, and is the frequency appearing in the dial settings of RF equipment intended for *single sideband* or *independent sideband transmission.*   This frequency does not necessarily correspond to any frequency in an *emission.*   Also see *authorized frequency; frequency allocation; frequency assignment.*

assigned frequency band.   A *frequency band* the center of which coincides with the frequency assigned to a *station* and the width of which equals the *necessary bandwidth* plus twice the absolute value of the *frequency tolerance.*

assignment.   See *demand assignment; frequency assignment; routing indicator assignment.*

assignment access plan.   See *demand-assignment access plan; preassignment access plan.*

assignment plan.   See *frequency assignment plan.*

assistance switchboard.   See *dial service assistance (DSA) switchboard.*

assisted call.   See *operator-assisted call.*

assumed value.   A value within the range of values, *parameters,* or *levels* assumed for a mathematical model, hypothetical *circuit,* or *network,* from which analyses, additional estimates, or calculations will be made.   The range of values, while not measured, represents the best engineering judgment and is generally derived from values found or measured in real circuits or networks of the same generic type, and includes projected improvements.   Also see *design objective.*

assurance.   See *quality assurance.*

astigmatism.   An *aberration* of a *lens* or *lens system* that causes an off-axis point on an *object* to be *imaged* as two separated lines perpendicular to each other.

astronomy.   See *radio astronomy.*

astronomy service.   See *radio astronomy service.*

astronomy station.   See *radio astronomy station.*

asymmetrical modulator.   See *unbalanced modulator.*

asynchronous communication system.   A *data communication system* in which extra *signal* elements are appended to the data for the purpose of *synchronizing* individual *data characters* or *blocks.*   The time spacing between successive data characters or blocks may be of arbitrary duration.   In such *data transmission systems,* each group of code elements corresponding to an *alphabetical signal* is preceded by a *start signal* that serves to prepare the receiving mechanism for the reception and registration of a character, and is followed by a *stop signal* that serves to bring the receiving mechanism to rest in preparation for the reception of the next character.   Primary application is in *alphabetic telegraphy* and *tape relay systems* using *start-stop transmission.*   Also see *start-stop system; stepped start-stop system.*

asynchronous digital computer.   A *digital computer* in which each event or the execution of each *instruction* starts as a result of a *signal* generated by the completion of the previous event or operation.   The next operation or event may proceed on the availability of the parts or components required for the operation.   Also see *synchronous digital computer.*

asynchronous network.   See *nonsynchronous network.*

asynchronous operation.   **1.** A sequence of operations in which each operation is executed out of time coincidence with any event.   **2.** An operation that occurs without a regular or predictable time relationship to a specified event, for example the calling of an error diagnostic routine that may receive control at any time during the execution of a *computer program.*   A *signal* indicating the completion of an event is *gated* to start the next event.   *Clocks* are usually not involved in asynchronous operation.   Synonymous with *asynchronous working*.   See *bit-by-bit asynchronous operation*.

asynchronous signals.   A set of *signals,* such as in *bit stream transmission,* arranged in such a manner that between any two *significant instants* in the same group there is always an *integral* number of *unit intervals.*   Also, between two significant instants in different groups there is not always an integral number of unit intervals.   In *data transmission,* a group is a *block* or *character;* in *telegraphy,* a group is a character.   *Asynchronous* signals often begin each group with a *start signal,* such as the start of each character in *start-stop telegraphy.*   In an *asynchronous counter* for example, the change of *output* state of each flip-flop is dependent on the previous stages having changed state, that is the flip-flops do not all change state synchronously since it takes a finite time for changes to *propagate* through the *circuits.*   Also see *synchronous signals.*

asynchronous time-division multiplexing (ATDM).   An *asynchronous transmission mode* that makes use of *time-division multiplexing.*   Also see *synchronous time-division multiplexing.*

asynchronous transmission.   *Data transmission* in which the time of occurrence of a specified *significant instant* in each *byte, character,* word, block, or other unit of *data,* usually the leading edge of a *start signal,* is arbitrary and occurs without necessarily being dependent on preceding signals on the *channel.*   *Lightwave communication systems* may be operated in both *synchronous* or asynchronous *transmission modes.*   It is a *transmission* process such that between any two *significant instants* in the same group there is always an *integral* number of *unit intervals.*   In *data* transmission this group is a *block* or a *character;* in *telegraphy,* this group is a character.   Between two significant instants located in different groups there is not always an integral number of unit intervals.   Also see *anisochronous transmission; synchronous transmission.*

asynchronous working.   See *asynchronous operation.*

ATDM.   *Asynchronous time-division multiplexing.*

atmosphere.   **1.** The envelope of air surrounding the earth and bound to it by the earth's gravitational attraction, extending from the solid or liquid surface of the earth to an indefinite height, its density asymtotically approaching that of interplanetary space.   **2.** A unit of pressure equal to 101,325 newtons per m^2 or 14.70 lbs per in^2, representing the atmospheric pressure of mean sea level under standard conditions.   Also see *ionosphere; stratosphere; tropopause; troposphere.*

atmosphere laser.   See *longitudinally-excited atmosphere laser; transverse-excited atmosphere laser.*   See Figure A-10.

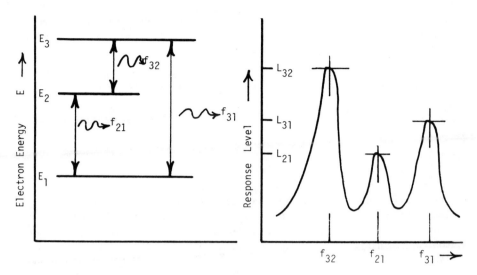

A-10. For an **atmosphere laser,** electrons returning to lower energy levels after excitation emit *photons* at energy levels (shown at left) producing the *spectral response* (at right) when the energies are summed over their average number per unit time for each level.

atmospheric duct. A *layer,* usually in the lower atmosphere, occasionally of great horizontal extent, in which the vertical *refractive index gradients* are such that *radio signals* are guided or *focused* within the duct and tend to follow the curvature of the earth with much less than normal attenuation.

atmospheric noise. *Radio noise* caused by natural atmospheric processes, primarily by lightning discharges in thunderstorms.

atom. See *radioactive atom.*

atomic defect absorption. In *lightwave transmission media,* (such as *optical fibers* and *integrated optical circuits* made of glass, silica, plastic, and other materials), the *absorption* of *light* energy caused by atomic changes that are introduced into the media, during or after their fabrication, by exposure to high radiation levels. For example, titanium doped silica can develop losses of several thousand db/km when the *optical fibers* are *drawn* under high temperature, and conventional *fiber optic* glasses can develop losses of 20,000 db/km during and after exposure to gamma radiation of 3000 *rads.*

atomic laser. A type of *laser* in which the *active medium* is an element in atomic form. Contrast with *molecular laser.*

attack. See *NAK attack.*

attack time.   In an *echo suppressor,* the time interval between the instant that the *signal* level at the *receiver* exceeds the suppression activate point and the instant when the suppression loss is introduced.

attack-time delay.   See *receiver attack-time delay; transmitter attack-time delay.*

attempt.   See *access attempt; block transfer attempt; disengagement attempt.*

attention sign.   In *semaphore communications,* the *flag* positions used as a *preliminary call* and to establish *communication.*

attenuation.   The decrease in power of a *signal, light beam,* or *lightwave,* either absolutely or as a fraction of a reference value. The decrease usually occurs as a result of *absorption, reflection, diffusion, scattering, deflection,* or *dispersion* from an original level and usually not as a result of *geometric spreading,* i.e., the inverse square of the distance effect. In an *optical fiber,* attenuation is undesirable for *transmission* purposes but desirable for prevention of leakage or clandestine detection.   Optical fibers have been classified as *high-loss* (over 100 db/km), *medium loss* (20 to 100 db/km), and *low-loss* (less than 20 db/km).   See *cloud attenuation; echo attenuation; optical dispersion attenuation; path attenuation; precipitation attenuation.*   Also see *attenuation term.*   See Figure A-11.   Also see Figure H-1.

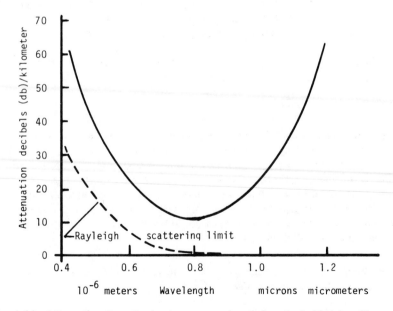

A-11.   **Attenuation** *(insertion loss)* versus *wavelength* for a typical *low-loss fiber.*

attenuation factor.   See *dispersion attenuation factor.*

attenuation-frequency distortion.   See *frequency distortion.*

attenuation term.   In the *propagation* of an *electromagnetic wave* in a *waveguide,* the term *a* in the expression for the exponential variation characteristic of guided waves: $e^{-pz} = e^{-ihz - az}$, that represents the *attenuation* or *pulse amplitude* diminution experienced per unit of propagation distance, *z,* of the wave. In a given guide, the phase term *h* is initially assumed to be independent of the attenuation term *a,* which is then found separately, assuming *h* does not change with losses, for an optical fiber. The attenuation term *a* is supplied by the manufacturer since it can be measured experimentally. Also see *phase term; propagation constant.*

attenuation test.   In an *optical fiber, bundle,* or *cable,* a test to measure the *attenuation factor,* usually in *decibels* per kilometer, at a specified *wavelength* (e.g., 0.907 microns or 907 nanometers). Usually the attenuation test is performed by measuring the attenuation in an entire reel or spool of fiber.

attenuator.   A device that has an *output signal* that is a function of, and less than, its *input signal.* The *attenuation* is expressed as a *transfer function* and often in negative *decibels.* If the output is greater than the input, that is if there is a *gain* in signal strength, the "attenuator" is an *amplifier.* See *continuous variable optical attenuator; fixed optical attenuator; optical attenuator; stepwise variable optical attenuator.*

at-the-dip.   In *flaghoist communications,* the *signaling condition* that exists when the flaghoist is hoisted (raised) three-fourths of the way up towards the point of hoist. Also see *close-up; flaghoist; hauled-down.*

attitude.   See *satellite attitude.*

attribute.   In *display systems,* a property or characteristic of any of its components or aspects. For example, the intensity, color, shape, or size of a *display element, group, image, segment, file, surface,* or *device.*

audio frequency (AF).   A *frequency* in the range from about 20 Hz to 20,000 Hz. *Electromagnetic waves* cannot be *detected* by the human ear, but *sound waves* in this range can. Also see *voice frequency.*

audio-frequency wave.   A *wave* with a *frequency* lying in the region of frequencies detectable by the human ear. It is assumed that the waves are *sound waves* of sufficient *intensity* to be heard. An audio-frequency wave has a frequency in the range of 20 to 20,000 Hz. *Lightwaves* as *carriers* can be *modulated* at audio frequencies and *transmitted* in *optical fibers, bundles,* and *cables.*

audio-visual.   Pertaining to the application and utilization of electrical, chemical, mechanical, and *optical* media to record or reproduce *audible signals* and *visual images*. Also see Figure D-5.

audit.   To conduct an independent review and examination of *system* records and activities in order to test for adequacy of system performance, compliance with policy, and areas of operations improvement. See *external security audit; internal security audit; security audit.*

audit trail.   A record of *system* activities that enables reconstruction, review, and examination of the sequence of activities that has occurred during operation of a system.

aural radio range.   See *visual-aural radio range.*

aurora.   The sporadic *radiant emission* from the upper *atmosphere* over middle and high latitudes. It is believed to be due primarily to emission from the nitrogen molecule, N_2; its molecular ion N_2^+; and atomic oxygen, O. Auroras are related to magnetic storms and the influx of charged particles from the sun. The exact details of the nature of the mechanisms involved are still being investigated. The aurora is most intense at times of magnetic storms, when it is also observed farthest toward the equator, and shows a periodicity related to the sun's twenty-seven-day rotation period and the eleven-year *sunspot* cycle. The distribution with height shows a pronounced maximum near 100 km. The lower limit is probably near 80 km. In northern latitudes, auroral displays are called aurora borealis, aurora polaris, or northern lights. In southern latitudes they are called aurora australis.

auroral display.   A particular visible occurrence of an *aurora* in one or more of its many shapes and colors, including arcs (bands of *light* extending across the sky, the highest point of the arc being in the direction of the magnetic meridian); *rays* (single lines, like a searchlight *beam* or bundle of lines); draperies or curtains (a curtainlike appearance, sharp at the bottom and tenuous at the top); crown or corona (rays appear to spread out from a single point in the sky); bands (similar to arcs, but less structured); streamers extending to great heights; and other shapeless, dynamic, and sun-lit forms. The auroral display can last from several seconds to several hours, with various levels of brightness and colors, and often pulsating at low frequencies of the order of 0.2 to 2.0 Hz. Displays appear as billowing or blowing curtains or areas of brightness running across the northern or southern night sky.

auroral zone.   1. The latitudes of the arctic, extending around the earth from Central Alaska, through James Bay, Southern Greenland, Iceland, Northern Norway, and along the Siberian coast, in which the aurora borealis (northern lights) occurs about 250 times per year; and the latitudes of the antarctic where the aurora australis (southern lights) occurs with a somewhat lower frequency. 2. A region in which a particular characteristic of an aurora occurs, such as extreme height, specific shapes, increased brightness, longer-lasting effects (in zones farther south), or particularly more or less frequent auroral displays.

authenticate.   1. An imperative request for a validation of a *communication* by use of an appropriate *authenticator*.   2. To issue an *authenticator*.

authentication.   1. A *communication security* measure designed to protect a *communication system* against acceptance of a fraudulent *transmission* or *simulation* by establishing the validity of a transmission, *message*, or *originator*.   2. A means of identifying *stations, users,* or equipment and verifying their eligibility to receive specific categories of *information*.   3. Evidence by proper signature or seal that a document is genuine or official.   4. The identification, verification, or validation of a *station, originator,* or *user* of a *system* or component thereof. See *challenge-and-reply authentication; message authentication; net authentication; self-authentication; transmission authentication.*

authentication equipment.   Equipment designed to provide protection against fraudulent *transmission* and *communication deception* or to establish the authenticity of a *transmission, message, station, originator, user,* or equipment.

authentication system.   1. A *system* designed for purposes of *authentication* and to serve as a secure means of establishing the authenticity of a *transmission* or *message,* or of challenging the identity of a *station*.   2. A *cryptosystem* or *cryptographic* process used for *authentication*.   3. A technique designed to provide effective *authentication*.

authenticator.   1. The means used to identify or verify the elegibility of a *station, originator,* or person to access specific categories of *information*.   2. A sequence of *characters* arranged in a predetermined manner that is inserted in a *message* for the purpose of *authentication*.   The authenticator may be a letter, numeral, group of letters or numerals, or both letters and numerals, selected or derived in a prearranged manner and usually inserted at a predetermined point within a *transmission* for the purpose of *authenticating* the message or transmission.

authority.   See *maritime air control authority; PTT authority.*

authorization.   The granting of a *user* (person, program, process, or equipment) the right of *access* to a *system.*

authorized frequency.   1. A *frequency* that is *allocated* and *assigned* by a competent authority to a specific *user* for a specific purpose.   2. A portion of the *radio spectrum,* normally with a width equal to the *necessary bandwidth* of *emission* plus twice the prescribed *frequency tolerance,* assigned to a user.

autocontrol. See *radio autocontrol.*

autocorrelation. The time integral of the product of a given *signal* and a time-delayed replica of itself. In mathematical notation:

$$A.C. = \int_{O}^{t} s(t) \cdot s(t - \tau)dt$$

where $s(t)$ is a function of time and $s(t - \tau)$ is a replica of $s(t)$ delayed by the time τ. In the process of correlating two or more interrelated signals or other phenomena, autocorrelation is the special case of *cross correlation* in which the functions are identical in shape but occur at different times. Also see *cross correlation.*

AUTODIN. A worldwide automatic *communication network* of the U.S. Defense Department for *transmission* of *digital data.* It is an acronym for automatic digital network.

AUTODIN operation. Mode 1: A *duplex synchronous message transmission network* operation with automatic error and channel controls allowing independent and *simultaneous two-way message transmission.* **Mode 2:** A *duplex asynchronous network* operation, without automatic error and channel controls, allowing simultaneous two-way message transmission. **Mode 3:** A duplex synchronous network operation with automatic error and channel controls utilizing one-way message transmission. The *backward direction* is used exclusively for error control and *channel* coordination purposes. The Mode 3 channel is reversible on a message basis. **Mode 4:** A unidirectional asynchronous network operation with a send only or a receive only capability and without error control and without channel coordination. The Mode 4 channel is nonreversible. **Mode 5:** A duplex asynchronous network operation allowing independent and simultaneous two-way message transmission. *Control characters* are used to acknowledge receipt of messages and perform limited channel coordination.

AUTODIN user. A person, installation, or activity having access to the *AUTODIN network* through an AUTODIN *switching center.*

automatic answer-back code exchange. Automatic identification of stations in which each *communication terminal* or *data terminal equipment* transmits its own *answer-back code.*

automatic answering. *Answering* by which the called *data terminal equipment (DTE)* automatically responds to the *calling signal.* The *call* may be established whether or not the called DTE is attended by a human *operator.*

automatic branch exchange. See *private automatic branch exchange (PABX).*

automatic calling. A facility by which *selection signals* must be entered contiguously at the full *character rate.* The *address* characters will be generated by the *data terminal equipment (DTE).* A limit may be imposed on the system to prevent more than a permitted number of unsuccessful *call* attempts to the same address within a specified period.

automatic charge indication. The automatic indication of the charge of a *call* given by a *communication system* to the paying *terminal* either prior to the release of the paying terminal, or by recall at a convenient time.

automatic continuous-tape relay switching. See *semiautomatic continuous-tape relay switching.*

automatic data processing (ADP). An interacting group of procedures, processes, methods, personnel, and equipment that is used to automatically perform a series of *data processing* operations that change the *input data.*

automatic data processing equipment (ADPE). *Data processors,* associated *input-output* devices, and auxiliary equipment using electronic circuitry to perform arithmetic and logic operations automatically by means of internally stored *programs.*

automatic data processing system (ADPS). In *communications* and *teleprocessing, automatic data processing equipment (ADPE)* linked together by *communication* and *data transmission* equipment to form an *integrated system* for the *processing* and *transfer* of *data.*

automatic date-and-time indication. In a *communication system,* the automatic indication of date and time of the commencement of a *call* or *message* to the *calling terminal* or to both the calling and *called terminals.*

automatic digital switching. See *tactical automatic digital switching (TADS).*

automatic duration indication. The automatic indication of the chargeable time of a *call* given by a *communication system* to the paying *terminal* either prior to the release of the paying terminal, or by recall at a convenient time.

automatic error detection. 1. The automatic *detection* and indication of an *error* in a *transmitted signal.* 2, Pertaining to the *detection* of *errors* in the *messages* of a *communication system* by automatic means.

automatic error detection and correction system. 1. A *system* that uses an *error-detecting code* so conceived that any false or incorrect *signal* initiates a repetition of the *transmitted character* incorrectly received.   2. A *system* in which *errors* that occur in *transmission* are *detected* and corrected automatically, through the use of error-detection equipment and error-detection codes without initiating a request for repetition.   Error-correcting codes are usually *redundant codes.*

automatic exchange.   A *telephone system* in which *communication* between *users* is effected without the aid of an *operator* by means of *switches* set in operation by the originating user's equipment.   Also see *data switching exchange; switching center.*

automatic gain control (AGC).   A feature of an *active device* that enables its *output signal* strength or *intensity* to be **(a)** a desired function of its *input* signal strength or **(b)** independent of its input signal strength or intensity, thus maintaining a more constant level of ouptut strength or intensity when the input signal strength fluctuates, without losing the intelligence in the *modulating signal.*   Automatic gain control is usually applied to amplifiers, *antennas,* and *light sources.*   See *instantaneous automatic gain control.*

automatic identification.   The automatic *transmission* of the identification of the *calling terminal* or *station* to the *called terminal* or station, or vice versa, or the identification of terminals and stations to one another.   Automatic identification may be established when a *connection* is made.   See *terminal automatic identification.*

automatic message switching.   A method of automatically handling *messages* through a *switching center,* either from local *users* or from other switching centers, whereby a distant electrical *connection* is established between the *calling* and *called stations,* or a *store-and-forward data transmission system* is used.

automatic multilevel precedence.   The automatic sensing and application of *precedence procedures* in accordance with established criteria to include several levels of *preemption* and override capability in an automatic *data transmission* or *telephone switching network.*

automatic numbering equipment.   Equipment that automatically generates and *transmits* the *transmission identification number* for each *message.*

automatic numbering transmitter.   An automatic *transmitter* that automatically *transmits* a serial number before each *message.*

automatic preemption.   A *telephone network* or *data transmission system facility* that permits a *user* to enter the *precedence* assigned to a *call* at the time the call is placed, *dialed,* or *keyed.*   The system processes the call with the assigned precedence and automatically *preempts* circuits with lower precedence calls when required or as necessary in accordance with the preemption criteria.

automatic programming. The process of using a *computer* to assist in generating (preparing) a *computer program.*

automatic radio relay plane. An aircraft that contains the necessary equipment to perform the function of automatically relaying *radio messages* intended for other aircraft.

automatic receiver. A *radio receiver* that performs automatic *tuning,* slowly *sweeps* the *frequency spectrum,* alerts the operator when a *signal* is picked up, and records the pickup. Also see *panoramic receiver.*

automatic recovery quotient (ARQ). An *automatic error detection and correction system,* used in *telegraph systems,* in which the *backward channel* is used to obtain repetition of corrupted *signals* until they are received uncorrupted.

automatic relay equipment. See *telegraph automatic relay equipment (TARE).*

automatic relay system. A *system* that contains the means of *switching* that causes automatic equipment to record and retransmit *messages.* Also see *semi-automatic relay system.*

automatic request-repeat (ARQ). A *system* of *error control* for *data transmission* in which the *receiver terminal* is arranged to detect a transmission error and automatically *transmit* a *request-repeat signal* to the transmitter terminal. The transmitter terminal then retransmits the *character, block,* or *message* until it is either correctly received or the error persists beyond a predetermined number of repeated transmissions. Synonymous with *decision-feedback system; error-detecting-and-feedback system; request-repeat system.*

automatic retransmission. A recording of *received signals* followed immediately by their *automatic transmission.*

automatic retransmitter. Equipment that automatically records and *retransmits signals* that it receives.

automatic search jammer. An *intercept* (search) *receiver* and a *jamming transmitter* that can search for *signals* that have specific characteristics and then automatically *jam* them. The search may be performed in the *frequency, time, space, polarization,* and other *domains.*

automatic secure voice communication system. See *AUTOSEVOCOM System.*

automatic send-receive teletypewriter. A *teletypewriter* arranged for automatic *transmission* and *reception* of *messages.* Also see *keyboard send-receive (KSR) teletypewriter; receive-only (RO) teletypewriter.*

automatic sequential connection. A *facility* provided by a *public data network service* to connect automatically, in a prearranged sequence, the *data terminal equipment (DTE)* at each of a set of specified *addresses* to a single DTE at a specified address.

automatic spot jammer. A *spot jammer* with a *noise* generator, having a *frequency bandwidth* that is small in comparison to the operating band, that automatically tracks frequency and sets the jammer center frequency to the frequency being *tracked.* Single and multiple spot jammers use a *look-through* period with rapidly sweeping receivers to detect and analyze *signals.* In these jammers, the jamming *transmitter* operates between the look-through intervals. These jammers are limited by fixed transmission time, *time sharing,* and *signal delay* in *reception* and *transmission.*

automatic switching. A method of *communication system* operation that effects the automatic interconnection of *channels, circuits,* and *trunks* and the handling of *traffic* through a *switching facility.*

automatic switching equipment. *Switching equipment* that has the capability of automatically processing *traffic* without operator intervention. For example, it can recognize *dial* and pushbutton (touch-tone) *signaling; switch* from *line*-to-line, *trunk*-to-trunk, trunk-to-line, and line-to-trunk; and automatically *route calls,* handle *precedences,* and dispose of incomplete calls.

automatic system. See *Wheatstone automatic system.*

automatic tape relay. A *system* of *tape relay* that embodies *automatic switching.*

automatic telegraph transmitter. A *telegraph transmitter* in which the forming of *signals* is not controlled by an *operator* but is actuated step-by-step from a signal *storage* device, usually a *perforated tape* and a *tape reader.*

automatic telegraphy. *Telegraphy* in which manual operations are effectively reduced or eliminated by the use of automatic equipment.

automatic telephone system. A *switching system* through which *telephone calls* are *routed* automatically under control of the *calling party's* instrument.

automatic traffic overload protection. A *communication system* operating procedure in which automatic equipment is used to reduce the volume of *line, trunk,* or *switch traffic* in accordance with specified line *load* control categories when demands for service exceed the *capacity* to meet the demand. For example, automatically delaying *dial tone* or denying *originating user* call privileges on certain lines. The protection is based on line load control designations.

automatic voice network. An *automatically-switched telephone network.* See *AUTOVON.*

AUTOSEVOCOM System. A worldwide *secure voice transmission system* of the U.S. Defense Department. It has *cryptosecure telephones* connected to *wideband switchboards* interconnected by *narrowband trunks.* AUTOSEVOCOM is an acronym for automatic secure voice communication.

AUTOVON. A worldwide *automatic voice-grade communication network* for end-to-end *circuit-switched* voice connections of the U.S. Defense Department. *Message-switched digital traffic* of the *AUTODIN* is carried between switching centers of the AUTOVON. AUTOVON is an acronym for automatic voice network.

AUTOVON user. A person, installation, or activity having access to the *AUTOVON network* through an AUTOVON *switching center.*

autumnal equinox. The line of intersection of the celestial equatorial and *ecliptic* planes at which the sun passes from the northern into the southern hemisphere. It occurs about the 22nd of September, bringing autumn to the northern hemisphere and spring to the southern hemisphere.

auxiliary channel. In *data transmission,* a *secondary channel* whose direction of *transmission* is independent of the *primary channel* and is controlled by an appropriate set of secondary control interchange *circuits.*

auxiliary operation. An *offline* operation performed by equipment not under the direct control of some other reference or given equipment, for example an operation performed by a *front-end* or *communication computer.*

auxiliary power. An alternate source of electric *power,* serving as backup for the *primary power* at the station main bus or prescribed subbus. An offline unit provides electrical isolation between the primary power and the *critical technical load;* an *online* unit does not provide electrical isolation between the primary power and the critical technical load. A Class A power source is a primary power source, that is, a source that assures an essentially continuous supply of power. Types of auxiliary power service include: Class B, a standby power plant to cover extended outages (days); Class C, a quick start (10 to 60 seconds) unit to cover short-term outages (hours); Class D, an uninterruptible (no-break) unit using stored energy to provide continuous power within specified *voltage* and *frequency* tolerances. Also see *primary power.*

availability. A measure of the degree to which a *system,* subsystem, or device is operable and in a committable state at the start of a mission when the mission is called for at an unknown or random instant of time. The conditions determining operability and committability must be specified. Also see *unavailability.*

available-at-action-office time. See *message available-at-action-office time.*

available-for-delivery time. See *message available-for-delivery time.*

available line length. In *facsimile transmission,* the portion of the *scanning line* that can be used specifically for *picture signals.* Synonymous with *useful line.*

available point. An *addressable point,* in the *display space* on the *display surface* of a *display device,* at which one or more characteristics of a *display element, display group,* or *display image* color, intensity, on/off condition, shape, or orientation may be changed. The characteristics that may be changed are usually changed by the operator or controlling *computer program.*

avalanche multiplication. In *semiconductors,* the sudden or rapid increase in the number or density of *hole-electron* pairs (carriers for conduction) that is caused when the semiconductor is subjected to high (near breakdown) electric fields. The increase in carriers causes a further increase. Incident photons of sufficient energy can still further increase multiplication of the carriers. These effects are used in *avalanche photodetectors.*

avalanche photodetector. A *photodetector* that uses the avalanche multiplication effect to increase the photocurrent. Also see *avalanche photodiode.*

avalanche photodiode (APD). A *photo-detecting* diode that is sensitive to incident *light* energy by increasing its *electrical conductivity* by exponentially increasing the number of *electrons* in its *conduction band energy levels* through the *absorption* of the *photons* of energy, electron interaction, and an applied bias voltage. The *photodiode* is designed to take advantage of *avalanche multiplication of photocurrent.* As the reverse-bias voltage approaches the breakdown voltage, *hole* electron pairs created by absorbed photons acquire sufficient energy to create additional hole-electron pairs when they collide with *substrate* atoms. Thus, a multiplication effect is achieved. Also see *avalanche photodetector.* See Figure A-12.

A-12. A silicon **avalanche photodiode** with integral *light pipes*. *Operating parameters* include an average *photocurrent* density of 5 mA/mm², a *quantum efficiency* of 85%, and a *responsivity* of 75 A/W at 900 *nanometers wavelength*. (Courtesy of RCA Electro-Optics and Devices.)

avalanche photodiode coupler. A *coupling* device that enables the coupling of *light* energy from an *optical fiber* onto the photosensitive surface of an *avalanche photodiode* (APD) of a *photodetector* (photon detector) at the receiving end of an *optical fiber data link*. The coupler may be only a fiber *pigtail* epoxied to the APD. Synonymous with *APD coupler*.

average block length. The average value of the total number of *bits* in *blocks transferred* across a *user-communication* functional *interface*. The average *block length* is specified by the *communication system operator* and is used in determining values for the block-oriented performance *parameters*. In systems where the information transferred across the functional interface is not delimited into blocks, the *data signaling rate* is used instead of the average block length.

average error rate. In a *transmission system*, the ratio of the number of incorrect *bits, characters, words, blocks,* or other *data units* received to the total number of bits, characters, words, blocks, or other data units sent correctly.

average information content. See *character mean entropy.*

average information rate. The *mean entropy* per *character* per unit of time. The average information rate may be expressed in a unit such as a *shannon* per second.

average power. In a *pulsed laser,* the energy per pulse (joules) times the *pulse repetition rate* (Hertz), usually expressed in watts.

average ratio. See *peak-to-average ratio.*

average terrain. See *antenna height above average terrain.*

average transinformation content. See *mean transinformation content.*

average transinformation rate. The *mean transinformation content* per *character* per unit of time. The average transinformation rate may be expressed in a unit such as a *shannon* per second.

average transmission rate. See *effective transmission speed.*

averaging. See *frequency averaging.*

aviation instructional station. A *land station* or *mobile station* in the *aeronautical mobile service* used for *radiocommunication* for instructions to students or pilots while actually operating aircraft or engaged in training flights.

avoidance routing. A *survivability* feature of a *communication system* in which *messages* are *routed* so as to avoid critical areas, such as congested areas, disaster areas, or obstacles.

avoidance system. See *terrain avoidance system.*

AVPO. *Axial vapor-phase oxidation process.*

axial bundle. A cone of *electromagnetic rays* that emanate from an *object* point that is located on the *optical axis* of a *lens system.* Also see *aperture stop.*

axial misalignment loss. See *angular misalignment loss.*

axial-ratio polarization. See *elliptical polarization.*

axial vapor-phase oxidation process (AVPO). A *vapor-phase oxidation (VPO) process* for making *graded-index (GI) optical fibers* in which the glass *preform* is grown radially rather than longitudinally as in other processes. The *refractive index* is controlled in a spatial domain rather than a time domain. The chemical gases are burned in an oxyhydrogen flame, as in the outside vapor-phase oxidation *(OVPO) process,* to produce a stream of soot particles to produce the graded refractive index.

axis. See *optical axis; primary axis; secondary axis; signal communication axis.*

axis of signal communication. See *signal communication axis.*

axis paraboloidal mirror. See *off-axis paraboloidal mirror.*

azimuth. 1. A given horizontal angular direction from a specified reference direction, measured in a clockwise direction (looking vertically downward) from the reference direction. 2. A direction expressed as a horizontal angle usually in degrees or mils and measured clockwise from north. Thus, azimuth will be true azimuth, grid azimuth, or magnetic azimuth depending upon which north is used. 3. The angle at the zenith between the observer's celestial meridian and the vertical circle through a heavenly body. Also see *altitude-over-azimuth; back azimuth; reciprocal bearing; reciprocal heading.*

azimuth-over-altitude. Pertaining to an *antenna* mount in which the altitude (elevation) axis is primary and is fixed to earth. The azimuth drive is secondary and is variable. The mount is used in equatorial regions for drifting equatorial *satellites.* Synonymous with *azimuth-over-elevation.*

azimuth-over-elevation. See *azimuth-over-altitude.*

B

back. See *call back; ring back.*

back azimuth. A direction opposite to an *azimuth,* that is, 180° from a given azimuth. Also see *azimuth; reciprocal bearing, reciprocal heading.*

back-bias gain-control circuit. See *detector back-bias gain-control circuit.*

backbone. **1.** The high *traffic* denisty portion of a *communication network.* **2.** In a *communication network,* a primary *forward direction path* traced sequentially through two or more major *relay* or *switching stations.* A backbone consists of *switches* and interswitch *trunks.* **3.** The *route* between two principal *terminal microwave stations.*

back focal length (BFL). The distance measured from the vertex of the back surface of a *lens* to its rear *focal point.*

background. See *display background.*

background-limited infrared detector. An *infrared detector* that is background *radiation noise* limited in its sensitivity when viewing an *ambient temperature* background. The limitation is primarily due to its inherent inability to shield itself from all *ambient infrared noise.* The background radiation tends to saturate the detector, that is, create such a large signal that infrared signals that do occur cannot be detected. For example, the infrared from an aircraft approaching a detector from the direction of a brightly visible sun cannot be detected because the infrared from the sun obliterates the infrared from the aircraft; or an infrared personnel detector may not function when exposed to the radiation of the noonday sun.

background noise. The total *system noise* in the absence of *data transmission.* It is usually independent of the presence or absence of a *signal.*

back lobe. In the *radiation pattern* of an *antenna* or *light source,* a lobe — or the *radiant* energy density corresponding to the lobe — that is directed opposite to the *main lobe.* The back lobe is usually extremely small compared to the main lobe. The energy density is far lower at a given distance from the *source.*

backlog. See *significant backlog.*

backscatter. **1.** To *scatter* or randomly *reflect electromagnetic waves* in such a manner that a component is directed back toward the *antenna* or *light source* that *emitted* the waves. Backscatter normally occurs to lightwaves and radio waves.

2. The components of *electromagnetic waves* that are directed back toward their *source* when resolved along a line from the source to the point of *deflection.* Back-scattering occurs in *optical fibers* due to reflecting surfaces of particles or occlusions in the *transmission medium,* resulting in *signal attenuation.* The term scatter can be applied to *reflection* or *refraction* by relatively uniform media but it is usually taken to mean *propagation* in which the *wavefront* and direction are modified in a relatively disorderly fashion. Backscatter also occurs in *atmospheric scattering* and *ionospheric scattering.* Also see *forward scatter.*

back scattering. In *radio wave* and *lightwave propagation,* that form of *wave scattering* in which at least one component of the scattered wave is directed opposite to the *incident wave.* A back-scattered wave is often referred to as *backscatter.* Also see *forward scatter; scatter.*

back-surface mirror. An *optical mirror* on which the highly *reflective coating* or reflecting surface is applied to the back surface of the mirror, i.e., not to the surface of first *incidence* of *light.* The *reflected ray* of light must pass through the *substrate* twice, once as part of the incident light and once as the reflected light. Also see *front-surface mirror.*

back-tell. *Information transfer* from facilities at a higher to a lower operational level or echelon of command or administration.

back-to-back connection. A direct *connection* between the *output* of a *transmitter* and the *input* of an associated *receiver.* This eliminates the effects of the *transmission channel* or *transmission medium.*

backward channel. **1.** The *channel* of a *data circuit* that *transmits data* in a direction opposite to that of its associated *forward channel.* The backward channel is usually used for transmission of *supervisory, acknowledgement,* or *error-control signals.* The direction of flow of these *signals* is in the direction opposite to that in which *user information* is being *transferred.* The *bandwidth* of this channel is usually less than that of the *forward channel* (information channel). The direction of transmission in the backward channel is restricted by the interchange circuit that controls the direction of transmission in the primary channel. If information is simultaneously transferred in both directions, the momentary *data sink* to *data source* direction determines which shall be called the backward channel. **2.** In *data transmission systems,* a secondary *channel* in which the direction of *transmission* is constrained to be opposite to that of the primary or *forward channel.* The same *optical fiber* can be used for the forward and backward channel at the same time. The backward channel can be used for control *signals.* Also see *forward channel.*

backward direction. **1.** In a *communication system,* the direction from a *data sink* to a *data source.* **2.** The direction from an *addressee* to a *message originator.* **3.** The direction from a *called party* to a *calling party.* Also see *forward direction.*

backward ionospheric scatter. See *backward propagation ionospheric scatter.*

backward propagation ionospheric scatter. *Ionospheric scatter* in the *backward direction.* Synonymous with *backward ionospheric scatter.*

backward signal. A *signal* sent in the direction from the *called* to the *calling station,* from a *data sink* to a *data source,* or from a *called party's end-instrument* to a *calling party's* end-instrument.

backward supervision. The use of *supervisory signals* from a *secondary station* to a *primary station.* Also see *secondary station.*

balance. See *earth radiation balance; hybrid balance; line balance; line filter balance; longitudinal balance.*

balanced. Pertaining to electrical symmetry.

balanced amplitude modulation. *Suppressed carrier modulation* in which the *modulator* suppresses the carrier by means of a *balanced circuit,* such as a modulator in which the modulating *voltage* enters a *transformer primary* with an *amplifier* connected to each secondary end and the carrier *signal* is fed through the center tap of the transformer in a push-pull connection. The resulting signal can be either a *single-sideband* or a *double-sideband amplitude-modulated signal.* Since either sideband can be suppressed as well as the carrier, all the intelligence is contained in one of the sidebands and none is contained in the carrier. There will be no *direct-current (DC)* component in the *antenna feed* signal. Also see *phase exchange keying.*

balanced code. In *pulse code modulation (PCM),* a *code* whose *digital* sum variation is finite. Balance codes have no *direct-current (DC)* component in their *frequency spectrum.* Also see *pulse-code modulation.*

balanced line. A *transmission line* consisting of two *conductors* in the presence of a *ground,* capable of being operated in such a way that when the *voltages* of the two conductors at all transverse planes are equal in magnitude and opposite in polarity with respect to ground, the currents in the two conductors are equal in magnitude and opposite in direction.

balanced link-level operation. The operation of *data links* at the link level that make use of *balanced lines.*

balanced modulation. A method of suppressing the *carrier* in an *amplitude modulated wave* so that only *sideband signals* appear in the wave and there is approximately equal *power* in each sideband, that is in the *upper* and *lower sidebands.*

balanced signal pair. See *balanced line.*

balanced station. A *station* that can perform *balanced link-level operations.* A balanced station generates commands, interprets responses, interprets received commands, and generates responses.

balancing.   See *power balancing.*

balancing network.   **1.** A *circuit* used to *simulate* the *impedance* of a uniform two-wire *cable* or open-wire circuit over a selected range of *frequencies.* **2.** A device used between a *balanced line* or device and an *unbalanced line* or device for the purpose of transforming from balanced to unbalanced or from unbalanced to balanced operation.

ball.   See *control ball.*

balsam.   See *Canada balsam.*

balun.   A *radio frequency (RF) balancing network* for *coupling* between balanced and unbalanced lines or devices.   It is normally used between equipment and *transmission lines* or between transmission lines and *antennas.*

band.   **1.** In *communications,* the *frequency spectrum* between two defined limits. **2.** A group of tracks on a *magnetic recording medium,* such as a magnetic drum, magnetic disk, or *magnetic card.*   See *assigned frequency band; baseband; conduction band; energy band; F-band; frequency band; frequency guard band; G-band; I-band; infrared band; J-band; K-band; M-band; multiphonon band; narrow band; pass-band; phonon band; Q-band, single-band; subband; stop-band; time guard band; valence band; V-band; vestigial sideband; X-band.*

band compaction.   See *variable-tolerance-band compaction.*

band edge absorption.   In *optical fiber* glass, *absorption* that occurs in the *visible* region that extends from the *ultraviolet* region of the *spectrum.*   It is usually caused by oxides of silicon, sodium, boron, calcium, germanium, and other elements, and by the hydroxyl ion.

band-elimination filter.   See *band-stop filter.*

band-gap energy.   The difference between allowable energy levels of the electrons of an atom.   An electron that absorbs a *photon* absorbs the band-gap energy. When an electron loses band-gap energy a photon with energy equal to the band-gap energy is emitted.

banding.   See *rubber-banding.*

B-AND-NOT-A gate.   A two-*input, binary,* logic coincidence *circuit* or device capable of performing the *logic operations* of B AND NOT A.   Thus, if A is a statement and B is a statement, the result is true only if B is true and A is false. For the other three combinations of A and B, the result is false.   Synonymous with *B-except-A gate* and with *negative (B-implies-A) gate.*   See Figure B-1.

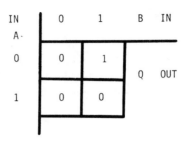

B-1. A table showing the *input* and *output digits* of a **B-AND-NOT-A gate.**

band-pass filter. A device that *transmits* a *band* of *frequencies* and blocks or *absorbs* all other frequencies not in the band. The band has a finite upper limit and a nonzero lower limit. If the lower limit is zero frequency and there is a finite upper limit, the filter is a *low-pass filter*. If the upper limit is infinitely high and there is a finite lower limit, it is a *high-pass filter*. Most *optical filters* are extremely narrow band-pass filters in that they transmit a very narrow band of frequencies, i.e., are *monochromatic*. Also see *high-pass filter; low-pass filter*.

band-rejection filter. See *band-stop filter*.

bandspreading technique. In *electromagnetic transmission,* the artificial dispersion of a *signal* over a substantially wider *bandwidth* than that of the original signal. *Modulation* is normally performed according to a prearranged, *coded*, high speed, *digital* process. The resulting signal will have a *noise*-like, *wideband* structure and can only be received and decoded by the use of a *correlation* process. *Synchronization* must be maintained with the prearranged code. Also see *code division multiple access; spread spectrum multiple access*.

band-stop filter. A *filter* having a single continuous *attenuation band,* neither the upper nor lower *cut-off frequencies* being either zero or infinite. Synonymous with *band-elimination filter; band-rejection filter; band-suppression filter*.

band-suppression filter. See *band-stop filter*.

bandwidth. **1.** A range of *frequencies,* usually specifying the number of *hertz* of the *band* or the upper and lower limiting frequencies. **2.** The range of *frequencies* that a device is capable of generating, handling, passing, or allowing, usually the range of frequencies in which the *responsibility* is not reduced greater than 3 *dB* from the maximum response. It is the difference between the limiting *frequencies* of a continuous frequency *band* in which performance with respect to some characteristic falls within specified limits. See *Carson bandwidth; facsimile bandwidth; necessary bandwidth; nominal bandwidth; occupied bandwidth; radio frequency bandwidth; spectral bandwidth*.

bandwidth limited. **1.** In *transmission circuits,* pertaining to an ability to pass *signals* with *frequency* components that lie only within certain limits. An *optical* *filter* that passes only a narrow *frequency band* — for example, in the blue or red region only — is bandwidth limited. Many *light sources* and *photodetectors* are bandwidth-limited because of the characteristics of the materials used in their construction. **2.** In a communication system, pertaining to a signal with spectral components that extend only between specified frequencies. If a signal is passed through a certain filter with a transfer function of 1 for frequencies equal to or less than the maximum frequency, the signal will be transmitted without distortion. Signals that are not themselves originally bandwidth limited may be passed through filters that introduce band limiting at either high or low frequencies. Hence, distortion is introduced. **3.** In a communication system, pertaining to the situation that exists when the total traffic capacity is limited by the allocated available bandwidth or assigned frequency bandwidth.

bandwidth product.   See *gain-bandwidth product.*

bandwidth rule.   See *Carson bandwidth rule.*

bank.   See *channel bank; data bank.*

bar.   See *writing bar.*

Barker code.   A *binary code* suitable for *pulse code modulation* and *synchronization.*   It has optimal *correlation* properties and relative immunity to *phase displacement* caused by *random pulses* immediately adjacent to the patterns compared to other codes, such as a *pure binary numeration system code.*   It is also relatively immune to phase displacement by errors in the *transmitter.*

barrage jammer.   A *jammer* that can spread its *radiated electromagnetic* energy over a wide *frequency band* and is therefore capable of jamming several *transmitters* simultaneously. It is also capable of preventing escape from jamming simply by shifting the transmission frequency of the transmitter being jammed. The jammer is normally *tunable* over a wide *frequency spectrum.*   However, spreading the energy over a wide frequency spectrum results in less *power* at a particular frequency.

barrage jamming.   *Jamming* accomplished by *transmitting* a *band* of *frequencies* that is large with respect to the *bandwidth* of a single *emitter.*   Barrage jamming may be accomplished by presetting multiple *jammers* on adjacent frequencies or by using a single *wideband transmitter.*   Barrage jamming makes it possible to jam emitters on different frequencies simultaneously and reduces the need for operator assistance or complex control equipment. These advantages are gained at the expense of reduced jamming power at any given frequency.

barrage jamming radar display.   See *spot-barrage jamming radar display.*

barred.   See *call barred.*

barred facility.   See *calls barred facility.*

barred signal. See *access-barred signal.*

barrel distortion. In *display systems,* a *distortion* of the *image* of an *object* in such a manner that the *display element, display group,* or *display image* of an otherwise straight-sided square or rectangular object has its sides bowed out (i.e., *convex*) relative to the object. Contrast with *pincushion distortion.*

barrier-layer cell. See *photovoltaic cell.*

base. See *data base.*

baseband. The *band* of *frequencies* associated with or comprising an original *signal* from a *modulated source.* In the process of modulation, the baseband is occupied by the aggregate of the transmitted signals used to modulate a carrier. In demodulation, it is the recovered aggregate of the transmitted signals. The term is commonly applied to cases where the ratio of the upper to the lower limit of the frequency band is large compared to unity. See *multiplex baseband; radio baseband.*

baseband receive terminal. See *multiplex baseband receive terminal; radio baseband receive terminal.*

baseband send terminal. See *multiplex baseband send terminal; radio baseband send terminal.*

baseband signal. A *digital data stream* that *transmits information* in the form of a *voltage level* or *signal amplitude.*

basecom. *Base communications.*

base communications (basecom). *Communication services* provided for the operation of a military post, camp, installation, station, or activity. Basecom includes the installation, operation, maintenance, augmentation, modification, and rehabilitation of communication networks, systems, facilities, and equipment that provide local and intrabase communications, including off-post extensions. Synonymous with *communication base section.*

baseline. In a *display device,* a line representing a reference level, usually zero, on which a scale, such as a time, *frequency,* or distance scale is placed, for the display of *signal,* waves, or other events. Display devices that exhibit a baseline include the cathode ray tube, vidicon, reflectometer, spectroscope, and fiberscope. See *direction-finding baseline.*

base station. A *land station* in a *land mobile service* carrying on a *communication service* with *land mobile stations.* A base station may also communicate with other base stations incident to communication with land mobile stations.

BASIC. A *computer programming language* with simple *syntax* (grammar) and *semantics* (mnemonic instructions) designed for ease of learning. It is used for conversational mode, numeric computations, and *string* handling. The name is derived from Beginner's All-purpose Symbolic Instruction Code. Many variations (dialects) are in use.

basic group.   1. In *frequency division multiplexing* of wideband systems, a number of voice *channels,* either within a *supergroup* or separately, that is normally composed of up to 12 voice channels occupying the *frequency band* from 60 to 108 kHz. Each basic group of 12 may be subdivided into four 3-channel *pregroups.* This is CCITT Basic Group B. Basic Group A in *carrier telephone systems,* is an assembly of 12 channels, occupying *upper sidebands* in the 12 to 60 kHz band. **2.** In *signaling,* a group of *characters* to which suffixes or prefixes may be added to form signal groups for specific signaling purposes. See *channel basic group.*

basic mode. See *laser basic mode.*

basic mode link control. The control of a *data link* at the data link level rather than at higher *layers* (levels) such as in *high-level data link control (HDLC).*

basic status. In *data transmission,* the state of readiness or capability of a *secondary station* to send or receive a *frame* containing an *information field.*

basket grip. A device for gripping a *cable* so that the pulling force is transferred to the sheath.

batch processing.   1. The *processing* of *data* or the accomplishment of jobs accumulated in advance in such a manner that each accumulation thus formed is processed or accomplished in the same *run.* **2.** The *processing* of *data* accumulated over a period of time. **3.** Loosely, the execution of *computer programs* serially. **4.** Pertaining to the technique of executing a set of *computer programs* such that each is completed before the next program of the set is started. **5.** Pertaining to the sequential *input* of *computer programs* or *data.*

bathtub curve. A curve, shaped like the cross-sectional profile of a bathtub, that characterizes failure rates of large populations or large numbers of components, such as are used in communication systems, as a function of time. The curve shows an *early failure period* with a high failure rate that weeds out defective items; followed by a nearly *constant failure period* with a low failure rate based on statistical failures; followed by a *wear-out failure period* with a rapidly rising failure rate as the life of each component expires. Also see *component life.* See Figure B-2.

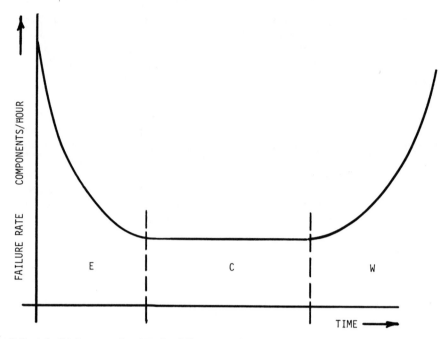

B-2. A **bathtub curve** showing the failure rate of *components* as a function of time in a *system* consisting of many components. E is the *early failure period,* C is the *constant failure period,* and W is the *wearout failure period.*

battery. See *common battery; local battery; station battery.*

battery exchange. See *common-battery exchange.*

battery signaling. See *common-battery signaling.*

battery signaling exchange. See *common-battery signaling exchange.*

baud. The basic unit of *modulation* rate or *signaling speed.* One baud corresponds to a rate of one *unit interval* per second, where the modulation rate is expressed as the reciprocal of the duration in seconds of the smallest unit interval — i.e., of the shortest *signal element.* Thus, if the shortest signal-element unit interval is 20 msec, the modulation rate is 50 baud; in *Morse code,* if a *dot* is 10 msec, the speed is 100 baud. As a result, the speed in baud is the number of shortest discrete conditions or signal events per second. In bilevel signaling, the baud rate is always equal to or greater than the *bit* rate, since several signal elements may be required to represent a bit. It is an instantaneous rate, not an average rate. It can change from instant to instant depending on the manner of *transmission* and signal representation of *pulses* or bits.

Baudot code. A five-unit *synchronous code,* developed about 1880, that has been replaced by the *start-stop asynchronous International Telegraph Alphabet Number 2.* The term Baudot code should not be used to identify ITA Number 2.

bay. See *coaxial patch bay; direct-current (DC) patch bay; group patch bay; patch bay; U-link bay.*

BCD. *Binary coded decimal.*

BCH code. *Bose-Chaudhuri-Hocquenghem code.*

beacon. A *light* or electronic *source* that emits a distinctive or characteristic *signal* used for the determination of bearings, courses, or location. See *crash locator beacon; fan marker beacon; marker beacon; nondirectional beacon; personnel locator beacon; radar beacon; radar homing beacon; satellite beacon; search-and-rescue beacon; z-marker beacon.*

beacon frequency. See *search-and-rescue beacon frequency.*

beacon navigation system. A navigation system that employs *electromagnetic* energy to establish a *signal* pattern that can be followed or used as a guide in as much as the direction of motion relative to a line from present position to the source can be measured.

beacon precipitation gage station. See *radar beacon precipitation gage station.*

beacon station. See *aeronautical marker beacon station; aeronautical radio beacon station; marine radio beacon station; radio beacon station.*

beam. A shaft or column of *electromagnetic radiation* consisting of parallel, converging, or diverging rays. See *diverging beam; fan beam; Gaussian beam;* laser beam; *radio beam; spot beam; telecommunication laser beam.*

beam-angle-between-half-power-points. See *emission beam-angle-between-half-power-points.*

beam antenna. See *narrow-beam antenna; wide-beam antenna.*

beam diameter. In an *electromagnetic beam,* the lateral distance between the two points at which the *optical power density* or energy density is a specified fraction, typically $1/2$, $1/e$, $1/e^2$, or $1/10$ of the peak density. Also see *beam width.*

beam divergence. In an *electromagnetic beam,* the increase in beam diameter with increase in distance from the *source* — for example, in a light beam, a *laser's* exit *aperture.* The *divergence,* usually expressed in milliradians, is measured at specified points, where *optical power density* or energy density is $1/2$ or $1/e$ of the maximum value. It can be specified as a half angle or a full angle of divergence. Also see *divergent light.*

beaming. See *multiple beaming.*

beam lobe switching. A method of determining the direction to a remote object by comparison of the *signals* from the object corresponding to two or more successive *beam* angles that differ slightly. Beam switching may be either continuous or discontinuous (periodic).

beam radar. See *narrow-beam radar; wide-beam radar.*

beam-riding guidance system. A guidance system in which an object is made to follow a directionally controlled *radio beam.*

beam satellite antenna. See *global beam satellite antenna.*

beam-split radar. See *conical beam-split radar.*

beam splitter. An *optical* device for dividing a *light beam* into two separated *beams.* A simple beam splitter may be a plane parallel plate, with one surface coated with a *dielectric* or metallic coating that *reflects* a portion and *transmits* a portion of the *incident* beam; i.e., part of the light is deviated through an angle of $90°$, and part is unchanged in direction. A beam splitter may be made by coating the hypotenuse face of a $45°-90°$ prism and cementing it to the hypotenuse face of another. The thickness of the metallic beam splitting *interface* will determine the proportions of the light reflected and transmitted. In metallic beam splitters, an appreciable amount of light is lost by absorption in the metal. It may also be necessary to match the reflected and transmitted beam for *brightness* and for *color.* In these cases, it is necessary to use a material at the *interface* that gives the same *color* of light by *transmission* and *reflection.* Where color matching at the surface or interface cannot be accomplished, a correcting color *filter* may be placed in one of the beams.

beam station. See *radar-beam station.*

beam tilt. The angular tilt of the *main lobe* of the vertical *radiation pattern* above or below $0°$ elevation. The tilt must be referred to the *free space* pattern unless the actual vertical radiation pattern approaches free space conditions, that is, unless it is free from *ground reflection* effects.

beamwidth. The angular difference between the direction in which *radiant power density* is a prescribed fraction of the peak density, the fraction often being expressed as $1/2$, $1/e$, $1/e^2$, or $1/10$ of the peak power density.

bearer. In *communication sytems,* a *facility* or *transmission medium* for *messages.* For example, *land lines, cables, microwaves* between towers, *radio relay, high-frequency radio, ionospheric reflection, tropospheric scatter,* and *satellites.*

bearer channel. See *information bearer channel.*

bearing. The direction of a point from another point. Bearings are usually expressed in degrees, from 001 to 360. It is usually the *bearing* from true north of a *station* requesting the bearing measured from the *direction-finding* station. See *gyro bearing; jamming bearing; reciprocal bearing; relative bearing; uncoordinated bearing.*

bearing classification. An evaluation of the precision with which the *bearing* of a *station* is measured by a *direction-finding* station or stations. Bearings are classified as Class A, B, C, etc., or are unclassified, depending upon the precision with which the bearing is determined. Class A is the most precise. The class of a position or bearing is specified by the direction-finding station. For example, a Class A bearing might be estimated to be accurate to within $\pm 2°$, a Class B bearing to within $\pm 5°$, and a Class C bearing to within $\pm 10°$.

bearing cut. In *direction finding,* the angle of intersection of two *bearings,* the angle being opposite or facing the *baseline.* Each bearing is taken from two different locations on the baseline. Unless bearing cuts are between $30°$ and $150°$, the results will be inaccurate. Also see Figure I-8.

bearing discrimination. A measure of the precision with which a *bearing* (direction or *azimuth*) can be measured. *Radar* has high *range discrimination,* but low bearing discrimination. *Radio* also has a low bearing discrimination since precision to only a few degrees of bearing corresponds to large distances at the large operating ranges involved in direction-finding operations. Also see *detection discrimination; range discrimination.*

bearing intersection. A method of determining the location of a stationary or moving *signal source* by means of *direction finding* from two or more locations. Also see *running fix.*

beat-frequency oscillator. An *oscillator* that produces a desired *frequency* by combining two other frequencies. The frequency may be an *audio frequency* produced by combining two *radio* frequencies, or it may be some desired radio frequency, such as the *intermediate frequency* of a *superheterodyne circuit.* Synonymous with *heterodyne oscillator.*

bed. See *plotter bed.*

Beer's law. In the *transmission* of *electromagnetic radiation* through a liquid solution (nonabsorbing nonscattering solvent containing an *absorbing* or *scattering* solute), the *attenuation,* reduction, decay, or diminution of *electromagnetic field* *intensity* or *optical power density* is an exponential decay function of the product of the concentration of the solute, c; the spectral absorption/scattering coefficient per unit of concentration per unit of distance, a, and the thickness, x, given by the relationship; $I = I_0 e^{-cax}$ where I is the power density at distance x and I_0 is the power density at $x = 0$. Also see *Bouger's law; Lambert's law.*

beginning-of-tape mark.   A *mark* on a *magnetic tape* used to indicate the beginning of the permissible recording area. For example, a photoreflective strip or a transparent section of tape.

bel.   A unit of *power* ratio equal to 10 *decibels.* The number of bels is the common (decimal) logarithm of the power ratio. Mathematically, bels = $\log_{10} P_1/P_2$.

bell.   See *extension bell; margin bell.*

bell (BEL) character.   A *transmission control character* that is used when there is a need to *call* for *user* or *operator* attention in a *communication system,* and that usually activates an *audio* or *visual alarm* or other attention-getting device.

Bell integrated optical device.   An *integrated optical circuit* with *active* and *passive* elements to be used as logic elements and control elements in *optical* memories, *pulse* shapers, *optical switches, differential amplifiers, optical amplifiers, logic gates (AND* and *OR* gates), and other elements, depending on how they are interconnected during fabrication.

belt.   See *Van Allen belt.*

bend.   See *cold bend.*

bending loss.   In an *optical fiber,* the *radiation emitted* at bends due to the escape of discrete *beams* of the *transmitted light* as they zigzag around the bend. Microbending loss in a *step-indexed fiber* is approximately inversely proportional to the cube of the *relative refractive index* difference. Ordinary bending loss is inversely proportional to the *relative refractive index.*

bend test.   See *hot bend test.*

BER.   *Bit error rate.*

beta particle.   See *electron.*

between failures.   See *mean-time-between-failures (MTBF).*

between outages.   See *mean-time-between-outages (MTBO).*

between-the-lines entry.   Unauthorized *access* to a momentarily inactive *terminal* of a legitimate *user* assigned to a *communication channel.* The access is obtained through the use of *active wiretapping* by an unauthorized user.

B-except-A gate.   See *B-AND-NOT-A gate.*

BFL.   *Back focal length.*

bias.   **1.** A systematic deviation of a value from a reference value. **2.** The amount by which the average of a set of values departs from a reference value. **3.** Electrical, mechanical, or *magnetic* force that is applied to a relay, vacuum tube, or other device, to establish an electrical or mechanical reference level to operate the device. **4.** The effect on *telegraph signals* produced by the electrical characteristics of the *terminal equipment.* See *internal bias; marking bias; spacing bias.*

bias distortion.   **1.** *Distortion* affecting a two-condition *(binary) modulation* in which all the *significant intervals* corresponding to one of the two *significant conditions* have uniformly longer or shorter durations than the corresponding theoretical durations. **2.** *Distortion* due to the lengthening of either the *mark* or *space* elements by lack of symmetry in the *transmitting* or *receiving* equipment. Also see *internal bias.*

bias gain-control circuit.   See *detector back-bias gain-control circuit.*

biconditional gate.   See *EXCLUSIVE-NOR gate.*

bidirectional cable.   In *fiber optics,* a *cable* that can handle *signals* simultaneously in both directions and that has the necessary components to operate successfully and avoid *crosstalk.*   Components that are used in or connected to bidirectional cables include *beam splitters,* entrance and exit *ports, mixing rods* and *boxes,* couplers, and interference filters.

bidirectional coupler.   **1.** In *optical fiber circuits,* a *coupling* device that permits *signals* to *propagate* through the fibers in both directions. **2.** A *directional coupler* that has *terminals* for *sampling waves* in both directions in a *transmission line.*

bifocal.   In *optics,* pertaining to a system or component that has, or is characterized by, two or more *optical focuses.*

bifurcation connector.   See *tee coupler.*

B-IGNORE-A gate.   A two-*input, binary,* logic coincidence *circuit* or device whose normal operation can be interrupted by a *control signal* that enables the *gate* to function so as to pass the B *input* signal and completely disregard the A input signal. The *output* signal is therefore the same as the B input signal and independent of the A input signal during the controlled period. This behavior is usually temporary, normal operation being that of an *OR gate.*   See Figure B-3.

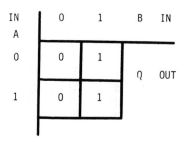

B-3. A table showing the *input* and *output digits* of a **B-IGNORE-A gate.**

bilateral control.   See *bilateral synchronization.*

bilateral synchronization.   A *synchronization* control *system* between exchanges A and B in which the *clock* at exchange A controls that at exchange B, and the clock at exchange B controls that at exchange A.   Synonymous with *bilateral control.*

billboard antenna.   A *broadside antenna array* with flat *reflectors.*

B-implies-A gate.   See *A-OR-NOT-B gate.*

binary.   Pertaining to a choice or condition that has two and only two possible different values or states; e.g., a numeration system having a *radix* of two, a *flip-flop,* or a *coded* on-off *condition* of *lightwaves* in an *optical fiber* for the representation and *transmission* of *information.*

binary adder.   A device capable of obtaining the sum of two or more *binary numbers.*   See Figure B-4.

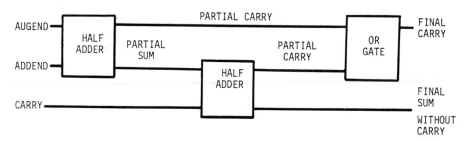

B-4. A block diagram of a **binary adder.**

binary channel.   See *symmetric binary channel.*

binary character.   Either of the *characters* of a *character set* consisting of two characters, for example, a *binary digit.*

binary code. A *code* composed by selection and configuration of an entity that can assume either one of two possible states. See *dense binary code; fixed-weight binary code; modified reflected binary code; non-return-to-zero (NRZ) binary code; pseudo-binary code; return-to-zero (RZ) binary code; symmetrical code; unit disparity binary code.*

binary-coded decimal (BCD). Pertaining to a numeration system in which each of the decimal *digits* is represented by a *binary numeral.* For example, in *binary-coded decimal* notation that uses the weights 8-4-2-1, the number twenty three is represented by 0010 0011. This is compared with 10111 in the *pure binary numeration system.*

binary-coded decimal interchange code. See *extended binary coded decimal interchange code (EBCDIC).*

binary counter. A *counter* that *displays* its results in the form of a *binary numeral.* Also see *ring counter; modulus counter.*

binary digit. One of the members of a set of two in the *binary* numeration system; e.g., either of the digits 0 or 1. In *lightwave communication systems,* the presence or the absence of a *pulse* of *light* at a particular place and instant of time may be used to represent binary digits, patterns or sequences of which can be used to *code characters* in the same manner as electrical pulses in wires or *electromagnetic* pulses in *free space.* The digit may be the individual light or electrical pulse itself. In the binary system of numbering, each digit can have only one of two values instead of one of ten values as in the decimal system. The binary digit is a member selected from a binary set, a set of two and only two items. The words 'binary digit' are abbreviated as 'bit.' The word 'bit' should not be used for *pulse, signal,* or *element.* Thus, 'unit element' should be used in a two-condition *start-stop system,* and *'shannon'* should be used for the *binary unit* of *information content.* The bit is a unit of information equal to one binary decision or the designation of one of two possible and perhaps equally likely states of anything used to store, convey, or simply represent *information.*

binary half adder. A device or circuit composed of *combinational logic elements* that is capable of forming the *modulo-two sum bit* and the carry bit at *output terminals* when a bit is present at both of two *input terminals.* The combinational logic element (binary half adder) has two *input channels* for inserting two *input signals* simultaneously, each representing a *binary digit,* that is, an addend and an augend. There are two *output channels* for two simultaneous *output signals,* one for the *logical sum* digit (modulo-two sum bit) and the other for the carry digit. If A and B are the input digits, the table (see Figure B-5) shows the sum without carry, S, and the carry, C, digits of the half adder. The logic diagram shows one method of assembling a binary half adder using *logic elements.* Two half adders are used to make a full adder. The Boolean expressions show the logic performed by the elements of the half adder. The carry digit is delayed for use in the next stage of a full serial adder. Also see *quarter adder.*

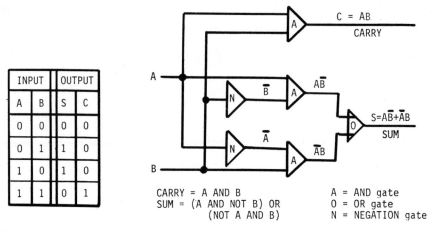

INPUT		OUTPUT	
A	B	S	C
0	0	0	0
0	1	1	0
1	0	1	0
1	1	0	1

CARRY = A AND B
SUM = (A AND NOT B) OR
      (NOT A AND B)

A = AND gate
0 = OR gate
N = NEGATION gate

B-5.   The *combinational logic elements* that comprise the **binary half-adder** and the table of *input* and *output digits.*

binary modulation.   The process of varying a *parameter* of a *carrier* as a function of two finite and discrete states.

binary notation.   A scheme for representing numbers characterized by the arrangements of *binary digits* in sequence, usually with the understanding that successive digits are interpreted as coefficients of successive powers of the base 2.   Also see *pure binary numeration system.*

binary number.   A number expressed in *binary* notation.

binary numeration system.   See *pure binary numeration system.*

binary sequence.   See *pseudo-random binary sequence.*

binary serial signaling rate.   In the particular case of serial two-state *transmission,* the reciprocal of the *unit interval* measured in seconds and expressed in *bits* per second.

binary signaling.   *Signaling* in which one *voltage, current,* or other condition, such as on versus off, up versus down, or open versus closed, represents a 0 and the other represents a 1.   It is the most fundamental and widely used form of *digital* signaling.   Despite its popularity, however, it has limitations, and in some signaling environments it is not an effective method of representing or conveying *data.*   In some environments *coding* techniques must be employed that take into account *signal spectral* characteristics, the requirements or limitations of *channels,* signal *synchronization* capabilities, *error detection* capabilities, *interference, noise* immunity, cost, and complexity.   Voice *(analog), ternary,* and direct picture *(fiberscope) transmission* are examples of nonbinary signaling.

binocular instrument. An *optical* instrument that makes use of, or allows a person to use, two eyes at the same time by providing for convergence of the *optical axis* of each of its two *optical systems* on the same *object* in order to produce the effect of a single *image* in the brain. For example, most field glasses and range finders are binocular, whereas hand-held telescopes are often *monocular instruments.*

BIOD. *Bell integrated optical device.*

Biot-Savart law. The *magnetic field intensity,* H, and hence the *magnetic flux density,* B, in the space surrounding an *electric current,* is directly proportional to the magnitude of the *electric current.* They are given by:

$$dB = \mu dH = \mu I dl sin\beta/4\pi r^2$$

where μ is the *magnetic permeability* of the surrounding medium; I is the electric current in the elemental *conductor dl;* β is the angle between the elemental conductor (direction of I) and a *vector* from the elemental conductor to the point at which the magnetic field is being determined; and r is the distance from the elemental conductor to the point. Also see *Fleming's rule; magnetic field.*

biphase coding. *Coding* in which there are two *phases,* that is, plus and minus $90°$ *phase-shift keying.* If a 1 is represented by a plus $90°$ phase shift from a reference, a zero is represented by a minus $90°$ phase shift from the same reference. Thus, the 0's and 1's are *sinewaves* or *pulses* shifted 180 electrical degrees from each other. They are, therefore, opposite in electrical polarity.

biphase-level coding. A form of *biphase signal coding* in which a change of state (amplitude) in the original *binary baseband signal* is represented by a change of *phase* in the biphase signal.

biphase mark coding. A form of *biphase signal coding* that has a *signal transition* at the beginning of every *bit* period, a 1 producing a second *transition* in the biphase signal a *significant interval* (one-half bit) later and a 0 producing no second transition. Biphase mark coding is generated by using conditioned signals (conditioned on 0) and *EXCLUSIVE OR*-ing the conditioned signals with the *system clock.* The advantage of conditioning the biphase signal is that any ambiguity in the *detected* signal is removed. The *spectrum* for conditioned biphase signaling is the same as that for conventional biphase. Synonymous with *conditioned biphase coding.*

biphase modulation. See *phase-shift keying.*

biphase signaling. *Signaling* in which *binary digits* are represented by *sine waves* that are $180°$ out of *phase* with each other, that is, shifted by 180 *electrical degrees.* For example, if 1 is represented by one cycle of *sin x,* 0 is represented by $-sin x.$ Biphase signaling has many forms, such as *biphase level, biphase mark,* and *biphase space.* Biphase is one of the source formats (NRZ, biphase, and delay modulation) most commonly used in *radio* applications. Biphase is generated by passing the *binary signal* and the *system clock signal* through an *EXCLUSIVE-*

OR gate. It is *decoded* by passing the biphase signal sequence and the recovered clock through an EXCLUSIVE-OR gate. The biphase signal *spectrum* has a low *direct-current (DC)* content, which is the major advantage of the code. It has high energy levels up to a *frequency* of twice the *bit rate.* Therefore, biphase is not unduly affected by *high-pass filtering,* but has a low tolerance to *low-pass* filtering. Biphase requires a *wideband,* typically 0.08 to 0.75 times the bit rate. This is the major disadvantage. For a 16 kb/sec data rate, the *bandwidth* is 10.8 kHz, extending from 1280 Hz to 12 kHz. *Non-return-to-zero signaling* requires only 8 kHz.

biphase space coding.   A form of *biphase signal coding* that, like *biphase mark coding,* has a *signal transition* at the beginning of every *bit* period, a 0 being represented by a transition half a bit later and a 1 by no second transition. Generation of biphase space coding is the same as for biphase mark except that the data is conditioned on 1's.

bipolar.   Pertaining to a method of *transmitting a signal* with the use of both positive and negative *voltages* in the signal. For example, a *mark* could be represented by a voltage or *current* in one direction and a *space* by a voltage or current in the opposite direction, with or without the use of the zero condition. Also see *unipolar.*

bipolar coding.   A form of *binary signal coding* in which each 'off' *bit* is represented by 0 and each 'on' bit is represented by the opposite polarity from the previous one, thus allowing three levels: positive, zero, and negative. Bipolar coding can be either *full-baud bipolar (FBB),* or *half-baud bipolar (HBD).* An FBB coding process consists of representing binary 0's by zero levels, and binary 1's by alternate positive or negative *pulses,* in the bipolar *signal* sequence. These pulses remain at their respective levels for the entire *baud* length, whereas HBB pulses return to the zero level at the midpoint of the baud. Bipolar is a *ternary signal* coding scheme and thus has a greater susceptibility to *noise* errors than does binary. The bipolar *spectrum* has an energy null at DC, as does *biphase,* but requires less *bandwidth* than biphase. Bipolar coding is an inherent *error detecting code* in that if a pulse is decoded improperly the bipolar pulse alternation rule will be violated (if not compensated by a pair of errors) and the error will be detected. Bipolar coding is generated by conditioning *non-return-to-zero signals,* delaying this sequence one bit period, and adding the delayed version and the undelayed version. Synonymous with *alternate mark inversion (AMI) coding* and with *alternating binary coding.* See *full-baud bipolar coding; half-baud bipolar coding.*

bipolar signal.   See *alternate mark inversion (AMI) signal.*

bipolar telegraphy.   See *double-current signaling.*

bipolar transmission.   See *double-current signaling.*

bipolar violation.   See *alternate mark inversion (AMI) violation.*

biquinary code. A *code* in which a *decimal digit, n,* is represented by the pair of numbers *a* and *b,* where $n = 5a + b$. The *a* may be a 0 or a 1 and the *b* may be a 0, 1, 2, 3, or 4. Examples of biquinary codes using a binary form of representation and a decimal form of representation are shown in Figure B-6.

DECIMAL DIGIT	BIQUINARY	
	BINARY FORM	DECIMAL FORM
0	01 00001	00
1	01 00010	01
2	01 00100	02
3	01 01000	03
4	01 10000	04
5	10 00001	10
6	10 00010	11
7	10 00100	12
8	10 01000	13
9	10 10000	14

B-6. Examples of **biquinary code.**

birefringence. The *splitting* of a *light beam* into two *divergent* components upon passage through a *doubly-refracting transmission medium,* with the two components *propagating* at different velocities in the medium. Also see *double refraction.*

bistable circuit. See *flip-flop.*

bit. *Binary digit.* See *added bit; check bit; deleted bit; delivered overhead bit; erroneous bit; error-correction bit; error-detection bit; framing bit; incorrect bit; information bit; overhead bit; parity bit; synchronization bit; user information bit.*

bit-by-bit asynchronous operation. In *data transmission systems,* a *mode* of operation in which rapid manual, semiautomatic, or automatic shifts in the *data modulation rate* are accomplished by *gating* or *slewing* the *clock modulation rate.* For example, the equipment may be operated at 50 b/s (bits per second) one moment and at 1200 b/s the next moment.

bit byte. See *n-bit byte.*

bit-count integrity. The preservation of the precise number of *bits* that are originated per *message* (in message *transmission systems*) or per unit of time (in *user*-to-user connections). This is not to be confused with *bit integrity* which requires that the bits delivered are in fact as they were originated. Also see *added bit; bit inversion; character-count integrity; deleted bit; digital error.*

biternary transmission. A *mode* of *digital transmission* in which two *binary pulse trains* are combined for transmission over a *system* in which the available *band-*

width is only sufficient for transmission of one of the two pulse trains when in binary form. The *biternary signal* is generated from two *synchronous* binary signals operating at the same *bit rate*. The two binary signals are adjusted in time to have a relative time difference of one-half the binary interval and are combined by linear addition to form the biternary signal. Each biternary signal element can assume any one of three possible states, corresponding to +1, 0, and −1. Each biternary signaling element contains *information* on the state of the two binary signaling elements as defined in the following truth table:

Bit 1	Bit 2	Biternary
0	0	−1
0	1	0
1	0	0
1	1	+1

The method of addition of Bit 1 and Bit 2 as described above does not permit the biternary signal to change from −1 to +1 or +1 to −1 without an intermediate biternary signal of 0. Since there is half a unit interval time difference between the binary signals for Bit 1 and Bit 2, only one of them can change its state during the biternary unit interval. This makes it possible in the *decoding* process to ascertain the state of the binary signal that has not changed its state, and thus avoid ambiguity in decoding a biternary signal of 0.

bit error rate (BER).   In the transmission of a single or parallel stream of *binary digits* in any *optical fiber,* wire, line, *channel, circuit, trunk,* or other path, the number of bits that are in error at one point divided by the total number of bits transmitted at another point. The BER is usually expressed as the number of erroneous bits per million introduced between the specified points. Two examples of bit error rate are the *transmission* BER, that is the number of erroneous bits received divided by the total number of bits transmitted; and the *information* BER, that is the number of erroneous decoded (corrected) bits divided by the total number of decoded (corrected) bits. The BER is usually expressed as a pure number (dimensionless), for example as 25 erroneous bits out of 1,000,000, or 25 in 10^6, or 25×10^{-6}, or 25 bits per million.

bit integrity.   Preservation of the value of a *bit* during *processing, storage,* and *transmission.* Also see *bit inversion.*

bit interval.   1. In a *bit stream,* the time or distance between corresponding points on two consecutive *signals,* each representing a bit. **2.** In the *transmission* of a single bit, the time or distance allowed or required to represent the bit.

bit inversion.   The deliberate or fortuitous changing of the state of a bit to the opposite state. Also see *bit-count integrity; character-count integrity; bit integrity; digital error.*

bitoric lens.   A *lens* with both surfaces ground and polished in a cylindrical form or in a toroidal shape.

bit pairing.   The practice of establishing, within a code, a number of subsets of two *characters* each that have an identical *bit* representation except for the state of a specified bit.   For example in the American National Standard Code for Information Interchange *(ASCII)* and in the *International Telegraph Alphabet Number 5,* the uppercase letters are related (paired) to their respective lowercase letters by the state of bit six.

bit rate.   In a *binary digital communication system,* the number of *bits transmitted* per unit time, usually expressed as bits per second.   See *multiplex aggregate bit rate.*

bit-rate-length product.   For an *optical fiber* or *cable,* the product of the *bit rate* that the fiber or cable is able to handle and the cable length for tolerable dispersion.   The product is usually stated in units of megabits-kilometers/second.   Typical bit-rate-length products for *graded index fibers* with a *numerical aperture (NA)* of 0.2 is 1000 mb-km/sec for research fibers and 200 mb-km/sec for production fibers.   Plastic *clad fibers* with an NA of 0.25 are 30 mb-km/sec for both research and production fibers.   The product is a good measure of fiber performance in terms of *transmission* capability.

bit-sequence independence.   In a *digital path* or digital section of a *pulse-code modulation (PCM) system* operating at a specified *bit rate,* a measure of the capability to permit any sequence of bits at that rate, or the equivalent, to be *transmitted.*   Practical transmission systems that are not completely bit-sequence independent may be described as quasi-bit-sequence independent.   In such cases the limitations should be clearly stated.

bit sequential.   A type of *data transmission* in which the *signal elements* are successive in time.

bits per second (b/s).   The number of *bits* occurring at or passing a point per second.   Values of modulation rate in *baud* and in *bits* per second are numerically the same if, and only if, all of the three following conditions are met: 1. All *pulses* (bits) are the same length.   2. All pulses (bits) are equal to the *unit interval* (the time element between the same two *significant instants* of adjacent pulses).   3. *Binary* operation is used.   In *n-ary* operation, the b/s equals the *modulation rate* in *baud* multiplied by the logarithm to the base 2 of N, where N is the number of distinct states used in the digital modulation process.   A distinct state might be the *amplitude, phase,* or *frequency.*   Also see *data signaling rate.*

bit stepped.   Operational control of *digital* equipment in which a device is stepped one bit at a time at the applicable *modulation rate.*

bit stream.   An uninterrupted sequence of *pulses* representing *binary digits transmitted* in a *transmission medium.*   For example, a continuous sequence of *bits* in a *wireline* or *optical fiber.*   See *mission bit stream.*   Also see *data stream.*

bit-stream signaling. See *random bit-stream signaling.*

bit-stream transmission. The *transmission* of *characters* at fixed time intervals without *stop* and *start elements.* The *bits* make up the *characters* following each other in sequence without interruption.

bit string. A linear sequence of *bits.*

bit stuffing. A *synchronization* method used in *time-division multiplexing* to handle *bit stream transmission* over which the *multiplexer clock* has no control. The *modulation rate* is somewhat higher than the sum of the incoming *bit rates* because of the adding of bits to the bit stream. Each incoming *signal* has enough *pulses* added to it to give it a rate compatible with the multiplexer clock. The number of bits stuffed into the individual incoming signals is varied to take care of variations in the incoming rates. The multiplexer inserts a *code* as part of the stuffing to tell the *demultiplexer* what pulses to de-stuff so that the signal delivered to the outgoing circuit has exactly the same number of pulses as that received. Synonymous with *justification; positive justification; positive pulse stuffing.* Also see *destuffing; nominal bit stuffing rate; padding.*

bit stuffing rate. See *nominal bit stuffing rate.*

bit-synchronous operation. In *data transmission systems,* a *mode* of operation in which *data circuit-terminating equipment (DCE), data terminal equipment (DTE),* and *transmitting circuits* are all operated in *bit synchonism* with an accurate *clocking system,* that is, they are all *synchronous* with the clock. *Clock pulses* are delivered at twice the *modulation rate,* and one bit is released during one clock cycle. Bit synchronous operation is sometimes erroneously referred to as digital synchronization.

black. See *noisy black; nominal black; picture black.*

black-and-white facsimile telegraphy. See *document facsimile telegraphy.*

blackbody. A body that is capable of *absorbing* all the *radiation* that is *incident* upon it. When heated by external means, the spectral energy distribution of radiated energy would follow curves shown on *optical spectrum* charts. The ideal blackbody is a perfectly absorbing body. It reflects none of the energy that may be incident upon it. It radiates (perfectly) at a rate expressed by the *Stefan-Boltzmann law* and the *spectral* distribution of radiation is expressed by *Planck's radiation* formula. When in thermal equilibrium, an ideal blackbody *absorbs* perfectly and *radiates* perfectly at the same rate. The radiation will be just equal to absorption if thermal equilibrium is to be maintained. Synonymous with *ideal blackbody.* Also see *Planck's law.*

black concept.   See *red-black concept.*

black designation.   A *security* designation applied to all *wirelines, optical fiber cables,* components, equipment, and *systems* that handle only *encrypted* or security unclassified *signals;* and to physical areas in which no unencrypted, security classified signals occur.   Also see *red-black concept; red designation.*

black facsimile transmission.   1. In an *amplitude modulated facsimile system,* that form of *transmission* in which the maximum *transmitted power* corresponds to the maximum density (black) area of the object copy or document.   **2.** In a *frequency modulation system,* that form of *transmission* in which the lowest *transmitted frequency* corresponds to the maximum density (black) area of the object copy or document.   Also see *white facsimile transmission.*

black noise.   In a *spectrum* of *electromagnetic wave* frequencies, a *frequency spectrum* of predominantly zero power level at all frequencies except for a few narrow *bands* or spikes.   For example, a spectrum that might be obtained when scanning a black area in *facsimile transmission systems* where there are a few white or colored spots or speckles on the surface.   Thus, in the *time domain,* a few random *pulses* occur at a point in space, such as on a *transmission* line.   In the frequency domain, only a few frequencies occur, depending on the *color* in the case of *light.*   Also see *blue noise; white noise.*

blackout.   In *communications,* a complete disruption of *communication* capability due to conditions that occur in the *transmission media.*   For example, the disruption of *radiotelephone communication* due to effects that are caused by *sunspots, solar flares,* or *ionospheric disturbances.*

black recording.   1. In *facsimile systems* using *amplitude modulation,* that form of recording in which the maximum received *power* corresponds to the maximum density (black) area of the *recording medium.*   **2.** In a *facsimile system* using *frequency modulation,* that form of recording in which the lowest received frequency corresponds to the maximum density (black) area of the *recording medium.* Also see *white recording.*

black signal.   In *facsimile systems,* the *signal* resulting from the *scanning* of a maximum density (black) area of the object copy or document.   The magnitude may be an *amplitude, frequency, phase-shift,* or other *signal parameter* variation maximum.   Also see *white signal.*

blanket.   See *thermal blanket.*

blanking   1. Preventing or suppressing the *display* of one or more *display elements, display groups,* or *display images* in the *display space* on the *display surface* of a *display device.*   Display surfaces particularly capable of blanking are *CRT* screens, *fiberscope faceplates,* and *LED* and *gas panels.*   **2.** In *infrared scanning systems,* the receipt of a *pulse* of such magnitude as to saturate (overdrive) *circuits* and therefore prevent *signal resolution, frequency discrimination,* and *direction finding.* A *laser* pulse can cause blanking in an *infrared scanning* device. Also see *clipping.* See *pulse interference suppression and blanking; sidelobe blanking.*

blemish. An area in a *fiber* or *fiber bundle* that has a reduced *light transmission* capability due to defective or broken fibers, foreign substances, or other spoilage.

blind area. A region of space not reached, that is, not *illuminated,* by a *radar signal.* Blind areas may be caused by *directional antennas* that *radiate* so as not to reach certain regions, by shadows caused by obstructions or land features, or by ground clutter in which an object (target) may be obscured. Since a blind area cannot be seen by radar or *direction-finding (DF)* equipment, *high-frequency line-of-sight radiation* cannot be obtained from sources in these areas nor can objects (targets) be identified in them. Synonymous with *shadow area.*

blind cone. See *antenna blind cone.*

blind range. See *radar blind range.*

blind speed. See *radar blind speed.*

blind transmission. *Transmission* without obtaining a receipt from the intended *receiving station.* Blind transmission may occur or be necessary when security constraints, such as *radio silence,* are imposed; technical difficulties with a sender's *receiver* or receiver's *transmitter* occur; or lack of time precludes the delay caused by waiting for receipts.

blinking. An intentional, usually regular or *periodic,* change in the intensity of a *display element, display group,* or *display image* in the *display space* on a *display surface* of a *display device.* Contrast with *flicker.*

blip. **1.** In *display systems,* a *mark,* spot, or *symbol* that appears in the *display space* of the *display surface* of a *display device;* e.g., in *radar* displays, a bright spot representing the polar coordinate position of a plane, target, or missile. **2.** An optical mark used for counting *film frames* by automatic means. See *document mark.*

block. **1.** A group of *bits,* or *n-ary digits, transmitted* as a unit. An *encoding* procedure is generally applied to the group of bits of n-ary digits for *error control* purposes. **2.** A finite *string* of records, *words,* or *characters* formed for technical or logic reasons to be treated as an entity. **3.** A set of things, such as *words, characters,* or *digits* handled as a unit. **4.** A collection of contiguous records recorded as a unit. *Blocks* are separated by *interblock gaps* and each block may contain one or more records. **5.** In *flaghoist communication systems,* the pulley or loop at the top of a mast or pole for raising a *flag, pennant,* or *panel* on a *lanyard.* **6.** In a *computer programming language,* a sequence of one or more declarations or *instructions* that may be treated as a unit.   **7.** In a *computer program,* a group of *instructions* that may be treated as a unit.   See *added block; deleted block; delivered overhead block; digital block; erroneous block; horizontal terminating block; incorrect block; lost block; misdelivered block; time block; user information block; vertical terminating block.*

blockage.   See *antenna blockage.*

block cancel character.   A *cancel character* used to indicate that the portion of the *block* back to the last block mark, that is, the most recently occurring block mark, is to be ignored or deleted.

block check   1. A *system* of *error control* based on the observance of preset rules for the formation of *blocks.*   **2.** The part of an *error control* procedure used for determining whether or not a *data block* is structured according to given rules.

block check character.   In an *error detection system,* a *character* added at the end of a *message* or *transmission block* to facilitate error detection.

block code.   A *code* in which the *block* of *digits* generated by the *encoder* during any particular time depends on the block of *input message* digits in that time. The block code was one of the earliest codes to be investigated. Also see *convolutional code.*

block correction efficiency factor.   In *data transmission systems* employing *error control,* a performance evaluation *parameter* given by the ratio of the number of *blocks* that have been received without error in a given time period times 100 to the total number of blocks received in the same time period, and expressed as a percentage.   Expressed mathematically, $BCEF = (100 \ BRC)/BR$, where $BCEF$ is the block correction efficiency factor, BRC is the number of blocks received correctly, and BR is the total number of blocks received in the same time period.

block delivery.   See *successful block delivery.*

block efficiency.   The average ratio of *user information bits* to total bits in successfully transferred *blocks.*

block-error probability.   The ratio of incorrect *blocks* received to the total number of blocks received during a specific measurement period.

blocking.   1. The forming of *blocks* for purposes of *transmission, storage, checking,* or other function.   **2.** Denying *access* to or use of a *facility, system,* or component.   Also see *access denial; access failure; system blocking signal.*   See *insulation blocking.*

blocking cement.   An adhesive used to bond *optical* elements to blocking tools. It is usually a *thermoplastic* material such as resin, beeswax, pitch, or shellac.

blocking probability. In a *communication system,* the probability that an *access attempt* will result in an *access failure.* For example, when expressed as a percentage, it implies the number of calls that can be expected not to be completed out of 100 calls that are attempted. Also see *nonblocking.*

blocking signal. See *system blocking signal.*

block length. See *average block length.*

block loss probability. The ratio of the number of lost *blocks* to the total number of *block transfer attempts* counted during a specific measurement period.

block misdelivery probability. The ratio of the number of *misdelivered blocks* to the total number of *block transfer attempts* counted during a specific measurement period.

block probability. See *added-block probability.*

block rate efficiency. The ratio of the product of the *block transfer rate* and the *average block length* to the *signaling rate.*

block reek. A chainlike *scratch* accidently occurring during the polishing of *optical elements.*

block transfer. See *successful block transfer.*

block transfer attempt. A coordinated sequence of *user* and *communication system* activities undertaken to effect *transfer* of a *block* from a *source user* to a *destination user.* A block transfer attempt begins when the first *bit* of the block crosses the functional interface between the source user and the communication system. A block transfer attempt ends either in *block transfer success* or in *block transfer failure.* Also see *block transfer success; block transfer time.*

block transfer failure. A failure to deliver a block successfully, that is, an unsuccessful *block transfer.* Normally the principal block transfer failure situations are *lost block, misdelivered block, incorrect block,* and *added block.*

block transfer rate. The number of *successful user information block transfers* during a performance measurement period divided by the duration of the period.

block transfer success. The transfer of a correct, nonduplicate, *user information block* between a *source user* and the intended *destination user.* Block transfer success occurs at the moment when the last bit of the transferred block crosses the functional interface between the *communication system* and the intended destination user. Block transfer success can only occur within a defined maximum *block transfer time* after initiation of a *block transfer attempt.* Also see *block transfer attempt; block transfer time.*

block transfer time. The elapsed time between the start of a *user information block transfer attempt* and *block transfer success.* Also see *block transfer attempt; block transfer success.* See *maximum block transfer time.*

blooming. The formation of trapped gas pockets in an *optical fiber.*

blowback. See *reenlargement.*

blowback ratio. The ratio of a linear dimension of an enlarged *image* of an *object* to the linear dimension of the original image of the same object before enlargement.

blue noise. In a *spectrum* of *electromagnetic wave frequencies,* a region in which the *spectral density* is proportional to the frequency (sloped), rather than independent of frequency (flat), as in white noise that is more of a uniformly distributed, constant amplitude frequency spectrum. Also see *black noise; white noise.*

board. See *secure voice cord board.*

boating. See *motor boating.*

body. See *blackbody.*

body problem. See *n-body problem; restricted circular three-body problem; three-body problem; two-body problem.*

body signal. See *ground-to-air visual body signal.*

Boehme equipment. **1.** *Transmitting* equipment used for sending *international Morse code characters* by passing *Wheatstone tape* through a *keying* head. **2.** Receiving equipment used for recording *international Morse code characters* on a moving paper tape using ink-syphon equipment.

Boehme tape. See *Wheatstone tape.*

bolometer. An electrical instrument for measuring *radiant* energy by measuring the changes in *electrical conductivity* or resistance of a blackened *temperature-*sensitive device exposed to the *radiations.*

Boltzmann's constant. The coefficient of *temperature* in the exponent of the *Boltzmann emission law,* equal to 1.38×10^{-23} joules/kelvin. The constant is usually designated by a lowercase k, in contrast to an uppercase K, which designates temperature, T, in *kelvin.* The quantity kT expresses energy.

Boltzmann's emission law. The ratio of the number of *electrons* in *energy level* n to the number in level m is an exponential function of the energy level difference between levels n and m, the *temperature,* and a proportionality constant, expressed mathematically as $N_n/N_m = e^{(E_m - E_n)/kT}$, where N_n is the number of electrons in energy level n; N_m is the number of electrons in energy level m; E_m is the energy of level m; E_n is the energy of level n; k is *Boltzmann's constant;* and T is the absolute temperature.

bombardment resistance.   See *neutron bombardment resistance.*

bond frequency.   The natural *frequency* of vibration due to thermal *(infrared)* excitation of the electronic bonds of molecules in a material. These vibrations give rise to *electric* and *magnetic fields* that interact with the electric and magnetic fields of *propagating electromagnetic waves* resulting in an *absorption* of energy from the propagating waves. In glass, the thermal vibrations of the oxides of silicon result in absorption of specific frequencies. Also see *infrared absorption.*

book.   See *code book.*

booked call.   In *telephone switchboard operation,* a *call* that is recorded so that the *operator* can call the *calling party* when the call has been set up, that is, when the *connections* are made.   Calls are booked when delays are encountered in order to preclude a calling party from remaining on the *line* for extended periods. Also see *delayed call.*

book message.   A *message* that is destined for two or more *addressees* and is of such nature that the *originator* considers that no addressees need to be informed of any other addressees. Each addressee should be indicated as an *action addressee* or an *information addressee.*

bootstrap.   1. A technique, device, or *computer program* designed to bring itself into a desired state by means of its own action.   **2.** An existing version, perhaps a primitive version, of a *computer program* that is used to establish another version of the program.   **3.** That part of a *computer program* used to establish another version of the program.

borescope.   See *fiber borescope.*

B-OR-NOT-A gate.   A two-*input, binary,* logic coincidence circuit or device capable of performing the logic operation of B OR NOT A, which is the same at A OR NOT B except that the variables are reversed. Thus, if A is a statement and B is a statement, the result is false only when A is true and B is false. For the other three combinations of A and B, the result is true. Synonymous with *A-implies-B gate; if-A-then-B gate; implication gate; inclusion gate.* See Figure B-7.

IN A	0	1	B IN
0	1	1	
			Q OUT
1	0	1	

B-7. A table showing the *input* and *output digits* of a **B-OR-NOT-A gate.**

Bose-Chaudhuri-Hocquenghem (BCH) code.   A multilevel, cyclic, *error-correcting, digital code* constructed of many lengths and with the ability to correct errors up to about 25% of the total number of *digits.*   BCH codes are not limited to binary codes, but may be used with multilevel *phase-shift keying* whenever the number of levels is a prime number or a power of a prime number, for example, 2, 3, 4, 5, 7, 8, 11, 13, . . . , etc. A BCH code in 11 levels has been used to represent the ten *decimal digits* plus a sign digit.

both-way communication.   See *two-way-simultaneous communication.*

Bouger's law.   In the *transmission* of *electromagnetic radiation* through a material or *transmission medium,* the *attenuation,* reduction, decay, or diminution of *electromagnetic field* intensity or *optical power density* is an exponential function of the product of a constant coefficient, dependent upon the material, and the thickness, given by the relationship: $I = I_0 e^{-ax}$, where I is the intensity at distance x, I_0 is the intensity at $x = 0$, and a is a material constant coefficient that depends upon the *scattering* and *absorptive* properties of the *transmission medium.*   If only *absorption* takes place, a is the *spectral absorption coefficient* and is a function of wavelength.   If only scattering takes place, it is the *scattering coefficient.*   If both absorption and scattering occur, it is the *extinction coefficient,* being then the sum of the absorption and scattering coefficients.   Also see *Beer's law; Lambert's law.*

boule.   An assembly of fused *optical fibers* from which *fiber faceplates* may be sliced. Also see *fiber faceplates.*

boundary-layer photocell.   See *photovoltaic cell.*

boundary limit marker.   See *drop-zone boundary limit marker.*

bounds checking.   See *storage bounds checking.*

bounds register.   A *register* that holds an *address* that signifies a storage boundary.

box.   See *optical fiber distribution box; optical mixing box; stunt box.*

bpi.   *Bits* per inch.

bps.   *Bits* per second.

branch.   **1.** In a *data network,* a direct *path* joining two *adjacent nodes* in the network.   **2.** A set of *instructions* that is executed between two successive decision instructions.   **3.** In the execution of a *computer program,* to select one from a number of alternative sets of *instructions.*   **4.** To select a route from among the members of a set of routes.   **5.** Loosely, a conditional jump or departure from the implicit or declared sequence in which instructions are being executed.   **6.** In a multiconductor *cable,* the portion that breaks out or departs from the remaining *conductors.*

branched cable.   A multiple-wire, multiple-*fiber,* or multiple-*bundle cable* that contains one or more breakouts or divergences, i.e., *branches.*

branch exchange.   See *private automatic branch exchange (PABX).*

branch exchange tie trunk.   See *private branch exchange tie trunk.*

branch feeder cable.   A *cable* that *conducts signals* to or in a *branch* in a *communication network.*

branching network.   An electrical *network* used for the *transmission* or the *reception* of *signals* over two or more *channels.*

branching repeater.   A *repeater* that *drives* several output *channels* or *circuits* from one input channel or circuit.

breadboard.   **1.** An assembly of *circuits* or parts used to prove the feasibility of a device, *circuit, system,* or principle with little or no regard to the final configuration or packaging of the parts.   **2.** To make, create, or prepare a device, *circuit,* or *system* with little or no regard to the final configuration or packaging of the parts.

break.   **1.** In a *communication circuit,* an action in which the *destination user* interrupts the *source user* and takes control of the circuit.   Breaking is performed when operating *half-duplex telegraph circuits* and two-way *telephone* circuits equipped with voice-operated devices.   **2.** In *radiotelephone systems,* the separation of the text from other portions of a *message.*   **3.** An interruption in *transmission.*   See *percent break.*

breaker.   See *circuit breaker; molded-case circuit breaker; power circuit breaker.*

break-in procedure. In *radiotelegraph communication,* a method whereby a *receiving station* may interrupt a *transmission* to request the *transmitting station* to perform some specified function, such as wait, shift *frequency,* repeat, or receive. A series of *dashes* are usually used to break in.

break lock. See *angle break lock.*

break-out chain. A set of *relays* in a relay *circuit* of a *telephone exchange dialing system* operated in such a manner that when the first relay of the set is energized any others in the set are prevented from being energized.

breakout point. The point where a *branch* meets, merges, or joins with or diverges from the main *cable* or *harness run.* The *convergence* or *divergence* is the breakout point of the *optical fiber.*

bremsstrahlung. A *pulsed ray* or *beam.*

brevity code. A *code* that makes use of *prosigns, prowords,* and other brief codes to represent a complete *message* or *instruction.* Brevity codes are used to save time and energy. The *originator* and *addressee* must have an a priori knowledge of the code. It is not used to maintain *communication security.*

brevity list. A list of the *brevity codes* in use, usually arranged for lookup *access* to entries in the list.

Brewster angle. The angle, measured with respect to the normal, at which an *electromagnetic wave incident* upon an *interface* surface between two dielectric media of different *refractive indices,* is totally transmitted into the second *medium.* The magnetic component of the incident wave must be parallel to the interface surface. The Brewster angle is given by: $\tan B = (\epsilon_2 / \epsilon_1)^{1/2}$, where B is the Brewster angle, ϵ_1 is the *electric permittivity* of the *incident* medium, and ϵ_2 is the electric permittivity of the *transmitted* medium. The Brewster angle is a convenient angle to transmit all the energy in an *optical fiber* to an outside *detector.* There is no Brewster angle, for which there is total transmission and therefore zero reflection, when the *electric field* component is parallel to the interface, except when the permittivities are equal, in which case there is no interface. Also, for entry into a more dense medium, such as from air into an *optical fiber:* $\tan B = (n_2 / n_1)$, and from a more dense medium into a less dense medium, such as fiber to air: $\tan B = (n_1 / n_2)$, where n_1 and n_2 are the *refractive indices* of the air and fiber, respectively.

Brewster's law. When an *electromagnetic wave* is *incident* upon a surface and the angle between the *refracted* and *reflected ray* is $90°$, maximum *polarization* occurs in both rays. The reflected ray has its maximum polarization in a direction normal to the plane of incidence, and the refracted ray has its maximum polarization in the plane of incidence.

bridge transformer.   See *hybrid coil.*

bridging.   The use of two or more *telephone instruments* connected in parallel across a single *line.*

bridging connection.   A parallel *connection* by means of which some of the *signal* energy in a *circuit* may be withdrawn, usually with imperceptible effect on the normal operation of the circuit.

bridging loss.   The *loss,* at a given *frequency,* resulting from connecting an *impedance* across a *transmission line.*   Expressed as the ratio (in decibels) of the *signal power* delivered to that part of the *system* behind the bridging point before bridging, to the signal power delivered to that same part after the bridging.

brightness.   An attribute or visual perception in accordance with which a *source* appears to *emit* more, or less, *light.*   Since the eye is not equally sensitive to all colors brightness cannot be a quantitative term. It is used in nonquantitative statements with reference to sensations and perception of light.   See *image brightness.*

brightness conservation.   See *radiance conservation.*

Brillouin diagram.   A diagram showing allowable and unallowable *frequencies* or *energy levels* of *electromagnetic waves* that can pass through certain materials that have *periodic* microstructures.   When an *electric field* is applied to the material, electrons experience periodic attractive and repulsive forces as they approach and depart from atomic nuclei in their path as they move through the material. The resulting electron vibration results in a field that interacts or resonates with electromagnetic waves, causing energy from the waves to be absorbed by the electrons at the resonant frequencies.   The net result is that electromagnetic waves of the resonant frequencies are absorbed, while the others are passed.   Crystals and certain glasses have the periodic microstructure, and therefore Brillouin diagrams can be drawn for them.

Brillouin scattering.   The *scattering* of *lightwaves* in a *transmission medium* caused by thermally driven density fluctuations that cause *frequency* shifts of several gigahertz at room *temperature.*

broadband.   See *wideband.*

broadband system.   See *wideband system.*

broadcast.   The *transmission* method whereby any number of organization, unit, *ship, aircraft,* or other *stations* may receive *messages transmitted* from a designated station.   Transmission is usually in the form of *radio, television,* or *radiotelephone signals.*   See *routine meteorological broadcast; special meteorological broadcast; time-signal standard-frequency broadcast.*

broadcast area. 1. One of the twelve numbered areas in which the world has been divided for purposes of operating the *merchant ship broadcast system.* **2.** The geographical area covered by the *signals* from a *radio station* or a *television station.*

broadcast area radio station. See *ship broadcast area radio station.*

broadcast communication method. 1. A method of *transmitting messages* or *information* to a number of *receiving stations* that make no receipt. **2.** A method of *communication* in which a *message* is *broadcast* and the *addressee* does not furnish a receipt. This method allows the *receiver* to maintain *radio silence.* It is used by *shore stations* to transmit messages to ships at sea, to aircraft in flight, or to units in the field. Synonymous with *broadcast method.* Also see *intercept communication method; receipt communication method; relay communication method.*

broadcast communication net. See *maritime broadcast communication net.*

broadcast frequency. The *frequency* used to *broadcast messages* and programs by *radio.* For example, the frequency used to broadcast messages from a *shore station* to *ship stations.*

broadcasting service. A *radiocommunication service* in which the *transmissions* are intended for direct *reception* by the general public. This service may include *sound, television,* or other types of transmission.

broadcasting station. 1. A *station* in a *broadcasting service* that *broadcasts* only in *sound (radio).* **2.** A *station* in a *broadcasting service* that *broadcasts* in *video* and *sound (television).* See *aeronautical broadcasting station; international broadcasting station.*

broadcast method. See *broadcast communication method.*

broadcast net. See *maritime patrol air broadcast net.*

broadcast operation. The *transmission* of *information* so that it may be received by *stations* that usually make no acknowledgement of receipt.

broadcast repeater. A *repeater* connecting several *channels,* one incoming and the others outgoing.

broadcast schedule. See *ship broadcast schedule.*

broadcast shift. See *area broadcast shift.*

broadcast station. See *area broadcast station; marine broadcast station.*

broadcast system. See *merchant ship broadcast system (MERCAST)*.

broadside antenna array. A group of parallel *dipole antennas* placed in a single, usually straight, line.

browsing. Searching through a *storage* (memory) to locate or acquire *information* without knowing necessarily of the existence or the format of the information being sought.

b/s. *Bits* per second.

bubble. A minute quantity of trapped free gas, or a small vacuum, in a *transmission medium* or *optical element*. A bubble usually consists of air or carbon dioxide, nitrogen, or water vapor. Bubbles, which are usually spherical, are formed when the medium, such as glass or plastic, is in the molten state because, in accordance with Pascal's principle, pressure is exerted equally in all directions against the surface tension of the molten medium. Bubbles cause *dispersion, reflection, deflection, diffusion, absorption,* and *scattering* of *lightwaves*.

budget. See *error budget; optical power budget; power budget*.

buffer. **1.** To allocate, schedule, or use a *computer program* or *storage* to compensate for a difference in the rate of flow of data, or time of occurrence of events, when *transferring* data from one device to another. **2.** An *isolating circuit* used to prevent a driven circuit from influencing the driving circuit, for example, an *OR gate*. Also see *first-in first-out; queue traffic*. See *data buffer; fiber buffer*.

buffer gate. See *OR gate*.

buffer. See *fiber buffer*.

buffer storage. A functional unit capable of storing *data* and usually used to compensate for a difference in the flow rate of data or for a disparity in time of occurrence of events when data are being transferred from one device to another. For example, when data are being transferred from a computer to a *display device* or from a high-speed *communication channel* to several slow-speed terminal devices.

bug. **1.** A small hidden listening device used for eavesdropping. **2.** A semiautomatic *telegraph key*. **3.** A mistake in a *computer program* or a *malfunction* of a part in a device.

building out. The process of adding a combination of *electrical inductance, capacity,* and *resistance* to a *paired cable* so that its electrical length may be increased by a desired amount to control *impedance* characteristics.

buildout. See *line buildout*.

bulk encryption. The *process* whereby two or more channels of a *communication system* are *encrypted* by a single unit of *cryptoequipment.* In the application of *bulk encryption* to multichannel systems, more than one unit of cryptoequipment may be required.

bulkhead connector. An *optical fiber connector* that enables the *connection* of a *cable* on one side of a barrier to a cable on the other side, usually with a *butted,* epoxied, *optical fiber interface* between the fiber ends. Typically, bulkhead connectors are used to pass through the sides of cabinets, aircraft, missiles, houses, or other structures. See Figure B-8.

B-8.   A Siecor *optical connector* for ordinary *terminations* or for use as a **bulkhead connector.**
The *insertion loss* is less than 1 *db.* (Courtesy of Siecor Optical Cables, Inc.)

bulk material absorption. The *lightwave power absorption* that occurs per unit volume of the basic material used to form an *optical fiber core, cladding,* or *jacket.* Measurement is made of bulk material absorption prior to use in forming *optical waveguides.* Absorption is usually expressed in decibels/kilometer (i.e., as an *attenuation*).

bulk material scattering. The *lightwave* power that is *scattered* per unit volume of the basic material used to form an *optical fiber core, cladding,* or *jacket.* Measurement is made of bulk material scattering prior to use in forming *optical waveguides.* Scattering follows a *Rayleigh* distribution which is characteristic of a *transmission medium* whose *refractive index* fluctuates over small distances compared to the wavelength of the *incident light.* Scattering losses are usually expressed in decibels/kilometer.

bulk optical glass. Large quantities of glass suitable in purity for making *optical elements.* Such elements include *lenses, prisms, mirrors,* and particularly *optical fibers.*

bulk optical plastic. Large quantities of plastic suitable in purity for making *optical elements.* Such elements include *lenses, prisms, mirrors,* and particularly *optical fibers.*

bunched frame alignment signal. A *frame alignment signal* in which the signal *elements* occupy consecutive *digit* positions. Also see *distributed frame alignment signal.*

bunching strip. In *telephone switchboard operation,* a strip of *jacks* connected in parallel in some types of *switchboards* to facilitate the *connection* of *multiple calls.*

bundle. A group of conductors associated together, usually in a single sheath. *Fiber bundles* are usually considered to be in a random arrangement and are used or considered as a single *transmission medium.* See *axial bundle; coherent bundle; incoherent bundle; optical fiber bundle; ray bundle.* Also see Figure S-9.

bundle cable. See *multiple-bundle cable; multichannel bundle cable; single-channel single-bundle cable.*

bundle cable assembly. See *multiple-bundle cable assembly.*

bundle jacket. The outer protective covering applied over a bundle of *optical fibers.* Also see *cladding.*

bundle of rays. See *ray bundle.*

bundle resolving power. The ability of a *coherent optical fiber bundle* to *transmit* the details of an *image,* usually stated in lines per millimeter.

bundle transfer function. See *fiber bundle transfer function.*

buoy. See *sonobuoy; fog buoy.*

buoyant antenna. An *antenna* designed to operate when floating on the surface of the sea, or when streaming submerged at listening depth when towed by a submerged submarine and, therefore, not visible from above the surface.

burn-through range. The maximum range from a given *radar* (being *jammed*) to an object at which a radar jammer can no longer *mask* the *echoes* from the object to the given radar. Consider the relative positions of the given radar, its object (target), and the jammer. At long range, the jammer is at an advantage since it can launch a *pulse* stronger than the object (target) echo and thus mask the echo on the screen of the radar being jammed. As the range to the object (target) decreases, the echo becomes stronger while the *jamming signal* remains the same, unless *jamming power* is increased or the jammer moves in closer to the radar being jammed. As the range diminishes the echo is no longer masked, that is, it propagates (burns) through the masking and is detected. The object (target) at that range is no longer masked by the jamming signals and becomes visible to the radar which until then was being jammed and now is no longer considered jammed, even though *interference* may be visible on the *screen.*

burn-through range equation. See *self-screening range equation.*

Burrus LED.   See *surface-emitting LED.*

burst.   1. In a *data communication system,* a sequence of *signals* counted as a unit in accordance with some specific criterion or measure.   **2.** To separate continuous-form paper into discrete sheets.   **3.** To separate multipart paper.   See *error burst.*

burst isochronous.   See *isochronous burst transmission.*   (The use of the term burst isochronous is deprecated.)

bursty transmission.   *Transmission* of *data* characterized by long periods of idleness between relatively short periods of transmission.   For example, the transmission of three-second *bit streams,* each stream separated by no transmission for 1 to 3 minutes.

bus.   1. One or more *conductors* that serve as a common *connection* for a related group of devices.   **2.** One or more *conductors* used for *transmitting power* or *signals.*   Also see *highway.*   See *data bus; power bus.*

bus coupler.   See *data-bus coupler.*

bus driver.   A *circuit* that *amplifies* a *signal* on a *bus* to assure *reception* of the signal at the destination, for example, an amplifier that energizes a bus.

busy.   In *communication systems,* the condition that exists when a system component is fully occupied and cannot undertake an additional task.   If an *access attempt* is made, a *busy signal* is obtained.   See *camp-on-busy.*

busy circuit.   See *pilot make-busy (PMB) circuit.*

busy hour.   Any 60-minute period during which the *communication traffic load* in a given 24-hour period is a maximum.   If the service time interval is less than 60 minutes, the busy hour is the 60-minute interval whose center is the maximum load service time interval.   In cases where more than one busy hour occurs in a 24-hour period, the busy hour or hours most applicable to the particular situation are used.   More than one busy hour can occur during *saturation,* that is, when a communication system is operating at its *traffic capacity* during two or more time intervals separated by operation at less than traffic capacity (nonsaturation operation).   Synonymous with *peak busy hour.*   Also see *erlang; traffic intensity; traffic load.*   See *group busy hour; network busy hour; switch busy hour.*   See Figure B-9.

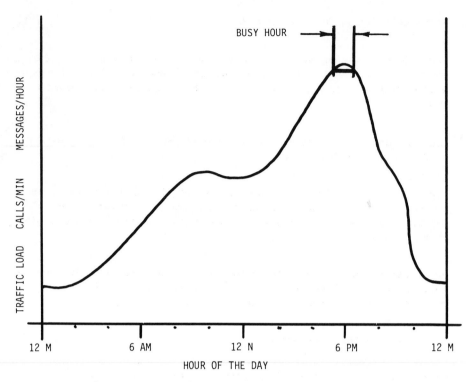

B-9. A *communication traffic load* curve showing the **busy hour.**

busy line. See *call forwarding busy line.*

busy party. A *user* of a *communication system* that is actively using a *terminal station* or *end instrument,* such as a *telephone.*

busy signal. A *signal* sent in the *backward direction* indicating to a *source user (calling party)* that a *destination user's (called party) access line* is *transmitting (busy).* Also see *engaged tone; terminal-engaged signal.* See *camp-on-busy signal.*

butt coupling. The coupling of one *optical fiber* or *optical element* to another, by placing the end or face of one against the end or face of the other so that an *electromagnetic wave* can be *transmitted* with a minimum of loss of power and a maximum *transmission coefficient* at the *interface.* The interface is usually either transverse to the direction of *propagation* or at the *Brewster angle* for maximum *coupling* and total transmission, i.e., zero *reflection,* from *optical element* to optical element. Synonymous with *face-to-face coupling.*

button. See *virtual push button.*

byte. A group of *binary digits* handled as a unit and usually used to represent a *character.* The byte may be a group or *string* of *pulses.* Bytes are used to constitute *alphanumeric characters,* for example, to represent decimal digits or letters. The American National Standard Code for Information Interchange *(ASCII)* and *International Telegraph Alphabet Number 5* use 7-bit bytes (8-bit bytes including the *parity bit)* to represent the *characters* and *control signals.* See *n-bit byte.*

C

Cable. 1. A *jacketed bundle* or jacketed *fiber* in a form that can be *terminated*. 2. A group of *conductors* that are bound together, usually with a protective sheath, a strength member, and *insulation* between individual conductors and for the entire group. See *aerial cable; aerial optical cable; air dielectric coaxial cable; bidirectional cable; branched cable; branch feeder cable; central strength-member optical cable; coaxial cable; distribution cable; duct optical cable; fiber optic cable; fiber optic telecommunication cable; flat optical cable; foam dielectric coaxial cable; intrusion-resistant communication cable; monofilament cable; multichannel bundle cable; multichannel cable; multichannel single-fiber cable; multifilament cable; multipaired cable; multiple bundle cable; paired cable; peripheral strength-member optical cable; plow-in optical cable; quadded cable; Siecor cable; single-channel single-bundle cable; single-channel single-fiber cable; special optical cable; spiral-four cable; submerged cable; symmetrical pair cable; twin cable; wire cable.* See *message.*

cable address code. A *code,* usually registered with all commercial *telecommunication carriers,* used as the address for messages to specific organizations in foreign countries. For example, the cable address code for the *International Organization for Standardization* in Geneva, Switzerland, is 23 887/ISO CH for *Telex* and ISORGANIZ for telegrams.

cable assembly. A *cable* terminated and ready for installation. See *multiple bundle cable assembly; multiple-fiber cable assembly.*

cable code. A variation of the *Morse code,* commonly used in submerged *cables,* in which *dots, dashes,* and *spaces* all have equal durations in time but differ in polarity.

cable core. The portion of a *cable* inside a common covering.

cable driver. See *optical cable driver.*

cable jacket. The outer protective covering applied over the internal *cable* elements.

cable retention. In an *optical transmission system,* the ability of a *connector to* hold or retain its *optical cable* against a specified pulling force on the cable when the connector is held fixed.

cable run. The portion of a *branched cable* or *harness* where the cross-sectional area is largest. Synonymous with *harness run.*

106

calendar.   See *Julian calendar.*

calibration factor.   See *transmitter calibration factor.*

call.   1. The sequence of events begun when a *user* causes a calling *signal* to be given at an exchange and asks for a connection, and concluded when conversation with the *called user (party)* is finished and all the *connections* have been removed.   2. To cause a *calling signal* to be given at an exchange or to cause a *user's* bell or other alarm signal device to operate.   3. A *transmission* identifying the *transmitting station* and the station for which the transmission is intended.   4. An attempt to reach a *user* whether or not successful, that is, a valid request for service.   See *booked call; completed call; conference call; data call; direct call; distress call; emergency call; finished call; follow-on call; junction call; local call; long-distance call; lost call; meet-me conference call; multiple call; nonprecedence call; number call; operator-assisted call; person-to-person call; precedence call; preliminary call; private call; progressive conference call; redirected call; single call; station-to-station call; ticketed call; toll call; trunk call; unsuccessful call; virtual call.*

call-accepted signal.   A *call control signal* sent by the called *data terminal equipment (DTE)* to indicate that it accepts the incoming *call.*   The *call-accepted signal* is sent in the *backward direction* also indicating that the call can be completed if the *called party* answers.   Normally, the call will be automatically charged to the *calling party.*   Also see *call-not-accepted signal.*

call address.   The part of the *call selection signal* that indicates the destination of the *call.*

call area.   See *maximum call area.*

callback.   The positive identification of a calling *terminal* by disconnecting and reestablishing the *connection* by having the called terminal *dial* the number of the calling terminal.   For example, a *computer system* could dial the number of the *calling party.*

call barred.   A *facility* that permits *terminal equipment* to make outgoing *calls* or to receive incoming calls only, but not both.

call capability.   See *virtual call capability.*

call collision.   Contention that occurs when *data terminal equipment (DTE)* and *data circuit-terminating equipment (DCE)* simultaneously transfer a call request *packet* and an incoming call packet, specifying the same *logical channel.*   The DCE will normally proceed with the call request and cancel the incoming call. Also see *clear collision.*

call completion objective.   Policy established within a *telephone network* concerning the manner in which an operator-assisted *call* will be handled.   For example, to process and complete a call without releasing the *calling party,* or not to hold a calling party when the *called party line* is *busy* or the called party is unavailable.

call control character. A *character* of an *alphabet,* or a part of a character, that is used for *call* control. It may be used in conjunction with defined *signal* conditions on other interchange circuits.

call control procedure. The entire set of interactive procedures necessary or required to establish, maintain, and release a *call.*

call control signal. A member of the set of interactive *signals* necessary to establish, maintain, and release a *call.*

call-directly code (CDC). A *code* contained in the first part of *calls* and *messages* so that all *stations* on a *line* can listen to all codes but a *receiver* responds only to its own code. If *broadcast* or group CDCs are used, called stations usually answer before the *transmitting* station begins sending the message. Also see *transmitter start code.*

called-line identification facility. A *facility* provided by a *network* that enables a *calling terminal* to be notified by the network of the *address* to which the calling terminal has been connected. Also see *calling-line identification facility.*

called-line identification-request indicator. An *indicator (signal)* sent in the *forward direction* indicating whether or not the *called-line* identity should be included in the *response message.*

called-line identification signal. A sequence of *characters transmitted* to *calling data terminal equipment* to permit identification of the *called line.*

called-line identity. *Information* sent in the *backward direction* consisting of a number of *signals* indicating the *address* of the *called line.*

called party. The organization or individual *(user)* to which a *call* is placed. Also see *calling party.*

called-party camp-on. A *communication system* function that enables the system to complete an *access attempt* in spite of the issuance of a *user blocking signal.* Communication systems that provide this feature monitor the *busy user* until the user blocking signal ends, and then proceed to complete the *access request.* This feature permits *holding* an incoming *call* until the *called party* is free. Also see *access attempt; calling-party camp-on; queue traffic.*

called station. The *station* to which a *message* is *routed,* a *transmission* is directed, or a *call* is placed.

called user.   In *telephone switchboard operation,* the *user* to whom a *calling party* wishes to be or has been *connected.*

caller.   See *calling party.*

call facility.   See *virtual call facility.*

call-failure signal.   A *signal* sent in the *backward direction* indicating that a *call* cannot be completed due to *time-out,* a *fault,* or a condition that does not correspond to any other particular signal.

call filing time.   The time at which a *call* is accepted by an *operator* for placement.   The *filing time* and date may be recorded on the *call ticket* for *callback* or other purposes.

call forward.   The operation that enables a *user* to forward an incoming *call* that was completed only insofar as it was received, to another *terminal* on the user's own *switching equipment.*   This will probably be preceded by a *call hold* to allow the user to establish that another user is available.

call forwarding.   A service feature available in some *switching systems* where *calls* can be rerouted automatically from one *line, station* number, user, or attendant to another.   This service feature is usually manually activated by the *user.* Also see *call forwarding busy line; call forwarding don't answer.*

call forwarding busy line.   A service feature in some *switching systems* in which an incoming *call* is automatically routed to an attendant when both the *called* and alternate *lines* (numbers) are *busy.*   Also see *call forwarding.*

call forwarding don't answer.   A *service* feature in some *switching systems* in which an incoming *call* is automatically routed to an attendant after a predetermined number of *rings* or seconds.   Also see *call forwarding.*

call hold.   A *telephone service* feature in some *switching systems* in which a *user* is able to leave a first *connection* temporarily in order to answer or make a second *call.*

call indicator.   See *redirected-call indicator.*

calling.   The process of *transmitting* a *selection signal* to establish a *connection* between *stations.*   See *automatic calling; double call-sign calling; group abbreviated address calling; offnet calling; single call-sign calling.*

calling area.   See *maximum calling area (MCA).*

calling facility.   See *manual calling facility; multiaddress calling facility.*

calling frequency. The *frequency* that a *radio station* uses to *call* another station. Also see *answering frequency; crossband radiotelegraph procedure; radiotelegraphy distress frequency; working frequency.*

calling-line identification facility. **1.** A *facility* provided by a *network* that enables a called *terminal* to be notified by the *network* of the *address* of the calling terminal, which may be an intermediate terminal, not necessarily the terminal from which the *call* has originated. **2.** A *facility* provided by a *network* that enables a called *terminal* to be notified by the network of the *address* from which the *call* has originated. Also see *called-line identification facility.*

calling-line identification-request indicator. *Information* sent in the *backward direction* indicating whether or not the *calling-line identity* should be sent forward in a *calling-line identity message.*

calling-line identification signal. A sequence of *characters* transmitted to the *called party* (called *data terminal equipment (DTE)*) to permit identification of the *calling party* (calling data terminal equipment) *line.*

calling-line identity. *Information* sent in the *forward direction* consisting of a number of *address signals* indicating the complete identity of the *calling party* (calling *data terminal equipment*).

calling-line identity message. A *message* sent in the *forward direction* containing the identity of the *calling party* (calling *data terminal equipment*). This message is sent subsequent to an address message that does not contain the identity of the calling party (calling data terminal equipment).

calling net. A *communication network* that is normally associated with *ship-shore communications* and normally used by *ship stations* to *call shore stations* in a *shore net.*

calling party. **1.** The *user* (person, organization, *station, activity, computer, program*) that places a *call.* **2.** In *telephone switchboard operation,* the *user* who originates a *call.* Synonymous with *caller.* Also see *called party.*

calling-party camp-on. A *communication system* function that enables the *system* to complete an *access attempt* in spite of the temporary unavailability of *system transmission* or *switching facilities* required to complete the *access request.* Systems that provide this feature *monitor* the system facilities until the necessary facilities become available and then proceed to complete the access request. Such systems may issue a *system blocking signal* to apprise the *originating user* of the *access* delay. Also see *access attempt; called-party camp-on; queue traffic.*

calling plug. In *telephone switchboard operation,* the *plug,* of the two normally associated with any *cord circuit,* that is the nearer to the *operator* and that is normally used to *call* another *switchboard* or *user.*

calling signal.   1. The *signal transmitted* over a *circuit* to indicate that a *connection* is desired.   **2.** In *telephone switchboard operation,* a visible or audible indication at a *switchboard* that a *user* wishes to speak to the *operator* or to another user, or that the operator wishes to speak to a user.

calling station.   1. The *station* initiating a *transmission.*   **2.** The *station* preparing a *tape* for *transmission.*

call message.   See *multiple-call message; single-call message.*

call-not-accepted signal.   A *call control signal* sent by the called *data terminal equipment (DTE)* to indicate that it does not accept the incoming *call.*   The call-not-accepted signal is sent in the *backward direction* indicating that the call cannot be completed.   Normally there will be no charge to the *calling* or *called party.* Also see *call-accepted signal.*

call-pending indication.   A *signal* indicating to a called and *busy user* that another *calling party* is waiting.

call progress signal.   1. A *call control signal* that is *transmitted* by the called *data-circuit terminating equipment (DCE)* to the calling *data terminal equipment (DTE)* to report the progress of a *call* (the state reached in the establishment of a *connection*) or the reason why the connection could not be established (negative call progress signal).   **2.** For *packet* services, a *call control signal* for *virtual call* service to inform the calling and called DTE's of the reason why a *call* has been cleared.   **3.** For *permanent virtual circuit* service, a *call control signal* to inform the DTE's of the reason why the permanent virtual circuit has been reset.   **4.** For *datagram* service, a *call control signal* to inform the source DTE about the delivery or nondelivery of a specific datagram or about general operation of the DTE-DCE datagram interface or service.

call release time.   In *telephone systems,* the time from initiation of a *clearing signal* by *data terminal equipment (DTE)* until the free circuit condition appears on the originating DTE.

call request time.   In the establishment of a *connection* or the setup of a *call* (placement of a call), the elapsed time from the initiation of a *calling signal* to the receipt of a *proceed-to-select signal,* such as a *dial tone,* by the *calling party.* Also see *call-setup time.*

calls barred facility.   A *facility* that permits *data terminal equipment (DTE)* either to make outgoing *calls* or to receive incoming calls, but not both.

call-second.   A unit of *communication* traffic equal to one *user communicating* with another for a duration of 1 sec.   For example, 150 call-seconds would result from one user making two 75-sec calls on one *channel,* or using two *data channels* for 75 sec each; or two users on two channels, each making a 75-sec call; or two users using the same data channel for 75 sec. *Multiplexing* increases the number of call-seconds available on a single channel or *circuit*. Since a larger unit than the call-second is generally needed, the CCS *(hundred-call-second)* was introduced. Thus, 3600 call-seconds = 36 CCS = 1 call-hour. Thus, 3600 call-seconds per hour = 36 CCS per hour = 1 call-hour per hour = 1 *erlang* = 1 *traffic unit*.

call selection time.   In the establishment of a *connection* or the placement of a *call*, the elapsed time from the receipt by the calling party of a *proceed-to-select signal (dial tone)*, until all the *selection signals* have been *transmitted* (*dialing* has been completed). Also see *call setup time*.

call setup.   The establishment of a *circuit-switched connection* between two *users* or between two sets of *data terminal equipment (DTE)*.

call setup time.   1. The overall length of time required to establish a *circuit-switched call* between *users*.   **2.** For *data communications*, the overall length of time to establish a *circuit-switched call* between two sets of *data terminal equipment (DTE)*, that is, the time from the initiation of a *call request* to the beginning of the call message. It is the summation of: (1) the *call request time*, or the time from initiation of a *calling signal* to the delivery of the *proceed-to-select signal* to the *calling party;* (2) the *call selection time*, or the time from the delivery of the *proceed-to-select signal* until all the *selection signals* have been *transmitted;* and (3) the *post selection time*, or the time from the end of the transmission of the selection signals until the delivery of the *completed call signal* to the *originating DTE*.

call sign.   A *station* or *address designator* represented by a combination of *characters* or pronounceable *words* that is used to introduce or identify a *communication facility, station,* command, authority, activity, or unit, and is used primarily for the establishment and maintenance of communication. See *aircraft call sign; collective call sign; indefinite call sign; individual call sign; international call sign; military call sign; military ship international call sign; net call sign; permanent voice call sign; ship call sign; ship collective call sign; visual call sign.*

call-sign allocation plan.   The table of allocation of *international call sign* series contained in the current edition of the *International Telecommunication Union (ITU)* Radio Regulations. The first two *characters* of each *call sign*, whether two letters or one number and one letter, in that order, identify the nationality of the station. In certain instances where the complete alphabetical block is allocated to a single nation, the first letter is sufficient for national identity. Individual assignments are made by appropriate national assignment authorities from the national allocation. Future expansion may require a new series for allocation to individual nations. For example, the new series might have as its first three national identity characters a letter, a number, and a letter, in that order. Certain combinations would remain unused.

call-sign calling.   See *double call-sign calling; single call-sign calling.*

call-sign linkage.   The association of a new *call sign* and *address group* of an activity or organization with the old call sign and address group of the same activity or organization.

call tape.   In *radiotelegraph communication systems* using automatic *broadcast* equipment, a *tape* on which the standard signals for initiating a broadcast are recorded for automatic *transmission.*

call ticket.   A record of a *call,* perhaps indicating the time and duration of the call, the *called* and *calling party* numbers, the date, the charges, and the *operator's* initials.

call tracing.   A *facility* that permits an entitled *user* to be informed about the *routing* of *data* for an established *connection,* identifying the entire route from the origin to the destination.   There are two basic types of call tracing; *permanent call tracing,* concerning all calls, and *on-demand call tracing,* in which a certain call is traced upon request immediately after it is disconnected.   See *on-demand call tracing; permanent call tracing.*

call transfer.   1. In a *telephone system,* to disconnect an incoming *access line* from one outgoing line and connect it to another outgoing line.   The user may *signal* the *operator* and request that an incoming call be transferred to another number served by the same *switchboard* or *private branch exchange (PBX).*   **2.** A service feature in which a *user* is able to arrange *call selections* personally.

call-up signal.   One of the members of a set of *signals* used by a *radio station* to establish contact with another station.   When confidential call signs are used in the call-up signals, their meanings in *message headings* should not be used.   See *preliminary call-up signal.*

call-without-selection signal.   See *direct call.*

calspar.   See *Iceland spar.*

camp-on.   1. A *communication system* feature that permits *holding* an incoming *call* until the *called party* is free.   The *busy party* hears a tone indicating that a *calling party* is waiting.   When the called party hangs up on the original call, the *phone* will ring and will automatically be connected to the calling party that has been waiting.   **2.** The *holding* by a *network* of a *call attempt* that was unsuccessful due to the *called terminal* being *busy,* with subsequent connection as soon as the called terminal becomes free.   Synonymous with *connect-when-free.*

camp-on-busy.   A *telephone* calling procedure in which a *calling party* is allowed to remain on the *line* until the *called party* is free.   Also see *call-pending indication.*

camp-on-busy signal.   1. A *telephone signal* that informs a *busy party* that another *calling party* is waiting for a *connection.*   **2.** A *teleprinter exchange facility signal* that automatically causes a *calling station* to retry the *called party's* number after a given interval when the *called party's* teleprinter is occupied or the circuits are busy. Synonymous with *speed-up tone.*

camp-on-with-recall.   A *camp-on* with the release of the *calling party's terminal* until the *called party* terminal becomes free. Thus, the calling party can establish other *calls* until the *recall signal* is obtained, rather than simply wait until the called party's *line* is free.

CAN.   Cancel character.

Canada balsam.   An adhesive used to cement *optical elements.*

cancel character (CAN).   A *transmission control character* used to indicate that the *data* with which it is associated are in *error* or are to be ignored. See *block cancel character.*

cancellation.   See *side-lobe cancellation.*

candela (cd).   The *luminous intensity* of 1/600,000 m^2 of a *blackbody radiator* at the *temperature* of solidification of platinum, 2045 *kelvin.* One candela emits 4π lumens of *light* flux.

candlepower.   A unit of measure of the *illuminating* power of any *light source,* equal to the number of international standard candles (candela) of the source of light. A *flux* density of 1 lumen of light flux per *steradian* of solid angle measured from the source is produced by a point source of 1 candela emitting equally in all directions.

capability.   See *multilevel precedence capability; virtual call capability.*

capacitance.   See *capacity.*

capacitive coupling.   The *coupling* of *signals* or *noise* in which one *conductor* is linked to another by means of the electrical *capacity* between them. Electric charge concentrations on one side of the capacity induce charge concentrations on the other side. The cumulative charges produce voltages and their migrations constitute *currents.* The coupling may be deliberate, as in the case of a capacitive coupled amplifier circuit, or unintentional, as in the case of *crosstalk.*

capacitive reactance.   The opposition to the flow of *alternating electric current* when an alternating *voltage* is applied to a *capacitor.* When a voltage is applied to the capacitor, electric charges accumulate on it, causing its voltage to rise. When the capacitor is fully charged, the capacitor voltage is equal to the applied voltage and no more current will flow. Thus, the current is reduced to zero. Then the applied voltage reverses, discharging the capacitor to zero charge and zero voltage. The applied voltage reverses polarity again and the cycle repeats.

The capacitive reactance, X_c in ohms, is given by $X_c = 1/2\pi fC$, where f is the frequency in *hertz,* and C is the capacity in farads. The capacity is a function of geometry and materials. The current, I_c, in amperes, is given by $I_c = V/X_c$, where V is the applied voltage in volts and X_c is the capacitive reactance in ohms. Also see *impedance; inductive reactance.*

capacitor.   An electrical device that has the capability of storing or holding an *electrostatic* charge and, therefore, electric energy.

capacity.   **1.** The ability of material media to store an electrical charge, usually measured in farads, microfarads, or picofarads.   **2.** The property of a *capacitor* that determines the amount of electrical energy that can be stored in it by applying a given voltage.   For example, $E = (1/2)CV^2$ where E is the energy, C the capacity, and V is the voltage.   Also: $Q = CV$, where Q is the stored charge, C is the capacity, and V is the voltage.   When rapidly vibrating over finite distances, the charge produces an oscillating *electric field* that can be used to launch an *electromagnetic wave,* such as a *lightwave* or a radio wave.   Synonymous with *capacitance.*   See *channel capacity; load capacity; storage capacity; traffic capacity.*   Also see Figure O-4.

capture effect.   An effect associated with the reception of *frequency modulated signals* in which, if two signals are received on the same frequency, only the stronger of the two *received* signals will appear in the *output.*   The complete suppression of the weaker *carrier* occurs at the receiver *limiter* where it is treated as *noise* and rejected.

card.   See *edge-notched card; flash card; key card; magnetic card; punch card.*

card code.   A *code* in which the set of *coded characters* is a set of patterns of holes punched in a card, each pattern corresponding to a character of an *alphabet,* such as the letters of the English (Roman) alphabet or the decimal numbers 0 through 9.   For example, the code used on the standard 80-column *punch card,* in which a column of 12 holes is used to represent a character.

card dialer.   An automatic *dialer* combined with a *telephone* that makes use of *coded* numbers recorded on a card.   The recording may be made with punched holes, *magnetic* recording, printed bar codes, or other means.

card punch.   A device that punches a pattern of holes in a card to represent *information.*

carriage return.   **1.** A *machine function* that controls horizontal movement of the carriage of *teletypewriter-teleprinter* equipment to the left margin of the paper.   This movement is accomplished by use of the *carriage return (CR) character key* or corresponding perforation in paper tape being read.   **2.** The return to the starting position of a line on a page.

carriage return (CR) character. A *format effector* that causes the print or *display position* to move to the first position on the same line of print.

carrier. 1. A *wave, pulse train,* or other *signal* suitable for *modulation* by an information-bearing signal to be *transmitted* over a *communication system.* **2.** An unmodulated *emission.* A *carrier* is usually a *sinusoidal wave,* a recurring series of *pulses,* or a *direct-current (DC) signal.* **3.** An organization that provides a transport service to the public, such as a railroad company, an airline company, a steamship company, a communication company, or a trucking company. Also see *center frequency.* See *commercial communication common carrier; common carrier; communication common carrier; continuous carrier; double-sideband suppressed carrier; full carrier; pulse carrier; reduced carrier; single-sideband suppressed carrier; subcarrier; suppressed carrier; telecommunication carrier; two independent-sideband carrier; virtual carrier.*

carrier controlled approach (CCA). A communication and control system for directing the approach of aircraft to an aircraft carrier. CCA is used in search and rescue operations and military operations for controlling the approach to the aircraft carrier. It is also used to assist in *homing.*

carrier dropout. A loss of the *carrier wave* as a result of *noise,* maintenance activity, *system fault,* system *degradation,* or other cause.

carrier frequency. 1. The *frequency* of an unmodulated *carrier wave.* **2.** A *frequency* capable of being *modulated* by an information-bearing *signal* of another frequency or frequencies. In *frequency modulation,* the carrier frequency is also referred to as the center frequency.

carrier frequency shift. See *subcarrier frequency shift.*

carrier frequency stability. A measure of the ability of a *transmitter* to maintain (remain on) an *assigned frequency.*

carrier-interrupt signaling. See *digital carrier-interrupt signaling.*

carrier leak. The portion of the *carrier* that remains after carrier *suppression* in a *suppressed-carrier transmission system.*

carrier level. The *power level* of a *carrier wave* at a particular point in a system, usually expressed in relation to some reference level in *decibels,* or in watts, milliwatts, microwatts, or picowatts.

carrier multiplex. See *frequency division multiplex.*

carrier noise level. The *noise* level that results from undesired variations of a *carrier* in the absence of any intended or desired *modulation signal.* Synomymous with *residual modulation.*

carrier pigeon. A *homing* pigeon trained to carry *messages* from a given site to its home destination.

carrier power. The average *power* supplied to an *antenna transmission line (feeder)* by a *radio transmitter,* averaged during one *radio frequency* cycle when there is no *modulation.* This does not apply to *pulse modulated* or *frequency-shift keying emissions.*

carriers. The *electrons* and *holes* in a *semiconducting* material that result when some electrons have been thermally excited into the *conduction band* from the *valence band.* Thermal *ionization* creates *hole-electron* pairs. One hole is created for each free (i.e., excited) electron. Both the hole and the electron are capable of transporting a charge; hence, they are collectively called "charge carriers" or, simply "carriers." The moving carriers constitute *electric currents* in *lasers, light emitting diodes, photodetectors,* diodes, and transistors. Electrons excited to higher *energy levels* cause *photon absorption.* When moving to lower energy levels, photons *(lightwaves)* are emitted.

carrier shift. 1. A method of *keying* a *radio carrier* for *transmitting binary data* or *teletypewriter signals* that consists of *shifting* the *carrier frequency* in one direction for a *mark signal* and in the opposite direction for a *space signal.* **2.** A condition resulting from imperfect *modulation* whereby the positive and negative excursions of the *envelope* pattern are unequal. This effects a change in the *carrier power.* There can be a positive or a negative carrier shift.

carrier-to-noise power ratio. The ratio of the *power* of the *carrier wave* to that of the *noise* measured at a *receiver* of defined *bandwidth* before any nonlinear *signal* processing, usually expressed in *decibels.* Examples of nonlinear signal processing are *amplitude* limiting (clipping) and *detection* (rectification or demodulation). In *lightwave communication systems,* noise is introduced by *light sources, coupling* with adjacent *channels,* the *transmission media,* and other sources of *interference.*

carrier-to-noise (C/N) ratio. 1. The ratio of the *amplitude* value of the *carrier* to that of the *noise* in the *receiver intermediate frequency (IF) bandwidth* before any nonlinear process such as amplitude *limiting* and *detection* takes place. **2.** The ratio of the *received signal* level to the *receiver noise* level. If *power* values are used, 10 times the logarithm to the base 10 of the ratio converts the ratio to *decibels;* if *current* or *voltage* values are used, 20 times the logarithm to the base 10 converts the ratio to *decibels.*

carrier-to-receiver noise density. In *satellite communications,* the ratio of the *received carrier power* (C), to the *received noise power density (kT),* where k is *Boltzmann's constant* and T is the *receiver system noise temperature* in *kelvin;* that is, the carrier-to-receiver noise density ratio is C/kT. Taking the logarithm to the base 10 of the ratio and multiplying by 10 converts the ratio to *decibels.*

carrier transmission. See *full-carrier transmission; suppressed-carrier transmission.*

carrier wave. A *wave* capable of being *modulated* in some fashion in order to be able to transmit *data, information,* or intelligence in the form of *signals.* Usually *electromagnetic,* it can also be a sound or elastic wave. Types of modulation include *frequency, phase, amplitude,* or *pulse code.* The *carrier wave* has its own frequency. It may be any electromagnetic wave such as radio waves, *lightwaves, gamma radiation,* X rays, or *microwaves.* Modulated lightwaves may be conducted in *optical fibers, bundles,* or *cables.*

Carson bandwidth. The *transmission bandwidth* required for a *frequency-modulated signal* as determined by the *Carson bandwidth rule.*

Carson bandwidth rule. A rule defining the approximate *bandwidth* requirements of *communication system* components for a *carrier signal* that is *frequency modulated* by a continuous or broad *spectrum* of frequencies rather than a single frequency. The Carson *bandwidth* rule is expressed in mathematical notation as C.B.R. = $2(\Delta f + f_m)$, where Δf is the carrier peak deviation frequency, and f_m is the highest modulating frequency. Bandwidth requirements for modulated carriers and equipment capabilities impose limits on the extent of *multiplexing* that can be accommodated. The Carson bandwidth rule is often applied to *transmitters, antennas, light sources, receivers, photodetectors,* and other communication system components.

Cartesian lens. A lens with one surface that is a Cartesian oval and which thus can be an *aplanatic lens.*

cascading. The forming of a linear *string* of entities, each entity interacting only with its neighbors. For example, a single sequence of *nodes* forming a one-*path network,* a series of *amplifiers* with each *output* connected to the *input* of another amplifier except the last, or a series of *circuits* connected end to end. Also see *tandem.*

case. See *figure case; letter case.*

case circuit breaker. See *molded-case circuit breaker.*

case shift.   1. In *data* equipment, the change from letters to numerals, or vice versa.   **2.** In typewriting or typesetting, the change from lowercase letters to uppercase letters, or vice versa.   **3.** The changeover of the mechanism of *telegraph* receiving equipment from letter case to figure case, or vice versa.

Cassegrain.   See *uniform-illumination Cassegrain.*

Cassegrain antenna.   An *antenna* that *radiates electromagnetic waves* by radiating from a primary source to a *reflector* that shapes the *beam* into a desired *directivity pattern (lobe).*

catastrophic degradation.   The rapid reduction of a *system's* or *component's* capability to perform its intended function; usually a total failure to function. For example, in *laser diodes,* the sudden reduction in *optical power output* due to facet failure caused by intense optical fields that bring about local disassociation of the material, to the point of fracturing or cracking.   The critical damage is measurable in watts per centimeter of facet.   Catastrophic degradation has occurred in solid-state (semiconductor) *lasers* of all types.   The reduction in optical power output usually occurs as a decrease in light flux density or a decrease in light pulse strength.   Also see *gradual degradation.*

category.   See *access category; emergency category.*

catenation.   See *tandem.*

catheter.   See *fiber-optic catheter.*

cathode.   An emitter of negatively-charged particles or a source of electrons, such as the heated filament in a vacuum or *cathode ray tube,* or the *photoemissive* surfaces of some *photodetectors.*   Synonymous with *emitter.*

cathode ray tube (CRT).   A vacuum tube consisting essentially of an electron gun that produces a concentrated stream of high-speed electrons (an electron beam or cathode ray) that impinges on a phosphorescent coating on the back of a viewing face *(screen).*   The excitation of the phosphor produces *light.*   The *intensity* of the light is controlled by regulating the flow rate of the electrons.   *Deflection* of the *beam* is achieved either electromagnetically, by *currents* in coils outside the tube, or electrostatically, by *electric fields* produced by *voltages* on pairs of deflection plates (horizontal and vertical) between which the beam passes inside the tube on its way to the phosphor-coated screen.   See Figure C-1.

C-1. An *operator* and a **cathode ray tube** (CRT) used for *display* of sales *information.* (Courtesy of Wyle Laboratories Corporate Communications Department.)

cavity. See *optical cavity; resonant cavity; selective cavity.*

cavity combiner. A *combiner* in which one or more *resonant bandpass* selective cavities are used to achieve a combining of two or more *frequencies.* Cavity combiners are placed in the *transmission lines* leading from a number of *transmitters* to a single *antenna.*

CCA. *Carrier controlled approach.*

cch. *Connections per circuit hour; hundred circuit-hours.*

CCIR. The International Consultative Committee for Radio, a committee of the *International Telecommunication Union (ITU),* Geneva, Switzerland.

CCITT. The International Consultative Committee for Telegraphy and Telephony, a committee of the *International Telecommunication Union (ITU),* Geneva, Switzerland.

CCS. *Hundred-call-seconds.*

CDF. *Combined distribution frame.*

CDM. *Color-division multiplexing.*

CDMA. *Code-division multiple access.*

celestial equator. The great circle of the *celestial sphere* whose plane is perpendicular to the axis of the earth's rotation. The celestial equator divides the celestial sphere into northern and southern hemispheres.

celestial latitude. The angle measured north or south from the *ecliptic* along a secondary great circle perpendicular to it.

celestial longitude. The angle measured from the *vernal equinox* along the *ecliptic* to the secondary great circle passing through the point at which the longitude is being determined.

celestial mechanics. The branch of astronomy concerning the translational, rotational, and deformational motions of bodies under the influence of forces such as gravitational forces, forces due to the resistance of media to the motion of bodies, and *light* pressure. It also treats the motion of artificial celestial bodies in unpowered phases of flight. Much of celestial mechanics is devoted to studies of the translational motion of the planets, satellites, meteors, and other elements of the solar system under mutual attraction according to the law of gravitation.

celestial meridian. The great circle on the *celestial sphere* that passes through the north and south points, the observer's *zenith* and *nadir,* and the celestial poles. The celestial meridian plane is parallel to that of the earth meridian that passes through the observation points on earth.

celestial pole. One of the points on the *celestial sphere* at which it is intersected by the celestial axis. Consequently, there is a north and a south celestial pole.

celestial sphere. In celestial mechanics, a sphere of near-infinite radius with a point of observation at its center. Since its radius is so large, any point on earth may serve as its center. Its maximum radius approaches that of the known universe; its minimum radius is the distance to the nearest star.

cell. See *index-matching cell; Kerr cell; photoemissive cell; photovoltaic cell; Pockel cell; radar resolution cell.*

cement. An adhesive used to bond *optical elements* together or to bond optical elements to holding devices. Three general types of cement used in the optical industry are blocking cements, mounting cements, and optical cements. See *blocking cement; mounting cement; optical cement; thermoplastic cement; thermosetting cement.*

cemented doublet. A *compound lens* consisting of two lenses joined together by *optical cement.*

center.   See *alarm center; circuit-switching center; communication center; filing communication center; filter center; gateway switching center; internal message distribution center; message center; nodal switching center; scattering center; signal center; signal communication center; storage center; store-and-forward switching center; switching and message distribution center; switching center; tandem center; telecommunication center.*

center frequency.   **1.** In *frequency modulation,* the resting *frequency* or initial frequency of the *carrier* before *modulation.* **2.** In *facsimile systems,* the *frequency* midway between *picture black* and *picture white* frequencies.   Also see *carrier.*

center sampling.   A method of *sampling* a *digital data stream* at the center of each *signal element.*

centimetric wave.   An *electromagnetic wave* with a *wavelength* between 1 centimeter and 10 centimeters, and hence a *frequency* of 3 to 30 gigahertz; that is, a wave in the *superhigh frequency (SHF) range.*   Also see *frequency spectrum designation.*

central battery exchange.   See *common battery exchange.*

centralized computer network.   A *computer network* in which all of the *data processing* capability required by *users* is located at one *node.*

centralized operation.   Operation of a *communication network* in which *transmission* may occur between the *control station* and *tributary stations,* but not between tributary stations.

central office.   See *switching center.*

central office side.   See *equipment side.*

central primary control.   The selection and management of the *control station* of a *communication network* from a given single *node* in the *network.*

central processing unit (CPU).   A unit of a *computer* that includes *circuits* that control the interpretation and execution of instructions.   Synonymous with *central processor* and with *main frame.*   CPU is also used as an abbreviation for *communication processor unit.*

central processor.   See *central processing unit.*

central strength-member optical cable.   A cable containing optical fibers that are wrapped around a high tensile-strength material and having crush-resistant jacketing. Examples of high tensile-strength materials are stranded steel and nylon. Also see *peripheral strength-member optical cable.*

cesium clock second.   See *second.*

CFAR.   *Constant false alarm rate.*

chad.   The material separated from a *punched tape* or a *punched card* produced when forming a hole.

chadless perforation.   A method of cutting a tape in which the cuts are only partial and do not form a hole, the chads or cuttings remaining attached (hinged) to the tape.

chadless tape.   Punched tape that has been punched in such a way that pieces are not separated from the tape, chad is not formed, only a partial perforation is made, and what would be chad remains attached to the tape. This is a deliberate process and should not be confused with imperfect chadding. Chadless tape is used on mechanically-sensed paper tape readers, rather than on optically-sensed readers.

chad tape.   Punched tape used in *telegraphy-teletypewriter* operation. The perforations, called chad, are severed from the tape and the patterns of holes thus formed represent *characters.* The characters are not normally printed on chad tape.

chaff.   A *resonant* piece of metal or conductive-coated material used to reradiate *electromagnetic* energy to create a *radar echo.* It is most effective as a *reflector* at a length of one-half *wavelength.* It is used to screen objects (targets), confuse search radar, and cause radar to break *lock-on.*

chain.   The sequence of *binary digits* used to generate a *chain code.* See *breakout chain; tandem; visual responsibility chain.*

chain code.   A *code* derived from a given *binary-digit* sequence in such a fashion that the *code groups* are related to their neighbors and are based on the given sequence. For example, the code set derived by taking a binary-digit sequence and deriving *n-bit bytes* by taking n-bits at a time from the sequence, each time moving (displacing) one bit to the right. If the sequence is 011010, the codes would be 011, 110, 101, 010, 100, and 001. Note that all the codes are different and the combination 000 does not occur. If it does occur, this could be interpreted as an error in an error detection scheme. Chain codes are frequently made using *unit distance codes.* See Figure C-2.

DECIMAL	00010111 CHAIN CODE
0	000
1	001
2	010
3	101
4	011
5	111
6	110
7	100

C-2. A 3-bit **chain code** and possible *decimal digit* equivalents.

chaining.   See *daisy chaining.*

challenge.   Any process carried out by a unit or person with the objective of ascertaining the identity of another unit or person. The answer to the challenge is called a *reply*. The *challenge and reply* combination is to be known only to those who are designated to be friendly. If the reply does not match the challenge, the challenger can assume that the replying unit or person is not friendly and take measures accordingly.

challenge and reply.   **1.** A prearranged procedure in which one *station* requests authentication of another station (the *challenge*) and the latter station, by a proper *reply* establishes its authenticity.   **2.** A procedure in which a calling *station* identifies itself (challenge), requests the identity of another station *(called station)*, and then the called station identifies itself *(reply)*, in accordance with a *code* in which the reply must match the challenge.

challenge-and-reply authentication.   In *communication* involving *messages,* a prearranged procedure in which one *message originator* places a request for *authentication* from another communicator *(addressee)* and the latter's validity or identity is established by proper *reply* to the *challenge.*

change.   See *non-return-to-zero change (NRZ-C).*

change coefficient.   See *phase change coefficient.*

changed-address interception.   The *interception,* usually by automatic means, of a call to an obsolete *address* in which the *calling party terminal* is advised of the new address, followed either by call redirection to the new address or by *release* of the calling party terminal.

change in operational control (CHOP).   In the course of a voyage or flight, the transfer of a ship or aircraft from one operational control authority (OCA) to another.   A shift in *radio guard* may take place at the same time.   The CHOP and shift times are usually prescribed in sailing or departure orders to enable the new OCA to *communicate* with the ship or aircraft.

channel. **1.** In *data transmission,* a means of performing *simplex transmission* in one preassigned direction. **2.** A single unidirectional or bidirectional *path* for transmitting or receiving *electrical signals.* In one-way-at-a-time transmission, the single channel may be used for two-way transmission. **3.** A single path in a *transmission medium,* each path separated by some means; e.g., physical separation, such as in a multipair cable, or by *multiplex* separation, such as *frequency* or *time division multiplexing.* **4.** A *connection* between two *nodes* in a *network.* **5.** In moving *magnetic storage* devices (discs, drums, tapes, or cards), that portion of the magnetic medium that is accessible to a reading or writing head. **6.** A path along which *signals* can be sent; e.g., a *data* channel, an input channel, or an output channel. **7.** In *communication theory,* that part of a *communication system* that connects a *data source* to a *data sink,* the source or sink being determined by the momentary direction of transmission. **8.** A complete *facility* for *telecommunications* on a system or *circuit;* e.g., a *television channel, radio channel,* or *facsimile* channel. The number of independent channels available in a system depends on the number of separate communication facilities that can be provided by them. See *adjacent channel; analog data channel; auxiliary channel; backward channel; data channel; data transmission channel; deep channel; digital data channel; drop channel; engineering channel; forward channel; frequency-derived channel; idle channel; information bearer channel; information channel; logical channel; network control channel; nonsynchronous data transmission channel; one-way-only channel; primary channel; radio channel; rescue control channel; secondary channel; status channel; symmetrical channel; symmetric binary channel; synchronous data transmission channel; telegraph channel; time-derived channel; transmission channel; voice frequency channel.* See Figure C-3 (p. 126).

channel allocation. See *adaptive channel allocation.*

channel-associated signaling. *Signaling* in which the *signals* necessary for the *traffic* carried by a single *channel* are transmitted in the channel itself or in a signaling channel permanently associated with it. Also see *in-band signaling.*

channel bank. A part of a *carrier-multiplex terminal* that performs the first step of *modulation.* It multiplexes a group of channels into a higher *frequency band* and, conversely, *demultiplexes* the higher frequency band into separate channels. Also see *wideband system.*

channel basic group. In *frequency-division multiplexed wideband systems,* a group of *channels;* usually 12 channels in the US and Canada.

channel bundle cable. See *multichannel bundle cable.*

channel cable. See *multichannel cable.*

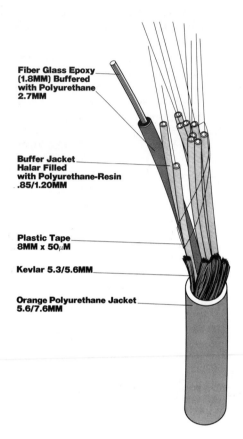

Fiber Glass Epoxy
(1.8MM) Buffered
with Polyurethane
2.7MM

Buffer Jacket
Halar Filled
with Polyurethane-Resin
.85/1.20MM

Plastic Tape
8MM x 50μM

Kevlar 5.3/5.6MM

Orange Polyurethane Jacket
5.6/7.6MM

C-3. A Siecor all-*dielectric* 10-*fiber cable* (filled *buffer*) for *duct* installation. Each fiber pair is capable of providing 672 *voice* **channels** for a Fort Wayne, Indiana, interoffice trunk. (Courtesy of Siecor Optical Cables, Inc.)

channel capacity. A measure of the maximum possible *information* rate that a channel can handle, based on specified constraints. Channel capacity is measured as the ability of a given *channel,* subject to specified constraints, to transmit *messages* from a specified *message source.* It is expressed either as the maximum possible *mean transinformation content* per character or as the maximum possible *average transinformation rate* that can be achieved. An arbitrarily small probability of error is allowed and an appropriate *code* is used.

channel gate. A device that connects a *channel* to a *highway (bus),* or a highway (bus) to a channel, at specified times under appropriate controls.

channel group. One of the assemblies of a number of *channels,* such as a *basic group, supergroup, mastergroup,* or *jumbogroup.*

channel increment. See *radio frequency channel increment.*

channeling equipment. See *channel translation equipment.*

channel interference. See *adjacent channel interference; cochannel interference.*

channelization. The method of using a single *wideband* facility to *transmit* many relatively *narrow-bandwidth signals* by subdividing the *frequency spectrum* used in the wideband channel. Also see *channel; wideband system.*

channel jumbogroup. In *frequency-division multiplexed wideband systems,* a group of *mastergroups;* usually 6 six-hundred *channel* mastergroups in the US and Canada.

channel loading. See *idle-channel loading.*

channel mastergroup. In *frequency-division multiplexed wideband systems,* a group of *supergroups.* In most *communication systems* in the US and Canada, a *mastergroup* is composed to 10 sixty-channel supergroups or 600 *voice channels.* Some mastergroups that are used in terrestrial *telephone systems* carry 300 or 900 channels that are formed by *multiplexing* 5 or 15 sixty-channel supergroups, respectively.

channel mode. See *satellite channel mode.*

channel noise. See *idle channel noise; total channel noise.*

channel noise level. 1. The *ratio* of the *channel noise* at any point in a *transmission system* to some arbitrary amount of *noise* chosen as a reference level, usually expressed in *decibels* above the specified reference level, abbreviated *dBrn,* signifying the reading of a *circuit noise meter;* or in adjusted decibels, *dBa,* signifying circuit noise meter reading adjusted to represent an interfering effect under specified conditions. 2. The *noise power density spectrum* in the *frequency range* of interest. 3. The average *noise power* in the *frequency range* of interest. 4. The indication on a specified instrument of the *noise* in a *channel,* the characteristics of the instrument being determined by the type of noise to be measured and the use being made of the channel. Also see *signal-to-noise ratio.*

channel operation. See *drop channel operation.*

channel packing. A technique for maximizing the number of lower *frequency* or lower-speed *data signals* into a single higher frequency or higher-speed *data stream* for *transmission* over a single *channel.* An *optical fiber, cable,* or *bundle* can be used to provide one channel or many channels, by means of *multiplexing,* as well as can other *transmission media.*

channel patching jackfield. A *patching jackfield* consisting of a rack of *telephone jack patch panels* that facilitate the *connection* of *user* discrete *channels* to channeling equipment by *jack* and *plug* connection. For example, a channel patching jackfield is used in *earth stations* to enable *patching* of *traffic* channels to *multiplex* equipment on a day-to-day basis for *fault* location purposes, and to allow *access* to traffic *paths* for monitoring and test purposes.

channel reliability. The percent of time that a channel may be expected to be available for use. It is calculated as the percent of time that a *channel* was available for use in a specific direction during a specified period of scheduled availability. Channel reliability, CR, is given in percent by $CR = 100(1 - T_O/T_s) = 100T_a/T_s$, where T_O is the channel total *outage* state time (outage period), T_s is the channel total scheduled time, and T_a is the channel total available time. Also see *circuit reliability*.

channel restoration. The repair or reconnection of an existing *channel*.

channel selectivity. See *adjacent channel selectivity*.

channel signaling. See *common-channel signaling; separate channel signaling*.

channel single-bundle cable. See *single-channel single-bundle cable*.

channel single-fiber cable. See *multichannel single-fiber cable; single-channel single-fiber cable*.

channel supergroup. In *frequency-division multiplexed wideband systems,* a group of *basic groups;* usually 5 twelve-channel basic groups in the US and Canada.

channel time slot. A time period starting at a particular instant in a *frame* and allocated to a *channel* for *transmitting* a *character, signal,* or other *data.* For example, a *telephone* channel *time slot* for *multiplexing calls*.

channel translation equipment. Equipment used for the *frequency translation* of *audio channels,* for their assembly into *channel groups,* and for performing the reverse process, that is, for *multiplexing* and *demultiplexing*. Synonymous with *channeling equipment*.

channel vocoder. See *channel voice encoder*.

channel voice encoder. A voice *encoding* and *decoding* device that uses *speech spectrum compression* of up to 90% by separation of the speech *frequency band* into a number of subband channels by rectifying the *signal* in each *channel*. The resulting *direct-current (DC)* signal represents a time-varying average signal for the subband. These *outputs* are *multiplexed* with a separate channel conveying the fine structure characteristics of the original speech necessary in order to reconstitute the original voice by decoding at the receiver. Synonymous with *channel vocoder*.

character. 1. One member of a set of elements used for the organization, control, or representation of *data*. Agreement must have been reached as to its use or meaning. Characters may be letters, *digits,* punctuation marks, *control signals,* or other signs and *symbols* often represented in a spatial arrangement of adjacent or connected strokes, or in the form of other physical *conditions* or events, such as time or space sequences of electrical pulses or patterns of magnetized spots, or punched holes in cards, tapes, or other *data media.* Characters are used to represent data, which, in turn, represent *information* when meaning is assigned to the data. Characters are used for the organization, control, representation, *transmission,* and storage of information. In most *communication systems,* characters are represented as strings or sequences of *pulses* or as graphic symbols on a *display surface.* Characters are represented in *optical fiber systems* as *light pulses* in single fibers or as a *picture element* in *optical cables.* 2. A *symbol,* such as a letter, numeral, punctuation mark, and by extension, a nonprinting *control character,* such as a *space, shift, carriage return,* or *line-feed character.* See *acknowledge character; bell character; binary character; block cancel character; block check character; call control character; cancel character; carriage return (CR) character; check character; code character; code extension character; control character; data link escape (DLE) character; delete (DEL) character; device control character; end-of-medium (EOM) character; end-of-selection (EOS) character; end-of-text (EOT) character; end-of-transmission (EOT) character; end-of-transmission block (ETB) character; enquiry (ENQ) character; escape (ESC) character; facility request separator character; font change character; form feed (FF) character; gap character; horizontal tabulation character; idle character; inactive character; line feed (LF) character; negative acknowledge (NAK) character; new line (NL) character; nonlocking code extension character; null (NUL) character; shift-in (SI) character; shift-out (SO) character; space character; special character; start-of-heading (SOH) character; start-of-text (STX) character; start-stop character; stuffing character; substitute (SUB) character; synchronous idle (SYN) character; transmission control character; vertical tabulation character; who-are-you (WRU) character.*

character check. A method of *error detection* in which preset rules are used for the formation of *characters.*

character count integrity. The preservation of the precise number of *characters* that are originated per *message* or per unit time in a *user*-to-user connection. This is not to be confused with *character integrity* that requires that the characters delivered are, in fact, as they were originated. Also see *added bit; bit inversion; deleted bit; digital error.*

character display device. A *display device* that gives a representation of *data* only in the form of *characters.*

character fill. To add meaningless *characters* to a *string* solely for the purpose of achieving a specified total, such as a specified number of characters stored in a given *storage medium* or *frame,* or a specified number of characters *transmitted* in a given *time frame,* or to complete a fixed string length when the meaningful data do not complete the *data unit,* such as a *word* or *block.*

character generator. 1. A device or *functional unit* used to control a *display writer* during the generation of a *graphic character* in the *display space* on the *display sur-face* of a *display device.* 2. A *functional unit* that converts the *code* for a graphic *character* into a character suitable for *display* in accordance with prescribed conventions. See *dot-matrix character generator; stroke character generator.*

character integrity. Preservation of a *character* during *processing, storage,* and *transmission.*

character interval. The total number of *unit intervals,* including intervals for *synchronizing, information, error checking,* or *control bits,* required to *transmit* any given *character* in any given *communication system.* Extra *signals* that are not associated with individual characters are not included. An example of an extra signal that is excluded is the character added in the time interval between the end of the *stop element* and the beginning of the next *start element* as a result of a *transmission* speed change, *buffering,* or other cause. This additional time is a part of the *intercharacter interval.* Also see *intercharacter interval.*

characteristic. See *halftone characteristic; loading characteristic.*

characteristic distortion. *Distortion* caused by *signal transients* that are present in the *transmission channel* as a result of *modulation.* Its effects are not consis-tent. Its influence upon a given *transition* is to some degree dependent upon the remnants of signal transients from previous *signal elements.*

characteristic frequency. A *frequency* that can be easily identified and measured in a given *emission.* Also see *reference frequency.*

characteristic impedance. The *impedance* that a *transmission line* would present at its *input terminals* if it were infinitely long. A line will appear to be infinitely long if terminated in its characteristic impedance, hence there will be no *reflec-tions* from the end of the line. The characteristic impedance applies only to lines having approximate electrical uniformity. For other lines or structures the *itera-tive impedance* must be used.

character mean entropy. The *mean entropy* per *character* for all possible *mes-sages* from a *stationary message source.* In mathematical notation, if H_m is the entropy of the set of all sequences of m characters from the source, then the mean entropy per character, H, is given by $H = \lim m \to \infty H_m/m$. The mean entropy per character may be expressed in an information content unit such as a shannon per character. The limit of H_m/m may not exist if the source is not stationary. Synonymous with *average information content; information rate; mean infor-mation content.*

character mean transinformation content. The mean per *character* of the *transinformation content* for all possible messages from a *stationary message source*. In mathematical notation, the character mean transinformation content, *CMTC*, is given by $CMTC = \lim m \rightarrow \infty \ T_m/m$, where T_m is the *mean transinformation content* for all pairs of corresponding *input* and *output* sequences of characters, and m is the number of characters. The mean transinformation content per character may be expressed in an *information content* unit such as a *shannon* per character.

character recognition. The identification of a given *character* from a known set of characters by automatic or manual means. See *magnetic ink character recognition; optical character recognition.*

character set. A finite, and usually ordered, set of different *characters* upon which agreement has been reached and that is considered complete for some purpose. For example, each of the character sets in International Standard (IS) 646, 6- and 7-Bit Coded Character Sets for Information Processing Interchange; the 26 letters of the Roman alphabet; Boolean 0 and 1; and the 128 ASCII characters. See *alphabetic character set; alphabetic coded character set; alphanumeric character set; alphanumeric coded character set; coded character set; numeric character set; numeric coded character set.*

character signal. A set of *signal elements* that are used to represent a *character.*

character stepped. Pertaining to operational control of *start-stop teletypewriter* equipment in which a device is stepped one *character* at a time. The step interval is equal to or greater than the character interval at the applicable *modulation rate.*

character subset. A selection of *characters* from a *character set,* comprising all characters that have a specified common feature. For example, in the character set of International Standard (IS) 646, the digits 0 through 9 constitute a character subset, as do the letters in the ASCII. See *alphabetic character subset; alphanumeric character subset; numeric character set.* See *numeric character subset.*

charge. See *electronic charge.*

charge indication. In *telephone system* operations, the indication by a *network,* upon request of the paying station, of the monetary charge of a call. It is issued prior to the *release* of the paying station, or after release by recall at a convenient time. See *automatic charge indication.*

chart. See *radio organization chart; routing chart; Smith chart; time conversion chart.*

Chaudhuri-Hocquenghem code. See *Bose-Chaudhuri-Hocquenghem (BCH) code.*

check. See *block check; character check; continuity check; echo check; marginal check; modulo-n check; parity check.*

check bit. A *binary digit* used for *error detection.* Also see *parity bit; service bit.*

check character. A *character* used for checking purposes and usually redundant. The check character is usually determined by some set of rules and appended to the set of *data* to which the rules were applied. If the rules are applied to the data and the same character is not generated, there is a high probability that there is an error in the data. See *block check character.*

check coding. See *parity check coding.*

check digit. A *digit* used for checking purposes and usually redundant. For example, if the digits of the numeral 106242370 were to be summed, modulo-9, the result would be 7, since their arithmetic sum is 25, which, when summed again, is 7. Also, the sum of the four digits from the left is 9, the next three digits sum to 9, and only 7 remains, the same as before, Thus, casting out nines is the same as a modulo-9 check. The 7 could then be appended to the number as a check digit. The check digit could be attached to a *date-time group,* a position number, or any other number to insure the accuracy of *reception* of the number to a high probability.

check group. A *transmitted* group of *digits* or *characters* that, by giving the *information* in a second form, or as a repetition, serves as a check on the proper *reception* of the original group.

checking. See *storage bounds checking.*

chemical vapor deposition (CVD) process. A method of making *optical fibers* in which silica and other glass-forming oxides and *dopants* are deposited at high *temperatures* on the inner wall of a fused silica tube, which is then collapsed into a short, thick *preform* from which a long thin fiber is *drawn* at a high softening temperature using a *fiber-pulling machine.* See *modified chemical vapor deposition process; plasma-activated chemical vapor deposition process.* See Figures C-4 − C-6.

chemical vapor phase oxidation (CVPO) process. A process for the production of low-loss (less than 10 db/km); high-*bandwidth* (greater than 300 MHz-km), *multimode, graded index* (GI), *optical fiber,* involving either the *inside vapor phase oxidation (IVPO) process,* the *outside vapor phase oxidation (OVPO) process,* the *modified chemical vapor deposition (MCVD) process,* the *plasma-activated chemical vapor deposition (PCVD) process,* or the *axial vapor phase oxidation (AVPO) process,* or a combination or variation of these, by *soot* deposition on a glass substrate followed by oxidation and drawing of the fiber. Synonymous with *soot process.*

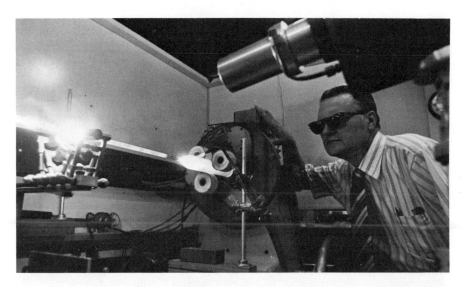

C-4. Fabrication of a *low-loss optical fiber* using a **chemical vapor deposition process.** Gases pass through the tube, which rotates as it is heated by four burners (heat is sensed by *infrared detector,* top right) moving along the length, causing gases to react and fuse on inner wall until tube collapses into a solid rod. (Courtesy of Bell Laboratories.)

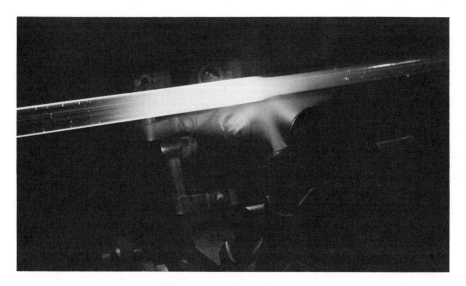

C-5. A step in a type of **chemical vapor deposition process** for fabricating *low-loss* glass *optical fibers* using a tube *(preform)* of fused silica heated to a high *temperature,* while silica and other glass-forming oxides and *dopants* are deposited on the tube's inner wall. (Courtesy of Bell Laboratories.)

C-6. The making of Corning *optical waveguide fiber* beginning with the *doped*-deposited-silica type of **chemical vapor deposition process.** (Copyright 1979, Corning Glass Works. Reprinted by permission from Corning Glass Works, Telecommunications Products Department.)

chicken wire.   An *optical fiber* blemish that appears as a grid of lines along fiber boundaries in a *multifiber bundle.*

chief operator.   See *chief supervisor.*

chief ray.   The central *ray* of a bundle of rays of *light.*

chief supervisor.   The person responsible for directing, assisting, and instructing the *switchboard operators* in the performance of their duties, insuring that maintenance is carried out, duty schedules are prepared, and *telephone traffic* is effectively *routed* at all times. Synonymous with *chief operator.*

chip.   1. In *micrographic* and *display systems,* a relatively small and separate piece of *microform* that contains *microimages* and coded information for search, identification, and retrieval purposes.   2. A minute piece of material cut from a single crystal on which electronic or *optical circuit active* and *passive* elements are mounted, usually by an etching and deposition or diffusion process to form an *integrated circuit.* See *flip-chip; large-scale integrated (LSI) chip; microimage chip.* See Figure C-7. Also see Figures M-1 and S-5.

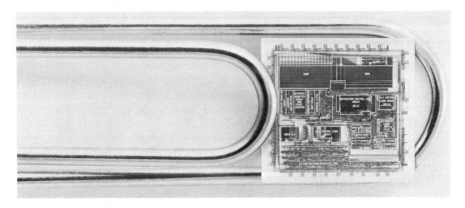

C-7. A one-**chip** *computer* for *telecommunication* applications compared to a paper clip. (Courtesy of Bell Laboratories.)

chip frequency. In *spread-spectrum systems,* one of the *frequencies* from a *frequency hopping generator.* The single frequency output occurs during *chip time* of the *spread spectrum code-sequence generator.*

chip time. In *spread-spectrum systems,* the duration of one of the *frequencies* of a *signal-hopping generator.*

chirp. A *pulsed frequency modulated signal.* See *source chirp.*

chirp modulation. See *pulse-frequency modulation.*

choledochoscope. See *fiber optic choledochoscope.*

CHOP. *Change in operational control.*

chopper. See *optical chopper.*

chopper bar. See *writing bar.*

chromatic aberration. *Image* imperfection caused by *light* of different *wavelengths* following different paths through an *optical system* due to *dispersion* caused by the optical elements of the system.

chromatic dispersion. *Dispersion* or *distortion* of a *pulse* in an *optical waveguide* due to differences in *wave velocity* caused by variations in the *refractive indices* for different portions of the guide. The *propagation* velocity varies inversely with the refractive index. The propagation time from the beginning to a point in the guide varies directly as the length, the rate of change of refractive index with respect to *wavelength,* and the spectral width of the *source.* The differences in delay causes the distortion.

chromatic resolving power.   The ability of an instrument to separate two *electromagnetic waves* of different *wavelengths.* It is equal to the ratio of the shorter wavelength divided by the difference between the wavelengths. Resolving power normally refers to the ability of *optical* components to separate two or more *object* points close together.   See *grating chromatic resolving power; prism chromatic resolving power.*

chromaticity.   The *frequency* composition of *electromagnetic waves* in the *visible region* of the *spectrum.* Chromaticity is normally characterized by the dominant frequencies or *wavelengths,* which describe the quality of *color.* It affects *transmission* in *filters, attenuation* in *optical fibers,* and the sensitivity of photofilm.

cifax.   **1.** The application of *cryptography* or *ciphony* to *facsimile signals.* **2.** *Facsimile signals* that have been *enciphered* to preserve the confidentiality of the transmitted material.   Synonymous with *ciphax.*   Also see *ciphony; civision; cryptoinformation; cryptology; cryptomaterial.*

cine-oriented mode.   A manner of recording *images* on strip or roll film in which the top edge of each image, when viewed normally for reading, is perpendicular to the long edge of the film.   For example, if successive *frames* of pictures were recorded on *microfilm* from the *faceplate* on the end of a *coherent bundle* of *optical fibers,* the film would move from top to bottom with respect to the normal orientation of the images.   Contrast with *comic-strip-oriented mode.*

ciphax.   See *cifax.*

cipher equipment.   Equipment that converts *plain text* to *cipher,* and vice versa. Cipher devices are usually operated manually, while cipher machines require sources of power.   See *literal cipher equipment.*

cipher group.   A group of letters or numbers that have been converted to *cipher text.*   Cipher text is arranged in cipher groups with a fixed number of *characters* for ease of *transmission* and for ease in performing the *encryption-decryption* processes.

cipher mode.   In *secure radiotelephone communication systems,* a *mode* of operation in which voice *transmissions* are *enciphered* and *deciphered* automatically by the *ciphony* equipment.

cipher system.   Any *cryptosystem* that requires the use of a *key* to convert, unit by unit, *plain* or *encoded text* or *signals* into an unintelligible form for confidential *transmission.*   The capability to *decipher* must also be available.

cipher text. *Text* or *signals* produced through the use of *cipher systems* that preserve the confidentiality of the enciphered *information* by rendering the signals unintelligible to any recipient without the *key*.

ciphony. **1.** The application of *cryptography* to *telephone communication*. **2.** Speech *signals* that have been *enciphered* to preserve the confidentiality of the transmitted *information*. **3.** The process of *enciphering* and *deciphering telephone* (speech) conversations and *messages*. Synonymous with *cyphony*. Also see *cifax; civision; cryptoinformation; cryptomaterial; cryptology*.

ciphony communication system. A *radiotelephone, wire*, or *optical fiber communication system* in which *messages* are *enciphered* to maintain confidentiality of the *transmitted information*.

ciphony-protected net. A *radiotelephone system* in which *communication* is secured with equipment that automatically *enciphers* and *deciphers* voice *messages* when *synchronism* has been established between sending and receiving equipment.

circle. See *aiming circle; great circle*.

circuit. **1.** In *communication systems*, an electronic, electrical, or *electromagnetic* path between two or more points capable of providing a number of *channels*. **2.** A number of elements connected together in a closed loop for the purpose of carrying an electrical current. **3.** The complete *path* between two *end-terminals* over which one-way or two-way *communication* may take place. **4.** A *data circuit* that is either a physical circuit or a *virtual circuit*. Also see *transmission channel*. See *approved circuit; clamping circuit; closed circuit; combinational circuit; common user circuit; composite circuit; conditioned circuit; conditioned voice-grade circuit; conference circuit; cord circuit; data circuit; data transmission circuit; decision circuit; dedicated circuit; detector back-bias gain-control circuit; differentiating circuit; direct-current (DC) restoration circuit; disturbed circuit; disturbing circuit; divider circuit; driving circuit; duplex circuit; engineering circuit; exclusive-user circuit; express engineering circuit; external liaison circuit; four-wire circuit; gating circuit; ground-return circuit; half-duplex circuit; homogeneous multiplexed circuit; hybrid optical fiber circuit; integrated circuit; integrated optical circuit; integrating circuit; interchange circuit; line adapter circuit; link engineering circuit; lithium niobate integrated circuit; local engineering circuit; logical circuit; maintenance control circuit (MCC); multipoint circuit; open circuit; permanent circuit; permanent virtual circuit; phantom circuit; pilot make-busy (PMB) circuit; point-to-point circuit; preemphasis circuit; printed circuit; radio circuit; reference circuit; ringdown circuit; self-repairing circuit; self-testing circuit; sequential circuit; side circuit; simplex circuit; simplexed circuit; sole user circuit; squelch circuit; switched circuit; switched hot-line circuit; telecommunication circuit; telegraph circuit; telephone cord circuit; temporary circuit; thin-film circuit; transfer circuit; trunk circuit; two-wire cir-*

cuit; unbalanced wire circuit; video discrimination circuit; virtual circuit; voice-grade circuit.

circuit activity.   See *mean circuit activity.*

circuit breaker.   A manual or automatic protective device for closing and opening a *circuit* between separable contacts under both normal and abnormal operating conditions.   When the breaker opens while *electric current* is flowing, the arc across the interruption gap may be forced to occur in liquids or gases, such as oil and air, or in *magnetic fields,* to snuff the arc quickly and with low dissipation of energy.   See *molded case circuit breaker; power circuit breaker.*

circuit-breaker switchgear.   See *low-voltage enclosed air circuit-breaker switchgear.*

circuit connection.   See *data circuit connection.*

circuit current.   See *metallic circuit current.*

circuit designator.   A set of standard *characters* (letters, numerals, special symbols) that represent *information* concerning a *circuit,* such as its *frequency* of operation, its application, or the types of *channels.*   Also see *emission designator; net glossary.*

circuit discipline.   The maintaining of *message security* and *integrity;* the proper use of *communication equipment;* adherence to *authorized frequencies* and operating procedures; the use of remedial action; the exercise of *net control;* proper monitoring; and the proper training of *operators* and maintenance personnel.

circuit filter-coupler-switch-modulator.   See *integrated-optical circuit filter-coupler-switch-modulator.*

circuit group congestion signal.   See *national circuit group congestion signal.*

circuit-hour.   See *connections per circuit-hour (CCH); hundred circuit-hours.*

circuit log.   In a *radiotelephone, telephone,* or *telegraph net,* a record of *transmitted* and *received traffic* and operating conditions for each day on each *circuit* or *channel,* including such *data* as opening and closing time, delays, *frequency* changes, procedure and security violations, and other significant events.

circuit multiplex set.   See *engineering circuit multiplex set.*

circuit noise level.   At any point in a *transmission system,* the ratio of the *circuit noise* at that point to some arbitrary amount of circuit noise (usually expressed in *dBm* with dBmO chosen as a reference point.)   The ratio is usually converted to *decibels* above reference noise, *dBrn,* signifying the reading of a circuit noise *meter,* or in dBrn adjusted, *dBa,* signifying circuit noise meter readings adjusted to represent an *interference* effect under specified conditions. Also see *dBrnC; noise.*

circuit quality control. The actions taken to assure proper performance of *circuits*. Examples include circuit evaluation, reporting of poor quality circuits, and removal of unusual circuits.

circuit-released acknowledgement signal. A *signal* sent in the *forward direction* in response to a *circuit-released signal* indicating that a *circuit* has been *released*.

circuit-released signal. A *signal* sent in the *forward direction* and in the *backward direction* indicating that a *circuit* has been *released*.

circuit reliability. The percent of time that a circuit may be expected to be available for use. It is calculated as the percent of time that a *circuit* was available to a *user* during a specified period of scheduled availability. The circuit reliability, *CR*, is given by:

$$CR = 100(1 - T_o/T_s) = 100T_a/T_s$$

where T_o is the circuit total *outage* state time (outage period), T_s is the circuit total scheduled time, and T_a is the circuit total available time. Synonymous with *time availability.* Also see *channel reliability.*

circuit restoration. The process by which another *communication circuit* is established between two *users* after disruption or loss of the original circuit. Circuit restoration is usually performed in accordance with planned procedures and priorities.

circuitry. A complex of *circuits* used for establishing *connections* among components of a *system* and among systems.

circuit security. See *telephone circuit security*.

circuit signaling. See *telephone circuit signaling*.

circuit-switched connection. **1.** A *circuit* that is established and maintained, usually on demand, between two or more *stations* or sets of *data terminal equipment,* in order to allow the exclusive use of the circuit until the *connection* is *released.*

circuit-switched data transmission service. A *communication service* that requires *circuit switching* to establish a *connection* before *data* can be *transferred* between *users* or their *data terminal equipment.*

circuit switching. **1.** A process that, usually on demand, connects two or more *users* or their *data terminal equipment,* and that permits the exclusive use of a circuit between them until the *connection* is *released.* **2.** A method of handling *traffic* through a *switching center,* either from local *users* or from other *switch-*

ing centers, whereby a *connection* is established between the *calling party station* and the *called party* station.

circuit switching center (CSC).   A complex of *communication circuits* and supporting facilities that can be interconnected and *released* for establishing and disestablishing *connections* between *users.*

circuit switching unit (CSU).   Equipment used for establishing direct *connections* between *data terminals,* between a *data terminal* and a *store-and-forward switching center,* or between any components of a *communication system,* for *user-to-user data transfer.*

circuit terminating equipment.   See *data circuit-terminating equipment (DCE).*

circuit transparency.   See *data circuit transparency.*

circuit unavailability procedure.   A procedure to be followed by *telephone operators* when *circuits* are *busy,* for example when backlogs occur, when other facilities are to be used, when *callbacks* are requested, or when *precedence* calls are to be handled.

circular dielectric waveguide.   A *waveguide* consisting of a long tube of concentric circular *dielectric* materials, capable of sustaining and guiding an *electromagnetic wave* in one or more *propagation modes.*   For example, most optical fibers are circular dielectric waveguides that are capable of conducting *lightwaves.*   See Figure C-8.

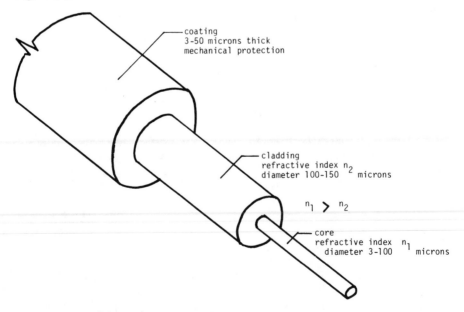

C-8.   A typical **circular dielectric waveguide** *optical fiber.*

circularly symmetric fiber.   An *optical fiber* of circular cross section whose *refractive index* and other material *parameters* are independent of the angular displacement of the central angle and the longitudinal coordinate, although the parameters are a function of the distance from the center, i.e., the *transmission media* parameters are the same in all radial directions at any cross section.

circular polar diagram.   In *radio communications,* a circle indicating that the *intensity* of *radiation* is nearly the same in all horizontal directions. Thus, a completely *omnidirectional antenna* would exhibit a circular polar diagram, in contrast to a *directional antenna,* which concentrates its *power* in certain directions.

circular polarization.   *Polarization* of the *electric* and *magnetic field vectors* in a *uniform plane-polarized electromagnetic wave* (such as a *lightwave* or a *radiowave*), in which the two arbitrary sinusoidally varying rectangular *components* of the electric field vector are equal in magnitude, but are out of the time *phase* by $90°$. This causes the electric field vector to rotate, with the direction of rotation depending on which component leads or lags the other, i.e., the tip (head) of the electric field vector rotates in a circle. The magnetic vector is at the center of the circle and perpendicular to the plane of the circle. Also see *linear polarization; elliptical polarization; left-hand circular polarization; right-hand circular polarization.*

circular scan.   1. In *satellite communication systems,* an *earth station antenna* search pattern in which the *directional antenna* is rotated about a usually vertical or horizontal axis. It is used after initial pointing to the predicted satellite position. This enables acquisition of the *down-link signals* prior to automatic *tracking.* **2.** In *radar systems,* the continuous rotation of a *directional antenna* usually about a vertical axis. The rotation may be full circle or only a sector.

circular shift.   In *data processing,* a process in which vacant positions at one end of a *code word* are filled in strict sequence by the *bits* dropped off the other end. For example, for a *register* 32 bits long, a circular shift of 32 places results in zero net change in the contents.   The circulation may be to the right or to the left. For example, the number 106242370 right circular shifted four places would become 237010624. Synonymous with *cyclic shift; end-around shift.*

circular three-body problem.   See *restricted circular three-body problem.*

circulator.   A *passive junction* of three or more *ports* in which the ports are placed in such a sequence that when *power* is fed into any port it is *transmitted* to the next port, in sequence, the first port following the last, in cyclic fashion. See *microwave circulator.*

civil day.   A 24-hour day of 86,400 seconds (236 seconds longer than the *sidereal day*) that relates to an imaginary sun and earth whose relative motion is uniform. Synonymous with *mean solar day.* Also see *true solar day.*

civil fixed telecommunication network. A *network* of commercial and government *telecommunication facilities* for *transmission* of *messages* on a worldwide basis by *radio, cable,* and *satellite links* that sends the *traffic* to specific *addressees,* usually via their nearest *station.* Also see *military fixed telecommunication network.*

civil communication network. A nonmilitary *communication network* owned and operated by a public authority or a private company.

civision. **1.** The application of *cryptography* to *television signals.* **2.** *Television signals* that have been *enciphered* to preserve the confidentiality of the *transmitted information.* Also see *cifax; ciphony; cryptoinformation; cryptology; cryptomaterial.*

cladded-fiber. See *doped-silica cladded fiber.*

cladded slab dielectric waveguide. See *doubly-cladded slab dielectric waveguide.*

cladding. An *optical conductive* material, with a *refractive index* lower than that of the *core,* placed over or outside the core material of an optical *waveguide* that serves to reflect or refract lightwaves in order to confine them to the core. The cladding also serves to protect the core. Synonymous with *coating.* See *extramural cladding.* Also see *bundle jacket; core.* Also see Figure S-3.

cladding eccentricity. The ratio of the minimum *cladding* thickness to the maximum cladding thickness.

cladding-guided mode. In an *optical waveguide,* a *transmission mode* supported by the *cladding;* i.e., a mode in addition to the modes supported by the *core* material. It is usually *attenuated* by *absorption* by using *lossy cladding media* to prevent reconversion of energy to core-guided modes and thus reduce *dispersion.*

cladding mode stripper. **1.** A material applied to *optical fiber cladding* to allow *light* energy being *transmitted* in the cladding to leave the cladding of the fiber. **2.** A piece of *optical* material that can support only certain *electromagnetic wave* propagation *modes.* In particular, it does not support the *propagation modes* in the cladding of a cladded optical fiber, slab dielectric waveguide, or integrated optical circuit. The stripper effectively removes the cladding modes without disturbing the core-supported *propagation modes.*

clad silica fiber. See *low-loss FEP-clad silica fiber; plastic-clad silica fiber.*

clad switchgear. See *metal clad switchgear.*

clamper. See *clamping circuit.*

clamping circuit. A *circuit* that prevents the *voltage level* of another circuit from shifting above or below predetermined levels. A diode and a constant voltage source can be used as a clamping circuit in *lasers, photodetectors, amplifiers, gates, optical integrated circuits,* and other circuits. *Infrared scanning system circuits* are usually equipped with a clamping circuit to reduce *blanking* by *laser pulses.* Synonymous with *clamper.*

class. See *service class; telephone service class; user service class.*

classification. See *bearing classification; position classification.*

classified. See *security classified.*

class indicator. See *user-class indicator.*

classmark. A designator used to indicate the type of service, kind of privilege, and nature of restriction allowed to a *user* of a *communication system,* for example, the type of *lines accessing* a *switching center,* the *precedence level* allowed, conference privileges granted, security level allowed, and zone restrictions imposed. Synonymous with *class-of-service mark.* Also see *service class.*

class-of-service mark. See *classmark.*

clear. **1.** In *telephone switchboard operation,* to cause a *clearing signal* to be given at an *exchange,* either by replacing the handset or by *ring off.* The *user* thus indicates to the *switchboard operator* that the *call* is *finished.* **2.** In *telephone system operation,* to take down *connections* at an *exchange,* thereby freeing lines for other *calls.* Synonymous with *clear down.* See *double clear; false clear; single clear.*

clearance. See *path clearance.*

clear collision. *Contention* that occurs when *data terminal equipment (DTE)* and *data circuit-terminating equipment (DCE)* simultaneously *transfer* a *clear request signal* or *packet* and a *clear indication signal* or packet specifying the same logical *channel.* In this case the DCE will function as if the *clearing* is completed and will not transfer a DCE *clear confirmation signal* or packet. Also see *call collision.*

clear confirmation. **1.** An *interrogation signal* or *message* to determine if a *circuit* has been *cleared.* **2.** The *signal* or *message,* in *response* to an interrogation, confirming that a *circuit* has in fact been *cleared.*

clear confirmation signal. A *call control signal* to acknowledge *reception* of the *data terminal equipment (DTE) clear request signal* by the *data circuit-terminating equipment* (DTE) or the reception of the DCE *clear indicator by the DTE.*

clear down. See *clear.*

clear-forward signal. In semiautomatic and automatic *telephone systems,* a *signal transmitted* in a *forward direction* on *termination* of a *call* by a *telephone* *operator* or when a *user* replaces the *receiver* or handset (hangs up) thus freeing the *circuit* at all points. An exception may occur where the *signaling system* includes a *switching release guard signal.* Synonymous with *forward clearing signal.*

clear indicator.   A *signal* or *message* indicating that a *circuit* has just been *cleared.*

clearing.   A sequence of events that disconnects a *circuit* after a *call* is finished and returns the circuit to the ready state for other use.   See *negative clearing; positive clearing.*

clearing indicator shutter.   See *fallen clearing indicator shutter.*

clear message.   1. A *message* sent in the *forward direction* and the *backward direction* containing a *circuit-released signal* or *circuit-released-acknowledgement signal.*   The *clear message* will normally contain an indication whether the message is in the *forward* or the *backward direction.*   2. A *message* in *plain language,* that is, not *enciphered.*   See *modified clear message.*

clear request signal.   A *signal* appearing in the *forward direction* and the *backward direction* in the *data channels* between *exchanges.*   It is usually sent by the *user terminals.*   Also see *data terminal equipment (DTE) clear request.*

clear signal.   See *data circuit-terminating equipment (DCE) clear signal.*

clear-to-send signal.   A *signal* generated by a device to indicate that it is ready to *transmit data.*   Also see *request-to-send signal.*

clear traffic.   *Traffic* that has not been *encrypted, scrambled,* or in any way deliberately made unintelligible.

clipper.   A *circuit* or device that limits the instantaneous value of its *output signal amplitude* to a predetermined maximum value, regardless of the amplitude of the *input signal.*   Also see *blanking; clipping; compander; compressor; expander; limiter; peak limiting.*

clipping.   The limiting of the *amplitude* of a *signal* to a specified value, particularly in *pulse circuits* to prevent overdrive of circuit elements.   In *integrated optical circuits, photodetectors,* and *light sources,* lightwave pulses are often clipped because of the limitations of the component.   For example, in pulse circuits it is a means of reducing the amplification of *frequencies* below a specified frequency or removing the tail of a pulse after a fixed time; in *telephone circuits,* it is the perceptible mutilation of signals or speech syllables during *transmission.*   It can result in the loss of the beginnings or endings of *signal elements* or speech syllables.   These modes of clipping are called initial clipping and final clipping.   In *analog systems,* clipping is an intentional *signal processing* action to reduce the dynamic range of an *analog signal.* Synonymous with *scissoring.* Also see *limiting.*

clock. 1. A reference source of *timing signals* for equipment, machines, or systems. 2. Equipment that provides a time base used in a *transmisison system* or a *computer* to control the timing of certain functions such as the control of the duration of *signal elements,* the *sampling rate,* or the execution of *instructions.* 3. A device that generates periodic *signals* used for *synchronization.* Also see *timing signal.* See *Department of Defense (DOD) master clock; equipment clock; independent clock; master clock; reference clock; station clock; synchronized clock.*

clock control. See *direct clock control; indirect clock control.*

clock difference. The time difference between two *clocks,* that is, a measure of the separation between their respective *time signals.* Clock differences should be represented as algebraic time quantities measured on the same time scale with the reference clock indicated. For example, a clock difference may be expressed as $-0.9\ \mu s \pm 0.2\ \mu s$, GMT.

clock phase slew. The changing in relative *phase* between a given *clock signal* and a phase-stable reference signal. The two signals are generally at or near the same *frequency* or have an *integral* multiple frequency relationship.

clock pulse-length modulation. See *suppressed-clock pulse-length modulation.*

clock second. See *cesium clock second.*

clock stability. A measure of the ability of a device to produce the same number of equally spaced *timing pulses* in equal and relatively large time intervals. Clock stability is usually expressed in parts per million, that is, in parts per 10^6. For example, the stability could be cited as correct within 2.4 parts per million. It might also be expressed as $+2.4 \times 10^{-6}$. This would indicate that there are 2.4 excess timing pulses per million of a standard reference clock.

clock track. On a *data medium,* such as a drum, disk, tape, or card, a track on which a pattern of *signals* is or can be recorded to provide a *timing signal* or timing reference during use, such as during reading and writing.

clockwise helical polarization. See *right-hand helical polarization.*

clockwise polarized electromagnetic wave. See *right-hand polarized electromagnetic wave.*

close. In *display systems,* to restore continuity in a specific sequence of graphic or *display commands* after inserting additional commands. Contrast with *open.*

close-confinement junction. See *single heterojunction.*

closed circuit. **1.** In *radio* and *television transmission,* a *circuit* that *transmits* directly to specific *users* and does not *broadcast* for general use. **2.** A completed *electrical circuit.*

closed code. See *cyclic code.*

closed orbit. A simple elliptical *orbit,* that is, an orbit that the orbiting body repeats. Thus, *parabolic orbits* and *hyperbolic orbits* are not closed orbits. Synonymous with *elliptical orbit.*

closed user group. A group of *users* of a *public data network* that has a *facility* that permits the users to *communicate* with each other, but does not allow them to communicate with all other users of the network. User *data terminal equipment* may belong to more than one closed user group. Also see *special-network service.* See Figure C-9.

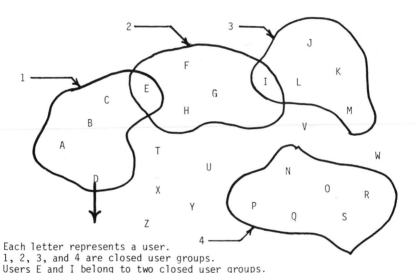

Each letter represents a user.
1, 2, 3, and 4 are closed user groups.
Users E and I belong to two closed user groups.
User D in closed user group 1 has outgoing access.
Users T-Z are not in a closed user group

C-9. *Users* in **closed user groups** with and without *outgoing access* in a *data network.*

closed user group with outgoing access. A *closed user group* that has a *user* with a *facility* that enables that user to *communicate* with users of a *public data network transmission service* that are not in the same closed user group and to users that have *data terminal equipment* connected to other public data networks. See Figure C-9.

closed waveguide. A *waveguide* that has electrically *conducting* walls, thus permitting an infinite but *discrete* set of *propagation modes* of which relatively few are practical. Each discrete mode defines the *propagation constant.* The field at any point is describable in terms of these modes. There is no *radiation field.* Discontinuities and bends cause *mode conversion* but not radiation. For example, a metallic rectangular cross-section pipe is a closed waveguide. Also see *open waveguide.*

close-up. In *flaghoist communication systems* on ship and on shore, the condition that exists when the *flaghoist* top is touching the block at the point of hoist, that is, when it is raised all the way up. The *signal*-originating *(transmitting) station* normally raises *flags, pennants,* and *panels* close-up. Also see *at-the-dip; flaghoist; hauled-down.*

cloud attenuation. The *attenuation* of *electromagnetic signals* due to *absorption* and *scatter* by water or ice particles in clouds. The amount of attenuation depends on many factors, including the density, particle size, turbulence, and distance.

cluster. A *pyrotechnic signal* in which all the stars or flares of a group burn at the same time.

clutter. See *ground clutter.*

C-message weighting. A *noise weighting* used in a *noise measuring set* to measure noise on a line that would be *terminated* by a 500-Type Noise Measuring Device or similar instrument. The meter scale reading is in *dBrn (C-message)* or in *dBrnC.*

CMRR. *Common-mode rejection ratio.*

C/N ratio. See *carrier-to-noise (C/N) ratio.*

coast station. A *land station* in the *maritime mobile service.* The coast station normally *communicates* with *ship stations.* A coast station may secondarily communicate with other coast stations incident to communication with ship stations.

COAT. See *coherent optical adaptive technique.*

coated optics. The use of *optical elements* or components whose optical *refracting* and *reflecting* surfaces have been coated with one or more layers of *dielectric* or metallic material for the purpose of reducing or increasing reflection from the surfaces, either totally or for selected *wavelengths,* and of protecting the surfaces from abrasion and corrosion. Antireflection materials that can serve as optical coating material include magnesium fluoride, silicon monoxide, titanium oxide, and zinc sulfide.

coating. See *antireflection coating; highly-reflective coating; optical fiber coating; optical protective coating.*

coaxial cable. A *cable* consisting of an insulated central *conductor* surrounded by a cylindrical conductor with additional *insulation* on the outside and covered with an outer sheath. For example, an electrical or *electromagnetic transmission* line consisting of one conductor (usually a small copper tube or wire) within and insulated from another conductor, using a *dielectric* as an insulator; the outer conductor usually consists of copper tubing or copper braid and may be grounded. The inside diameter of the outer conductor is sufficiently larger than the outside diameter of the inner conductor so as to allow space for the insulating material between them. Synonymous with *coaxial line; concentric line; concentric cable.* See *air dielectric coaxial cable; foam dielectric coaxial cable.* See Figure C-10.

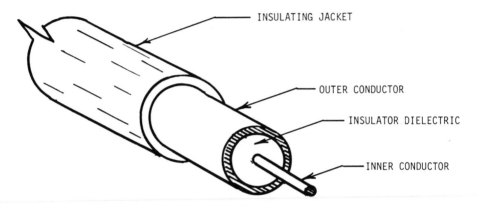

INSULATING JACKET

OUTER CONDUCTOR

INSULATOR DIELECTRIC

INNER CONDUCTOR

C-10. A **coaxial cable** can serve as a *waveguide* or *uniform transmission line.*

coaxial line. See *coaxial cable.*

coaxial patch bay. A *patch bay* that is served by *coaxial cable circuits.*

COBOL. A *computer* general-purpose *programming language* in which English words are used rather than mathematical notation. It is principally used for record and file handling. The name is derived from Common Business-Oriented Language.

cochannel interference. *Interference* that results from two or more *transmissions* occurring simultaneously in the same *channel.*

code. 1. A set of unambiguous rules and conventions specifying the manner in which *data* may be represented in *discrete* form, such as by means of individual *signals, binary digits,* punched holes, magnetized spots on a surface, or *lightwave* or radio wave *pulses.* 2. Any set of correspondences between *data* items on two lists that may be used to convert *information* represented by the items on one list to the same information expressed in items of the other list. The reverse process can be performed so as to recover the original representation and not lose the meaning. 3. Any *system* of *communication* in which groups of symbols represent *data* or *information* in a symbolic form for the *transmission* of plain *text* or in *scrambled* form for *security* reasons. **4.** To represent *information* in a symbolic form, such as might be acceptable to a *communication system,* computer, or data processor. **5.** To represent data or a *computer program* in a symbolic form that can be accepted by a *data processor.* Also see *decode; encode.* See *access code; alphabetic code; alphanumeric code; answer-back code; area code; balanced code; Barker code; Baudot code; binary code; biquinary code; cable address code; cable code; call-directly code; card code; chain code; composite code; convolutional code; cyclic code; data code; dense binary code; equal-length code; error-correcting code; error-detecting code; excess-three code; extended binary coded decimal interchange code (EBCDIC); fixed-weight binary code; gold code; Gray code; Hagelbarger code; Hamming code; Hollerith code; illegal code; interlock code; international Morse code; international signal code; international visual signal code; instruction code; language code; linear-sequence code; line code; lock code; minimum distance code; mnemonic code; modified non-return-to-zero-level code; modified reflected binary code; Morse code; m-out-of-n code; n-ary code; network code; non-return-to-zero (NRZ) binary code; numeric code; operation code; paired disparity code; panel code; prearranged message code; privacy code; pseudo-binary code; pulse code; pyrotechnic code; redundant code; return-to-zero (RZ) binary code; self-demarcating code; signaling panel code; symmetrical binary code; syncopated code; telegraph code; time code; transmitter start code; unit disparity binary code; unit distance code; walking code; zip code.*

code alphabet.   See *n-unit code alphabet.*

code book.   A book containing codes arranged in systematic order and a vocabulary made up of arbitrary meanings (letters, syllables, words, phrases, or sentences) each accompanied by one or more groups of *symbols* used as equivalents to the *plain text messages.*   The book is arranged so that messages can be *encoded* and *decoded.*

CODEC.   An assembly or device that consists of an *encoder* and a *decoder.*

code character.   The representation of a discrete value or symbol in accordance with a *code.*   Also see *digital alphabet.*

code combination.   A set of *significant conditions* formed by means of an *n-unit code* in which each element assumes a given significant condition.

code conversion.   **1.** Conversion of *signals* or groups of signals that represent *characters* in one *code* into corresponding signals or groups of signals in another code. **2.** A process for converting a *code* of some predetermined *bit* structure, for example 5, 7, or 14 bits per *character,* into a second code usually with approximately the same number of bits per character.   No *alphabetical* significance is necessarily assumed in this process.   Also see *pulse-code modulation.*

code converter. A *data converter* that changes the representation of data using one *code* in the place of another code or one *coded character set* in the place of another coded character set.

coded character set. A *character set* derived from a set of unambiguous rules that establishes the character set and the one-to-one relationships between the characters of the set and their *coded* representations. See *alphabetic coded character set; alphanumeric coded character set; numeric coded character set.*

coded decimal. See *binary-coded decimal (BCD).*

coded decimal interchange code. See *extended binary-coded decimal interchange code (EBCDIC).*

code-dependent system. A *system* that depends for its correct functioning upon the *character set* or code used for *transmission* of *data.* Synonymous with *code-sensitive system.* Also see *code independent system.*

coded-image space. See *image storage space.*

code division multiple access (CDMA). A form of *modulation* in which *digital information* is *encoded* in an expanded *bandwidth* format. Several *transmissions* can occur simultaneously within the same bandwidth and the *mutual interference* can be reduced by the degree of orthogonality of the unique codes used in each transmission. It permits a high degree of energy dispersion in the emitted bandwidth. In some *satellite communication systems,* it is used as an *access* method that permits *carriers radiated* from different *earth stations* to go through the same satellite *transponder.* On reception at an earth station, each carrier can be distinguished from the others. In CDMA, each carrier is identified by a specific *modulation code.* The system allows for simultaneous reception, by a satellite transponder, of multiple signals that overlap in frequency and in time. Some *spread spectrum multiple access systems* also make use of CDMA.

coded representation. 1. The representation of an *item* of *data* by a *code.* 2. The representation of a *character* established by a *coded character set.* For example, the letters IAD that represent the Washington, DC's Dulles International Airport in the three-letter identification code for international airports; or the 7 *binary* digits that represent the *delete character* in the 7-bit coded character set for information interchange *(ASCII).* Synonymous with *code value.*

coded speech. The *output* of any device that converts a *signal* derived from plain speech into another type of signal.

code element. One of a finite set of *data items* or *signals* used to compose the *characters* in a given *code.*

code exchange. See *automatic answer-back code exchange.*

code extension character. A *control character* that is used to indicate that one of the succeeding coded representations is to be interpreted according to a different code or according to a different *coded character set.* See *nonlocking code extension character.*

code group. In a *coding system,* a group of *symbols,* such as letters, numbers, or other special signs in combination, assigned to represent an element of *plain text.*

code identifier. 1. A *code* or *signal* that is used to identify another particular code from a set of available codes for use in a given situation or application. 2. In *visual signaling systems,* an identifier used to identify an object, for example a configuration of *panels* used to identify a *drop zone* or landing zone.

code-independent. Pertaining to a *communication,* computing, or data processing system, whose correct and proper functioning does not depend upon any particular *code* used to represent alphanumeric or control *characters.* However, limitations or dependency on mechanical, electrical, and *pulse* configurations may exist. Synonymous with *code transparent.*

code-independent data communication. A *mode* of *data communication* that uses a *code-independent protocol* for *data transmission.* It does not depend for its correct functioning on the *character set* or *code* used. Synonymous with *code-transparent data communication.* Also see *data transmission.*

code-independent system. A *system* that does not depend for its correct functioning upon the *character set* or *code* used for the *transmission* of *data.* Synonymous with *code-insensitive system* and with *code-transparent system.* Also see *code-dependent system.*

code indicator. See *destination code indicator; Morse code indicator.*

code-insensitive system. See *code-independent system.*

code line index. In *micrographics,* a visual index consisting of a pattern of transparent and opaque bars parallel to the long edge of a *microfilm* roll and located between the *frames.*

code modulation. See *differential pulse-code modulation (DPCM); code modulation; pulse-code modulation.*

code modulation multiplexing. See *pulse-code modulation multiplexing.*

coder. 1. An *analog-to-digital converter,* that is, a device for converting continuously varying *signals* into *discrete* signals. 2. An *encoder* or *decoder.* See *analog-to-digital encoder; channel voice encoder; pattern-matching voice coder; vocoder.*

code repertoire. See *instruction code.*

code repertory. See *instruction code.*

code-sensitive system. See *code-dependent system.*

code sequence. See *maximal code sequence.*

code sequence generator. See *Mersenne code sequence generator; modular spread-spectrum code-sequence generator; spread-spectrum code-sequence generator.*

code set. The complete set of representations of a *code* or *coded character set.* For example, the set of three-letter identification groups for international airports. Also see *digital alphabet.*

code transparent. See *code-independent.*

code-transparent data communication. See *code-independent data communication.*

code-transparent system. See *code-independent system.*

code value. See *coded representation.*

code word. **1.** A *word* that is used to convey a prearranged meaning other than its conventional one. It is used for maintaining security and confidentiality of *messages.* **2.** A *word* assigned or used to identify sensitive intelligence *data.* **3.** A *word* or term used to establish a condition, an alert, or the equivalent; or to initiate the implementation of a plan or operation. It is usually assigned a classification and a classified meaning to safeguard intentions and *information* regarding a classified plan or operation. See *inactive code word.*

coding. A process used to alter the characteristics of a *signal* to better fit an intended application. For example, coding can be used to modify the *signal spectrum,* increase the *information content,* provide *error detection* and *error correction,* and provide *data security.* Any single coding scheme usually does not provide all of these capabilities but each *code* has advantages and disadvantages compared to other codes. See *adaptive predictive coding (APC); biphase coding; biphase-level coding; biphase-mark coding; biphase-space coding; bipolar coding; dipulse coding; duobinary coding; full-baud bipolar coding; half-baud bipolar coding; linear predictive coding; non-return-to-zero coding; parity check coding; return-to-zero coding; three-condition coding.*

coding compaction. See *floating-point coding compaction; variable precision coding compaction.*

codress message. In *military communication systems,* a *message* in which the entire *address* is *encrypted* along with the message text.

codress message address. An *address* that is *encrypted* in the *text* of a *message.*

coefficient. See *absorption coefficient; electrooptic coefficient; phase change coefficient; reflection coefficient; reference coefficient; scattering coefficient; spectral absorption coefficient; transmission coefficient.*

COGO. A *computer programming language* used primarily for geometric problems, *network topology,* and similar applications. The name is derived from coordinate geometry.

coherence. Pertaining to the similarity of two *signal wave* forms in regard to a given particular feature, for example, the same *polarization* or the same *frequency.* Also see *correlation.*

coherency. In a *spread-spectrum communication system,* a synchronized and *phase*-matched condition between a *receiver's* reference and the desired *signal.*

coherent. Pertaining to an *electromagnetic wave* in which the *electric* and *magnetic field vectors* are uniquely and specifically definable within narrow limits.

coherent bundle. A *bundle* of *optical fibers* in which the spatial coordinates of each fiber are the same or bear the same spatial relationship to each other at the two ends of the bundle. Synonymous with *aligned bundle.* Also see *incoherent bundle.*

coherent detector. A *signal detector* that uses both *phase* and *amplitude information* in the received or *input signal* by using a reference signal for phase determination; e.g., a *photodetector* or *demodulator.* It removes out-of-phase *noise.*

coherent light. *Light* of which all parameters are predictable and correlated at any point in time or space, particularly over an area in a plane perpendicular to the direction of *propagation* or over time at a particular point in space. See *space-coherent light; time-coherent light.*

coherent moving target indicator. A moving target indicator (MTI) in which a *radar reference frequency oscillator* is used in the *receiver* for *phase* comparison with the return *signals* for determining the radial component of the velocity of an object.

coherent optical adaptive technique (COAT). A technique used to improve the *optical power density* of *electromagnetic wave fronts* propagating through turbulent *atmosphere,* using approaches such as *phase conjugation, compensating phase shift, aperture tagging,* and *image sharpening.* Used in *wavefront control.*

coherent pulse operation.   A method of *pulse* operation in which a fixed *phase* relationship of the *carrier wave* is maintained from one pulse to the next.

coherent repeater jammer.   A *repeater jammer* that produces a *jamming signal* that maintains a fixed relationship with the signal that it receives. The signal that it *transmits* is made to be identical to a signal that would be *reflected* from a target if there were a target. The *signal strength*, shape, *PRR*, and *frequency* is adjusted for deception.

coherent signals.   Two or more *signals* that are locked in *phase* or bear a fixed time relationship to each other.

coil.   See *hybrid coil; loading coil; repeating coil.*

coincidence circuit.   See *AND gate.*

coincidence gate.   See *AND gate.*

coincidence unit.   See *AND gate.*

cold bend.   The alternate cyclic bending of an *optical fiber, bundle,* or *cable* using a specified device at a specified *temperature* (usually room temperature).

colinear antenna array.   An arrangement of *dipole antennas* in which the dipole antennas are all mounted in a single line that is an extension of their long axes. The arrangement is usually in a vertical line so as to produce an *antenna gain* in the horizontal direction at the expense of vertical gain. When stacking the antennas, doubling their number produces a 3 dB increase in gain.

collate.   To place two or more sets of items in a prescribed single sequence, such as placing two lists of words each of which is in *alphabetical* order into a single alphabetical list.

collect.   In a *communication system,* a prefix in a *message* indicating that the charges for the message were not paid at the *source* and are to be collected at the destination, for example, from the *addressee.* Also see *prepaid.*

collection.   See *data collection.*

collection angle.   See *acceptance angle.*

collection facility.   See *data collection facility.*

collective address group. An *address group* that represents two or more organizations, authorities, activities, units, persons, or any combination thereof, the *addressees* usually being the heads of the organizations.

collective call sign. 1. A *call sign* that represents two or more facilities, commands, authorities, or units. 2. In a *radio communication system* or *net, a call sign* that identifies a predetermined group of *stations.* Also see *individual call sign; net call sign.* See *ship collective call sign.*

collective lens. A *lens* of *positive power,* used in an *optical system* to *refract* the *chief rays* of *image*-forming bundles of rays, so that these rays will pass through subsequent *optical elements* of the system. If all the rays do not pass through an optical element, a loss of *light* ensues, known as *vignetting.* Sometimes used incorrectly to denote any lens of positive power. Also see *converging lens.*

collective routing. Routing in which a *switching center* automatically delivers *messages* to a specified list of destinations. This avoids the need to list each single *address* in the *message heading. Major relay stations* usually *transmit* messages bearing collective routing indicators to *tributary, major,* and *minor relay stations.*

collective routing indicator. A group of *symbols,* usually letters, that identifies a group of *stations,* for example, all the stations of a given *relay network* in a specified geographical area, or all the *minor* and *tributary stations* of a *major relay station.*

collimated light. A bundle of *light rays* in which the rays emanating from any single point in the *object* are parallel to one another; e.g., the light from an infinitely distant real *source,* or an apparent source, such as a *collimator reticle.* Synonymous with *parallel light.*

collimated transmittance. *Transmittance* of an *optical waveguide* in which the *lightwave* at the ouptut has *coherency* related to the coherency at the input.

collimation. 1. The process of aligning the *optical axis* of *optical systems* to the reference mechanical axes or surfaces of an instrument, or the adjustment of two or more optical axes with respect to each other. 2. The process of making *light rays* parallel. 3. The extent to which an *electromagnetic wave* is uniformly constant in *phase* in a plane perpendicular to the *direction of propagation.* A high degree of collimation is obtainable from a *laser* that oscillates in a single *lowest-*

order transverse mode. The output has essentially a uniform and constant phase distribution across the entire *output aperture.* A *divergence* of 2×10^{-4} radians is typical. Also see *divergent light.*

collimator. An *optical device* that renders *diverging* or *converging light rays* parallel. It may be used to simulate a distant target or *object,* align the *optical axes* of instruments, or prepare rays for entry into the end of an *optical fiber, fiber bundle,* or *optical thin-film.*

collision. **1.** In a *data transmission system,* the situation that occurs when two or more simultaneous demands are made on equipment that can handle only one at any given instant. *Protocol* is used to resolve the *contention* that immediately follows the instant of collision. **2.** In a *computer,* the situation that occurs when the same *address* is obtained and attempted to be used for two different *data items* that are to be stored at that address, such as might occur when calculating hash-addresses. See *call collision; clear collision.*

color. **1.** The sensation produced by *light* of different *wavelengths* in the *visible spectrum.* Color-related properties of *light* include *chromatic aberration* and *color,* shape, and number of *Newton's rings* present when two *optical* surfaces are placed together multiples and submultiples of wavelength apart. **2.** A given *frequency* of a *lightwave* in the *visible region* of the *electromagnetic frequency spectrum.* **3.** The sensation produced by a given *frequency,* or combination of frequencies, when *incident* upon the retina of the eye.

color-division multiplexing (CDM). In *optical communication systems,* the *multiplexing* of *channels* on a single *transmission medium;* e.g., using each *color* in a transmitted polychromatic light beam as a channel in one *optical fiber* or *bundle of fibers.* Color division multiplexing in the visible region of the *electromagnetic frequency spectrum* is the same process as *frequency division multiplexing* in the nonvisible region of the spectrum. Each color corresponds to a different *frequency* and a different *wavelength.*

colored-light transmission. *Transmission* in which an arrangement of *colored lights* is *displayed* in accordance with a prearranged *code.*

colorimeter. An *optical* instrument used to compare the *color* of a sample with a source reference or synthesized stimulus. For example, in a three-color color-imeter, the synthesized stimulus is produced by mixtures of three colors of fixed *chromaticity* but variable *luminance.* See Figure C-11.

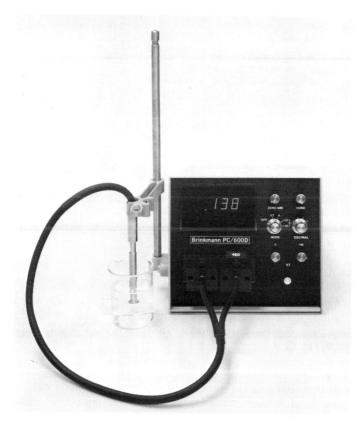

C-11. Brinkman *digital* dipping probe **colorimeter** with *fiber optic lightwave guide.* (Photo courtesy of Brinkman Instruments, Inc., subsidiary of Sybron Corporation.)

colors.   See *false colors.*

color temperature.   For a given body, the thermal *temperature* of a *blackbody* that *emits light* of the same *color* as the given body.   The color temperature is also expressed in *kelvin,* as is the thermal temperature.

COM. 1. *Computer-output microfilm.* **2.** *Computer-output microform.* **3.** Computer-output microfilming. **4.** Computer-output microfilmer.

coma.   An *aberration* of a *lens* that causes oblique pencils of *light rays* from an *object* point or source to be *imaged* as a comet-shaped blur.

combat-net radio. In *military communication systems,* a *radio net* used primarily for command and control in tactical situations. Usually a single *frequency* is employed in a *radio network* that uses *half-duplex operation.*

combination. See *code combination.*

combinational circuit. **1.** A *logic device* whose output values at any given instant depend on a set of input values at that instant; i.e., a special case of a *sequential circuit* without storage capability. For example, an *AND, OR,* or *NEGATION gate* as used in *optical integrated circuits.* **2.** A device that has at least one *output channel* and zero or more *input channels,* all characterized by *discrete* states, such that at any instant the state of each output channel is completely determined by the states of the input channels at the same instant. For example, an *AND, OR,* or *NEGATION gate* as used in an *optical integrated circuit.* Synonymous with *combinational logic element; logic element.* Also see *gating circuit; sequential circuit;* Figure B-5.

combinational logic element. See *combinational circuit.*

combined communications. The common use of *communication facilities* by two or more military services, each belonging to a different nation. Such use might be specified by a combined communications-electronics board. Also see *joint communications.*

combined distribution frame (CDF). A *distribution frame* that combines the functions of the *main* and the *intermediate distribution frames.* The frame contains both the *vertical terminating blocks* for terminating the permanent outside lines entering the station, and the *horizontal terminating blocks* for terminating *inside plant* equipment. This arrangement permits the association of any *outside line* with any desired *terminal equipment.* These *connections* are made with *twisted-pair jumper wire* or the equivalent. In *telephone* control facilities, the vertical side may be used to terminate equipment as well as outside lines. The horizontal side is then used for *jackfields* and *common battery terminations.* Also see *horizontal terminating block; intermediate distribution frame; main distribution frame; vertical terminating block.*

combined station. In *high-level data link control (HDLC) operation,* the *station* that is normally responsible for performing *balanced link level operations* and that generates *commands,* interprets *responses,* interprets received commands, and generates responses.

combiner. A device that enables two or more *transmitters* operating at different *frequencies* to simultaneously use a single *antenna.* It eliminates the need for separate antennas for each frequency or for each transmitter. The combiner should minimize *antenna insertion loss* and minimize *intermodulation noise.* See *cavity combiner; diversity combiner; equal-gain combiner; linear combiner; maximal-ratio combiner; post-detection combiner; selective combiner.*

combining. See *digital combining; dual diversity combining; linear diversity combining; predetection combining; pregroup combining; quadruple diversity combining; radio frequency combining.*

combining method. See *maximal ratio-square diversity combining method.*

comic-strip-oriented mode. A manner of recording *images* on strip or roll film so that the top edge of each image, when viewed normally for reading, is parallel to the long edge of the film. For example, if successive *frames* of pictures were being recorded on *microfilm* from the *faceplate* on the end of a *coherent bundle* of *optical fibers,* the film would move from left to right with respect to the normal orientation of the images. Contrast with *cine-oriented mode.*

COMINT. *Communication intelligence.*

COMJAM. *Communication jamming.*

command. **1.** In *data transmission,* an *instruction* or *control signal* usually sent from a *primary station* to a *secondary station* instructing the secondary station to perform a specific function or operation. **2.** In *high-level data link control (HDLC) operation,* the content of the *control field* of a *command frame* sent by the primary station or *combined station* to perform some specific *link level* function. **3.** That part of a *computer instruction word* that specifies the operation to be performed by the computer. See *disconnect command (DISC); display command; telemetry command; theater-area command; unnumbered command.*

command and control system. The personnel, facilities, *communication equipment,* and procedures essential to a commander for planning, directing, and controlling operations.

command-control-communication network. See *air defense command-control-communication network.*

command frame. **1.** In *data transmission,* a *frame* that contains a *command* transmitted by a *primary station.* **2.** In *high-level data link control (HDLC) operation,* a *frame* that is *transmitted* by a *primary station* or a *combined station,* and that has the remote (receiving) combined station *address.*

command fuzing. Fuzing in which a device is detonated only when directed to detonate. For example, a *computer* may be used to determine relative position between a missile and a target. When the computed distance is a minimum or below a threshold distance, the fuze is ordered to detonate.

command guidance. A guidance system in which intelligence *transmitted* to a missile from an outside *source* causes the missile to take a directed flight path.

command guidance system. A guidance system based on *signals transmitted* from the ground, the air, or the sea to a controllable object, such as a spacecraft, missile, aircraft, ship, or land vehicle. The *surface station* or the *aircraft station* transmits to the *mobile station* which converts the *command signals* to maneuvering control signals.

command net. A *communication network* that connects an echelon of command or control to some or all of its subordinate echelons.

command post. See *airborne command post.*

command station. See *telemetry command station; tracking-telemetry-command station.*

commercial communication common carrier. A privately owned organization, usually a corporation, that provides *communication services* to the public.

commercial communication service. A specific *service class* or type available from a *commercial communication common carrier.* For example, *user*-to-user service, user to nonuser service, public *message* service, full rate *facsimile* service, or overnight *telegram* service.

commercial refile. In *military communication systems,* the processing of a *message* from a given *network,* such as a *tape relay network,* a *point-to-point telegraph network,* or a *radio-telegraph network,* to a commercial communication network or system. Commercial refiling of a message normally will require a reformatting of the message, particularly the *heading.*

common-address multiple lines. A *facility* that permits a *user* to receive *calls* to a single *address* on more than one *circuit.*

commonality. The characteristic of *systems* for command, control, and *communications* that have the quality that a given component in the system has parts that are similar and interchangeable with parts of another component of the same system. Equipment and systems have commonality when each can be operated and maintained by personnel trained on the others without additional specialized training; and when repair parts, components, subassemblies, and consumable items are interchangeable between them. Also see *compatibility; interchangeability; interface; interoperability; transparency; transparent interface.*

common battery. 1. A battery that serves as a central source of energy for many *circuits.* In many *telecommunication* applications, the common battery is 48 volts. 2. An electrical *power* supply concept in which all *direct-current (DC)* energy for a unit of a *telephone system,* such as a *switching center,* is supplied by one source.

common battery exchange. In a *telephone system,* a *manual* or *automatic telephone exchange* in which the *power* needed for operating *supervisory signals* and *user's* calling signals, and also the power required to enable the user to speak over the line, are supplied from a battery situated at the exchange. Synonymous with *battery exchange.*

common battery signaling. A *telephone* or *telegraph system* in which the *signaling power* is supplied by a battery at the servicing *switchboard* or *switching center.* Switchboards may be manual or automatic. The power that enables the *user* to speak over the *line* may be supplied by either a *common* or a *local battery.*

common battery signaling exchange. A *manual* or *automatic switching exchange* that provides *supervisory* or *user signaling power* from a battery situated at the exchange. The power required to enable the user to speak over the *line* is provided by *local batteries* installed on the user's premises, or by dry cells in the user's *telephone* instrument.

common carrier. A public service organization closely regulated by a government. In the U.S., *telephone, telegraph,* railroad, and airline companies are common carriers whose rates, routes, and operating procedures are government regulated. See *commercial communication common carrier; communication common carrier.*

common-channel signaling. 1. A *signaling method* using a *link* common to a number of *channels,* for the control, accounting, and management of *traffic* on these channels. 2. A *signaling* technique in which signaling *information* relating to a multiplicity of *circuits,* and *information* for *network* management, are conveyed over a single channel by *addressed messages.*

common control system. An *automatic switching system* in which common equipment is used to establish a *connection.* After a connection is established, the common equipment then becomes available to establish other connections. Also see *communication system.*

common emergency frequency. See *military common emergency frequency.*

common frequency. See *convoy common frequency.*

common-mode interference. *Interference* that appears or occurs between *signal* leads or between the *terminals* of a measuring device and *ground.*

common-mode rejection ratio (CMRR). The ratio of the *common-mode interference voltage* at the *input* of a *circuit* to the interference voltage at the *output* of the circuit.

common-mode voltage. 1. Any uncompensated combination of generator or receiver *ground potential difference (voltage),* generator common return offset voltage, and longitudinally-coupled peak *random noise* voltage measured between the receiver circuit ground and receiver *cable* with the generator ends of the cable short-circuited to ground. 2. The algebraic mean of the two voltages appearing at the *receiver input terminals* with respect to the receiver *circuit ground.*

common return. A return path that is common to two or more *circuits* and that serves to return *currents* to their source or to ground.

common-return offset voltage. The *direct-current (DC) common return potential difference* of a *line.*

common trunk line. In *lightwave communication systems,* an *optical transmission channel* connected between a *transmitter (light source)* and a *receiver (photodetector),* with each transmitter and receiver located at a station or *node* in a *communication network* and being capable of accepting and ejecting *wavelength frequency division multiplexed* or *time division multiplexed signals* at various points along its length.

common user. Pertaining to *communication facilities* and *services* provided to essentially all *users* in an area served by a *communication system.* This is in contrast to facilities assigned to one or a relatively small number of users.

common-user circuit. A *circuit* designated to furnish *communication facilities* and services to a number of *users.*

common-user communications. *Communications* in which *communication services* are provided to many *users.*

common-user communication service. A *communication service* established to provide *communication service* and support to a group of *users* that have a common interest, such as a group of users in a single organization. Also see *dedicated communication service.*

common-user network. A *network* in which *circuits* or *channels* are allocated to furnish *communication paths* between *switching centers* to provide *communication facilities* and services on a common basis to all connected *stations* or *users.* Synonymous with *general purpose network.*

common-user service. A type of *communication service* that is provided by a *common-user network.*

communication. **1.** The transfer of *information* between a *source (transmitter, light source),* and a *sink (receiver, photodetector)* over one or more *channels* in accordance with a protocol and in a manner suitable for interpretation or comprehension by the receiver. **2.** A method or means of conveying information of any kind from one person or place to another, except by direct unassisted conversation or corrrespondence. See *code-independent data communication; data communication; dedicated communication; duplex communication; ground-to-air communication; long-haul communication; one-way communication; public relations communication; radiotelegraph communication; radiotelephone communication; surface-to-air communication; teletypewriter communication; two-way-alternate communication; two-way-simultaneous communication.* Synonymous with *message.*

communication agency. A *facility* that uses personnel and equipment to provide *communication services* to public or private organizations or to the general public, and performs other communication-related functions such as allowing communication-related charges to be appended to *telephone* bills, such as for the sending of *telegrams* or flowers or the purchasing of theater tickets.

communication axis. See *signal communication axis.*

communication base section. See *base communications.*

communication cable. See *intrusion-resistant communication cable.*

communication center. A *facility* that receives, *transmits,* and *delivers messages.* Also see *signal center.* See *filing communication center.*

communication common carrier. An organization, agency, or system that operates as a *common carrier* and that provides *communication services* to public and private organizations and to the general public. See *commercial communication common carrier.*

communication control character. See *transmission control character.*

communication control procedure. See *data communication control procedure.*

communication copy watch. See *radio communication copy watch.*

communication cover. See *radio communication cover.*

communication deception. **1.** In *military communication-electronic systems,* the *radiation,* reradiation, or *reflection* of *electromagnetic* energy in a manner intended to mislead, confuse, or harass *communications.* **2.** The introduction of deceptive *emissions* into *radio communication channels* with the intent of misleading operating personnel or *users.* **3.** The *transmission,* retransmission, alteration, *absoption,* or *reflection* of *telecommunication signals* in a manner intended to cause a misleading interpretation of these signals. See *manipulative communication deception.*

communication device. See *low-power communication device.*

communication emergency frequency. See *air-ground communication emergency frequency.*

communication equipment. See *data communication equipment; high-performance communication equipment; low-performance communication equipment; mobile communication equipment; transportable communication equipment.*

communication exercise. The *transmission, reception,* or *processing* of *information* directed specifically to evaluate the efficiency of *communication facilities,* procedures, personnel, and training.

communication facility. An installation or equipment that provides *communication services.* See *internal communication facility; record communication facility.*

communication guard. See *radio communication guard.*

communication intelligence (COMINT). Technical intelligence *information* derived from *communication systems* by other than the intended *users* or recipients of the *communication services.* COMINT is obtained using communication systems, procedures, and equipment to *intercept transmissions.* Also see *electronic intelligence; signal intelligence.*

communication intercept. A *reception* of a *signal* in which the *operator* is able to read *words,* letters, or numbers, or understand *codes,* such as the *international Morse code,* that were not intended for the operator.

communication jamming (COMJAM). 1. The portion of *electronic jamming* that is directed against *communication circuits* and *systems.* **2.** The prevention of successful *radio communications* by the use of *electromagnetic signals. Jamming* is the deliberate *radiation,* reradiation, or *reflection* of *electromagnetic* energy with the objective of impairing the effective use of *electronic communication systems.* The aim of communication jamming is to prevent communication by electromagnetic means or at least to degrade communications sufficiently to cause delays in *transmission* and *reception.* Jamming may be used in conjunction with *deception* to achieve an overall *electronic countermeasure (ECM) plan* implementation.

communication line. A land, sea, or air *route* that connects an operating unit with one or more bases of operations and along which supplies and reinforcements may move. For example, it may be the *path,* means, and media of *communication* maintained in support of operations. Lines of communication are maintained between higher and lower echelons of control, between supporting and supported elements, and among other elements involved in a given situation or operation, such as a rescue, fire fighting, medical evacuation, or military operation.

communication means. A *system* or *mode* of *communication* usually identified by the *transmission medium, coding* method, *service class,* or operating organization. Examples include *telephone, telegraph, wire, radio, television, visual,* messenger, *teletypewriter,* military, and commercial means.

communication method. See *broadcast communication method; intercept communication method; receipt communication method; relay communication method.*

communication net.   An organization or group of *stations* capable of direct *communication* with each other usually on a common *channel* or *frequency*.   Also see *communication network.*   See *alternate communication net; distress communication net; maritime amphibious communication net; maritime broadcast communication net; maritime distress communication net; maritime ship-shore communication net; maritime tactical air operations communication net.*

communication network.   **1.** A group of *stations* connected or in *communication* contact so that *messages* can be *transmitted* among them, although not necessarily on the same *channel.*   **2.** Two or more interrelated *circuits, switches,* or terminals for *communications.*   **3.** A combination of *switches, terminals,* and *circuits* that serve a given purpose.   **4.** A combination of terminals and circuits in which *transmission facilities* interconnect the *user stations* directly, there being no switching, control, or *processing centers* involved.   **5.** A combination of *circuits* and *terminals* serviced by a single *switching* or *processing center.*   See *air defense command-control-communication network; hybrid communication network; military fixed communication network.*

communication operation instruction.   See *signal operation instruction.*

communication operating instruction.   See *standing communication operating instruction (SCOI).*

communication organization.   See *area communication organization.*

communication plan.   A plan stating *communication* requirements in terms of equipment, *communication nets,* personnel, *facilities,* policies, and procedures.

communication plan format.   The arrangement, layout, or sequence of *data items* or topics that are included in a *communication plan.*

communication precedence system.   See *Joint Uniform Telephone Communication Precedence System (JUTCPS).*

communication processor unit (CPU).   The *message* control and *processing* unit of a *switching center.*   CPU is also used as an abbreviation for *central processing unit* in *computers.*

communication publication.   A publication containing *information* concerning *communication* personnel, intelligence, operations, and logistics.   Communication publications particularly contain information concerning communication systems, networks, and equipment, including their acquisition, operation, and maintenance.

communication reliability.   The probability that *information transmitted* from the *communication station* serving the *originator* of a *message,* a *calling party,* or other *source user,* to the communication station serving the *addressee, called party,* or other *destination user,* will arrive in a timely manner without loss of meaning.

communications.   The branch of science and technology that is concerned with the process of representing, *transferring,* interpreting, or *processing data* among persons, places, or machines. It is essential that the meaning assigned to the data is preserved during the process. See *air-air communications; air defense communications; air-ground communications; air traffic control communications; airways-air communications; base communications (BASECOM); combined communications; common-user communications; control communications; convoy communications; convoy internal communications; distress communications; fiber-optic communications; free-space optical communications; intelligence communications; joint communications; lateral communications; lightwave communications; maritime air communications; military communications; optical fiber communications; rescue communications; scene-of-action communications; search-and-rescue communications; secure communications; ship communications; ship-shore communications; signal communications; sound communications; tactical communications; weather communications; wireline communications.*

communication satellite.   An oribiting vehicle that relays *signals* between *communication stations.* They are of two types, namely *active communication satellites* and *passive communication satellites.* See *active communication satellite; passive communication satellite.*

communication satellite earth station.   An *earth station* in the *communication satellite service.*

communication satellite service.   A *communication service* between (1) *earth stations* using *active* or *passive satellites* for the exchange of *messages* in a *fixed* or *mobile service;* or (2) an earth station and stations on active satellites for the exchange of messages in a mobile service, with a view to their retransmission to or from stations in the mobile service, for example from train to train, truck to truck, ship to ship, aircraft to aircraft, ship to aircraft, and all other combinations.

communication satellite space station.   A *space station* on an *earth satellite* in the *communication satellite service.*

communication security.   1. The protection resulting from the application of measures that deny unauthorized persons access to *information* transferred in a *communication system.*   2. The protection of a *communication system* from unauthorized access to, *information* in, or information concerning the system (e.g., *codes,* location of equipment, *frequencies,* and protocol). *Optical circuits* provide security due to reduced leakage *radiation* and difficulty of *tapping* without detection. *Lightwaves* are not *electric currents.* They are easily prevented from leaking from an *optical fiber* or cable by a thin opaque sheath. However, electric currents in conventional wires produce *electric* and *magnetic fields* that are not stopped by simple coverings on the wires. These fields are detectable at large distances from the wires. In order to tap an optical fiber, a coupling device must be attached. The presence of the *coupler* is easily detectable at the receiving end. Also see *electronic security; emission security; signal security.*

communication security equipment.   Equipment designed to provide *security* to *telecommunication systems* by converting *information* to a form that is unintelligible to an unauthorized interceptor and by reconverting such information to its original form for authorized recipients. Equipment designed specifically to aid in the conversion process and equipment that is an essential element of the conversion process are also included, such as *cryptoequipment,* cryptoancillary equipment, cryptoproduction equipment, and *authentication* equipment. Also see *security.* See *integrated communication security equipment.*

communication security information.   *Information* that concerns *communication security, communication security material,* and communication security *systems.* Also see *cryptoinformation.*

communication security material.   All documents, devices, equipment, or systems, including *cryptomaterial,* used in establishing, maintaining, or authenticating *secure communications.*

communication security policy.   The overall policy applicable to all areas of *communication security,* including communication security monitoring, control systems, analyses, equipment, materials, *information,* custodianship, codes, aids, surveillance, surveys, and others.

communication security profile.   An identification of all *communication security* measures and materials available for a given operation, *system,* or organization. It includes a determination of the amount and type of use of these measures and materials.

communications-electronics.   The field of technology devoted to the design, development, and use of electronic devices and *systems* for the acquisition, acceptance, *processing, storage, display, analysis, protection,* and *transmission* of *data* and *information.* It applies to and includes (1) the wide range of responsibilities and actions relating to electronic devices and *systems* that are used in the *transfer* of ideas and perceptions; (2) electronic sensors and sensory systems that are used in the acquisition of information; (3) electronic devices and systems that are intended to allow operation in a hostile environment; and (4) the denial or prevention of use of *electromagnetic* resources by other individuals or organizations. Also see *theater director of communications-electronics.*

communication service.   A service or *facility* provided to *users* that enables them to *communicate* with each other. For example, *telephone, telegraph,* and *facsimile transmission* are communication services normally provided by *commu-*

nication common carriers. See *commercial communication service; common-user communication service; dedicated communication service.*

communication silence. The avoidance of any type of *transmission, emission,* or *radiation* by any means, even by *receiving* equipment. For example, during communication silence, *listening watch* may be maintained only if the receivers do not radiate *electromagnetic* energy. Also see *radio silence.*

communication sink. **1.** A device that receives *data, control, timing,* or other *signals* from *communication sources,* e.g., a device that accepts *data* from a *communication system.* **2.** A place where energy from one or more sources is collected or drained away. **3.** A *power* dissipating device, such as the load in a *circuit.* Also see *communication source.*

communication source. A device that generates *information, control,* or other signals destined for *communication sinks.* Also see *communication sink.*

communication standard plan. See *aircraft communication standard plan; ship-fitting communication standard plan.*

communication subsystem. A major functional part of a *communication system,* usually consisting of *facilities* and equipment essential to the operation of the system.

communication survivability. The capability of a *communication system* to continue to operate effectively even though portions may suffer physical damage or destruction. Methods for maintaining system survival include dispersing *routing facilities,* utilizing different *transmission* methods, employing redundant equipment, and using sites hardened against *radiation.* Also see *electromagnetic survivability.*

communication system. A *system* or *facility* capable of providing *information transfer* between persons and equipment. The system usually consists of a collection of individual *communication networks, transmission systems, relay stations, tributary stations,* and *terminal equipment* capable of interconnection and interoperation so as to form an integrated whole. These individual components must serve a common purpose, be technically compatible, employ common procedures, respond to some form of control, and generally operate in unison. See *air defense communication system; air-ground worldwide communication system; asynchronous communication system; AUTOSEVOCOM system; ciphony communication system; flashing light communication system; hybrid communication system; integrated communication system; optical communication system; satellite communication system; space communication system; strategic military communication system; tactical communication system; visual communication system; wideband communication system.*

communication system abbreviations. See *aeronautical communication system abbreviations.*

communication system consolidation.   A combination of two or more existing autonomous *communication facilities* into a single entity with all or most of the original capability and some of the original autonomy remaining. Communication system consolidation is a facet of system rationalization.

communication system management.   The planning, organizing, coordinating, directing, controlling, and supervising of *communication systems* and *networks.* It includes the authority and responsibility for executing all applicable network planning functions, including formulation, review, and revision of the applicable management information system.   It includes the issuance and enforcement of standing operating procedures, *standing communication operating instructions,* and technical directives; the development of routine logistical processes, including maintenance, supply, and replacement of equipment; development of procedures for advice and assistance visits by representatives of other authorities; programming for acquisition of equipment or modifications to improve system efficiency and reliability; development of manning and training criteria for system personnel; and preparing budgetary policies within the established rules. Management control is a long-term support function and may not always respond instantaneously to unforeseen situations.

communication system saturation.   The condition that exists in a *communication system* when the system is handling *traffic* at its maximum capacity.

communication test.   The *transmission* or *reception* of *information* specifically intended to evaluate the efficiency of *communication media* or facilities.

communication theory.   Theory dealing with the probabilistic characteristics of the *transmission* of *data* in the presence of *noise.*   Mathematics of communication theory was considerably developed and advanced by Quine, who developed theories in combinational logic; Shannon, who contributed to advances in information theory; and Wiener, who contributed to advances in cybernetics, i.e., control theory.

communication traffic.   1. The totality of *transmitted* and *received messages.*   2. The streams of *messages* transmitted within and among *networks,* including *user* and *system operator* messages.

communication traffic volume.   A measure of the number of calls, messages, words, or other *data* units handled by a *communication system* per unit time. Also see *erlang.*

communication watch.   To monitor one or more *communication lines, frequencies,* or *channels* for the purpose of obtaining *information* by listening to or receiving all *transmissions* on them; and to *transmit* and receive *messages* as required. See *continuous communication watch.*

communication zone.   In *military communication systems,* the part of a theater of operations that contains the *communication lines,* activities for supply and

evacuation, and other agencies required for the immediate support and maintenance of field forces in a combat zone.

community of interest. In *communications,* a grouping of *users* who share a
common interest, who generate a majority of their *traffic* in *calls* to each other,
and who are usually located relatively near each other. The community may be
related to a geographic area, an administrative organization, a project or field of
endeavor, or other common interest.

commutation. **1.** The sampling of two or more *channels, circuits, sources,* or
quantities in a cyclical or repetitive manner for *transmission* over a single *channel*
using a *multiplexing* method for *transmission.* **2.** The process of converting *alternating current* to *direct current* in a direct-current generator.

compaction. See *curve-fitting compaction; data compaction; fixed-tolerance
band compaction; floating-point coding compaction; frequency analysis compaction; incremental compaction; probability-analysis compaction; sample-change
compaction; slope-keypoint compaction; storage compaction; variable precision
coding compaction; variable tolerance band compaction.*

compander. A device that combines the functions of a *compressor* with that of
an *expander.* In a *communication system,* it is a combination of a compressor at
one point in a *communication path* for reducing the volume range of *signals,* followed by an expander at another point for restoring the original volume range.
Usually its purpose is to improve the *signal-to-noise ratio* entering the path between the compressor and expander. It permits the *transmission* of a signal that
has a small volume range. Usually the compressor and expander may be used independently. Also see *clipper; compressor; expander; image processing; peak
limiting.*

companding. In a *communication system,* the process of improving the *signal-
to-noise ratio* by *compressing* the *amplitude* or volume range of the *signal* with a
compressor at the *transmitter* and restoring the range at the *receiver* or *detector*
with an *expander.* The process of dynamic range compressison of *analog signals*
is used extensively in *frequency modulated (FM)* systems to improve the *signal-
to-noise ratio* of weak signal components and to give a more constant *modulator*
loading. Companding techniques are applied to speech channels prior to *multiplexing.* They involve a compressor at the *transmitter* and an expander at the
receiver. Also see *compressor; image processing.* See *instantaneous companding;
logarithmic companding; syllabic companding.*

comparator. **1.** In *analog computing* and *communication systems,* a device that
compares two *analog variables* and indicates the result of the comparison. Some
comparators indicate whether the variables are the same or different. Others indicate which is the greater. If their difference is indicated, it is a *subtracter.* **2.**
In *digital computing* and *communication systems,* a device that uses *combinational circuits (gates)* to determine whether or not two numbers are identical and
to indicate the results of the comparison. Also see *subtracter.*

compartmentalization. The isolation of components, *programs,* and *informa-tion* in order to provide protection against unauthorized *access.*

compatibility. **1.** The characteristic of *systems* for command, control, and *com-munication* in which *information* can be exchanged directly in usable form. *Sig-nals* can be exchanged between them without the addition of devices for the spe-cific purpose of achieving workable *interface connections;* and the equipment or systems being interconnected possess comparable *radiation* characteristics. **2.** The capability of two or more items or components of equipment or material to exist, function, or be connected in the same *system* or environment without *mu-tual interference.* Also see *commonality; interchangeability; interoperability.* See *electromagnetic compatibility (EMC); frequency compatibility.*

compatibility analysis. See *electromagnetic compatibility (EMC) analysis.*

compatible sideband transmission. That method of *independent sideband trans-mission* in which the *carrier* is deliberately reinserted at a lower level after its normal suppression to permit *reception* by conventional *amplitude modulation (AM) receivers.* The normal method of *transmitting compatible sideband elec-tromagnetic waves* is to *transmit* the carrier plus the *upper sideband.* Synony-mous with *amplitude modulation equivalent (AME); compatible SSB.*

compatible SSB. See *compatible sideband transmission.*

compensated optical fiber. An *optical fiber* whose *refractive index profile* has been so controlled that *light rays* traveling in the high *refractive index core* or cen-ter (thus traveling a shorter distance at lower speeds due to the high index mate-rial) and the rays traveling in the outer lower index material (undergoing *internal reflection* or bending back and forth and thus traversing a longer path but travel-ing faster due to the lower index) arrive at the end of the fiber at the same time and at the same place along with the *skew rays* that traveled a *helical path,* thus reducing *modal dispersion* perhaps to zero. Also see *over-compensated optical fiber; under-compensated optical fiber.*

compensating equalizer. See *line temperature-compensating equalizer.*

compensating phase shift. A *coherent optical* adaptive technique used to im-prove the *power density* of *electromagnetic wavefronts* by changing the *shape, phase,* or character of the wavefront with *optical systems* or *fields* in order to adjust for unwanted variations of these parameters introduced by *transmission media* and *system components,* such as *optical fibers, connectors, couplers, lenses,* or the atmosphere.

compensation. See *luminance compensation; wavefront compensation.*

compile. **1.** To *translate* a *computer program* expressed in an *application-oriented language* into a *computer-oriented language.* **2.** To prepare a *machine language program* using a *computer program* written in another *programming language* and using various methods, such as by making use of the overall logic structure of the program or by generating more than one computer *instruction* for each symbolic statement as well as performing the function of an *assembler*. Also see *machine language*.

compiler. 1. A *computer program* that converts computer programs written in a *procedure-oriented language* into a form suitable for execution on a *computer*. Thus, a computer program that, when executed, produces another computer program with new features, such as a capability to be directly executed by a computer as a *machine language program*. **2.** An *artificial language* used to generate, express, or write *computer programs*.

complementary wave. A *wave* with a *polarization* that is obtained or derived from the polarization or *modulation* of another wave. The repolarization of the *signal* is accomplished in order to avoid *interference*. If *circular* or *elliptical polarization* is used, the complementary *wavefront* is at right angles to the given wavefront.

completed call. A *call* for which *connections* have been established and the *calling party* and *called party* are in *communication*. Also see *finished call*.

completion objective. See *call completion objective*.

complex-pulse radar. A *radar* that has an *output signal* that is best described, for precise analytical purposes, in terms of a complex mathematical function. For example, the shape of the *pulse* may be described as a complex function of time with the general equation $s(t) = x(t) + jy(t)$ where $s(t)$ is the complex signal function of time, $x(t)$ is the real part, $y(t)$ is the imaginary part, and j is the imaginary component (quadrature component, $j = (-1)^{1/2}$) operator.

complex transfer function. A *transmission transfer function* that includes the *phase* transformation, as well as the *attenuation* transformation, that occurs to a *signal* traveling in a *medium*. For example, the complex transfer function may be determined from a Fourier transform analysis of a 100-*psec* recorded pulse entered into and received from a length of optical fiber.

component. 1. An assembly, or part thereof, that is essential to the operation of some larger assembly. It is a subdivision of the assembly to which it belongs. Thus, a *radio receiver* may be considered to be a component of a complete *radio station* consisting of a *transmitter* and *receiver*. The *intermediate frequency (IF) amplifier* section would be a component of the receiver but not of the radio station. Similarly, a resistor, capacitor, vacuum tube, *transistor,* or other item in a *circuit* within the IF amplifier section would be a component of that section. **2.** One of the elements of a *vector,* which, when summed with others, forms a whole vector quantity. For example, the part of a vector directed in a given reference direction, such as the part of a vector parallel to the x-axis of a Cartesian coordinate system. See *electric field component; magnetic field component; quadrature component*. Also see Figure Q-1.

component life. The period of acceptable usage of a *component,* part, or device after the expiration of which the likelihood of failure sharply increases. In the interest of achieving a high level of reliability, components are removed from service prior to the expiration of their component life. See *indefinite component life; inphase component life; out-of-phase component life.* Also see *bathtub curve; wear-out failure period.*

composite circuit. A *circuit* that can be used simultaneously for *telephony, direct-current (DC) telegraphy,* or *signaling.* Separation between the two is accomplished by *frequency division multiplexing.* Synonymous with *voice-plus circuit.* Also see *speech-plus-duplex operation; speech-plus-signaling; speech-plus-telegraph.*

composite code. In a *spread-spectrum system,* a *code* that is obtained from two or more other distinct codes. For example, a *gold code.*

composite signaling (CX). A *signaling* arrangement that provides for *direct-current (DC) signaling* and *dial pulse* generation beyond the range of *loop* signaling methods. Composite signaling, like *direct-current signaling (DX),* permits *duplex operation* in that it provides simultaneous two-way signaling. Synonymous with *CX signaling.* Also see *direct-current signaling (DX).*

composite two-tone test signal. A *test signal* used for *intermodulation distortion* measurements. The two tones, of *frequencies* f_1 and f_2, are of equal level. The main *intermodulation products* are $2f_1 - f_2$ and $2f_2 - f_1$.

compound-glass process. See *double-crucible process.*

compound lens. A *lens* composed of two or more separate pieces of glass or other *optical* material. The component pieces or elements may or may not be cemented together. A common form of compound lens is a two-element *objective,* one element being a *converging lens* of *crown glass* and the other a *diverging lens* of *flint glass.* The combination of suitable glasses or other optical materials (plastics, minerals) properly ground and polished, reduces *aberrations* normally present in a *single lens.* Contrast with *single lens.*

compressed dialing. A *dialing facility* that permits the use of a shortened directory with shorter *telephone numbers* to obtain frequently called *parties.*

compression. See *data compression; facsimile data compression; luminance range compression; optical fiber pulse compression; radar pulse compression.*

compression and expansion. See *linked compression and expansion (LINCOM-PEX).*

compression radar. See *pulse compression radar.*

compressor. **1.** An *amplifier,* usually forming part of a *signal transmitter,* whose *gain* always decreases with increasing *input signal level* in order to partly compensate for *amplitude* variation. This action reduces the dynamic range of variation for *transmission,* the process perhaps being reversed by an *expander* at the *receiver.* **2.** A device with a *nonlinear gain* characteristic that acts to reduce the *gain* more on larger input signals than it does on smaller input signals. The compressor is usually used to allow signals with a larger dynamic amplitude range to be sent through devices and circuits with a more limited range. Also see *clipper; compander; companding; expander; image processing.*

compromise. **1.** The availability, exposure, or *transfer* of *information* to unauthorized persons through any means, such as loss, *photography,* theft, and breaking of *codes.* **2.** In *communication security,* any occurrence that results in, or can be presumed to have resulted in, unauthorized persons gaining *access* to protected *information.* **3.** The known or suspected exposure of *protected information,* installations, personnel, materials, or other assets to an unauthorized person.

compromise equalizer. See *fixed compromise equalizer.*

compromising emanation. **1.** *Radiation* from a *communication circuit* that can disclose security classified or proprietary *information* being *transmitted* in the circuit to unauthorized persons or equipment. *Optical fibers* radiate less than wires. **2.** An unintentional *data* or intelligence-bearing *signal* that, if *intercepted* and analyzed, will disclose to unauthorized persons the *protected information* being *transmitted, received,* handled, or otherwise *processed* by any *information processing* or *communication* equipment. Also see *red-black concept; tempest.*

compute mode. The operating mode of an *analog computer* during which the solution is present or in progress at the *output.* Synonymous with *operate mode.*

computer. **1.** A device capable of accepting and processing *data* and supplying results. It usually consists of *input, output, storage,* arithmetic, logic, and control units. **2.** A *data processor* that can perform computation, such as arithmetic or logic operations, without intervention by a human *operator.* See *analog computer; asynchronous digital computer; digital computer; front-end computer; host computer; synchronous digital computer.*

computer-based office work. See *office automation.*

computer-dependent language. See *assembly language.*

computer graphics The science, technology, methods, and techniques devoted to the conversion of *data* to or from *display elements, display groups,* or *display images* in the *display space* on the *display surface* of a *display device,* through the use of computers. For example, the screen of a *CRT,* surface of an *LED* or *gas panel,* or *faceplate* on the end of a *coherent bundle* of *optical fibers* of a *fiberscope.* See Figure C-12.

C-12. An application of **computer graphics** in which *codes,* used to *store* and *transmit* a *simulated* advertisement, are checked. (Courtesy of Bell Laboratories.)

computer interface.   See *host computer interface.*

computer net.   A *communication net* designed for the *transfer* of *computer*-generated *data* taken directly from the computer *output terminals* or devices.

computer network.   Two or more *computers* connected together by a *communication network.*   See *centralized computer network; decentralized computer network.*

computer-oriented language.   **1.** A *programming language* that is dependent upon or reflects the structure of a given *computer* or class of computers. **2.** A *programming language* that has *words* and *syntax* designed for use on a specific group or class of *computers.*   Also see *assembly language.*

computer-output microfilm (COM).   In *display systems, microfilm* that contains *data* that are recorded directly from computer-generated *signals.*   The signals may be used to deflect and *modulate* the *electron beam* of a *CRT,* energize the electrodes of an *LED* or *gas panel,* or energize the LEDs or *lasers* that illuminate a *coherent bundle* of *optical fibers* that lead to the *faceplate* of a *fiberscope.*   The abbreviation COM is also used for the technique (computer-output microfilming) and for the device (computer-output microfilmer). If *microforms* in general are indicated, COM also implies computer-output microform.

computer-output microform (COM).   In *display systems, microform* that contains *data* that are recorded directly from *computer*-generated *signals.*   The signals may be used to deflect and *modulate* the *electron beam* of a *CRT,* energize the electrodes of an *LED* or *gas panel,* or energize the LEDs or *lasers* that illuminate a *coherent bundle* of *optical fibers* that lead to the *faceplate* of a *fiberscope.*   The abbreviation COM is also used for the technique (computer-output microforming) and for the device (computer-output microformer). If only *microfilm* is indicated, COM also implies computer-output microfilm.

computer patch.   See *computer program patch.*

computer peripheral device.   An auxiliary device under direct or indirect control of a *computer,* such as a *card punch, card reader,* high-speed printer, *magnetic tape* unit, or an *optical character reader.*

computer program.   A sequence of imperative, interrogative, or declarative statements, *commands, instructions,* or orders in a form acceptable to a *computer* or *data* processing machine.   Most programs are instructions to be executed by a computer.   Also see *routine.*

computer programming.   1. The planning, designing, writing, and testing of *computer programs.*   **2.** The art and science of planning the solution of problems and using a *computer* for assisting in solving these problems.   **3.** The process of setting up a *computer* for a specific automatic *operation* or series of operations.

computer program patch.   A temporary change in a *computer program, routine,* or *subroutine,* such as a section of new *instructions* added to an existing program normally using transfer or *branch* instructions to go to or from the patch. The patch allows the use of old programs to handle new situations or changes in situations.   The patch may become a permanent part of the program, though, if there are too many, the program may be rewritten.

computer routine.   A sequence of *computer instructions* that has general use and that is designed for some specific task that may have to be performed repeatedly.   For example, a computer routine might be created to solve a specific mathematical function, such as a series expansion of sin x; to retrieve a file from bulk storage; or to update a payroll record.

computer simulation.   The use of a *programmed computer (digital* or *analog)* to represent or model the features or behavior of a physical or abstract *system* so as to make the computer produce the same results as would the system being simulated.   Many systems can be simulated using the same computer, changing only the *software.*   For example, the behavior of a high-*traffic communication* *system,* the flight of a missile or satellite, the economy of a country, war games, a railroad network, or another computer, all can be simulated on a computer. Also see *emulator; simulator.*

computer systems. See *heterogeneous computer systems; homogeneous computer systems.*

computer tape. A strip of material that may be punched or coated with *magnetic* or *optically* sensitive substances, and used for *data input, storage,* or *output. Data* recorded in or on the tape is arranged to be read by a *computer,* and a computer can record data in or on the tape.

computer terminal. A device that enables an *operator* to interact with a *computer.* Also see *data processing terminal.*

computer time. The time scale used in or by a *computer* for the solution of a problem or the execution of a *computer program.* Computer time may be different from problem time and from *real time.* For example, in the computation of a *parameter* as a function of time, such as points in the trajectory of a satellite or missile, if the parameter is computed for say 2 second intervals of flight *(problem time)* and if the value of 2 is inserted by the program in the flight equation every 5 milliseconds (real time), the computer *time scale* unit is smaller and computer time is faster, that is, the satellite motion is computed 400 times faster than the satellite actually moves.

computer word. In computing equipment, a sequence of *bits* or *characters* that occupies one *storage* location, is usually of constant length in a given *computer,* and is treated by computer *circuits* as a unit, that is, it is stored, retrieved, transferred, or operated upon as a unit.

concatenation. See *tandem.*

concave. Pertaining to a hollow curved surface of a given material. If a *lens* is imbedded in a medium and one lens surface is concave, the contiguous surface of the medium is *convex.* Also see *convex.*

concave lens. See *diverging lens.*

concavo-convex lens. See *meniscus.*

concealment. The hiding of sensitive *information* and the preservation of its confidentiality by embedding it in irrelevant *data.*

concentrating equipment. In *communication systems,* equipment that performs the functions of a *data concentrator,* that is, equipment that permits a common *transmission medium* to serve more *data sources* than there are *channels* currently available within the transmission medium. The concentration, or merging and *buffering* of *data streams,* is usually performed by *multiplexing,* rather than by *compaction* or *compressing.*

concentrator. In *communication systems,* a *functional unit* that permits a common *path* to handle more *data sources* than there are *channels* currently available within the path. A concentrator usually provides communication capability between many low-speed, usually *asynchronous channels* and one or more high-speed, usually *synchronous* channels. Usually different *signaling (transmission) speeds,* different *codes,* and different *protocols* can be accommodated on the low-speed side. The low-speed channels usually encounter *contention* and hence require *buffering.*   See *data concentrator; optical fiber concentrator; telegraph concentrator.*

concentric cable. See *coaxial cable.*

concentric lens. A *lens* in which the centers of curvature of the surfaces coincide and thus have a constant radial thickness in all zones.

concentric line. See *coaxial cable.*

concept. See *red-black concept.*

condensing lens. A *lens* or *lens system* of *positive lens power* used for condensing (i.e., converging) *radiant energy* from a *source* onto an *object* or surface.

condition. See *decibel above isotropic condition; exception condition; modulation significant condition; not-ready condition; prelasing condition; ready condition; reeling condition; significant condition; steady-state condition; trunk-free condition; trunk-seized condition.*

conditional information entropy. In Shannnon's information theory, the mean of the measure of the *information content* conveyed by the occurrence of one of a finite set of mutually exclusive and jointly exhaustive events, each with definite conditional probabilities, given the occurrence of another set of mutually exclusive events. Synonymous with *mean conditional information content; average conditional information content.*

conditional information content. The *information content* conveyed by the occurrence of an event of definite conditional probability, given the occurrence of another event. See *conditional entropy.*

conditioned baseband representation. See *non-return-to-zero mark (NRZ-M).*

conditioned biphase coding. See *biphase mark coding.*

conditioned circuit. A *circuit* that has conditioning equipment to obtain the desired characteristics for *analog* (voice) or *digital data transmission.*

conditioned diphase modulation. A method of *modulation* that employs both *diphase modulation* and *signal* conditioning to eliminate the *direct-current (DC) component* of a *signal,* to enhance timing recovery, and to facilitate *transmission* over *video frequency (VF) circuits* or *coaxial cable* facilities.

conditioned loop. A *loop* that has *conditioning equipment* to obtain the desired *line* characteristics for *analog* (voice) or *digital data transmission.*

conditioned voice-grade circuit. A *voice grade circuit* that has *conditioning equipment* to equalize *envelope* or *phase-delay response* so as to improve *data transmission* through the *circuit.* Synonymous with *data grade circuit.*

conditioning equipment. **1.** Equipment at junctions of *circuits* to accomplish *transmission leveling, impedance matching,* and *equalization* between *facilities.* **2.** *Networks* used to equalize the *insertion loss* versus *frequency* characteristic and the *envelope delay distortion* over a desired *frequency range* in order to improve *data transmission.*

condition mode. See *initial condition mode.*

condition number. See *significant condition number.*

conductance. A measure of the ability of a material to conduct or carry an *electrical current* in relation to the magnitude of the applied *voltage.* It is the reciprocal of the resistance (ohms) and is expressed in mhos (ohms spelled backward). The greater the conductance, in mhos, the greater the current that can be carried for a given *potential difference,* whereas the greater the resistance (ohms) the less the current. Mathematically, $J = \sigma_1 E$ and $I = \sigma_2 V,$ where J is the *current density* in amperes per meter square, E is the *electric field intensity* in volts per meter, I is the total current in amperes, V is the potential difference in volts, σ_1 is the electrical conductivity in mhos per meter, and σ_2 is the conductance in mhos.

conducted interference. **1.** *Interference* resulting from *radio noise* or unwanted *signals* entering a device by *direct coupling.* **2.** An undesired *potential difference (voltage)* or *electric current* generated within a *receiver, transmitter,* or associated equipment and appearing at *antenna terminals.*

conduction. See *acoustical conduction; optical conduction.*

conduction band. **1.** In a *semiconductor,* the range of *electron* energy, higher than that of the *valence band,* possessed by electrons sufficient to make them free to move from atom to atom. When they leave the valence band, they are free to move under the influence of an applied *electric field* and thus they constitute an *electric current.* **2.** In the atomic structure of a material, a partially filled or empty *energy level* in which electrons are free to move, thus allowing the material to conduct an electric current upon application of an *electric field* by means of an *applied voltage.*

conductivity. See *electrical conductivity.*

conductor. 1. In *fiber optics,* a *transparent medium* that is capable of *transmitting* or conveying *lightwaves* a useful distance. 2. In electric circuits, a material that readily permits a flow of *electrons* through itself upon application of an *electric field.* Electrical conductors include copper, aluminum, lead, gold, silver, and platinum. The conductivity is specified by: $J = \sigma E$, where J is the current density in amperes/square meter for *SI* units, E is the applied *electric field* in volts/meter, and σ is the conductivity in reciprocal ohms/meter. Contrast with *dielectric.* See *electrical conductor; fortuitous conductor, optical conductor.*

conductor loss. See *connector-induced optical conductor loss.*

conduit. 1. A protective tube, usually installed externally to walls and foundations, designed to house, and usually installed with, wire or *optical fiber cables.* 2. See *incoherent bundle.*

cone. See *acceptance cone; antenna blind cone.*

cone of silence. The cone-shaped region of *space* with its apex at an *antenna,* in which the *signals* from the *antenna* are greatly reduced in *amplitude.* The near-zero or zero portions of the antenna *radiation lobe* may be an inverted cone-shaped space directly over the antenna, particularly if the antenna is a *dipole* or *stacked dipole antenna.* In this region signals are greatly reduced in amplitude. The cone of silence occurs directly over the antenna towers of some forms of *radio beacons.*

conference. See *preset conference; random conference; telecommunication conference.*

conference call. A *call* in which more than two *access lines* are connected. Also see *multiple call.* See *meet-me conference call; progressive conference call.*

conference circuit. A *circuit* that permits simultaneous *communication* between two or more *stations* for conference purposes. All stations can originate and receive *messages* when connected by a conference circuit.

conference operation. 1. In a *telephone system,* that type of operation in which more than two *stations* can carry on a conversation. 2. In *telegraph* or *data transmission,* that form of *simplex* or *half-duplex operation* in which more than two *stations* may simultaneously exchange *information,* carry on conversations, or pass *messages.* In *radio systems,* the stations receive simultaneously, but must *transmit* one at a time. The common modes are *push-to-talk (telephone)* and *push-to-type (telegraph* and *digital data transmission).* A simple form of conference operation may be carried on by a *radio net.*

conference repeater. A *repeater,* connecting several *circuits,* that *receives telephone* or *telegraph signals* from any one of the circuits and automatically retransmits them over all the others. Also see *data conferencing repeater.*

configurable station. In *high-level data link control (HDLC) operation,* a *station* that has a *mode*-setting capability of being more than one type of *logical station* at different times. For example, it may be a *primary station, secondary station,* or *combined logical station* at different times.

configuration. See *network configuration; relay configuration.*

confirmation. See *clear confirmation; delivery confirmation.*

confirmation signal. See *clear confirmation signal.*

confirmation signaling. In *telephone systems,* a method of *signaling* on *trunks* to ensure error-free *transmission* of *dialed information.* As each *digit* is sent over the trunk, confirmation is accomplished by returning a unique digit-dependent *signal* from the far end of the trunk.

congestion. See *frequency spectrum congestion; reception congestion.*

congestion signal. See *international congestion signal; national circuit group congestion signal; national switching equipment congestion signal.*

congruency. The ability of a *facsimile transmitter* or *receiver* to perform in a manner identical to the manner in which the equipment of another *facsimile system* performs.

conical beam-split radar. A *radar* that has an *antenna* with an *output beam* that is spun about an axis so as to describe a cone in space and that distributes energy in two or more directions at any given instant. This mode combines the advantages of *conical scanning* with *multiple beaming.* Also see *conical scanning; multiple beaming.*

conical fiber. See *optical taper.*

conical scanning. In *radar systems,* a target *scanning* technique in which *lobing* consists of movement of the *antenna* axis and sampling of the *echo signal* at various points in the *image* plane. The scanning is accomplished by rotating the antenna axis so as to describe a cone with its apex at the radar antenna site and its base at the object (target), thus providing an echo signal. The signal can be made symmetrical during a single rotation thus indicating that the antenna is on the object (target) and the direction of the object can be determined. Conical scanning permits automatic *tracking* and eliminates the necessity of manual tracking by an *operator* who must obtain a balance of two pulses that become unequal when the antenna moves off the object. Also see *conical beam-split radar; paired lobing; sequential lobing.*

conjugation. See *phase conjugation.*

conjunction. The situation in which two or more *satellites* are in line with their parent body, for example, when two earth satellites and the earth's center are in one straight line; when the moon, an artificial satellite, and the earth are in one straight line; or when the sun, earth, mars, and venus are in one straight line. See *phase conjugation.*

conjugation gate. See *AND gate.*

conjunctive address group. An *address group* that has an incomplete meaning and must be used in combination with one or more other address groups.

connected network. See *fully connected network.*

connected station. See *directly connected station.*

connection. A provision for a *signal* to *propagate* from one *circuit, line,* or *component* to another. See *automatic sequential connection; back-to-back connection; bridging connection; circuit-switched connection; cross connection; data circuit connection; data connection; dedicated connection; laser service connection; logical connection; multipoint connection; point-to-point connection; ring connection; star connection; virtual connection.*

connection-in-progress signal. A *call control signal* at the *data circuit-terminating equipment (DCE)* and the *data terminal equipment (DTE) interface* that indicates to the DTE that the establishment of the *data connection* is in progress and that the *ready-for-data signal* will follow.

connections per circuit-hour (CCH). In a *communication system,* a unit of *traffic* measurement, that is, the number of *connections* established at a *switching center* per *circuit-hour.* For example, if there are 500 *circuits* at a switching center and 7,000 connections are made per hour at the center, then 14 connections per circuit-hour are being made.

connectivity. See *network connectivity.*

connector. In *fiber optics* and *wirelines,* a device that permits the *coupling* of *signals* from one *optical fiber* or *cable* to another. See *bulk-head connector; dimpled connector; double-eccentric connector; fixed fiber-optic connector; free fiber-optic connector; grooved fiber-alignment connector; laser connector; optical fiber active connector; tapered-plug connector.* Also see *coupler;* Figure B-8.

connector-induced optical conductor loss. That part of *connector insertion loss* due to impurities or structural changes to the *optical conductors* caused by *termination* or the handling of signals within the *connector.* Usually expressed in *decibels.*

connector insertion loss. The *power* loss sustained by a *transmission medium* (such as a wire, *coaxial cable, optical fiber cable,* or *integrated optical circuit component*) due to the insertion of a *connector* between two elements, which would not occur if the *media* were continuous without the *connector* (i.e., if there were no *reflected, absorbed, dispersed,* or *scattered power*). The *power* loss, usually expressed in *decibels,* is often due to insertion of a mated connector onto a *cable.*

conservation. See *radiance conservation.*

CONSOL. A specific *long-range radio navigational aid,* the *emissions* of which, by means of their *audio frequency modulation* characteristics, enable *bearings* to be determined. CONSOL is operated such that one line of bearing is obtained from one *station* on any *low-frequency receiver.* Thus, at least two stations are required for position *fixing* by obtaining crossed bearings, that is by *resection.* Certain charts are necessary for aid in interpreting the *information* received.

console. 1. In *communication systems,* a control device with *access* to a *communication network switch* installed so as to control *access lines* and instruments in a local area. 2. In *automatic data processing,* the part of a *computer,* process controller, or operations controller that is used for *communication* between the *operators* or service personnel and the *system.* The console usually contains a panel for lights, keys, *switches,* and related circuits for man-machine communication. It may be a desklike unit, permitting the seating of personnel. It may be used for *error control, error detection, error correction,* mounting *display registers* and *counters,* revising *storage* contents, checking *data flow,* diagnosing *faults* and *malfunctions,* and generally for *monitoring* and *supervising* operations. See *display console.*

consolidation. See *communication system consolidation.*

constant. See *abbe constant; Boltzmann's constant; fast time constant; ground constant; logarithmic fast time constant (logFTC); propagation constant; time constant.*

constant-current modulation. A method of *amplitude modulation* in which a *source* of constant *electrical current* supplies a *radio frequency* generator and a *modulation amplifier* in parallel. Thus, current variations in one can cause equal and opposite variations in the other, resulting in modulation of the *carrier output.*

constant failure period. In a device with a large number of *components,* the period of the *life* of the device following the *early failure period,* characterized by a lower fairly constant failure rate as each component statistically reaches the end of its life. Also see *bathtub curve.*

constant false alarm rate (CFAR). The rate at which false alarms occur in a *radar system,* that is, the rate at which targets that do not exist are indicated as being present due to *noise, interference,* or *jamming.* An alarm is the indication of a target. CFAR techniques in radar systems are intended to maintain a constant noise level at the *input* of an *automatic data processor.* CFAR techniques do not usually permit the indication of a target if the *signal* from the target is weaker than noise, interference, or jamming. These techniques do remove some of the confusing effects caused by noise, interference, and jamming.

constant-watch ship. In *radiotelegraph communications* at sea, *a ship station* that is on *listening watch,* is *transmitting,* or is *receiving transmissions* on a continuous basis.

constant-watch station. In *radiotelegraph operations,* a *station* that is operational (on *listening watch, transmitting,* or *receiving*) on a continuous basis, especially in shore-ship operations. Also see *operator-period station.*

constitutive relations. A set of three relations pertaining to the properties of a *transmission medium* in which *electric and magnetic fields, electric currents,* and *electromagnetic waves* exist and *propagate.* The relations are given in their simplest form as: $D = \epsilon E$, $B = \mu H$, $J = \sigma E$, where D is the *electric flux density* or electric displacement vector, E is the *electric field intensity,* B is the *magnetic flux density,* H is the *magnetic field intensity,* J is the *electric current density,* ϵ is the *electric permittivity,* μ is the *magnetic permeability,* and σ is the *electric conductivity.* In some substances, they assume a complex form and are represented as vectors or tensors when operating upon *vector* field and current values in the constitutive relations shown, instead of the *scalar* values shown above. Also see *Maxwell's equations.*

contact. See *optical contact.*

contamination. See *data contamination.*

content. See *character mean transinformation content; conditional information content; decision content; information content; joint information content; mean transinformation content; mutual information content; natural unit of information content (nat); signaling information content; transinformation content.*

contention. In a *communication* or computer *system,* the condition that occurs when two or more devices demand at the same time the services of another device, which can handle only one demand at a time. For example, two or more *data sources* demanding the use of a single one-way *channel* at the same time. A *contention* can occur in *data communications* particularly when no *station* is designated a *master station.* The condition can arise when two or more data stations attempt to *transmit* at the same time over a shared *channel,* or when two data stations attempt to transmit at the same time in *two-way alternate communication.* When in contention, each station monitors signals and waits for a quiescent condition before initiating a bid for master status. Contention can arise in a *computer* that can deal with only one *data source* at a time, such as when attempting to place different data in the same *storage* location at the same time.

continuity check. 1. A check made of a *circuit* to verify that a *communication path* for *signals* exists. 2. A check made to determine if *conduction* can occur between two points.

continuity failure signal. A *signal* sent in the *backward direction* indicating that a *call* cannot be completed due to failure of the continuity check in the *forward direction.*

continuous carrier. 1. A signal in which the *transmission* of the *carrier* is continuous, that is, not *pulsed* on and off. 2. A *radio wave* of constant *amplitude* and constant *frequency.* A continuous carrier signal may be amplitude, *phase,* or *frequency modulated.* The carrier wave is transmitted without interruption caused by a modulating signal. Thus, it cannot be pulse-code modulated, since in this case it is turned on and off in accordance with the modulating pulses, as in *Morse code* transmission. Synonymous with *continuous wave (CW).* Also see *continuous emission.*

continuous communication watch. A *communication watch* on a 24-hours-a-day basis, normally accomplished when there are at least 3 *operators* available at a *station* to maintain the watch. Also see *single-operator period watch; two-operator period watch.*

continuous emission. The *transmission* of an uninterrupted *signal,* such as an unending *dash* in *radiotelegraphy,* or a 1,000-hertz *audio signal* in voice transmission. For example, before abandonment of a ship or aircraft, the *radio transmitter* should be set for continuous emission. Also see *continuous carrier.*

continuous variable optical attenuator. A device that when inserted into an *optical waveguide link, attenuates* the *intensity* of *lightwaves,* over a continuous range of decibels, depending upon a setting or control *signal.*

continuously-variable-slope delta (CVSD) modulation. *Delta modulation* in which the size of the steps of the approximated *signal* can be progressively increased or decreased as required to make the approximated signal closely match the *input analog wave* form. For example, modulation in which an analog (voice) signal is converted into a *digital* signal, achieving economy of *bandwidth* and a high *bit rate* while maintaining low *distortion.* It can be used for providing the digital (voice) input to voice *encryption* devices.

continuous operation. In *data transmission,* a type of operation in which the *master station* need not stop for a reply after transmitting each *message* or transmission *block.*

continuous receiver. In *facsimile systems,* equipment that records line-by-line on a *data medium* that moves with a constant pitch between consecutive lines so as to record several *messages* in succession without the need for the *operator* to change the medium between consecutive messages.

continuous spectrum. A *frequency spectrum* in which all *frequencies* within a *band* are present. Also see *white noise.*

continuous-tape relay switching.   See *semiautomatic continuous-tape relay switching.*

continuous time system. A *system* in which *input* and *output signals* can change at any instant of time. The system operation may be modeled by the use of differential equations. Also see *discrete time.*

continuous wave (CW). See *continuous carrier; Morse continuous wave.*

continuous wave jamming. See *unmodulated continuous wave jamming.*

continuous wave radar. A *radar system* in which a continuous flow of *radio frequency* energy is *transmitted* to the object (target) which *scatters* and *reflects* the *incident* energy and returns a small fraction of it to a *receiving antenna.*

contract developmental station. See *experimental contract developmental station.*

contrast. In *display systems,* the relation between (1) the intensity of *color,* brightness, or shading of the area occupied by a *display element, display group,* or *display image* in the *display space* on the *display surface* of a *display device,* and (2) the intensity of an area not occupied by elements, groups, or images. The contrast is said to be large or great when a large or great difference in intensity between these occupied and unoccupied areas is sensed by the human eye or a sensing device. The contrast may also be indicated as a ratio of the intensities of the occupied and unoccupied areas of the display space. See *accentuated contrast; facsimile signal contrast; maximum contrast; signal contrast.*

contrast transfer function. See *modulation transfer function.*

control. See *access control; automatic gain control; basic mode link control; central primary control; change in operational control (CHOP); circuit quality control; direct clock control; electromagnetic emission control; electromagnetic interference (EMI) control; electromagnetic radiation control; emission control; error control; failure control; fast automatic gain control; frequency control; function control; guided missile control; high-level control; high-level data link control (HDLC); indirect clock control; instantaneous automatic gain control (IAGC); line load control; low-level control; operational network control; packet flow control; port radio transmission control; pulse-jet control; quality control; radio control; radio transmission control; receiver intermediate-frequency gain control; remote control; right-through control; sensitivity time control; synchronous data-link control; transmit flow control; wavefront control.*

control authority. See *maritime air control authority.*

control ball. A captive ball that, when manually rotated, controls the movement of *display elements, display groups,* or *display images* in the *display space* on the *display surface* of a *display device.* It is usually mounted in the surface panel of a *display console* of the display device. It performs functions similar to that of a *joystick.* Synonymous with *track ball.*

control channel. See *network control channel; rescue control channel.*

control character. A *character* that can, when it occurs in a particular context, initiate, modify, or stop a function, or control operation. Such a character may be recorded for use in a subsequent action and it may have a *graphic* representation in some circumstances. See *call control character; device control character; transmission control character.*

control circuit. See *maintenance control circuit (MCC).*

control-communication network. See *air defense command-control-communication network.*

control communications. The branch of science and technology devoted to *communication facilities* and personnel used specifically for control purposes, such as for controlling industrial processes; movement of operational resources; electric power generation, distribution, and utilization; *communication networks;* and transportation networks, such as air, rail, truck, bus, taxi, and steamship lines. See *air traffic control communications.*

control designation. See *line load control designation.*

control equipment. See *remote control equipment.*

control facility. See *technical control facility (TCF).*

control field. In *high-level data link control (HDLC) operation,* the sequence of eight (or sixteen, if extended) *bits* immediately following the *address field* of a *frame.* The content of the control field is interpreted by the receiving *secondary station* designated by the address field as a *command* instructing the performance of some specific function. The content of the control field is interpreted by the receiving *primary station* as a *response* from the secondary station designated by the address field to one or more commands. The control field is also interpreted by the receiving *combined station* as a command instructing the performance of some specific function if the address field designates the receiving station as a combined station. Finally, the control field is also interpreted by the receiving combined station as a response to one or more transmitted commands if the address field designates a remote combined station.

control field extension. In standard *high-level data link control (HDLC) operation,* an enlargement of the *control field* to include additional control *information.*

control flow.   The sequence in which *instructions, routines,* and subroutines are executed when a *computer program* is executed.

control function.   An action that affects the recording, processing, *transmission,* or interpretation of *data.*   For example, the action of starting or stopping a process, such as a *carriage return,* font change, rewind, or transmisison. Synonymous with *control operation.*

controllable coupler.   See *electronically-controllable coupler.*

control language.   See *job control language.*

controlled access.   See *access control.*

controlled accessibility.   See *access control.*

controlled approach.   See *carrier controlled approach (CCA).*

controlled approach landing.   See *ground controlled approach (GCA) landing.*

controlled approach system.   See *ground controlled approach (GCA) system.*

controlled area.   In *communication security,* a physical area to which *security* controls are applied to provide protection to an *information processing system* and communication *lines* at a level equivalent to that required for the information *transmitted* through the system.

controlled not-ready signal.   A *signal* sent in the *backward direction* indicating that a *call* cannot be *completed* because the *called line* is in a controlled not-ready condition rather than in an uncontrolled not-ready condition.

controller.   See *network controller; system controller.*

control net.   A communication net that may be used for the direction and control of activities, systems, organizations, operations, or processes.

control operation.   See *control function.*

control phase.   See *network control phase.*

control point.   See *secondary control point.*

control procedure.   See *call control procedure; data communication control procedure; flow control procedure.*

control service.   See *aerodrome control service; approach control service.*

control signal.   See *call control signal.*

control signaling.   **1.** *Signaling* used for purposes of effecting control of a *communication system.*   **2.** The use of *directory numbers* of *users, operators,* and maintenance personnel for effecting control of an *automatic telephone system.*

control station.   **1.** In a *data network,* the *station* that selects the *master station* and *supervises* operational procedures such as *polling, selecting, interrogating,* and *recovery.*   The control station controls the orderly operation of the network. A control station also initiates recovery in the event of abnormal conditions on the network.   The designation of a particular station as a control station is usually not affected by the control procedures. **2.** In a *multipoint* or *point-to-point connection,* using *basic mode link control* procedures, the *terminal installation* that nominates the *master station* and supervises *polling, selecting, interrogating,* and *recovery.*   Also see *primary station; secondary station; slave station; tributary station.*   See *master net control station (MNCS); net control station (NCS).*

control system.   See *command and control system; common control system.*

control tower.   A *facility* provided for the control of aircraft and vehicles operating on and around an airport (aerodrome), landing zone, or landing area.   The tower is usually equipped with *communication facilities.*   Its height is to afford direct visibility of the surrounding area.

control unit.   See *teletypewriter control unit.*

control-warning system.   See *aircraft control-warning system.*

control zone.   The *space* that surrounds equipment used to process sensitive *information* that is under sufficient physical and technical control to prevent unauthorized entry or *compromise.*

convergence.   The bending of *light rays* toward each other, as by a *convex* or *converging lens.*   Contrast with *divergence.*

convergence angle.   The angle formed by the lines of sight of both eyes in *focusing* on any line, corner, surface, or part of an *object.*   Synonymous with *convergent angle.*

convergent angle.   See *convergence angle.*

convergent lens.   See *converging lens.*

converging lens.   A *lens* that adds *convergence* to an *incident* bundle of *light rays.*   One surface of a converging *lens* may be spherically convex and the other plane (plano-convex).   Both may be convex (double-convex, biconvex) or one surface may be convex and the other *concave* (converging meniscus).   Synonymous with *convergent lens; convex lens; collective lens; crown lens; plus lens; positive lens.* Also see *collective lens.*

conversation. See *telegraph conversation.*

conversational mode. A *mode* of operation of a *system* or systems similar to a conversation between two persons, that is, a mode of operation similar to a dialogue. *Computers* can operate in a conversational mode with each other and with persons. *Communication systems* are used to support the dialogue and often make it possible for the participants to be at a distance from each other while they converse.

conversion. See *code conversion; double conversion; frequency translation; mode conversion.*

conversion chart. See *time conversion chart.*

convert. To change the representation of *data* from one form to another without changing the *information* they convey. For example, to convert one *radix* to another; one code to another, as in *code conversion;* to convert *analog data* to *digital data* using an *analog-to-digital (A–D) converter;* or to convert data on *cards* to data on *tapes* without loss of meaning, accuracy, or precision. Also see *translation.*

converter. **1.** A section of a *superheterodyne radio receiver* that converts the desired incoming *radio frequency signal* to a lower frequency, known as the *intermediate frequency.* **2.** A rotating machine consisting of an electric motor driving an electric generator to change *alternating current (AC)* to *direct current (DC)* or to change alternating current at one frequency to alternating current at another frequency. **3.** A *facsimile* device that changes the type of *modulation* delivered by its *scanner.* **4.** A facsimile device that changes *amplitude modulation* to *audio frequency-shift modulation,* often called a *redemodulator.* **5.** A device that changes audio frequency-shift modulation, to amplitude modulation, generally called a *discriminator.* **6.** A *transducer* in which the *output* frequency is the sum of the input frequency and a *local oscillator* frequency. **7.** In computers, a unit that changes the representation of *data* from one form to another without changing the meaning *(information)* that they convey, for example a tape-to-card or card-to-printer converter. See *analog-to-digital (A–D) converter; code converter; digital-to-analog (D–A) converter; down converter; facsimile converter; parallel-to-serial converter; serial-to-parallel converter; signal converter; up-converter.*

convex. Pertaining to a continuous surface to which more than one tangent plane can be drawn. For example, the surface of a solid sphere or the outside surface of an intact orange rind. A *reflective* convex surface will cause the reflected *rays* of an *incident beam* of parallel rays to diverge.

convex lens. See *converging lens.*

coordinate. See *absolute coordinate; device coordinate; real-world coordinate; relative coordinate; screen coordinate.*

convolutional code. A *code* in which the *block* of n *digits* generated by an *encoder* depends not only on the block of k *message* digits in the same time interval, but also depends on the block of message digits within a previous span of (n − 1) units (n larger than 1), k and n usually being small *integers.* For example, a *parity bit* may be the *modulo-2 sum* of several past *data* and parity bits. Logical analysis of successive parity bits allows identification of the erroneous bit and facilitates correction of the data. Also see *block code.*

convoy common frequency. A *frequency* that can be used by all *ship stations* of a convoy. For example, the *convoy radiotelegraph frequency* of 500 kHz, or a voice *radiotelephone* frequency for use within a convoy as might be prescribed by a convoy commander or commodore.

convoy communications. The branch of *communications* concerned with methods, *systems,* and equipment used for *transmission* of *messages* to, from, and within land and maritime convoys. It is concerned with transmission of *information* for controlling convoy formations, routes, and procedures. It is also concerned with transmission and reception of information to and from convoys, particularly from *fixed land stations* to *mobile stations* and their formations.

convoy internal communication. *Communication* among the elements of a land or maritime convoy, including *radio, visual,* and *sound transmission. Radio* intervehicle and intership communication is usually by *radiotelephone,* using the receipt method of operation. The convoy commander's vehicle or ship usually has the *net control station* aboard. Usually a single *frequency* is used for convoy internal communication.

convoy radiotelephone frequency. The *radio frequency* common to all vehicles or ships in a convoy, usually for *radiotelephone transmission.*

cooperation factor. In *facsimile transmission systems,* the product of the total *scanning line length* and the *scanning density.* Mathematically, the cooperation factor, *CF,* is given by $CF = L\sigma$, where L is the line length and σ is the density, both in compatible units. For example, for a 20 cm line and a density of 6 scanning pitches per cm, the cooperation factor would be 120. Also see *drum factor.*

cooperation index. In *facsimile transmission systems,* the quotient of the *cooperation factor* divided by π. In the case of a *drum transmitter* or *receiver,* the cooperation index is equal to the product of the drum diameter and the *scanning density.* Mathematically, the cooperation index, *CI,* is given by $CI = D\sigma$ where D

is the drum diameter and σ is the scanning density, both in compatible units. For example, for a drum diameter of $20/\pi$ cm, and a σ of 6 scanning pitches per cm, the cooperation index would be $120/\pi$ and the cooperation factor would be 120. The relationship is based on the line length being the circumference of the drum, and thus the line length is π times the drum diameter. Synonymous with *diametral cooperation index.* Also see *drum factor.*

coordinate data. *Data* that represents positions or locations on the *display surface (CRT screen, fiberscope faceplate, plotter bed,* or *LED* or *gas panel)* of a *display device.* Coordinate data may be either *absolute coordinate data* or *relative coordinate data.* Coordinate data may be used to control or perform *operations* such as moving *display elements, display groups,* or *display images; rubberbanding; scissoring; clipping; zooming;* or *scrolling.* See *absolute coordinate data; relative coordinate data.*

coordinated time scale. A *time scale,* generated by electronic or mechanical devices such as electronic *clocks* driven (controlled) by crystal or atomic *oscillators,* that is coordinated by international agreement to approximate *Greenwich mean time (GMT).* This coordinated universal time is referred to as UTC (Universal time, coordinated). Also see *Greenwich mean time; leap second.*

coordinate graphics. In *display systems,* the methods and techniques devoted to the generation of *display elements, display groups,* or *display images* in the *display space* on the *display surface* of a *display device* using *display commands* and *coordinate data.*

coordinate position. In *display systems,* a single location in the *display space* on the *display surface* of a *display device* specified by *absolute* or *relative coordinate data.* In a *fiberscope,* each *fiber* or *fiber bundle* can be assigned a *coordinate position* and the relative position of each fiber in the bundle can be maintained, giving rise to a *coherent bundle.*

coordinates. See *world coordinates.*

coordination. See *frequency coordination.*

coordination distance. In *satellite communication systems,* the distance between an *earth station* and fixed or mobile service stations within which there is a possibility that (1) the use of a given *transmitting frequency* at this *earth station* will cause harmful *interference* to stations in the *fixed* or *mobile service* that share the same *frequency band;* or (2) the use of a given frequency for reception at this earth station will cause reception of harmful interference from stations in the fixed or mobile service.

coordination net. A *communication net* designed for the free and rapid exchange of *information* normally associated with the control of particular processes, activities, organizations, or programs, including *communication systems.*

coordinator.   See *line traffic coordinator (LTC)*.

copier.   See *microform reader-copier.*

copy.   **1.** To receive a *message.*   **2.** A recorded *message.*   **3.** A duplicate of a re-corded *message.*   **4.** In *radio communications,* to maintain a continuous *radio receiver watch* and to keep a complete *radio log.*   **5.** To read data from a *source,* leaving the source *data* unchanged at the source, and to write the same data else-where though it may be in a physical form that differs from that of the source. For example, to copy the contents of a deck of *punched cards* onto a *magnetic tape,* that is to convert the data from cards to tape.   The degree of editing that may be performed at the same time depends upon the circumstances in which the copying is performed.   **6.** To understand a *transmitted message.*   See *hard copy; soft copy.*

copy watch.   A *radio* or *video communication watch* in which an *operator* is required to maintain a continuous *receiver watch,* keeping a complete *log.*   Also see *guard watch; listening watch.*   See *radio communication copy watch.*

cord.   See *plug-ended cord.*

cord board.   See *secure voice cord board.*

cord circuit.   A *switchboard circuit,* terminated in two plug-ended wires or *op-tical fibers (cords),* used to establish *connections* manually between *user lines* or between *trunks* and user lines.   A number of cord circuits are furnished as part of a *switchboard's position* equipment.   The cords may be referred to as front cord and rear cord (trunk cord and station cord).   In modern *cordless switchboards,* the cord circuit is *switch* operated.   See *telephone cord circuit.*

cord lamp.   In telephone systems, a lamp associated with a *cord circuit* that in-dicates *supervisory* conditions in the *connection* established by the circuit.

cordless switchboard.   A *telephone switchboard* in which manually operated *keys,* rather than *cord circuits* with manually operated *plug-ended cords,* are used to make *connections.*

core.   The central primary *light-conducting* region of a material medium, such as an *optical fiber,* the *refractive index* of which must be higher than that of the *cladding* in order for the *lightwaves* to be *internally reflected* or *refracted.*   Most of the *optical power* is in the *core.*   Core material in an *optical fiber* is usually glass, fused silica, or plastic.   See *cable core; fiber core; magnetic core.*   Also see *cladding;* Figures A-6, C-8 and T-14.

core diameter.   See *fiber core diameter.*

core fiber.   See *liquid core fiber.*

core radii. See *mismatch-of-core-radii loss.*

core storage. A device that stores *data* by magnetizing *discrete* stationary pieces of material, such as toroidal rings, deposited thin films, or slugs. The direction of magnetization determines whether a 0 or a 1 is stored in each core. Residual magnetism provides the retention of digits.

core wrap. A material placed around the *lightwave* conducting or electrical conducting elements of a *fiber optic cable* for mechanical protection, *dielectric* insulation, heat insulation, and reduction of strain in flexure. Also see *stuffing.*

Corguide. An *optical cable* produced by Siecor Optical Cables, Inc., Horseheads, New York. One Corguide *cable* has seven *fibers* per *cable,* with 12 or 20 dB/km *attenuation;* another has 20 dB/km attenuation; and another has six pairs of *waveguides* capable of handling 50,000 simultaneous conversations at 2 dB/km.

corner-cube reflector. See *triple mirror.*

corner reflector. See *triple mirror.*

corrected lens. A *lens* designed to be relatively free from one or more *aberrations.* For example, a *simple lens* with an aspheric surface, or a *compound lens* consisting of several *optical* elements and different glasses.

correcting code. See *error-correcting code.*

correcting system. See *error-correcting system.*

correction. See *forward error correction; synchronous correction.*

correction bit. See *error-correction bit.*

correction efficiency factor. See *block correction efficiency factor.*

correction request. A *service message* to a *calling station* requesting correction of all or part of a *message* that is in *error.* Errors may be, for example, incorrect groups, incorrect code group counts, omitted portions, and similar errors that the *communication system* is capable of detecting. Certain types of *garbling* or mutilation may not be correctable by the system, since the system is not designed to detect them.

correction signal. See *synchronization correction signal.*

correction system. See *automatic error detection and correction system.*

corrective maintenance. Tests, measurements, and adjustments made to remove or correct a *fault.* The maintenance is performed specifically to overcome existing faults. Also see *preventive maintenance.*

correlation. The process of comparing a common characteristic of two or more interrelated phenomena. For example, if there is a time shift between two *signal* sequences, the set of correlation values plotted as a function of time is called the time correlation function. The variable quantity may, however, be the spatial separation between the points of signal measurements, yielding a spatial correlation function. See *autocorrelation; cross correlation; track correlation.* Also see *coherence.*

correlator. In a *spread spectrum system,* the part that compares a *received signal* with a local reference to check for agreement.

correlation. See *autocorrelation; cross correlation.*

cosine emission law. The energy emitted in any direction by an *electromagnetic-radiator* is proportional to the cosine of the angle that that direction makes with the normal to the *emitting surface,* namely: $N = N_0 \cos A$, where N is the *radiance,* N_0 is the *radiance* normal to an *emitting surface,* and A is the angle between the viewing direction and the normal to the surface. Emitters that radiate according to this law are referred to as *lambertian radiators* or *sources.* Synonymous with *Lambert's emission law.*

cosmic noise. See *galactic noise.*

cosmic velocity. See *third cosmic velocity.*

Costas loop. A *phase-lock loop demodulator circuit* in which *symbol synchronization* need not be known and *integrators* in the *tracking* loop are replaced by arbitrary *filters.* The circuit is used particularly in *spread-spectrum systems.* Costas loops are generally used in *pulse-amplitude modulated (PAM)* and *binary phase-shift key (PSK) loop circuits.* A variation of the Costas loop is the *squaring loop* that includes a *square-law* device. Also see *squaring loop.*

coulomb (C). The *SI* practical meter-kilogram-second unit of electrical charge. It is equal to the quantity of electricity transferred by a current of 1 A flowing for 1 sec, equivalent to 6.2418×10^{18} electrons per second.

Coulomb's law. The universal law of attraction and repulsion of electric charges, namely $F = q_1 q_2 / 4\pi\epsilon r^2$, where F is the force of attraction, if the charges are of opposite polarity, or the force of repulsion, if they are of like polarity; q_1 and q_2 are the magnitudes of the charges, usually expressed in coulombs; ϵ is the *electric permittivity* of the surrounding medium in which the charges are imbedded; and r is the distance of separation of q_1 and q_2. The charges are assumed to be points compared to their distance of separation. Also see *electric field; electric field force.*

count. See *fiber count; peg count; raster count.*

counter. See *binary counter; modulo-n counter; modulus counter; reversible counter; ring counter; synchronous counter; zero-crossing counter.*

counterclockwise polarized electromagnetic wave. See *left-hand polarized electromagnetic wave.*

counter-countermeasure. See *electronic counter-countermeasure (ECCM); infrared jamming electronic counter-countermeasure; radio relay electronic counter-countermeasure.*

countermeasure. See *absorption electronic countermeasure; active electronic countermeasure; active optical countermeasure; electronic counter-countermeasure (ECCM); electronic countermeasure (ECM); infrared jamming electronic counter-countermeasure; optical countermeasure.*

counterpoise. A *conductor* or system of conductors used as a substitute for *earth* or *ground* in an *antenna system.* Also see *earth; ground.*

count integrity. See *bit-count integrity; character-count integrity.*

count register. See *peg-count register.*

country-network identity. In a *communication system, information* sent in the *backward direction* consisting of *address signals* that indicate the identity of a country or a *network* to which a *call* has been *switched.*

coupled modes. In a *waveguide* (such as an *optical fiber, coaxial cable,* or metal pipe), *propagation modes* that coexist, whose fields are interrelated and whose energies are mutually interchanged.

coupled power. See *source-to-fiber coupled power.*

coupled reperforator tape reader. A *perforated-tape retransmitter* that ensures the retransmission of all *signals* recorded by perforation, including the last one. Synonymous with *fully-automatic reperforator transmitter distributor (FRXD).*

coupler. In *optical transmission systems,* a component used to interconnect three or more *optical conductors.* See *access coupler; acoustic coupler; antenna multicoupler; bidirectional coupler; data bus coupler; directional coupler; electronically-controllable coupler; fiber-optic multiport coupler; fiber-optic rod coupler; laser diode coupler; light-emitting diode coupler; non-reflective star coupler; optical directional coupler; optoelectronic directional coupler; positive-intrinsic-negative photodiode coupler; reflective star-coupler; tee coupler; unidirectional coupler.* Also see *connector.*

coupler loss. See *source-coupler loss.*

coupler-switch-modulator. See *integrated-optical circuit filter-coupler-switch-modulator.*

coupling. The connection, attachment, or binding of *optical elements,* electric *circuit* elements, *electric* and *magnetic fields, propagation modes,* or *electromagnetic wave components* (such as *surface waves* and *evanescent waves*) to internal waves in *waveguides, dielectric slabs,* or other interdependent associations and interactions of events and materials in a system. For example, two *optical fibers* or certain elements in an *integrated optical circuit* may be coupled together in some manner to preserve *signal* continuity. It is the means by which *signals* are transferred from one *conductor,* including a *fortuitous conductor,* to another. See *butt coupling; capacitive coupling; cross coupling; crosstalk coupling; direct coupling; end-fire coupling; evanescent field coupling; fiber-detector coupling; furcation coupling; inductive coupling; lens coupling; reference coupling; resistance coupling; source-fiber coupling; tangential coupling.* Also see *crosstalk.*

coupling coefficient. A measure of the electrical *coupling* that exists between two *circuits.* The coupling coefficient is given by $CC = Z_m/(Z_1 Z_2)^{1/2}$ where Z_m is the mutual *impedance* and Z_1 and Z_2 are the self-impedances of the coupled circuits, all impedances being of the same kind, for example, *capacitive, inductive,* or *resistive.* It is also given by $CC = M/(L_1 L_2)^{1/2}$ where M is the mutual *inductance* and L_1 and L_2 are the self-inductances of the coupled circuits. Also see *coupling efficiency.*

coupling efficiency. In *optical fiber transmission,* the ratio of the *optical power* on one side of an *interface* to the optical power on the other side. For example, the ratio of the power developed by a *light source* to the power accepted by a *bundle* of *fibers,* or the power received at the end of a bundle of fibers to the power that impinges on a *photodetector.* For light sources with *emitting* areas larger than *fiber core* diameters, the product of fiber *numerical aperture* (N.A.) and core diameter is a good indicator of maximum coupling efficiency. For other sources, such as small *laser* diodes with emitting areas smaller than the fiber core diameter, the N.A. alone is a relevant indicator of coupling efficiency. Synonymous with *coupling coefficient.* See *source coupling efficiency.*

coupling loss. See *aperture-to-medium coupling loss; connector insertion loss.*

couriergram. A *message* that normally would be sent by electrical means, but if *circuits* are not available, is carried over all or part of its *route* by a messenger or agency that is not necessarily a part of the *communication system* accepting the message for *transmission.*

courier service. A method of *transmission* based on the use of persons who carry *messages* between persons, *stations,* commands, organizations, or places. For example, a daily two-way transfer of messages between a subordinate unit and its higher headquarters, using a motorcycle, a rider, and a message pouch.

course. See *heading; vector.*

cover. See *horizontal cover; radio communication cover; vertical cover.*

coverage. See *earth coverage; jammer area coverage.*

coverage diagram. See *radio coverage diagram; vertical coverage diagram.*

cover watch. See *radio communication cover.*

cpi. *Characters* per inch. For example, the number of characters recorded on an inch of *magnetic tape,* an inch of magnetic disk track, an inch of *microfilm,* an inch of printed line, or an inch of paper tape.

cps. *Characters* per second.

CPU. *Central processing unit; communication processor unit.*

CR. *Carriage return.*

crack. See *microcrack.*

craft frequency. See *emergency craft frequency.*

crash locator beacon. An automatic *radio beacon* that can identify the location of a crash site by means of *direction finding.*

creeping code. See *walking code.*

critical angle. The angle, with the *normal,* at which an *electromagnetic wave incident* upon an *interface surface* between two *dielectric* media, at which *total reflection* of the *incident ray* first occurs as the *incidence angle* is increased from zero, and beyond which *total internal reflection* continues to occur although with increased *attenuation* at a rate determined not only by the *electromagnetic* parameters of the *transmission medium,* but also by the *frequency* and the incidence angle.. The *wave* is guided along the reflecting surface with no average transport of energy into the second medium, and the intensity of the reflected wave is exactly equal to the intensity of the incident wave. The wave in an *optical fiber* will be confined to the fiber for all incidence angles greater than the critical angle. The critical angle is given by:

$$\sin \theta_c = (\epsilon_2 / \epsilon_1)^{1/2}$$

where θ_c is the critical angle and ϵ_2 and ϵ_1 are the *permittivities* of the transmitted (outside) and *incident* medium (inside), respectively, and where ϵ_1 is always greater than ϵ_2; e.g., the case for an optical fiber (conducting a wave), and air. In terms of *refractive indices,* the critical angle is the incidence angle from a denser medium, at an interface between the denser and less dense medium, at which all of the light is *refracted* along the interface, i.e., the angle of refraction is 90°. When the critical angle is exceeded, the *light* is totally reflected back into the denser medium. The critical angle varies with the refractive indices of the two media with the relationship, $\sin \theta_c = n_2/n_1$, where n_2 is the refractive index of the less dense medium, n_1 is the refractive index of the denser medium, and θ_c is the critical angle, as above. In terms of total internal reflection in an optical fiber, the critical angle is the smallest angle made by a *meridional ray* in an optical fiber that can be totally reflected from the innermost interface and thus determines the *maximum acceptance angle* at which a meridional ray can be accepted for *transmission* along a fiber. Also see *total internal reflection*. See Figure C-13.

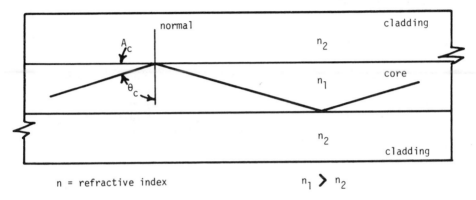

n = refractive index $n_1 > n_2$

C-13. For a *step-index fiber,* with *refractive indices* of n_1 = 1.500 and n_2 = 1.485, the **critical angle** complement, A_c, for *total internal reflection* is about 6°. The critical angle, given by $\theta = \sin^{-1} 1.485/1.500$ is about 84°.

critical frequency. 1. In the *propagation* of *electromagnetic waves,* the limiting *frequency* below which a *wave* component is reflected by *ionospheric reflection,* and above which it propagates or is *transmitted* through an *ionospheric layer* at a specified *incidence angle.* **2.** The limiting *frequency* below which a *wave component* is *reflected* by and above which it penetrates through an *ionospheric layer* at a zero *incidence angle* (vertical angle). The existence of the critical frequency is the result of electron limitation in the ionospheric layer, that is, the inadequacy of the existing number of free electrons to support *reflection* at higher *frequencies.*

critical radius. 1. The radius of curvature of an *optical fiber,* containing an axially *propagated electromagnetic wave,* at which the *field* outside the fiber detaches itself from the fiber and *radiates* into space because the *phase-front velocity* must increase to maintain a proper relationship with the guided wave inside the fiber. This velocity cannot exceed the velocity of *light,* as the wavefront sweeps around the outside of the curved fiber. This causes *attenuation* due to a *radiation* loss. The field outside the fiber decays exponentially in a direction transverse to the direction of propagation. **2.** The radius of curvature of an *optical fiber* at which there is an appreciable *propagation mode conversion loss,* due to the abruptness of the transition from straight to curved. For a radius of curvature greater than the critical value, the fields behave essentially as in a straight guide. For radii smaller than the critical value, considerable mode conversion takes place.

critical technical load. That part of the total *technical load power* requirement that is required for *synchronous communication equipment* and *automatic switching equipment.*

cross-band radiotelegraph procedure. A *radiotelegraph network* operational procedure in which *calling stations,* such as *ship stations,* call other stations, such as *shore stations,* using one *frequency,* and then shift to another frequency to *transmit* their *messages.* The *called stations* answer using a third frequency. Also see *simplex radiotelegraph procedure; calling frequency; working frequency; answering frequency.*

crossbar switch. A *switch* that has a plurality of vertical *paths,* a plurality of horizontal paths, and electromagnet-operated mechanical means (relays) for interconnecting any one of the vertical paths with any one of the horizontal paths. The same *logical function* may also be achieved using *coincidence circuits (gates)* made from *semiconductor* devices.

crossbar system. An *automatic switching system* that consists of *crossbar switches,* selecting mechanisms, and common *circuits* to select and test the *switching paths* and control the operation of the selecting mechanism. The switching *information* is received and stored by control mechanisms that determine the operations necessary to establish a *connection* in a *communication system.*

cross connection. A *connection* between *terminal blocks* on the two sides of a *distribution frame* or between terminals on a terminal block. A *connection* between *terminals* on the same block is also called a *strap.* Also see *strap.*

cross correlation. The time *integral* of the product of one *signal* and another related, but time-delayed, signal. In mathematical notation:

$$C.C. = \int_{O}^{t} f(t)\, g(t - \tau)dt$$

in which $f(t)$ and $g(t)$ are the two signals or arbitrary functions of time, and τ is the time $g(t)$ is delayed in relation to the occurrence of $f(t)$. The process of correlating two or more interrelated phenomena involves finding the similarity between two different *symbols.* Also see *autocorrelation.*

cross coupling. The *coupling* of a *signal* from one *channel, circuit,* or *conductor* to another. Cross coupling results in undesired signals, such as *crosstalk.*

crossfire.   See *sending-end crossfire.*

crossing counter.   See *zero-crossing counter.*

cross-level.   Pertaining to one axis of a three-axis *antenna* mount, one axis in each Cartesian direction, often used by an *earth station* on board a ship.

cross-linking.   In *satellite communications,* the direct *transmission* from *satellite* to satellite.   The two satellites are *geostationary satellites* separated by approximately 90° of longitude (100,000 km) and carry *narrow-beam antennas* pointed at each other.   *Long-haul communication traffic* passing through them avoids the *atmospheric attenuation* associated with a double *hop.*

cross-modulation.   *Intermodulation* due to the *modulation* of a *carrier* of a desired *signal* by an undesired signal.

cross-office trunk.   A *trunk* with *terminations* that are within a single *facility,* such as a *central office, switching center,* or *exchange.*

cross-polarized operation.   The use of two *transmitter-receiver* pairs operating on the same *frequency,* with one transmitter-receiver pair using *vertically-polarized electromagnetic waves* and the other pair using *horizontally-polarized electromagnetic waves.*

cross-section.   See *radar cross-section; scattering cross-section.*

cross-site link.   In a *satellite communication system,* the *signal power* and control *connections* between the *components* of an *earth station.*   For example, a link between *transmitter* and *antenna* or between control *terminal consoles* and transmitters.

cross strapping.   Connecting two or more points in a *circuit* or device with a short piece of wire or metal.   For example, connecting together resonator segments having the same polarity in a multicavity magnetron to suppress undesired *modes* of *oscillation,* or connecting *terminals* on the same *block* of a *distribution frame.*

crosstalk.   **1.** The unwanted *transfer* of energy from one *circuit (disturbing circuit)* to another circuit *(disturbed circuit).*   **2.** The phenomenon in which a *signal transmitted* on one *circuit* or *channel* of a *transmission system* is detectable or creates an undesirable effect in another circuit or channel.   **3.** In an *optical transmission system,* leakage of *optical power* from one *optical conductor* to another.   The leakage may be due to frustrated *total reflection,* inadequate *cladding* thickness, or low *absorptive* quality.   Also see *coupling.*   See *far-end crosstalk; fiber crosstalk; intelligible crosstalk; interaction crosstalk; near-end crosstalk; unintelligible crosstalk.*

crosstalk coupling. The ratio of the *power* in one *circuit (disturbing circuit)* to the *power* induced in another circuit *(disturbed circuit)* observed at definite points in the circuits under specified *terminating* conditions. Crosstalk coupling is usually expressed in *decibels (dB)*. Synonymous with *crosstalk coupling loss*. Also see *loss*.

crosstalk coupling loss. See *crosstalk coupling*.

crosstalk resistance. In a *multiplexed communication system* or component, the ability to prevent transfer of *noise* or unwanted *signals* from one *channel* to another.

cross-tell. See *lateral-tell*.

crown glass. An *optical* glass, made of alkaline-lime silicate, that has a relatively low *refractive index,* low *dispersion attenuation factor,* and low *absorption factor,* compared to other glasses.

crown lens. See *converging lens*.

CRT. Cathode-ray tube.

crucible process. See *double-crucible process (DC)*.

crush. **1.** A small scratch, or series of small scratches, on the surface of an *optical element,* usually caused by mishandling, scuffing, scraping, or rubbing. Synonymous with *rub*. **2.** The damage done to an *optical fiber, bundle,* or *cable* by a compressive force.

cryogenics. The field of science and technology devoted to the behavior of materials at or near absolute zero *temperature* (i.e., at or near zero *kelvin*). For example, the reduction of *thermal noise* in materials at very low temperatures, as in the cooling of preamplifiers to reduce *intrinsic noise*. Cooling is usually accomplished by circulating liquid helium or liquid nitrogen through or around the *amplifier*.

cryptanalysis. The study of *encrypted texts,* including a study of the steps, operations, and procedures involved in converting encrypted *messages* into *plain text* without prior knowledge of the *cryptokey* employed in the *encryption* process. Synonymous with *cryptographic analysis*. Also see *cryptology*.

crypto. Pertaining to *cryptography, cryptanalysis,* and *cryptology,* and to the materials, systems, procedures, *information,* and operations related to these areas.

cryptochannel. A complete *cryptocommunication system* established between two *users.* For example, a basic cryptochannel for cryptocommunication includes (1) the *cryptographic* aids prescribed; (2) the holders of the cryptographic aids; (3) the indicators or other means of identification; (4) the areas in which the *channel* is effective; (5) the special purpose, if any, for which the crypto-channel is provided; and (6) pertinent notes, distribution, and usage. The crypto-channel is analogous to a *radio circuit.* Synonymous with *cryptographic channel.*

cryptoequipment. Equipment used to *encrypt messages.* Synonymous with *cryptographic* equipment.

cryptogram. A *message,* such as a *telegram,* that has been *encrypted.*

cryptographer. One who *encrypts* or *decrypts messages,* or who creates components for *cryptosystems.*

cryptographic analysis. See *cryptanalysis.*

cryptographic channel. See *cryptochannel.*

cryptographic information. See *cryptoinformation.*

cryptographic key. See *cryptokey.*

cryptographic net. See *cryptonet.*

cryptographic operation. See *offline cryptographic operation; online cryptographic operation.*

cryptographic security. See *cryptosecurity.*

cryptographic system. See *cryptosystem.*

cryptography. 1. The branch of science and technology devoted to the design, operation, maintenance, and use of *cryptosystems.* 2. The art or science that deals with the principles, means, and methods for converting *plain text* into unintelligible form and converting apparently unintelligible *ciphered* text into intelligible form, usually by means other than *cryptanalysis.*

cryptoinformation. *Information* that can be used for or that would make a significant contribution to the *cryptanalytic* conversion of encrypted text, or that would contribute to the operation of a *cryptosystem.* Synonymous with *cryptographic information.* Also see *cifax; ciphony; civision; cryptology; cryptomaterial.*

cryptokey. The *cipher* or *code* used to set or adjust *cryptoequipment* at a *transmitting station* and a *receiving station* in order that *messages* can be *enciphered (encrypted)* at the transmitting station and *deciphered (decrypted)* at the receiving station. The cryptokey permits the *cryptoequipment* to be set, changed, or adjusted periodically. The cryptokey remains in effect for a specified period unless it is known to be *compromised.* For example, the 64-bit cryptokey, containing 56 independent bits and 8 parity bits, that functions with the Federal Information Processing Standard Publication 46, dated January 15, 1977. Also see *data encryption standard.*

cryptologic. Pertaining to *cryptology.*

cryptology. The science that deals with the hidden, disguised, or *encrypted* meanings in *messages.* Also see *cifax; ciphony; civision; cryptoinformation; cryptomaterial.*

cryptomaterial. All material, including documents, devices, or equipment, that contains *cryptoinformation* and is essential to the *encryption, decryption,* or *authentication* of *messages.* It includes information pertaining to *communication* procedures involving the safeguarding of encryption and decryption devices, *facilities, codes, cryptokeys,* and related matters. Synonymous with *cryptographic information.* Also see *cifax; ciphony; civision; cryptoinformation; cryptology.*

cryptonet. An organization of *stations* capable of direct *communication* on a common *cryptochannel.* Two or more activities that have a *cryptosystem* in common and possess a means of communication can form a cryptonet. Synonymous with *cryptographic net.*

cryptooperation. See *synchronous cryptooperation.*

cryptosecurity. The part of *communication security* that deals with the provision of *secure communication systems,* as well as sound and practicable communication security operating procedures. Cryptosecurity results from the proper use of these systems.

cryptosystem. A *system* composed of *cryptomaterial* and used as a unit for *encryption* and *decryption* of *messages* to provide *communication security.* Synonymous with *cryptographic system.* See *literal cryptosystem.*

crystal. See *doubly-refracting crystal; multirefracting crystal.*

crystal optics. The study of the *propagation* of *radiant energy* through crystals, especially *anisotropic* crystals, and their effects on *polarization* of *electromagnetic waves,* particularly *lightwaves.*

CSU. *Circuit switching unit.*

cue. See *prompt.*

current. See *alternating current (AC); dark current; direct current (DC); disturbance current; electrical current; metallic circuit current; photocurrent; pulsat-*

ing direct current; stationary direct current; stray current; current modulation. See *constant-current modulation.*

current position. 1. In *display systems,* the present position of a *display element, display group,* or *display image* in the *display space* on the *display surface* of a *display device,* expressed in *user coordinates* or *device coordinates.* 2. The present position of an *object,* whose *image* is *displayed* on the *display surface* of a *display device,* expressed in *real-world coordinates.*

current telegraph system. See *neutral direct-current telegraph system.*

cursor. A movable, usually visible, mark or symbol used to indicate a position in the *display space* on the *display surface* of a *display device,* and which may be moved by a *pointer.*

curvature. In the measurement or specification of *lenses,* the amount of departure from a flat surface. It is specified as the reciprocal of the radius of curvature. See *field curvature.*

curve. See *absolute luminosity curve; bathtub curve; luminosity curve.*

curve-fitting compaction. A method of *data compaction* accomplished by substituting an analytical expression for the *data* to be stored or *transmitted.* For example, if the curve to be stored or transmitted can be broken into a series of straight line segments, it may only be necessary to specify the slope, intercept, and range for each segment; or a mathematical expression such as a polynomial or a trigonometric function and a single point on the curve could be specified instead of the graphic curve or a series of points on it.

curve generator. A *functional unit,* (such as a *display device* or *computer program*) that generates curves, usually consisting of a connected sequence of *dots* or of very short *vectors* or *line* segments, that are either tangent to the smoothed curve or are cords to the smoothed curve. A *vector generator* might produce the tangent line segments or short cords.

custodian. See *security custodian.*

customer identification. See *user identification.*

customer set. See *user set.*

cut. See *bearing cut; runner cut.*

cutoff frequency. 1. In a *waveguide,* (such as a hollow rectangular cross-section pipe or an optical fiber) the frequency below which a specified *mode* of propagation fails to exist. In a *cladded optical fiber,* a mode is cutoff when the *field* no longer decays in the *cladding.* 2. The *frequency* above which, or below which, the *output electric current* in a *circuit,* such as a *line* or a *filter,* is reduced to a specified level.   **3.** The *frequency* below which a *transmitted electromagnetic wave* fails to penetrate a *layer* of the *ionosphere* at the *incidence angle* required for transmission between two specified locations by *reflection* from the layer.

cutting tool.   See *fiber-cutting tool.*

CVD.   Chemical vapor deposition.

CVPO.   Chemical vapor-phase oxidation.

CVSD modulation.   *Continuously-variable-slope delta (CVSD) modulation.*

CW.   **1.** *Continuous wave.*   **2.** Pertaining to a *pulse-code-modulated carrier wave,* such as is used in *international Morse code radio telegraphy.*

CX signaling.   See *composite signaling.*

cybernetics.   The branch of science and technology devoted to theories and studies of *communication* and control in living organisms and in machines.

cycle.   See *display cycle; duty cycle; sun-spot cycle.*

cycle of saros.   Approximately 223 lunar months (18 years, 11 days), after which both the moon and the line of nodes return practically to their original positions relative to the sun.   *Eclipses* tend to recur after this interval.   Accurate astronomical measurements show that there is a difference of 0.46 day between the time of return of the moon nodes to the same position relative to the sun and the return of the moon to the same point in its *orbit* after 223 lunar months.   A complete cycle of saros lasts about 1,200 years before the moon and the line of nodes return exactly to their original positions relative to the sun.

cyclic binary unit-distance code.   See *Gray code.*

cyclic code.   A *unit distance code* of finite length in which the representation of the largest quantity is one unit distance away from the code that represents zero. Cyclic codes include *reflected codes.* Synonymous with *closed code.*

cyclic distortion.   In *telegraphy, distortion* that is periodic and that is neither characteristic, biased, nor fortuitous. Causes of cyclic distortion might be irregularities in the duration of contact time of the brushes of a *transmitter distributor,* or *disturbing alternating currents.*

cyclone.   See *anticyclone.*

cylindrical lens.   A *lens* with a cylindrical surface. *Cylindrical lenses* are used in range finders to introduce *astigmatism* in order that a pointlike source may be *imaged* as a line of light.   By combining cylindrical and spherical surfaces, an *optical system* can be designed that gives a certain *magnification* in a given azimuth of the *image* and a different magnification at right angles in the same image plane.   Such a system is designated *anamorphic.*   See *microcylindrical lens.*

cylindrical microlens.   See *microcylindrical lens.*

cyphony.   See *ciphony.*

D

D. See *D-star.*

D–A converter. See *digital-to-analog (D–A) converter.*

daisy chaining. A method of *transmitting signals* along a *bus* to which a series of devices are sequentially connected in such a manner that devices not requesting a given signal allow it to pass on to the first device that requested, or is designated to receive, the signal. This device *responds* by performing the requested action and breaking the continuity to the devices that are on the bus beyond it. The scheme permits assignment of priorities based on electrical position on the bus.

damage. See *optical fiber radiation damage.*

damping. The progressive diminution of certain quantities characteristic of a phenomenon, for example, the progressive decaying with time of the *amplitude* of the free (natural) oscillations in an *electrical circuit.*

dark adaptation. The ability of the human eye to adjust itself to low levels of *illumination.*

dark current. The *current* that flows in a *photodetector* when there is no *radiant energy* or *luminous flux incident* upon its sensitive surface, i.e., when there is total darkness. Dark current generally increases with increased *temperature* for most photodetectors. For example, in a *photoemissive photodetector,* the dark current is given by:

$$I_d = A T^2 e^{q\phi/kT}$$

where A is the surface area constant, T is the absolute *temperature, q* is the electron charge, ϕ is the work function of the photoemissive surface material, and k is *Boltzmann's constant.*

dark resistance. The *electrical resistance* of the *photoconductive* material of a *photodetector* when there is no *radiant* energy or *luminous flux incident* upon its sensitive surface. Dark resistance generally decreases with increases in *temperature* for most photodetectors. See *infrared detector dark resistance.*

dark-trace tube. A *CRT* that creates dark lines on the *display surface* of its brightened screen. The *display element, display group,* or *display image* is made visible by *illumination* in such a manner that it appears as a dark trace on the display surface. Such *images* can easily be transmitted in a *coherent bundle* of *optical fibers* directly from the face of the tube or after proper collimation to assure proper *bundle acceptance angles.*

darlington.   See *photodarlington.*

darlington pair.   A base-driver or emitter-follower *transistor circuit,* usually consisting of a *voltage amplifier* followed by a *power* amplifier connected in cascade offering high-*input impedance* and increased power gain with high stability. Commonly used in electronic and *integrated circuits.*

dash.   In the *international Morse code,* a *signal element* of *mark* condition and of duration of three *unit intervals* followed by a signal element of *space* condition having a duration of one unit interval.   The duration of a dash is usually equal to the duration of three *dots.*

data.   Representation of facts, concepts, or instructions in a manner suitable for *communication,* interpretation, or *processing* by human, manual, semiautomatic, or fully-automatic means.   The *characters* used as data may assume any form or pattern to which meaning may be assigned in order to represent *information.* Data may be transferred or transported from place to place, such as from city to city; from position to position, such as from *coordinate position* to coordinate position in the *display space* on the *display surface* of a *display device* as *display elements, display groups,* or *display images;* or from location to location, such as in computer or *buffer storage* as *characters* or *words.*   Data may be holes in tapes or cards; magnetized spots on discs, drums, tapes, cards, or chips; electrical current or voltage *pulses* in a wire; or *modulated electromagnetic waves* in free space or in *optical fibers.*   Data may be presented on a *CRT* screen, a *LED* or *gas panel,* a *fiberscope faceplate* at the end of a *coherent bundle* of *optical fibers,* or other surface suitable for data *display.*   See *absolute coordinate data; alphanumeric data; analog data; coordinate data; digital data; numeric data; relative coordinate data; static data.*

data alphabet.   A set of correspondences established by convention that indicates the relationship between *data characters* and the *coded signals* that represent them.

data bank.   A comprehensive collection of *data.*   For example, a complete set of the records that form the collection of files used by an organization.   The data in a data bank is usually organized and structured.   Also see *data base.*

data base.   A set of *data* that is required for a specified purpose or that is fundamental to a *system,* project, enterprise, or business.   For example, all the data concerning the items stored in a warehouse whether in an organized file or not; or all the distriubted data concerning the ecology of a country. Also see *data bank.*

data buffer. A *data storage* device used to compensate for a difference in the rate of flow of data or to compensate for the difference of time of occurrence of events. Thus, the data *buffer* can accept short bursts of high-speed data flow and emit a continuous lower speed data flow; or it can accept data at a low rate of flow and emit the data in short higher speed bursts, perhaps interleaved *(multiplexed)* with high-speed bursts from other buffers. In any case, the buffer must temporarily store data. Synonymous with *speed buffer.*

data bus. 1. A *bus* that is specifically intended to carry *data,* for example a *daisy chain* at a single site, or a single *conductor* that connects a *data source* to several devices. 2. In an *optical communication system,* an *optical waveguide* used as a *common trunk line* to which a number of *terminals* can be interconnected using *optical couplers.* Also see *power bus.*

data bus coupler. A *connector* that connects a device to a *data bus.* For example, in an *optical communication system,* a *component* that interconnects a number of *optical waveguides* and provides an inherently bidirectional system by mixing and splitting all *signals* within the component.

data call. A *call* established and used for the pupose of transferring *digital data* or *analog data,* but not voice *signals.*

data channel. A *channel* that allows one-way *transmission* of *data.* See *analog data channel; digital data channel.*

data circuit. A means of two-way *transmission* of *data,* comprising associated *transmit* and *receive* capability at both ends. The data circuit may include data *circuit-terminating equipment* between *data switching exchanges,* depending on the type of *interface* used at the data switching exchange. The data circuit between the *data terminal installation* and a data switching exchange *or concentrator* includes the *data circuit-terminating equipment* at the data terminal installation location. It may also include equipment similar to data circuit-terminating equipment at the data exchange or concentrator location. Physical or *virtual circuits* may be established. The data circuit may consist of a pair of associated data *channels* permitting *transmission* in both directions between two locations. Also see Figure D-1.

data circuit connection The interconnection of a number of *data links* or *trunks,* on a *tandem* basis, by means of *switching equipment* to enable *data transmission* to take place among *data terminal installations.*

data circuit-terminating equipment (DCE). The *interface* equipment that *couples data terminal equipment (DTE)* to a *transmission circuit* or *channel* and a transmission circuit or channel to a DTE. The equipment is usually installed at a *user's* premises. It provides all the functions that are required to establish, maintain, and terminate a *connection.* It also provides the *signal conversion* and *coding* between the DTE and the *line.* It may be an *integral* part of another unit or it may be a separate piece of equipment. A simplified form of DCE, called a network terminating unit, may be provided in a specialized *data network.* Also see *data terminal equipment;* Figure D-1.

data circuit-terminating equipment (DCE) clear signal. A *call control signal* that is *transmitted* by a DCE to indicate that it is *clearing* a call.

data circuit-terminating equipment (DCE) waiting signal. A *call control signal* at the DCE–DTE *(data terminal equipment) interface* that indicates that the DCE is waiting for another event in the *call* establishment procedure (sequence).

data circuit transparency. The capability of a *data circuit* to *transmit* all *data* without changing the *information content* or structure. For example, a measure of the ability of a circuit to handle many *alphabetic codes* or to function at a wide range of *pulse repetition rates.*

data code. In *communications,* a set of rules and conventions according to which *messages* or the *signals* that represent *data* are to be formed, *transmitted, received,* and *processed.*

data collection facility. A *facility* for gathering and organizing *data* from a group of *data sources.*

data collection station. See *data input station.*

data communication. Two-way *data transfer* between *data source* and *data sink* via one or more *data channels* or *links.* Usually the data transfer takes place according to a *protocol.* Also see *data transmission.* See *code-independent data communication.*

data communication control character. See *transmission control character.*

data communication control procedure. A means used to control the orderly *communication* of *information* among the *stations* in a *data communication network.*

data communication equipment. Any equipment used in a *communication system* or as stand-alone equipment for communication purposes.

data compaction.   The reduction of space, *bandwidth,* cost, and time for the generation, *transmission,* and *storage* of *data* without loss of *information* by employing techniques designed to eliminate redundancy, remove irrelevancy, and employ special *coding.*   Some data compaction methods employ *fixed tolerance bands, variable tolerance bands, slope-keypoints, sample changes, curve patterns, curve fitting, floating-point coding, variable precision coding, frequency analysis,* and *probability analysis.*   Simply squeezing noncompacted data into a smaller space, for example by increasing packing density or by transferring data on *punched cards* onto *magnetic tape,* is not considered as data compaction.   Also see *data compression.*

data compression.   1. A method of increasing the amount of *data* that can be stored in a given space or contained in a given *message* length.   2. A method of reducing the amount of *storage* space required to store a given amount of *data* or reducing the length of *message* required to transfer a given amount of *information.*   Also see *data compaction.*   See *facsimile data compression.*

data concentrator.   1. Equipment that permits a *data transmission medium* to serve more *data sources* than there are *channels* currently available within the medium.   2. *Switching equipment* that enables *connections* between *circuits* and *stations* to be established and severed as required.   The number of *data circuit-terminating equipment* units always exceeds the number of stations.

data conferencing repeater.   A device that enables a group of *users* to operate such that if any one user *transmits* a *message* it will be *received* by all others in the group.   Synonymous with *technical control hubbing repeater.*   Also see *conference repeater.*

data connection.   The *connection* of a number of *data circuits* on a *tandem* basis by means of *switching equipment* to enable *data transmission* to take place between *data terminal equipment* units.   One or more of the interconnected data circuits may be a *virtual circuit* connected by a *virtual connection.*   The overall connection includes the data circuit-terminating equipment at the respective *data station* locations.

data contamination.   A change in the *integrity* of *data,* or the process that results in such change.

data delimiter.   A *mark, signal,* or *character,* such as a separator, that is used to separate *data* in a *data stream* into *data units* or groups of data units, for example, to separate characters into *words.*

data element.   The name given to a class or category of *data items.*   For example month, date, day of week, or name of person.   Thus, January is a data item for the data element month.   Also 01 could be the *data code* for the data item January.

data encryption standard. A standard procedure for *enciphering plain text*. For example, the *cryptographic algorithm* designed to *encipher* and *decipher 8-byte blocks* of *data*, using a 64-bit *cryptokey*, as specified in Federal Information Processing Standard Publication 46, dated January 15, 1977. Also see *cryptokey*.

data grade circuit. See *conditioned voice grade circuit*.

datagram. 1. In a *packet-switching network*, a finite-length *packet*, with destination *host address* and *source address*, that can be exchanged in its entirety between hosts. The datagram usually has a maximum length of 1000 to 8000 bits. 2. In a *data network*, a self-contained, independent entity of data carrying sufficient *information* to be *routed* from the *data source data terminal equipment (DTE)* to the *data sink* DTE without reliance on earlier exchanges between the source or sink DTEs and the network.

datagram service. A *transmission service* whereby a *datagram* is *routed* to the destination identified in its *address field* without reference by the *data network* to another *datagram* previously sent or likely to follow. It is possible that datagrams may be delivered to a destination address in a different order from that in which they entered the network. It may be necessary for *users* to provide procedures to insure delivery of datagrams to the *destination user* (destination *addressee*). In *packet mode operation*, a datagram is usually conveyed as a single *packet*.

data input station. A *user terminal* primarily used for the insertion of *data* into a *data processing system* or a *communication service*. Synonymous with *data collection station*.

data integrity. The preservation of the validity of *data* when it is *converted*, *translated*, or *transferred*, or when it is stored and retrieved.

data item. A unit of recorded *data* representing a unit of *information* that usually can be identified or classified by a name *(data element)*. For example January would be a data item for the data element month; Tuesday would be a data item for the data element day of the week; and Helen Harrison would be a data item for the data element person's name. The data item is often represented by a *data code*, such as 01 for January. Usually only the code needs to be transmitted, if the data item and the data element are understood by the *users*.

data keyboard. A device comprising an array of *keys* that is used to control a *telegraph transmitter* or other *data source*.

data link. 1. A *communication link* suitable for *transmission* of *data*. The data link does not include the *data source* and the *data sink*. 2. Two *data stations* and their connecting *network*, operating in such a manner that *information* can be exchanged between the stations. For example, data-terminal installations and their connecting *circuit.* See *fiber optic data link; logical data link; signaling data link.* See Figure D-1. Also see Figures F-5, M-5, U-2, and V-2.

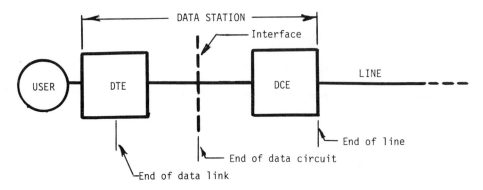

D-1. Components of a **data link,** showing the *data-circuit terminating equipment (DCE)* and the *data terminal equipment (DTE).*

data link control. See *high-level data link control (HDLC); synchronous data-link control.*

data link escape (DLE) character. A *transmission control character* that changes the meaning of a limited number of contiguously following *characters* or *coded* representations, and that is used to provide supplementary transmission control characters.

data link layer. In *open systems architecture,* the *layer* that provides the functions, procedures, and *protocol* needed to establish, maintain, and *release data link connections* between the *data stations* of a *network.* It is a conceptual level of *data processing* or control logic existing in the hierarchical structure of the data station that is responsible for maintaining control of the data link. Data link layer functions provide an *interface* between the station high-level logic and the data link. These functions include *bit injection* at the *transmitter* and *bit extraction* at the *receiver; address* and *control field* interpretation; *command-response* generation; *transmission* and interpretation; and *frame check sequence* computation and interpretation. Also see *layer.*

data logging. The recording of *data* about events that occur in time sequence.

data medium. 1. The material in or upon which a specific physical variable may be used either as *data* or to represent data statically or dynamically; e.g., film, wire, cards, discs, drums, paper, *optical fibers, CRT* screens, *LED* and *gas panels,* and *fiberscopes. Modulated electromagnetic waves* in transit in *free space* — e.g., between the earth and moon — may be considered as using the free space as a data medium, even though no physical material may be present. Contrast with *transmission medium*. **2.** The physical quantity, material, or substance that may be varied to represent *data*.

data mode.   The state of *data circuit-terminating equipment* when connected to a *communication channel* and not in the *dial mode*. Also see *dial mode*.

data multiplexer.   A *functional unit* that permits two or more *data sources* to share a common *transmission medium* so that each data source has its own *channel*.

data network.   **1.** The assembly of *functional units* that establishes *data circuits* between *data terminal equipment* at *data stations*. **2.** A *network* that *transfers data* among a group of interconnected stations. See *public data network (PDN); synchronous data network*. See Figure D-2.

D-2. The Dataphone® for use in a **data network** or a *telephone network*. (Reproduced with permission of AT&T Co.)

data part. See *header part.*

data phase. A *phase* of a *data call* during which *data signals* may be transferred between *data terminal equipment* units that are interconnected via a *network.*

data processing. The systematic execution of *operations* upon *data;* e.g., merging, sorting, transferring, storing, computing, and comparing. See *automatic data processing; distributed data processing; optical data processing.*

data processing equipment. See *automatic data processing equipment (ADPE).*

data processing node. A *node* in a *network* at which *processors, controllers, data terminals,* and other *data processing equipment* and their associated *software* are located.

data processing station. 1. A *station* at a *data processing node* in a *network* that has *input-output* devices that serve the needs of the *user.* 2. An *input-output* device at a *data processing node* that serves the needs of *users.*

data processing system. See *automatic data processing system; distributed data processing system.*

data processing terminal. A device that enables an *operator* to interact with a *data processing system.* Also see *computer terminal.*

data security. Protective measures, including procedures and actions, designed to prevent the unauthorized disclosure, transfer, modification, or destruction, either accidental or intentional, of *data.*

data set. A set or group of *data items,* usually stored, retrieved, or organized as a unit of *data.* For example, the collection of data constituting a file or a record concerning one person.

data service. A *communication service* devoted to the handling of relatively large volumes of *data,* such as in *facsimile* or *digital data transmission,* or *telemetry,* in contrast to *voice* or *video transmission* by *telephone* or *television.* Also see *voice-data service.*

data shift. To justify the position of *data* so that *symbols* line up with some reference, such as a margin. For example, to eliminate all zeros at the right-hand or left-hand end of a *data word.* An algebraic shift to the left accomplishes the same result as multiplication and to the right, division. The amount of multiplication or division depends on the *coding* used, the *base* or *radix* of the data, and the amount of the shift. Thus, a three-place shift to the left in a *binary number* is the same as multiplication by eight. The shift can occur in a *register* where data flow is obtained by shifting bits from cell to cell. Shifting produces serial flow, at least internally, although the rate of *input* shifting and *output* shifting may differ, and, indeed, either the input or the output may be parallel. The register may be used as a *buffer* to change data speeds or to convert serial to parallel flow or vice versa.

data signaling rate. The aggregate *signaling rate* in the *transmission* path of a *data transmission system.* Mathematically:

$$D.S.R. = \sum_{i=1}^{m} (1/T_i)\log_2 n_i$$

where *m* is the number of parallel *channels,* T_i is the minimum time interval for the *i*th channel expressed in seconds, *n* is the number of *significant conditions* of the *modulation signal* in the *i*th channel. Thus, for a single channel, it reduces to $(1/T)\log_2 n$. With a two-condition channel, $n = 2$, it is $1/T$. For a parallel transmission with equal minimum intervals and equal number of significant conditions on each channel, it is $(m/T)\log_2 n$. In *synchronous binary signaling,* the data signaling rate in bits per second is numerically the same as the *modulation rate* expressed in *baud. Signal processors,* such as four-phase *modems,* cannot change the data signaling rate, but the modulation rate depends on the *line* modulation scheme. For example, in a 2400 *b/s* 4-phase sending modem, the signaling rate is 2400 b/s on the serial input side, but the modulation rate is only 1200 baud on the 4-phase output side.

data signaling rate transparency. A *communication network* characteristic that enables the *transfer* of *data* between one user and another without placing any restriction in regard to a specific data *signaling rate* except that it lies within certain limits. One method of achieving data signaling rate transparency in fixed-rate systems is to use *stuffing pulses.*

data sink. In a *communication system,* equipment that accepts *data* after *transmission* and perhaps checks the data and originates *error-* and *system*-control *signals.* Also see *data source.*

data source. In a *communication system,* equipment that supplies *data* to be *transmitted* and perhaps originates *system*-control and *error-checking signals.* Also see *data sink.*

data station. An installation comprising the *data terminal equipment (DTE),* the *data circuit-terminating equipment (DCE),* and any intermediate equipment, such as an *interface.* In some instances, the DTE may be connected directly to a *data processor* or another *communication network,* or it may be an *integral* part of these. Synonymous with *data terminal installation.* Also see Figure D-1.

data stream. A sequence of *characters* or *pulses* used to represent *information* during *transmission.* Also see *bit stream.* See *serial data stream.*

data subscriber terminal equipment (DSTE). A general purpose *AUTODIN terminal* device consisting of all the equipment necessary to provide *interface* functions, perform *code* conversion, and transform *messages* on various *data media,* such as *punched cards, magnetic tape,* and paper tape, to *electrical signals* for *transmission.* Also included is the equipment necessary to convert received electrical signals to data on various data media.

data switching. See *digital data switching.*

data switching exchange (DSE). The equipment installed at a single location, such as a *switching center,* to *switch data traffic.* The DSE may provide only *circuit switching,* only *packet switching,* or both.

data system. A *system* designed to *process* or *transfer data,* for example, an *automatic data processing system* or a *communication system.*

data terminal equipment (DTE). 1. The equipment comprising the *data source,* the *data sink,* or both. **2.** Equipment, consisting of *digital end-instruments,* that converts *user information* into *data signals* for *transmission,* or reconverts the received data signals into user information. **3.** The *functional unit* of a *data station* that serves as a *data source* or a *data sink* and provides for *data communication* control to be performed in accordance with *link protocol.* The DTE may consist of a single piece of equipment that provides all the required functions necessary to permit *users* to *communicate,* or it may be an interconnected subsystem of multiple pieces of equipment, including *communication security* equipment, which performs all the required functions. Also see *data circuit-terminating equipment.* Also see Figure D-1.

data terminal equipment (DTE) clear request signal. A *call control signal* sent by *data terminal equipment* to initiate clearing. Also see *clear request signal.*

data terminal equipment (DTE) waiting signal. A *call control signal* at the *data circuit-terminating equipment* and data terminal equipment (DCE-DTE) *interface* that indicates that the DTE is waiting for a call control signal from the DCE. Also see *data terminal equipment (DTE).*

data terminal installation. See *data station.*

data transaction. See *interactive data transaction.*

data transfer. See *request data transfer.*

data transfer phase. In a *call,* the *phase* during which *user data* is actually transferred between a *source user* and a *destination user.* Other phases are the *call setup phase* and the *call termination phase.* Also see *information transfer phase.*

data transfer rate. The number of *data units* passing per unit time between specified equipment, usually corresponding equipment, in a *data transmission sys-*

tem. It is usually expressed in terms of bits, characters, blocks, or other data units per second, minute, or hour. The corresponding equipment should be indicated, such as *modems, data sources, data sinks,* or *intermediate equipment.* Also see *data signaling rate.* See *effective data transfer rate.*

data transfer request signal. A *call control signal transmitted* by *data circuit-terminating equipment (DCE)* to *data terminal equipment (DTE)* to indicate that a distant DTE is ready and requests to exchange *data.*

data transfer time. The time that elapses between the initial offering of *user data* to a *network* by transmitting *data terminal equipment* and the complete delivery of that data to receiving data terminal equipment.

data transmission. The sending or conveying of *data* from one place to another by means of *signals* over a *channel* or *data circuit.* Also see *code-independent data transmission; data communication.* See *store-and-forward data transmission.*

data transmission channel. A *channel,* including the *transmission media* and related equipment, used in the transfer of *data* between *data terminal equipment (DTE)* at different locations. A data transmission channel includes *signal conversion* equipment. A data transmission channel may support the transfer of information in one direction only, in either direction alternately, or in both directions simultaneously. When the DTE has more than one speed capability associated with it, for example 1200 bits per second transmission in the *forward direction* and 150 bits per second transmission in the *backward direction,* a channel is defined for each speed capability. See *nonsynchronous data transmission channel; synchronous data transmission channel.*

data transmission circuit. A *circuit,* including the *transmission media* and the intervening equipment, used in the *transfer* of *data* between *data terminal equipment* at different locations. A data transmission circuit includes the *signal conversion* equipment. A data transmission circuit may support the transfer of information in one direction only, in either direction alternately, or in both directions simultaneously.

data transmission control character. See *transmission control character.*

data transmission interface. In a *data transmission system,* a shared boundary identified by a distinguishing or transition characteristic, such as a functional change, physical interconnection, *signal* transformation, or change in *data medium.*

data transmission service. A service, usually provided to the public by a *recognized private operating agency* or an *administration,* that enables the *transmission* of *data* from one *user* to another. Also see *public data transmission service.* See *circuit-switched data transmission service; leased circuit data transmission service; packet-switched data transmission service; public data transmission service.*

datawire. The *channel* or path in a *communication system* used to *transmit* the *data* for which the system was designed and built. Also see *orderwire.*

date. An instant in the passage of time, identified with desired precision by a *clock* and a calendar. For example 23 seconds after midnight on February 9, 1926. This date might be represented by the recommended international standard as 1926Feb090023, or simply as 192602090023EST. In a *message,* the date is represented by a *date-time group.* See *Julian date.*

date-and-time indicator. See *automatic date-and-time indicator.*

date-time group (DTG). A set of *characters* usually in a prescribed format used to express day of the month, hour, minute, time zone, month, and possibly year, in that order, in a *message.* For example, 081330Z AUG 85 indicates 1:30 PM *Greenwich mean time (GMT)* on the 8th day of August of the year 1985. The DTG of a message may indicate either the date and time when the message was dispatched by the *transmitting station,* or the date and time when the message was handed into a communication facility by a *user* or *originator* for *transmission.* The DTG is normally expressed as six *digits* (two for the day of the month and four for the time), followed by a *time zone* suffix and the month expressed by the first three letters. The year need not always be included. Seconds or fractional minutes should be clearly indicated after the minute digits, such as 1330.8 to indicate eight tenths of a minute after 1:30 PM. The DTG can be used as a message identifier, particularly if each DTG is unique. The DTG should not be used to compute *message processing* or delay time. See *true date-time group (TDTG).*

dating format. 1. The particular arrangement for specifying or representing the date. For example, the time of an event on the *Greenwich mean time system* given in the sequence hours, day, month, year, for example 1030GMT 24 Feb 1984. 2. In automatic data processing, the time of an event given in the sequence year, month, day, hour, minute, and second in that order, for example 1984 Feb 24 1635.7. The hour is designated for a 24-hour clock.

day. See *civil day; radio day; sidereal day; true solar day; undisturbed day.*

dB. *Decibel.*

dBa. *Weighted noise power* in *decibels* referred to 3.16 *picowatts* (−85 dBm), which is 0 dBa. When using an F1A-line or HA-1 receiver, weighting should be indicated in parentheses as required. A one *milliwatt,* 1000 Hz tone will read +85 dBa, but the same *power* as *white noise,* randomly distributed over a 3 kHz *band* (nominally 300 to 3300 Hz), will read +82 dBa, due to the *frequency weighting.* Synonymous with *dBrn (adjusted).* Also see *dBm (psoph); noise weighting.*

dBa(F1A). *Noise power* in *dBa,* measured by a *noise measuring set* with *F1A-line weighting.*

dBa(HA1). *Noise power* in *dBa,* measured across the *receiver* of a Western Electric 302 Type or similar instrument, by a noise measuring set with *HA1-receiver weighting.*

dBa0. *Noise power* in *dBa* referred to or measured from a *zero transmission level (reference) point (OTLP).* The OTLP is the point of zero *relative transmission level (0 dBr).* It is usually preferred to convert noise readings from *dBa* to dBa0, as this makes it unnecessary to know or state the relative transmission level at the point of actual measurement.

dBm. *Decibels* referred to one *milliwatt.* It is used in *communications* as a measure of *absolute power* values. Zero dBm equals one *milliwatt.* In some American practice, unweighted measurement is normally understood as being applicable to a certain *bandwidth* that must be stated or implied. In European practice, *psophometric weighting* may be implied, as indicated by context. This is equivalent to *dBm0p,* which is preferred.

dBm0. *Noise power* in *dBm* referred to or measured at a *zero transmission level (reference) point (OTLP).* The OTLP is the point of *zero relative transmission level (0dBr).* In some international documents, *dBm0* is used to mean *noise power* in *dBm0p (psophometrically weighted dBm0).*

dBm0p. *Noise power* in *dBm0,* measured by a *psophometer* or *noise measuring set* having *psophometric weighting.* Also see *dBm (psoph); noise weighting.*

dBm (psoph). A unit of *noise power* in *dBm,* measured with *psophometric weighting.* For conversion to other weighted units, dBm(psoph) = $[10 \log_{10} (pWp)] - 90 = dBa - 84$, where *pWp* is the *picowatts psophometrically weighted* and *dBa* is the *weighted noise power.* Also see *dBa; dBm0p; psophometric weighting; pWp.* Synonymous with *psophometrically weighted dBm.*

dBr. The *electrical power* difference, expressed in *decibels,* between any point and a reference point selected as the *zero transmission level (reference) point (OTLP),* used to express relative *transmission power* levels. Any power expressed in dBr does not specify the *absolute power.* It is a relative measurement only. For example, a pilot tone of −10 dBm0, when measured at a +17 dBr point, gives a power level of −10 + 17 = +7 dBm; or a carrier leak of −17 dBm, when measured at −37 dBr point, is equivalent to a level of −17 + 37 = +20 dBm0. Also see *absolute power; transmission level point.*

dBrn. The number of *decibels* above reference *noise.* It is the weighted *noise power* in *decibels* referred to one *picowatt.* Thus, 0 dBrn = −90 *dBm.* Use of *144-line weighting, 144-receiver* or *C-message weighting,* or *flat weighting* is indicated in parentheses as required. With C-message weighting, a one *milliwatt,*

1000 Hz tone will read +90 dBrn, but the same *power* as *white noise,* randomly distributed over a 3 kHz *bandwidth* will read approximately +88.5 dBrn due to the *frequency weighting.* It is usually rounded off to +88 dBrn. With 144-line weighting, a 1 mw, 1000 Hz tone will also read +90 dBrn, but the same 3 kHz white noise power will read only +82 dBrn, due to the different frequency weighting. Also see *noise weighting.*

dBrn (adjusted).   See *dBa.*

dBrnC.   *Noise power* in *dBrn,* measured by a *noise measuring set* with a *C-message weighting.*   Also see *circuit noise level.*

dBrnC0.   *Noise power* in *dBrnC* referred to or measured from a *zero transmission level (reference) point (OTLP).*

dBrn($f_1 - f_2$).   *Flat noise power* in *dBrn,* measured over the *frequency band* between frequencies f_1 and f_2. Also see *flat weighting; noise weighting.*

dBrn (144-line).   *Noise power* in *dBrn,* measured by a *noise measuring set* with a *144-line weighting.*

dBv.   *Decibels* relative to one volt peak-to-peak.   This unit is usually used for *television video signal* level measurements.

dBw.   *Decibels* referred to one watt of *power.*

dBx.   *Decibels* above *reference coupling.*   This unit is used to express the amount of *crosstalk* coupling in *telephone circuits.*   It is measured with a *noise measuring set.*

DC.   *Direct current.*

DCE.   *Data circuit-terminating equipment.*

DC patch bay.   See *direct-current (DC) patch bay.*

DCPSK.   *Differentially-coherent phase-shift keying.*

DC restoration circuit.   See *direct-current (DC) restoration circuit.*

DC signaling.   See *direct-current (DC) signaling.*

DDD.   *Direct distance dialing.*

dead reckoning.   To calculate a present position using the last known position and the movements that have been made since leaving the last known position. For example, to use the *integrated* velocity with respect to time and the initial coordinates to obtain new coordinates. In *radionavigation*, dead reckoning may have to be used if *radio transmission* or *reception* is lost.

dead-reckoning position. In navigation, the position calculated by *dead reckoning*.

dead sector. 1. In *facsimile systems,* the portion of the surface of a *drum transmitter* whose *scanning* time cannot be used for *picture signal transmission.* 2. In *facsimile systems,* the elapsed time between the end of *scanning* of one line and the start of scanning of the following line.

dead space. The area, zone, or volume of space that is otherwise within range of a *radio, radar,* or other *transmitter* but in which a *signal* is not detectable and therefore cannot be received.

dead-zone unit. A device that has an *output analog variable* that is constant over a specified range of the *input analog variable.*

debug. To detect, trace, and eliminate *mistakes, errors,* or *malfunctions* in *hardware (communication systems* and *computers)* or *software (protocols* and *computer programs).*

decametric wave. An *electromagnetic wave* in the *high-frequency (HF)* subdivision of frequencies, ranging from 3 to 30 MHz. Also see *frequency spectrum designation.*

decay time. See *pulse decay time.*

DECCA. A *radio phase*-comparison system that uses a *master* and *slave stations* to establish a *hyperbolic* lattice and provide accurate position-fixing capabilities. It is a long-range *hyperbolic navigational system* that operates in the 70 to 130 kHz frequency band. It is a *continuous-wave* system in which the *receiver* measures and *integrates* the relative *phase* difference between the *signal* received from two or more synchronized ground stations. One master station and three slave stations are usually arranged in a fixed formation. Operational range is about 250 miles (400 km).

decentralized computer network. A *computer network* in which the *data processing* capability required by *users* is distributed over two or more *nodes.*

deception. See *communication deception; electronic deception; manipulative communication deception; manipulative electronic deception; radar scan-rate modulation deception; radio deception.*

deception jammer. A *jammer* that is used to induce false indications in the *system* that it *jams.*

deception repeater. A device that can *receive* a *signal;* amplify, delay, or otherwise manipulate it; and retransmit it for the purpose of *deception.* See *radar deception repeater.*

decibel (dB). A *gain* or *attenuation factor* measured as 10 times the logarithm to the base 10 of a *power* ratio, or as 20 times the logarithm to the base 10 of the *voltage* or *current* ratio with reference to 1-ohm *impedance.* The ratio consists of a reference value as the ratio denominator and the value to be defined or measured as the numerator. If the logarithm is positive a *gain* is represented by decibels that are positive and if *loss* or *attenuation* is defined or measured, the decibels are negative. For example, if the ratio of *optical power* at the end of an *optical fiber* to the power at the beginning is 0.500, the loss is expressed as 10 log 0.500 = −3.0103 dB, i.e., 3 dB down. Since the individual component gain or loss ratios introduced by serially connected *cables, amplifiers, optical fibers,* and other *circuit* or *optical elements* are multiplicative, the decibel gains and losses need only be added or subtracted according to sign. Thus, the mathematical relationships are:

$$dB = 10 \, log_{10} \, (P_1/P_2)$$
$$= 10 \, log_{10} \, (E_1{}^2/R_1)/E_2{}^2/R_2)$$
$$= 10 \, log_{10} \, (I_1{}^2 R_1)/I_2{}^2 R_2)$$

If $R_1 = R_2$, then:

$$dB = 10 \, log_{10} \, (E_1{}^2/E_2{}^2) = 10 \, log_{10} \, (I_1{}^2/I_2{}^2)$$
$$= 20 \, log_{10} \, (E_1/E_2) \qquad = 20 \, log_{10} \, (I_1/I_2)$$

where *P* is the *power*, *E* is the *electrical voltage*, *I* is the *electrical current*, and *R* is the *resistance* or like *impedance* and the subscripts identify the two points of comparison of power, voltage, or current. The *dB* is one tenth the size of a bel, which is too large for convenient use.

decibel above isotropic (DBI) condition. An *antenna gain* unit of measure used instead of *dB.* DBI and dB have the same numerical value.

decimal. See *binary-coded decimal (BCD).*

decimal digit. One of the digits 0, 1, 2, 3, 4, 5, 6, 7, 8, and 9 when used in the *decimal numeration system.*

decimal interchange code. See *extended binary coded decimal interchange code (EBCDIC).*

decimal unit of information content. See *hartley.*

decimetric wave. An *electromagnetic wave* in the *ultrahigh frequency (UHF)* subdivision of *frequencies,* ranging from 300 to 3000 MHz. Decimetric waves have a *wavelength* between 10 and 100 centimeters. Also see *frequency spectrum designation.*

decimillimetric wave. An *electromagnetic wave* in the *tremendously high frequency (THF)* subdivision of *frequencies,* ranging from 300 to 3000 GHz or 3 THz. Decimillimetric waves have a *wavelength* between 10 and 100 thousandths of a centimeter, hence the name decimillimetric.

decipher. To *convert* an *enciphered text* into its equivalent *plain language* by means of a *cipher system.* This does not include solution by *cryptanalysis.* Also see *decipher; decode; decrypt.*

decision circuit. 1. A *circuit* that measures the probable value of a *signal element* and produces a *signal* if a specified *threshold* is reached. 2. A *circuit* that generates an *output signal* representing a decision based on *input signals* past or present. For example, a *combinational circuit,* such as an *AND gate.*

decision content. A measure of the number of possible decisions needed to select a given event from among a finite number of mutually exclusive events. In mathematical notation, this measure is H = log n, where n is the number of events. The base of the logarithm determines the unit used. The decision content is independent of the probabilities of the occurrence of the events. However, in some applications, it is assumed that these probabilities are equal. Also see *hartley; natural unit of information content (NAT); shannon.*

decision feedback. See *error-detection and feedback.*

decision-feedback system. See *automatic request-repeat (ARQ).*

decision instant. In the *reception* of a *digital signal,* the instant at which a decision is made by a receiving device as to the probable value of a *signal element.* Synonymous with *selection position.* Also see *significant instant.*

deck log. See *ship deck log.*

declaration. In a *programming language* or *computer program,* an expression that influences the interpretation of other expressions in that language. For example, in PL/1, the establishing of an identifier as a name or the construction of a set of attributes of the named item.

declination parallel. Any small circle of the celestial sphere whose plane is parallel to the plane of the *celestial equator* and perpendicular to the celestial axis.

decode. 1. To *convert data* by reversing the effect of some previous *encoding.* 2. To interpret a code. 3. To *convert encoded language* into its equivalent *plain language* by means of a *code.* This does not include solution by *cryptanalysis.* 4. The section of a *code book* in which the *code groups* are in alphabetical, numerical, or other systematic order, in order to convert *coded language* into *plain language.* Also see *code; decipher; encode.*

decoder. 1. A device that *decodes data.* 2. A device that has a number of *input lines,* of which any number may carry *signals,* and a number of *output lines,* of which not more than one may carry a signal at any given instant. There is usually a one-to-one correspondence between the combinations of input signals and the output signals. Also see *coder; encoder.*

decoding. See *analog decoding.*

decollimation. In a *lightwave guide,* the spreading or *divergence* of *light* due to internal and end effects. Such effects include curvature, irregularities of surfaces, erratic variations in *refractive indices,* occlusions, and other blemishes that may cause *dispersion, absorption, scattering, deflection, diffraction, reflection,* and *refraction.*

decrypt. 1. To convert an *encrypted message* into *plain language* by reversal of the *encryption* process. This does not include solution by *cryptanalysis.* 2. To *convert encrypted language* into its equivalent *plain language* by means of a *cryptosystem.* Also see *decipher; decode.*

dedicated circuit. 1. A *circuit* provided for the sole use or private use of certain *users* to serve a preassigned purpose. 2. A *circuit* designated for the exclusive use of only two *users.* Also see *exclusive-user circuit; leased-circuit data transmission service.*

dedicated communication. *Communication* between specified *users.* The communication is usually for particular purposes and is under the direct control of the users.

dedicated communication service. A *communication service* devoted to the exclusive use of one *user, user group, system,* or subsystem. Also see *common user; common-user communication service.*

dedicated connection. A *user-to-user connection* that is automatically set up on some simple *command,* such as a *key* depression or short *dialing* by one *user.* This type of connection will normally incorporate a *preemption facility* to ensure an adequate *service grade.*

dedicated mode. The operation of a *system* or *component* by a specific group of *users,* for a specific application or use, or for a specific class of *information.*

deducible directory. A *directory* constructed in such a manner that *users* (customers, subscribers) can deduce the *directory numbers* of other users (customers, subscribers) using defined rules and fixed lookup tables. This might enable a subscriber to form a directory number for most of the subscribers in a *closed user-group.* The rules should be simple and capable of being easily memorized.

de-emphasis. In *frequency modulation,* a process of reducing the *amplitude* of the *high frequencies* after their detection to restore the frequency *components* to their original relative level. Also see *pre-emphasis.*

de-emphasis network. A *network* inserted into a *system* in order to decrease the *amplitude* of *electromagnetic waves* or *signals* in one *frequency range* with respect to the amplitude in another range. Also see *pre-emphasis network.*

deep channel. A *channel* used to *communicate* into or within *deep space.*

deep space. 1. *Space* at distances from the earth greater than the distance between the earth and the moon. 2. *Space* at distances from the sun greater than that of the farthest planet from the sun. Also see *outer space.*

defect. See *interstitial defect; vacancy defect.*

defect absorption. See *atomic defect absorption.*

defense command-control-communication network. See *air defense command-control-communication network.*

defense communications. See *air-defense communications.*

defense communication system. See *air-defense communication system.*

defense master clock. See *Department of Defense (DOD) master clock.*

definition. In *facsimile systems,* the distinctness or clarity of detail or outline in a *record sheet,* object copy, or other reproduction.

deflection. 1. A change in the direction of a traveling particle, usually without loss of particle kinetic energy, representing a velocity change without a speed change. 2. A change in the direction of a *wave, beam,* or other entity, such as might be accomplished by an *electric* or *magnetic field* rather than by a *prism (refraction),* a *mirror (reflection),* or *optical grating (diffraction).*

degenerate waveguide mode. A member of a set of *waveguide modes* that have the same *propagation constant* for all *frequencies* of interest.

degradation. The deterioration or decrease in the quality, level, or standard of performance of a *functional unit.* See *catastrophic degradation; gradual degradation; partial degradation.*

degraded service state. A *communication service* condition that exists during any period over which the established limiting values for at least one of the performance *parameters* is worse than its specified *threshold.* Also see *outage state.*

degauss. To remove the magnetization from a *magnetic data medium,* usually by raising and then lowering an alternating *magnetic field* in the magnetic material.

degree. See *electrical degree; spatial degree.*

delay. The lost or waiting time introduced because a call cannot be connected immediately or because a *message* or *signal* cannot be transmitted immediately, usually due to a queue on the required *line* or *circuit.* See *absolute delay; absolute signal delay; operator delay; phase delay; propagation time delay; receive-after transmit time delay; receiver attack-time delay; receiver release-time delay; transmit-after-receive time delay; transmitter attack-time delay; transmitter release-time delay.*

delay distortion. The *distortion* caused by the difference between the maximum and minimum *propagation time delay* of the *electromagnetic waves* with different *frequencies* within a *signal (pulse).* The distortion is caused by the difference in arrival time of each of the different frequency *components* at the *output* of a *transmission medium, circuit,* or *system.* Thus, the *output* signal wave shape is not the same as the *input* wave shape. Synonymous with *phase distortion* and with *time-delay distortion.* See *group-delay distortion; waveguide delay distortion.*

delay element. A device that yields an *output signal* essentially similar to a previously introduced *input signal.* The time interval between the signals is the *delay time.*

delay equalizer. A corrective *circuit* that is designed to make the *envelope phase delay* of another circuit or *system* substantially constant over a specified *frequency range.* Thus, the *network* is designed to compensate for *group-delay frequency distortion.* It is the *transmission time* that is made substantially constant for all frequency components within the specified *frequency band.* Synonymous with *delay frequency equalizer; phase equalizer.* Also see *absolute delay; group delay; phase-frequency equalizer.*

delay line. 1. A real or *artificial transmission line* or equivalent device designed to introduce *delay* into the *propagation* of a *signal.* 2. A *sequential circuit* or device designed with one *input channel* in which the channel *output* state at a given instant, t, is the same as the channel input state at the instant t − n, that is, the input signal sequence undergoes a delay of n time units. There may be additional taps on the delay line that yield ouput states with smaller values of n. Also see *absolute delay; electromagnetic delay line.* See *optical fiber delay line.*

delay modulation (DM). *Modulation* achieved by introducing different forms of delay in a *signal element.* It is a form of signal modulation that is most commonly found in *radio* applications. DM provides a compromise waveform between *non-return-to-zero (NRZ)* and *biphase.* It produces a *spectrum* that has less *low-frequency power* than NRZ and less *high-frequency power* than biphase. DM *encodes* the *binary data* into one of four *symbols* according to the following three rules: (1) A 1 *(mark)* is represented by a *transition* from either level, that is from either high or low level to the other level in the center of the *bit interval,* and thus the DM 1 can be *encoded* into either of the biphase symbols; (2) A 0 *(space)* is represented by no transition except in the case of two or more consecutive 0's (spaces), in which case transitions are placed at the ends of the interval and thus the DM 0 can be encoded into either of the two NRZ symbols; and (3) there is no transition at the end of a bit interval when a 0 (space) is followed by a 1 (mark), or vice versa.

delay operator. In *telephone switchboard operations,* an *operator* specifically assigned to deal with all *booked calls* or *lines* over which *delay working* is in progress.

delay spread.   See *multimode group-delay spread.*

delay time.   See *group delay time; round-trip delay time.*

delay working. In *telephone switchboard operation,* a method of operation intended to ensure fair distribution of the time of a *line* or lines among groups of callers. For example, the line or lines could be withdrawn from general use and placed under the control of a *delay operator.* Under this arrangement, the other operators book their call demands on *tickets* that are passed to the delay operator for *connection* in the order in which they are booked. See *trunk delay working.*

DEL character.   See *delete (DEL) character.*

delete (DEL) character. A *transmission control character* used primarily to obliterate an erroneous or unwanted *character.* On *perforated tape,* this character consists of a code hole at each punch position. Synonymous with *erase character* and with *rub-out character.*

deleted bit. A *bit* that is not delivered to the intended *destination user.* Also see *added bit; bit-count integrity; character-count integrity.*

deleted block. A *block* that is not delivered to the intended *destination user.* Also see *added block.*

delimiter.   See *data delimiter.*

delineation map.   See *routing indicator delineation map.*

delineation table.   See *routing indicator delineation table.*

delivered overhead bit. A *bit* that is transferred to a *destination user,* but whose primary functional effect or purpose is within the *communication system.*

delivered overhead block. A successfully transferred *block* that contains no *user information bits.*

delivery. See *successful block delivery.*

delivery confirmation. *Information* returned to the *message originator* or *source user* indicating that a given unit of *information* has been delivered to the intended *addressee* or *destination user.*

delivery time. In a *communication system,* the *date* and *time* at which a *message* is delivered into the hands of an *addressee* or *destination user.*

Dellinger effect. An effect that causes *electromagnetic sky wave signals* to disappear rapidly as a result of greatly increased *ionization* in the *ionosphere* due to increased *solar noise* caused by solar storms. The effect lasts from ten minutes to several hours. For example, the effect will cause *fading* of *short-wave radio communication* because of the formation of a highly absorbing *D-layer,* which is lower than the regular *E-layer* and *F-layer* of the *ionosphere.* On the occasion of a burst of hydrogen particles from eruptions associated with *sunspot* activity, this effect is particularly disturbing to *radio communication.* Synonymous with *Dellinger fade-out* and with *Dellinger fading.*

Dellinger fade-out. See *Dellinger effect.*

Dellinger fading. See *Dellinger effect.*

delta modulation. A technique for converting an *analog signal* to a *digital signal.* The technique approximates the analog signal with a series of segments. The approximated signal is compared to the original analog signal to determine an increase or decrease in relative *amplitude.* A *decision circuit* establishes the state of successive *binary digits* determined by this comparison. Only the change of *information,* that is, an increase or decrease of the signal amplitude from the previous sample, is sent. Thus, a 'no change' condition remains at the same 0 or 1 state of the previous sample. There are several variations to this simple delta modulation system. See *continuously-variable-slope delta (CVSD) modulation.*

delta sigma modulation (DSM). A form of *signal modulation* in which the *information*-bearing signal, $s(t)$, is first *integrated* and then subjected to delta modulation in such a manner that the *input* to the *modulator,* $E(t)$, is the difference between the integrated information-bearing signal, integral $s(t)dt$, and the integrated output pulses, integral $p(t)dt$. In mathematical form:

$$E(t) = \int s(t)dt - \int p(t)dt = \int [s(t) - p(t)]dt$$

This special case of delta modulation results in a flat load capacity spectrum with increasing signal frequency rather than the 6 dB per octave reduction that is characteristic of ordinary delta modulation.

demand.   In telephone switchboard operation, any request made to an operator by a user (subscriber, customer) or by another operator.

demand assignment.   An operations technique in which various *users* share a *satellite communication system capacity* on a *real-time* demand basis.   A *user* (subscriber, customer) needing to *communicate* with another user of the *network* activates the required *circuit*.   Upon completion of the *call*, the circuit is deactivated and the capacity is available for other users.   This service is analogous in many ways to a *telephone switching network* that provides a *common user trunk* for many users through a limited size *trunk group* on a demand basis.

demand-assignment access plan.   In *satellite communication system* operations, a variable *communication channel access* plan in which the allocation of *accesses* or the number of *channels* per access is varied by demand, as opposed to a preassigned (fixed) access plan.   Also see *preassignment access plan.*

demand factor.   1. The ratio of the maximum actual *power* demand on a *system* to the total power that would be absorbed if the entire load were connected to the system.   2. The ratio of the maximum integrated power (kW) absorbed from a system over a specified time interval to the maximum volt-amperes (kVA) integrated over a time interval of the same duration, though not necessarily during the same period.   The maximum demand is usually the integrated maximum kW demand over a 15 or 30 minute interval rather than the instantaneous or peak demand.

demand load.   1. The total *power* required by a *facility*.   The demand load is the sum of the operational and nonoperational demand loads.   It is determined by applying the proper *demand factor* to each of the connected loads and a *diversity factor* to the total sum.   2. In a *communication system,* the power required by all *automatic switching, synchronous,* and *terminal equipment* operated simultaneously *online* or on standby; all control and *keying* equipment; and lighting, ventilation, and air conditioning equipment required to maintain full continuity of *communication services.*   3. The *nontechnical load,* that is, the power required for ventilating equipment, shop lighting, and other support items that may be operated simultaneously with the technical load.   4. Operationally, the sum of the *technical* and *nontechnical loads* of an operating *facility.*   5. In a *receiver facility,* the *power* required for all receivers and auxiliary equipment that may be operated on prime or spare *antennas* simultaneously, those in standby condition, *multicouplers,* control and *keying* equipment, plus lighting, ventilation, and air conditioning equipment required for full continuity of *communication services.*   6. In a *transmitter facility,* the *power* required for all *transmitters* and auxiliary equipment that may be operated on prime or spare *antennas* or dummy loads simultaneously, those in standby condition, control and *keying* equipment, plus lighting, ventilation and air conditioning equipment required for full continuity of *communication services.*

democratically synchronized network.   A mutually *synchronized network* in which all *clocks* in the network are of equal status and exert equal amounts of control on the others. The network operating *frequency* is the mean of the natural (uncontrolled) frequencies of the population of clocks. Also see *despotically synchronized network; frequency averaging; hierarchically synchronized network oligarchically synchronized network.*

demodulation. 1. To undo or reverse the effects of *modulation;* i.e., to remove the intelligence-bearing *signal* from a modulated *carrier* or to reconstitute the signal that performed the modulation. **2.** The process in which a *modulated wave* is processed to derive a wave having substantially the characteristics of the original modulating wave. Also see *restitution.* See *synchronous demodulation.*

demodulation linearity. See *modulation-demodulation linearity.*

demodulator. A unit that converts a *modulation product* into a *signal* suitable for *processing,* thus performing *demodulation.* See *modulator-demodulator; redemodulator; telegraph demodulator.*

demultiplex (DEMUX). The inverse of *multiplex,* that is, the process of separating two or more *signals* that were previously combined *(multiplexed)* by a compatible *multiplexer* and *transmitted* over a single *channel.* Also see *multiplex.*

DEMUX. *Demultiplex.*

denial. See *access denial; disengagement denial.*

denial probability. See *access denial probability; disengagement denial probability.*

denial ratio. See *disengagement-denial ratio.*

denial time. See *access-denial time.*

dense binary code. A *binary code* in which all possible patterns of *binary digits* of a fixed number of digits are used. For example, a *pure binary representation* for sexadecimal digits using all sixteen patterns, or an octal representation using all eight patterns, in contrast to a binary representation of *decimal numbers* using four binary digits of which only 10 of the possible 16 patterns are used. If a *binary code* is not dense, the unused patterns can be used to *detect errors* inasmuch as they should only occur if there is a malfunction.

density. In a *facsimile system,* a measure of the *light transmission* or *reflection* properties of a material. It may be expressed as the *luminous flux* through a specific area or as the common logarithm of the ratio of *incident* to *transmitted* or *reflected light intensity* per unit area. There are many types of density that will usually have different numerical values for a given material. For example, *diffuse density,* double diffuse density, and *spectral density.* The relevant type of density depends upon the characteristics of the *optical system* in which the material is used.   See *carrier-to-receiver noise density; diffuse density; electro-magnetic energy density; internal optical density; luminous density; magnetic flux density; noise power density; optical density; optical energy density; optical power density; packing density; power density; raster density; spectral density; scanning density; uniform density.*

Department of Defense (DOD) master clock.   The U.S. Naval Observatory *master clock,* designated as the DOD master clock, to which DOD *time* and *frequency* measurements are referenced.   This clock is also the standard time reference for the U.S. Government in accordance with Federal Standard 1002.   Synonymous with *DOD master clock.*

departure angle.   The angle between the axis of the *main lobe* of a *transmitting antenna pattern* and the horizontal plane at the antenna location.   Synonymous with *takeoff angle.*

dependent system.   See *code-dependent system.*

deposition process.   See *chemical vapor deposition (CVD) process; modified chemical vapor deposition (MCVD) process; plasma-activated chemical vapor deposition (PACVD) process.*

depression angle.   An angle, in a vertical plane, between a horizontal plane and a line from a point in the vertical plane (observation point, origin, or vertex) to a point (object) below the horizontal plane, measured from the point in the vertical plane.

depth.   See *focus depth; listening depth.*

derived channel.   See *time-derived channel; frequency-derived channel.*

desensitization.   See *receiver desensitization.*

design.   See *antenna design.*

designation.   See *black designation; frequency spectrum designation; line load control designation; precedence designation; red designation.*

designator.   See *address designator; circuit designator; emission designator; precedence designator; special-handling designator.*

design margin.   See *RF power margin.*

design objective.   A desired electrical, mechanical, or *optical* performance characteristic for *communication circuits* and related equipment that is based on engineering judgement but is not yet considered feasible to establish as a *system* standard.   Examples of reasons for designating a performance characteristic as a design objective rather than as a standard are: (1) It may be bordering on an advancement in the state of the art. (2) The requirement may not have been fully confirmed by measurement or experience with operating circuits. (3) It may not have been demonstrated that it can be met considering other constraints such as cost and size. A design objective may be considered as guidance in the preparation of specifications for development or procurement of new equipment or systems that can be used if they are technically and economically practical. Also see *assumed values; system standards.*

despun antenna.   See *electrically despun antenna; mechanically despun antenna.*

destination address.   In a *communication system, data* sent in the *forward direction* consisting of a number of *signals* indicating the complete *address* of the *destination user* (*called party,* customer, subscriber).

destination code indicator.   In a *communication system, data* sent in the *forward direction* indicating whether or not the destination *code* that refers to the country or *network* is included in the *destination address.*

destination dialing.   A *facility* provided by an *automatically switched communication system* that employs *automatic trunk routing.* Users (subscribers, customers) are not required to define, or have knowledge of, the route to the *called party (destination user).*

destination office.   The office, such as a *switching center* or central office, that *routes* a *call* or *message* directly to a *destination user.* Also see *originating office.*

destination user.   A *user* designated to receive *source user information.* Normally the information is to be delivered during a particular *information transfer transaction.* Synonymous with *message sink* and with *sink user.* Also see *source user.*

destuffing.   The controlled deletion of *digits* from a *stuffed digital signal* to recover the original signal that existed prior to stuffing. The deleted data is *transmitted* via a separate low *traffic capacity time slot.* Synonymous with *negative justification; negative pulse stuffing.* Also see *bit stuffing; nominal bit stuffing rate.*

despotically synchronized network.   A *synchronized network* in which a unique *master clock* has the full power to control all other clocks in the network. Also see *democratically synchronized network; hierarchically synchronized network; oligarchically synchronized network.*

detectable element.   A *display element* that can be detected by a *pointer.* Also see *detectable group.*

detectable group.   A *display group* that can be detected by a *pointer.* Also see *detectable element.*

detecting system. See *error-detecting system.*

detection. The separation of a *modulating signal* from its *modulated carrier* in such a manner that only the positive portion of the *signal envelope* remains. See *automatic error detection; light-pen detection; passive detection; pitch detection; radio detection.*

detection and correction system. See *automatic error detection and correction system.*

detection and feedback. See *error-detection and feedback.*

detection combiner. See *postdetection combiner; predetection combiner.*

detection combining. See *predetection combining.*

detection discrimination. The ability of a *receiver* to distinguish, separate, identify, and *detect* a given *signal* or signal source from all other *incident* signals, *noise, interference,* or environmental effects. Also see *bearing discrimination; range discrimination.*

detection equipment. See *airport surface detection equipment.*

detection range. See *maximum detection range.*

detection resolution. In *communication systems,* the *precision* or *accuracy* with which *signal parameters* can be measured or determined. Signal parameters include *frequency, pulse width, phase, amplitude,* or *shape.* The resolution is expressed in terms of time and spatial aspects. Also see *range resolution.*

detection system. See *active detection system; passive detection system.*

detection-tracking. See *passive detection-tracking.*

detectivity. The reciprocal of *noise equivalent power (NEP),* i.e., $D = 1/\text{NEP}$, where NEP is usually measured in watts.

detector. A device responsive to the presence of a stimulus. See *background-limited infrared detector; coherent detector; external photoeffect detector; infrared point-source flash detector; internal photoeffect detector; optical detector; photodetector; photon detector; pitch detector; video optical detector.*

detector back-bias gain control circuit. A *circuit* that performs instantaneous *response automatic gain control* by operating on the *detector* rather than on the *intermediate frequency (IF) amplifier.*

detector bandwidth. See *postdetector bandwidth.*

detector coupling. See *fiber-detector coupling.*

detector dark resistance. See *infrared detector dark resistance.*

detector noise-limited operation. In *optical communication system operations,* the situation that occurs when the *amplitude* of *pulses,* rather than their *width,* limit the distance between *repeaters.* In this regime of operation, the losses are sufficient to *attenuate* the amplitude of the pulse to such an extent, in relation to the *detector noise* level, that an intelligent decision based on the presence or absence of a pulse in the *signal* is not possible. Also see *dispersion-limited operation.*

detector signal/noise ratio. See *postdetector signal/noise ratio.*

determination. See *isochrone determination; radio determination; radio position line determination.*

determination service. See *radio determination service.*

determination station. See *radio determination station.*

deterministic routing. A method of *switching* within a *network* in which the *routes* between a pair of *nodes* are decided (determined) in advance.

detonation. See *proximity fuze detonation.*

developmental station. See *experimental contract developmental station; experimental developmental station.*

deviation. See *frequency deviation; phase deviation.*

deviation angle. 1. The angular change in direction of a light ray after crossing the *interface* between two different *transmission media.* 2. The angle through which a *ray* of *light* is bent by *reflection* or *refraction.*

deviation ratio. In a *frequency modulated signaling system,* the ratio of the maximum *frequency* deviation to the maximum *modulating* frequency of the *system* under specified conditions.

device. See *active device; active infrared device; antisinging device; Bell integrated optical device; character display device; computer peripheral device; display device; fiber-optic interface device; incidental radiation device; infrared device; input-output (I-O) device; intelligent display device; logic device; low-power communication device; optoelectronic device; passive device; passive infrared device; pattern recognition device; photoconductive device; radio-wire integration (RWI) device; square-law device; telephone traffic metering device; trunk encryption device.*

device control character. A *control character* used for the control of ancillary, auxiliary, and peripheral devices associated with a *data processing, computer,* or *communication system.* For example, a *character* used to select a device from a set of devices or a character used to *switch* a device on or off.

device coordinate. In *display systems,* a coordinate in a coordinate system physically marked on a *display device* that identifies a physical location on the *display surface* of the display device; e.g., a *screen coordinate.* Also see *real-world coordinate; user coordinate.*

devitrification. The changing of glass from the vitreous state to a crystalline state, thus greatly changing most of its *optical* properties, usually for the worse. For example, reduced *light transmission* in *optical fibers* and *integrated optical circuits.*

dewpoint. The *temperature* at which air that is mixed with a given amount of water vapor (gas), usually expressed as partial pressure, begins to condense into droplets visible as fog. At the dewpoint, the relative humidity is 100%. At that temperature, the air cannot hold additional moisture in gaseous form. Dew forms, and, in effect, it rains.

DF. *Direction finder; direction finding.*

DFB laser. *Distributed feedback laser.*

DFSK. *Double-frequency-shift keying.*

diad. See *dibit.*

diagnostic program. A *computer program* that recognizes, locates, and explains either a *fault* in equipment, an *error* in input data, or a *mistake* in itself or in another computer program.

diagram. See *Brillouin diagram; circular polar diagram; logic diagram; polar diagram; radio coverage diagram; routing diagram; vertical coverage diagram.*

dial. 1. In *telephone systems,* a calling device on a *user* (subscriber, customer) instrument or on a *switchboard.* It is in the form of a rotatable disk that, when rotated an amount corresponding to a desired digit and released, generates *signals* that control equipment at an *automatic exchange* and allow any required *party number* connected to the automatic exchange to be obtained without the assistance of an *operator.* When rotated and released, it generates a sequence of *pulses* used to establish the *connection* corresponding to the sequence of generated numbers. The term dial is often used to designate or refer to all calling devices, including mechanical *keyboards,* touch keyboards, and *switch* panels, that generate signals used for establishing *telephone* connections. 2. Any device that generates *signals* used for selecting and establishing *connections.*   **3.** To use a device that generates signals used for establishing *connections.*   See *rotary dial.*

dialer.   See *card dialer; repertory dialer.*

dialing.   The act or process provided at a *telephone* instrument or *switchboard* that enables the *directory number* of a *called party* (subscriber, customer) to be inserted into an *automatically switched telephone system.*   Also see *loop-disconnect pulsing system.*   See *compressed dialing; destination dialing; direct distance dialing (DDD); direct outward dialing; network in-dialing (NID); push-button dialing; route dialing.*

dialing key.   In most *manually-operated telephone switchboards,* a *key* that must be actuated before *dialing* commences in order that the dial can be heard. The dialing key must not be restored until the dial has come to rest after dialing the last *digit.*   If it becomes necessary to *clear* and redial on the same *line,* the *operator* must restore the dialing key before reconnecting, otherwise the *dial tone* will not be heard in most systems.

dialing system.   See *long-distance direct-current (DC) dialing system.*

dial mode.   A manner of operating *data circuit-terminating equipment* so that *circuits* directly associated with *call* origination are connected to the *communication channel.*   Synonymous with *talk mode.*   Also see *data mode.*

dial service assistance (DSA) switchboard.   A *telephone switchboard* associated with *switching center* equipment to provide *operator* services such as *information, interception, conferencing,* and *precedence* calling assistance.

dial signaling.   *Signaling* in which *pulse trains* are *transmitted* to a *receiving terminal* to operate *automatic line selection* equipment.   The sequence of the *dial pulses* is determined by an *operator.*   The duration of the pulses is predetermined by equipment adjustments.

dial through.   A technique applicable to *access lines* and *circuits* that permits an outgoing *call* to be *dialed* by the *private branch exchange (PBX) user* after the PBX *operator* has established the initial *connection.*

dial tone.   In *telephone system operation,* an audible *signal* indicating that a *circuit* connected to an *automatic exchange* is ready for *dialing signals.*

diamagnetic.   Pertaining to a substance, such as bismuth or silver, that is always repelled by a magnet and has a *magnetic permeability* slightly less than that of air.   A length of diamagnetic material tends to take a position at right angles to the lines of *magnetic flux* when it is placed in a *magnetic field,* whereas *paramagnetic* material aligns itself parallel to the lines of magnetic flux.   Also see *ferromagnetic; paramagnetic.*

diameter.   See *beam diameter; fiber core diameter; fiber diameter.*

diametral cooperation index.   See *cooperation index.* Also see *drum factor.*

diathermy equipment.   See *medical diathermy equipment.*

dibit.   A group of two *bits.* The four possible states for a dibit are 00, 01, 10, and 11. Synonymous with *diad.*

dichroic.   Pertaining to the quality of *dichroism.*

dichroic filter.   An *optical filter* capable of *transmitting* all *frequencies* above a certain *cutoff frequency* and *reflecting* all lower frequencies, thus being either a *high-pass* or *low-pass filter.*

dichroism.   In *anisotropic* materials, the *absorption* of *light rays* propagating in only one particular plane relative to the crystalline axes of the material. As applied to *isotropic* materials, *dichroism* refers to the selective *reflection* and *transmission* of *light* as a function of *wavelength* regardless of the plane of *propagation.*   The *color* of such materials, as seen by *transmitted light,* varies with the thickness of the material examined.   Synonymous with *dichromatism; polychromatism.*

dichromatic radiation.   See *polychromatic radiation.*

dichromatism.   See *dichroism.*

dielectric.   Pertaining to material composed of atoms whose *electrons* are so tightly bound to the atomic nuclei that *electric currents* are negligible even under applied high *electric fields.*   That is, scarcely any electrons of the material are in the *conduction band;* most remain in the *valence band,* even when high electric fields are applied, thus qualifying the material to be called an insulator. *Conduction* currents in dielectrics are nearly zero.   Charges that might accumulate in one place tend to remain for relatively long periods of time.   Most *optical elements* and *optical fibers* are dielectric.   A transient *polarization* current occurs only when an electric field is applied or removed, due to dipole rotation and alignment and polarization.   Polarization and polarization currents are specified in *Maxwell's equations* by the *electric permittivity,* ϵ, of dielectric materials. Contrast with *conductor.*

dielectric coaxial cable.   See *air dielectric coaxial cable; foam dielectric coaxial cable.*

dielectric constant.   See *electric permittivity.*

dielectric film.   See *multilayer dielectric film.*

dielectric optical waveguide. See *slab-dielectric optical waveguide.*

dielectric waveguide. See *circular dielectric waveguide; doubly-cladded slab dielectric waveguide; slab dielectric waveguide.*

diel-guide feed antenna. An *antenna* with a cone of *dielectric* foam between the *antenna horn feeder* and the *subreflector.* The dielectric material confines the *rays* by total *internal reflection.* This results in low *spillover.* Another advantage is that the dielectric cone can support the subreflector and thus eliminate the need for the usual support legs.

difference. See *clock difference; phase difference; potential difference.*

difference gate. See *EXCLUSIVE-OR gate.*

differential encoding. *Data transmission encoding* using *phase-shift keying (PSK)* in which the *information* is not conveyed by the *phase* of the *signal,* but by the difference between phases of successive *symbols.* This eliminates the requirement for a phase reference at the *receiver.* Also see *relative phase telegraphy.*

differentially-coherent phase-shift keying (DCPSK). A method of *modulation* in which *information* is *encoded* in terms of *phase* changes rather than absolute phases. The *signal* is *detected* by comparing phases of adjacent *bits.* The *carrier pulses* are of constant *amplitude, frequency,* and duration, but are of different relative phase. In detection, a phase comparison is made of successive samples. Information is conveyed by the phase *transitions* between carrier and pulses rather than by the absolute phases of the pulses relative to a *synchronizing signal.*

differentially-encoded baseband. See *non-return-to-zero mark (NRZ-M).*

differential mode interference. **1.** *Interference* that causes a change in electric *potential difference* between one side of a *signal transmission path* and the other side. **2.** *Interference* resulting from an interference *electric current path* that coincides with the *signal path.*

differential modulation (DM). *Modulation* in which the choice of the *significant condition* for any *signal element* is dependent on the choice for the previous signal element. For example, *data modulation.*

differential phase-shift keying (DPSK). *Modulation* that is used for *digital transmission* in which each *signal element* is a change in the *phase* of the *carrier* with respect to its previous *phase angle.* DPSK systems are designed so that the carrier can assume only two different phase angles. Each change of phase of the signal element carries one *bit* of *information,* that is, the *bit rate* equals the *modulation rate.* If the number of recognizable phase angles is increased to 4, then 2 bits of information can be *encoded* into each signal element. Likewise, 8 identifiable phase angles can encode 3 bits in each signal element. The 2 bits (dibit) can be used to count from 0 to 3. Thus, it can represent 4 different *characters*. The 3 bits *(triad)* can be used to represent 8 different characters.

differential pulse code modulation (DPCM). A *phase code modulation (PCM)* used in *data transmission systems* in which *quantized* differences between successive samples are used for *transmission*. The *modulating signal* is *sampled*, and the difference between two successive samples is quantized and then *coded* into a defined number of equal-duration *binary digits*.

differential quantum efficiency. The slope at a point in an *output* versus *input* curve of a device, such as a *photodetector*. Changes in input energy or *power* that cause changes in output energy or power, are usually plotted with input as the abscissa and output as the ordinate. The differential quantum efficiency at any operating point is measured as a small change in output divided by the corresponding small change in input that caused the output change. Synonymous with *incremental quantum efficiency*.

differentiating circuit. An *electrical circuit*, with one *output* and one *input*, that operates in such a manner that the *output* is the time rate of change *(derivative)* of the *input signal*, that is, at any instant the ouptut signal value is proportional to the rate at which the signal is changing at that instant. Thus, if the input to the differentiating circuit is a square (rectangular) *wave (pulse)* the output is a short, high-amplitude pulse *(spike)*. The spikes corresponding to one square pulse are a pair of opposite polarity spikes. For a positive square pulse, the first spike will be positive and the second spike will be negative, each spike occurring when the pulse changes its value. See Figure D-3.

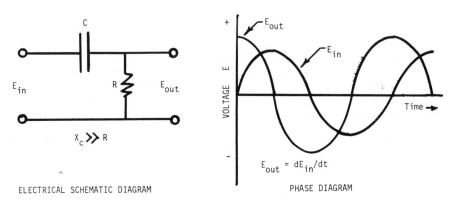

ELECTRICAL SCHEMATIC DIAGRAM   PHASE DIAGRAM

D-3. In the **differentiating circuit,** the *phase angle* of the *output voltage* leads the phase angle of the *input voltage* by nearly 90° *(electrical degrees)*.

differentiation. In the calculus, a process that determines the rate at which a mathematical function is changing with respect to a variable in the function. The function might describe a process or phenomenon. It is the reverse of *integration,* and it yields the slope of a curve as a function of the variables and other parameters. For example, if $f(x) = ax^2$, then the derivative of $f(x)$ is $f'(x) = 2ax$. At the point x_1 in the function, the slope of the function is equal to $2ax_1$. A *differentiating circuit* can perform the process, yielding the derivative of the *input* function. If the input to the circuit is a given *signal* as a function of time, the *output* of the differentiating circuit will be the time derivative of the input signal. The integral or a derivative may differ from the original function only by a constant. The derivative of an integral always yields the original function. Also see *integration.*

differentiator. A device that performs the process of *differentiation.* For example, in *analog systems,* a device that has an *output analog variable* that is the derivative of an *input analog variable* with respect to time or a variable other than the input variable. Also see *integrator.*

diffraction. **1.** The process by which the *propagation* of *radiant waves* or *lightwaves* are modified as the waves interact with *objects* or obstacles. Some of the *rays* are deviated from their path by *diffraction* at the objects, whereas other rays remain undeviated by diffraction at the objects. As the objects become small in comparison with the *wavelength,* the concepts of *reflection* and *refraction* become useless, and *diffraction* plays the dominant role in determining the redistribution of the rays following *incidence* upon the objects. Diffraction results from the deviation of light from the paths and *foci* prescribed by the rectilinear propagation laws of *geometrical optics.* Thus, even with a very small, distant source, some *light,* in the form of bright and dark bands, is found within a geometrical shadow because of the diffraction of the light at the edge of the object forming the shadow. *Diffraction gratings,* with spacings of the order of the wavelength of the incident light also cause diffraction that results in the formation of light and dark areas called "diffraction patterns." Such gratings can be ruled grids, spaced spots, or crystal lattice structures. **2.** The bending of *radio, sound,* or *lightwaves* around an object, barrier, or *aperture* edges.

diffraction grating. An array of fine, parallel, equally spaced *reflecting* or *transmitting* lines that mutually enhance the effects of *diffraction* at the edges of each so as to concentrate the *diffracted light* very close to a few directions characteristic of the spacing of the lines and the *wavelength* of the diffracted light. If I is the *incidence angle,* D the angle of diffraction, S the center-to-center distance between successive rulings, and N the *diffraction grating spectral order,* the wavelength is:

$$L = (S/N) \, (\sin I + \sin D)$$

If there is a large number of narrow, close, equally spaced rulings upon a *transparent* or *reflecting substrate,* the *grating* will be capable of *dispersing incident light* into its *frequency* component *spectrum.*

diffraction grating spectral order.   The *integers* that distinguish the different directions of each member of a family of *light rays* emerging from a *diffraction grating;* e.g., when a *beam* of parallel rays of *monochromatic light* passes through a diffraction grating.   The emergent rays that have remained undeviated belong to the zero spectral order, but the light flux in the family of deviated rays that emerge after diffraction at the grating exhibit pronounced maxima, along well-defined and enumerable directions, on each side of the undeviated beams. The integers that are assigned to distinguish these directions mark the spectral orders. Also see *diffraction grating; grating chromatic resolving power.*

diffraction region.   The region that is beyond the *radio* or *radar horizon.*

diffused waveguide.   See *planar diffused waveguide.*

diffusant.   *Dopant* introduced into a material by the process of *diffusion.*

diffuse density.   The logarithm to the base 10 of the reciprocal of *diffuse transmittance.*

diffused optical waveguide.   An *optical-wavelength electromagnetic waveguide* consisting of a *substrate* into which a *dopant* has been diffused to a depth of a few *microns,* thus producing a lower *refractive index* on the outside. The result is an optical *waveguide* with a *graded* refractive index. *Diffused optical waveguides* can be made from single crystals of zinc selenide or cadmium sulfide. Dopants include cadmium for the zinc selenide and zinc for the cadmium sulfide. See *strip-loaded diffused optical waveguide.*

diffuse reflectance.   1. The ratio of *light flux reflected* diffusely in all directions to the total flux at *incidence, specular reflection* excluded. **2.** The *reflectance* of a sample relative to a perfectly diffusing, perfectly reflecting standard, with a 45° *incidence angle* and observation along the perpendicular to the surface. Synonymous with *total diffuse reflectance.*

diffuse reflection.   *Reflection* of an *incident,* perhaps *coherent,* group of *light rays* from a rough surface, such that different parts of the same group are reflected in different directions, as *Snell's laws* of *reflection* and *refraction* are microscopically obeyed at each undulation of the rough surface. Diffuse reflection prevents the formation of a clear *image* of the *light* source or of the *illuminated object.* Contrast with *specular reflection.* Also see *reflection.*

diffuse transmission.   The *propagation* of *lightwaves* in a *transmission medium* with a high level of *attenuation* resulting from *diffusion* of the waves. Clear *images* are not *transmitted.* Diffuse transmission is not desirable in *optical waveguides,* since excessive attenuation of *signals* would result. Contrast with *spectral transmission.*

diffuse transmittance. **1.** The *transmittance* measured with *diffusely incident flux.* **2.** The ratio of the *flux diffusely transmitted* in all directions to the total *incident flux.*

diffusion. In *electromagnetic wave transmission,* the deviation of different *rays* of different bundles or *beams* due to obstacles in their path. *Diffusion* can be forward, sideways, or backward, depending on *incidence angles* with the scattering surfaces and their *transmission* and *reflection coefficients,* and on the relative magnitudes and directions of the *reflection* components. For example, fog, frosted glass, a rough surface, the *ionosphere,* or occlusions in a *transmission medium,* can diffuse a *light* beam.

digit. A *symbol, numeral,* or *graphic character* that represents an *integer.* For example, one of the *decimal characters* 0 to 9, or one of the *binary characters* 0 or 1. In a given numeration system, the number of allowable different *digits,* including zero, is always equal to the *radix.* A digit is usually a member selected from a finite set of whole numbers, that is, *integers.* A digit might be represented by a *signal element.* In *storage,* a digit may be represented by a specified physical condition, such as the direction of *magnetic* polarization of a ferrite core. Synonymous with *numeric character.* See *access digit; binary digit; check digit; decimal digit; n-ary digit.*

digital. Pertaining to representation of *data* or physical quantities by means of *digits* or *discrete* quantities. Strings of *light pulses,* in temporal or spatial sequence in an *optical fiber,* is an example of digital data generation and transmission. Contrast with *analog.* Also see *discrete.*

digital alphabet. **1.** A *coded character set* in which the *characters* of an *alphabet* have a one-to-one relationship with their *coded* representations. **2.** A table of correspondences between *characters* or functions and the *bit* patterns or combinations that are used to represent them. Also see *code character; code set.*

digital block. In *communication system hardware,* a set of *multiplexed* equipment that includes one or more *data channels* and associated circuits. *Digital blocks* are usually designated in terms of *signaling speed,* for example, a 134.5 *baud* digital block.

digital carrier-interrupt signaling. *Telephone system signaling* in which *direct-current (DC) pulses* are used to *key* a *carrier* on and off.

digital combining. A method of interleaving *digital data signals* that are either *synchronous* or *asynchronous* without converting the *data* into an *analog signal.* The combining is accomplished by interleaving *baseband,* independently *clocked,* digital data into one combined *data stream* containing the *information* from the individual independently clocked sources. Digital data containing timing corrections for these sources are added to the data stream. Also see *diversity combiner.*

digital compression. See *digital speech compression.*

digital computer. A *computer* in which *discrete* representations of *data* are used. The digital computer operates on discrete data by performing arithmetic and logic processes on these data using *combinational circuits (logic elements).* Accuracy is not limited by the precision with which parts are manufactured. Also see *analog computer.* See *asynchronous digital computer; synchronous digital computer.*

digital converter. See *analog-to-digital converter.*

digital data. **1.** *Data* represented in *digital* form; e.g., a sequence of *light pulses* in an *optical fiber.* **2.** *Data* represented by *discrete* or *integral* values or conditions, as opposed to *analog data.* **3.** A *discrete* representation of a *quantized* value of a variable, that is, the representation of a number by *digits,* perhaps with *special characters* and the *space character.*

digital data channel. A one-way *path* for *data signals* that includes a *digital channel* and associated *interface equipment* at each end.

digital data switching. *Switching* in which *connections* are established by operations directly on *digital signals* without converting them to *analog signals.*

digital encoder. See *analog-to-digital (A–D) converter.*

digital error. An inconsistency between the existing representation of a *digit* and the representation that it should be. For example, a single-digit inconsistency between a *signal* actually received and the signal that should have been received, or between a digit stored at a given location and the digit read from that location. Also see *bit-count integrity; bit inversion; character-count integrity.*

digital filter. A *filter* that substitutes a *programmed digital* process for an *analog filter network* or device; e.g., a filter in an *optical system.* Digital filters have the advantages of *accuracy,* stability, reliability, and flexibility, although not simplicity, over normal (analog) filters. In their simplest form, digital filters consist of *sampling circuits, analog-digital converters,* digital pattern filters, or *comparators, digital-analog converters,* and first-order *hold circuits.* Accuracy depends on pattern-filter *word length,* not on *electric circuit R–L–C parameters. Response* can be changed simply by changing parameters in the *program,* such as the filter word pattern. Also see *discrete-time filtering system.*

digital frequency modulation. The *transmission* of *digital data* using *frequency modulation* of a *carrier.* For example, the modulation performed in *binary frequency-shift keying (FSK).*

digital information link. See *tactical digital information link (TADIL).*

digital interface. See *high-level digital interface.*

digital interpolation. See *digital speech interpolation.*

digital mark-space signaling. A *telephone system binary signaling* scheme in which signaling *pulses* or *bits* may be *time-division multiplexed* into the *output data stream* of a *digital vocoder.*

digital modulation. The process of varying one or more *parameters* of a *carrier wave* as a function of two or more finite and *discrete* states of a *signal.* For example, the *ternary signal coding modulation* technique in which two independent *bipolar coding* sequences are interleaved. The digital modulation *power spectrum* nulls at a *direct-current (DC)* level and again at one-half the *bit rate.* This requires less *bandwidth* than *non-return-to-zero (NRZ) signals* and provides better *low-frequency response* than *return-to-zero (RZ)* signals. The main disadvantage in using digital modulation is its low tolerance of poor *signal-to-noise* conditions, that is, low signal-to-noise ratios. Digital modulation can also be accomplished by *coding* the *data,* delaying it two *bit* intervals, and then adding.

digital signal. 1. A nominally discontinuous electrical *signal* that changes from one state to another in *discrete* steps. 2. A *signal* that is timewise discontinuous, is *discrete,* and can assume a limited set of values. The electrical signal could be changed in its *amplitude* or polarity. *Analog signals* may be *converted* to digital signals by *sampling* and *quantizing.* See *n-ary digital signal.*

digital signaling. A method of *transmitting signaling information* over a *digital transmission system.* Information is usually transmitted as *characters coded* as digital patterns.

digital slip. When two *data streams* that are *asynchronous* with each other are compared in *phase,* the situation that occurs when one of the data streams gains or loses a digit interval with respect to the other data stream.

digital speech interpolation. The utilization of inactivity periods or constant periods in *digital speech transmission* in order to increase the efficiency and lower operational cost. The constant (inactive) periods of a *pulse code modulation signal* are compressed, transmitted, and reconstituted using complementary *algorithms* on both ends. Synonymous with *digital interpolation; digital compression.* Also see *analog speech interpolation.*

digital switch. *Switching equipment* designed, designated, or used to connect *circuits* between *users* for *transmission* of *digital signals.*

digital switching. A process in which *connections* are made by using *digital signals* without *converting* them to *analog signals.* Selection and decision-making are performed using *combinational circuits.* The interconnection of *input* and *output lines* is accomplished with a matrix that transfers digital signals between the lines. See *tactical automatic digital switching (TADS).*

digital synchronization. An erroneous term for *bit synchronous operation.*

digital-to-analog (D–A) converter. A device that *converts* a *digital input signal* to an *analog output signal* representing equivalent *information.* It converts the electrical *pulses* that represent *digital data* to *analog voltages* or *electric currents* thereby converting digital data (representation) to analog data (representation). Also see *analog-to-digital (A–D) converter;* Figure A-7.

digital transmission group. A number of *voice channels,* a number of *data channels,* or both, the data in which are combined into a single *digital data stream* for *transmission* using various *communication* means or *transmission media.*

digital voice transmission. The *transmission* of *voice analog signals* that have been *converted* into *digital signals.* For example, the transmission of voice analog signals using *pulse code modulation (PCM)* of the *analog signals.*

digital voltage level. The peak-to-peak *amplitude* excursion or height of a *digital signal* usually expressed in volts or millivolts.

digitize. To *convert* an *analog signal* into a *digital signal.* For example, to express or represent in a digital form *data* that are not *discrete* data, thereby obtaining a digital (numeric) representation of the magnitude of a physical quantity from an *analog* representation of that magnitude.

digitized speech. See *digitized voice.*

digitized voice. Electrical *analog* (continuously variable) *speech signals* that have been *converted* into *discrete* (separate *pulses* or *voltage* levels) for *digital transmission.* *Pulse-code modulation (PCM)* may be used to digitize speech signals. Synonymous with *digitized speech.*

digitizer. 1. A device that converts the position of a *stylus* on a surface into *coordinate data.* For example, the *faceplate* on a *coherent bundle* of *optical fibers* connected to *digital* logic that generates digital data corresponding to the cartesian coordinate position of the fiber or group of fibers in the bundle currently or momentarily illuminated by a *light pen;* or a *tablet* and stylus that generate coordinate data according to the position of the stylus on the tablet. 2. A device that *converts* an *analog signal* to a *digital signal.*

digit position. The position in time or space into which a representation of a *digit* may be placed. For example, a position occupied by a digit in a *time slot* of a *data stream,* a position occupied by a digit in a *register* or *storage* unit, a position occupied by a digit in a printed line, or a position occupied by a digit in a number.

digit time slot. In a *bit stream,* the time interval allocated to or occupied by a single *digit.*

dimension.   See *recorded spot x-dimension; recorded spot y-dimension.*

dimensional stability.   The capability of an *optical fiber, bundle,* or *cable* to retain its original dimension when stimulated by environmental factors such as heat, humidity, and water immersion.   See *fiber dimensional stability.*   See Figure D-4.

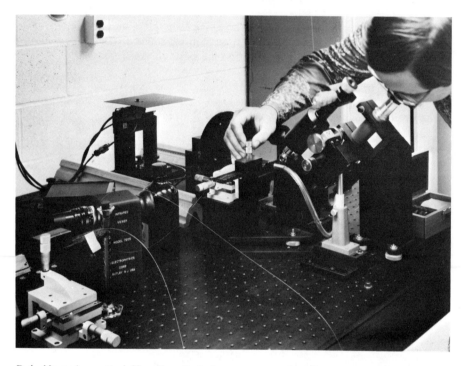

D-4. Measuring *optical fibers* for physical *parameters* such as **dimensional stability.**   (Copyright 1979, Corning Glass Works.   Reprinted by permission from Corning Glass Works, Telecommunications Products Department.)

dimpled connector.   An *optical cable connector* in which the *fiber* end-surfaces lie in a concave surface at the cable end.   Thus, *divergent rays* from a *driving light source* can enter each fiber within its individual, and perhaps small, *acceptance angle.*   This arrangement insures increased *coupling.*

DINA jammer.   A barrage jammer in which direct noise amplification (DINA) is used.

diode.   See *double heterojunction diode; five-layer four-heterojunction diode; four-heterojunction diode; injection laser diode; large optical-cavity diode; laser diode; light-emitting diode; monorail double-heterojunction diode; pin diode;*

photodiode; positive-intrinsic-negative diode; restricted edge-emitting diode; stripe laser diode; superluminescent diode (SLD).

diode coupler. See *avalanche photodiode coupler; laser diode coupler; light-emitting diode coupler; positive-intrinsic-negative photodiode coupler.*

diode laser. See *semiconductor laser.*

diopt. See *diopter.*

dioptic power. The refractive *power* of an *optical element* expressed in *diopters.*

diopter. A unit of *refractive power* of a *lens* or *prism,* equal to the reciprocal of the *focal length* in *meters.* Abbreviated as *diopt.*

dip. See *at-the-dip.*

diphase modulation. See *conditioned diphase modulation.*

diplexer. A *multicoupler* device that permits the *connection* and simultaneous use of several devices, such as several *transmitters* or several *receivers,* to a common or single device, such as an *antenna* or *channel.* The diplexer itself does not permit simultaneous *transmission* and *reception.* It does allow the simultaneous transmission of two or more *signals* using the same *circuit,* such as an *antenna feed,* without *interference.* Also see *duplexer.*

diplexing. See *radar diplexing.*

diplex operation. The simultaneous one-way *transmission* or *reception* of two or more independent *signals* using a common element, such as a single *antenna* or *channel.* For example, the operation of two or more *radio transmitters* on different *frequencies* using one antenna. Also see *duplex operation.*

diplex telegraphy. See *four-frequency diplex telegraphy.*

dipole antenna. A straight, center-fed, one-half *wavelength antenna.* See *half-wave dipole antenna; lossless half-wave dipole antenna; multielement dipole antenna.*

dipulse coding. The *coding* of 1's and 0's in a *message* in such a manner that one full cycle of a *square wave* is *transmitted* when the message bit is a 1. Nothing is transmitted when the message bit is a 0. In dipulse coding, a *binary* 1 is represented by a positive *pulse* followed by a negative pulse in the same bit period (interval). No pulse is generated for a 0. A dipulse signal can be generated by *encoding* the data into 50% *return-to-zero (RZ) unipolar data* and sending it through an *AND gate* with the *system clock pulse.* This RZ *bit stream* is then delayed one half-bit period (interval) and added to the undelayed RZ stream. This produces the final dipulse waveform. The dipulse *power spectrum* is similar to that of *biphase* except dipulse has a *pulse repetition rate* equal to the *bit rate.*

direct access.   In *data processing* operations, pertaining to the entering of *data* into or the obtaining of data from a *storage* device in such a way that the process depends only on the location of that data and not on the location of data previously entered or obtained.

direct call.   A *call* that is handled by a *facility* that avoids the use of *addresses* or *address selection signals* by having the *network* interpret the call request signal as an *instruction* to establish a *connection* with a single destination address previously designated by the *user.*   This facility may reduce *call set-up time.*   No special priority is implied over other users of the network in establishing a connection. The designated address is usually assigned for an agreed period. Synonymous with *call-without-selection signal.*

direct clock control.   In *digital data transmission, clock control* in which a *clock* at twice the *modulation rate* is used, rather than a higher modulation rate, such as 4, 8, or 128 times the modulation rate as is done in *indirect clock control.*

direct coupling.   The *coupling* or *conduction* of *signals* or *noise* from one *conductor* to another by means of a direct *hardwire* contact or an *optical fiber* to fiber direct *interface.*   Direct coupling can be achieved in *optical waveguides,* such as *optical fibers* and *integrated optical circuits,* by the transfer of *electromagnetic energy* from *source* to *guide,* or from guide to guide, by *butting* the source directly up against the *sink.*   For example, butting an *LED* up against a fiber or *fiber bundle.*   The input *coupling coefficient* by *direct coupling* is proportional to the square of the *numerical aperture,* with values ranging from 0.14 to 0.50.   Also see *lens coupling.*

direct current (DC).   An *electric current* of constant direction (polarity). If the current is of constant strength it is called *stationary direct current.*   If it changes periodically it is called *pulsating direct current.*   See *pulsating direct current; stationary direct current.*

direct-current (DC) dialing system.   See *long-distance direct-current (LDDC) dialing system.*

direct-current (DC) patch bay.   A *patch bay* in which *direct-curent (DC) circuits* are grouped.

direct-current (DC) restoration circuit.   A *circuit* that forces a *voltage* level back to its normal value after it has deviated from the normal level because of some *disturbance, interference, malfunction,* or excessive *signal input* (overdrive). For example, *infrared scanning systems* need to be equipped with such circuits to reduce *blanking* by *laser pulses.*

direct-current (DC) signaling (DX). In *telephone systems,* a method in which the *signaling circuit E&M leads* use the same pair of *conductors* as the *voice circuit.* No *filter* is required to separate the *signaling currents* from the *voice currents* during *transmission* because of the great disparity in *frequency.* Synonymous with *DX signaling.* Also see *composite signaling (CX).*

direct-current (DC) telegraph system. See *neutral direct-current (DC) telegraph system.*

direct distance dialing (DDD). A *telephone* service that enables a *user* (subscriber, customer) to *dial* directly the *telephones* that are outside the local area without the assistance of an *operator.* Synonymous with *subscriber trunk dialing (STD).*

directed-beam scan. See *directed scan.*

directed net. A *radio net* in which no *station* other than the *net control station* may *communicate* with any other station except for the *transmission* of *emergency, urgent,* or *distress messages,* without first obtaining permission of the net control station. The directed net is established by the net control station. The net control station may restore the net to a *free net.* Also see *free net.*

directed scan. In *display systems,* a technique in which *display elements, display groups,* or *display images* are generated, recorded, or displayed in any sequence, as directed by an *operator,* a *computer program,* or a program stored in the *display device.* Synonymous with *directed-beam scan; random scan.* Contrast with *flying-spot scan; raster scan.*

direction. See *backward direction; forward direction; scanning direction.* Also see *heading.*

directional antenna. An *antenna* that *radiates* or receives *electromagnetic* energy in such a manner that more energy is radiated in, or received from, some directions than others. The directional antenna is capable of *transmitting,* or *receiving, radio signals* with greater *power* in certain directions and lesser or zero power in other directions. Antenna radiated *power* transmission and reception sensitivity, a *vector* quantity, is confined to a given solid angle. Also see *omnidirectional antenna.*

directional coupler. 1. A *transmission coupling* device for obtaining separate samples, through a known *coupling loss* introduced by the sampling device used for measuring purposes, of either the forward *(incident)* or the backward *(reflected)* wave in a *transmission line.* A directional coupler may be used to excite either a forward or backward wave in the transmission line. A unidirectional coupler has available *terminals* or connections for sampling only one direction of transmission. A bidirectional coupler has terminals for sampling signals traveling in both directions. 2. Two *waveguides coupled* in such a manner that a portion of the energy fed into one end of either guide is *transferred* to only one end of the other guide. A portion of the energy fed into the other end of the first guide is transferred to the other end of the second guide. Also see *coupling.* See *optical directional coupler; optoelectronic directional coupler.*

directional signaling system. A *signaling system* in which the *signals* are *transmitted* with increased intensity or *power density* in the range of a small (narrow) solid angle. For example, by means of a *narrow-beam searchlight*, a *spot-light*, or a *directional antenna.* Also see *omnidirectional signaling system.*

directional transmission. The concentration of *electromagnetic wave* energy of an *antenna* or *light source* in a given direction rather than being spread in many or all directions. Directional transmission may be accomplished by such devices as *lasers, collimators, parabolic reflectors,* or *mirrors.* For example, directional *transmission* may be accomplished by a *parabolic antenna* that transmits electromagnetic energy in a *narrow beam* (parallel rays), or by an *antenna array* designed to *transmit* all of its *power* seaward.

direction finder. (DF). A device that indicates or measures the *bearing* of a *source* of *electromagnetic radiation* from a given reference direction and from a given point. If the true, magnetic, grid, or relative bearings of an electromagnetic source from two or more known points can be determined, the position of the source can be determined provided the source is not on the same line as the known points. Conversely, if the bearings to two or more sources of known location are measured from an unknown point, the position of the unknown point can be determined. The former method of direction finding is known as *intersection* and the latter is known as *resection.* Either method is considered as *triangulation.* Also see *direction finding (DF).*

direction finding (DF). The process of determining the *bearing* of a *source* of *electromagnetic radiation.* Two or more bearings can be used for such purposes as *fixing* the point at which the bearings are taken, or fixing a source of radiation. Coupled with time and distance, the velocity and acceleration of sources and points of measure can also be determined. With two or more stations, a fix can be made on a source of radiation. If a *station* (requesting station) position is to be determined, it can request its bearing from another station. Direction finding may make use of any *vector* quantities that can be received or transmitted, such as *electromagnetic waves, electrostatic fields, magnetic fields, sound waves,* pressure gradients, water waves, vibrations, and gravitational fields. Also see *direction finder (DF).* See *radio direction finding (RDF); simultaneous direction finding.*

direction-finding (DF) base line. The line joining two or more *direction-finding stations,* used as a base for determining the *bearings,* and hence position, of a *transmitter* by *intersection.* The base line is chosen for maximum *triangulation* accuracy and reception advantage. *Groundwave, VHF, UHF,* and *SHF* direction finding (receiving) stations need to be as close as possible to the area of the transmitter whose location is to be determined. *Skywave* and *HF* stations can be further away from the transmitter whose location is to be determined. UHF and SHF stations practically need *line-of-sight* contact with the unknown transmitter. Also see Figure I-7.

direction-finding (DF) equipment. See *radio direction-finding equipment.*

direction-finding (DF) message. In *distress* and *rescue communications,* a *message* that is sent immediately after the *distress message.* This permits *direction-finding stations* to *fix* the position of the requesting station. The message is repeated as frequently as required. Specific procedures are established in international standards. For example, in *radiotelegraph* and *radiotelephone* procedure, two *dashes* of approximately 10 seconds each followed by the station's *call sign* are sent. In *voice transmission,* suitable *signals* followed by the station's call sign or other identification are sent.

direction-finding (DF) picket. A ship, aircraft, or vehicle with DF equipment aboard that is stationed at a distance from an area, population, or force, to provide a DF capability to elements within the area, population, or force, or to elements that need the DF capability to reach the area, population, or force. For example, a DF station outside an army area, a DF *aircraft station* near an air force in flight, or a DF *ship station* near a fleet.

direction-finding (DF) recorder. See *airborne direction-finding recorder.*

direction-finding (DF) service. A service that is established for the purpose of providing *bearing* (direction, course) or position information to a *transmitting* or a *receiving station.* *Direction-finding stations* may operate singly or in pairs, providing bearing, direction, course, or position *information* to requesting stations, such as *ship stations, aircraft stations,* or *mobile land stations.*

direction-finding (DF) station. See *radio direction-finding station.*

direction-finding unit. See *airborne direction-finding unit.*

directive gain. In *radiation* from a *light source* or an *electromagnetic wave antenna,* the ratio of 4π times the *power* delivered per *unit solid angle (steradians)* in a given direction to the power delivered to 4π steradians, i.e., total power in all directions. The directive gain is usually expressed in *decibels,* as 10 times the logarithm to base 10 of the preceding ratio. This yields the gain in a given direction relative to an *isotropic antenna,* i.e., one that radiates equal power density in all directions. The electromagnetic power delivered to 4π steradians is the total power radiated. For *optical fiber coupling,* all power should be delivered in a small angle (i.e., a narrow *beam*), resulting in an extremely high directive gain. Also see *antenna gain; high-gain antenna.*

directivity pattern. A diagram that relates *power density, electric field strength,* or *magnetic field strength* to direction from an *antenna* at a constant distance from the antenna. The patterns are normally *polar plots* in the horizontal plane, but may also be three dimensional, and usually refer to planes or the surface of a cone containing the antenna. They are usually normalized to the maximum value of the power density or field strengths (electric or magnetic). Also see *main lobe; radiation pattern.* See Figure D-5.

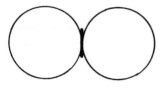

VERTICAL DIRECTIVITY PATTERN   HORIZONTAL PATTERN   HORIZONTAL OR VERTICAL DIRECTIVITY
VERTICAL DIPOLE ANTENNA   VERTICAL DIPOLE ANTENNA   PATTERN OF A PARABOLIC ANTENNA

D-5. The **directivity pattern** shows the distribution of *electromagnetic* energy *radiated* by an *antenna* as a function of direction.

direct line. In *telephone system operation,* a *line* connecting two *switchboards* that does not pass through an intervening *exchange* or an intervening *switchboard.*

directly connected station. In a *communication network,* a *station* connected to another station by means of a *dedicated circuit* or by means of a *direct line.*

direct mode. In a *radionavigation system,* the operation or use of the several *transmitters* of the *radionavigation service* as a single *system* without consideration of the value of individual transmitters as *radio beacons* for *direction finding.* Also see *indirect mode.*

director. See *telephone exchange director.*

director of communications-electronics. See *theater director of communications-electronics.*

directory. In *communication system operations,* a list of *users* (customers, subscribers) whose *end instruments* are connected to an *exchange.* The directory usually contains only essential information to assist in identifying the users, such as their titles or appointments, addresses, and their numbers. Directories are circulated or distributed to the users. Copies are also kept at the exchange or *switchboard. Alphanumeric symbols* are used to identify uniquely each user (equipment, process, person, or program) in a *communication network.* The sequence of entries in the directory may be alphabetical by name, by title, by organization, or by area. Often it is a combination of these. Some directories are arranged to allow for memorization or deduction of entries. In a *fixed directory* the number assigned to each user remains fixed regardless of the location of that user. This feature allows freedom of movement of users without directory changes and serves as an aid to calling parties. In an *appointment directory* each number designates the appointment, title, function, or assignment of that user. Personnel changes do not affect the updating of such a directory though reorganizations do affect it. See *appointment directory; deducible directory; field directory; fixed directory; inverted directory; routing directory; telephone directory.*

directory service. In *telephone system operation,* a service in which *calls* may be placed and answered not necessarily by number. The *caller* describes the *called party* to the *operator,* referring to location, function, title, name, organization, services needed, or other matters. For example, a service that responds to a call for police, fire, medical, rescue, the mayor, or other important persons or services, without the operator referring the calling party to the *information operator* who will only furnish a number.

direct outward dialing (DOD). A *telephone system service* in which outgoing *calls* are placed directly by *dialing* an initial *digit (access digit)* and then the desired number without the assistance of an *operator.*

direct ray. A *ray* of *electromagnetic radiation* that follows the *path* of least possible *propagation* time between a *transmitting antenna (source)* and a *receiving antenna (sink).* The least time path is not always the shortest distance path. Also see *direct wave.*

direct recording. *Facsimile recording* in which a visible record or *image* is produced without subsequent processing in *response* to the *received signals.*

direct-sequence modulation. In *spread-spectrum systems, modulation* in which a sequence of *binary pulses* is used to directly modulate a *carrier,* usually by *phase-shift keying.* Synonymous with *direct-spread modulation.* See *frequency-hopper direct-sequence modulation.*

direct-spread modulation. See *direct-sequence modulation.*

direct wave. 1. A wave that arrives at a point via a direct path through the *transmission medium* without *reflection* or *scattering* from surrounding objects, including the earth, *ionosphere,* or surrounding objects. It may be refracted by the *atmosphere.* 2. A *wave* that travels directly between the *transmitting antenna (source)* and *receiving antenna (sink)* without *reflecting* from any object. The direct wave usually consists of *direct rays.* Also see *direct ray; indirect wave; surface wave.*

direct working. In *radio communication net* operation, the direct two-way *transmission* of *messages* between pairs of *stations* or from any one station to a group of stations of the same or other *net.*

direct-working local net.   In *radio communication local net* operation, the direct *transmission* of *messages* between *stations* or from one station to a group of stations in the same (local) *net.*

disabling signal.   A *signal* that prevents the occurrence of a specific event that normally would or could occur if the *signal* were not present.   Also see *enabling signal.*

disabling tone.   A selected tone that is *transmitted* over a *communication path* to control equipment that is normally used to place an *echo suppressor* in a non-operative condition during *data transmission* over a *telephone circuit.*

disaster communications.   See *distress communications.*

DISC.   *Disconnect command.*

discernible signal.   See *minimum discernible signal.*

discipline.   See *circuit discipline.*

disconnect.   In *telephony,* the *release* of a *switched circuit,* that is, the disassociation of two *stations* or of a *calling party* and a *called party* after a *call* is *finished.*

disconnect command (DISC).   In a *data communication network,* an unnumbered *command* used to terminate the operational *mode* previously established.   It is used to inform the *secondary station* that the *primary station* is suspending operation.   No *information field* is permitted with the DISC command.   Prior to instituting the command, the secondary station confirms the acceptance of the DISC by the *transmission* of a *response.*   Previously *transmitted frames* that are unacknowledged when this command is instituted remain unacknowledged.

disconnecting switch.   See *fuse disconnecting switch.*

disconnection.   See *line disconnection.*

disconnect switch.   In a *power system,* a *switch* used to close, open, or change the *connections* in a *circuit* or *system.*   For example, for isolating purposes.   It may not have an interrupting capacity rating since it is not used to interrupt a circuit that is bearing or conducting an *electric current.*   It is intended to be operated only after the circuit has been opened by some other means.   Also see *interrupting switch.*

disconnect system.   See *loop disconnect system.*

discontinuity.   See *optical impedance discontinuity.*

discrete. Pertaining to distinct, separable elements. For example, pertaining to the representation of *data* by distinct elements, such as *pulses, bits, bytes,* and *characters* or pertaining to physical quantities that have only distinct *integral* values. Also see *analog; digital.*

discrete-time filtering system. A *filtering system* in which *input* and *output signals* change only at *discrete* instants. They do not vary continuously. The filtering system may be modeled by the user of difference equations. Also see *digital filter.*

discrete-time system. A *system* in which *input* and *output signals* change only at *discrete* instants. They do not vary continuously. The system may be modeled by the use of difference equations. Also see *continuous time system.*

discrimination. See *bearing discrimination; detection discrimination; range discrimination.*

discrimination circuit. See *video discrimination circuit.*

discriminator. A *circuit* that extracts the desired *signal* from an incoming *frequency-modulated wave* by changing *frequency* variations into *amplitude* variations. See *telegraph discriminator.*

disengagement. See *successful disengagement.*

disengagement attempt. The process by which one or more *users* interact with a *communiction system* in order to end a *call,* an *access success,* or an established access.

disengagement denial. *Disengagement* that is prevented (by design or malfunction) by a *communication system* for an excessive period of time. Disengagement denial may result from either a valid system action or a *system malfunction,* whereas *disengagement failure* is a result of system malfunction only.

disengagement-denial probability. The *disengagement-denial ratio* measured using acceptable statistical sampling techniques and criteria. Also see *disengagement-denial ratio.*

disengagement-denial ratio. The ratio of the number of *disengagement attempts* that result in *disengagement denial* to the total number of disengagement attempts counted during a measurement period. The ratio can be converted to a percentage by multiplying by 100. Also see *disengagement denial; disengagement-denial probability.*

disengagement failure. The failure of a *disengagement attempt* to return the *circuit* of the participating *user* to the *idle state* within a specified *maximum dis-*

engagement time. Disengagement failure is a result of *system malfunction* only, whereas *disengagement denial* may result from either valid system action or system malfunction. Also see *successful disengagement.*

disengagement originator. In a *communication system,* the functional entity that is responsible for initiating a particular *disengagement attempt.* A disengagement attempt can be initiated by either the *source user* or the *destination user.* In the case of systems with *preemption* the *communication system* itself can originate a disengagement. Also see *access originator.*

disengagement phase. In a *communication system,* the third *phase* of an *information transaction* and the phase during which *disengagement success* occurs. Also see *access phase; information transfer phase; successful disengagement.*

disengagement request. A *control signal* issued by a *disengagement originator* for the purpose of initiating a *disengagement attempt.* Also see *successful disengagement.*

disengagement success. A *disengagement attempt* that results in success.

disengagement success ratio. The ratio of the number of *disengagement attempts* that result in *disengagement success* to the total number of disengagement attempts. The ratio can be converted to a percentage by multiplying by 100. Also, the disengagement success ratio plus the *disengagement denial ratio* equals 1. Therefore, only one or the other ratio needs to be measured if the total number of disengagement attempts are counted.

disengagement time. The elapsed time between the start of a *disengagement attempt* and *disengagement success.* See *maximum disengagement time.*

disjoint signals. *Signals* that are not overlapping, coincident, or superimposed in time or in space. For example, *frequency-division multiplexed signals* and *time-division multiplexed signals* are disjoint in the *time domain,* whereas *space-division multiplexed signals* are disjoint in the *space domain.*

disjunction gate. See *OR gate.*

disk. See *optical disk; optical video disk; shared disk.*

disparity. In *pulse code modulation (PCM),* the *digital* (algebraic) sum of a set of *signal elements.* If there are as many positive elements as there are negative elements the disparity will be zero and there will be no cumulative or drifting polarization. Also see *paired-disparity code; pulse-code modulation.*

disparity binary code. See *unit disparity binary code.*

disparity code.   See *paired disparity code.*

dispatch time.   See *message dispatch time.*

dispersal.   See *frequency dispersal.*

dispersion.   1. The process by which *rays* of *light* of different *wavelength* are deviated angularly by different amounts; e.g., as with *prisms* and *diffraction gratings.*   2. Phenomena that cause the *refractive index* and other *optical* properties of a *transmission medium* to vary with *wavelength.*   Dispersion also refers to the *frequency* dependence of any of several *parameters,* for example, in the process by which an *electromagnetic signal* is distorted because the various frequency components of that signal have different propagation characteristics and paths. Thus, the components of a complex *radiation* are *dispersed* or separated on the basis of some characteristic.   A *prism* disperses the components of *white light* by deviating each wavelength a different amount.   For example, 2.5 nsec/km might be a maximum allowable dispersion for an 18.7 Mbit/sec pulse repetition rate with 10-km repeater spacing.   3. The allocation of *circuits* between two points over more than one geographic or physical route.   Synonymous with *route diversity.* See *chromatic dispersion; fiber dispersion; material dispersion; modal dispersion; optical multimode dispersion; pulse dispersion; waveguide dispersion.*

dispersion attenuation.   See *optical dispersion attenuation.*

dispersion attenuation factor.   A factor that, when multiplied by an initial value of *optical power,* yields the value of optical power at another point in an *optical system,* with the reduction in power due only to *dispersion.*   The dispersion attenuation factor is given by:

$$D.A.F. = e^{-df^2}$$

where d is a material constant, including substance and geometry, and f is the *frequency component* (of the *signal*) being *attenuated.*   Also see *optical dispersion attenuation.*

dispersion equation.   An equation that indicates the dependence of the *refractive index* of a *transmission medium* on the *wavelength* of the *light* conducted or *transmitted* by the medium.   The adjustment of the index for wavelength permits more accurate calculation of angles or paths that are dependent upon the index.   Often, it is necessary to obtain a value of the rate of change of the refractive index with respect to the wavelength.   The *dispersion* equation attributed to Hartmann is:

$$N = N_0 + C/(L - L_0)$$

That attributed to Cauchy is:

$$N = A + B/L^2 + C/L^4$$

A more complicated one derived by Sellmeier is:

$$N^2 = 1 + \sum_{i=0}^{m} A_i L^2 / (L^2 - L_i^2)$$

An extension of the Sellmeier equation is useful for covering more than one *absorption* region. Finally, Helmholtz included an additional term to the Sellmeier equation, namely:

$$B_i / (L^2 - L_i^2)$$

It is useful within *absorption regions* as well. In all equations, L is the wavelength, N is the refractive index, and the other symbols are material dependent and empirically determined. Usually, some of the terms of the summation are replaced by a constant. In practice, one of the preceding expressions is often used. Then, a more accurate fit is found by an appropriate curve-fitting technique, such as the method of least squares.

dispersion gate. See *NAND gate.*

dispersion-limited. In *optical fiber transmission systems,* pertaining to the limitations placed on the *pulse* repetition rate caused by *intersymbol interference* due to *dispersion* at the end of the *transmission line.* For example, in certain *step index fibers* in which $n_1 = 1.51$ and $n_2 = 1.49$ *(core* and *cladding refractive indices),* the dispersion-limited repetition rate is 18 *Mbps* for a 1-km length, 9 *Mbps* for a 2-km length, and so on.

dispersion-limited operation. In *optical communication system* operations, the situation that occurs when the *dispersion* of a *pulse,* rather than its *amplitude,* limits the distance between *repeaters.* In this regime of operation, *waveguide* and material dispersion are sufficient to preclude an intelligent decision based on the presence or absence of a *pulse* in the intelligence *signal.* Also see *detector noise-limited operation.*

dispersion wavelength. See *zero material dispersion wavelength.*

dispersive lens. See *diverging lens.*

displacement. 1. The movement of an *object* or *image* from one position to another; e.g., the movement of a *cursor* in a *display device* from one *coordinate position* to another in the *display space* on the *display surface* of the device, or the movement of a *light pulse* from one point to another in an *optical field.* 2. The actual represented distance, from one point to another, usually indicated as a vector that is equal to the difference between two position vectors. Synonymous with *translation*. See *frequency displacement*.

displacement loss. See *lateral displacement loss*.

display 1. A visual presentation of *data*. 2. To present *data* visually, using a *display device;* e.g., a *CRT*, the end-face or *faceplate* of a *coherent bundle* of *optical fibers*, a *light-beam* projection of an *image* from a film onto a *screen*, puffs of smoke against a blue sky, or an *LED* or *gas panel*. See *auroral display; radar display; raster display; spot-barrage jamming radar display; spot-continuous wave jamming radar display*. Also see Figure E-3.

display background. In *display systems*, the fixed portion of a *display image* that cannot be changed by an *operator* or user during a particular application. For example, a *form flash* or *form overlay* might provide a display background. Contrast with *display foreground*.

display column. In a *display system*, the column of *display positions* that constitutes a full-length sequence of vertical positions on the *display surface* of a *display device*. In display systems, "vertical" is defined as perpendicular to the direction of right to left when the *display image* is viewed by an observer. Synonymous with *addressable vertical positions*. Contrast with *display line*.

display command. In *display systems*, a command that can be used to control a *display device*. Synonymous with *display order*.

display console. A control device that includes a *display device* and usually one or more *input* units, such as an *alphanumeric keyboard, function keys*, a *joystick*, a *control ball*, or a *light pen*. The device is usually equipped for use by a human operator. The *display surface* of the display device may be a *CRT* screen, an *LED* or *gas panel*, a *fiberscope faceplate* at the end of a *coherent bundle* of *optical fibers*, or the surface of a *plotter bed* or *tablet*.

display cycle. In *display systems*, the sequence of events needed to *regenerate* a *display element, display group*, or *display image* on the *display surface* once, if and when such regeneration is necessary to preserve the presentation of the element, group, or image.

display device. A device capable of forming a *display element, display group*, or *display iamge* in the *display space* on its *display surface*. A *CRT* screen, a *fiberscope faceplate*, a plotter bed, and an *LED* or *gas panel* are *display surfaces*. The device provides a visual representation of *data*. Usually the data are displayed temporarily; however, arrangements may be made for making a permanent record. See *character display device; intelligent display device*. See Figure D-6. Also see Figure V-2.

D-6. A **display device** consisting of an electronic blackboard, including a remote monitor that *displays* handwriting from the board, with a portable conference *telephone,* used for *audiovisual communications.* (Courtesy of Bell Laboratories.)

display element. A basic graphic element that can be placed in the *display space* on a *display surface* of a *display device* to produce or construct a *display group* or *display image* (e.g., a graph, drawing, picture, or word). Examples of display elements are dots, line segments, arcs, squares, and crosses. Collection of associated display elements can be used to form *images* that can be manipulated as a unit. Also see *display group.*

display field. A specified part of the *storage space* of a *display buffer* or a specified area on a *display surface* that contains or displays a set of *characters* that can be manipulated or operated upon as a unit.

display file. In *display systems,* a sequence of *instructions* similar to a *computer program* to be executed by the processor in a *display device.*

display foreground. In *display systems,* the variable portion of a *display image* that can be changed by an *operator* or user during a particular application. For example, a *computer program* or *pointer* may be used to change the display foreground. Contrast with *display background.*

display frame. In *display systems,* a specified portion of the area of the *display surface* available for viewing; e.g., a specified portion of the area of a *microform* available for viewing a *microimage.*

display group. A group of *display elements* that can be manipulated or processed as a unit (e.g., *transferred, converted, translated, rotated,* or *tumbled*). Composed of display elements, they are used to form larger groups or *display images*. Synonymous with *display segment*.

display image. A collection of *display elements* or *display groups* associated together at one time in the *display space* on the *display surface* of a *display device*. For example, an assembly drawing, a picture, a graph, or a narrative text on a *CRT* screen or on the *faceplate* on the end of a *coherent bundle* of *optical fibers*.

display line. In *display systems*, the row of *display positions* that constitutes a full-length horizontal line in the *display space* on the *display surface* of a *display device* (e.g., a *fiberscope*). "Horizontal" is defined as the direction of right to left, left to right, or the direction or reading of lines of English text, when the *display image* is viewed by an observer. Synonymous with *display row; addressable horizontal positions*. Contrast with *display column*.

display order. See *display command*.

display position. In the *display space* on the *display surface* of a *display device*, an addressable location that may be occupied by a *character, display element*, or other symbol.

display row. See *display line*.

display segment. See *display group*.

display space. The part of a *display surface* upon which a *display image* may be placed. The display space may be equal to, but is usually less than, the display surface area. For example, only that portion of the *faceplate* of a *fiberscope* upon which an *image* can be formed due to the limitations imposed by a frame at the source; i.e., at the opposite end of a *coherent bundle* of *optical fibers* transmitting an image; or only that portion of a *CRT* screen can be used to *display* an image; or only that portion of a sheet of drawing paper available to the writing *stylus* of a plotter. Synonymous with *operating space*.

display surface. The *data medium* of a *display device* on which *display elements, display groups*, or *display images* may be made to appear; e.g., the entire screen or a *CRT* or the surface of the *faceplate* at the end of a *coherent bundle* of *optical fibers* forming a *fiberscope*. The entire display surface may not be available for the display elements, groups, or images. The part of the display surface available for display is called the *display space*.

display system. Any *system* whose primary purpose is to present *data* in a form that is visible or legible to the human eye. For example, a system that has a *display surface* for the presentation of *display images*, such as the *faceplate* of a *fiberscope*, a *CRT* screen, an *LED* or *gas panel*, or the display surface of a *plotter*. See *interactive display system*. Also see Figures C-1 and S-11.

display writer. Parts of a *display device* specifically used to create visible marks or traces in the *display space* on the *display surface* of the device. For example, *light pens, laser beams, electron* guns and *beams,* and *plotter* pens with their holders.

dissector. See *image dissector.*

distance. See *coordination distance; down-wind distance; signal distance; skip distance; transmission loss distance.*

distance code. See *minimum distance code; unit distance code.*

distance dialing. See *direct distance dialing (DDD).*

distance gate. See *EXCLUSIVE-OR gate.*

distance measuring equipment. A *radionavigation aid* in the *aeronautical radionavigation service* that determines the distance of an *interrogator* from a *transponder* by measuring the *transit time* of a *pulse* to and from the transponder.

distance square law. See *inverse distance square law.*

distortion. In a *signal transmission system,* the amount by which an *output* waveform or *pulse* differs from the *input* waveform or pulse. It may be expressed as the change in *amplitude, frequency* composition, *phase,* shape, or other *attribute* of the *signals.* See *amplitude distortion; aperture distortion; barrel distortion; bias distortion; characteristic distortion; cyclic distortion; delay distortion; early distortion; end distortion; envelope delay distortion; fortuitous distortion; frequency distortion; group-delay distortion; group-delay frequency distortion; harmonic distortion; intermodulation distortion; isochronous distortion; late distortion; optical distortion; modulation frequency harmonic distortion; modulation frequency intermodulation distortion; nonlinear distortion; optical distortion; phase-amplitude distortion; phase-frequency distortion; pincushion distortion; quantization distortion; radial distortion; significant instant distortion; single-harmonic distortion; start-stop distortion; telegraph distortion; teletypewriter signal distortion; total harmonic distortion; waveguide delay distortion.*

distraction. An extraneous audible *signal* appearing on a *circuit* during a *telephone* conversation, consisting of *crosstalk, echo, noise, interference,* or other unwanted *disturbance.*

distress call. In *distress* and *rescue communications,* a *call* that combines the *distress signal* with the *call sign* of the *calling station* or *party.* It usually has priority over all other *transmissions.* It should not be *addressed* to a particular *station* nor is acknowledgement or receipt to be given before the *distress message* that follows it is sent. All stations that hear a distress call should immediately cease any transmission that might interfere with the *distress traffic.* They should continue to listen on the *frequency* used for emission of the distress call. In *CW transmission,* the distress call is SOS followed by the call sign of the *mobile station* in distress. In *voice transmission,* the distress signal is MAYDAY followed by the call sign or other identification of the mobile station in distress. MAYDAY is usually said in groups of three. See Figure D-7.

MODE	DISTRESS CALL		
	DISTRESS SIGNAL	DISTRESSED STATION	MESSAGE
VOICE	MAYDAY (3 times)	NAME (3 times)	DISTRESS MESSAGE
CODE	SOS (3 times)	CALL SIGN (3 times)	DISTRESS MESSAGE

D-7. The structure of **distress calls** for *voice* and *code transmission.*

distress communication net. A *communication net* used exclusively for the *transmission,* control, and coordination of *distress calls* and *messages.* See *maritime distress communication net.*

distress communications. *Communication* methods, *systems,* and equipment used for *transmission* of *messages* that contain *information* about emergency or distress situations. *Distress messages* are sent to or from a specific emergency or disaster area for the purpose of directing, controlling, reporting, or assisting in survival or recovery operations. It particularly includes the transmission of messages related to the immediate assistance required by a *station* that is in distress. Transmissions include *alarm signals, distress signals, distress calls, distress messages,* and *direction-finding transmissions.*

distress frequency. A *radio frequency* that is used exclusively for emergency or *distress calls* and *messages.* The following are examples of some distress frequencies that have been established by international agreement for emergency and distress purposes:

   500   KHz International distress calling (MF).
 2182   KHz International distress and calling (HF).
 8364   KHz International lifeboat, lifecraft, survival craft (HF).
  121.5 MHz Aeronautical emergency (VHF).
  243.0 MHz Survival emergency (UHF).
  156.8 MHz International calling and safety (VHF).

These radio frequencies are designated for use by *mobile stations* or survival craft for handling *distress traffic.* For example, the first *transmission* by an aircraft in distress should be made on the frequency in use by that aircraft. If no response is obtained, 121.5 KHz or 243.0 MHz should be used for distress and emergency traffic. For *radiotelegraphy,* 500 KHz should be used. Synonymous with *emergency frequency.* See *international radiotelegraph distress frequency; international radiotelephone distress frequency; radiotelegraph distress frequency; radiotelephone distress frequency.*

distress message. In *distress* and *rescue communications,* the *message* that contains the details of the distress situation. The distress message should follow the *distress call* as soon as possible. The message, usually following the *distress signal* (SOS, MAYDAY) and the name or other identification of the ship, aircraft, or unit in distress, contains the particulars of its position, the nature of the distress, the kind of assistance required, and any other *information* that might facilitate the rescue. A common practice is that the distress message is repeated at one-quarter before and after the hour in some areas at 500 KHz, and on the hour and half-hour in other areas at 2182 KHz. As a general rule, a ship signals its position in latitude and longitude using degrees and minutes suffixed by north, south, east, or west. In *CW,* the *signal* AAA is used to separate the degrees from the minutes. If possible, the true *bearing* and the distance in *nautical miles* from a known geographic point should be given. Conventions are published by the *International Telecommunication Union (ITU).* Also see *emergency message.*

distress period. The specific time period during which a continuous *listening watch* is to be maintained on the international *distress* and calling *frequencies* and during which *communication silence* should be maintained. For example, international distress periods are 15–18 and 45–48 minutes past the hour for 500 KHz and 00–03 and 30–33 minutes past the hour for 2182 KHz *distress frequencies.*

distress signal. In *distress* and *rescue communications,* a *signal* that indicates that the unit *(station)* sending the signal is threatened by grave or imminent danger and requests immediate assistance. It is sent before the *distress call* and at the beginning of the *distress message.* In *CW transmission,* the distress signal is SOS; in *voice transmission* it is (MAYDAY). See *pyrotechnic distress signal.*

distress traffic. All *messages* relevant to the assistance required by a *mobile station* that is in distress or is experiencing an emergency. The *distress signals* SOS or MAYDAY should accompany all messages for as long as the *emergency category* is that of distress. Elements of *distress traffic* include *alarm signals, distress signals, distress calls, distress messages,* and *direction-finding transmissions.*

distributed data processing. *Data processing* in which the data processing functions, such as *program* execution, *storage,* control, and *input-output* functions, are performed at two or more *nodes* of a *network.*

distributed data processing system. In *open systems architecture,* two or more *computers* or *data processors* interconnected for a specific purpose. The interconnections may be made at corresponding *layers* in each *system.*

distributed-feedback (DFB) laser. A *laser* with part of its *output* fed back to its input using more than one *propagation mode* in the feedback path for controlling *mode* generation and mode conversion. Usually uses periodically inhomogeneous thin films, periodically inhomogeneous *substrate* guides, or *thin-film waveguides* with periodic surfaces. The DFB laser operates more efficiently when feedback and direct waves are in the same mode.

distributed frame-alignment signal. A *frame-alignment signal* in which the *signal elements* occupy digit positions that are not consecutive. Also see *bunched frame-alignment signal.*

distributed parameter. Pertaining to a *communication, power,* or other *circuit* in which the electrical *components* (parameters) of *resistance, inductance,* and *capacity* (R–L–C) are spatially distributed, that is, they cannot be considered to be located or concentrated at a single point. Thus, an input *electrical signal* affects various interconnected components at different times depending on the *propagation* speed of the signal through the circuit. Also see *lumped parameter.*

distributed thin-film waveguide. See *periodically-distributed thin-film waveguide.*

distribution. See *fading distribution; lambertian distribution; mean-power-of-the-talker volume distribution; Poisson distribution; Rayleigh distribution; uniform lambertian distribution.*

distribution box. See *optical fiber distribution box.*

distribution cable. In a *communication system,* a *cable* that leads from a *distribution frame* to a *destination user terminal.*

distribution center. See *internal message distribution center; switching and message distribution center.*

distribution frame. A structure with *terminations* for connecting the permanent *wires, circuits, optical fibers,* or *buses* in such a manner that interconnection by cross connection may be made. See *combined distribution frame (CDF); fiber distribution frame (FDF); group distribution frame (GDF); high-frequency distribution frame (HFDF); intermediate distribution frame (IDF); main distribution frame (MDF); supergroup distribution frame (SGDF).*

distribution substation. An electrical *power* unit that modifies electrical energy. For example, a distribution substation might transform the *voltage* to lower levels for use by electrical equipment at *user* installations.

distribution system. See *local distribution system; primary distribution system; protected optical fiber distribution system; protected wireline distribution system.*

distribution voltage drop. The decrease in *potential difference,* that is, the *voltage* drop, between any two defined points of interest in a *power distribution system.*

distributor. A device that accepts a *data stream* from one *line* and places a sequence of signals, one or more at a time, on several lines, thus performing a *spatial multiplexing* of the original stream. The device may be a mechanical unit with *input* to a rotor and *output* through many contacts wiped by the rotor, or it may be a set of *combinational circuits* (logic elements), such as a series of *AND gates* that are *sequentially enabled* by a set of *pulses* and that are all connected to a common *bus* carrying the *input signals.*

disturbance. See *ionospheric disturbance; sudden ionospheric disturbance.*

disturbance current. The *electrical current* produced by a *disturbance voltage.* Together with the disturbance voltage, it constitutes the *disturbance power.*

disturbance power. The unwanted extraneous *power* from natural or man-made sources, associated with *transmission,* and tending to limit or interfere with the interchange of *information.* Disturbance power degrades or otherwise interferes with normal operation of a *communication system.* For example, it may produce a false *signaling noise* in a *telephone,* cause a noise in a *radio receiver,* or *distort* a *received signal.*

disturbance voltage. The unwanted extraneous *voltage* from natural or man-made sources associated with *transmission,* and tending to limit or interfere with the interchange of *information.* Disturbance voltage degrades or otherwise interferes with normal operation of a *communication system.* For example, it may produce a false *signaling noise* in a *telephone,* cause a noise in a *radio receiver,* or *distort* a *received signal.*

disturbed circuit. 1. A *circuit* in which *crosstalk* is generated by *disturbance power* from a *disturbing circuit.* 2. A *circuit* that generates *noise* in itself. For example, a *component* that vibrates in the earth's *magnetic field* and induces a *disturbance voltage* and *current* in itself, or a circuit that is experiencing *microphonics.*

disturbing circuit. A *circuit* that generates *crosstalk* in another circuit by transferring *disturbance power* to it. For example, the power from the disturbing circuit may be transferred to the *disturbed circuit* by *conduction* (current leakage), by induction *(inductive coupling* by *magnetic fields),* by *electrostatic fields (capacitive coupling),* by *electromagnetic wave coupling* (the disturbing circuit behaving as a *transmitting antenna* and the disturbed circuit behaving as a *receiving antenna*), by *optical coupling* (*light* leakage), or by other means.

dither. In *spread-spectrum systems,* a *phase shift* of the *clock signal* supplied to the *receiver* by a controlled amount so as to generate an *error signal* for *clock control.* The shift is usually only for the period of time corresponding to a fraction of a *bit.* Synonymous with *tau-jitter.* See *frequency multidither; polystep dither.*

diurnal. Pertaining to the variation with time of day of an environmental element, physical quantity, or other entity, such as *temperature,* atmospheric pressure, magnetic declination, or height of the *ionosphere* (and therefore *skip distance*).

divergence. The bending of *electromagnetic waves* away from each other; e.g., by a *concave* or minus *lens,* a *convex mirror,* or a parabolic dishlike *antenna.* In a *binocular* instrument, divergence is the horizontal angular disparity between the *images* of a common *object,* as seen through the left and right systems. Divergence is positive when the right image is to the right of the left image. Contrast with *convergence.* See *beam divergence.*

divergent lens. See *diverging lens.*

divergent light. A *beam* of *light* consisting of a *bundle* of *rays* that are propagating in such a direction as to depart from one another; i.e., they are not parallel to each other and are spreading. Thus, a point source, or a *concave lens* that receives *collimated light,* produces *divergent light.* Also see *beam divergence; collimation.*

divergent meniscus lens. A *lens* with one *convex* and one *concave* surface, the latter having the smaller radius of curvature and hence the greater power. The lens behaves generally like a *concavo-concave lens.* Synonymous with *diverging meniscus lens; negative meniscus.*

diverging beam. A *beam* of *light* that is not *collimated;* e.g., one whose *wavefront* is spherical. A high degree of collimation (i.e., minimal *divergence*) is required to *couple* energy into an *optical fiber waveguide. Lasers* produce beams with a high degree of collimation and uniform *phase,* as though the *monochromatic* light was emanating from a distant source.

diverging lens. A *lens* that causes parallel *light rays* to spread out. One surface of a *diverging lens* may be *concavely* spherical and the other plane *(plano-concave).* Both may be *concave* (double concave) or one surface may be concave and the other *convex* (concavo-convex, divergent-meniscus). The diverging lens is considered to have a negative focal length, measured from the *focal point* toward the *object.* Synonymous with *concave lens; dispersive lens; divergent lens; minus lens; negative lens.*

diverging meniscus lens. See *divergent meniscus lens.*

diverse routing. A survivability feature of a *communication system* in which access *lines* or *channels* serving the same *station* or *facility* are *routed* over geographically separated *circuits.* It also includes the use of two or more *radio nets.*

diversity. See *angle diversity; frequency diversity; polarization diversity; spaced antenna diversity; space diversity; time diversity; tone diversity.*

diversity combiner. A *circuit* for combining two or more *signals* that carry the same *information received* via separate *paths* or *channels* with the objective of providing a single resultant signal that is superior in quality to any of the contributing signals. Also see *digital combining; equal gain combiner; linear combiner; maximal-ratio combiner; postdetection combiner; predetection combiner; selective combiner.*

diversity combining. See *dual diversity combining; quadruple diversity combining.*

diversity combining method. See *maximal-ratio-square diversity combining method.*

diversity factor. In a *power* distribution *system* with its electrical load, the ratio, to the maximum demand of the whole system, of (1) the sum of the individual maximum demands, (2) the sum of the individual maximum possible demands, or (3) the sum of the individual component rated power, of the various electrical components connected to a power distribution system. The diversity factor is always greater than unity.

diversity gain. In *high-frequency communications,* the ratio of the *signal strength* or *power density* obtained by *diversity combining,* to the signal strength obtained by a single *path* or *channel.* The gain is usually expressed in *decibels.*

diversity gate. See *EXCLUSIVE-OR gate.*

diversity order. 1. The number of independently *fading propagation paths* or *frequencies,* or both, used in *diversity reception.* 2. The number of *signals* simultaneously *combined* and *detected* through the use of *space, frequency,* or *time division multiplexing; polarization; modulation* characteristics; or their combination. Also see *diversity reception; dual diversity combining; quadruple diversity combining.*

diversity reception. *Reception* in which a resultant *signal* is obtained by a combination or selection, or both, of two or more independent *sources* of received signal energy that carry the same *modulation* or *information.* The signals may vary in their *fading* characteristics at any given instant. Diversity reception is used to minimize the effects of fading. The amount of *diversity gain* or signal improvement is directly dependent on the independence of the fading characteristics of the *transmission media.* Synonymous with *diversity system.* Also see *diversity order; polarization diversity; quadruple diversity; tone diversity.*

diversity system. See *diversity reception.*

diversity transmission. *Transmission* in which two or more *signals* with the same *modulation* or bearing the same *information* are independently transmitted over different *paths* or *media* in order that their recombination can result in an improved signal. Diversity transmission is used to obtain reliability and signal improvement, for example to overcome *fading, outages,* or *circuit failures.*

divider. See *analog divider; frequency divider.*

divider circuit. A *filtering circuit* that provides for the separation of simultaneous multiple-frequency *signals,* arriving on a single *transmission path,* into separate paths for each *frequency* or group of frequencies.

division. See *frequency division; space division; time division.*

division multiple access. See *code division multiple access (CDMA).*

division multiplexing. See *color-division multiplexing; frequency-division multiplexing; optical space-division multiplexing; synchronous time-division multiplexing; time-division multiplexing; wavelength-division multiplexing.*

D-layer. The region of the *ionosphere* from 50 to 90 km in altitude. It causes most of the *attenuation* of *radio waves* in the 1 to 100 MHz *band.* It exists only during daylight hours. Synonymous with *D-region.*

DLE. The *data link escape transmission control character.*

DLE character. See *data link escape (DLE) character.*

DM. *Delay modulation; differential modulation.*

document. A *data medium* and the *data* recorded on it. It generally has permanence and can be read by a person or a machine.

documentation. 1. The management of documents, including the actions of identifying, acquiring, processing, storing, and disseminating them. 2. A collection of documents on a given subject, for a given organization, for a given purpose, in a given container, on a given *data medium,* or otherwise grouped by some other criterion.

document facsimile system. See *group-one document facsimile equipment group; three document facsimile equipment; group-two document facsimile equipment.*

document facsimile telegraphy. *Facsimile telegraphy* intended primarily for the *transmission* of documents that have only two levels of density. Synonymous with *black-and-white facsimile telegraphy.*

document mark. In *micrographics,* an *optical* mark used for counting *display frames* automatically. Synonymous with *blip.*

DOD. *Direct outward dialing.*

DOD master clock.   See *Department of Defense (DOD) master clock.*

domain.   1. In *distributed networks,* all of the *hardware* and *software* that is under the control of a specified set of one or more *host processors.*   2. The independent variable used to express a function, such as a *time domain, frequency domain, spatial domain,* or *complex domain.*

domain network.   See *multiple-domain network.*

domains.   See *adjacent domains.*

dominance.   See *fault dominance.*

dominant mode.   The *mode* of *operation* of an *electromagnetic waveguide* that is designed and operated to support only one *wavelength.*   For example, a rectangular cross-section waveguide that operates in the TE_{10} *mode* (operates with a *transverse electric wave* at a *frequency* just above the cutoff frequency that can be *propagated*).   Therefore, it can operate at only one wavelength and hence only in one mode.   Also see *lowest order transverse mode; mode conversion.*

donor.   In an intrinsic *semiconducting* material, a *dopant* that has nearly the same electronic bonding structure as the intrinsic material, but with one more *electron* among its valence electrons than that required to complete the intrinsic bonding pattern, thus leaving one "extra" or "excess" electron for each impurity (dopant) atom in the structure.   The dopant (i.e., the donor) atoms are relatively few and far apart and hence do not interfere with the electrical *conductivity* of the intrinsic material.   Arsenic can serve as a dopant for germanium and silicon. The extra electron moves or wanders from atom to atom more freely than the bound electrons that are required to complete the bonding structure, although interchanges actually occur with the bound electrons.   The extra electrons move about more freely than the *holes* created by *acceptors.*   Hence, the electrons are more mobile than the holes.   Under the influence of *electric fields,* the electrons and holes move in the direction of the field according to their sign.   Also see *acceptor; hole.*

don't answer.   See *call forwarding don't answer.*

door.   See *trap door.*

dopant.   A material mixed, fused, amalgamated, crystallized, or otherwise added to another material in order to achieve desired characteristics of the resulting material.   For example, the germanium tetrachloride or titanium tetrachloride used to increase the *refractive index* of glass for use as an *optical fiber core* material; the gallium or arsenic added to silicon or germanium to produce a doped *semiconductor* for achieving *donor* or *acceptor,* positive or negative, material for *diode* and *transistor* action.

doped-silica cladded fiber. An *optical fiber* consisting of a *doped* silica *core* with doped silica *cladding,* usually produced by the *chemical vapor deposition process.* The fiber has a very low *loss* and moderate *dispersion.* It is a *step-indexed fiber.*

doped-silica graded fiber. An *optical fiber* consisting of a silica fiber in which the *doping* varies in order to produce a decreasing *refractive index* from the center toward the outside, thus eliminating the necessity of *cladding.* The refractive index profile is *graded* and tailored to reduce *multimode dispersion,* since the nonaxial *rays* of *light,* although traveling further, travel faster in the outer *transmission medium* where the refractive index is lower; thus the axial rays arrive at the end of the fiber the same time as the nonaxial or *paraxial rays.*

Doppler. See *radio Doppler.*

Doppler effect. A change in observed *frequency* of a *wave* caused by the time rate of change of the radial component of relative velocity between the *source* of the wave and the point of observation. For example, the increase in observed frequency of a *light* or sound wave from a *source* of constant frequency increasing its speed toward an observer. If the source continues to accelerate closer, the observed frequency increases, and if it accelerates away, the frequency will continue to decrease; e.g., the red shift of the stars, or the approach and departure of a constant-speed constant-frequency train whistle to an observer standing a significant distance from a straight track. Also see *radio Doppler.*

Doppler navigation system. A *navigation system* that uses *electromagnetic waves* to measure the radial component of velocity by measuring *phase* and *frequency shifts* of *transmitted* or *reflected signals.*

Doppler radar. *Radar* that *detects* the radial component of the velocity of a distant object (target) relative to the *radar antenna* by means of the *Doppler effect.* See *pulse Doppler radar.*

Doppler shift. The change in observed *frequency* of a *wave* from a *source* that is moving with a radial component of velocity relative to the observer or *antenna* making the measurement.

dosimeter. See *fiber optic dossimeter.*

dot. **1.** In the *international Morse code,* a short *signal* (on-key) interval represented as a short burst of *carrier* energy, a short pulse of applied *modulating* *voltage,* a short burst of *audio* or *visual* energy, a short interval between clicks, or some such similar physical representation. The dot is often used as the unit of duration to specify the duration of other *signaling* intervals, such as the length or duration of *dashes* and *spaces.* Since the length of a dot is basic, its time or space length is arbitrary but usually constant in any given *system* or *mode* of operation.   2. In *Morse code,* a *signal* element of *mark* condition and of duration of one *unit interval* followed by a *signal element* of *space* condition having the same duration.

dot frequency.   1. In *facsimile transmission systems,* half the number of contiguous *picture elements transmitted* in a second.   A *mark* followed by a *space* may be considered as two picture elements.   2. The *fundamental frequency* of the *signal* representing alternately black and white *picture elements* along a *scanning line.*   Also see *picture element.*

dot matrix.   A pattern of dots in two-dimensional *space* that can be used for constructing *display images,* either directly or through the use of *display elements* or *display groups.*   The display elements or display groups may themselves be constructed of dot matrices.   Each dot can be transmitted, for example, by one or more *optical fibers.*   The dot matrix can be used to form *characters,* such as letters, *numerals,* or other special signs or *symbols.*

dot-matrix character generator.   A *character generator* that generates *characters* composed of dots for presentation in the *display space* on the *display surface* of a *display device.*   The characters are usually formed from an array of dot positions, and the presence or absence of a dot at each position is used to form the character.   Dot matrices can readily be formed and transmitted in *coherent bundles* of *optical fibers.*   In this case, the display surface is the *faceplate* of a *fiberscope* on the end of the coherent bundle of optical fibers.

double call-sign calling.   A method of establishing and conducting *communications* in which the *call sign* of the *called station* is followed by the call sign of the *calling station.*   The call signs are separated by a letter group or word meaning "this is."

double clear.   In *telephone switchboard operation,* a *double supervisory working signal* that indicates a *clearing* condition.

double conversion.   In *satellite communication systems,* the two-stage process involved in *up-converter* and *down-converter frequency conversion.*

double-crucible (DC) process.   A process of producing *optical fibers* in which two concentric crucibles are used, one for the *core* glass and one for the *cladding* glass.   The *cladded fiber* is drawn out the bottom, and diffusion of the *dopant* materials in the glasses to each of the glasses produces a *graded index (GI) fiber.*   Synonymous with *compound-glass process; ion-exchange process.*   See Figure D-8.

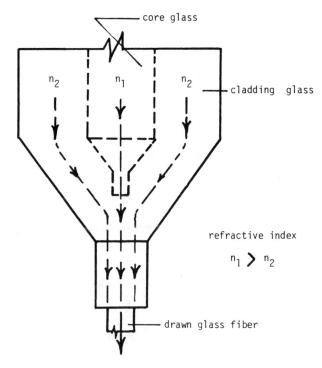

core glass

n_2 n_1 n_2 cladding glass

refractive index

$n_1 > n_2$

drawn glass fiber

D-8. A **double crucible process** of *drawing optical fibers.*

double-current signaling. A *telegraph signaling* method in which *marks* and *spaces* are represented by *electric currents* of opposite polarities rather than by a current and no current. It is *binary transmission* in which positive and negative *direct currents (DC)* denote the *significant conditions.* Some advantages of double-current signaling are (1) fast operation of sensitive polarized receiving relays, (2) fast cut-off (disabling) of *combinational circuits,* (3) no *bias* is required, and (4) the system operates in a *neutral condition* when there are no *signals.* Synonymous with *bipolar telegraphy; bipolar transmission; double-current telegraphy; double-current transmission; mark-space signaling; polar direct-current telegraph transmission; polar transmission.* Also see *unipolar.*

double-current telegraphy. See *double-current signaling.*

double-current transmission. See *double-current signaling.*

double-eccentric connector. An *optical fiber connector* with an eccentric center in each mating pair so that relative rotation between the mating pair compensates for eccentricity of the *fiber cores* and permits core-to-core alignment for improved *coupling.*

double-ended control.   See *double-ended synchronization.*

double-ended synchronization.   A *synchronization* control system between two *exchanges* in which the *phase error signals* used to control the *clock* at one exchange are derived from comparison of the *phase* of the incoming *digital signal* and the phase of the *internal clock* at both exchanges. Synonymous with *double-ended control.*

double-frequency-shift keying (DFSK).   A *multiplex system* in which two *telegraph signals* are combined and *transmitted* simultaneously by a method of *frequency shifting* among four different frequencies.

double heading.   See *message readdressal.*

double heterojunction.   In a *laser diode,* two *heterojunctions* in close proximity, resulting in full *carrier* and *radiation* confinement as well as improved control of *recombinations.*

double heterojunction diode.   A *laser diode* that has two different *heterojunctions,* the difference being primarily in the stepped changes in *refractive indices* of the material in the vicinity of the *P–N junction.* The double heterojunction laser diode is widely used for *pulse-code (CW)* operation. See *monorail double-heterojunction diode.*

double image.   Pertaining to the doubling of an *image* caused by *optical* imperfections in an *optical system.*

double refraction.   The *refraction* displayed by certain materials in which a single *incident beam* of *light* is refracted into two internally *transmitted* beams as though there were two distinct *refractive indices* operating in the material at the same time. Also see *birefringence.*

double sideband.   In an *amplitude-modulated carrier,* the *frequencies* that are above and below the *carrier frequency.* They are caused by the *audio frequency modulation* of the *carrier wave.* The *audio frequency wave* is the intelligence *(information)* bearing signal.

double-sideband suppressed-carrier.   The *carrier* used in *double-sideband suppressed-carrier transmission systems* in which, after *modulation* of the carrier by an intelligence (information-bearing) signal, the carrier is fully or partially suppressed and only both of the symmetrical *sidebands* are *transmitted.*

double-sideband suppressed-carrier transmission.   *Transmission* in which the *radio frequency electromagnetic waves* that are the result of *amplitude modula-*

tion are symmetrically spaced (in the *frequency spectrum*) above and below the *carrier frequency* and transmitted at full *power*. The carrier power level is reduced to a predetermined level below that of the transmitted *sidebands*.

double-sideband suppressed-carrier transmission system. A *transmission system* that uses *amplitude modulation* in which the *electromagnetic waves* produced by the modulation are symmetrically spaced (in the *frequency spectrum*) above and below the *carrier frequency*. The carrier power level is reduced to a predetermined level below that of the transmitted *sidebands*.

double-sideband transmission. A method of *sideband transmission* in which both sidebands are transmitted at full *power*. It is a method of transmission in which the *electromagnetic waves* produced by *amplitude modulation* are symmetrically spaced (in the *frequency spectrum*) above and below the carrier frequency and are *transmitted* along with the *carrier wave,* all at full power.

double supervisory working. In *telephone switchboard operation,* a *supervisory system* in which two *supervisory signal keys (switches)* are provided for each *cord circuit* and are arranged on a *switchboard* keyshelf (panel) to correspond with the arrangement of the *cords*. The back signal of each pair, that is, the *answering supervisory signal,* is associated with the *answering plug* of a *cord*. This constitutes the answer-back unit. The front signal of each pair, that is, the calling supervisory *signal,* is associated with the *calling* (front) *plug* of a cord. Either the front or back signal indicates that the *user* (subscriber, customer) or the *exchange* has left the circuit by restoring the *telephone instrument receiver* to its rest, cradle, or on-hook condition, or by *exchange* disconnection.

doublet. 1. A *byte* composed of two *binary digits* or *pulses*. 2. In *optics,* a *compound lens* consisting of two elements. If an airspace exists between the elements, it is called an "airspaced doublet". If the inner surfaces are cemented together, it is called a *cemented doublet.* See *cemented doublet.*

doubly-cladded slab dielectric waveguide. A *slab dielectric waveguide* with a *core* surrounded by two layers of *dielectric* material, the core having the highest *refractive index,* the inside cladding layer having the lowest index, and the outermost layer having an intermediate index.

doubly-refracting crystal. A *transparent* crystalline substance that is *anisotropic* with respect to the velocity of *light* propagating within it in two different directions. The velocity of light is different in one direction than the other because the *refractive index* is different in one direction than the other. Light travels slower in a material with a higher refractive index than in a material with a lower refractive index.

down-converter. A device that converts an *input signal* with a given *frequency* to an *output signal* with a lower frequency. It is the opposite of an *up-converter*.

downrange site. An area that lies in a direction away from a launch site of a missile or projectile. If the area is not a target, it usually has sensing and *tracking* equipment, observation stations, and *communication equipment* on it. If the site is a target area, it may have test objects and other instrumentation for terminal ballistic testing.

down-the-hill radio relay. A short-range high-capacity *radio relay station* for extending *radio relay trunks* from a complex radio relay site to the local *communication center*.

downtime. The time during which a *functional unit* is inoperable due to a *fault*. Downtime can result from a fault within the functional unit or from an environmental fault. In the latter case, the functional unit is operable except for the environmental fault that prevents it from being operated. For example, a unit might be in an operable condition, but it cannot be operated because there is no *power* or there is no *operator*. See *system downtime*.

downwind distance. The distance in the direction of the wind from the point of a nuclear explosion to a point where fallout from the exploded nuclear bomb would no longer be dangerous. However, *communications* may still be disrupted. One common standard specifies the downwind distance of a one megaton detonated nuclear bomb as a unit of measure.

DPCM. *Differential pulse code modulation.*

DPSK. *Differential phase-shift keying.*

drafter. See *message drafter*.

dragging. In *display systems, picking* a *display element, display group*, or *display image* in the *display space* on the *display surface* of a *display device* and *translating* it so that all points on the element, group, or image continuously move in a path parallel to that taken by the *picking* device.

drawing. See *fiber drawing*.

drawn glass fiber. A glass *fiber* formed by pulling a heat-softened glass strand from a *preform* through a die or mandrel with a *pulling machine*. See Figure D-9. Also see Figure D-8.

D-9. A **drawn glass fiber.** (Courtesy of Bell Laboratories)

D-region.   See *D-layer.*

drift.   1. The slight variation of the *frequency* of an *electromagnetic wave* caused by the variation of the frequency of the *source* generator, such as a crystal-controlled *oscillator* in a *transmitter.* **2.** The variation of the *voltage* or *current* level at a point in a *circuit,* usually caused by a buildup or accumulation of charges. **3.** The horizontal displacement of an object caused by the wind or tide. For example, the sideways movement of a ship caused by the wind or the tide, the sideways movement of an aircraft due to a sideways wind component, or the movement of chaff after it is dispensed. See *frequency drift.*

drive circuit.   In *optical fiber transmission systems,* the *electrical circuit* that drives the *light-emitting* source, *modulating* it in accordance with an intelligence-bearing *signal.*

driver.   See *bus driver; optical cable driver.*

drone.   A pilotless radiocontrolled aircraft.

drop.   1. The portion of a device that is directed toward the internal station facilities or extended local *users.* For example, a four-wire *switch,* a *switchboard,* or a *switching center.* **2.** The *central office* side of *test jacks.* See *distribution voltage drop.*

drop-and-insert. A process in which a part of the *data* carried in a *transmission system* is terminated (dropped) at an intermediate point on a *transmission line, channel,* or *circuit,* and different data is entered (inserted) for subsequent or continued transmission in the same *space, time, frequency,* or *phase* position previously occupied by the terminated data.

drop channel. A *channel* in a multichannel *transmission path* or *branch* that is *terminated* at an intermediate point between the beginning and end of the path or branch. *Data* that is in the channel exists at that point.

drop channel operation. Operation of a multichannel *transmission system* in a manner such that one or more *channels* are *terminated* (dropped) at intermediate points between the end points of a *path* or *branch.* The data in the drop channels exit at these termination points.

drop message. A *message* that is dropped from a higher to a lower altitude, such as a message dropped from an aircraft in flight to the ground.

dropout. **1.** In a *communication system,* a momentary loss in *signal,* usually due to the effect of *noise, propagation* anomalies, or *system malfunction.* For example, *fading* in *radio communications.* **2.** A *failure* to read a *binary digit* from *storage.* This failure is usually caused by defects in the *data media,* or by a *malfunction* of the recording or reading mechanism. **3.** In *magnetic data media,* a recorded *signal* whose *amplitude* on reading is less than a predetermined percentage of a reference signal. See *carrier dropout.*

drop zone. An area designated to serve as a receiving area for dropping objects, such as *drop messages,* equipment, supplies or persons.

drop-zone boundary limit marker. A marker, such as a *panel, light,* contrasting objects, or footprints, used to indicate the boundary of the usable *drop zone.*

drop-zone impact point. The point in a *drop zone* where the first of a series of dropped objects or persons should land.

drop-zone indicator. A previously agreed upon *signal* used to mark the boundary of a *drop zone.*

drum factor. In *drum transmitters* and *receivers* for *facsimile systems,* the ratio of the *usable scanning length* of the drum to the diameter of the drum. In facsimile systems that do not use drums, it is the ratio of the equivalent dimensions of the scanned surface.

drum receiver. In *facsimile systems,* a *receiver* in which the *recording medium,* such as sensitized or photosensitive paper, is fastened to a rotating drum and *scanned* helicoidally by a recording head that moves in a straight line along an element of the drum cylinder.

drum speed. The angular speed of a *facsimile transmitter* drum or *receiver* (recording) drum, usually measured in revolutions per minute.

drum transmitter. In *facsimile systems,* a *transmitter* in which the original document, whose contents are to be *transmitted,* is fastened to a rotating drum and *scanned* helicoidally by a recording head that moves in a straight line along an element of the drum cylinder.

dry glass. Glass from which as much water as possible has been driven out; e.g., glass with a water concentration about 1 *ppm.* Drying is accomplished primarily to reduce hydroxyl-ion *absorption loss.* Drying can be accomplished by many days of drying of *starting powders* in a 250°C vacuum oven, followed by many hours of dry-gas melt bubbling to dry out water to extremely low levels.

DSA switchboard. *Dial service assistance (DSA) switchboard.*

DSE. *Data switching exchange.*

DSM. *Delta sigma modulation.*

D-star. *Detectivity* of a *photodetector* multiplied by the square root of the detector area and the square root of the detector *bandwidth.* The concept of D-star is useful because the *noise equivalent power (NEP)* of many detectors is proportional to the square root of the product of detector area and *bandwidth.* Thus, D-star normalizes the detectivity to these *parameters.* The unit of D-star is:

$$(\text{Meters} - \text{Hertz}^{1/2})/\text{Watt}$$

DSTE. *Data subscriber terminal equipment.*

DTE. *Data terminal equipment.*

DTG. *Date-time group.*

DTMF. *Dual-tone multifrequency signaling.*

dual access. **1.** The *connection* of a *user* (customer, subscriber) *end-instrument* to two *switching centers* by separate *access lines* using a single *message routing indicator* or *telephone number.* **2.** In *satellite communication systems,* the *transmission* of two *carriers* simultaneously through a single *communication satellite repeater.* **3.** Pertaining to the availability of *voice transmission* and *digital transmission* from the same *station* or *terminal.* Also see *multiple access.*

dual-access tributary station. A *tributary station* with a *user* (subscriber, customer) *access line* normally used for *voice communication* but that has special *circuits* or equipment for use as a *digital transmission circuit.* Synonymous with *voice-data tributary station; voice-graphics tributary station.*

dual-diversity combining. The simultaneous *combining* of, or selection from, two independently *fading signals,* and their *detection* through the use of *space, frequency, phase, time,* or *polarization* characteristics. Also see *diversity order; frequency diversity; quadruple-diversity combining.*

dual homing. The *connection* of a *terminal* so that it is served by either of two *switching centers.* This service uses a single *directory number.* It provides for increased reliability and survivability. Also see *multiple homing.*

dual-precedence message. A *message* that contains two *precedence designations.* The higher one is used for all *action addressees* and the lower one for all *information addressees.* Also see *single-precedence message.*

dual-tone multifrequency signaling (DTMF). A *signaling* method that employs fixed combinations of two specific *voice frequencies,* one of which is selected from a group of four low frequencies, and the other from a group of either three or four relatively high frequencies. *Users* (customers, subscribers) or *private branch exchanges (PBX)* make use of DTMF to indicate *telephone address digits, precedence designation,* and end-of-*signaling,* if their *switchboards* or *end-instruments* enable them to do so. *Telephones* equipped with DTMF normally have 12 *key* positions, the ten *decimal digits* and the # and *, the latter being primarily reserved for special purposes. For example, *AUTOVON* telephones have 16 positions, the extra 6 above the 10 decimal digits are primarily used for military purposes, such as precedence designation. DTMF signals, unlike *dial pulses,* can pass through the entire *connection* to the *called party,* and therefore lend themselves to various schemes, such as remote control or *tone-coded data transmission,* after the connection is established. Also see *key pulsing.*

dual-use access line. A *user* (customer, subscriber) *access line* that can be used for *voice communications* and has special equipment for use as a *digital transmission circuit* or *channel.*

duct. A permanent tube or tunnel, usually installed inside of walls and foundations, or underground, through which *cables* may be pulled or *threaded* for installation or replacement. See *atmospheric duct; elevated duct.*

ducting. The *trapping* of a *wave,* caused by a layering of *transmission media,* in which a layer of material of a given *refractive index* is bounded on both sides by layers of material of lower refractive index, thus trapping a wave in the higher refractive index material. For the case of *sound waves,* the surrounding walls of the duct can be sound-reflective rather than sound-absorbing. The phenomenon is useful in the operation of *optical fibers* to keep *signals* confined to the fiber.

Ducting also occurs in layers of the atmosphere. Also see *trapped electromagnetic waves.*

duct optical cable. An *optical cable* designed for use in *underground ducts.*

dummy character. See *null character.*

dummy group. In *cryptosystems,* a *code group* that has the appearance of a valid *code* or *cipher group,* but has no *plain text* significance.

dummy load. A dissipative *impedance-matched circuit element* used at the end of a *transmission line* to absorb all *incident power* and thus avoid *reflections.* The incident energy is converted to heat. The actual useful load plus the dummy load is usually equal to the *characteristic impedance* of the line.

duobinary coding. A form of *binary coding* in which a 0 in the *input* sequence of *binary digits* is represented by a 0 in the *output* sequence of duobinary digits, whereas a binary 1 in the input sequence of binary digits might cause a change in the output duobinary sequence *pulse* level, this change depending on the number of 0's since the last 1 occurred in the input binary sequence. If the number of 0's since the last 1 is even, no change occurs, if the number of 0's since the last 1 is odd, a change occurs in the duobinary pulse to the appropriate level at which it was last positioned. The duobinary *bandwidth* is about half of that required for *non-return-to-zero (NRZ).* It requires about 6.5 KHz to pass 16 *kbps data.* Duobinary is a *ternary signal* and thus has a poorer *signal-to-noise ratio* than regular binary. However, this loss is offset by its increased data handling capacity. Duobinary is encoded by conditioning the data, delaying it one bit interval, inverting it, and then adding it to the undelayed version.

duobinary signal. A *pseudo-binary coded signal* in which a 0 *bit* is represented by a zero-level *electric current* or *voltage;* a 1 bit is represented by a positive-level current (voltage), if the quantity of 0 bits since the last 1 bit is even, and by a negative-level current (voltage), if the quantity of 0 bits since the last 1 bit is odd. Also see *pseudo-binary code.*

duplex. See *semiduplex; two-frequency half-duplex.*

duplex circuit. In a *communication system,* a *circuit* or *transmission path* capable of *transmitting* or *conducting signals* in both directions simultaneously. A single *optical fiber* can handle *lightwaves* in both directions at the same time, but a single wire cannot handle *direct currents* both ways at the same time. Synonymous with *full-duplex circuit.* See *half-duplex-circuit.* Also see *duplex operation.*

duplex communication. *Transmission* between two points in both directions simultaneously. Synonymous with *full duplex.* Also see *speech-plus-duplex operation.* See *two-way-simultaneous communication.* See Figure D-10.

D-10. The Dataphone Switched Digital Service® for 56 000 *bps* for full **duplex communication,** *synchronous transmission,* and retention of *data* in *digital* form. (Reproduced with permission of AT&T Co.)

duplex equipment. Equipment that comprises *transmitting* and *receiving components* arranged for *duplex operation.* Also see *half-duplex equipment.*

duplexer. 1. A device that allows the simultaneous use of a *transmitter* and a *receiver* in *connection* with a common element such as an *antenna system.* Thus, the *duplexer* allows the same antenna to be used for *transmission* and *reception* at the same time. **2.** In radar, a *transmitter-receiver switch* that automatically *couples* an *antenna* to a *receiver* during the *receiving* period and to a *transmitter* during the *transmitting* period. Also see *diplexer; duplex operation.*

duplexing. See *time-division duplexing.*

duplex operation. Operation of *transmission equipment* in such a manner that simultaneous two-way conversations may be held or *messages* may be passed between two given points. Synonymous with *full-duplex operation; two-way simultaneous operation.* Also see *diplex operation; duplex circuit; duplexer; half-duplex operation.* See *speech-plus-duplex operation; two-way-simultaneous communication.*

duplex transmission. *Transmission* over a *circuit* in both directions at the same time. See *half-duplex operation.*

duration. See *outage duration; significant interval theoretical duration.*

duration indication. In *telephone system operation,* the indication, upon request by the *network* to the paying *station,* that the time of a *call* is chargeable, and that the chargeable time is to be indicated prior to the *release* of the paying station or by recall at a more convenient time. See *automatic duration indication.*

duress signal. In *communication systems,* a prearranged *signal* used to indicate to the *addressee* or *destination user* that the *operator* is being forced to *transmit* the particular *message* in which the signal occurs.

duty cycle. In *radio transmission,* the daily schedule of a *transmitting station.*

duty factor. The product of *pulse duration* and *pulse* repetition *rate* from a wave consisting of *periodic pulses.*

DX. *Direct-current (DC) signaling.*

DX signaling. *Direct-current (DC) signaling.*

DX signaling unit. A *direct-current (DC) duplex* unit that applies *E-and-M lead signals* into a *cable* consisting of two *double-current* leads. These signals are *transmitted* on the same *cable pair* that transmits the *message.* Also see *E-and-M lead signaling.*

dynamicizer. See *parallel-to-serial converter.*

dynamic range. **1.** In a *transmission system,* the ratio, usually expressed in *decibels,* between the *noise* level of the *system* and its overload level. **2.** The ratio, usually expressed in *decibels,* between the overload level and the minimum acceptable *signal* level in a *system* or a *transducer.* **3.** The ratio, usually expressed in *decibels,* of the maximum *power* that can be *transmitted* by a *communication system* without *distortion* to the minimum power that can be transmitted without *signal* degradation due to *noise.*

dynamics. See *antenna dynamics.*

dynamic scanning. In *optical fiber transmission systems,* a technique in which a *fiber bundle* is vibrated about a fixed point with reference to the impressed *image* in order to render the *fiber pattern* less visible at the *output* end.

dynamic variation. A short time variation that is outside of the *steady state* condition in the characteristics of *power* delivered to *communication equipment.* Synonymous with *transient.*

E

E-and-M lead signaling. A *signaling* technique in which *communication* between a portion of a *circuit* and a separate signaling unit is accomplished using two leads, namely the 'E' lead that rEceives open or *ground signals* from the signaling unit, and the 'M' lead that transMits battery or ground signals to the signaling unit. Also see *DX signaling unit; pulse-link repeater.*

early distortion. *Distortion* that is due to advanced arrival of parts of a *signal.* Signal parts are *transmitted* in a given sequence, each part in a specific *time slot.* A part that arrives ahead of the proper instant causes early distortion. Synonymous with *negative distortion.*

early failure period. In a device with a large population of *components,* the period that immediately follows the initial use or turn-on. The period is characterized by a *failure rate* that is higher than the rate that occurs during the following period, called the *constant failure period.* The high failure rate is primarily caused by defects in the failing components. Also see *bathtub curve.* Synonymous with *infant mortality period.*

early warning. See *airborne early warning.*

early warning net. See *airborne early warning net.*

early-warning radar. *Long-range radar* that provides range, direction, and elevation *information* as far as the *radar horizon,* and at *slant ranges* beyond the *atmosphere.* It provides the earliest possible data on the position and movement of objects (targets) in space, including missiles, aircraft, and *satellites.* Also see *long-range radar.*

earth. In an *electric circuit,* a point in the circuit that is connected by a zero *resistance* path directly into or under the ground. For example, a point connected to a heavy copper stake driven deeply into a salted and wetted area in the ground, or to a metal water pipe that is buried in the ground. The earth can also be used as one part of a circuit, as in a *ground return.* A perfect earth is at zero potential; it never rises above zero potential no matter how much current is driven into it; it is of infinite *capacity;* and the *connection* to it is of zero resistance and infinite *conductance*. Earth is often used as a synonym for ground, though a distinction should be made. Also see *ground*. See *smooth earth*.

earth coverage. In *satellite communications*, the condition that exists when a *radio, video, microwave,* or *optical beam* is sufficiently wide to cover *(illuminate)* the surface of the earth that is exposed to the *satellite*. The beam is assumed *propagating* from the satellite to the earth. The entire earth facing the satellite is assumed to be illuminated for all *elevation angles* from the earth to the satellite above the minimum at which *reception* and *transmission* is possible.

earth radiation. The totality of *electromagnetic radiation* that emanates from the earth.

earth radiation balance. The balance of thermal *radiation* (*infrared* radiation) as determined by the difference between *solar radiation* absorbed by the earth surface-*atmosphere system,* and the earth surface-atmosphere radiation at a given point. The annual average radiation balance of the whole surface of the earth equals zero. The principal varying factors are cloudiness, *albedo,* and the *temperature* of the underlying surface. The radiation balance of the earth at a point has a latitudinal, diurnal, and annual variability. Near the equator the balance is always positive, in the high latitudes it is nearly always negative. The annual average value of radiation balance of the earth in the zone $0-10^0$ N is $40.3 - 34.7 = 5.6$ cal/m^2-min. At $80-90^\circ$ N it is $10.6 - 24.5 = -13.9$ cal/m^2-min.

earth radius. See *effective earth radius*.

earth satellite. A *satellite* that *orbits* the earth. See *synchronous earth satellite*.

earth station. In *satellite communications,* a *space communication station* in the *space service* that is located either on the earth's surface (land or sea) or in the air. It may be aboard a land vehicle, fixed to the ground, on board a ship, in an aircraft, or in a balloon. It differs from the ground *stations* that maintain *communications* without the use of *spacecraft*. In the space service, an earth station is an equipment complex that contains all of the radio and support equipment for communication with, and control of, a *satellite*. For a satellite communication earth station this complex may not include all the *baseband signal* processing equipment necessary for *channeling* and *interfacing* with terminal equipment or with other terrestrial communication networks. See *communication-satellite earth station; fixed earth station; meteorological-satellite earth station; mobile earth station; radionavigation-satellite earth station; space research earth station; space telecommand earth station; space telemetering earth station; space tracking earth station.* See Figure E-1. Also see Figure S-2.

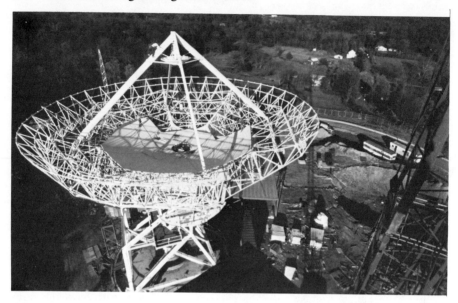

E-1. An earth station for a nationwide *satellite telecommunication network*. (Reproduced with permission of AT & T Co.)

earth station engineering control center. The part of an *earth station* that contains *control consoles* for *switching, monitoring, patching,* and *supervising transmission* and *reception* equipment.

earth terminal. See *satellite earth terminal.*

earth-width pulse. A *pulse* generated by a device in a *satellite* that can sense or detect *radiation* from the earth. It is used to determine satellite attitude (orientation). For a spin-stabilized satellite, it has a duration *(pulse length)* depending on the time that a portion of the earth is in the sensor field of view as the satellite spins on its axis.

eavesdropping. The interception of *information* using methods other than *wire-tapping.*

EBCDIC. *Extended binary-coded decimal interchange code.*

eccentric connector. See *double-eccentric connector.*

eccentricity. See *cladding eccentricity.*

ECCM. *Electronic counter-countermeasure.*

echo. A *wave* that has been *reflected* or otherwise returned toward its *source* with sufficient magnitude and delay to be perceived. Echoes are frequently measured in *decibels* relative to the directly *transmitted* wave at the point of measure. See *permanent echo; radar echo.*

echo area. See *scattering cross-section.*

echo attenuation. In a *circuit*, such as a two-wire or four-wire circuit, in which the two directions of *transmission* can be separated from each other, the *attenuation* of the *signals* that return to the *input* of the circuit. It is the ratio of the echo *power* received to the power transmitted. It is usually expressed in *decibels*.

echo check. A method of checking the accuracy of *transmission* of *data*, by which the received data are returned to the *transmitter* or *source* for comparison with the data that were transmitted. Also see *information feedback*.

echo effect. In *facsimile* or *video transmisison*, a defect in reproduction due to *transmission* anomalies consisting of the appearance of a second outline, or several other outlines, of the scanned object. The *image* outlines are displaced in the scanning direction from the outline of the normal picture. For example, in *television* transmission, the extra outlines may be due to reflections from objects in or near the transmission path from the *transmitter* to the *receiver*.

echo noise. See *feeder echo noise*.

echoplex. An *echo check* applied to *network terminals* operating in the *two-way simultaneous transmission mode*.

echo sounder. A device that determines water depth or distance to an *object* by measuring the time it takes sound, elastic, or *electromagnetic waves* of known velocity to *reflect* from the bottom of the water body or from the distant object. Echo sounders usually employ *damped CW transmission*.

echo suppressor. A voice-operated device that, when connected to a two-way *telephone circuit*, attenuates *echo signals* propagating in one direction caused by telephone signals propagating in the other direction. See *half echo suppressor*.

eclipse. Any obscuration of *light* from a *source* by an intervening body. In celestial mechanics, it is the obscuration of light from one celestial body by another body that lies between the source and an observer or photodetector. For example, an eclipse of the sun by a planet, called a *transit* of the planet, occurs when the planet prevents light from the sun from reaching an observer, usually on earth. An eclipse of the sun by the moon is called a *solar eclipse*, and an eclipse of the moon by the earth is called a *lunar eclipse*. See *lunar eclipse; solar eclipse*.

ecliptic. The great circle traced on the celestial sphere annually by the sun. The inclination of the ecliptic plane to the *celestial equatorial* plane is about 23.5^0. Also see *equinox*.

ecliptic obliquity. The inclination of the ecliptic plane to the equatorial plane of the earth. The approximate value is 23.5^0. The accurate value for any date is obtainable from almanacs.

ECM. *Electronic countermeasure.*

edge. See *reference edge.*

edge absorption. See *band edge absorption.*

edge-emitting diode. See *restricted edge-emitting diode.*

edge-emitting LED. A *light-emitting diode,* with a *spectral output* emanating from between the heterogeneous layers. It usually has a higher output *intensity* and greater *coupling efficiency* to an *optical fiber* or *integrated optical circuit* than the *surface-emitting LED,* but not as great as the *injuction laser diode.* Surface-emitting and edge-emitting LED provide several milliwatts of power in the 0.8–1.2 *micron* spectral range at drive *currents* of 100–200 mA. Diode lasers at these currents provide tens of milliwatts. Also see *surface-emitting LED.*

edge notched card. 1. A card into which notches that represent *data* are punched around the edges. 2. A card that is punched with hole patterns in *tracks* along the edges. Usually the hole patterns are in the same *codes* that are used in punched paper tape.

edge-response. The ability of an *optical fiber bundle* to form, maintain, and resolve an *image* of a sharply outlined *object* or other image, such as a *knife-edge.*

edge test. See *Foucault knife-edge test.*

EEP. *Electromagnetic emission policy.*

effect. See *acoustooptic effect; capture effect; Dellinger effect; Doppler effect; echo effect; electrooptic effect; fluid immersion effect; flywheel effect; Kendall effect; knife-edge effect; magnetooptic effect; night effect; photoconductive effect; photoelectric effect; photoelectromagnetic effect; photoemissive effect; photovoltaic effect; piezoelectric effect; skin effect; speckle effect; Stark effect; thermoelectric effect; Zeeman effect.*

effective antenna length. The ratio of the *open-circuit voltage* of an *antenna* to the *electric field intensity* in volts per unit length, such as volts per meter.

effective area. See *antenna effective area.*

effective data transfer rate. The average number of *bits, characters, blocks,* or other designated unit of *data,* per unit time transferred from a *data source* and accepted as valid and correct by a *data sink,* within a prescribed maximum permissible error rate.

effective earth radius. The radius of a hypothetical earth for which the distance to the *radio horizon,* assuming rectilinear *propagation* (propagation in a geometric straight line), is the same as that for the actual earth with an assumed uniform vertical gradient of *refractive index.* For the standard *atmosphere,* the effective radius is 4/3 that of the actual earth. Also see *Fresnel zone; K-factor; path clearance; path profile; path survey; propagation path obstruction.*

effective height. 1. The height of the center of *radiation* of an *antenna* above the effective ground level. 2. In low frequency applications involving loaded or nonloaded vertical antennas, the moment of the current distribution in the vertical section divided by the *input current.* For an antenna with symmetrical current distribution, the center of *radiation* is the center of distribution. For an antenna with asymmetrical current distribution, the center of radiation is the center of current moments when viewed from directions near the direction of maximum radiation.

effective input noise temperature. The source or input noise *temperature* in a two-port *network* or *amplifier* that will result in the same output noise power as that of the actual network or amplifier. It is assumed that *noise*-free equipment and *sources* are used to make the measurements. Also see *effective noise temperature.*

effective isotropic radiated power. The *power* that is supplied to an *antenna* multiplied by the *directive gain* of the antenna, that is, the gain in a given direction relative to an *isotropic antenna.* Also see *effective radiated power.*

effective noise temperature. The *temperature* that corresponds to a given *noise* level from all sources, including *thermal noise, source noise,* and induced noise *(interference).* The effective noise temperature, T_n, is given by $T_n = 290(N.F. - 1)$ where 290K is the standard noise temperature in *kelvins* and *N.F.* is the *noise figure.* Also see *effective input noise temperature.*

effective radiated power (ERP). 1. The *power* supplied to an *antenna* multiplied by the *directive gain,* that is, the *power gain* of the antenna in a given direction relative to an *isotropic antenna.* 2. The *power* supplied to an *antenna* multiplied by the *power gain* of the antenna in a given direction relative to a standard *dipole* antenna. The ratio of the *power gain* referred to an *isotropic* antenna and that referred to a standard *half-wave dipole* antenna is equivalent to 2.15 dB. Also see *effective isotropic radiated power (EIRP).*

effective transfer rate. The average number of *binary digits, characters,* or *blocks* transferred between two points and accepted as valid at the receiving point per unit of time, that is, the average number of error-free *data units* transferred per unit of time.

effective transmission speed. The long-term rate at which *data* is processed by a *transmission facility.* It is determined by dividing the number of transmitted *data units,* such as *binary digits, characters,* or *blocks* in a significantly long time period, by the length of the significantly long time period, thereby obtaining an average number of data units per unit of time, such as characters per minute averaged over several hours. Synonymous with *average transmisison rate.* Also see *efficiency factor; instantaneous transmisison speed; throughput.*

effector. See *format effector (FE).*

effects on electronics. See *transient radiation effects on electronics (TREE).*

efficiency. See *block efficiency; block rate efficiency; coupling efficiency; differential quantum efficiency; luminous efficiency; luminous radiation efficiency; optical power efficiency; radiant efficiency; response quantum efficiency; source coupling efficiency; transmission efficiency.*

efficiency factor. In *telegraph communications,* the ratio of the time to *transmit* a text automatically at a specified *modulation rate,* to the time actually required to receive the same text with an error rate less than a specified maximum. All the *communication facilities* are assumed to be in a normal condition of adjustment and operation. Telegraph communication systems may have different efficiency factors for the two directions of *transmission.* The conditions of measurement should be specified such as the duration and the *error detection* criteria. Also see *effective transmission speed; instantaneous transmission speed; throughput.* See *block correction efficiency factor.*

efficiency test. See *termination efficiency test.*

EFL. Equivalent focal length.

eigenvalue. A constant in an equation or expression that can assume any one of a set of finite values and still have the equation or expression be a solution of an *integral, differential,* or other equation or function. Thus, in the solution of the *wave equation,* each eigenvalue produces another *propagation mode* that is allowable for a particular *waveguide.* The allowable eigenvalues are determined by physical factors such as waveguide dimensions, and for a given guide may be simply multiples of π or of *wavelength.* Also see *mode; wave equation.*

either-way communication. See *two-way-alternate communication.*

elastic. See *photoelastic.*

elastic wave. A *wave* that consists of a series of *pulses* of elastic deformation traveling in a *medium.* Its *propagation* speed and *attenuation* depend upon the elastic properties of the medium.

E-layer. An *ionized layer* of the *ionosphere* about 175 km in altitude. Synonymous with *Heaviside layer; Kennelly-Heaviside layer; E-region.*

electric.   Pertaining to the natural phenomena of the motion, effects, and characteristics of the electron and other charged particles that exhibit attraction and repulsion in accordance with *Coulomb's law.*

electrical conductivity.   A *transmission medium* parameter that defines the ability of a material to conduct an *electric current* when under the influence of an applied *electric field.*   The conductivity is the constant of proportionality in the *constitutive relation* between the electrical *current density* and the applied electric field intensity.   It is expressed mathematically as:

$$J = \sigma E$$

where J is the current density, σ is the conductivity, and E is the electric field intensity.   For example, if J is in amperes per square *meter* and E is in volts per meter, the conductivity is given as $\sigma = J/E$ ampere/volt-meter or (ohm-meter)$^{-1}$.

electrical conductor.   A material in which large numbers of atoms whose *electrons* are easily excited into the *conduction band* from the *valence band* and hence are easily moved in large quantities upon application of small *electric fields.* In a conductor, it is difficult to maintain a large potential difference (i.e., voltage) between two points because of the large currents, which prevent the buildup or segregation of charges at any specific point.   In many devices, electrical conductors are used to provide equipotential surfaces between points or *terminals* because of the high conductivity or extremely low resistance to flow.   Normally, good electrical conductors are poor *light* conductors (light conduits), and vice versa.

electrical signal.   See *electronic signal.*

electrical degree.   A 1/360 of a cycle of a *wave.*   A complete cycle is measured from a point in one wave to the corresponding point in the next wave, such as from crest to crest or from a zero crossing from negative to positive value to the next zero crossing from negative to positive.   Also see *spatial degree.*

electrical delay line.   See *electromagnetic delay line.*

electrical interface.   A boundary between two electrical *systems,* where the interconnection that enables them to interoperate is specified.   The specifications usually include the type, quantity, and function of the interconnection *circuits,* and the type and form of signals to be interchanged via those circuits.

electrical length.   A length that is expressed in *wavelengths, radians,* or *degrees.* When expressed in angular units, it is the distance expressed as the number of whole wavelengths, or fraction of a wavelength, multiplied by 2π to obtain radians, or by 360 to obtain degrees.   The length may be a *phase shift,* a *phase delay* introduced by a *delay line,* the *length* of a *pulse,* or the distance, in degrees or radians, between two *significant instants* of a *wave*. It may be converted to time when *frequency*, angular velocity, or *propagation* velocity is known.

electrically-despun antenna.   An *antenna* without moving mechanical parts that can electrically direct its *main lobe* in a given direction while the platform on which it is mounted pitches, rolls, and sways. For example, a *phased-array antenna* that is mounted on a spinning *satellite* and can fix its *main beam* in the direction of the earth at all times. Also see *mechanically-despun antenna*.

electrically-powered telephone.   A *telephone* in which the operating *power* is obtained either from batteries located at the telephone (local battery) or from a telephone *central office* (common battery). Also see *sound-powered telephone*.

electrical transmission.   1. The *transmission* of *messages* by electrical means, such as by wire, *radio*, or *optical fiber*. For example, a message sent by *telephone, telegraph, facsimile*, or *television*. *Flashing lights, infrared,* and colored lights may be quasi-electrical means, whereas mail, messenger, handflags, smoke, *pyrotechnics, panels,* and *flaghoists* are considered nonelectrical means. 2. A *message transmitted* by electrical means.

electric current.   The amount of electrical charge that passes through a given cross-sectional area per unit time. Thus, the total drift of electrons or other charges past a point per unit of time. The SI unit of current is the ampere, which is equal to 1 coulomb per second.

electric field.   The effect produced by the existence of an electric charge, such as an electron, ion, or proton, in the volume of space or medium that surrounds it. Each of a distribution of charges contributes to the whole field at a point on the basis of superposition. A charge placed in the volume of space or in the surrounding medium has a force exerted on it. The magnitude of the force is the product of the strength of the field and the magnitude of the charge. Thus, $E = F/q$, where E is the electric *field strength* and F is the force it exerts on the charge q. The direction of the force is in the same direction as the field for positive charges, and in the opposite direction for negative charges. Moving an electric charge with an applied force against the electric field requires work (energy), and increases the potential energy of the moving charge. The field strength is measurable as force per unit charge or as potential difference per unit distance. It is also expressible as electric lines of flux per unit of cross-sectional area. It is a *vector* quantity. Also see Figure I-1.

electric field component.   The part of an *electromagnetic wave* that consists of a time-varying *electric field* whose interaction with a *magnetic field* gives rise to the *propagation* of a field (i.e., energy) in a direction perpendicular to both fields. *Reflection, refraction,* and *transmission* that occur at *media interfaces* depend upon the direction of the electric field *component* and the *magnetic field component* relative to the direction of the *interface surface* as well as the *refractive indices, permittivities, permeabilities,* and *conductivities* of the transmission media on both sides of the interface surface. Also see *Maxwell's equations; wave equation.*

electric field force. **1.** The force exerted by an *electric field* upon an electric charge placed in the field. **2.** The force of attraction or repulsion between two electric charges, each subject to the other's *electric field.* Like charges (both positive or both negative) repel each other, whereas opposite charges (one negative and one positive) attract each other. Also see *Coulomb's law.*

electricity. See *static electricity.*

electric permittivity. A *transmission medium parameter* that serves as the constant of proportionality between the magnitude of the force exerted between two point charges of known magnitude separated by a given distance. It is defined by the relation:

$$F = Q_1 Q_2 / 4\pi \epsilon d^2$$

where Q_1 and Q_2 are the charges, F is the force between them, d is their distance of separation, ϵ is the electric permittivity of the medium in which they are imbedded, and π is 3.1416. The electric permittivity, along with the *magnetic permeability*, determines the *refractive index*, thus having an influence on *reflection, refraction,* and *transmission* at interface surfaces. Also see *constitutive relations; Maxwell's equations; Snell's law.* Synonymous with *dielectric constant.*

electric vector. A representation of the *electric field* associated with an *electromagnetic wave,* and hence with a *lightwave,* that specifies the direction and *amplitude* of this electric field. Also see *magnetic vector.*

electric wave. See *transverse electric wave.*

electroluminescence. The direct conversion of electrical energy to *light energy.*

electromagnetic delay line. A sequence of *distributed* or *lumped electric circuit parameters* (elements) that introduces a delay in a *signal* due to the *propagation time delay* of the signal from one point in the sequence of elements to another. The *time constants* of the elements introduce the delay in each element as the signal propagates. A *rectangular pulse* introduced at one end usually has the higher *frequencies attenuated* so that the *output signal* is less square than the *input signal.* The *line* can be used to bring about exact coincidence or synchronism at *combinational logic elements* by delaying the earlier signals. Synonymous with *electrical delay line.*

electromagnetic emission control. *Emission control* applicable to *electromagnetic radiation, signal transmission,* and related *communication-electronic* emissions only. Also see *emission control.*

electromagnetic emission policy (EEP). Policy that governs the operation of equipment that *emits electromagnetic, electrostatic, magnetostatic,* or *electromagnetostatic field* energy. It concerns the *bands* of *frequencies* and the use of the equipment on which *transmission* is permitted. Synonymous with *electronic emission policy.* Also see *emission control.*

electromagnetic energy density. The amount of energy contained per unit volume of space or *transmission medium* at a point at which an *electromagnetic wave* is *propagating* or *standing.* The density is scalar and is a function of the *electric* and *magnetic field intensities* at the point. When the velocity is considered, the energy density can be considered as the energy per unit volume times distance per unit time, thus becoming the vector quantity of energy per cross-sectional area per second, i.e., the *power density.*

electromagnetic environment. The space and time distribution in various *frequency* ranges of the *radiated* or *conducted electromagnetic emission power* levels that may be encountered by equipment when performing its assigned function. The electromagnetic environment of equipment may also be expressed in terms of the local *electric field strength* in the immediate vicinity of the equipment.

electromagnetic field. A field characterized by both *electric* and *magnetic field vectors* that usually interact with each other rather than exist independently of each other as in *electrostatic, staticmagnetic,* and *electromagnetostatic fields.* The electromagnetic field varies with time and propagates as a *wave* far from its *source,* whereas the others, although they may be made to vary, do not *propagate* very far from their sources and decay rapidly with distance. Also see *wave equation.*

electromagnetic hazard. See *electromagnetic radiation hazard; hazards of electromagnetic radiation to fuel (HERF); hazards of electromagnetic radiation to ordnance (HERO); hazards of electromagnetic radiation to personnel (HERP).*

electromagnetic interference. *Interference* caused or generated in a circuit by *electromagnetic radiation* energy *coupling.* The radiation may be *lightwaves, radio waves, gamma rays,* high-energy neutrons, *x-rays,* or *microwaves.* Sources include artificial *transmissions* and *emissions* as well as natural sources, such as cosmic and solar sources. The phenomenon of *interference* is considered to occur when *electromagnetic* energy causes an unacceptable or undesirable *response, malfunction, degradation,* or interruption of the intended operation or performance of electronic equipment. It includes any *electronic emission, radiation,* or *induction* that endangers the functioning of *radionavigation* or other safety services. The potential to degrade, obstruct, or interrupt a *communication-electronic circuit* or *system* is also included.

electromagnetic interference (EMI) control. The control of *radiated* and *conducted electromagnetic* energy such that *emissions* unnecessary for *system,* subsystem, or equipment operation are minimized or eliminated. Electromagnetic radiated and conducted emissions regardless of their origin within the equipment, subsystem, or system are held to a level of acceptability for specific purposes, such as prevention of *interference, compromise,* and loss of energy. Successful EMI control, along with *susceptibility* control, leads to *electromagnetic compatibility (EMC).*

electromagnetic pulse (EMP). A *broadband,* high-intensity, short-duration burst of *electromagnetic* energy, such as might occur from a nuclear detonation. In the case of a nuclear detonation, the electromagnetic pulse *(signal)* consists of a *continuous spectrum* with most of its energy distributed throughout the lower *frequencies* between 3 Hz and 30 kHz. Also see *pulse.*

electromagnetic radiation. *Radiation* that is made up of oscillating and interacting *electric* and *magnetic fields.* The radiation is *propagated* with a *phase velocity* of $v_p = \lambda f = c/n$ where λ is the *wavelength, f* is the *frequency, c* is the *velocity of light* in a vacuum (approximately 3×10^8 m/s), and n is the *refractive index* of the *transmission medium.* It includes *gamma radiation, x-rays, ultraviolet, visible,* and *infrared radiation.* It also includes *radar* and *radio waves* as well as *microwaves.* Also see *radiation pattern; radiation scattering.*

electromagnetic radiation control. **1.** An operational plan to minimize the use of *electromagnetic radiation* in the event of an emergency, an impending attack, or possible use as an aid to attacking aircraft, missiles, or other devices. The control of all electromagnetic radiation, useful and nonuseful, with an aim toward its reduction, redistribution, minimization, elimination, change *(frequency, modulation, power level, spreading),* or *repolarization* is also included in electromagnetic radiation control when the main purpose is *security,* particularly against missile *homing, interception, jamming,* or *navigation.* **2.** To insure *electromagnetic radiation* lies within prescribed limits.

electrochemical recording. Recording by means of a chemical reaction brought about by the passage of a *signal*-controlled *electric current* through the sensitized portion of the *recording medium.* The technique can be used in *facsimile receiving systems.*

electrolytic recording. *Electrochemical recording* in which the chemical change is made possible by the presence of an electrolyte.

electromagnetic compatibility (EMC). The condition that exists when *communication equipment* is collectively performing its individual designed functions in a common *electromagnetic* environment without causing or suffering unacceptable *degradation* due to electromagnetic *interference* from other *communication-electronic equipment* in the same environment. It includes the capability of electronic equipment to be operated in the intended environment at designed levels of efficiency without degradation due to unintentional interference. EMC encompasses the utilization of the full flexibility of equipment as well as the ability of the *operators* to deal with interference if and when it occurs.

electromagnetic compatibility (EMC) analysis. An investigation of the *electromagnetic compatibility* of *communication-electronic (C-E) system components* for operation in the environment created by the totality of other electronic systems. For example, in 1952, during the development of the EDVAC (Electronic Discrete Variable Automatic Computer) at the Aberdeen Proving Ground, Maryland, an electromagnetic compatibility analysis revealed that *radar beams* from radars being locally tested caused the computer to *malfunction* when the beams were focused on the computer thus creating *errors* in computed results which caused unprogrammed halts in computer operation. Also see *electromagnetic radiation hazard.*

electromagnetic radiation hazard. The exposure to danger that can be brought about by *electrostatic, magnetostatic, electromagnetostatic,* and *electromagnetic fields* of sufficient *strength* (intensity) to produce *electric currents, voltages,* or molecular structural changes in material media that can cause harmful effects to personnel and materiel. For example, the *radiation* can cause detonation of explosive materials, ignition of combustible materials, damage to electronic *circuits,* damage to the cells of living tissue, and *malfunction* of equipment. These fields can be produced by high-power *communication equipment, radar,* and other electronic devices installed in *ship, aircraft,* and *land stations.* Synonymous with *electromagnetic hazard.* Also see *electromagnetic compatibility (EMC) analysis.*

electromagnetic spectrum. 1. All the *frequencies* (or *wavelengths*) present in given *electromagnetic radiation.* A given *spectrum* could include a single *frequency,* a wide range of frequencies, or a group of *narrow bands,* depending on the amount of *power* of each frequency. **2.** The entire range of *wavelengths,* extending from shortest to longest or vice versa, that can be generated physically. This range of electromagnetic wavelengths extends almost from zero to infinity and includes the visible portion of the *spectrum* known as *light.* Also see *frequency spectrum; visual spectrum.*

electromagnetic surveillance. A search for, and identification of, *electromagnetic signals* in a specified area or at a specified point (location). See *exploratory electromagnetic surveillance.*

electromagnetic survivability. The ability of a *communication system* to resume functioning without evidence of *degradation* following temporary exposure to an adverse *electromagnetic environment,* such as excessive *sunspot activity,* high-intensity *jamming, infrared* or *untraviolet* exposure, or an atomic blast. The system may be *degraded* during the exposure, but survivability is a measure of the extent to which there is no *component* destruction or *degradation* significant enough to preclude successful *operation.* Also see *optical fiber radiation damage.*

electromagnetic theory.   The theory of *propagation* of energy by combined *electric* and *magnetic fields.*   Much of the theory is embodied in *Maxwell's equations.*

electromagnetic wave (EMW).   The effect obtained when a time-varying *electric field* and a time-varying *magnetic field* interact, causing electrical and magnetic energy to be *propagated* in a direction that is dependent upon the spatial relationship of the two interacting fields that are interchanging their energies. The most common EMW consists of time-varying electric and magnetic fields that are directed at right angles to each other, thus defining a plane in which they both lie, i.e., the *polarization plane.*   The direction of energy propagation is perpendicular to this plane, and the wave is called *plane polarized.*   A plane-polarized wave may be *linearly, circularly,* or *elliptically polarized* depending on the *phase* relationship between the varying electric and magnetic fields. When launched initially, the interacting and interrelated time-varying electric and magnetic fields are produced by an electric current, consisting of moving electric charges that oscillate in time and space, such as might oscillate in a wire, called an *antenna.* If an electric field is made to vary in time in a *conductive* medium in order to produce an oscillating current, an electromagnetic wave will be launched that can propagate energy through material media and a vacuum. If the time and spatial distributions of currents are given, the electromagnetic field intensities, power flow rates, and energy densities can be determined everywhere in space, provided also that the parameters of the material in the space are known. *Lightwaves* are electromagnetic waves that can travel in *optical fibers* where they can be trapped and guided, and can be made to energize *photodetectors.*   See *horizontally-polarized electromagnetic wave; left-hand polarized electromagnetic wave; plane-polarized electromagnetic wave; right-hand polarized electromagnetic wave; transverse electromagnetic wave; trapped electromagnetic wave; uniform plane-polarized electromagnetic wave; vertically-polarized electromagnetic wave.*   Also see *elliptical polarization.*

electromagnetic wave transmission.   See *low-detectability electromagnetic wave transmission.*

electromagnetic wave velocity.   The velocity of an *electromagnetic wave* in a *given transmission medium.*   For a vacuum, the velocity is approximately 3×10^8 m/sec, designated as c. In other media, the velocity is c/n, where n, the *refractive index,* is about 1.003 for air. 1.33 for seawater, 9 for distilled water, and 1.5 to 2.0 for certain types of glass and plastics.

electromagnetostatic field.   A field of force in which both *electrostatic fields* and *magnetostatic fields* exist at the same point and are produced by time-independent *currents* flowing in a conducting region whose *electric conductivity* is so low that the *electric field intensity* in the conducting region cannot be neglected. Each *field vector* is nonzero. The electrostatic and magnetostatic fields are *coupled* by the electric current density given as:

$$J = \sigma E$$

where σ is the *electric conductivity* and E is the *electric field intensity,* the current giving rise to the *magnetic field* in accordance with Ampere's law. Thus, the electromagnetostatic field has coupled time-invariant fields, while the *electromagnetic wave* has coupled time-variant *electric* and *magnetic fields.*

electromechanical recording. Recording accomplished by means of a *signal-*actuated mechanical device.

electromotive force (EMF). 1. The driving force of an *electric field* equal to the *electric field intensity* (a gradiant) integrated over any path between two points. Thus, it is equal to the *potential difference,* or the difference between the *absolute potentials* of two points. 2. The *voltage* at a point with respect to a reference point. See *psophometric electromotive force.*

electron. A basic negatively charged particle with a charge of 1.6021×10^{-19} C and a mass of 9.1091×10^{-31} kg. It is outside the nucleus of the chemical elements, exists with different *discrete* energy levels in a given chemical element, differentiates the elements by its population outside the nucleus, and is the moving matter that contributes the most to the formation of *electric currents* and *voltages.* Synonymous with *beta particle.*

electron-beam recording. A method of recording on film in which a *beam* of *electrons* impinging on the *screen* of a *CRT* is used to expose film. Contrast with *fiberscope recording.*

electron energy. See *emitted electron energy.*

electronic. Pertaining to the effects, motion, and behavior of electrons under the influence of *electric* and *magnetic fields,* chemical reaction, physical force (sound, vibration, shock, gravity), bombardment by atomic particles and photons, and other forms of excitation. Control of the flow of electrons allows for *power transmission* and *communications.* Since moving electrons produce *electromagnetic waves, electromagnetic wave propagation* is also included in electronics.

electronically-controllable coupler. An *optical element* that enables other optical elements to be coupled to, or uncoupled from, each other, in accordance with an applied electrical *signal.* For example, two parallel *slab dielectric waveguides* with an optical material between them whose *refractive index* can be altered by application of an electronic signal, thus turning the coupling of the waveguides on or off according to the signal. See Figure E-2.

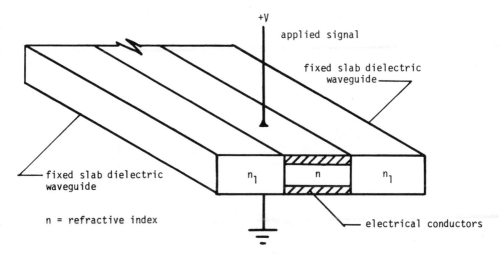

E-2. An **electronically-controllable coupler** (ECC) between two *slab dielectric* (planar) *waveguides.*

electronic charge.   The quantity of charge represented or possessed by one *electron,* equal to 1.6021×10^{-19} *coulombs.*

electronic counter-countermeasure (ECCM).   A *countermeasure* taken to insure the effective use of the *electromagnetic spectrum* despite opposition to such use; or a measure taken to render an *electronic countermeasure* ineffective. See *infrared jamming electronic counter-countermeasure; radio relay electronic counter-countermeasure.*

electronic countermeasure (ECM).   A measure taken to prevent or reduce the effective use of the *electromagnetic spectrum,* particularly for such purposes as *communication,* navigation, *radar,* and control. See *absorption electronic countermeasure; active electronic countermeasure.*

electronic deception.   The deliberate *radiation,* reradiation, alteration, *absorption,* or *reflection* of *electromagnetic* energy in a manner intended to mislead or cause misinterpretation or misuse of *information* received by electronic systems. For example, to insert false data into a *communication system. Deception* and *jamming* can be used in combinations. Deception is normally used first and jamming is used subsequently if deception is not effective. Deception may be used in *electronic warfare* to deliberately create a false appearance of activity. See *manipulative electronic deception (MED).*

electronic device.   See *optoelectronic device.*

electronic directional coupler.   See *optoelectronic directional coupler.*

electronic emission policy. See *electromagnetic emission policy.*

electronic emission security. The totality of measures taken to protect all transmissions from interception and analysis.

electronic exchange. An *automatic telephone exchange* that makes use of *solid state switching* and *computing equipment.*

electronic intelligence (ELINT). The intelligence *information* obtained from activities engaged in the collection and processing of *electromagnetic radiation* received from sources other than *radioactive sources,* such as nuclear detonations, and other than *message traffic* itself. Also see *signal intelligence.*

electronic jamming. An *electronic countermeasure* in which the deliberate *radiation,* reradiation, or *reflection* of *electromagnetic* energy is used to impair the use of electronic devices, equipment, or systems. For example, the *jamming* can be accomplished by radiating or reradiating electromagnetic energy at the *frequency* that the receiver to be impaired uses. Usually the jamming *emission* is *modulated* so as to *mask,* interfere with, or otherwise prevent full use of the equipment to be impaired. See *antielectronic jamming.*

electronic line scanning. In *facsimile* and *video (television) transmission systems, scanning* in which the motion of the *scanning spot* along the *scanning line* is accomplished by electronic means.

electronic reconnaissance. The detection, identification, evaluation, and location of *electromagnetic radiation* emanating from sources other than *radioactive sources* such as nuclear detonations, radioactive waste, or radioactive materials used for medical diagnostic or therapeutic purposes. The reconnaissance is devoted primarily to *communication, radar,* and *control guidance* sources.

electronics. See *communications-electronics; optoelectronics; theater director of communications-electronics; transient radiation effects on electronics (TREE).*

electronic search. An investigation of the distribution of *signals* in the *electromagnetic spectrum,* or portions thereof, in order to determine the existence, *sources,* and characteristics of the *electromagnetic radiation.*

electronic security (ELSEC). 1. The *security* that results from all measures taken to deny unauthorized persons *information* of value that might be derived from interception and study of *electromagnetic radiation.* Information obtained from the *transmission* of *messages* and their interception is not included in ELSEC. 2. The protection that results from all measures designed to deny to unauthorized persons *information* that might be derived from interception and study of electromagnetic radiation from electronic equipment, such as *radiation* from *radio, video,* wire, *optical fiber, microwave, radar, sonar,* and missile systems. Also see *communication security; signal security.*

electronic signal. A *signal* consisting of an *electrical current* (i.e., a flow of electrons) that varies with time or space in accordance with specified conditions or parameters. Synonymous with *electrical signal.*

electronic silence. The prevention of any form of *electromagnetic emission,* including *radio transmission, radar transmission, sonar transmission, electronic sounding,* missile or aircraft *control signaling,* and *emanations* from other equipment such as *receivers* and ignition systems that *radiate electromagnetic* energy. When electronic silence is in effect, all equipment capable of electromagnetic *radiation* is usually kept inoperative. *Frequency bands* and types of equipment affected usually are specified.

electronic surveillance. The receipt, analysis, and evaluation of *signals* obtained from *scanning* a designated volume of space with electronic equipment such as *receivers, radars,* and *infrared scanners.* Electronic surveillance devices may be ground-based or airborne, or may be side-looking, forward-looking, or area-searching. They are used to *monitor, intercept,* classify, and analyze all *electromagnetic transmisison* and *radiation* from or in a given area.

electronic switch. See *semielectronic switch.*

electronic switching system. A *switching system* with *components* that utilize *semiconductor* devices, such as *transistor combinational circuits (logic elements),* semiconductor *diode* matrices, and *integrated circuits* to perform the *selection* and *switching* of *circuits.* Also see *semielectronic switch.*

electronic warfare (EW). The use of *electromagnetic* energy to determine, exploit, reduce, or prevent use by others of the electromagnetic *spectrum* for such purposes as *communication, radar, sonar,* or *control guidance.* EW includes actions taken to retain the use of the electromagnetic spectrum for similar purposes. EW also includes *electronic countermeasures (ECM), electronic counter-counter-measures (ECCM),* and other supporting measures. Also see *radio deception.*

electron lens. A *lens* capable of converging or diverging an *electron beam* by means of *electric* or *magnetic fields* or both.

electron microscope. An *electron-optical* instrument that can produce an enlarged *image* of a *small object* on a fluorescent screen or photographic plate by *focusing* an electron *beam* by means of an *electron lens.* See *scanning electron microscope.*

electron optics. The area of science devoted to directing and guiding *electron beams* using *electric* or *magnetic fields* in the same manner as *lenses* are used on *light beams.* For example, in *image*-converter tubes and *electron microscopes,* pertaining to devices whose operation relies on modification of a material's *refractive index* by *electric fields.* In a *Kerr cell,* the index change is proportional to the square of the electric field, and the material is usually a liquid. In a *Pockel cell,* the material is a crystal whose index changes linearly with the electric field.

electron-volt (eV).   A unit of energy equal to the amount of energy released or acquired when an electric charge equivalent to the charge of one *electron* moves through a *potential difference* of one volt. The unit is convenient to use when expressing energies of charged particles under the influence of *electric* and *magnetic fields.* The electric charge of an electron is usually expressed in *coulombs.* It is equal to 1.6021×10^{-19} coulombs.

electrooptic.   Pertaining to the conversion of *electrical power* or energy into *optical power* or energy, such as the conversion of an *electrical signal* to an *optical signal.* Also see *optoelectronic.*

electrooptic coefficient.   A measure of the extent to which the *refractive index* changes with applied high *electric field,* such as several parts per 10 thousand for applied fields of the order of 20 V/cm. Since the phase shift of a *lightwave* is a function of the refractive index of the *transmission medium* in which it is propagating, the change in index can be used to *phase-modulate* the lightwave by shifting its phase at a particular point along the *guide,* by changing the propagation time to the point. Also see *electrooptic phase modulation.*

electrooptic effect.   The change in the *refractive index* of a material when subjected to an *electric field.* It can be used to *modulate* a *light beam* in a material since many light propagation properties are dependent upon the refractive indices of the *transmission medium* in which the light travels.

electrooptic (e–o) modulator.   A *modulator* that uses the *electrooptic effect* to modulate a *lightwave carrier.*

electrooptic frequency response.   The *response* obtained when an *electrooptic* device is electronically driven by a *signal* consisting of many *frequencies.* For example, the *output* signal *amplitude,* plotted as a function of the frequency of a fixed-amplitude *input* signal, obtained from a Bragg-type surface interaction device that launches *surface waves* on a *piezoelectric* ZnO thin-film *elastooptic waveguide* section using electromechanical *coupling.* The response is specified as the amplitude, or other parameter of the output *signal* of a device, as a function of the frequency of the applied (input) signal.

electrooptic phase modulation.   *Modulation* of the *phase* of a *lightwave* in accordance with an applied *field* serving as the *modulating signal.* For example, changing the *refractive index* and thus the velocity of propagation and the phase at a point in the *transmission medium* in which the wave is propagating. Also see *electrooptic coefficient.*

electrooptics. The field of science and technology devoted to the study and application of the interrelationship of electronics and *optics,* particularly the generation and control of *lightwaves* by electronic means.

electrooptic transmitter. A *transmitter* that accepts an *electrical signal* and converts it to an *optical signal* for *transmission* over an *optical cable.*

electrostatic field. 1. In *electromagnetic field theory,* the electromagnetic field of a *radiating antenna* or *source* of *electromagnetic radiation* that lies in close proximity to the *antenna* or *source.* The electrostatic field varies inversely as the cube of the distance from the antenna or source. It is the electric field intensity of an electric dipole if the time dependence is suppressed. Electrostatic fields surround electric charges. They are a field of force, such that a force is exerted on an electric charge placed in them. Synonymous with *near field.* 2. The field of force produced by the existence of an electric charge, such as an *electron* or proton. The *field intensity* is measured in terms of the force that it exerts on a unit electric charge placed in it. The electrostatic field is usually considered not to vary with time, or to vary slowly relative to field *propagation* times to points in the field far from the electric charge causing the field. The electrostatic field is *uncoupled* from any other field. If the antenna has a maximum overall dimension that is not large compared to the *wavelength* of the *transmitted wave,* this field region may not exist. For an antenna focused at infinity, the radiating electrostatic field is referred to as the *Fresnel zone.* Synonymous with *near field; near zone.* Also see *electric permittivity; induction field; radiation field.*

electrostatic recording. Recording by means of a *signal-controlled electrostatic field* that produces chemical action on the *recording medium.*

electrothermal recording. Recording that is produced principally by *signal*-controlled thermal action on a thermally sensitive *recording medium.*

element. See *code element; combinational logic element; data element; delay element; detectable element; display element; message element; n-ary information element; optical element; picture element (PEL); receiving element; signal element; stop element; thin-film laser element; transmitting element; unit element.*

elemental area. In *facsimile transmission systems,* any segment of a *scanning line* of the subject (object) *copy* whose dimension along the line is equal to the *nominal line width.* The elemental area is not necessarily the same as the area of the *scanning spot.*

elevated duct. An *atmospheric duct* consisting of a high-density air layer that starts at high altitudes and continues upward or remains at high altitudes. Elevated ducts primarily affect *very-high frequency (VHF) transmission.*

elevation. The distance from a reference point, such as a point on the earth's surface, to another point radially away from the center of the earth, that is, the vertical *component* of distance between them.

elevation angle. An angle, in a vertical plane, between a horizontal plane and a line from a point in the vertical plane (observation point, origin, or vertex) to a point (object) above the horizontal plane, measured from the point in the vertical plane.

elevation-over-azimuth. See *altitude-over-azimuth.*

ELF. *Extremely low frequency.*

ELINT. *Electronic intelligence.*

elliptical orbit. See *closed orbit.*

elliptical polarization. *Polarization* of the *electric* and *magnetic field vectors* in a *uniform plane-polarized electromagnetic wave* in which the two arbitrary sinusoidally-varying rectangular *components* of the electric field vector are not equal in magnitude, and there is a *phase* angle between them; i.e., one leads or lags the other by an arbitrary *time phase* or *phase angle.* If the phase angle is not 90°, the ellipse will be inclined to both of the rectangular components. When the phase angle is zero, the ellipse flattens to a straight line, and the wave is *linearly polarized.* If the vectors are equal and 90° out of phase with each other, the wave is *circularly polarized.* In elliptical polarization, the tip of the electric field vector describes an ellipse; thus, the electric vector varies in magnitude and angular velocity as it rotates. Also see *circular polarization; linear polarization.* Synonymous with *axial-ratio polarization.*

ELSEC. *Electronic security.*

EM. The *end-of-medium character.*

emanation. See *compromising emanation.*

emanation security (EMSEC). 1. The protection that results from all measures taken to deny unauthorized persons information of value that might be derived from interception and analysis of *compromising emanations* from electronic equipment. Usually *telecommunication cryptographic systems,* and their *message traffic,* are not included in emanation security. 2. The security that results from all measures taken to deny unauthorized persons *information* of value that might be derived from interception and analysis of *emanations* from *communication systems,* including from cryptoequipment. Synonymous with *emission security.* Also see *communication security.*

EMC. *Electromagnetic compatibility.*

EMC analysis.   *Electromagnetic compatibility (EMC) analysis.*

emergence.   Pertaining to the trigonometric relation between an *emergent ray* and the surface of a *transmission medium.*   See *grazing emergence; normal emergence.*

emergency call.   A *call* used to establish *communications* during an emergency, distress, or disaster.   Also see *emergency message; emergency signal.*

emergency category.   A level (degree) of emergency indicating the extent of danger, urgency, or probability of loss of life or property.   For example, the categories, in descending order of precedence, of distress, urgent, and safety.   These three levels indicate the *precedence* (priority) of *messages.*   Also see *precedence designation.*

emergency communications.   See *distress communications.*

emergency craft frequency.   An international *distress* and *emergency frequency* for survival purposes.   For example, *frequencies* for emergency craft position-indicating *radio beacons,* distress and emergency situations, and *direction-finding transmissions* for search and rescue operations.   Frequencies for distress, safety, emergency, search, and rescue operations are assigned by the *International Telecommunication Union (ITU),* Geneva, Switzerland.

emergency frequency.   See *aircraft emergency frequency; air-ground communication emergency frequency; distress frequency; international aeronautical emergency frequency; military common emergency frequency.*

emergency message.   A *message* that contains *information* pertaining to an emergency, and that is *transmitted* to or from the *station* that is experiencing the emergency.   For example, the emergency message might contain information concerning the nature of the emergency or the type of assistance that is required.   Also see *distress message; emergency call; emergency signal.*

emergency meteorological warning.   A warning of an urgent nature that is of interest to all units (aeronautical, maritime, and land based), usually in a broad area and *broadcasted* on several *frequencies.*   Meteorological warnings include *information* concerning wind, rain, lightning, hail, tidal waves, earthquakes, and tides.   The information covers location, direction, area, and severity.   An emergency meteorological warning could be dispatched to specific units by special means.   The warnings are for the preservation of life, property, and *communication* continuity.   Also see *routine meteorological broadcast; special meteorological broadcast.*

emergency signal.   In *communication system operations,* a *signal* used to alert *listening stations* to suspend operations to the degree necessary to hear the message that follows.   For example, in order of accepted descending *precedence,* the *emergency categories* are distress, urgent, and safety. In *voice communication systems,* these may be *signaled* by speaking three times, respectively for each category, the words MAYDAY, PAN, or SECURITE (pronounced say-coor-ee-tay). Also see *emergency call; emergency message.* See *ground-air visual emergency signal.*

emergency signal alarm. In *communication system* maintenance, a *signal* that is used for attracting attention to some abnormal condition in an emergency, such as a lamp and a loud-ringing bell that alerts *central office* personnel to serious troubles. The troubles that might be signaled automatically include high *voltages,* major fuse blowing, circuit-breaker operation, or *ringing* machine failure.

emergent ray. A *ray* of *light* emerging from a *transmission medium,* in contrast to an entering or *incident ray.*

EMF. *Electromotive force.*

EMI. *Electromagnetic interference.*

EMI control. *Electromagnetic interference (EMI) control.*

emission. Electromagnetic energy propagated from a *source* by *radiation* or conduction. See *continuous emission; interference emission; parasitic emission; spontaneous emission; spurious emission; stimulated emission.*

emission-beam-angle-between-half-power-points. The angle centered on the *optical axis* of a *light*-emitter within which the *radiant power density* is equal to or greater than half the maximum power density (on the optical axis).

emission control. The control of *electromagnetic* and *sonic radiation* for the purpose of preventing or minimizing their use by unintended recipients. All types of radiation are included, including *radio, video, radar, sonar,* and *microwave.* It is the implementation of the *emission policy* formulated to obtain the maximum practical advantage of a particular situation. This may be achieved by the management of emissions in accordance with plans that may authorize, restrict, or prohibit the operation of specified equipment. Limitations may be imposed by organizational unit, type of equipment, components, power, or frequency, including the sonic *spectrum.* It includes the selective control of emitted electromagnetic or sonic energy to minimize *interference,* prevent undesired detection, and improve the performance of installed *sensors. Electrostatic, magnetostatic,* and *magnetoelectrostatic* emanations are also included. Also see *electromagnetic emission control; electromagnetic emission policy; emission policy.*

emission designator. A set of standard *characters,* such as letters, numerals, and special *symbols,* that are used to designate a type or class of *transmitting stations* or *communication networks.* The emission designator normally consists of an approved basic functional *word* with approved prefixes and suffixes. Also see *circuit designator; net glossary.*

emission intercept range. A range at which a specified *emission* or *transmitted signal* can be received, interpreted, or analyzed. The maximum range at which emissions may be intercepted depends upon the *emitter* characteristics, *transmission medium* conditions, and the *receiver* type and location.

emission law. See *Boltzmann's emission law; cosine emission law.*

emission of radiation. See *microwave amplification by stimulated emission of radiation.*

emission policy. Policy concerning the controls and limitations imposed upon or used in an organization pertaining to *electromagnetic,* sonic, and other forms of *emission, transmission, radiation,* or emanation by any means including conduction. Forms of emission include *radio, video, sonar, visible light, infrared,* or any other electromagnetic, *electrostatic, magnetostatic, magnetic,* or sonic means. It includes policies concerning the operation of radio or *radar receivers* that emit radiation when operated. See *electromagnetic emission policy (EEP).*

emission security. See *emanation security.*

emissivity. The ratio of the *radiant emittance* or *radiated flux* of a *source* to the radiant emittance or radiated flux of a *blackbody* having the same *temperature.* It is usually a function of *wavelength.* See *total emissivity.*

emittance. See *luminous emittance; radiant emittance; spectral emittance.*

emitted electron energy. In a *photoemissive detector,* the remaining energy, E_e, of an electron that escapes from the emissive material due to the energy imparted to it by an *incident photon,* expressed mathematically as:

$$E_e = hf - q\phi$$

where h is *Planck's constant,* f is the photon *frequency,* q is the charge of an electron, ϕ is the work function of the emissive material (hf is the photon energy and $q\phi$ is the energy required for an electron to escape from the emissive material, namely, to overcome the boundary effects).

emitter. See *optical emitter; victim emitter.*

emitting diode. See *light-emitting diode; restricted edge-emitting diode.*

emitting diode coupler. See *light-emitting diode coupler.*

emitting LED. See *edge-emitting LED; surface-emitting LED.*

emitting surface. A surface from which waves emerge; e.g., *electromagnetic waves (lightwaves, radiowaves, microwaves, x-rays, gamma rays)* or particles (*electrons,* ions, protons, neutrons). Light sources, such as *LEDs, lasers,* lamps, and receiving-end surfaces of *optical fibers,* have emitting surfaces.

EMP. *Electromagnetic pulse.*

emphasis. The intentional alteration of the *amplitude, phase, frequency,* or *shape* characteristics of a *signal* to reduce adverse effects of noise in a *communication system.* For example, pre-emphasis may be used in the *transmission* of a *frequency modulated wave.* The higher *frequency signals* are emphasized in order to produce a more equal *modulation index* for the *transmitted frequency spectrum* and therefore a better *signal-to-noise ratio* for the entire frequency range. Also see *de-emphasis; pre-emphasis.*

emphasis circuit. See *pre-emphasis circuit.*

emphasis network. See *pre-emphasis network.*

EMP resistance. The ability of a *communication system* or *component* to withstand the effects of a high-energy *electromagnetic pulse* such as might be produced by a nuclear blast.

empty medium. A *data medium* that does not contain *data* other than format controls or *indicators* such as fixed frame, legend, or position marks. For example, a preprinted (blank) form, a paper tape punched only with feed holes, or a *magnetic tape* that has been erased.

EMSEC. *Emanation security.*

emulator. A device that is capable of operating in such a manner that it appears to have all of the characteristics of another device. For example, a *hardware* and *software* combination that enables one *computer* to execute *programs* written for another computer, or a device that produces the same set of *outputs* for a given set of *inputs* as does another device. Also see *computer simulation; simulation; simulator.*

EMW. *Electromagnetic wave.*

enabling signal. A *signal* that permits the occurrence of a specific event that would not occur if the signal were not present. For example, a signal that would allow an *AND gate* to perform its normal function only when the signal is present.

encipher. To convert *plain text* into an unintelligible form by means of a *cipher* system. Also see *decipher; encode; encrypt.*

enciphered telephony. See *ciphony.*

enclosure. See *shielded enclosure.*

encode. 1. To apply a *code,* usually one consisting of *binary digits* that represent individual *characters* or groups of characters in a *message.* 2. To substitute letters, *numerals,* or *characters* to hide the meaning of a *message* except to certain *users* (recipients) who know the conversion scheme. 3. To *convert* plain text into an unintelligible form by means of a *code.* For example, to convert a *plain text message* into a *coded message.* 4. The section of a *code book* in which the *plain text* equivalents or the *code groups* are in *alphabetical,* numerical, or other systematic order. 5. To *convert data* by the use of a *code* or a *coded character set* in such a manner that reconversion to the original form is possible, even if exact reconversion is not possible.

encoded recording. See *phase-encoded recording.*

encoder. 1. A device that *encodes data.* 2. A device that has a number of *input lines,* of which not more than one may carry a *signal* at a given instant, and a number of *output lines* of which any number may carry signals, there being a one-to-one correspondence between the input signals and the combinations of output signals. Also see *decoder.* See *analog-to-digital (A–D) encoder; channel voice encoder.*

encoding. See *analog encoding; differential encoding; segmented encoding; uniform encoding.*

encoding law. The law that defines the relative values of the quantum steps that are used in *quantizing* and *encoding signals.* Also see *segmented encoding.*

encrypt. To convert *plain text* into an unintelligible form by means of a *cryptosystem.* Also see *encode; encipher.*

encrypted voice. A *voice transmission* that is *secured* against *compromise* through the use of an approved *ciphony system.* Synonymous with *secure voice.*

encryption. The conversion of *plain text* into a disguised or unintelligible form by means of a *cryptosystem.* See *bulk encryption; link encryption; multiplex link encryption; reencryption; superencryption; variable-spacing encryption.*

encryption algorithm. A set of mathematically expressed rules for rendering *data* unintelligible by effecting a series of conversions controlled by the use of a *key.*

encryption device. See *trunk encryption device.*

encryption standard. See *data encryption standard.*

end. See *local end.*

end crossfire. See *sending-end crossfire.*

end crosstalk. See *far-end crosstalk.*

end distortion. In *start-stop systems,* the *shifting* of the ends of all *mark pulses* from their proper *positions* in relation to the beginnings of the *start signals.*

end-finish. See *optical end-finish.*

end-fire coupling. *Optical fiber* and *integrated optical-circuit (IOC) coupling* between two *waveguides* in which the waveguides are *butted* up against each other. It is a more straightforward, simpler, and more efficient coupling method than *evanescent field coupling. Mode* pattern matching is required and is accomplished by maintaining unity cross-sectional area *aspect ratio,* axial alignment, and minimal lateral axial displacement. Also see *evanescent field coupling.*

ended cord. See *plug-ended cord.*

ending. 1. In a *message,* the parts that follow the *text.* 2. In *radiotelephone system messages,* the part of the message that consists of the *date-time group,* final instructions, and ending sign. The ending normally follows the *break* that follows the *text.* See *transmission ending.*

end instrument. A device that is connected to the *terminal* of a *circuit* and used to *convert data* into electrical *signals* or electrical signals into useful *information.* For example, a *telephone, teleprinter, teletypewriter, keyboard,* or *display device.* The end instrument normally belongs to the *user* rather than to the *communication agency* or *administration.* It is usually on the user's (customer's, subscriber's) premises, though it is still considered as part of the communication system to which it is connected. See Figure E-3. Also see Figures U-1 and V-2.

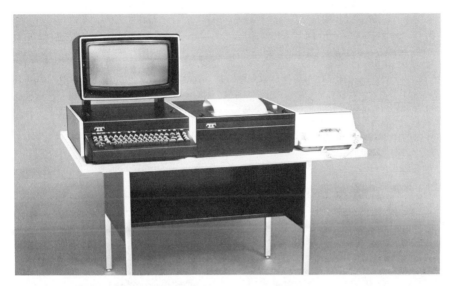

E-3. A *user* **end-instrument** consisting of the Dataspeed® Printer with table-top *keyboard display printer.* (Reproduced with permission of AT&T Co.)

end-of-medium (EM) character. A *control character* that may be used to identify either the physical end of a *data medium,* the end of the usable or used portion of a data medium, or the end of the wanted portion of *data* that is recorded on a data medium.

end-of-message function. In *tape relay* procedure, the letter and *key functions,* including the *end-of-message indicator,* that comprise the last *format line.*

end-of-message indicator. In *tape relay communication systems,* an *indicator* that is used to *signal* the end of a *message* or the termination of a *transmission.* For example, one end-of-transmission indicator that is used is NNNN.

end-of-selection (EOS) character. The *character* that is used to indicate the end of the *selection signal.*

end-of-tape mark. A *mark* on a *magnetic tape* that indicates the end of the permissible recording area. For example, a photo reflective strip, a transparent section of tape, a punched hole in the tape, or a particular *bit* pattern, each of which excites a sensing mechanism.

end-of-text (ETX) character. A *transmission control character* that is used to terminate the *reading, transmission, reception,* or *recording* of *text.*

end-of-transmission-block (ETB) character. A *transmission control character* that indicates the end of the *transmission* of a *block* of *data* when data are divided into blocks for transmission purposes.

end-of-transmission (EOT) character. A *transmission control character* that indicates the conclusion of a *transmission* that may have included one or more *texts* and associated *message headings.*

end-of-transmission function. In *tape relay* procedure, the letters and *machine functions,* including the *end-of-message indicator,* that signify the termination of *transmission.*

end-of-transmission (EOT) group. A standardized, uninterrupted sequence of *characters* and *machine functions* that is used to terminate a *transmission,* disconnect the *circuit,* and turn off the transmitting equipment.

endoscope. An *optical* instrument used to view and to take pictures of the internal parts of a *system,* such as the internal cavities and organs of the human body. Endoscopes often use *optical fiber bundles* as *transmission cables.*

endpoint node. **1.** A *node* at the end of a *path.* **2.** A *node* connected to one and only one *branch.*

end-to-end transport layer. In a *layered communication system,* the set of functions and *protocols* that pertain to the control of *integrity* and *errors* in the functions performed by the *transmission layer* to assure accuracy in the *application layer.*

energy. See *band-gap energy; emitted electron energy; radiant energy.*

energy band. A specified range of *energy levels* that a constituent particle or component of a substance may have. The particles are usually *electrons,* protons, ions, neutrons, atoms, or molecules. Some energy bands are allowable and some are unallowable for specific particles. For example, electrons of a given element at a specific *temperature* occupy certain energy bands. Examples of energy bands are the higher and lower level ranges of the *conduction* and *valence bands.*

energy density. See *electromagnetic energy density; optical energy density.*

energy level. The *discrete* amount of kinetic and potential energy possessed by an orbiting *electron.* A quantum of energy is *absorbed* or *radiated* depending on whether an electron moves from a lower to a higher energy level or vice versa.

engaged signal. See *terminal-engaged signal.*

engaged signaling. See *visual engaged signaling.*

engaged test. In *telephone switchboard operation,* a *test* to determine whether or not a *line* is in use. The test applies only to *switchboards* with two or more *positions.* It may be accomplished manually by touching the bust of the *jack* with the tip of the *calling plug.* A click will be heard if the line is in use, provided the associated key is actuated.

engaged tone. In *telephone switchboard operation,* an *audible signal* indicating that either the *called line, called party,* or the *intermediate equipment* required for setting up a particular *connection* is in use. Also see *busy signal.*

engagement clip. See *quick-engagement clip.*

engineering. See *software engineering; traffic engineering.*

engineering channel. A *voice* or *data channel* that is used by technical control, operating, maintenance, and attendant personnel for coordination and control activities related to activation, deactivation, change, rerouting, reporting, establishment, operation, and maintenance of *communication system services,* facilities, and equipment. Synonymous with *order channel; service channel; speaker channel.*

engineering circuit. A *voice* or *data circuit* that is used by technical control, operating, maintenance, and attendant personnel for coordination and control activities related to activation, deactivation, change, rerouting, reporting, establishment, operation, and maintenance of *communication system services,* facilities and equipment. In *satellite communication systems,* these circuits are set aside from *user traffic* circuits to provide engineering *links* between the technical managing organizations at each *earth station* and *switching center* in the system. Synonymous with *engineering orderwire (EOW); order circuit; orderwire; speaker circuit.* Also see *maintenance control circuit (MCC).* See *express engineering circuit; link engineering circuit; local engineering circuit.*

engineering circuit multiplex set. A *multiplex carrier* set specifically designed to carry *engineering circuit (orderwire) traffic* as opposed to one designed to carry *user* (subscriber, customer) traffic. Synonymous with *orderwire multiplex set.*

engineering path. In *communication networks,* a *path* consisting of *engineering channels* and *engineering circuits.* These paths are used for *voice, data,* or both. They are provided to facilitate the installation, maintenance, restoral, or deactivation of segments of a *communication system* by *operators,* attendants, and control personnel.

enlargement. In *display systems,* an enlarged copy of a *display element, display group,* or *display image.* For example, an enlarged copy of a *microimage* or a positive print larger than the *photographic* negative from which it was made. Also see *reduction; scale; zooming.*

ENQ. The *enquiry character.*

enquiry. A question, that is, a request for a *response.* Synonymous with *query.*

enquiry (ENQ) character. A *transmission control character* that is used as a request for a *response* from the *station* with which a *connection* has been set up. The response may include *station identification,* the type of equipment in service, and the status of the station.

E/N ratio. In the *transmission* of a *pulse* of an *electromagnetic wave,* representing a *bit,* the ratio of the energy per bit, E, divided by the *noise energy density* per *hertz, N.* Since E is normally expressed in joules/bit and N is expressed in watts/hertz, the ratio is hertz-seconds/bit, or "per bit." Since a joule is a watt-second and a hertz is a cycle per second, the ratio is actually cycles per bit; however, if a cycle is a bit, then the quantity is dimensionless and is usually considered to be dimensionless.

enroute guard station. See *secondary station.*

entrance pupil. 1. In an *optical system,* the *image* of the limiting *aperture stop* formed in the *object* space by all optical elements of the system preceding the limiting aperture stop. 2. The *aperture* of the *objective* when there are no other limiting stops following it in an *optical system.* Also see *input aperture.*

entrapment. In *communication system security,* the deliberate planting of apparent flaws in a *system* for the purpose of detecting attempted *penetrations.* Also see *pseudo-flaw.*

entropy. See *character mean entropy; conditional information entropy; information entropy; relative entropy.*

entry. See *between-the-lines entry; piggy-back entry; remote job entry.*

envelope 1. In a representation of a *modulated carrier wave,* the function that describes the extent of variation of the carrier that is caused by the modulation *signal,* as a function of time. For example, if a high-*frequency sinusoidal wave* is *amplitude modulated* by a low-frequency sinusoidal wave and the resultant signal is plotted versus time, the line joining the peaks of the modulated carrier is the envelope. 2. The boundary formed by a family of curves obtained when a parameter is varied. 3. In *digital data transmission,* a group of *pulses* representing *binary digits* forming a *byte,* with the additional bits required for *transmission system* operation, such as *start* and *stop pulses.* See *permanently locked envelope.*

envelope delay distortion. 1. In a given *passband* of a device or a *transmission facility,* the maximum difference of the *group delay time* between any two specified *frequencies.* 2. The *distortion* that occurs when the rate of change of *phase* *shift* with *frequency* of a *circuit* or system is not constant over the frequency range that is required for the *transmission*. Envelope delay distortion is usually expressed as half the difference between the two extremes of frequency that define the *channel* used.

envelope power.   See *peak envelope power (PEP)*.

environment.   The totality of *radiated electromagnetic power* in all *frequencies* as a function of time surrounding a point in space. See *electromagnetic environment*.

environmental file.   See *system environmental file*.

environmental loss time.   The *downtime* due to a *fault* that is outside of the *functional unit* whose time is being measured. Synonymous with *external loss time*.

environmental security.   1. The *security* that is inherent in the physical surroundings in which a *facility* or *functional unit* is located. For example, shipboard, airborne, and underground locations by their nature provide a certain amount of protection against exploitation of *compromising emanation* even before other protective measures are implemented. 2. The application of electrical, acoustic, physical, and other safeguards to an area to minimize the risk of unauthorized *interception* of *information* from the area.

e–o.   *Electrooptic.*

EOMI.   *End-of-message indicator.*

ephemeris.   1. A tabulation of the location of celestial bodies at specific intervals. 2. A tabulation of the location of *artificial satellites* at specific intervals.

EOS.   The *end-of-selection character*.

EOT.   The *end-of-transmisison character*.

epitaxial growth.   A growth of crystals formed in layers, such as the growth of crystals for *LEDs* and *lasers*.

E-propagation.   See *sporadic E-propagation*.

equal-gain combiner.   A *diversity combiner* in which the *signals* on each *channel* are added together. The channel *gains* are all equal and can be made to vary equally so that the resultant signal is approximately constant.

equality gate.   See *EXCLUSIVE-NOR gate*.

equalization.   The process of reducing the *frequency distortion* or the *phase distortion,* or both, of *signals* in a *circuit* by the introduction of *electric circuits* or *networks* to compensate for the difference in *attenuation* or time delay that occurs to the various *frequency components* of the signals in the circuit.

equalizer.   See *amplitude equalizer; delay equalizer; fixed compromise equalizer; line residual equalizer; line temperature-compensating equalizer; phase-frequency equalizer; slope equalizer.*

equal-length code.   A *telegraph* or a *data code* in which all the *words* or *code groups* are composed of the same number of unit elements, each element having the same duration or spatial length. Thus, each word or code group has the same time duration or spatial length, and usually the same number of *characters.*

equal-level patch bay.   See *patch bay.*

equation.   See *one-way radio equation; radar line-of-sight equation; self-screening range equation; two-way radar equation.*

equator.   See *celestial equator.*

equinox.   Either of two points on the celestial sphere where the *ecliptic* circle and the *celestial equatorial* plane intersect. The ecliptic is the great circle traced on the celestial sphere annually by the sun. Its inclination to the celestial equator is about 23.5°. The *vernal equinox* is where the sun crosses the equator from south to north on or about March 21, bringing spring to the northern hemisphere and autumn to the southern hemisphere. At the *autumnal equinox,* the sun crosses the equator from north to south on or about September 22, at which time autumn begins for the northern hemisphere and spring begins for the southern hemisphere. When the sun is at either point, the day is only slightly longer than night. See *autumnal equinox; vernal equinox.* Also see *ecliptic.*

equipment.   See *airport surface detection equipment; authentication equipment; automatic data processing equipment (ADPE); automatic numbering equipment; automatic switching equipment; Boehme equipment; channel translation equipment; cipher equipment; communication security equipment; concentrating equipment; conditioning equipment; data circuit-terminating equipment (DCE); data communication equipment; data subscriber terminal equipment (DSTE); data terminal equipment (DTE); distance measuring equipment; duplex equipment; group-one document facsimile equipment; group-three document facsimile equipment; group-two document facsimile equipment; half-duplex equipment; high-performance communication equipment; industrial RF heating equipment; industrial-scientific-medical RF equipment; intermediate equipment; limited-protection voice equipment; literal cipher equipment; low-performance communication equipment; medical diathermy equipment; mobile communication equipment; off-line equipment; online equipment; peripheral equipment; radio direction-finding equipment; remote control equipment; start-stop equipment; switch-*

ing equipment; telegraph automatic relay equipment (TARE); telegraph error-rate measuring equipment; terminal equipment; through-group equipment; through-supergroup equipment; time-division multiplex equipment; transportable communication equipment; ultrasonic equipment.

equipment clock. A *clock* that satisfies the particular needs of equipment and in some cases may control the flow of *data* at the equipment *interface*.

equipment congestion signal. See *national switching equipment congestion signal*.

equipment intermodulation noise. *Intermodulation noise* that is introduced into a *system* by a specific piece of equipment.

equipment mobility. In *communications*, pertaining to the capability of communication equipment to be moved from place to place. Fully mobile implies the ability to fulfil its primary mission, that is, perform communication operations, such as *transmit* and *receive*, while on the move. Transportable does not imply the ability to fulfil its primary mission while on the move.

equipment side. In *communications*, the portion of a *communication* device that is connected to the *station* equipment. Synonymous with *station side* and with *central office side*. Also see *line side*.

equivalence gate. See *EXCLUSIVE-NOR gate*.

equivalent focal length (EFL). 1. The distance from a principal point to its corresponding *principal focus point*. 2. The *focal length* of the equivalent *thin lens*. The size of the *image* of an *object* is directly proportional to the equivalent focal length of the *lens* forming it.

equivalent isotropically-radiated power. The product of the *power* supplied to an *antenna* and the *antenna gain* relative to an *isotropic antenna*.

equivalent network. 1. In a *communication system*, a *network* that may replace another network without altering the performance of the portion of the system external to the network. 2. A theoretical representation of an actual *network*. 3. A *network* that has one or more characteristics that are the same as another network.

equivalent noise resistance. A quantitative representation in *resistance* units of the *spectral density* of a *noise voltage* generator at a specified *frequency*. The relation between the equivalent noise resistance, R_n, and the spectral density, W_n, of the noise making generator is $R_n = \pi W_n / k T_o$ where k is *Boltzmann's constant* and T_o is the *standard noise temperature* of 290 K ($k T_o = 4.00 \times 10^{-21}$ W-s). The equivalent noise resistance, R_n, in terms of the mean-square noise-generator voltage, e^2, within a *frequency* increment, Δf, is $R_n = e^2 / 4 k T_o \Delta f$.

equivalent noise temperature. The physical (thermal) *temperature (kelvin)* of a *matched resistance* at the *input* of an assumed noiseless device *(amplifier)* that would account for the measured *output noise.*

equivalent PCM noise. By means of a comparative test, the amount of *thermal noise power* on a *frequency-division multiplexed (FDM) channel* that is necessary to approximate the same judgement of speech quality created by *quantizing noise* in a *pulse-code modulated (PCM) channel.* Generally, 33.5 dBrnC ±2.5 dB is considered to be the approximate equivalent PCM noise of a *7-bit* PCM *system.*

equivalent power. See *noise equivalent power.*

equivocation. The *conditional information entropy* of the occurrence of specific *messages* at the *message source* given the occurrence of specific messages at a *message sink* that is connected to the message source by a specific *channel.* The equivocation is the mean additional *information content* that must be supplied per message at the message sink to correct the received messages affected by a noisy channel.

erase. 1. To obliterate *data* from any *storage* medium. For example, to clear, remove, or overwrite data that is stored. 2. To remove all previous *data* from *magnetic storage* by changing the magnetic material to a specified condition that may be an unmagnetized state or a predetermined magnetized state that represents zero or no stored *information.*

erase character. See *delete character.*

erasure signal. A *signal* that is used for the purpose of invalidating a previous signal without actually erasing or deleting the original signal.

erect image. In an *optical system,* an *image,* either real or *virtual,* that has the same spatial orientation as the *object.* The *image* obtained on the retina with the assistance of an optical system is said to be erect, in contrast to inverted, when the orientation of the image is the same as seen with the unaided eye.

erect position. In *frequency translation* performed in *frequency-division multiplexed channels,* a *position* or condition in which an increasing *signal frequency* in the untranslated *channel* causes an increasing signal frequency in the translated channel. Synonymous with *upright position.* Also see *inverted position.*

E-region. See *E-layer.*

erlang. An international, dimensionless unit of the average *traffic intensity* (i.e., occupancy) of a *facility* during a period of time, such as a *busy hour,* equal to the ratio of the cumulative occupied time to the cumulative available time, 1 erlang being the maximum for a single facility, such as a *register, trunk, circuit,* or *channel.* For example, if a facility can handle 10^8 *call-seconds* in a given hour, but only 10^7 call-seconds are used, the average traffic intensity for the hour is 0.1 erlang. The number of erlangs is the ratio of the time during which a *facility* is occupied (continuously or cumulatively) to the time this facility is available for occupancy. Most facilities, such as *switch registers, trunks,* and *circuits,* are usually shared by many *users. Communication traffic* measured in erlangs and offered to a group of shared facilities, such as a *trunk group,* is equal to the sum of the *traffic intensity* (in erlangs) of all individual sources, such as *telephones, teleprinters,* and remote *data terminals,* that share, and are served exclusively by, the group of facilities. Synonymous with *traffic unit.* Also see *busy hour; call-second; communication traffic volume; group busy hour; traffic intensity; traffic load.*

ERP. *Effective radiated power.*

erroneous bit. A *bit* that is not what it should be according to some criterion. For example, a 1 that should be a 0, or vice versa.

erroneous block. A *block* of *data* in which there are one or more *erroneous bits.*

error. The difference between a computed, estimated, or measured value or condition and the true, specified, or theoretically correct value or condition. For example, the inversion of the letters "at" in "thta" when the correct spelling is "that," the letter A in the social security number 106-2A-2370, or a wrong character in a *computer program instruction word.* Also see *failure; fault; mistake.* See *digital error.*

error budget. The distribution of allowable or required *bit error rates (BER)* among the components that are in spatial (i.e., consecutive) sequence in a *channel* or *circuit.* A *bit error rate* requirement is allocated to each of the segments or operations of a *circuit,* such as *trunks, switches, access lines,* and *terminal* devices, in a manner that permits the specified end-to-end error rate requirements to be satisfied for the *traffic* to be *transmitted* over the circuit. The circuit may be a postulated reference circuit, but it is usually a typical circuit in which the *components* are utilized.

error burst. In *data communication,* a group of *bits* or a sequence of *signals* that contains one or more *errors* but is considered as a unit, in regard to errors, in accordance with some criterion of measure. One such criterion might be that if at least three correct bits follow an erroneous bit, the particular error burst is considered terminated. This criterion, in general, would identify an error burst as a group of bits in which two successive erroneous bits are always separated by less than a given number, n, of correct bits. The last erroneous bit in a burst and the first erroneous bit in the following burst are accordingly separated by n correct bits or more. The number n should be specified when describing an errror burst. Stated otherwise, the error burst becomes the group of bits between two consecutive error-free intervals of length n or greater.

error control. The improvement of *communications* through the use of techniques designed to reduce, eliminate, or prevent *errors,* such as *error detection,* forward-acting *error correction,* and use of *block codes.* For example, it may be the part of a *protocol* that controls the detection, and possibly the correction, of errors.

error-correcting code. A *code* in which each *group* of *characters* or *signals* conforms to specific rules of construction so that departures from this construction in the received signals can be automatically detected and some or all of the *errors* can be automatically corrected. Such codes require more *signal elements* than are necessary to convey the basic *information,* and more signal elements than are necessary for *error detection* only. The code makes use of *redundant characters* to assist in the restoration of the *word* that has been mutilated. Only certain kinds of errors may be corrected if the *redundancy* is less than 100 percent. The redundancy is usually arranged so that the mutilated word when wholly or partially corrected resembles the original word more closely than any other valid representation of another possible word in the vocabulary. If an error occurs that the code is not designed to correct the adjustment that is made may be erroneous. In most applications, the code is in the form of additional *digits* appended to the word that is *transmitted.* See Figure E-4.

EVEN PARITY

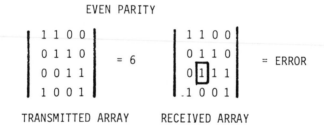

TRANSMITTED ARRAY   RECEIVED ARRAY

E-4. In the **error-correcting code** used to represent *decimal* 6, the *bit* in the third row and second column is an *erroneous* bit, since *even parity* is not satisfied. It may be automatically corrected to a 0.

error-correcting system. A *system* that employs an *error-correcting code* and is so arranged that some or all *signals* detected as being in error are automatically corrected at the receiving *terminal* before delivery to the *data sink.* In a *packet-switched data service,* the error-correcting system might result in the retransmission of at least one or more complete *packets* should an error be detected.

error correction. See *forward error correction.*

error-correction bit. One of a group of *bits* that is inserted into a *bit stream* at the end of a *block* of *bits* to enable the receiving equipment to *detect* and correct the *errors* that may exist in a block.

error-detecting-and-feedback system.   See *automatic request-repeat (ARQ)*.

error-detecting code.   A *code* in which each group of *characters* or *data signals* must conform to specific rules of construction so that departures from this construction in the received signals can be automatically *detected*. Such codes require more *signal elements* than are necessary to convey the basic *information*. For example, the use of a *parity bit* enables the detection of most *errors*, particularly one-*bit* errors. It is possible that if two errors occur in the group to which the parity bit is appended, the errors can go undetected.

error-detecting system.   A *system* that employs an *error-detecting code* and is so arranged that any *signal* that is in *error* can be *detected* and identified to a high order of probability. The signal detected as being in error can either be deleted from the data delivered to the *data sink (destination user)* or be retained with an indication that the signal is in error.

error detection.   See *automatic error detection*.

error detection and correction system.   See *automatic error detection and correction system*.

error-detection and feedback.   An *error control* technique that employs an *error-detecting code* and in which a *signal detected* as being in error automatically initiates a request for retransmission of the signal. Synonymous with *decision feedback; request-repeat*.

error detection bit.   One of a group of *bits* that are periodically inserted into a *bit stream* that enables the equipment at the receiving end to determine if errors are likely to exist in the *data* that is received immediately preceding these bits.

error probability.   See *block error probability*.

error rate.   The ratio of the number of *bits, elements, characters,* or *blocks* received with *erroneous bits* in them to the total number of bits, elements, characters, or blocks sent during a specified time interval. See *average error rate; bit error rate (BER); residual error rate*.

error-rate measuring equipment.   See *telegraph error-rate measuring equipment*.

ESC.   The *escape character*.

escape (ESC) character.   A *code extension character* that is used to indicate by means of some convention or agreement that the *coded* representations of the *character* or group of characters following it are to be interpreted according to a different code or according to a different *coded character set.* Also see *figures shift; letters shift.*

escort jamming. *Jamming* that is accomplished with equipment that is aboard a ship, aircraft, truck, or other vehicle that is accompanying the group that is being protected.

estimated time of arrival (ETA). In *radio communications,* the time at which a *mobile station,* such as an *aircraft, ship,* or *land vehicle station,* is expected or calculated to arrive at a specified location.

ETA. *Estimated time of arrival.*

etalon. A device used for spectral analysis of *light beams,* operating from *infrared* to *ultraviolet,* tunable or fixed, usually with *piezoelectric* crystals, *cavities, mirrors,* and gimbal mounting, using *interferometer* techniques to accomplish the analysis.

ETB. The *end-of-transmission block transmission control character.*

ETX. The *end-of-text transmission control character.*

eV. *Electron-volt.*

evanescent-field coupling. *Optical fiber* or *integrated optical-circuit (IOC) coupling* between two *waveguides* in which the waveguides are held parallel to each other in the *coupling* region, with the *evanescent waves* on the outside of the waveguide entering the coupled waveguide, bringing some of the light energy with it into the coupled waveguide. Close-to-*core* proximity or fusion is required. The *evanescent field* of the *core modes* can be made available by etching away the *fiber cladding* or locally modifying the *refractive index.* Also see *tangential coupling.*

evanescent wave. In a *waveguide* conducting a *transverse electromagnetic wave,* the wave on the outside of the guide. It will *radiate* away at sharp bends in the guide if the radius of the bend is less than the *critical radius.* It usually has a *frequency* smaller than the *cutoff frequency* above which true *propagation* occurs and below which the waves decay exponentially with distance from the guide. Evanescent *wavefronts* of constant *phase* may be perpendicular or at an angle less than $90°$ to the surface of the guide. See Figure E-5. Also see Figure P-14.

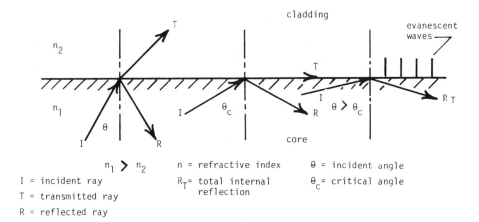

E-5. *Total internal reflection* occurs when the angle of θ is greater than the *critical angle*, which has sine n_2/n_1. **Evanescent waves** are produced in the *cladding*.

evasion. See *frequency evasion*.

even parity. *Parity* in which the number of 1's *(mark)* in a group of *binary digits*, such as those that comprise a *character* or a *word*, is always maintained as an even number, including the *parity bit*. However, the electrical representations of 1's and 0's are often interchanged due to the inversion and reversion that occurs in *signal processing* electronic circuitry. Also see Figure E-4.

evident code. See *self-evident code*.

EW. *Electronic warfare; early warning.*

exalted-carrier reception. A method of receiving either *amplitude* or *phase modulated signals* in which the *carrier* is separated from the *sidebands, filtered*, and *amplified*, and then *combined* (in a *diversity combiner*) with the sidebands again at a higher level prior to *demodulation*.

exception condition. In *data transmission*, the condition assumed by a *secondary station* when it receives a *command* that it cannot execute. For example, in *high-level data link control (HDLC) operation*, the condition assumed by a *station* upon receipt of a *control field* that it cannot execute due either to a transmission *error* or to an internal processing failure.

excess-three code. A *code* for representing *binary-coded decimal digits* in which the decimal digit n is represented by the *straight binary* equivalent of n + 3. In this code, the nines complement of a decimal digit is formed simply by changing all 1's to 0's and all 0's to 1's in any given digit. This is convenient since any bank of *flip-flops* forming a *register* always has available a number and its complement, considering both sides of each flip-flop. The complements are needed in performing arithmetic operations. See Figure E-6.

EXCESS-THREE	PURE BINARY	DECIMAL
0 0 1 1	0 0 0 0	0
0 1 0 0	0 0 0 1	1
0 1 0 1	0 0 1 0	2
0 1 1 0	0 0 1 1	3
0 1 1 1	0 1 0 0	4
1 0 0 0	0 1 0 1	5
1 0 0 1	0 1 1 0	6
1 0 1 0	0 1 1 1	7
1 0 1 1	1 0 0 0	8
1 1 0 0	1 0 0 1	9

E-6. The *decimal* and *pure binary* equivalents to the **excess-three code**.

exchange. All of the *telephone* equipment in a room or building equipped so that telephone *lines* terminating there may be interconnected as required. The equipment may include *manual* or *automatic switching equipment*. See *automatic answer-back-code exchange; automatic exchange; common-battery exchange; common-battery signaling exchange; data switching exchange (DSE); electronic exchange; magnetic exchange; manual exchange; private automatic branch exchange (PABX); terminal exchange; trunk exchange; zone exchange.*

exchange director. See *telephone exchange director.*

exchange keying. See *phase exchange keying.*

exchange line. 1. In *telephone switchboard operation*, a *line* that joins a *user's* (customer's, subscriber's) *end-instrument* in a *closed user group*, or a *switchboard*, to an *exchange*. 2. A *line* that connects one *exchange* to another.

exchange process. See *double-crucible process.*

exchange signaling. See *frequency exchange signaling.*

exchange tie trunk. See *private branch exchange tie trunk.*

excitation. See *impulse excitation.*

excited atmosphere laser. See *longitudinally-excited atmosphere laser; transverse-excited atmosphere laser.*

excited state. Any *orbital* kinetic and potential energy state that an *electron* can have above the *ground state.* An atom emits a *quantum* of energy when one of its electrons moves from an excited state to the ground state. Also see *ground state.*

exclusion gate. See *A-AND-NOT-B gate.*

exclusive message. A *message* that is appropriately marked and that is to be delivered only to the person or authorized representative of the person, whose name or designator appears immediately following the appropriate marking in the *address* component of the *message.*

EXCLUSIVE-NOR gate. A two-*input, binary, combinational circuit* or device that is capable of performing the logic operation of exclusive-NOR. In this operation, if A is an input statement and B is an input statement, the output statement is true when both A and B are true or when both A and B are false. Thus, the result is false when A and B differ. Synonymous with *equivalence gate; biconditional gate; equality gate; identity gate; match gate.* See Figure E-7.

IN A	0	1	B IN
0	1	0	
1	0	1	Q OUT

E-7. A table showing the *input* and *output digits* of an **EXCLUSIVE-NOR gate.**

EXCLUSIVE-OR. A logic operator having the property that if P is a statement and Q is a statement, then P EXCLUSIVE-OR Q is true if either but not both statements are true, and false if both are true or both are false.

EXCLUSIVE-OR gate. A two-*input, binary,* logic, *combinational circuit* or device capable of performing the logic operation of exclusive-OR. In this opera-

tion, if A is an input statement and B is an input statement, the output statement is true when A is true and B is false or when A is false and B is true. Thus,
the result is false when A and B are both true or when A and B are both false.
Synonymous with *add-without-carry gate; anticoincidence gate; anticoincidence
unit; difference gate; distance gate; diversity gate; exjunction gate; nonequality
gate; nonequivalence gate; partial-sum gate; symmetric difference gate.*   See
Figure E-8.

IN A	0	1	B IN
0	0	1	A OUT
1	1	0	

E-8. A table showing the *input* and *output digits* of an **EXCLUSIVE-OR gate.**

exclusive-user circuit. A preset or programmed *circuit* between specified *users*
(customers, subscribers) or groups of users for their full-time use. Also see *dedicated circuit; leased-circuit data transmission service; sole-user circuit; switched
hot-line circuit.*

exempted addressee. An organization, activity, or person included in the *collective address group* of a *message* and deemed by the *originator* as having no need
for the *information* in the *message.* Exempted addressees may be explicitly excluded from the collective address group for the particular message to which the
exemption applies. Also see *action addressee; information addressee.*

exempt information. *Information* that is exempted from public disclosure by
law. It does not include information that is *security* classified in accordance
with executive orders, proprietary information, and information covered by privacy statutes.

exercise. See *communication exercise.*

exitance. See *radiant exitance.*

exit angle. When a *light ray* emerges from a surface, the angle between the *ray*
and a normal to the surface at the point of emergence. For an *optical fiber,* the
angle between the output ray and the axis of the fiber or *fiber bundle.*

exit pupil. In an *optical system,* the *image* of the limiting *aperture stop* formed
by all *lenses* following this stop. In photographic *objectives,* this image is *virtual*

and is usually not far from the iris diaphragm. In telescopes, the *image* is real and can be seen as a small, bright, circular disc by looking at the eyepiece of the instrument directed toward an illuminated area or *light* source. In telescopes, its diameter is equal to the diameter of the *entrance pupil* divided by the *magnification* of the instrument. In Galilean telescopes, the exit pupil is a *virtual image* between the *objective lens* and *eyepiece* and acts as an out-of-focus *field stop*. Also see *aperture stop; field stop; output aperture.*

exjunction gate. See *EXCLUSIVE-OR gate.*

expander. An amplifier, usually forming part of a *signal receiver,* whose gain increases with increasing input signal *amplitude* according to a specified law, function, or relationship. The expander may be used to undo the effects of a *compressor* at the *transmitter,* compensate for *transmission distortion,* or provide for other types of *image processing* techniques. The expander has a *nonlinear gain* characteristic that acts to increase the gain more on larger *input* signals than it does on smaller input signals. It is usually used to restore the original *dynamic range* of a signal that was compressed for transmission. Also see *clipping; compander; compressor, image processing; peak limiting.*

expansion. See *linked compression and expansion (lincompex); luminance range expansion.*

expendable jammer. An *electronic jamming transmitter,* normally designed for one-time use and unattended operation, that is placed in the vicinity of the equipment to be *jammed.*

experimental contract developmental station. A contractor-operated *experimental station* that is used for evaluation or testing of electronic equipment or systems in a design or development stage.

experimental developmental station. An *experimental station* that is used for the evaluation or testing of electronic equipment or systems that are in a design or development stage.

experimental export station. An *experimental station* that is intended for export and is to be used for the evaluation or testing of electronic equipment or systems that are in a design or development stage.

experimental research station. An *experimental station* that is used in basic studies and scientific investigation for the advancement of *radio communications.*

experimental station. A *station* that utilizes *radio waves* in experiments for the advancement of science and technology. Amateur stations are not included. The current experimentation is performed primarily in the 10 MHz to 3000 MHz *bands.*

experimental testing station.   An *experimental station* that is used for the evaluation or testing of *electronic* equipment or systems, including site selection and *transmission path surveys,* that have been developed for operational use.

exploratory electromagnetic surveillance.   *Electromagnetic surveillance* in an unknown environment.

export station.   See *experimental export station.*

exposure.   In a risk-bearing situation, the monetary value of an item multiplied by the probability of occurrence of its loss. For example, if the value of a *mobile station* is 10^6 dollars and the probability of its complete destruction in a given situation is 10^{-4}, that is one chance in 10,000, then the exposure is 100 dollars for this situation. If there is a probable salvage value in a given situation, then the monetary value is adjusted accordingly. In a sequence of mutually exclusive risk-bearing situations, the exposures may be added as long as the total exposure remains small compared to the actual value. For example, if an aircraft valued at 10^7 dollars has a probable total loss of 2×10^{-6}, 4×10^{-6}, and 3×10^{-6} in three consecutive hops of a given flight, then the total exposure for the flight is 90 dollars.

express engineering circuit.   A permanently connected *voice circuit* between selected *stations* for technical control purposes. Synonymous with *express orderwire.*

express orderwire.   See *express engineering circuit.*

extended binary-coded decimal interchange code (EBCDIC).   A set of 256 different *characters,* each character represented by a unique eight-*bit byte* (octet). The code is used for *data* representation in *storage* and *transmission.* There is no *parity bit* and letters are collated before numerals. The code is similar to the *ASCII* except that the bit patterns that correspond to the alphanumeric characters are not the same for each of the characters.

extensible language.   A *computer programming language* that readily permits a *user* to define new elements, such as new control structures, *data* types, and operational statements.

extension.   In *telephone switchboard operation,* a *telephone* that is directly connected to a *switchboard* or an *exchange.* See *address field extension; control field extension; offnet extension; threshold extension.*

extension bell.   In *telephone switchboard operation,* an *audible signal* on a *user's* (customer's, subscriber's) *telephone* that indicates there is an incoming *call* from the *switchboard* or *exchange.* The extension bell sounds when the exchange is *ringing.*

extension character. See *code extension character; nonlocking code extension character.*

extension facility. A means of providing *communication access* to a *user* (subscriber, customer) or group of users geographically isolated from a given *communication station.*

external heading. The parts of a *message* that precede the heading, such as a special handling *instruction* given prior to the standard heading. Also see *message heading; message text.*

external liaison circuit. An *engineering circuit* from a *facility control, switching control,* or *earth station* to a remote facility control, switching control, or earth station.

external loss time. See *environmental loss time.*

external noise. The *noise* from outside a *communication system,* that is, from external *sources,* such as *galactic, sun-spot, ionospheric, tropospheric, atmospheric,* and *ground* or *earth noise,* as well as artificial *interference* from man-made sources. Noise from internal sources, such as *thermal noise* and *circuit noise,* is not included.

external optical modulation. *Modulation* of a *lightwave* in a *transmission medium* by application of *fields,* forces, *waves,* or other energy forms upon a transmission medium *conducting* a *light beam* in such a manner that a characteristic of either the medium, or the beam, or both are modulated in some fashion. External *optical modulation* can make use of such effects as the *electrooptic, acoustooptic, magnetooptic,* or *absorptive* effect.

external photoeffect. The emission of *photon*-excited electrons from the surface of a material after overcoming the energy barrier at the surface of a *photoemissive* material.

external photoeffect detector. A *photodetector* in which the energy of each *photon incident* on the detector surface is sufficient to liberate one or more *electrons;* i.e., *Planck's constant* times the frequency, which is the energy of the photon, is sufficient to overcome the work function of the material, and the liberated electrons move under the influence of an applied *electric field. Photoemissive* devices make use of the external *photoeffect.* Also see *internal photoeffect detector.*

external security audit. A *security audit* of a *system* by an organization (agency) independent of the organization operating the system.

extinction coefficient. The sum of the *absorption coefficient* and the *scattering coefficient.* Also see *Bouger's law.*

extra bit. See *added bit.*

extra block. See *added block.*

extra block probability. See *added block probability.*

extramural absorption. The *absorption* of *light, transmitted* radially through the *cladding* of an *optical fiber,* by means of a dark or *opaque* coating placed over the cladding. It may be accomplished by any light-absorbing material, such as secondary coatings, interstitial *fibers,* or other *jackets.*

extramural cladding. A layer of dark or *opaque* absorbing coating placed over the *cladding* of an *optical fiber* to increase *internal reflection,* protect the smooth reflecting wall of the cladding, and absorb *scattered* or escaped stray *light* that might penetrate the cladding.

extraordinary ray. A *light ray* that has a *nonisotropic* velocity in a *doubly refracting crystal.* An extraordinary ray does not necessarily obey *Snell's law* upon *refraction* at the crystal surface.

extremely high frequency (EHF). A *frequency* that lies in the *range* from 30 GHz to 300 GHz. The *alphabetic designator* of the range is EHF. The *numeric designator* of the range is 11. Also see *frequency spectrum designation.*

extremely low frequency (ELF). A *frequency* that lies in the *range* from 30 Hz to 300 Hz. The *alphabetic designator* of the range is ELF. The *numeric designator* is 2. Also see *frequency spectrum designation.*

extrinsic internal photoeffect. An internal *photoeffect* involving the *dopants* or other impurities in a basic (intrinsic) material. Also see *intrinsic internal photoeffect.*

eye pattern. An *oscilloscope* pattern that is used for examination of *digital signal distortion.* An open eye pattern corresponds to minimal signal distortion. Distortion of the signal waveform due to *intersymbol interference, noise,* or other causes makes the eye pattern close.

eyepiece. In a *lens system,* the *lens* closest to the eye when using the system; hence, it is usually farthest from the *object* being viewed and from the *objective lens.* The eyepiece is used to *focus* the *image* either on a screen or to allow, in conjunction with the lens of the human eye, the image to be focused on the retina. For example, an objective lens, a *bundle* of *optical fibers,* and an eyepiece can be used to form a flexible *fiberscope, endoscope,* or *fiber-optic choledochoscope.*

eyes only. A *message* marker for a *special category message* that is intended for delivery to a specific person or authorized representative only and no one else.

F

Fabry-Perot interferometer. A high-resolution multiple-*beam interferometer* consisting of two *optically* flat and parallel glass or quartz plates held a short fixed distance apart, the adjacent surfaces of the plates or interferometer flats being made almost totally *reflecting* by a thin silver film or multilayer *dielectric* coating.

face change character. See *font change character*.

faceplate. See *fiber faceplate*.

face-to-face coupling. See *butt coupling*.

facilities request signal. The part of the *selection signal* that identifies required *facilities*.

facility. An operational capability or the means of providing a capability. Facilities include *hardware* and *software*. They do not include persons. See *called-line facility; calling-line identification facility; calls barred facility; communication facility; data collection facility; extension facility; information facility; internal communication facility; manual answering facility; manual calling facility; multiaddress calling facility; multimode facility; packet assembly-disassembly (PAD) facility; patch and test facility; priority facility; technical control facility; trouble-desk facility; user facility; virtual call facility; whisper facility*.

facility control. See *switching center*.

facility request separator character. The *character* that separates the different individual *facility request signals* in the facilities request signal of a *selection signal*.

facsimile. Pertaining to the *transmission* and *reception* of *data* in *graphic* form. Also see Figures T-1 and T-7.

facsimile bandwidth. In a given *facsimile system*, the difference in *frequency* between the highest and lowest frequency *components* that are required for adequate *transmission* of the *facsimile picture signals*. The *bandwidth* is expressed in *hertz*.

facsimile converter. A *facsimile* device that either changes the type of *modulation* from *frequency shift modulation* to *amplitude modulation* at a *receiver* or changes the modulation from amplitude modulation to frequency shift modulation at a *transmitter*.

facsimile data compression. A technique in which *redundancy* is removed from a *facsimile picture signal* before *transmission* to reduce the *bandwidth* requirement for transmission.

facsimile equipment. See *group-one document facsimile equipment; group-three document facsimile equipment; group-two document facsimile equipment.*

facsimile frequency shift. In a *frequency-shift facsimile system,* the numerical difference between the *frequency* that corresponds to a *white signal* and the frequency that corresponds to a *black signal* at any point in the system. The frequencies are expressed in *hertz.*

facsimile picture signal. A *signal* that results from the *scanning* of a document on a *facsimile transmitter.*

facsimile receiver. A *facsimile* device that *converts* the *facsimile picture signal* from the *communication channel* into an *image* of the subject (object) copy on a *recording medium.*

facsimile receiver aperture. The final opening through which the *light* from a local *source* that has been *intensity modulated* by the received *facsimile picture signal* passes. After passing through the aperture, the light is *focused* on a *photosensitive recording medium.*

facsimile recorder. The part of a *facsimile receiver* that *converts* the *facsimile picture signal* to an image of the subject (object) copy on the *recording medium.*

facsimile service. A *communication system,* public or private, that is devoted to the *transmission* and *reception* of fixed *images,* such as photographs, charts, maps, drawings, and printed pages.

facsimile signal contrast. The ratio between the *facsimile signal* level obtained when *optically scanning* a white area and the signal level obtained when scanning a black area on the subject (object) copy, fixed *image,* or document. The ratio is usually expressed in *decibels.*

facsimile signal level. The instantaneous *facsimile signal power* or *voltage* that can be measured at any point in a *facsimile system.* It is used to establish the operating levels in a *facsimile system.* It is often expressed in *decibels* with respect to a standard value such as 1 mw. Thus, the unit of measure can be *dBm.*

facsimile system. A *communication system* that is capable of *transmitting* fixed *images* and *receiving* them in a permanent form such as *hard copy.* A facsimile system usually has a *scanner,* a *transmission* medium, and a *receiver*-printer. Since most facsimile scanners use a spot of *light,* the scanning *signal* can be ampliied and then transmitted directly over *optical fiber cables*. Fixed images include pictures, maps, drawings, and printed pages. It includes a *scanning system* that may or may not have the capability of handling half-tones. Wirephoto and Telephoto are *facsimile* via wirelines. Radiophoto is facsimile via *radio*. Synonymous with *FAX*. See Figure F-1.

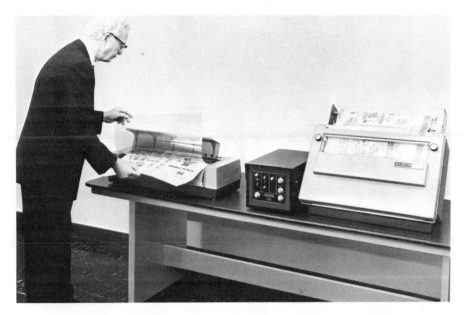

F-1. A **facsimile system** for large-size documents. (Courtesy of Alden Electronic and Impulse Recording Equipment Company, Inc.)

facsimile telegraphy.   *Telegraphy* in which the surface of the source document is systematically *scanned* on sending and synthesized on *reception* to produce on a *recording medium* an *image* that is geometrically similar to the image on the original document. The reproduction may be either in two density states, generally black and white; it may have intermediate shades of black and white (half-tones); or it may be in *color*. See *document facsimile telegraphy; picture facsimile telegraphy.*

facsimile transmission.   See *black facsimile transmission; white facsimile transmission.*

facsimile transmitter.   A *facsimile* device that converts the subject (object) copy, fixed *image*, or document content into a *facsimile picture signal* that is suitable for delivery to the *communication channel* for *transmission* to the *facsimile receiver*. See Figure F-2.

F-2. A **facsimile transmitter** and receiver *(transceiver)* that conforms to CCITT standards, and features *automatic dialing, transmission,* and *polling.* (Courtesy of 3M Business Communication Products Division.)

facsimile transmitter aperture. An opening through which a constant, controlled, nonmodulated *beam* of *light* passes and which effectively controls the size of the *scanning spot* of a *facsimile transmitter.*

factor. See *activity factor; block correction efficiency factor; cooperation factor; demand factor; dispersion attenuation factor; diversity factor; drum factor; duty factor; efficiency factor; feedback factor; FM improvement factor; K-factor; load factor; modulation factor; noise factor (NF); pulse duty factor; radiation absorption factor; reflection factor; shape factor; spot noise factor; time scale factor; transmitter calibration factor; work factor.*

fade. 1. In *radar operations,* to disappear from the *radar display.* 2. In *radio communications,* a reduction of *signal strength* at the *receiving antenna input. Fading* is normally due to *atmospheric propagation* conditions, such as *scattering, ducting, absorption, dispersion,* and *refraction,* and *ionospheric* conditions, that change continuously. Changes in *transmitted power* are not considered as fading, though the effect at the *receiver* is the same.

fade margin. 1. In a *communication system,* an allowance that is provided in *system gain* (sensitivity) to accommodate expected *fading* to insure that a required *communication service grade* is maintained for a specified percentage of the time. 2. The amount by which a received *signal* level may be reduced without causing the *system* or *channel output* to fall below a specified *threshold.* Synonymous with *fading margin.* Also see *RF power margin.*

fading. In the *propagation* of *electromagnetic waves* in *transmission media,* the fluctuation in *intensity* or *propagated power density* due to changes in parameters of the transmission media. Electromagnetic waves include *lightwaves, radio waves, radar pulses, microwaves,* and *gamma rays.* The relative *phase* of any or all *frequency components* of a received *signal* may also change due to changes in the characteristics of the *propagation path* with time and thus result in fade at the *receiver.* Also see *fade margin.* See *flat fading; multipath fading; phase interference fading; Rayleigh fading; selective fading.*

fading distribution. The probability that the amount of *signal* level *fade* will exceed a certain value relative to a specified reference level *(threshold).* In the case of *phase interference fading,* the time distribution of the instantaneous *field intensity* approximates a *Rayleigh distribution* a large part of the time. This occurs when at least several *signal elements* of equal amplitude occur. Also see *Rayleigh fading.*

fail-safe. The automatic protection of *transmission, programs,* and *components* when a failure occurs in a *computer* or *communication system.*

fail-safe operation. A *control operation* or *function* that prevents improper *system* functioning or *catastrophic degradation* in the event of *circuit* or *operator failure.*

fail-soft. The termination of selected lower-priority operations when a *hardware* or *software failure* is *detected* in a *system* in order to prevent *catastrophic degradation.*

failure. The undesired termination of the ability of a *functional unit* to perform its required function. It is usually the result of a *fault.* For example, the termination of the ability of a *tape reader* to correctly sense the data on tape because of a low voltage condition in a *bias power* supply. Catastrophic failures are both sudden and complete. Degradation failures are gradual and partial. Synonymous with *malfunction.* Also see *disengagement denial; error; fault; mistake.* See *access failure; block transfer failure; disengagement failure; mean-time-between-failures (MTBF); radio failure.*

failure access. An unauthorized or inadvertent *access* to *data* that results from a *hardware* or *software failure* in a *system.*

failure control. Control used to provide *fail-safe* or *fail-soft* recovery from *hardware* and *software failures* in a *computer* or *communication system.*

failure-fraction-automatically-switched. In a *communication system,* the fraction of all *failures* that are immediately bypassed by *automatic switching* to another *component,* such as *channel, line,* or *data terminal equipment.* Also see *mean-time-between-outages.*

failure period.   See *constant failure period; early failure period; wear-out failure period.*

failures.   See *mean-time-between-failures (MTBF).*

failure signal.   See *call-failure signal; continuity-failure signal.*

fallen clearing indicator shutter.   In a *single-supervisory* electromechanical *telephone switchboard,* a *clearing indicator* that is in the form of a shutter or lever that drops down to indicate that a *user* (customer, subscriber) has *finished* a *call.*

fallout message.   A *message* that indicates the time and the location of a nuclear explosion; the direction, speed, and extent of the fallout zone; and related *data* for use in the affected area.   Also see *preburst message.*

fall time.   See *pulse decay time.*

false alarm rate.   See *constant false alarm rate (CFAR).*

false clear.   In *telephone switchboard operation,* a *clearing signal* that is accidentally caused by means other than normal disconnection, a *ring-off,* or a *user* (customer, subscriber) replacing the *telephone receiver* on its hook, cradle, or contact (hanging up).

false colors.   In *visual signaling systems,* a *flag* or marking of a country other than the country of registry of the ship, aircraft, spacecraft, or vehicle from which the flag is flown or on which the marking is placed.

family.   See *frequency family.*

fan beam.   A *radar beam radiation pattern* that is broad in two Cartesion dimensions and narrow in the third.   For example, a *beam* pattern with large vertical and narrow horizontal coverage.   It is used normally with *search radars.*

fan marker beacon.   A *radio beacon* that *radiates* with a *radiation pattern* that is a *fan beam* pattern.   The *signal* can be *keyed* for identification purposes.

Faraday effect.   See *magnetooptic effect.*

far-end crosstalk (FEXT).   *Crosstalk* that is *propagated* in a *disturbed channel* in the same direction as the propagation of the *signal* in the *disturbing channel.* The *terminals* of the disturbed channel at which the far-end crosstalk is present, and the energized terminals of the disturbing channel, are usually remote from each other.   For example, in *optical fibers, bundles,* and *cables,* the FEXT is the *optical power* measured at the *receiving* end of a given fiber when optical power is inserted into an adjacent fiber at its *transmitting* end.

far-field region. See *radiation field region.*

far infrared. Pertaining to *electromagnetic wavelengths* from 30 to 1000 *microns.*

far zone. See *radiation field region.*

fast automatic gain control. *Automatic gain control* that has a very short *response* time. It can be used as an *electronic counter-countermeasure (ECCM).*

fast select. A *facility* that is applicable to *virtual calls* and that allows *data terminal equipment (DTE)* to increase the possibility of *transmitting data* in *call setup* and *call-clearing packets* beyond the basic capabilities of a virtual call.

fast time constant (FTC). A *time constant* of comparatively short duration. Fast time constants are used in *radar signal processing* to reduce the effects of certain types of undesired *signals.* Fast time constants are used to *emphasize signals* of short duration to produce *discrimination* against low *frequency components* of *clutter* in *radar.* To obtain a fast time constant in an electric *circuit,* a low product of *resistance* and *capacitance* (RC), or a low ratio of *inductance* to resistance (L/R) is used. If these circuit elements are of proper magnitude and are properly connected in relation to *input* and *output,* the resulting circuit *output* is the derivative of its input. This fast time constant protects against *interference* of either *frequency* or *amplitude modulated* signals. The *differentiating circuit (differentiator),* inserted between the *detector* and *video amplifier,* will pass individual *pulses* but not the *modulation frequencies.* Circuits of this type shorten the length of the observed pulse and should be switched on only when interference makes it necessary. Such differentiating circuits are of real value so long as the *intermediate frequency (IF) amplifier* is not overloaded. See *logarithmic fast time constant (logFTC).*

fault. An accidental condition that causes a *functional unit* to fail to perform its required function. For example, a short circuit. A fault is reproducible. This is contrasted with an *error* which is normally not reproducible. A fault is considered reproducible if it occurs consistently under the same circumstances. Also see *error; failure; mistake.* See *loophole.*

fault dominance. If x and y are two *faults* that can occur in a *system,* then fault x is said to dominate fault y if and only if every test to determine if y has occurred is also a test to determine if x has occurred.

fault masking. If x and y are two *faults* that can occur in a *system,* then fault x is said to mask fault y if no test for the occurrence of y is a test for the joint occurrence of faults x and y.

FAX. *Facsimile system.*

F-band. *Frequencies* that are in the range from 3 to 4 GHz. It comprises 10 numbered *channels* of 100 MHz width each.

FDM. *Frequency division multiplexing.*

FE. 1. *Format effector.* 2. The *format effector transmission control character.*

feature. See *spill-forward feature.*

Federal telecommunication standard. One of a series of standards developed by the *National Telecommunications System,* Washington, DC 20305 and published by the General Services Administration (GSA), Washington, DC 20405. For example, Federal Standard 1037, Glossary of Telecommunication Terms; and Federal Standard 1033, Data Communication Performance Assessment.

Federal Telecommunications System (FTS). A U.S. Government *communication system* administered by the General Services Administration (GSA), Washington, DC 20405 covering the 50 states, Puerto Rico, and the Virgin Islands. It provides services for *voice, teletypewriter, facsimile,* and *data transmission.*

feed. See *antenna feed; line feed; prime focus feed.*

feed antenna. See *diel-guide feed antenna.*

feedback. 1. The return of a portion of the *output* energy of the device or *circuit* to the *input.* In positive feedback, the portion of the output *signal* that is fed back adds to the input signal. In negative feedback, the portion of the output signal that is fed back subtracts from the input signal. Positive feedback leads to instability, whereas negative feedback leads to stability. 2. The energy, *signal,* or *information* that is returned to the originating *source.* See *error detection and feedback; information feedback; video integrator feedback.* Also see Figure T-8.

feedback factor. The fraction of the *output signal* of a device that is returned and combined with the *input signal* at the *input terminal.* The factor may be a complex function, since both magnitude and *phase* are involved. For example, if there is no *phase shift* in the signal that is fed back, the feedback is positive. If the phase shift is 180° (electrical), the feedback is negative. The factor can lie between these values. Also see *transfer function.*

feedback laser. See *distributed-feedback (DFB) laser.*

feedback shift register. A *shift register* that is made to generate a sequence of *binary* combinations by feeding back functions of the state of the register to its *input.* The *binary* combinations that are generated do not necessarily follow the *pure* (straight) *binary* counting sequence. Synonymous with *twisted ring counter.*

Also see *spread-spectrum code-sequence generator.* See *linear feedback shift register; nonlinear feedback shift register.*

feedback tap. In a *spread-spectrum code-sequence generator,* an *output* tap of one of the *flip-flops* of the *code-sequence generator register.* In a simple generator, the tap is connected to one of the *inputs* of an *EXCLUSIVE-OR gate* (modulo-two summer). The output tap of the last flip-flop is connected to the other input of the gate, and the gate output is connected to the input of the first flip-flop. More complex arrangements can be made to produce special effects and pseudorandom modification of the generator itself. Also see Figure S-14.

feed character. See *form feed (FF) character; line feed (LF) character.*

feeder. A means whereby *radio frequency* energy can be transmitted between a *radio transmitter amplifier output* and an *antenna.* For example, a rectangular metal *waveguide* or *coaxial cable* that connects the amplifier output to the antenna at a *radio station.*

feeder cable. See *branch feeder cable.*

feeder echo noise. *Noise* that is caused by *reflected electromagnetic waves* in a *transmission line* that is many *wavelengths* long and mismatched at both the generator *(transmitter)* and load *(receiver)* ends. The noise results in *signal distortion.*

feed harness. The set of electrical and mechanical elements that conducts electrical energy from a *transmitter output* to an *antenna* and from the *antenna input terminal* to the actual *connections* or *terminals* on the invidual *radiators* of the *antenna array.* It includes all *impedance-matching transformers* and *connectors.*

feed horn. See *scalar feed horn.*

feed system. See *five-horn feed system; four-horn feed system; monopulse antenna feed system.*

FEP-clad silica fiber. See *low-loss FEP-clad silica fiber.*

Fermat's principle. A *ray* of *light* follows the path that requires the least time to travel from one point to another, including *reflections* and *refractions* that may occur. The *optical* path length is an extreme path in the terminology of the calculus of variations. Thus, if all *rays* starting from point *A* and traveling via a medium arrive at the same point *B*, the *optical paths* from *A* to *B* are the same length. In fibers, since different rays take different paths, they arrive at the end at different points, giving rise to *dispersion.* Synonymous with *least-time principle.*

ferrite switch. A *passive switch* that uses the *phase-shifting* properties of a high *magnetic permeability* ferrite at *microwave frequencies* to connect either of two outputs to either of two inputs by *switching* the *electromagnetic wave fields*.

ferromagnetic. Pertaining to material with a *magnetic permeability* very much greater than that of air or a vacuum. Ferromagnetic materials act like good conductors of *magnetic* lines of *flux* when placed in a *magnetic* field, tend to draw the lines of flux inside, and tend to take a position with their long axes parallel to the lines of magnetic flux with a strong force compared to other materials. Also see *diamagnetic; paramagnetic.*

ferrous shield. A low-*resistance electric-current* conducting material that contains iron and therefore provides a low-*reluctance*, high-*permeability*, *magnetic* path. *Incident electromagnetic waves* are absorbed in the shield. They do not penetrate deeply and, therefore, are not *transmitted* through the material.

fetch protection. A restriction to prevent a *user* (subscriber, customer) from gaining *access* to another user's *information* that is stored or *transmitted* in a *computer, communication,* or other *system.*

FEXT. *Far-end crosstalk.*

FFL. *Front focal length.*

fiber. See *air-supported fiber; circularly symmetric fiber; compensated fiber; doped silica cladded fiber; doped-silica graded fiber; drawn glass fiber; graded index fiber; high-loss fiber; inhomogeneous fiber; jointed fiber; jumbo fiber; liquid core fiber; low-loss FEP-clad silica fiber; low-loss fiber; medium loss fiber; multimode fiber; optical fiber; overcompensated fiber; plastic-clad silica fiber; self-focusing fiber; SEL fiber; SELFOC fiber; single fiber; single-mode fiber; step-index fiber; transition fiber; triangular-cored fiber; undercompensated optical fiber; uniform-index-profile fiber; W-type fiber.*

fiber absorption. In an *optical fiber,* the *lightwave* power *attenuation* due to *absorption* in the *fiber core* material, a loss usually evaluated by measuring the power emerging at the end of successively shortened known lengths of the fiber.

fiber acoustic sensor. See *optical fiber acoustic sensor.*

fiber active connector. See *optical fiber active connector.*

fiber-alignment connector. See *grooved fiber-alignment connector.*

fiber borescope. A device capable of viewing the interior of a device or machine with an *optical fiber* that both *illuminates* and obtains the *reflected image,* such as an optical fiber embedded in the housing of a turbine to view the blade clearance.

fiber buffer. The material surrounding and immediately adjacent to an *optical fiber* that provides mechanical isolation and protection. Buffers are generally softer materials than *jackets*. Also see *stuffing*. See Figure F-3.

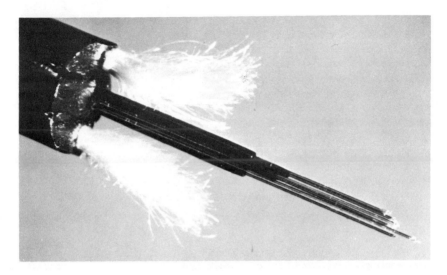

F-3. An early six-*fiber optical waveguide cable* with two fuzzy arimid yarn *strength members*. Each fiber is in an individual **fiber buffer** tube. (Copyright 1979, Corning Glass Works. Reprinted by permission from Corning Glass Works, Telecommunication Products Department.)

fiber bundle. See *optical fiber bundle*.

fiber bundle transfer function. The function that produces the *output signal* waveform when it operates upon the *input* signal waveform for an *optical fiber bundle*. For example, the *transfer function* might assume the form:

$$FBTF = A(f)e^{j\theta(f)}$$

where $A(f)$ is the amplitude portion and $\theta(f)$ is the *phase* portion of the fiber bundle transfer function (FBTF), and j is the complex operator.

fiber cable. See *multiple-fiber cable; multichannel single-fiber cable; single-channel single-fiber cable*.

fiber cable assembly. See *multiple-fiber cable assembly*.

fiber circuit. See *hybrid optical fiber circuit*.

fiber cladding. A *light-conducting* material that surrounds the *core* of an *optical fiber* and that has a lower *refractive index* than the core material.

fiber coating. See *optical fiber coating.*

fiber communications. See *optical fiber communications.*

fiber concentrator. See *optical fiber concentrator.*

fiber core. The central *light-conducting* portion of an *optical fiber.* The core has a higher *refractive index* than the *cladding* that surrounds it.

fiber core diameter. In an *optical fiber,* the diameter of the higher *refractive index* medium that is the primary *transmission medium* for the fiber.

fiber count. The number of *optical fibers* in a *bundle,* given approximately by:

$$N = 0.907(D/d - 1)^2$$

where D is the bundle diameter and d is the fiber diameter.

fiber coupled power. See *source-to-fiber coupled power.*

fiber coupling. See *source-fiber coupling.*

fiber crosstalk. In an *optical fiber,* exchange of *lightwave* energy between a *core* and the *cladding,* between the cladding and the ambient surrounding, or between differently-*indexed* layers. Fiber *crosstalk* is usually undesirable because *refractive* differences in path length and *propagation* time can result in *dispersion,* thus reducing *transmission* distances. Therefore, *attenuation* is deliberately introduced into the cladding by making it a *lossy medium.*

fiber-cutting tool. A special cutting tool designed to prepare the ends of *fibers* for *splicing* or *connecting* by bending the fiber under tension and using a sharp-edged blade to initiate a *microcrack,* which fractures the fiber and produces a smooth flat cleavage.

fiber delay line. See *optical fiber delay line.*

fiber-detector coupling. In *fiber-optic transmission systems,* the transfer of *optical signal power* from an *optical fiber* to a *detector* for conversion to an electrical signal. Many optical fiber detectors have an *optical fiber pigtail* for connection by means of a splice or a connector to a *transmission* fiber.

fiber diameter. The diameter of an *optical fiber,* normally including the *core,* the *cladding* if *step-indexed,* and any adherent *coating* not normally removed when making a connection (such as by a *butted* or *tangential coupling*).

fiber dimensional stability.   A measure of the constancy of the physical dimensions, particularly diameter and length, of a *fiber* under the stress and *temperature* changes that occur during *pulling* and operating.

fiber dispersion.   The lengthening of the width of an *electromagnetic-energy pulse* as it travels along a *fiber* caused by *material dispersion,* due to the *frequency* dependence of the *refractive index; modal dispersion,* caused by different *group velocities* of the different *modes;* and *waveguide dispersion,* due to frequency dependence of the *propagation constant* of that mode.

fiber distribution box.   See *optical fiber distribution box.*

fiber distribution frame (FDF).   An *optical fiber connector panel* for *splicing* or connecting distribution *cables* and jumper cables, usually of one fiber each, to the *optical transmitters* and *optical receivers.*   See Figure F-4.

F-4. Checking *single-fiber jumpers* in a *light guide* or **fiber distribution frame** at an Illinois Bell *central office.*   (Courtesy Bell Laboratories.)

fiber distribution system. See *protected optical fiber distribution system.*

fiber drawing. The controlled pulling of a *fiber*, in a melted or softened state, through an aperture, causing it to elongate and thus to reduce its diameter as it cools. Also see Figure F-7.

fiber faceplate. A *coherent* array or *bundle* of fused *optical fibers* used as a cover for a light source, such as an *LED* or a vacuum or gas tube, usually cut from a *boule*. Also see *boule.*

Fiberguide. An *optical fiber* produced by Times Fiber Communications, Inc.

fiber gyroscope. A gyroscope that uses *optical fibers* to conduct *signals* representing tilt forces as part of the control system for maintaining stability and for conveying signals from perturbations. It is characterized by low power consumption, high sensitivity to perturbations, and high reliability.

fiber hazard. See *optical fiber hazard.*

fiber jacket. See *optical fiber jacket.*

fiber jumper. An *optical fiber* that directly connects two points. Also see Figure F-4.

fiber junction. See *optical fiber junction.*

fiber light-guide. See *optical fiber.*

fiber link. See *TV optical fiber link.*

fiber loss. See *source-to-fiber loss.*

fiber merit figure. See *optical fiber merit figure.*

fiber-optic. Pertaining to *optical fibers* and the *communication systems* in which they are used.

fiber-optic arteriovenous oximeter. A device using a *fiber-optic catheter* for continuous prolonged *in vivo* measurement of blood oxygen content, tension, or saturation.

fiber-optic bloodflow meter. A bloodflow meter mounted in a catheter, introduced *in vivo* into a vein, that uses a single *optical fiber* to transmit *light* into, and obtain *scattered light* from, the moving erythrocytes, and uses *optical mixing* spectroscopy and *Doppler shift* to measure bloodflow rate.

fiber-optic cable. *Optical fibers* incorporated into an assembly of materials that provides tensile strength, external protection, and handling properties comparable to those of equivalent-diameter *coaxial cables. Fiber-optic* cables (light guides) are a direct replacement for conventional coaxial cables and wire pairs. The glass-based *transmission* facilities occupy far less physical volume for an equivalent transmission capacity, which is a major advantage in crowded underground ducts. Manufacturing, installation, and maintenance costs are less. These advantages, with the reduced use of critical metals, such as copper, is a strong impetus for the use of fiber-optic cables. Also see Figures L-5, M-7, M-8 and M-9.

fiber-optic choledochoscope. A device for viewing the bile duct using *optical fibers* for *illuminating* and viewing the interior of the duct.

fiber-optic communications (FOC). *Communication, systems,* and components in which *optical fibers* are used to carry *signals* from point to point.

fiber-optic connector. See *fixed fiber-optic connector; free fiber-optic connector.*

fiber-optic data link. An *optical link* capable of handling *data* in *digital* form. See Figures F-5 and F-6. Also see M-5.

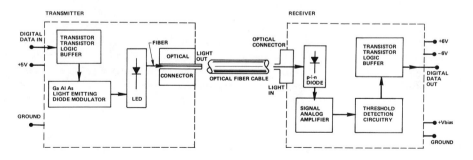

F-5. *Components* of a **fiber-optic data link.** (Courtesy of RCA Electro-optics and Devices.)

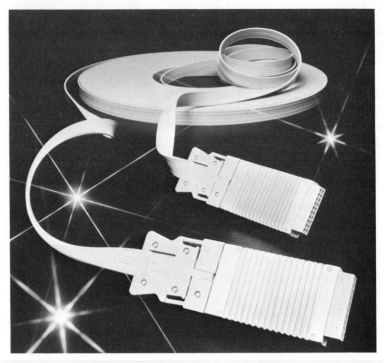

F-6. A **fiber optic data link** that consists of two *transceivers* that can be used in a card cage without modification, and a pre*terminated duplex cable.* (Courtesy of 3M Business Communication Products Division.)

fiber-optic dosimeter. A dosimeter for measuring cumulative exposure to high-energy *radiation* or bombardment by measuring the *degradation* or increased *attenuation* introduced into an *optical fiber* from exposure to the bombardment. Also see *optical-fiber radiation damage.* Examples of high-energy radiation are gamma radiation and high-energy neutrons.

fiber-optic interface device. A device capable of (1) accepting electrical *signals* and converting them to *lightwave* signals for *transmission* in an *optical fiber, bundle, cable,* or *slab dielectric waveguide* or (2) accepting lightwave *pulses* and converting them to electrical signals for transmission over electrical conductors. For example, a *full-duplex asynchronous data-transmission* unit capable of handling a *data signaling rate* of 0 to 20 *Kbps* using *fiber-optic cable* transmission and maintaining a *BER* of less than 10^{-9}. Synonymous with *fiber-optic modem.*

fiber-optic modem. See *fiber optic interface device.*

fiber-optic multiport coupler. An *optical* unit, with at least one *input* and two outputs or two inputs and one *output,* that can be used to *couple* various sources to various receivers. The ports are usually *optical fibers.* If there is only one input and one output port, it is simply a *connector.* Most fiber-optic multiport couplers consist simply of a solid chamber of optical material. Operation depends upon *scattering* or *diffusion.*

fiber-optic myocardium stimulator. A device capable of delivering *impulses* directly into the heart muscles (myocardium) to initiate periodic contraction at appropriate instants in strategic places in the heart muscles to overcome blocking of normal neuronal conduction. It consists of a heart pacemaker, control circuits, a *light source, optical fibers,* and *photodetectors.*

fiber-optic nuclear hardening. Design allowances made to prevent or ameliorate the effects of *gamma* or high-energy neutron *radiation* or bombardment, which causes some fibers to darken, increase *attenuation,* or depart from normal operating parameters. *Light sources,* such as *LEDs* and *lasers,* and *photodetectors* also need to be hardened to prevent similar malfunction.

fiber-optic probe. A flexible probe made up of a *bundle* of fine-glass *fibers* optically aligned to *transmit* an *image.*

fiber-optic reflective sensor. A sensor that *illuminates* an *object* with a *light source* and senses *reflections* from the object, using *optical fibers* to conduct the light both ways; the final output is an electrical *signal* from a *photodetector* proportional to the *intensity* or *color* of the *reflected light.* The output signal may be sequential from each fiber or the signal may represent a scanned *image* of the object *focused* on a screen. A hand-held *optical scanner* is an example of a fiber-optic reflective sensor.

fiber-optic rod coupler. A *graded-index,* cylindrically shaped section of *optical fiber* or rod with a length corresponding to the pitch of the undulations of *light-waves* caused by the *graded refractive index.* The *light beam* is injected via fibers at an off-axis endpoint on the radius. The undulations of the resulting wave vary periodically from one point to another along the rod. *Half-reflection* layers at the 1/4 pitch point of the undulations provide for *coupling* between input and output fibers. Also see *half-reflection.*

fiber-optic rod multiplexer-filter. A *graded-index*, cylindrically shaped section of *optical fiber* or rod with a length corresponding to the pitch of the undulations of lightwaves caused by the *graded refractive index*. The *light beam* is injected via fibers at an off-axis endpoint on the radius. The undulations of the resulting wave varying periodically from one point to another along the rod. *Interference* layers at the 1/4 pitch point of the undulations, provide for *multiplexing* or *filtering*, as desired.

fiber optics (FO) 1. As first defined by Kapany in 1956, the art of the *active* and *passive* guidance of *light (rays* and *waveguide modes)* in the *ultraviolet, visible,* and *infrared* regions of the *spectrum* along *transparent fibers* through predetermined paths. **2.** The technology of guidance of *optical power,* including *rays* and *waveguide modes* of *electromagnetic waves* along *conductors* of electromagnetic waves in the *visible* and near-visible region of the *frequency spectrum,* specifically when the *optical energy* is guided to another location through thin *transparent* strands. Techniques include conveying *light* or *images* through a particular configuration of glass or plastic *fibers. Incoherent optical fibers* will transmit light, as a pipe will transmit water, but not an image. *Coherent optical fibers* can transmit an image through perfectly aligned, small (10–12 *microns*), clad, optical fibers. Specialty fiber optics combine coherent and incoherent aspects. See *ultraviolet fiber optics.*

fiber-optic scrambler. Similar to a *fiberscope* except that the middle section of loose *fiber* is deliberately disoriented as much as possible. When potted and sawed, each half is then capable of *coding* a picture that can be decoded by the other half.

fiber-optic splice. A nonseparable junction joining one *optical conductor* to another. Also see Figures F-8, L-9, and P-11.

fiber-optic telecommunication cable. A long-haul *optical fiber cable* usually with *optical fiber bundles, strength members, stuffing, electrical conductors, insulation, jacketing,* and protective sheathing for maximum *protection* and *security* in rugged and wet overhead, buried, and *conduit* installations.

fiber-optic terminus. A device, used to terminate an *optical conductor,* that provides a means to locate and contain the optical conductor within a *connector.*

fiber-optic transmission system (FOTS). A *transmission system* using small-diameter *transparent fibers* through which *light* is *transmitted. Information* is transferred by *modulating* the transmitted *light*. These modulated *signals* are detected by light-sensitive devices (i.e., *photodetectors*). See *laser fiber-optic transmission system*.

fiber-optic visible-infrared spin-scan radiometer. A device for measuring and recording the *intensity* of *visible* and *infrared electromagnetic radiation* from many directions simultaneously, using *optical fibers* to conduct the received radiation from the scanned directions. For example, the radiometer may be a fixed or tilting device used to create a terrestrial map based on infrared radiation from the earth received by a satellite.

fiber-optic waveguide. A relatively long thin strand of *transparent* substance, usually glass, capable of *conducting* an *electromagnetic wave* of *optical wavelength (visible* or near-visible region of the *frequency spectrum)* with some ability to confine longitudinally directed, or near-longitudinally directed, *lightwaves* to its interior by means of *internal reflection*. The fiber-optic waveguide may be homogeneous or radially inhomogeneous with *step* or *graded* changes in its *refractive index*, the indices being lower at the outer regions and the *core* thus being of an increased refractive index.

fiberoptronics. **1.** An abbreviation of *fiber optics* and *optoelectronics*. **2.** The branch of science and technology devoted to electronically *modulating* a *light source* in order to impress *information* on a light *beam* and to guide the beam through *optical fiber cables* to an *electrooptical detector* where the impressed information is recovered in electronic form.

fiber pattern. In the *faceplate* of a *fiberscope*, on the end of a *bundle* of *optical fibers*, the arrangement of the ends of the individual optical fibers that comprise the end surface. Inspection of the *image* on the end surface might reveal the fiber pattern, thus making the image appear as a mosaic of individual *picture elements*. Also see *picture element*.

fiber preform. See *optical fiber preform*.

fiber-pulling machine. A device capable of drawing an *optical fiber* from a *preform* heated to fusion *temperature*. The increased temperature provides for ductility and fusion of *dopants* to control the *refractive index profile*. The cross section decreases and the length increases as drawn fiber is wound on a spool or drum. See Figure F-7.

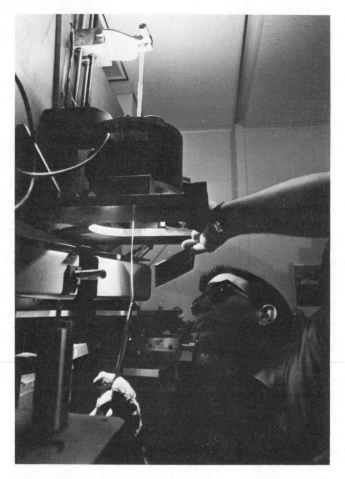

F-7. Hand-starting of an *optical fiber* for *drawing* by a **fiber-pulling machine.** The first strand is connected to a rotating drum for winding. (Courtesy of Bell Laboratories.)

fiber pulse compression.   See *optical fiber pulse compression.*

fiber radiation damage.   See *optical fiber radiation damage.*

fiber ribbon.   See *optical fiber ribbon.*

fiber ringer.   See *optical fiber ringer.*

fiber scattering. In an *optical fiber,* the *coupling* or leaking of *lightwave power* out of the *core* of the fiber by *Rayleigh scattering* or *guide* imperfections. Such imperfections include *dielectric* strain, compositional or physical discontinuities in the core or *cladding,* irregularities and extraneous inclusions in the core-cladding *interface,* curvature of the *optical axis,* or *tapering. Scattering* losses are measured in all directions as an *integrated* effect and expressed in *decibels*/kilometer.

fiberscope. A device consisting of an entry point, at which a *bundle* of *optical fibers* can enter, and a *faceplate* surface on which the entering fibers can uniformly terminate, in order to *display* the *optical image* received through the fibers. The bundle of fibers *transmit* a full *color image* that remains undisturbed when the bundle is bent. By mounting an *objective lens* on one end of the bundle and an *eyepiece* at the other, the assembly becomes a flexible fiberscope that can be used to view *objects* that are otherwise inaccessible for direct viewing. See *hypodermic fiberscope.*

fiberscope recording. A method of recording on film in which the light emerging from the *faceplate* of a *coherent bundle* of *optical fibers* is used to expose film. Contrast with *electron-beam recording.*

fiber source. See *optical fiber source.*

fiber strain. The percent or per unit elongation of an *optical fiber* when subjected to a given stress or force. Fracture occurs at approximately 1%. Operating strains on installation are held to about 0.2%.

fiber system. See *integrated optical fiber system.*

fiber tensile strength. See *optical fiber tensile strength.*

fiber transfer function. See *optical fiber transfer function.*

fiber trap. See *optical fiber trap.*

fiber video trunk. See *optical fiber video trunk.*

fiche. See *ultrafiche.*

fidelity. The degree to which a *system* or a *functional unit* accurately reproduces the essential characteristics of an *input signal.* Also see *linearity.*

field. 1. A specification of a particular *vector* quantity in a given region or at a specific point in space, the existence of which is describable or manifested by a physical phenomenon, such as force or motion, in terms of other vector quantities and time. In *electromagnetic* theory, force fields and their gradients are manifested by stationary or moving charges within the fields, since these charges will have forces exerted upon them if the field exists. 2. A dimensional space, such as a line, surface, or volume. See *address field; aiming field; control field; display field; electric field; electrostatic field; gravitational field; induction field; information field; magnetic field; magnetostatic field; near field; radiation field; scanning field; signaling information field; view field.*

field component. See *electric field component; magnetic field component.*

field coupling. See *evanescent-field coupling.*

field curvature. In *optics,* an *aberration* of actions that causes a plane *image* to be *focused* onto a curved surface instead of a flat plane.

field directory. 1. A *directory* specially designed for use by a military force during a tactical situation. 2. A directory specially designed for use by *communication system* maintenance personnel outside *central offices.*

field extension. See *address field extension; control field extension.*

field force. See *electric field force; magnetic field force.*

field lens. In an *optical* system or instrument, a *positive lens* used to collect the *chief rays* of *image*-forming *bundles* so that entire bundles, or sufficient portions of them, will pass through the *exit pupil* of the instrument. A field lens is usually located at or near the *focal point* of the *objective lens.* The field lens increases the size of the field that can be viewed with any given eyelens diameter.

field rays. In the *object* space of a symmetrical *optical system,* a *ray* that intersects the *optical axis* at the center of the *entrance pupil* of the *optical system.* In the *image* space, the same ray emerges from the *exit pupil.* In a *thick lens,* a field ray is a *principal ray.*

field splicing. The joining of the ends of two *optical cables* in a field environment without the use of detachable *connectors* and in such a manner that continuity across the splice is preserved in all elements of the cable such as *fiber*-to-fiber *coupling,* electrical continuity if any is required, and continuity of *jacketing,* sheathing, *stuffing,* insulation, waterproofing, and *strength members.* See Figures F-8 and F-9.

F-8. Temporary cover for use in short term protection of *optical fiber cable* **field splicing.** Cover is secured with Scotchmate hook 'n loop fasteners. (Courtesy of 3M Business Communication Products Division.)

F-9. A Siecor portable machine for laboratory or **field splicing** of *optical fibers.* (Courtesy of Siecor Optical Cables, Inc.)

field stop.   In an *optical system*, a limit or boundary placed on an *image* at some point in the system in order to limit the size or extent of the image and thus eliminate unwanted *diffused, deflected*, or *divergent light*.   Also see *aperture stop; exit pupil.*

field strength.   The *intensity* of an *electric* or *magnetic field* at a given point. The field strength is usually expressed as a gradient, such as volts per meter for electric fields and amperes per meter for magnetic fields.   Field strengths can also be indicated by the forces they exert upon electric charges (electric fields) or magnetic poles (magnetic fields) placed in them.   Their strength may also be indicated in terms of the number of lines of force or flux per unit cross-sectional area when the *dielectric* constant *(permittivity)* or the *magnetic permeability* is taken into account.   The field strength is a *vector* quantity.   Synonymous with *radio field intensity* and with *field intensity*.   Also see *electric field; magnetic field; Maxwell's equations.*

field switchboard.   A *telephone switchboard* that is specially designed and packaged to be used for *communication* in open country, either on or off vehicles.

FIFO.   *First-in-first-out.*

figure.   See *optical-fiber merit figure.*

figure case.   **1.** In the *teletypewriter code* for *tape relay systems*, the *machine function* that produces or interprets a hole pattern on tape or a *pulse* pattern on wires, *fibers*, or *cables* as one of the arabic *numerals* 0 through 9, a punctuation mark, or a special sign or *symbol*.   The figure case is obtained by actuating a special *function key*.   Synonymous with *upper case*.   Also see *letter case.*   **2.** One of the groups into which the *characters* and the *machine functions* of a *code* are placed.   The figure case contains the numbers 0 through 9.

figure indicator.   In *visual signaling systems*, a *panel signaling indicator* that consists of a single panel appropriately placed to mean that the characters that follow are to be interpreted as *numerals* rather than as letters.

figure shift.   In *teletypewriter operations*, a *case shift* that results in the *translation* of *signals* into another group of *characters* that is predominantly *numerals* and *machine functions* rather than the letters group that was being used or interpreted before the shift occurred.   Also see *escape character; letter shift.*

figure-shift signal.   The *signal* that conditions a *telegraph receiver* to *translate* all *received* or *transmitted signals* as the *figures case* (numerals or machine *functions*) rather than as the *letters case* that was in use before the figure-shift signal occurred.

filament.   See *monofilament.*

file. An organized collection of related *data* for a specific purpose and treated as a unit. The file may be recorded on any *data medium*. See *display file; system environmental file.*

file protection. The processes and procedures that are designed to prevent unauthorized *access, contamination,* or elimination of a file.

file time. See *message file time.*

filing. In a *communication system,* the entering or handing in of a *message* at a *communication center* for *processing* and *transmission.* Also see *filing time; refile message.*

filing communication center. The *communication center* at which an *originator's message* is first accepted for *transmission.*

filing time. 1. In *communication system operation,* the *date* and time a *message* is received, that is, handed in for *transmission* by an *originator* at a *communication center.* The *time-date group* is usually shown as a *Julian date* immediately followed by hour and minutes in *digits. Greenwich mean time* is usually used for international *transmission* without the time zone suffix, Z, such as 0401215, which would be 15 minutes past 12 noon, GMT, on the 40th day of the year. The filing time for *refile messages* is the date and time the message is received by a communication center for refile. 2. In *telephone switchboard operation,* the time at which a *call* is placed or *booked.* For *booked calls,* the filing time is placed on the *call ticket.* See *call filing time.*

fill. See *character fill; interframe time fill; zerofill.*

film. See *multilayer dielectric film; optical thin film; photoconductive film.*

film frame. The area on film specifically dedicated to the recording of a *display image;* e.g., the area on film exposed each time the film is in place on the *faceplate* of a *fiberscope* when a succession of images is being recorded on *microfilm.* Synonymous with *recording area.*

film optical modulator. See *thin-film optical modulator.*

film optical multiplexers. See *thin-film optical multiplexers.*

film optical switch. See *thin-film optical switch.*

film optical waveguide. See *thin-film optical waveguide.*

film waveguide. See *periodically distributed thin-film waveguide.*

filter.   **1.** An electrical *network* that passes certain *frequencies* but greatly *attenuates* other frequencies. For example, a device for use on *power lines* or *signal lines,* specifically designed to pass only selected frequencies and to attenuate all other frequencies or to attenuate selected frequencies and pass all other frequencies. There are two basic types of filters: *active filters,* that require the application of power to perform their filtering action; and *passive filters,* that do not require the application of power to perform their filtering function. **2.** In an *optical system,* a device, with the desired characteristic of selective *transmittance* and *optical* homogeneity, used to modify the *spectral* composition of *radiant light flux.* A filter is usually of special glass, gelatin, or plastic optical parts with plane-parallel surfaces that are placed in the path of *light* through the optical system of an instrument to selectively *absorb* certain *wavelengths* of light, reduce glare, or reduce light intensity.   *Colored, ultraviolet,* neutral density, and *polarizing* filters are in common use.   Filters may be separate elements or integral devices mounted so that they can be placed in or out of position in a system as desired. See *active filter; band-pass filter; bandstop filter; dichroic filter; fiber optic rod multiplexer filter; high-pass filter; low-pass filter; notch filter; optical filter; passive filter; preselection filter; roofing filter; security filter; video filter.*

filter balance.   See *line filter balance.*

filter center.   A *communication center* in which *information* from different *data sources* is checked and perhaps *encrypted* prior to further dissemination.

filter-coupler-switch-modulator.   See   *integrated-optical   circuit   filter-coupler-switch, modulator.*

filtering.   The removal of specific components, features, or characteristics from an entity; e.g., removal of certain *frequencies* from a *beam* of *light* containing many frequencies.   Filtering is one of the processes that can be accomplished on *light-waves* in *integrated optical circuits* and *optical fibers.*   Examples of processes that usually involve some form of filtering include *coupling, switching, modulating,* and *image restoration.*   See *inverse filtering; Kalman filtering; pseudo-inverse filtering.*

filtering system.   See *discrete-time filtering system.*

final modulation.   The last state of the *modulation* of a *carrier* prior to *transmission* to the *antenna* to be *radiated* into *space.*

finder.   See *direction finder (DF); height finder.*

finding.   See *direction finding (DF); radio range finding; simultaneous direction finding.*

finding equipment.   See *radio direction-finding equipment.*

finding station.   See *radio direction-finding station.*

finish. See *optical end-finish.*

finished call. A *call* in which the *calling* or *called party* no longer desires to *communicate* and thus *rings-off,* returns the *receiver* to the *hook,* or returns the handset to the cradle (hangs up). Also see *completed call.*

finished lens. *Lens* with both surfaces ground and polished to a specific *dioptric power* or *focus.*

firmware. 1. *Software* that has been built into *hardware.* Examples of firmware include *computer programs, display files,* and *segments* that have been permanently stored in a fixed, *read-only storage* that is permanently wired to contain specific unchangeable words. Such firmware can be created by constructing a set of orthogonally intersecting wires with a *magnetic core* at each intersection and then removing the cores where the zeros of a *binary number* are to be stored permanently, whereas the ones of the number are stored where the cores remain. The same effect can be obtained by thin-film, evaporative deposition, printed, or integrated circuit techniques. In a *data* processing or *communication system, firmware* is permanently installed or wired into the system either in pluggable or nonremovable circuits capable of executing arithmetic and logic operations, such as executing specific built-in sequences of computer-program *instructions,* performing *code* or *language translations, compiling* instructions, or performing other *software* operations such as *communication system store-and-forward, switching,* or control *operations* automatically. The use of firmware permits more rapid execution of built-in instructions, since the instructions need not be obtained from storage, interpreted, and then executed by general-purpose logic circuits. Some flexibility is lost through the use of firmware. There are no clear-cut boundaries between hardware, firmware, and software inasmuch as they occupy different realms. 2. A *computer program* that is implemented in hardware; e.g., a *read-only storage* or a permanently wired set of *logic circuits* designed to execute a specific set of *instructions.* Contrast with *hardware; software.* Also see *hardwire.*

first-in-first-out (FIFO). A queueing discipline in which entities that arrive at a point assemble in the time order in which they arrive and leave in the same order in which they arrived. Thus, service is offered first to the entity that has waited the longest. For example, in *message switching,* an order of precedence for processing *message traffic* based on the queue position of messages such that *messages* are dispatched from the point in the same order in which they are received at the point. The message waiting the longest is the first to be dispatched. Synonymous with *push-up.* Also see *buffer; last-in-first-out (LIFO); queue traffic.*

first out. See *first-in-first-out (FIFO); last-in-first-out (LIFO).*

first principal point. In an *optical system,* the first significant point in the system nearest the *object;* e.g., the geometric center of an *objective lens.*

five-horn feed system.   In *radar systems,* a *monopulse* or *pseudomonopulse antenna feed system* in which four elements act in the *receive mode* for *signal tracking* and a separate element acts in the *transmit mode.*   Also see *four-horn feed system.*

five-layer four-heterojunction diode.   A *four-heterojunction laser diode,* consisting of two pairs of heterojunctions, that has five layers of *step-indexed* material (i.e., five layers of material with a sudden transition of *refractive index* at the *interface* between layers).   The *emitted light* is confined to a narrow *beam* for optimum *coupling* to an *optical fiber, fiber bundle,* or *integrated optical circuit.* Usually, only three different refractive indices are involved, since there may be a pair of identically indexed outside layers, a pair of identically indexed inside layers on opposite sides of a center layer, each pair and center layer being of different refractive index.   The lower refractive indices are toward the outside, resulting in a layered cross-section with *step-indices* of $n_1:n_2:n_3:n_2:n_1$, with $n_1 < n_2 < n_3$. Thus, almost all of the generated and emitted light is confined to the center layer by *internal reflection.*

fix.   A successful *triangulation* in *direction finding.*   See *radio fix; request fix; running fix.*

fixed communication network.   See *military fixed communication network.*

fixed compromise equalizer.   A fixed *circuit* or *network* that is connected to a *transmission line* to compensate for the different *impedances* encountered by the different *frequencies* that usually occur.   Since each frequency requires a different *balancing, matching,* or *terminating impedance,* a compromise impedance is used that best fits all the frequencies that are encountered.   This will minimize *reflections,* obtain maximum *power* transfer, or accomplish other specific purposes.

fixed directory.   A *telephone directory* in which the number assigned to each *user* (customer, subscriber), equipment, *program,* or process remains fixed regardless of where the user's instrument or terminal is connected to the *systems* within the area covered by the directory.   Personnel changes affect updating; entries are *alphabetical* by user's name.   Also see *appointment directory.*

fixed earth station.   An *earth station* intended to be used at a specified fixed ground location.   It is neither *mobile* nor *transportable.*

fixed fiber-optic connector.   A connector that permits connection of *optical fiber* components that are to be associated on a permanent basis.   Fixed fiber-optic connectors can be used to connect source to *optical conductor,* optical conductor to optical conductor, or optical conductor to *detector.*   They are usually part of the devices being connected.

fixed focus.   Pertaining to instruments that are not provided with a means of *focusing.*

fixed function generator. A *function generator* in which the *function* that it generates is determined by construction and cannot be altered by the *user.* In *analog systems,* the function is usually an *analog electric current* or *voltage* that is a function of time or space coordinates.

fixed horizontal polarization. In a *horizontally-polarized electromagnetic wave propagating* in *free space* or in a *transmission medium, polarization* of the *electric field vector* such that it remains horizontal always and everywhere and hence does not change from a horizontal direction with time or distance along the propagation path. The *magnetic field vector* may change with time or distance, thus governing the angle of *elevation* with the horizontal that the wave is propagating at a particular point in space or time. Also see *fixed vertical polarization; horizontally-polarized electromagnetic wave.*

fixed logic. A permanent, *hard-wired,* interconnected set of *combinational circuits (logic elements).* Fixed logic can be changed by exchanging *pluggable* units, by resetting *connectors* or *switches,* or by rewiring, but not by *software* changes. Also see *programmable logic.*

fixed magnetron. A fixed-*frequency transmitter* tube that produces *pulses* of *ultra-high frequency (UHF)* energy. The flow of *electrons* is controlled by an applied *magnetic field.* In operation, electrons are released from a large *cathode* and forced to gyrate in an axial *magnetic field* before reaching the *anode.* Their energy is collected in a series of slot resonators in the face of the circular anode. It serves as a *radio frequency electromagnetic wave* generating device. The *output power pulses* are taken from a small *coupling circuit* and *transmitted* to an *antenna* to be *radiated.*

fixed optical attenuator. A device that *attenuates* the *intensity* of *lightwaves* a fixed or given number of decibels when inserted into an *optical waveguide* link. For example, a standard fixed single attenuation of 3, 6, 10, 20, or 40 dB for each attenuator is common.

fixed optics. The development and use of *optical* components whose characteristics do not change during their operational use, except perhaps for minor adjustments of *focus* for *accommodation* of the human eye, such as in *telescopes, microscopes,* and *magnifying* glasses. Contrast with *active optics.* Synonymous with *inactive optics; passive optics.*

fixed-reference modulation. *Modulation* in which the choice of the *significant condition* for any *signal element* is based on or makes use of a fixed reference. For example, the fixed reference may be a *timing pulse* or it may be a *carrier* fixed *frequency.*

fixed service. In *radio communications,* a service between specified fixed locations. This is in contrast to the *mobile service.* See *aeronautical fixed service.*

fixed station.   In *radio communications,* a *station* in the *fixed service.* A fixed station may, as a secondary service, *transmit* to *mobile stations* on its normal frequencies.   See *aeronautical fixed station; hydrological and meteorological fixed station; telemetering fixed station.*

fixed storage.   *Storage* whose contents during normal operation are unalterable by a *user.* Fixed storage may be modified only by physical modification. There is an implied restriction on the ability or authority of persons to effect modification of the storage contents. Changes to the storage content cannot be made by means of a *program.* Synonymous with *nonerasable storage; permanent storage; read-only memory (ROM).*

fixed telecommunication network.   See *civil fixed telecommunication network.*

fixed-tolerance-band compaction.   *Data compaction* in which *stroage* or *transmission* of *data* only becomes significant and is stored or *transmitted* when the data deviate beyond preordained limits. For example, in a *telemetering system,* transmission of the *temperature* will not take place unless the temperature is above or below preestablished *threshold* limits. Thus, the recipient of the transmission is to assume that the value is in range unless a *signal* to the contrary occurs. Since the value is in range most of the time, transmission requirements are considerably reduced. Redundant information is not transmitted continuously. Care must be taken to make the system *fail-safe,* as is always the case when information is based on nontransmission. See Figure F-10.

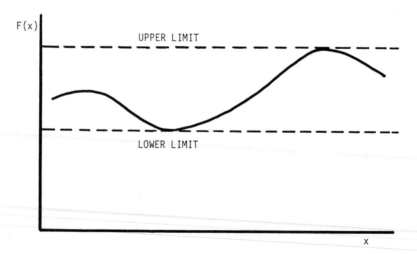

F-10. *Transmission* need only occur if and when the *parameter* exceeds the *thresholds* in **fixed-tolerance-band compaction.**

fixed vertical polarization. In a *vertically-polarized electromagnetic wave propagating* in free space or in a *transmission medium, polarization* of the *electric field vector* such that it remains vertical always and everywhere and hence does not change from a vertical direction with time or distance along the propagation path. The *magnetic field vector* may change in direction with time or distance, thus governing the horizontal direction or azimuth that the wave is propagating at a particular point in space or time. Also see *fixed horizontal polarization; vertically-polarized electromagnetic wave.*

fixed-weight binary code. A *binary code* that has a fixed number of 1's in each *word*, for example two binary 1's out of five *digits*. The scheme can be used in *error detection* and *error correction.*

fixer network. A combination of *radio* or *radar direction-finding* installations that operate in conjunction and are capable of plotting the position relative to the ground of an aircraft that is in flight, either by obtaining *fixes* on its *transmitter* or by obtaining *radar azimuths.*

fixing aid. See *radio fixing aid.*

flag. 1. In *data transmission,* an *indicator,* such as a *signal, symbol, character,* or *digit* used for identification. For example, a *word mark,* a *group mark,* or a letter that *signals* the occurrence of some condition or event, such as the end of a *word* or *block.* Synonymous with *sentinel; tag.* 2. In *visual signaling systems,* a *symbol* or emblem usually made of colored cloth and raised by a *halyard* on a pole for *signaling* purposes. See *alphabetic flag; numeral flag; special flag; turning flag.*

flaghoist. See *inferior position flaghoist; superior position flaghoist.*

flaghoist signaling. A *visual signaling system* in which colored *pennants* or *flags* are hung from a hoist (flat pole) and are used to represent letters, *numerals,* and *words* for the *transmission* of *messages.* Flaghoist signaling is used on ship and on shore. Also see *at-the-dip; close-up; hauled down; inferior-position flaghoist; superior-position flaghoist.*

flaghoist transmission. *Transmission* of *messages* by means of *flags* or *pennants* that are *displayed* from *halyards.* Although this is a rapid and accurate method of *visual transmission,* its use is usually limited to daylight hours and to short distances compared to *telecommunication systems.*

flag lockers. A container for holding all the necessary *flags* for *flaghoist signaling.* Flag lockers are normally placed near the *halyard* mast for immediate hoisting when required.

flag sequence. 1. In *data transmission,* the sequence of *bits* that are employed to delimit the beginning (opening) and the end (closing) of a *frame.* For example, in one standard *data transmission system,* the eight-*bit* sequence 01111110 is used as a flag sequence. 2. In *high-level data link control (HDLC) operation,* the specific 8-*bit* sequence 01111110. It is employed to delimit the opening and closing of a *frame.*

flag signaling. See *Morse flag signaling.*

flag transmission. See *hand-flag transmission.*

flare. A *high intensity source* of *light* that is produced by chemical reaction, such as combustion, and is used for *signaling* or *illumination.* See *solar flare.*

flash. 1. In *telephone switchboard operation,* to *oscillate* the *supervisory signal* that is associated with a *user's line* in a connected *call* with the intention of attracting the *operator's* attention. A user can often effect this by alternately depressing and releasing the *switch* on which the handset normally rests when not in use. 2. In *military communication systems,* a *precedence designation* of the highest urgency. See *index flash; form flash.*

flash card. In *micrographics,* a document that is introduced during recording on *microfilm* to facilitate indexing.

flash detector. See *infrared point-source flash detector.*

flashing-light communication system. A *visual signaling system* in which a *light* that is turned on and off, or *blanked* and unblanked (masked and unmasked) is used to *transmit messages.* Usually the *international Morse code* is used to accomplish the *transmission* of *messages.*

flashing-light ship signaling. *Visual signaling* to and from a ship by means of a *flashing-light communication system.*

flashing-light transmission. In *visual signaling systems,* the *transmission* of *messages* by turning a light on and off or by *blanking* and unblanking (masking or unmasking) a *light* that is on continuously. Flashing-light transmission equipment has been built for both directional and nondirectional operation. The use of directional flashing light reduces the possibility of undesirable *interception* and increases the transmission distance for a given power level. The available *power* is concentrated in one direction usually with the use of *reflectors.* When *security* is required, highly directional (high *directive gain*) is usually used. Its *intensity (brilliancy)* may be the minimum necessary to provide *communication.* Nondirectional transmission permits simultaneous transmission to *stations* in any direction but affords little security from interception, particularly at night, if this is required. Flashing light systems usually use the *international Morse code.* Transmissions may be *enciphered.*

flash-override precedence. The *precedence designation* that is reserved for *messages* of greater importance, emergency, or criticality than *flash messages.* The designation can be used only when specifically authorized by the highest authority.

flash precedence. The *precedence designation* that is reserved for *messages* of extreme urgency, such as critical military action messages.

flatbed plotter. A *plotter* that draws or otherwise creates an *image* on a *display surface* that is usually flat. Usually a moving plotting head draws or creates the image.

flat-bed transmitter. A *facsimile transmitter* that *scans* the subject (object) *document* while it is lying on a flat surface. The scanning is usually accomplished *line* by line by a moving *optical* reading head while the document remains stationary.

flat fading. *Fading* in which the *amplitude* of all *frequency components* of a *radio signal* vary by fading in the same proportion simultaneously.

flat-noise power. *Noise power* that is constant over a *band* of *frequencies*, that is, the *noise power* per *hertz* is inversely proportional to the *frequency.* Expressed mathematically, $p/f = a/f$ where p is the power at any given frequency, f is the frequency, and a is the constant of proportionality. This implies that $p = a$ where a is a constant. Thus, the power at any one frequency is the same as the power at any other frequency.

flat optical cable. In *fiber optics,* a *cable* consisting of a group of *slab dielectric waveguides* or *optical fibers* arranged in a rectangular (Cartesian) coordinate system or array, the relative position of each guide remaining constant throughout the cable, the cable being of rectangular cross section with rectangular *connectors* on the ends. Also see *optical fiber ribbon.*

flat weighting. In a *noise measuring set,* an *amplitude-frequency* characteristic that is flat over a specified *frequency range* and that must be explicitly stated. *Flat noise power* may be expressed in *dBrn($f_1 - f_2$)* or in *dBm($f_1 - f_2$).* Flat weighting may also be designated as 3 KHz flat weighting and 15 KHz flat weighting. These are used for characteristics that are flat from 30 Hz to the upper *frequency* indicated. Also see *dBrn($f_1 - f_2$).*

flaw. See *loophole.*

F-layer. A region of the *ionosphere* between 175 and 400 km in altitude. The F_1 layer, at about 175 to 250 km in altitude, exists only during the daylight hours. The F_2 layer, at about 250 to 400 km in altitude, is the principal *reflecting* layer for *high-frequency electromagnetic waves* used in *long-distance telecommunications.* Synonymous with *F-region.*

Fleming's rule. If the thumb of the right hand points in the direction of an *electric current,* then the fingers point in the direction of the *magnetic field* that encircles the current. If the fingers of the right hand describe the *electric current* in a solenoid, the thumb points in the direction of the *magnetic field* inside the solenoid. Synonymous with *right-hand rule.* Also see *Biot-Savart law.*

flicker. An undesirable pulsation or temporary variation in intensity of a *display image* on a *display surface* usually caused by *voltage* or *current* variations or by low *regeneration* rates in those types of display images that must be regenerated to prevent loss of intensity by electric charge leakage or *radiation* decay. Contrast with *blinking.*

flight phase. See *passive-flight phase; powered-flight phase.*

flight telemetering land station. A *telemetering land station* that is used for *telemetering data* to a balloon, booster, or rocket, excluding a booster or rocket in *orbit* about the earth or in *deep space,* or to an aircraft, excluding a *station* that is used in the flight testing of an aircraft.

flight telemetering mobile station. A *telemetering mobile station* that is used for *telemetering data* from a balloon, booster, or rocket, excluding a booster or rocket in *orbit* about the earth or in *deep space,* or from an aircraft, excluding a *station* that is used in the flight testing of an aircraft.

flight test station. An *aeronautical station* that is used for the *transmission* of essential *messages* in connection with the testing of aircraft or major *components* of an aircraft.

flint glass. A heavy brilliant glass, containing lead oxide, that has a relatively high *refractive index* and is used for *optical* structures more than *optical elements.*

flip chip. In *fiber-optic circuits* and *integrated optical circuits (IOC),* an *optical switch* designed to control *light conduction* paths into and out of a *junction.* Also see *optical switch.*

flip-flop. A *circuit* or device that contains active elements and that is capable of assuming either one of only two stable states at a given time. The *transition* states from one stable state to the other stable state are not stable.

floating-point coding compaction. Numerical *data compaction* that makes use of exponents to specify the scale, range, or magnitude of numbers. The exponent indicates the location of the decimal point in numbers. Thus, each number has two parts, namely the coefficient or fractional part, and the exponent part. The coefficient is to be multiplied by a power of ten indicated by the exponent part. For example, the number 12190000 may be expressed in floating point notation as 1219×10^4, or as 1219(4), or as 12194, in which the 4 indicates the number of 0's to be appended to the 1219. If the number is rounded to $122 \times$

10^5, it might be written as 1225, or as 126, in which the last digit indicates the number of 0's. Thus only 3 positions are required instead of 8 to represent the number in *storage* or in a message, which is only 37.5% of the original space and time requirement.

flow. See *control flow; pdeudo-flow.*

flow control. See *packet flow control; transmit flow control.*

flow control procedure. In *switching systems,* the procedure for controlling the *data transfer rate* between two specified points in a *data network.* For example, flow control between *data terminal equipment (DTE)* and a *data switching exchange,* or between two DTE's.

flow meter. See *fiber-optic bloodflow meter.*

flow security. See *traffic flow security.*

fluid immersion effect. In *optical fibers, bundles* and *cables,* the effect on *transmission medium parameters* when immersed in a given fluid for a specified period of time; e.g., the ratio of *transmitted power* before and after immersion for the same *input power* or the change in *pulse dispersion* as a result of immersion.

fluorescence. The *emission* of *electromagnetic radiation* by a material during *absorption* of electromagnetic radiation from another *source.* Also see *phosphorescence.*

flutter. **1.** The *distortion* that is due to the variation in loss that results from the simultaneous *transmission* of a *signal* at another *frequency.* **2.** The *distortion* that is due to the variation in *loss* that results from *phase distortion.* **3.** In recording and reproducing, the deviation of *frequency* that results from irregular motion that occurs during recording, duplication, or reproduction. **4.** In *radio transmission,* the rapidly changing *signal amplitude* levels together with variable *multipath* time delays, caused by the *reflection* and possible partial *absorption* of the *radio* signal by aircraft flying through the *beam* or *scatter* volume. **5.** The effect of the variation in the *transmission* characteristics of a *loaded telephone circuit* caused by the action of *direct currents* on the loading coils. **6.** Fast-changing variation in received *signal strength,* such as may be caused by *atmospheric* variations, *antenna* movements in a high wind, or interaction with another *signal.* Also see *distortion.*

flux. *Radiant flux* or *luminous flux.* See *luminous flux; radiant flux.*

flux density. See *magnetic flux density.*

flux reversal. See *phase flux reversal.*

flux rise time. In an *LED* or *laser,* the time required for the output *radiation* level to rise from 10% to 90% of the maximum level during the *pulse* from the time of onset or median value of the leading edge of the driving pulse. The flux rise time is usually specified in *nanoseconds* or *picoseconds.*

flying-spot scan. In *display systems,* a technique in which the intensity of *light* from a *beam* reflected from any point in the *display space* on the *display surface* of a *display device* is measured at any instant, thus providing a capability of reading a *display image* by light reflection rather than light transmission. Contrast with *directed scan; raster scan.*

flying-spot scanner. In *display systems,* a device that makes use of a moving beam of *light* to scan an *object* or *image* so that a *photodetector* can generate *signals* from variations in intensity of *transmitted* or *reflected* light that represent the object.

flywheel effect. The characteristic of an *oscillator* that enables it to sustain oscillations after removal of the control stimulus. The effect may be desirable, as in the case of *phase-locked loops* employed in *synchronous systems;* or undesirable, as in the case of a *voltage*-controlled *oscillator* that is to be turned on and off abruptly by a *pulse.* Synonymous with *flywheeling.*

flywheeling. See *flywheel effect.*

FM. *Frequency modulation.*

FM improvement factor. The *signal-to-noise* ratio at the *output* of a *receiver* divided by the *carrier-to-noise* ratio at the *input* of the receiver. This improvement is obtained at the same time as an increased *bandwidth* requirement for the receiver and the *transmission path.*

FM improvement threshold. The point in a *frequency modulated (FM) receiver* at which the peaks in the *radio frequency (RF) signal* equal the peaks of the *thermal noise* generated in the receiver. A *baseband signal-to-noise ratio* of about 30 dB is typical at the improvement *threshold.* This ratio improves 1 dB for each *decibel* of increase in the signal above the threshold.

F-number. A number expressing the effectiveness of the *aperture* of a *lens* in relation to the *brightness* of the *image* of an *object* such that, the smaller the number, the brighter the image and therefore the shorter the exposure time required for a given amount of *incident* energy, such as to expose a given film emulsion. Also see *aperture ratio.*

FO. *Fiber optics.*

foam dielectric coaxial cable. A *coaxial cable* with plastic foam *insulation* between the inner and outer *conductors.*

FOC. *Fiber-optic communications.*

focal length. The distance from a *mirror*, or a *lens*, or some point therein, to the *image* of a small, infinitely distant *source* of *light*. This *image point* is referred to as the *focal point*. See *back focal length; equivalent focal length; front focal length.*

focal plane. In an *optical system*, a plane through the *focal point* perpendicular to the *principal axis* of the system, such as a *lens* or *mirror*. For example, the film plane in a camera *focused* at infinity.

focal point. 1. In an *optical system*, the point at which a *bundle* of *rays* form a sharp *image* of an *object*. 2. The point at which an *object* in an *optical system* must be placed for a sharp *image* to be obtained. Synonymous with *principal focus.*

focus. To make an adjustment in an *optical system* so that a sharp, distinct *image* is registered. For example, to adjust the eyepiece or objective of a *microscope*, telescope, or camera. See *fixed focus; focal point.*

focus depth. In *coupling lightwaves* in and out of an *optical fiber*, the distance the *light source* or *photodetector* is placed from the ends of the fiber. The depth of *focus* is given by:

$$D = d/2\tan\theta$$

where θ is the *acceptance angle* and d is the desired resolution diameter or *image* size. Also see *numerical aperture.*

focus feed. See *prime focus feed.*

focusing optical fiber. See *self-focusing optical fiber.*

focus point. See *principal focus point.*

fog buoy. A device that is towed by a ship in a fog or heavy (thick) weather as a marker to assist *ship* and *aircraft stations* in maintaining their proper position (station) or their relative position in a convoy. The buoy contains a *transmitter.*

follow-on call. The establishment of a *connection* for a new *call* without completely *releasing* the *call selection* chain established for the preceding call. For example, *holding* an international *circuit* connection to establish a subsequent connection for another *called party* in the same called country.

FOMS. *Fiber optic myocardium stimulator.*

F1A-line weighting. A *noise weighting* that is used in a set to measure the *noise* on a *line* that would be terminated by a 302-Type or similar noise measuring instrument. The meter scale readings of the measuring set are in *dBa(F1A)*.

font. A family, group, or assortment of graphic *characters* of given size and style, some of which are available for typewriters, printers, and *display devices.* For example, elite, pica, italic, or 8-point Bodoni Modern.

font change character. A *control character* that is used to select and make a change in the specific shape, or size, or shape and size, of the *graphics* for a set of *graphemes.* The *character* itself remains unchanged. For example, a character that denotes a change from roman to italic font. Synonymous with *face change character.*

foot-candle. A unit of *illuminance* equal to 1 *lumen incident* per square foot. It is the *illuminance* of a curved surface, all points of which are placed 1 foot from a *light source* having a *luminous intensity* of 1 candle or *candela.*

footprint. The portion of the earth's surface that is *illuminated* by a *narrow beam* from a *satellite transmitter.* It is less than *earth coverage.* Also see *earth coverage.*

for. The *indicator* of the *addressee* of a *message.* When it is used it does not necessarily limit the distribution to any other addressees.

forbidden code. See *illegal code.*

forbidden landing-point marker. In *air-to-ground visual communication systems,* a large 45 ft. x 45 ft. (15 m x 15 m) cross displayed in the center of a landing strip, site, zone, or point that is not to be used for landing purposes. Synonymous with *no-landing marker.*

force. See *electric field force; electromotive force (EMF); magnetic field force; magnetomotive force (MMF); psophometric electromotive force.*

forces radio service. See *Armed Forces Radio Service.*

forecast. See *long-term ionospheric forecast; short-term ionospheric forecast.*

forecasting. See *ionospheric forecasting.*

foreground. See *display foreground.*

formal message. A *message* in which the *format* is rigidly controlled in order to facilitate *transmission,* handling, and distribution.

format. 1. The distribution, arrangement, or layout of *data elements* on or in a *data medium.* 2. The arrangement of *bits* or *characters* within a group, such as within a *word, message,* or *language.* **3.** The shape, size, and general makeup of a document and its contents. See *communication plan format; dating format; ionospheric message format; packet format; radio telegraph message format.*

format effector (FE). One of a group of *control characters* used to control the positioning of printed, *displayed,* or recorded data.

formation radar jamming. *Jamming* a *radar system* by flying aircraft in a formation that causes the radar system to experience difficulty in ascertaining *azimuth* and *elevation* angles. For example, jamming by causing *strobes* to overlap on a *radar scope* so that the *operator* cannot tell where one strobe starts and another stops.

format line. A *line* of printed *characters* in a *message* that starts with or consists of some *format effector* or *indicator.* For example, a line that starts with to, from, *information,* or a *break symbol.* In some *tape relay systems,* there are as many as 16 possible format lines for messages. In some *communication systems,* there are mandatory format lines. The format lines are used to assist in *switching* and *routing* messages. Also see *message format.*

form feed (FE) character. A *format effector* that causes the *data medium* to be moved so that the *print* or *display position* occurs at a predetermined spot on the next *line,* the next form, the next page, or the equivalent.

form flash. In *display systems,* the projection of a *form overlay* on the *display surface* of a *display device;* e.g., the placement of a grid or projection of a *data* form on the *faceplate* of a *fiberscope.*

form overlay. In *display systems,* a pattern used as *display background* for a *display image;* e.g., a form, grid, map, graph, or outline. A data form for blocking out various areas on the *display surface* of a *fiberscope faceplate* to allocate certain areas for identifying specific *data.*

FORTRAN. An international standard *computer programming language* that is used primarily for numeric, arithmetic, and algebraic operations. Many versions (dialects) of FORTRAN exist most of which are extensions of the standard. The name is derived from Formula Translation.

fortuitous conductor. A *conductor* that may provide an unintended *path* for intelligible *signals.* For example, water pipes, wire, cable, or metal structural members that are associated with, are in close proximity to, or are in any way *coupled* to a *communication system* may serve as fortuitous conductors.

fortuitous distortion. *Distortion* of *signals* that result from causes generally subject to random laws. For example, accidental irregularities or *current* surges that occur in the operation of *communication system components* and their moving parts. These random *disturbances* will affect *transmission* in any *channel* coupled to the source of the disturbance.

forward.   See *call forward; spill forward; store-and-forward.*

forward channel.   In *data transmission systems*, a *channel* in which the direction of transmission is the same as that in which *data* are being transferred; i.e., the channel that transmits *information* (i.e., the forward *signals*) from the *source* to the *sink.* The forward channel is usually the data transmission channel in which the direction of transmission coincides with that in which *user* information is being transferred.   If information is simultaneously transferred in both directions, the momentary *data source* to *data sink* determines the forward channel. Also see *backward channel.*

forward clearing signal.   See *clear-forward signal.*

forward data transmission.   See *store-and-forward data transmission.*

forward direction.   1. In a *communication system,* the direction from a *data source* to the *data sink.*   2. The direction from a *message originator* to an addressee. 3. The direction from the *calling party* to the *called party.*   Also see *backward direction.*

forward error correction.   A system of *error control* for *data transmission* wherein the receiving device has the capability to detect and correct any *character* or *code block* that contains a predetermined number of erroneous *bits.*   It is usually accomplished by adding error-detection and error-correction bits to each transmitted character or code block using a predetermined *algorithm.*

forward feature.   See *spill-forward feature.*

forwarding.   See *call forwarding.*

forwarding busy line.   See *call forwarding busy line.*

forwarding don't answer.   See *call forwarding don't answer.*

forward ionospheric scatter.   See *forward propagation ionospheric scatter.*

forward propagation ionospheric scatter.   *Ionospheric scatter* in the *forward direction.*   Synonymous with *forward ionospheric scatter; ionospheric forward scatter.*

forward scatter   1. To scatter or randomly reflect *electromagnetic waves,* so that a *component* is directed away from the *antenna* or *light source* that *emitted* the waves, when the waves at the point of scatter are resolved along a line from the source to the point of scatter.   2. The *components* of *waves* that are directed forward when resolved along a line from the source to the point of scatter.   Forward scattering of *electromagnetic waves* occurs in *optical fibers* due to *reflecting* surfaces of particles or occlusions in the *transmission medium* resulting in *attenuation* since *transverse* components are lost. *Sound waves, radio waves, lightwaves,* and *elastic waves* are examples of waves that are subject to forward scatter. **3.** The *deflection,* by *reflection* or *refraction,* of an *electromagnetic wave or signal* in such a manner that a *component* of the deflected *wave* is deflected in the direction of *propagation* of the *incident wave* or *signal.* The term scatter can be applied to *spectral reflection* or *refraction* by relatively uniform media, but it is usually taken to mean propagation in which the *wavefront* and direction of propagation are modified in a more disorderly fashion. Also see *back scattering; backscatter.*

forward signal. A *signal* that is sent in the *forward direction,* that is, from the *calling station* to the *called station* or from a *data source* to the *data sink.* The forward signal is *transmitted* in the *forward channel.* See *clear-forward signal.*

forward switching center. See *store-and-forward switching center.*

forward-tell. *Information transfer* from *facilities* at a lower to a higher operational level or echelon of command.

FOT. 1. *Optimum traffic frequency.* **2.** *Frequency of optimum traffic.*

FOTS. *Fiber optic transmission system.*

Foucault knife-edge test. A method of determining the *errors* in an *image* of a *point source* by partially occluding the *light* from the image by means of a *knife edge.* The same *test* may be used to measure the errors in *refracting* or *reflecting* surfaces.

four-cable. See *spiral four-cable.*

four-color theorem. Every planar map can be colored with not more than four *colors* under the restriction that any two areas with a contiguous border must be colored differently.

four-frequency diplex telegraphy. *Frequency-shift telegraphy* in which each of the four possible *signals* obtainable in two *telegraph channels* is represented by a different *frequency.* It is used in *radio telegraphy.* Synonymous with *four-frequency duoplex telegraphy; twinplex telegraphy.*

four-frequency duoplex telegraphy. See *four-frequency diplex telegraphy.*

four-heterojunction diode. A *laser-diode* with two *double heterojunctions,* i.e., two pairs of *heterojunctions* to provide improved control of direction of *radiation* and radiative *recombination.* Synonymous with *symmetrical double-heterojunction diode.* See *five-layer four-heterojunction diode.*

four-horn feed system.   In *radar systems,* a *monopulse antenna feed system* for *signal tracking* in which a *diplexer* allows simultaneous *transmission* and *reception.* Also see *five-horn feed system.*

Fourier analysis.   The definition of a periodic phenomenon or arbitrary *wave shape,* such as a square wave, in terms of a group of *sine waves* with *frequencies* that are multiples of the *fundamental frequency* of the periodic phenomenon such as the square wave. Each sine wave has an *amplitude* such that when all the waves are added the shape of the periodic phenomenon (square wave) is obtained. The representation is an approximation. A given *circuit* may discriminate against certain of the frequencies resulting is *distortion* of the wave. The analysis (representation) is particularly well suited for *communication* equipment design (synthesis), and for analysis of performance of a given design. Also see *sine wave; sinusoidal function.*

four-wire circuit.   A two-wire *circuit* that uses two *paths* arranged in such a manner that the *signals* in the circuit are *transmitted* in one direction only by one path and in the other direction only by the other path.

four-wire repeater.   A *repeater* for use in a *four-wire circuit* in which there are two *amplifiers,* one that is used to amplify the *signals* in one direction of the four-wire circuit and another that is used to amplify the signals in the other direction of the four-wire circuit.

four-wire subset user service.   A *telephone service* in which a *user's* (customer's, subscriber's) *instrument* is connected directly into a *switching center* of a *telephone network* without going through a *private branch exchange (PBX)* or a *private automatic branch exchange (PABX).* Care is usually taken to insure that overseas *calls* are controlled and *precedence* is not abused.

four-wire terminating set.   A set of equipment that is used to *terminate* the *transmit* and *receive channels* of a *four-wire circuit* and to interconnect four-wire and two-wire circuits. Also see *hybrid set.*

fox message.   A standard test *message* that includes all the *alphanumeric characters* on a *teletypewriter* and also some *function characters* such as *space, figures shift, letters shift,* and punctuation marks. One such message is "THE QUICK BROWN FOX JUMPED OVER THE LAZY DOG'S BACK 1234567890."

fraction.   See *packing fraction.*

fraction-automatically-switched.   See *failure-fraction-automatically-switched.*

fraction loss.   See *packing fraction loss.*

frame.   1. In *data transmission,* the sequence of contiguous *bits* that are bracketed by and that include opening (beginning) and closing (ending) *flag sequences.* A typical frame may consist of a specified number of bits between flags and may contain an *address field,* a *control field,* and a *frame check sequence.* A frame may include an *information field.* For example, in *high-level data-link control (HDLC) operation* a valid frame contains at least 32 bits between flags. **2.** In the *multiplex* structure of *pulse-code modulation (PCM) systems,* a set of consecutive *digit time slots* in which the position of each digit time slot can be identified by reference to a *frame alignment signal.* The frame alignment signal does not necessarily occur in whole or in part in each frame. **3.** In *time-division multiplexing,* a repetitive group of *signals* resulting from a single sampling of all *channels.* The group also includes *synchronizing,* checking, and *control signals.* In-frame is the condition that exists when there is a channel-to-channel and bit-to-bit correspondence between all the inputs of a time-division *multiplexer* and the *output* of its associated *demultiplexer.* **4.** In *facsimile systems,* a rectangular area, the width of which is the *available line* and the length of which is determined by the service requirements. See *combined distribution frame; command frame; display frame; fiber distribution frame; film frame; group distribution frame (GDF); high-frequency distribution frame (HFDF); intermediate distribution frame; main distribution frame (MDF); main frame; response frame; supergroup distribution frame; time frame.*

frame alignment. The extent to which the *frame* of the *receiving* equipment is correctly phased or synchronized with respect to the frame of the received signal.

frame alignment recovery time. See *reframing time.*

frame alignment signal. **1.** In *transmission systems,* the *signal* that enables the proper *frame alignment.* **2.** In *facsimile transmission,* a *signal* that is used for the adjustment of the picture to a desired position in the direct line of progression. Synonymous with *framing signal.* Also see *multiframe alignment signal.* See *bunched frame-alignment signal; distributed frame-alignment signal.*

frame alignment time slot. A *time slot* that starts at a particular *phase* or instant in each *frame* and is allocated to the *transmission* of the *frame alignment signal.*

frame check sequence. In *high-level data-link control (HDLC) operation,* the *field* that immediately precedes the closing *flag sequence* of a *frame* and that contains the *bit* sequence that provides for the *detection* of *transmission errors* by the *receiving station.*

frame frequency. The number of *frames* per unit time that are *transmitted* from or received at a point in a *transmission system.* For example, 500 frames per second *transmitted* in a single *channel.*

frame multiplex structure. A set of consecutive *digit time slots* in which the position or timing of each digit time slot can be identified by reference to a *frame alignment signal.* The frame alignment signal need not necessarily occur in whole or in part in each *frame.*

frame pitch. 1. The distance, time, or number of *bits* between corresponding points *(significant instants)* on two consecutive *frames.* 2. The distance between corresponding points on two contiguous or successive *film frames* on a recording or *data medium,* such as a *microfilm* or a *michofiche.* Synonymous with *pulldown.*

frame synchronization. A technique for *synchronizing* the *receive circuits* with the incoming *bit stream* to properly interpret the incoming *data.* Frame synchronization can also be used in *time-division multiplex (TDM) systems* for identifying the individual *channels.*

frame synchronization pattern. In *digital communication systems,* a prescribed recurring pattern of *bits* or *pulses* that is *transmitted* for the purpose of enabling the *receiver* to achieve *frame synchronization.* Synonymous with *address pattern.*

framing. 1. The process of partitioning a *data signal* into separate entities by interleaving repetitive signals into the *data stream.* In *digital transmission,* framing is the process of inserting *marker digits* into a *digit stream* so that *communication system components* are able to identify digital groupings, such as *blocks* and *messages,* or are able to identify *channels* in a *time-division multiplexed bit stream.* 2. In *facsimile systems,* the adjustment of the facsimile picture to a desired position in the direction of *line* progression.

framing bit. 1. A *bit* that is used for *frame synchronization.* 2. A *bit* at specific intervals in a *bit stream* that is used to determine the beginning or end of a *frame.* Framing bits are non-information-carrying bits that are used to make possible the separation of *characters* in a bit stream into separate groupings, such as *lines,* paragraphs, or *channels.* Frames in a digital data stream are usually repetitive.

framing signal. See *frame alignment signal.*

Fraunhofer region. The *radiation field* region for an *antenna* that is *focused* at infinity.

free condition. See *trunk-free condition.*

free fiber-optic connector. A *connector* that permits connection of *optical fiber* components and that also permits easy disconnection. Free fiber-optic connectors can be used to connect source to *optical conductor,* optical conductor to optical conductor, or optical conductor to *detector.* They may be *cable*-mounted, but are independent of components.

free-line signaling. In *telephone switchboard operations, signaling* in which the lighting of a lamp is used to indicate that the first of a group of outgoing *trunks* is no longer engaged. This facility relieves the *operator* from performing the *engage test.*

free net. A *radio net* in which any *station* may *communicate* with any other *station* in the net without first obtaining the permission of the *net control sta-*

tion. Permission to operate as a free net is granted by the net control station until such time as a *directed net* is established by the net control station. Also see *directed net.*

free space.   A theoretical concept of space devoid of all matter. In *communications,* the concept includes the notion of remoteness from material objects that could influence the *propagation* of *electromagnetic waves,* such as cause *dispersion, reflection,* or *absorption.*

free space loss.   The *signal attenuation* that would result if all *scattering, reflecting, diffusing, absorbing,* and *diffracting* influences were sufficiently removed so as to have no effect on *propagation.* Free space loss is primarily caused by *beam* divergence. The *signal* energy is spread over larger areas at increased distances from the *source.* Also see *geometric spreading.*

free-space optical communications.   *Communications* using *lightwaves* that *propagate* in unbounded *transmission media* and are not confined to *waveguides,* such as *optical fibers, slab dielectric waveguides,* and *integrated optical circuits,* but travel in such *media* as *outer space,* the *atmosphere,* the *ionosphere,* or the ocean.

F-region.   See *F-layer.*

FRENA system.   *Frequency-and-amplitude (FRENA) system.*

frequency.   The number of recurrences per unit time of a *periodic* phenomenon. For example, the number of *wave* crests per second of an *electromagnetic wave* passing a point in space or a point along the length of an *optical fiber transmitting* such a wave. In specifying the frequency of an electromagnetic wave the unit of time is the second. *Radio frequencies* are normally expressed in kilohertz(KHz) at and below 30000 kilohertz. The frequency above this frequency is usually expressed in megahertz (MHz). One *hertz* (Hz) is equivalent to one complete oscillation per second, formerly called a cycle, thus giving rise to the now obsolete terms of kilocycles and megacycles (per second.) The reciprocal of the frequency is the time in seconds for one complete *wavelength* or the period of one oscillation. The wavelength in *meters* is obtained by dividing the speed of *light* in the given *transmission medium* in meters per second by the frequency in hertz. The frequency of a *plane polarized electromagnetic wave* is the number of times per second one of the *field vectors,* electric or magnetic, reaches its peak value in a given direction. See *aircraft emergency frequency; air-ground communication emergency frequency; alternative frequency; answering frequency; assigned frequency; audio frequency (AF); authorized frequency; bond frequency; broadcast frequency; calling frequency; carrier frequency; center frequency; characteristic frequency; chip frequency; convoy common frequency; convoy radiotelephone frequency; critical frequency; cut-off frequency; distress frequency; dot frequency; emergency craft frequency; extremely high frequency (EHF); extremely low frequency (ELF): frame frequency; fundamental frequency; guarded frequency; high frequency (HF): infralow frequency (ILF); intermediate frequency (IF); international aeronautical emergency frequency; international radiotelegraph dis-*

tress frequency; international radiotelegraph lifecraft frequency; international radiotelephone distress frequency; lowest usable frequency; lowest useful high frequency (LUF); low frequency (LF); maritime mobile radiotelephone frequency; maximum keying frequency; maximum modulating frequency; maximum usable frequency; medium frequency (MF); military common emergency frequency; normalized frequency; optimum traffic frequency (OTF); picture frequency; precise frequency; primary frequency; protected frequency; radio frequency; radiotelegraph distress frequency; radiotelephone distress frequency; reference frequency; resonant frequency; scene-of-air-sea-rescue frequency; search-and-rescue beacon frequency; search-and-rescue frequency; secondary frequency; super-high frequency (SHF); taboo frequency; transition frequency; transmission frequency; tremendously high frequency (THF); ultrahigh frequency (UHF); very-high frequency (VHF); very-low frequency (VLF); victim frequency; video frequency; working frequency; voice frequency (VF).

frequency accuracy.   The degree of conformity of a periodic phenomenon to a specified *frequency* value.

frequency agile radar.   A *radar* whose operating *frequency* can be changed readily.   For example, the frequency may be changed to avoid *jamming*, reduce *mutual interference* with other *sources*, enhance *echoes* from objects (targets), or produce necessary patterns for *electronic countermeasures* or *electronic counter-countermeasure radiation*.   Frequency agility includes *signal processing* in the *video* portion of the receiver after the *phase information* has been removed from the signal.   It acts on the *amplitude* information only as *noncoherent* signal processing.   The process reduces *clutter* and results in *range resolution* improvement.

frequency agility.   The capability to change the *frequency* of a *receiver, transmitter,* or other device quickly and easily.   As an *electronic counter-countermeasure (ECCM)* for *radar*, some systems may have the capatibility to *shift* frequency within their operating *bands* on a *pulse-to-pulse* basis.   For *communication systems*, frequency agility is used to avoid *jamming*, prevent *interference*, and reduce *noise*.   Frequency shifting is usually performed by shifting the frequency above and below the *assigned frequency.*

frequency allocation.   **1.** The assignment of a part of the *frequency spectrum* to a specified category of *users*.   For example, the allocation of *narrow bands* in the 30–3000 MHz very high frequency (VHF) and ultrahigh frequency range to the public safety, citizens' radio, industrial, land transportation, and maritime mobile bands.   **2.** The planning process of establishing *radio frequency bands* or designating *radio frequencies* for the performance of specific functions.   **3.** The process of designating *radio frequency bands* for use by specific *radio communication services*.   The allocation of frequencies is accomplished by international and national agreements.   International frequency allocation is conducted under the auspices of the *International Telecommunication Union (ITU)*, Geneva, Switzerland, in accordance with current international agreements. National allocations are accomplished by the individual governments within their respective international allocation by the ITU.

frequency allocation plan. A plan that indicates the *electromagnetic frequencies* that are to be used in particular areas or by particular countries without specifying the *stations* to which the frequencies are to be assigned. Also see *frequency assignment plan.*

frequency-analysis compaction. *Data compaction* that uses an expression composed of a number of different *frequencies* of different magnitudes to represent a particular curve. For example, a *Fourier analysis* of a periodic or aperiodic function makes use of a set of frequencies of different amplitudes to represent a *function* or *wave shape.* Thus, the amplitude of the *fundamental frequency* and the amplitude coefficients of the *harmonics,* and the fundamental frequency, are all that is needed to describe a particular wave shape. The sum of the fundamental and the harmonics is all that is needed to reconstitute the function (wave shape) at every point. The shape can thus be readily stored and *transmitted* in this compacted form.

frequency-and-amplitude (FRENA) system. A *system* of *transmission* in which the *frequency* and *amplitude components* of a *signal* are *transmitted* separately and recombined at the *receiver.*

frequency assignment. 1. The process of authorizing a specific *frequency,* group of frequencies, or *frequency band* to be used at a certain location under specified conditions, such as specified *bandwidth, power, azimuth, duty cycle,* or *modulation.* 2. The *frequency band* or frequency designated for use at a *given station.* The *International Frequency Registration Board (IFRB),* a permanent organization of the *International Telecommunication Union,* maintains the *Master International Frequency Register (MIFR).* The MIFR is a master list of all international frequency registrations. Specific assignments within national allocations are made by national frequency management organizations in each country or group of countries. Also see *assigned frequency; authorized frequency; frequency allocation; frequency spectrum.*

frequency assignment plan. A plan that indicates the *electromagnetic frequencies* that are to be used by specified *stations* and organizations. Also see *frequency allocation plan.*

frequency averaging. A process in which *network synchronization* is achieved by the use of *oscillators* (at all *nodes*) that adjust their *frequencies* to the average frequency of the *digital bit streams* received from all connected nodes. All oscillators are assigned equal weight in determining the ultimate operating network frequency inasmuch as there is no *reference frequency* oscillator. Also see *democratically synchronized network.*

frequency band. 1. A continuous and contiguous group of *frequencies* that are defined or limited by some means, such as the type of *user*, specific limiting frequencies, or the name of a specific range of frequencies (e.g., the citizens band, police band, 400–500 MHz band, *VHF* band, or *optical* or visible band). 2. The frequencies that an electrical *circuit* element, *optical fiber*, or *filter* can pass or block; e.g., the frequency band that an optical *band-pass filter* can *transmit* with minimal *attenuation*. See *assigned frequency band.*

frequency bandwidth. See *radio frequency bandwidth.*

frequency-change signaling. *Signaling* in which one or more specific *frequencies* correspond to each *signaling condition* of a *code.* The *transition* from one set of frequencies to another may be either a continuous or discontinuous change in frequency or *phase.*

frequency channel increment. See *radio-frequency channel increment.*

frequency characteristic. See *insertion-loss versus frequency characteristic.*

frequency code modulation. *Digital frequency modulation* in which several *discrete frequencies* are used as a *binary* representation of *data.* The scheme may be used for defining *instructions* or *commands* from a *remote terminal.* A number of such *frequency-coded command bits* may be sent in *parallel.*

frequency combining. See *radio frequency combining.*

frequency compatibility. A measure of the extent to which *communication-electronic* devices will operate in their intended operational environment at design levels of performance. For example, a random selection of *channel frequencies* without consideration of equipment characteristics usually results in unacceptable *interference* on a number of *channels.* This results in a reduction of frequency compatibility.

frequency control. The regulation of the *frequency* generated by a *source*, that is, the maintenance of the precise frequency of a source to within a desired degree of *error* at each instant of time.

frequency conversion. See *frequency translation; single-frequency translation.*

frequency coordination. Coordination among public and private agencies for the purpose of minimizing *electromagnetic interference* through cooperative use of the *electromagnetic frequency spectrum.* To be effective, the coordination must extend through the planning, proposal, and actual use phases of the cooperative effort.

frequency-derived channel. A *channel* that is obtained by *frequency-division multiplexing* a *line, circuit,* or other *channel.* Also see *time-derived channel.*

frequency deviation. 1. In *frequency modulation,* the greatest difference between the instantaneous *frequency* of a *modulated wave* and the *carrier frequency.* The carrier frequency is present when there is no *modulation.* The frequency deviation is the maximum value of the *frequency shift* that corresponds to the maximum modulation *signal amplitude* in a frequency modulated wave. 2. The instantaneous value of the difference between the actual *frequency* at which a *transmitter* is *transmitting* and the *assigned* or desired frequency. Synonymous with *frequency settability.* Also see *frequency stability.*

frequency dispersal. An *electronic counter-countermeasure (ECCM)* in which *communication net* operating *frequencies* are widely separated from each other. This causes a requirement to spread *jamming power* over wider *frequency bands* and thus compels a reduction of available jamming power on any single *channel* (frequency). It might also cause a requirement for more jamming power or more jamming equipment.

frequency displacement. The overall *shift* in *frequency* that may result from independent *frequency translation errors* in a *circuit* or sequence of circuits. Also see *frequency translation.*

frequency distortion. 1. *Distortion* that is caused by nonuniform *attenuation* or *gain* of the different *frequencies* in a *signal.* Most devices react differently to different frequencies. For example, the *response* to different frequencies is different. *Resonance* causes certain frequencies to be passed and others to be blocked, and *multimode* effects add and remove certain frequencies *(wavelengths).* In most instances, the *impedance* to different frequencies is different. Except for the theoretical pure *resistance,* impedance is a *function* of frequency. 2. An undesired variation with respect to *frequency* of the ratio of the magnitude of the *fundamental component* of the *response* to a *sinusoidal excitation,* to the magnitude of the excitation. Synonymous with *amplitude-frequency distortion; amplitude versus frequency distortion; attenuation-frequency distortion; gain-frequency distortion.* See *group-delay frequency distortion; phase-frequency distortion.*

frequency diversity. The use of two or more *electromagnetic wave frequencies* to *transmit* the same *information* to achieve *reliability* and avoid loss of information by deliberate or inadvertent *noise* or *interference.* It is a method of *diversity transmission* and *reception* in which two or more *signals* with the same *modulation* or bearing the same information are transmitted and received simultaneously on two or more independent *carrier* frequencies. The technique is used to overcome *fading,* provide reliability, and improve reception. It can also be used as a *communication electronic counter-countermeasure (ECCM)* that involves the use of various types of equipment that operate in widely separated *frequency bands.* If one group of *channels* is *jammed,* a shift may be made to other equipment that performs similarly but operates on different frequency *bands.* Also see *dual diversity; spread spectrum.*

frequency divider. A device that produces *output power* at a *frequency* that is an exact *integral* submultiple of the *input* frequency, such as one-half, one-third, or one-fourth of the input frequency.

frequency division. In *communications,* the use of *frequency* to obtain separation between *channels.* For example, several *messages* can be handled by the same *circuit* at the same time, each message being transmittdd at a different frequency. Also see *space division; time division.*

frequency-division multiple access (FDMA). In *satellite communication systems,* the use of *frequency-division multiplexing* to provide multiple and simultaneous *transmission* to a single *transponder.* Thus, it is one of several *access* methods that permits *carrier waves* that are *radiated* from different *earth stations* to use the same satellite transponder. It allows each carrier to be distinguished from the others when received at an earth station. In FDMA, the available *repeater bandwidth* is divided into nonoverlapping *frequency bands.* Each carrier is assigned one of these bands. *Modulation* must occur within the band. Also see *frequency guard band.*

frequency-division multiplex (FDM). A method of deriving two or more simultaneous, continuous *channels* from a *transmission medium* that connects two points by assigning separate portions of the available *frequency spectrum* to each of the individual channels. The frequency range is usually divided into *narrow bands.* Each band is used as a separate channel. See *wavelength-division multiplex.*

frequency-division multiplex combining. See *radio frequency combining.*

frequency-division multiplexing (FDM). A *multiplexing* system in which the available *transmission frequency* range is divided into narrower *bands,* each used as a separate *channel.* When an *optical fiber transmits* more than one frequency at the same time, each frequency can be modulated with a different intelligence-bearing signal. Also see *frequency sharing; wavelength-division multiplexing.* See Figure F-11.

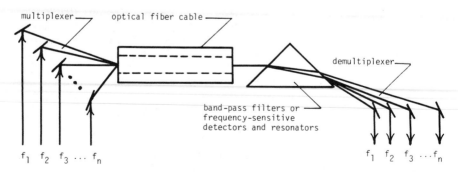

F-11. **Frequency-division multiplexing** by *transmitting* all *frequencies* in the same *fiber.*

frequency drift. A slow, undesired change in the operating *frequency* of *oscillators, transmitters, receivers,* or other equipment. Frequency drift applies to devices that generate *waves* as well as devices that process them.

frequency equalizer. See *phase-frequency equalizer.*

frequency evasion. An *electronic counter-countermeasure (ECCM)* that consists of changing *frequency* to avoid a *jamming signal.*

frequency exchange signaling. A *frequency-change signaling* method in which the change from one *signaling significant condition* to another is accompanied by a decay in the *amplitude* of one or more *waves* each with a different *frequency,* and by a buildup in amplitude of one or more waves that have other frequencies. Synonymous with *two-source frequency keying.*

frequency family. A group of *frequencies* that are assigned to specific sites or geographical areas. Frequency families have been developed for the *ultrahigh frequency (UHF) range* with 100 KHz, 50 KHz, and 25 KHz spacings. The number of usable *channels* at a given site or in a given area is limited to the channel separation that is required to prevent *interference.*

frequency frogging. 1. The interchanging of *carrier frequencies* in a *channel* in order to prevent *singing,* reduce *crosstalk,* and correct for *line slope.* It is accomplished by having the *modulators* in a *repeater translate* a low-frequency group to a high-frequency group, and vice versa. This frequency inversion or alternation process will cause a channel to appear in the low group for one repeater section and in the high group for the next repeater section. Frequency translation is used to accomplish this. It results in nearly constant *attenuation* as a *function* of frequency over two successive repeater sections and eliminates the need for large slope *equalization* and adjustment. In addition, *singing* and *crosstalk* are minimized because the high level *output* of a repeater is at a different frequency than the low level input to other repeaters. 2. The alternate use of *waves* of two different *frequencies* at *repeater* sites of *line-of-sight microwave systems.* Also see *heterodyne repeater.*

frequency gain control. See *receiver intermediate-frequency gain control.*

frequency generator. See *master frequency generator.*

frequency geographical sharing. A method of *frequency sharing* in which two or more *stations* do not *transmit* in certain sections or areas so as to avoid *interference* among their *signals.* Also see *frequency time-sharing.*

frequency guard band. A *frequency band* that is not used between two *channels,* thereby providing a margin of safety against *mutual interference.* The width of the guard band is the difference between the highest frequency used by one channel and the lowest frequency used by the next higher adjacent channel. Also see *frequency-division multiple access (FDMA); time guard band.*

frequency harmonic distortion. See *modulation frequency harmonic distortion.*

frequency hopper. In *spread-spectrum communication systems,* an *electromagnetic wave signal source* that generates a *wide-band* signal by changing from one *frequency* to another over a large number of usually fixed-frequency choices pseudo-randomly selected by a *code-sequence generator.* The *receiver* is *tuned* by the same code sequence.

frequency-hopper direct-sequence modulation. In *spread-spectrum systems,* a combination of *frequency-hopping modulation* and *direct-sequence modulation* of a *signal.*

frequency hopping. *Frequency shift keying* in which a large number of *frequencies* are selected by means of a *spread-spectrum code-sequence generator.* It can be used for *security,* privacy, or as an *electronic counter-countermeasure (ECCM).* It is a technique in which the instantaneous *carrier frequency* of a *signal* is periodically changed, according to a predetermined *code,* to other *positions* within a *frequency spectrum* that is much wider than that required for normal *message transmission.* The *receiver* uses the same code to keep itself in *synchronism* with the hopping pattern.

frequency-hopping generator. A device that allows the *gating* of different *frequencies* in rapid succession for immediate *transmission.* Also see *spread-spectrum code-sequence generator.*

frequency interference. See *radio frequency interference (RFI); single-frequency interference.*

frequency intermodulation. See *radio frequency intermodulation.*

frequency intermodulation distortion. See *modulation-frequency intermodulation distortion.*

frequency management. The control of functions, activities, policies, and procedures that govern the satisfaction of *user* requirements that are related to the assignment and use of the *electromagnetic frequency spectrum.*

frequency meter. An instrument that is designed to determine the *frequency* of an *electromagnetic wave* that falls within its range of perception. The meter is calibrated to indicate the frequency of the wave that it is *tuned* to *receive* and *amplify.*

frequency modulated signal. See *pulsed frequency modulated signal.*

frequency modulation. The *modulation* of the *frequency* of an *electromagnetic, elastic, sound,* or other *wave* serving as a *carrier,* with another wave serving as the *modulating signal,* such that the frequency excursions of the carrier are proportional to a parameter of the modulating signal bearing the intelligence to be *transmitted.* It is a form of *angle modulation* in which the instantaneous frequency of a *sine wave carrier* is caused to depart from the carrier frequency by an amount that is proportional to the instantaneous value of the modulating signal. Combinations of *phase* and frequency modulation are also considered as frequency modulation. Also see *phase modulation.* See *digital frequency modulation; pulse-frequency modulation (PFM).*

frequency modulation improvement factor. See *FM improvement factor.*

frequency modulation improvement threshold. See *FM improvement threshold.*

frequency modulation integrator. A device that has an *output signal* that is the time *integral* of the *frequency modulated input signal.* It provides a means of achieving *integration* of *functions* and of *wave shapes.* The FM integrator is more sophisticated than the *video* integrator and it allows the use of higher *feedback factors* (backward gains).

frequency multidither. In an *optical system,* a method of obtaining and tagging perturbations consisting of an ensemble of *sine waves* of different *amplitudes* and *frequencies.* Also see *polystep dither.*

frequency octave. The logarithm to the base 2, or 3.322 times the logarithm to the base 10, of the ratio of two *frequencies.* If the frequency ratio is 16 to 1, they would be 4 octaves apart. *Wideband receivers* that can cover entire frequency octaves are used to augment normal *tunable receivers* for *monitoring* and *recording transmissions* in a *wide band* of frequencies. (Though the term octave is used, it is apparently a misnomer. It is related to 8 only in the sense that if one frequency is 8 times the other, there are 3 octaves. A single octave implies a frequency doubling.)

frequency offset. The fractional *frequency* deviation of one frequency with respect to another frequency. Mathematically, the frequency offset, *FO* is given by $FO = \Delta f/f_2 = (f_1 - f_2)/f_2$ where Δf is the difference between the two frequencies, f_1 and f_2, and f_2 is the reference frequency with respect to which the offset is taken. If f_2 is greater than f_1, the offset is negative. For example, the difference between the frequency of the *National Bureau of Standards (NBS) Primary Frequency Standard* and the quartz-crystal controlled *oscillators* from which the NBS *broadcast signals* are derived. These offsets may be on the order of one part in 10^{12}. Also see *primary frequency standard.*

frequency power margin. See *radio-frequency power margin.*

frequency prediction. A prediction of the *maximum usable frequency (MUF),* the *optimum traffic frequency,* and the *lowest usable frequency (LUF)* for *transmission* between two specific locations or geographical areas during various times throughout a 24-hour period. The prediction is usually indicated by means of a graph for each frequency plotted as a *function* of time.

frequency priority. The right of an organization to use a specific *frequency* for authorized purposes so as to remain potentially free of harmful *interference* that might be caused by *signals* from *stations* of other organizations in the same priority area (jurisdiction).

frequency pulse. See *radio frequency pulse.*

frequency range. A continuous range or *spectrum* of *frequencies* that extends from one limiting frequency to another. The frequency range for given equipment specifies the frequencies at which the equipment is operable. For example, *filters* pass or stop certain *bands* of frequencies. The frequency range for propagation indicates the frequencies at which *electromagnetic wave propagation* in certain *modes* or *paths* is possible over given distances. *Frequency allocation,* however, is made in terms of bands of frequencies. There is little if any conceptual difference between a range of frequencies and a band of frequencies.

frequency record. A record of *frequency allocation* agreements, *assignments,* and regulations, and *frequency management* procedures for an organization, nation, or other entity or area. For example, the radio regulations published by the *International Telecommunication Union,* Geneva, Switzerland.

frequency register. See *Master International Frequency Register (MIFR).*

frequency registration board. See *International Frequency Registration Board (IFRB).*

frequency response. See *electrooptic frequency response; insertion loss versus frequency characteristic.*

frequency response curve. A plot of the *gain* or *attenuation* of a device, such as an *amplifier* or a *filter,* as a *function* of *frequency.* A flat curve indicates a uniform gain or attenuation over the *range* of frequencies that the curve is flat. Most *amplifiers,* for example, will have a *flat response* up to a certain maximum frequency at which the gain is reduced. A *filter* has a peak or a trough as a response curve.

frequency-response test. In an *optical fiber, bundle* or *cable,* a measure of the *pulse rise time,* the 3 dB cutoff *frequency, dispersion,* or other *parameter* that is a function of frequency (i.e., is frequency dependent).

frequency scanning. Conducting a search for *signals* over a *band* or *range* of *frequencies* by means of a *manual* or *automatically-tuned receiver.* The *tuning* (frequency change) rate may be fixed or variable, or it may be performed mechanically (low speed) or electronically (high speed). The technique may be used to enable *radar* to *transmit* on a clear (no *interference*) frequency by searching a *frequency band* and then tuning the system to a clear portion of that band.

frequency-selective waveguide. On a *dielectric slab,* a center *waveguide* with slotted or periodically-varying-thickness waveguides on each side, one slotted with a pitch of $\lambda_1/n,$ the other $\lambda_2/n,$ where the λ's are *wavelength.* If the parallel waveguides are the proper distance apart, *coupling* will take place between them on a highly selective basis since only a narrow *frequency band* will *propagate* and *transfer* to the central waveguide and to the other slotted guides.

frequency series. A group of several harmonically-related *electromagnetic wave frequencies.* For example, a *fundamental frequency* and a group of *harmonics* that are multiples of the fundamental frequency.

frequency service. See *standard frequency service.*

frequency settability. See *frequency deviation.*

frequency sharing. A *frequency management* arrangement in which the use of the available *frequency spectrum* is distributed among the elements of an organization. Frequency sharing is accomplished by means of *time sharing* or *geographical (space) sharing.* Also see *frequency-division multiplexing; time sharing.* See *geographical frequency sharing.*

frequency shift. 1. Any change in the *frequency* of a *wave* from a *source,* such as a change in the frequency of an *electromagnetic wave* from a *radio transmitter.* 2. In *facsimile systems,* a *frequency modulation system* in which one frequency represents *picture black* and another frequency represents *picture white.* Frequencies between these two limits may represent shades of gray. 3. The number of *hertz* difference in a *frequency modulation system.* For example, in *frequency-shift keying,* the difference between the two frequencies used to *code binary data.* 4. A change of a *transmitter, receiver, oscillator,* or other electrical *circuit* to a different operational *frequency.* 5. A *system* of *radioteletypewriter* operation in which the *mark* and *space signals* are represented by different *frequencies.* See *facsimile frequency shift; signal frequency shift; subcarrier frequency shift.*

frequency-shift keying (FSK). 1. A form of *frequency modulation* in which the *modulating signal* shifts the *output frequency* between predetermined values and in which the *output signal* has no *phase* discontinuity. The instantaneous frequency is shifted between two *discrete* values that are often called *mark* and *space* frequencies. 2. A *signaling* method in which different *frequencies* are used to represent different *characters* to be *transmitted.* For example, using one frequency to represent a *binary* zero and another frequency to represent a binary one, with a smooth *phase transition* between them if practical or necessary. The method is characterized by continuity of phase during the transition from one signaling condition to another. *Frequency change signaling* is similar to frequency-shift keying but may involve a discontinuous change in frequency and change in phase with *signaling condition transitions.* Synonymous with *frequency-shift* *modulation; frequency-shift signaling.*   Also see *two-tone keying.*   See *double frequency-shift keying (DFSK); multiple frequency-shift keying (MFSK); narrow-shift frequency-shift keying; wide-shift frequency-shift keying.*

frequency-shift modulation.   See *frequency-shift keying.*

frequency-shift signaling.   See *frequency-shift keying.*

frequency-shift telegraphy.   *Telegraphy* that makes use of *frequency modulation* in which each *significant condition* is characterized, under *steady-state* conditions, by a specified *frequency* of oscillation or *sinusoidal wave.*   The *telegraph signal* shifts the frequency of the *carrier* between predetermined values. There is usually *phase* continuity during the shift from one frequency to the other.   Also see *four-frequency diplex telegraphy.*

frequency signal.   See *standard time-frequency signal.*

frequency spectrum.   The array of *frequency* components present in a given *electromagnetic, elastic,* or *sound wave, pulse,* or other recurring phenomenon. The spectrum is usually *displayed* in order of increasing or decreasing frequency, with the *amplitude* of the plot proportional to the energy in each of the *bands* indicated.   Also see *electromagnetic spectrum; frequency spectrum designation.*

frequency spectrum congestion.   The situation that occurs when many *stations transmit* simultaneously using *frequencies* that are close together, that is, with insufficient width of frequency *guard bands* or *channel* spacing. This causes difficulty in *discrimination* by *tuning;* overlap in *sidebands* and main *signal;* and *interference,* such as occurs when frequencies shift slightly or are phase-shifted by *ionospheric reflection.*

frequency spectrum designation.   A method of referring to a *band (range) of frequencies.*   The designator is a two or three letter abbreviation of the name of the band (USA). The designator is also a one or two digit number (ITU). The designated bands (ranges) are as follows:

Frequency Range	Letter Designator	Numeric Designator
0–30 Hz	DC (Direct Current) (approximate)	1
30–300 Hz	ELF (Extremely Low Frequency)	2
300–3000 Hz	ILF (Infra-Low Frequency)	3
3–30 kHz	VLF (Very Low Frequency)	4
30–300 kHz	LF (Low Frequency)	5
300–3000 kHz	MF (Medium Frequency)	6
3–30 MHz	HF (High Frequency)	7
30–300 MHz	VHF (Very High Frequency)	8
300–3000 MHz	UHF (Ultra High Frequency)	9
3–30 GHz	SHF (Super High Frequency)	10
30–300 GHz	EHF (Extremely High Frequency)	11
300–3000 GHz	THF (Tremendously High Frequency	12

The lower limit is exclusive; the upper limit is inclusive. The first three numeric designators are not normally used. The upper limit is given as 3×10^n, where n is the numeric designator. Synonymous with *spectrum designation of frequency*. Also see *frequency spectrum; radio frequency*.

frequency stability. 1. An inverse measure of the extent of undesired variation of the *frequency* of an *oscillator, transmitter, receiver, filter,* or other *tuned* or controlled frequency *source* or *circuit,* from its mean frequency over a specified period of time. The less the frequency deviation the greater the stability. 2. A measure of the ability of a *circuit* or device to operate at a constant frequency. Also see *frequency deviation.* See *carrier frequency stability.*

frequency standard. A stable *frequency* source *(oscillator)* that is used for frequency calibration of equipment. The *output* of an accepted standard is usually established by authority as describing the specified frequency. It usually generates a *fundamental frequency* with a high degree of accuracy. *Harmonics* of this fundamental frequency are used to provide other reference frequencies to serve as reference points in the *frequency spectrum.* See *primary frequency standard.*

frequency standard accuracy. The degree to which the *frequency* of any given *frequency standard* agrees with a specified primary frequency standard or with a stated frequency value.

frequency standard precision. An exact measure, with a specified tolerance, of the degree to which a *frequency standard* reproduces the same frequency each time it is placed in operation regardless of whether or not maintenance has been performed.

frequency standard stability. The degree to which a continuously operating *frequency* standard retains its initial frequency within a specified time interval.

frequency station. See *standard frequency station.*

frequency switch. See *laser frequency switch.*

frequency synthesizing. A method of generating multiple *frequencies* with great stability using only a single stable *oscillator.*

frequency time sharing. *Frequency sharing* in which *stations* in the same geographical area operate on schedules in such a manner that two stations do not use the same, or nearly the same, frequency at the same time. *Time sharing* is an effective method of avoiding interference. It is somewhat limited in its application. For example, in some municipal operations, a community usually requires full-time use of its *allocated* and *assigned frequencies.* Time sharing generally becomes an unacceptable burden on the *communication system.* Also see *frequency geographical sharing.*

frequency tolerance.   1. The maximum permissible departure from the *assigned frequency* of the center *frequency* of the *occupied bandwidth* of an *emission*. **2.** The maximum departure of the characteristic frequency of an emission from a reference frequency. This includes both the initial-setting tolerance and excursions that are related to short term *frequency stability*, long term frequency stability, and aging. The frequency tolerance may be expressed as parts per 10^n, where n is any positive *integer* greater than 1. It may be expressed in *hertz*. It also may be expressed as a percentage of the assigned frequency or some other reference frequency.   Frequency tolerances are established by international agreement.   They may vary according to the assigned frequency, the type of *transmitter* (fixed or mobile), or the *power* of the transmitting *station*.

frequency translation.   The transfer or conversion of a set of *signals* that occupies a definite *frequency band*, such as the signals in a *channel* or group of channels, from one position in the *frequency spectrum* to another, in such a way that the arithmetic frequency difference of the signals within the band is unaltered. Synonymous with *frequency conversion*.   Also see *frequency displacement*.   See *single-frequency translation*.

frequency weighting.   The adjustment that needs to be made to meter readings because of *frequency* distribution in a set of signals or in noise when measuring signal or noise energy in an *electrical circuit*.

Fresnel equation.   An equation that defines the *reflection* and *refraction (transmission) coefficients* at an *optical interface* when an *electromagnetic wave* is *incident* upon the *interface surface*.   Also see *reflection coefficient; transmission coefficient*.

Fresnel reflectance loss.   See *Fresnel reflection loss*.

Fresnel reflection loss.   The *power loss* incurred at an *interface* surface when an *electromagnetic wave* is *incident* upon it and part of the incident power is *reflected*. The reflection loss depends on many factors, including the *refractive indices* of the incident and *refracting* media, the *wavelength*, the *incidence angle*, and the *incident light polarization* relative to the interface.   Reflection losses that are incurred at the input and output of an *optical fiber* are due to the difference in refractive index between the fiber and the *transmission medium* from which the *light* enters and to which it leaves. Synonymous with *Fresnel reflectance loss*. Also see *reflection coefficient; transmission coefficient*.

Fresnel zone.   The circular zone about the direct *path* between an *electromagnetic wave transmitter* and *receiver* in an unbounded *transmission medium* free of radiation *sources*.   The zone is of such radius that the distance from a point on the circular perimeter to the receiver has a path length that is some multiple of one-half *wavelength* longer than the direct path from transmitter to receiver. The zone is actually in the form of a cigar-shaped shell of circular cross section surrounding the path. Thus, for the first Fresnel zone, the distance from the transmitter to any point on this shell and on to the receiver is one half-wavelength longer than the direct path; for the second Fresnel zone, two half-wavelengths longer than the direct path, and so on. Also see *effective earth radius; K-factor; path clearance; path profile; path survey; propagation path obstruction.*

fringe. In *optics,* a *light* or dark band, region, or area caused by *interference* of two or more *electromagnetic waves,* usually *lightwaves,* so that areas (bands) of reinforcement and cancellation occur. See *Newton's fringes.*

frogging. See *frequency frogging.*

front-emitting LED. See *surface-emitting LED.*

front-end computer. A processor that can relieve a *host computer* from *line* control, *message* handling, *code* conversion, *error* control, *terminal* control, and other processing tasks that are usually nonapplication oriented. It may perform these tasks for a *communication system,* a *computer network,* or another computer.

front-end noise temperature. An indication of the *thermal noise* level in the first stage of a *receiver.*

front-end processing. 1. The preprocessing of *data* prior to the main *processing* operation. 2. The *processing* of *data* that is always performed for each *application computer program* or for each *message transmission,* that is independent of the programs or messages, and that is required by *system protocol* rather than by the *user.* For example, *serial-to-parallel conversion, packetizing, multiplexing, concentration, network access, signaling supervision, protocol conversion, error control,* and *diagnostic programming.*

front-end processor. A *programmed-logic* or *stored-program* device that *interfaces data communication* equipment, *data processing systems,* or other pieces of major equipment with an *input-output bus* or *storage* device and a *data processing computer.* It is designed to perform nonapplication-oriented or nonuser-oriented administrative or overhead services, such as *serial-to-parallel conversion, packetizing, multiplexing, concentration, network access, signaling supervision, protocol converting, error control,* and *diagnostic programming.*

front fed. See *prime focus feed.*

front focal length (FFL). In a *lens* of an *optical system,* the distance measured from the *principal* focus, located in the front space, to the *first principal point* on the lens.

front sign. In *semaphore communications,* the *flag positions* that are used after the *attention sign* to indicate the *operating signal* and other signs.

front-to-back ratio. In *communication systems*, a ratio of *parameters* that is used in connection with *antennas, rectifiers,* or other devices, in which *signal strength, resistance,* or another parameter in one direction of *transmission* or *electric current* flow is compared with that in the opposite direction.

front-surface mirror. An *optical mirror* on which the *reflecting* surface is applied to the front surface of the mirror instead of the back (i.e., to the surface of first *incidence*). The *reflected light* does not pass through any *substrate*. Also see *back-surface mirror.*

front velocity. See *phase-front velocity.*

FSK. *Frequency-shift keying.*

FTC. See *logarithmic fast time constant (log FTC).*

FTS. *Federal Telecommunication Standard. Federal Telecommunication System.*

full-baud bipolar coding. A *coding* process that consists of representing a 0 by a zero level *voltage* in the *bipolar* sequence of *pulses* and a 1 by alternate positive or negative pulses in the bipolar sequence of pulses. The pulses remain at their respective levels for the entire *baud* length, that is, unit interval. *Bipolar coding* has an inherent *error detection* capability because of the alternate polarity pulses. Also see *half-baud polar coding.*

full carrier. A *carrier wave* that is *transmitted* at a *power* level that has not dropped more than a specified amount from the *peak envelope power,* such as not more than 3 dB or not more than 6 dB. *Double-sideband* and *single-sideband amplitude modulated transmissions* normally comprise a *full carrier* with a power level that is exactly 6 dB below the peak envelope power at 100% modulation.

full-carrier transmission. *Transmission* in which a *modulated full carrier* is *transmitted,* that is, the *amplitude* of the *carrier* never drops more than a specified amount below the *peak envelope power,* such as not more than 6 dB.

full duplex. See *duplex.*

full-duplex circuit. See *duplex circuit.*

full-duplex operation. See *duplex operation.*

Fullerphone. An instrument that makes use of a very low *direct current (DC)* in the *line* but converts this direct current into an intermittent current of *audio frequency* at the *receiver.* This enables hand speed *Morse telegraphy* to take place over good or bad lines with the least chance of remote *interception.* The system uses buzzer *signals* for *keying* and reception by listening. Direct currents are used for actual *telegraphic transmission* thus making the system somewhat untappable.

full modulation. In an *analog-digital converter*, the condition in which the *input signal amplitude* has just reached the *threshold* at which *clipping* begins to occur.

fully-automatic reperforator-transmitter-distributor. See *coupled reperforator tape reader.*

fully connected network. A *network* in which each *node* is directly connected to every other *node*. Thus, each node is connected to $n - 1$ branches where n is the number of nodes in the network. The number of branches is given by $n(n-1)/2$. See Figure F-12.

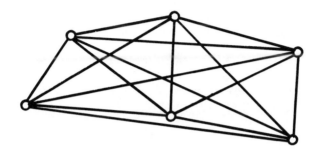

F-12. A **fully connected network.**

function. See *complex transfer function; control function; end-of-message function; end-of-transmission function; fiber bundle transfer function; harmonic function; machine function; modulation transfer function; optical fiber transfer function; sectorial harmonic function; sinusoidal function; spherical harmonic function; tesseral harmonic function; zonal harmonic function.*

functional signaling link. A *communication link* together with its *transmission control functions* and other associated controls.

functional unit. Any *hardware, software,* or *firmware* that has a specific purpose or is capable of performing a specific function, such as a *data processing system, computer program,* or *fiberscope.*

function control. The control of an operation *(control function)* to be performed by a *system,* such as a *telegraph, data recording,* or *data processing* device, other than recording or printing a letter, *numeral,* punctuation mark, or the *graphic symbols* that are contained in a *message* or other *data stream.* For example, the control of *line feed, carriage return, shifting,* or *spacing.*

function generator. A *functional unit* that has an output variable that is a function of its input analog variables. See *fixed function generator; variable function generator.*

function key. 1. A specific *key* on a *keyboard* that provides for *function control.* For example, a key on a *teletypewriter* keyboard that is marked LTRS,

CR, LF, or FIGS, and that when operated causes the teletypewriter to perform the identified *machine function* of *letters shift, carriage return, line feed,* or *figures (numerals) shift,* respectively. These functions enable a *message* to be *transmitted, received,* and *recorded* in proper form. **2.** In *display systems,* a button or *switch* that may be used to generate and dispatch a *signal* identifying, or corresponding to, the button or switch that is actuated, selected, or depressed. The signals can be used to control a *display device* directly or through the use of a *computer program.*

function keyboard.   A *keyboard* that contains a set of *function keys* for initiating, activating, or causing *control functions.*   For example, in *display systems,* a set or *panel* of associated *function keys* that might, for example, be mounted on a *display console* to form part of an *input* unit for a *display device.*

function signal.   A set of *signal elements* that is used to *transmit* or represent a *function control character* that actuates a *control function,* such as *carriage return, line feed, letters shift,* or *figures shift,* that is to be performed by a *teletypewriter (teleprinter), typewriter,* or other *communication* device.

fundamental frequency.   The basic or lowest *frequency* in a *wave* or periodic phenomenon.   It is the repetition rate of the repeated phenomenon.   For example, in a square wave, it is the repetition rate of the complete square wave.   A pure *sine wave* has one frequency.   If it is distorted it may be conceived to consist of other higher frequencies that are multiples of the original undistorted wave.   The fundamental frequency remains the same as long as the distortion is limited.   In a *Fourier analysis* representation of an arbitrarily-shaped periodic wave, the higher frequencies are multiples of the fundamental frequency.   Each frequency has a specific *amplitude,* such that when all the frequencies are added, the original distorted or arbitrary wave is obtained.   The multiples of the fundamental are called *harmonics,* beginning with the second harmonic.   The first harmonic is the fundamental frequency itself.

fundamental keying frequency.   See *maximum keying frequency.*

furcation coupling.   The mixing of *signals* from several separate *optical fibers* by passing them through a common single *fiber rod,* thus obtaining a signal containing all the *components* of the several signals.   The mixing of several *colors* can take place in this manner.

fuse.   A protective device with a *circuit*-opening part that, when heated to a prescribed *temperature* by an *electric current* passing through it, severs (opens) the circuit in which it is a part.

fuse disconnecting switch.   A disconnecting *switch* in which a *fuse* forms a part of, or is connected to, a blade assembly that forms the circuit continuity contacts.   When the fuse and blade assembly are removed from the circuit, the circuit is open and current flow is either interrupted or prevented.

fusion splicing. In *optical transmission systems* using solid *transmission media,* the joining together of two media by *butting* them, forming an *interface* between them, and then removing the common surfaces so that there be no interface between them when a *lightwave* is propagated from one medium to the other. Thus, no *reflection* or *refraction* at the former interface can occur.

fuze detonation. See *proximity-fuze detonation.*

fuzing. See *command fuzing.*

G

gage station. See *radar beacon precipitation gage station.*

gain. In an active device or *system,* the ratio between an *output* quantity and an *input* quantity given as a pure number (dimensionless), a percent, or in *decibels* when the input and output units are the same. For example, if the ratio of the output *signal power* to the input signal power is greater than unity (over 100%), or is measured in positive *decibels,* it is considered a *gain.* If less than unity (less than 100%), or negative decibels, it is considered *attenuation.* The gain may be in power, *voltage, current, field intensity,* or other units depending on the system and the quantity being considered. Examples of gain in *communications* are *antenna gain, power gain, directive gain, diversity gain,* and process gain. Directive gain is a significant attribute of a *light source* when *coupling lightwaves* to *optical fibers.* See *antenna gain; antenna power gain; directive gain; diversity gain; height gain; insertion gain; loop gain; net gain; power gain; process gain; Q-gain.*

gain antenna. See *high-gain antenna.*

gain-bandwidth product. The product of the *gain* of an *active device* and a specified *bandwidth.* For an *avalanche photodiode,* the gain-bandwidth product is the gain times the *frequency* of measurement when the device is biased for maximum obtainable gain.

gain combiner. See *equal-gain combiner.*

gain control. See *automatic gain control; instantaneous automatic gain control (IAGC); receiver intermediate-frequency gain control.*

gain-control circuit. See *detector back-bias gain-control circuit.*

gain factor. See *photoconductive gain factor.*

gain-frequency distortion. See *frequency distortion.*

gain-to-noise temperature (G/T). See *antenna gain-to-noise temperature (G/T).*

galactic noise. *Noise* or *interference coupled* into a *communication system,* originating from *sources* outside our solar system, mainly from certain areas of the Milky Way. Antennae pointed toward the center of our galaxy sense many *noise* sources. Another smaller noise peak occurs when antennae point in the direction of the galactic arm. Galactic noise is random. Its characteristics are similar to *thermal noise.* It is experienced at frequencies above 15 MHz. Extragalactic noise also comes from *emission* nebulae in other galaxies and from the remnants of supernovae. Synonymous with *cosmic noise; galactic radio noise.*

galactic radio noise. See *galactic noise.*

Galite. An *optical fiber* produced by Galileo Electro-Optics Corporation available in single and multiple *fiber cables* with small and large fiber *cores.*

galvanic series. A sequence of metal elements and alloys that indicates their relative electrochemical activity or affinity for replacing one another in electrolytic chemical action and, thus, corroding each other. For example, when constructing *communication* equipment, such as *antennas* and structural members, metals in contact should be as close together as possible in the galvanic series. For example, copper or brass lugs should be zinc plated before connection to aluminum. Copper or brass should not be placed in contact with aluminum. Platings or coatings should be used to prevent their physical contact. See Figure G-1.

```
              GALVANIC SERIES
  1  Magnesium        7  Steel              13 Brass
  2  Zinc             8  Stainless Steel    14 Copper
  3  Aluminum         9  Lead-Tin Solders   15 Monel Metal
  4  Aluminum Alloys  10 Lead               16 Silver
  5  Cadmium          11 Tin                17 Gold
  6  Iron             12 Nickel             18 Platinum

  Relative Position of Metals and Platings Commonly Used in Communication
                     Equipment.
```

G-1. During **galvanic series** action, metal flows from low numbered metals to high numbered metals. The lower number metal becomes the anode. Metals in contact should be as close together in the series as possible since this lowers the potential difference between them.

gamma photon. A fundamental particle (quantum) of *gamma radiation,* with an energy equal to hf, where h is *Planck's constant* and f is the *frequency* of the *radiation (photon).*

gamma radiation. *Electromagnetic waves,* of a *frequency* higher than *lightwaves* and higher than *x-rays,* that can only be absorbed by dense materials such as lead and depleted uranium. They cannot be confined to, or guided in, *optical fibers* and are usually produced by nuclear reaction or high-power *lasers,* since gamma radiation is produced only when transitions occur from very high to very low *energy bands.* The *photon* energy of gamma radiation is destructive to living tissue, causing changes in molecular structures.

gamma ray. A *ray* of *electromagnetic radiation* from a *source* that *radiates* in the 10^{10} to 10^{12} GHz *band.* It is a ray of *electromagnetic radiation* with a frequency between 10^{10} and 10^{12} GHz. Such rays are *emitted* by atoms that are undergoing *energy band transitions,* that is, by atoms that are *radioactive.* These rays are destructive to living tissues and organisms.

gap. See *interblock gap.*

gap character. A *character* that is included in a *word* for technical purposes and that does not represent *information* being *transmitted* for a *user.* For example, if a fixed-length word is 24 characters long and the word is to be used for a person's name that contains only 20 characters, 4 gap characters are inserted to complete the word. This satisfies a character count on reading and recording in some *transmission, storage,* and *data processing systems.*

gap energy. See *band-gap energy.*

gap loss. In a *fiber-optic system,* a *power loss,* usually expressed in *decibels,* due to the longitudinal deviation from optimum spacing between the *light* source and the *fiber junction,* between *fiber* and fiber junction, or between fiber and *photodetector* junction.

gap switch. See *horn gap switch.*

garble. In *communication systems,* an undesired result of an *error* in *transmission, reception, recording, encryption,* or *decryption* that renders a *message* or a portion of a message incorrect or undecipherable. Garbled *text* usually appears as a random sequence of letters that may result from such causes as transposing, omitting, substituting, or adding letters or other characters; from using wrong *keys* when *deciphering;* from *dropout pulses* on reading, recording, or transmitting; or from equipment *failures* or *operator mistakes.*

garble table. A table, chart, or other aid that may be used to assist in the correction of a *garble.*

garnet source. See *YAG/LED source.*

gas laser. A *laser* in which the active medium is a gas. Types of lasers include the atomic laser, such as the helium-neon laser; the ionic laser, such as the argon, krypton, and xenon lasers; the metal-vapor laser, such as the helium-cadmium and helium-selenium lasers; and the *molecular laser,* such as the carbon-dioxide, hydrogen-cyanide, and water-vapor lasers. See *mixed-gas laser.*

gas panel. The part of a *display device* that consists of a *display surface* beneath which is a grid of electrodes or wires in a flat gas-filled envelope wherein the energizing of a group of electrodes causes the electrons in the gas molecules to attain higher energy levels at specific locations. Upon returning to normal levels, photons are emitted at those locations, thus creating an *image* of light. Synonymous with *plasma panel.*

gate. A device that has one *output channel* and one or more *input channels.* It is constructed in such a manner that the output channel state is completely determined by the input channel states except during *switching transients.* It is a *combinational circuit (logic element).* It is used for making logical decisions by performing a *gating* logic function.   See *A-AND-NOT-B gate; A-EXCEPT-B gate; A-IGNORE-B gate; AND gate; A-OR-NOT-B gate; B-AND-NOT-A gate; B-OR-NOT-A gate; channel gate; EXCLUSIVE-NOR gate; EXCLUSIVE-OR gate; GENERATOR gate; NAND gate; NEGATION gate; NEGATIVE A-IGNORE-B gate; NEGATIVE B-IGNORE-A gate; NOR gate; NULL gate; OR gate; range gate.*

gate stealing.   See *range-gate stealing; velocity gate stealing.*

gateway.   1. A *node* at which two or more *networks* are connected, with the fundamental role of serving as the boundary between the internal *protocols* of the connected networks.   2. The collection of *hardware* and *software* that is required to effect an interconnection between two or more networks to enable *users* in different networks to *communicate* with each other.   Also see *port; terminal port.*

gateway interface.   An *interface* between two dissimilar *communication systems* in which *switching centers* are provided that enable *switching, signaling, supervisory,* and *transmission* functions to be performed on *calls* from a *user* (customer, subscriber) in one system to a user in another system.   The gateway interface switching functions may be under the control of an *operator* or may be performed automatically under the control of a *programmed computer.*   Usually only a limited number of users in both systems are permitted *access* to the other system via the gateway interface.

gateway switching center.   An *automatic telephone network switching center* that is part of a *gateway* and provides interconnections among *communication systems* and *networks.*   For example, a switching center that provides *connections* to networks in foreign countries or overseas.

gating.   1. The process of selecting only those portions of an *electromagnetic* or *electrical wave* or *pulse* that meet specified criteria, such as portions of the wave that lie between certain instants of time or between selected *amplitude* limits. 2. The controlling of *signals* by means of *combinational circuits (logic elements).* The control process is one in which a predetermined set of conditions, when established, permits some event or process to occur.

gating circuit.   A *circuit* used to limit *input signals* to another circuit, either in time or space, to prevent *interference,* commutate *pulses, multiplex,* perform logic decisions, limit *output operations* during receiving operations, prevent *blanking* or *saturation,* or perform other signal *processing* functions.   For example, *infrared scanning systems* are equipped with gating circuits to reduce *blanking* by *laser pulses* by admitting pulses only during certain time intervals or when specified conditions are met.   They are used in *radars* to examine *echoes* only at certain times after launching a *signal.*   They are used in *computers* to perform arithmetic and logical operations.   Also see *combinational circuit.*

Gaussian beam.   A *beam* whose *light intensity* across its diameter is somewhat proportional to a Gaussian distribution curve (i.e., the bell curve), in which the maximum intensity occurs in the center and the intensity diminishes toward the edges, the cross section normally being symmetrical in intensity.

Gaussian-shaped pulse. A *pulse* that has the shape of a Gaussian or normal distribution curve. In the time domain, the shape is defined by:

$$R_t = Be^{-at^2}$$

where *a* and *B* are constants and *t* is time. A similar expression could hold in the *frequency* domain with *t* replaced by *f*.

G-band. *Frequencies* from 4 to 6 GHz comprising 10 numbered *frequency bands* of 200 MHz width each. These frequencies overlap parts of the obsolete S-band, C-band, X-band, and J-band.

GBH. *Group busy hour.*

Gbps. *Gigabits/second,* i.e., 10^9 bits/second.

GCA landing. *Ground controlled approach (GCA) landing.*

GCA system. *Ground controlled approach (GCA) system.*

GDF. *Group distribution frame.*

general message. A *message* that has a wide standard distribution, such as to all *stations* in a *network,* to all ships at sea, to all ships in a given convoy, to all ships under one command, to all ships in a given ocean area or of a given nation, to all aircraft, police patrols, or forest rangers, or to all of the civilian population of a country or area.

general-purpose language. A *computer programming language* used in a broad class of applications.

general-purpose network. See *common user network.*

general-purpose user service. A *telephone service* in which *users* (customers, subscribers) are connected to a telephone *network* through a *private branch exchange (PBX),* a *private automatic branch exchange (PABX),* or a *console* with direct *access* to a *switching center.*

generation. In recording and reproduction systems, a measure of the remoteness, in succession, of a copy from the original *image.* A first-generation copy is a copy made from the original; a second-generation copy is made from the first-generation copy; and so on. For example, if a *microfilm* is made from a *display element, display group,* or *display image* in the *display space* on the *display surface* of a *fiberscope faceplate* at the end of a *coherent bundle* of *optical fibers,* the microfilm would be the first-generation copy, and another microfilm, or a *blowback* made from the microfilm, would be the second generation.

generator. See *character generator; curve generator; dot-matrix generator; fixed function generator; frequency-hopping generator; function generator; key vari-*

able generator; master frequency generator; Mersenne code sequence generator; modular spread-spectrum code-sequence generator; signal generator; shift-register generator; spread-spectrum code-sequence generator; stroke character generator; variable function generator; vector generator.

GENERATOR gate. A *circuit* or device that produces a continuous *string* or *stream* of *pulses* or conditions that represent a sequence of 1's in a given *system.* Thus, the GENERATOR gate may be considered as a special case of a *combinational circuit* that produces 1's regardless of the *input* or with no input. It is the reverse of a *NULL gate.* See Figure G-2.

G-2. A table showing the *input* and *output digits* of a **GENERATOR gate.**

geographic address group. In a *message,* an *address group* that represents a geographic location or area and must be used in combination with another address group in order that a message can be *routed* from *source user (originator)* to *destination user (addressee).*

geographical frequency-sharing. The sharing of the *electromagnetic frequency spectrum* among all *users* that are located in a given geographical area. It is one of the most effective methods of *frequency sharing.* In determining the necessary separation for the use of the same or adjacent frequencies, a number of factors must be considered. Some of these factors are the *receiver selectivity* and *sensitivity, transmitter* and receiver separation distances, terrain features, *transmission medium propagation* characteristics for the frequency ranges involved, environmental factors, transmitter and receiver siting, and *emission bandwidths.* Geographical frequency-sharing can often be achieved or enhanced by the use of *directional antennas.*

geographical mile. The distance along the equator that corresponds to one minute of longitude, that is, 6087.15 ft, or 1855.4 m. It is often confused with the *nautical mile,* that is, 6076.1 ft or 1852 m.

geographical sharing. See *frequency geographical sharing.*

geographic reference system. See *worldwide geographic reference system.*

geometric image. Pertaining to the location and shape of the *image* of a particle as predicted by the use of *geometric optics* alone. The geometric image is distinguished from the *diffraction image,* determined from both physical and geometric optics. For example, the geometric image of two points is also two points, but the diffraction image may suggest the presence of an *object* comprised of two small particles. The diffraction image more closely resembles the object.

geometric optics. **1.** The *optics* of *light rays* that follow mathematically defined paths in passing through *optical* elements, such as *lenses* and *prisms,* and *optical transmission media* that *refract, reflect,* or *transmit electromagnetic radiation.* **2.** The branch of science that treats *light propagation* in terms of *rays* considered as straight or curved lines in *homogeneous* and nonhomogeneous *media.*

geometric spreading. In a wave *propagating* in a *transmission medium* in which there are no *sources,* the decrease in *power density* as a function of distance in the direction of propagation. As a curved *wavefront,* such as for *divergent electromagnetic waves,* moves in the direction of *propagation,* the available power at one point must be spread over a larger area at the next point in space; e.g., a point source of *light* has its light energy spread over larger and larger spherical surfaces as the distance from the source increases. Also see *free space loss; inverse-square law.*

geostationary satellite. A satellite that has a circular orbit, lies in the plane of the earth's equator, and moves about the earth's polar axis in the same direction and with the same period as the earth's rotation. Thus, the satellite remains above a fixed point on the earth's equator. Synonymous with *stationary satellite.* See *nongeostationary satellite.*

geostationary satellite height. The elevation above the surface of a rotating celestial body (earth) at which a satellite in its equatorial plane will remain directly above a given point on its equator without requiring an internal force to overcome gravity to remain in position. At this height the centrifugal force (radial outward force of acceleration) equals the centripetal force (radial inward force of gravitational attraction between the body and its satellite). The earth geostationary satellite height is 35 787 km above the equator. Such a satellite in equatorial circular orbit has a period of 24 hours. Thus it appears to be stationary to an observer anywhere on earth. Synonymous with *synchronous equatorial satellite height.*

ghost image. A spurious single or multiple *image* of *objects,* seen in *optical* instruments, caused by *reflections* from optical surfaces. By coating optical surfaces with low reflection films, the ghost images are greatly reduced.

GHz. Gigahertz.

gigabits/second (Gbps) signaling rate. A *signaling rate* of 10^9 bits/second; i.e., 1000 million bits/second or a billion (U.S.) bits/second.

gigahertz (GHz). A unit of frequency that denotes one billion (U.S.) Hz, that is, 10^9 Hz.

glass. See *magnifier; bulk optical glass; crown glass; dry glass; flint glass.*

glass fiber. See *drawn glass fiber.*

glass laser. A *solid-state laser* whose *active laser* medium is glass.

glass powder. Pulverized glass resulting from the industrial glass production process. When in the molten state, the glass is purified for making *optical fiber preforms.* See Figure G-3.

G-3. Stages in production of *optical fibers,* including **glass powder,** glass disk, cylindrical block, rod, tube *(preforms),* and fibers. (Courtesy of Bell Laboratories.)

glass window. The *interface* that lies between a *light source* and a glass *optical element* such as a *microcylindrical* lens or an *integrally grown lens.*

glide path-slope station. A *radionavigation land station* in the *aeronautical radio-navigation service* that provides vertical guidance in connection with an *instrument landing system.* In certain instances, a glide path-slope station may be placed on board a ship, such as an aircraft carrier.

G-line. *Goubau line.*

global beam satellite antenna. An *antenna* on board a *satellite* that emits a *conical beam* that provides, at the intended *orbit* height, complete coverage of all the area of the earth that faces the satellite to the *radio horizon* in all directions. The area of coverage might be described as the area inside the circle of tangency of a cone, inside of which the earth is fitted, with the satellite at the apex.

glossary. See *net glossary.*

GMT. *Greenwich mean time.*

gnomonic map. A map made by projecting from the center of the earth onto a plane that touches the earth's surface at the point of tangency. This map can show only a limited portion of the earth's surface without severe distortion at the edges. Also see *orthodromic map.*

go-ahead message. See *go-ahead notice.*

go-ahead notice. In a *tape-relay communication system,* a *service message,* to a *relay station* or to a *tributary station,* that contains a request to the *operator* to resume *transmitting* over a specified *channel* or channels. Synonymous with *go-ahead message; start message; start notice.* Also see *stop notice.*

gold code. In *spread-spectrum systems,* a *code* that is generated by adding, *modulo-two,* the *outputs* of two *spread-spectrum code-sequence generators.*

goniometer. 1. In a *radar system,* a device for *electrically* shifting the characteristics of a *directional antenna.* 2. The *antenna system* of a *radio direction-finding* set. 3. An electrical device that is used to determine the *azimuth* of a received *signal* by combining the outputs of individual elements of an *antenna array.* The *radiating* individual elements of the antenna have specific *phase* relationships among them.

goniometry. See *radio goniometry.*

Goos-Haenchen shift. The *phase shift* that occurs in a *lightwave* when it is *reflected,* the magnitude of shift being a function of the *incidence angle.* This shift occurs with every *internal reflection* that occurs in an *optical fiber.*

Goubau line. A single-wire open *waveguide.* The Goubau line is capable of guiding an axial cylindrical *surface wave.* Synonymous with *G-line.*

GPSS. A *computer programming language* based on *block diagrams* and used primarily for *digital simulation.*

graceful degradation. See *gradual degradation.*

grade. See *service grade.*

graded fiber. See *doped-silica graded fiber.*

graded-index fiber. An *optical fiber* with a variable *refractive index* that is a function of the radial distance from the fiber axis, the refractive index getting progressively lower away from the axis. This characteristic causes the *light rays* to be continually *refocused* by refraction into the *core.* As a result, there is a designed continuous change in refractive index between the core and *cladding* along a fiber diameter. Also see *uniform index profile*. Synonymous with *gradient-index fiber*.

graded-index profile. The condition of having the *refractive index* of a material, such as the glass of an *optical fiber*, vary continuously from one value at the *core* to another at the outer surface.

gradient. See *refractive index gradient*.

gradient-index fiber. See *graded-index fiber*.

gradual degradation. A *system* operating condition that is characterized by a gradual or slow reduction in operational capabilities. The system continues to provide a reduced or partial service but in a degraded *mode*. The system does not fail completely, suddenly, or catastrophically. It is the slow reduction of a *system's* or *component's* capability to perform its intended function; e.g., in a *light-emitting diode (LED)*, a reduction in the externally measured *quantum efficiency*. In a *laser diode*, the *threshold current density* increases, and the resulting *incremental quantum efficiency* decreases, resulting in reduced power output for given current density without evidence of facet damage. However, the *power* output level can usually be restored by an increase in the current density. Also see *catastrophic degradation*. Synonymous with *graceful degradation*.

granular noise. See *quantizing noise*.

grapheme. A *graphic* representation of a *semanteme*, such as x-former for *transformer*, x-mission for *transmission*, and x-roads for crossroads.

graphics. 1. The branch of science and technology that is devoted to the transport of *information* through arrays of symbols, such as graphs, letters, *numerals*, lines, drawings, and pictures. It includes nonvoice *analog information* devices and systems such as *facsimile, photographics, television, Wirephoto*, and *radiophoto*. 2. The *symbols* that are formed by connected or adjacent strokes, such as the letter A on this page. See *computer graphics; coordinate graphics; interactive graphics; passive graphics*.

graphic service. A *communication service* or *system* that makes use of *graphics*, that is, a system that *receives* and *transmits data* in pictorial form, such as pictures, graphs, letters, *numerals*, lines, and drawings. For example, *facsimile, wirephoto, radiophoto*, and *television*.

grass. *Random noise* in a *radar receiver* that is due to *atmospheric* disturbances, thermal agitation, *interference*, or other sources. It can be seen on a *radar screen*. It is so named because of its appearance on an A-scan *display*. Grass appears as illumination that is displayed on a radar screen when the *gain* control is set so high that the screen displays the noise that occurs in the radar set itself without receiving *antenna signal input* other than interference and *cosmic noise*.

grating. See *diffraction grating*.

grating chromatic resolving power. The *resolving power* that determines the minimum *wavelength* difference for any *spectral order* that can be distinguished as separate. The *chromatic resolving power* for *diffraction gratings* is usually stated for cases in which parallel *rays* of *light* are *incident* upon the grating and is numerically equal to the number of lines or ruled spacings per unit distance in the grating. Also see *diffraction grating spectral order.*

grating spectral order. See *diffraction grating spectral order.*

gravitational field. The field of force, established by the existence of a mass of material matter, such that material masses attract one another. The field is said to exist in the space surrounding matter. Thus, an infinitesimally small element of matter produces a gravitational field that varies inversely as the square of the distance from the element and extends to infinity at which it is zero. The field at a given point is the sum (integral) of all the contributions of the individual elements. Mutual gravitational attraction is expressed mathematically as $F = Gm_1 m_2/d^2$, where F is the force of attraction, G is the gravitational constant (proportionality constant), m_1 and m_2 are the masses of the attracting bodies, and d is the distance between their centers of gravity (which, for homogeneous substances, are their geometric centroids).

gray code. A *cyclic binary unit distance code* in which a *positional binary code* system for consecutive numbers is used such that in two consecutive numbers of the code the digits are the same in every place *(digit position)* except one, and in that place the digits differ by one unit. Thus the Hamming *(signal) distance* between consecutive numbers in the code is one. The code proves valuable for *encoding* devices since only one *digit* changes at a time. This provides for smooth operation and reduced ambiguities at change points. Instead of many digits changing at the same time, such as when counting in *pure binary* from 1111 to 10000, or in *decimal* from 999 to 1000, only one digit changes at these transition points. In order to convert from pure binary to the gray code, one may proceed as follows: Starting from the left end of the pure binary number, copy any initial 0's and the first occurrence of a 1. If the next binary digit is different from 1, that is, is a 0, write a 1. If it is the same, that is, is a 1, write a 0. If the next digit is different from the previous digit write a 1, if the next digit is the same as the previous digit write a 0. Thus, each time the next digit in the pure binary number changes, write a 1, each time the next digit is the same as the previous digit, write a 0 for the gray code. Thus, each time the next digit in the pure binary sequence changes, write a 1 and each time the next digit is the same write a 0 until the end of the pure binary number. For example, 1011011 in pure binary is 1110110 in gray code. In order to convert the gray code back to pure binary, start counting the gray code 1's from the left. If the count is odd, write a 1. As long as the count remains odd as position by position (digit by digit) is passed continue to write 1's for the pure binary. Whenever, and for as long as, the count remains even, write 0's. Thus, write 1's for an odd count and 0's for an even count until the end of the number. For example, given the gray code code number 1110110, the pure binary number equivalent will be 1 for the first 1 in the gray code number, 0 for the second 1 because the count of 1's is now even, 1 for the third 1 because the count of 1's is now odd, 1 again because the count of 1's is still odd in the gray code number, now 0 because the count is again even, and so on to yield 1011011 in pure binary. The entire code may be constructed in a cyclic reflected fashion. Begin with 0,1 written in a column as:

0
1

Then reflect the 0 and 1 by writing its mirror image under it, that is, in reverse sequence, to obtain:

0
1
1
0

Prefix the forward sequence with 0's and the reflected (reverse) sequence with 1's to obtain:

00
01
11
10

With this as the forward sequence reflect it by writing the reverse sequence under it to obtain:

00
01
11
10
10
11
01
00

Prefix the forward sequence with 0's and the reflected (reverse) sequence with 1's to obtain:

000
001
011
010
110
111
101
100

This process may be continued indefinitely. To obtain the table of equivalences, simply number the gray code sequence with binary numbers. To construct an (n + 1)-bit gray code from an n-bit gray code write the n-bit sequence forward and then in reverse (reflected). Prefix the forward sequence with 0's and the reverse sequence with 1's. Synonymous with *cyclic binary unit-distance code; reflected binary unit distance code; CP code.* Also see *unit distance code.* See Figure G-4.

DECIMAL	PURE BINARY	GRAY CODE
0	0 0 0 0	0 0 0 0
1	0 0 0 1	0 0 0 1
2	0 0 1 0	0 0 1 1
3	0 0 1 1	0 0 1 0
4	0 1 0 0	0 1 1 0
5	0 1 0 1	0 1 1 1
6	0 1 1 0	0 1 0 1
7	0 1 1 1	0 1 0 0
8	1 0 0 0	1 1 0 0
9	1 0 0 1	1 1 0 1

G-4. The **gray code** equivalent to *decimal* and pure *binary numbers.*

gray scale. Discrete *light intensity* levels between zero and a maximum level, usually when referring to *diffused light* from a rough or frosted surface. It is not a measure of intensity, but more a measure of the proportionate distribution of black spots on a white surface or white spots on a black surface. For example, in *facsimile systems,* the scale is made in *discrete* steps between all white and all black by introducing an array of small black dots on a white area and increasing their size until they cover all the area. No dot is white. The dot density is increased by increasing their size rather than their number until the area is black.

grazing emergence. In *optics,* a condition in which an *emergent ray* makes an angle of 90° to the normal of the emergent surface of a *transmission medium.* Also see *emergence; normal emergence.*

grazing incidence. Pertaining to *light rays incident* at 90° to the normal to the incident surface. Also see *normal incidence.*

great circle. A circle on the surface of a sphere, the plane of which passes through the center of the sphere. It has the same radius and center as the sphere itself. It is the intersection of a plane that passes through the center of the sphere with the surface of the sphere. A great circle is the shortest surface distance between two points on a sphere. The term is used for earth measurements as though the earth were a sphere rather than a spheroid. All lines of longitude are great circles, but of the lines of latitude, only the equator is a great circle. The true *bearing* of one point from another is the angle between true north and the great circle passing through the points and measured at the observing point.

Greenwich mean time (GMT). The mean solar time at the meridian (longitude 0°) of Greenwich, England. It is used as a basis for standard time measurement and expression throughout the world. GMT is normally expressed in four *numerals* to the nearest minute from 0000 (midnight) to 2359. Synonymous with *Greenwich civil time; universal time.* Also see *coordinated time scale.*

Griffith microcrack model. A *microcrack model* for glass described by Griffith in which the crack is described by the relation:

$$s_t = s_f(1 - 2x/y)$$

where s_t is the ultimate tensile strength of the material, and s_f is the failure stress for a given crack of depth x and surface width y.

grip. See *basket grip.*

grooved fiber-alignment connector. An *optical fiber connector* that holds fibers in grooves cut in split blocks of material to assure proper alignment of fibers between the mating pair of the connector. The connector can be made of nearly any opaque plastic. Polyvinyl chloride and styrofoam are commonly used.

grooved waveguide. An *optical slab dielectric waveguide* for supporting and conducting *lightwaves* in certain *propagation modes* in narrow grooves (a few *microns* wide); particularly used in *integrated optical circuits.*

ground. A *conducting connection,* whether intentional or accidental, by which a point in an *electric circuit* is connected to the *earth* or to some conducting body of relatively large extent that can serve in place of the earth. The point may be connected to a single point that is common to many circuits, such as the frame or cabinet containing the electric circuits, and thus may serve as a return path or as a reference point for all the circuits. The ground *terminal* may be connected to the earth via a low resistance path or it may never be connected to the earth at all. If it is not connected to the earth it is said to be floating, as in the case of an automobile or perhaps a small power supply. Ideally, ground is a zero *resistance* (infinite *conductance*) path to a capacitor with an infinite *capacity.* It is usually considered to be at zero *absolute potential (voltage).* Also see *earth.* See *neutral ground.*

ground-air net. A *communication net* that is established for one-way communication from *earth stations* to *aircraft stations.*

ground-air visual emergency signal. 1. A pattern, figure, letter, or *graphic symbol* to which measning has been assigned and that can be used for *signaling.* It is usually formed by straight lines of contrasting material on the ground for ground-to-air signaling in an emergency. 2. A *symbol* made of straight lines of material that is used by survivors and search parties to send *coded messages* to aircraft. The symbol may be made of sticks, stones, trampled sod, footprints in sand, or any other material. 3. Any signal that can be used to attract attention in an emergency, such as a *panel,* a flare, smoke, *reflected light,* a *flag,* or a fire. For example, by prearrangement, a single straight line on the ground made with anything available might mean that medical attention is required; two parallel lines might mean food and water only.

ground clutter. A large distribution of *radar echoes* that extends a few miles in all directions from a *radar* site. They are caused by radar *signal reflections* from the earth's surface and fixed objects, such as buildings and trees. The pattern on a radar screen (planned position indicator (PPI) or A-scope) is approximately circular, is constant, and is near the origin of the *screen coordinates.*

ground communication emergency frequency. See *air-ground communication emergency frequency.*

ground communications. See *air-ground communications.*

ground constant. An *electric* or *magnetic* constant of the earth, such as *electrical conductivity, electric permittivity,* or *magnetic permeability.* The values of these *parameters* vary with the chemical composition of the earth, physical material distribution, and the *frequency* of the *signals.* They influence the *propagation* of *ground waves, surface waves,* and *evanescent waves.* Also see *constitutive relations.*

ground controlled approach (GCA) landing. The landing of an aircraft by a pilot who is given landing instructions by *radiotelephone* from a *ground station* that can determine the precise instantaneous position of the aircraft in relation to the landing strip, landing zone, or runway.

ground controlled approach (GCA) system. A ground *radar system* that provides *information* needed by pilots of aircraft as they approach a landing zone, landing strip, or runway. Information is *transmitted* to the pilot during approach by *radiotelephone, signals* from the *ground station* to the *aircraft station,* and by radar. The system is used to accomplish *ground controlled approach landing* with or without pilot visibility. Though it is usually accomplished by radar, radiotelephone, and signals from the ground station, some systems can also control the aircraft with a pilot override capability.

ground-link subsystem. See *space-ground-link subsystem.*

ground potential. The *absolute potential* of the earth, usually taken as a zero level of absolute potential. *Voltages (potential differences)* are usually indicated as relative to *ground potential.*

ground return. **1.** In *wire communication systems,* the *circuit* arrangement in which one line *conductor* is replaced by a *connection* to *earth* at each end of the other conductor. This forms a complete circuit consisting of one *insulated* conductor and a return path through the earth. This requires that the *transmitter output terminal* and the *receiver input terminal* must be connected to the earth or to a ground. **2.** In any *electrical system,* an arrangement of *power* and *signal* distribution in which all *return paths* for currents are via a common *bus,* such as a copper strip, a cabinet, a frame, a chassis of the instrument, or the *earth.* **3.** In *radar operations,* a *wave* or *echo* obtained by *reflection* from the ground, trees, buildings, or other objects fixed to the ground.

ground-return circuit. A *circuit* in which the *earth* serves as one *conductor* of a pair. Thus, the wire conductor may be considered as the *forward path* and the *ground* or *earth* as the *return path,* or vice versa. See Figure G-5.

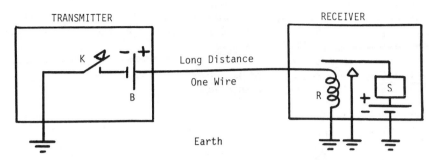

TRANSMITTER

RECEIVER

Long Distance

One Wire

Earth

G-5. Depressing *key* K will cause *local battery* B at the *telegraph transmitter* to send *current* through *relay* R to sounder S at the *telegraph receiver*. The current returns through the *ground* (earth) portion of the *ground-return circuit* to the transmitter.

ground segment. 1. In *satellite communications,* all of the *earth stations* in a satellite communication *system.* 2. In *electric circuits,* all the *ground return paths* in a set of ground return circuits. Also see *space segment.*

ground state. The lowest orbital kinetic and potential energy state that an *electron* of a given element can have. An electron *absorbs* a *quantum* of energy when it moves from the ground state to an *excited state.* Also see *excited state.*

ground-to-air communication. One-way *communication* from ground *stations* (fixed or mobile) to *aircraft stations.*

ground-to-air visual body signal. A *signal* formed by arm, leg, and body position and movement for sending *messages* from the ground to an aircraft. The signals can be used to direct the landing of aircraft, send *emergency messages,* indicate all is clear, or send other simple messages.

ground wave. An *electromagnetic wave* that *propagates* close to the earth, land or sea; is *coupled* to the earth; interacts with it; is *absorbed* by it; travels within it; and can emerge from it at certain distances from the *source.* Ground waves are usually heavily *attenuated,* although other *surface waves* are not. *Low-frequency* waves are propagated principally by surface waves, particularly ground waves, which do not depend on *ionospheric reflection.* The *frequency* of *light-waves* is too high to function as surface waves such as ground waves. A *radio wave* that is *propagated* just above the earth's surface is often locked to, and affected by the presence of, the ground. It is affected by changes in the *electric conductivity, electric permittivity,* and *magnetic permeability* of the ground and the lower *atmosphere.*

ground worldwide communication system. See *air-ground worldwide communication system.*

group. See *address group; address indicating group (AIG); channel basic group; channel group; check group; cipher group; closed user group; code group; col-*

lective address group; conjunctive address group; date-time group; detectable group; digital transmission group; dummy group; end-of-transmission group; graphic address group; high-usage trunk group; international address indicating group; jumbo group; national address indicating group; peer group; phantom group; signal group; synchronized transmitter group; supergroup; through group; true date-time group (TDTG); trunk group.

group abbreviated address calling. In *telephone operations,* the establishment of a *connection* to a group of destinations, *stations,* or *addressees* by using a single *abbreviated address.*

group allocation. See *address group allocation; address indicating group allocation.*

group busy hour (GBH). The *busy hour* of a given *trunk group.* Also see *network busy hour; switch busy hour; traffic load.*

group congestion signal. See *national circuit group congestion signal.*

group delay. In the *propagation* of an *electromagnetic wave* consisting of several *frequencies* in a *dispersive medium,* the difference in *transmission* time between the highest and lowest frequency *components* in the wave. For a wave with a certain frequency, in a group of waves of different frequency, it is the first derivative with respect to frequency of the *phase shift* between two given points. In a transmission system where phase shift is proportional to frequency, the group delay is constant. Also see *distortion; delay equalizer; group delay frequency distortion; phase-frequency equalizer.*

group-delay distortion. In the *propagation* of a *signal,* the *distortion* that is caused by the *transmission medium* due to the difference in *propagation* velocity (and hence propagation time) among the different *frequencies* that comprise the signal. Thus, the resulting *dispersion* will make the shape of the received signal be different from that of the dispatched signal. The result is a spreading of the signal during transmission in the medium, as different parts of the signal arrive in a time sequence relatively different from the sequence in which they were dispatched. One method of compensating for group delay distortion is to require the different frequencies to travel a different path length. This method of compensation can be readily accomplished in *optical fibers* and *integrated optical circuits.*

group-delay frequency distortion. An undesired variation of the rate of change with respect to *frequency* (first derivative with respect to frequency) of the difference in *phase angle* between a *sinusoidal* excitation and the *fundamental frequency component* of the received *signal.* It is a combination of group delay distortion and *frequency distortion* caused by undesired frequency and phase shift variations between the carrier and its *modulating waves.*

group-delay spread. See *multimode group-delay spread.*

group delay time.   The time interval that is required for the crest of a group of *waves* to travel through a device or *transmission facility* in which the component wave *trains* have different individual frequencies. Any other *significant instant* may be chosen rather than the crest. Thus, there is a rate of change of the total *phase shift* with angular velocity through a device or transmisison facility. If the phase shift is an angle, θ, and the *angular velocity* is ω, the group delay time is expressed as $\Delta\theta/\Delta\omega$, or $d\theta/d\omega$, which has the units of time (seconds); θ is normally expressed in radians and ω in radians/second. The angular velocity is given as $\omega = 2\pi f$, where f is the frequency. The changes are taken over the length of the *transmission medium.*

group distribution frame (GDF).   In *frequency-division multiplexing,* a *distribution frame* that provides (1) *terminating* and *connecting facilities* for the *modulator output* and *demodulator input circuits* of the *channel* transmitting equipment, and (2) modulator input and demodulator output circuits for the group *translating* equipment.   Equipment may operate in the *basic spectrum* of 60 kHz to 108 kHz. See *supergroup distribution frame.*

group equipment.   See *through-group equipment.*

grouping.   In *facsimile systems,* a periodic *error* in the *spacing* of *recorded lines.* See *line grouping.*

group-one document facsimile equipment.   Document *facsimile* equipment in which *double sideband modulation* is used without *signal frequency compression,* and that is suitable for the *transmission* of *International Organization for Standardization (ISO)* Size A4 documents at a nominal 4 lines per millimeter in about 6 minutes via a *telephone channel.* Equipment in this group may be designed to operate at a lower *definition* (resolution) that is suitable for the transmission of documents of this size in from 3 to 6 minutes. Synonymous with *group-one document facsimile telegraph apparatus.*

group-one document facsimile telegraph apparatus.   See *group-one document facsimile equipment.*

group patch bay.   A *patch bay* that is used specifically for a group of *circuits,* such as a number of *basic groups, mastergroups,* or *jumbogroups.*

group selector.   In an *automatic telephone exchange,* a *selector* that, in response to an appropriate *control signal (character),* connects one *input path* to one of a number of *output paths.* A group selector may be more specifically designated as a *code, tandem, numeral,* or final selector.

group-three document facsimile equipment.   Document *facsimile* equipment in which redundant *signals* are reduced before *modulation* so as to obtain a *transmission* time of about 1 minute or less for a typical *International Organization for Standardization (ISO)* Size A4 document via a telephone channel. The equipment may make use of *signal frequency compression.* Synonymous with *group-three document facsimile telegraph apparatus.*

group-three document facsimile telegraph apparatus.   See *group-three document facsimile equipment.*

group-two document facsimile equipment.   Document *facsimile* equipment in which *signal frequency compression* is used in order to obtain a *transmission time* of about 1 to 3 minutes for the transmission of an *International Organization for Standardization (ISO)* Size A4 document at a nominal 4 lines per millimeter via a *telephone channel.* Signal frequency compression includes *encoding* and *vestigial sideband transmission.*   Synonymous with *group-two document facsimile telegraph apparatus.* See Figure G-6.

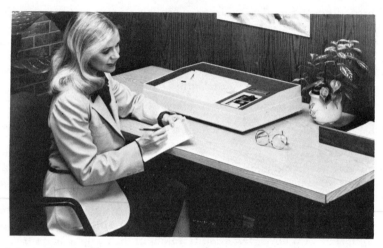

G-6. A *facsimile transceiver* that has two-minute *transmission* of 8 1/2 x 11 inch document capability and compatibility with *CCITT* standard group one and **group-two document facsimile equipment.** (Courtesy of 3M Business Communication Products Division.)

group-two document facsimile telegraph apparatus.   See *group-two document facsimile equipment.*

group velocity.   The velocity of *propagation* of the *envelope* produced when an *electromagnetic wave* is *modulated* by (i.e., mixed with) another wave of slightly different *frequency.*   The group velocity is the velocity of information propagation and, loosely, of energy propagation. It is the velocity of *transmission* of energy associated with a progressing wave consisting of a group of *sinusoidal components;* i.e., the velocity of a certain feature of the wave envelope, e.g., the crest. The group velocity differs from the *phase velocity.* Only the latter varies with frequency. In general, the group velocity, represented as:

$$v_g = d\omega/d\beta$$

is less than the phase velocity, represented as:

$$v_p = \omega/\beta$$

where ω is the *carrier angular velocity*, and $d\omega$ is the signal angular velocity. β is the phase change coefficient at the *carrier* frequency. βL is the carrier *phase delay* for a line *L meters* long. The angular velocity is $2\pi f$, where f is the frequency. In *nondispersive* media, the group velocity and the phase velocity are equal. Also see *phase velocity.*

group with outgoing access. See *closed user group with outgoing access.*

growth. See *epitaxial growth.*

G/T. *Gain/noise-temperature.* See *antenna gain-to-noise temperature (G/T).*

guard. In *radio, radar,* and *sonar communication systems,* to maintain a continuous *receiver watch* with *transmitter* ready for immediate use. Usually a complete *radio log* is kept. The radio listening watch may be maintained on one or more *frequencies* thereby maintaining radio contact with specifid *fixed* or *mobile* stations. See *primary guard; radio communication guard; radio guard.*

guard band. See *frequency guard band; time guard band.*

guarded frequency. A *transmission frequency* that is not to be *jammed* or interfered with because of the value of the *information* being derived from it. For example, a guarded frequency may be jammed when the potential operational gain is weighed against the loss of the tactical, strategic, and technical information that can be obtained. Also see *protected frequency; taboo frequency.*

guard ring. A specifically *doped* peripheral region designed to prevent leakage *currents* that cause gain saturation in surface-dominated *avalanche photodiodes (APD),* such as lattice-matched InGaAsP APDs. For example, the guard ring improves performance in the 1.0-to-1.3-*micron detection* range for 0.01-to-0.02-mm diameter APDs operating at less than 5 μA.

guard ship. A *ship station* that is designated to maintain any one of the various types of *receiver watches* on a definite *frequency* on behalf of another ship station. A complete *radio station log* is usually kept by the guard ship station.

guard station. See *primary guard station.*

guard time. In *time-division multiplexing (TDM)* and in *time-division multiple-access (TDMA) systems,* the time between the end of one *burst* of *signals* and the beginning of the next burst of signals.

guard watch. 1. A *radio communication watch* in which the *operator* is required to maintain a continuous *receiver watch.* Usually a complete *radio station log* is kept and the *transmitter* is kept ready for instant use. A guard watch may be any one of several types or may be a combination of several types. The guard watch is performed by a *guard station.* A *ship station* or a *land station* may be designated as a guard station. 2. In *communication networks* of any type, the *monitoring, copying,* and *relaying* of *calls* or *messages* that are intended for another *station.* A guard watch is not the only type of watch that may be performed by a guard station. Also see *copy watch; listening watch; radio communication cover; radio communication guard.*

guidance navigation system. See *terminal-guidance navigation system.*

guidance radar. *Radar* that is used to *track* an aircraft or a missile in order to obtain position *information* that is to be used with other position information to calculate *instructions* that are needed to steer the aircraft or missile from its present position to a desired fixed or moving position.

guidance system. A *system* that is designed and operated for the purpose of guiding an object, such as a spacecraft, missile, aircraft, ship, or land vehicle, from its present position to another specific position in space and time. See *homing guidance system; noninertial guidance system.*

guide. See *light guide; ultraviolet light guide; waveguide.*

guided missile control. The control of guided missiles through (1) the use of *communication* equipment (flight control); (2) the control of guided missile organizational elements (command control); and (3) the control of procurement, movement, receipt, storage, repair, maintenance, and salvage of guided missiles, missile systems, components, and repair and replacement parts (supply control).

guided mode. See *cladding-guided mode.*

guide edge. See *reference edge.*

gyro bearing. 1. A *bearing* or direction that is determined or measured by means of a gyrocompass. 2. The initial *bearing* or reference direction at which a gyrocompass is initially or originally set. 3. The mechanical bearings on which a gyrocompass rotates.

gyroscope. See *fiber gyroscope.*

H

Hagelbarger code. An efficient *burst-correcting binary code* that is used for *data transmission* through a *telephone network.*

half-adder. See *binary half-adder.*

half-baud coding. A modified *full-baud bipolar coding* process that consists of representing a 0 by a zero level *voltage* in the *bipolar sequence* of *pulses* and a 1 by alternate positive or negative pulses in the bipolar sequence. These pulses return to the zero level at the midpoint of the *baud,* that is, the midpoint of the *unit interval.* Bipolar coding *(half-baud)* is similar to full-baud bipolar coding except for the pulse levels returning to the zero voltage level at the midpoint of each baud. Bipolar coding has an inherent *error detection* capability because of the alternate polarity pulses. Also see *full-baud bipolar coding.*

half-duplex. See *two-frequency half-duplex.*

half-duplex circuit. 1. A *transmission path* or *circuit* capable of transmitting *data* or *information* in only one direction. 2. A *data circuit* capable of transmitting in either direction, i.e., one direction at a time. Also see *duplex circuit; push-to-talk operation; push-to-type operation.*

half-duplex equipment. Equipment that comprises a transmitting and receiving part that is arranged to allow for *transmission* in both directions but not simultaneously. Also see *duplex apparatus.*

half-duplex operation. 1. An operation that makes use of a *half-duplex circuit.* The operating method may employ a *circuit* that is designed for duplex operation but can only be operated alternately in each direction because of the limitations of the *terminal equipment.* 2. Pertaining to an alternate, one-way at a time *transmission mode* of operation. Synonymous with *one-way reversible operation; two-way alternate operation.*

half-duplex transmission. *Transmission* in either direction but only in one direction at a time. Also see *push-to-talk operation; push-to-type operation.*

half echo suppressor. *Telephone echo suppression* equipment in which *speech signals* in one *path* control suppression of *reflected waves (echoes)* in the other path, but the action is not reciprocal.

half-power point. Any point at which *power* is determined to be one-half of what it is at some other reference point in a given system or component. For example, at particular distances and directions from a *source* of *electromagnetic radiation,* a point at which the *power density* or *signal strength* squared is one-half of the maximum density at that distance but in some other direction; or when moving radially outward from the center of a narrow circular cross-section *beam,* the point at which the *luminous power density* is one-half of the power density at the center of the beam, regardless of the distance from the source at which the cross-section is taken.

half-power points.   See *emission-beam-angle-between-half-power-points.*

half-reflection.   The *reflection* that occurs at the *interface* between one *transmission medium* and another when half of the *optical power* of the *incident* wave is reflected and half is *transmitted.* A half-reflection *coupler* permits half of the *light* energy to be *coupled* out of an *optical fiber, bundle,* or *cable,* and half to be available for transmission beyond the coupler. The reflecting surface makes an angle of about 45° to the axis of the fiber or *fiber optic rod coupler.* Also see *fiber-optic rod coupler.*

halftone characteristic.   In *facsimile systems,* a relation between the *density* of the *recorded copy* (received) and the density of the *subject (object) copy* (transmitted document). It is the ratio of the facsimile *signal strength* to the density of the subject (object) copy or of the recoded copy when only a portion of the system is considered. In a *frequency-modulated facsimile system,* an appropriate *parameter,* such as the *frequency shift* value that corresponds to the *halftone* levels of copy density, may be used instead of the *amplitude* (strength) of the *facsimile signal.*

halftone picture.   A picture that has a range of tones or shades of gray that lie between the limits of *picture black* and *picture white.*

halfwave dipole antenna.   An *antenna* that is straight and is one-half *wavelength* long. It is center fed so as to have equal *current* distribution in both halves. When it is mounted vertically it produces a volumetric doughnut-shaped *radiation pattern* that is circular in the horizontal plane and double-*lobed* in a vertical plane through the antenna's long axis. It is an antenna that can be easily constructed and mounted. It has some inherent *losses.* When used as an *antenna gain* reference, the halfwave dipole antenna has a power gain of 0 dB. The ratio of the *power gain* referred to an *isotropic source (antenna)* and that referred to the standard halfwave dipole antenna is equivalent to 2.15 dB. Also see *dipole antenna.* See *lossless halfwave dipole antenna.*

halyard.   In *flaghoist signaling systems,* a rope, wire, or chain on which *signaling flags* or *pennants* are attached for hoisting up a pole or mast.

Hamming code.   A *digital data transmission code* that provides for multiple *error detection* and single *error correction.*

Hamming distance.   See *signal distance.*

hand-flag transmission.   The *transmission* of *messages* by means of one or two *flags* that are held in the *operator's* hands. The position or movement of the flags represent letters and *numerals.* For example, transmission by means of *semaphore, wig-wag,* and *Morse flag signaling.*

handshake. In *communication system* operation, a method of *error control* in which *data transmitted* over a *forward channel* are returned over a *backward channel* and checked with the stored data originally transmitted, usually on an immediate and continuous basis.

handshaking. An exchange of predetermined *characters* or *signals* between two *stations.* The exchange provides for control or *synchronism* after a *connection* is established, particularly during the *information transfer phase* of a *call.*

hangover. See *tailing.*

hard copy. A permanent copy of a *display image* that can be read directly by human beings or machines and that usually is easily or handily transported; e.g., a display image recorded on a piece of paper. Hard copy can be produced by direct contact of photographic film or paper on the ends of *optical fibers.* Contrast with *soft copy.*

hardening. See *fiber-optic nuclear hardening.*

hard limiter. See *limiter circuit.*

hard limiting. A *limiting* action with negligible variation in output in the range where the *amplitude, power,* or other characteristic of the *output signal* is limited (controlled) when there is a wide variation of *signal input* value.

hardness. See *limiter hardness.*

hardware. A *functional unit* consisting of physical equipment, as opposed to *computer programs* such as utility *routines, compilers, translators, procedures,* drawings, *instruction* manuals, or other *software.* Contrast with *firmware; software.* See *off-the-shelf hardware.*

hardware reliability. A measure of the ability of a product to continue to perform its intended function under either normal or adverse conditions. For example, the probability that a *system* will function without *failure* over a specified time period, that is, the probability that the system will not fail in the time from zero to time *t,* given the assumed *Poisson* model that the probability of failure, *P,* is given by $P = e^{-\lambda t}$ where λ is the constant component failure rate in parts per unit per second. Also see *software reliability.*

hardwire. 1. To permanently connect equipment or *components* in contrast to using *switches, plugs,* or *connectors.* 2. In a *computer, data processing, communication,* or other *electrical* or electronic *system,* the wiring of *fixed-logic* or *fixed storage* (fixed contents) that cannot be altered by *programmed* changes, that is, by *software.* Also see *firmware.*

harmful interference. Any *emission, radiation,* or *induction* that endangers the functioning or seriously degrades, obstructs, or repeatedly interrupts a *communication service,* such as a *radionavigation service,* a *search and rescue communication,* or a *weather service.* It is assumed that these services are operating in accordance with approved standards, regulations, and procedures. Harmful interference causes *circuit outages* and *message* losses, as opposed to interference that is merely a nuisance or annoyance that can be overcome by appropriate measures.   In order to be harmful interference it must seriously degrade the performance of the *communication, radar,* or other *electrical* or electronic *system.*

harmonic.   An integral multiple of a *fundamental frequency.* See *single harmonic.*

harmonic distortion.   The presence of *waves* of certain *frequencies* at the *output* of a device that are caused by nonlinearities within the device. The frequencies are usually *harmonics* of the single or multiple frequencies that are applied to the *input* of the device. The frequency of the first harmonic, that is, the *fundamental frequency,* is the input frequency when the input is a *periodic* function with a fundamental frequency, such as a pure *sine wave* or a square wave. See *modulation frequency harmonic distortion; single harmonic distortion; total harmonic distortion.*

harmonic function.   A mathematical function that can be used to describe the curves used to represent *waves,* whose *amplitudes* at particular constant intervals of time, distance, or other abscissa *parameters* have a specific constant value; e.g., a *sine wave.* Combinations of harmonic functions may also be harmonic functions, such as occurs in a *Fourier analysis.* The oscillations of the *electric* and *magnetic fields* in *plane-polarized electromagnetic waves* may be described by harmonic functions as well as exponential functions. See *sectorial harmonic function; spherical harmonic function; tesseral harmonic function; zonal harmonic function.*

harness.   See *feed harness; optical harness; vehicle harness.*

harness assembly.   See *optical harness assembly.*

harness run.   See *cable run.*

hartley.   A unit of logarithmic measure of *information content* that is equal to the *decision content* of a set of ten mutually exclusive events that are expressed as a logarithm to the base 10. For example, the decision content of a *character set* of 8 characters equals 0.903 hartley. It is obtained from $\log_{10} 8$. Synonymous with *decimal unit of information content.* Also see *decision content.*

hauled-down.   In *flaghoist communications,* the situation that exists when a *flaghoist* is returned (lowered) to the deck or ground. Usually the moment of hauling down is the moment of execution of the *instruction, command,* or order that was specified by the flaghoist when it was raised. Also see *at-the-dip; close-up; flaghoist.*

hazard.   See *electromagnetic radiation hazard; laser hazard; optical fiber hazard.*

hazards of electromagnetic radiation to fuel (HERF).   The exposure to *electromagnetic radiation* that may cause spark or electrical ignition of volatile combustible materials, such as aircraft fuels, hydrogen, propane, carbon monoxide, or other critical mixtures, including powders and dusts.

hazards of electromagnetic radiation to ordnance (HERO). The exposure to *electromagnetic radiation* that may cause spark or electrical detonation of explosives, such as munitions, *fuzes,* or blasting materials. For example, the premature actuation of electroexplosive devices by exposure to electromagnetic radiation such as is produced by *communication* and *radar transmitters.* Electromagnetic radiation can damage or trigger *solid-state circuits,* cause erratic readings in test sets, and set off electrical blasting caps, any of which may be part of a munitions detonating device. There is a high potential for munitions or electroexplosive devices to be adversely affected by electromagnetic radiation.

hazards of electromagnetic radiation to personnel (HERP). The exposure to *electromagnetic radiation* that may produce harmful biological effects in humans. Particular damage can occur to the retina of the eye and to abdominal tissue at *microwave frequencies* and above. *X-ray* and *gamma radiation* can destroy living tissue cells and cause genetic disorders.

HA1-Receiver weighting. A *noise weighting* that is used in a noise measuring set to measure *noise* across the HA1-Receiver of a 302-Type or similar instrument. The meter scale readings are in *dBa(HA1).*

HDLC. *High-level data link control.*

head. See *keying head; laser head; tape reading head.*

header part. In a *packet,* the part that contains the *information* that is required for the packet to be *routed* to its destination. The header part may consist of both user *overhead information* and *system overhead information.* Synonymous with *data part.*

heading. 1. The portion of a *message* that contains the *information* necessary to enable a *communication system* to deliver the message to the intended *destination user* (*addressee,* customer, subscriber) in a manner that is consistent with the desires of the *originator* of the message. For example, the desires of the originator may relate to *security, precedence,* and *transmission speed.* 2. The direction in which a ship, aircraft, or other mobile object is either pointed or moving with reference to a true, magnetic, compass, grid or other reference direction. Headings (courses, bearings) are usually given as true or *magnetic* headings unless otherwise specified. Synonymous with *course.* See *external heading; message heading; reciprocal heading; supplementary heading.* Also see *direction.*

heading character. See *start-of-heading (SOH) character.*

heading sense. One of the two opposite directions that are associated with a given *heading* (course, direction) as determined by a *direction-finding (DF) station* or stations. Unless otherwise stated, the *calling station,* that is the station that desires to know its heading, will assume that sense was determined by the DF station and therefore the proper forward heading is given in the response. Thus the 180° ambiguity has been removed. If the *mobile station* that is requesting the heading were to proceed in the direction of the bearing given by the DF station, it would arrive at the DF station. If two successive requests by a mobile station result in a determination of actual heading by a mobile station, the DF station will report the actual heading (course) being taken by the mobile station. In normal usage, heading is the direction in which an object is moving relative to a reference direction, whereas bearing is the direction from an object to another object relative to a reference direction. Both must be established in the proper sense in regard to the 180° ambiguity.

hearing threshold. In *audiometry,* the *sound* energy level below which a person with normal hearing capability cannot hear the sound. The *threshold amplitude* varies with *frequency.*

heating equipment. See *industrial RF heating equipment.*

Heaviside layer. See *E-layer.*

heavy seeding. Pertaining to a condition in an *optical transmission medium,* such as glass, in which the fine and coarse *seeds* are very numerous, such as 25 or more to the square inch.

hectometric wave. An *electromagnetic wave* that is in the *medium frequency (MF)* subdivision of the *frequency spectrum,* ranging from 300 to 3000 kHz. Also see *frequency spectrum designation.*

height. See *effective height; geostationary satellite height; synchronous height.*

height above average terrain. See *antenna height above average terrain.*

height finder. 1. A device, such as *radar,* that is located on the earth's surface and can measure the altitude of an object above the ground or above the site at which it is located. 2. A device, such as a *radar,* that is located in an aircraft, *satellite,* balloon, or other object and can measure its own height above the earth's surface, usually the height above the surface directly below it.

height gain. For a given *propagation mode* of an *electromagnetic wave,* the ratio of its *field strength* or *power density* at a specified height to that at the earth's surface.

height indicator. See *range-height indicator.*

helical polarization. See *left-hand helical polarization; right-hand helical polarization.*

heliograph. In *visual signaling systems,* a mirrored device for *signaling* by means of *reflected rays* of the sun.

helix. In *facsimile systems,* a rotating part that is used in *continuous receivers,* comprising a helicoidal rib, the intersection of which with the *scanning line,* defines the *position* of the *picture element* on this line at a given instant.

hellschreiber system. See *hell system.*

hell system. *Mosaic telegraphy* in which a *telegraph code* is used that represents each *character* by a fixed, unique number of unit elements. The received characters are formed with a rotating spiral that is continuously inked and that is brought into contact with a moving paper tape under the control of the unit elements. Synonymous with *hellschreiber system*.

Helmholtz equations. The set of equations that describe uniform plane *electromagnetic waves* in an unbounded loss-less (nonabsorptive) *source*-free *transmission medium* when (1) the *wave equations* are expressed in Cartesian (rectangular) coordinates, (2) the components of the *electric* and *magnetic fields* in the direction of *propagation* are identically equal to zero, and (3) the transverse first derivatives ($\partial/\partial x$ and $\partial/\partial y$ when the wave is propagating in the z-direction) are also identically zero; namely:

$$d^2 E_x/dz^2 - \gamma^2 E_x = 0 \qquad\qquad d^2 E_y/dz^2 - \gamma^2 E_y = 0$$

$$d^2 H_x/dz^2 - \gamma^2 H_x = 0 \qquad\qquad d^2 H_y/dz^2 - \gamma^2 H_y = 0$$

where E is the scalar electric field component and H is the scalar magnetic field component in the direction indicated by subscript, for a z-direction propagating wave. These equations specifically apply to propagation in *optical elements* under certain geometrical conditions. These equations are solutions of the vector Helmholtz equations:

$$\nabla^2 E - \gamma^2 E = 0 \qquad\qquad \nabla^2 H - \gamma^2 H = 0;$$

where γ^2 is a complex function equal to $-\omega^2 \mu\epsilon + j\omega\mu\sigma$, and the parameters are the angular velocity, *magnetic permeability*, *electric permittivity*, and the *electrical conductivity*, respectively.

HERF. *Hazards of electromagnetic radiation to fuel.*

HERO. *Hazards of electromagnetic radiation to ordnance.*

HERP. *Hazards of electromagnetic radiation to personnel.*

hertz. The unit of *frequency* equivalent to one cycle per second. It is the frequency of a *periodic* phenomenon of which the period is one second. It is the *Systeme International d'Unites (SI)* unit for frequency.

Hertzian wave. An *electromagnetic wave* that has a *frequency* that is lower than 3000 GHz and that is *propagated* in *free space* without a *waveguide*. Also see *radio wave*.

heterochronous. A relationship between two *signals* such that their corresponding *significant instants* do not necessarily occur at the same time. Thus, two *signals* that have different nominal *signaling rates* and do not stem from the same *clock* or from *homochronous* clocks, are usually heterochronous. Also see *anisochronous; homochronous; isochronous; mesochronous; plesiochronous*.

heterodyne. The process of combining two *electromagnetic waves* of different *frequency* in a nonlinear device in order to produce frequencies that are equal to the sum and difference of the combining frequencies.

heterodyne repeater. A *repeater* in which the received *signals* are *converted (translated)* to an *intermediate frequency, amplified,* and reconverted (retranslated) to a new frequency *band* for *transmission* over the next repeater section. Synonymous with *intermediate frequency (IF) repeater.* Also see *frequency frogging.*

heterodyne oscillator. See *beat frequency oscillator.*

heterodyning. The mixing of an *electromagnetic wave* of one *frequency* with a *wave* of another frequency to produce one or more additional frequencies. Usually the sum and difference frequencies will be produced when waves of two different frequencies are combined in a nonlinear device, such as a nonlinear *amplifier.*

heteroepitaxial optical waveguide. An *optical-wavelength electromagnetic waveguide* consisting of an optical-quality crystal *substrate* upon which are deposited one or more layers of substances with different *refractive indices.* The deposited layers have closely matched lattice structures and indices of refraction less than that of the substrate, so that the layers themselves do not act as ordinary *waveguides* with total *internal reflection. Optical propagation* of *leaky modes* does occur, with *attenuation* losses inversely proportional to the square of the *wavelength.* For example, the waveguide may be made of cubic zinc sulfide layered upon a calcium arsenide substrate; or zinc selenide on a gallium arsenide substrate.

heterogeneous computer systems. *Computer systems* with distinctive structural, *electrical,* operational, or other characteristic differences.

heterogeneous multiplexing. Multiplexing a *channel* in such a manner that the information-bearing channels resulting from the multiplexing do not all operate at the same *data-signaling rate.* Thus, it is multiplexing of channels in which some of the information-bearing channels operate at different data-signaling rates.

heterogeneous network. A *network* of dissimilar or incompatible components, such as *computers* of different manufacture, different *electrical* characteristics, or different mechanical features.

heterojunction. In a *laser diode,* a boundary surface at which a sudden transition occurs in material composition across the boundary. For example, in a *semiconductor,* a change in the *refractive index* as well as a change from a positively-doped (p) region to a negatively-doped (n) region; or a positively-doped region with a rapid change in doping level, i.e., a high concentration gradient of *dopant* versus distance. In most heterojunctions, change in geometric cross-section occurs across which a voltage or voltage barrier exists. Heterojunctions provide a controlled level and direction of *radiation* confinement. There usually is a step in the refractive index level at each heterojunction. See *double heterojunction; single heterojunction.* Contrast with *homojunction.*

heterojunction diode. See *double heterojunction diode; five-layer four-hetero-junction diode; four-heterojunction diode; monorail double-heterojunction diode.*

HF. *High frequency.*

HFDF. *High-frequency distribution frame. High-frequency direction-finding.*

hidden line. In *display systems* in which there is a two-dimensional projection of a three-dimensional *object* in the *display space* on the *display surface* of a *display device,* a representation of an object edge that is obscured by the object itself, or by another object, when the object is viewed. Hidden lines are used to represent the shape of the object. They are usually in a format different from that of edges that are not obscured by the object when it is being viewed. Usually, hidden lines are represented as a sequence of short line segments. Edges of an object occur at abrupt or discontinuous changes in surface direction, such as at intersections of surfaces, or occur as boundaries or perimeters of images of objects.

hierarchical computer network. A *computer network* in which *processing* and control functions are performed at several *layers* (levels) by *computers* that are specially suited for performing such application-oriented functions as *communication network* control, industrial process control, inventory control, *data base* control, or hospital automation.

hierarchically synchronized network. A *mutually synchronized network* in which some of the *clocks* exert more control than others. The *network operating frequency* becomes the weighted mean of the frequencies of the population of clocks in the network. Also see *democratically synchronized network; despotically synchronized network; oligarchically synchronized network.*

hierarchical network. A *network* in which processing and control functions are performed at several *layers* by *computers* that are specially designed to perform the functions at each layer.

hierarchical structure. A system configuration in which groups of elements (components) that form a class are *layered* above or below other groups of elements (components) in a laminar fashion. For example, the hierarchical structure in the *open systems architecture* concept of a layered system, or the hierarchical structure in a *tree network.*

high frequency (HF). **1.** A *frequency* that lies in the range from 3 MHz to 30 MHz. The *alphabetic* designator of the range is HF. The *numeric* designator of the range is 7. **2.** Generally, a *radio, radar,* or *video frequency* that is above 3 MHz. Also see *frequency spectrum designation.* See *extremely high frequency (EHF); lowest usable frequency (LUF); lowest useful high frequency (LUF); superhigh frequency (SHF); tremendously high frequency (THF); ultrahigh frequency (UHF); very high frequency (VHF).*

high-frequency distribution frame (HFDF). A *distribution frame* that provides *terminating* and interconnecting *facilities* for the combined *supergroup modulator output* and the combined supergroup *demodulator input circuits* that occupy the *baseband spectrum* from 12 kHz to 2540 kHz.

high-frequency omnidirectional radio range. See *very-high frequency omnidirectional radio range.*

high-frequency radio. A *radio* in which *electromagnetic waves* at *frequencies* above 3 MHz are used for *communication* purposes. The higher frequencies are used to obtain greater *propagation* distances than the lower frequencies, usually by *ionospheric reflection.* Synonymous with *shortwave radio.*

high-gain antenna. An *antenna* with an antenna *power gain* that is achieved by confining its *radiated* power to a smaller solid angle than is obtained in other antennas. Also see *directive gain.*

high-grade cryptographic system. See *high-grade cryptosystem.*

high-grade cryptosystem. A *cryptosystem* that is designed to provide long-lasting *security,* that is, a cryptosystem that is inherently resistant to solution for a comparatively longer period of time than lower grade cryptosystems. It is a system in which security lasts almost indefinitely, that is, infinitely long.

high-level control. In *data transmission,* the level of *processing* or *control functions* that exists in the *hierarchical structure* of a *communication station* or *network* and that is above the *data link layer* (level). It is a level upon which the performance of data link layer (level) functions, such as device control, *buffer* control, buffer allocation, and *station* management, depend. In the *open systems architecture* concept of a communication network, the high levels are considered to be the *application, presentation, session, transport,* and *network layers;* whereas the *data link* and *physical layers* are considered to be the low levels. Also see *high-level data link control (HDLC); low-level control.*

high-level data link control (HDLC). The *high level control* that may be applied to a *data link.* The level of control is above the data link layer (level). Also see *high-level control.*

high-level digital interface. An *interface* between two sets of *station* equipment, such as between *data terminal equipment* and *data circuit-terminating equipment,* that is designed to operate at relatively high *electrical voltages* and *currents.* For example, interface equipment that operates at 60 V and 20 mA, or at 130 V and 20 or 60 mA, direct current (DC).

high-level language. 1. A *computer programming language* that neither reflects nor depends upon the structure of any one class of *computers* or any one computer. **2.** A *computer programming language* in which a notation scheme is used that is convenient and readily understood by a *user* (programmer) and is independent of the *computer* that will execute *programs* written in the language.

high-level protocol (HLP). A rule or procedure that is used in a *computer distributed network* to direct or control its *communication* and *data processing* resources for the purpose of accomplishing assigned tasks. Particular emphasis is placed on directing the computing and data processing operations in the system.

highlighting. In *display systems,* any method or scheme for emphasizing a specific *display element, display group,* or *display image* in the *display space* on the *display surface* of a *display device;* for example, by thickening lines, increasing luminous intensity above normal, increasing background intensity, converting from light-on-a-dark background to dark-on-a-light background, underscoring, surrounding with a halo, or causing the element, group, or image to *blink* regularly.

high-loss fiber. An *optical fiber* having a high energy *loss* per unit length of fiber, usually measured in *decibels*/kilometer at a specified *wavelength.* High-loss is usually considered to be above 100 dB/km *attenuation* in *amplitude* of a *propagating wave.* The attenuation is caused primarily by *scattering* due to metal ions and by *absorption* due to water in the OH radical form, although all causes of loss are included when rating a given fiber, including *Rayleigh scattering.*

highly-reflective coating. A broad class of single or multilayer coatings that are applied to an *optical* surface for the purpose of increasing its *reflectance* over a specified range of *wavelengths.* Single films of aluminum or silver are common, but multilayers of at least two *dielectrics* are utilized when low *absorption* is imperative. Other parameters, such as *incidence angle* and *radiant intensity,* are also significant.

high-pass filter. A device that passes all *frequencies* above a specified value and removes, blocks, rejects, *absorbs,* or *attenuates* all other frequencies of *electrical currents* or *electromagnetic waves.* Also see *band-pass filter; low-pass filter.*

high-performance communication equipment. *Communication* equipment that has sufficiently exacting characteristics to permit use in *trunks, links,* or *circuits;* that is designed primarily for use in global and tactical applications in which maximum performance capabilities are required under abnormal conditions; and that is relatively immune to *electromagnetic interference.* Requirements for global and tactical equipment are dependent upon the specific applications.

high-probability-of-intercept receiver. A *receiver* that has a high probability of *detecting* any *electromagnetic* energy that *illuminates* its *antenna* within the *frequency range* that it is designed to cover. Also see *low-probability-of-intercept receiver.*

high selectivity. In *communications systems,* such as *wavelength-division multiplexed lightwave communication systems* using *optical fibers,* the ability to select, separate, and amplify wanted *signals* and reject unwanted energy such as *crosstalk, noise,* and *interference.*

high sensitivity. The capability of electronic equipment to accept weak *incident signals* and render them useful.

high-speed Morse. The *international Morse code transmitted* at speeds that are over 80 *words* per minute. High-speed Morse should be used only when time is critical, such as during search and rescue operations or military situations, and when the higher probability of *errors* in transmission, reception, and interpretation has been considered.

high-technology office. See *office automation.*

high-usage trunk group. A group of *trunks* for which an alternate *route* has been provided in order to absorb the relatively high volume of overflow *traffic* whenever it occurs.

highway. 1. A *bus* that is capable of carrying a *digital serial-coded bit stream* with *time slots* allotted to each *call* on a sequential basis. 2. A common *path*, or a set of parallel paths, over which *signals* from many *channels* can pass. Separation of *calls* and *messages* is achieved by *time-division multiplexing.* Also see *bus.*

hit. 1. In *data transmission*, a *transient disturbance* that affects a *transmission medium.* 2. In *data processing*, the situation that occurs when specified conditions are met, such as when two items of *data* are being compared and they are identical. See *amplitude hit; phase hit.*

HLP. *High-level protocol.*

Hocquenghem code. See *Bose-Chaudhuri-Hocquenghem (BCH) code.*

Hogg-horn antenna. An *earth station antenna* that has a somewhat higher *antenna* efficiency and lower *noise* pick-up than a *prime focus feed antenna* or a *cassegrain antenna.* It is relatively bulky and expensive.

hold. See *call hold; mark hold; space hold.*

holding. See *line holding.*

holding time. 1. The total length of time that a *trunk* or *channel* is occupied by a *call.* For example, the elapsed time that a *telephone call* occupies equipment, measured from the time a demand for service is initiated until the restoration of an *idle line condition.* Holding time is usually measured in *call-seconds.* 2. The time of a *telephone call hold.*

hold mode. The operating *mode* of an *analog computer* during which *integration* is stopped and all variables are held at the value that they had when the mode was entered.

hold unit. See *track-and-hold unit.*

hole. In a *semiconducting* material containing a *dopant* that has one less *electron* for each atom than that required to complete the intrinsic bonding structure, a site at which an electron is missing to complete the bonding structure. Initially, the hole is created by the impurity atoms, but if an electron from a neighboring atom moves in to "fill" the hole, the neighboring atom will have a hole; thus, the hole can be considered to have migrated. Also see *acceptor; donor.*

Hollerith code. A set of hole patterns punched in a card and corresponding to a set of *alphanumeric characters,* usually the 26 letters of the English *alphabet,* the set of ten *decimal digits,* and a set of punctuation marks and special signs and symbols, such as the dollar sign, hyphen, comma, period, and question mark. Each specific pattern of holes is placed in a column on the card, each column corresponding to a character. The original Hollerith code-hole pattern was designed for the widely used 80-column, 12-row *punched card.* The columns on the card are numbered consecutively 1 through 80 from left to right. The rows are labeled X, Y, and 0 through 9 from top to bottom. For example, letters are represented on the card by a hole in the X, Y, or 0 row and also in one of the numbered rows 1 through 9, both holes being in the same column for one letter. The decimal digits are represented by a single hole in the row that corresponds to the digit. Other special combinations of two and three holes are used to represent other signs and symbols. The card has 960 punch positions, and, therefore, a capability to represent 2^{960} (approximately 10^{280}) different patterns. If every different pattern were to be placed on a different card there would not be enough material matter in the known universe to make the 10^{280} cards that would be required. Avogadro's number is only 6.03×10^{23}. The potential of the 80 column card to represent *data* is not nearly used. Also see *punch card.*

hologram. An in-depth apparent three-dimensional *image* with great realism produced by *illuminating* an *object* field with two interrelated *coherent light beams,* one directly from a *light source* and the other slightly delayed, thus giving the three-dimensional appearance. The image can be recorded and recreated using similar techniques. Damage to a spot on the holographic film results only in a slight reduction in *resolution* or *brightness,* not a loss of a *picture element.* A *scanning* technique permits recording on film, which can later be recovered and displayed. The recording is not intelligible without reversing the holographic process.

home optical transceiver. An *optical fiber photodetector-transmitter* and *transmitter-light-source* in the home that transmits *lightwave signals* to, and receives lightwave signals from, an *optical fiber distribution box,* via optical fibers. Synonymous with *home optical transmitter-receiver.*

home optical transmitter-receiver. See *home optical transceiver.*

homer. A *homing station* that serves as a *radionavigation aid* by making use of *direction-finding* equipment.

homing. **1.** A process in which a *mobile station* is directed (or directs itself) toward an *electromagnetic,* thermal, sonic, or other source of energy, whether primary or reflected, or follows a *vector* force field or a gradient of a scalar force field.   **2.** In *radio direction finding,* the locating of a moving *signal source* by a moving direction-finding *station* that has a mobile advantage.   **3.** The act of approaching a *source* of *electromagnetic radiation* in which the approaching vehicle is guided by a *receiver* with a *directional antenna.*   **4.** Seeking, finding, intercepting, and engaging an object (target), fixed or mobile, that may or may not contain a *signal source.*   See *active homing; dual homing; multiple homing; request homing; semiactive homing; split homing.*

homing adapter.   A device that can produce *audio* or *visual signals* and indicate the direction of a *transmitting radio station* with respect to the *heading* or orientation of the device.   For example, a device used with an aircraft radio receiver to indicate the direction from which received *signals* are coming with respect to the heading or with respect to the frame of the aircraft.

homing beacon.   See *radio beacon.*

homing guidance system.   A *guidance system* that is based on the use of a device that seeks a *source* of energy, such as an *electromagnetic radiation source* or an *acoustic (sound) source.*   *Infrared sources* are included as well as *illuminated reflecting sources.*

homing procedure.   A *procedure* that is used to accomplish a rendezvous of *stations* at least one of which is *mobile.*   For example, procedures that are used to enable an aircraft to reach a ship.   The ship might use *radar* to determine the position of the aircraft and then issue *heading instructions* to the aircraft, or the aircraft might head in the direttion of signals being received from the ship.   Homing procedures make use of *radio, radar, beacon,* and other specialized *direction-finding (DF)* equipment.   Types of homing procedures include those in which (1) the relatively *fixed station (ship station* or *land station)* to be homed on by a relatively *mobile station (aircraft station* or *land vehicle station) transmits* a scheduled *signal* the direction of which can be determined by the mobile station for homing purposes, this procedure being nearly always used for aircraft stations to home on ship stations or land stations; (2) the mobile station transmits a signal and the relatively fixed station obtains a bearing of the signal and transmits the proper bearing (course, heading) for the mobile station to arrive at the fixed station or at some other predetermined location; and (3) a station to be homed on simply transmits a signal, such as a beacon signal or its *call sign,* and any mobile station desiring to home on it or obtain a bearing on it may do so with appropriate direction-finding equipment.

homochronous.   The relationship between two *signals* such that their corresponding *significant instants* are displaced by an interval of time that remains constant.   Also see *anisochronous; heterochronous; isochronous; mesochronous; plesiochronous; synchronous system.*

homogeneous computer systems.   *Computer systems* that have similar *architecture* or *layering* in order that similar layers can be readily or routinely interconnected or interrelated.

homogeneous medium.   In *optical systems,* a *transmission medium* whose *light-transmission parameters,* such as the parameters of the *constitutive relations,* are spatially constant and not a function of space coordinates, although they may vary as a function of time, *temperature,* pressure, humidity, or other parameter uniformly throughout the medium.

homogeneous multiplexed circuit.   A *multiplexed circuit* in which all the *information channels* operate at the same *data signaling rate.*

homogeneous multiplexing.   *Multiplexing* in which all of the *information bearing channels* in a *communication system* operate at the same *data signaling rate.*

homogeneous network.   A *network* of similar or *compatible computers,* such as computers of one model manufactured by a given manufacturer.

homojunction.   In a *laser diode,* a single junction; i.e., a single region of shift in *doping* from positive to negative majority *carrier* regions, or vice versa, and a change in *refractive index,* at one boundary, and hence one energy-level shift, one barrier, and one refractive-index shift. Contrast with *heterojunction.*

hook.   See *off-hook; verified off-hook.*

hook service.   See *off-hook service.*

hook signal.   See *off-hook signal.*

hop.   One excursion of a *radio wave* from the earth to the *ionosphere* and back. The number of hops indicates the number of *reflections* from the ionosphere. Also see *skip distance; skip zone.*

hopper.   See *frequency hopper.*

hopping.   See *frequency hopping; time hopping.*

horizon.   See *radar horizon; radio horizon.*

horizon angle.   For an antenna, the angle, in a vertical plane, that lies between a horizontal line extending from the center of the antenna and a line extending from the same point to the radio horizon. A horizontal line is a line that is tangent to the earth's average surface, which is the same as a line that is perpendicular to a vertical line. The horizon angle is usually an angle of depression, since the radio horizon is usually lower than the antenna, particularly for antennas that are on ship's masts, aboard aircraft, or on towers or mountains.

horizon range.   See *radio horizon range (RHR).*

horizon cover.   The horizontal angle (azimuth) that an electromagnetic wave source (emitter, antenna) is capable of scanning or illuminating. Also see *vertical cover.*

horizontally-polarized electromagnetic wave.   A *uniform plane-polarized electromagnetic wave* in which the *electric field vector* is always and everywhere horizontal while *propagating* in space or in a *transmission medium;* e.g., a *lightwave* or *radio wave.* The *magnetic field vector* may be inclined at any angle of *elevation* to the horizontal plane. If it is vertical, the wave will be propagated horizontally. If the magnetic field vector is horizontal, the wave will be propagated vertically; if inclined at 45°, the propagation will be at 45°, to the horizontal, all depending on the *antenna* configuration or the time *phasing* of the electric and magnetic fields. Thus, if the wave is propagating vertically, the magnetic field will be horizontal. If the wave is propagating horizontally, the magnetic field will be vertical. However, in any case, the electric field must be horizontal regardless of the direction of the magnetic field or the direction of propagation. Also see *vertically-polarized electromagnetic wave.*

horizontal polarization.   See *fixed horizontal polarization.*

horizontal tabulation character.   A format effector that causes the print position or the display position on a printer to move forward to the next of a series of predetermined positions along the same line. The next predetermined position is normally more than one character space away when the horizontal tabulation character is used. If the next position is only one space away, the space character may be used. Also see *space character.*

horizontal terminating block.   In a *switching center,* a group of *electrical terminals* at which contact can be made with *inside plant equipment.* Also see *combined distribution frame.*

horn.   See *scalar feed horn.*

horn antenna.   An *antenna* that has the shape of a tube with a cross-sectional area that increases toward the open end and through which *radio waves* may pass. Horn antennas may be large *earth station* antennas, small *radio link* antennas, or *electrically* and *mechanically despun antennas.*

horn feed system.   See *five-horn feed system; four-horn feed system.*

horn gap switch.   A *switch* that is provided with arcing horns and that is used for breaking the *electrical* charging *current* when disconnecting overhead *transmission power* distribution *lines.*

horse.   See *Trojan horse.*

host.   In a *packet switching network,* the collection of *hardware* and *software* that makes use of *packet switching* to support *user-to-user* (end-to-end) *communication,* interprocess communication, *distributed data processing,* and other user services.

host computer.   A *computer* at a *node* in a *network* that provides *application program* direct support functions, such as computation, *data base access,* utility programs, and *programming languages.* Synonymous with *host processor.*

host computer interface.   The *interface* between a *host computer* and a *network.* It may be a *front-end computer.*

host interface. The *interface* between a *data processing network* and a *host computer* or a host processor. It may be a *front-end computer* or a *communication computer.*

host node. In a *user application network,* a *node* at which the *host computer* or host processor that controls a *domain* is located.

hot bend test. In an *optical fiber, bundle,* or *cable,* a test to discover the effect on *parameters,* such as *attenuation, dispersion,* and particularly breaking point, during and after repeated alternate bend flexure at elevated *temperatures.*

hot-line circuit. See *switched hot-line circuit.*

hour. See *busy hour; connections per circuit-hour (CCH); group busy hour (GBH); network busy hour (NBH); switch busy hour; year worst hour.*

housekeeping information. See *service information.*

housekeeping signal. See *service signal.*

housing. See *laser protective housing.*

hundred-call-seconds (CCS). A unit of communication traffic or system utilization equal to 100 *call-seconds.* Also see *hundred-circuit-hours (cch).*

hundred-circuit-hours (cch). A unit of measure of the use or time of a *communication circuit* or group of circuits. For example, if 6 circuits are in use for 168 hours, the total usage would be 1008 circuit-hours. This would be equivalent to 10.08 cch. The cch could be used to specify total *outage,* loss due to *preventive maintenance,* or other types of circuit time. In cch, the initial c is the Roman *numeral* for 100. Also see *hundred-call-seconds (CCS).*

hunting. 1. In *automatic switching systems,* pertaining to the *operation* of a selector or similar device that is engaged in finding and establishing a *connection* with a given or prescribed *circuit* in a given group of circuits. 2. Pertaining to the *failure* of a device to achieve a state of equilibrium, usually by alternately overshooting or undershooting the point of equilibrium or some other desired or prescribed point. 3. The process of seeking and finding a specified state that involves some oscillation about a specified position or operating condition. Hunting ceases when equilibrium is reached and oscillation about an operating point ceases.

hybrid. In *electrical, electronic,* or *communication systems,* a device, *circuit,* apparatus, or system that consists of two or more *components,* each of which is normally used in a different application and not usually combined to meet a particular requirement. For example, a hybrid may be an electronic circuit that has both vacuum tubes and *transistors;* a mixture of *thin-film semiconductor integrated circuits* with circuits with *discrete* lumped circuit elements; a *computer* that has both an *analog* and a *digital* capability; or a *transformer* or combination of transformers, *resistors,* and *gates* affording *paths* to three branches (circuits)

A, B, and C, but connected in such a manner that A can send signals to C, B can receive signals from C, but A and B are isolated from each other.

hybrid balance. A measure of the degree of balance between two *impedances* that are connected to the two conjugate sides of a *hybrid set*. It is given by the formula for *return loss.*

hybrid coil. A single *transformer* that has three windings and is designed to be connected to four branches of a *circuit* so as to make them conjugate pairs. Synonymous with *bridge transformer.*

hybrid communication network. A *communication system* in which a combination of *trunks, loops,* or *links* are used, some of which are capable of *transmitting* and *receiving* only *analog* or *quasianalog signals* and some of which are capable of transmitting and receiving only *digital signals.*

hybrid communication system. A *communication system* that can accommodate both *digital* and *analog signals.*

hybrid optical fiber circuit. An interconnection of *optical fibers* (for transmission) and *integrated optical circuits* (for decision and control operations).

hybrid ranging. In *spread spectrum systems,* a ranging *(radar)* method in which short *code* sequences are combined with a constant *frequency synchronous* tone to give faster acquisition of objects (targets) than is obtainable with longer sequences but longer range than is obtainable with short sequences alone. *Spread spectrum* techniques are employed in *communication* and *radar systems* in order to provide some *security* and to provide some *antijamming* capability.

hybrid set. Two or more *transformers* that are interconnected to form a *network* that has four pairs of accessible *terminals* to which four *impedances* may be connected so that the branches containing them may be made interchangeable. Also see *four-wire terminating set.*

hydrographic information. *Information* that concerns hydrography, which deals with the measurement and description of the physical features of the oceans, seas, lakes, rivers, and their coastal areas. Particular reference is made to their development and use for navigation purposes.

hydrographic message. A serially-numbered *broadcasted message* that contains navigational and hydrographic *information.* Synonymous with *hydrolant.*

hydrolant. See *hydrographic message.*

hydrological and meteorological fixed station. A *fixed station* used for the *automatic transmission* of either hydrological or meteorological *data,* or both.

hydrological and meteorological land station. A *land station* used for the *automatic transmission* of either hydrological or meteorological data, or both.

hydrological and meteorological mobile station. A *mobile station* used for the *automatic transmission* of either hydrological or meteorological data, or both.

hydroxyl ion absorption. The *absorption* of *electromagnetic waves,* particularly *lightwaves,* in *optical glass* due to the presence of trapped hydroxyl ions remaining from water as a contaminant. See Figure H-1.

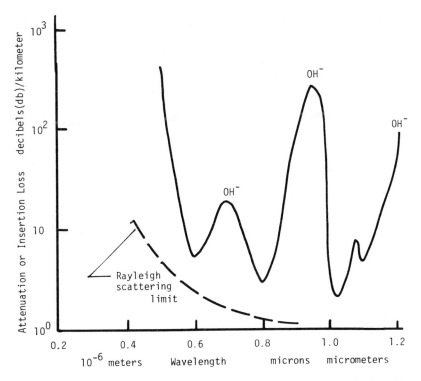

H-1. The *attenuation* or *insertion loss* for a *low-loss fiber* showing peaks of **hydroxyl ion absorption.**

hydroxyl ion overtone absorption. *Absorption* caused by the presence of the hydroxyl (OH^-) ion, giving rise to *fundamental* vibrations and hence an *absorption band* centered at 2.8 *microns wavelength,* with *harmonics* of the fundamental vibrations at 1.4, 0.97, and 0.75 *microns.* The OH^- originates primarily from water as a contaminant in *optical* glass.

hyperbolic navigation system. A *navigation system* in which *electromagnetic waves* are employed to establish a grid of intersecting waves that can be used by a *receiving station* located in the grid to determine its position without transmitting any *signals.* The grid is in the form of intersecting hyperbolas, since two *transmitters* are used to establish the grid and *signal strength* varies inversely as the square of the distance from the *antenna*.

hyperbolic orbit.   An *orbit* that has the shape of a hyperbola and therefore is not a *closed orbit.*   It might be described as a hyperbolic trajectory.   Circular and elliptical orbits are closed.   Parabolic and hyperbolic orbits are not closed. Also see *parabolic orbit.*

hypodermic fiberscope.   A *fiberscope* consisting of a *light source* for *illumination;* a single *optical fiber* of the order of 4 to 8 *microns* in diameter for *forward transmission* of the illumination for the *object* field and *backward transmission* of the *reflected* light from the object field; and a device for *displaying* the reflected *image* from subcutaneous tissue.

Hz.   *Hertz.*

I

IAGC. *Instantaneous automatic gain control.*

I-band. The band of *frequencies* in the range from 8 to 10 GHz, comprising ten numbered *channels* each of which is 200 MHz wide. These frequencies overlap parts of the old X-band and H-band.

Iceland spar. A *transparent* variety of the natural uniaxial crystal calcite that displays very strong *double refraction*. Chemically, Iceland spar is calcium carbonate crystallized in the hexagonal rhombohedral crystallographic system. Synonymous with *calspar*.

ICS. *Integrated communication system.*

ICW. *Interrrupted continuous wave.*

ideal blackbody. See *blackbody*.

identification. See *aircraft signature identification; automatic identification; line identification; subscriber identification; terminal automatic identification; transmission identification*.

identification facility. See *called-line identification facility; calling-line identification facility*.

identification friend-or-foe (IFF). A system in which electronic *transmissions* are used to identify equipment in one group to equipment in another group by means of automatic *responses* to the transmissions. For example, one piece of equipment will emit a *pulse* pattern that is received and checked by another piece of equipment. A satisfactory check will cause a *signal* confirming the success of the check back to the equipment that originally emitted the pulse pattern. It is an automatic method of determining the identity or character of an *aircraft station, ship station,* or *ground station* by means of electronic equipment at both the *challenging* and *replying* station. Synonymous with *radio recognition and identification*.

identification-not-provided signal. In a *telephone* or a *telegraph system,* a *signal* that is sent in *response* to a request for *calling* or *called line* identification when the corresponding facility is not provided in the *source user* or in the *destination user network*.

identification-request indicator. See *called-line identification-request indicator; calling-line identification request indicator*.

identification signal. See *called-line identification signal; calling-line identification signal.*

identifier. In *communication* and *data processing systems,* a *character* or a group of characters that is used to identify or name an *item* of *data* and to indicate certain properties of that data. See *code identifier.*

identity. See *called line identity; calling line identity; country-network identity.*

identity gate. See *EXCLUSIVE-NOR gate.*

identity message. See *calling line identity message.*

idle channel. A *channel* that is momentarily not being used, though it is in a state of readiness to use at any instant at electronic speeds. *Idle characters* may be passing through it. Idle channels are selected for use in *time-assignment speech interpolation (TASI) systems.*

idle-channel loading. Meaningless *signals,* special *codes,* or *noise* deliberately applied to individual unused *multiplexed channels* to maintain a desired level of *modulator* loading.

idle-channel noise. *Noise* that is present in a *communication channel* when *signals* are not applied to the channel. The conditions and *terminations* must be stated for the measured value of the noise (noise level) to be significant.

idle character. A *control character* that is *transmitted* when there is no *information* to be *transmitted.* See *synchronous idle (SYN) character.*

idle condition. See *idle state.*

idle line termination. An *electrical network* that is controlled by a *switch* and that maintains a desired *impedance* at a *trunk* or *line terminal* when that terminal is in the *idle state.*

idle state. The *telecommunication service* condition that exists when *user messages* are not being *transmitted* but the service is immediately available for use. Synonymous with *idle condition.*

IF. *Intermediate frequency.*

IF amplifier. See *linear-logarithmic intermediate frequency (IF) amplifier.*

if-A-then-B gate. See *B-OR-NOT-A gate.*

if-A-then-not-B gate. See *NAND gate.*

if-B-then-A gate. See *A-OR-NOT-B gate.*

if-B-then-not-A gate. See *NAND gate.*

IFF. *Identification friend-or-foe.*

IFRB. *International Frequency Registration Board.*

ignore gate.   See *A-IGNORE-B gate.*

IIL.   *Integrated injection logic.*

ILF.   *Infralow frequency.*

illegal code.   A *code element, character,* or *symbol* that appears or purports to
be a proper element because it possesses features that are required of the proper
elements of the code, but is in fact not a proper member of the defined *alphabet*
or *language* of the *code.*   For example, an illegal code might be one of the six
4-*bit bytes* that are not needed to represent the ten *decimal digits* by means of
4-bit bytes, since sixteen different bytes are possible using 4 bits in each byte.
Since these may not be used, they may be declared illegal and their occurrence
forbidden.   Should one of these patterns occur it may be assumed that a *malfunction* or *failure* has occurred and the matter can be brought to the attention
of the *operator.*   Synonymous with *forbidden code; improper code.*

illuminance.   *Luminous flux incident* per unit area of a surface.   Illuminance is
expressed in *lumens* per square *meter.*   Synonymous with *illumination.*

illuminate.   To cause *electromagnetic* energy to become *incident* upon a surface.

illumination.   See *illuminance.*

illumination cassegrain.   See *uniform-illumination cassegrain.*

ILS.   *Instrument landing system.*

image.   In an *optical system,* a representation of an *object* produced by means
of *light rays.*   An *optical element* forms an image by collecting a *bundle* of *light
rays diverging* from an *object point* and transforming it into a bundle of rays that
converge toward, or diverge from, another point.   If the rays *converge* to a point, a
real image of the object point is formed; if the rays diverge without intersecting
each other, they appear to proceed from a *virtual image.*   See *display image; double image; erect image; geometric image; ghost image; real image; reflection image;
reverted image; virtual image; wire-frame image.*

image antenna.   A hypothetical, *mirror-image antenna* that is located as far below
ground as the actual *antenna* is above ground and in an inverted position as if it
were a *reflection* of the actual antenna.   Since the surface of the ground may be
considered as an equipotential surface, image methods can be used in the calculation and analysis of antenna *radiation patterns.*   For the above ground *electromagnetic fields,* it can be assumed that both antennas are *transmitting* to produce
the resultant *field* at a point.

image aspect.   The spatial orientation of an *image;* e.g., normal, canted, inverted,
reverted, rotated, or *displaced* (translated).

image brightness.   In an *optical system,* the apparent *brightness* of an *image* as
seen through the optical system.   This brightness depends on the brightness of

the *object,* the *transmission, magnification, distortion,* and diameter of the *exit pupil* of the instrument.

image dissector.   In *fiber optic systems,* a *bundle* of *fibers* with a tightly packed end on which an *image* may be *focused,* in which the fibers may be separated into groups, each group *transmitting* part of the image, each part remaining *coherent.*

image intensifier.   A device, capable of increasing the *luminance* of a low-intensity *image* or source; e.g., an *electrooptic* tube with a fiber-optic faceplate.

image inverter.   In *fiber optic systems,* an *image* rotator that rotates the image $180°$.

image jump.   The apparent displacement of an *object* due to a *prismatic* condition in an *optical system.*

image method.   An analytical method for analyzing and calculating *field* distribution patterns *(radiation patterns)* emanating from a *radiating source.* The method assumes that a given charge distribution produces a field in the region outside a plane-bounded *conducting* region as though there were a mirror image of the same charge distribution inside the plane-bounded conducting region, but of opposite polarity and inverted as though the distribution were a mirror image of the actual distribution. The method holds for line and point charge distributions such as occur on a vertical straight *antenna.* See Figure I-1.

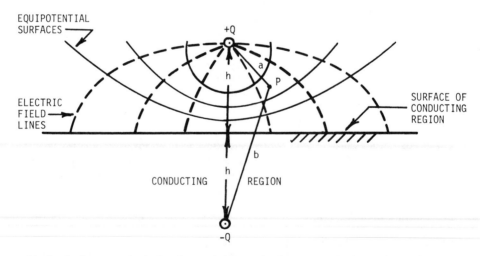

I-1. In the **image method,** the *electric field* at point P may be calculated as though charge ⁻Q also existed and the *conducting* region did not exist. The field is the result of the *vectorial* additive effects of the charge +Q and the charge −Q and the distances a and b.

image plane. The plane in which an *image* lies or is formed, perpendicular to the *optical axis* of a *lens*. A *real image* formed by a converging lens would be visible upon a screen placed in this plane.

image point. In *optical systems* capable of forming *images*, any point or location, *coordinate position*, or place in the image *display space* on the *display surface* of a *display device* that is also on an image displayed on that display surface.

image processing. The performance of operations on an *image* by an *optical system;* for example, image formation, *image restoration*, image *filtering*, or *wavefront control*, by *phase conjugation, aperture tagging, wavefront compensation, image sharpening*, or other process. Also see *compander; compressor; expander.*

image quality. A measure of how closely an *image* resembles the *object* from which it is made. Characteristics of a *lens* or *optical system* that affect image quality primarily include resolving power and contrast. Abberations contribute to poor image quality. Errors of construction and defects in materials adversely affect image quality. Characteristic effects of aberrations on image quality make it possible to distinguish between their effects and those of accidental errors of workmanship, such as nonspherical surfaces, poor polish, scratches, pits, decentering, defects on cementing, and *scattered light,* all of which contribute to deterioration of the image. Defects in glass such as *bubbles, stones, striae,* crystalling bodies, cloudiness, strain, *seeds, chicken-wire,* and *opaque* minerals play a part in poor image quality.

image restoration. The process or technique used to convert a distorted *image* to a less distorted image.

image rotator. In a *fiber optic system,* a *coherent bundle* of *fibers,* the *output* end of which can be rotated with respect to the input end. Thus, twisting the bundle along its length and rotating the output image permits image rotation.

imagery. In *display systems,* the representation and sensing of *objects* produced electronically, *optically,* or by other means on film, *screens, plotters,* or other *display surfaces* of *display devices.*

image sharpening. **1.** In *image processing* by an *optical system,* the increasing of the spatial *light intensity* gradients of an *image* on a *display surface* in order to increase the contrast at boundaries of *components* of the image to more clearly distinguish individual *object points* from which the image was made. Sharpening may be accomplished by improved *object illumination, focusing, wavefront control, filtering,* or other *image restoration* techniques. **2.** In *image restoration,* a method of *wavefront control* in which *transition* gradients from light to dark regions are increased in order to increase the clarity of the elements of an *image.*

image storage space. In *display systems* and *computer graphics, storage* locations that are used to store, or are occupied by, *coded images.* Synonymous with *coded-image space.*

imaging system. A *display system* that is capable of forming *images* of *objects;* e.g., *lens systems, optical fiber* systems, *computer*-controlled *CRT* or *fiberscope terminals,* and film systems.

imitation. See *signal imitation.*

immediate precedence. The *precedence designation* that is reserved for *messages* that gravely affect the *security* of national forces or populations and that require delivery to the *addressee* without delay.

immersion effect. See *fluid immersion effect.*

impact point. See *drop-zone impact point.*

impact test. In *optical fibers, bundles,* and *cables,* a measure of the ability to (1) withstand impact loading without loss of design capabilities or (2) withstand breaking.

impedance. The total passive opposition offered to the flow of an *alternating electric current.* It consists of a combination of *resistance, inductive reactance,* and *capacitive reactance,* each theoretically ranging from 0 to infinity in value. Their value is usually expressed in ohms. The magnitude of an impedance consisting of *lumped circuit elements* connected in series is given by $Z = [R^2 + (X_L - X_C)^2]^{1/2}$. The vector value is given by $R + jX_L - jX_C$, where R is the resistance, X_L is the inductive reactance, X_C is the capacitive reactance, and j is the quadrature (imaginary) operator ($j = (-1)^{1/2}$). The admittance is the reciprocal of the impedance. In parallel circuits, the admittances are added to obtain the total admittance of the parallel combination of elements. See *characteristic impedance; input impedance; iterative impedance; terminal impedance.*

impedance discontinuity. See *optical impedance discontinuity.*

impedance matching. The *connection* of an additional *impedance* to an existing one in order to improve the performance of an *electric circuit* or to produce a specific effect. For example, to *terminate* a *transmission line* in its *characteristic impedance* in order to prevent *reflections,* or to adjust the impedance of a functioning device in order to obtain maximum *power transfer* from a connected power source.

implication gate. See *A-OR-NOT-B gate; B-OR-NOT-A gate.*

improper code. See *illegal code.*

improvement. See *angle modulation noise improvement; pre-emphasis improvement.*

improvement factor. See *FM improvement factor.*

improvement threshold. See *FM improvement threshold.*

impulse. A surge of *electrical* energy, usually of short duration and usually of a nonrepetitive nature. Also see *pulse.*

impulse dialing.   See *loop-disconnect pulsing system.*

impulse excitation.   The production of an *electrical current* surge *(impulse)* in a *circuit* that is obtained by impressing a *voltage* on the circuit for a relatively short period compared with the duration of the electrical current that is produced by the voltage. Synonymous with *shock excitation.*

impulse noise.   1. *Noise* that consists of random occurrences of energy *impulses* that have random *amplitudes* and *bandwidths* and that can be a major cause of *errors* in a *data channel.* Impulse noise is due primarily to disturbances that have abrupt changes of short duration in *electric current* or *voltage.* 2. In *telephone operations, noise* that is characterized by transient disturbances that are separated in time by quiescent intervals. These impulse noises may not have systematic *phase* relationships. The same source may produce impulse noise in one *system* and *random noise* in a different system.

impulse response.   The amplitude-versus-time *output* of a device, *circuit,* or other *transmission facility* in *response* to an *impulse.*

impurity absorption.   In *lightwave transmission media,* the *absorption* of *light* energy from a *traveling* or *standing wave* by foreign elements in the medium. Examples of such elements include iron, copper, vanadium, chromium, hydroxide, and chloride ions; if concentrations of these elements can be held below 8, 9, 18, and 28 ppb, respectively, less than 20 db/km losses can be obtained at *band* center. *Power absorption* occurs predominantly from foreign substances, such as transition metal ions (e.g., iron, cobalt, and chromium). *Slab dielectric waveguides* are included.

impurity level.   An *electron* energy level of a material outside the normal energy levels of the material, caused by the presence of impurity atoms in the material. Such levels are capable of making an insulator *semiconducting.* The impurity atom may be a *donor* or an *acceptor.* If a donor, the impurity induces electronic conduction through the transfer of an electron to the *conduction band.* If an acceptor, the impurity can induce *hole* conduction through the acceptance of an electron from the *valence band.*

inactive character.   A *character* that is *transmitted* in the *information transfer phase* of a *call* as a *stuffing character.* It does not represent any information.

inactive code word.   A *code word* that has been placed in use but which has been subsequently replaced by another word that has the same meaning.

inactive optics.   See *fixed optics.*

in-band noise power ratio.   For *multichannel* equipment, the ratio of the *mean noise power* (level) measured in any *channel* with all channels *loaded* with *white noise,* to the mean noise power (level) measured in the same channel with all channels but the channel being measured loaded with white noise.

in-band signaling.   *Signaling* in which *frequencies* or *time slots* are used that are within the *bandwidth* of the *information channel.* In-band signaling makes use of the *frequency band* or *bit stream* that is normally allocated for *user traffic.* In-band signaling has also been used for *supervisory, control,* and *status signaling.* Also see *channel-associated signaling.*

incandescence. The *emission* of *light* by thermal excitation, which brings about *energy level* transitions that produce quantities of *photons* sufficient to render the source of *radiation* visible.

incidence. The act of falling upon or affecting, as a *ray* of *light* upon a surface. The ray is in the direction of *propagation* and perpendicular to the *wave-front,* which contains the *electric* and *magnetic vectors* of a *transverse electromagnetic wave.* See *grazing incidence; normal incidence.*

incidence angle. In *optics,* the angle between the *incident ray* and the normal to a *reflecting* or *refracting* surface at an *optical interface.* Synonymous with *angle of incidence; incident angle.*

incidence sounding. See *oblique-incidence sounding.*

incidental radiation device. A device that *radiates electromagnetic* energy during its *operation* although the device is not intentionally designed or intended to generate electromagnetic energy. For example, a *radio receiver* or *direction-finding* equipment.

incident angle. See *incidence angle.*

incident ray. A *ray* of *light* that falls upon, or strikes, the surface of any *object.* The ray is said to be incident to the surface.

inclusion. Extraneous substance within a *transmission medium.* For example, foreign material such as bubbles, *seeds, striae,* metal ions in glass, or OH⁻ in glass.

inclusion gate. See *A-OR-NOT-B gate; B-OR-NOT-A gate.*

inclusive-NOR gate. See *NOR gate.*

inclusive-OR gate. See *OR gate.*

incoherent bundle. A *bundle* of *optical fibers* in which the spatial coordinates of each fiber do not bear the same relationship to each other at the two ends of the bundle. Thus, an incoherent bundle cannot be used to transmit a picture since the input *image* will be destroyed during the *transmission* as the fibers in the bundle change their relative positions, thus scrambling the image as each fiber carries its *picture element* to a relative *image point* different from the corresponding relative object point. The incoherent bundle is usually in a single sheath, the fibers are randomly placed, and the bundle is considered as a single *transmission medium,* path, or *channel.* The entire bundle is usually used simply as a means of guiding *light,* with no concern for spatial relationships of picture elements. Synonymous with *light conduit; noncoherent bundle; unaligned bundle.* Also see *coherent bundle.*

incorrect bit. A received *bit* that has a *binary* value that is the complement of the bit that was transmitted, that is, it is a wrong bit and not the bit that was intended.

incorrect block. A *block* that is *successfully delivered* to the intended *destination user* (customer, subscriber) but has one or more incorrect *bits,* has additional or unwanted bits, or lacks bits that it should have or that were sent.

increment. See *radio frequency channel increment.*

incremental compaction. A method of *data compaction* in which only the initial value and all subsequent changes are stored or *transmitted.* For example, if a *line voltage* or a speed measurement is to be recorded or transmitted at specific time intervals or independent variable interval, only the initial, standard, or normal value need be processed along with the deviations. Thus, instead of transmitting the values 102, 104, 105, 103, 100, 104 and 106, only the values 102, +2, +1, −2, −3, +4, and +2, or only the values 100, +2, +4, +5, +3, 0, +4, and +6 need be sent, depending on the system used. These *transmissions* require much less time and space than transmitting the *absolute values.*

incremental magnetic permeability. The limit of the ratio of the change in *magnetic flux density,* ΔB, produced in a material, to the change in *magnetic field intensity,* ΔH, required to produce the ΔB at a given point in the material. Mathematically, $\mu_{inc} = dB/dH$. Thus, the incremental magnetic permeability is the slope of the magnetization curve of B plotted versus H. Also see *absolute magnetic permeability; relative magnetic permeability.*

incremental phase modulation (IPM). In *spread-spectrum systems, phase modulation* in which one *binary code* sequence is *shifted* with respect to another, usually for the purpose of conducting a synchronizing search, that is, a search to discover if the two sequences are the same, and perhaps thereby enabling two *data streams* to be *synchronized.*

incremental quantum efficiency. See *differential quantum efficiency.*

incremental vector. See *relative vector.*

increment size. The spatial distance between adjacent *addressable points* within a *display space.* For example, the distance between centers of adjacent *optical fibers* in the *faceplate* of a *fiberscope,* or the minimum displacement that can be drawn by a plotter (i.e., the *plotter step size*).

indefinite call sign. **1.** A *call sign* that represents a group of *facilities, commands,* authorities, *activities,* or units rather than one of these. **2.** In *radio communications,* a *call sign* that does not identify a *station* and that is used in the call-up or in a *message* that has the station's call sign *encrypted* in the *text.*

indefinite component life. The life of a *component* that is expected to remain in a satisfactory operational and serviceable condition during the entire life of the *system* of which it is a part.

independence.   See *bit-sequence independence.*

independent.   See *code-independent.*

independent clock.   A *clock* that *emits timing signals* that are not regulated by any other device except the reference that keeps the clock *frequency* fixed, such as its own internal crystal *oscillator.* Also see *synchronized clock.*

independent sideband.   A *sideband* in a *sideband transmission system* in which the separate sidebands are used to convey independent or different *information.*

independent-sideband carrier.   See *two-independent-sideband carrier.*

independent-sideband transmission.   *Double-sideband transmission* in which the *information* carried by each of the *sidebands* is different. It is a method of transmission in which the *modulated frequencies* on the opposite sides of the *carrier* frequency that are produced by the modulation are not related to each other. They are related separately to two sets of modulating signals. In such transmission systems, the carrier may be *transmitted, suppressed,* or partially suppressed. Synonymous with *twin-sideband transmission.*   See *sideband transmission; two-independent-sideband transmission.*

index.   See *absolute refractive index; absorption index; code line index; cooperation index; modulation index; radiation transfer index; refractive index; relative refractive index; surface refractive index.*

index fiber.   See *graded-index fiber; step-index fiber.*

index flash.   In *visual signaling systems,* a single *panel* that indicates the top of *numerals* or *words* formed with *signaling panels.* It is placed first and removed last when *signaling* from ground to air.

index gradient.   See *refractive-index gradient.*

index-matching cell.   A container, usually filled with a liquid whose *refractive index* can be made equal to the refractive index of an inserted *optical fiber.* Since the *reflection coefficient* for *normal incidence* is given by $(n_1 - n_2)/(n_1 + n_2)$, the *reflected power* will be zero, and hence independent of the end surface of *the fib*er, when $n_1 = n_2$.

index-matching materials.   *Light-conducting* materials used in intimate contact to reduce *optical power* losses by using materials with *refractive indices* at *interfaces* that will reduce *reflection,* increase *transmission,* avoid *scattering,* and reduce *dispersion.*

index of refraction.   See *refractive index.*

index profile.   See *graded-index profile; parabolic-index profile; radial refractive index profile; step-index profile; uniform index profile.*

in-dialing.   See *network in-dialing (NID).*

indicating group.   See *address indicating group (AIG); international address indicating group; national address indicating group.*

indicating group allocation.   See *address indicating group allocation.*

indication.   See *automatic charge indication; automatic date-and-time indication; automatic duration indication; call-pending indication; charge indication; clear indication; duration indication.*

indicator.   1. A device that may be set into a prescribed state based on the result of a previous process or on the occurrence of a specified condition and gives a *signal* announcing the existence of the prescribed state or occurrence of the specified condition.   Usually the indicator may be used to determine a selection from among a group of alternatives, such as a *message routing indicator* or an *instrument status indicator.*   2. A *symbol, signal,* or group of symbols or signals that serves to identify a specific item, such as a *message* from a specified *source* or the specific *cryptosystem key* used to *encrypt* or *authenticate* a message or *transmission.*   See *alternative-routing indicator; called-line identification-request indicator; calling-line identification-request indicator; coherent moving target indicator; collective routing indicator; destination-code indicator; drop-zone indicator; end-of-message indicator; figure indicator; letter indicator; message alignment indicator; mobile unit routing indicator; Morse code indicator; moving target indicator (MTI); panel signaling indicator; panoramic indicator; planned position indicator (PPI); radar planned position indicator; range-height indicator; routing indicator; signal unit indicator; special purpose routing indicator; start-of-message indicator; user-class indicator.*

indicator allocation.   See *routing indicator allocation.*

indicator assignment.   See *routing indicator assignment.*

indicator delineation map.   See *routing indicator delineation map.*

indicator delineation table.   See *routing indicator delineation table.*

indicator shutter.   See *fallen clearing indicator shutter.*

indirect clock control.   In *digital data transmission, clock* control in which a clock at a higher *modulation rate,* such as 4, 8, and 128 times the basic modulation rate, is used, rather than no more than twice the modulation rate as is done in *direct clock control.*

indirect mode.   In a *radionavigation system,* the operation or use of the several *transmitters* of the *radionavigation service* simply as *radio beacons* for *direction finding* rather than as part of a radionavigation system such as *LORAN* or *hyperbolic navigation systems.*

indirect wave.   A *wave,* such as a *lightwave, radio wave,* or *sound wave,* that arrives at a point in a *transmission medium* by *reflection* or *scattering* from surrounding objects, rather than directly from the *source.*   In *optical fiber transmis-*

sion, indirect waves arriving later will combine with direct waves, causing *delay distortion.* Also see *direct wave.*

individual call sign. In a *radio communication system* or *net,* a *call sign* that identifies a single *station.* Also see *collective call sign; net call sign.*

individual normal magnification. The apparent *magnification* produced by a magnifier, such as a *lens* or a *mirror.* The individual normal magnification is usually different from the absolute magnification. The apparent magnification depends on the extent of myopia or hyperopia (hypermetropia) possessed by the individual.

induced optical conductor loss. See *connector-induced optical conductor loss.*

induction. The generation of an *electromotive force (voltage)* by a time rate of change of *magnetic flux.* Expressed mathematically, $e = Nd\phi/dt = -l\ di/dt$, where e is the electromotive force (voltage) generated in a closed *circuit* through which there is a time rate of change of magnetic flux linkages, $d\phi/dt$; N is the number of conductor turns in the circuit; L is the inductance, a function of the geometry and materials; and di/dt is the time rate of change of *electric current* in the circuit.

induction field. In *electromagnetic field theory,* the electromagnetic field of a *radiating antenna* or *source* of *electromagnetic radiation* that lies between the *radiation field* and the *electrostatic field.* The induction field strength varies inversely as the square of the distance from the antenna. It obeys and is predictable from the *Biot-Savart law* of the elemental magnetic field due to the existence of an elemental *electric current. Integration* over all the distributed elemental electric currents produces the *magnetic flux density* at a specified point. The induction region is a transition region that lies between the near field region and the far field region. In this field region the *electric field strength* of an *electromagnetic wave* developed by a *transmitting antenna* is dependent upon the inverse distance and the inverse cube of the distance as well as the inverse squared distance from the antenna. It may be considered as any distance between 0.1 and 1.0 of the *wavelength,* for an *antenna equivalent length* that is small compared to this distance. Synonymous with *intermediate field* and with *intermediate zone.* Also see *electrostatic field; radiation field; transition zone.*

inductive coupling. The *coupling* of *signals* or *noise* in which a *conductor* is linked to another by means of changing *magnetic flux* linkages that are created by *electrical currents* in one conductor and that induce *voltages* in the other.

inductive reactance. The opposition to the flow of *alternating electric current* that is produced by configurations of *conductors* such as straight wires, coils, and other shapes when an alternating voltage is applied. The changing current (alternating current) produces a changing *magnetic field,* the changing *flux* linkages induce an *electromotive force* in the configuration that opposes the flow of current producing the flux linkages. This creates the opposition to the flow of current produced by the applied alternating *voltage.* The inductive reactance is thus the ratio between the applied voltage and the resultant current. In a pure reactance the *electrical resistance* is 0. The inductive reactance is given by $X_L = j2\pi fL$ where j is the quadrature operator ($j = (-1)^{1/2}$), π is 3.1416, f is the *frequency (hertz)*, *and L* is the inductance (henries). *L* is purely a function of geometry and materials. The current is given as $I = V/X_L$ where V is the voltage and X_L is the inductive reactance. Using hertz and henries, X_L is in ohms. Using V in volts and X_L in ohms the current I will be in amperes. Also see *capacitive reactance; impedance.*

industrial RF heating equipment. Equipment in which a *radio frequency (RF) oscillator* or other *radio frequency* generator is used to control the generation of RF energy for industrial heating operations in manufacturing or production processes, such as for the annealing of copper tubing.

industrial-scientific-medical RF equipment. *Radiation* devices that use *electromagnetic waves* for industrial, scientific, or medical (ISM) purposes. It includes the *transfer* of energy by *radio* though not necessarily used, nor intended to be used, for *communications.* For example, equipment that develops *radio frequency (RF)* energy for induction heating, *microwave (dielectric)* heating, diathermy, and *infrared* heating.

inertia. The characteristic of matter (mass) to remain at rest or to remain at a constant velocity (constant speed and constant direction) unless acted upon by an outside force. The outside (applied) force produces acceleration, a *vector* quantity. The force f, mass m, and acceleration a, are related in Newtonian mechanics by the equation $f = ma$. The equation applies as long as the speeds involved are small compared to the speed of *light.* For curvilinear motion at constant speed the acceleration a is replaced by v^2/r where v is the speed and r is the radius of curvature, thus obtaining $f = mv^2/r$.

inertial guidance system. A guidance system that is based on the principle of *inertia.* An accelerometer, such as a spring-loaded mass, and *integration* can be used to obtain velocity and distance, provided that the initial conditions are known. Also see *noninertial guidance system.*

inferior position flaghoist. A *flaghoist signaling message* that is to be read after a *superior position flaghoist* message. Also see *flaghoist signaling.*

information. 1. The meaning that humans or machines assign to *data,* using certain conventions for the representation and interpretation of the data, thus enabling *communication* between humans and machines. 2. In *communication* and *teleprocessing systems,* any *transmission* of *signals* via *telecommunication channels.* The signals that represent *information* may take the form of *data* or *text messages.* See *cryptoinformation; exempt information; hydrographic information; overhead information; perishable information; protected information; raw radar information; security information; sensitive information; service information; signaling information; system overhead information; user information; user overhead information.*

information addressee. The organization, activity, or person deemed by the *message originator* to require the *information* in a *message* but not required to take the action specified in the message. Also see *action addressee; exempted addressee.*

information bearer channel. A *channel* for *data transmission* that is capable of carrying all the necessary *information* to enable *communication* between *users* (subscribers, customers) to take place, including *user's data, synchronizing* sequences, and *control signals.* It may operate at a greater *data signaling rate* than that required solely for the user's data.

information bit. A *bit* that is generated by a *data source* and delivered to a *data sink* and is not used by the *data transmission system.* See *user information bit.*

information block. See *user information block.*

information channel. The *transmission media* and the intervening equipment that is used for the *transfer* of *information* in a given direction between two *stations.* The information channel usually includes the *modulator, demodulator, error control* equipment, and *backward channel.*

information content. **1.** In *information theory,* a measure of the *information* that is conveyed by the occurrence of an event of definite probability. This measure, $I(x_i)$, for the event x_i is normally expressed as the logarithm of the reciprocal of the probability, $p(x_i)$, that the particular event will occur. Expressed in mathematical notation, $I(x_i) = log\ (1/p(x_i)) = -log\ p(x_i)$. Thus, if there are 2 characters, x and y, among others in a *message,* and the probability of x occurring in the message is 0.5, and the probability of y occurring in the message is 0.25, then the information content of x is $\log_2 2 = 1$ *shannon,* $\log_{10} 2 = 0.301$ *hartley,* and ln 2 = 0.693 *natural unit.* The information content of y is 2 shannons, 0.602 hartley, and 1.386 nats, since these are the logarithms of 1/0.25, that is, of 4. **2.** The *information* that is represented by a given set of *characters.* For example, the meaning that is assigned to the *data* in a *message.* See *conditional information content; joint information content; mutual information content; natural unit of information content (nat); signaling information content; transinformation content.*

information content binary unit. See *shannon.*

information entropy. The mean value of the *information content* that is conveyed by the occurrence of any one of a finite number of mutually exclusive and jointly exhaustive events of definite probability of occurrence. See *conditional information entropy.*

information facility. In a *communication system,* a *facility* that enables a *user* (customer, subscriber) to send a predetermined *address* from a *data station* and gain *access* to *information* regarding available *data communication services.* For example, access may be provided for *directory* (inquiry) *service,* for charge information service, or for *fault* reporting. Synonymous with *inquiry facility.*

information feedback. The sending of *data* back to the *source* or *transmitter* usually for the purpose of checking the *accuracy* of *transmission* of the data. The data that are received back at the transmitter are compared with the data that were originally transmitted. Also see *echo check.*

information field. In *data transmission,* a part of a *message* that is assigned to contain *user information.* The contents of the information field is not interpreted at the *link level* in most systems.

information link. See *tactical digital information link (TADIL).*

information measure. **1.** In *information theory,* a function of the probability of occurrence of an event or sequence of events out of a set of possible events. For example, the probability of occurrence of a specified member of a set, the probability of occurrence of a specified *character* or a specified *word* in a given position in a *message,* or the probability of occurrence of a specified *bit* pattern in a *bit stream.* **2.** An *indication* of the amount or volume of *information* that is represented by a given set of *data* in a particular situation or environment. *Coding* of the information must also be taken into account when determining the volume.

information rate. See *average information rate; character mean entropy.*

information security. The protection of *information* for the purpose of preventing unauthorized disclosure, transfer, modification, or destruction whether by accident or diabolical intent.

information separator. In an *information system,* a *control character* that is used to *delimit data units* in a hierarchical arrangement of *data.* The name of the information separator does not necessarily indicate the unit of data that it separates. Synonymous with *separating character.*

information source. See *source user.*

information theory. The branch of learning that is concerned with the study of measures and properties of *information.* Also see *communication theory.*

information transfer. **1.** The result of *data transmission,* such as the result of moving a *message* from a *data source* to a *data sink.* **2.** The process of moving *data* from one point to another. The information transfer rate may not exceed the *modulation rate.* Also see *isochronous burst transmission.*

information transfer phase. In a *communication system,* the second phase of an *information transfer transaction* and the phase during which *user* (customer, subscriber) *information* is transferred from the *source user* to the *destination user.* Also see *access phase; data transfer phase; disengagement phase; successful disengagement.*

information transfer transaction. In a *communication system,* a coordinated sequence of *user* and *system* activities that ultimately results in user *information*

being *transferred* from a *source user* to a *destination user.* An information transfer transaction is typically divided into three consecutive phases, namely the *access
phase,* the *information transfer phase,* and the *disengagement phase.* Also see
access phase; disengagement phase; transfer phase.

infralow frequency (ILF). A *frequency* that lies in the range from 300 Hz to
3 kHz. The *alphabetic* designator of the range is ILF. The *numeric* designator
of the range is 3. Also see *frequency spectrum designation.*

infrared (IR). *Electromagnetic radiation* in the range of *frequencies* that extends
from the visible red region of the *spectrum* to the *microwave* region, the frequency being lower and the *wavelength* longer than that of visible red. The *band*
of infrared electromagnetic wavelengths lies between the extreme of the visible
part of the spectrum, about 0.75μ *(microns)* and the shortest *microwaves,* about
1000μ. The IR region is often divided as near infrared, 0.75 to 3μ; middle infrared, 3 to 30μ; and far infrared, 30 to 1000μ. The sun, moon, earth, and all bodies
having a *temperature* above absolute zero are sources of infrared radiation. *Absorption* of *light* energy in a *transmission medium,* such as an *optical fiber* or
integrated optical circuit, can result in the production and dissipation of infrared
radiation – namely, as heat, which may be removed by *conduction,* convection,
or radiation. See *far infrared; middle infrared; near infrared.*

infrared absorption. In a material such as *optical fiber* glass, the *absorption*
caused by the motion of thermally excited ionic bonds (i.e., *electric dipoles*),
which interact with the *electric* and *magnetic fields* of *propagating lightwaves,*
resulting in a transfer of energy from the fields to the structure. Infrared absorption is particularly significant beyond a 1.5-*micron wavelength,* which is not in
the *visible* region. Also see *bond frequency.*

infrared angle tracker. In an airborne *infrared (IR) receiver,* a device that gives
the *look-angle* to the *IR radiation source,* such as an aircraft, missile, missile
launch, fire, factory, or *electric power* generating plant; the look-angle change
rate (angular velocity); and the *radiation intensity* of the received infrared radiation. Also see *infrared point-source flash detector.*

infrared band. The *band* of *electromagnetic wavelengths* between the extreme
of the visible part of the *spectrum,* about 0.75μ *(microns),* and the shortest
microwaves, about 1000μ. The IR region is sometimes subdivided into *near infrared,* 0.75–3μ; *middle infrared,* 3–30μ; and *far infrared,* 30–1000μ.

infrared detector. See *background-limited infrared detector.*

infrared detector dark resistance. The *electrical resistance* of the *photoconductive (infrared sensitive)* material of an *infrared detector* when no *infrared radiation* is *incident* upon it.

infrared device. A device in which *radiation* in the *infrared* region of the *electromagnetic spectrum* is used. Infrared (IR) radiation has a *wavelength* slightly

infrared jamming electronic counter-countermeasure. A measure that is designed to reduce the effectiveness of *infrared (IR) active* and *passive devices* by the use of IR antijamming techniques, such as changing *wavelengths,* increasing *scanning* rates to produce higher *modulation frequencies,* using *frequency modulation (FM)* rather than *amplitude modulation (AM),* reducing *bandwidths,* using *squelch systems,* and using multifrequency systems.

infrared point-source flash detector. In an *infrared (IR) receiver* that accepts and *displays* IR energy, a *detector*-warning device that gives an indication of a *point-source* of IR radiation, such as an aircraft, missile launch, or fire, and the *azimuth* and *elevation angles* at which the source lies with respect to the location of the detector. Also see *infrared angle tracker.*

infrared radiation (IR). *Radiation* that is in the *infrared* region of the *electromagnetic spectrum,* that is, radiation with a *wavelength* slightly greater than that of *visible light.* The radiation has a wavelength greater than 900×10^{-9} meters, 900 millimicrons (millimicrometers), or 9000 angstrom units. The *frequency* is just below that of visible light, that is, just below 3.33×10^{14} Hz or 333 Thz.

infrared radiation suppression. The reduction of *infrared radiation* by means of *shielding,* baffling, *temperature* reduction, use of nonthermal (cool) devices, cooling, and flame reduction.

infrared saturation jamming. *Infrared (IR) jamming* in which a high-intensity *infrared source* is used to drive the *guidance* and *control system* of the object being jammed into the nonlinear portion of its *operating* characteristic. This deprives the system being jammed of effective (useful) guidance *information.* Thus, the system is "blinded" with high-intensity IR radiation.

infrared sensor. See *photoconductive infrared sensor.*

infrared spin-scan radiometer. See *fiber optic visible-infrared spin-scan radiometer.*

infrared transmission. The *transmission* of *messages* or *data* using *infrared radiation,* i.e., *electromagnetic waves* with a *frequency* just below that of *visible light.*

infrared viewer. A device for viewing *infrared light,* particularly from the end of an *optical fiber* carrying infrared *radiation* from a *laser source,* which would be invisible without the viewer. Direct viewing of infrared radiation, such as from the end of an optical fiber, can cause damage to the retina of the eye.

inhibiting signal. A *signal* that prevents the occurrence of an event. For example, a signal that is used to *disable* an *AND gate,* thus preventing any signals from passing through it as long as the inhibiting signal is present.
longer and a *frequency* slightly lower than *visible light.* Also see *active infrared device; passive infrared device.*

inhomogeneous fiber. An *optical fiber* with a *refractive index* that is not constant throughout the fiber with respect to spatial coordinates.

initial condition mode. The operating mode of an *analog computer* during which the *integrators* are inoperative and the initial conditions are set. Synonymous with *reset mode.*

initial warning radar. A *radar* that is used to obtain the first indication of the existence of an object (target). Initial warning is usually obtained from a *long-range radar* that may be an *early warning* radar. However, if the warning is not in time to permit planned reaction, it cannot be considered as an early warning though it may be an initial warning.

injection laser. See *semiconductor laser.*

injection laser diode. A *diode* operating as a *laser* producing a *monochromatic light modulated* by injection of *carriers* across a P–N *junction* of a *semiconductor* with narrower spatial and *wavelength emission* characteristics for longer-range higher-data-rate systems than the *LEDs* that are more applicable to larger diameter and larger *numerical aperture fibers* for lower information *bandwidths.* See Figure I-2.

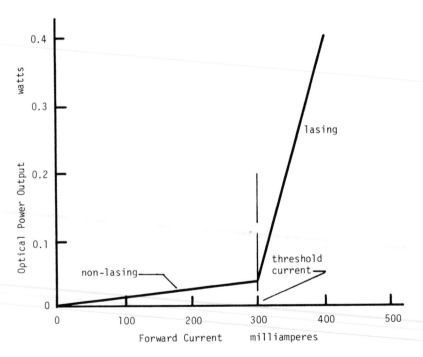

I-2. *Power-current* relationship for a typical **injection laser diode** *light source.*

injection logic. See *integrated injection logic.*

ink character recognition. See *magnetic ink character recognition.*

inking. In *display systems,* the drawing of a *line* from one *display position* to another in the *display space* on the *display surface* of a *display device,* leaving a trail behind the *display writer,* in the manner of a pen drawing a line on paper. Inking may be accomplished by manual control or by automatically directed control of the display writer.

ink vapor recording. In *facsimile systems,* recording in which vaporized ink particles are directly deposited upon the *recording sheet.*

inphase component life. The life of a *component* that can be placed into the *maintenance* or *service* cycle of the *system* of which it is a part. Also see *out-of-phase component life.*

input. **1.** In *data processing systems,* pertaining to a device, process, or *channel* involved in the process of entering *data* into an entity, or pertaining to the *data* involved in the process. The data that is entered may be *signals, pulses, impulses, modulated waves* or any similar form of representation of *information.* Though the word input is often unqualified, it may mean the *data,* the *terminal,* or the *channel.* **2.** The *electric current, voltage,* or *power* that is entered into a *circuit* or device. **3.** The *terminals,* contacts, or other *access ports* that are used to enter *signals* into a device or *system.* **4.** In *computers,* the *data* that is *transferred* into a computer or into its *storage* unit. **5.** Any *data* that is to be *processed* or *operated* upon. For example, the operands in an arithmetic or logical operation. **6.** The state or sequence of states or *signals* that occur or are made to occur on a specific *channel.* **7.** A device or set of devices that is used for inserting *data* into another device or set of devices. **8.** The state of the *terminals* at which *signals* are entered into a *combinational circuit.* **9.** The *data* obtained by a *transmitter* for *transmission* or the data received by a *receiver.* When devices are in tandem, the *output* of one is the input to the next in sequence. Also see *output.*

input aperture. The *aperture* at the point of entrance to an *optical system.* It is usually equal to the aperture of the *objective.* Also see *entrance pupil.*

input device. See *input unit.*

input impedance. The ratio of *voltage* to *current* at the *input terminals* of a device, such as an *antenna, transmission line,* or *amplifier,* when all sources of voltage inside the device are shorted or nonexistent.

input noise temperature.   See *effective input noise temperature.*

input-output (I-O) device.   In *communication* and *data processing systems,* a device that introduces *data* into, or extracts data from, a *system.*   The device may be a *terminal, channel,* or *port.*   The data may be in the form of *signals, pulses, impulses,* or states.   The systems may be *computers, storage* units, *buffers, communication networks,* or *data processing systems.*

input station.   See *data input station.*

input unit.   A *functional unit* that can introduce *data* into a *system,* such as a *data processing, computing,* or *communication system.*

inquiry facility.   See *information facility.*

inquiry station.   A *user terminal* that is used primarily for the interrogation of a *communication* or a *data processing system.*

insert.   See *aerial insert; drop-and-insert.*

insertion gain.   In a *communication system,* the change, usually the increase, in *signal level* resulting from the insertion of a *component* in a *transmission circuit.* It is expressed as a percent, *decibel,* or per unit coefficient or fraction. The gain may be positive or negative, i.e., greater or less than unity, although, if less than unity (i.e., negative), it is called an *insertion loss.*

insertion loss.   1. In a *communication system,* the change, usually the decrease, in *signal* level that results from the insertion of a *component* in a *transmission circuit.*   It is expressed as a percent, in *decibels,* or as a per unit coefficient or fraction.   The loss may be positive or negative, that is, greater or less than unity when expressed as a ratio (per unit fraction or coefficient). If the insertion loss is negative it is considered as a *gain.*   When it is expressed as a fraction, ratio, or per unit, it is the decrease in signal level caused by the insertion divided by the signal level before insertion.   2. In an *optical fiber,* the *optical power loss* due to all causes, usually expressed as *decibels*/kilometer. Causes of loss may be *absorption, scattering, diffusion, leaky modes, dispersion, microbending,* or other causes or methods of *coupling* power outside the fiber. 3. In *lightwave transmission systems,* the power lost at the entrance to a *waveguide* due to any and all causes, such as *Fresnel reflection, packing fraction,* limited *numerical aperture, axial misalignment, lateral displacement,* initial *scattering,* or *diffusion.* See *connector insertion loss.* See Figure I-3.

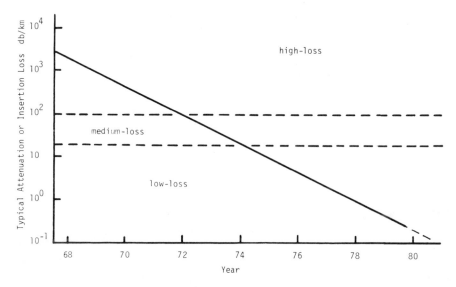

I-3. Approximate reduction in *optical fiber* **insertion loss** *(attenuation)* achieved primarily by improved *optical* glass purification and forming methods during the years shown. The lower limit may be due to such causes as *Rayleigh scattering, infrared absorption, overtone absorption,* and Si-O *bond frequency.*

insertion loss versus frequency characteristic. The *amplitude transfer function* characteristic of a *system* or *component* as a function of *frequency* of operation. The amplitude *response* to the insertion of the component into the system may be stated as an actual *gain, loss, amplification,* or *attenuation,* or as the ratio of any one of these quantities at a specified frequency to that at a reference frequency. Synonymous with *amplitude frequency response; frequency response.*

inside plant. 1. In *radio, television,* and *radar systems,* the fixed ground *communication-electronic (C-E)* equipment that is permanently located inside of buildings in contrast to equipment that is outside, buried, or otherwise exposed to weather. **2.** In wire, *cable,* and *optical fiber* systems, fixed ground *communication-electronic* (C-E) equipment that extends inward inside a building from the *main distribution frame (MDF).* For example, *central office equipment, switching equipment, teletypewriters, switchboards, display devices,* and other *data terminal equipment* inside a building. Wire, *cable,* and *fibers* that lead from the MDF outward to the outside, though they may be still inside, all buried and outside equipment, and equipment at *user's* (customer's, subscriber's) premises are considered as *outside plant.*

inside vapor-phase oxidation process (IVPO). A *CVPO process* for production of *optical fibers,* in which *dopants* are burned with dry oxygen and a fuel gas to form an oxide *(soot)* stream. The stream is deposited on the inside of a rotating glass tube and then sintered to produce a doped layer of higher *refractive index* glass on the inside; the tube is then drawn into a solid fiber. Also see *outside vapor phase oxidation process; chemical vapor phase oxidation process; modified inside vapor-phase oxidation process.*

inspection.   See *tempest inspection.*

installation.   See *radio installation.*

instant.   See *decision instant; significant instant.*

instantaneous automatic gain control (IAGC).   The *automatic gain control* of an *amplifier* in which the *response time* is equal to or less than the received *pulse length.* In *radar systems,* IAGC can be used an an *electronic counter-counter-measure (ECCM)* against long-pulse *interference* or *jamming.* It is the portion of the radar system that is capable of automatically adjusting the *gain* of an *amplifier* for each pulse it receives in order to obtain substantially constant *output pulse* peak *amplitude* with different *input* pulse peak amplitudes. The *circuit* is fast enouth to act during the time that a pulse is passing through the amplifier.

instantaneous companding.   A process that reduces the *quantizing noise* on *pulse-code modulated signals* by passing the *analog signals* through a *compressor* before quantizing. At the *receiver,* the reverse process must be applied by using an *expander* after the *decoding operation.*

instantaneous transmission speed.   The short-term rate at which *data* is processed by a *transmission facility.* It is determined by dividing the number of *transmitted data units,* such as *binary digits, characters,* or *blocks,* in a short time period without their being interrupted, by the length of the short period, thus obtaining an instantaneous number of data units per unit time, such as characters per minute. The average or effective transmission speed is less than the instantaneous transmission speed, when the instantaneous speed varies with time in a given *circuit.* Also see *effective transmission speed; efficiency factor; throughput.*

instant distortion.   See *significant instant distortion.*

instruction.   In a *computer programming language, computer program, data processing system,* or *communication system,* an expression that specifies an *operation.* It includes both the *operator* and the *operand.* For example, the instruction "add A and B" produces the sum of A and B when it is executed. The instruction may be written in many ways, depending on the *languages* and the *systems.* The example instruction may be written as "ADD A,B"; as "+A,B"; as "A + B"; or as "A,B+". The instruction may specify the *addresses* of *storage* locations where the operands are stored rather than the operands themselves. The instruction may also include the address where the result of the operation is to be stored, or it may include the address of the next instruction. The instruction may specify that nothing be done, or simply to stop executing further instructions, or jump to another specified instruction in a given sequence of instructions rather than execute the next instruction in the sequence. See *macroinstruction; signal operation instruction (SOI); standing communication operating instruction (SCOI); transmission instruction.*

instructional station.   See *aviation instructional station.*

instruction code.   In *computing, data processing,* and *communication systems,* a *code* that is used to represent the *instructions* that a *system* is capable of executing.   The code is used to prepare a program, such as a *computer program,* for execution.   The program, consisting of a sequence of instructions selected from the code that the system is capable of executing, is entered into the system, stored, and executed.   The code itself is interpreted by the system, usually converted to a *machine language* code and executed.   The codes are usually written in a somewhat *mnemonic common language,* such as *COBOL* or *FORTRAN.* For example,   MPY might be interpreted as multiply, converted to machine language by the system or by a *compiler,* and executed.   The instruction repertory is the complete set of instruction codes that a system is capable of accepting and executing.

instruction passing.   The forwarding or *relaying* of an *instruction* over a *communication system,* such as from *station* to *station,* point to point, or ship to ship, in order that it may arrive at its ultimate destination.

instrument.   See *binocular instrument; end instrument; monocular instrument; terminal instrument.*

instrument landing system (ILS).   A *radionavigation system* that provides aircraft *stations* with horizontal and vertical guidance before and during landing and that indicates the distance to a landing reference point.   Also see *localizer.*

insulated.   In *electric circuits,* the state that exists at a point that does not have a *path* to another point for other than negligible currents due to separation from other conducting points by extremely high *resistance* materials, such as plastic, rubber, fabric, tar, or other *dielectric* materials that are nonconductors.   For example, an insulated conductor would be wrapped in a nonconducting material. However, *electrostatic, magnetic, electromagnetic,* and *magnetostatic coupling* may still occur between *conductors* in spite of their being insulated, in which case they are not *isolated.*   Also see *isolated.*

insulation blocking.   The ability of the *jacket, sheath,* or other outside cover of an *optical fiber cable* to withstand elevated *temperatures* without sticking to itself on adjacent turns or layers when coiled or wound on spools or reels.

integral.   1. In the calculus, the result of the process of *integration.* Thus, the integration of an *integrand* produces an integral. For example, the integral of $12x^2 + 6x$ is $4x^3 + 3x^2$ when integrated from 0 to x.   **2.** Pertaining to a whole number *(integer).*   **3.** Pertaining to a *component* that is a permanent part of a *system.*

integral-lens LED.   An *LED,* such as a *side-emitting (edge-emitting)* high-radiance *double-heterostructured   diode,* that is *coupled* to *multimode* glass *fibers* via a photolithographically etched and regrown *converging microlens* structure on the emitting surface of the *semiconductor.* Typical *brightness* is 75 W/*steradian*-cm^2 at a current density of 3.5 kA/cm^2. Also see Figure L-3.

integrand.   In the calculus, the mathematical function *(operand)* upon which the process of *integration* operates. Thus, integration of the integrand results in the *integral.* For example, if the integrand is $12x^2 + 6x$, then the integral is $4x^3 + 3x^2$ when integrating from 0 to x. The derivative of the integral will yield the integrand, since differentiation is the inverse of integration.

integrated chip.   See *large-scale integrated (LSI) chip.*

integrated circuit.   An electronic *circuit* that consists of many individual circuit elements, such as *transistors, diodes, resistors, capacitors, inductors,* and other *active* and *passive semiconductor devices,* formed on a single chip of *semiconducting* material and mounted on a single piece of *substrate* material. Also see Figure S-5.

integrated communication system (ICS).   1. A *communication system* created by the consolidation of two or more existing originally autonomous communication systems into a single system with none of the original autonomy remaining, i.e., the complete interconnection and interoperation of separate systems. **2.** A *communication system* that *transmits analog* and *digital traffic* over the same *switched network.*

integrated injection logic (I^{2}L).   An *integrated optical circuit* containing *injection laser diodes, waveguides, switches, gates,* and related circuitry. I^{2}L's use less power, are more stable and cheaper, can be easily mass produced, and are two orders of magnitude faster than transistor-to-transistor logic (TTL).

integrated optical circuit (IOC).   A *circuit,* or group of interconnected circuits, consisting of miniature *solid state optical* components. Examples of such components include *light-emitting diodes, optical filters, photodetectors* (active and passive), and *thin film optical waveguides* on *semiconductor* or *dielectric substrates.* Components on an IOC chip might include *semiconductor injection lasers, modulators, filters, lightguides, switches, couplers, logic gates, pulse* shapers, *differential amplifiers,* and *optical memories.* Synonymous with *optical integrated circuit.* See Figure I-4. Also see Figure R-7.

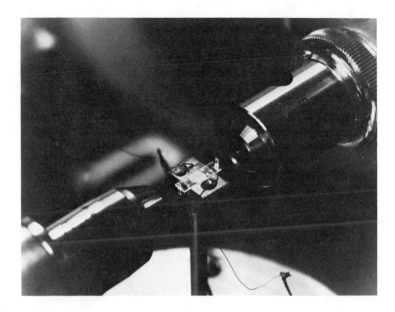

ı-4. An **integrated optical circuit** for *signal processing* in *lightwave communication* and *data-processing systems.* It contains an *optical waveguide* version of a *Fabry-Perot resonator* in which nonlinearity is produced by driving an *electrooptic* element with the *output* of a *photodetector* that *samples* the *transmitted light.* (Courtesy of Bell Laboratories.)

integrated-optical circuit filter-coupler-switch-modulator. Two or more *optical waveguides* fabricated on a minute piece of material, such as lithium niobate, whose *light-propagating* characteristics and energy interaction can be varied, in order to perform the four major functions found in a *radio receiver* — namely, *filtering, coupling, switching,* and *modulating.* Special electrodes that apply a voltage across a section of a *waveguide* alone, or across a section of a waveguide shared by two or more waveguides, control the performance of the various functions.

integrated optical device. See *Bell integrated optical device.*

integrated optical fiber system. A *communication system* or *network* consisting of wire and *microwave links* connected to *optical fiber links.* For example, the Fort Wayne, Indiana, *fiber optic link,* which handles 672 simultaneous *telephone* conversations on a single pair of glass strands when connected to the telephone *network.*

integrated optical spectrum analyzer. An *integrated optical circuit* that performs *electromagnetic spectral analysis* by executing *coherent optical signal processing operations,* such as Fourier transform analysis, Fourier transform integration, and related correlation and convolution functions. The integrated optical circuits are monolithic structures of alloy compositions of gallium-arsenide formed by liquid-phase epitaxial techniques, energized molecular beam processes, or *chemical vapor deposition* processes.

integrated optics. The design, development, and operation of *circuits* that apply the technology of integrated electronic circuits produced by planar masking, etching, evaporation, and crystal film growth techniques to microoptical circuits on a single planar *dielectric substrate.* Thus, a combination of electronic circuitry and optical waveguides are produced for performing various *communication, switching,* and *logic* functions, including *amplification, gating, modulating, light generation, photodetecting, filtering, multiplexing, signal processing, coupling,* and *storing.*

integrating circuit. An *electrical circuit,* with one *output* and one or more *inputs,* that operates in such a manner that the output is the time *integral* of all of the inputs. See Figure I-5.

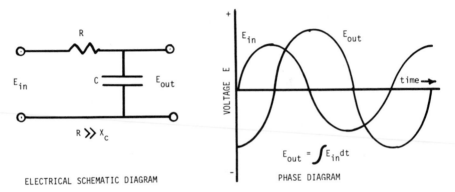

ELECTRICAL SCHEMATIC DIAGRAM   PHASE DIAGRAM

I-5. In the **integrating circuit,** the *phase angle* of the *output voltage* lags the phase angle of the *input voltage* by nearly $90°$ *(electrical degrees).* E_{out} is not to same scale as E_{in}.

integration. In the calculus, a process of summation in which an infinite number of infinitesimally small values are added to produce the whole. For example, the process, when applied to a mathematical function curve, obtains the area that lies between the curve and an axis and between defined limits of the coordinates of that axis. The process of integration operates on a mathematical function *(integrand)* to yield a result *(integral).* Thus, the integration of the function ax^2 between 3 and 6 yields $63a$. Expressed mathematically.

$$\int_3^6 ax^2\,dx = a(6^3 - 3^3)/3 = 63a.$$

The integral is exact since the limits are given. The $63a$ represents the area under the curve between the limits of $x = 3$ and $x = 6$. An *integrator* can perform the process of integration. Also see *differentiation.* See *radio-wire integration.*

integration device. See *radio-wire integration (RWI) device.*

integrator. A device that performs *integration.* For example in *analog systems,* a device that has an *output analog variable* that is the *integral* of an *input analog variable* with respect to time or another input variable. Also see *differentiator.* See *frequency modulation integrator; summing integrator.*

integrator feedback. See *video integrator feedback.*

integrity. See *bit-count integrity; bit integrity; character-count integrity; character integrity; data integrity; system integrity.*

intelligence. See *communication intelligence (COMINT); electronic intelligence (ELINT); photographic intelligence (PHOTINT); signal intelligence (SIGINT).*

intelligence communications. *Communication* methods, systems, and equipment that are used for the *transmission* of *messages* that contain foreign military or *security information.*

intelligent display device. 1. In *display systems,* a *display device* containing a *computer,* a processor, or other arithmetic or *logic* unit that is capable of performing certain local operations within itself (e.g., generate *characters,* move *display elements, display groups,* or *display images* by shifting *device coordinates,* store *data* in a buffer, control *scrolling,* or control the *scissoring* of data in its *buffer storage*). 2. A *display device* directly supported by a computer that allows certain operations to be performed locally.

intelligent terminal. A *terminal* that can execute certain fixed or variable *programs* for its *user* without continous intervention by the user during their execution.

intelligibility. See *voice intelligibility.*

intelligible crosstalk. *Crosstalk* that consists of *signals* or *sounds* that are capable of being interpreted by a person or a machine.

intensifier. See *image intensifier.*

intensity. See *luminous intensity; mean spherical intensity; peak radiant intensity; radiant intensity; traffic intensity.*

interaction crosstalk. *Crosstalk* that is caused by *coupling* between *carrier* and noncarrier circuits. The crosstalk may, in turn, be coupled to another carrier *circuit.* Also see *coupling.*

interactive data transaction. A single (one-way) *message* that is *transmitted* via a *data channel* and to which a reply is required in order for work or a conversation between two persons, a person and a machine, or two machines, to proceed logically.

intensity modulation. See *analog-intensity modulation.*

interactive display system. A *display system* that can be used in a conversational mode; i.e., a *user* can enter *display commands* or inquiries and the system can respond as in a conversation by changes in *display elements, display groups,* or *display images* in the *display space* on the *display surface* of a *display device* that is a part of the system. An interactive display system is usually supported by a computer or data processing system, *computer programs,* a *menu,* display commands, and the *display device,* such as a *CRT* or *fiberscope* and console.

interactive graphics. In *display systems,* the field of application and study in which *display devices,* their *components,* and associated equipment are used in an *interactive mode,* i.e., a sequence of alternating entries and *responses* takes place between the display devices, their components, or associated equipment in a manner similar to a dialogue between two persons. Contrast with *passive graphics.*

interactive mode. In *display systems,* a *mode* of *operation* of a *display device* in such a manner that a sequence of alternating entries and *responses* takes place between the device and a *user* similar to a dialogue between two persons, usually so that a user can alter or interact with a *display element, display group,* or *display image* in the *display space* of the *display surface* of the device. Synonymous with *conversational mode.* Contrast with *passive mode.*

interblock gap. An area on a *data medium* that may be used to indicate the end of a *block* or the end of a physical record. For example, a *space* between blocks of *data* on *magnetic tape.*

intercept. See *communication intercept.*

intercept communication method. A method of *communication* in which a *station transmits* a *message* to another station that repeats the message, thus transmitting it to a third station that may not transmit at all and that cannot receive messages directly from the station that originated the message. Also see *broadcast communication method; receipt communication method; relay communication method.*

interception. See *airborne interception; changed-address interception.*

intercept radar. See *airborne intercept radar; track-while-scan airborne intercept radar.*

intercept receiver. A *receiver* that is designed to *detect electromagnetic waves* and provide visual or aural indication of the received *emissions* that occur within the particular portion of the electromagnetic *spectrum* to which it is *tuned.* The tuning may be fixed or variable, but the *frequency band* is narrow compared with a *panoramic receiver.*

intercept tape storage. In a *communication system,* a method that provides temporary *storage* on paper or *magnetic tape* for enroute *message traffic* that is destined for nonoperating or backlogged (saturated) *channels.*

interchangeability. A condition that exists when two or more items possess such functional and physical characteristics as to be equivalent in performance and durability. They must be capable of being nonselectively substituted one for the other in their operational environment without alteration of the items themselves, their adjoining items, or the system in which they are placed. They may be only adjusted for fit and performance. Also see *commonality; compatibility; interoperability.*

interchange circuit. 1. A *circuit* that is part of the intermediate equipment at a *data station* and is connected between the *data terminal equipment (DTE)* and the *data circuit-terminating equipment (DCE)* for exchanging *data* and *signaling information.* Control signals, *timing signals, common return* functions, and other service features may also be included in the functions of an interchange circuit. **2.** A *circuit* that provides for the interchange of *traffic* between an element of one *communication system* and an element of another system. For example, a circuit between a military and a nonmilitary communication system.

interchange code. See *extended binary-coded decimal interchange code (EBCDIC).*

intercharacter interval. The time interval between the end of the *stop signal* of one *character* and the beginning of the *start signal* of the following *character.* This interval may be of any length. The signal sense of the intercharacter interval is always the same as the sense of the stop signal, that is, both are always a 1 or *mark* signal, or always a 0 or space signal. Also see *character interval.*

interco. In the *international signal code,* the *proword* that is used to precede, announce, or introduce the use of the code.

intercom. A device that enables a *closed user group* of persons to converse with one another. Usually the members of the group are not within direct audio range but belong to a group with some element of commonality, such as belonging to the same organization, office, shop, ship, or *station.* Synonymous with *intercommunication equipment; interphone.*

intercommunication equipment. See *intercom.*

interdiction. In *communication system security,* the denying of the use of a *system's* resources to a *user* or a group of users.

interest. See *community of interest.*

interface. 1. A shared boundary between two identifiable entities. For example, the boundary or a point that is common to two or more similar or dissimilar *systems,* subsystems, devices, or other entities, across which *information* or *control flow* may take place; or a shared boundary between two pieces of equipment, such as the interconnection between two *electronic* devices, two *layers* of a layered *communication system,* or between *data circuit-terminating equipment (DCE)* and *data terminal equipment (DTE);* or in *open systems architecture,* the *connection* between adjacent layers at the same *node* or between corresponding layers at different nodes in a *network*. The boundary is defined primarily by functional, interconnection, and *signal* characteristics in communication systems. The interface must allow the entities to be interconnected and to interoperate. In order to adequately define the interface requirements, the type, quantity, and function of the interconnecting *circuits,* the type and form of signals that are to be interchanged via those circuits, and the mechanical details of *plugs,* sockets, pin numbers and the like, must be specified. 2. To interrelate two or more dissimilar *circuits* or *systems.* 3. In *layered systems,* the set of *protocols* that is applicable to the interaction between any two *layers* within a single system, such as a *computer, data processing,* or *communication system.* Also see *commonality.* See *data transmission interface; electrical interface; gateway interface; high-level digital interface; host computer interface; host interface; radio-wire interface (R WI); transparent interface.* Also see Figure D-1.

interface device. See *fiberoptic interface device.*

interface processor. 1. In *communication systems,* a *processor* that serves as the *interface* between a *network* and another processor or *terminal.* 2. A *processor* that is used to control the flow of *data* into or out of a *network.* Synonymous with *communication computer.*

interface surface. In *optical systems* and *fiber optics,* the surface over which a discontinuity occurs in the *refractive index, electrical permittivity, electrical conductivity, magnetic permeability,* or other *parameter* of a *transmission medium.* Interface surfaces exist in *step-indexed optical fibers, couplers, integrated optical circuits,* and surfaces of *lenses, prisms,* and *back-surfaced mirrors* or wherever there is an abrupt change in those parameters of the material that affect the transmission of a *light beam propagating* in the medium. For example, if a lens is immersed in a *transparent* material with the same *refractive index,* and the material "wets" the surface, the lens will have no effect on a lightwave passing from the material to the lens; i.e., to the lightwave, the lens is not there and there is no interface surface. Note that in the expression for the *reflection coefficient,* if $n_1 = n_2$, and since according to *Snell's law,* the angles of *incidence* and *refraction* are equal in this case, the reflection coefficient reduces to zero and the *transmission coefficient* becomes unity. Thus, there is no interface surface.

interference. 1. In *lightwave transmission,* the systematic reinforcement and *attenuation* of two or more lightwaves when they are superimposed. Interference is an additive process. (The term is applied also to the converse process in which a given wave is split into two or more waves, for example, by *reflection* and *refraction* at *beam splitters.*) The superposition must occur on a systematic basis between two or more waves in order that the *electric* and *magnetic fields* of the waves can be additive and produce noticeable effects such as *interference patterns.* For example, the *polarization planes* should nearly or actually coincide, or the *wavelengths* should nearly or actually be the same. Also see *Fabry-Perot interferometer.* 2. In a *communication system,* extraneous *power* entering or induced in a *channel* from natural or man-made *sources* that might *interfere* with reception of desired *signals,* or the disturbance caused by the undesired power. See *adjacent channel interference; antenna interference; cochannel interference; common-mode interference; conducted interference; differential-mode interference; electromagnetic interference (EMI); harmful interference; intersymbol interference; mutual interference; radio frequency interference (RFI); single-frequency interference; single-tone interference.* Also see *static.*

interference emission. An *emission* of *electromagnetic radiation* that results in an *electrical signal* being *propagated* into and *interfering* with the proper *operation* of *electronic* equipment. The *frequency range* of such *interference* may be taken to include the entire *electromagnetic spectrum.*

interference limit. In *radio transmission,* the maximum permissible *interference* as specified in recommendations of recognized authorities, such as the International Special Committee on Radio Interference.

interference pattern. In *data display systems,* a defect in the reproduced *images.* The defect may assume the form of regularly spaced curved or straight lines that are superimposed on the *display image.* The interference pattern is caused by recurring *interference signals* and is usually man-made.

interference report. *Information* that concerns the type of *interference* that is being received, its source, the *transmitter* or *receiver* being interfered with, the receiving station that is experiencing the interference, and other relevant information.

interference suppression and blanking. See *pulse interference suppression and blanking.*

interferometer. An instrument employing the *interference* of *lightwaves* for purposes of measurement, such as the *accuracy* of *optical* surfaces by means of *Newton's rings,* the measurement of optical paths, and linear and angular displacements. See *Fabry-Perot interferometer; speckle interferometer; Twyman-Green interferometer.*

interframe time fill. In *data transmission,* the sequence of *bits* that are transmitted between *frames.* Time fill within a frame is not considered as interframe time fill.

interior communications. See *internal communications.*

interlacing. See *interleaving.*

interleaving. 1. The arranging of the members of one sequence of items or events so that they alternate with members of one or more other sequences of items. Each original sequence retains its identity, that is, its ordering sequence. 2. In *communications,* the *transmission* of *pulses* from two or more *digital sources* in *time-division* sequence over a single *path.* The technique can be used in conjunction with *error-correcting codes* in order to lower the error rates of communication *channels* that are characterized by *error bursts.* In the interleaving process, *code symbols* are reordered before transmission in such a manner that any two successive code symbols are separated by *I-1* symbols in the transmitted sequence, where *I* is the degree of interleaving. Upon reception, the interleaved code symbols are reordered into their original sequence using the same degree of interleaving. This spreads or randomizes the errors (in time) and enables an improvement in the error-correcting capability of an error-correcting code. Synonymous with *interlacing.*

interlock code. In a *communication system,* a *code* sent in the *forward direction,* and in some circumstances in the *backward direction,* that indicates that a *closed user group* is involved in a *call.*

intermediate distribution frame (IDF). In a *telephone switching center,* a *frame* that has the primary purpose of cross-connecting the *user* (customer, subscriber) *line cable* to the user line *circuit.* In a *private branch exchange (PBX),* the IDF is used for similar purposes. The IDF is also used as a distribution point for multipair cables from the *main distribution frame (MDF)* or *combined distribution frame (CDF)* to individual cables for equipment in areas that are remote from the frames. The IDF is usually connected between the MDF and the *switching* apparatus or switching circuits. Also see *combined distribution frame (CDF); main distribution frame (MDF).*

intermediate equipment. At a *data station,* the auxiliary equipment, such as an *interchange circuit,* that may be inserted between the *data terminal equipment (DTE)* and the *data circuit-terminating equipment (DCE)* or the *signal* conversion equipment, and can perform certain additional functions before *modulation* or after *demodulation.* All *input* and *output* circuits and signals of the intermediate equipment must conform to the established standards for the *interface* between the DTE and the DCE.

intermediate field. See *induction field.*

intermediate frequency (IF). In a *heterodyne circuit* such as is used in a *radio receiver,* the *frequency* that is produced when the frequency of a *local oscillator* is mixed with the *audio frequency (AF) modulated* incoming *radio frequency (RF) signal.* The IF is usually higher than the AF and lower than the RF and thus can be effectively processed by the receiver circuits.

intermediate frequency (IF) repeater. See *heterodyne repeater.*

intermediate frequency (IF) amplifier. See *linear-logarithmic intermediate frequency (IF) amplifier.*

intermediate-frequency gain control. See *receiver intermediate-frequency gain control.*

intermediate node. In a *network,* a *node* that is directly connected to at least two other nodes by means of *branches* and is therefore not an *endpoint node.*

intermediate switchboard. In *telephone switchboard operations,* any *switchboard* that is situated or connected between the switchboard that is serving a *calling party* and the switchboard that is serving a *called party.*

intermediate zone. See *induction field.*

intermittent-timing transmission. See *random bit-stream signaling.*

intermodulation. In *communication systems,* the *modulation* of the *frequency components* of an *electromagnetic wave,* producing waves having frequencies equal to the sums and differences of *integral* multiples of the component frequencies of the original waves, such as by mixing or the use of nonlinear *circuits.* Intermodulation occurs more in *frequency-* or *wavelength-division multiplexed* systems than in *time-division multiplexed* systems. Each frequency modulates all the others. See *radio frequency intermodulation.*

intermodulation distortion. *Distortion* of a *signal* caused by *intermodulation.* In *communication systems,* it is usually considered as *nonlinear distortion* that is characterized by the appearance of *frequencies* in the *output* of a *system, circuit,* or device, such as a *channel* or an *amplifier,* that are equal to the sums and differences of *integral* multiples of the component frequencies present in the *input. Harmonic components* are components that define the *signal shape.* They are also present in the *output* but are not considered as part of the intermodulation distortion. They are part of the desired signal. The nonlinear distortion is the resultant response to simultaneous (coexistent) *sinusoidal* excitation, that is, they are *intermodulation products.* See *modulation-frequency intermodulation distortion.*

intermodulation noise. In a *transmission path,* the *noise* that is the result of *modulation, demodulation,* and any nonlinear characteristics of the *electrical components* or the *transmission media.* See *equipment intermodulation noise; path intermodulation noise.*

intermodulation noise loss. The difference between the actual *output power* and the theoretical output power of a wanted *signal* from a nonlinear *circuit.* The power loss is attributable to the total power losses that are due to unwanted *intermodulation products* that are generated by nonlinearities in the circuit.

intermodulation product. The *frequencies* in an *output signal* produced by *intermodulation,* equal to the sums and differences of *integral* multiples of the frequencies present in the *input* signal. Intermodulation products are caused by *nonlinear distortion.*

internal absorptance. The ratio of *light flux absorbed* between the entrance and emergent surfaces of a *transmission medium,* to the flux that has penetrated the entrance surface. The effects of interreflections between the two surfaces are not included. Internal absorptance is numerically equal to unity minus the *internal transmittance*.

internal bias. In a *start-stop teletypewriter* receiving mechanism, the marking or spacing *bias* that has the same effect on the *margin* of *operation* as a bias that is external to the *receiver*. Also see *bias distortion*.

internal communication facility. An electrical, acoustical, or mechanical *communication system* that interconnects the various operational compartments or spaces within a specified area, such as on a ship, or in an aircraft, vehicle, or building. Synonymous with *interior communications*. See *convoy internal communications*.

internal message distribution center. A special *communication service center* that provides *communication services* within an organization, such as a headquarters. It contains *message* distribution equipment and other support facilities. Delivery of incoming messages is accomplished automatically, semiautomatically, or manually by recognition of the *address designator* or *addressee,* the message subject matter, or a subject matter discriminator or descriptor.

internal optical density. The logarithm to the base 10 of the reciprocal of the *internal transmittance*. Synonymous with *transmission factor*.

internal photoeffect. The changes in characteristics of a material that occur when *incident photons* are *absorbed* by the material and excite the *electrons* in the various *energy bands*. Characteristic changes include changes in *electrical conductivity, photoemissivity,* and electric potential development. For example, electrons may move from a *valence band* to a *conduction band* for both intrinsic material and impurities, or to or from the valence bands of the intrinsic material and impurities; (i.e., *dopants* and other impurities). Thus, both intrinsic and extrinsic *photoeffects* may be involved in the internal photoeffect. See *extrinsic internal photoeffect; intrinsic internal photoeffect*.

internal photoeffect detector. A *photodetector* in which *incident photons* raise *electrons* from a lower to a higher energy state, resulting in an altered state of the electrons, *holes,* or electron-hole pairs generated by the transition, which is then detected. Most *semiconductors* make use of the internal photoeffect for *signal* detection at the end of an *optical fiber*. Also see *external photoeffect detector*.

internal reflection. In an *optical element* in which an *electromagnetic wave* is *propagating,* a *reflection* at an outside surface from the inside such that a wave that is *incident* upon the surface is reflected wholly or partially back into the element itself. *Optical fibers* depend on internal reflection for the successful *transmission* of *lightwaves* in order that the waves do not leave and depart from the fiber; namely, the wave energy is confined to or bound to the fiber. Also see *total internal reflection*. See Figure I-6.

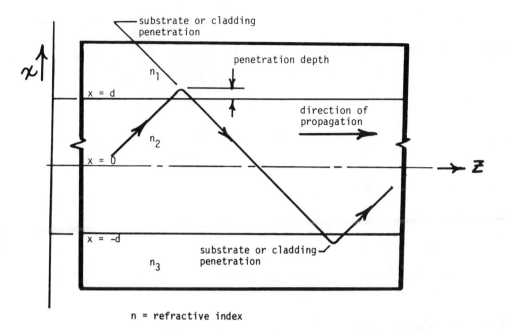

n = refractive index

I-6. **Internal reflection** in a *slab dielectric* (planar) *waveguide,* where n_1 and n_3 are less than n_2.

internal reflection angle. See *critical angle.*

internal security audit. A *security audit* of a *system* that is conducted by persons who are not repsonsible to the organization or agency that operates the system.

internal transmittance. The ratio of the *flux transmitted* to the second surface of a *transmission medium* to the corresponding flux that has just passed through the first surface, i.e., the *transmittance* from the first surface to the second surface. Internal transmittance does not include the effects due to interreflection between the two surfaces.

internal address indicating group. An *address indicating group (AIG)* that is assigned for international use. From the block of AIG's that are allocated to each nation, each nation may use each AIG as appropriate. The AIG may be either permanent or temporary. Also see *national address indicating group.*

international aeronautical emergency frequency. The nominal 121.5 MHz *frequency band* that is used internationally for *emergency messages* by *aircraft stations, ship stations,* and *aeronautical land stations* that are primarily concerned with safety and regulation of travel along international routes and lanes, particularly international civil air routes and international shipping lanes. The emergency frequency band lies in the range from 118 MHz to 132 MHz.

international broadcasting station. A *broadcasting station* that employs *frequencies* that are allocated to the *broadcasting service.* International broadcasting *transmissions* usually lie between 5950 kHz and 26,100 kHz. The transmissions are considered as *short wave* broadcasts. The transmissions in this band are intended to be received directly by the general public in foreign countries.

international call sign. A *call sign* that is assigned in accordance with the rules of the *International Telecommunication Union.* These call signs are intended to permit a *receiver* to identify a *radio station.* Also see *military call sign; military ship international call sign; ship international call sign.*

international congestion signal. In an international *communication system,* a *signal* that is sent in the *backward direction* to indicate the failure of a *call* setup attempt (unsuccessful *access attempt*) due to the congestion (saturation, contention) that is being encountered in the international *network* or in the destination national network.

international frequency register. See *Master International Frequency Register (MIFR).*

international cooperation index. See *diametral cooperation index.*

International Frequency Registration Board (IFRA). A permanent organization of the *International Telecommunication Union (ITU)* that implements *frequency assignment* policy and maintains the *Master International Frequency Register (MIFR).*

international Morse code. A *code* in which letters and *numerals* are represented by specific groupings of *dots* and *dashes.* The international Morse code is used especially in *radio telegraph* and *visual communication systems.* See Figure I-7.

I-7. The **international Morse code.**

International Organization for Standardization (ISO). An international organization whose members are the national standards bodies of most of the countries of the world. The organization is responsible for the development and publication of standards in various technical fields, after developing a suitable consensus. It is affiliated with the United Nations. Member bodies of the ISO include, for example, the Association Francaise de Normalisation (AFNOR), the British Standards Institution (BSI), the American National Standards Institute (ANSI), and the Standards Council of Canada. The headquarters of the ISO is at 1, rue de Varembe, Geneva, Switzerland. International standards may also be obtained from ANSI, 1430 Broadway, New York, NY 10018.

international radiotelegraph distress frequency. The nominal 500 kHz *frequency band* that is used internationally for *distress radiotelegraph messages* that are sent by *ship stations, aircraft stations,* and *survival craft stations* when requesting assistance. The distress frequency band range is from 405 kHz to 535 kHz. Assistance is usually requested through the stations of the *maritime mobile service* and the *aeronautical mobile service.* The frequency is used only for *distress calls, distress traffic, distress messages, urgency messages,* and *safety signals.*

international radiotelegraph lifecraft frequency. The nominal 8364 kHz *band* that is used internationally for *radiotelegraph distress messages* sent by lifeboat, lifecraft, and *survival craft stations.* These stations are usually equipped to *transmit* on *frequencies* that are between 4000 kHz and 27500 kHz. Assistance is usually requested through stations of the *maritime mobile service* and the *aeronautical mobile service.* The *calls* and *messages* are used only for establishing and conducting *search-and-rescue communications.*

international radiotelephone distress frequency. The nominal 2182 kHz *frequency band* that is used internationally for *radiotelephone distress messages* from *ship stations, aircraft stations,* and *survival craft stations.* These stations are usually equipped to use frequencies in the 1605 kHz to 4000 kHz band when requesting assistance through stations of the *aeronautical mobile service* and the *maritime mobile service.* The international radiotelephone distress frequency is used for *distress calls, distress messages, distress traffic, urgency signals, urgency messages,* and *safety signals.*

international signal code. A *signaling code* and its related *systems* and procedures for international use, consisting of signs, *symbols,* letters, numerals, *prowords,* and control *signals,* that have been accepted for use by international agreement. The international signal code is used particularly when communicating with *ship stations. Code groups* in *messages* should be preceded by the special *pennant* that identifies the code or by the proword *interco.*

International System of Units (Systeme International d'Unites). See *SI.*

International Telecommunication Union (ITU). A civil international organization established to promote standardized *telecommunications* on a worldwide basis in such matters as communication procedures and practices, *frequency allo-*

cations, and radio regulations. The CCIR (International Consultative Committee on Radio) and the CCITT (International Consultative Committee on Telephone and Telegraph) are permanent committees of the ITU. Main offices of the ITU are in Geneva, Switzerland. It is older than the United Nations. It is recognized by the UN as the specialized agency for telecommunication matters.

International Telecommunication Union (ITU) regulations. *Telecommunication* standards that are published by the ITU.

International Telecommunication Union (ITU) world region. A subdivision of the world area for purposes of *communication,* particularly for *distress signaling.* The Western Hemisphere is roughly Region 2. The South Pacific (China, East Indies, Australia, New Zealand and Southern Japan) is roughly Region 3, and the remainder of the world (Eurasia, Africa, and North Atlantic) is Region 1.

International Telegraph Alphabet Number 1 (ITA-1). An *alphabet* in which a two-condition five-unit *code* is used. It is used in Baudot *synchronous telegraphy.* This alphabet is specified by Article 16 of the Telegraph Regulations of the *International Telecommunication Union,* Geneva, Switzerland, 1958.

International Telegraph Alphabet Number 2 (ITA-2). An *alphabet* in which a two-condition five-unit *code* is used. This alphabet is specified in CCITT (International Consultative Committee on Telephone and Telegraph) *International Telecommunication Union* Recommendation F.1. In *tape relay systems,* a two-condition *(binary) code* is the set of correspondences between *impulses* or patterns of holes at each row on tape, and the letters, figures (numerals), special signs and *symbols,* or *operating signals* and *machine functions* that the patterns represent. The early five-unit *telegraph* alphabet was developed about the year 1895.

International Telegraph Alphabet Number 3 (ITA-3). An *alphabet* in which a two-condition seven-unit constant-ratio *code* is used. This *alphabet* is specified in CCITT (International Consultative Committee on Telephone and Telegraph) Recommendation S.13, 1972, or by CCIR (International Consultative Committee on Radio) Recommendation 342-2, 1970, of the *International Telecommunication Union,* Geneva, Switzerland.

International Telegraph Alphabet Number 4 (ITA-4). An *alphabet* in which a two-condition six-unit *code* is used for *time-division multiplex synchronous telegraphy.* The code is comprised of two code combinations corresponding to permanent positive and negative polarity in order that the *multiplexed channel* can be operated in a *switched network.*

International Telegraph Alphabet Number 5 (ITA-5). An *alphabet* in which a different seven *binary digit* pattern is assigned to each different letter, *numeral,* special sign and *symbol,* and *control character* in the code. The code is used for effecting *information* interchange. International agreement has been reached on the code. The code is a result of a joint agreement between the CCITT (International Consultative Committee on Telephone and Telegraph) of the *Interna-*

tional Telecommunication Union, and the *International Organization for Standardization (ISO).* The code is published as CCITT Recommendation V3 and as ISO 646. It has also been adopted by NATO for military use. In the code, 12 of the seven binary digit patterns are unassigned to any letter, numeral, or control character. These are open for use in a given country that may have unique language requirements, such as monetary symbols, diacritical marks (tilde, umlaut, circumflex, dieresis), or other requirements. The United States' adaptation of ITA-5 is the *ASCII* (American Standard Code for Information Interchange) published by the American National Standards Institute. The alphabet actually includes a two-condition (binary) eight digit pattern that consists of seven primary binary digits and a *parity check bit.* The code includes upper and lower case letters, ten *decimal* numerals, special signs and symbols, diacritical marks, *data delimiters,* and *transmission control characters.*

international visual signal code. A *code* that has been adopted by many nations for international *visual communication.* The code contains combinations of letters that are assigned to *words,* phrases, and sentences. The letters may be transmitted by the hoisting of internationally standardized *alphabet flags* and *pennants,* by *flashing lights* or *wigwag* using the *international Morse code,* or by other *signaling systems* designed to transmit internationally standardized letters by visual means.

interoperability. The ability of *communication systems* or equipment to function together. It is the condition that is achieved among *communication-electronic (C-E) systems* or equipment when information or services can be exchanged directly between them or their *users* (customers, subscribers), or both. The degree of interoperability should be defined when referring to specific situations. *Interface* devices may be placed between devices or systems in order to achieve a desired degree of interoperability. Also see *commonality; compatibility; interchangeability.*

interphone. See *intercom.*

interpolation. See *analog speech interpolation; digital speech interpolation.*

interposition trunk. 1. A *connection* between two *positions* of a *switchboard* in order that a *line* on one position can be connected to a line on another position. **2.** *Connections* that are *terminated* at *test points* for testing and *patching* between testboards and *patch bays* within a *technical control facility.*

interrogating. The process of *transmitting* and *receiving* a *message* that is in the form of a question or that requires a *response.* For example, the process in which a *signal* or combination of signals is intended to trigger a response, or the process in which a *station,* such as a *master station,* requests another station, such as a *slave station,* to indicate its identity or status.

interrogator. In *satellite communications,* a *pulse transmitter* that is used exclusively for exciting a *transponder.*

interrupt signaling. See *digital carrier-interrupt signaling.*

interrupted continuous wave (ICW). A *modulation* technique in which on and off *keying* of a *continuous carrier* is used. Also see *continuous carrier.*

interrupted isochronous transmission. See *isochronous burst transmission.*

interruption rate. In a *telephone system* in which *direct current (DC)* is used for control *signals,* the rate at which a DC source is interrupted for *signaling* purposes.

interruption switch. In an *electric power* distribution *system,* a *switch* that has the capability of opening (interrupting) a *circuit* that is *conducting* an *electric current.* The switch usually has an interrupting capacity, usually specified in amperes, before opening, and a *voltage* rating to ground or between contacts, specified in volts, after opening; that is, it can be opened or closed under *load* within specified voltage and current limits. Also see *disconnecting switch.*

intersection. *Direction finding* by *triangulation* in which the location of a single *source* of *radiation,* such as a *radio transmitting antenna* or an observed forest fire, is determined by obtaining bearings of the source of radiation from two known locations and determining the point on a map at which they cross. Also see *resection.* See *bearing intersection; space intersection.* See Figure I-8.

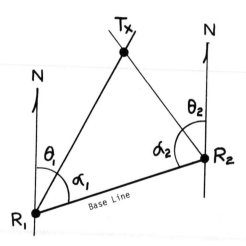

I-8. Receivers R_1 and R_2 of known location may be used to determine the *azimuths (bearings)* with North, or the angles with the *base line,* to determine the position of the *transmitter* T_X by the **intersection** method of *triangulation.*

intersection gate. See *AND gate.*

intership radio teletypewriter. A *ship-to-ship radio communication system* in which a *teletypewriter* is used for the *transmission* and *reception* of *messages.*

interstitial defect. In the somewhat ordered array of atoms and molecules in *optical fiber* material, a site at which an extra atom or molecule is inserted in the space between the normal array.   The defect can serve as a *scattering center,* causing *diffusion,* heating, *absorption,* and resultant *attenuation.*   Also see *vacancy defect.*

interswitch trunk.   A *trunk* that connects two *switching centers* directly.

intersymbol interference.   **1.** In a transmission system, the overlapping of successively transmitted *signals* at the end of a *transmission line* primarily caused by *dispersion* of the *frequencies* comprising the signal.   **2.** Extraneous energy that originates from a signal in one or more *keying* intervals *(character time slots)* and that interferes with the reception of the signal in another keying interval.   **3.** The disturbance that results when a *character* in one *time slot* or *keying* interval causes *interference* in the time slot or keying interval of another character.

interval.   See *bit interval; character interval; intercharacter interval; Nyquist interval; service time interval; significant interval; unit interval.*

interval modulation.   See *pulse interval modulation.*

interval theoretical duration.   See *significant interval theoretical duration.*

interworking.   A process in which *data terminal equipment (DTE)* that belongs to one *user service class* communicates with a DTE that belongs to a different user service class.

intranodal.   In a *communication network,* pertaining to any matter, such as an event, *transmission,* or *message exchange,* that takes place entirely within the equipment at a single *node.*

intrinsic absorption.   In *lightwave transmission media,* the *absorption* of *light energy* from a *traveling* or *standing wave* by the medium itself, causing *attenuation* as a function of distance, material properties, *mode, frequency,* and other factors.   Intrinsic absorption is primarily due to charge transfer bands in the *ultraviolet* region and vibration or *multiphonon bands* in the near *infrared,* particularly if they extend into the region of *wavelengths* used in *fiber communications,* namely, 700 to 1100 nm.   Intrinsic absorption normally occurs in *optical fibers* and *integrated optical circuits* made of glass, silica, or plastic.

intrinsic internal photoeffect.   An *internal photoeffect* involving the basic material rather than any *dopants* or other impurities.   Also see *extrinsic internal photoeffect.*

intrinsic negative photodiode.   See *positive-intrinsic-negative photodiode.*

intrinsic-negative photodiode coupler.   See *positive-intrinsic-negative photodiode coupler.*

intrinsic noise.   In a *transmission path* or device, *noise* that is inherent to the *path* or device and that is not dependent upon *modulation.*   For example, *thermal noise* in a *resistor,* domain rotation noise in a *ferromagnetic* material, or *microphonic* noise in an *amplifier* (due to mechanical vibration).

intrusion-resistant communication cable. A *cable* that is designed to provide substantial physical protection, electrical isolation, and the capability of reducing the possibility of clandestine *coupling,* of the wires or *fibers* in the cable that contain *information*-bearing *signals.* Protective measures and specialized equipment are used to detect slight changes in the physical or *electrical* state of the cable. These provide visible or audible indications at a central control point of attempts at intrusion. Synonymous with *alarmed cable.*

inverse-square law. The *radiant intensity,* that is, the *power* per unit area in the direction of *propagation,* of a spherical *wavefront* varies inversely as the square of the distance from the *source.* For example, the power radiated from a *point source,* an *omnidirectional (isotropic) antenna,* or from any source at very large distances from the source compared to the size of the source, must spread itself over larger and larger spherical surfaces as the distance from the source increases. *Diffused* and noncoherent *radiation* is similarly affected. It also must spread over larger spherical surfaces as it moves away from the source. Also see *geometric spreading.*

inverse filtering. An *image restoration* technique in which the distorted *image* is processed in a manner that reverses the transformations that caused the original *distortion.* If S is an *operator* that maps g into $h,$ in which h is a distorted image of the *object g,* then the inverse filter is the operator S^{-1} that operates on h to form a less distorted or more true image of $g.$ The operator S is the *point-spread-function,* and S^{-1} performs the reverse. For example, if the elements of an image of an object are shifted in one direction proportionally by $S,$ then S^{-1} operating on the distorted image would shift the image elements (e.g., *display elements, display groups,* and *display images*) proportionally in the opposite direction, thus obtaining the original, undistorted, or at least less distorted, image of the object. See *pseudo-inverse filtering.*

inversion. See *bit inversion; population inversion.*

inversion signal. See *alternate mark inversion (AMI) signal.*

inversion violation. See *alternate mark inversion (AMI) violation.*

inverted directory. In a *telephone system,* a listing in numerical order of *telephone numbers,* each number followed by the name of the *user* (customer, subscriber, person, process, equipment, place, organization). Also see *telephone directory.*

inverted position. In *frequency translation* performed in *frequency-division multiplexed channels,* a position or condition of a translated *channel* in which an increasing signal frequency in the untranslated channel causes a decreasing signal frequency in the translated channel. Also see *erect position.*

inverter. **1.** A device in which *direct current (DC)* is changed to *alternating current (AC).* **2.** In *digital computers,* a device or *circuit,* such as a *transformer* or a *NEGATION gate,* that inverts the polarity of a *pulse.* **3.** In *analog systems,* a device that has an *output analog variable* that is equal in magnitude to its *input* *analog variable* but is of opposite algebraic sign. Synonymous with *negation circuit.* See *image inverter.*

IOC. See *integrated optical circuit.*

I-O device. See *input-output (I-O) device.*

ion. A charged particle that is usually formed when there is an excess or deficiency of *electrons* forming a parent atom or molecule. For example, a sodium atom with its outermost electron missing is a positive ion; a chlorine atom with one extra electron in its outermost shell is a negative ion. The movement of electrons and ions constitute *electric current.*

ion absorption. See *hydroxyl ion absorption.*

ion-exchange process. See *double-crucible (DC) process.*

ionization. A process in which *ions* are produced by the removal or addition of *electrons* to atoms or molecules. The ionized layers of the *stratosphere* cause *reflection, refraction,* and *dispersion* of *electromagnetic waves* that are *incident* upon them. This enables *radio communication* over great distances around the surface of the earth. Also see *ionosphere.*

ion laser. A *gas laser* involving ionization of certain gases, such as argon, krypton, and xenon.

ionosphere. The region of the *atmosphere* that extends from approximately 50 km to 400 km in altitude and in which there is appreciable *ionization,* that is, appreciable *ion* density as might be measured in ions per unit volume. The presence of the charged particles in this region profoundly affects the *propagation* of *electromagnetic waves* of long *wavelength,* such as *radio* and *radar waves.* The ionosphere consists of several identifiable layers, some of which are called the D, E, and F layers. Other planets also have ionospheres. Also see *atmosphere; ionization; stratosphere; tropopause; troposphere.*

ionospheric disturbance. A sudden increase in the *ionization* density of the *D-layer* of the *ionosphere.* It is usually caused by *solar flares* and results in greatly increased *radio wave absorption,* that is, *radio blackout.* Also see *sudden ionospheric disturbance.*

ionospheric forecast. See *long-term ionospheric forecast; short-term ionospheric forecast.*

ionospheric forecasting. The forecasting of *ionospheric* conditions and the preparation and distribution of *electromagnetic wave propagation data* that is derived from the forecasting.

ionospheric forward scatter. See *forward propagation ionospheric scatter.*

ionospheric message format. The arrangement of *data* in a *message* that contains *information* on the condition of the *ionosphere.* For example, a message that contains a series of dates on which *propagation* disturbances will begin, to continue over the next 30 days, followed by a date up to which a 7-day daily forecast is given, followed by a 7-digit code in which each digit represents one of 9 propagation conditions that range from "useless" to "excellent," followed by the time-date group. An example of such a message might be 1–2 Aug, 10–12 Aug, up to 7 Aug 3455666, DTG 020001Z.

ionospheric reflection.   A bending by *reflection* and *refraction* of *electromagnetic waves* back toward the earth as they strike successive *ionized layers* of the *ionosphere.* The amount of bending depends on the extent of penetration which is a function of *frequency, incidence angle,* direction of *polarization* of the wave, and ionospheric conditions, such as the *ionization* density (*ion* density in number of ions per unit volume), and the height of the ionosphere. The minimum distance from a *ground station* to the point on the earth's surface where a radio wave returns after reflection from the ionosphere is known as the *skip distance.*

ionospheric scatter.   The *propagation* of *electromagnetic waves* by means of *scattering* that is due to irregularities, turbulence, and discontinuities in the *ionosphere.* See *backward propagation ionospheric scatter; forward propagation ionospheric scatter.*

ionospheric turbulence.   A permanent ongoing turbulence or disturbance in the *ionosphere* that has the effect of *scattering incident electromagnetic waves.* Ionospheric turbulence results in irregularities in the composition of the ionosphere that change with time. This causes changes in *reflection* properties. These, in turn, cause changes in *skip distance, fading,* local intensification, and *distortion* of the *incident waves.*

ion overtone absorption.   See *hydroxyl ion overtone absorption.*

IOS.   *International Organization for Standardization.* (Properly abbreviated in all languages as *ISO.*)

IPM.   *Incremental phase modulation.*

irrelevence.   In *information theory,* the conditional info*rmation entropy* measured as the occurrence of specific *messages* at a *message sink* given the occurrence of specific messages at the *message source* connected to the message sink by a specified *channel.* Synonymous with *prevarication; spread.*

IR.   *Infrared.*

irradiance.   **1.** The *power* per unit area of *incident light* upon a surface. **2.** The *radiant flux* incident upon a unit area of surface. It can be measured as watts per square *meter,* as for any form of *electromagnetic waves,* or as *lumens* per square meter when *visible light* is incident upon a surface. Previously, it was measured in foot-candles. Synonymous with *radiant flux density.* See *spectral irradiance.*

irradiation.   The product of *irradiance* and time; therefore, *radiant energy* received per unit area.

ISO. *International Organization for Standardization.* (The proper abbreviation in all languages.)

isochrone. A line on a map or chart joining points associated with a constant time difference from the *transmitter* to *receiver* of *electromagnetic waves,* such as *lightwaves* or *radio waves,* at all points along the line.

isochrone determination. *Radiolocation* in which a position line is determined by the difference in the *propagation times* of *signals* from the same *source* but propagating along two different *paths.*

isochronous. **1.** A characteristic of a *periodic signal* in which the time interval that separates any two corresponding *significant instants* or *transitions* of *signal* level is equal to the *unit interval* or to a multiple of the unit interval. **2.** Pertaining to *data transmission* in which corresponding significant instants (signal level transitions) of two or more sequential signals have a constant *phase* relationship with each other. Also see *anisochronous; heterochronous; homochronous; mesochronous; plesiochronous.*

isochronous burst transmission. In a *data network, transmission* that is performed by interrupting at controlled intervals the *data stream* that is being transmitted. The method of transmission enables communication between *data terminal equipment (DTE)* and data networks that operate as dissimilar *data signaling rates.* The transmission method may be used where the *information bearer channel* signaling rate is higher than the *input* data signaling rate. The *binary digits* being transferred are transmitted at the *digit* rate of the information bearer channel and the transmission in interrupted at controlled intervals in order to produce the required mean data signaling rate. The interruption is always for an equal number of digit periods *(character time slots).* Isochronous burst transmission has particular application where *envelopes* are being transmitted and received by the *data circuit-terminating equipment (DCE)* and only the *bytes* contained within the envelopes are being transmitted between the DCE and the *data terminal equipment (DTE).* Synonymous with *burst isochronous; burst transmission; interrupted isochronous transmission.* Also see *information transfer.*

isochronous distortion. The difference between the measured *modulation rate* and the theoretical modulation rate in a *digital system.* It is measured as the ratio of the maximum measured difference between the actual and theoretical intervals that separate any two *significant instants* of *modulation* or *demodulation,* and the *unit interval.* The difference is taken without regard to sign. The significant instants occur at *signal level transition* points in the transmitted signal. These significant instants will not necessarily be consecutive. The ratio is usually expressed as a percentage. The result of the measurement should be accompanied by an indication of the limited period during which the measurement was made. For a prolonged modulation or demodulation it is useful to consider the probability that an assigned value of the degree of *distortion* will be exceeded.

isochronous modulation. *Modulation* or *demodulation* in which the time interval that separates any two *significant instants* is theoretically equal to the *unit interval* or to a multiple of the unit interval.

isochronous restitution. *Telegraph restitution* in which each *significant interval* has a duration that is equal to a *unit interval* or to an *integral* multiple of this interval.

isochronous transmission. A *transmission* process in which there is always an *integral* number of *unit intervals* between any two *significant instants.* The transmission is characterized by a constant *pulse* rate, a constant time interval or multiples thereof between *voltage* or *electromagnetic field intesnsity transitions,* and a *gating* by a controlled *clock.*

isolated. In *electric circuits* and *communication systems,* the state that exists at a point such that the state of the point cannot be changed or influenced by any stimulus from outside itself.   Thus, the point is not subject to the influence of any *electrostatic, magnetic, magnetostatic,* or *electromagnetic field.*   It is subject only to its self-influence.   It is therefore also insulated, that is, it is inaccessible to *electric currents* and *voltages* as well as fields.   The state is somewhat achievable by means of certain nonconducting *insulators* and certain types of conducting *shields,* such as metal containers.   Also see *insulated.*

isolator.   See *optical isolator; optoisolator; waveguide isolator.*

ISO seven-bit code.   See *International Telegraph Alphabet Number 5 (ITA-5).*

isothermal region.   See *stratosphere.*

isotropic antenna.   See *isotropic source.*

isotropic condition.   See *decibel above isotropic condition.*

isotropic material.   A substance that exhibits the same property when *tested* along an axis in any direction.   For example, a *dielectric* material with the same *permittivity* or a glass with the same *refractive index* in all directions.

isotropic radiated power.   See *effective isotropic radiated power.*

isotropic radiator.   See *isotropic source.*

isotropic source.   A theoretical *antenna, light source,* or sound source that *radiates* with equal *power density* in all directions and that can only be approximated in actual practice.   Truly isotropic sources do not exist physically, but they represent convenient reference sources for comparing and expressing the directional properties of actual sources such as radio antennas.   They have a hypothetical *directive gain* of unity in all directions.   The ratio of the *power gain* when referred to an isotropic source (antenna) and that referred to a standard *half-wave dipole antenna* is equivalent to 2.15 dB.

isotropic space loss.   The ratio of the available *power* from a loss-free standard receiving *antenna* and the power radiated by an identical transmitting antenna.

The *transmission medium* is *free space,* that is, there is no *atmospheric attenuation, scattering, reflection,* or *absorption.* The ratio is measured at a specified *frequency.*

ITA. *International telegraph alphabet.*

item. See *data item.*

iterative impedance. In a pair of *terminals* of a four-terminal *network,* the *impedance* that will *terminate* the other pair of terminals in such a way that the impedance that is measured at the first pair is equal to this terminating impedance. The iterative impedance of a *uniform transmission line* is the same as its *characteristic impedance.*

ITU. *International Telecommunication Union.*

IVPO. See *inside vapor-phase oxidation process.*

I^2L. *Integrated injection logic.*

J

jack. In a *telephone switchboard,* a socket, hole, or receptacle mounted on the face of the switchboard into which a *plug* can be inserted to complete a *connection.* See *monitor jack.*

jacket. See *bundle jacket; cable jacket; optical fiber jacket.*

jacket leak. A measure of the imperviousness of an *optical cable jacket,* measured by such techniques as the water-submerge-and-vacuum method and the gas-detection-and-vacuum method.

jackfield. A group of terminals that is used for making *connections* to *jacks.* See *channel patching jackfield; patching jackfield.*

jam. 1. To deliberately prevent the successful operation of a *communication system* by interfering with the *transmission* of *signals* in the system by using other signals to cause the *interference.* 2. To cause a halt to the dynamic interaction of moving parts of a mechanical system by a forced interference in the fitting of the parts. 3. The binding caused by a forced interference of the mechanical parts of a system. A jam can be removed by removing the interference fit, by lubrication, by adjustment, or by other means.

jammer. A *transmitting system* that is designed specifically for *jamming* purposes. See *airborne radar jammer; automatic search jammer; automatic spot jammer; barrage jammer; coherent repeater jammer; deception jammer; DINA jammer; expendable jammer; locked-pulse radar jammer; manual spot jammer; multipurpose jammer; noise jammer; preset jammer; reflecting jammer; repeater jammer; search-and-lock jammer; spot jammer; sweep jammer; swept jammer; swept-repeater jammer.*

jammer analyzer. A device in which *signal processing* methods are used to determine specific characteristics of received jamming signals, such as the identity of the *source,* the type of *modulation,* and the *power* level of a received *jamming* signal. A jammer analyzer may be used to control an *antijamming* device.

jammer area coverage. The geographical area in which a *jammer* is capable of producing an effective *jamming signal.*

jammer modulation. The specific *modulation* of the *carrier wave* that is *transmitted* by a *jammer.* For example, *random noise modulation, locked-pulse modulation, swept-frequency CW modulation (sweep jamming), frequency-hopped modulation,* and *spread-spectrum modulation.* The latter two forms of modulation require a variable *carrier frequency.*

484

jammer out-tuning.   Changing the *tuning* of a *radio, radar,* or *video receiver* so as to reduce the effects of *jamming* at a particular *frequency.*   Out-tuning may be accomplished either by selecting a faster tuning rate than a *spot jammer* can follow or by tuning to a portion of the *frequency band* that the jammer cannot reach.

jammer polarization.   The *electromagnetic wave polarization* that is used in a particular *jammer.*

jammer receiver.   The part of a *jammer* that can receive *signals* and ascertain their exact *frequency, bearing,* and *strength.*

jammer transmitter.   The part of a *jammer* that generates, amplifies, and sends the *jamming signal* to a *transmitting antenna,* which also may be considered as part of the transmitter. The transmitter is normally *tunable* to the *frequency* of the signal that is being jammed, whether *spot, barrage,* or *hopping jamming* is performed.

jamming.   The deliberate introduction of *interference* into a *communication channel* with the intent of preventing *error*-free *reception* of *transmitted signals. Lightwaves* confined to an *optical fiber* are difficult to jam except by direct access to the *core* of the fibers with a compatible or *coherent light source.* Jamming involves the *radiation,* reradiation, or *reflection* of *signals* with the object of impairing the use or reducing the effectiveness of electronic devices. The primary purpose is to either obliterate or obscure the *information* that is contained in signals. See *antielectronic jamming; antijamming; barrage jamming; communication jamming (COMJAM); electronic jamming; escort jamming; formation radar jamming; infrared saturation jamming; mechanical jamming; noise jamming; periodic wave-form jamming; pulse-modulation radar jamming; reflective jamming; self-protection jamming; sequential jamming; side-lobe jamming; slow-sweep noise-modulated jamming; spoof jamming; spot jamming; spot noise jamming; spot off-frequency jamming; standoff jamming; support jamming; sweep jamming; synchronous jamming; unmodulated continuous-wave jamming.*

jamming antenna.   An *antenna* that is used for *jamming* purposes. The design of a jamming antenna includes the *frequency, directivity, gain, polarization, power,* and *beam pattern* requirements of the *jamming signal.*

jamming bearing.   The angle, measured by an observer with equipment at a given point, between a reference direction, such as true or grid north, and the direction that a *jamming signal* is observed to be coming from.

jamming electronic counter-countermeasure.   See *infrared jamming electronic counter-countermeasure.*

jamming margin.   The level of *interference (jamming)* that a *system* is able to accept and still maintain a specified level of performance, such as maintain a specified *bit error rate* even though the *signal-to-noise ratio* is decreasing. See *antijamming margin.*

jamming modulation. *Modulation* used by a *jammer,* such as *noise, pulse, pulse repeater, CW, AM, tone,* and *multitone modulation.*

jamming power. The *radio frequency (RF) power* that a *jammer* can develop. The power may be the total *emitted* power, the power emitted at a specific *frequency* or within a specified *frequency band,* the power at a given point in space in terms of *power density* or *signal strength,* or any other specified form of power.

jamming radar display. See *spot-barrage jamming radar display; spot-continuous wave jamming radar display.*

jamming report. A report prepared by *radar, radio, video,* or other *station operators* that contains *information* on *detected jamming.* The report normally identifies the *frequency, channel,* or *band* that is being jammed; the type of *jamming signal;* the time and duration of the *jamming;* the jamming *signal strength;* the *jammer bearing;* the *antijamming measure* that was taken by the reporting station; and the reaction of the jamming *source* to the antijamming measure that was taken.

jamming signal. A *modulated* or unmodulated *carrier signal* that is *transmitted* for the purpose of *electronic jamming.* The *jamming signal* may be used to accomplish other purposes, such as transmit *information,* provide guidance *signals,* or serve as a *homing beacon.*

jamming-to-signal ratio. The ratio of the *jamming signal power* to the useful power, that is, the reciprocal of the *signal-to-noise ratio.* The point in space or in the *circuits* of a *system,* such as a *radio, radar, beacon,* or *video system,* where the ratio is measured and the condition under which it is measured must be specified for the ratio to have any real significance. For example, the ratio of the *jamming power* to the *information-bearing signal* power at the *terminal* of a *receiving antenna.*

J-band. The band of *frequencies* in the range from 10 GHz to 20 GHz. It comprises 10 numbered *channels,* each 1 GHz wide. These frequencies overlap parts of the obsolete X-band, K-band, and M-bands. Frequencies in the range 5.30 GHz to 8.20 GHz overlap parts of the old C-band, G-band, X-band and H-bands, which are also obsolete.

JCL. *Job control language.*

jet control. See *pulse-jet control.*

jinking. The flying of an aircraft in a path in which there is a continual change in altitude, *heading (azimuth),* and sometimes air or ground speed.

jitter. 1. Relatively rapid or jumpy undesired movement of *display elements, display groups,* or *display images* about their normal or mean positions in the *display space* on the *display surface* of a *display device.* For example, the movement of a display image on the *faceplate* of a *fiberscope* when the *image* source at the opposite end of the *coherent bundle* of *optical fibers* is vibrated relative to the connecting coherent bundle of optical fibers, or the movement of an image on the screen of a *CRT* when the bias *voltage* on the deflecting plates oscillates at, for instance, 5 to 10 Hz. If the jitter rate exceeds about 15 Hz, or if the persistence of the *CRT screen* is long, the jitter will cause the image to appear blurred. Contrast with *swim*. **2.** The variation in time of a received *signal* compared to the instant of its *transmission* or compared to a fixed *time frame* at the *receiver*. Examples of jitter sources include *signal*-pattern-dependent *laser* turn-on delay jitter, *noise* induced jitter on a *gating* turn-on point, gating hysteresis jitter, and gating jitter that accumulates in a *data link*. The signal variations are usually abrupt and spurious. They include variations in *pulse length, amplitude* of successive cycles, *frequency* of successive pulses, or *phase* of successive pulses. Since the jitter may occur in time, amplitude, frequency, phase, or other parameter, there should be an indication of the measure that was made, such as average, *RMS, peak-to-peak,* or maximum. Also see *phase perturbation*. See *longitudinal jitter; phase jitter; time jitter.*

jittered pulse repetition rate. A *random* or quasirandom variation of the *pulse repetition rate* of a transmitting system, such as a *radio, radar,* or *video transmitter.* When performed deliberately as an *electronic counter-countermeasure (ECCM),* a jittered pulse repetition rate provides some *discrimination* capability against *repeater jammers* due to the difficulty they may experience in following the jitter variations.

job control language (JCL). An *artificial language* that is designed specifically to identify and describe jobs to a *computer* and to control the execution of the *programs* that are specified for the jobs.

job entry. See *remote job entry.*

Johnson noise. See *thermal noise.*

join gate. See *OR gate.*

joint communications. The common use of *communication facilities* by two or more military services that belong to the same nation. Also see *combined communications.*

joint-denial gate. See *NOR gate.*

jointed fiber. A *fiber* consisting of several lengths joined in sequence, such as a fiber 10 km long made up of ten 1-km lengths. The *coupling* may be accomplished by a *splice* or a *connector.* The joints introduce *reflection, absorption,* and other *insertion losses.*

joint information content. In *information theory,* the *information content* that is conveyed by the occurrence of two events of definite joint probability.

joint uniform telephone communication precedence system (JUTCPS). A *precedence system* of the US armed services. The system is used in such *communica-*

tion systems as *AUTOVON, AUTODIN,* and *AUTOSEVOCOM.* It applies to *messages* and *calls.*

JOVIAL. A *procedure-oriented computer programming language* that is derived from *ALGOL.* Specific application has been in command and control systems, such as *satellite* maneuver control. *Data* in the system can be controlled by the *byte* or by the *bit.* The language has also been used in commercial and scientific applications. The name is derived from Jule's (Schwartz) own version of the international algorithmic language. The language was developed by the System Development Corporation.

joystick. A manually operated lever used to control the movement of *display elements, display groups,* or *display images* to other or new *display positions* in the *display space* on the *display surface* of a *display device;* to generate or enter *coordinate data;* to select *symbols, characters* or other items from a *menu;* to indicate a selection from a set of options or choices; to simply indicate a *display position;* or to perform other such functions.

Julian calendar. The calendar that was introduced by Julius Caesar in which the year consisted of 365 days, every fourth year having 366 days. The calendar was introduced in Rome in 46 BC and established the 12-month year. The months each had 30 or 31 days, except for February which had 28 days. In the 366-day years (leap years) February had 29 days, as does the Gregorian calendar of today.

Julian date. A chronological date in which the days of the year are numbered consecutively, that is the first day of the year is numbered 001, the second day is numbered 002, and so on, until the last day of the year, which is numbered 365 (366 in leap years).

jumbo fiber. A relatively large, single *optical fiber* of the order of 500-*micron core diameter* or larger, used to replace *bundles* in *cables* and capable of *transmitting* sufficient *optical power* for *ringing* or electronic *circuit operation,* including *repeater* operation, in addition to *information transmission.* Synonymous with *macrofiber.*

jumbogroup. In *telecommunication carrier telephony,* a grouping of six *mastergroups.* Synonymous with *supermastergroup.* See *channel jumbogroup.*

jump. See *image jump.*

jumper. See *fiber jumper.*

jumper wire. A wire that makes a direct electrical *connection* between two points in order that they are maintained at the same *electrical potential (voltage)* with respect to a reference, that is, the jumper assures that no *potential difference* occurs between the points that it connects.

junction. See *double heterojunction; heterojunction; optical fiber junction; single heterojunction.*

junction call. In *telephone switchboard operation,* a *call* that requires that a *connection* be made between two or more *switchboards.* The switchboards would be connected by a *trunk.* Synonymous with *trunk call.*

junction point. See *node.*

junction stage. A stage in the *electrical* layout of a system that represents a characteristic point that is identifiable and is accessible to a stage in the same or another *system.* For example, a stage of *voice frequency channels,* an *intermediate frequency (IF)* stage in a *radio receiver,* a stage of groups of channels (primary group or secondary group), or a *radio frequency* stage in an *amplifier* that may have several stages of amplification.

justification. See *bit stuffing.*

justify. 1. To *shift* the contents of a *register* so that the *character* at a specified end of the *data* that has been stored in the register is at a specified *position* in the register. 2. To control the *printing positions* of *characters* on a page so that the left-hand, right-hand, or both, margins of the printing are regular. The printing on this page is right and left justified. See *left justify; right justify.*

JUTCPS. *Joint uniform telephone communication precedence system.*

K

k. In *tape relay system operations,* the *message prosign* that is used to indicate an invitation to *transmit.* It is placed at the end of a *transmission* and indicates that a *response* is implied, necessary, requested, or expected. See *Boltzmann's constant.*

K. Abbreviation for *kelvin,* the SI unit for *temperature.*

Kalman filtering. In *image restoration,* a recursive *filtering* technique using a linear time-varying *discrete-*time inverse *filter* function that provides a least-mean-square *error* estimate of a discrete-time *signal* based on *noisy* observations and that makes use of an adaptive *algorithm,* such as a *computer program* or segment, suitable for direct evaluation by a *digital computer.* If the Kalman filter is restricted to be time-invariant, it becomes a *Wiener filter.*

K-band. The band of *frequencies* that are in the range from 20 GHz to 40 GHz and that comprise 10 numbered *channels* that are 2.00 GHz wide each. These frequencies overlap parts of the obsolete P- and K-bands, which comprised frequencies in the range from 10.90 GHz to 36.00 GHz between the old X- and Q-bands, and overlapping parts of the old X- and P-bands. The old K-band was divided into 12 subbands each designated by a distinctive letter. There were other subdivisions of the old K-band that differed in the US and the UK.

kbps. *Kilobits/second.*

keeping. See *station keeping.*

kelvin (K). The unit of *temperature,* formerly called the degree kelvin, or $^{\circ}$K. The datum of the Kelvin temperature scale is absolute zero kelvin, at which all molecular motion stops, which is 273.16 kelvins below the triple point of water. The increment of temperature of 1 kelvin is the same as the increment of 1°C, establishing 100 units between the melting (or freezing) and the boiling point of water at 1 atmosphere of pressure.

Kelvin temperature scale. The *temperature scale* in the International System of Units *(SI).* The *kelvin (K)* is the fraction 1/273.16 of the thermodynamic *temperature* of the triple point of water. The temperature 0 K is called absolute zero. All thermodynamic activity stops at this temperature. Absolute zero is equivalent to -273.16°C and also to -459.69°F. The Celsius degree is a temperature interval of one *kelvin.* The term "degree kelvin" is incorrect, since the kelvin is the unit. For example, a room temperature of 20°C or 68°F is approximately 293 K. The conversion relationship between degrees Fahrenheit and degrees Celsius is F = 9C/5 + 32, or C = 5(F−32)/9. To convert to kelvin, simply add 273 to the degrees C, algebraically. Also see *temperature.*

490

Kendall effect. In *facsimile systems,* a spurious pattern or other *distortion* in a *facsimile record* that is caused by unwanted *modulation products* that arise from the *transmission* of a *carrier signal* and appear in the form of a *rectified baseband* that interferes with the *lower sideband* of the carrier. The effect occurs particularly when the *single sideband* width is greater than half of the facsimile *carrier frequency.*

kernel. See *security kernel.*

Kerr cell. A substance, usually a liquid, whose *refractive index* change is proportional to the square of the applied *electric field.* The substance is configured so as to be part of another system, such as an *optical* path, and the cell thus provides a means of *modulating* the *light* in the optical path.

key.   1. To manually enter a representation of a *digit,* letter, or other *character* into a device. For example, to push a button on a *keyboard* or actuate a *switch.* **2.** A device that when actuated connects a *signal source* to a *transmission line.* The signal source is usually a *code* generator and the device is usually a manually operated contact that is actuated by a finger. **3.** In *cryptography,* a *symbol* or sequence of symbols, or an electrical or mechanical correlate of a symbol or sequence of symbols, that controls the operations of *encryption* and *decryption.* It normally consists of a set of *characters.* **4.** A set of *characters* within a set of data that represents *information* about the *data* in the set. It also identifies the set, as does a label, but a label is outside the set. See *cryptokey; dialing key; function key; Morse key.*

keyboard.   1. On an *input* device, an array of *keys* that are mounted on a *panel* and are connected to a set of *pulse code* sources. Each key and its connected source corresponds to a letter, number, other *symbol,* or *control character.* When a key is depressed, the source that generates the particular *pulse* pattern that corresponds to the actuated key is connected to the outgoing *line.* Thus, each key depression is equivalent to a selection of a *code* that represents a *character.* **2.** A set of keys systematically arranged for ease of selection of individual keys that are used to control a *telegraph transmitter, data source, data storage* device, *computer input* device, *communication system,* or other equipment. See *data keyboard; function keyboard; motorized keyboard; sawtooth keyboard; storage keyboard; telegraph keyboard.* Also see Figure E-3.

keyboard perforator. A *perforator* that is provided with a *keyboard* and that is used to control the perforation of *data media* such as paper tape.

keyboard send-receive teletypewriter. A combination that consists of a *teletypewriter transmitter* and a *teletypewriter receiver* with *input* at the *keyboard* only and *output* at the printer. It does not have a punched paper tape send-and-receive capability. Also see *automatic send-receive (ASR) teletypewriter; receive-only (RO) teletypewriter.* See *function keyboard.*

key card.   1. A card that contains a pattern of punched holes that establishes the *key* for a *cryptosystem* during a *cryptoperiod.* **2.** A card on which is recorded a *code.* When the bearer inserts the card into a reading device, the reader will actuate another device, such as a lock to a vault or to a *controlled area.*

keying. The forming of *signals* by the interruption or *modulation* of an otherwise steady *signal* or *carrier. Keying* may control *amplitude, phase, frequency,* or other *parameters* of the *carrier.* See *differential phase-shift keying (DPSK); differentially-coherent phase-shift keying (DCPSK); double frequency-shift keying (DFSK); frequency-shift keying (FSK); low-level keying; multiple frequency-shift keying (MFSK); multiple phase-shift keying (MPSK); narrow-shift frequency-shift keying; phase exchange keying; phase-shift keying (PSK); phase-reverse keying; quadrature phase-shift keying (QPSK); remote keying; two-tone keying; wide-shift frequency-shift keying.*

keying frequency. See *maximum keying frequency.*

keying head. A device that reads *(detects)* hole patterns on tape and converts the patterns into *electrical pulses* that represent the same *information* as the hole patterns represent. The *pulse trains* that are formed are usually obtained as a group of *parallel bits* for each row of holes. They may be serialized for *transmission* on a single line, in which case the pattern of bits in time sequence still constitute a *character* with appropriate *start* and *stop elements.*

keying material. In *cryptosystems, cryptomaterial* that describes the arrangements and settings of *cryptoequipment* that is used in the *encryption* and *decryption* process. It also describes the *code* sequences, *messages,* and *signals* that are used for command, control, and *authentication.* It indicates the code sequences that can be used in messages. Key lists and *instructions* for the use of cryptomaterials are changed as often as may be required in order to maintain *security.* Also see *cryptokey.*

keying-off. To halt the process of *keying-on.*

keying-on. To initiate, and continue to dispatch, a *signal* by actuating (depressing) a *key* or *switch,* that is, to turn on a switch. The signal thus generated is used to cause another device to perform a specific function until the key is released. For example, to depress a key, thus closing a circuit and thereby causing a transmitter to transmit a modulated carrier signal for as long as the key is held depressed; or to cause a telegraph transmitter to send a dot or a dash until the key is released.

key list. A publication that contains the *keys* for a *cryptosystem.* It specifies the keys and the periods that they are to be in use.

keypoint compaction. See *slope-keypoint compaction.*

key protection. See *lock-and-key protection.*

key pulsing. A *system* of sending *call signals* in which the *digits* of the call signal are transmitted by *operation* of push-pull buttons on a *keyboard.* The key pulsing that is used by both *users* (customers, subscribers) and *private branch ex-*

change *(PBX)* operators is usually a form of *dual-tone multifrequency signaling.* Each push button causes the generation of a unique pair of tones. In some systems, pushbuttons are also provided for additional signals, such as *precedence indication.* Also see *dual-tone multifrequency signaling.*

key variable. A *digital word* that is used by *cryptokey* generators to obtain the same pseudorandom key stream for their associated *communicating terminals.*

key variable generator. A device that can produce electronic *cryptokeys* for use in *communication security.*

keypunch. A *keyboard*-actuated device that punches holes in a *punch card* or in paper tape.

K-factor. In *tropospheric electromagnetic wave propagation,* the ratio of the *effective earth radius* and the actual earth radius. The K-factor is approximately 4/3. In ionospheric electromagnetic wave propagation calculations, it is a correction factor that is applied in the calculations that involve a curved layer of the *atmosphere* or *ionosphere.* It is a function of the distances involved and the real height of the point of *ionospheric reflection.* Its use takes into account the effects of *ducting.* Also see *effective earth radius; Fresnel zone; path clearance; path profile; path survey; propagation path obstruction.*

kHz. *Kilohertz.*

kilobits/second (kbps). A *signaling rate* of 10^3 bits per second, i.e., 1000 bits per second.

kilohertz (kHz). A unit of *frequency* that denotes one thousand *hertz,* that is, 10^3 hz.

klystron. An electron tube in which an electron beam is *velocity-modulated* to generate or amplify energy at *microwave frequencies.*

knife-edge effect. In the *propagation* of *electromagnetic waves,* the *diffraction* or *deflection* that occurs when a wave is cut transverse to its direction of propagation by a sharp edge of material, such as a razor edge, a leaf, or a mountain peak. The uncut portion of the wave, or light beam, continues, but the edges spread into the volume that would have been occupied by the wave had it not been cut, giving rise to a *diffraction pattern* such that the knife-edge acts as a new source from which waves emanate. The knife-edge effect causes the *transmission* of *radio, radar, video,* and other electromagnetic waves into the *line-of-sight* shadow region by means of the diffraction that occurs at the edge of an obstacle.

knife-edge test. See *Foucault knife-edge test.*

kpps. *Kilopulses per second.*

kT. The product of *Boltzmann's constant* and the *equivalent noise temperature.* Also see *noise power density.*

L

label. **1.** One or more *characters* that are within or attached to a set of *data* and represent *information* about the set, including its identification. **2.** In *communications,* the information in a *message* used to identify specific system *parameters,* such as the particular *circuit* to which the message is related. Messages that do not relate to *call* control should not contain a label. **3.** In computer programming, an identifier of an *instruction.*

lambert. A unit of *luminance,* equal to $10^4/\pi$ candles per square *meter.* The *SI* unit of luminance is the *lumen* per square meter, where in 4π lumens of *light flux* emanate from 1 *candela.*

lambertian distribution. A *radiance* distribution that is uniform in all directions. See *uniform lambertian distribution.*

lambertian source. An *emitter* that *radiates electromagnetic waves* according to the *cosine emission law.*

Lambert's emission law. See *cosine emission law.*

Lambert's law. In the *transmission* of *electromagnetic radiation* when *propagating* in a *scattering* or *absorptive medium,* the *internal transmittance,* T_2, of a given thickness, d_2, is related to the known transmittance, T_1, of a known thickness, d_1, by the relationship:

$$T_2 = T_1{}^{d_2/d_1}$$

Also see *Beer's law; Bouger's law.*

lamp. See *cord lamp; signaling lamp.*

landing. See *ground-controlled approach (GCA) landing.*

landing aid. See *radio landing aid.*

landing marker. See *no-landing marker.*

landing-point marker. See *forbidden landing-point marker.*

landing system. See *instrument landing system (ILS).*

land mobile service. A *radio communiccation service* that provides *communication* among *base stations* and *land mobile stations.*

land station. A *station* in the *mobile service* that is not intended for *operation* while in motion. Land stations usually *communicate,* on a secondary basis, with *fixed stations* or other land stations of the same category. See *aeronautical mul-*

ticom land station; aeronautical telemetering land station; aeronautical utility land station; flight telemetering land station; hydrological and meteorological land station; radiolocation land station; radionavigation land station; radionavigation test land station; radiopositioning land station; telemetering land station.

language.   A set of *symbols,* conventions, and rules that are used for representing and conveying *information* between persons and machines. The rules are used for combining the symbols *(characters)* into larger groups, such as *words,* phrases, and sentences, and for their arrangement into *messages* to achieve specific and perhaps profound meanings. See *application-oriented language; artificial language; extensible language; general-purpose language; job control language (JCL); machine language; natural language; plain language; problem-oriented language; procedure-oriented language; special-purpose language; symbolic language; user language.*

language code.   In a *communication system,* an *address digit* that permits an originating *operator* to request the asssitance of an operator in a desired *language* on an international call.

language override.   See *plain-language override.*

lapping.   In *optical transmission systems,* the use of *tangential coupling* in order to transmit *lightwaves* from one *optical element* to another, such as from one *optical fiber* to another.

large optical-cavity diode (LOC).   A *laser diode* in which the P-N *junction* is placed between two *heterojunctions,* thus providing for a wide *optical cavity* for *lasing* action, the wider cavity having a higher *refractive index* than the material on either side of the cavity. The *output beam* is wider and the output *power* is greater than that of an LED.

large-scale integrated (LSI) chip.   An *integrated circuit* that has many circuit elements that are formed from a single piece of *semiconducting* material. It is used for performing *logic functions.*   For example, several thousand interconnected *transistors* and other circuit elements forming *logic gates* formed on a one square inch silicon *chip.*

laser.   Abbreviation for *light amplification by stimulated emission of radiation.* See *atomic laser; distributed-feedback (DFB) laser; gas laser; glass laser; liquid laser; mixed-gas laser; molecular laser; multiline laser; Q-switched repetitively-pulsed laser; multimode laser; semiconductor laser; solid-state laser; telecommunication transverse-excited atmosphere laser; tunable laser.*

laser basic mode.   The primary or lowest order fundamental *transverse propagation mode* for the *emitted lightwave* of a *laser.* The emitted energy normally has Gaussian (bell-shaped) distribution in space, and all the energy is in a single *beam,* with no *side lobes.*

laser beam.   A *collimated,* highly directional bundle of *monochromatic light rays,* with nearly zero *divergence* and exceptionally high *optical power density,* emitted from materials that are undergoing *lasing* action. See *telecommunication laser beam*.

laser connector. An active *connector* that uses a *laser* as the active *semiconducting* device to convert an incoming *electrical signal* to a *lightwave* signal.

laser diode (LD). A *junction diode,* consisting of positive and negative *carrier* regions with a P-N transition region *(junction),* that *emits electromagnetic radiation* (*quanta* of energy) at *optical frequencies* when injected *electrons* under forward *bias* recombine with *holes* in the vicinity of the junction. In certain materials, such as gallium arsenide, there is a high probability of *radiative recombination* producing *emitted light,* rather than heat, at a frequency suitable for *optical waveguides.* Some *light* is *reflected* by the polished ends and is trapped to stimulate more emission, which further excites, overcoming losses, to produce *laser* action. See *injection laser diode; stripe laser diode.*

laser diode coupler. A *coupling* device that enables the *coupling* of *light energy* from a *laser diode (LD)* source to an *optical fiber* or *cable* at the *transmitting* end of an *optical data link.* The coupler may be an *optical fiber pigtail* epoxied to the LD. Synonymous with *LD coupler.*

laser element. See *thin-film laser element.*

laser fiber-optic transmission system. A system consisting of one or more *laser transmitters* and associated *fiber-optic cables.* During normal operation, the *laser radiation* is limited to the cable. Thus, laser systems that employ *fiber-optic transmission* shall have *cable* service connection that requires a tool to disconnect if such cable connections form part of the protective housing. Consideration should also be given to incorporating mechanical *beam attenuators* at *connectors.* Safety aspects peculiar to fiber optics are an important consideration.

laser frequency switch. A *switch* that enables selection of *laser* output *frequency* by electronically driving an *electrooptic* crystal in order to produce changes in the laser *resonant cavity* length, thus enabling control of laser frequency. For example, driving a deuterated ammonium dehydrogen phosphate crystal inside of a dye laser cavity with low-voltage *pulses* causing time-dependent variations in the *refractive index* of the electrooptic element to produce the changes in the resonant cavity length that will change the laser operating frequency.

laser hazard. An injury-causing feature of a *laser.* For example, a gallium arsenide laser emits *invisible infrared radiation* from a *glass window* on its top that can cause eye damage. Precautions include observation only by indirect methods, such as through *filters* or by use of shielding.

laser head. A module containing the *active laser medium, resonant cavity,* and other components within one enclosure; it does not necessarily include a *power* supply.

laser linewidth. In the operation of a *laser,* the *frequency* range over which most of the *laser beam's energy* is distributed.

laser protective housing. A protective housing for a *laser* to prevent human exposure to laser *radiation* in excess of an allowable, established, or statutory emission limit. Part of the housing that can be removed or displaced and not interlocked may be secured in such a way that removal or displacement of the parts requires the use of special tools.

laser pulse length. The time duration of the burst of *electromagnetic energy emitted* by a *pulsed laser*. It is usually measured at the *half-power points,* i.e., on a plot of pulse power developed versus time, the laser pulse length is the time interval between the points that are at 0.5 of the peak of the power curve. Synonymous with *laser pulse width.*

laser pulse width. See *laser pulse length.*

laser service connection. An access point in a *laser-to-fiber-optic transmission system* that is designed for service and that, for safety, should require a special tool to disconnect.

laser sonar. A ranging or *communication system* in which *modulated laser beams* are fired into a *transmission medium* to launch sound waves or *phonons* for detection at other places for communication or for reflection from objects for ranging. Laser sonar is usually used under water or under ground. See *long-range laser sonar; short-range laser sonar.*

lasing. Phenomenon occurring when *resonant frequency*-controlled energy is *coupled* to a specially prepared material, such as a uniformly-*doped semiconductor* crystal that has free-moving or highly mobile loosely-coupled *electrons.* As a result of *resonance* and the imparting of energy by collision or close approach, electrons are raised to highly *excited energy states,* which, when they move to lower states, cause *quanta* of high-energy *electromagnetic radiation* to be released as *coherent lightwaves.* This action takes place in a *laser.*

lasing medium. See *active laser medium.*

last-in first-out (LIFO). A *queueing traffic* discipline in which entities that arrive at a point assemble in the time order in which they arrive and leave in the opposite order from that in which they arrived. Thus, service is offered first to the entity that has waited the least time. For example in a file, the item that was entered last, or placed on top, is the first to be retrieved, such as in a spike file or an in-box in which correspondence placed on top is taken out first. Synonymous with *push-down.* Also see *buffer; first-in first-out (FIFO); queue traffic.*

late distortion. *Distortion* that is due to the delayed arrival of parts of a *signal.* Signal parts are *transmitted* in a given sequence, each part in a specific *time slot.* A part that arrives after the proper instant of its time slot causes late distortion. Synonymous with *positive distortion.*

lateral communications. *Communications* between *facilities* that are at the same operational level or echelon of command.

lateral displacement loss.   In an in-line *(butt)* splice of an *optical fiber,* the loss of *signal power* caused by a sidewise *displacement* of the *optical axes* of the two fiber ends that are joined.

lateral magnification.   The ratio of the linear size of an *image* to that of the *object,* as when an *enlarging lens* is used.

lateral tell.   *Information transfer* that occurs between *facilities* that are at the same operational level or echelon of command.

latitude.   See *celestial latitude; terrestrial latitude.*

launch angle.   **1.** The *beam divergence* of a *light source.*   **2.** The *beam divergence* from any *emitting* surface, such as an *LED laser, lens, prism,* or *optical fiber* end. **3.** The angle at which a *light beam* emerges from a surface.   **4.** In an *optical fiber* or *fiber bundle,* the angle between the input *radiation* vector, i.e., the input *light chief ray* and the *axis* of the fiber or fiber bundle.   If the ends of the fibers are perpendicular to the axis of the fibers, the launch angle is equal to the *incidence angle* when the *ray* is external and the *refraction angle* when initially inside the fiber.   See Figure L-1.

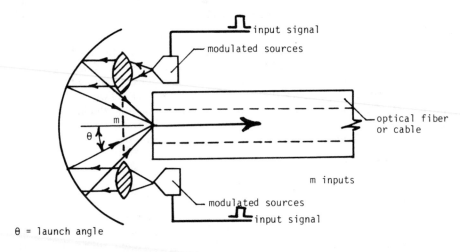

θ = launch angle

L-1. *Multiplexing n modulated input signals into a single optical fiber* or *cable,* showing the **launch angle.**

launching.   See *single-mode launching.*

law.   See *Beer's law; Biot-Savart law; Boltzmann's emission law; Bouger's law; Brewster's law; cosine-emission law; encoding law; inverse-square law; Lambert's law; Planck's law; reflection law; Richardson's law; Snell's law.*

layer.   In *network configuration* and in *open system architecture,* a group of related functions that comprises one level of a hierarchy of functions.   In specifying and performing the functions of each layer, the assumption is made that the functions that are specified for the layers below are performed. See *application layer; data link layer; D-layer; E-layer; end-to-end transport layer; F-layer; Heaviside layer; presentation layer; network layer; physical layer; session layer; transmission layer; transport layer.* See Figure L-2.

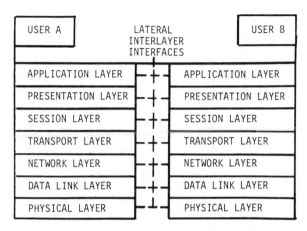

L-2. Each **layer** of a *network, computer,* or *station* in the *open systems architecture* concept may be laterally associated through *connections* and *protocols* with layers of other stations, computers, and networks in order that *user end-instruments* may be interconnected.

layered protocol. In *network architecture (configuration),* particularly in *open systems architecture, protocol* that is distributed over two or more *layers* of a *network.*

layered system. A *system* in which *components* are grouped in a hierarchical arrangement in such a manner that *lower layers* provide functions and services that support the functions and services of *higher layers.* Various systems, particularly *communication systems* and *computing systems,* of ever-increasing capability can be built by superimposing the layers one above the other, or by adding layers below to improve capability, each layer using the facilities below and supporting the layers above. The concept particularly allows for using the components that are in place while still improving the capability of the overall system. Also see *layer; open systems architecture.*

layer protocol. In *network architecture,* the *protocol* that is applicable to the group of functions of a *layer.*

LD. *Laser diode.*

LD coupler. See *laser diode coupler.*

LDDC dialing system. *Long-distance direct-current dialing system.*

leader. See *magnetic tape leader.*

lead signaling.   See *E-and-M lead signaling.*

leak.   See *carrier leak; jacket leak.*

leakage loss.   See *light-leakage loss.*

leaky mode.   An *electromagnetic wave propagation mode* in a *waveguide* that *couples* considerable or significant energy into *leaky waves,* usually being the higher-order modes. Also see *eigenvalue.*

leaky wave.   In an *optical waveguide,* an *electromagnetic wave* that is *coupled* to *transmission media* outside the waveguide, such as in the *cladding* or beyond. Leaky waves are no longer guided, become detached, and usually stem from *modes* that have a large skew component. They are of higher order and are beyond cutoff. Low-order modes may normally remain bound to the *fiber core.* Efforts are usually made to reduce leaky waves to a minimum in *optical fibers, slab-dielectric waveguides,* and *optical integrated circuits.* Also see Figure P-14.

LEA laser.   *Longitudinally-excited atmosphere laser.*

leap second.   A *second* that is added to *Greenwich mean time (GMT) (universal time)* about once a year to adjust the GMT in accordance with the *coordinated time scale.* Also see *coordinated time scale.*

leased-circuit data transmission service.   A *communication service* in which a *data circuit* of a *public data network* is made available to a *user* or group of users for their exclusive use. When only two sets of *data circuit-terminating equipment (DTE)* are involved, it is known as a *point-to-point facility.* When more than two are involved, it is known as a *multipoint facility.*

least privilege.   In *computer* and *communication system security,* the granting of the minimum *access* authorization that is necessary for the performance of required tasks.

least-time principle.   See *Fermat principle.*

LED.   *Light-emitting diode.*   See *edge-emitting LED; integral lens LED.*

LED coupler.   *Light-emitting diode coupler.*

left-circular polarization.   See *left-hand circular polarization.*

left-hand circular polarization.   Circular polarization of an *electromagnetic wave* in which the *electric field vector* rotates in a counterclockwise direction, as seen by an observer looking in the direction of *propagation* of the wave. Synonymous with *left-circular polarization.*

left-hand helical polarization.   *Polarization* of an *electromagnetic wave* in which the *electric field vector* rotates in a counterclockwise direction as it advances in the direction of *propagation,* as seen by an observer looking in the direction of propagation.   The tip of the electric field vector advances like the thread of a left-hand screw when entering a fixed nut or tapped hole.

left-hand polarized electromagnetic wave.   An *elliptically* or *circularly polarized electromagnetic wave* in which the direction of rotation of the *electric vector* is counterclockwise, as seen by an observer looking in the direction of *propagation* of the wave.   Synonymous with *anticlockwise polarized electromagnetic wave; counterclockwise polarized electromagnetic wave.*

left justify.   1. To *shift* the contents of a *register,* if necessary, so that the *character* at the left-hand end of the *data* that is stored in the register is at a specified *position* in the register.   2. To control the printing *positions* of *characters* on a page so that the left-hand margin of the printing is regular.

legend.   See *accounting legend.*

length.   See *available line length; average block length; back focal length; effective antenna length; electrical length; equivalent focal length; focal length; front focal length; optical path length; pulse length; register length; scanning line length; scanning line usable length; total scanning line length; word length.*

length discrimination.   See *pulse length discrimination.*

length discriminator.   See *pulse length discriminator.*

length modulation.   See *pulse length modulation.*

length selection.   See *packet length selection.*

lens.   1. An *optical* component, having curved surfaces and made of one or more pieces of a material *transparent* to the *radiation* passing through, that is capable of forming an *image,* either *real* or *virtual,* of the *object* source of the radiation, at least one of the curved surfaces being convex or concave and normally spherical but sometimes aspheric.   See *collective lens; compound lens; converging lens; diverging lens.*   2. A *transparent optical* element, usually made from optical glass, having two opposite polished major surfaces of which at least one surface is *convex* or *concave* in shape.   In most lenses, the concave or convex surface or surfaces are usually spherical.   The polished major surfaces are shaped so that they serve to change the amount of *convergence* or *divergence* of the *transmitted rays.*   See *achromatic lens; aplantic lens; bitoric lens; cartesian lens; concentric lens; condensing lens; corrected lens; cylindrical lens; divergent meniscus lens; electron lens; field lens; finished lens; microcylindrical lens; plane lens; planoconcave lens; planoconvex lens; single lens; tapered lens; telephoto lens; thick lens; thin lens; zoom lens.*

lens coupling.   In *optical waveguides,* the *transfer* of *electromagnetic energy* from *source* to guide, or from guide to guide, by means of a *lens* placed between the source and *sink.   Coupling loss* can be reduced to *packing fraction loss, axial* *misalignment loss,* and *axial displacement loss* when a lens is used. Also see *direct coupling.*

lens LED.   See *integral-lens LED.*

lens measure.   A mechanical device for measuring surface curvature in terms of *dioptric power.*

lens speed.   Property of a *lens* that affects the *illuminance* of the *image* it produces.   Lens speed may be specified in terms of the *aperture ratio, numerical aperture, T-stop,* or *F-number.*

lens system.   Two or more *lenses* arranged to work in conjunction with one another.

lens watch.   A dial depth gauge graduated in *diopters.*

Le Systeme International d'Unites.   The International System of Units *(SI).*   See *SI.*

letter case.   **1.** In the *teletypewriter code* for *tape relay systems,* the *machine function* that produces or interprets a hole pattern on tape or a *pulse pattern* on wires or *optical fibers* as one of the 26 letters of the English *alphabet.*   The letter case is obtained by actuating a special *function key,* usually marked LTRS.   **2.** One of the groups into which the *characters,* particularly the letters, of a *character set,* are placed.   Synonymous with *lower case.*   Also see *figure case.*

letter indicator.   A *panel signaling indicator* that consists of a single *panel,* is appropriately placed, and means that the following *message* is to be read as letters. The panels that are *coded* to represent numbers are used to represent letters in such a manner that the numbers 1–26 are used to represent the letters A–Z. Thus, words can be spelled using the panels.

letters.   See *signal letters.*

letter shift.   In *teletypewriter operations,* a *case shift* that results in the *translation* of *signals* into another group of *characters,* a group that consists primarily of letters and *machine functions,* rather than the figures group that was being used or interpreted before the shift.   Also see *escape character; figure shift.*

letter-shift signal.   The *signal* that conditions a *telegraph receiver* to *translate* all received or transmitted signals as the *letter case,* which is a group of signals that primarily represent letters and *machine functions,* rather than as the *figure case* that was in use before the letter-shift signal occurred.

level.   See *ambient noise level; carrier noise level; carrier level; channel noise level; circuit noise level; cross-level; digital voltage level; energy level; facsimile signal level; impurity level; link level; noise level; optical level; peak signal level;*

power level; quantization level; relative transmission level; signal level; single-sideband reference level; standard telegraph level (STL); transmission level; zero relative level.

level alignment. In *transmission system data links,* the adjustment of the levels of single links and links in *tandem* in order to prevent their overloading or the overlapping of the *transmission system* and its connected *components.*

level code. See *modified non-return-to-zero-level code.*

level coding. See *biphase level coding.*

leveling. See *power leveling.*

level operation. See *balanced link-level operation.*

level point. See *transmission level point.*

LF. Low frequency.

LF character. See *line feed (LF) character.*

LHOTS. *Long-haul optical transmission set.*

liaison circuit. See *external liaison circuit.*

life. See *component life; indefinite component life; inphase component life; out-of-phase component life.*

lifecraft frequency. See *international radio telegraph lifecraft frequency.*

LIFO. *Last-in first-out.*

light. 1. *Electromagnetic waves* of *radiant energy* of *wavelengths* from about 0.3 to 30 μ *(microns),* thus including the *visible* wavelengths from 0.38 to 0.78 μ and those wavelengths, such as *ultraviolet* and *infrared,* that can be handled by the *optical* techniques used for the visible region. 2. *Radiant electromagnetic energy* within the limits of human visibility and therefore with *wavelengths* to which the human retina is responsive, approximately 0.38 to 0.78μ. 3. A *source* of *illumination* in the *visible spectrum.* See *coherent light; collimated light; divergent light; monochromatic light; polarized light; pyrotechnic light; space-coherent light; time-coherent light; ultraviolet light; velocity of light; white light.* Also see *lightwave communications; wavelength.*

light absorption. The conversion of *light* into other forms of energy upon traversing a *transmission medium,* thus weakening the *transmitted light beam.* Energy *reflectance* R, *transmittance* T, *absorption* A, and *scattering* S, obey the law of the conservation of energy, R + T + A + S = 1.

light adaptation.   Ability of the human eye to adjust itself to a change in the *intensity* of *light*.

light amplification by stimulated emission of radiation (laser).   A *coherent-light* generator in which molecules of certain substances can *absorb incident electro-magnetic* energy at specific *frequencies*, store the energy for short periods in higher *energy-band levels* and then release the energy, upon their return to the lower energy levels, in the form of *light* at particular frequencies in extremely narrow frequency bands.   The release of energy can be controlled in time and direction so as to generate an intense highly directional narrow *beam* of electromagnetic energy that is *coherent*, i.e., the electromagnetic *fields* at every point in the beam are uniquely and specifically definable.   One form of *laser* consists of a rod of crystallized aluminum oxide with an admixture of metallic chromium (synthetic ruby).   The ends of the rod are optically plane parallel, with one end totally reflecting and the other partially reflecting.   The rod is surrounded by a spiral gas-discharge tube which, when energized, generates light energy of the proper frequency to energize the ruby's chromate molecules.   In a subsequent cascade discharge, the molecules return to their original energy levels and in so doing radiate the stored energy in a narrow intense beam of coherent light in the *infrared* region of the *electromagnetic spectrum*.

light analyzer.   For *incident light,* a *polarizing element* that can be rotated about its *optical axis* to control the amount of *transmission* of *incident plane polarized light,* or to determine the *polarization plane* of the *incident light*.

light antenna.   A system of *reflecting* and *refracting* components arranged to guide or direct a *beam* of *light*.

light button.   See *virtual push button*.

light communication system.   See *flashing-light communication system*.

light conduit.   See *noncoherent bundle*.

light detector.   See *photodetector*.

light-emitting diode (LED).   A diode that operates similar to a *laser diode,* with the same total *output power level,* the same output limiting *modulation* rate, and the same operational *current densities*.   The high current densities of thousands of amperes per square centimeter, cause *catastrophic* and *graceful degradation*. Compared to the laser diode, the LED possesses greater simplicity, tolerance, and ruggedness, and about 10 times the *spectral* width of its *radiation*.   Typical *peak spectral power* output for a gallium arsenide *LED source* occurs at 0.910 μ

(microns), with a spectrum about 0.050-μ wide. An aluminum arsenide LED source operates at 0.820 μ at a 10-MHz-wide spectrum. Both operate at roughly 1-mW spectral power output and a 50-mA driving current. See Figure L-3. Also see Figure O-7.

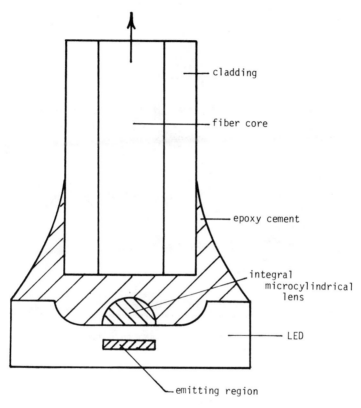

L-3. A *butt coupling* of an *optical fiber* and **light-emitting diode (LED)** *source,* showing the *spherical integral lens* for *coupling optical power* from the *emitting* area into the *fiber core.*

light-emitting diode coupler. A *coupling* device that enables the coupling of *light energy* from a *light-emitting diode (LED)* source to an *optical fiber* or *cable* at the *transmitting* end of an optical *fiber data link.* The coupler may be an *optical fiber pigtail* epoxied to the LED. Synonymous with *LED coupler.*

light guide. An assembly of *optical fibers* and other *optical elements* mounted and finished in a component that is used to *transmit light.* See *ultraviolet light guide.* See Figure L-4.

L-4. An undersea **light guide** capable of *operating* as a *submerged cable* one inch in diameter with 12 hair-thin glass *optical fibers.* (Courtesy of Bell Laboratories.)

light gun. See *light pen.*

lighting. See *highlighting.*

light-leakage loss. *Light energy* loss in a *light transmission system,* such as in a *light conduit, optical fiber cable, connector,* or *optical integrated circuit,* due to any means of escape, such as imperfections at *core-cladding* boundaries, breaks in *jackets,* and less-than-*critical-radius* bending.

lightning. The sudden discharge of an *electrical voltage (static electricity)* that builds up between clouds and between clouds and the earth. Also see *static electricity.*

light pen. A *stylus,* usually hand-held, that is *light*-sensitive or is a *light source.* It may be used to identify *display elements, display groups,* or *display images* in the *display space* on the *display surface* of a *display device;* detect the light generated within an *aiming symbol;* provide or generate *coordinate data* in the display space on the display surface of a display device; make selections from a *menu* of items; indicate one or more choices from selectable alternatives; or perform similar functions. For example, a light pen can be used to illuminate specific *fibers* that terminate on the *faceplate* of a *coherent bundle* of *optical fibers* of a *fiberscope* in order to energize or enable specific logic gates in a *digital* system. Synonymous with *selector pen; light gun.*

light pencil. In *optics,* a narrow *ray bundle diverging* from a *point source* or *converging* toward an *image point.*

light-pen detect. See *light-pen detection.*

light-pen detection. In *display systems,* the sensing of the light, using a *light pen,* from a *display element, display group,* or *display image,* in the *display space* on the *display surface* of a *display device.* Synonymous with *light-pen detect; light-pen hit; light-pen strike.*

light-pen hit. See *light-pen detection.*

light-pen strike. See *light-pen detection.*

light pipe. 1. An *optical element* that *conducts light* from one place to another, such as an *optical fiber* or *slab-dielectric waveguide.* 2. A hollow tube with a *reflecting* inner wall that guides *lightwaves* in its hollow center. 3. A synonym for *optical fiber.*

light quantity. The product of *luminous flux* and time.

light ray. A line, perpendicular to the *wave-front* of a *lightwave,* indicating its direction of *propagation* and representing the lightwave itself. Also see *optical ray.*

light-repeating ship. In *visual signaling systems,* a *ship station* that is designated to repeat *flashing light signals* that originate from other ships in order to *relay messages* to other ships that may be the *destination addressees* of the messages represented by the signals or that may repeat the signals.

light request. In *visual signaling systems,* a special *message* that requests the activation of certain navigational lights for specific purposes, such as identification, message exchange, course indication, and safety.

lights. See *northern lights; plugging-out lights.*

light source. A device that produces or emits *lightwaves,* such as a *light-emitting diode,* a *laser,* or a lamp.

light transmission. See *colored light transmission; flashing-light transmission.*

light valve. See *optical switch.*

lightwave. An *electromagnetic wave* in the *visible spectrum.*

lightwave communications. That aspect of *communications* and *telecommunications* devoted to the development and use of equipment that uses *electromagnetic waves* in or near the *visible* region of the *spectrum* for communication purposes, including *light-detectors, converters, integrated optical circuits,* and related devices, used for generating and processing lightwaves. The term *optical communications* applies to optical equipment whereas the term *lightwave communications* is oriented toward the *signal* being processed. Synonymous with *optical communications.* Also see *light.* See Figure L-5.

L-5. A *cable* of glass *optical fibers* for a **lightwave communication** system by which messages are *communicated* by *light pulses.* (Reproduced with permission of AT&T Co.)

limit. See *accommodation limit; interference limit.*

limited. See *bandwidth limited; dispersion-limited; power limited.*

limited infrared detector. See *backgroung-limited infrared detector.*

limited operation. See *detector-noise-limited operation; dispersion-limited operation; quantum-limited operation; thermal-noise-limited operation.*

limited protection. A form of short-term *communication security* that is applied to the *electromagnetic* or *acoustic transmission* of *information* that warrants a degree of protection against simple analysis and easy exploitation.

limited-protection voice equipment. Equipment that provides *limited protection* of *voice information* for purposes of *security* and *privacy.*

limited scanning. In *facsimile transmission,* the *scanning* at double or other *integral* multiples of the *scanning pitch.* It is used to shorten the *transmission time* at the possible expense of picture quality.

limiter. A device in which the *current, voltage, power, frequency, phase,* or other *parameter* of an *output signal* is automatically prevented from exceeding a specified value. In normal *operation,* a limiter yields a proportional output for varying instantaneous *inputs* below a certain value. For inputs above this value, the output is at a constant peak value. Also see *clipper; peak limiting.*

limiter circuit. A *circuit* that consists of nonlinear elements and restricts the excursion of *electrical current, voltage, power,* or some other characteristic of a *signal* in accordance with some specified criteria.

limiter hardness. A measure of the extent to which a *limiter* restricts the excursion of its *output signal* in comparison with excursions of the *input signal.* For example, if the *gain* is severely reduced for large input signal increments at high input signal levels, it is considered as a hard limiter, that is, it provides a sudden, sharp limit or maximum at the output. If the gain is not severely reduced for incremental variations of input at high input signal levels, it is considered as a soft limiter. If the gain is constant for all values of input signals, there is no limiting function being performed.

limiting. A process in which the *voltage, current, power, frequency, phase-shift,* or other *parameter* of an *output signal* of a device is prevented from exceeding a predetermined value. Also see *clipping; limiter; peak limiting.* See *hard limiting; soft limiting; video amplitude limiting.*

limiting resolution angle. The angle subtended by two points or lines that are just far enough apart to permit them to be distinguished as separate. The ability of an *optical* device to *resolve* two points or lines is called *resolving power* and quantitatively is inversely proportional to the limiting resolution angle.

limit marker. See *drop-zone boundary limit marker.*

lincompex. *Linked compression and expansion.*

line. 1. In *communication systems,* the portion of a *data circuit* that is external to *data circuit-terminating equipment (DCE)* and connects the DCE to a *data switching exchange (DSE)* or to one or more other DCE's, or connects two DSE's. 2. A *connection* or *channel* between *data circuit-terminating equipment (DCE)* at one *data station* and a DCE and a *user terminal,* device, or *end instrument* at another. 3. A device for *transferring* electrical energy from one point to another, such as a *transmission line.* 4. In *facsimile, television, wirephoto,* and *telephoto systems,* an element on a document or object that is *scanned.* 5. The path or trace of a moving spot on a *screen.* 6. A *communication channel.* 7. A horizontal sequence of *symbols,* such as *characters,* on a printed page. 8. A mark, path, or trace drawn between two points. See *access line; artificial transmission line; balanced line; baseline; call forwarding busy line; common trunk line; delay line; direction-finding baseline; direct line; display line; dual-use access line; electromagnetic delay line; exchange line; format line; Goubau line; hidden line; long-distance line; long line; marked-access line; network access line; offline; online; optical fiber line; party line; position line; private line; scanning line; special* *grade access line; transmission line; unbalanced line; uniform transmission line.* Also see Figure D-1.

line adapter circuit. A specific *circuit* that is used at the *station* end of a *user* (customer, subscriber) *access line* to connect to a *four-wire circuit* for a *telephone.*

linear analog control. See *linear analog synchronization.*

linear analog synchronization. *Synchronization* in which the functional relationships that are used to obtain *synchronization* are of simple proportionality. Synonymous with *linear analog control.*

linear combiner. A *diversity combiner* that can add two or more *receiver outputs.* Also see *diversity combiner.*

linear diversity combining. *Diversity combining* in which the *outputs* of two or more *receivers* that operate in a *diversity mode* are combined in an adder.

linear feedback shift register. A *shift register* that has *modulo-two feedback* and that can generate *pseudo-random binary* sequences. The register is amenable to mathematical theory and *information theory* in much the same ways as linear networks (circuits). Also see *nonlinear feedback shift register.*

linear feedback shift register. See *nonlinear feedback shift register.*

linearity. Pertaining to a relationship, over a designated range, between two variables, such as the *input* and the *output* of a device, such that the ratio of the two variables is a constant. For example, if the *gain* of a device is constant over all values of *input signal amplitudes, frequencies,* and *phase shifts* at all times, it is considered linear. If the *input/output* ratio of only one of the *parameters* is a constant, then it is linear only with respect to that parameter and nonlinear with respect to other parameters. See *modulation-demodulation linearity.*

linear-logarithmic intermediate frequency (IF) amplifier. An *intermediate frequency (IF) amplifier* with a *gain* characteristic that varies linearly as a function of lower input signal amplitudes, frequency changes, or phase shifts, and logarithmically as a function of higher *input signal amplitudes, frequency* changes, or *phase shifts.* The linear-logarithmic IF amplifier may be used to increase the *dynamic range* of a *radar receiver* in order to maintain a *constant false-alarm rate* at the *output* of the receiver.

linear polarization. The *polarization* of a uniform *plane-polarized electromagnetic wave* in which two arbitrary *sinusoidally*-varying rectangular *components* of the *electric field vector* are exactly in *phase;* i.e., their relative phase angle is zero, although their magnitudes may differ depending on the orientation of the electric field vector with reference to a coordinate system. Also see *circular polarization; elliptical polarization; plane polarization; right-hand circular polarization.*

linear predictive coding (LPC). **1.** A *narrow band analog-to-digital conversion* or *coding* technique in which a one-level or multilevel *sampling system* is used and in which the value of the *signal* at each *sample time* is predicted to be a particular linear function of the past values of the *quantized signal.* LPC is related to *adaptive predictive coding (APC)* in that adaptive predictors are used in both. However, more prediction coefficients are used in LPC in order to permit a lower *information bit rate* (about 2.4 to 4.8 kbps) than in APC. However, LPC requires a more complex *processor* for *voice signals.* **2.** *Coding* that consists of a *digital bit stream* that is *modulated* by an *analog (voice) signal.* **3.** *Coding* that is produced by a *vocoder* that is smaller than a *channel* vocoder and that has an improved voice quality. *Solid-state* electronic *components* are used. It is sensitive to channel errors and requires performance improvement at high *frequencies.* Also see *adaptive predictive coding.*

linear receiver. A *receiver* that has an *output signal* that varies in direct proportion to its *input signal,* that is, it has a constant *gain (transfer function)* regardless of changes in the *frequency, phase,* or *amplitude* of the *input signal.* The output signal value divided by the input signal value is a constant.

linear-sequence code. The sequence of *binary digits* that are produced by a *spread-spectrum code-sequence generator,* that uses only linear addition *combinational circuit* elements, such as *modulo-two adders.*

line balance. The degree of *electrical* similarity of the two *conductors* of a *transmission line.* Proper balancing reduces *coupling* of extraneous *signals, interference, noise,* and disturbances of all kinds, including *crosstalk.* With proper balancing, a disturbance in one *conductor* produces a cancellation of the disturbance in the other conductor.

line buildout. The result that is obtained by the process of adding a combination of electrical *inductances, capacitances,* and *resistances* to a line, such as a *paired cable,* so that its electrical length may be increased by a desired amount in order to control its *impedance* characteristics.

line character. See *new line (NL) character.*

line circuit. See *switched hot-line circuit.*

line code. A table of equivalences between a set of *digits* that are generated by a *data processing system* or *data processing system components,* such as a *terminal,* and the *pulse* patterns that are selected to represent that set of digits for *transmission* in a *line.* Consideration is given to the characteristics of the *transmission medium* when choosing a line code.

line determination. See *radio position line determination.*

line disconnection. The interruption of the continuity or *transmission* capability of a *line,* such as by physically removing a *plug* from a *jack,* opening a *relay,* or *disabling* a *logic gate.* Line disconnection is usually performed at a *private branch exchange (PBX), a private automatic branch exchange (PABX),* or a *switching center,* either by an *operator* or by automatic equipment.

line equipment. See *offline equipment; online equipment.*

line feed.   1. The movement (displacement) of the paper on a page printer from one line of printing to the next in the vertical (downward or upward) direction without horizontal (right or left) movement.   2. A machine function that controls the vertical (downward or upward) movement of paper in a printer to allow line-by-line printing.

line feed (LF) character.   A format effector that enables or causes the print or display position to move to the corresponding position on the next line.

line filter balance.   An electrical network (circuit) that can maintain a balance in a phantom group when one side of the group is equipped with a carrier system, that is, is transmitting a modulated carrier signal.   Since it must balance the phantom group for audio frequencies, its configuration is simple compared with the filter that it is capable of balancing.

line function.   In a formatted message, the purpose or use that is made of a particular line in the heading, text, or ending of the message.

line grouping.   The connection to one switch of a group of users (customers, subscribers) with a common interest.   The line to each user is grouped with all the others in such a manner that an incoming call to a busy line is routed to a free line of the group in a preferred sequence.   Thus, when in a line grouping condition, a call that is destined for a particular user is directed to that user.   If the user is busy, the call is directed to the next free line in the preferred sequence. If all the lines in the group are busy, a busy signal is returned to the calling party, unless preemption or precedence is invoked.   Thus, if a high precedence call is directed to a line in the group and that line is busy, preemption is not usually invoked unless all other lines of the group are also busy.

line holding.   A continuation of *line seizure.*

line identification.   An identification of a *line* that is furnished by a *communication network* at the request of two *parties* that are connected.

line identification facility.   See *called-line identification facility; calling-line identification facility.*

line identification-request indicator.   See *called-line identification-request indicator; calling-line identification-request indicator.*

line identification signal.   See *called-line identification signal; calling-line identification signal.*

line identity.   See *called-line identity; calling-line identity.*

line identity message.   See *calling line identity message.*

line index.   See *code line index.*

line length.   See *available line length; scanning line length; total scanning line length.*

line load control. A control of the *traffic load* on a *line,* usually by selective denial of *call* origination to a specified *access line* when excessive demands for service are required of a *switching center.* Selective denial may be accomplished by delaying the *dial tone* on certain groups of lines according to specified criteria. Each line may be assigned a line load control designation. For example, one group might be the first group to be denied a dial tone when circuits are overloaded. Other groups may have a higher *precedence* and therefore will be denied a dial tone only if *circuits* are still overloaded. One group may never be denied a dial tone. Synonymous with *line traffic load control.*

line load control designation. In a *communication system,* one of the set of *precedences* that may be used to determine the sequence (priority order) in which specific groups of *users* will have their *communication service* degraded in order to provide full services to users with more essential needs. *Line load control* is used to provide a degree of *automatic traffic overload protection* during *saturation* conditions or when *facilities* are limited.

line loop. See *local loop.*

line of sight (LOS). In *communications,* a direct *propagation path* that does not go below the *radio horizon.*

line-of-sight (LOS) equation. See *radar line-of-sight (LOS) equation.*

line-of-sight (LOS) link. 1. In *radar, radio, video,* and *microwave systems,* a *link* in which *line-of-sight* conditions exist between the *antennas* of the transmitting and receiving sites. 2. In *optical transmission systems,* a direct non-waveguided *beam transmission path* from point to point; e.g., a *microwave link* between two towers or a *laser beam link* between an earth station and a satellite.

line-of-sight (LOS) propagation. *Electromagnetic wave propagation* in the *atmosphere* in a manner such that the *intensity* decreases because of the spreading of the energy of the wave according to the *inverse-square law* and with relatively minor effects due to the composition and structure of the atmosphere. Line-of-sight propagation is considered to be unavailable when any *ray* from the transmitting *antenna* or *light source refracted* by the atmosphere will encounter the earth or any other opaque object, such as a mountain, that prevents the ray from proceeding directly to the receiving antenna. A path that is found by atmospheric or ionospheric refraction alone is still considered line of sight regardless of the geometric shape of the path.

line period. See *scanning line period.*

line rate. See *reading line rate; recording line rate; scanning line rate.*

line recovery. See *offline recovery.*

line residual equalizer. An *electrical network (circuit)* that reduces the *attenuation* and *frequency distortion* that remains in a *transmission medium* after other equalizers have been adjusted to their optimum condition.

line-route map. In *signal communication operations,* a map or overlay that shows the actual *routes* and types of *communication circuits* in a *communication system.* It may include the locations of other communication *facilities,* such as *switchboards, telegraph stations, radio stations,* and *message centers.*

lines. See *common-address multiple lines.*

line scanning. See *electronic line scanning.*

line segregation. See *routing-line segregation.*

line side. The portion of a device, such as a *user end-instrument,* that is connected to the *transmission path, channel, loop,* or *trunk.* Also see *equipment side.*

line seizure. In a *communication system,* the prevention by a *user* of further use of a *line* by any other user or by an *operator.*

line signaling. See *free-line signaling.*

line slope. The rate of change, with respect to *frequency,* of the *attenuation* of a *transmission line* over the *frequency spectrum.* Normally the attenuation is greater at high frequencies than at low frequencies.

line temperature-compensating equalizer. An *equalizer network* that is used with a *transmission line* to compensate for changes in *attenuation* and *frequency distortion* that are caused by changes in the *temperature* of the line.

line termination. See *idle line termination.*

line traffic coordinator (LTC). The *processor* in a *switching center* that is designated and used to control and coordinate *line traffic.*

line traffic load control. See *line load control.*

line usable length. See *scanning line usable length.*

line weighting. See *F1A-line weighting.*

line width. See *nominal line width.*

link. 1. In a *communication network,* the *communication facilities* between two *adjacent nodes* of the *network.* 2. A portion of a *circuit* that is designed to be connected in *tandem* with other portions. 3. A *radio path* between two points. The radio link may be *unidirectional, half-duplex,* or *full-duplex.* The *signals* at each end of the link are of the same *mode* of *transmission,* such as *modulation, polarization,* or *frequency,* except as might be altered by *propagation path anomalies.* 4. In *computer programming,* the part of a *computer program* that passes control and *parameters* between separated portions of the program. The link may be a single *instruction* or a single *address,* or it may be a sequence of instructions or addresses. See *cross-site link; data link; down-link; fiber optic data link; functional signaling link; line-of-sight link; logical data link; long-haul optical* *link; multiplex link; multipoint link; optical link; point-to-point link; radio link; repeatered optical link; satellite link; satellite optical link; signaling data link; signaling link; tactical digital information link (TADIL); TV optical fiber link; up-link.*

linkage.   See *call-sign linkage.*

link bay.   See *U-link bay.*

link control.   See *basic mode link control; high-level data link control (HDLC); synchronous data link control.*

linked compression and expansion (lincompex).   *Companding* in which *data links* are used to interconnect the *functional units* of a *compander.*

link encryption.   The application of *online cryptooperations* to a *link* of a *communication system* so that all *data* that pass over the link are entirely *encrypted.* See *multiplex link encryption.*

link engineering circuit.   A *voice* and *data communication circuit* that connects adjacent communication facilities and that is used by system personnel and components for control of *link* activities and functions.   Synonymous with *link orderwire.*

link escape character.   See *data link escape character.*

linking.   See *cross-linking.*

link layer.   See *data link layer.*

link level.   In *data transmission,* the level of control of *data processing logic* that exists in the *hierarchical structure* of a *primary* or *secondary station* that is responsible for maintaining control of the *data link.* The link level functions provide an *interface* between the station high-level logic and the data link. These functions include *bit* injection *(stuffing)* at the *transmitter,* bit extraction *(destuffing)* at the *receiver, address field* and *control field* interpretation, *command* generation, *response generation, transmission, data* interpretation, and *frame check-sequence* interpretation and computation.

link-level operation.   See *balanced link-level operation.*

link orderwire.   See *link engineering circuit.*

link protocol.   The set of rules by which a *logical data link* is established, maintained, and *terminated.*   It includes the *format* and rules by which control *information* is exchanged and interpreted in order to *transfer data* across the link. The protocol is usually specified in terms of a *transmission code,* a *transmission mode, flow control procedures,* and *recovery processes.*

link repeater.   See *pulse link repeater.*

link subsystem.   See *space-ground-link subsystem.*

link threshold power. In *satellite communication systems,* the minimum *earth station transmitter carrier power* that is necessary to maintain the received *signal* at the *demodulator* above a *threshold* level. The received signal demodulator is at the *destination addressee* earth station, not in the *satellite.* The system conditions under which the threshold is specified must also be defined.

liquid-core fiber. An *optical fiber* consisting of *optical* glass, quartz, or silica tubing filled with a higher *refractive index* liquid that typically has *attenuation* troughs less than 8 dB/km at 1.090, 1.205, and 1.280-*microns.* The higher *refractive index core* is a liquid that is pumped in after pulling or *drawing.* For example, tetrachloroethylene is used as a liquid core in optical fibers.

liquid laser. A laser whose *active medium* is in liquid form, such as organic dye and inorganic solutions. Dye lasers are commercially available. They are often called "organic dye" or "tunable dye" lasers.

LISP. A *computer programming language* that is used primarily for list *processing.* The name is derived from list processing.

list. See *access list; brevity list; key list; traffic list.*

listening depth. The depth at which a submarine is able to receive *messages* over a specified *communication system* or *network,* such as the *submarine operations and distress net.* Listening depth varies with weather conditions, the *signal strength* at the surface, the type of *antenna,* the *signal-to-noise ratio, operator* experience, and other factors. Synonymous with *reception depth.*

listening silence. 1. The condition of a *station* when it is only receiving a *transmission,* or when it is standing by ready to receive a *transmission,* without transmitting. 2. The condition of a *station* when neither a *receiver* nor a *transmitter* is turned on, in order to eliminate *radiation* by both *transmitters* and *receivers.*

listening watch. 1. A *radio communication watch* in which an *operator* is required to maintain a *continuous receiver watch* that is established for the *reception* of *messages* that are *addressed* to, or are of interest to, the listening station. Normally a *log* is kept. Synonymous with *loudspeaker watch.* 2. In *radio telephone ciphony net operations,* the period of time that equipment and an *operator* at a *station* are ready to receive a *message* should there be one. Listening watches that are established in the *cipher-mode* at directed times are usually conducted in the cipher *standby* condition. At other times, listening watches may be conducted in the *plain mode.* Also see *copy watch; guard watch; radio communication cover.*

literal cipher equipment. *Cipher* equipment that is designed to accept letters of the *alphabet,* and sometimes *space characters, numerals* (0–9), or other *symbols* that are normally used in a *language*. The equipment is normally designed to produce *encrypted text* consisting of only letters of the alphabet.

literal cryptosystem.   A *cryptosystem* that is designed for literal *communication*, that is, communication in which the *plain text characters* are primarily letters. In some *systems, numerals* (0–9) and perhaps other *symbols* that are normally used in a *language* are also used.

lithium niobate integrated circuit.   An *integrated circuit* that performs *filtering, coupling, switching,* and *modulation* of *lightwaves* on a lithium niobate *chip*.

load.   1. The volume of *traffic* that is carried by a *communication system* or *component* during a specified time period or per unit time.   **2.** The *power* that is consumed by a device or *circuit* when it is performing its intended functions.   **3.** A *power*-consuming device that is connected in a *circuit*.   **4.** To place *computer programs* or *data* into a *register, computer,* or *storage* device.   **5.** To place machine-readable *data media* on or into a sensing device. For example, to place a *magnetic tape* reel on a tape drive or to place cards into the card hopper of a card reader. See *critical technical load; demand load; dummy load; noncritical technical load; nonoperational load; nontechnical load; operational load; station load; tactical load; traffic load.*

loaded diffused optical waveguide.   See *strip-loaded diffused optical waveguide.*

load factor.   The ratio of the *average power load* during a designated period of time to the *peak power load* that occurs during that period.

loading.   1. The adding of *traffic* to a *communication system* or *component*.   **2.** The insertion of additional *impedance* so as to increase the real or reactive power in a *circuit*.   **3.** In *multichannel.telephony systems,* the *power* that is required as a function of the number of *channels*. The power may be the *equivalent mean power* or the *peak power*.   **4.** The *equivalent power* of a *multichannel group* or *composite signal* referred to the *zero transmission level point (OTLP)*.   **5.** In *multichannel communication systems,* the insertion of *white noise* or equivalent dummy *traffic* at a specified volume in order to *simulate* a *traffic load* and evaluate system performance. See *idle-channel loading; system loading.*

loading characteristic.   In *multichannel telephone systems,* the equivalent mean *power* plotted as a function of the number of *voice channels*. The equivalent power of a multichannel signal, usually referred to the *zero transmission level point (OTLP)*, is a function of the number of channels and has a specified mean channel power.

loading coil.   A coil that does not provide *coupling* with any other *circuit* but that is inserted into a circuit to increase its *inductance*.

load resistance.   An *electrical resistance* that is used to accept *electrical current* from a *source* or to cause a *voltage* drop when it is conducting a current. For example, *infrared (IR) photoconductive sensors* are connected to a *load resistance;* reducing the load resistance increases the *sensitivity.*

load test.   See *tensile load test.*

lobe.   1. A *polar diagram* of the energy *intensity* at a particular range in each direction from an *emitter (antenna).* The central axis of the lobe is the line from the antenna to a point at a particular range (the range for which a lobe is drawn) where the power density is a maximum.   2. In a *beam,* the locus of points where the *power density* is one-half of the peak value at a given range but not in a given direction.   See *antenna lobe; back lobe; main lobe; side lobe.*   Also see *radiation pattern.*

lobe blanking.   See *side-lobe blanking.*

lobe cancellation.   See *side-lobe cancellation.*

lobe jamming.   See *side-lobe jamming.*

lobe-on-receive-only (LORO).   *Passive scanning* in which a steady *beam* is used to *illuminate* an *object (target)* while a separate receive *antenna* is scanned either *conically* by *lobe switching* or by *unidirectional beams.* The steady illuminating beam is usually of the nonscanning type.   LORO permits an improved *electronic counter-countermeasure* capability by reducing *interference.*

lobe switching.   See *beam lobe switching.*

lobing.   In *radar systems,* making use of the variation of energy levels of different parts of a *lobe* while *illuminating* an object (target).   Also see *conical scanning.*   See *paired lobing; sequential lobing.*

LOC.   *Large optical-cavity diode.*

local battery.   1. In *telephone systems* and *telegraph systems,* the *battery* that actuates the *station* recording instruments, as distinguished from the battery that furnishes *electric current* to the *line.*   2. In *telephone systems,* an arrangement in which each *telephone* has its own individual source of *power.*

local call.   In *telephone switchboard operations,* a *call* in which the *calling party* and the *called party* are both directly connected to the same *exchange,* in contrast to a *long distance call* in which case at least two exchanges are involved in the call.   Also see *long-distance call; number call; person-to-person call; station-to-station call.*

local distribution system.   In *communications,* a *system* that serves a group of *users* (customers, subscribers) that have a fixed, local association.   See Figure L-6.

L-6. A *telephone communication operator* and a **local distribution system.** (Courtesy of Wyle Laboratories Corporate Communications Department.)

local end. In *telegraph systems*, the *telegraph key, line, telegraph repeater,* control units, *power* sources, and other *components* at the end of a *transmission line*. It is also a point at which transmission quality can be measured.

local engineering circuit. A *communication circuit* that is between a *technical control facility* and selected *terminal* or *repeater facilities* within a communication *system*. In *multichannel radio communication systems*, the local engineering circuit is usually a handset *connection* at the *radio station* location. Synonymous with *local orderwire*.

localizer. A *directional radio beacon* that provides an *aircraft station* with an indication of its lateral position relative to a specific runway centerline while landing. Also see *instrument landing system*.

localizer station. A *radionavigation land station* in the *aeronautical radionavigation service* that provides *signals* for the lateral guidance of *aircraft stations* with respect to a runway centerline. It employs an *instrument landing system localizer*.

local line. See *local loop*.

local loop. A *communication channel* between a *switching center* unit and a customer, subscriber, or *user* instrument. Local loops normally occur between *distribution frames* and *data terminals, telephones,* and *facsimile* units. It is a single *connection* from a *switching center* or an individual *message distribution point* to the *terminals* of a *user* (customer, subscriber) *end-instrument.* For example, it may be the portion of a *radio,* wire, or *optical fiber communication circuit* that connects a user end-instrument to a *central office exchange* or *switching center.* Synonymous with *line loop; local line; subscriber line;*

local net. In *radio net operations,* the *radio net* to which a *station* belongs and within which it operates.

local orderwire. See *local engineering circuit.*

local oscillator. An *oscillator* in a piece of electronic equipment that is usually used as a *source* of *electromagnetic wave frequencies* for mixing with other *frequencies* that the equipment is handling. It is usually a crystal-controlled fixed frequency oscillator, though it may be *tunable.* It is usually an inherent part of *radar, radio,* or *television* equipment, particularly *receivers.* Though its *output* may be used for many purposes, its prime purpose is to provide frequencies for local use. For example, in a *heterodyne receiver,* the oscillator that produces a frequency that is mixed with the incoming *radio frequency (RF)* to produce the *intermediate frequency (IF)* that is to be processed in the receiving circuits; or in television receivers, an oscillator that will produce the *sweep frequencies* for *scanning* purposes. See *stabilized local oscillator.*

local oscillator off. A *radar* operating condition in which the *local oscillator* is turned off in order to reduce the effects of *jamming.* It is an *electronic countercountermeasure (ECCM)* used during *barrage jamming.* Turning the local oscillator off will cause the barrage jamming not to be seen on the *radar scope* but objects (targets) that are on the *jammer azimuth* can be seen. Targets that are not on the jammer azimuth cannot be seen because the local oscillator is off. For these targets other arrangements must be made, such as using an automatic azimuth *switch* or another *receiver display system.*

local oscillator tuning. The capability of changing the *frequency* of a *local oscillator* in electronic equipment, such as a *radar, radio,* or *television receiver.* The capability can be used for *signal tuning* for improved *reception,* for reduction of *interference,* reduction of *jamming* effects, and other pruposes.

local record. In *communication systems,* a *display* or *hard copy* of a *transmitted message* made on a *receiver* that is associated with or connected to the *transmitter* and that is at the transmitting *station.*

local ship-shore station. A shore-based *station* equipped with low-powered *transmitters,* usually operated at *low frequency (LF)* or *medium frequency (MF)* but is occasionally operated at *very-high frequency (VHF)* or *ultra-high frequency (UHF),* and provides communication with ships in and around ports, harbors, and other local areas such as bay areas and estuaries.

local side. That portion of a *communication* device, such as a *user end-instrument,* that is connected to the *internal station facilities* of a communication *system.*

locating. In *display systems,* generating *coordinate data* corresponding to specific locations, in the *display space* on the *display surface* of a *display device,* by using a *cursor,* cross-hairs, or *stylus* guided by a *control ball, thumb wheel, joystick,* or other manual control device. Synonymous with *positioning.*

location. See *radiolocation.*

location land station. See *radiolocation land station.*

location loss. See *receiver location loss.*

location mobile station. See *radiolocation mobile station.*

location station. See *radiolocation station.*

locator. In *display systems,* a device that is used as an *ijput* device for *computers* and *communication systems* and provides *outputs* that represent *coordinate positions.*

locator beacon. See *personnel locator beacon.*

lock. See *angle break-lock; transfer lock.*

lock-and-key protection. *Protection* that makes use of a *password* or *key* that is matched to an *access* requirement in order to obtain *information* from a *system* or to use a system.

lock code. A *code* used in a *system,* such as a *computer,* a *data processing system,* or a *communication system,* to provide *protection* against improper use of *components* in the system, such as *storage* areas, *input-output* files, *input-output* devices, *communication channels,* and *switching systems.*

locked envelope. See *permanently locked envelope.*

locked-pulse radar jammer. A *repeater-jammer* that returns an *echo* to the *jammed receiver* that is different from the normal echo in range, *bearing,* and number of echoes. The *pulses* that are returned by the jammer are locked to the *radar transmitter* that is being jammed. They are timed to arrive at the *jammed radar* at the same time as the echo to give the impression of a larger target. They are also timed to arrive early, late, and on time to give the impression of many targets. They are timed and powered to enter *side lobes* to give wrong *bearings.* They are made to appear as a normal echo from specific types of targets to give the impression that these targets exist when in fact they do not exist.

lockers. See *flag lockers.*

locking. The function of a *code extension character* in a *communication system* that has the characteristic that the change in the interpretation of *characters* following the character applies to all *coded* representations that follow, or to all coded representations in a given class, until the next appropriate code extension character occurs.

locking code extension character. A *code extension character* that indicates that the *character* change that is signaled by the character applies to all the succeeding characters that follow until the next appropriate *extension* or *escape character,* that is, it does not apply to just the one character that follows or to a specific number of characters that follow. See *nonlocking code extension character.*

lock jammer. See *search-and-lock jammer.*

lock loop. See *phase-lock-loop.*

lock-on. The fixation of a *radar tracking antenna* on a specific object. The *tracking* is automatically maintained by feeding the return signal *(echo)* from the object (target) being tracked through a control *feedback loop* so as to optimize the *amplitude* of the echo. The lock-on condition in a *radar system* indicates that the system is continuously tracking an object in *range, azimuth,* and *elevation.* Also see *relock; transfer lock.*

lockout. 1. In a *telephone circuit* that is controlled by two voice-operated devices, a circuit condition that results in the inability of one or both *users* (customers, subscribers) to get through to the other because of excessive local *circuit noise* or because of continuous speech from either or both users. 2. In *mobile communications,* an arrangement of control *circuits* in which only one *receiver* can feed *signals* (voice or data) into the *system* at one time. Synonymous with *receiver lockout system.* 3. In *telephone systems,* to automatically disconnect from the *switching* equipment a *user's* (subscriber's) *line* that is in trouble or is in a permanent *off-hook* condition.

log. See *aeronautical station master log; aeronautical telecommunication log; circuit log; operator log; position log; ship deck log; ship radio log; station log.*

logarithmic companding. *Companding* in which the *transmitted signal* is a logarithmic function of the *amplitude* of the *input* signal to the transmitting *compressor* portion of the *compander.*

logarithmic fast time constant (log FTC). In *radar systems,* a combination of a logarithmic function and a *fast (short) time constant.* The combination is produced by a logarithmic (nonlinear) *intermediate frequency (IF) amplifier* that has an *output* that is fed into a fast time constant (FTC) *circuit.* The log-FTC combination is effective in removing variations in *output noise* level, particularly in *video systems,* that might be caused by *spot noise, wideband noise,* and *slow-sweep noise modulated jamming* or by other forms of *interference.*

logarithmic intermediate frequency (IF) amplifier. See *linear-logarithmic intermediate frequency (IF) amplifier.*

logarithmic receiver. In *radar, radio, video,* and *microwave systems,* a *receiver* that has a large *dynamic range* of *automatic gain control (AGC)* and that provides protection against *saturation* by strong *interference* or *jamming signals.* The receiver is useful in *communication systems* against weather, *clutter, chaff, spot jamming* and many other forms of interference.

log FTC. *Logarithmic fast time constant (log FTC).*

logging. See *data logging.*

logic. See *fixed logic; integrated injection logic; programmable logic.*

logical channel. In *packet mode operation,* a means of *two-way simultaneous transmission* across a *data link* that is comprised of associated transmit and receive *channels.* A number of logical channels may be derived from a data link by *packet* interleaving, that is, by *time-division multiplexing* (time sharing). Several logical channels may exist on the same data link.

logical circuit. In *packet mode operation,* a means of *two-way simultaneous transmission* across a *data link* that is comprised of associated transmit and receive *circuits.* A number of logical circuits may be derived from a data link by *packet* interleaving, that is, by *time-division multiplexing* (time sharing). Several logical circuits may exist on the same data link.

logical connection. In a *communication network,* a *path* that is established between a *source user* and a *destination user* and in which *logical circuits* are used.

logical data link. A *data link* that is created by means of *logical circuits.* For example, a data link that is established by *time-division multiplexing* or by interleaving packets on a physical (actual) data link.

logical diagram. See *logic diagram.*

logical station. A *data station* that is created by means of *multiplexing* and that is located at the end of a *logical data link* or at the end of a *logical circuit.*

logical sum. A sum of two *binary numbers* in which carry *digits* are ignored, that is, a sum produced by an *EXCLUSIVE-OR gate.* For example, the logical sum of 110101 and 011011 is 101110.

logic device. A device capable of executing *logic operations;* i.e., operations that follow the rules of symbolic logic, such as the Boolean operations, of *AND, OR,* and *NEGATION. Integrated optical circuits* can be designed and used to perform the logic operations.

logic diagram. A *graphic* representation of the interconnected logic, that is, the interconnected decision-making *logic circuits,* of a *system,* such as a *computer,* a *data processing system,* a *control system,* or a *communication system.* For example, a diagram of interconnected *gates* and control *flip-flops* in symbolic form, perhaps including *counters, registers, encoders, decoders, storage* units, and their interconnecting *signal lines.* Usually only the functional elements are shown in the logic diagram, rather than supporting elements such as power supplies, illumination wiring, and disconnect switches. The mechanical structural elements, *grounding,* air conditioning, and actual circuit elements, such as tubes, *transis-*

tors, diodes, resistors, capacitors, transformers, and *inductors* are not shown. Even a *clock pulse network* for signal timing and shaping is not shown. Special sets of *symbols* are used to express the logic events and to show the flow path of *data* and decision-making control signal paths through the system. Synonymous with *logical diagram.* See Figure L-7.

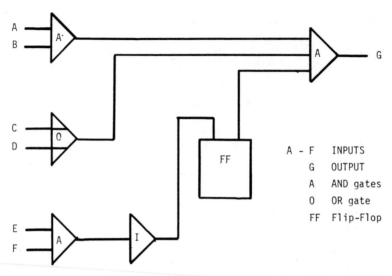

L-7. A **logic diagram** of a six-*input* one-*output sequential circuit* consisting of 3 *AND gates,* an *OR gate,* an *INVERTER,* and a *flip-flop.*

logic element. See *combinational circuit.*

logic product gate. See *AND gate.*

logic sum gate. See *OR gate.*

logic variable. See *switching variable.*

log-off. The *procedure* that is followed by a *user* in ending a period of *terminal operation,* that is, in terminating a *session.*

log-on. The *procedure* that is followed by a *user* in beginning a period of *terminal operation,* that is, in starting a *session.*

log-periodic antenna. A *wideband,* multi-element, unidirectional *narrow-beam antenna* that has a *frequency response curve* (characteristic) that is repeated at frequencies that are equally spaced in the *frequency spectrum.* The value of the frequency spacing is determined by the logarithm of the ratio that is used to determine the physical length and physical spacing of the elements of the antenna.

long-distance call. In *telephone system operation,* a *call* on a *long distance line,* that is, a call in which a *trunk* that connects two *switching centers* is used. It is a call to a *user* (customer, subscriber) at the far end of one or more trunks from the end that the *calling party* is calling from. Also see *local call.*

long-distance direct current (LDDC) dialing system. A *long-distance telephone dialing system* in which *direct current* is used for *transmission* and *signaling.* The British Post Office Telephone System makes use of it.

long-distance line. A *line* that, because of its electrical length, its physical length, its *traffic load,* or the number of *connections* that it has, requires one or more *trunks* between *switching centers* or *exchanges.*

long-haul communication. *Communication* occurring over long distances, usually nationwide or worldwide. Compared to *tactical communication systems,* long-haul communication systems are characterized by the higher levels of commands that they serve, such as national authorities, the more stringent performance requirements that they have (higher quality *circuits,* at least in some respects), the longer distances between the *users* they serve (worldwide), the higher traffic volume and density (larger size *switches* and *trunk* cross sections) that they have, and the fact that they constitute fixed or recoverable assets. Also see *long line.*

long-haul optical link. An *optical link* capable of *transmitting lightwave signals* over *optical cables* for long distances; e.g., between *telephone distribution frames* or *switching centers.* Synonymous with *long-haul optical transmission set.*

long-haul optical transmission set. See *long-haul optical link.*

longitude. See *celestial longitude; terrestrial longitude.*

longitudinal balance. The *electrical* symmetry of the two wires of a pair with respect to *ground.* Thus, from an *electrical* standpoint, the two wires cannot be distinguished from each other by any electrical test, such as *impedance, transmitted wave* form *distortion* for identical waves, or other electrical tests.

longitudinal jitter. In *facsimile transmission,* the effect that is due to the irregularity of the *scanning speed.* The speed irregularity may occur from many causes, such as the irregular rotation of the drum or helix that causes slight waviness or breaks in the *lines* of the reproduced *image,* lines that were straight on the original object (document).

longitudinally-excited atmosphere laser (LEA). A *gas laser* in which the *electric field* excitation of the *active medium* is longitudinal to (in the direction of) the flow of the active medium. This type of *laser* operates in a gas pressure range lower than that required for *transverse-excitation.* Contrast with *transverse-excited atmosphere laser (TEA).*

longitudinal resolution. 1. In a *facsimile transmitter,* the dimension along a *scanning line* of the smallest recognizable detail of an *image* that is reproduced by the shortest signal transmitted by the *transmitter* under specified conditions. In *phototelegraphy,* the transmission resolution includes the dimensions and effective *luminance* of the finest detail in question. In *document facsimile telegraphy,* assuming that the contrast of the finest detail is adequate, the transmitted *signal* must correspond to either *nominal black* or *nominal white*. 2. In a *facsimile receiver,* the dimension along a *scanning line* of the smallest recognizable detail of the *image* that is produced by the shortest *signal* capable of actuating the receiver under specified conditions. In *phototelegraphy,* the longitudinal and transverse dimensions of the finest detail correspond to those of the *picture element.* In *document facsimile telegraphy,* the longitudinal resolution is determined by the length of the line that is produced by the shortest *nominal black* or shortest *nominal white* signal that is capable of actuating the receiver. The *transverse resolution* is equal to the width of the *scanning pitch.* Synonymous with *longitudinal definition.*

long line. A physical *conductor* that is used for *communication* purposes, such as open wire systems, underground and overhead wire, *optical,* and *coaxial cables, submarine cables,* but not local connections, and that usually covers long distances. A 1-mile-long trunk between *switching centers* or a transatlantic cable are long lines, but a 20-mile-long local loop to a *user* (customer, subscriber) *end-instrument* is not considered under the concept of long lines. Long lines are used in *long-haul communication systems.* They constitute the transmission elements of the *long-distance telephone networks* and they may also contain *radio relay systems, radio* and *microwave links,* and *satellite communication systems* when these are *integrated* with the wire and *optical fiber systems.* Also see *long-haul communication.*

long-range aid to navigation (LORAN). *Radionavigation* equipment that consists of a fixed *transmitter* and a mobile *receiver* capable of selecting one hyperbolic line of position from *information* that is contained in one *channel.* For point position *fixing,* information from two channels is necessary in order to provide an intersection of two hyperbolas, that is, two crossing lines, using specially prepared charts. The LORAN position fixing system uses the time difference of reception of *pulse transmissions* from two or more *stations* that are fixed. Their transmissions are synchronized. The name is derived from long-range radio (or electronic) navigation or long-range aid to navigation.

long-range laser sonar. A *sonar* device for long-range applications in which a *laser* is used for forming separate and identifiable *beams,* that is, for forming a *pulse-coded frequency-modulated (FM) wave.*

long-range radar. *Radar* that is capable of determining the range and direction *(azimuth* and *elevation)* of objects (targets) at great distances. Also see *early-warning radar.*

long-term ionospheric forecast. A three months or more forecast of *ionospheric* conditions. The forecast is usually distributed in printed pamphlet form. Also see *short-term ionospheric forecast.*

long-term security. In *cryptographic communication systems,* the *protection* that results from the use of a *cryptosystem* that will protect *encrypted communication traffic* from successful *cryptanalysis* for as long as the traffic has intelligence value.

LO off. *Local oscillator off.*

look angle. The angle between a direction of sight and a reference direction. For example, the angle between the direction from an aircraft to a *radiation source* and the longitudinal axis of the aircraft frame.

look through. In *electronic warfare systems,* the irregular interruption of a *jamming signal* for short periods, usually extremely short periods, in order to allow for monitoring of the signal that is being jammed.

lookup table. A tabular arrangement of *data* such that on the basis of a multiple entry into the table, a single or unique location in the table will permit an identification of a particular item in the table (array). A single entry usually permits a set of items to be selected. Another entry permits the selection of another set, and an element common to both sets can then be selected. For example, a *code* table, a logarithm table, a periodic chemical elements table, a mileage table, or a transportation system time-table. The table may be arranged in chart form, with guiding lines to entries and elements, such as the *Smith chart* that is used for *transmission line* analysis.

loop. 1. The go and return *conductors* of an *electrical circuit,* that is a closed circuit when the circuit elements are connected. 2. A closed path that is established as such by a *resistance* measurement test. 3. An *antenna* that is in the shape of a circle and that is used extensively in *direction-finding equipment.* 4. In *computers,* a single repetition of a group of *instructions* in a *computer program.* See *conditioned loop; Costa's loop; local loop; phase-lock loop; squaring loop; test loop; unrepeatered loop.*

loop back. In *communication systems,* pertaining to a *transmission* test of *access lines* from the serving *switching center* to a *user* (customer, subscriber) end-instrument. The loop-back test does not require the assistance of the user. In the test, a connection is made over one access line from the serving switching center, through the transmission test equipment, and back to the serving switching center over another access line.

loop dialing. See *loop-disconnect pulsing system.*

loop-disconnect pulsing system. An extension of the loop-disconnect system that allows numbers to be *dialed* into an *automatic telephone exchange* as a series of *direct-current (DC) pulses.* A standard *pulse repetition rate* is 10 pps. This method of *telephone signaling* makes use of *break pulses* in a *loop circuit.* The break pulses are generated by a cam-operated *dial* spring *switch.* Synonymous with *impulse dialing; loop dialing.*

loop-disconnect system. A *telephone signaling system* that is used with *manual exchanges* and in which a handset rest switch (cradle switch, gravity switch, hook switch) applies a short circuit to the line *paired cable* when the *telephone* is not in use.

loop gain. 1. The total usable *power gain* of a *carrier amplifier* or a two-wire *repeater.* The maximum usable gain is determined by, and may not exceed, the losses in the closed path. **2.** The product of the gain values, or their sum if expressed in *decibels,* that act upon a *signal* as it travels around a closed path.

loophole.   In *communication security,* an error of omission or oversight in *software* or *hardware,* or on the part of personnel, that permits the circumvention of the *access control* process in a *communication system.*

loop network.   A *network configuration* in which each *node* is directly connected to two and only two nodes both of which are adjacent to it. Thus, one and only one *path* connects all nodes, there are no *endpoint nodes,* but one or more nodes may serve as a *port* or connection to other networks. Also see *ring network.* See Figure L-8.

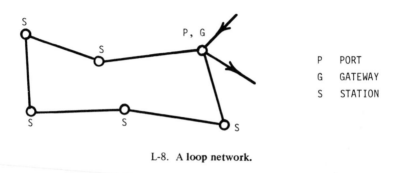

P   PORT
G   GATEWAY
S   STATION

L-8. A **loop network.**

loop noise.   The *noise* that originates in or that is contributed by the *local loops* in a *communication system.*

loop test.   **1.** A test that is used to locate a *fault* in the *insulation* of a *conductor* when the conductor can be arranged to form part of a closed *loop.* **2.** A test of a *local loop* by applying a short circuit (or loop) at a remote end of the loop, or by closing the *circuit* with an *impedance* of known value. **3.** The *coupling* of a *signal* from the transmitting path back to the local receiving path for test purposes. The looped path may include the whole of the *transmitter* and *receiver.* In a *satellite system,* the loop may extend through the *satellite transponder* and return to earth. A physical link at appropriate intermediate points in the transmitting and receiving equipment may also be included in the test.

loop translator.   See *test loop translator.*

loose-tube splicer.   A glass tube with a square hole used to splice two *optical fibers.* The curved fibers are made to seek the same corner of the square hole, thus holding them in alignment until the *index-matching* epoxy, already in the tube, cures, thus forming an aligned, low-loss *butted* joint. Also see *precision-sleeve splicer; tangential coupling.* Synonymous with *square-tube splicer.* See Figure L-9.

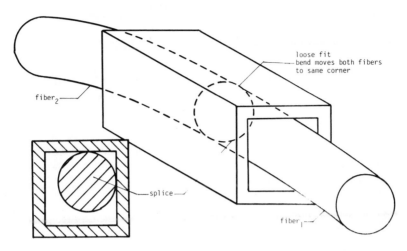

L-9. A loose-tube splicer.

LORAN. *Long-range aid to navigation.*

LORO. *Lobe-on-receive only.*

LOS. *Line of sight.*

LOS propagation. *Line-of-sight propagation.*

loss. **1.** In *communication systems,* the amount of electrical *attenuation* in a *circuit,* or the *power* that is consumed in a circuit *component.* **2.** The energy that is dissipated without accomplishing useful work. In communications, it is usually expressed in *decibels.* Also see *crosstalk coupling.* See *absorption loss; angular misalignment loss; aperture-to-medium coupling loss; bending loss; bridging loss; connector-induced optical conductor loss; connector insertion loss; coupling loss; free space loss; Fresnel reflection loss; gap loss; insertion loss; intermodulation noise loss; isotropic space loss; lateral displacement loss; light-leakage loss; microbending loss; misalignment loss; mismatch-of-core-radii loss; modal loss; net loss; packing fraction loss; path loss; receiver location loss; reference loss; refractive-index-profile mismatch loss; return loss; scattering loss; source-coupler loss; source-to-fiber loss; splicing loss; transmission loss.*

loss distance. See *transmission loss distance.*

lossless halfwave dipole antenna. A theoretical *halfwave dipole antenna* that has a *directivity power gain* of 2.15 dB over an *isotropic antenna.* When used as a gain reference, the lossless halfwave dipole antenna has a power gain of 0 dB.

loss probability. See *block loss probability.*

loss time. See *environmental loss time.*

loss variation.   See *net loss variation.*

loss versus frequency characteristic.   See *insertion loss versus frequency characteristic.*

lossy medium.   A *wave transmission medium* in which a significant amount of the energy of the wave is *absorbed* per unit distance traveled by the wave. For example, in an *optical fiber cladding,* lossy material is used to attenuate by *absorption* the energy that has leaked outside the *fiber core.*

lost block.   In a *communication system,* a *block* that is successfully *transferred* across the *source user* (customer, subscriber) *interface* into the system, but that is not delivered to any user within the specified *maximum (end-to-end) block transfer time.*

lost call.   A *call* that has not been *completed* for any reason other than the instances in which the *called party* is *busy.*

lost time.   In a *facsimile transmission system,* the portion of the *scanning line* period that cannot be used for *picture signal transmission.* In a *drum transmitter,* the lost time is the *dead sector scanning time.*

loudspeaker.   In *communications,* a device that converts *electrical* energy into *sound* energy. The device accepts *electrical voice signals* or electrical sound signals and converts them into sound signals that can be heard a considerable distance away from the device. For example, the final stage of a *radio receiver.* Its primary *components* are an electromagnet and a vibrating diaphragm attached to an armature that is vibrated by the variations of *electric current* in the electromagnet.

loudspeaker watch.   See *listening watch.*

loupe.   See *magnifier.*

low-detectability electromagnetic wave transmission.   A *communication transmission system* that is designed to provide an enhanced *signal-to-noise ratio* at the intended *receiver,* while at the same time exhibiting a low or less-than-unity signal-to-noise ratio (negative in *decibels*) at potential *narrowband* clandestine intercept receivers.

lower case.   See *letter case.*

lower sideband.   The *sideband* that has a lower *frequency* than the *carrier* frequency. Its frequency is also lower than the *upper sideband* if there is no carrier, that is, if the carrier is suppressed. Also see *upper sideband.*

lowest-order transverse mode.   The lowest-*frequency electromagnetic wave* that can *propagate* in a given *waveguide* that can support more than one *transverse electric (TE) mode* or more than one *transverse magnetic (TM) mode,* the limitation in the number of modes being imposed by the boundary conditions and the geometrical shape of the waveguide as well as the frequency. Solution of

Maxwell's equations with the boundary conditions for a rectangular waveguide operating in the TM mode yields the following relationship:

$$\omega^2 \mu\epsilon > [(m\pi/a)^2 + (n\pi/b)^2]$$

where ω is the angular velocity $(\omega = 2\pi f)$, μ is the *magnetic permeability* of the material in the waveguide, ϵ is the *electric permittivity* of the material in the waveguide, a and b are the cross-section dimensions, and m and n are the whole numbers introduced when solving Maxwell's equations. Solutions of Maxwell's equations for both transverse magnetic (TM) and transverse electric (TE) modes of propagation yield modes identified as TM_{mn} and TE_{mn}, except that for *TM* modes neither m nor n can be zero, and for *TE* modes, m or n, but not both, can be zero, since these conditions result in a zero field. Therefore, the lowest order mode for *TE* is TE_{10} and the lowest order of *TM* is TM_{11}. The TE_{10} mode, called the *dominant mode,* is obtained by designing a waveguide with a width-to-height ratio of about 2, and using an operating frequency above the TE_{10} cutoff frequency, given by:

$$f_c = c/2a$$

where c is the *velocity of light* in the *medium* in the guide, but below the next higher cutoff frequency. Higher-order modes occur at higher frequencies. Also see *dominant mode; mode conversion.*

lowest usable frequency (LUF). In *electromagnetic wave transmission,* such as is used in *radio, video, microwave,* and *satellite communication systems,* the lower limit of the *frequencies* that can be used with good results between two specified points and that involves *propagation* by *reflection* from the regular *ionized layers* of the *ionosphere.* The LUF is a median frequency, that is applicable to 90% of the days of a month, as opposed to 50% for the *maximum usable frequency (MUF).* Also see *maximum usable frequency (MUF).* Synonymous with *lowest useful frequency.*

lowest usable high frequency. See *lowest useful high frequency (LUF).*

lowest useful frequency. See *lowest usable frequency (LUF).*

lowest useful high frequency (LUF). The lowest *frequency* in the *high-frequency band* at which the *field intensity* at a *receiver* is sufficient to provide the required *signal-to-noise ratio* on 90% of the *undisturbed days* of the month. Synonymous with *lowest usable high frequency.*

low frequency (LF). The *frequency* range from 30 kHz to 300 kHz. The *alphabetic* designator of the range is LF. The numeric designator of the range is 5. Also see *frequency spectrum designation.* See *extremely low frequency (ELF); infralow frequency (ILF); very low frequency (VLF).*

low-level control. In *data transmission,* the *processing* or control functions that occur at or below the *data link layer* in the *hierarchical structure* of a *communication station* or *network.* The low-level control functions include *bit stuffing* (injection) and *destuffing* (extraction), *address* interpretation, *response* generation, and *frame check sequence* computation. In the *open system architecture* concept of a *communication network,* the data link layer and the *physical layer* are low levels.

low-level keying. In *telegraph systems,* the *keying* of *electrical currents* and *voltages* in which the currents and voltages are at the lowest possible values; usually not more than 6 volts occurs between the keying contacts. Purposes of low-level keying include a reduction of the possibility of unauthorized *detection* of *digital data* and *telegraph transmissions,* a reduction of *crosstalk* and *interference* to other *channels,* and a reduction of *high-frequency harmonics* that are caused by the sudden interruption of currents and voltages, since sharp-edged waveforms are equivalent to the existence of high frequency *components* in the *signals.* Typical low-level keying values are 2 volts at 70 μa or less, or 6 volts at 1 ma or less.

low-level protocol (LLP). In the *open systems architecture* concept of a *communication system,* a *protocol* at the *lower layers* of the system, such as at the *data link layer* and the *physical layer.* The low-level protocol places particular emphasis on the *communication processes* and the *transmission operations.*

low-level signaling. *Signaling* in which the levels of *voltages* on *signal lines* do not exceed a specified value, such as 6 volts.

low-loss (FEP)-clad silica fiber. An *optical fiber* consisting of a pure fused silica *core* and a perfluoronated ethylene-propylene (FEP) (a commercial polymer) *cladding.* FEP-clad silica *fibers* have *refractive indices* of 1.458 and 1.338 for the core and cladding, respectively, and a *transmission* loss of 2 to 3 dB/km at the present time, with an *ultraviolet* capability at 0.546 *microns* of 360 dB/km.

low-loss fiber. An *optical fiber* having a low energy loss, due to all causes, per unit length of fiber, usually measured in *decibels*/kilometer at a specified *wavelength.* Low-loss is usually considered to be below 20 dB/km. In low-loss fiber, *attenuation* of a *propagating wave* is caused primarily by *scattering* due to metal ions and intrinsic fiber material (Rayleigh scattering), and by *absorption* due to water in the OH radical form. Also see Figure H-1.

low-noise amplifier. An *amplifier* in which its *noise temperature* is the primary cause of internally generated *noise,* that is, the main cause of noise is thermally *excited electrons.*

low-pass filter. A device that passes all *frequencies* below a specified value and removes, blocks, rejects, or *absorbs* all other frequencies of *electrical currents* or *electromagnetic waves.* Also see *band-pass filter; high pass filter.*

low-performance communication equipment. 1. *Communication* equipment that has insufficiently exacting characteristics to permit use of the equipment in *trunks* or *links.* Such equipment may be used in *loops* whenever loop performance requirements are met by the equipment. 2. Tactical ground and airborne equipment whose size, weight, and complexity must be kept to a minimum and whose primary requirement is to operate in *nets* with performance standards that are similar to those of the equipment.

low-power communication device.   A *communication* device that has a severely restricted low *radiation power output* capability. *Conducted* or *guided* output power devices, such as *waveguides, coaxial cables,* and *optical fiber cables,* are not included. Low-power *radiation* devices are usually used for short-range communication or control purposes. For example, wireless *microphones, phonograph oscillators, radio*-controlled garage door openers, *television receiver* remote *channel* selectors, and model aircraft radio controllers.

low-probability-of-intercept receiver.   A *receiver* in which *directional antennas* are used or in which variable *frequency tuning* is used and that will not *detect incident electromagnetic power* unless the frequency, direction, and *polarization* of the *receiver* are in proper coincidence with the *transmitter* at the instant of *transmission.* If the ratio between the time during which the transmission *illuminates* the receiver, and the time taken by the search system to cover the complete frequency *band* and spatial sector of search of the antenna, is greater than unity, then the search system becomes a *high-probability-of-intercept system.* In both instances a *sampling* process is used. Also see *high-probability-of-intercept receiver.*

low-speed Morse.   The *international Morse code* transmitted at speeds that are lower than normal speeds, such as speeds of less than 18 *words* per minute. Maritime and aeronautical *radio* organizations tend to limit *signaling speeds* to less than 18 words per minute.

low-voltage enclosed air-circuit-breaker switchgear.   *Switching equipment* that is designed for service at low *voltages,* usually not to exceed 600 v for *alternating-current (AC) circuits* and not to exceed 750 v for *direct-current (DC)* circuits. The air circuit breakers are contained in individual compartments with controlled access, are controlled remotely, or are controlled from front *panels* (control *consoles*). Only dead-front *switchgear* assemblies are used, that is, no power is available at the front panel. All power is at the back panel or remote from the control area.

L-pad.   In *electrical systems,* a device that is used for volume control and that has the same *impedance* at all settings. It consists essentially of an electrical *network* arranged so that its elements are adjusted simultaneously from one actuator.

LSI chip.   *Large-scale integrated (LSI) chip.*

LTC.   *Line traffic coordinator.*

Lucal code.   See *modified reflected binary code.*

LUF.   *Lowest usable frequency. Lowest useful frequency. Lowest useful high frequency.*

Lukasiewicz notation.   See *prefix notation.*

lumen (lm).   The *SI* unit of *light flux* corresponding to $1/(4\pi)$ of the total light flux emitted by a *source* having an *intensity* of 1 *candela*, thus being equal to the flux issuing from $1/60 \text{ cm}^2$ of opening of the standard source, and included in a solid angle of 1 *steradian*.

lumen-hour (lm-hr).   The unit quantity of *light* equal to 1 lm of *luminous flux* flowing for 1 hr.

lumen-second (lm-sec).   The unit quantity of *light* equal to 1 lm of *luminous flux* flowing for 1 sec.

lumerg.   The centimeter-gram-second (cgs) unit of *luminous* energy, equal to 10^{-7} lumen-second.

luminance.   The ratio of the *luminous intensity emitted* by a *light source* in a given direction by an infinitesimal area of the source, to the projection of that area of the source upon the plane perpendicular to the given direction. Luminance is usually stated as *luminous intensity* per unit area, or *luminous flux emitted* per unit solid angle projected per unit area upon which the *flux* is *incident,* the areas being perpendicular to the direction in which the *lightwave* is propagating.

luminance compensation.   In the *transmission* of pictures, whether by facsimile, phototelegraph, or *lightwave* systems using *optical fibers,* compensation introduced at the *receiver* by the *image*-recording medium so as to exactly reproduce the *luminance range* present in the *object*.

luminance range.   The difference between the lowest *luminous intensity* and the highest luminous intensity that are obtained from an object *(reflected)* or from a *light source* (directly).

luminance range compression.   In *lightwave, facsimile, or phototelegraphic transmission systems,* a reduction in the *luminance* range of the *signals* in the *transmission medium* or in the *display image* from the luminance range of the *object*.

luminance range expansion.   In *lightwave, facsimile, or phototelegraphic transmission systems,* an increase in the luminance range of the *signals* in the *transmission medium* or in the *display image* over and above the *luminance range* of the object, such as the subject document or picture being transmitted. Thus, the luminance range of the image is greater than that of the original object. The expansion could occur accidentally or be deliberate.

luminance temperature.   The *temperature* of an ideal *blackbody* that would have the same *luminance* as the source for which the luminance temperature is desired for some narrow *spectral* region.

luminance threshold.   See *absolute luminance threshold*.

luminescence.   The process whereby matter *emits electromagnetic radiation,* which, for certain *wavelengths* or restricted regions of the *spectrum,* is in excess of that attributable to the thermal state of the material and the *emissivity* of its surface.   The *radiation* is characteristic of the particular luminescent material, and occurs without outside stimulation. Also see *phosphorescence*.

luminescent diode.   See *superluminescent diode*.

luminosity.   The ratio of *luminous flux* to the *radiant flux* in a sample of radiant light flux; e.g., *lumens* per watt of *radiant energy*.   Synonymous with *luminous efficiency*.

luminosity curve.   The curve obtained by plotting *luminous efficiency* against the *wavelength* of a *lightwave*.   See *absolute luminosity curve*.

luminous density.   The *luminous energy* per unit volume of an *electromagnetic (light) wave*.

luminous efficiency.   The ratio of the *luminous flux* emitted to the power consumed by a *source* of *light;* e.g., *lumens* per watt-applied-at-the-source.

luminous emittance.   The total *luminous flux emitted* by a unit area of an extended surface, in contrast to a point or line *source*.

luminous flux.   The quantity that specifies the capacity of the *radiant flux* from a *light* source to produce the attribute of visual sensation known as *brightness*. *Luminous flux* is *radiant flux* evaluated with respect to its *luminous efficiency* of *radiation*.   Unless otherwise stated, luminous flux pertains to the standard photopic observer.

luminous intensity.   The ratio of the *luminous flux emitted* by a *light source,* or an *element* of the source, in an infinitesimally small cone about the given direction, to the solid angle of that cone, usually stated as luminous flux emitted per unit solid angle.

luminous radiation efficiency.   See *luminosity*.

luminous transmittance.   The ratio of the *luminous flux transmitted* by an *object* to the *incident luminous flux*.

lumped parameter.   In an *electrical communication, power,* or other *circuit,* pertaining to a situation in which the electrical *components,* such as *resistance, inductance, capacitance, semiconductor junctions, thermocouples, photosensitive* materials, and *connector* surfaces, are each considered as being located at a single point in the circuit in which they are connected.   An electrical *signal* is considered to *propagate* instantly through each component.   If the *propagation time* is considered or is appreciable, the component is considered as *distributed* rather than lumped.   A circuit consisting of resistance, capacitance, and inductance elements that are linear can be modelled by ordinary differential equations.   In lumped parameter circuits the input *wavelength* is large compared to the dimensions of the components.   Usually no energy is considered lost by *radiation*.   Also see *distributed parameter*.

lunar eclipse. An *eclipse* of the moon by the earth as the earth *(obstruction)* moves between the sun *(source)* and the moon *(reflector).* It occurs only during a full moon.

lux. A unit of *illuminance;* equal to a *lumen incident* per square meter of surface normal to the direction of *propagation.*

M

MAA. *Maximum acceptance angle.*

mach. A factor that is used to express the speed of a body moving in a given medium. Given a particular set of conditions, such as *temperature* and pressure, the mach number is the number of times the speed that sound would have traveling in the same medium under the same conditions as the body whose speed is being expressed. Thus, $M = v_b/v_s$, where v_b is the actual speed of a body relative to a medium, v_s is the speed that sound would have traveling in the same medium under the same conditions, and M is the mach number. Typically, the speed of a body traveling at 2160 ft/s in air at $0°C$ at sea level (dry) would be moving at mach 2, since the speed of sound in air under those conditions is about 1080 ft/s. There is about a 1 ft/s increase in the speed of sound in air at sea level for each *kelvin* above $0°C$. Thus, the body would have to move faster in warmer air if it is to remain at mach 2.

machine. See *fiber-pulling machine.*

machine code. 1. Any *code* that a machine, such as a *computer* or a *communication system* can recognize, sense, read, or interpret. 2. A set of *coded instructions* that a machine can sense, interpret, and execute. Thus, *machine languages, machine functions,* and machine *instructions* are described or written in machine code.

machine function. 1. An *operation* that is performed by equipment. 2. The *signal* that causes equipment to perform an operation. For example, a shift or a carriage return.

machine instruction code. See *instruction code.*

machine language. A *computer-oriented language* that has *instruction codes* that are executed directly by a machine *(computer)*. A machine language is usually based on, or is part of, the internal electronic circuitry *(hardware)* design of a computer. A programmer need not necessarily be aware of the machine language. It is an *artificial language.* A machine language *program* is *compiled* by the computer itself from the *high-level language* instructions cited by the programmer.

machine system. See *man-machine system.*

macrofiber. See *jumbo fiber.*

macroinstruction. A *computer instruction* that can be replaced by a specific sequence of instructions in the same *language*. The macroinstruction usually provides the *parameters* that are required for its own execution. It may also designate the *machine language* instructions for performing a specified task.

magnetic. 1. Pertaining to the phenomenon that causes certain materials that are found in nature to attract or repel one another independently of their *electric* attraction or repulsion and independently of gravitational attraction. **2.** Pertaining to the field of force that exhibits polarity and can be created by *electric currents* consisting of moving electric charges. See *ferromagnetic*. See Figure M-1.

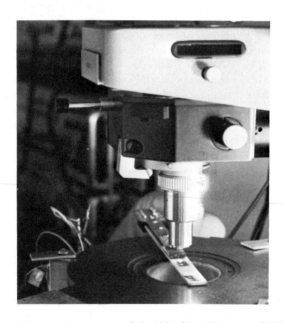

M-1. Making final adjustments on a **magnetic** bubble *chip*. (Courtesy of Bell Laboratories.)

magnetic card. A card with a magnetizable surface layer on which *data* can be stored by a magnetizing *field* and read by a sensing device.

magnetic core. A configuration of magnetizable material placed in relationship to *current*-carrying *conductors* such that the polarity of its magnetization can be reversed by selection of the proper conductors. The direction of magnetization, or its reversal, can be used to store and read *binary data* and perform *logic operations*. It may be made of magnetic materials such as iron, ferrite, or iron oxide, and it may come in such shapes as wires, tapes, toroids, rods, *thin films,* slugs, or beads.

magnetic field. A *field* that is created by an electric charge that is in motion. The field is identified and quantified by (1) the force exerted on a magnetic pole placed in it, (2) by the *electromotive force (voltage)* induced in a *conductor* moved relative to and transverse to it, provided the magnetic field produces magnetic flux and the number of flux linkages around the *circuit* in which the *current* is flowing changes with respect to time, or (3) by the force exerted on an electric charge moving transverse to it. Also see *Biot-Savart law.*

magnetic field component. In an *electromagnetic wave,* the part of the wave that consits of a time-varying *magnetic field,* whose interaction with an *electric field* gives rise to the *propagation* of a field of force or energy in a direction perpendicular to both fields. *Reflection, refraction,* and *transmission* that occur at a *media interface* depend upon the direction of the magnetic field component and the *electric field component* relative to the direction of the *interface surface* as well as the *refractive indices, permittivities, permeabilities,* and *conductivities* of the *transmission media* on both sides of the interface surface. Also see *Maxwell's equations; wave equation.*

magnetic field force. 1. The force of attraction or repulsion exerted on two *magnetic* poles, or the force exerted on one magnetic pole situated in a magnetic field. The force, $\mathbf{F}$, is given by $\mathbf{F} = (\mu m_1 m_2 / r^2)\mathbf{a_r}$ where μ is the *magnetic permeability* of the medium in which the magnetic poles are imbedded, m_1 and m_2 are the magnetic pole strengths, $\mathbf{a_r}$ is a unit vector in the direction joining the two poles, and r is their distance of separation. 2. The force exerted on a magnetic pole or on an electric current-carrying wire properly oriented and situated in a *magnetic field.* The elemental force, $d\mathbf{F}$, on a wire perpendicular to a magnetic field is given by $d\mathbf{F} = \mathbf{B} \times i d\mathbf{L}$, where $\mathbf{B}$ is the *magnetic flux density, i* is the electric current, and $d\mathbf{L}$ is the elemental length of *conductor* carrying the current *i.* The flux density is given by $\mathbf{B} = \mu\mathbf{H}$, where $\mathbf{H}$ is the magnetic field intensity and μ is the *magnetic permeability* of the medium in which the conductor is imbedded.

magnetic flux density. 1. The number of *lines* of *magnetic flux* passing through a unit area perpendicular to the direction of the magnetic lines, that is $\mathbf{B} = \phi/A$, where $\mathbf{B}$ is the magnetic flux density, ϕ is the magnetic flux, and A is the area perpendicular to ϕ. Thus, $\mathbf{B}$ is the number of magnetic lines per unit area. 2. The *magnetic permeability* times the *magnetic field intensity.* Thus, $\mathbf{B} = \mu\mathbf{H}$, where $\mathbf{B}$ is the magnetic flux density, μ is the magnetic permeability, and $\mathbf{H}$ is the magnetic field intensity. 3. The *magnetomotive force (mmf)* divided by the *magnetic reluctance, R,* of the magnetic path over which the mmf is exerted, and divided by the cross-sectional area of the path. Thus, $\phi = \text{mmf}/R$, where ϕ is the total magnetic flux, **mmf** is the magnetomotive force, and R is the reluctance of the path; and $\mathbf{B} = \phi/A$, where $\mathbf{B}$ is the magnetic flux density and A is the cross-sectional area of the path. The mmf is proportional to the ampere-turns of current-carrying conductor that is producing the magnetic field. The reluctance is directly proportional to the length of the magnetic path, inversely proportional to the cross-secitonal area of the path, and inversely proportional to the *magnetic permeability* of the path material.

magnetic ink character recognition (MICR). The recognition of *characters* that are printed with ink that contains particles of *magnetic* material. The characters can be read by a magnetic reading head and by persons.

magnetic permeability. A *transmission medium parameter* that defines the characteristic of the medium that serves as the constant of proportionality in the *constitutive relation* between the applied *magnetic field* and the *magnetic flux density* obtained in the material; i.e., $\mathbf{B} = \mu\mathbf{H}$, where μ is the magnetic permeability and $\mathbf{B}$ and $\mathbf{H}$ are the magnetic flux density and the magnetic field intensity, respectively. The permeability is also the constant of proportionality in the equation expressing the force of attraction of two unlike magnetic poles a given distance apart. The magnetic permeability of most materials is nearly the same as free space, except the ferrous metals exhibiting very much larger values. Magnetic permeability and *electric permittivity* in a given medium are related by the relation:

$$1/\sqrt{\mu\epsilon} = c$$

where c is the *velocity of light* in the medium. For a *lightwave* entering electrical nonconductors (*dielectric* materials) from free space, the *refractive index* for the material relative to free space is:

$$n = \sqrt{\mu_r \epsilon_r}$$

where the permeability and permittivity are relative to free space. See *absolute magnetic permeability; incremental magnetic permeability; relative magnetic permeability.*

magnetic recording. See *NRZI magnetic recording.*

magnetic reluctance. The *resistance* of a path to the establishment (flow) of *magnetic flux*. The *magnetic reluctance, R,* is given by $R = mmf/\phi$, where R is the magnetic reluctance of the magnetic path that is followed by the magnetic flux, *mmf* is the *magnetomotive force* that is causing the *magnetic field intensity*, and ϕ is the total magnetic flux in the path. The magnetic reluctance is also given by $R = L/\mu A$, where L is the length of the path, μ is the *magnetic permeability* of the path material, and A is the cross sectional area of the path. Reluctances in a magnetic path may be combined like the *resistances* in an *electric circuit*. Also see *magnetomotive force.*

magnetic tape. A tape that has a surface layer of *magnetic* material on which *data* can be stored by means of *magnetic recording*. The data is stored in the form of magnetized areas at typical *packing densities* of 800 and 1600 *bpi* in each of several *tracks*. Since the *bits* for each *character* are in parallel tracks, the packing density for the characters is the same as for the bits. Many *modes* of recording are used, such as *non-return-to-zero (NRZ)* and *return-to-zero (RZ)*.

magnetic tape leader. The portion of *magnetic tape* that precedes the *beginning-of-tape mark* and that is used to thread the tape on a tape handler or on a reel.

magnetic tape trailer. The portion of *magnetic tape* that follows the *end-of-tape mark* and that is used to retain the tape on the reel or on the tape handler.

magnetic vector. A representation of the *magnetic field* associated with an *electromagnetic wave*, and hence with a *lightwave*, that specifies the direction and amplitude of this magnetic field. Also see *electric vector.*

magnetic wave. See *transverse magnetic wave.*

magnetism. See *residual magnetism.*

magneto exchange. See *magneto switchboard.*

magnetohydrodynamics (MHD). The study of the flow of electrically conducting fluids while under the influence of *electric* and *magnetic fields.*

magnetomotive force (mmf). The driving force that creates a *magnetic field intensity* at a point in space and materials. It is due to an *electric current.* It is proportional to the ampere-turns presented by an *electrical conductor* carrying a current. For example, the mmf produced by a long coil of wire is given by *mmf = 0.4πNI,* where *N* is the number of turns, *I* is the electric current in amperes, and π is 3.1416. The mmf is not dependent upon the *magnetic permeability* but the magnetic flux and the flux density is dependent on the material in which the coil is imbedded. Also see *magnetic reluctance.*

magnetooptic effect. The rotation of the *polarization plane* of *plane-polarized lightwaves* in a *transmission medium* brought about when subjecting the medium to a *magnetic field* (Faraday rotation). The effect can be used to *modulate* a *light beam* in a material, since many properties, such as *conducting* velocities, *reflection* and *transmission coefficients* at *interfaces, acceptance angles, critical angles,* and *transmission modes,* are dependent upon the direction of *propagation* at *interfaces* in the media in which the light travels. The amount of rotation is given by:

$$A = VHL$$

where *V* is a constant, *H* is the magnetic field strength, and *L* is the propagation distance. The magnetic field is in the direction of propagation of the *lightwave.* Synonymous with *Faraday effect.*

magnetooptic (m-o) modulator. A *modulator* that uses the *magnetooptic effect* to *modulate* a *lightwave carrier.*

magnetostatic field. The *field* of force produced by moving electric charges. The strength of a magnetostatic field can be measured in terms of the force it exerts on a magnetic pole of known strength placed within it. The magnetostatic field is usually considered not to vary with time, or to vary slowly relative to events of interest occurring within it. The field is *uncoupled* from any other field. Synonymous with *staticmagnetic field.*

magnetostriction. The phenomenon exhibited by some materials in which dimensional changes occur when the material is subjected to a *magnetic field,* usually becoming longer in the direction of the applied field. The effect can be used to launch a shock or *sound wave* each time the field is applied or changed, possibly giving rise to *phonons* that could influence energy levels in the atoms of certain materials such as *semiconductors* and *lasers* and thereby serve as a *modulation* method. Along with *photon* or *electric field* excitation, the phonon energy could provide threshold energy to cause electron *energy level* transitions, causing photon *absorption* or *emission.*

magneto switchboard. A *manually-operated telephone exchange* in which the *users* (customers, subscribers) and *operators call* and *clear* by means of hand-cranked magneto generators that serve as the source of *signaling (calling* and *clearing) power.* The *signaling* is called *ring* and *ring-off.* Synonymous with *magneto exchange.* See *single-position magneto switchboard.*

magnetron. See *fixed magnetron.*

magnification. The relationship between the linear dimension of an *image* and the corresponding dimension of an *object* when the image is larger than the object. For example, if an image is four times the size of the original object, the magnification may be expressed as 4X, 4:1, or 300% larger. Usually magnification pertains to a given *optical system.* See *absolute magnification; angular magnification; individual normal magnification; magnifying power.*

magnifier. An *optical system* capable of forming a magnified *virtual image* of an *object* placed near its *front focal point. Magnifications* usually range from 3X to 20X. Synonymous with *loupe; magnifying glass; simple microscope.*

magnifying glass. See *magnifier.*

magnifying power. The measure of the ability of an *optical* device to make an *object* appear larger than it appears to the unaided eye. For example, if an optical element or system has a *magnification* of 2-power (2X), the object will appear twice as wide and high. The magnification of an optical instrument is equal to the diameter of the *entrance pupil* divided by the diameter of the *exit pupil.* For a telescopic system, the magnification is also equal to the *focal length* of the *eyepiece.* Another expression for the magnification of an instrument is the tangent of an angle in the apparent field divided by the tangent of the corresponding angle in the true field. Synonymous with *magnification.*

main beam. See *main lobe.*

main distribution frame (MDF). The *distribution frame* for the internal *lines* and the external lines of a *telephone exchange.* The MDF can serve as the *interface* between a *network* and a *user facility.* One part of the MDF terminates the permanent *outside lines* entering the exchange, central office, or communication building. The other part terminates the *user* (customer, subscriber) *lines* and *trunk cabling.* The MDF is used for associating any outside line with any other outside line or with any cabling terminal. It usually carries the central office protective devices. It functions as a test point between line and central office. In a *private branch exchange (PBX),* the MDF is used for similar purposes. The outside lines include *radio, video, microwave, satellite, optical fiber,* or other *circuits* as appropriate. Usually for *telephone systems,* the MDF carries all outside lines and their protective devices on the *vertical terminating block* side of the frame. All connections to central equipment that may be assigned to particular outside lines are carried on the horizontal side of the frame. When used in *communication systems* other than telephone systems, all station lines and equipment terminate on the vertical side of the MDF and all *patch fields terminate* on the horizontal side of the MDF. Synonymous with *main frame.* Also see *combined distribution frame; intermediate distribution frame.*

main frame. See *central processing unit; main distribution frame.*

main lobe. The lobe of an *antenna electromagnetic radiation pattern* that describes or includes the largest amount of *power* or highest *radiant power density,* i.e., radiated power per *unit solid angle.* For a *light source* energizing an *optical fiber, bundle,* or *cable,* the main lobe is directed into the fibers. Synonymous with *main beam.* Also see *directivity pattern; radiation pattern; side lobe.*

maintainability. A measure of the ease with which maintenance of a *functional unit (hardware* or *software)* can be performed in accordance with prescribed requirements. It is a characteristic of design and installation that is expressed as the probability that an item will be retained in or restored to a specified condition within a given period of time, when the maintenance is performed in accordance with prescribed procedures and resources.

maintenance. An activity or any group of activities, such as tests, measurements, replacements, adjustments, and repairs, that is intended to eliminate *faults* or to keep a *functional unit* in a specified state or restore it to a specified state. Also see *corrective maintenance; preventive maintenance.*

maintenance control circuit (MCC). In *communication system maintenance,* a voice *circuit* that is used for coordination of maintenance personnel. This circuit is usually not available to *technical control facility* or operations personnel. Also see *engineering circuit.*

maintenance panel. A *connection, display,* or *control panel* or *console* that is used by maintenance personnel for their interaction with the equipment that is being maintained.

maintenance test land station. See *radionavigation maintenance test land station.*

major. In *optics,* a piece of glass to which a piece of glass of a different *refractive index* will be fused to make a *multifocal lens.*

major relay station. In *tape relay systems,* a *tape station* that is connected to two or more *trunk circuits* and that provides alternate *routing* in order to meet *communication system* performance requirements.

make-busy circuit. See *pilot make-busy (PMB) circuit.*

malfunction. See *failure.*

management. See *communication system management; frequency management.*

maneuvering signals. A *signal* transmitted to *stations* on ships, aircraft, spacecraft, land vehicles, or other mobile units for the purpose of controlling or directing their movement. The *transmission* may be accomplished by any means of *communication,* such as *voice, radio, flaghoist, colored lights,* or *hand signaling.*

Mangin mirror. A *negative meniscus lens* whose second, or *convex,* surface is silvered. *Spherical aberration* can be corrected for any given position of the *image* by carefully choosing the radii.

manipulative communication deception (MCD). The controlled insertion of misleading *information* into a *communication system* for the purpose of presenting a false *traffic* picture. MCD is designed to mislead *communication monitors* by transmitting false *data* over communication *circuits* and *channels.* Communication system *operators* or *users* can be the *deception traffic originators.* The alteration or *simulation* of *electromagnetic* communication *radiation* is intended to falsify the *information* that can be obtained from analysis of the radiation.

manipulative electronic deception (MED). The use of *electromagnetic radiation* in such a manner as to falsify the *information* that can be obtained from analysis of the *electromagnetic radiation.* The alteration or *simulation* of electromagnetic radiation or the reradiation, *absorption,* or *reflection* of electromagnetic radiation to accomplish *deception* is included in MED.

man-machine system. A system in which the functions of a person and a machine are interrelated.

manual answering facility. A *facility* that is used to establish a *call* only if the *called party* indicates a readiness to receive the call by means of a manual *operation* or manually-generated *signal.*

manual calling facility. A *facility* that is manually operated by a *calling party* and that enters *selection signals* into a *communication system* at an undefined (nonspecific) *data signaling rate.* The *signaling characters* may be generated at the *data terminal equipment (DTE)* or at the *data circuit-terminating equipment (DCE).*

manual exchange. An *exchange* in which the *connections* between incoming and outgoing *lines,* that is, between outside lines, are manually controlled by an *operator.*

manual relay system. A *communication system* in which *messages* are *relayed* manually from *point-to-point.* For example, a *tape-relay system* in which messages received at a *data station* are torn off the *receiver* and manually moved to a unit for transmitting to a final station or to another intermediate station for further relay.

manual spot janner. A *spot jammer* that can concentrate its *transmitted power* at a given *frequency* or *channel* by manually selecting the *frequency.* The frequency can be continuously varied over a wide *spectrum.*

manual telegraphy. Any method of *telegraph operation* in which the *signal elements* are *keyed* individually by an *online operator* from a knowledge of the *code* and in which the signals are immediately *transmitted* without *storage* at the *transmitter.*

map. See *gnomic map; line-route map; orthodromic map; routing indicator delineation map.*

margin. **1.** In *communication systems,* the maximum degree of *signal distortion* that can be tolerated without affecting their *restitution,* that is, without interpreting them incorrectly. **2.** The allowable *error rate,* deviation from normal, or degradation of performance of a system. **3.** The allowance, such as the margin on this page, that is made to insure that *data* in or on a *data medium* does not exceed the limits of the medium. See *antijamming margin; fade margin; jamming margin; net margin; nominal margin; radio frequency power margin; singing margin; start-stop margin; synchronous margin; synchronous receiver margin; telegraph receiver margin; theoretical margin.*

marginal check. See *marginal test.*

margin bell. A *machine function* that controls a bell *(audio signal)* that indicates that the end of a printing or typing *line* is being approached. Margin bells are used on manual typewriters, *input keyboards, teletypewriters,* and *teleprinters.*

marginal test. A test or check in which certain operating conditions, such as *voltage* or *frequency,* are varied about their nominal values in order to detect and locate incipient *faults* in a *system.* Synonymous with *marginal check.*

marine broadcast station. A *coast station* that makes scheduled *broadcasts* of time, meteorological *information,* and hydrographic *information.*

marine radio beacon station. A *radio beacon navigation land station* that is in the *maritime radionavigation service* and that *transmits* for the benefit of ships at sea. The *emissions* of the station are intended to enable a *ship station* to determine its *bearing* (direction) in relation to the marine radio beacon station.

maritime air communications. *Communication systems,* procedures, *operations,* and equipment that are used for *message traffic* between *aircraft stations* and *ship stations* in the *maritime service.* Commercial, private, naval, and other ships are included.

maritime air control authority. An organization that is responsible for the control of air operations that are performed by air and sea units.

maritime air radio organization. A worldwide air *radio communication system* in which *high-frequency (HF) Morse code* is used for controlling and reporting maritime patrol aircraft operations.

maritime air telecommunication organization. An organization for satisfying the *communication* requirements for the control and reporting of maritime patrol aircraft operations and for the transmitting of air *safety messages.*

maritime broadcast communication net. A *communication net* that is used for area meteorological *broadcasts, facsimile transmission,* merchant ship communications, or other broadcasting purposes on behalf of maritime units.

maritime distress communication net. A *communication net* that is used for *international distress calling,* including *international lifeboat, lifecraft,* and *survival-craft high frequency (HF); aeronautical emergency very high frequency (VHF); survival ultrahigh frequency (UHF); international calling and safety very high frequency (VHF);* combined scene-of-search-and-rescue; and other similar and related purposes. Basic *international distress calling* is performed at either *medium frequency (MF)* or at *high frequency (HF).*

maritime mobile service. A *communication service* for messages between *ship stations* and *coast stations* and between ship stations.

maritime patrol air broadcast net. A *broadcast net* that is used to control maritime aircraft patrol units and to *transmit information* to *aircraft stations.*

maritime patrol air reporting net. The two-way *communication link* that is established between aircraft patrol units and their controlling maritime headquarters. The net may also be used for communication between *aircraft stations* and *ship stations.*

maritime radionavigation service. A *radionavigation service* that is intended for the use of *ship stations,* particularly to enable a ship station to determine its position or its *bearing* (direction, course) in relation to reference points or directions.

maritime ship-shore communication net. A *communication net* that is primarily used for long-distance *ship-shore communication,* such as for command and control communication between *ship stations* and *shore stations.*

maritime tactical air operations communication net. A *communication net* that is used for coordination of maritime air movements, helicopter control, maritime air patrol reporting, joint air support, air homing, or other maritime air related purposes.

mark. 1. In *communication systems,* one of the two *significant conditions* of *modulation,* that is, of a *signal* level or condition. Synonymous with *marking pulse; marking signal.* 2. A *symbol* that indicates the beginning or the end of a *field, word, data item,* or set of *data,* such as a file, record, or *block.* 3. In *Morse code,* the designation that is given to one of the two *significant signal conditions,* the other condition being designated as a *space.* Also see *modulation significant condition.* See *beginning-of-tape mark; document mark; end-of-tape mark.*

mark-active. In *telegraph systems,* pertaining to a *signal* in which a *mark* is represented by a *pulse* of an on-*condition,* such as a *direct current (DC)* flowing condition or a fixed-*frequency* tone that is sounding, and a *space* is represented by the off-condition, that is, there is no *current* flowing, the tone is not sounding, or a *circuit* is open and nothing is happening in it.

mark coding. See *biphase mark coding.*

marked-access line. In *telephone systems,* a *line* that has been marked for special *access.* A method of marking is used to provide a *preemption* capability to the *private branch exchange (PBX)* or other *switchboard operator*. Certain lines are marked with *priority, immediate,* or *flash precedence* so that the operator can use the line marked for the corresponding level of precedence of the call that is being placed. In some systems, the only special marking that might be used is priority.

marker. In *display systems,* a *symbol* that can be *displayed* in the *display space* on a *display surface* of a *display device* and that has a recognizable shape and usually an obvious center or index point; e.g., a circle, square, caret, bracket, or underscore.   See *drop-zone boundary limit marker; forbidden landing-point marker; no-landing marker; range marker.*

marker beacon. A *transmitter* in the *aeronautical radionavigation service* that *radiates* a distinctive vertical pattern for providing *position information* to aircraft. See *fan-marker beacon; Z-marker beacon.*

marker beacon station. See *aeronautical marker beacon station.*

mark hold. In a *telegraph system,* a no-*traffic* condition in which a steady *mark* is *transmitted.* Also see *space hold.*

marking. See *multiple peg marking; position marking.*

marking bias. In a *telegraph system,* the uniform lengthening of the duration of *mark pulses* at the expense of the duration of the *space pulses.*

marking panel. A sheet of material that is *displayed* on the ground for *visual signaling* to an *aircraft staion.*

marking pulse. See *mark; teletype marking pulse.*

marking signal. See *mark.*

mark inversion signal. See *alternate mark inversion (AMI) signal.*

mark inversion violation. See *alternate mark inversion (AMI) violation.*

mark scanning. The automatic *optical sensing* of *marks* that are usually recorded manually on a *data medium.*

mark sensing. The automatic sensing of *conductive marks* that are usually recorded manually on a nonconductive *data medium.*

mark signal. 1. In *telegraph* and *teleprinter operations,* the *signal* that corresponds to the inactive condition in a teleprinter. Normally the *mark* is the *signaling condition* that produces a *stop signal* when using the *International Telegraph Alphabet Number 2 (ITA-2).* 2. The signal that corresponds to an on-key or *transmit* condition.

mark-space signaling. See *digital mark-space signaling; double-current signaling.*

m-ary code. See *n-ary code.*

m-ary digit. See *n-ary digit.*

m-ary digital signal. See *n-ary digital signal.*

m-ary information element. See *n-ary information element.*

m-ary signaling. See *n-ary signaling.*

maser. Abbreviation for *microwave amplification by stimulated emission of radiation.* See *optical maser.*

mask. **1.** In *communication systems,* to cover up, obliterate, or otherwise prevent *information* from being derived from a *signal.* The masking is usually performed by means of another signal, such as by *noise, jamming, static,* or other forms of *interference.* Thus, to mask is not the same as to *erase* or to delete. **2.** In *computing* and *data processing systems,* a pattern of *characters* that is used to retain or eliminate portions of another pattern of characters.

masking. **1.** The use of *transmitters* to hide or obliterate a particular *transmission,* particularly to obscure the *source,* purpose, or *information* value of a transmission. **2.** The blocking or preventing of a *signal* from reaching a *receiver* by means of *deflection, reflection, absorption, dispersion, refraction,* or *attenuation* that is caused by an intervening object. **3.** The obliteration of *transmission* in certain directions by means of a directed jamming *signal.* **4.** In *computing* and *data processing,* the use of a pattern of *characters,* such as a *string* of *characters,* to retain or eliminate portions of another pattern of characters. See *fault masking; radar masking.*

master clock. A *clock* that generates accurate *timing signals* for the control of other clocks and perhaps also other equipment. Also see *reference clock.* See *Department of Defense (DOD) master clock.*

master frequency generator. In *frequency-division multiplexing (FDM),* a generator that provides *system* end-to-end *carrier frequency signals* for *synchronization* and that provides frequency-accurate tones for transmission over the system. There are many different types of *oscillators* in use in *communication systems.* For example, a master oscillator as an *integral* part of a *multiplexer set,* a submaster oscillator or slave oscillator as an integral part of a multiplexer set, an external master oscillator that has extremely accurate and stable frequency and *amplitude* characteristics, or an oscillator with a continuously-variable frequency capability for *frequency modulated* systems. Synonymous with *master frequency oscillator.*

master frequency oscillator. See *master frequency generator.*

mastergroup. In *frequency-division multiplexing,* a grouping of *supergroups.* In most *communication systems* in the US and Canada, a *mastergroup* is composed of 10 supergroups or 600 *voice channels.* Some mastergroups that are used in terrestrial *telephone systems* carry 300 or 900 channels that are formed by *multiplexing* 5 or 15 supergroups, respectively. See *channel mastergroup.*

Master International Frequency Register (MIFR). A master list of all *frequency* registrations of *transmitting stations* throughout the world.

master log. See *aeronautical station master log.*

master net control station (MNCS). A *control station* that directs *operational* aspects of an operational network, including direction of the net control station and control of *network* equipment, usually for a unique or special communication system that involves *common user* or *dedicated facilities.*

master oscillator. An *oscillator* that is used for *frequency* control in a *communication system.* For example, an oscillator that is arranged to establish the *carrier frequency* for the *output signal* of a *transmitter,* or an oscillator that provides or controls *modulator* frequencies for a number of channels or groups of channels in a *frequency modulated* communication system or in a *frequency-division multiplexed system.*

master-slave timing system. A *system* in which one *station* or *node* of a *network* supplies the *timing signal* for all other interconnected stations or nodes in the network.

master station. In a *data network,* the *station* that has been requested by the *control station* to ensure that *data transfer* to one or more *slave stations* occurs in a proper manner. There can be only one master station that has control of one or more *data links* of the data network at a given instant. The assignment of master status to a given station is temporary and is controlled by the control station according to the procedures set forth in the operational *protocol.* Master status is normally conferred upon a station so that it may *transmit* a *message,* but a station need not have a message to send in order to be selected as the master station. This arrangement is used particularly in *basic mode link control procedures.*

match gate. See *EXCLUSIVE-NOR gate.*

matching. See *antenna matching; impedance matching.*

matching cell. See *index-matching cell.*

matching materials. See *index-matching materials.*

matching voice coder. See *pattern-matching voice coder.*

material. See *communication security material; isotropic material; keying material.*

material absorption. See *bulk material absorption.*

material dispersion. 1. The variation in the *refractive index* of a *transmission medium* as a function of *wavelength,* in *optical* transmission media used in *optical waveguides;* e.g., *optical fibers, slab dielectric waveguides,* and *integrated optical circuits.* Material dispersion contributes to *group-delay distortion,* along with *waveguide-delay distortion* and *multimode group-delay spread.* **2.** The part of the total *dispersion* of an *electromagnetic pulse* in a *waveguide* caused by the changes in properties of the material with which the waveguide, such as an *optical fiber* is made, due to changes in *frequency.* As *wavelength* increases, and frequency decreases, material dispersion decreases. At high frequencies, the rapid interactions of the *electromagnetic field* with the waveguide material *(optical fiber)* renders the *refractive index* even more dependent upon frequency.

material dispersion wavelength.   See *zero material dispersion wavelength.*

material scattering.   See *bulk material scattering.*

materials.   See *index-matching materials.*

matrix.   See *dot matrix; route matrix; switching matrix.*

maximal code sequence.   In *spread-spectrum systems,* a *binary digit code* sequence that is the longest that can be generated by a given *spread-spectrum code-sequence generator* before the sequence is repeated.   The longest code sequence for a single linear binary code sequence *feedback shift-register* generator is *2n-1,* where *n* is the number of stages (flip-flops) in the register of the generator.   Also see *spread-spectrum code-sequence generator.*

maximal ratio combiner.   A *diversity combiner* in which the *signals* from each *channel* are added together.   The gain of each channel is made proportional to the root-mean-square *(rms) signal* and inversely proportional to the rms *noise* in that channel.   The same proportionality constant is used for all channels.   Synonymous with *ratio-squared combiner.*   Also see *diversity combiner; selective combiner.*

maximal-ratio-square diversity combining method.   A method for combining the *signal power outputs* of two or more *receivers* that are operating in a *diversity mode* in which the combined output power squared equals the sum of the squares of the *input* signal powers.   Thus, the root-mean-square (rms) output power is the rms value of the input powers.

maximum acceptance angle (MAA).   The maximum angle between the longitudinal *axis* of an *optical* transmission system or *transmission medium* and the normal to an entering *wave-front* in order that there be *total internal reflection* of the portion of the *incident light* that is transmitted through the system or medium *interface.*   For example, in an *optical fiber,* the angle between the *transmitted ray* and the normal to the inside surface of the *cladding* is greater than the *critical angle.*   The sine of the maximum acceptance angle is given by the square root of the difference of the squares of the *refractive indices* of the *fiber core* glass and the cladding.   The square root of the difference of the squares is called the *numerical aperture* (N.A.).   In mathematical notation:

$$\text{N.A.} = (n_2{}^2 - n_1{}^2)^{1/2}$$

$$\text{MAA} = \sin^{-1} \text{N.A.}$$

maximum access time. In a *communication system,* the maximum allowable waiting time between initiation of an *access attempt* and *access success.*

maximum block transfer time. The maximum allowable waiting time between initiation of a *block transfer attempt* and *successful block delivery.*

maximum call area. See *maximum calling area.*

maximum calling area. The geographical area or the calling limits of a particular *communication network.* It is the area in which a given *user* (customer, subscriber) can place a *call* without special authorization or arrangements. Usually calling limits are not assigned. They are based on the requirements for the particular *line.* Such limits are imposed for *network* control purposes and for operating efficiency.

maximum contrast. The ratio of the *luminance* of the brightest portion of an *object* or *image* to the darkest portion, i.e., the range of minimum to maximum luminance.

maximum detection range. In *radio reception,* the range that corresponds to the minimum *field strength* that a *signal* can have and still be separated from *noise* and restored to the form in which it was transmitted by a specified *transmitter* that is transmitting under specified conditions, such as *power, direction,* and *modulation.* The maximum range of a radio signal depends upon such factors as the *transmitting power, propagation* conditions, and characteristics of the *receiver.* Maximum range can only be considered in terms of a transmitter and receiver pair, not in terms of either transmitter or receiver alone.

maximum disengagement time. The maximum allowable waiting time between initiation of a *disengagement attempt* and successful disengagement *(disengagement success).*

maximum justification rate. See *maximum stuffing rate.*

maximum keying frequency. In *facsimile transmission systems,* the *frequency* in *hertz* that is numerically equal to the *spot speed* divided by twice the *scanning spot x-dimension.* Synonymous with *fundamental scanning frequency.* Also see *recorded-spot x-dimension.*

maximum modulating frequency. The highest *picture frequency* that is required for a given *facsimile transmission system.* The maximum *modulating frequency* and the maximum *keying frequency* are not necessarily equal.

maximum pulse rate. In *optical waveguides* and metallic conductors in which *pulse dispersion* is the limiting factor on pulse repetition rate, the pulse rate that is just sufficient to create a specified *bit error rate,* the maximum pulse rate being expressed mathematically as:

$$P_m = AL^{-\Upsilon}$$

where A is determined by *line* characteristics that fix the value of Υ and L is the length.   Normally $\Upsilon = 1/2$ for *single mode* glass *fibers*.   For *multimode fiber guides*, $1/2 < \Upsilon < 1$. For wires, $\Upsilon = 2$.

maximum user signaling rate. The maximum rate, in *bits* per second, at which *binary data* can be *transferred* in a given direction between *users* (customers, subscribers) over *telecommunication system facilities* that are *dedicated* to a particular *information transfer transaction,* under conditions of continuous *transmission* and no *overhead information.*   The single *channel signaling rate* is expressed mathematically as $SCSR = (1/\tau)log_2\,\eta$, where $SCSR$ is the single channel signaling rate in bits per second, η is the number of *significant conditions* of *modulation* of the channel and τ is the minimum time interval in seconds for which each level of *voltage, current, frequency, phase,* or other *parameter* must be maintained.   In the case in which an individual end-to-end telecommunication service is provided by *parallel* channels, the parallel channel signaling rate is given by:

$$PCSR = \overset{w}{\underset{i=1}{\Sigma}}(1/\tau_i)log_2\,\eta_i$$

where $PCSR$ is the total signaling rate for all w channels, w is the number of parallel channels that are being included in determining the rate, τ_i is the minimum interval for the i-th channel, and η_i is the number of significant conditions of modulation for the i-th channel. In the case in which an end-to-end communication service is provided by *tandem* channels, the end-to-end signaling rate is limited by the channel with the lowest signaling rate. In this latter case, the end-to-end signaling rate is the signaling rate of the slowest channel.

maximum stuffing rate. The maximum rate at which *bits* can be inserted into or deleted from a *data stream.* Synonymous with *maximum justification rate.*

maximum usable frequency (MUF). The upper limit of a *band* of *frequencies* that can be used for *communication* because of a limiting factor. Such limiting factors include system frequency response limit, ionospheric limitation, excess loss or leakage, and *critical radius* limit. In *radio transmission,* the MUF is the upper limit of the frequencies that can be used with good results at specified times between two points and involving *propagation* by *reflection* from the regular *ionized layers* of the *ionosphere.*   The MUF is a median frequency that is applicable to 50% of the days of a month, as opposed to 90% for the *lowest usable frequency (LUF)* and the *optimum traffic frequency (OTF,* also abbreviated as *FOT).* Also see *lowest usable frequency (LUF).*

Maxwell's equations. A group of basic equations, in either integral or differential form, that (1) describe the relationships between the properties of *electric* and *magnetic fields,* their sources, and the behavior of these fields at material *media interfaces;* (2) express the relations among electric and magnetic fields that vary in space and time in material media and free space; and (3) are fundamental to the *propagation* of *electromagnetic waves* in material media and free space. The equations are the basis for deriving the *wave equation* that expresses the *electric* and *magnetic field vectors* in a propagating electromagnetic wave in a *transmission medium* such as the *lightwave* in an *optical fiber*. Maxwell's equations in differential form are:

$$\nabla \times \mathbf{E} = -\partial \mathbf{B}/\partial t$$

$$\nabla \times \mathbf{H} = \mathbf{J} + \partial \mathbf{D}/\partial t$$

$$\nabla \cdot \mathbf{B} = 0$$

$$\nabla \cdot \mathbf{D} = \rho$$

where **E, H, B,** and **D** are the electric field intensity, the magnetic field intensity, the magnetic flux density, and the electric flux density (electric displacement) vectors, respectively, **J** is the electric current density, and ρ is the electric charge density, the Δ is the "del" space derivative operator, expressing differentiation with respect to all distance coordinates, the $\Delta \times$ being the curl and the $\Delta \cdot$ being the divergence. The partial derivatives are with respect to time. These equations are used in conjunction with the *constitutive relations* to obtain useful practical results given actual sources of charge and current in real media. These are only valid when the field and current vectors are single-valued, bounded, continuous functions of position and time, and have continuous derivatives.

MAYDAY. The *distress signal* that is used in *voice communications*. The distress signal is the first part of a *distress call*. After the distress signal is repeated three times, it is followed by the *call sign* of the *mobile station* in distress. The call sign is also repeated three times. The *distress message* then follows the call signs.

M-band. The band of *frequencies* in the range from 60 GHz to 100 GHz, comprising ten numbered *channels* that are each 4 GHz wide. The old M-band comprised frequencies in the range from 10 GHz to 15 GHz, overlapping parts of the old X-band and the old P-band.

Mbps. *Megabits/second*, i.e., 10^6 bits/second.

MCA. *Maximum calling area.*

MCVD. See *modified chemical-vapor deposition process.*

mean circuit activity. The ratio of the total time to the time that a *circuit* is occupied by necessary *signals*. Necessary signals include *speech, data,* and *control signals*. A typical value of the mean circuit activity is 25%. With the greater incentive to use high-cost international circuits more intensively, 37% is the typical value for transatlantic *links*. Mean circuit activity is an important factor in the use of *time-assignment speech interpolation (TASI)* and in the use of *digital speech interpolation systems* for *long-distance communication trunks*.

mean entropy. See *character mean entropy.*

mean information content. See *character mean entropy.*

mean power. In *radio, video, radar,* and *microwave transmission systems,* the *power* that is supplied to the *antenna transmission line* by a *transmitter* during normal *operation,* averaged over a time that is sufficiently long compared with the period of the lowest *frequency* (longest *wavelength*) that is encountered in the *modulation.* A time of 0.1 second during which the mean power is the greatest is normally selected.

mean-power-of-the-talker volume distribution. The *mean-power-talker* volume less a conversion constant to convert from *volume units (vu)* to *decibels* referenced to 1 milliwatt (dBm). The constant is taken as 3.9 dB by some authorities and 1.4 dB by others. In the US Department of Defense, 2.9 dB is used. Also see *mean-power talker.*

mean-power talker. A talker that represents the average of the *powers* of a group of talkers measured at a given location or in a given environment. It is the value of an ordered set of values below which and above which there are an equal number of values. Synonymous with *mean volume talker.* Also see *mean-power-of-the-talker volume distribution.*

mean repair time. See *mean-time-to-repair.*

mean solar day. See *civil day.*

mean spherical intensity. The average value of *intensity* of an *electromagnetic* source of *radiation,* such as a *light* source, with respect to all directions.

mean time. See *Greenwich mean time (GMT).*

mean-time-between-failures (MTBF). For a stated period in the *component life* of a *functional unit,* the mean value of the lengths of time between consecutive *failures* under stated conditions and criteria for failure determination. Thus, for a particular interval during the total functioning life of a population of items, the total number of failures that occur within the population during a particular measurement interval divided by the duration of the measurement interval. The functioning life may be measured in any reasonable unit, such as time (minutes, hours, days), cycles, miles, or events.

mean-time-between-outages (MTBO). The mean time between equipment *failures* that result in loss of capability that satisfies the criteria for defining an *outage,* such as loss of *system* continuity or unacceptable degradation, as expressed by the equation $MTBO = MTBF/(1 - FFAS)$ where $MTBO$ is the mean-time-between-outages, $MTBF$ is the nonredundant mean-time-between-failures, and $FFAS$ is the *failure-fraction-automatically switched.* Also see *failure-fraction-automatically-switched (FFAS).*

mean-time-to-repair (MTTR). The total *corrective maintenance* time divided by the total number of corrective maintenance actions during a given period. It is thus the average time required for a corrective maintenance action. It is applied to a specific system or population of components, such as a *communication system,* a *computer,* or a *data station.* Synonymous with *mean repair time.*

mean-time-to-service-restoral (MTTSR). The total time that is required to restore service following all system *failures* divided by the number of *outages* that result from the failures. The time to restore service includes all the time from the instant of failure (beginning of outage) until restoral of service (end of outage). The time to restore is usually longer than the repair time, since it includes *fault* detection, fault location, and fault correction (repair).

mean transinformation content. The average of the *transinformation content* that is conveyed by the occurrence of any one of a finite number of mutually exclusive and jointly exhaustive events, given the occurrence of another set of mutually exclusive events. It is equal to the difference between the *entropy* of one of the two sets of events and the *conditional information entropy* of this set relative to the other. For example, in the *transmission* of one *message,* the difference between the entropy at the *message source* and the *equivocation* is equal to the difference between the entropy at the *message sink* and the *irrelevance.* Mathematically, the mean transinformation content is given by $MTC = H_x - H_{x/y} = H_y - H_{y/x}$ where H_x is the entropy of the message at the source, $H_{x/y}$ is the equivocation, H_y is the entropy at the sink, and $H_{y/x}$ is the irrelevance. Synonymous with *average transinformation content.* See *character mean transinformation content.*

mean volume talker. See *mean-power talker.*

measure. See *addressability measure; information measure; lens measure; repeatability measure.*

measurement period. See *performance measurement period.*

measurement unit. See *noise measurement unit.*

measuring equipment. See *distance measuring equipment; telegraph error-rate measuring equipment.*

mechanical jamming. *Jamming* that is accomplished by using devices, such as *chaff,* that r*eradiate* or *reflect signals* to produce *clutter* or other extraneous *signals* that tend to *saturate* or degrade *radar systems* and confuse and deceive radar *operators.*

mechanically-despun antenna. An *antenna* that is mounted on an articulating platform and that is driven to maintain a constant *antenna* pointing direction. For example, an antenna that is mounted on gimbals on a spinning *satellite* and that constantly points toward the earth; or a gun barrel that is mounted in a tank running over rough terrain and always points toward a fixed object, such as a terrain feature or a target.

mechanical optical switch. A manually or electromechanically operated *optical switch* capable of allowing or preventing *lightwave propagation* in a given *circuit* or allowing selection of alternate *paths*. *Switching* times are currently of the order of tens of milliseconds and are practical for light path coupling and decoupling in the same manner as electrical microswitches.

mechanics.   See *celestial mechanics*.

MED.   *Manipulative electronic deception*.

medical diathermy equipment.   Equipment that generates and *transmits radio frequency electromagnetic waves* for medical therapeutic or diagnostic purposes. Such equipment can create *interference* in *communication equipment*, particularly at receiving ends where the *signal-to-noise ratios* are low.

medical RF equipment.   See *industrial-scientific-medical RF equipment*.

medium.   In *optics*, any substance or space through which *light* can *propagate* or stand.   See *data medium; empty medium; homogeneous medium; lossy medium; record medium; sensitized medium; transmission medium; virgin medium*.

medium coupling loss.   See *aperture-to-medium coupling loss*.

medium frequency (MF).   A *frequency* that lies in the range from 300 kHz to 3000 kHz.   The *alphabetic* designator of the range is MF.   The numeric designator of the range is 6.   Also see *frequency spectrum designation*.

medium-loss fiber.   An *optical fiber* having a medium-level energy loss, due to all causes, per unit length of fiber, usually measured in *decibels*/kilometer at a specified wavelength.   Medium-loss is usually considered to be between 20 and 100 dB/km. In medium-loss fiber, *attenuation* in amplitude of a propagating wave is caused primarily by scattering due to metal ions and by *absorption* due to water in the OH⁻ radical form.   Attenuation is also caused by *Rayleigh scattering*.

medium-power talker.   The *talker,* of a log-normal distribution, whose *power* lies at the medium power of all talkers that determine the power distribution at the point of interest.   When the distribution follows a log-normal curve, with the values expressed in dB, the mean and standard deviation can be used to compute the medium-power talker.   The talker power distribution follows a log-normal curve and the medium-power talker is uniquely determined by the average talker power.   The standard deviation is computed using the equation $V = V_o + 0.115$ σ^2 where V is the power that corresponds to the average-power talker expressed in *volume units* (vu), V_o is the average of the talker power distribution, and σ is the standard deviation of the distribution.   Synonymous with *medium-volume talker*.   Also see *mean-power-of-the-talker volume distribution; mean-power talker*.

medium volume talker.   See *medium power talker*.

meet-me conference call.   A *conference call* in which the *operator* notifies each conferee of the number to call at a specified time, prior to which the operator sets up all the necessary *bridging circuits* so that when the conferees place their calls they will all be connected together, including the conference originator (requestor). Also see *progressive conference call.*

megabits/second (Mbps) signaling rate.   A *signaling rate* of 1 million bits/second.

meniscus.   A *lens* having a convex and a *concave* surface.   Synonymous with *concavo-convex lens.*   See *divergent meniscus lens.*

megahertz (MHz).   A unit of *frequency* that is equal to one million *hertz*, that is, 10^6 Hz.

memory.   See *storage; range rate memory.*

memory bounds checking.   See *storage bounds checking.*

menu.   In *display systems,* a set of *display elements, display groups,* or *display images,* usually *displayed* on the *display surface* of a *display device,* one of which can be chosen, by means of *picking,* to indicate one or more subsequent actions.

MERCAST.   *Merchant ship broadcast system.*

merchant ship broadcast system (MERCAST).   A maritime *shore-to-ship broadcast system* in which the ocean areas are divided into primary *broadcast areas* each covered by a high-powered *shore radio station* that broadcasts simultaneously on one *medium frequency (MF)* and one or more high frequencies (HF) for *routing messages* to ocean-going ships.   In some instances, *ship broadcast coastal radio stations* may repeat the *messages.*

merging.   The combining of two or more ordered sets of items into one ordered set while preserving the original ordering of the items that existed in the sets that were combined to form the new set.

meridian.   See *celestial meridian.*

meridian plane.   Any plane that contains the *optical axis* of an *optical system;* e.g., a plane that contains the optical axis of a round *optical fiber.*

meridional ray.   In an *optical fiber,* a *light ray* that passes through the axis of the fiber while being *internally reflected* and that is confined to a single plane, called the *meridian plane.*   Also see *skew ray.*

merit figure.   See *optical fiber merit figure.*

Mersenne code sequence generator.   A *maximal code sequence generator* in which the length of the code sequence is a prime number of code elements, such as *bits.*   Such a sequence is significant when *cross-correlation* is a major factor of consideration.   The generator is used in *spread-spectrum transmission* and *reception systems.*

mesh network.   A *network configuration* in which there is more than one *path* between any two *nodes* and thus there are no *endpoint nodes.*   See Figure M-2.

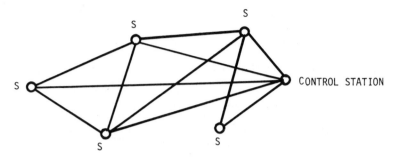

M-2. A **mesh network** with *control station.*

mesochronous. The relationship between two *signals* such that their corresponding *significant instants* occur at the same average rate. Also see *anisochronous; heterochronous; homochronous; isochronous; plesiochronous.*

message. 1. In *communication systems,* any thought or idea that is expressed in *plain* or *encrypted text* and that is prepared in a form that is suitable for *transmission* by any means. A complete message normally has three parts. There must be an indication of an *addressee,* there must be the *information* to be *communicated,* and there must be an indication of the sender. Therefore, a message must have a *heading,* a *body,* and an *ending.* These three entities may be accomplished many ways, for example, the ending might be only an *end-of-message mark.* A *transmission* starts with a *start-of-transmission control function,* whereas a message begins after a *start-of-message indicator,* such as ZCZC in *tape relay systems.* 2. *Information* and control *bit* sequences that are *transferred* as an entity. 3. In *alphabetic telegraphy* and in *data transmission,* a group of *characters* and control *signal* sequences that are *transferred* as an entity from a *transmitter* to a *receiver.* The arrangement of the characters is determined at the transmitter. 4. In *information theory* and in *communication theory,* an ordered arrangement of *characters* that are intended to convey *information.* Synonymous with *signal, transmission, communication, cable, wire, telegram,* and *line.* (The use of these words as synonyms for message is not recommended, however. They have other more specific meanings.) See *address message; amplifying message; amplifying switch message; book message; calling line identity message; clear message; codress message; direction-finding message; distress message; drop message; dual-precedence message; emergency message; exclusive message; fallout message; formal message; fox message; general message; hydrographic message; multiaddress message; multiple-part message; multiunit message; plaindress message; preburst message; proforma message; refile message; response message; safety message; service message; signal message; single-call message; single-precedence message; straggler message; switch message.*

message address. The *address component* of a *message.* It usually consists of one or more *identifiers* for the *originator, action addressees, information addressees,* and *exempted addressees.* See *codress message address.*

message alignment. The process of placing *messages* or their parts in or on a *medium.*   Specified time and space relationships are usually maintained among the various *data* media that are used as well as among the messages and their various parts.

message alignment indicator. *Data* that is contained in a *signal message,* that is, *transferred* between the *user part* and the *message transfer part* of a *communication system,* and is used to identify the boundaries of the signal message. Also see *signal message.*

message authentication. A *communication security* measure that is designed to establish the authenticity of a *message* by means of an *authenticator* within the message and that is derived from certain predetermined elements of the message itself. The measures and procedures are adopted to protect a communication system against the acceptance by a receiving *station* of a fraudulent message. Authentication procedures are normally placed in effect by appropriate authorities.

message available-at-action-office time. The time that a *message* is received by the *action office* or by the office of the *action addressee.*

message available-for-delivery time. The time that a received *message* is ready for distribution from the receiving *communication center* to the *action addressee.*

message backlog. In a *communication facility,* all of the *messages* or *data* that are awaiting *transmission* or *processing.*   Synonymous with *message queue; queue.*

message center. The part of a *communication center* that is responsible for the acceptance and *transmission* of outgoing *messages* and for the receipt and delivery of incoming messages.

message character. See *end-of-message (EOM) character.*

message code. See *prearranged message code.*

message dispatch time. The date, which includes the time, when a *message* is dispatched to an *addressee* or to a *communication agency.*

message distribution center. See *internal message distribution center; switching and message distribution center.*

message drafter. The person or machine that composes a *message* for approval and release by the *originator* or by the *releasing officer.*

message element. Any part of a *message.*   For example, *accounting symbols, address designators, routing indicator groups, address groups, address indicating groups, call signs, originator designator,* the *text* written by the *originator,* or an *ending.*

message file time. The time that a *message* is brought into a *message center* for *processing,* or in the case of automated remote entry devices, the time that the

‎‎

message is released to the *communication system* for *transmission*. Synonymous with *time-of-file (TOF)*.

message format. A predetermined or prescribed spatial or time-sequential arrangement of the parts of a *message* when it is represented or recorded in or on a *data medium*. *Electrical* messages are usually composed on a printed blank form with spaces for each part of the message and for administrative entries. Also see *format line*. See *ionospheric message format; radiotelegraph message format*.

message heading. The *message part* or parts that precede the *text* (body) in time or space according to established conventions. *Message headings* may include *data items* such as *address groups, routing indicators, action addressee designators, information addressee designators, exempted addressee designators, prosigns, prowords, clear indicators, date-time groups, originator designators, special instructions,* and *protocol symbols*. Some of these may comprise a *preamble*. Also see *external heading; message text*.

message indicator. See *start-of-message indicator*.

message originator. The commander, authority, agency head, person, or organization by whose authority a *message* is drafted, approved, and released for *transmission*. The originator is responsible for the functions of the *message drafter* and the *releasing officer*.

message part. 1. In *radiotelephone system messages,* one of the three major subdivisions of a *message,* namely the *heading,* the *text,* or the *ending*. Each part may have separate *components* and each component may have elements and contents. 2. In *cryptosystems,* one of the parts that result from the division of a long *message* into several shorter messages of different lengths as a *transmission security* measure. Message parts are usually prepared in such a manner as to appear unrelated externally. Statements that identify the parts for assembly at reception are *encrypted* in the *texts*.

message preparation time. 1. From a *communication system* point of view, the time that is required for a *message* to be processed for entry into a *communication system*. For manually *operated* systems, this includes the time during which *transmission media,* such as tape, are prepared and made ready for transmission. For automatic *terminals,* such as *remote entry terminals,* it is the time during which the message is read by the automatic message processing equipment. 2. From a *message originator* point of view, the time that is required to write and prepare a message on a *data medium,* such as on a message form or on a remote terminal, for acceptance by a *communication system message center* or by a communication system.

message processing time. The total time interval that is used to *transmit* a *message* from the *message drafter* (writer) to the *destination addressee* (reader). The time interval may be divided as (1) for the drafter, from the *message release time* to the *message file time* at a *communication facility;* (2) for the *communication system operators,* from the message file time at the originating communication facility to the *available-for-delivery time* at the receiving *addressee communica-tion facility,* including the processing at both the originating and terminating communication facilities in addition to the total *transmission time;* and (3) for the *addressee,* from the *available-for-delivery time* at the receiving addressee communication facility to the *time of receipt* by the *designated addressee.*

message queue.   See *message backlog.*

message readdressal.   The adding of a new *addressee* to a *message* by the *origi-nator,* by an initial addressee, or by another authority, without changing the ad-dressees or *text* of the previously *transmitted* message.   Synonymous with *dou-ble heading.*

message relay.   To send, that is, to retransmit, a *message* that has been received.

message release time.   The actual time at which an authorized *releasing officer* authorizes a *message* for *transmission.*

message releasing officer.   The person who authorizes the dispatch of a *message* for, or in the name of, an organization or command and in behalf of the *message originator.*

message sink.   See *destination user.*

message source.   The part of a *communication system* from which a *message* is considered to have originated.   See *source user; stationary message source.*

message switching.   The process of *routing messages* by receiving, storing, and forwarding complete *messages* within a *data network,* each message being an *in-formation* unit, from *user* to user.   It is a method of handling message *traffic* through a *switching center,* either from local *users* or from other switching cen-ters.   A connection is established between the *calling station* and the *called sta-tion,* or messages are forwarded or stored and forwarded through the center. The *message heading* determines the routing and destination.   In message switch-ing there is no *dial-through.*   Also see *circuit switching; packet switching; queue traffic; store-and-forward switching center; switching center; switching system.* See *automatic message switching.*

message text.   The *message part* that represents the thought or idea that the *originator* wants to send.   Also see *external heading; message heading.*

message time objective.   The overall handling time that *communication system* personnel attempt to achieve for a *message.*   It is normally measured as the time from the moment that a message is accepted for dispatch at a communication fa-cility to the moment of *available-for-delivery time* or to the moment of receipt by the *addressee.*   For example, a message time objective of 10 minutes or less might be established for a *flash precedence* message.

message transfer part.   The functional part of a *channel signaling system* that *transfers signal messages* and performs the necessary related functions, such as *error control* and signaling *link security* actions.   Also see *user part.*

message verification. The determination of the *validity* of all or certain portions of a *message* when the recipient believes that the *text* that was received is not what the *message originator* intended to send. Verification of the entire message is equivalent to repetition of the entire message. Normally, only the doubted portions need to be verified.

message weighting. See *C-message weighting.*

metal clad switchgear. An indoor or outdoor metal structure that contains *switching equipment* and other associated equipment, such as *circuit breakers,* instrument *transformers, buses,* and *connectors.* The transformers, buses, and connectors are *insulated* and placed in separate *grounded* metal containers. Circuit breakers are equipped with self-coupling disconnecting devices and are arranged with a position-changing mechanism for moving the breaker vertically or horizontally in sequence from the connected position to a test or disconnected position. Interlocks are provided to insure the proper and safe sequence of *operations* during the insertion or withdrawal of removable elements.

metallic circuit. An *electrical circuit* in which *conductors* that are made of metal are used for the entire *circuit* and in which *ground* or *earth* does not form a part of the circuit.

metallic circuit currents. *Electric currents* that flow in a metallic circuit. When the circuit consists of a pair of wires, the current flow is in opposite directions in the two wires of the pair.

meteorological aids service. A *radio communication service* that is used for meteorological and hydrological observation and exploration.

meteorological broadcast. See *routine meteorological broadcast; special meteorological broadcast.*

meteorological fixed station. See *hydrological and meteorological fixed station.*

meteorological land station. See *hydrological and meteorological land station.*

meteorological mobile station. See *hydrological and meteorological mobile station.*

meteorological organization. See *World Meteorological Organization (WMO).*

meteorological-satellite earth station. An *earth station* that is in the *meteorological satellite service.* The meteorological-satellite earth station is always a *receiving station.*

meteorological-satellite service. In *satellite communications,* a *telemetering space service* in which the results of meteorological observations are made by instruments that are on *earth satellites* and the results are *transmitted* to *earth stations* by *space stations* on these satellites.

meteorological-satellite space station. A *telemetering space station* that is in the *meteorological-satellite service* and that is located on an *earth satellite.*

meteorological warning. See *emergency meteorological warning.*

meter.   1. Originally established by Napoleonic scientists as one ten millionth, that is, 10^{-7}, of the distance between a pole and the earth's equator. Now it is established as a specific number of *wavelengths* of the *emission* from *radioactive* krypton. It has been recorded as the distance between two fine lines engraved on a platinum bar held at the International Bureau of Weights and Measures near Paris, France.   **2.** A device that is capable of measuring a *parameter's* value and indicating the result of the measurement. See *fiber-optic bloodflow meter; frequency meter; par meter; phase meter; photoconductive meter; photovoltaic meter.*

metering device. See *telephone traffic metering device.*

method. See *broadcast communication method; frequency code method; image method; intercept communication method; maximal-ratio-square diversity combining method; radio telegraph operating method; receipt communication method; relay communication method.*

metric radar. A *radar* set that operates in the 1 to 10 meter *wavelength band,* that is, in the *very-high frequency (VHF)* range, which is from 30 MHz to 300 MHz.

metric system. A *decimal system* of weights and measures that is based on the meter, the kilogram, and the second. The modern version of this system uses the International System of Units (Systeme International d'Unites), that is the *SI* units. For example, in the SI system of units, the meter is used for length, the kilogram for mass, the second for time, the ampere for electric current, the *kelvin* for *temperature,* and the *candela* for *luminous intensity.* Many derived terms have also been standardized in the SI system of units, such as the *hertz.* The following prefixes are used with metric units:

Prefix	Abbreviation	Value	Prefix	Abbreviation	Value
tera	T	10^{12}	centi	c	10^{-2}
giga	G	10^{9}	milli	m	10^{-3}
mega	M	10^{6}	micro	μ	10^{-6}
kilo	k	10^{3}	nano	n	10^{-9}
hecto	h	10^{2}	pico	p	10^{-12}
deka	da	10	femto	f	10^{-15}
deci	d	10^{-1}	atto	a	10^{-18}

For example, megahertz is abbreviated MHz and means 10^{6} hertz; picofarad is abbreviated pF and means 10^{-12} farad; nanosecond is abbreviated ns and means 10^{-9} second; centimeter is abbreviated cm and means 10^{-2} meter; kilometer is abbreviated km and means 10^{3} meters; millivolt is abbreviated mV and means 10^{-3} volts; and microampere is abbreviated μA and means 10^{-6} ampere.

metric wave. An *electromagnetic wave* with a *wavelength* that is between 1 m and 10 m, that is, a wave that has a *frequency* of 30 MHz to 300 MHz and therefore lies in the *very-high frequency (VHF)* range. Also see *frequency spectrum designation; radio frequency.*

MF. *Medium frequency.*

MFSK. *Multiple-frequency shift keying.*

MHD. *Magnetohydrodynamics.*

MHz. *Megahertz.*

MICR. *Magnetic ink character recognition.*

microbending loss. In an *optical fiber,* the *loss* or *attenuation* in *signal power* caused by small bends, kinks, or abrupt discontinuities in direction of the fibers, usually caused by fiber *cabling* or by wrapping fibers on drums. Microbending losses usually result from a *coupling* of *guided modes* among themselves and among the *radiation modes.*

microcrack. In *optical transmission media,* a minute crack that may be enlarged by moisture, bending, twisting, tensile stress, thermal gradients, vibration, and other environmental factors, such as corrosive *atmospheres.*

microcrack model. See *Griffith microcrack model.*

microcylindrical lens. An extremely small *lens,* usually made by an etching and crystal regrowth process that attaches it to a *light source* or *photodetector* on a monolithic basis; e.g., the cylindrically shaped *lens* on an *integral-lens LED.* Its purpose is to assist in controlling the *divergence* of a *beam* in one dimension. Synonymous with *cylindrical microlens.*

microfiche. A *microform,* consisting of film in the form of separate sheets, that contains *microimages* usually arranged in a grid pattern for location of *images* by means of Cartesian coordinates. Each microfiche usually has a title that can be read without *magnification.* Also see *ultrafiche.*

microfilm. A *microform* consisting of film as a *data medium,* usually in the form of a roll or strip, that contains *microimages.* The images are usually in a sequential arrangement that is either in a *cine-oriented mode* or in a *comic-strip-oriented mode,* rather than in rows or columns as on *microfiche.* See *computer-output microfilm.*

microform. Any *data medium* that contains *microimages,* for example *microfiche, microfilm,* and *microimage chips.* See *computer-output microform.*

microform reader. 1. A device that has a *blowback ratio* large enough to permit *microimages* to be viewed by the unaided human eye; e.g., an *optical-fiber fiberscope* enlarger. 2. A device that can *scan* and sense *data* directly from *microimages* and dispatch these data to another device.

microform reader-copier. A device that can perform the functions of a *micro-form reader* and in addition produce a *hard-copy enlargement* of selected *micro-images.* Synonymous with *microform reader-printer.*

microform reader-printer. See *microform reader-copier.*

micrographics. The branch of science and technology devoted to those methods and techniques that are used for converting *data* to or from a *microform* or that are used to process data that are on a microform.

microimage. An *image* that is too small to be interpreted by the human eye under ordinary *light* without *magnification.*

microimage chip. A microform consisting of a small piece of material on which is recorded an *image* that requires the use of a *high-powered optical system* to render the *image* legible to the human eye. For example, a copy of the entire Bible, Koran, and Torah on one side of a 1-in.^{2} surface of photofilm.

microlens. See *microcylindrical lens.*

micrometer (μm). See *micron.*

microminiaturization. In *electrical engineering,* the technology of constructing *electrical circuits* and devices in such a manner as to include a large number of circuit elements, such as *transistors, diodes, resistors, capacitors,* and *inductors* in extremely small packages. For example, the miniaturization that is accomplished in the technology of *large-scale integrated (LSI) circuits* and of *integrated optical circuits (IOC).*

micron (μ). A unit of length in the metric system equal to one-millionth of a meter. Synonymous with *micrometer.*

microphone. A device that converts variations in *sound* pressure *(sound waves)* into correlated *electrical currents* or *voltages,* that is, a sound wave to electrical wave *transducer.*

microphonics. The generation of *noise* in an *electrical circuit* element or *component* due to its own mechanical vibration. For example, a *conductor* vibrating in a *magnetic field* in such a manner that the *magnetic flux* linkages change has a *voltage* induced in it; or a *capacitor* that changes its *capacity* as a result of vibration alters the current in the *circuit* in which it is connected with an applied voltage. A *microphone* makes use of microphonics in order to function.

microprocessor. 1. An arithmetic, logic, or control unit that is constructed on a single *large-scale integrated (LSI) chip.* 2. A *processor* that executes microinstructions, that is, executes simple instructions, such as add, compare, and shift. 3. A processor that is constructed of microelectronic circuits.

microscope. See *electron microscope; magnifier; scanning electron microscope.*

microsecond. One-millionth of a *second,* i.e., 10^{-6} seconds.

microwave. **1.** An *electromagnetic wave* that has a *wavelength* of about 0.3 cm to 3 m, thus covering wavelengths from very high *frequency* (VHF) to extremely high frequency (EHF). **2.** The portion of the *electromagnetic spectrum* between 0.003 to 3 m. **3.** Pertaining to equipment and *communication* in the 0.003- to 3-m band of the *electromagnetic spectrum.* Microwave equipment is used in *long-haul telephone networks.* These wavelengths are much longer than those of visible *electromagnetic radiation (light)* used in *fiber optics.* However, the term is loosely applied to those electromagnetic wavelengths that are sufficiently short so as to exhibit some of the properties of light. For example, they are easily concentrated into a *beam.* Microwave commonly applies to frequencies from about 0.1 GHz to 100 GHz.

microwave amplification by stimulated emission of radiation (MASER). A low-noise radio-frequency amplifier whose *emission energy* is stored in a molecular or atomic system by a *microwave* power supply stimulated by the input *signal.*

microwave circulator. A lossless *junction* that is used to *couple* an *antenna* to a *transmitter* in one direction and to a *receiver* in the other direction. For example, a *diplexer.*

middle infrared. Pertaining to *electromagnetic wavelengths* from 3 to 30 *microns.*

MIFR. *Master International Frequency Register.*

mile. See *geographical mile; nautical mile (nmi); radar mile; statute mile.*

military call sign. A *call sign* that is used by and for units that are under military control. Also see *international call sign.*

military common emergency frequency. A *frequency* that is used by all military units that are equipped to operate at that frequency or in the *band* in which that frequency lies. The military common emergency frequency band is also used internationally by *survivalcraft stations* and survivalcraft equipment.

military communications. The means that are used by military commanders to exercise command and control over forces and areas that are widely distributed. Military communication systems are used to facilitate and expedite the transfer of instructions, orders, and information among persons and machines in military units. Military communications support administration, intelligence, operations, logistics, and related activities that are essential to the exercise of command and to mission accomplishment.

military communication system. See *strategic military communication system.*

military fixed communication network. In *military communications,* a *network* of *fixed stations.* Each station, normally a *land station,* can *communicate* with a number of stations in other areas by means of *point-to-point nets.* Each net normally consists of two stations that *relay messages* when stations are not in direct contact. The net stations handle *traffic* into and out of local areas. They relay messages over the military fixed communication worldwide network that they form. Also see *civil fixed communication network*.

military ship international call sign.   An international call sign that is used by and for ships that are under military control.

millimeter (mm).   One-thousandth of a meter, i.e., 10^{-3} meters.

millimetric wave.   An *electromagnetic wave* that has a *wavelength* between 1 mm and 10 mm (1 cm), that is, a *frequency* between 30 GHz and 300 GHz, which is the *extremely-high frequency (EHF) range*.   Also see *frequency spectrum designation; radio frequency*.

millimicron.   See *nanometer*.

millimicrosecond.   See *nanosecond*.

millisecond.   One-thousandth of a *second*, i.e., 10^{-3} seconds.

minimum discernible signal.   In *radar systems*, the lower limit of power level that can be useful to a *radar receiver*.   The minimum discernible signal is determined by the *signal-to-noise ratio* at the output of the *receiving antenna* and by the *signal* characteristics and capability of the antenna and *receiver system*.   Also see *radar sensitivity*.

minimum distance code.   A *binary code* in which the *signal distance* does not fall below a specified value and which therefore can be interpreted under *noise* conditions.   For example, a code with a minimum *signal distance* of 3 is constructed so that at least three *bits* must be changed to convert one valid code *word* to another.   Thus, a great many words (binary combinations or binary patterns) are unusable and therefore invalid for *transmission*.   They are thus recognized as erroneous words when they are received.

minimum interval.   In *data transmission*, the duration of the shortest *significant interval* when the durations of the significant intervals are not all multiples of a *unit interval*.

minimum mean square error restoration.   An *image-restoration* technique in which an estimate, f_e, is made of the actual original *light-intensity* distribution, f_o, of an *image*.   The error in the estimate is defined as:

$$e = f_o - f_e$$

The total error of estimation is made a minimum over the entire ensemble of all possible images.   Synonymous with *Wiener filtering; MMSE filtering*.

minor relay station.   In a *tape relay communication system*, a *relay station* that cannot provide an alternate *route* in either direction.

minus lens.   See *diverging lens*.

mirror. 1. A flat surface *optically* ground and polished on a reflecting material, or a *transparent* material that is coated to make it reflecting, used for reflecting light. A *beam-splitting* mirror has a lightly deposited metallic coating that *transmits* a portion of the *incident light* and reflects the remainder. 2. A smooth, highly polished plane or curved surface for reflecting light. Usually a thin coating of silver or aluminum on glass constitutes the actual reflecting surface. When this surface is applied to the front face of the glass, the mirror is a front-surface mirror. See *back-surface mirror; front-surface mirror; Mangin mirror; off-axis paraboloidal mirror; paraboloidal mirror; triple mirror.*

mirroring. In *display systems,* the *reflecting* of all or part of a *display element, display group,* or *display image,* in such a manner that the element, group, or image appears to have been rotated 180° about a line in the plane of the *display surface.* Each point on the image is *translated* perpendicularly to a point on the opposite side of the line as far from the line as it was originally. The line may be considered as the "plane of the mirror" projected on the display surface. The element, group, or image will thus be reversed with respect to the direction perpendicular to the line.

misalignment loss. See *angular misalignment loss.*

misdelivered block. A *block* that is received by a *user* other than the one intended by the *message originator.*

misdelivery probability. See *block misdelivery probability.*

mismatch loss. See *refractive-index-profile mismatch loss.*

mismatch-of-core-radii loss. A loss of *signal power* introduced by an *optical fiber splice* in which the radii of the *cores* of the two fibers that are joined are not equal. The loss is usually expressed in *decibels.*

missile control. See *guided missile control.*

mission traffic. The *traffic* for which a *communication system* was designed, constructed, and installed.

mission bit stream. The total *user* (customer, subscriber) *information bits* that are being passed through a *communication system channel.* Though *framing, stuffing,* control, and *service bits* are not user information bits (mission bits), they are a part of the *bit stream.*

mistake. An action that is performed by a person and that produces an unintended result. For example, the use of a wrong *call sign* in the *heading* of a *message,* the misspelling of a *word,* or the use of the wrong *circuit* or *channel* to *transmit* a message. Also see *error, failure; fault.*

MIVPO. *Modified inside-vapor phase-oxidation process.*

mixed-gas laser. An *ion laser* that uses a mixture of gases as the *active medium.* A mixture of argon and krypton is often used in mixed-gas lasers.

mixed net. In *radiotelephone communication systems,* a *net* in which one or more *stations* are equipped with *ciphony* capabilities or *compatible cryptokey* capability and the others in the net are not so equipped. Mixed net *operations* are also applicable to ciphony nets in which one or more stations have had, but for some reason have lost, the capability to *communicate* in the *cipher mode.*

mixer. See *turn-around mixer.*

mix gate. See *OR gate.*

mixing. See *optical mixing.*

mixing box. See *optical mixing box.*

mixing rod. See *optical mixing rod.*

MLP. *Multilevel precedence.*

mm. *Millimeter.*

μm. *Micrometer; micron.*

MMSE filtering. See *minimum mean square error restoration.*

MNCS. *Master net control station.*

mnemonic. Pertaining to the memory or to the quality of being easily remembered. For example, pertaining to the use of *symbols* or combinations of symbols that are specifically chosen to aid the memory of a person when recall becomes necessary. For example, the use of the word *tiger* to help one remember that *t*rees, *g*rass, and *r*agweed pollinate in that order each season, or GI for *gov*ernment *i*ssued.

mnemonic code. A *code* that can be remembered comparatively easily and that aids its *user* in recalling the information it represents. For example, the mnemonic code *ROY G. BIV* aids in remembering the colors of the spectrum: *R*ed, *O*range, *Y*ellow, *G*reen, *B*lue, *I*ndigo, *V*iolet. A mnemonic code in one *natural language* is usually not a mnemonic code in another language. Mnemonic codes are widely used in computer programming and communication system operations to specify instructions. The systems can be designed to be responsive to arbitrary sets of symbols, but the mnemonic codes are used to help the programmers and operators remember the codes for the instructions. For example, upon receipt of the letter group MPY, the computer is designed to execute a multiply instruction. See Figure M-3.

GERMAN INSTRUCTION	MNEMONIC CODE	SCHLÜSSEL CODE	MNEMONIC CODE	ENGLISH INSTRUCTION
WAGENRÜCKLAUF	WRL	0 0 1	CR	CARRIAGE RETURN
RECHTSVERSCHIEBUNG	RVS	0 1 0	RS	RIGHT SHIFT
LINKSVERSCHIEBUNG	LVS	0 1 1	LS	LEFT SHIFT
DRUCKBEFEHL	DBF	1 0 0	PR	PRINT
LOCHKARTENLESEN	LKL	1 0 1	RC	READ CARDS
SPRUNGBEFEHL	SBF	1 1 0	JP	JUMP
WEITERSCHALTEN	WSN	1 1 1	CF	COUNT FORWARD

M-3. A **mnemonic code's** value depends on the *language* that is familiar to the *user.*

m–o. *Magnetooptic.*

mobile communication equipment. *Communication* equipment that is installed in or on a vehicle and that can be operated while the vehicle is in motion. If the equipment is mounted, loaded, or installed in or on a vehicle, but the equipment can only be operated when the vehicle is stationary, the equipment is considered as *transportable* rather than mobile. Thus, a mobile unit can *transmit* and *receive messages* and *signals* while it is moving.

mobile earth station. An *earth station* that can be used while it is in motion and during halts.

mobile radiotelephone frequency. See *maritime mobile radiotelephone frequency.*

mobile service. A *radio communication service* in which *mobile stations* and *fixed stations,* or only mobile stations, *communicate* with each other. See *aeronautical mobile service; land mobile service; maritime mobile service.*

mobile station. A *station* in the *mobile service* that is intended to be used while in motion. See *aeronautical multicom mobile station; aeronautical telemetering mobile station; aeronautical utility mobile station; flight telemetering mobile station; hydrological and meteorological mobile station; radiolocation mobile station; radionavigation mobile station; radiopositioning mobile station; telemetering mobile station.*

mobile unit routing indicator. A *message routing indicator* that is assigned to a *mobile station,* such as a *ship station,* an *aircraft station,* or a *mobile land station.*

mobility. See *equipment mobility.*

modal dispersion. In the *propagation* of an *electromagnetic wave* or *pulse* in a *waveguide,* the changes introduced in the relative magnitudes of the *frequency components* of the wave or pulse. The guide is capable of supporting or introducing only a fixed number of frequencies depending on its geometry and material parameters, such as *permeability, permittivity,* and *conductivity.*

modal loss. In an *open waveguide,* a loss of energy on the part of an *electromagnetic wave* due to obstacles outside the waveguide, abrupt changes in direction of the waveguide, or other anomalies, that cause changes in the *propagation mode* of the wave in the waveguide. Also see *propagation mode.*

mode. 1. A specific condition or arrangement of *electromagnetic waves* in a *transmission medium,* particularly in a *waveguide.* The total number of *modes* that a step-index *optical fiber* can support, *couple* to, or *radiate* into is given by:

$$I = 2\pi^2 a^2 \ (n_1{}^2 - n_2{}^2)/\lambda^2$$

where *a* is the fiber radius, n_1 and n_2 are the *refractive index* values of *core* and *cladding,* and λ is the *wavelength.* Also see *eigenvalue.* 2. In *communication systems,* a form or medium for *transmission* of voice, *image, digital data,* or other *signals.* Also see *multimode facility.* See *cine-oriented mode; cipher mode; cladding guided mode; comic-strip-oriented mode; compute mode; conversational mode; data mode; dedicated mode; degenerate waveguide mode; dial mode; direct mode; dominant mode; hold mode; indirect mode; initial condition mode; interactive mode; laser basic mode; leaky mode; passive mode; plain mode; propagation mode; satellite mode; set mode; static test mode; TE mode; TM mode.*

mode conversion. In *electromagnetic wave transmission,* the changing from one *propagation mode* to another, either intentionally or unintentionally. Also see *dominant mode; lowest-order transverse mode.*

mode fiber. See *single-mode fiber.*

mode interference. See *common-mode interference.*

model. See *Griffith microcrack model.*

mode launching. See *single-mode launching.*

mode link control. See *basic mode link control.*

modem. *Signal* conversion equipment that includes both a *modulator* and a *demodulator.* It is a combination of equipment that (1) changes the type of *modulation,* (2) *modulates* an incoming *signal,* (3) *demodulates* an incoming signal, (4) *converts digital signals* into *quasi-analog signals* usually for *transmission,* or (5) *converts quasi-analog signals* into *digital signals* usually for further *processing.* It is normally part of a *terminal installation* and is connected to a *data ceannel.* It is used for the transmission and reception of *data* at either or both ends of a circuit or channel. It may include *clocks* and signal generators but normally does not contain error control equipment. It may be considered as a signal processor. Many additional functions may be added to a modem or may be considered to be part of a modem in order to provide *user* (customer, subscriber) services or communication system control features. See *narrowband modem; wideband modem.*

modem patch.   A *patch* that electrically connects two points, two *paths,* or two *conductors* by means of two *modems* that are connected *back-to-back.*

mode operation.   See *packet mode operation.*

modes.   See *coupled modes.*

mode stripper.   See *cladding mode stripper.*

mode terminal.   See *packet mode terminal.*

mode volume.   The number of *modes* that a *waveguide* can support or propagate.   For large values, the number of modes, or mode volume, is expressed as:

$$N = (1/2)f_n{}^2$$

where f_n is the *normalized frequency.*   For example, if $f_n = 4$, then 8 modes will propagate.   Also see *normalized frequency; propagation mode.*

modified alternate mark inversion (MAMI) signal.   An *alternate mark inversion (AMI) signal* that does not conform exactly with bipolar coding criteria but allows violations of alternate coding in accordance with a defined set of rules. Also see *alternate mark inversion (AMI) signal.*

modified chemical vapor deposition process (MCVD).   A *modified inside vapor phase oxidation process* for production of *optical fibers* in which the burner travels along the glass tube.   The *soot* particles are created inside the tubing rather than in the burner flame as in the *OVPO process.*   The chemical reactants, such as silicon tetrachloride, oxygen, and *dopants,* are caused to flow through the rotating tube of glass at a pressure of about 1 atm.   The high *temperature* causes the formation of oxides (soot) and a glassy deposit on the inside tube surface. The tube is then drawn into a solid fiber.   Synonymous with *modified inside vapor phase oxidation process.*   Also see *chemical vapor phase oxidation process.*

modified clear message.   A message that contains combinations of clear text and encrypted text.

modified inside vapor phase oxidation process (MIVPO).   See *modified chemical vapor deposition process.*

modified non-return-to-zero level (MNRZ-L) code.   A variation of the basic *non-return-to-zero (NRZ) code.*   The basic NRZ code should actually be called a non-return-to-zero level (NRZ-L) code.   The MRZ-L code, a modification of the NRZ-L code, represents the *binary* states of 0 and 1 as *voltage transitions,* rather than as voltage levels as do the NRZ-L codes, such as the *non-return-to-zero mark (NRZ-M) code* and the *non-return-to-zero space (NRZ-S) code.*

modified reflected binary code.   A *code* that is formed by adding an extra *even parity bit* to the right-most position of each *reflected binary word.*   It is used because of its *error detection* properties in some arithmetic operations, but it requires two to three times as many *combinational circuit elements* as the conventional *binary adder.* Synonymous with *Lucal code.*

modular spread-spectrum code-sequence generator. In *spread spectrum systems,* a *spread-spectrum code-sequence generator* in which each *flip-flop* in the *code sequence register* is followed by a *modulo-two adder.*

modulated jamming. See *slow-sweep noise-modulated jamming.*

modulated signal. See *pulsed frequency modulated signal.*

modulation. 1. The variation of a characteristic or *parameter* of a *wave* in accordance with a characteristic or parameter of another wave. For example, a variation of the *amplitude, frequency,* or *phase* of a *carrier wave* in accordance with the wave form that represents intelligence by means of superposition or mixing. The carrier may be a continuous *direct-current (DC) signal* or a continuous alternating signal such as a *sinusoidal wave.* The carrier is used as a means of *propagation.* The superimposed or mixed *signal* is used as the intelligence bearing signal. The variation of the *modulated carrier* is *detected* at the *receiver.* The *information* or intelligence *frequencies* are normally called the *baseband.* 2. The process, or the result of the process, of varying certain features, characteristics, or *parameters* of one *signal* by means of another signal. For example, in *continuous carrier modulation,* the *modulated signal* is always present. In *pulsed carrier modulation,* there is no signal between *pulses.* 3. In *lightwave communications,* the variation of a characteristic or *parameter* of a *lightwave* in order to superimpose an intelligence-bearing *signal* on a *carrier wave.* For example, a variation of the *amplitude, frequency,* or *phase* of a lightwave by an *analog* or *digital signal* that is first coded to bear intelligence, then *transmitted,* and finally recovered by a *photodetector* at the receiving end of an *optical cable.* The carrier is usually a continuous or *sinusoidal wave* when it is not modulated. See *absorptive modulation; amplitude modulation; analog modulation; analog intensity modulation; angle modulation; balanced-amplitude modulation; balanced modulation; binary modulation; conditioned diphase modulation; constant-current modulation; continuously-variable-slope delta (CVSD) modulation; cross modulation; delta modulation (DM); delta sigma modulation (DSM); demodulation; delay modulation (DM); differential modulation (DM); differential pulse code modulation (DPCM); digital frequency modulation; digital modulation; direct-sequence modulation; electrooptic phase modulation; external optical modulation; final modulation; fixed-reference modulation; frequency code modulation; frequency-hopper direct-sequence modulation; full modulation; incremental phase modulation (IPM); intermodulation; isochronous modulation; jammer modulation; jamming modulation; multilevel modulation; non-return-to-zero (change) modulation; non-return-to-zero (change-on-ones) modulation; percentage modulation; phase modulation; polarization modulation; pulse-amplitude modulation (PAM); pulse-code modulation; pulse-interval modulation; pulse length modulation; pulse modulation; pulse position modulation; pulse time modulation; reference modulation; start-stop modulation; suppressed-clock pulse-length modulation; synchronous demodulation; telegraph modulation; 100% modulation.* See Figure M-4.

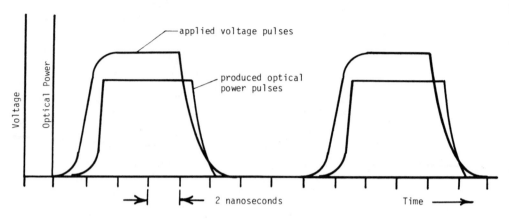

M-4. **Modulation** of a *light source,* such as a *laser* or *LED,* with a *modulating pulse.*

modulation deception.   See *radar scan-rate modulation deception.*

modulation-demodulation linearity.   A measure of the presence or absence of *harmonics* of the *frequency* of the *modulating signal* in the signal that results from the *modulating* or *demodulating* process.

modulation factor.   1. In *amplitude modulation,* the ratio of the peak-to-peak variation of an *electromagnetic wave* that is actually used, to the maximum design variation in a given type of *modulation.*   In conventional amplitude modulated waves, the maximum design variation is that for which the instantaneous *amplitude* of the *modulated signal* just reaches zero.   When zero is reached, there is *100% modulation.*   **2.** The ratio of half the difference between the maximum and minimum *amplitudes* to the average amplitude of an *amplitude modulated wave.*   **3.** The ratio of half the difference between the maximum and minimum *frequencies* to the average frequency of a *frequency modulated wave.*   Synonymous with *modulation depth.*   Also see *modulation index; unbalanced modulation.*

modulation-frequency harmonic distortion.   A constituent of *nonlinear distortion* that consists of the production of *sinusoidal components* whose *frequencies* are *integral* multiples of the frequency of the *modulating signal.*   The distortion occurs particularly in the *modulation-frequency response* of equipment to a *sine-wave modulated carrier.*

modulation-frequency intermodulation distortion.   A constituent of *nonlinear distortion* that consists of the production of *sinusoidal components (intermodulation products)* whose *frequencies* are linear combinations (sums and differences) of the frequencies of the sinusoidal components of the *modulating signal.*

modulation index. In *angle modulation,* that is, in *phase* or *frequency modulation,* the ratio of the *frequency* deviation of the *modulated signal* to the frequency of a *sinusoidal modulating signal.* Also see *modulation factor.*

modulation integrator. See *frequency modulation integrator.*

modulation multiplexing. See *pulse code modulation multiplexing.*

modulation noise improvement. See *angle modulation noise improvement.*

modulation product. **1.** One or more of the new *frequencies* that are obtained when one *signal modulated* another. **2.** The entire *output* product *(signal* and *noise)* that results from *modulation.*

modulation radar jamming. See *pulse modulation radar jamming.*

modulation rate. The reciprocal of the measure of the shortest nominal *unit interval* between successive *significant instants* of the *modulated signal.* If this measure is expressed in *seconds,* the *modulation rate* in *baud* (bauds) is obtained.

modulation significant condition. A condition such as *voltage, current, frequency,* or *phase,* that is assumed by an appropriate device and that corresponds to the *quantization* values of the characteristics that are chosen to form the *modulation.* Also see *mark; restitution.*

modulation transfer function. In *optics,* the function describing the *modulation* of the *image* of a sinusoidal *object* as the *frequency* increases. The transfer function is usually described by means of a graph or an equation. Synonymous with *sine wave response.* Contrast with *transfer function.*

modulator. A device that accomplishes *modulation,* that is, has the capability of varying one *signal* in accordance with the variations of another signal. Thus, it converts a basic signal into a *modulation product.* In *transmission systems,* the *modulated signal* is *transmitted* to a *receiver* that *demodulates* the signal to recover the original intelligence that was represented by the *modulating signal.* See *acoustooptic (a-o) modulator; demodulator; electrooptic (e-o) modulator; integrated-optical circuit filter-coupler-switch-modulator; magnetooptic (m-o) modulator; telegraph modulator; thin-film optical modulator; unbalanced modulator.*

modulator-demodulator. See *modem.*

module. **1.** In *electrical circuits,* an interchangeable *hardware* plug-in unit that contains one or more *circuit* elements. For example, a *printed circuit* board with *combinational circuits (logic gates), transistors, resistors, capacitors,* and *inductors.* **2.** In *computer programming,* a *software* unit that is *discrete* and identifiable with respect to *compile, load,* execute, and other *programming* functions. See Figure M-5. Also see Figure T-12.

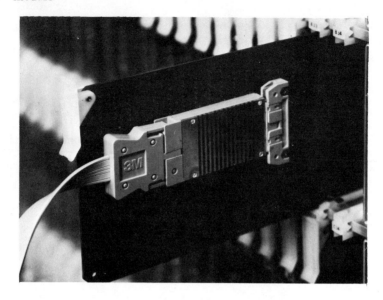

M-5. A *transceiver* **module** used in a *fiber optic data link.* (Courtesy of 3M Business Communication Products Division.)

modulo. In mathematics, pertaining to the remainder after the division of any *integer* by another specified integer. For example, 26 modulo 8 is 2.

modulo-n arithmetic. Conventional arithmetic that is performed in the usual manner, except that *modulo* values are used instead of the normal operands in the conventional arithmetic. The value of n may be any *integer.* For example, in modulo-5 arithmetic, the product of 59 and 38, modulo 5, is 2, since 59 modulo 5 is 4, 38 modulo 5 is 3, and 4 times 3 is 12, and 12 modulo 5 is 2. Also, 59 X 38 is 2242, and 2242 modulo 5 is also 2. Modulo-n arithmetic is used in *checking systems* for *data storage* and *transmission* in *computers* and *communication systems.* Also see *modulo-n check.*

modulo-n check. A check for verifying a computation, though with limited certainty, by repeating the arithmetic operations to be checked using *modulo-n arithmetic* and comparing the results with the results obtained using the original *operations.* In modulo-n arithmetic, no number is allowed to become larger than n-1. All numbers are cyclic. A number is congruent to another number modulo-n if the remainder after dividing each number n, is the same. Thus 5 and 23 are congruent modulo-9 and modulo-6, but are not congruent modulo-8 and modulo-4. Also see *modulo-n arithmetic.*

modulo-two adder. See *EXCLUSIVE-OR gate.*

modulo-two addition. The addition of *binary* quantities or *signals* without a carry action. This is accomplished by an *EXCLUSIVE-OR gate* (anticoincidence gate, antiequivalence gate), that is, a gate that produces a 1 when either input is a 1 and that produces a 0 when both inputs are a 1 and produces a 0 when both inputs are 0. For example, in normal binary addition $11010 + 11100 = 110110$, but modulo-two addition of the same operands produces 00110. Carries are ignored.

modulo-two-sum gate. See *EXCLUSIVE-OR gate.*

modulo-n counter. A *counter* in which the number that is represented by the counter reverts to zero in the sequence of counting one at a time after reaching a maximum value of n-1.

modulus. The quantity of permissible numbers that can occur in a counting system. For example, if only the numbers from -128 to $+128$ are allowed, the modulus is 257.

modulus counter. A *counter* that produces an *output pulse* after a certain number, or multiple of this number, of *input pulses* are applied. The total count possible is based on the number of *stages (digit positions).* A *binary modulo-8* counter with 3 *flip-flops* (stages) will produce an output pulse, that is, *display* a 1, after 8 input pulses have been counted (applied). This assumes that the counter started in the zero condition. The only output is that count of 1 each time the counter has counted 8. At the ninth pulse, the output is 0, and it remains 0 until 8 pulses have been counted again, that is, it remains 0 for 7 counts and remains 1 for every eighth count.

moire. See *interference pattern.*

molded case circuit breaker. A *circuit breaker* that is assembled as an *integral* part in a supporting and enclosing housing of *insulating* material. Molded case circuit breakers are usually used on systems in which a rating of 600 V or less may be used.

molecular laser. A type of *gas laser* whose *active medium* is a molecular substance (compound); e.g., a carbon dioxide, hydrogen cyanide, or water vapor *laser.* Contrast with *atomic laser.*

molecular stuffing process (MS). A process of making *graded refractive index optical fibers* using five broad steps, namely, glass melting, phase separation, leaching, *dopant* introduction, and consolidation.

monitor. See *variation monitor.*

monitoring. See *off-the-air monitoring, technical monitoring.*

monitor jack. A *jack* that provides *access* to a *communication circuit* for the purpose of observing the *signal conditions* on the circuit without interrupting the *communication service* or function that is provided by the circuit.

monitoring. 1. In *communication systems,* the act of *detecting* the presence of *electromagnetic waves* and measuring them with instruments. 2. The act of listening to, reviewing, or recording *transmissions* particularly for the purposes of maintaining standards, improving communication system performance, obtaining reference *signals,* or *intercepting information.*

monochromatic. Pertaining to a composition of one *color.* Purely monochromatic *light* has all its *energy* confined to one *frequency,* i.e., one *wavelength.*

monochromatic light. *Electromagnetic radiation,* in the *visible* or near visible *(light)* portion of the *spectrum,* that has only one *frequency* or *wavelength.*

monochromatic radiation. *Electromagnetic radiation* that has one *frequency* or *wavelength,* usually in the *visible frequency spectrum.* Also see *polychromatic radiation.*

monochromator. An instrument for isolating narrow portions of the *frequency spectrum* by means of *dispersion* of *light* into its component *colors.*

monocord switchboard. In *telephone systems,* a small, usually magneto-operated *switchboard,* in which each *loop* is principally a *cord,* a *jack,* a *drop,* and a two-way level-type *key.* On most monocord switchboards, *conference connections* are made by plugging the *originating user's* (subscriber's, customer's) *plug (cord)* into the first *called user's* jack, the first called user's plug (cord) into the second called user's jack, and so on. Four- to twelve-cord boards are typical, particularly in military and field installations.

monocular instrument. An *optical* instrument having one *optical axis* and *one eyepiece* that makes use of, or allows the use of, one eye at a time. In such instruments, there is no requirement to provide for *convergence* in order to accomodate two eyes. Examples include hand-held telescopes, magnifying glasses, monocles, some microscopes, and jewelers' *loupes.*

monofiber cable. See *monofilament cable.*

monofilament cable. An *optical cable* containing a single strand of *optical fiber.* Synonymous with *monofiber cable.* See Figures M-6, M-7, M-8 and M-9.

M-6. A Siecor-133 **monofilament cable** for *trays, conduits,* or *ducts.* (Courtesy Siecor Optical Cables, Inc.)

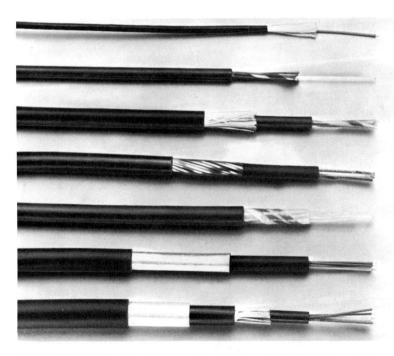

M-7. General cable *monofilament* and *multifilament* general and *special-purpose optical-fiber* **multichannel cables.** (Courtesy of General Cable Company, a division of GK Technologies, Inc.)

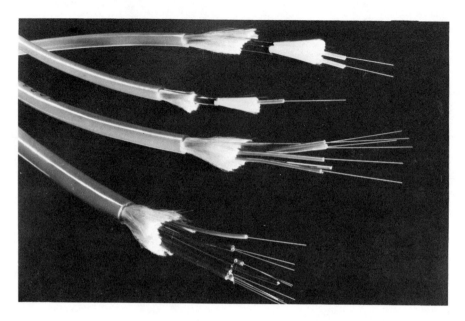

M-8. Siecor 1-, 2-, 6-, and 10-filament general-purpose *optical-fiber* **multichannel cables.** (Courtesy of Siecor Optical Cables, Inc.)

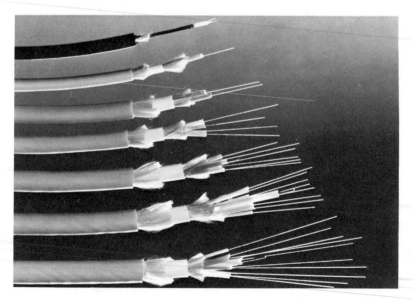

M-9. Corning *monofilament* and *multifilament* general-purpose *optical-fiber* **multichannel cables.** (Copyright 1979 Corning Glass Works. Reprinted by permission from Corning Glass Works, Telecommunication Products Department.)

monopulse antenna feed system. An *antenna feed system* that has two or more partially overlapping *radiation lobes,* that is used to deduce directional *information,* and in which the sum and difference *channels* in a *tracking receiver* compare the *amplitude* or *phase* of the *antenna output signals.* The antenna design makes use of two or more *feeds* and one *reflector.* Corresponding antenna *beams* with a small angular displacement between them are thus obtained. The antenna is used primarily in *tracking radars* in which an *error signal* to control the antenna is derived from the difference of signals received from the offset antenna beams.

monopulse tracking system. See *pseudo-monopulse tracking system.*

monorail double-heterojunction diode. A *laser diode* with a *double-hetero-junction* and a shift and return-to-level of the *refractive index profile* that has the spatial-plot appearance of a *square wave* of step-function on both sides of the *junction.*

morpheme. An element in a *language* that indicates the relationship between *semantemes* in the language and that contains no smaller meaningful part. For example, the words but, and, if, or, with, not. The words forthcoming, always, and *communication* would not be considered as morphemes. Also see *semanteme.*

Morse. 1. Samuel F. B. Morse, inventor of the *telegraph.* 2. Pertaining to *systems,* devices, and techniques that make use of the *dot* and *dash code* and the type of *telegraph* equipment invented by Samuel F. B. Morse. See *high-speed Morse; low-speed Morse.*

Morse code. A two-*condition telegraph code* in which *characters* are represented by groups of *dots* and *dashes.* Each unique group represents a letter or *digit* and each group is separated by a *space.* See *international Morse code.*

Morse code indicator. In *visual signaling systems,* a *panel signaling indicator* that consists of two panels that form an open V. When the panels are placed above the *index flash* the use of *Morse code* is indicated.

Morse continuous wave. A method of *telegraph operation* in which the *signals* are formed in accordance with the *Morse code.* The two basic methods of operation include *direct-current (DC)* interruption or *carrier-wave* interruption to form the *dots* and *dashes.* Synonymous with *Morse CW.*

Morse CW. See *Morse continuous wave.*

Morse flag signaling. *Visual signaling* in which a *dot* is indicated by raising both arms vertically overhead. A *dash* is indicated by spreading both arms horizontally to the sides. Dot-dash separation is indicated by placing both arms before the chest. Both arms are lowered to a 45° angle from the ground to indicate the separation of letters. Circular motions of arms and hands overhead means repeat or erase. Quick vertical movement of arms in front of the body means end of transmission. Also see *semaphore signaling; wigwag signaling.*

Morse key. A device that can be used to form *Morse telegraph signals* by manual *operation.* It consists basically of a spring-loaded contact that when depressed makes a *connection* and when released breaks the contact. Spark suppressors, relays, and other circuits and devices may be added for improved performance. The key is used to *modulate* a *carrier.*

Morse printer. A device that accepts *Morse code signals* and prints the *characters* that correspond to the *signals.*

Morse telegraphy. Any method of *telegraph operation* in which the *signals* are formed in accordance with the *Morse code.* It includes the *transmission* and *reception* of *international Morse code signals,* and the use of *Morse keys* and semi-automatic and automatic devices associated with them. Thus, any form of *alphabetic telegraphy* using the Morse code is included.

mosaic telegraphy. Any method of *telegraph operation,* such as *alphabetic telegraphy,* in which the patterns that form the *characters* are made up of units that are transmitted as separate *signal elements.*

motor boating. *Singing* that occurs in a *circuit* at a *very low frequency,* usually as result of *feedback* and often at *power* frequencies.

motorized keyboard. A *keyboard* in which the energy that is required to move the combination bars into the *position* that is selected by depression of a *key* is derived from a motor that drives the instrument of which the keyboard is a part.

mount. See *nonorthogonal antenna mount; X-Y mount.*

mounting cement. An adhesive used to hold *optical* elements in their mounts. It may be either a *thermoplastic, thermosetting,* or chemical-hardening material.

mouse. A hand-held device that may be moved in contact with a flat surface in order to generate desired *coordinate data.* It may be used with a *tablet,* have an index *mark,* and perhaps a *light source.* It is usually small and can be made to move about with a minimum of *inertia* so as to permit the following of curves on paper placed on the tablet. For example, if the mouse is a light source and the surface is the *faceplate* of a *coherent bundle* of *optical fibers,* the selection of a specific fiber to be *illuminated,* or a group of contiguous fibers to be illuminated, can result in the generation of *digital coordinate data* that corresponds to the position of the illuminated fiber or fibers by *enabling* a set of *logic gates* that will generate the digital coordinate data. Also, a mouse can be made that will perform the functions of a *joystick.* The coordinate data can be used to control or perform display operations, such as translating *display elements, rubber-banding, scissoring,* or *tracking.*

m-out-of-n code. A *binary code* that has a fixed *weight* assigned to each *digit position* and in which every n-digit word has exactly m digits that are the same. The word is a pattern or *string* of binary digits that may form a *character* or a group of characters. For example, a 2-out-of-5 code in which every 5-bit word *(byte)* has exactly two 1's and three 0's. If this rule is violated an *error* is indicated. The *error detector* need only be a *modulo-n counter* in which n = 3.

moving target indicator (MTI). A *radar display* that shows only objects (targets) that are in motion. *Signals* from stationary objects are subtracted from the return *(echo) signal* by the *output* of a suitable *storage circuit*. There are two basic types of MTI, noncoherent and coherent. Both systems are used to remove *ground clutter* and slow-moving target returns (echoes). Both systems depend on a pulse-to-pulse comparison and subsequent cancellation of fixed or slow-moving target echoes. Cancellation can take place in either *intermediate frequency (IF)* or *video stages*. Coherent MTI, however, makes use of *Doppler information* from an object in a clutter environment thus providing subclutter visibility that is not available in noncoherent MTI. The radar displays only those objects that have a radial component of velocity in relation to the radar site. A radial change in distance (range) causes a *shift* in *frequency, amplitude,* or *phase* between two adjacent returns (echoes) from the object. In some MTI radars, the return signal is fed into two *channels*. One of these is a normal *amplifier*. It amplifies the signal to video level. The other channel is a delay circuit. The outputs are compared with a new return signal to determine any amplitude, frequency, or phase change in a *discriminator*. The *output* of the discriminator presents to the radar display unit only those targets in which above-*threshold* changes have occurred. See *coherent moving target indicator*.

MPSK. *Multiple phase-shift keying.*

MS. *Molecular stuffing process.*

MTBF. *Mean-time-between-failures.*

MTBO. *Mean-time-between-outages.*

MTI. *Moving target indicator.*

MTTF. *Mean-time-to-failure.*

MTTR. *Mean-time-to-repair.*

MTTSR. *Mean-time-to-service-restoral.*

multiaddress calling facility. A *facility* or process that permits a *user* (customer, subscriber) to use more than one *address* for the same *message* or *data,* or to *call* more than one *party* or *data station* at the same time. The *communication system* may undertake this either sequentially or simultaneously, perhaps at the option of the user. The procedure for using this facility may be the same as for a *direct call*. A special *code* or codes may be used to designate all the required destinations or to indicate the individual full or *abbreviated address* of each *destination user*. This facility may also be used with *delay working* procedures.

multiaddress service. A *communication service* that provides for the delivery of a *message* that is destined for more than one *addressee.* Multiaddress service differs from *broadcast service* in that a multiaddress *message* need not be *transmitted* simultaneously to all addressees and the service is addressee selective.

multichannel bundle cable. In *optical fiber systems,* two or more *single-bundle cables* all in one outside *jacket.*

multichannel cable. In *optical fiber systems,* two or more *cables* combined in a single *jacket, harness, strength-member,* cover, or other unitizing element. Also see Figures M-7, M-8 and M-9.

multiband radar. *Radar* that *transmits* at more than one *frequency* simultaneously and that uses only one *antenna.* This radar allows for many sophisticated forms of *video processing.* It provides for improved performance, overcomes some forms of *interference,* and as an *electronic countermeasure,* it requires that a *jammer* must *jam* all the *frequencies (channels)* at the same time.

multichannel optical analyzer. A device capable of analyzing the *components* or content of *electromagnetic radiation,* such as a *vidicon tube* with a sensing area and an electron gun for reading *signals* representing an *image focused* on its *screen.*

multichannel single-fiber cable. In *optical fiber systems,* two or more *single-fiber cables* all in one outside *jacket.*

multichannel voice frequency telegraph (MCVFT). *Telegraph* in which two or more *carrier current signals* are used that have *frequencies* that are within the *voice frequency* range, that is, in the range between 300 Hz and 3 000 Hz.

multicom. See *aeronautical multicom land station; aeronautical multicom mobile station; aeronautical multicom service.*

multicoupler. See *antenna multicoupler.*

multidither. See *frequency multidither.*

multidrop network. A *network configuration* in which one or more *intermediate nodes* are on a *path* between *endpoint nodes.* See Figure M-10.

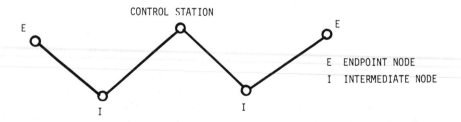

M-10. A **multidrop network** with *control station.*

multielement dipole antenna. An arrangement of a number of *dipole antennas.* By varying the arrangement *(array)* and the phasing in which they are driven, various directional radiation patterns may be obtained. Also see *phased-array antenna.*

multifiber cable. See *multifilament cable.*

multifilament cable. An *optical cable* with more than one strand of *optical fiber.* Synonymous with *multifiber cable.* Also see Figures M-7, M-8 and M-9.

multifocal. In *optics,* pertaining to a system or component, such as a *lens* or *lens system,* that has, or is characterized by, two or more *foci.*

multiframe. In *pulse-code modulation (PCM) systems,* a set of consecutive *frames* in which the *position* of each frame can be identified by reference to a *multiframe alignment signal* for the group of consecutive frames. The multiframe alignment signal does not necessarily occur, in whole or in part, in each and every multiframe.

multiframe alignment signal. A *frame alignment signal* that serves as a *timing* (reference) *signal* for a specified group of consecutive *frames.* Also see *frame alignment signal.*

multifrequency pulsing. See *multifrequency signaling.*

multifrequency (MF) signaling. A *signaling* method in which a combination of *frequencies* for *signaling* purposes is used, such as two-out-of-six (MF 2/6) or two-out-of-eight (MF 2/8) *audio frequencies* that are used to indicate *telephone number (address) digits, precedence,* control *signals,* such as *line-busy* or *trunk-busy* signals, and other required signals. Thus, each separate digit is represented by two different frequencies, each frequency being one of a possible six or a possible eight in these examples. Thus, a maximum of 36 or 64 possible codes may be obtained in these cases. For the case of 8 frequencies, two at a time but different frequencies for each code element, there are 56 possible codes. If permutations are not permitted but only combinations, and the frequencies must be different, only 28 variations are available. For 6 frequencies, the corresponding values are 30 and 15. See *dual-tone multifrequency signaling (DTMF).*

multilevel modulation. See *n-ary signaling.*

multilevel precedence (MLP). Pertaining to *communication systems* and *components* that can handle more than one *precedence designation.* See *automatic multilevel precedence.*

multilevel precedence capability. In *automatically-switched telephone networks,* the capability of handling *traffic* at more than one *precedence designation* level. For example, the capability of handling *flash override, flash, immediate, priority,* and *routine traffic* all in the same *network* and all within the specified precedence level definition limits. Normally a *preemption* procedure is used.

multiline laser. A *multimode gas laser.*

multilink.   1. In a *communication system,* pertaining to a multiplicity of *data links.*   **2.** A group of *data links* that are obtained by means of *multiplexing,* that is, *multiplexed* data links.   **3.** In a *data network,* pertaining to a *branch* that lies between two *nodes* and that consists of two or more *data links.*

multimeter.   A test instrument that is used for measuring *electric voltages, currents,* and *resistances* that may lie within a number of different ranges. The range may be selected to obtain optimum measurement precision. Synonymous with *volt-ohm-milliammeter.*

multimode dispersion.   See *optical multimode dispersion.*

multimode facility.   In *communication systems,* a *facility* that is capable of handling more than one *transmission mode,* such as *telephone, telegraph, radio,* or *facsimile.*

multimode fiber.   An *optical fiber waveguide* that will allow more than one *mode* to *propagate.* Multimode optical fibers have a much larger *core* (25 to 75 *microns*) than single-mode fibers (2 to 8 *microns*) and thus permit *nonaxial rays* or modes to propagate through the core compared with only one mode through a single-mode fiber.

multimode group-delay spread.   In an *optical waveguide,* the variation in *group delay,* due to differences in *group velocity,* among the supported *propagating modes* at a single *frequency.* Multimode group-delay spread contributes to *group-delay distortion,* along with *material dispersion* and *waveguide-delay distortion.* The spread in arrival time of the edges of a *light pulse* at the end of an *optical waveguide* is caused by the different time delays, or *propagation* times, of the various *waveguide modes.* The modes can be visualized as different *optical* paths of different lengths; e.g., *photons* or *waves* propagating along the fiber axis reach the end of the fiber before *photons* or waves that propagate along semihelical off-axis paths, causing *optical pulse spreading* (increase in width) and resulting *intersymbol interference* beyond the *bit-rate-length* capacity of the fiber. Reduction of spreading can be accomplished by having the longer paths be in a lower-refractive-index medium so that the wave can travel faster in longer paths.

multimode laser.   A *laser* that *emits radiation* at two or more *wavelengths.* In *gas lasers,* these are also called *multiline lasers.*

multimode operation.   In *analog systems,* the use of a common *circuit* or a single *transmission medium* for both *analog* and *digital data.* For example, *voice, binary coded data, facsimile,* and *Morse code* all on one circuit though not necessarily at the same time. Simultaneous *transmission* in more than one *mode* at the same time can be accomplished using *multiplexing* techniques.

multimode waveguide.   A *waveguide* capable of supporting more than one *electromagnetic wave propagation mode.*

multinode network.   In *communication systems,* a *communication network* in which *users* (customers, subscribers) may be interconnected through more than one *node.*

multipaired cable. A *paired cable* that has two or more pairs of *conductors,* such as two or more *twisted pairs.*

multipath. Pertaining to the *propagation* phenomenon that results in *transmitted electromagnetic waves* reaching the *receiving antenna* by two or more *paths.* Multipath may be due to many causes, such as *atmospheric ducting, ionospheric reflection,* and reflection from terrestrial objects such as mountains and buildings. Multipath affects *signals* as the waves combine in a variety of ways from constructive reinforcement to destructive cancellation during *propagation* and at the receiving antenna. Also see *propagation; Rayleigh fading.*

multipath fading. *Fading* due to the *propagation* of an *electromagnetic wave* over many different *paths,* dissipating energy and causing *distortion,* particularly by *signal* cancellation at the destination because of differences in arrival time due to the different paths. Multipath fading occurs to both *radio waves* and *lightwaves.* Synonymous with *multiple-path fading.*

multiphonon band. The group or range of acoustic, elastic, or vibrational *frequencies* associated with a number of *phonons* with energies lying in a given range, the range usually containing phonons of many different energies and therefore different frequencies.

multiple access. 1. In *communication systems,* the connection of a *user* (customer, subscriber) *end-instrument* to two or more *switching centers* by using separate *access lines* and by using a single *message routing indicator* or *telephone number.* 2. In *satellite communications,* the capability of a *communication satellite* to function as a portion of a *communication link* between more than one pair of *satellite earth stations* simultaneously. The method involves passing a number of separately *modulated carriers,* perhaps from different earth stations, through a single *satellite transponder.* Three basic types of multiple access are employed with communication satellites. These are *code-division, frequency-division,* and *time-division multiple access.* See *code-division multiple access (CDMA); frequency-division multiple access (FDMA); pulse-address multiple access (PAMA); satellite-switched time-division multiple access (SS-TDMA); space-division multiple access (SDMA); spread-spectrum multiple access (SSMA); time-division multiple access (TDMA).*

multiple-access-rights terminal. A *terminal* that may be used for more than one *user service class.* For example, a situation in which different groups of *users* have *access* rights to certain classes of data and not to other classes of *data.*

multiple-address message. A *message* that is destined for two or more *addressees.* In most *communication systems,* each addressee is informed of all addressees. Each addressee should be indicated by the *originator* as an *action, information,* or *exempted addressee.*

multiple beaming. In *radar systems,* the *transmission* of two or more *beams* from an *antenna,* each in a different direction at any given instant. Also see *conical beam-split radar.*

multiple-bundle cable. A number of *jacketed optical fiber bundles* placed together in a common, usually cylindrical, envelope.

multiple-bundle cable assembly. A *multiple-bundle optical fiber cable* terminated and ready for installation.

multiple call. 1. In *telephone switchboard operation,* a *call* from one *user* (customer, subscriber) to several others. Synonymous with *conference call; bunched call.* 2. In *radiotelegraph transmission,* a *call* in which two or more *call signs* are *transmitted.* The call signs may be individual *station, net,* or *collective call signs.* Call signs may be transmitted twice under difficult operating conditions. Also see *conference call.*

multiple-call message. A *message* that contains *routing indicators* that require segregation at intermediate *relay stations.* Also see *routing-line segregation.*

multiple-domain network. A *network* that has two or more *host nodes.*

multiple-fiber cable assembly. A *multiple-fiber cable* terminated and ready for installation.

multiple frequency-shift keying (MFSK). A *modulation* system in which a different discrete *transmission frequency* is used for each *digital data* input code; e.g., 10 different frequencies for the 10 different *numerals* in the decimal system of notation. The system may utilize several frequencies that are transmitted concurrently or sequentially.

multiple homing. In *telephone systems,* the *connection* of a *terminal facility,* using a single *directory number,* so that it can be served by one of several *switching centers;* or the connection of a terminal facility to more than one switching center by separate *access lines,* separate directory numbers being used to access each switching center. Also see *dual homing.*

multiple lines. See *common-address multiple lines.*

multiple-part message. A *message* that is *transmitted* in separate parts.

multiple-path fading. See *multipath fading.*

multiple peg marking. In *telephone switchboard operation,* a *system* of color-coded pegs, some with numbers, that are used to indicate the status of the *jack* into which the peg is inserted. For example, plain black may be used to indicate a spare *line,* no *telephone* connected, or not in use; plain red may be used to indicate out-of-order.

multiple phase shift keying (MPSK). A *modulation system* in which there are as many *phase states (positions, conditions)* of a *carrier* as there are *digital information input code elements* to represent. For example in a *quaternary code,* that is, a *code* in which there are four *conditions,* each perhaps representing one of the digits 0, 1, 2, and 3, there would be four different *phase positions* of the *carrier.*

multiple-selection signal code. See *network multiple-selection signal code.*

multiple-spot scanning. In *facsimile systems, scanning* in which two or more *scanning spots* scan simultaneously, each one reading its fraction of the total scanned area of the subject copy.

multiplex (MUX). 1. Pertaining to the use of a single or common *channel* or path in order to make two or more channels, such as by *sharing* the *time* of the channel *(time-division multiplexing)* or superimposing many *frequencies* at the same time *(frequency-division multiplexing)* in order that many *signal sources* and *sinks* may *communicate* during a given time period. 2. To use one *channel* for connecting two or more *communication source* and *sink* pairs. Also see *demultiplex.* See *heterogeneous multiplex; orthogonal multiplex; space-division multiplex; teleprinter-on-multiplex.*

multiplex aggregate bit rate. The *bit rate* in a *time-division multiplexer* that is equal to the sum of the *input channel data signaling rates* that are available to the *user* plus the rate of the *overhead bits* that are required. Mathematically, the multiplex aggregate bit rate is given by:

$$MABR = R(\sum_{i=1}^{m} n_i + H)$$

where *MABR* is the multiplex aggregate bit rate, R is the repetition rate of the *frame* of the *output channel, m* is the maximum number of input channels to the *multiplexer* (including nonworking channels, equipped channels, or both), n_i is the number of *bits* per *multiplex frame* associated with the i-th channel, and H is the number of overhead bits per multiplex frame of the output channel. The number of bits in the multiplex frame is assumed to be constant.

multiplex baseband receive terminal. The point in the *baseband circuit* that is nearest to the *multiplex* equipment and from which *connection* is normally made to the *radio, video, optical,* or *line baseband receiving terminals* or intermediate *facility.*

multiplex baseband send terminal. The point in the *baseband circuit* that is nearest to the *multiplex equipment* and from which *connection* is normally made to the *radio, video, optical,* or *line baseband transmitting terminals* or intermediate *facility.*

multiplexed circuit. See *homogeneous multiplexed circuit.*

multiplexer. See *data multiplexer; thin-film optical multiplexer; trunk group multiplexer.*

multiplexer-filter. See *fiber-optic rod multiplexer-filter.*

multiplexing. In *communication systems,* the creation of *data links, circuits,* or *channels* by using a given set of equipment and applying various means of increasing the *capacity* of the physical equipment to carry *messages.* For example, *mul-*

tiplexing may be accomplished by *timesharing, frequency division, time division, space division, phase shifting,* or other means. See *asynchronous time-division multiplexing (ATDM); color-division multiplexing; frequency-division multiplexing; heterogeneous multiplexing; homogeneous multiplexing; optical-division multiplexing; pulse code modulation multiplexing; space-division multiplexing; statistical multiplexing; statistical time-division multiplexing; synchronous time-division multiplexing; time-division multiplexing; wavelength-division multiplexing.* Also see Figure L-1.

multiplex link. A *link* that enables *data terminal equipment (DTE)* to have several *access channels* to a *network* over a single *circuit. Interleaving* methods that may be used in a multiplex link are *packet* interleaving, *byte* interleaving, and *bit* interleaving. Any form of *multiplexing* may be used to establish the link.

multiplex link encryption. *Encryption* in which a single *cryptographic* device, that is, a single piece of *cryptoequipment,* is used to *encrypt* the *data* in all of the *channels* within a *multiplex link.*

multiplex operation. *Operation* of a *communication path,* such as a *circuit, channel,* or *link,* in such a manner that there is simultaneous *transmission* of two or more *messages* in either or both directions over the transmission path.

multiplex set. See *engineering circuit multiplex set.*

multiplex structure. See *frame-multiplex structure.*

multiplier. See *analog multiplier.*

multiplication. See *avalanche multiplication.*

multipoint. Pertaining to the ability to interconnect three or more devices, such as sets of *data circuit-terminating equipment (DCE),* without intervening *switchboards* or *switching centers,* in order to obtain satisfactory *operation.* Also see *point-to-point.*

multipoint circuit. A *circuit* that provides simultaneous *communication* among three or more separate points.

multipoint connection. 1. A *connection* between two *data stations* via one or more other (intermediate) *stations. 2.* A *connection* among three or more *data stations* in order to accomplish *data transmission* among them. The connection may include *switching facilities.*

multipoint link. A *data communication link* that is used to connect three or more *data stations.*

multiport coupler. See *fiber-optic multiport coupler.*

multiprocessor. A *computer* with two or more *processors* that have access to a common *storage.*

multipurpose jammer. A *jammer* that is capable of *jamming* multiple *frequencies* throughout a wide *band* of frequencies simultaneously; or that is capable of combining two or more *electronic countermeasures (ECM)*, such as *barrage jamming* and *deception jamming* simultaneously; or that is capable of accomplishing two or more other types of jamming.

multiposition switchboard. In *telephone switchboard operation,* a *switchboard* that is built to accommodate more than one *operator* and is therefore equipped with more than one *position.*

multirefracting crystal. A *transparent* crystalline substance that is anisotropic with respect to the velocity of *light* traveling within it in different directions (i.e., with respect to its *refractive index* in different directions).

multiunit message. A *message* in which more than one *signal unit* is used when it is *transmitted.*

multivibrator. A relaxation *oscillator* that comprises two *stages* that are *coupled* so that the *input* of each stage is derived from the *output* of the other.

Murray code. See *International Telegraph Alphabet Number 2 (ITA-2).*

mutual information content. See *transinformation content.*

mutual interference. The *interference (noise)* that is obtained, created, or induced in one device when it is operating in conjunction with another device, and vice versa. For example, two *antennas* that are *radiating* simultaneously, particularly in the same *frequency band* and in close proximity, are likely to experience an interchange of energy *(mutual interference)* because of the *electrostatic, magnetostatic, magnetic,* and *electromagnetic coupling* that occurs between them.

mutually synchronized network. A *communication network,* in which *synchronization* is obtained by an arrangement in which each *clock* in the network exerts some control on all the other clocks in the network.

MUX. *Multiplex.*

myocardium stimulator. See *fiber-optic myocardium stimulator.*

myriametric wave. An *electromagnetic wave* in the range from 3 kHz to 30 kHz, that is, in the *very low frequency (VLF) band.* Also see *frequency spectrum designation; radio frequency.*

N

N.A. *Numerical aperture.*

nadir. The point on earth that is directly under an observer, that is, from the observer, in a direction toward the center of the earth, and at the surface or at any other point on this line. This is opposed to the *zenith,* a point that is on a line directly away from the center of the earth.

NAK. The *negative acknowledge (NAK) transmission control character.*

NAK attack. In *communication security systems,* a *security penetration* technique that makes use of the *negative acknowledge transmission control character* and capitalizes on a potential weakness in a *system* that handles *asynchronous transmission* interruption in such a manner that the system is in an *unprotected* state against unauthorized *access* during certain periods of time.

naming. 1. In *communication systems,* the selection and assignment of *identifiers,* that is, titles, to an *addressee* for purposes of *message* delivery. For example, the assignment of "Personnel Coordinator" to a person, or "Room 835" to a place, or "Traffic Control" to a function, for purposes of message delivery. 2. In a *display system,* the assignment of a name or label to a *segment, display file, computer program,* or other *software* used for operating the display system.

NAND element. See *NAND gate.*

NAND gate. A *binary logic combinational circuit* or device that is capable of performing the NAND (negative AND) logic operation. In this operation, if A is a statement, B is a statement, C is a statement, ... , the NAND of A, B, and C, . . . , is false if all the statements are true, and true if any one or more of the statements are false. The NAND gate behaves like the *AND gate* when the *output* of the AND gate is simply negated. In terms of binary notation with 0's and 1's as *input digits,* the NAND will yield an output of 0 when all the inputs are 1, and a 1 when at least one input is a 0. Synonymous with *Sheffer stroke gate; if-B-then-NOT-A gate; if-A-then-NOT-B gate; negative AND gate; nonconjunction gate; NOT-AND gate; NOT-both gate; alternative denial gate; dispersion gate; NAND element.* See Figure N-1.

IN A	0	1	B IN
0	1	1	Q OUT
1	1	0	

N-1. A table showing the *input* and *output digits* of a **NAND gate**.

nanometer (nm). One-thousandth of a millionth of a *meter*, i.e., 10^{-9} meters. The nanometer is a convenient unit for designating the *wavelength* of *visible electromagnetic radiation* (namely, the wavelength of *light*). The wavelengths extend from about 750 nm at the highest *infrared* energy level *(near-infrared)* down to 390 nm lowest energy *ultraviolet*. The decrease in wavelength corresponds to the increase in *frequency* and increase in *photon (quantum)* energy. The nanometer is also equal to 10 angstroms. Synonymous with *millimicron*.

nanosecond (nsec). One-thousandth of a millionth of a *second*, i.e., 10^{-9} seconds. Synonymous with *millimicrosecond*.

narrative traffic. *Messages* that consist of *plain* or *encrypted text* of a *natural language*. For example, *teletypewriter messages* that are placed on paper tape, *transmitted*, and on *reception converted* back to a printed page in accordance with standardized procedures.

narrowband. Pertaining to a group of *frequencies* that lie within a relatively restricted range of frequencies. For example, at 100 kHz, a *band* that is 1 kHz wide would be considered wide. At 100 MHz the 1 kHz would be considered narrow. At 100 MHz, a 10 MHz band would be considered wide, but at 100 THz the same 10 MHz might be considered narrow. Less than 0.1% of the operating frequency is considered to be narrowband; greater than 0.1% is considered *wideband*.

narrowband modem. **1.** A *modem* whose *modulated output signal* has a *frequency spectrum* that is limited to that which can be wholly contained within, and faithfully *transmitted* through, a *voice channel* with a nominal 4 kHz *bandwidth*. The 4 kHz bandwidth is arbitrary. Other widths have been proposed to imply narrowband, such as 20 kHz. **2.** A modem in which a narrow *bandwidth* is used or that has a narrow bandwidth capability.

narrowband signal. Any *analog signal,* or analog representation of a *digital signal,* that has a *spectral* content limited to a narrow *band*. For example, a digital signal that has a spectral content limited to that which can be contained in a *voice channel* of nominal 4 kHz *bandwidth*. The 4 kHz is arbitrary. Other bandwidths have been proposed to imply narrowband, such as 20 kHz for a voice channel.

narrow-beam antenna. An *antenna* that has a high *directive gain,* that is, its *radiated* energy is confined to a small solid angle and thus has a narrow *main lobe.* It generally has comparatively small *side lobes.* In *radar systems,* narrow-beam antennas are well suited for *tracking.* They are less subject to *interference* because of their directional capability. They are more difficult to *jam* than *wide-beam antennas* or *omnidirectional antennas.*

narrow-beam radar. A *radar* that emits a *signal* that has its energy confined to a small solid angle or to a small angle in *elevation* or *azimith.* It uses a *narrow-beam antenna.* The *antenna radiation pattern* usually has relatively small *side lobes* compared to the narrow *main lobe.* The narrow beam is similar to that of a *spotlight* or the *light* from a *parabolic reflector.* Also see *wide-beam radar.*

narrow-shift frequency-shift keying. In *radiotelegraph communication systems, frequency-shift keying* in which the *frequency shift* accomplished by the *modulating signal* is small compared to the *frequencies* being used. The frequency-shift is used to distinguish the *mark* from the *space,* such as to distinguish 1's from 0's, to distinguish *dots* and *dashes* from spaces, or to distinguish tone from silence. For example, a shift of +425 Hz could be used for the mark and a shift of −425 Hz could be used for the space, both with reference to the *assigned frequency.* Also see *wide-shift frequency-shift keying.*

n-ary code. A *code* in which each *code element* may be any of n distinct kinds or values, where n may be any integer. For example, *binary, ternary,* and *quaternary signal codes.* The n designates the number of stable states, such as *amplitude* levels, *phase positions,* or *frequencies,* that are required to implement the code depending on the type of *modulation* that is used. Synonymous with *m-ary code.*

n-ary digit. A *digit* or member selected from an *n-ary code.* For example, a 1 in a *binary code* consisting of 0 and 1, or a 3 in a *quaternary code* consisting of 0, 1, 2, and 3. Synonymous with *m-ary digit.*

n-ary digital signal. A *digital signal* in which a *signal element* may assume n *discrete* states, where n may be any *integer.* For example, a *ternary digital signal* element could have any one of three stable states, *conditions,* or *levels,* such as +V, 0, and −V where V may be any number of volts. Synonymous with *m-ary digital signal.*

n-ary information element. An *information element* that enables the representation of n distinct states, conditions, or levels, where n may be any *integer.* For example, a ternary information element *(data element)* has three and only three possible *data items,* such as masculine, feminine, and neuter as data items for the data element gender. Synonymous with *m-ary information element.*

n-ary signaling. The *transmission* of *digital data* in such a way that the *pulses* can assume with equal probability any of n stable states at any given instant, such as any of n *amplitude* levels, any of n *frequencies,* or any of n *phase positions* relative to a reference where n is any *integer.* Thus, this multilevel or multiple decision system implies that there must be n *conditions* that are *transmitted* and *detected.* Each condition must be held within its permitted *dynamic range* of variability. Each *discrete position* or condition represents a decision or selection of the n possible positions or conditions. Synonymous with *m-ary signaling* and with *multilevel modulation.*

nat.   *Natural unit of information content.*

national address indicating group.   An *address indicating group (AIG)* that is assigned for use within a specific nation. Also see *international address indicating group.*

national circuit-group-congestion signal.   In international *communications,* a *signal* that is sent in the *backward direction* and that indicates that the *call setup* attempt was unsuccessful due to *congestion* encountered on a *circuit group* in a national *network,* that is, that the *access attempt* ended in *access failure.*

national switching-equipment congestion signal.   In international *communications,* a *signal* that is sent in the *backward direction* and that indicates that the *call setup* attempt was unsuccessful due to *congestion* encountered at a *switching center* in a national network, that is, that the *access attempt* ended in *access failure.*

natural language.   A *language* in which the *symbols,* conventions, and rules for its use are based on current usage and were not specifically or explicitly prescribed prior to its use. Also see *artificial language.*

natural unit of information content (nat).   A unit of logarithmic measure of *information content* that is expressed as a Naperian (natural) logarithm, that is, a logarithm to the base e, where e = 2.71828, approximately. For example, the *decision content* of a *character set* of eight characters equals ln 8, or 2.079 nat. Also see *decision content.*

nautical mile (nmi).   The fundamental unit of distance that is used in navigation. The international nautical mile is 1853 m, 6076.1 ft, or 1.15 statute miles. The nautical mile is frequently confused with the geographical mile, which is equal to 1 min of arc on the earth's equator, that is 6087.15 ft. The US Department of Defense and the US Department of Commerce adopted the international nautical mile in 1954. The geographical mile is 1855.4 m. The statute mile is 5280 ft or 1609 m.

navigation.   See *long-range aid to navigation (Loran); radar navigation; radionavigation; short-range aid to navigation (SHORAN).*

navigation aid.   See *radionavigation aid.*

navigation and ranging.   See *sound navigation and ranging (SONAR).*

navigation land station.   See *radionavigation land station.*

navigation service.   See *maritime radionavigation service.*

navigation system. See *beacon navigation system; hyperbolic navigation system; terminal-guidance navigation system.*

n-bit byte. A *byte* that is composed of n *binary digits,* where n can assume any positive *integral* value. Normally n is not greater than 16, while 4 and 8 are common.

n-body problem. A class of problems in classical *celestial mechanics* that treats the relative motion of an arbitrary number, n, of point masses that are only under their mutual gravitational attraction. It is assumed that the bodies are released under a set of initial conditions, that is, initial velocities and initial distances of separation, and that there are no forces acting on the *system* other than their own inertial forces and their forces of attraction. The problems are encountered in *satellite systems.* Also see *restricted circular three-body problem; three-body problem; two-body problem.*

NCS. *National Communication System. Net control station.*

near-end crosstalk. *Crosstalk* that is *propagated* in a *disturbed channel* in the direction opposite to the direction of *propagation* of the *electric current* in the *disturbing channel.* The *terminals* of the disturbed channel, at which the near-end crosstalk is present, and the energized terminal of the disturbing channel, are usually near each other.

near field. See *electrostatic field.*

near-infrared. Pertaining to *electromagnetic wavelengths* from 0.75 to 3 *microns.*

near zone. See *electrostatic field.*

necessary bandwidth. In *electromagnetic wave transmission,* and depending upon *emission* characteristics such as type of *modulation, carrier suppression,* and *sideband suppression,* the minimum value of the *occupied bandwidth* that is sufficient to insure the transmission of *data* at the rate and quality that is required under specified conditions. *Frequencies* that are useful for the proper functioning of the receiving equipment, such as the emission that corresponds to the carrier of a reduced carrier system, are included in the necessary bandwidth. The necessary bandwidth is normally used to determine *frequency assignments.* Also see *nominal bandwidth; occupied bandwidth; radio frequency (RF) bandwidth.*

negation circuit. See *inverter.*

NEGATION gate. A device that is capable of producing the state other than the *input* state at any given moment in a two-state variable system such as a *binary digital* logic system, that is a *combinational logic gate* that converts a 1 into a 0 and a 0 into a 1.

negative acknowledge (NAK) character. A *transmission control character* that is sent to a *transmitter* by a *receiver* to indicate the receipt of a *block* that contains one or more *errors*. Receipt of the NAK will cause the transmitting station to retransmit the block of *information*. Also see *acknowledge (ACK) character.*

NEGATIVE A-IGNORE-B gate. A two-*input binary logic combinational circuit* or device that is capable of performing the logic operation of NEGATIVE (A IGNORE B). In this operation, if A is a statement, and B is a statement, then the result of NEGATIVE (A IGNORE B) is true when A is false and false when A is true. Thus, the result is independent of B. The output of the gate is simply the inverse of A. The gate is the same as an A IGNORE B gate that has its *output* negated. This behavior is usually temporary and controllable. Normal operation might be that of a NOR gate, which, upon *signal,* is converted to the NEGATIVE (A IGNORE B) gate. See Figure N-2.

IN A	0	1	B IN
0	1	1	Q OUT
1	0	0	

N-2. A table showing the *input* and *output digits* of a **NEGATIVE (A IGNORE B) gate.**

negative (A implies B) gate. See *A-AND-NOT-B gate.*

negative-AND gate. See *NAND gate.*

NEGATIVE (B-IGNORE-A) gate. A *combinational logic gate* that is the same as the NEGATIVE (A-IGNORE-B) gate except that the two *binary input* variables are reversed, that is, they are simply renamed. If the input *line* identities are to remain unchanged, only the terminals need to be interchanged. The gate's behavior is the same as that of the *NEGATIVE (A-IGNORE-B) gate.* See Figure N-3.

IN A	0	1	B IN
0	1	0	Q OUT
1	1	0	

N-3. A table showing the *input* and *output digits* of a **NEGATIVE (B IGNORE A) gate.**

negative (B implies A) gate. See *B-AND-NOT-A gate.*

negative clearing. In *double supervisory working* of *telephone switchboards, clearing* in which a *light* disk, or other indicator associated with a *plug* that is in use, turns on (appears) when a *connection* is set up. When a *user* (customer, subscriber) clears, the associated indicator is turned off (disappears), thus giving a negative indication of the clearing. Also see *positive clearing.*

negative distortion. See *early distortion.*

negative justification. See *destuffing.*

negative lens. See *diverging lens.*

negative meniscus. See *divergent meniscus lens.*

negative-OR gate. See *NOR gate.*

negative photodiode. See *positive-intrinsic-negative photodiode.*

negative photodiode coupler. See *positive-intrinsic-negative photodiode coupler.*

negative pulse stuffing. See *destuffing.*

negative scanning shift. In *facsimile transmission systems,* a relative *shift* of the *scanning* device with respect to the document being scanned when the surface of the document is scanned along the *lines* from right to left and from top to bottom. In a drum scanning apparatus, helicoidal scanning towards the right is a negative scanning shift.

NBH. *Network busy hour.*

neither-NOR gate. See *NOR gate.*

NEP. See *noise equivalent power.*

neper. A standard unit for expressing *gain, loss,* and other relative ratios that are dimensionless. It is similar to the *bel,* except that the natural logarithm, ln, is used. For the bel and *decibel,* the logarithm to the base 10 is used. For the neper, the logarithm to the base e, approximately 2.718, is used. The neper is equal to the natural logarithm of the scalar ratio of two currents or two voltages, while the bel is the common logarithm of the ratio of two powers. The number of nepers is expressed mathematically as $N = ln(I_1/I_2) = ln(V_1/V_2)$. One neper (N) is equal to 8.686 dB = (20/ln10) dB. The units decineper (N/10) and the centineper (N/100) are also used.

net. An organization of stations capable of conducting *communication* operations in accordance with a protocol and usually on the same *channel.* See *airborne early warning net; alternate communication net; answering net; calling net; ciphony-protected net; command net; communication net; computer net; control net; coordination net; direct-working local net; directed net; distress communication net; free net; ground-air net; local net; maritime amphibious* *communication net; maritime broadcast communication net; maritime distress communication net; maritime patrol air broadcast net; maritime patrol air reporting net; maritime ship-shore communication net; maritime tactical air operations communication net; mixed net; operation net; radio net; relay net; reporting net; ship-air net; ship-shore net; ship-to-air net; ship-to-ship net; ship-to-shore net; shore net; triangulation net; warning net; working net.*

net authentication. An *authentication* procedure in which a *net control station* authenticates itself and all other stations in the net systematically establish their authenticity.

net call sign. In a *radio net,* a *call sign* that uniquely identifies each *station* in the net. Also see *collective call sign; individual call sign.*

NETCONSTA. *Net control station.*

net control station (NCS). A *station* that maintains control of an operational *network* that consists of two or more *facilities.* The NCS controls *traffic* and enforces *circuit* discipline within a given *net.* The NCS is responsible to the MNCS and assumes control of the overall *communication system* or portion of the system as directed by the MNCS. Synonymous with *NETCONSTA.* See *master net control station (MNCS).*

net gain. In *communication systems,* the overall *gain* of a *transmission circuit.* It is measured by applying a *test signal* of some convenient *power* at the beginning of a circuit and measuring the power delivered at the other end. The ratio of these powers is the net gain of the circuit. The net gain may be expressed in *decibels* as $10 \, log(P_o/P_i)$ where P_o is the *output* power and P_i is the *input* power of the circuit. If the output power is greater than the input power there is a greater than unity or positive *decibel gain.* If the input power is greater than the output power there is a less than unity or negative decibel gain, which is also called a *net loss.* Also see *net loss.*

net glossary. An organized cross-referenced functional list of *communication network* titles of all *nets,* such as police, fire, rescue, medical emergency, military, naval, coast guard, and forestry nets, available for use or contact by an organization. Also see *circuit designator; emission designator.*

net loss. In *communication systems,* the overall *loss* of a *transmission circuit.* It is measured by applying a *test signal* of some convenient *power* at the beginning of a circuit and measuring the power delivered at the other end. The ratio of these powers is the net loss of the circuit. The net loss may be expressed in *decibels* as $10 \, log(P_i/P_o)$ where P_i is the *input* power and P_o is the *output* power of the circuit. If the output power is less than the input power there is a greater than unity or positive decibel loss. If the output power is greater than the input power there is a less than unity or negative decibel loss, which is also called a *net gain.* Also see *net gain.*

net loss variation. The maximum change in *net loss* that occurs in a specified portion of a *communication system* during a specified period.

net margin. In *telegraph operation,* the *margin* of the *telegraph* apparatus when the *modulation rate* at the *input* of the apparatus is the standard rate.

net operation. The *operation* of an organization of *stations* that are capable of direct *communication* on a common *channel* or *frequency. Net* operations are characterized by ordered conferences whose participants have common *information* needs or like functions to perform; by adherence to *standard operating instructions (SOI);* and by responsiveness to a common *supervisor,* called the network controller at a *net control station.* Functions of the net controller include permitting *access* to the net and maintaining circuit discipline.

net radio interface. See *radio-wire interface.*

netting. In *radiotelegraph communication,* the *tuning* of the *frequency* of two or more *stations,* such as when establishing a *net,* when stations join a net, or when operating a net. Netting is accomplished under the direction of a *net control station.* See *radar netting.*

netting station. See *radar netting station.*

network. 1. In *communications,* an organization of *stations* that are capable of interstation *communication* but not necessarily on the same *channel* or *circuit.* **2.** Two or more interrelated *circuits.* **3.** A combination of *swtiches, terminals,* and *circuits* in which *transmission facilities* interconnect *user stations* directly, that is, there are no *switching,* control, or *processing* centers in the combination. **4.** A combination of *switches, terminals,* and *circuits* that serves a given purpose. **5.** A combination of *circuits* and *terminals* that are serviced by a single *switching* or *processing* center. **6.** In topology, an interconnected group of *nodes.* The interconnections are accomplished by *branches.* See *active network; administrative network; air defense command-control-communication network; application network; automatic voice network; balancing network; branching network; centralized computer network; civil fixed telecommunication network; civil communication network; common-user network; communication network; computer network; data network; decentralized computer network; deemphasis network; democratically synchronized network; despotically synchronized network; equivalent network; fixed network; fully-connected network; heterogeneous network; hierarchical computer network; hierarchically synchronized network; hierarchical network; homogeneous network; hybrid communication network; loop network; mesh network; military fixed communication network; multidrop network; multinode network; multiple-domain network; mutually synchronized network; nodal network; nonsynchronous network; oligarchically synchronized network; passive network; preemphasis network; public data network (PDN); radiotelephone network; shaping network; single-domain network; single-node network; star network; switched network; synchronous data network; synchronous network; teletypewriter network; transparent network; tree network; weighting network.*

network access line. A *line* that connects the *communication facility* of an organization to a *communication network.* For example, a tie-line to a *private branch exchange (PBX).*

network architecture. 1. The design principles, physical structure, functional organization, *data format,* operational procedure, and other features used as the basis for the design, development, and *operation* of a *user application network.* 2. The structure of a *network,* including the operating procedures and *data formats.*

network automatic identification. The automatic identification of a *station* or of a *user* in which the *answer-back code* is provided by the network.

network busy hour (NBH). The *busy hour* for an entire *network.* Also see *group busy hour; switch busy hour; traffic load.*

network configuration. A schematic presentation of the elements of a *network.* In particular, it is the arrangement of the *nodes* and *branches* of a network. Synonymous with *network topology.*

network control. See *operational network circuit.*

network control channel. In a *communication network,* a *channel* between *nodes* that carries *information* concerning the status of the network.

network controller. In *communication systems,* a device, usually controlled by a *programmed computer,* that directs the *operation* of the *data links* of a *communication network.*

network control phase. In a *data call,* the phase during which *network* control *signals* are exchanged between *data terminal equipment (DTE)* and the network. The network control phase occurs during the three phases of a call, namely the *access phase,* the *information transfer phase,* and the *disengagement phase.*

network connectivity. The topological description of a *network* that specifies the interconnection of the *nodes* of the *network* in terms of *circuit parameters,* such as location, *termination,* and quantity.

data collection. In *communication systems,* a *facility* for gathering *data* from a group of *addressees,* assembling the data within the communication system, and delivering the data in the form of *messages* to specified addressees.

network identity. See *country network identity.*

network in-dialing (NID). In an *automatically-switched telephone network,* the capability of *dialing* an *extension* number at the *called party* installation from the *calling party* (customer, subscriber, user) *end-instrument,* and obtaining a *ring* and an answer without *operator* intervention at all, or without operator intervention at the called party's *switching center, switchboard,* or *exchange.* Also see *network out-dialing.*

network layer. In *open systems architecture,* the *layer* that provides the functions, procedures, and *protocol* that are needed to control the *transfer* of *data* in a specified *transmission medium.* The network layer *masks* the *routing* and *switching* characteristics of the *data link layer* and of the *physical layer* from the layers that are above the network layer.

network multiple-selection signal code. One of the several *codes* that may be accepted by a *network* as a *selection signal.* For example, in the use of *International Telegraph Alphabet Number 2 (ITA-2),* and in the *International Telegraph Alphabet Number 5 (ITA-5),* the choice of *code* may be either fixed or optional for a given *user* (customer, subscriber) for each *access attempt.*

network out-dialing (NOD). In an *automatically-switched telephone network,* the capability of enabling a *user* (customer, subscriber) to directly *dial* all user numbers by dialing through the local *switchboard* and obtaining a *called party ring* and answer without *operator* intervention at all or without operator intervention at the *calling party's switching center,* switchboard, or *exchange.* Also see *network in-dialing (NID).*

network security. The measures that are taken to protect a *network,* including its *hardware, software,* and *operators,* against unauthorized *access,* accidental or unauthorized willful interference with operations, destruction, or bodily injury.

network service. See *special network service.*

network supplement. In *tape-relay communication networks,* the alteration of the *format* of a *message* or group of messages by adding control or *information symbols* to the message. Alteration of the format should be avoided as much as possible.

network terminating unit. A simplified form of *data circuit-terminating equipment (DTE)* that *terminates* a *circuit* in a specialized *data network.*

network topology. The branch of science and technology that is devoted to the study and analysis of the *configuration* and properties of *networks.*

neutral. In an *electric circuit,* pertaining to a point that is not polarized relative to other points in the circuit. For example, the common point of a balanced three-phase star-connected network. Neutral points are usually connected to *ground.* See *thermoneutral.*

neutral direct-current (DC) telegraph system. A *telegraph system* in which an *electric direct current (DC)* flows during *mark* intervals and no current flows during *space* intervals for the *transmission* of *signals* over the *line.* The direction of current flow is immaterial for *neutral systems.* Synonymous with *single-current system; single-current transmission system; single-Morse system.*

neutral ground. In *electrical networks* and *circuits,* a *ground* that is applied to the electrically *neutral conductor* or to the neutral point of a circuit, *transformer,* machine, apparatus, or other *component* of a *system,* or to the system itself.

neutral operation. In *teletype transmission systems,* a method of *teletype* equipment *operation* in which *mark signals* are formed by *electric current pulses* of one polarity, either positive or negative, and *space signals* are formed by reducing the current to zero or nearly zero.

neutral relay.   A relay in which the movement of the armature does not depend upon the direction of the *electric current* in the magnetic coil circuit that controls the armature.

neutral telegraphy.   See *single-current telegraphy.*

neutral transmission.   See *single-current signaling.*

neutron bombardment resistance.   In *optical transmission systems,* the ability of an *optical element* to continue to perform its designed function when subjected to high-energy neutrons.   For example, an *optical fiber* subjected to a 3×10^9 neutron/cm^2 *beam* can result in an increase in *attenuation* of 0.005 dB/km per 10^8 *incident* neutrons/cm^2, resulting from a 5% to 10% increase in *scattering* losses, although a 50% recovery occurs 5 min. after cessation of bombardment.

new address signal.   See *redirected-to-new-address signal; redirect-to-new-address signal.*

new line (NL) character.   A *format effector* that causes the print or *display* portion of a printer to move to the first print or display *position* on the next *line.*

newton.   The SI unit of force.   A force of 1 newton (1 N) produces an acceleration of 1 m/sec^2 on a 1 kg mass.

Newton's fringes.   See *Newton's rings.*

Newton's rings.   The series of rings, bands, or fringes formed when two clean polished surfaces are placed in contact with a thin air film between them, and *reflected,* usually *chromatic, beams* of *light* from the two adjacent surfaces interfere with each other, causing alternate cancellation and reinforcement of *light* as the distance between the surfaces are multiples or submultiples of the *wavelength.*   By counting these bands from the point of actual contact, the departure of one surface from the other is determined.   The regularity of the fringes maps out the regularity of the distance between the two surfaces.   This is the usual method of determining the fit of a surface under test to a standard surface of a test glass.   Synonymous with *Newton's fringes.*

NF.   *Noise factor.*

NID.   *Network in-dialing.*

night effect.   The variations in the state of *polarization* of *electromagnetic waves* that are *reflected* by the *ionosphere.*   The variations sometimes result in *errors* in *direction finding (DF) bearings.*   The effect is most frequent and most pronounced at nightfall.

niobate integrated circuit.   See *lithium niobate integrated circuit.*

NL.   *New line character.*

nm. *Nanometer.*

nmi. *Nautical mile.*

NOD. *Network out-dialing.*

nodal point. See *node.*

nodal switching center. A *switching center* that is within a *telephone network* of an *integrated communication system,* employs *circuit switching* techniques, and contains *communication-electronic* equipment that is designed to interconnect *terminals* with other circuits in the network.

node. 1. In a *data network,* a point at which one or more *data transmission lines* are interconnected. 2. In *network topology,* a *terminal* (end) of any *branch* of a *network* or a *terminal* that is common to two or more branches of a network. 3. In *switched communication networks,* a switching point that may include *patching* and control *facilities.* 4. In a *data network,* the location of a *data station* where one or more *functional units* interconnect *transmission lines* or *data links.* Synonymous with *junction point; nodal point; vertex.* 5. A point in a *standing wave* (stationary wave) at which the *amplitude* of the wave is a minimum. The wave should be identified as a *voltage wave* or a *current wave* for the case of *electrical* waves. Nodes may also occur in *acoustic waves* and in *elastic waves,* such as in vibrating bodies. See *antinode; data processing node; endpoint node; host node; intermediate node.*

nodes. See *adjacent nodes.*

nodeless network. A *communication network* in which all *connections* are direct between all *users* (customers, subscribers).

noise. In a *communication system,* the sum of unwanted or disturbing energy introduced into the system from natural or man-made *sources,* such as unwanted *lightwaves coupled* into an *optical fiber.* Noise may be audible in *voice* or *sound communication* equipment and visible in *visual systems,* such as *radar* and *television.* In visual systems, noise has been given various descriptive names, such as snow, rain, stripes, and running rabbits. Also see *antenna noise temperature, circuit noise level; precipitation static.* See *acoustic noise; atmospheric noise; background noise; black noise; blue noise; equipment intermodulation noise; equivalent PCM noise; external noise; feeder echo noise; galactic noise; idle-channel noise; impulse noise; intermodulation noise; intrinsic noise; loop noise; notched noise; path intermodulation noise; pseudorandom noise; quantizing noise; random noise; reference noise; shot noise; sky noise; solar noise; spot noise; thermal noise; triangular random noise; total channel noise; white noise.*

noise density. See *carrier-to-receiver noise density.*

noise-equivalent power (NEP). 1. In *communication systems,* the value of *radiated power* that produces an *rms singal-to-noise ratio* of unity in a *detector.* It is usually measured with a *blackbody radiation source* at 500 kHz and a *band-*

width of 1 or 5 hz. The *modulation* rate varies with the type of detector and is usually between 10 hz and 1000 hz. It is essential that the measurement conditions be specified when indicating a value of NEP. **2.** In *optics,* the *rms* value of *optical power* required to produce unity rms *signal-to-noise ratio.* NEP is a common parameter in specifying *detector* performance. NEP is useful for comparison only if *modulation frequency, bandwidth, detector area,* and *temperature* are specified. Typically the reference bandwidth is 1 Hz and the modulation frequency is a few hundred hertz. NEP is indicated in watts/hertz$^{1/2}$. The *total NEP* is usually indicated in watts, microwatts, or picowatts.

noise factor. The amount of *noise* added by *signal*-handling equipment to the noise existing at its input, usually expressed in *dB,* thus being equal to the *signal-to-noise ratio* at *input* divided by the signal-to-noise ratio at *output.* In a *transducer,* it is the ratio of the *output noise power* to the portion thereof that is attributable to *thermal noise* at the *input terminal* at a standard *noise temperature* of 290 K. The noise factor is thus the ratio of the actual output noise to that which would remain if the transducer itself was noiseless. It is also a measure of the deterioration of the *signal-to-noise power density ratio* that occurs in the process of *amplification.* In this case, it is equal to the actual noise power at the *output* divided by the noise power that is calculated assuming the device itself is noiseless, that is, it is always greater than unity. The value depends on the level of *input* noise. Unless otherwise stated, the input noise is assumed to be that which would be due to a *matched resistor* at the input at room *temperature* (290 K). In *heterodyne* systems, output noise power includes spurious contributions from *image frequency* transformations, but the portion that is attributable to thermal noise in the input termination at standard noise temperature includes only that which appears in the output via the principal frequency transformation of the system, and excludes that which appears via the image frequency transformation. The noise factor is expressed mathematically as $NF = (T_n + 290)/290$ where T_n is the *effective noise temperature.* Synonymous with *noise figure.* See *spot noise factor.*

noise figure. See *noise factor.*

noise improvement. See *angle modulation noise improvement.*

noise jammer. A *jammer* that *emits* a *signal* in which the *power* is randomly distributed over a wide *band* of *frequencies.*

noise jamming. *Jamming* in which the *carrier wave* is *modulated* by *noise* or in which noise at the desired *output frequencies* is *amplified* and *radiated* without a *carrier.* Noise jamming is usually accomplished in *radar* and *communication systems* by means of a *signal* that has many different and usually random frequencies such as *white noise* or *spot noise.* See *spot noise jamming.*

noise level. The *noise power* in a *system* or at a point. It is usually measured in *decibels,* and often referred to a reference, such as 1 watt, *milliwatt,* or *picowatt.* In these cases, the unit of measurement would be the *dBw, dBm,* or *dBp.* See *ambient noise level; carrier noise level; channel noise level; circuit noise level.*

noise-limited operation. See *detector noise-limited operation; thermal noise-limited operation.*

noise loss. See *intermodulation noise loss.*

noise measurement unit. A unit of *noise power* measurement, either relative or absolute. The *decibel* is the most common unit for noise power measurements. The *picowatt* is also commonly used. To obtain an absolute unit when expressing noise levels in dB, a suffix is added to indicate the reference level. A suffix is also added to indicate a particular measuring instrument or other specific qualities or conditions of the measurement. Examples of noise measurement units include *dBa, dBa(F1A), dBa(Ha1), dBa0, dBm, dBm0, dBm(Psoph), dBmop, dBrn, dBrn(144-line), dBrnC, dBrn($f_1 - f_2$), pW, pWp, and pWp0.* Also see *noise weighting.*

noise power density. The *noise power* in a *bandwidth* of 1 Hz, that is, the noise power per hertz. The noise power density of the internal noise that is contributed by a receiving system to an incoming *signal* is expressed as the product of Boltzmann's constant, *k,* and the equivalent noise temperature, T_n. Thus, the noise power density of often expressed simply as *kT.* Synonymous with *kT.*

noise-modulated jamming. See *slow-sweep noise-modulated jamming.*

noise power. **1.** In *transmission systems,* the mean power of the *noise* that is supplied to an *antenna transmission line* by a *radio transmitter* when it is *loaded* with *white noise* that has a Gaussian (normal bell curve) distribution of *amplitude* rather than a constant distribution of amplitude. **2.** The *power* that is developed by unwanted *electromagnetic waves* from all *sources* in the *output* of a device, such as a *transmission channel* or *amplifier,* expressed as a function of the noise *voltage* squared and the equivalent source resistance. Noise power is usually the total noise power of waves with *frequencies* within the *passband* of the system or device. *Crosstalk, distortion,* and *intermodulation products* are usually classed as noise. **3.** In *information theory,* a *disturbance* that does not represent any *information* from the *message* or *signal source.* See *flat-noise power; received noise power.*

noise power ratio. See *carrier-to-noise power ratio; inband noise power ratio; single-sideband noise power ratio.*

noise ratio. See *carrier-to-noise (C/N) ratio; signal-plus-noise to noise (S+N)/N ratio.*

noise resistance. See *equivalent noise resistance.*

noise strobe. **1.** In *radar systems,* a *scan* for the purpose of determining *noise* levels as a function of *azimuth* or *elevation.* **2.** A *display* of *noise* that is obtained by a *radar strobe pulse.* **3.** In *electronic warfare systems,* a *scanning* of the *frequency spectrum* for *noise* levels.

noise suppression. A *receiver circuit* arrangement that automatically reduces the *noise output* of a device, such as an *antenna, transmission line, amplifier,* or *channel,* during periods when a *carrier* is not being received or transmitted. Also see *squelch circuit.*

noise temperature. See *antenna gain-to-noise temperature (G/T); antenna noise temperature; effective input noise temperature; effective noise temperature; equivalent noise temperature; front-end noise temperature; receiving-system noise temperature; standard noise temperature.*

noise weighting. A specific *amplitude-frequency characteristic* that permits a measuring set to give numerical readings that approximate the *interference* effects to any listener using a particular class of *telephone* instrument. Noise weighting measurements are made in *lines* that are *terminated* either by the measuring set or an end instrument. The noise weightings generally used were established by agencies that were concerned with public telephone service, and are based on characteristics of specific commercial telephone instruments, representing successive stages of technological development. The coding of commercial apparatus appears in the nomenclature of certain weightings. The same weighting nomenclature and units are used in military versions of commercial noise measuring sets. Also see *dBa; dBm0p; dBrn; dBrn(f_1 - f_2); noise measuring unit; psophometric voltage; pWp; weighting network.*

noise window. A trough in the *noise frequency spectrum* characteristic of a device, such as a *transmitter, receiver, channel,* or *amplifier,* from external sources or internal sources. The trough is usually represented as a *band* of lower *amplitude* noise in a wider band of higher amplitude noise.

noisy black. In *facsimile* or other *display systems,* such as *television,* a nonuniformity in the black area of a document, picture, or *image* that is due to a *signal level* change caused by *noise.* For example, a signal that is supposed to represent a black area but whose noise content causes the creation of white spots would be considered as noisy black. Also see *noisy white.*

noisy white. In *facsimile* or other *display systems,* such as *television,* a nonuniformity in the white area of a document, picture, or image that is due to a *signal level* change caused by *noise.* For example, a signal that is supposed to represent a white area but whose noise content causes the creation of black spots would be considered as noisy white. Also see *noisy black.*

no-landing marker. See *forbidden landing-point marker.*

nominal bandwidth. In *communication systems,* the widest *band* of *frequencies,* inclusive of *guard bands,* that is assigned to a *channel.* Also see *necessary bandwidth; occupied bandwidth; radio frequency (RF) bandwidth.*

nominal black. In *display systems,* such as *facsimile, television,* and *radar,* a characteristic or value, such as *signal* level or *frequency,* that corresponds to the darkest black that can be transmitted by a particular *transmitter.* Also see *nominal white.*

nominal line width. In *facsimile systems,* the average separation between the centers of adjacent *scanning* or *recording lines.*

nominal margin.   In *communication systems,* the minimum value that is set for the effective operating *margin* of a device, such as a *receiver, detector,* or *transducer,* while operating under standard adjustment conditions.

nominal white.   In *display systems,* such as *facsimile, television,* and *radar,* a characteristic or value, such as a *signal level* or *frequency,* that corresponds to the brightest white that can be transmitted by a particular *transmitter.*

nonblocking.   Pertaining to a *communication system* in which 100% of all *access attempts (calls)* are *completed.* Also see *blocking probability.*

noncentralized operation.   In *communication systems,* a control discipline for *multipoint data communication links* in which *transmission* may be between *tributary stations* or between the *network control station* and tributary stations.

nonconjunction gate.   See *NAND gate.*

noncritical technical load.   In a *communication system,* that part of the total *technical load power* requirement that is not required for *synchronous operation* and for *automatic switching equipment.* Also see *critical technical load.*

nondirectional beacon.   A *radionavigation aid* that consists of *transmitters, receivers,* and *antennas* for *direction finding.* The range of the beacon varies with the *power output* of the transmission source, but rarely exceeds 500 km. Single *bearing* lines are obtained from individual beacons. The bearings from two beacons are necessary for *resection.* Short ranges are necessary to achieve accuracy. Nondirectional implies omnidirectional.

nondisjunction gate.   See *NOR gate.*

nonerasable storage.   See *fixed storage.*

nonequality gate.   See *EXCLUSIVE-OR gate.*

nonequivalence gate.   See *EXCLUSIVE-OR gate.*

nongeostationary satellite.   A *satellite* that does not *orbit* the earth from west to east at such a speed in the equatorial plane as to remain fixed over a given point on the earth's equator at approximately 35,900 km altitude, making one revolution around the earth in 24 hours in exact *synchronism* with the earth's rotation. Thus the *geostationary satellite* orbit is an equatorial orbit in which the satellite revolves about the primary body at the same angular rate as the primary body rotates on its axis. The satellite thus appears to be stationary from any point on the primary body. A stationary orbit must be synchronous, but a synchronous orbit need not be stationary. For example, if a satellite's orbit is not in the equatorial plane, yet it maintains synchronism with the earth's rotation, the satellite would maintain a constant meridian of longitude. It might appear to oscillate back and forth but it might never set on an observer at certain locations. Any satellite that does not meet all the necessary conditions for a geostationary satellite is a nongeostationary satellite.

noninertial guidance system. A *guidance system* that does not make use of the principle of *inertia.* For example, it does not use the doubly-*integrated* output of an accelerometer to obtain distance but uses other means such as *command guidance, beam-riding,* and *homing guidance systems.* These examples of guidance systems are subject to *interference* and *jamming.* Some types of noninertial guidance systems, such as preprogrammed systems or logging systems, are not subject to interference or to *electronic countermeasures,* such as jamming. Also see *inertial guidance system.*

nonlinear distortion. *Distortion* that is a deviation from a linear relationship between specified *signal parameters* as the signal passes through equipment or *system components.* For example, the distortion that occurs because the *gain* of an *amplifier* is not constant over all values of signal *amplitude* or all values of *frequency;* or the distortion that occurs because *attenuation* is not the same for all amplitudes and frequencies of waves traveling in a *transmission medium* or in an electrical component. Transmission medium distortion can occur because the *constitutive-relation constants,* such as the *electric permittivity,* change with *frequency, electric current density, electric field intensity, magnetic field intensity,* or direction of *propagation* of an *electromagnetic wave.*

nonlinear feedback shift register. A *shift register* in which the *feedback* elements are not necessarily reducible to *modulo-2* functions. Multiple *feedback* loops and special *networks* are used to create the nonlinear feedback shift register. Also see *linear feedback shift register.*

nonlocking code extension character. A *code extension character* that has the characteristic that the change in interpretation that is to be made of the *characters* that follow applies only to a specified number of the *coded* representations (characters) that follow the code extension character. Usually the nonlocking code extension character applies only to the character that immediately follows it.

nonoperational load. In a *communication system,* the *power* that is required for the administration, support, and housing of the system. Synonymous with *utility load.* Also see *operational load.*

nonorthogonal antenna mount. In *radar systems,* an *antenna* mount in which two axes of rotation are not at right angles. These mounts have advantages for particular situations where fast *tracking* may be required.

nonprecedence call. **1.** In *telephone system operations,* a *routine precedence call* in networks in which a *precedence system* is used. **2.** A *call* in a *telephone system* in which *precedences* are not assigned to *calls.* **3.** A *call* to which a *precedence* has not been assigned. Also see *precedence call.*

nonradiative recombination. In an *electroluminescent diode* in which *electrons* and *holes* are injected into the P-type and N-type regions by application of a forward *bias,* the recombination of injected minority *carriers* with the majority *carriers* in such a manner that the energy released upon recombination results in heat which is dissipated primarily by *conduction* and some thermal *radiation*. Energy released by nonradiative *recombination* in LEDs does not contribute to *light energy* for *optical* use such as energizing *optical fibers* or driving *integrated optical circuits*. Also see *radiative recombination*.

nonreflective star coupler.   An *optical fiber coupling* device that enables *signals* in one or more *fibers* to be *transmitted* to one or more other fibers by entering the *input* signal fibers into an optical fiber volume without an *internal reflecting* surface so that the *diffused* signals pass directly to the *output* fibers on the opposite side of the fiber volume for *conduction* away in one or more of the output fibers. The optical fiber volume is a shaped piece of the optical fiber material to achieve transmission of two or more inputs to two or more outputs. Synonymous with *transmitting star-coupler*.   Also see *reflective star-coupler; tee coupler*.

nonresonant antenna.   See *aperiodic antenna*.

non-return-to-zero (NRZ).   Pertaining to a *signal* that represents a sequence of *digits,* such as *binary, ternary,* or *n-ary digits,* in which the *signal* level does not return to a zero *amplitude,* or to a value that represents a zero level, between the digits.   Thus, if the varying *parameter* is a *phase shift,* the signal would not return to a zero phase shift between digits; if the parameter is an *electric current* or *electric field intensity,* it would not return to a zero value between digits. There are four basic forms of NRZ data, namely *NRZ-change, NRZ-level, NRZ-mark,* and *NRZ-space*.   NRZ data in *binary* form has successive 1's and 0's following one another and the *signal* does not return to the zero level between each digit.   For example, as long as there is a series of consecutive 1's, the voltage level could be up, until the first 0, at which time it could go to zero level and remain there for as long as there is a series of 0's and then return to the high level at the next occurrence of a 1 and again remain there until the next 0 occurs.

non-return-to-zero (NRZ) binary code.   A *code* in which there are two and only two states of a *signal parameter* that is used to represent *data,* a state that is termed 0 and a state that is termed 1, and no other state is possible, such as a neutral or rest condition.   *Transitions* are direct from one stable state to the other.   Also see *return-to-zero code*.

non-return-to-zero change (NRZ-C).   Pertaining to a *binary signal stream* in which a *signal level* or *condition transition* occurs whenever there is a change from a state that represents a 1 to a state that represents a 0, and a transition in the reverse direction occurs when the state that represents 0 changes to the state that represents 1.   As long as the *digits* remain the same, there are no transitions.   It is the transition, rather than a stable state, that represents the *data*.

non-return-to-zero (change) modulation.   The *modulation* of a *signal parameter* that is used in a *bit stream* in which one of the *binary digits,* say the 1's, are represented by a *transition* to a specified *signal condition* from a given condition, such as *magnetization, electric field intensity, magnetic field intensity,* or *electric current* or *voltage amplitude (level);* and the other binary digit, in this case the 0's, are represented by a transition from the specified condition back to the given condition. The two conditions may be a finite value of a *signal parameter* and a zero value, two finite values, two polarities, or opposite directions. This *mode* is called change modulation because the signal condition changes only when the bits in a bit stream change from a 0 to a 1 or from a 1 to a 0. Thus, only the change is significant. It indicates that the digit has changed. See Figure N-4.

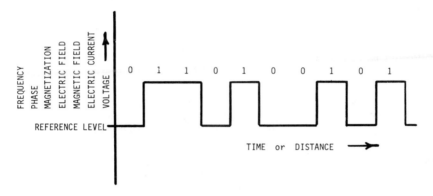

N-4. In **non-return-to-zero (change) modulation,** the physical *parameter* does not change except when the *digit* changes.

non-return-to-zero (change-on-ones) modulation. The *modulation* of a *signal parameter* that is used in a *bit stream* in which one of the *binary digits,* say the 1's, is represented by a change in the *signal condition* and the other binary digit, in this case the 0's, is represented by the absence of a change. The signal parameter that changes condition might be the *magnetization, electric field intensity, magnetic field intensity, electric current* or *voltage level, phase,* or *frequency,* or any other parameter. This modulation mode is also called *mark* because only the 1's (or only the 0's) are actually explicitly recorded. See Figure N-5.

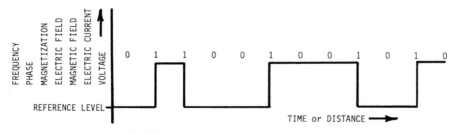

N-5. In **non-return-to-zero (change-on-ones) modulation,** the physical *parameter* changes from its previous state each time a *binary* 1 occurs.

non-return-to-zero coding. *Coding* using electrical or *lightwave pulses* that do not return to a zero level *condition* of *power, current, voltage, phase, light intensity,* or other *parameter* between each pulse-on condition. For example, the *binary digits* 111001 would be represented by an on-condition for three time intervals, an off-condition for two time intervals, and an on-condition for one time interval. There would be no returning to the off-condition between the *binary* ones. Also see *return-to-zero coding.*

non-return-to-zero level (NRZ-L). Pertaining to a *binary signal stream* in which the *signal level* or *condition,* such as the *voltage, electric current, phase, frequency, electric field intensity,* or any other *signal parameter,* remains in one state, say high, for as long as there are just 1's in the *bit stream* of the *data* that is being represented and, in this case, low for as long as there are just 0's in the bit stream; or 0 could be high and 1 could be low. The *level shift* corresponds exactly to the *binary code.* The condition of the signal parameter remains in a given condition for as long as there are digits in the stream that correspond to that condition. It is obvious for long strings of 1's or for long strings of 0's, NRZ data often contains *direct current (DC)* and *low frequency components* and perhaps little energy at *high frequencies.* This would cause the *data* to degrade rapidly under *high-pass filtering* in which the low frequency components of the signal could not get through. It retains its *integrity* under *low pass-filtering.* Therefore, in order to pass NRZ data, the *transmission channel* must be able to accept and transmit low frequencies, even down to direct current (DC).

non-return-to-zero level code. See *modified non-return-to-zero level code.*

non-return-to-zero mark (NRZ-M). Pertaining to a *binary signal stream* in which a *signal parameter,* such as *electric current* or *voltage,* undergoes a change in its condition or level every time that a 1 occurs, but when a 0 occurs, it remains the same, that is, no transition occurs. (The transitions could also occur only when 0's occur and not when 1's occur.) If the condition transition occurs on each 0, it is called non-return-to-zero space (NRZ-S). The signals are interchangeable. It is only necessary to maintain proper accounting in the electronic circuitry when distinguishing between NRZ-M and NRZ-S. Synonymous with *conditioned baseband representation; differentially-encoded baseband; non-return-to-zero one (NRZ-1); NRZ-B.*

non-return-to-zero one (NRZ-1). See *non-return-to-zero mark (NRZ-M).*

non-return-to-zero space (NRZ-S). Pertaining to a *binary signal stream* in which a *signal parameter,* such as *electric current* or *voltage,* undergoes a change in its *condition* or *level* every time that a 0 occurs, but when a 1 occurs, it remains the same, that is, no *transition* occurs. (The transitions could also occur only when 1's occur and not when 0's occur.) If the condition transition occurs on each 1, it is called *non-return-to-zero mark (NRZ-M).* The signals are interchangeable. It is only necessary to maintain proper accounting in the electronic circuitry when distinguishing between NRZ-S and NRZ-M.

nonsynchronous data transmission channel. A *data channel* in which no separate timing *information* is *transferred* between *data terminal equipment (DTE)* and *data circuit-terminating equipment (DCE)*.

nonsynchronous network. In *communication systems,* a *network* in which the *clocks* need be neither *synchronous* nor *mesochronous.* Synonymous with *asynchronous network.*

nontechnical load. In a *communication system,* that part of the total *operational load* that is used for general lighting, air conditioning, and other purposes, all of which are required for normal *operation* of the system. Also see *technical load.*

NOR gate. A *binary, logic combinational* (coincidence) *circuit* or device that is capable of performing the logic operation of NOR (negative OR). In this operation, if A is a statement, B is a statement, C is a statement, ... , the result of NOR A,B,C, . . . is false if at least one of the statements is true, and true only if all the statements are false. The behavior of the NOR gate is that of an *OR gate* (inclusive-or) with its output negated, that is inverted or reversed. Synonymous with *inclusive-NOR gate; negative-OR gate; neither-NOR gate; nondisjunction gate; joint denial gate; rejection gate; zero-match gate.* See Figure N-6.

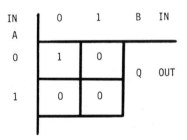

N-6. A table showing the *input* and *output digits* of a **NOR gate.**

normal emergence. In *optics,* a condition in which a *ray emerges* along the normal to the emergent surface of a *transmission medium.* Also see *emergence; grazing emergence.*

normal incidence. Pertaining to *light rays incident* at $90°$ to the incident surface.

normalized frequency. A *parameter* that can be used to calculate or express the number of *propagating modes* that a *step-indexed optical fiber* is capable of supporting, expressed mathematically as:

$$f_n = (2\pi a/\lambda)(n_1{}^2 - n_2{}^2)^{1/2}$$

where f_n is the *normalized frequency*, a is the *optical fiber core* radius, λ is the *wavelength*, and n_1 and n_2 are the *refractive indices* of the core and *cladding* of the optical fiber. For a large number of *modes*, the *mode volume* is given by:

$$N = (1/2)f_n{}^2$$

where N is the number of modes, or mode volume, and f_n is the normalized frequency above. Synonymous with *v-value.*

normalized power.   In *electric circuits,* the mean or average value of the *voltage* squared of a waveform that is defined as a voltage as a function of time and dissipated in a 1 ohm resistor. The dimension of the normalized power is voltage squared (V^2) rather than watts. It is only numerically equal to watts when the power is dissipated in a 1 ohm resistor. Sometimes the word normalized is dropped and reference is made only to power. It is given mathematically as:

$$P_n = (1/T)\int_O^T v(t)^2\, dt$$

where P_n is the normalized power, T is the time interval over which the average is taken, $v(t)$ is the voltage as a function of time, and t is time.

normal magnification.   See *individual normal magnification.*

northern lights.   *Aurora* borealis.

not-accepted signal.   See *call-not-accepted signal.*

NOTAL.   An *indicator* that is placed after a statement or reference in a *message heading* to indicate that the statement is neither intended for nor needed by all of the *addressees* of the message.

not-AND gate.   See *NAND gate.*

notation.   See *binary notation; postfix notation; prefix notation.*

not-both gate.   See *NAND gate.*

notch.   In a *frequency spectrum,* consisting primarily of *white noise* though not necessarily of uniform (constant) *amplitude,* a *narrow band* of the spectrum in which the amplitudes of the waves are low or zero, that is, they may not be present. Also see *notched noise.*

notch antenna.   An *antenna* that forms a *radiation pattern* by means of a *notch* or slot in a *radiating* surface. Its characteristics are similar to those of a properly proportioned metal *dipole antenna* and may be evaluated with similar techniques.

notched card.   See *edge-notched card.*

notched noise.   *Noise* that is distributed over a wide *frequency spectrum* and in which one or more *narrow bands* of *frequencies* have been removed.

notch filter. A *filter* that passes all *frequencies* except for a single extremely *narrow band.* The *frequency response curve* is constant over all frequencies, except at a narrow band, where the response curve dips to zero and recovers, giving the appearance-of a deep trough or valley (notch) in a long mountain chain or plateau.

notice. See *go-ahead notice; stop notice.*

not-if-then gate. See *A-AND-NOT-B gate.*

not-obtainable signal. In a *communication system,* a *signal* that is sent in the *backward direction* and that indicates that a *call* cannot be *completed* because the *called party's number (line)* is not in use or is in a different *user group* or different *user class.*

not-ready condition. In a *communication system,* a *steady-state condition* at the *data terminal equipment (DTE)* and *data circuit-terminating equipment (DCE) interface* that denotes that the DCE is not ready to accept a *call request signal* or that the DTE is not ready to accept an incoming *call.* The not-ready condition may be controlled or uncontrolled.

not-ready signal. See *controlled not-ready signal.*

NRZ. *Non-return-to-zero.*

NRZ-B. See *non-return-to-zero mark (NRZ-M).*

NRZ-C. *Non-return-to-zero change.*

NRZ coding. *Non-return-to-zero coding.*

NRZ-L. *Non-return-to-zero level.*

NRZ-M. *Non-return-to-zero mark.*

NRZ1 magnetic recording. A *non-return-to-zero change magnetic recording* in which 1's are represented by a change in *magnetic condition* and 0's are represented by no change.

NRZ-S. *Non-return-to-zero space.*

nuclear hardening. See *fiber-optic nuclear hardening.*

NUL. *Null character.*

null. See *node.*

null (NUL) character. **1.** In *transmission systems,* a *control character* that is used to accomplish a *media*-fill *(stuffing),* or a *time*-fill *(stuffing)* in *storage* or in *data transmission* and that may be inserted and removed from a series of *characters* without affecting the meaning of the series. However, the control of equipment or the *format* of *messages* may be affected by the null character. **2.** In *cryptosystems,* a letter that is inserted into an *encrypted message* in order to delay or prevent its solution, to complete *encrypted* groups for *transmission,* or for *transmission security* purposes.

NULL gate. A device that produces a *signal,* or a sequence of signals, that represents *strings* of 0's in a given *system,* using a specified convention of representation, for as long as the *power* is on. The null gate output may be controlled or uncontrolled by an *input* control on-off signal. The NULL gate is the inverse of a *GENERATOR gate.* See Figure N-7.

IN A	0	1	B IN
0	0	0	
			Q OUT
1	0	0	

N-7. A table showing the *input* and *output digits* of a **NULL gate.**

null string. A *string* in which the number of entities in the string is reduced to zero.

number. In *communication systems,* an *identifier,* such as a *string* of *numerals,* assigned to an *end-instrument.* See *binary number; F-number; prime number; significant condition number; spot number; telephone number; T-number; wave number.*

number call. A *telephone call* to a *user's* (customer's, subscriber's, *called party's) number* rather than the the user's name. Calls to a number usually speed service. An *operator* can proceed to other business as soon as anyone at the number answers, thus allowing the *calling party* to seek the proper person at the destination (called) number. Also, in an *automatically-switched system, operator* assistance is not required. This is usually called a *station-to-station call.* Also see *local call; person-to-person call; station-to-station call.*

numbering equipment. See *automatic numbering equipment.*

numbering transmitter. See *automatic numbering transmitter.*

number sequence. See *pseudorandom number sequence.*

number-unobtainable tone. In *telephone switchboard operations,* an audible indication that a *dialed number* is unobtainable for some reason other than that the *number (line)* is *busy* or that the number *(called party)* does not answer.

numeral. A *graphic* or *discrete* representation of a number. For example, the number of fingers on a person's hand may be represented by the *numeral* five (a *word* in the English language), by the numeral 5 (an Arabic numeral in the *decimal* numeration system), by the numeral V (a Roman numeral), and by the numeral 101 (a numeral in the *pure binary numeration system*). See *ship radio-telephone numeral.*

numeral flag. In *visual communication systems,* a *flag* that is used to represent one of the *numerals* from 0 through 9. The numeral flag is square. On it, a pattern of colors is used to represent the numerals. Each of the 10 numeral flags has a different color pattern. Also see *numeral pennant.*

numeral pennant. In *visual communication systems,* a *pennant* that is used to represent one of the *numerals* from 0 through 9. The pennant is elongated and tapered and flown or hung with the base of the taper at the *halyard.* On it, a pattern of colors is used to represent the numerals. Each of the 10 numeral pennants has a different color pattern. Also see *numeral flag.*

numeral sign. In *semaphore communications,* the *flag position* that is used before and after each group of *numerals,* or groups of mixed letters and numerals, in the *text* of a *message.* The numeral sign is used to indicate that the group of mixed numerals and letters, or numerals only, is to be considered and recorded as a single group. This is particularly important when *codes* are being used in order that each *code group* is separately identifiable.

numerical aperture (N.A.). A measure of the *light*-accepting property of an *optical fiber.* For example, glass; given by:

$$\text{N.A.} = (n_1{}^2 - n_2{}^2)^{1/2}$$

i.e., the square root of the difference of the squares of the *refractive indices* of the *core, n_1,* and the *cladding, n_2.* If n_1 is 1.414 (glass) and n_2 is 1.0 (air), the *numerical aperture* is 1.0 and all *incident rays* will be trapped. The numerical aperture is a measure of the characteristic of an *optic conductor* in terms of its acceptance of impinging *light.* The degree of openness, light-gathering ability, *angular acceptance,* and *acceptance cone* are all terms describing the characteristic. It may be necessary to specify that the *refractive indices* are for *step index fibers* and for *graded index fibers;* n_1 is the maximum index in the core and n_2 is the minimum index in the cladding. As a number, the N.A. expresses the lightgathering power of a fiber. It is mathematically equal to the sine of the acceptance angle. A method of measuring the N.A. is to excite the fiber in the *visible* region and *display* the light emerging from the end perpendicularly on a *screen* about 10 to 30 cm away. The measured diameter of the projected circle of light divided by twice the distance from the fiber end to the screen is the numerical aperture. The numerical aperture is also equal to the sine of the half-angle of the widest *bundle* of *rays* capable of entering a *lens,* multiplied by the refractive index of the *medium* containing that bundle of rays, i.e., the incident medium. Typical numerical apertures for *plastic clad fused silica optical fibers* range from 0.25 to 0.45. Also see *focus depth.* See Figure N-8.

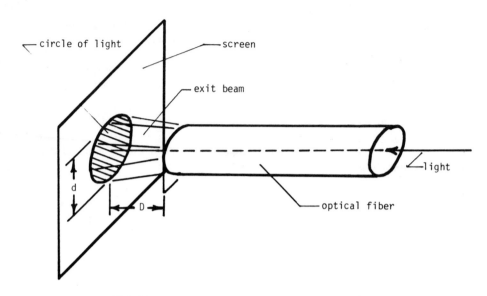

N-8. Measurement of **numerical aperture** as $NA = d/2D$.

numeric character set. A *character set* that contains *digits* and that may contain *control characters, special characters,* and the *space character,* but not letters.

numeric character subset. A *character subset* that contains *digits* and that may contain *control characters, special characters,* and the *space character,* but not letters.

numeric code. A *code* in which a *numeric character set* is used to represent *data.*

numeric coded character set. A *numeric character set* that is used to *code characters* that may be *numeric* characters, or nonnumeric characters, such as letters, special signs and *symbols,* the *space character,* or *control characters.* For example, the character set of a *binary coded decimal code,* or the character set of the *International Telegraph Alphabet Number 5 (ITA-5)* from which the *ASCII* code is derived and in which patterns of binary digits are used to represent the characters. Thus, each character of the set is represented by a *numeral.*

numeric data. *Data* that is represented entirely by *numerals.*

numeric representation. A *discrete* representation of *data* in which only *numerals* are used.

numeric word. A group of *digits* that represents *data* and to which meaning has been assigned. It normally consists of *digits* and possibly the *space character* and other *special characters* such as the parentheses and the decimal point or comma. For example, the numeric word 61(03) = 20 is used in the Universal Decimal Classification to mean any medical encyclopedia in English.

n-unit code. A *code* in which the *signals* or groups of *digits* that represent *coded items,* such as *characters,* have the same number of *signal elements* or digits, namely n elements or digits, where n may be any positive *integer.* For example, the *International Telegraph Alphabet Number 5 (ITA-5)* from which the *ASCII* code is derived, is a 7-unit code (8-unit with parity). Each character is represented by a pattern of 7 *binary digits.* The units may also be characters or other special signs. For example, in some *cryptosystems* a 5-unit code is used, each *code group* consisting of 5 characters, such as letters.

nutation. The nodding of the axis of a spinning top about the cone of precession. The effect is caused by *impulses* or rearrangement of the masses of the top. Special equipment for *damping* this effect is normally fitted to *satellites* that use spin stabilization.

nu value. See *abbe constant.*

Nyquist interval. The maximum time interval that must be allowed between regularly spaced *samples* of a *signal* in order that the signal waveform can be completely determined. The Nyquist interval, expressed in *seconds,* is equal to the reciprocal of twice the *bandwidth,* expressed in *hertz,* of the *sampled signal,* that is, in seconds per sample.

Nyquist noise. See *thermal noise.*

Nyquist rate. A minimum theoretical *sampling rate* for a *signal* waveform that allows recovery of the signal at a point that is distant from the *transmitter.* It is equal to the reciprocal of the *Nyquist interval* and thus is expressed in samples per *second.* The Nyquist interval is expressed in seconds per sample.

O

object. In an *optical system,* the figure viewed through or *imaged* by the optical system. It may consist of natural or artificial structures or targets, or may be the *real* or *virtual image* of an object formed by another optical system. In the field of *optics,* an object should be thought of as an aggregation of points. See *sine-wave object.*

objective. In an *optical system,* the *optical component* that receives *light* from the *object* and forms the first or primary *image.* In cameras, the image formed by the objective is the final image. In telescopes and microscopes, when used visually, the image formed by the objective is *magnified* by use of an *eyepiece.* See *call completion objective; design objective.*

object plane. In an *optical system,* the plane that contains the *object* points lying within the field of view.

object point. In an *optical system,* any point on an *object* that is usually also identifiable on an *image* of the object.

oblate spheroid. The surface that is obtained by spinning an ellipse about its minor axis. The shape of the earth approximates that of an oblate spheroid, namely it bulges at the equator. The primary distortion of the oblate spheroid is the pear-shape, that is, the southern hemisphere is slightly larger than the northern hemisphere. The polar radius is 6357 km and the equatorial radius is 6378 km.

oblique-incidence sounding. The *transmission* of an *electromagnetic wave* obliquely to a surface and back again, particularly to the *ionosphere* and back. The *incidence angle* with the normal to the surface of the ionosphere that is used in ionospheric sounding (measuring the height) is of the order of $20°$ to $40°$.

obliquity. See *eliptic obliquity.*

obstruction. See *propagation path obstruction.*

occluder. In *optics,* a device that completely or partially limits the amount of *light* reaching the eye.

occultation. An *eclipse* of a celestial body by the moon. A special case is the solar eclipse, in which the sun is eclipsed by the moon as observed from a point on earth.

occupied bandwidth. In *electromagnetic wave transmission,* the *frequency band-width* that is bounded by limits such that below its lower limit and above its upper limit the mean power *radiated* are each equal to 0.5% of the total mean power that is radiated. Thus, it is the band of frequencies that is occupied by an *emission* comprising 99% of the total radiated power. It includes any *discrete* frequency at which the power is at least 0.25% of the total radiated power. For example, in *multichannel frequency-division multiplexing systems,* use of the 0.5% limits may lead to certain difficulties in the practical application of the criteria for the occupied bandwidth and the *necessary bandwidth.* In such cases a different set of criteria may prove useful. These considerations are used in determining *frequency allocations* and *assignments.* Also see *necessary bandwidth; nominal bandwidth; radio frequency bandwidth.*

occurrence time. In *communication systems,* the *date* of an event when it is referred to a particular *time scale.* (The date is an instant on a particular time scale.)

octave. See *frequency octave.*

octet. A group or *byte* that consists of eight *binary digits* and is usually operated upon as a single entity. An octet, or 8-bit byte, is used in the *International Telegraph Alphabet Number 5 (ITA-5),* from which the *ASCII* is derived, to represent each *character,* including the *parity bit.*

octet alignment. The temporal and spatial positioning of an *octet* with respect to a *time frame* or a spatial frame of reference.

octet timing signal. A *signal* that identifies each *octet* in a contiguous sequence of *serially transmitted* octets. It usually identifies the first *bit* in each octer.

odd-even check. See *parity check.*

odd parity. *Parity* in which the number of 1's, or marks, in a group of *binary digits,* or in a group of *mark* and *space signaling elements,* such as those that comprise a *character* or *word,* is always maintained as an odd numer, including the *parity bit* itself. Thus, the 1's in a group, such as a 7-bit *byte,* are counted. If the number is even, a 1 bit is added to the byte, making it an 8-bit byte with an odd number of 1's. During *processing* or *transmission* at various points in a *system,* the number of 1's is counted in each byte. The count must always be odd or an *error* will be indicated.

off-axis paraboloidal mirror. A *paraboloidal mirror* that has a paraboloidal surface through which the *optical axis* does not pass.

off-frequency jamming. See *spot off-frequency jamming.*

off-hook. 1. In *telephone operations,* the conditions that exist when the *receiver* or handset of a *telephone* instrument, or other piece of equipment that is similarly operated, is removed from its *switch,* that is, it is changed from its rest or non-use condition. 2. One of the two possible *signaling* states, such as tone or no tone, *ground connection* or battery connection, or on or off, that is opposite to the *on-hook* condition. 3. The active state *(closed-loop)* of a *user* (subscriber, customer) *loop* or a *private branch exchange (PBX)* user loop. Also see *on-hook*. See *verified off-hook*.

off-hook service. 1. In *telephone systems,* the automatic establishment of a *connection* between specified *users* (customers, subscribers) that is made as a result of lifting the handset off the hook, that is, off its rest or cradle. 2. A type of *telephone service* that is based on a situation in which a single action on the part of one *user* (customer, subscriber) automatically establishes a *connection* directly and immediately with another user or set of users. For example, the lifting of a handset off its cradle, hook, or rest position, immediately causes a prearranged *number* or group of numbers to *ring*. The service makes use of two *signaling* states, such as tone or no tone, ground or battery, or on and off.

off-hook signal. In *switching systems,* a *signal* that indicates a *seizure* of a *line,* a request for service, or a *busy* condition. The signal is usually transmitted when a *user* actuates a *switch* on an *end-instrument,* such as by lifting a *telephone receiver* off of its cradle, hook, or rest position.

office. See *destination office; originating office.*

office automation. The organization and integration of several applications of *computers* and *networks* to accomplish office work. For example, word-processing (dictation and document preparation), *computer*-based filing *(information storage* and retrieval and *data banking), communication* (electronic mail, electronic *message service,* and *teleconferencing*), financial accounting (electronic funds transfer), management information systems, and computerized commerce are some of the applications of office automation.

officer. See *message releasing officer; senior ship radio officer.*

officer-of-the-watch. See *radio officer-of-the-watch.*

office trunk. See *cross-office trunk.*

off-line. In *communication systems,* pertaining to the *operation* and use of devices and *components* that are not directly connected to the system and therefore are not available for immediate use on demand by the system without human intervention. Inasmuch as these devices do not form part of the system relative to which they are off-line, they are not subject to the same controls as those devices that are *online*. These devices may be operated independently of the system relative to which they are considered to be off-line and they may be operated independently of each other.

off-line cryptographic operation. *Cryptosystem operation* in which the processes of *encryption* and *transmission,* or *reception* and *decryption,* are performed in separate steps rather than automatically and simultaneously with transmission and reception. Encryption and decryption in *off-line cryptographic operation* is usually performed as a self-contained operation, similar to the use of hand machines that are not connected to the line. The encryption process is not associated with any *transmission mode* and therefore the resulting *cryptogram* can be transmitted by any means.

off-line equipment.   1. In *data transmission,* equipment that provides *data* to, or accepts *data* from, intermediate *storage* and not directly to or from a *transmission line*.   2. In *communication systems,* equipment that is not connected to a transmission line. Thus, *signals* cannot pass to or from the equipment and the *line* without *operator* intervention.   3. In *computing* and *data processing systems,* equipment that is not under the direct or continual control of a computer or a data processing system.

off-line recovery.   In a *communication system,* the process of recovering non-protected *message traffic* by use of an *off-line processor.*

off-net calling.   In *communications,* calling in which *calls* that originate from, or are destined for, *users* in nonnetwork entities, are handled by a given communication *network.*   For example, the handling of a call from a private local *telephone* network by a military telephone network to a *party* in the military network, or the handling of a call from a military network to a party in a commercial network; or the use of a private or commercial telephone network from a *user* in a military network to a user in the same military network but at a great distance away.

off-net extension.   Relative to a given *communication network,* such as a *telephone* or *telegraph network,* the ability of an *exchange* or *switching center* to extend an incoming *call* into another network.   Normally *off-net calling* from outside-the-net *calling parties* may not be within the mission requirements of the *local net.*   Off-net extension accomodation rests with the local net authority.

offset.   See *frequency offset.*

offset prime-focus feed.   A specialized arrangement for *coupling* a *transmitter output signal* to an *antenna.*

offset voltage.   See *common-return offset voltage.*

off-the-air monitoring.   1. In *radio net communication operations,* the *monitoring* by the *net control station* of the *transmissions* of stations in the net, particularly to check the quality of their transmissions.   The monitoring is usually performed during periods when the net control station is not transmitting. 2. The act of a *station's* listening to its own *transmission* by receiving the *signal* that has been transmitted from the transmitting *antenna,* in order to discover the quality of the signal that is being transmitted to other stations or is being *broadcasted.* To be off-the-air, the received signal must have traveled through the air some distance from the transmitting antenna and not be a signal that is *tapped* on its way to the transmitting antenna internal to the station or in the antenna *transmission line* or *feeder.*

off-the-shelf hardware. Equipment that has already been produced, is available, and is ready for use.

OFTF. *Optical fiber transfer function.*

oligarchically synchronized network. In *communication systems,* a *synchronized network* in which the *timing signals* of all *clocks* in the network are controlled by a few selected clocks. Also see *democratically synchronized network; despotically synchronized network; hierarchically synchronized network.*

omnidirectional antenna. An *antenna* that has a *radiation pattern* that is nondirectional in *azimuth,* that is, the *electric field intensity* measured some distance from the *antenna* is the same in all directions of azimuth. It may be a *transmitting* or *receiving antenna* that is capable of transmitting or receiving *electromagnetic signals* in many or all directions with nearly equal power in each direction. Also see *directional antenna.*

omnidirectional radio range. A *radionavigation aid* that creates an infinite number of paths in space throughout $360°$ of *azimuth* and *elevation angle.* Synonymous with *omnirange.* See *very-high frequency omnidirectional radio range.*

omnidirectional range station. A *radionavigation land station* that is in the *aeronautical radionavigation service* and provides a direct indication of its *bearing* from an aircraft.

omnidirectional signaling system. A *signaling system* in which *signals* are *transmitted* in nearly equal *intensity* or *power density* in all directions, or at least in a given plane such as the horizontal plane. For example, a *light* bulb without a *reflector* or a *dipole antenna.*

on black. See *phasing on black.*

on-call patching service. A *communication service* that is provided by a *communication system* between authorized *users* and in which a temporary *path* is created between them in order to fulfil an unanticipated or special communication request.

on-demand call tracing. *Call tracing* of a specific *call* that is performed on request, particularly during the *information transfer phase* of a call. It may also be performed during the *disengagement phase,* or after the *circuits* are disconnected.

one gate. See *OR gate.*

one-operator ship. In *radiotelegraph communications,* a *ship station* that has only one *radiotelegraph operator. Messages* for a specific one-operator ship station are received and held for that station during nonoperational periods and transmitted to that station during its *operational* period by other stations, which may be ship stations or *shore stations.* If ship stations, the guard watch can be rotated, particularly if they are in the same convoy or in immediate ocean areas.

one-way communication. *Communication* in which *information* can be *transferred* in only one preassigned direction.

one-way-only channel. A *channel* that is capable of *operation* in only one fixed direction and cannot be reversed. Synonymous with *unidirectional channel.*

one-way operation. In a *communication system,* pertaining to a *transmission operation* between two points such that transmission takes place only from one point to the other and not back, regardless of the transmission equipment capability to perform otherwise.

one-way radio equation. An equation that expresses the *signal power* at the receiving *antenna terminals* as a function of many constants and *parameters,* such as the transmitted *power,* receiving *antenna gain,* transmitting antenna gain, *wavelength, transmitter-to-receiver range, frequency,* and *bandwidth.* Also see *two-way radar equation; self-screening range equation.*

one-way reversible operation. See *half-duplex operation.*

one-way trunk. In *communication systems,* a *trunk* between *switching centers* that is used for *traffic* in one fixed preassigned direction. One-way trunks are normally used to collect a particular *switching center's* originating traffic for *transmission* to a particular destination. At the traffic originating end, the one-way trunk is known as an outgoing trunk. At the other end, it is known as an incoming trunk.

on-hook. **1.** In *telephone operations,* the conditions that exist when the *receiver* or handset of a *telephone instrument,* or other piece of equipment that is similarly operated, is resting on its *switch,* that is, is in its cradle in a rest or non-use condition. **2.** One of the two possible *signaling* states, such as tone or no tone, ground connection or battery connection, or on or off, that is opposite to the *off-hook* condition. **3.** The *idle state* (open-loop) of a *user* (subscriber, customer) *loop* or *private branch exchange (PBX)* user loop. Also see *off-hook.*

on-hook signal. In *switching systems,* a *signal* that indicates a disconnect, an unanswered call, or an *idle state.* The signal is usually *transmitted* when the *switch* on an *end-instrument* is allowed to remain undisturbed in its cradle, hook, or rest position.

online. **1.** In *communication systems,* pertaining to the direct *connection, operation,* and control of devices and *components* for immediate use on demand by a system, normally without human intervention. **2.** In *automatic data processing,* pertaining to *operations,* equipment, or devices that are under the direct control of, or in direct *communication* with, a *processor.* **3.** Pertaining to a condition in which devices or subsystems are connected to, form a part of, and are subject to the same controls as the other *components* of the system to which they are connected. **4.** In *transmission systems,* a method of transmission in which *signals* from *communication* equipment are passed directly to a *channel* or *circuit* to operate one or more *compatible* pieces of equipment at one or more distant *stations,* and usually, though not necessarily, without *operator* intervention. **5.**

In *cryptographic radio* and wire *teletype, telegraph,* and *secure voice communication systems,* pertaining to the capability of *encryption* and *decryption* of *messages* automatically at the send and receiving *stations* without *operator* intervention or copying the message in *encrypted* form.

online cryptographic operation. A method of *cryptosystem operation* that involves the use of *cryptoequipment* that is directly connected to a *line* and that makes *encryption* and *transmission,* or *reception* and *decryption,* or both, a single process. This method of operation involves an automatic method of encryption that is associated with a particular transmission system in which *messages* are encrypted and passed directly to a line to operate decryption equipment at one or more distant *stations.* The *user* of such a system may not be aware of the encryption-decryption process, but the user is aware of the *security* classification of the messages.

online equipment. 1. In *data transmission,* equipment that provides *data* directly to, or accepts data directly from, a *transmission line* without intermediate storage. 2. In a *communication system,* equipment, such as a *switch* or a *user end-instrument,* that is connected directly to the system. *Signals* can pass from the online equipment to the system and to other online equipment without *operator intervention.* 3. In *computing* and *data processing systems,* equipment that is under the direct or continual control of a computer or data processing system.

on white. See *phasing on white.*

opaque. 1. A quality of material that makes it impervious to *light,* and therefore reduces its *luminous transmittance* to zero. 2. A substance that is impervious to *light* applied to *transparent* or *translucent* substances. 3. To make impervious to *light.*

opcode. See *operation code.*

open. In *display systems,* to prepare a specific sequence of graphic or *display commands* in order that the segment may accept additional commands. Contrast with *close.*

open circuit. 1. In electrical engineering, a single electrical loop or path that closes on itself but that contains in infinite *impedance.* 2. In *communication systems,* a *circuit,* such as a *signal path, line,* or *channel,* that is available for use.

open systems architecture. The structure, *configuration,* or model of a *distributed data processing system* or *network* that enables system design, development, and operation to be described as a *hierarchical structure* or a *layering* of functions. In the concept, each layer provides a set of accessible functions that can be used by the functions in the layer above it. Thus, layers can be implemented without affecting the implementation of other layers. The concept is useful since it permits the alteration of system performance without disturbing the huge investment in existing equipment or procedures, since the alterations can be made at the higher levels or at the lower levels. For example, converting from wire to *optical fibers* at the *physical layer* need not affect the *data link layer* or *network layer* except to provide more *traffic capacity*. Also see Figures L-2 and P-15.

open systems interconnection (OSI). The interconnection of *data processing systems* and *communication networks,* usually using standard procedures.

open waveguide. A *waveguide* in which *electromagnetic waves* are guided by a *refractive index gradient* so that the waves are confined to the guide by *refraction* within, or *reflection* from, the outer surface of the guide. Thus, the electromagnetic waves propagate, without *radiation,* along the *interface* between different *media.* For example, an *optical fiber.* Also see *closed waveguide.*

open wire. *Electrical conductors* that are separately supported above the surface of the earth. They are not sheathed in *cables* and they may or may not be *insulated.*

operand. The object or variable that is operated upon by an *operator.* For example, in the expression A+B, the A and the B are operands. The + sign is an operator.

operate mode. See *compute mode.*

operating agency. In *communication system operations,* the agency or authority that is responsible for or that controls the *operation* of a *communication network* or communication system. See *telecommunication private operating agency (TPOA).*

operating instruction. See *standing communication operating instruction (SCOI).*

operating method. See *radiotelegraph operating method.*

operating signal. A group of *characters* that are used as necessary in *communication operations* to convey orders, *instructions,* requests, reports, or other *information* to facilitate communications. For example, operating signals may be groups of three letters that are sometimes followed by a *numeral* and that may begin with an 0 or a Z. They are used as a *brevity code* to express various stereotyped phrases that are encountered in the daily conduct of communication operations. In voice systems, they may be simple *prosigns* or *prowords,* such as OVER, ROGER, and OUT.

operating space. See *display space.*

operating time. See *system operating time.*

operation. 1. In *communication systems,* the method, act, process, or effect of operating a device or *system.* 2. In general, an action that, when applied to an entity, or combination of entities, produces a new entity. For example, the action of obtaining a result from one or more *operands* in accordance with a rule; a program step that involves the execution of an *instruction* in a *computer pro-*

gram to produce a result; the action that is performed by a *combinational logic element, logic gate,* or *logic circuit* to produce an output; or the insertion of a *switchboard plug* into a *jack* to create a *circuit* or connect a *line.* See *asynchronous operation; AUTODIN operation; auxiliary operation; balanced link-level operation; bit-by-bit asynchronous operation; bit-synchronous operation; broadcast operation; centralized operation; coherent pulse operation; conference operation; continuous operation; cross-polarized operation; detector noise-limited operation; diplex operation; dispersion-limited operation; drop channel operation; fail-safe operation; half-duplex operation; multiplex operation; multimode operation; net operation; neutral operation; noncentralized operation; off-line cryptographic operation; one-way operation; one-way reversible operation; on-line cryptographic operation; packet mode operation; parallel operation; polar operation; push-to-talk operation; push-to-type operation; quantum-limited operation; repetitive operation; sequential operation; speech-plus-duplex operation; synchronous cryptooperation; thermal-noise-limited operation; unidirectional operation.*

operational amplifier. In *analog computing systems* and in *communication systems,* a high-*gain amplifier* that is connected to external elements in order to perform specific *operations* or functions, such as multiplication by a constant.

operational control. See *change in operational control.*

operational load. See *nonoperational load.*

operational test land station. See *radionavigation operational test land station.*

operation instruction. See *signal operation instruction (SOI).*

operational network control. In a *communication network,* the control and implementation of functions that prevent or eliminate degradation of any part of the *network,* of the *response* to changes in the network to meet longe range requirements, and of the immediate response to demands that are placed on the network. Some of these functions are immediate *circuit* utilization action; continuous control of circuit quality; continuous control of equipment performance; development of procedures for immediate repair, restoration, or replacement of *facilities* or equipment; continuous liaison with network *users* and with representatives of other networks; and the rendering of advice and assistance in network use, including instruction in use and use restraint when appropriate.

operational load. In a *communication system,* the total *power* requirement for *communication facilities.* Also see *nonoperational load.*

operational service period. In *communication and telecommunication systems,* a *performance measurement period,* or succession of performance measurement periods, during which a *communication* or *telecommunication service* remains in an *operational service state.* An operational service period begins at the beginning of the performance measurement period in which the communication or telecommunication service enters the operational service state, and ends at the beginning of the performance measurement period in which the communication or telecommunication service leaves the operational service state.

operational service state. A *communication* or *telecommunication service* condition that exists during any *performance measurement period* over which the calculated values of specified supported *performance parameters* are equal to or better than their associated *outage thresholds.*

operation code (opcode). In *communication systems,* a *code* that is used for immediate and rapid *communication* during written and oral exchanges of *information* among operating, maintenance, and management personnel. The codes consist of *words* and phrases, with prearranged or assigned meanings, that are capable of being pronounced or spelled, usually both. Nearly all of them are contractions of terms in this dictionary. For example, the word opstate may be used for operational service state, the word zeezero (Z_o) might be used for the *characteristic impedance* of a *transmission line,* or the word disc for *disconnect command.*

operation net. In *tactical* or *strategic military communication systems,* a *communication net* that is used primarily for the exchange of *messages* that are in support of tactical or strategic military operations.

operations communication net. See *maritime tactical air operations communication net.*

operator. 1. In *telephone switchboard operation,* the person at a *switchboard position* who connects *calling parties* to *trunks* of *called parties,* sets up *multiple calls,* completes *call tickets,* and performs such other functions as may be required to handle *telephone traffic* and inquiries. 2. In a *communication system,* a person who interacts with the system to insure successful *operation* of the system, for example, a *teletype* operator, a *facsimile system* operator, or a *computer* operator. 3. In the description of a process, such as an arithmetic or logic *operation,* that which performs an action or indicates an action to be performed on an item or an object, called an *operand.* The operator may be a *symbol,* a person, a machine, or anything else capable of action. For example, the + sign in the arithmetic operation A+B, the OR in the Boolean operation A OR B as might be performed by an *OR gate,* the differentiating operator d/dt for taking the time derivative of a function of time, or the exponent in x^2. See *delay operator; radio operator; real-time operator; telecommunication system operator.* Also see Figures C-1 and L-6.

operator-assisted call. A *call* that is established with the help of a person *(operator)* rather than with the assistance of *automatic switching* and related equipment only.

operator delay. In a *communication system,* the time from a request for service by a *user* (customer, subscriber) for *operator* assistance until the operator commences to process the service request.

operator log. In a *communication system,* a chronological record of events that relate to the operation of a particular *system,* subsystem, or *component,* such as a *line, circuit, group, trunk, link, exchange, station, transmitter,* or *receiver.*

operator-period station. In *communication systems, a station* that is not operated on a continuous 168 hour/week basis. For example, a station that operates with a *single-operator period watch,* or a station that is not operated between sunset and sunrise. Also see *constant-watch station.* See *single-operator period watch; two-operator period watch.*

operator ship station. See *one-operator ship station.*

operator signaling. See *remote operator signaling.*

optic. See *acoustooptic; electrooptic; fiber-optic.*

optical. **1.** Pertaining to the field of *optics.* **2.** Pertaining to eyesight. **3.** Pertaining to systems, devices, or components that generate, process, and detect *lightwaves* or *light* energy, such as *lasers; lens systems; optical fibers, bundles,* and *cables;* and *photodetectors.*

optical adaptive technique. See *coherent optical adaptive technique.*

optical analyzer. See *multichannel optical analyzer.*

optical attenuator. In an *optical-fiber data link* or *integrated optical circuit,* a device used to reduce the *intensity* of the *lightwaves* when inserted serially into an *optical waveguide.* Three basic forms of *optical attenuators* have been developed—namely, a fixed optical attenuator, a stepwise variable optical attenuator, and a continuous variable optical attenuator. One form of attenuator uses a *filter* consisting of a metal film evaporated onto a sheet of glass to obtain the attenuation. The filter might be tilted to avoid reflection back into the input *optical* fiber or *cable.* See *continuous variable optical attenuator; fixed optical attenuator; stepwise variable optical attenuator.*

optical axis. **1.** The line formed by the coinciding *principal axes* of a series of *optical* elements comprising an *optical system.* **2.** The line passing through the centers of curvatures of the *optical* surfaces. **3.** The *optical* centerline.

optical cable. See *aerial optical cable; central strength-member optical cable; duct optical cable; flat optical cable; peripheral strength-member optical cable; plow-in optical cable; special optical cable.* Also see Figure S-9.

optical cable driver. A device, consisting of several modules, that accepts electrical *pulses* from a wire or *transmission medium,* converts them to *lightwave pulses,* and *couples* them to an *optical fiber, bundle,* or *cable.* The modules are amplifiers, *modulated light sources,* and *optical couplers.* The unit is usually capable of launching *modulated lightwaves* into an *optical cable* and usually consists of an input channel for modulating the *light source,* a *light source* capable of being modulated, such as an *LED* or *laser,* and an output *coupling* means, such as a connector or *optical fiber pigtail.*

optical cavity. A geometric bounded space in which *lightwaves* can *reflect* back and forth to thus produce *standing waves* of high intensity at certain *frequencies.* Such standing waves might be obtained in a ruby crystal *laser* with two plane or spherical *mirrors,* forming a cavity (i.e., the crystal itself between the mirrors) in which the molecules can be excited by an inert gas lamp, thus generating and emitting a *monochromatic light* of high intensity in the direction of the crystal axis. Some *light-emitting diodes* have large optical cavities.

optical cavity diode. See *large optical-cavity diode.*

optical cement. A permanent and *transparent* adhesive capable of withstanding extremes of *temperature.* Canada balsam is a classic *optical* cement, although it is being replaced by modern synthetic adhesives, such as methacrylates, caprinates, and epoxies.

optical character recognition (OCR). The use of *optical* means to identify optical *characters,* i.e., graphic characters. It particularly includes the machine identification of printed characters through the use of *light*-sensitive devices, such as *facsimile scanners* and other optical scanners.

optical chopper. A device for periodically interrupting a *light beam.* For example, a rotating disk with radial slots through which a *collimated beam* must pass, or an *electronically controllable coupler* that uses the *peizoelectric effect* to move a *mirror* or change the *refractive index* and thus interrupt a *lightwave.*

optical circuit. See *integrated optical circuit; lithium niobate integrated optical circuit.*

optical circuit filter-coupler-switch modulator. See *integrated-optical circuit filter-coupler-switch modulator.*

optical communication system. A *communication system* that makes use of *optical systems* and components such as *light sources, transmission media,* and *photodetectors,* perhaps in conjunction with *display systems* and conventional communication systems. *Visual signaling systems,* such as those that use *heliographs, semaphores,* ship *pennants,* ground *panels, flares,* or smoke signals, are not considered as optical communication systems. Contrast with *visual communication system.*

optical conduction. The *propagation* or *transmission* of *lightwaves* through a *transmission medium* in which the waves are guided from a *light source* to a *photodetector* with minimal loss of light energy by *absorption, dispersion, deflection, reflection,* or *diffusion,* such that the intelligence carried by the modulated lightwaves at the source can be recovered at the end of the transmission medium.

optical conductor. Materials that offer a low *optical attenuation* to *transmission of light* energy. Conductors may be arranged as *single fibers, bundles, single-channel single-bundle cables, multichannel single-fiber cables, single-channel single-fiber cables, multichannel bundle cables,* and *multichannel cables.*

optical conductor loss. See *connector-induced optical-conductor loss.*

optical contact. A condition in which two sufficiently clean and close-fitting surfaces adhere together without *reflection* at the *interface.* The *optically* contacted surface is practically as strong as the body of the glass.

optical countermeasure. A measure or action that is taken to deliberately prevent the use of the *visible spectrum,* that is the portion of the *electromagnetic spectrum* from *infrared* to *ultraviolet.* See *active optical countermeasure.*

optical data processing. The performance of *data-processing operations* that model or *simulate* actual *systems* that are represented by the mathematical functions and relationships governing the behavior of *light* passing through *optical elements,* such as by making use of *diffraction patterns, interference* patterns, *reflection* patterns, *transmission* through variously shaped optical elements, and *wavefront* transformation. For example, Fourier-transform optical-wave analysis can be used to perform ocean-wave analysis, *antenna pattern* analysis, *phased-array radar signal processing,* linear *frequency modulated* stepped-radar signal processing, *wideband* signal processing, *spread-spectrum* systems analysis, and folded *spectrum* applications, and for performing *filtering* and *image* and word *pattern recognition.*

optical density. The logarithm to the base 10 of the reciprocal of *transmittance.* See *internal optical density.*

optical detector. A device that converts the *optical power* or energy of a *signal* to other forms of power or energy representing the same signal or that controls other forms of energy or power in accordance with optical energy *incident* upon its sensitive surface. For example, an optical detector might convert a *lightwave pulse* to an electrical pulse. See *video optical detector.*

optical device. See *Bell integrated optical device.*

optical directional coupler. A *coupler* for use with *optical fibers, bundles,* and *cables* that operates on *lightwaves propagating* in one or both directions. Uses of the coupler include *tapping,* directional control of *propagation,* drop-inserting, monitoring, *branching, mixing,* and *wavelength multiplexing.* The directional coupler is used in *optical fiber communication systems,* such as CATV and *data-links* for optical fiber measurements, to combine or split optical *signals* at desired ratios by insertion into a *transmission* line; e.g., a three-or four-port unit with precise *connectors* at each *port* to enable inputs to be coupled together and transmitted via multiple outputs.

optical disk. A flat circular disk coated with a photosensitive medium on which *binary digits* in the form of light and dark spots may be stored by *modulation* of *light* from a *source* such as a *laser,* with *packing densities* of over 10^{10} bits per 30-cm-diameter disk, 10-Mbps recording rates, and 10^{-6} to 10^{-5} error rates.

optical dispersion attenuation. The *attenuation* of a *signal* in an *optical waveguide* caused by each *frequency component* of a launched *pulse* being attenuated such that higher frequencies are attenuated more than the lower frequencies, giving rise to attenuation distortion. The dispersion attenuation factor is given as:

$$D.A.F. = e^{-df^2}$$

where d is a material constant, including substance and geometry, and f is a frequency component of the signal being attenuated. Also see *dispersion attenuation factor*.

optical distortion.   An *abberation* of spherical-surface *optical systems* due to the variation in *magnification* with distance from the *optical axis*.

optical element.   A component or part of an *optical system*. For example, a *lens, prism, mirror, display device, LED, photodetector,* or *optical fiber, bundle,* or *cable*.

optical emitter.   A source of *optical power,* that is, a source of *electromagnetic radiation* in the *visible* and near-visible region of the *frequency spectrum*. See Figure O-1.

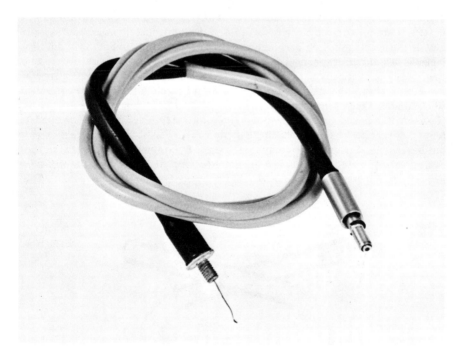

O-1. A high-speed gallium aluminum *infrared IR* **optical emitter** with an *integral fiber-optic output cable* and *connector,* designed to operate continuously at 200 mA producing 60μW of IR *optical power* with a 150-MHz *bandwidth.* (Courtesy of RCA Electro-optics and Devices.)

optical end-finish.   The surface condition at the face of an *optical conducting medium*.

optical energy density. The energy in a *light beam* passing through a unit area normal to the direction of *propagation* or the direction of maximum power gradient, expressed in joules/square meter.

optical fiber. A single discrete *optical transmission* element or *waveguide* usually consisting of a *fiber core* and a *fiber cladding* that can guide a *lightwave* and is usually cylindrical in shape. It consists either of a cylinder of *transparent dielectric* material of a given *refractive index* whose walls are in contact with a second dielectric material of a lower refractive index; or of a cylinder whose core has a refractive index that gets progressively lower away from the center. The length of a fiber is usually much greater than its diameter. The fiber relies upon *internal reflection* to *transmit light* along its *axial* length. Light enters one end of the fiber and emerges from the opposite end with losses dependent upon length, *absorption, scattering,* and other factors. A *bundle* of *fibers* has the ability to transmit a picture from one of its surfaces to another, around curves, and into otherwise inaccessible places with an extremely low loss of definition and light, by the process of *total internal reflection.* Each fiber transmits only one element of the composite emergent *image.* The definition in the output image depends on the size of each element composing it. It is desirable to keep the cross-section of the individual fibers as small as possible. If the spacing of the fibers increases toward the output end of the bundle, the image is *magnified;* if spacing is reduced, the image is reduced in size. By crossing the fibers systematically or randomly, the image is scrambled, and can be recovered by retransmitting the scrambled image backward through the same or equivalent fiber bundle. One optical fiber classification scheme is to divide them into plastic, glass, or plastic-clad fused silica fibers; then into step-index multimode, graded-index multimode, or step-index single mode fibers. Plastic is less brittle than glass but has increased *attenuation* compared to glass. Synonymous with *light pipe.* See *compensated optical fiber; over-compensated optical fiber; self-focusing optical fiber; triangular-cored optical fiber; undercompensated optical fiber.* See Figure O-2.

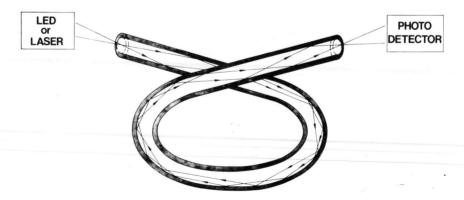

O-2. An **optical fiber** with *cladding.* (Courtesy of the Belden Corporation.)

optical-fiber acoustic sensor. A high-sensitivity device that senses *sound waves* by allowing the waves to impinge on a length of *optical fiber,* the waves causing variation in the *refractive indices* of the fiber which is used to *modulate light-waves,* usually from a *laser, propagating* in the fiber, to a *photodetector.* The sensor may be omnidirectional or unidirectional; for example, a wrapped ball of fiber would be omnidirectional and a planar mesh would be directionally sensitive.

optical-fiber active connector. An *optical connector* with a built-in *active device.* Examples of such devices include an electronically driven *LED,* a *laser,* a *photodetector,* or an electronic *transmitter.* The device is usually built into one of the mating elements of the connector, usually in the form of a *semiconductor chip* with an *optical fiber pigtail* for connection to a fiber. The connector is built to enable fiber-to-fiber or fiber-to-pigtail *coupling.* The combination results in an improved overall *coupling efficiency;* for example, one such connector provides 50 times normal coupling efficiency at 30 Mbps over a 1-km length. *Apertures* of the active semiconductors are about 0.20 mm for a 0.20-mm-diameter *core* with a *numerical aperture* of 0.48 and a 2-dB *insertion loss,* adaptable for *bulkhead* or printed-circuit-board mounting and *EMI* and *RFI* shielding.

optical-fiber bundle. Many *optical fibers* in a single protective *sheath* or *jacket.* The jacket is usually made of polyvinyl chloride (pvc). The number of fibers might range from a few to several hundred, depending on the application and the characteristics of the fibers.

optical-fiber circuit. See *hybrid optical fiber circuit.*

optical-fiber coating. A protective material bonded to an *optical fiber* over the *cladding,* if any, to preserve fiber strength and inhibit cabling losses by providing protection against mechanical damage, protection against moisture and debilitating environments, compatibility with fiber and cable manufacture, and compatibility with the *jacketing* process. Coatings include fluorpolymers, Teflon, Kynar, polyurethane, and many others. Application methods include dipcoating (for those in solution), extrusion, spray coating, and *electrostatic* coating.

optical-fiber communications. The use of physical *paths,* such as *lines, circuits,* and *links,* that are made of *optical fibers* between *terminals,* from terminals to *end-instruments,* between *exchanges* and *switching centers,* or between other *components* of a *communication system.* Also see *wireline communications.*

optical-fiber concentrator. A *communication system component* that *multiplexes* a number of separate incoming *optical fiber* communication *channels.* For example, a distribution box that accepts 3000 voice optical-fiber channels from *home optical transceivers, time-division multiplexes* them using ten 10-to-1 *multiplexers,* the output of each going into 30 more 10-to-1 multiplexers, the final output *modulating* a *lightwave carrier* in an *optical fiber;* or a unit that multiplexes 32 full duplex *digital data* channels on a single multiplexed *optical data link* or *cable.*

optical-fiber delay line. An *optical fiber* of precise length used to introduce a delay in a *lightwave pulse* equal to the time required for the pulse to *propagate* from beginning to end. The delay line may be used for operations such as *phase* adjustment, *pulse positioning, pulse interval coding,* or *storage.*

optical-fiber distribution box. A local *distribution box* used to connect *optical fibers* in *cables* from the *fiber distribution frame* to loops going to the *home optical transceiver* or other subscriber instrument.

optical-fiber distribution system. See *protected optical fiber distribution system.*

optical-fiber hazard. An injury-causing feature of an *optical fiber.* For example, flame-retardant treated *optical cables* can cause skin lesions; high-*radiation LEDs* or *lasers* can cause eye injury when staring at the output end; fragments of silica glass *core* or *cladding* can cause eye damage; and grinding and polishing residues of silica *powders* can cause respiratory tract damage. Precautions include use of gloves, goggles, and masks; during handling and processing operations frequent washing of all parts of the body is helpful.

optical-fiber jacket. The material that covers the buffered or unbuffered optical fiber.

optical-fiber junction. An *interface* formed by joining the ends of two *optical fibers* in a *coaxial* (in-line) *butt joint* for direct fiber-to-fiber *transmission.*

optical-fiber link. See *TV optical-fiber link.*

optical-fiber merit figure. A figure that indicates the ability of an *optical fiber* to handle high-*frequency signals* over given distances with specified *distortion* limits or *error rates.* For example, the *pulse repetition rate* times the fiber length when *pulse dispersion* is the specified limiting factor in signal distortion rather than *attenuation.* Another such figure of merit for *multimode fibers* is given by:

$$F_m = PL^{\Upsilon}$$

where $1/2 < \Upsilon < 1$, L is the length, and P is the pulse repetition rate.

optical-fiber preform. *Optical-fiber* material from which an optical fiber is made, usually by *drawing* or rolling. For example, a solid glass rod made with a higher *refractive index* than the tube into which it is slipped, to be heated and drawn or rolled into a *cladded* optical fiber; or four lower-refractive-index rods surrounding a higher-refractive-index rod heated and drawn into a *cladded fiber.*

The drawing process results in fiber many times longer than the preforms. See Figure O-3. Also see Figures C-5 and G-3.

O-3. **Optical fiber preforms.** A central rod, supporting plate, and tubing, all made of the same material, will be drawn into a *single optical fiber* several *microns* in diameter. (Courtesy of Bell Laboratories.)

optical-fiber pulse compression. In the *transmission* of *pulses* in *optical fibers,* the compression or shortening of certain *frequency-modulated* pulses arriving at the end of the fiber when longer *wavelengths* emitted later catch up with shorter wavelengths emitted earlier.

optical-fiber radiation damage. The increased *attenuation* caused by increased losses through *absorption, diffusion,* or *scattering* at *deflection* sites introduced into an *optical fiber* by exposure to high-energy bombardment; (e.g., *gamma radiation* or high-energy neutrons). Both *catastrophic* and *gradual degradation* can occur since the effects are cumulative and irreversible. Degradation can occur to fibers at dosage levels below *threshold* of damage to *photodiodes, LEDs,* and associated electronic circuits. Also see *fiber-optic dosimeter; electromagnetic survivability.*

optical-fiber ribbon. A row of *optical fibers* laminated in a flat plastic strip. Also see *flat optical cable.* See Figure O-4. Also see Figure W-1.

O-4. A 12-ribbon, 12-**optical-fiber-ribbon** 0.5-in-diameter, 50,000 simultaneous conversation *light-guide cable* alongside a 1200-pair *wire cable* that has one-third the *capacity* of the *optical cable*. (Courtesy of Bell Laboratories.)

optical-fiber ringer.   A *signaling system* for obtaining attention in which a *photodetector* and *transmitter* convert enough *lightwave* energy from *information*-bearing *modulated carrier optical fibers* into an audio tone for sound signaling, i.e., *ringing*. The *ringer power* may also be used for other electronic circuits such as *integrated optical circuits*. Also see *optoacoustic transducer*.

optical-fiber source.   A *light source* that can be *modulated* by an intelligence-bearing *signal* and of which the *output* is, or can be, *coupled* to an *optical fiber,* usually by means of a *pigtail* or a *connector* or *coupling*. Typical *power* output of such sources is 2 mW at a median *wavelength* of 0.910 *microns*.

optical-fiber system.   See *integrated optical-fiber system*.

optical-fiber tensile strength.   The maximum load that a short piece of *optical fiber* can sustain without breaking, normally calculated as:

$$T_s = E(r/r_{min})$$

where T_s is the safe tension stress; E is Young's modulus, about 10^7 lb./in.^{2} (7 $\times$ 10^9 kg/m^2); r is the radius of the fiber; and r_{min} is the minimum bending radius before breaking. The T_s obtained is approximate and must be adjusted for probabilistic fractures and cracks in long fibers.

optical-fiber transfer function (OFTF). The transformation that an *optical fiber* brings about on an *electromagnetic wave* that enters it, such that if the *input signal* composition is known, and the transfer function is known for the fiber, the *output* signal can be determined. For example:

$$OFTF = e^{-af^2}$$

where *OFTF* is the fiber transfer function, *a* is a constant for the fiber, and *f* is a *frequency* component of the signal, (i.e., of the wave).

optical-fiber trap. A hair-fine, nearly invisible, *optical fiber* that (1) breaks easily when strained, (2) can be placed on fences or in fields, and (3) can *signal* the location of a break and so cannot be cut without detection, and thus can be used to warn of trespassers. Synonymous with *security optical fiber.*

optical-fiber video trunk. A video *signal trunk* that uses *optical fibers, bundles,* and *cables* as the *transmission media* for video *signals.* *Color multiplexing* is practical over the full-color *spectrum* from *infrared* to *ultraviolet* inclusive. *Dispersion* may be used as a means of separating the colors; however, once separated, they must be individually *detected* and processed.

optical filter. A *component* or group of components placed in an *optical system* to reduce or eliminate certain selected *wavelengths* of *transmitted light* while leaving others relatively unchanged, or to modify the *intensity* or *polarization* of the light. Also see *polarizer.*

optical-frequency division multiplex. See *wavelength division multiplex (WDM).*

optical glass. See *bulk optical glass.*

optical harness. A number of multiple-*fiber cables* or *jacketed bundles* placed together in an array that contains branches. A harness is usually installed within other equipment and mechanically secured to that equipment.

optical harness assembly. An *optical harness* that is *terminated* and ready for installation.

optical impedance discontinuity. An abrupt spatial variation in the *refractive index, absorption, scattering, geometric,* or other parameters of an *optical waveguide,* such as an *optical fiber* or a *slab dielectric waveguide.* In addition to geometric factors, the *electric permittivity, magnetic permeability,* and the *electrical conductivity* contribute to the optical impedance, which is also a *function of frequency.*

optical integrated circuit. See *integrated optical circuit.*

optical isolator. An *optical transmission system,* such as a *fiber-optic link,* inserted into or between wire *communication systems* for the purpose of preventing electrical contact between systems or parts of systems.

optical lever. The means of amplifying small angular movements by *reflecting* a *beam* of *light* from a *mirror* or *prism.*

optical link. A *system* consisting of a *light source* as a *transmitter,* a *fiber-optic* cable, and a *photodetector* as a *receiver,* all connected in such a manner that *lightwaves* from the source can reach the receiver. Light from the transmitter is usually modulated by an intelligence-bearing *signal.* Synonymous with *fiber optic link; optocoupler.* See *long-haul optical link; repeatered optical link; satellite optical link.* See Figure O-5. Also see Figure T-6.

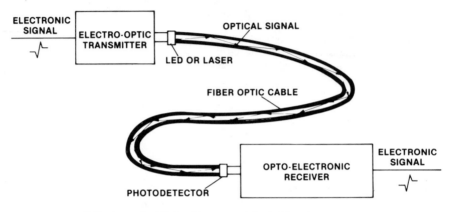

O-5. An **optical link.** (Courtesy of the Belden Corporation.)

optical maser. A source of nearly *monochromatic* and *coherent radiation* produced by the synchronous and cooperative *emission* of *optically* pumped ions introduced into a crystal host lattice, gas, or liquid atoms excited in a discharge tube, the radiation being a *lightwave* with a sharply defined *frequency* that *propagates* in an intense highly directional *beam.*

optical mixing. 1. The production of *dichromatic* or *polychromatic, radiation* from *monochromatic* radiation through use of a *mixing box, mixing rod,* or other means. 2. To produce an *electrical current* proportional to the *frequency* difference between two *monochromatic lightwaves incident* upon the same *photodetector.* See Figure O-6.

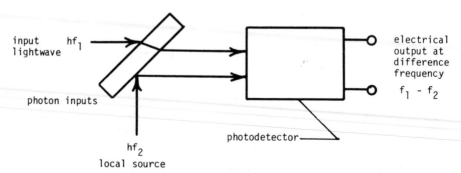

O-6. **Optical mixing** by means of a partially *reflecting* and *transmitting mirror* and a *photodetector.*

optical mixing box.   A *fiber-optic coupler* consisting of a piece of fiber-optic material that receives several *optical frequencies* and that mixes them to produce *dichromatic* or *polychromatic lightwaves* for dispatch via one or more *outputs* for *transmission* elsewhere and perhaps subsequent separation into the constituent frequencies to produce the original intelligence introduced by the modulation of each of the constituent frequencies.   The mixing box usually has *reflective* inner surfaces, except at the *ports*.   The lightwaves entering the box are usually a group of *monochromatic* waves each of a different frequency and each modulated separately.

optical mixing rod.   An *optical mixing box* that has the general shape of a right circular cylinder, usually with *pigtails* to serve as entrance and exit ports.   Also see Figure P-9.

optical modulation.   See *external optical modulation.*

optical modulator.   See *thin-film optical modulator.*

optical multimode dispersion.   A *dispersion* of the constituent frequencies of *pulses* in an *optical waveguide* caused by *mode* mixing when two or more *transmission modes* are supported by the same *fiber*.   Optical multimode dispersion is greatly reduced in *graded-index fibers* and somewhat reduced by using a *monochromatic light source* such as a *laser*.

optical multiplexer.   See *thin-film optical multiplexer.*

optical parametric oscillator.   A *tunable* device, usually a crystal, that varies the *wavelength* of a *light beam* from a *solid-state laser*.

optical path length.   In a *medium* of constant *refractive index, n,* the product of the geometrical distance and the refractive index.   If *n* is a function of position along the geometrical path, the optical path length is the integral of *nds,* where *ds* is an element of length along the path.   In mathematical notation:

$$L = \int nds$$

optical plastic.   See *bulk optical plastic.*

optical power budget.   In an *optical transmission system,* the distribution of the available power that is requried for *transmission* within specified *distortion* limits or *error rates*.   The distribution is usually in terms of *decibels* for each *component* of the system from *source* to *sink*.   Components include the *light source* module, *connectors, cable, detector* module, and *splices*.

optical power density.   The energy per unit time *transmitted* by a *light beam* through a unit area normal to the direction of *propagation* or the direction of maximum *power* gradient, expressed in watts per square *meter* or joules per second-(square meter).

optical power efficiency.   The ratio of *emitted electromagnetic power* of an *optical source* to the *electrical input power* to the *source*.

optical power output.   The *electromagnetic power* in the *visible region* of the *spectrum emitted* by a device.   It is usually measured in watts or in *lumens* per *second.*   See Figure O-7.   Also see Figure I-2.

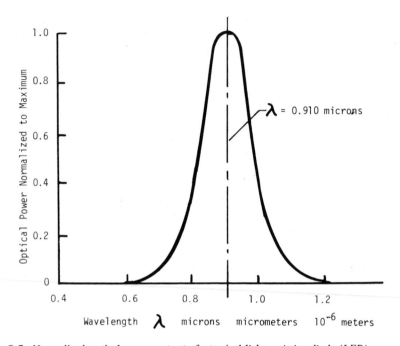

O-7.   Normalized **optical power output** of a typical *light-emitting diode (LED) source.*

optical protective coating.   Films that are applied to a coated or uncoated *optical surface* primarily for protecting the surface from mechanical abrasion, chemical corrosion, or both.   An important class of protective *coatings* consists of evaporated thin films of titanium dioxide, silicon monoxide, or magnesium fluoride.   A thin layer of silicon monoxide may be added to protect an aluminized surface to prevent corrosion.

optical range.   **1.** The direct *line-of-sight* distance between two points at given altitudes above the earth's surface.   **2.** The range that is achieved by a straight line from one point above the surface of the earth to another point above the earth and tangent to the earth at one point in between.

optical ray.   A representation of the direction of *propagation* of *electromagnetic radiation* as defined by directional *parameters.*   A ray is perpendicular to a *wavefront* and in the direction of the *Poynting vector.*

optical receiver. A *detector,* capable of *demodulating* a *lightwave,* that can be coupled to a *transmission medium* such as an *optical fiber.*

optical repeater. An *optical*/optical, optical/*electrical,* or electrical/optical *signal amplification* and *processing* device.

optical repeater power. In *optical cables, power* delivered to an *optical repeater* by an *electrical conductor* in the cable, a solar cell, a local battery, a commercial power outlet, or by tapping the *signal* power contained in the *optical fibers* without disturbing their *information content.* Also see *signaling path.*

optical rotation. 1. The angular displacement of the plane of *polarization* of *light* passing through a *medium.* 2. The azimuthal displacement of the field of view achieved through the use of a rotating *prism.*

optical scanner. A device used to *scan marks* such as bar *codes* or letters and containing a *light source* to *illuminate* the marks and a *reflection* sensor to develop the coded electrical signals representing the marks. For example, a device held like a writing pen and moved across marks on a *display surface,* or an oscillating *scanning head* that scans an entire page line by line.

optical signal. See *two-level optical signal.*

optical source. See *video optical source.*

optical space-division multiplexing (OSDM). The use of independent *fibers* contained in a *bundle* to provide *optical* paths for independent *channels.* Usually, the fibers are collected into a single *cable* with sheathing and *strength members.*

optical spectrum analyzer. See *integrated optical spectrum analyzer.*

optical speed. In *lens systems,* the reciprocal of the square of the *f-number,* being inversely proportional to twice the *numerical aperture.* Thus, the optical speed of an *optical fiber* is directly proportional to the numerical aperture squared.

optical surface. In an *optical system,* a *reflecting* or *refracting* surface of an *optical* element, or any other identified geometric surface in the system. Normally, optical surfaces occur at surfaces of discontinuity (abrupt changes) of *refractive indices, absorptive* qualities, *transmissivity,* vitrification, or other optical quality or characteristic.

optical switch. A *switching circuit* that enables *signals* in *optical fibers* and *integrated optical circuits (IOC)* to be selectively *switched* from one circuit or *path* to another or to perform *logic operations* with these signals by using *electrooptic effects, magnetooptic effects,* or other effects or methods that operate on *transmission modes,* such as *transverse-electric* versus *transverse magnetic modes,* type and direction of *polarization,* or other characteristics of *electromagnetic waves.* For example, a *multimode achromatic electrooptic waveguide switch* or an *optic polarization switch.* Synonymous with *light valve.* See *mechanical optical switch; thin-film optical switch.* Also see *flip switch.*

optical system.   A group of interrelated parts and equipment designed to accept, process, and utilize *lightwaves conducted* for the most part in material *media,* such as in *lenses, prisms, optical fibers,* and other *waveguides.*   The optical system for *communications* has a *light source* (such as a *laser* or *LED*), the *output* of which can be *modulated; a transmission medium,* such as an *optical fiber, bundle,* or *cable;* and a *photodetector,* to convert the *transmitted* lightwave to electrical current *signals* for audio or visual purposes.   Another optical system would be a *lens system* as used in a telescope, *microscope,* range finder or field glasses.

optical taper.   An *optical fiber* with a diameter that is a linear function of its length, thus having a conical shape, either increasing or decreasing in diameter in the direction of *propagation* of a *lightwave* in a longitudinal direction.   The taper can be used to increase or decrease the size of an *image* when the tapers are bundled.   Synonymous with *conical fiber.*

optical tapoff.   The removing of some of the *lightwaves propagating* in an *optical waveguide,* such as an *optical fiber, bundle,* or *cable,* a *slab dielectric waveguide,* or a *waveguide* on an *optical integrated circuit.*   Tapoff is usually accomplished by the use of *connectors, couplers,* and *branches.*

optical thin film.   A thin layer of an *optical transmission medium,* usually deposited or formed on a *substrate,* with a geometric shape and *refractive* quality so as to enable the *conduction* of *lightwaves* for specific purposes, usually to accomplish logical functions by forming *gates.*   For example, a *transparent* thin layer of an *optical conductor* in an *integrated optical circuit.*

optical time-domain (OTD) reflectometer.   A device that measures distance to a *reflection interface* surface by measuring the time it takes for a *lightwave pulse* to *reflect* from the surface.   Reflection interface surfaces include the ends of *cables* and breaks in *fiber.*   The reflectometer usually also *displays* the reflected waves on a time axis for precise reading of, e.g., the leading edges of the *transmitted* and reflected waves.   The reflectometer is capable of launching a *pulse* into a *transmission medium* and measuring the time required for its reflection to return by *backscattering* or end reflection, thus indicating the continuity, discontinuity, splicing loss, inhomogeneity, crack, fracture, break, or other *anisotropic* features of the medium.   See Figure O-8.

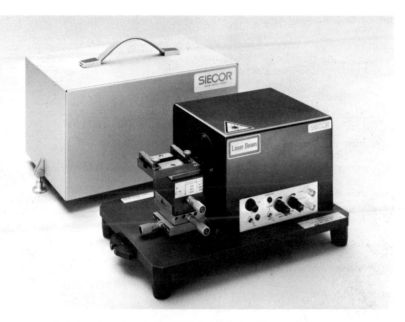

O-8. A Siecor **optical time-domain reflectometer** for determining *optical-fiber* length, *splice,* or *connector* continuity; measuring *attenuation;* assessing *fiber* homogeneity; and locating fractures. (Courtesy of Siecor Optical Cables, Inc.)

optical transceiver.   See *home optical transceiver.*

optical transimpedance.   In an *optical transmission system,* the ratio of the *output voltage* at the *detector* end to the *input current* at the *light source* end.

optical transmitter.   A *light source* capable of being *modulated* and *coupled* to a *transmission medium* such as an *optical fiber* or an *integrated optical circuit.*

optical video disk (OVD).   A disk on the surface of which *digital data* are recorded at high *packing densities* in concentric circles or in a spiral using a *laser beam* to record spots that are read by means of a *reflected* laser beam of lower intensity than the recording intensity. Up to 10^{11} bits are being recorded on a single disk, thus being suitable for an hour of *television* programming playback.

optical waveguide.   See *diffused optical waveguide; fiber-optic waveguide; hetero-epitaxial optical waveguide; slab-dielectric optical waveguide; strip-loaded diffused optical waveguide; thin-film optical waveguide.*

optic arteriovenous oximeter.   See *fiber-optic arteriovenous oximeter.*

optic bloodblow meter.   See *fiber optic bloodflow meter.*

optic bundle.   See *fiber-optic bundle.*

optic cable.   See *fiber-optic cable.*

optic choledochoscope.   See *fiber-optic choledochoscope.*

optic communications.   See *fiber-optic communications.*

optic connector.   See *fixed fiber-optic connector; free fiber-optic connector.*

optic data link.   See *fiber-optic data link.*

optic dosimeter.   See *fiber-optic dosimeter.*

optic-electronic device.   See *optoelectronic device.*

optic interface device.   See *fiber-optic interface device.*

optic modulator.   See *acoustooptic (a−o) modulator; electrooptic (e−o) modulator; magnetooptic (m−o) modulator.*

optic multiport coupler.   See *fiber-optic multiport coupler.*

optic myocardium stimulator.   See *fiber-optic myocardium stimulator.*

optic probe.   See *fiber-optic probe.*

optic reflective sensor.   See *fiber-optic reflective sensor.*

optic rod coupler.   See *fiber-optic rod coupler.*

optic rod multiplexer-filter.   See *fiber-optic rod multiplexer-filter.*

optics.   The branch of physical science concerned with the nature and properties of *electromagnetic radiation* and with the phenomena of vision. See *active optics; coated optics; crystal optics; electron optics; fiber optics; fixed optics; geometric optics; integrated optics; physical optics; ultraviolet fiber optics; woven-fiber optics.*

optic scrambler.   See *fiber-optic scrambler.*

optic splice.   See *fiber-optic splice.*

optic telecommunication cable.   See *fiber-optic telecommunication cable.*

optic terminus.   See *fiber-optic terminus.*

optic transmission system.   See *fiber-optic transmission system; laser fiber-optic transmission system.*

optic waveguide.   See *fiber-optic waveguide.*

optimum traffic frequency (OTF or FOT).   The highest *frequency* that is predicted to be available for *skywave transmission* over a particular *path* at a particular hour for 90% of the days of the month.   It is the most effective frequency for *ionospheric reflection* of *radio waves* between two specified points on earth. In the prediction of useful frequencies, the OTF is commonly taken as 15% below the monthly median value of the *maximum usable frequency (MUF)* for the specified time and path.   Synonymous with *optimum working frequency.*

optimum working frequency.   See *optimum traffic frequency (OTF or FOT).*

optoacoustics.   See *acoustooptics.*

optoacoustic transducer.   A device that converts an *audio frequency modulated lightwave* into a sound tone by causing a crystal to vibrate at the audio modulation frequency of the lightwave.   Also see *optical fiber ringer.*

optocoupler.   See *optical link.*

optoelectronic.   Pertaining to the *conversion* of *optical power* or energy into *electrical power* or energy, such as the conversion of an *optical signal* into an *electrical signal.*   Also see *electrooptic* and Figure O-5.

optoelectronic device.   **1.** A device that uses the *electromagnetic radiation* in the *visible, infrared,* or *ultraviolet spectral* regions of the *frequency spectrum;* emits or modifies *noncoherent* or *coherent electromagnetic radiation* in these same regions; or uses such electromagnetic radiation for its internal operation. The *wavelengths* handled by these devices range from approximately 0.3 to 30 *microns.*   **2.** Electronic devices associated with *light,* serving as *sources, conductors,* or *detectors.*   Also see *light.*   Synonymous with *optic-electronic device.*

optoelectronic directional coupler.   A *directional coupler* in which the *coupling* function is electronically controllable, usually with a *photodetector* that permits an electronic circuit to be driven by the coupler by *tapping* some of the passing *optical power.*

optoelectronic receiver.   A *receiver* that accepts an *optical signal* from an *optical cable* and converts it to an *electrical signal* for further *processing* or use.

optoelectronics.   The combination of pure and applied *electronics, optics,* and *lightwave* theory.   Also see *electrooptics.*

optoisolator.   An *optical transmission link,* consisting of an *optical line driver,* an optical waveguide, and a *photodetector,* to provide *electrical isolation* between two *communication systems* or components.   The optical waveguide serves as an *electrical insulator* as well as an optical *transmission line.*

OR.   See *EXCLUSIVE-OR.*

orbit. The *path* (trajectory) that is followed by a body moving with respect to, and usually under the influence of, another body. For example, the path of a *communication satellite,* or the path of the moon, around the earth. See *closed orbit; hyperbolic orbit; parabolic orbit; phased orbit; randomly-phased orbit; synchronous orbit.*

OR circuit. See *OR gate.*

order. See *absolute order; diffraction grating spectral order; diversity order; relative order.*

order channel. See *engineering channel.*

order circuit. See *engineering circuit.*

orderwire. The *channel* or *path* in a *communication system* used for *signals* to control, or direct the control of, system operations. For example, an *analog* voice orderwire may operate at 300 to 400 Hz; a *digital* orderwire, or *datawire,* at 16 kbps; and a telemetering orderwire at 2 kbps. In an *optical fiber cable,* the orderwire may be a metallic conductor, another fiber, or the same fiber used for regular communications. Also see *datawire; engineering circuit.* See *remote orderwire.*

orderwire multiplex set. See *engineering circuit multiplex set.*

ordinary ray. The *ray* that has an *isotropic* velocity in a *doubly refracting crystal,* obeying *Snell's law* upon *refraction* at the crystal surface.

ored. See *wire-ored.*

OR element. See *OR gate.*

organization. See *area communication organization; maritime air radio organization; maritime air telecommunication organization; World Meteorological Organization (WMO).*

organization chart. See *radio organization chart.*

OR gate. A device that is capable of performing the logical OR (inclusive) operation, namely, that if P is a statement, Q is a statement, R is a statement, . . . , then the OR of P, Q, R, . . . is true if at least one statement is true, and false if all statements are false. P OR Q is often represented as P + Q, P V Q. The OR gate can serve as a *buffer,* since all *input signals* are carried through to the *output* without having an input signal on any one *line* going back out on any other input line. Synonymous with *alternation gate; buffer gate; disjunction gate; inclusive-OR gate; join gate; logic-sum gate; mix gate; one gate; OR circuit; OR element; OR unit; positive-OR gate; union gate.* See Figure O-9.

IN A	0	1	B IN
0	0	1	
			Q OUT
1	1	1	

O-9. A table showing the *input* and *output digits* of an **OR gate.**

orientation. **1.** In *synchronous transmission systems,* a *systematic phase differ-ence* between the rotation of the *receiving distributor* and the rotation of the *transmitting distributor* in order to take into account the *propagation time* of the *signals* or the *response* of the receiving device. **2.** The position or direction of an *object* or *image* with respect to a frame of reference, such as a *coordinate system* or a reference direction.

orientation range. In *data transmission systems,* the *phase* difference that lies between the limits, in either direction, of the orientation of *receiving* and *trans-mitting distributors* that is *compatible* with the correct *translation* of *signals.*

oriented language. See *application-oriented language; problem-oriented lan-guage; procedure-oriented language.*

originating office. In a *communication system,* the *switching center* or *central office* at which a *message* or *call* is entered into the system. For example, the *office* from which a *calling party* places a call or the *message center* at which a *message originator* places a *message* for dispatch.

originating user. The *user* initiating a particular *information transfer transac-tion.* The originating user may be either the *source user* or the *destination user.*

originator. See *access originator; disengagement originator; message originator.*

orthodromic map. A map that is made by projecting all great circles as straight lines even though the angles between them are correct at only one point, namely the point of contact or tangent point. At other points a distorted angular scale must be used. For example, a gnomonic projection is formed by projecting from the center of the earth onto a plane that touches the earth's surface at the tan-gent point. This has the disadvantage that only a limited portion of the earth's surface can be shown on any one map. A map that covers an area 100 km on a side has noticeable distortion of shapes and angles at the edges.

orthogonal. **1.** Pertaining to being at right angles or mutually perpendicular. For example, pertaining to two *vector* functions that have the *integral* of their scalar product throughout space always and everywhere zero, inasmuch as the scalar product of two vectors is the product of their magnitudes times the cosine of the angle between them. If they are at right angles, this angle is $90°$, the cosine of which is 0. 2. The property of being independent and mutually exclusive.

orthogonal antenna mount. See *nonorthogonal antenna mount.*

orthogonal multiplex. A method of *time-division multiplexing* in which *pulses* with *orthogonal* properties are used so as to avoid *intersymbol interference.*

orthogonal signals. A pair of *signals* that at least theoretically are considered mutually noninterfering; for example, *frequency-modulated signals* and *amplitude modulated signals* are *orthogonal* to each other. Thus, orthogonality of signals is relative and not an intrinsic property of a single signal.

OR unit. See *OR gate.*

oscillator. A device that produces an *electrical signal* of relatively constant *frequency* and *amplitude.* The shape of the *wave* that is produced may be of any shape, though the initially-generated signal is usually a *sinusoidal wave.* Subsequent *processing,* such as *clipping* and *differentiating,* may convert the sine wave to a *rectangular wave* or to a series of *pulses* or *spikes* which become the final *output.* See *beat-frequency oscillator; local oscillator; master oscillator; optical parametric oscillator; stabilized local oscillator.*

oscillator off. See *local oscillator (LO) off.*

oscillator tuning. See *local oscillator tuning.*

oscilloscope. A laboratory instrument that is used to *display* representations of waveforms that are encountered in *electrical circuits.* It contains a *cathode-ray tube* with accessible deflecting plates or coils. *Signals* on these *deflectors* move an *electron beam* that impinges on a *screen,* thus enabling the waveforms to be displayed. Normally a sawtooth *sweep* is used for horizontal *deflection,* thus producing a *time scale.* The signal to be displayed is placed on the vertical deflector. Both are *synchronized* to show the wave shape. If other synchronized signals are placed on both deflectors, other shapes, such as ellipses (Lissajou figures), can be displayed.

OSDM. See *optical space-division multiplexing.*

OTDR. *Optical time domain reflectometer.*

OTF. *Optimum traffic frequency.*

out. In *voice communication systems,* the *word* that indicates the end of a *transmission* and that no reply is required or expected. See *time out.*

outage duration. In a *communication system,* the value of elapsed *user information transfer time* between the start and the end of an *outage period.*

outage period. In *communication systems*, a *performance measurement period*, or succession of performance measurement periods, during which a *communication service* remains in an *outage state*. An outage period begins at the beginning of the performance measurement period in which the *communication service* enters the outage state, and ends either at the beginning of the performance measurement period in which the communication service leaves the outage state, or on expiration of the *service time interval*, whichever occurs first. Similar outage periods may occur on equipment other than *communication equipment*, such as *telecommunication equipment, computing equipment, data processing equipment*, and *radar equipment*. Also see *performance measurement period*.

outage probability. In a *communication system*, the probability that the *outage state* will occur within a specified time period. In the absence of specific known causes of *outages*, the outage probability is the sum of all the outage durations divided by the overall time period of the measurement. Also see *performance measurement period*.

outages. See *mean-time-between-outages (MTBO)*.

outage state. In *communication systems*, a *communication service* condition during which a *user* (customer, subscriber) is completely deprived of service due to any cause within the communication system. Also see *degraded service state*.

outage threshold. In a *communication system*, a defined value for a supported *performance parameter* that establishes the minimum operational service performance level for that parameter. A measured parameter value "worse" than the associated outage threshold indicates that the *communication service* is in an *outage state*. The parameter is in a worse-than-threshold state when it is outside a specified range, above a specified maximum *threshold* value or below a specified minimum threshold value. Also see *performance parameter*.

out-dialing. See *network out-dialing (NOD)*.

outer space. The space that is beyond the earth's *atmosphere*. Also see *deep space*.

outgoing access. The capability of a *user* (customer, subscriber) in one *network* to *communicate* with a user in another network via the networks to which they are connected. See *closed user group with outgoing access*.

out-of-band signaling. *Signaling* in which *frequency bandwidths* or *bits* over and above that which are allocated for normal *traffic* are used, although *transmissions* are still within the established *frequency channels* or *time slots*. For example, signaling in which frequencies that are within the *guard band* between channels are used; signaling in which *bits* that are other than information bits are used in a *digital system;* or signaling in which only a portion of the channel *bandwidth* is provided by the *transmission medium*, such as the carrier channel, and the speech or intelligence path is denied by *filters*, resulting in a reduction of the effective available bandwidth.

out-of-frame alignment time. In a *data transmission system,* the time during which *frame alignment* is effectively lost. The out-of-frame-alignment time includes the time to *detect* the loss of *frame alignment* and the *reframing time.*

out-of-order signal. In a *communication system,* a *signal* that is sent in the *backward direction* indicating that a *call* cannot be *completed* because either the *called terminal* or the called terminal *access line* is in the *outage state,* is out-of-service, or has a *fault.*

out-of-phase component life. In a given *system,* the *life* of a *component* that cannot be placed into the *maintenance* or *service* cycle with the components that have an *in-phase component life.* Also see *in-phase component life.*

outpulsing. The process of transmitting *digital address information* over a *trunk* from one *switching center* or *switchboard* to another.

output. **1.** Pertaining to a device, process, or *channel* that is involved in the process of removing (extracting) data from an entity, or pertaining to the *data* involved in the process. Thus, the output may be the output *data,* the output *signal,* the output *terminal,* or the output *channel.* The usage should be made clear by the context if it is not explicitly stated. **2.** The *electric current, voltage, power,* or other form of driving force that is delivered by a *circuit* or device. **3.** The *terminals* or other places that the *electric current, voltage, power,* or other form of driving force is delivered by a *circuit* or device. **4.** In *computers, data transferred* from internal *storage* to external storage or to any device outside of the computer. **5.** *Data* that have been processed. **6.** The state or sequence of states or *signals* that occur on a *channel* at the receiving end. **7.** A device or collective set of devices that are used for taking *data* out of another device. **8.** A *channel* that is used for expressing the state of a device or *logic element,* such as the channel that indicates the result produced by a *logic gate.* **9.** The *data* obtained from a *transmitter* or from the end of a *communication line, channel,* or *link.* Also see *input.* See *optical power output; power output.*

output aperture. The *aperture* at the point of exit of an *optical system,* usually equal to the aperture of the final *lens,* such as the *eyepiece,* from which the *image* is projected and *focused* on a *screen* for viewing or for *input* to another system. Also see *exit pupil.*

output device. See *input-output (I-O) device; output unit.*

output power. See *rated output power.*

output rating. **1.** The *power* that is available at the *output terminals* of a device, such as a *transmitter,* when connected to the normal *load* or its equivalent. **2.** Under specified ambient conditions, the *power* that can be delivered by a device over a long period of time without overheating, or over a specified *duty cycle* (on-off periods). See *transmitter power-output rating.*

output unit. In *data systems,* a *functional unit* that extracts *data* from a *system,* such as a *communication, data processing,* or *computer system.* Synonymous with *output device.* Also see *input unit.*

outside plant. In a *communication system,* that portion of the system that extends from the *main distribution frame* outward to the *user end-instrument* or to the *terminal connections* for other user *components.*

outside vapor phase oxidation process (OVPO). A CVPO process for the production of *optical fibers,* in which the soot stream and heating flame are deposited on the outside surface of the rotating glass rod. Also see *inside vapor phase oxidation process; chemical vapor phase oxidation process.*

out station. In a *radio net,* a *station* that is listening and not *transmitting.* Out stations normally respond to a *call* in the *alphabetical* order of their *call signs.*

out-tuning. See *jammer out-tuning.*

outward dialing. See *direct outward dialing (DOD).*

OVD. *Optical video disk.*

over. In *voice communication systems,* the *word* that is used to indicate the end of a *transmission (message),* that a *response* is requested or expected, that the *calling station (party)* is ready to receive the response, and that the *called station (party)* should *transmit* immediately.

overcompensated optical fiber. An *optical fiber* whose *refractive index profile* is adjusted so that the higher-order *propagating modes* arrive ahead of the lower-order modes. In an *uncompensated fiber,* the higher-order modes arrive after the lower-order modes. The higher-order modes have higher *eigenvalues* in the solution of the *wave equations.* Also see *compensated optical fiber; undercompensated optical fiber.*

overdue report. In *communication systems,* a report that is expected by a listening *station* from a *mobile station* at a specified time, or at a time when a mobile station is expected to reach a specified position, and that has not yet been received by the listening station.

overflow. 1. In *communication systems,* the generation of potential *traffic* beyond the *capacity* of a *system* or subsystem. 2. A count of *telephone access attempts* that are made on *busy groups* of *trunks* or *access lines.* 3. *Traffic* that is handled by auxiliary equipment. 4. Intermediate *message storage,* such as *magnetic tape,* that serves as an extension of in-transit storage to preclude *system saturation.* 5. *Traffic* that exceeds the *capacity* of a *system component,* such as *switching equipment,* and is therefore lost. 6. In *computers* and *data processing,* the part of the *data,* such as a sum, that exceeds the capacity of the location in which it is stored, or the condition that caused the excess data.

overflow register. 1. In a *telephone system,* a device that records the number of *access attempts* that are made to contact *busy lines* or *busy trunks.* 2. In a *computer,* a *register* in which an *overflow* may be stored.

overhead bit. Any *bit* that is not an *information bit* and that is contained in a *message.* The bit may be a part of *user overhead* or it may be a part of *system* *overhead.* For example, a *check bit,* a *stuffing bit,* or a *transmission control bit.* Also see *service bit.* See *delivered overhead bit.*

overhead block. See *delivered overhead block.*

overhead information. *Digital information* that is *transferred* across the functional *interface* that separates a *user* and a *communication system* or that separates a *user end-instrument* and a communication system, for the purpose of directing or controlling the *transfer* of *user information.* The interface may also be between any two *functional units* within the communication system. Overhead information that is originated by the user is not considered as *system overhead information.* Overhead information that is generated within the system and not delivered to the user is considered as system overhead information. Thus, the *user throughput* is reduced by both overheads while *system throughput* is only reduced by *system overhead.* See *system overhead information; user overhead information.*

overlap. In *facsimile transmission systems,* a defect in reproduction by a *facsimile receiver* when the width of the *scanning line* is greater than the *scanning pitch.*

overlap tell. In *radar systems,* the *transfer* of *data,* to an adjacent *radar facility,* concerning objects (targets) that are *detected* in the area of responsibility of the adjacent radar facility.

overlay. 1. In a *computer program,* a segment of the *program* that is not permanently stored in internal *storage.* 2. The process of repeatedly using the same areas of internal *storage* during different stages of the execution of a *computer program.* 3. In the execution of a *computer program,* to *load* part of the computer program in a *storage* area that was occupied by parts of the program that are not currently, or are no longer, needed. See *form overlay; radarscope overlay.*

overload point. See *load capacity.*

overload protection. See *automatic traffic overload protection.*

overmodulation. In a *communication system,* a condition in which the mean level of the *modulating signal* is such that the peak value of the *signal* exceeds the value that is necessary to produce *100% modulation.* This results in *distortion* of the *modulated signal.* For example, overmodulation occurs when the *amplitude* of the modulating signal is greater than that required to bring the modulated signal to its zero value. Overmodulation may occur in *amplitude modulation, frequency modulation, phase modulation,* or any other type of *modulation.*

over-over communication. See *two-way alternate communication.*

over-over mode. See *two-way alternate communication.*

override precedence. See *flash-override precedence.*

overshoot.   1. In the *transmission* of *electromagnetic waves,* the result of an unusual *atmosphere* or *ionospheric* condition that causes the waves to be received where they are not intended.   **2.** In an *amplifier output,* the increased *amplitude* of a portion of a non*sinusoidal wave,* the increased amplitude being due to specific characteristics of the *circuit.*   In *transmission systems,* the overshoot may be valuable in decreasing the *response time* of a *signal,* but it causes *distortion* of the signal.   **3.** In the *transition* of any *parameter* from one value to another, the temporary value of the parameter that exceeds the final or target value.

overtone absorption.   See *hydroxyl ion overtone absorption.*

OVPO.   *Outside vapor-phase oxidation process.*

oxidation process.   See *axial vapor-phase oxidation process; chemical vapor-phase oxidation process; inside vapor-phase oxidation process; modified inside vapor-phase oxidation process; outside vapor-phase oxidation process.*

oximeter.   See *fiber optic arteriovenous oximeter.*

P

PABX. *Private automatic branch exchange.*

packet. **1.** A group of *characters* or *binary digits,* including *data* and control *signals, switched* as a composite whole in a *communication system.* **2.** A group of *frequencies* or *pulses,* such as those comprising a *photon* or group of photons. **3.** A finite sequence of *bits* or *characters* that represents *information* and usually consists of a *header part* and a *data part.* The *data,* all *control signals,* and possibly *error* control signals, are usually arranged in a specific *format.*

packet assembly-disassembly (PAD) facility. A *functional unit* that enables *data terminal equipment (DTE)* not equipped for a *packet switching mode* of *transmission (operation)* to operate with a *packet switching network.* Also see *packet-switched data transmission service.*

packet flow control. In *packet switching communication systems,* the procedure for controlling the *transfer* rate of data in *packets* between two specified points in a *data network.* For example, the control of the transfer rate between *data terminal equipment (DTE)* and a *data switching exchange (DSE),* or between two DTE's.

packet format. The structure or arrangement of the *user data* and the control *data* in a *packet.* The size and content of the various *data fields* in a packet are defined by a set of rules that are used to make up the packet.

packet length selection. A *user facility* in which *data terminal equipment (DTE)* is used to select a certain maximum user *data field* length from a specified set of fixed lengths.

packet mode operation. The *operation* of a *data network* in which *packet switching* is used.

packet mode terminal. *Data terminal equipment (DTE)* that can control the *formatting, transmission,* and *reception* of *packets.*

packet sequencing. The process of controlling the order in which *packets* are *processed* by a *communication system.* For example, the process of ensuring

656

that packets are delivered to the receiving *data terminal equipment (DTE)* in the same sequence as they were received by the sending DTE or in the same sequence as they were *transmitted* by the sending DTE.

packet switch. In a *network* that provides *packet-switched data transmission* service, the collection of *hardware* and *software* that is used to implement network procedures, such as *routing,* resource allocation, and *error-control.* The packet switch provides *access* to network *packet-switching services* via a *host-network interface.*

packet-switched data transmission service. A *communication service* that is provided to a *user* (customer, subscriber) and that includes the *transmission,* and perhaps the assembly and disassembly, of data in the form of *packets.* Also see *packet assembly-disassembly (PAD) facility.*

packet switching. The process of *routing* and *transferring data* in the form of *packets* in a *communication system* so that a *channel* is occupied during the *transmission* of the packet only; upon completion, the channel is made available for the transmission of other packets. A packet may consist of several *messages,* or an abnormally long message may require several packets. Messages are *user* units, and packets are communication-system units; hence, they can overlap each other or be made up of each other. The process consists of *routing, transmitting,* and *receiving data* in the form of *addressed packets. Packet mode operation* potentially increases the *channel traffic capacity.* In certain *communication networks,* the *data* may be *formatted* into one or more packets by *data terminal equipment (DTE)* or by other equipment within the network. The packets are formed for *transmission, multiplexing,* or other purposes. Also see *message switching.*

packing. See *channel packing.*

packing density 1. In a *bundle* of *fibers,* the end cross-sectional total *core* area per unit of cross-sectional area of the assembly of fibers whose cross-sectional core areas are counted. Packing density varies with size of fiber, core areas relative to total fiber, the geometric or spatial distribution of fibers, the overall size of fibers, tightness of packing, and other factors. 2. The number of *storage* cells per unit length, area, or volume of storage media; for example, the number of *bits* or *characters* storable per inch of *magnetic tape* or the number of bits stored on an *optical disk.*

packing fraction (PF). The ratio of the total active *core* cross-sectional area of a *fiber bundle* to the total end area of the bundle. It may be necessary to specify the conditions under which the packing fraction is to be measured. For example, the end area of a bundle or a *cable* might be the inside area of a termination or *coupler.* A packing fraction might be given as:

$$PF = N(A/D)^2$$

where N is the number of fibers, A is the diameter of the core in each fiber, and D is the diameter of the whole assembly.

packing fraction loss. The *power* loss, expressed in *decibels* (dB), due to the *packing fraction.*

PACVD. *Plasma-activated chemical vapor deposition process.*

pad. See *L-pad.*

PAD. *Packet assembly-disassembly.*

padding. 1. In a *communication system,* the appending of redundant *bits* to a *bit stream* in order to accomplish a specific purpose, such as to bring the *bit rate* up to a specified value or to maintain an *idle state* when there are no *data* to transmit. 2. In a *communication system,* the extraneous *text* that is added to a *message* for a specific purpose, such as to conceal its beginning, ending, or length.

page. 1. In *tape relay communication systems,* a single sheet of paper that contains, or has the capacity to contain, not more than a prescribed number of *lines* of printed material, such as 20 lines. 2. In a *storage system* for a *computer,* a fixed-length *block* of *data* that has an *address* and that can be *transferred* as a unit between storage units or to and from other units and storage.

page printer. An instrument that prints an array of *characters* that are arranged on a *page.*

paging rule. 1. In *tape relay communication systems,* a rule that governs the identification and *formatting* of *messages* that consist of two or more *pages.* 2. In *computer systems,* a rule that pertains to the *transfer* of *pages* between *storage* units, between other units and storage, or between other units.

pain threshold. In *audiometry,* the *sound* energy level above which the sound causes a person to feel pain in the ear receiving the sound.

pair. See *Darlington pair.*

pair cable. See *symmetrical-pair cable.*

paired cable. A *cable* that is made up of one or more separately *insulated twisted pairs* of *conductors* or *lines,* none of which are arranged with others to form *quads.* Also see *quadded cable.*

paired-disparity code. A *code* in which some or all of the *digits* or *characters* are represented by two assemblies of digits of opposite *disparity* that are used in a sequence so as to minimize the total disparity of a longer sequence of digits. For example, an *alternate mark inversion signal.* Synonymous with *alternating code.* Also see *alternate mark inversion signal; disparity.*

paired lobing.   In *radar systems,* an extension of *sequential lobing* in which *radar echo signals* that are received by the upper pair or right-hand pair of four horns symmetrically placed about the *radar antenna* axis are combined and compared with the combined signals that are received by the lower pair or left-hand pair of horns.   Also see *conical scanning; sequential lobing.*

pairing.   See *bit pairing.*

PAM.   *Pulse-amplitude modulation.*

pancratic lens.   See *zoom lens.*

panel.   **1.** In *visual signaling systems,* a large piece of background-contrasting material, such as cloth, canvas, paper, or plastic, usually laid on the ground, of specific shape or *color* that is used for sending *messages* to aircraft. Panels may be used for *position marking* or for *signaling.* They are usually *displayed* in accordance with a prearranged *code* to convey messages. **2.** A surface on which items may be mounted, such as a *switchboard,* an instrument board, or a *console.* See *gas panel; maintenance panel; marking panel; patch panel.*

panel code.   A prearranged *code* that makes use of *panels* that are designed for *visual communications* between the ground and aircraft. Synonymous with *surface code.* See *signaling panel code.*

panel signaling.   In *visual communication systems, signaling* by means of *panels* that are laid flat on the ground for *communication* with aircraft by means of a limited prearranged *code.* Panels may be made of flexible strips, pieces of wood, or markings on snow, ice, earth, grass, or sand. A standard panel that is used for ground to air signaling is a 6 ft by 2 ft rectangle, usually made of cloth or plastic.

panel signaling indicator.   In a standard *panel signaling system,* one of the four standard *signaling panel displays,* namely the *index flash,* the *letter indicator,* the *Morse code indicator,* and the *figure (numeral) indicator,* that is used to indicate the kind of *character* that is being represented by the remainder of the *display* in which the *indicator* occurs. Also see *signaling panel code.*

panel signaling sign.   See *special signaling sign.*

panel signaling vocabulary.   In *visual communication systems,* a set of correspondences between *numerals* (figures) and *messages* that may be sent from *ground stations* to *air stations* by means of *panel* arrangements that are to be read as numerals that correspond to the messages being sent. For example, the *index flash* is used alone, then the *numeral* (figure) 5 panel is *displayed.* It is to be read and *decoded* in a prearranged *vocabulary.* In this case the message might indicate a request for medical aid, based on the entries in the prearranged decoding list.

panoramic adapter.   In *radar systems,* an attachment that is designed to operate with a *search receiver* to provide a *visual* presentation on an *oscilloscope screen* of a *band* of *frequencies* that extends above and below the center frequency to which the search receiver is *tuned.*

panoramic indicator.   In *radar systems,* auxiliary equipment that is used with a *receiver* and that presents a visual indication of all *signals* that are contained within the *frequency* coverage of the associated *receiver.*

panoramic receiver.   In *radar systems,* a *receiver* of very wide *frequency* coverage with an *integral* or auxiliary *panoramic indicator.*   Normally, a panoramic *radio* receiver *tunes* automatically, rapidly *sweeps* the *frequency spectrum,* and has a visual presentation of picked-up signals.   It usually displays a *spike* or pip in a frequency baseline (abscissa axis).   It is usually used for general search and *monitoring* of *transmissions,* such as for *jammer* control.   Also see *automatic receiver.*

paper.   See *sensitized paper.*

parabolic antenna.   An *antenna* that consists of a *parabolic reflector* and a *radiating* or *receiving* element at or near its *focus.*   The reflector surface is parallel to the longitudinal axis of the radiating or receiving element, and it has a parabolic cross-section, that is, the intersection of the surface and a transverse plane is a parabola.   The *beam* is thin but spread, like a hand-held fan.   If the reflector is in the shape of a paraboloid of revolution, it is called a paraboloidal reflector. Cylindrical paraboloids and partial paraboloids are also used.   If it is a paraboloid of revolution, the beam is like a rod or pencil, with little divergence and a circular cross-section, similar to that of a spot light.

parabolic index profile.   In an *optical fiber,* the condition of having the *refractive index* vary radially as a parabolic function of the radius, namely, in such a manner that the refractive index at any radius, r, is given by:

$$n_r = n_0(1 - ar^2)$$

where r is the radial distance from the *fiber axis,* a is a constant, and n_0 is the refractive index at $r = 0$, i.e., at the center, and:

$$a = d/b^2$$

where:

$$d = 1 - (n_1/n_0)$$

where n_1 is the refractive index at the outer edge, and b is the value of r for which the index becomes uniform.   This formula is also written as:

$$n_r = n_0(1 - d(r/b)^2)$$

Synonymous with *quadratic index profile* and with *square-law index profile.* See Figure P-1.

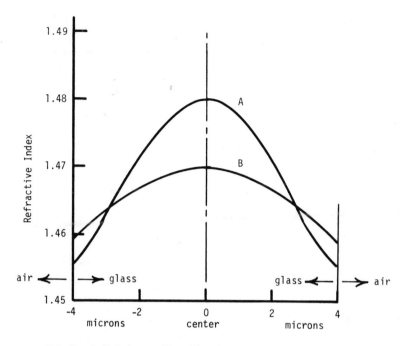

P-1. **Parabolic index profiles** of two 8-micron-diameter *optical fibers.*

parabolic orbit.   An *orbit* that has the shape of a parabola and therefore is not a *closed orbit.*   Circular and elliptical orbits are closed.   Like a parabolic orbit, a hyperbolic orbit is not closed.   Also see *hyperbolic orbit.*

paraboloidal mirror.   A *concave mirror* that has the form of a paraboloid of revolution.   If the paraboloidal mirror consists of only a portion of a paraboloidal surface through which the axis does not pass, it is known as an *off-axis paraboloidal mirror.*   All axial parallel *light rays* are *focused* at the *focal point* of the paraboloid without *spherical aberration;* conversely, all light rays emanating from an axial source at the focal point are *reflected* as a *bundle* of parallel rays without spherical abberation.   Paraboloidal mirrors are free from *chromatic aberration.* See *off-axis paraboloidal mirror.*

parallel.   See *declination parallel.*

parallel light.   See *collimated light.*

parallel operation.   In *data processing systems,* an operating *mode* in which *operations* are performed concurrently in one or more devices.   For example, to concurrently store while computing, to read while adding, or to *transfer data* concurrently over several wires or *optical fibers.*

parallel-to-serial converter. **1.** A device that accepts a group of *parallel inputs,* all of which are presented simultaneously, and converts them into a single corresponding time sequence of *signal elements.* **2.** A device that *converts* a spatial distribution of *signal* states that represent *data* into a corresponding time sequence of signal states. Each of the *parallel input signals* requires a separate channel while the *serial output* requires only a single channel. Synonymous with *dynamicizer; serializer.* Also see *serial-to-parallel converter.*

parallel transmission. The simultaneous *transmission* of a number of *signal elements.* For example, the use of a *code* in which each *signal element* is characterized by a combination of 3 out of 12 *frequencies* that are simultaneously transmitted over a 3-wire *channel;* or the use of a separate wire or *circuit* for each signal element of a *character* or *word* so that all of the signal elements of a single character or word are simultaneously *transmitted.* The most common form of parallel transmission is the transmission of all the *bits* that represent a single character, along with a *parity bit,* in parallel, that is transmitted simultaneously, over as many *conductors* as there are bits for the character, such as 8, including the parity bit, for the *International Telegraph Alphabet Number 5 (ITA-5),* which is implemented in the US as the *ASCII.*

paramagnetic. Pertaining to material with a *magnetic permeability* that is only slightly greater than that of air or that of a vacuum. Some materials that exhibit paramagnetism are nickel, cobalt, and chromium. The material is attracted by a magnet with a force that is weak compared to that of a *ferromagnetic* material such as iron. A length of paramagnetic material tends to take a position parallel to lines of *magnetic flux,* that is, it tends to align itself with the *field flux.* Also see *diamagnetic; ferromagnetic.*

parameter. See *distributed parameter; lumped parameter; performance parameter; signal parameter; wave parameter.*

parametric amplifier (paramp). An *amplifier* that has a very low *noise level* and in which the *output* of an *oscillator* that is *tuned* to the received *frequency* is amplified by making use of the energy that is generated by another pumping oscillator of a different frequency that periodically varies the *parameters (capacitance* or *inductance)* of the oscillatory *circuit.* Parametric amplifiers with a variable capacitance of the oscillator *semiconductor diode* are employed in *radar tracking* and *communication ground stations* for *earth satellites* and *deep space* flights. The *noise temperature* of paramps cooled to the *temperature* of liquid helium, about 5 K, is in the range of 20 K to 30 K. Their *gain* is about 40 dB.

parametric oscillator. See *optical parametric oscillator.*

paramp. *Parametric amplifier.*

paraphrase. In *communication systems,* to change the wording of a *message* without changing the meaning to the intended recipient.

parasitic emission. In a *communication system* using *electromagnetic sources,* *electromagnetic radiation* from a *source* that is not harmonically related or *co-*

herent with the *transmitted carrier,* usually caused by undesired oscillations or *energy level* transitions in the source. Parasitic emissions may consist of *light-waves, radio waves, microwaves, X rays,* or *gamma rays.*

paraxial ray. A *ray* of a group of rays that approaches the *chief ray* of that *bundle* as its limiting position. It is a ray in the sense of Gaussian or first-order *optics.* It is nearly parallel with the *optical axis.* For purposes of computation, the angle between paraxial rays and the optical axis is small enough for the sine of the angle to be replaced by the angle in radians without introducing significant *errors.*

parity. In *binary-coded data,* a condition that is obtained with a *check code* such that in any permissible *code* expression the total number of 1's, or 0's, is always odd or always even. For example, in the *ASCII code,* or the *International Telegraph Alphabet Number 5 (ITA-5)* as normally implemented, 7 *bits* are used for each *character,* the 8th bit is used as a *parity check bit.* See *even parity; odd parity.*

parity bit. A *check bit* that is appended to an array of *binary digits* to make the sum of all the binary digits, that is, the result obtained by adding all the 1's, including the *check* (parity) *bit* always odd or always even. Thus, the number of 1's in each array is made always odd or always even. The parity bit is usually associated with a *character, word,* or *block* for the purpose of providing a means for checking the accuracy of *transmission* or *storage* and retrieval. When using the *ASCII,* which is the US implementation of *International Telegraph Alphabet Number 5 (ITA-5),* the 8th bit is appended to each character so as to always have an odd or always an even number of 1's. Usually *odd parity* is used. Thus, the value of the pairty bit, 0 or 1, depends on the previous sequence and whether the system operates on odd parity or even parity. Also see *check bit; check digit.*

parity check. A check that tests whether the number of 1's (or 0's) in an array of *binary digits* is odd or even. *Odd parity* of 1's including the *parity bit* is standard for *synchronous transmission* and *even parity* for asynchronous transmission. Synonymous with *odd-even check.*

parity check coding. *Error-detecting coding* that consists of the addition of an extra bit, a *parity bit,* at the end of each *binary coded byte, character, word,* or *block* that is *transmitted* or stored. The extra bit is always chosen so as to make the number of 1's or 0's in each *code group* always odd or always even. For example, for *odd parity,* if the code group of say a *byte,* was 1011, it would become 10110 with the odd-parity check bit. If even parity were being used for the same byte, it would become 10111. The parity bit is always included in the count. The parity checking *circuit* adds all the bits, including the parity bit. The checking bit may be generated by a *modulo-two adder.*

par meter. A *display* meter that is used in the *peak-to-average ratio (P/A R)* measurement technique that was developed by the Bell Telephone Laboratories as a fast means of identifying degraded *telephone channels.* The measurement is very sensitive to *envelope delay distortion.* It is also useful for *idle channel noise, nonlinear distortion,* and *amplitude distortion* measurements.

Parseval's theorem. An extension of the superposition theorem, applied to non-periodic waveforms, for *power spectral density.* In the *periodic* case, the various *signals* are considered *orthogonal* over the period, but in the nonperiodic case, the interval of orthogonality extends over the entire time axis from minus to plus infinity.

part. See *address part; message part; message transfer part; user part.*

partial degradation. A condition in which a *system* does not fail completely or *catastrophically,* but continues to provide a partial service or operate with a reduced *capability.* It reaches the new reduced operating condition suddenly rather than *gradually* (gracefully).

partial response signal. A *signal* that has been processed in such a manner that though there is a controlled amount of *intersymbol interference* inherent in the signal design, there are desirable *spectral* properties at the *band* edges so that it is less susceptible to *filter* degradation.

partial-sum gate. See *EXCLUSIVE-OR gate.*

partial tone reversal. In *facsimile transmission,* a defect in which the *scanning output signal* does not have a smooth *transition* from white to black, but it goes from white to black and then towards white again, or vice versa, like a *damped oscillation.* One cause of the defect may be the incorrect setting of black and white limits in the *subcarrier frequency modulation.*

particle. See *alpha particle; radioactive particle.*

part message. See *multiple-part message.*

party. See *busy party; called party; calling party.*

party camp-on. See *called-party camp-on.*

party line. In *telephone systems,* an arrangement in which several *users'* (customers', subscribers', parties') *end-instruments,* particularly *telephones,* are all connected to the same *local loop (line).* Usually all users on a line are assigned the same *number.* They are distinguished by a different *ringing signal* for each user. For example, each party might have a different number of rings, or a unique combination of long and short rings. Party lines remain primarily in rural areas in which there are long loops. *Privacy* is limited on a party line and *congestion* occurs often. Also see *private line.*

PASCAL. A *block*-structured, general purpose, *computer programming language* that is used primarily for logical processes; *string,* record, and set handling; and numeric *operations.*

pascal. A unit of sound pressure variation, equal to 1 *newton* per square meter. The micropascal, equal to 10^{-6} N/m^2, is the standard unit of sound pressure variation.

pass-band. **1.** The *frequency band* of *electromagnetic waves* that a *filter* allows to pass. All other frequencies outside the pass-band are not allowed to pass. **2.** The number of *hertz* that expresses the difference between the limiting *frequencies* at which *output power* of the specified fraction, usually one-half of the maximum output power, is obtained from an *electric circuit* or a *component* in a *circuit,* such as from a *passband filter.* Also see *stop-band.*

passing. See *instruction passing.*

passive communication satellite. A *communication satellite* that only *reflects signals* from one *earth station* to another, or from several earth stations to several others. Also see *active communication satellite.*

passive detection. In *communication systems,* the process of *detecting electromagnetic radiation* by using the energy that is *emitted* by the *source* and without emitting radiation to perform the detection.

passive detection system. A *system* that does not *radiate electromagnetic* energy and that has the capability of determining the existence, location of *source,* and type, such as *modulation* and *polarization,* of received *electromagnetic radiation.* The location of the source is determined by *triangulation.* The range of *passive detection* equipment is variable, depending on *sensitivity,* site location of both *source* and *detector, directivity* of *antenna,* and other factors. Also see *active detection system.*

passive detection-tracking. In *radar systems,* the *detection* and *tracking* of *radar* or *jammers* by *triangulation* performed on *signals* that are received at two or more locations. By combining *azimuth data* on *jamming strobes* from several receiving *stations,* intersections are obtainable that indicate the position of jammers. Some passive detection-tracking systems may also provide an indication of the jammers' *average power output.*

passive device. A device that does not contain a *source* of energy, the *output* of which is a function of present or past *input signals.* For example, an *electrical resistor* or *capacitor;* a *diode;* an *optical fiber, bundle,* or *cable;* a wire; a *lens;* a *filter;* or an *optical connector.* Contract with *active device.*

passive filter. A *filter* that does not require *power* to perform its function. Also see *active filter.*

passive flight phase. In *satellite* launching, the part of *spacecraft* flight in which propulsion engines are shut off. The trajectory during this phase depends on the final stage of the preceding powered flight phase and on natural forces, such as *atmospheric* drag forces and gravitational forces. Also see *powered flight phase.*

passive graphics. In *display systems,* the field of application and study in which *display devices,* their *components,* and associated equipment, are used in a *passive mode* — i.e., without human interaction other than reading or transporting *data* — such as in the use of *plotters, microfilm* recorders, and outdoor fixed signs and billboards. Contrast with *interactive graphics.*

passive homing. A *guidance system* in which a *mobile station* tracks an object (target) and in which the mobile station does not *radiate* energy. The *radiation* from the object being tracked is used to guide the mobile tracking station to the object. For example, a missile-to-target guidance system in which the missile tracks the target without the use of radiation from itself, or its launcher, and uses radiation from the target, such as *radio waves, infrared radiation,* or *reflected* sunlight; or an *aircraft station* that uses *direction finding* to guide its way to an aircraft carrier *ship station* or island *land station.* Also see *active homing; semiactive homing.*

passive infrared device. A device that can *detect,* measure, or determine the direction of a *source* of *infrared radiation,* but does not itself contain a *source* of infrared radiation. Also see *active infrared device.*

passive mode. 1. A *mode* of *operation* of a *communication, data processing,* or other *system* or device that does not allow an *online user* to alter or interact with the system. 2. In *display systems,* a mode of operation of a *display device* in such a manner that a user cannot alter or interact with a *display element, display group,* or *display image* in the *display space* of the *display surface* of the device. Contrast with *interactive mode.*

passive network. A *network* that does not include a *power source.* Also see *active network.*

passive optics. See *fixed optics.*

passive repeater. In *microwave systems,* an unpowered device that is used to *route* a *microwave beam* over or around an obstruction. For example, two *parabolic reflectors* connected back to back, or a *flat reflector* used as a *mirror.*

passive sonar. *Sonar* that does not depend on the *reflection* of a *sound wave* that it launched, but does depend on *reception* of *sound* generated by a *source,* such as a sound source on an aircraft, ship, or submarine. Also see *active sonar.*

passive station. In a *multipoint connection,* a *tributary station* that is waiting to be *polled* or *selected.*

passive tracking. In *radar* and *sonar systems,* the *tracking* of a moving object (target) that is accomplished without the use of a launched and *reflected signal.* For example, tracking by using *infrared radiation* from the tracked object, by using sunlight reflected from the object, or by using sound energy from the object. Thus, in passive tracking, the object being tracked is the energy source and the tracking station does not *radiate* any energy.

passive wiretapping. The monitoring or recording of *data* that is being *transmitted* in a *communication line* or *circuit.*

patch. 1. In *communication systems,* to connect *circuits* together temporarily, such as by means of a *cord (cable)* known as a patch cord. 2. In *computers* and *data processing,* to add a set of new *instructions* to an existing *computer program.* See *computer program patch; modal patch; telephone patch.*

patch and test facility. An organic element of a *station* or *terminal facility* that functions as a supporting activity under the technical supervision of a designated *technical control facility (TCF).* The patch and test facility may perform many functions, such as quality control tests on *links, circuits,* and other equipment; troubleshooting; activation, changing, and deactivation of circuits; technical coordination; and reporting.

patch bay. In *communication systems,* an assembly of *hardware* so arranged that a number of *circuits,* usually of the same or similar type, are connected to *jacks* for monitoring, interconnecting, and testing purposes. Patch bays are used at many locations, such as *technical control facilities, patch and test facilities,* and *telephone exchanges.* Patch bays are used for special purposes, such as *direct-current (DC) circuits; group, coaxial,* and equal level *circuits; digital data circuits;* and *voice frequency (VF) circuits.* Also see *coaxial patch bay; direct-current (DC) patch bay; group patch bay.*

patching. 1. The connecting of *circuits* temporarily, such as by means of *cords* with *plugs* inserted into appropriate *jacks.* 2. The inserting of a *program, routine,* or subroutine into an existing *computer program.*

patching jackfield. In a *communication system,* a group of *jacks* that *terminate* permanent *input* and *output connections* to channeling equipment or that provide monitoring points to allow *circuits* to be set up by means of *plug-terminated cord circuits* to allow the connection of monitoring equipment. See *channel patching jackfield.*

patching service. See *on-call patching service.*

patch panel. In *communication systems,* one segment of a *patch bay.* For example, a board, *panel,* or *console* in which *circuits* are *terminated* in *jacks* mounted on the surface. The other end of the circuit is connected to various points in the communication system to permit monitoring or testing via the jacks.

path. In *communication systems* and *network topology,* a *route* between any two *nodes* of a *network.* See *engineering path; signaling path; virtual path.*

path attenuation. In a *transmission system, attenuation* that is measured in *decibels* or *nepers* and that is due to *losses* that are encountered by a *wave* in *transit* between a *transmitter* and a *receiver.* Also see *path loss.*

path clearance. 1. In *microwave line-of-sight communication,* the perpendicular distance from the *radio beam* axis to obstructions, such as trees, buildings, or terrain features. The required path clearance is usually expressed, for a particular *K-factor,* as a fraction of the first *Fresnel zone* radius. **2.** In *electromagnetic wave propagation,* the distance between the nearest point on a wave path and a *propagation* path obstruction. If the clearance exceeds 0.6 of the first Fresnel zone radius, the obstruction does not cause a significant loss. Also see *effective earth radius; Fresnel zone; K-factor; path profile; path survey; propagation path obstruction.*

path fading. See *multiple-path fading.*

pathfinder. In *radar systems,* a set of equipment that is used for navigating or homing to reach an objective or position when lack of visibility precludes accurate visual navigation. The lack of visibility may be due to precipitation, darkness, or other causes.

path length. See *optical path length.*

path loss. The decrease in *power* that occurs when a *signal* is *transmitted* from one point to another. It is usually expressed in *decibels.* In *radio systems,* it is the *loss* that occurs between the *transmitting antenna* and a *receiving antenna.* Also see *path attenuation.*

path intermodulation noise. *Noise* that is in a *transmission path* and enters a *signal* by *modulating* it, that is, by mixing with the signal and distorting it. The noise results from the nonlinear characteristics of the path. These nonlinear characteristics create noise from the signal energy. In addition, the various *frequencies* of the signal, and the noise, encounter different characteristics, such as *absorption, refraction, diffraction, dispersion, reflection,* and *scattering.* These effects cause more noise which further modulates the signal.

path obstruction. See *propagation path obstruction.*

path profile. A *graphic* representation of the *propagation path* of a *signal,* showing the surface features of the earth, such as trees, buildings, terrain, and other features that may cause obstruction, *reflection,* or *diffraction (knife-edge effect).* The profile is made in the vertical plane that contains the path and may be made for a path in any direction from an existing or projected *source.* Also see *Fresnel zone; K-factor; path clearance; propagation path obstruction; smooth earth.*

path-slope station. See *glide path-slope station.*

path survey. In *communication systems,* particularly *microwave systems,* the assembling of pertinent geographical and environmental *data* that concerns the existing or potential *paths* that a *signal* is or may be using. The data is usually used in the design of communication systems. Also see *Fresnel zone; K-factor; path clearance; path profile; propagation path obstruction.*

pattern. See *acceptance pattern; directivity pattern; eye pattern; fiber pattern; frame synchronization pattern; interference pattern; radiation pattern; test pattern.*

pattern-matching voice coder.   A *voice encoder* in which the short term *speech frequency spectrum* is compared with *spectral data* that are stored at specific *addresses.*   The appropriate address is then *transmitted* to a receiver that locates the same pattern that is stored at the receiving *speech synthesizer.*   Also see *vocoder.*

pattern plotter.   See *acceptance angle plotter; radiation pattern plotter.*

pattern recognition.   The identification of *objects* and *images* by their shapes, forms, outlines, *color,* surface texture, *temperature,* or other *attribute,* usually by automatic means.

pattern recognition device.   A device that is capable of sensing and interpreting (recognizing) *signal* shapes and components of complex *wave* forms.   The complex wave forms may be due to *reflections* from moving, spinning, oscillating, or vibrating objects, such as jet engine exhaust or speech vibrations.   The recognition is usually accomplished by comparing the signals with a library of previously stored signals, and finding the nearest match to the stored signals.   If the signals are *digitized,* stored digital patterns are used in the match test.   The device will select the nearest or closest stored pattern.   *Digital conversion* of the *analog signal* reduces the *bandwidth* required to handle the *baseband (original) signal.*   The stored patterns are identified with various waveforms from specific sources, thus permitting identification (recognition) of the source.   If objects are to be recognized, such as graphic patterns, the signals that are obtained by *scanning* the pattern are compared with a library of signal patterns, and the nearest pattern is selected.   The associated graphic pattern, such as the letter A, becomes the recognized pattern.   This is accomplished in *optical character recognition (OCR).*

patrol air broadcast net.   See *maritime patrol air broadcast net.*

patrol air reporting net.   See *maritime patrol air reporting net.*

paulin signal.   See *visual paulin signal.*

PBX.   *Private branch exchange.*

PBX tie trunk.   *Private branch exchange tie trunk.*

PBX trunk.   *Private branch exchange trunk.*

PCM.   *Pulse-code modulation.*

PCM noise.   See *equivalent PCM noise.*

PCS.   *Plastic-clad silica fiber.*

PD.   *Photodetector.*

PDN.   *Public data network.*

peak.   See *absorption peak.*

peak busy hour. See *busy hour.*

peak envelope power (PEP). The *average power* that is supplied to an *antenna feed transmission line* by a *radio transmitter* during one *radio frequency wave* cycle at the highest crest of the *modulation envelope,* and that is measured under normal operating conditions.

peak limiting. A process in which the absolute instantaneous value of a *signal parameter* is prevented from exceeding a specified value. Also see *clipper; compander; compressor; expander.*

peak power output. In *radio frequency transmission,* the *output power averaged* over the *radio frequency wave* cycle that has the largest peak value that can occur under any combination of *transmitted signals.* The peak power output may be obtained for any *electromagnetic wave frequency* and for any form of *modulation.*

peak radiant intensity. The maximum value of *radiant intensity* of a *lightwave.*

peak signal level. The maximum instantaneous *signal power, voltage,* or *current* as measured at any point in a *transmission path.*

peak spectral power. The maximum *optical power emitted* by a *light source,* usually occurring at a specific *wavelength* or in a specific range of wavelengths; e.g., a gallium arsenide *LED* emits its peak spectral power at a wavelength of 0.910 *microns.*

peak spectral wavelength. The *wavelength* at which a *light source emits* its maximum power. For example, the 0.910 *micron* wavelength of a gallium arsenide *LED* operating at a peak diode current of 50 mA at 1 mW of total *optical power,* with about 0.30 mW of the optical power *coupled* to an *optical fiber pigtail.*

peak-to-average ratio. The ratio of the instantaneous peak value of a *signal* to its time averaged value. Peak-to-average ratio can be determined for *voltage, current, power, phase* displacement, *frequency shift, pulse length* change, or other signal *parameter.*

peak-to-peak value. The algebraic difference between the extreme or limiting values of a varying quantity. For example, the difference between the most negative value and the most positive value of a *polarized wave.*

peak value. The maximum value that a varying value may have with respect to a given reference. For example, with reference to a zero level, the maximum value of the crest of a *sinusoidal wave.*

peak wavelength. The *wavelength* at which the *radiant intensity* of a *lightwave* is a maximum.

peer. In *open systems architecture,* a member of a *peer group.*

peer group. In *open systems architecture,* the group of *functional units* that are in a given *layer* of a *network.* The layer normally extends across all the *nodes* and *branches* of a network.

peg count. 1. In *communication systems,* a count that is made of the number of times that an event or *condition* occurs. 2. In a *telephone system,* the process that provides counts of the *calls* of different *service classes* that occur during intervals of such frequency as to reliably indicate the *traffic load.*   3. A count of the attempts to seize, or a count of the actual seizures that occur, of various types of *telephone trunks, access lines, switches,* or other equipment.

peg count register. A device that is used on *telephone trunks* to record the number of *calls* that are attempted, that is, the number of *attempted accesses.*

peg marking. See *multiple peg marking.*

PEL. *Picture element.*

pen. See *light pen; sonic pen.*

pencil. See *light pencil; voltage pencil.*

pending indication. See *call-pending indication.*

penetration. In *communication, computer,* and *data processing security systems,* a successful unauthorized *access* to a *system.* The access may be accidental or deliberate. See *technological penetration.* Also see Figure I-6.

penetration profile. In *system security,* a delineation of the activities that are required to effect a *penetration* of a *system.*

penetration reaction. See *real time penetration reaction.*

penetration signature. In *system security,* the description of a situation or a condition in which a *penetration* of a *system* could occur, or the set of events that indicates that a penetration is in progress. Most security systems are designed in such a manner that the penetration signature will reveal the fact that a penetration is in progress.

penetration test. In *system security,* to test the ability of a *system* to withstand *penetration* and to identify system weaknesses against penetration. In *communication system security,* a test usually consists of attempting *access* at various points and measuring *access successes* and *detection* successes.

pennant. In *visual communication systems,* an elongated and tapered flag on which colored patterns are used to represent *words,* letters, and *numerals.* See *numeral pennant; special pennant.*

penta prism. A *prism* having the unique property of being able to divert a *beam* of *light* 90° in the principal plane even if the beam does not strike the end faces exactly with *normal incidence.*

percent break. In *telephone dialing,* the ratio, expressed as a percentage, of the *open circuit* time to the sum of the open and closed circuit times that are allotted to a single *dial pulse* cycle.

percentage modulation. 1. In *angle modulation,* the fraction of a specified reference *modulation,* expressed in percent. 2. In *amplitude modulation,* the *modulation factor* expressed in percent. It is often convenient to express percentage modulation in *decibels* or *nepers* when they are below 100% modulation.

perforated tape. A tape in which patterns of holes are punched to represent *information.*

perforated-tape retransmitter. An automatic *retransmitter* comprising a *reperforator* that feeds a tape directly into an automatic *transmitter.*

perforation. See *chadless perforation.*

perforator. In *telegraph systems,* a device that is used for punching patterns of holes to represent *data* in paper tape for use on a tape *transmitter.* When the punching of holes is automatically controlled by incoming *signals,* the device is called a *reperforator* (receiving perforator or receiver-perforator). See *keyboard perforator; printing perforator; tape perforator.*

performance measurement period. In a *communication system,* the time period over which the values of *performance parameters* are measured. The duration of a performance measurement period is determined by required confidence limits (probability measurement) and may vary as a function of the observed parameter values. A *user's* (customer's, subscriber's) time may be divided into a succession of consecutive performance measurement periods to enable measurement of user *information transfer* reliability. Also see *outage period; outage probability.*

performance parameter. A quality that has numerical values and characterizes a particular aspect of communication system performance. For example, a peg count, a ratio of *access attempts* to *access successes,* the *mean time between failures,* and the *outage probability.* Also see *outage threshold.*

perigee. The point in a *satellite's orbit* at which the satellite is the least distance from the center of the gravitational field of the controlling (parent) body or bodies. Also see *apogee.*

period. See *access period; antenna rotation period; constant failure period; distress period; early failure period; operational service period; outage period; scanning line period; scanning period; synodic period; wear-out failure period.*

periodic. Pertaining to a phenomenon, such as a *wave,* that repeats itself during regular intervals that are equally spaced. It pertains to *electrical* and physical phenomena. A *frequency* or *repetition rate* is usually associated with periodic phenomena. The frequency is the reciprocal of the time interval that is required for one whole cycle of the repeating phenomenon. If the period is in seconds the frequency will be in *hertz,* or if the period is in *microseconds* the frequency will be in *megahertz,* if in *nanoseconds* then *gigahertz,* and so on. A signal is periodic if and only if any selected value is the same as a value taken a fixed time period later. Expressed mathematically, a signal $v(t)$ is periodic if and only if $v(t + T_c) = v(t)$, where $v(t)$ is a given signal parameter, such as voltage, current, or power, as a function of time; T_c is the smallest constant period of repetition, that is, the fundamental period; and t is the time, which varies from minus infinity to plus infinity.

periodically-distributed thin-film waveguide. A *slab dielectric waveguide* formed by evaporating, growing, etching, cementing, depositing, masking, or other techniques on *substrates,* usually on *integrated optical circuit chips,* of periodic structure such as *periodically* varying the width of the waveguide in order that only selected *modes* are supported and others are eliminated. See Figures P-2 and P-3.

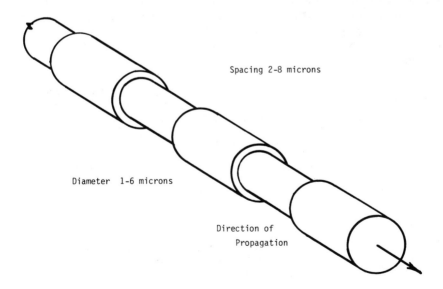

Spacing 2-8 microns

Diameter   1-6 microns

Direction of
Propagation

P-2. Circular *dielectric* **periodically-distributed thin-film waveguide.**

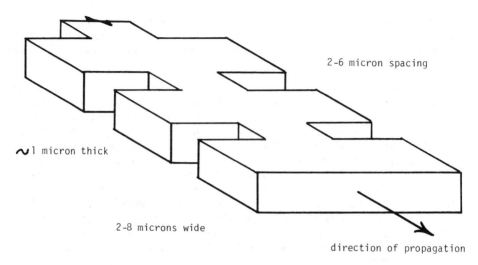

2-6 micron spacing

∿1 micron thick

2-8 microns wide

direction of propagation

P-3. Slab *dielectric* **periodically-distributed thin-film waveguide.**

periodic antenna. An *antenna* that is designed to have an approximately constant *input impedance* but only over a narrow range of *frequencies.* For example, a *dipole array antenna.* Synonymous with *resonant antenna.* Also see *aperiodic antenna; log-periodic antenna.*

periodic wave-form jamming. *Jamming* in which *periodic wave* forms, such as saw-toothed (triangular) or square waves, are used to *modulate* jamming *transmitters.* Usually *amplitude* or *frequency modulation* is used. In *radar systems,* the effect that is produced is to raise the jamming *signal level* in the *receiver,* thereby obliterating *echoes* reflected from objects (targets) or thereby producing *error signals* that indicate that there is a target when there in fact is none. Such signals will often produce an appearance on the *display* that is less dense than *noise.* Mixed noise and periodic signals can be used to modulate either the amplitude or frequency of a jamming *oscillator.*

period station. See *operator period station.*

period watch. See *single-operator period watch; two-operator period watch.*

peripheral device. See *computer peripheral device.*

peripheral equipment. 1. In a *data processing system,* any *online* or *off-line equipment* that is distinct from the main processor *(central processing unit)* and that may provide the system with additional *facilities.* **2.** In a *communication system,* any *off-line equipment* that is distinct from the communication system and is available to provide the system with additional capabilities.

peripheral strength-member optical cable. A *cable* containing *optical fibers* that are on the inside of a group of outer high tensile-strength material such as standard or solid contrahelical or longitudinal steel, nylon, or other material, with a crush-resistant *jacketing* (sheathing) on the outside of the cable. Also see *central strength-member optical cable.*

periscope antenna. An *antenna* that produces a vertical *radiation pattern* and above which is an antenna configuration that consists of a flat or parabolically curved *reflector* that is mounted in such a manner as to redirect the vertical *beam* into a horizontal *path* toward the receiving antenna. This configuration allows for path clearance of obstructions, reduces the weight at the top of a mast, and keeps the *waveguide antenna feed (transmission line)* to a minimum length. The active equipment is located at ground level for ease of maintenance. The reflector at the top of the mast is relatively simple and requires little or no maintenance. It is used normally in *microwave radio relay antenna* arrangements in which the feed and antenna are at the base of a tower and an angled *passive reflector* is at the top, aimed so as to reflect signals to the next tower.

permanent call tracing. *Call* tracing that is performed on all *calls* that are made through a given *line, trunk, switchboard, exchange, switching center,* or other specified equipment.

permanent circuit. In *communication systems,* a *circuit* that is permanently installed for use under all conditions.

permanent echo. In *radar systems,* any dense and fixed *radar returns* that are caused by the earth's surface features or other fixed or moving objects, such as swaying trees. A permanent echo is distinguishable from *ground clutter* by being *reflected* from identifiable locations rather than large areas.

permanently locked envelope. In *signal transmission,* an *envelope* that is always separated by a number of bits that correspond to an *integral* number of envelopes.

permanent storage. See *fixed storage.*

permanent virtual circuit. A *virtual circuit* that is used to establish a long-term association *(connection)* between two sets of *data terminal equipment (DTE)* and that in *operation* is identical to the *data transfer phase* of a virtual call. Permanent virtual circuits eliminate the need for repeated *call setup* (establishment) and *clearing* (disengagement).

permanent voice call sign. A *call sign* that is permanently assigned to a *station* or organization and that is to be used for *voice transmissions.* For example, RED FOX.

permeability. See *absolute magnetic permeability; incremental magnetic permeability; magnetic permeability; relative magnetic permeability.*

permittivity. See *electric permittivity.*

permutation table. In *communication cryptosystems* and other *security systems,* a table of *data items* that is designed for the systematic construction of *code* *groups* for *encoding* a *message.* It may also be used to correct *garbles* that occur in *coded* or *encrypted text.*

permuter. In *secure communication systems,* a device that is used in *crypto-equipment* to change the order in which the contents of a *shift register* are used in various *nonlinear combining circuits.*

personal call. See *private call.*

personal sign. In *communication systems,* a *call sign* that is composed of one or more letters, normally personal initials, that is used when endorsing *station* records and *messages* to indicate the responsible *operator* or *supervisor.*

personnel locator beacon. In *search and rescue communications,* a *beacon* that is capable of providing *homing signals* and is used to enable the location of personnel who are in distress.

personnel security. In *communication security,* procedures that are used to insure that persons who have requested access to sensitive *information* have the required authority and clearance for that information.

person-to-person call. A *call* that requires *operator* intervention, even in *automatically switched systems,* in order to verify that the *called party* who was explicitly requested by the *calling party* is in fact on the *line.* Also see *local call; number call; station-to-station call.*

perturbation. See *phase perturbation.*

PF. *Packing fraction.*

PFM. *Pulse frequency modulation.*

PTT. *Printing teletypewriter telegraphy.*

phantom circuit. A *circuit* that is derived from two suitably arranged pairs of *conductors (side circuits)* with each pair of conductors being a circuit in itself and at the same time acting as one leg *(conducting path)* of the phantom circuit. Also see *logical circuit; physical circuit; simplex circuit; simplexed circuit; simplex signaling; virtual circuit.*

phantom group. Three *circuits* that consist of two physical circuits *(side circuits, each consisting of a pair of conductors)* and a *phantom circuit* that is derived from them.

phase. In a *periodic* function, such as occurs in the variation of the *electric vector* in a *lightwave,* the instant or position at which a specified significant *parameter* of the function occurs relative to a given time reference; e.g., the angular *displacement* between the peak value of a given *sinusoidal* time-plot of a wave and another reference wave of the same *frequency.* In *optical fibers,* different frequencies are shifted in *phase* over given lengths of the fiber by different amounts due to different *propagation* velocities or path lengths giving rise to phase *distortion* in *signals* consisting of more than one frequency, such as a square wave. This can be compensated for by having the different frequencies travel different path lengths to reach the end of the fiber. The phase of a signal is considered as the position of a *significant instant* of the signal relative to a *time scale* or with respect to time *pulses.* See *access phase; data phase; data transfer phase, disengagement phase; information transfer phase; network control phase; passive flight phase; powered flight phase.*

phase-amplitude distortion. In a *nonlinear system,* a lack of constancy of the *phase* difference between the *output* and the *input* of the *system* at different *amplitudes* of the input. It is measured while the system is *operated* under *steady-state conditions* and usually with a *sinusoidal input wave* form. For example, an *amplifier* introduces some *phase shift,* somewhat like a *delay line.* The phase shift should be constant for all *frequencies* and their amplitudes of which a *signal* is comprised. If the phase shift is different for different amplitudes, the signal will be distorted. This distortion is phase-amplitude distortion. There may be other distortion, such as nonlinearity of *frequency* versus *gain.*

phase angle. The number of *electrical degrees* or other unit of measure of angle, between a reference point on a *frame* of reference and the angle that corresponds to a point on a *wave.* Thus, the phase angle of a wave is the number of electrical degrees from a reference to the point at which the wave crosses the zero reference level and is changing from negative to positive. The phase angle of a point on the wave is the number of degrees from the negative-to-positive zero crossover point to the point at which the phase angle is to be determined. See Figure P-4. Also see Figure D-3.

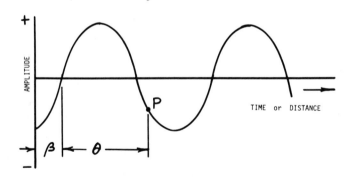

P-4. β is the **phase angle** of a *significant instant* of a *wave* relative to a fixed distance or *time frame.* θ is the phase angle of a point, P, on the wave relative to a significant instant. The wave need not be a sine wave. Both phase angles may be expressed in *electrical degrees,* radians, or time units.

phase change coefficient. At a given *frequency,* the *phase* change *(phase shift)* that is introduced per unit length of *transmission line.* The total phase change for a uniform line of length L is βL where β is the phase change coefficient. Synonymous with *phase shift coefficient.*

phase conjugation.   In *image restoration,* a method of *wavefront control* in which the shape of the wavefront, distorted by *phase* changes introduced during *propagation* in a *transmission medium,* is restored by using a conjugate, or reverse *phase shift,* to compensate for the phase changes that have occurred. Thus, if a point on the *wavefront* got shifted forward of a reference, conjugation results in having the point shifted backward in order to restore the original wavefront to its proper relative position.   The method makes use of the *information* obtained from *reflection* from the *object* to compensate for modification of the *beam* during propagation to the object.

phased array.   An arrangement of *antennas* of any type in which the *signal feeding* each *antenna* can be varied in such a way that *radiation* is reinforced in a desired direction and suppressed in undesired directions.   Rapid *scanning* in *azimuth* and *elevation* can be accomplished with such arrays.   For example, an *antenna array* of *dipoles* in which the *phase* of the *signal* that is fed to each dipole is varied in such a way that beams can be formed and directed very rapidly in azimuth and elevation without requiring physical movement of the antenna.   Also see *multielement dipole antenna.*

phase delay.   In the *transfer* of a *wave* of one *frequency* from one point to another in a *circuit,* circuit *component,* or an entire system of components, the time delay of that part of the wave that is used to identify the *phase.*   It is the *shift* in phase, that is, the time delay converted to a portion of the cycle of the wave.   The phase delay may be expressed by the ratio of the total *phase shift* in *seconds* to the frequency in *hertz,* that is, seconds per hertz (s/Hz), or it may be expressed in degrees, radians, or in *wavelengths,* such as a decimal fraction of a wavelength, for example, 2×10^{-6}.   Also see *absolute delay.*

phase deviation.   In *phase (angle) modulation,* the peak difference between the instantaneous angle of the *modulated wave* and the angle of the *carrier.*   In the case of a *sinusoidal modulating function,* the value of the phase deviation, expressed in radians, is equal to the *modulation index.*   Also see *phase modulation.*

phase difference.   The time, or the number of *electrical degrees,* by which one *wave* leads or lags another in *phase angle,* that is, the phase angle between them.

phase distortion.   See *delay distortion.*

phased orbit.   An *orbit* in a *system* employing a group of *satellites* in which the orbit or position of an individual satellite has a fixed or controlled relationship with one or more other satellites in the group.   Also see *randomly phased orbit.*

phase-encoded recording.   A method of recording on *magnetic tape* in which a 1 bit (or a 0) is a *magnetic flux* reversal to the polarity of the *interblock gap,* and a 0 bit (or a 1) is a magnetic flux reversal to the polarity opposite to that of the interblock gap, when reading in the *forward direction* (or in the *backward direction*).

phase equalizer.   See *delay equalizer.*

phase exchange keying.   In *phase modulation* of an *electromagnetic wave,* a transition from one *phase* state to another that is achieved by reducing the *amplitude* of the *carrier component* of one phase to zero while replacing it by the carrier component of the other phase. The phase and amplitude of the *output signal* is determined at any instant by the *vector* sum of the two components. In the case of a *transition* between two states that are separated by $180°$, one intermediate state is the exact cancellation of the two components. This results in an amplitude of zero. The method is a form of *balanced amplitude modulation*. It can be achieved by the presentation of a shaped *baseband signal* to a *balanced modulator* that is excited by the desired *carrier*. Synonymous with *phase exchange signaling*. Also see *balanced amplitude modulation; phase keying*.

phase exchange signaling. See *phase exchange keying*.

phase flux reversal. In *magnetic phase-encoded recording*, a *magnetic flux* reversal that is recorded at the nominal midpoint between successive 1 *bits* or between successive 0 bits to establish proper polarity.

phase-frequency distortion. *Distortion* in which the *phase-frequency* characteristic is not linear over the *frequency range* of interest, that is, the *phase shift* that is introduced by a *circuit, component,* or *system* is not the same for all frequencies of *input signal*. Thus, the zero-frequency intercept (y-axis intercept) of the phase-shift versus frequency characteristic of a device is neither zero nor an *integral* multiple of 2π radians. For example, an undesired variation with frequency of the *phase difference* between a *sinusoidal* excitation and the *fundamental* component of the *output* of a device. The phase shift is not the same for each frequency of the input signal. This introduces distortion in the output signal.

phase-frequency equalizer. A *network (circuit)* that is designed to compensate for *phase-frequency distortion* within a specified *frequency band*. Also see *delay equalizer; group delay*.

phase-front velocity. In an *electromagnetic wave*, the velocity of a *wavefront*, the wavefront being the surface in which the same *significant instant* occurs, such as the surface at which the peak value of the *electric vector* is a constant.

phase hit. In a *transmission system*, a momentary disturbance that is caused by a sudden *phase change* in a *signal*.

phase interference fading. The variation in *signal amplitude* that is produced by the interaction of two or more *signal elements* with different relative *phases*.

phase jitter. A rapid or repeated *phase perturbation*. Also see *phase perturbation*.

phase keying. A *signaling* method in which *ditital information* is *transmitted* by a representation of each of the possible *signaling* states that can be assumed by the *phase* of a *carrier*. In a practical system of limited *bandwidth*, an abrupt *transition* from one *phase condition* to another cannot be achieved while maintaining constant *amplitude*. Also see *phase shift keying; phase exchange keying*.

phase-lock loop. An electronic *circuit* that controls an *oscillator* so that it maintains a constant *phase angle* relative to a reference *signal source*. The *system* can be used in situations in which signals that are *shifted* in *phase* with respect to one another maintain a fixed phase relationship. In *spread-spectrum systems* a phase-lock loop is used to cause an oscillator internal to the *feedback loop* to oscillate at an incoming *carrier frequency*. The feedback, or servoloop, *circuit* utilizes the *output* of a *phase-sensitive detector*, via a *low pass filter*, to control the *frequency* of its own reference *signal*. The feedback loop is *damped* to permit *tracking* of the *carrier phase* changes at the *input*, but not tracking of the *modulation* changes. The arrangement also provides a low *noise threshold*.

phase meter. An instrument that may be used for measuring the difference in *phase* between two alternating quantities that have the same *frequency*. Its *output* is a *signal* that is proportional to the *phase angle*.

phase modulation (PM). *Angle modulation* in which the instantaneous *phase angle* of an unmodulated *sine wave carrier* is varied proportionally in accordance with the instantaneous value of the *amplitude* of a *modulating signal*. Also see *frequency modulation; phase deviation.*   See *electrooptic phase modulation; incremental phase modulation; quadriphase modulation.*

phase oxidation process. See *chemical vapor-phase oxidation process; inside vapor-phase oxidation process; modified inside vapor-phase oxidation process.*

phase shift. See *compensating phase shift.*

phase perturbation. The cause of a usually rapid *shifting* of the relative *phase* of a *signal*, or the momentary phase shifting itself. The shifting in phase may be random, cyclic, or a single shift. *Amplitude* perturbations also occur, due to superimposed *noise, spikes, transmission media* anomalies, and other causes. The amount of phase perturbation may be expressed in *electrical degrees* or radians. A cyclic (recurring) perturbation may be expressed in *hertz*. The perturbation may or may not be significant in a given *transmission system*. Also see *jitter; phase jitter.*

phase-reverse keying. *Phase shift keying* in which the phase of a *sinusoidal carrier wave* is *switched* plus or minus 90 *electrical degrees* by the *transitions* of a *digital data stream.*

phase-sensitive detector-demodulator. A *demodulator* in which a *local oscillator* reference voltage at the received *carrier frequency* is applied as a *parallel input* to a *diode balanced circuit*, with the *phase* of the reference voltage in *quadrature* to the *carrier signal* that is applied as a differential input. The *output*, for *phase differences* of less than 90 *electrical degrees* between a *modulated carrier input* and the reference, is proportional to the sine of the phase difference angle. If the reference voltage is arranged to be inphase with the received carrier, the circuit acts as an *amplitude detector.*

phase shift. In *transmission systems*, the change in *phase* of a *periodic signal* with respect to a reference. See *compensating phase shift.*

phase shift coefficient. See *phase change coefficient.*

phase-shift keying (PSK). In a *communication system,* a method of representing *bits* or *characters* by *shifting,* with respect to a reference, the *phase* of an *electromagnetic carrier wave,* an amount corresponding to each type of *character.* For example, the *phase shift* could be 0 for *transmitting* a 0 and 90° for transmitting a 1, or the phase shift could be −90° for a 0 and +90° for a 1, thus making the representations for 0 and 1 a total of 180° apart. The *transition* from one phase state to another is achieved by maintaining a constant *amplitude* while the *signal* passes through intermediate phases at an angular rate that is determined by the phase excursion involved and a shaping function that may be defined. Thus, PSK is *angle modulation* in which a *sinusoidal carrier* is *switched* between two phase states by the *transitions* of a *digital data stream.* It is actually *digital transmission* in which the phase of the carrier is discretely varied in relation either to a reference phase, or to the phase of the previous *signal element,* in accordance with the *data* that is to be *transmitted.* Synonymous with *biphase modulation; phase-shift signaling.* Also see *phase exchange keying; phase keying.* See *differential phase-shift keying (DPSK); differentially-coherent phase-shift keying (DCPSK); multiple phase-shift keying (MPSK); quadrature phase-shift keying (QPSK); quadriphase phase-shift keying (QPSK).*

phase-shift signaling. See *phase-shift keying.*

phase slew. See *clock phase slew.*

phase telegraphy. See *relative phase telegraphy.*

phase term. In the *propagation* of an *electromagnetic wave* in a *waveguide,* such as an *optical fiber* or metal pipe, the term h in the expression for the exponential variation characteristic of guided waves:

$$E = E_0 e^{-pz} = E_0 e^{-ihz - az}$$

where E_0 is the initial *field strength* at $z = 0$; a is the *attenuation constant* due to distance, caused by *absorption* or *scattering,* z is the distance in the direction of *propagation;* i is the complex coefficient $[i = (-1)^{1/2}]$ identifying the *quadrature phase component* of the exponent. The h represents the phase change per unit of *propagation* distance of the wave, causing *pulse distortion.* The phase term h is dependent upon the *permittivity* and *permeability* of the material filling the guide, the *frequency,* and the *modal* characteristics of the propagating wave. Also see *attenuation term; propagation constant.*

phase velocity. The velocity with which one particular point on a *sine wave* (e.g., the peak value of the *electric vector* of an *electromagnetic wave*) is *propagated* in a material *medium* or in *free space.* This concept can only strictly be applied to a single *frequency* wave, such as an *unmodulated carrier wave.* The phase velocity is the propagation velocity of a uniform plane sinusoidal wave, given as the *wavelength* times the *frequency* of the wave. The phase velocity is also the velocity at which an observer would have to move to make the wave characteristics appear to remain constant in phase in a given medium. The phase velocity in a given medium is equal to the velocity of propagation of the wave divided by the *refractive index* of the medium when the wave is an electromagnetic wave.

It is not the velocity of electromagnetic energy propagation, although it may be higher than the velocity of *light* in free space. For a given frequency, the wavelength is less in material media than in free space when electromagnetic waves are involved. In *nondispersive media,* the phase velocity and the *group velocity* are equal. Also see *group velocity.*

phasing. In *facsimile transmission,* the ensuring of the coincidence between a point on the *scanning field* at the *receiver* with the corresponding point at the *transmitter* so as to ensure that the *positioning* of the picture or *data* on the *record medium* is correct.

phasing on black. In *facsimile transmission, phasing* between the *transmitter* and *receiver* that is ensured by a phasing signal that corresponds to *nominal black.* The phasing is accomplished by a short interruption corresponding to nominal black that is transmitted during the *lost time.* Also see *phasing on white.*

phasing on white. In *facsimile transmission, phasing* between the *transmitter* and *receiver* that is ensured by a phasing signal that corresponds to *nominal white.* The phasing is accomplished by a short interruption corresponding to nominal white that is transmitted during the *lost time.* Also see *phasing on black.*

phasing signal. In *facsimile transmission,* a *signal* that is sent by a *transmitter* to the corresponding *receiver* to ensure that the proper *phase* relationship exists between the receiver and the transmitter. It insures that the receiver *scanner* is at the corresponding point on the *record medium* as the transmitter scanner is on the object (subject) copy or document field.

phon. A unit of subjective loudness level of *sound.* It is equal to the sound pressure level in *decibels* compared to that of an equally loud standard sound. The accepted standard is a pure 1 kHz tone or *narrowband noise* centered at 1 kHz. For example, a sound that is judged to be as loud as a 40 dB, 1 kHz tone has a loudness level equal to 40 phons. Also see *sone.*

phonation. A physiological process of opening and closing the vocal folds or cords 100 to 200 times per second *emitting* successive puffs of air that constitute voice.

phone. See *telephone.*

phone patch. See *telephone patch.*

phonetic alphabet. 1. A list of standard common *words* each corresponding to a letter of the *alphabet.* For example, the word 'echo' corresponds to the letter E in the military communication phonetic alphabet. Use of the alphabet promotes understanding when spelling is required or letter *codes* are *transmitted* by voice. Phonetic alphabets are also used for *numerals.* 2. A special *alphabet* in which each *character* represents a specific sound that is pronouncable by a person. For example, the symbol θ might represent the sound of the TH in the words thing, through, thread, or theta, and not the sound of TH in words such as the, these, those, that, or them. The initial vowel sound in the words southern and brother would be represented by the same symbol. Thus, words spelled with these symbols would be pronounced the same way by everyone who has learned to use the alphabet. Some of these alphabets have been standardized. See Figure P-5.

LETTER	WORD	PRONUNCIATION	LETTER	WORD	PRONUNCIATION
A	ALPHA	AL FAH	N	NOVEMBER	NOH VEM BER
B	BRAVO	BRAH VOH	O	OSCAR	AHS KAH
C	CHARLIE	CHAR LEE	P	PAPA	PAH PAH
D	DELTA	DELL TAH	Q	QUEBEC	KAY BECK
E	ECHO	ECK OH	R	ROMEO	ROH MEE OH
F	FOXTROT	FAHKS TRAHT	S	SIERRA	SEE AIRAH
G	GOLF	GAHLF	T	TANGO	TANG GO
H	HOTEL	HOH TELL	U	UNIFORM	YOU NEE FORM
I	INDIA	IN DEE AH	V	VICTOR	VICK TAH
J	JULIETT	JEW LEE ETT	W	WHISKEY	WISS KEE
K	KILO	KEE LOH	X	XRAY	ECKS RAY
L	LIMA	LEE MAH	Y	YANKEE	YANG KEE
M	MIKE	MIKE	Z	ZULU	ZOO LOO

P-5. The **phonetic alphabet** used for spelling *words* or citing letters in *voice transmission systems.*

phoneticised.   *Translated* into a *phonetic alphabet.*

phonon.   An acoustic energy packet similar in concept to a *photon,* being a function of the *frequency* of vibration of a sound *source.* Phonons are contained in or form a *sound wave.* The energy of a phonon is usually less than 0.1 eV. It is an order of magnitude less than the energy of a photon. However, when dealing with *band-gap energies* in *semiconductors,* the energy of a phonon is not negligible.

phonon band.   **1.** The group of acoustic, elastic, or vibrational *frequencies* associated with or that comprise a *phonon.*   **2.** The acoustic, elastic, or vibrational *frequencies* associated with a group of *phonons.*

phosphorescence.   The *emission* of *electromagnetic radiation* by a material after stimulation from an outside *source* ceases. The phosphorescence may continue during, for a short time after, or for a long time after the stimulation ceases. Also see *fluorescence; luminescence.*

PHOTINT.   *Photographic intelligence.*

photocell.   A device that produces a *current, voltage,* or *power* variation proportional to the *luminous intensity* of *light incident* upon a sensitive surface, using either *photovoltaic, photoconductive,* or *photoemissive effects.*

photoconduction.   An increase in the *electrical conduction* capability of a material resulting from the *absorption* of *electromagnetic radiation* by the material.

photoconductive cell.   A device for detecting or measuring *electromagnetic radiation intensity* by variation of the *conductivity* of a substance caused by *absorption* of the radiation. Synonymous with *photoresistive cell; photoresistor.*

photoconductive device.   A device that makes use of *photoconductivity,* such as a *photoconductive cell.*

photoconductive effect.   The phenomenon in which some nonmetallic materials exhibit a marked increase in *electrical conductivity* upon *absorption* of *photon energy.*   Photoconductive materials include gases (ionization) as well as crystals. They are used in conjunction with *semiconductor* materials that are ordinarily poor conductors but become distinctly conducting when subjected to *photon* absorption.   The photons excite electrons into the *conduction band* where they move freely, resulting in good electrical conductivity. The conductivity increase is due to the additional free *carriers* generated when photon energies are absorbed in energy transitions. The rate at which free carriers are generated and the length of time they persist in conducting states (their lifetime) determine the amount of conductivity change.

photoconductive film.   A film of material whose *electrical current*-carrying ability is enhanced when *illuminated* by *electromagnetic radiation,* particularly in the *visible* region of the *frequency spectrum.*

photoconductive gain factor.   The ratio of the number of *electrons* per *second* flowing through a *circuit* containing a cube of *semiconducting* material, whose sides are of unit length, to the number of *photons* per second of *incident electromagnatic radiation absorbed* in this volume.

photoconductive infrared sensor.   An *infrared electromagnetic radiation detector* that makes use of the *photoconductive effect;* i.e., a device that makes use of a material whose *electrical conductivity* is proportional to the *frequency* or *intensity* of *incident infrared electromagnetic waves.*

photoconductive meter.   An exposure meter in which a battery supplies *power* through a *photoconductive cell* to an *electrical-current* measuring device, such as a milliammeter, to measure the *intensity* of *electromagnetic radiation* of specific frequencies *incident* upon its active surface.

photoconductive photodetector.   A *photodetector* that makes use of the phenomenon of *photoconductivity* in its operation. It detects the presence of *electromagnetic radiation,* in the *visible* region of the *frequency spectrum,* by changing its *electrical resistance* in accordance with the *intensity* of the *incident radiation.* The current flow from an applied *bias voltage power source* is controlled by the changing resistance.

photoconductivity.   The increase in *electrical conductivity* displayed by many materials, particularly nonmetallic solids, when they *absorb electromagnetic radiation.*

photoconductor.   A material, usually a nonmetallic solid, whose *electrical conductivity* increases when it is exposed to *electromagnetic radiation.*

photocurrent. The *electrical current,* in a material *medium,* resulting from the *absorption* of *electromagnetic radiation,* such as *light* energy, by the material. A photocurrent is due more as a result of the *photovoltaic* or *photoemissive* effects than as a result of increased *conductivity.* However, if the electric current is a function of incident electromagnetic energy, the term may be applied in any case. Photocurrents occur in *photodiodes* and other *photodetectors.* The photocurrent is given by:

$$I_{ph} = \eta e P / h f$$

where η is the carrier collection quantum effiency, e is the *electron* charge, P is the *incident optical power,* h is *Planck's constant,* and f is the *frequency* of the *incident radiation.*

photodarlington. A combination of a *photodetector* and a *Darlington-pair transistor circuit.* The photodarlington is capable of *detecting* a *lightwave signal* and producing an amplified electrical version of the *signal.*

photodetector (PD). A device capable of extracting the *information* from an *optical carrier* (i.e., a thermal *detector* or a *photon detector,* the latter being used for *communications* more than the former). Synonymous with *light detector.* See *avalanche photodetector; photoconductive photodetector; photoelectromagnetic photodetector; photoemissive photodetector; photovoltaic photodetector.* Also see Figures A-2 and P-7.

photodetector responsivity. The ratio of the *RMS* value of the *output current* or *voltage* of a *photodetector* to the *RMS* value of the *incident optical power input.* In most cases, detectors are linear in the sense that the responsivity is independent of the *intensity* of the *incident radiation.* Thus, the detector output in amps or volts is proportional to the incident optical power in watts. Differential *responsivity* applies to small variations in optical power. *Optical detectors* are square-law detectors that respond to *optical intensity,* i.e., the square of the *electromagnetic field* associated with the optical *radiation.* They are linear in the sense that the response in volts or amps varies linearly with optical power input.

photodetector signal-to-noise ratio. The *signal-to-noise ratio* (SNR) obtained in a *photodetector,* expressed mathematically as:

$$SNR = (N_p / B)(1 - e^{-h f / k t})$$

where N_p/B is the number of *incident photons* per unit *bandwidth,* h is *Planck's constant,* f is the *frequency* of the incident photons, k is *Boltzmann's constant,* and T is the absolute *temperature.*

photodiode. A diode whose *conductivity* increases with increased *incident electromagnetic radiation.* The photodiode can serve as a *photodetector,* since the instantaneous *current* flowing through it can be a function of the instantaneous incident *electromagnetic power.* A source of *voltage* is required. See *avalanche photodiode; positive-intrinsic-negative photodiode.* See Figure P-6. Also see Figure S-11.

P-6. A high-speed silicon *fiber-optic* **photodiode** with *integral light pipe* designed for a maximum 100-μA reverse-bias *dark current,* a continuous *photocurrent density* of 5 mA/mm^2, a forward current of 10 mA, a *responsivity* of 0.6 A/W, *luminous* responsivity of 8.5 mA/lm, and a quantum efficiency of 83% all at 830 nanometers wavelength. (Courtesy of RCA Electro-Optics and Devices.)

photodiode coupler. See *avalanche photodiode coupler; positive-intrinsic-negative photodiode coupler.*

photoeffect. See *external photoeffect; internal photoeffect; extrinsic internal photoeffect; intrinsic internal photoeffect.*

photoeffect detector. See *external photoeffect detector; internal photoeffect detector.*

photoelastic. The property of a material in which the mechanical elasticity, or the coefficient of elasticity (stress/strain), at a point in the material is a function of the instantaneous *incident electromagnetic power density* at the point. The *incident electromagnetic power density* is the electromagnetic energy reaching per unit area per unit time.

photoelectric effect. 1. The changes in material *electrical* characteristics due to *photon absorption.* 2. The *emission* of *electrons* as the result of the *absorption* of *photons* in a material. The photons can be of any energy, and the electrons can be released into a vacuum or into a second material. The material itself may be solid, liquid, or gas. Thus, *photoconductive, photoelectromagnetic; photoemissive,* and *photovoltaic effects* are all photoelectric effects.

photoelectromagnetic effect. The production of a *potential difference* by virtue of the interaction of a *magnetic field* with a *photoconductive* material subjected to *incident radiation.* The incident radiation creates *hole-electron* pairs that *diffuse* into the material. The magnetic field causes the pair components to separate, resulting in a *potential difference* across the material. In most applications, the *light* is made to fall on a flat surface of an intermetallic *semiconductor* located in a magnetic field that is parallel to the surface; excess hole-electron pairs are created; and these *carriers diffuse* in the direction of the light but are *deflected* by the magnetic field to give a *current* flow through the semiconductor that is at right angles to both the light *rays* and the magnetic field. This is due to transverse forces acting on *electrons* and *holes* diffusing into the semiconductor from the surface. Synonymous with *photomagnetoelectric effect.*

photoelectromagnetic photodetector.   A *photodetector* that makes use of the *photoelectromagnetic effect;* i.e., uses an applied *magnetic field.*

photoemissive cell.   A device that *detects* or measures *radiant energy* by measurement of the resulting *emission* of *electrons* from a surface that has or *displays* a *photoemissive effect.*

photoemissive effect.   The ejection of *electrons* from a material, usually into a vacuum, as a result of *photon absorption.*   See Figure P-7.

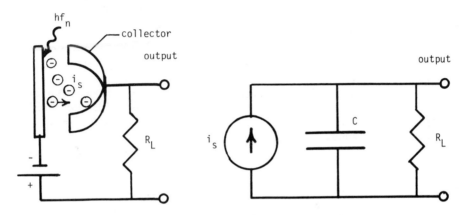

P-7. A *photodetector* using the **photoemissive effect** and its equivalent circuit.

photoemissive photodetector.   A *photodetector* that makes use of the *photoemissive effect.*   Usually an applied *electric field* is necessary to attract or collect the emitted *electrons.*

photoemissive tube photometer.   A *photometer* that uses a tube made of a *photoemissive material.*   It is highly accurate, but requires electronic amplification and is used mainly in laboratories.

photoemissivity.   The property of a substance that causes it to emit *electrons* when *electromagnetic radiation* in the *visible* region of the *frequency spectrum* is *incident* upon it.   Normally, an *electric field* is applied to collect the emitted electrons.

photographic intelligence (PHOTINT).   *Information* that is obtained from *photographs* or is on *photographic media,* and has been processed for use.

photography.   The branch of science and technology that is devoted to the creation of pictures, usually on *hard copy,* by exposing sensitive chemically-treated paper or other substances to an *image* composed of *electromagnetic radiation,* usually in the *visible region* of the *frequency spectrum,* though *infrared* and *ultraviolet waves* are also included. It also includes activities related to the making of pictures, such as finding, creating, or traveling to or near objects to photograph. Still and motion pictures are included, though the subdivision of motion pictures tends to be called cinematography.

photomagnetoelectric effect.   See *photoelectromagnetic effect.*

photometer.   A device that measures and indicates *incident light intensity.* See *photoemissive tube photometer.*

photometry.   The science devoted to the measurement of the effects of *electromagnetic radiation* on the eye.   Photometry is an outgrowth of psychophysical aspects and involves the determination of visual effectiveness by considering *radiated power* and the sensitivity of the eye to the *frequency* in question.

photomultiplier.   An *electron* tube that multiplies the effect of *incident electromagnetic radiation* by accelerating emitted electrons and using them to impinge upon other surfaces, knocking out additional electrons, until a large *electric current* is produced for low incident-radiation levels.   The electron tube contains a photocathode, one or more dynodes, and an output electrode.   Electrons emitted from the cathode are amplified by secondary emission from the dynodes.   The original electron emission is thus cascaded by the secondary electrodes.

photon.   A quantum of *electromagnetic energy.*   The energy of a photon is hf, where h is *Planck's constant,* and f is the *frequency* of the *radiation.*   Also see *Planck's law.* See *gamma photon.*

photon detector.   A device that responds to *incident photons;* i.e., a device capable of *signaling,* with some reasonable probability of being correct, the *absorption* of a *photon (quantum* of *light energy).*   The photon detector exhibits a change in property when it absorbs a photon; i.e., it is *photoemissive, photoconductive, photovoltaic,* or *photoelectromagnetic.*

photoresistive cell.   See *photoconductive cell.*

photoresistor.   See *photoconductive cell.*

photosensitive recording.   Recording by the exposure of a photosensitive surface to a *signal*-controlled *light beam* or spot, or to a projected *light image.*

phototelegraphy.   In *facsimile systems,* the *transmission* of pictures by *telegraphic* means in which a *photographic* process at the *receiver* produces a permanent *image* of the picture that was *scanned* by the *transmitter.*

phototronic photocell.   See *photovoltaic photocell.*

phototransistor.   A *transistor* that produces *electrical output signals* corresponding to input *incident lightwave* signals.   Phototransistors may be used in *photodetectors,* such as *photodarlington* circuits.

photovoltaic. Pertaining to the capability of generating a *voltage* as a result of exposure to *visible* or other *electromagnetic radiation.* Also see *radiovoltaic.*

photovoltaic cell. A device that *detects* or measures *radiant energy* by the production of a *source* of *voltage* proportional to the *incident radiation intensity.* It is possible to operate a photovoltaic cell without an additional source of voltage, since it develops a voltage. The cell detects or measures *electromagnetic radiation,* by generating a potential at a *junction* (barrier layer) between two types of material, upon *absorption* of *radiant energy.* Synonymous with *barrier-layer cell; barrier-layer photocell; boundary-layer photocell;* and *photronic photocell.*

photovoltaic effect. The production of an *electromagnetic force (voltage)* across a *semiconductor* P-N *junction* due to the *absorption* of *photon energy.* The potential is caused by the *diffusion* of *hole-electron* pairs across the junction potential barrier, which the *incident photons* cause to shift or increase, leading to direct conversion of a part of the absorbed energy into usable electric force (voltage). Usually the photovoltaic effect involves the production of a voltage in a nonhomogeneous semiconductor, such as silicon, or at a junction between two types of material.

photovoltaic meter. An exposure cell in which a *photovoltaic cell* produces a *current* proportional to the *light intensity* falling on the cell or to the area exposed. This current is measured by a sensitive current-measuring device, such as a microammeter.

photovoltaic photodetector. A *photodetector* that makes use of the *photovoltaic effect.* Usually a *source* of *voltage* is not needed for the photovoltaic photodetector, since it is its own source of voltage.

physical circuit. An actual *circuit* that is constructed with *hardwire* rather than by *multiplexing.* For example, a pair of wires, an *optical fiber,* or a *microwave transmitter* and *receiver.* In order to create *logical circuits, phantom circuits,* and *virtual circuits,* physical circuits must be available.

physical layer. In *open systems architecture,* the *layer* that provides the functions that are used or needed to establish, maintain, and *release* physical *connections,* and to *conduct signals* between *data terminal equipment, data circuit-terminating equipment,* and *switching equipment.* Also see *layer.*

physical optics. 1. The branch of *optics* that considers *light* as a form of *wave* motion in which energy is *propagated* by *wavefronts,* i.e., as a form of *electromagnetic radiation or waves.* 2. The branch of science that treats *light* as a *wave* phenomenon wherein light *propagation* is studied by means of *wavefronts* rather than *rays* as in *geometric optics.*

physical security. In *communication security,* the security and protection that is obtained from all physical measures that are taken to safeguard material and *information* from *access* or observation by unauthorized persons or *systems.* It includes measures that safeguard a *communication system,* such as classified document accounting procedures, the use of safes, security clearances of personnel, training for secure use of communication equipment, and the control of access to areas that are occupied by communication equipment and communication personnel.

picket. A ship, aircraft, vehicle, or troop, or groups of these, placed in a specific time and spatial relation to a larger group for a specific purpose. Formerly, a picket was only a detachment of soldiers or a single ship serving to guard an army or fleet from surprise, that is, a small outguard or patrol boat. See *direction-finding (DF) picket; radar picket.*

picking. In *display systems* using a *stylus,* to select, identify, or point to a coordinate position in the *display space* on the *display surface* of a *display device* that contains *display elements, display groups,* or *display images* on its *display surface.* Picking enables identification or selection of specific display images or parts thereof. Examples of styli include *light pens, sonic pens, tablet styli, voltage pencils, cursors,* and tracing needles attached to pantographs.

pick-off coupling. See *tangential coupling.*

picosecond. One-millionth of one-millionth of a *second,* i.e., 10^{-12} seconds.

picowatt. One millionth of one millionth of a watt, that is, 10^{-12} W.

picture. See *half-tone picture.*

picture black. In a *communication system,* the *signal* that corresponds to the darkest part (i.e., the spot with the lowest *illuminance*) of the *object* whose *image* is *transmitted.* Also see *picture white.*

picture element (PEL). 1. In *display systems,* a *display element* that can be used to construct a *display image,* or picture, in the *display space* on the *display surface* of a *display device.* For example, the *output* of a single *optical fiber terminating* on the *faceplate* at the end of a *coherent bundle* of optical fibers, or the output from a single separate piece of the mosaic that forms the *screen* of a *CRT* and whose output can be independently controlled by an *electron beam.* 2. In a *facsimile transmission system,* that area of the original document that coincides with the *scanning spot* at a given instant. 3. In a *facsimile transmission system,* the area of the finest detail that can be effectively reproduced on the *record medium.* Both the *mark* and the *space* may be considered as separate picture elements. Synonymous with *pixel.* Also see *dot frequency.*

picture facsimile telegraphy. *Facsimile transmission* in which the original object (subject) document is reproduced as a picture with graded tone densities, as in a black and white photo with shades of gray.

picture frequency. In *facsimile systems,* a *frequency* that results solely from *scanning* an object (document). A *frequency* that is part of a *modulated carrier signal* is not a picture frequency.

picture signal. See *facsimile picture signal.*

picture white. In a *communication system,* the *signal* that corresponds to the *brightest* part (i.e., the spot with the highest *illuminance*) of the *object* whose *image* is *transmitted.* Also see *picture black.*

pigeon. See *carrier pigeon.*

piece-wise linear encoding. See *segmented encoding law.*

piezoelectric effect. 1. The physical property demonstrated by certain natural and synthetic crystals by which they are mechanically deformed under the influence of an *electric field,* usually increased in length in the direction of the applied field. 2. The effect of producing a *voltage* when the stress, either compression, expansion, or twisting (torsional) is undergoing change on certain crystals, and conversely, producing a stress in certain crystals by applying a voltage to it. The voltage is produced only when the applied stress is changing.

piggy-back entry. In *computing, data processing,* and *communication system security,* an unauthorized *access* to a *system* via an authorized *user's* (customer's, subscriber's) legitimate *connection.*

pigtail. 1. In *fiber optics,* a length of *optical fiber* extending from an *optical connector* or *coupler* to which an optical fiber can be *spliced.* 2. A length of wire, usually flexible, extending from an *electrical circuit component,* such as a *resistor, capacitor, inductor, diode,* or *transistor,* used for *connection* to a *circuit terminal* or to another circuit *component.*

pilot. 1. In *transmission systems,* a *signal* that usually consists of a single-*frequency wave* and that is *transmitted* to accomplish a specific purpose other than to transmit *user information.* For example, a *supervisory, control, synchronization,* or *framing reference signal.* It may be necessary to use several independent pilot frequencies. Most *radio relay systems* use radio or continuity pilots of their own and also transmit the pilots that belong to the *carrier frequency-multiplexing* system. 2. In *tape relay systems,* the *instructions* that appear in *message format* relative to the *transmission* or handling of the message in which they are contained. See *synchronizing pilot; tape relay pilot.*

pilot make-busy (PMB) circuit. In *communication systems,* a *circuit* arrangement in which *trunks* that are provided over a *carrier system* are made *busy* to the *switching equipment* in the event of carrier system *failure,* or during *fading* of a *radio system.* A *busy signal* is preferable to the transmission of an unintelligible signal or a completely erroneous signal. The busy signal will prompt the *user* (customer, subscriber) into using other means of communication.

pilot regulation. See *two-pilot regulation.*

piloted vehicle. See *unretrievable remotely piloted vehicle.*

PIN. Positive-intrinsic-negative. See also *positive-intrinsic-negative photodiode.*

pincushion distortion. In *display systems,* a distortion of the *image* of an *object* in such a manner that the *display element, display group,* or *display image* of an otherwise straight-sided square or rectangular object has its sides bowed in, or concave, relative to the object. Contrast with *barrel distortion.*

PIN diode. A *junction diode* whose junction consists of three *semiconducting* materials joined in sequence in the forward current conducting direction; the first of the three materials is doped positive; the second is undoped (intrinsic) material; and the third is doped negative. PIN diodes are used extensively as *photodetectors* in *optical fiber* circuits and *integrated optical circuits.*

PIN photodiode. *Positive-intrinsic-negative photodiode.*

pip. See *spike.*

pipe. See *light pipe; voice pipe.*

pipelining. In *computer* and *communication system operations,* the fetching of the next *instruction* or the setting up for the next *operation* to be performed while the current instruction or the current operation is being performed.

pitch. See *frame pitch; scanning pitch.*

pitch detector. In a voice encoder *(vocoder),* a *circuit* that detects the overall volume and *frequency* of a *sound,* such as *speech* sound or *audio frequency* sound in electrical form. *Frequency information* is *transmitted* to the receiving synthesizer to *modulate* a *pulse* generator that provides the *carrier input* for modulation by the *spectral channels* in reconstituting the sounds, usually voiced sounds.

pixel. See *picture element.*

plaindress message. A *message* in which the *originator* and *addressee designations* are indicated externally of the *text.* The *address indicating group (AIG)* number or its address group usually appears on the *"TO" line* of a *message address.* Additional *action addressees* and *information addressees* will appear on the *"TO" line* or the *"INFO" line* as appropriate. If necessary, the originator's title will appear on the *"FROM"* or *"FM" line.*

plain language. 1. *Text* or *language* that is used to convey intelligible meaning in the language in which it is written with no *codes* used to deliberately hide or obscure the meaning. 2. The intelligible *text* that underlies *encrypted text.* Plain language text is written in intelligible text or uses *signals* that have generally understood meaning and that can be read and acted upon without the application of *decoding* or *decryption* devices. Synonymous with *plain text.*

plain language address designator. An *address designator* that is written in *plain language* rather than in the language that results from an *encryption* process.

plain language override. In *cryptosystems,* a capability that is built into certain *cryptoequipment* that permits *operators* to listen for *plain language signals* in the *frequency* to which they are *tuned* for *operations* and to receive signals in the *guard channel* when their equipment is set for reception of *ciphony transmis-*

sions. Under this arrangement operation is in the *cipher standby condition.* The arrangement is used primarily in *radiotelephone communication systems.* Synonymous with *plain text override.*

plain mode.   In *communication systems,* a nonsecure *transmission mode* of operating *ciphony* equipment in which voice *transmissions* are not *encrypted,* that is, *plain text* is *transmitted* as spoken.

plain text.   See *plain language.*

plain text override.   See *plain language override.*

plan.   See *aircraft communication standard plan; call-sign allocation plan; communication plan; demand-assignment access plan; frequency allotment plan; frequency assignment plan; preassignment access plan; ship-fitting communication standard plan.*

planar dielectric waveguide.   See *slab dielectric waveguide.*

planar diffused waveguide.   A thin-film *slab dielectric waveguide,* usually 1 to 10 *microns* thick, with a *refractive index profile,* usually linearly *graded,* constructed of diffused *dopants.*

Planck's constant.   A physical constant equal to 6.626×10^{-34} joule-*seconds.* Also see *Planck's law.*

Planck's law.   The *quantum* of *energy* associated with an *electromagnetic field* of *frequency f* is $E = hf$, where h is *Planck's constant* and E is the *photon* energy. The product of energy times the time is sometimes referred to as the *action.* Hence, H is sometimes referred to as the elementary quantum of action. Planck's law is the fundamental law of quantum theory and has direct application in *optical communications (lightwave communications).*   It describes the essential concept of the quanta of electromagnetic energy. Also see *blackbody.*

plane.   See *automatic radio relay plane; focal plane; image plane; meridian plane; object plane; polarization plane.*

plane lens.   A *lens* having no curved surface, or whose two curved surfaces neutralize each other, so that it possesses no net *refracting power.*

plane of polarization.   See *polarization plane.*

plane polarization.   **1.** In an *electromagnetic wave,* such as a *lightwave* or a *radio wave, polarization* of the *electric* and *magnetic field vectors* in such a manner that they remain in a plane that is perpendicular to the direction of *propagation.* The orientation of the plane is usually constant with respect to distance coordinates, and the orientation does not change with time except perhaps slowly with respect to the *frequency.* A slowly rotating *source* may be considered to be capable of producing plane-polarized waves at each instant of time. **2.** The *polarization* of a *plane-polarized electromagnetic wave.*

plane-polarized electromagnetic wave. An *electromagnetic wave* whose *electric field vector* is contained in a plane perpendicular to the direction of *propagation*. Also see *uniform plane-polarized electromagnetic wave.*

plan format. See *communication plan format.*

planned position indicator (PPI). A map or *display* that is usually in the form of a *polar diagram* in polar coordinates with the *user* or observer assumed to be at the origin, that indicates the position of an object relative to the observer or other objects. For example, a *radar planned position indicator.* Also see *polar diagram.* See *radar planned-position indicator.*

planoconcave lens. A *lens* with one plane and one *concave* surface.

plant. See *inside plant; outside plant.*

plasma-activated chemical vapor deposition process (PACVD). A *chemical vapor deposition (CVD) process* for making *graded-index* (GI) *optical fibers* by depositing a series of thin layers of materials of different *refractive indices* on the inner wall of a glass tube as chemical vapors flow through the tube, using a *microwave cavity* to stimulate the formation of oxides by means of a nonisothermal plasma generated by the microwave *resonant cavity.*

plasma panel. See *gas panel.*

plastic. See *bulk optical plastic.*

plastic-clad silica fiber (PCS). An *optical fiber* consisting of a pure silica glass *core* with plastic *cladding,* thus being a *stepped refractive-index fiber. Loss* and *dispersion* are generally higher in a *plastic-clad silica fiber* than in other types of fibers.

plesiochronous. In *time-division multiplexing (TDM),* pertaining to the relationship between two *signals* that exist when their corresponding *significant instants* occur at nominally the same rate and any variations are constrained to remain within a specified limit. Also see *anisochronous; heterochronous; homochronous; isochronous; mesochronous.*

plosive. A non*periodic* speech *sound* that is created by an explosive action, that is, a step-function or *pulse* of sound that is created by the speech forming mechanisms. For example, in English, plosives include the sounds involved in naming (pronouncing) the letters B, K, P, and T when reciting the alphabet, or when used in *words* in which they are not silent.

plotter. A *display device* that displays *data* on a *display surface,* usually on a point-by-point or *line*-segment-by-line-segment basis using a *stylus* or writing head placed at a *coordinate position* by a mechanical driving mechanism and thus making a permanent copy of an *image* on paper or film placed on a flat or cylindrical surface. See *acceptance pattern plotter; flatbed plotter; radiation pattern plotter.*

plotter bed.   The *display surface* of a *plotter.*

plotter step size.   The smallest *displacement* that can be drawn by a *plotter,* usually corresponding to the distance between adjacent *addressable points* within the *display space* of the plotter.

plow-in optical cable.   An *optical cable* designed specifically to be buried in the ground without any further preparation, treatment, or protection, usually by plowing a trench and laying the cable in it.

plug.   In *telephone switchboard operation,* a metal fitting that is connected to the *conductors* of a flexible *cord circuit* and is used to make a *connection* by inserting it into a *jack.*   See *answering plug; calling plug.*

plugboard.   A perforated board or *panel* on which is mounted an array of *jacks* into which pins, plugs, or jumpers may be inserted in order to create *circuits* to control equipment in a desired manner. For example, in *cryptoequipment,* an *electrical* device that may be used to introduce variations in *cryptooperations* and typically consists of a number of wires with plugs and an array of jacks into which the plugs may be inserted; or in an *analog computer,* a panel with an array of jacks in which pins, plugs with wires attached, or *jumpers* may be inserted to connect the various *components,* such as *summers, multipliers, integrators,* or *differentiators,* that are required for the solution of a problem.

plug connector.   See *tapered-plug connector.*

plug-ended cord.   A *conductor* with a *plug* on both ends that may be used to establish a *connection* between two *jacks* into which they are inserted. For example, a conductor with a plug on both ends used on a *telephone switchboard* to connect incoming *(calling) lines* to outgoing *(answering or called) lines.*

plugging-out lights.   In *telephone switchboard operation,* the deliberate *answering* of a *call* by inserting a *plug* into the *calling jack,* thereby causing the call *indicator light* to go out, and then removing the plug without any attempt to *complete* the call. Such action by an *operator* is invariably prohibited.

plus lens.   See *converging lens.*

PL/1.   A *general-purpose computer programming language* that is used primarily for numeric *operations, string* handling, record *processing,* and other logical processing operations.

PM.   *Phase modulation.*

PMB circuit.   *Pilot make-busy circuit.*

p-n junction.   In a *semiconductor* (solid-state) device, the *interface* between semiconducting material that has been *doped* positively — i.e., with an impurity material that produces *holes* (*acceptor* sites) on one side of the interface, and material that produces relatively free *electrons* (*donor* sites) on the other side. The junction is usually assumed to be abrupt or linearly graded in its transition region across the interface from a positive *carrier* (hole) *dopant* to a negative carrier (electron) dopant in the intrinsic semiconductor material such as germanium or silicon.

Pockel cell.   A material, usually a crystal, whose *refractive index* change is linearly proportional to an applied *electric field,* the material being configured so as to be part of another system, such as an *optical path;* the cell thus provides a means of *modulating* the *light* in the optical path.

point.   See *access point; addressable point; available point; dew point; dropzone impact point; first principal point; focal point; image point; object point; principal focus point; secondary control point; singing point; subsatellite point; test point; transmission-level point; viewpoint; visibility point.*

pointer.   In *display systems,* a manually operated *functional unit* used to conduct *interactive graphic* operations, such as selection of one member of a predetermined set or *menu,* of *display elements,* or indication of a *coordinate position* in the *display space* on the *display surface* of a *display device,* thus generating corresponding *coordinate data.*

pointing.   In *display systems,* indicating or *picking* one of several *symbols* reserved for a specific use without using *keyboard input, labels,* or *coordinate data.* For example, touching a *light-pen* to a *displayed* symbol for clearing the screen of a *CRT* or the *faceplate* of a *fiberscope,* or picking a symbol adjacent to a selected *display image* to indicate a *response* to a displayed *query.*

pointing angle.   In *satellite communication systems,* the *elevation angle* or the *azimuth angle* of an *earth station antenna* when it is directed toward a *satellite.*

point of train (POT).   In *infrared transmission systems,* a steady *infrared light* that is used to assist the *transmitter* in locating a *receiving station* and that is used for keeping the transmitting light pointed in the proper direction for satisfactory *reception.*

points.   See *emission-beam-angle-between-half-power-points.*

point source.   A *source* of *electromagnetic radiation* that is so distant from a point of observation or measurement of the radiation that the *wavefront* of the radiation is planar rather than a curved surface, regardless of the shape of the source. Thus, the size or shape of the source has no influence on the shape of the wavefront at the point of observation or measurement. The point source need not necessarily radiate with equal intensity in all directions to be considered a point source.

point-source flash detector.   See *infrared point-source flash detector.*

point-to-point.   In *communication systems,* pertaining to the interconnection of two devices, particularly *user end-instruments,* such as *telephones, display devices, remote terminals,* and *recorders,* without intervening *switchboards* or *switching centers* and with satisfactory *operation.* Also see *multipoint.*

point-to-point circuit. **1.** A *circuit* that is established between two *terminals,* including any intermediate *patching* or *switching facilities* connected on a long-term basis. **2.** A *circuit* that is established between only two adjacent *data stations* for *data transmission* between them.

point-to-point connection. In *communication systems,* a *connection* established between only two *terminals, nodes,* or *data stations,* not necessarily through *switching facilities.*

point-to-point link. In a *communication network,* a *communication link* that connects only two *stations, terminals,* or *nodes.*

point-to-point transmission. In a *communication system, transmission* between two *stations, terminals,* or *nodes* in the system.

Poisson distribution. A statistical distribution of values of a variable that differs from the normal bell curve (Gaussian) distribution only in that the variable cannot assume all values, but is limited to a particular and finite set of values. For example, a distribution of groups of *bits* that can occur only in certain patterns, a distribution of *pulses* that can occur only in certain ways or in certain groups, or the distribution that is involved in counting the number of blood cells that pass through an orifice while suspended in a liquid. The cells pass through in clusters with a finite number in each cluster according to a Poisson distribution. The clusters are counted by a resistance change across the orifice as the cluster passes through. The total number of cells is determined by the number of clusters counted and the statistical number of cells in each cluster.

polar diagram. A *display* on a relatively flat *display surface* of a *display device* in which distances or ranges from a reference, origin, or observation point are indicated as a straight line distance (radial) to the point observed, and *headings* or *azimuth* angles are indicated as angular displacements from a radial reference line. In most *radar* polar diagrams, the observation point is considered to be in the center of the polar diagram. Ranges are measured by concentric circles that indicate the radial distance to an object. A reference direction, such as true north or a ship's bow, is indexed to the *screen* for measuring azimuth. The arrangement is that of a polar coordinate system, in which the coordinates are ρ and θ, ρ being the radial distance outward from the origin at the center, and θ being the angular displacement from a reference direction. Also see *planned position indicator (PPI).* See *circular polar diagram.*

polar direct-current telegraph transmission. See *double-current signaling.*

polarential telegraph system. A *direct-current (DC) telegraph system* in which *double-current signaling (polar transmission)* in one direction, and a form of *duplex transmission* in the other, is used. There are two basic types of polarential systems in use. These are known as Type A and Type B. In *half-duplex operation* of a Type A polarential system, the direct-current balance is independent of *line resistance.* In half-duplex operation of a Type B polarential system, the direct current is substantially independent of the line leakage. Type A is better for *cable loops* where leakage is negligible but resistance varies with *temperature.* Type B is better for open wire loops where variable line leakage frequently occurs.

polariscope. A combination of a *polarizer* and an analyzer used to *detect birefringence* in materials placed between them or to detect rotation in the *polarization plane* caused by materials placed between them.

polarization. The direction of the *electric field vector* of an *electromagnetic wave,* such as a *lightwave.* It is the property of a *radiated* electromagnetic wave that describes the time-varying direction and *amplitude* of the electric field vector, that, together with the *magnetic field vector,* makes up the wave. It is specifically illustrated by the figure that is traced in space as a function of time by the extremity (tip) of the vector that represents the electric field with its base at a fixed point in space, as observed along the direction of *propagation.* In general, for a *plane polarized wave,* the figure is elliptical and it is traced in a clockwise or counterclockwise sense. *Circular polarization* and *linear polarization* are obtained when the ellipse becomes a circle or a straight line, respectively. Clockwise sense rotation of the electric field vector is designated *right-hand polarization,* and counterclockwise sense rotation is designated *left-hand polarization.* Sense of rotation is obtained by viewing the rotating electric field vector while facing in the direction of propagation. The direction of propagation is the direction of a right-hand screw obtained when the electric vector is rotated through the smaller angle into the magnetic vector, the direction of propagation being perpendicular to both fields, namely, the direction of the *Poynting vector.* See *circular polarization; elliptical polarization; fixed horizontal polarization; fixed vertical polarization; jammer polarization; left-hand helical polarization; left-hand polarization; plane polarization; right-hand polarization; rotating polarization; variable length polarization; variable polarization.*

polarization diversity. 1. Pertaining to the ability to change the direction of *polarization* of an *electromagnetic wave,* usually at the *source* of *radiation,* by changing the direction of the *polarization plane,* the *horizontal* or *vertical polarization,* or the *linear, circular, elliptical,* or *helical polarization.* 2. Pertaining to two or more types of *polarization.* 3. Any method of *diversity transmission* and *reception* in which the same *information signal* is *transmitted* and *received* simultaneously on *orthogonally polarized waves* with *fade*-independent propagation characteristics. Also see *diversity reception.*

polarization modulation. The *modulation* of an *electromagnetic wave* in such a manner that the *polarization* of the *carrier wave,* such as the direction of polarization of the *electric* and *magnetic fields,* or their relative phasing, to produce changes in polarization angle in *linear, circular,* or *elliptical* polarization, is varied according to a characteristic of an intelligence-bearing *input signal,* such as a *pulse*-or-no-pulse *digital signal.* In *optical fibers* or other *waveguides,* polarization shifts that are made in accordance with an input signal variation are a practical means of *modulation.*

polarization plane. In a *transverse,* or ordinary, *electromagnetic* (TEM) *wave,* the plane defined by the *electric* and *magnetic field vectors* of the wave; i.e., both *field vectors* at a point lie in, and therefore define, the polarization plane. The direction of *propagation,* or *power* flow, of the wave is perpendicular to both the electric and magnetic field vectors at the point, i.e., perpendicular to the polarization plane at that point. The *wavefront* lies in the polarization plane. ization

polarized electromagnetic wave. See *horizontally-polarized electromagnetic wave; left-hand polarized electromagnetic wave; plane-polarized electromagnetic wave; right-hand polarized electromagnetic wave; uniform plane-polarized electromagnetic wave; vertically-polarized electromagnetic wave.*

polarized light. A *light beam* whose *electric vector* vibrates in a direction that does not change, unless the *propagation* direction changes; i.e., it is in a plane perpendicular to the line of propagation. If the time-varying electric vector can be broken into two perpendicular components that have equal *amplitudes* and that differ in *phase* by 1/4 *wavelength,* the light is said to be *circularly polarized. Circular polarization* is obtained whenever the phase difference between the two perpendicular *components* is any odd, *integral* number of quarter wavelengths. If the electric vector is resolvable into two perpendicular components of unlike amplitudes and differing in phase by values other than 1, 1/4, 1/2, 3/4, 1, etc., wavelengths, the light beam is said to be *elliptically polarized.*

polarized operation. See *cross-polarized operation.*

polarized return-to-zero modulation. The *modulation* of a *binary signal* in which one of the *binary digits,* say the 1's, are represented by a *signal condition,* such as the *magnetization* direction, the *electric field intensity* polarity, the *magnetic field intensity* polarity, the *voltage* polarity, or the *electric current* flow direction, in one sense, and the other binary digit, in this case the 0's, are represented by a signal condition in the opposite sense. For each binary digit, there is a time or spatial condition of the signal that represents a zero level of the signal. See Figure P-8.

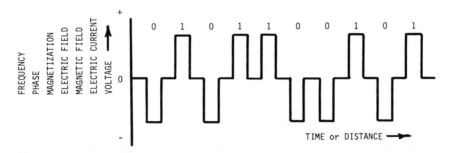

P-8. The physical *parameters* return to a zero state between each *binary digit* and opposite, complementary, or other nonzero *conditions* are used for the 0 and 1 digits in **polarized return-to-zero modulation.**

polarizer.   An *optical* device capable of transforming unpolarized (i.e., *diffused* or *scattered*) *light* into *polarized light,* or altering the *polarization* of polarized light. Also see *filter.*

polar operation.   A *transmission system* in which *mark signals* are formed by *electric current* or *voltage pulses* of one polarity and *space signals* are formed by electric current or voltage pulses of equal magnitude but of opposite polarity; or one polarity for one of the *binary digits,* say the 1's, and the other polarity for the other binary digits, in this case the 0's. For example, a positive pulse, represented by current flowing in one direction in a circuit, could be used to represent a *mark* or a 1, and a negative pulse, represented by current flowing in the opposite direction in the circuit, could be used to represent the *space* or a 0. The direction of electric current flow, or the polarity of a voltage, is not to be confused with the direction of *information* flow. Thus, a negative current pulse at the transmitting end means current flow from the receiving end, but the pulse never-the-less travels to the receiving end.

polar relay.   A relay consisting of a solenoid (electromagnet) and an armature that it can actuate in such a manner that the direction of movement of the armature depends upon the direction of *current* flow.

polar transmission.   See *double-current signaling.*

pole.   See *celestial pole.*

policy.   See *communication security policy; electromagnetic emission policy (EEP); emission policy.*

Polish notation.   See *prefix notation.*

polling.   **1.** In *communication systems,* a *network control system* in which a designated *control station* invites its *tributary stations* to *transmit* in the sequence specified by the control station. **2.** The requesting of a *response* from the members of a group. For example, the inviting of a group of *data stations* to *transmit* one at a time.

polychromatic radiation.   *Electromagnetic radiation* consisting of two or more *frequencies* or *wavelengths.*   Synonymous with *dichromatic radiation.*   Also see *monochromatic radiation.*

polychromatism.   See *dichroism.*

polyline.   In *display systems,* a *display element, display group,* or *display image* consisting of a set of connected lines, usually capable of being *operated* upon as a unit, such as *translating, rotating* and *scissoring* the set of lines.

polystep dither.   In *optical systems,* a method of obtaining and tagging perturbations consisting of *discrete* changes made consecutively on a fixed time schedule. Also see *frequency multidither.*

population inversion. 1. A redistribution of energy levels in a population of elements such that, instead of having more atoms with *lower-energy-level* electrons, there are fewer atoms with higher-energy-level *electrons*. That is, an increase in the total number of electrons in the higher *excited states* occurs at the expense of the energy in the electrons in the ground or lower state and at the expense of the *resonant* energy source (i.e., the pump). This is not an equilibrium condition. The generation of population inversion is caused by *pumping.* 2. A condition in a stimulated material, such as a *semiconductor,* in which the upper *energy level* of two possible electronic energy levels in a given atom, distribution of atoms, molecule, or distribution of molecules, has a higher probability (usually only slightly higher) of being occupied by an electron. When population inversion occurs, the probability of downward energy transition giving rise to *radiation,* is greater than the probability of upward energy transitions, giving rise to *photon absorption,* resulting in a net *radiation* level, thus obtaining stimulated emission − i.e., *laser* action.

port. 1. In an *optical fiber, bundle* or *cable,* a point at which *signals* can enter or leave. Also see *access coupler; coupler.* 2. In a *communication network,* a point at which *signals* can enter or leave the network enroute to or from another network. 3. A place of *access* to a device or *network* where energy may be supplied or withdrawn or where the device or network variables may be observed or measured. Also see *gateway.* See *terminal port.* See Figure P-9.

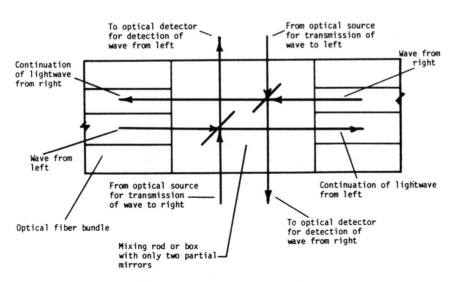

P-9. *Connection* of *fiber bundles* to *optical mixing rod* and entry and exit **ports.**

portable. See *air portable.*

port radio transmission control. Special controls that are imposed on *ship stations* while they are in port. For example, sealing *radio* equipment, restrictions against all *messages* except *distress messages,* and obtaining permission from local consular authority to *transmit.*

position. 1. In a *character string,* a location that may be occupied by a *character* and that may be identified by a serial number. 2. In a *communication system,* a certain point, location, or piece of equipment. For example, a *transmitter distributor* or a contact on it, an *operating position* at a *switchboard* or *control console,* a service clerk in a *message center,* a tape-cutting unit, a typing *reperforator,* or any other unit or place of work in a *communication facility.* See *coordinate position; current position; dead-reckoning position; digit position; display position; erect position; inverted position; print position; supervisor position; teletype position.*

position classification. In *direction finding systems,* an evaluation of the *precision* with which the location of a *station* is or can be measured by two or more *direction-finding stations.* For example, positions may be classified as a Class A, Class B, or Class C position. A Class A position might be a position measurement that is estimated to be accurate to within 5 nmi, a Class B position to within 20 nmi, and a Class C position within 50 nmi. The position classification is specified by the direction-finding station.

position flaghoist. See *superior position flaghoist.*

position indicator. See *planned position indicator (PPI); radar planned position indicator.*

positioning. In *display systems,* a technique in which a *stylus* or *display writer,* such as a *light-pen, sonic pen, laser* beam, electron gun, *voltage pencil, plotter stylus,* or *tablet stylus,* is used to indicate the location, in the *display space* on the *display surface* of a *display device,* where a specific *display element, display group, display image, character,* or picture is to be placed. Synonymous with *locating.*

positioning land station. See *radio positioning land station.*

positioning mobile station. See *radio positioning mobile station.*

position line. In *radiolocation,* a *line* that is drawn on a map at a *radiodetermined azimuth* through a known point, such as through the location of the *transmitting antenna* or the location of the *receiving antenna.*

position line determination.   See *radio position line determination.*

position log.   In a *radio* or *radar station position* (work station), a description of operating events that pertain to the position. The position log might include the *station identification,* the *position* identification, opening and closing time, date, *stations* communicated with, *operating frequencies,* tests performed, communication summaries, distress actions, safety actions, and any other significant actions or events pertaining to the position, such as operating difficulties, maintenance problems, and repairs or adjustments effected. Also see *aeronautical station master log.*

position marking.   In a military operational situation, marking for purposes of identification of personnel or equipment on the ground, such as the location of the most advanced elements of an advancing military unit, or the location of a forest fire fighting unit. In *visual signaling systems,* a small individual *panel* exposed on the ground, or a cloud of colored smoke, may be used for position marking.

position modulation.   See *pulse-position modulation.*

positive-AND gate.   See *AND gate.*

positive clearing.   In *double-supervisory working* of *telephone switchboards, clearing* in which a *light,* disc, or other indication associated with a *plug* in use, appears when a *user* (customer, subscriber) *clears* a connected *call* and remains *displayed* until the associated plug is disconnected. Also see *negative clearing.*

positive distortion.   See *late distortion.*

positive feedback.   See *regeneration.*

positive-intrinsic-negative (PIN) diode.   A *junction diode* doped in the forward direction positive, intrinsic (no *dopant*), and negative, in that order. PIN diodes are used as *photodetectors* in *fiber-optic* and *integrated optical circuits.*

positive-intrinsic-negative (PIN) photodiode.   A *positive-intrinsic-negative (PIN) diode* that changes its *conductivity* in accordance with the *intensity* and *frequency* of *incident light.*

positive-intrinsic-negative (PIN) photodiode coupler.   A coupling device that enables the coupling of *light energy* from an *optical fiber* or *cable* onto the photosensitive surface of a *positive-intrinsic-negative (PIN) diode* of a *photon detector (photodetector)* at the receiving end of an *optical-fiber data link.* The coupler may only be a *fiber pigtail* epoxied to the *photodiode.*

positive justification. See *bit stuffing.*

positive lens. See *converging lens.*

positive-OR gate. See *OR gate.*

positive pulse stuffing. See *bit stuffing.*

positive scanning shift. In *facsimile transmission systems,* a relative shift of the *scanning* device with respect to the surface of the document being scanned when the document is scanned along the *line* from left to right and where the *scanning lines* proceed from top to bottom. In a *drum facsimile transmitting* apparatus, helicoidal scanning toward the left is a positive scanning shift.

post. See *airborne command post.*

postal address. An *address* that is used for mail. For example, the postal address of the *International Organization for Standardization* is 1211 Geneve 20, Suisse.

postamble. *Characters* that follow a specified group of characters. For example, a sequence of characters that are recorded at the end of each *block* of *data* on *phase-encoded magnetic tape* for the purpose of *synchronization* when the tape is read backward, that is, in the reverse direction.

postdetection combiner. A *circuit* or device for combining two or more *signals* after *demodulation.* Also see *diversity combiner.*

postdetector bandwidth. The *bandwidth* of the *baseband channels* for the *signal output* of a *detector.* It is determined by the *bandpass* of the postdetection *filter.*

postdetector signal/noise ratio. The ratio of the *baseband signal power* to the total *noise power* in the *postdetector bandwidth,* expressed as a ratio, percentage, or in *decibels.*

postfix notation. A method of forming mathematical expressions in which each *operator* is preceded by its *operands* and indicates the *operation* to be performed on the operands or on the intermediate results that precede it. For example, AB+ indicates that the values of A and B are to be added, and ABX indicates that the values of A and B are to be multiplied. Synonymous with *reverse Polish notation; suffix notation.* Also see *prefix notation.*

post-selection time. In the establishment of a *connection* or the placement of a *call,* the elapsed time from the end of *transmission* of *selection signals* until the receipt of the *call-completed signal* at the *calling user's (calling party's) data terminal equipment (DTE).* For example, the time that elapses between the completion of *dialing* to the end of *ringing* or receipt of an *off-hook signal.* Also see *call setup time.*

POT.   1. *Point of train.*   2. *Potentiometer.*

potential.   See *absolute potential; ground potential.*

potential difference.   In *electrical* equipment, the difference between the *electric potential (absolute voltage)* of one point relative to another. For example, the 12 volts of *potential difference* between the *terminals* of an automobile battery, regardless of the *absolute potential* of one of the terminals. Synonymous with *voltage.*

potentiometer.   A spatially distributed *electrical resistance* that has a *terminal* on both ends and a movable contact that slides along the resistive element in such a manner that the *resistance* from either end to the sliding contact can be made to vary. The resistive element is usually circular and the moving wiper contact is rotated about the center of the circle. Usually a *potential difference* is connected across the two ends of the resistive element. A fraction of this potential difference will appear between either end and the wiper contact, its value depending on the fraction of resistance between one end and the wiper compared to the entire resistance. If not much current is drawn, the fraction will be proportional to the percent of the resistance between an end and the wiper contact. Adjustment can be made for electrical loading. The potentiometer has many applications in volume control, *bias* control, *circuit balancing,* and other areas. The potentiometer is often referred to simply as a pot or a *voltage* divider.

powder.   See *glass powder; starting powder.*

power.   1. The time rate of *transfer* or *absorption* of energy in a *system.*   2. In *optics,* a measure of the ability of an *optical* element to bend or *refract light,* usually measured in *diopters.* In a telescope, it is the number of times the instrument *magnifies* the *object* viewed. For example, if with a six-power instrument, an object 600 m away is enlarged six times, it appears as it would to the naked eye if it were at a distance of only 100 m. See *absolute power; average power; auxiliary power; bundle resolving power; carrier power; chromatic resolving power; disturbance power; effective isotropic radiated power; effective radiated power (ERP); equivalent isotropically-radiated power; flat-noise power; grating chromatic power; jamming power; link threshold power; magnifying power; mean power; noise equivalent power; noise power; normalized power; optical repeater peak envelope power (PEP); peak power; peak spectral power; primary power; prism chromatic resolving power; psophometric power; radiant power; rated output power; received noise power; resolving power; signaling power; source-to-fiber coupled power; theoretical resolving power; transmitted power.* See Figure P-10.

P-10. A 15 kVA uninterruptible **power** *system* for *computer* power *interface, telecommunication, security,* medical laboratory, and process control systems. (Courtesy of Clary Corporation.)

power balancing. **1.** In *communication systems,* the adjustment of individual *radiated power levels* in a *multipoint network.* For example, in a *satellite communication system,* to achieve optimum performance of each component of the network by distributing the available power among the *components;* or in a *radio network,* to adjust the transmitting (radiated) power of each *station* for optimum reception and minimum *interference* among all stations. **2.** In a *satellite communication system,* the optimizing of the available *down-link power* that is allocated to the individual *accessing signals,* depending on the number of accessing signals and their relative *up-link strengths.* The power levels are controlled by adjustment of *transmitter power* at the *earth stations.* Also see *power sharing.*

power budget. The allocation of *available power* in a *system* to the various functions that need to be performed. For example, in a *satellite communication system,* the distribution of the available power in a *satellite* for maintaining orientation, maintaining *orbit* control, and for the *reception* and *retransmission* of *signals*. Synonymous with *system budget*. See *optical power budget*.

power bus. A *conductor (bus)* that carries *electrical power* to a set of devices or *components*. The bus is usually maintained at a constant *voltage* and is considered to have zero *impedance* and be capable of supplying infinite *current*. A power bus is sometimes called an infinite bus. Also see *data bus*.

power circuit breaker. 1. A circuit breaker that is used on *power circuits* that supply *alternating-current (AC)* or *direct-current (DC)* to electrical equipment. They are characterized by an ability to interrupt large *currents* or *voltages* and usually have a voltage interrupt capability in excess of 1500 V and a current interrupt capability in excess of 100 A. **2.** The main or primary *switch* that is used to apply or remove *electrical power* to or from equipment.

power density 1. In an *electromagnetic wave,* the *power* flow rate, a vector quantity, that *propagates* in a specific direction at a particular point in a *transmission medium,* expressed as the energy per unit time (power) passing through a unit cross-sectional area that is perpendicular to the direction of propagation of the wave. The power density usually diminishes with distance from the *source,* due to *absorption, dispersion, diffusion, deflection, reflection, scattering, defraction,* and *diffraction,* as well as *geometric spreading.* **2.** A measure of the power that may be attributed to a particular *frequency band,* usually expressed in watts/ hertz. Also see *optical energy density.* See *noise power density; optical power density.*

powered. See *sound powered.*

powered telephone. See *electrically-powered telephone; sound-powered telephone.*

powered-flight phase. In the launching of a *satellite,* the part of *spacecraft* flight during which propulsion engines are developing thrust. In most cases the powered-flight phase ends when the required height has been reached and the launch vehicle is separated from the spacecraft *(satellite).* When launch conditions are such that the satellite cannot be propelled directly into the chosen orbit, the launch sequence consists of several powered-flight phases alternating with unpowered intervals with the engines shut off until the proper height and velocity are reached. Also see *passive flight phase.*

power efficiency. See *optical power efficiency.*

power gain. See *antenna power gain.*

power gain of an antenna. See *antenna gain.* Also see *antenna power gain.*

power level. In a *transmission system,* the ratio of the *power* at or passing a point in the system to the power at the *input* to the system or to some arbitrary amount of power, such as a milliwatt or a watt; it is represented as *dBm* or *dBW.*

power leveling. The process of adjusting the *power* delivered at the end of a *transmission medium* to a *load* whose *reactance* varies with *frequency*, particularly to avoid overloading, *reflections,* or *distortion.* Power leveling is usually accomplished at the receiving end of *transmission lines, cables,* and *waveguides.*

power limited. In a *communication system,* pertaining to the situation in which the total *traffic capacity* of the *system* is limited by the *power* that is available for allocation to the *signals* being processed and the *channels* being operated. Usually there is a limitation only of the *radio frequency (RF)* energy. The alternative to being power limited is to be *bandwidth limited.* This occurs when the total traffic capacity is limited by the limited frequencies that are available for use, that is, by the available *bandpass.* The situation for a communication system in regard to power and bandwidth limitation is somewhat analogous to the situation in an *automatic data processing system* that may be either *input-output* (bandwidth) limited or *processor* (power) limited. Also see *bandwidth limited.*

power margin. See *radio frequency power margin.*

power-of-the-talker volume distribution. See *mean-power-of-the-talker volume distribution.*

power output. See *optical power output; peak power output.*

power output rating. See *transmitter power output rating.*

power points. See *emission-beam-angle-between-half-power-points.*

power ratio. See *carrier-to-noise power ratio; inband noise power ratio; radiant power ratio; single-sideband noise power ratio.*

power sharing. The distribution of power among the *components* of a system. For example, in a *satellite communication system,* the fixed division of the available *satellite down-link power* among the individual *transponders* or separate pathways through the *satellite.* The allocation of power to individual *access signals* is a variable, the distribution depending on the number of accessing signals and the relative *up-link signal strengths,* controlled by adjustment of *transmitter power* at the *earth stations.* The controlled adjustment of distribution is called *power balancing.* Usually only *radio frequency (RF)* power is implied. Also see *power balancing.*

power talker. See *medium-power talker.*

Poynting vector. The *vector* obtained, in the direction of a right-hand screw from the cross product (vector product) of the *electric field vector* rotated into the *magnetic field vector* of an *electromagnetic wave.* The Poynting vector, with *transmission media parameters* and constants, gives the *power density* and direction of *propagation* of the electromagnetic wave. Mathematically:

$$\mathbf{P} = \mathbf{E} \times \mathbf{H} \quad \text{(vectors)}$$

PPI. *Planned position indicator.*

PPM. *Pulse-position modulator.*

ppm. Parts per million.

pps. *Pulses* per *second.*

pragmatics. The branch of philosophy that deals with the testing of the value and truth of ideas by their practical consequences or utility, including the study (discipline) concerned with the practical relationships between *symbols* or groups of *characters* and their *users* or interpreters.

preamble. A segment of *text* that appears or occurs in space or time before a larger body of text. For example, in *computers* and *communication systems,* a *component* of the *heading* of a *message,* including such items as the *precedence designation,* the *date-time group,* and *message instruction;* in *spread-spectrum systems,* a *binary code* sequence that is used for acquiring *synchronization,* particularly synchronization of the *spread-spectrum code-sequence generators;* and in *magnetic tape storage,* a sequence of *characters* that is recorded at the beginning of each *block* of *data* on a *phase-encoded magnetic tape* for the purpose of *synchronization.* In most instances, preambles are usually short compared to other *character* sequences or *codes.*

prearranged message code. A *code* that is adapted for use and that requires a special or technical vocabulary. It is usually composed exclusively of groups of *characters* that represent complete or nearly complete statements or messages.

preassignment access plan. In *satellite communication system operations,* a fixed *communication channel access plan,* as opposed to a *demand-assignment access plan* in which the allocation of *accesses* or the number of *channels* per access is varied in accordance with the demand. Also see *demand-assignment access plan.*

preburst message. A *message* that indicates the effective forward wind and the *down-wind distance* for a given geographical area. The *information* is to be used in the event of a nuclear explosion in that area. The information is of particular interest in regard to the effects in the downwind area from ground zero of a burst. Also see *fallout message.*

precedence. In *communication systems,* the level of urgency that an *originator* assigns to a *message.* The level is assigned according to the estimated effect on life and property that is caused by a delay in *transmission* of the message. See *automatic multilevel precedence; flash-override precedence; flash precedence; immediate precedence; multilevel precedence (MLP); priority precedence; routine precedence.*

precedence call. In *telephone switchboard operation,* a *call* with a *precedence* above *routine* in *networks* in which a *precedence system* is in effect. Also see *nonprecedence call.*

precedence capability.   See *multilevel precedence capability.*

precedence designation.   In *communication systems,* a designation that is assigned to a *message* by the *originator* to indicate the relative order in which *communication* personnel or equipment are to handle the message and the order in which the *addressee* is to handle the message relative to other messages.   The precedence designation indicates an estimate of the degree of urgency and an estimate of the adverse effects on life and property that may occur if the message is delayed.   Precedence designators that are used in *military communication systems* include *flash override, flash, immediate, priority,* and *routine,* in descending order of urgency.   Some of these categories are used in public and private communication systems.   Also see *emergency category.*

precedence designator.   A letter, group of letters, or *word* that is used to indicate the *precedence designation* of a *message,* that is, used to indicate the *precedence* that is assigned to a message.

precedence message.   See *dual-precedence message; single-precedence message.*

precedence responsibility.   The responsibility for assigning the *precedence* to a *message* or to a *call.*   The responsibility for *precedence designation* normally rests with the *originator.*

precedence system.   See *Joint Uniform Telephone Communication Precedence System (JUTCPS).*

precedence telephone system.   A *telephone system* that requires the use of *precedence designations* on all *calls* or on all calls over certain *trunks* in the system.

precession.   The effect that results from the application of an external torque to a spinning body in which the gryoscopic forces cause the resultant displacement caused by the torque to be *orthogonal* to the applied force and orthogonal to the *vector* representing the spinning mass.   The vector that represents the spinning mass is parallel to the axis of rotation and in the direction of a right-hand screw turning in the direction of spin.   The effect occurs in all spinning masses, from *electrons* to *satellites.*   The effect must be accounted for in spin-stabilized *communication satellites* in order to maintain proper orientation of communication equipment, particularly *antennas.*

precipitation attenuation.   The loss of the energy of an *electromagnetic wave* by *reflection, scattering, refraction,* and *absorption* during *propagation* through a volume of the *atmosphere* that contains precipitation such as dust, rain, snow, hail, sleet, or fog.   For example, it is the reflection of a *radar signal* from a volume of falling snow that enables it to be seen on a radar screen.   This indicates that at least a part of the signal is reflected and perhaps an *attenuated* part penetrates the snow volume.

precipitation gage station.   See *radar beacon precipitation gage station.*

precipitation static.   *Interference* that is experienced in a *receiver* during the times the precipitation, such as dust, rain, snow, hail, sleet, or fog, occurs between the receiver and a *transmitter antenna*. It is most often caused by charged particles in the precipitation impacting against the *receiver antenna*. Also see *noise*.

precise frequency. A *frequency* that is maintained to the known accuracy of an accepted *reference frequency standard*.

precise time. A time instant or a time interval that is known accurately with reference to an accepted reference time standard. In actual practice, the instant or interval is identified by a *mark* or *signal* and the moments of occurrence of the mark or signal are described with *precision* relative to the accepted standard reference *time scale*.

precision. 1. A measure of the ability to distinguish between nearly equal values. 2. The degree of agreement among repeated measurements of the same object or event. 3. A measure of the spread or deviations of the results of an *operation* that is repeated from the mean value. The distinction between precision and *accuracy* is illustrated by a situation in which an entry in a four-place table of values, such as a trigonometric or logarithmic table, is less precise than the corresponding entry in a six-place table but a properly (correctly) computed four-place entry may be more accurate than an improperly (incorrectly) computed six-place entry. Also see *accuracy*. See *frequency standard precision*.

precision coding compaction. See *variable precision coding compaction*.

precision-sleeve splicer. A round tube, with a round hole that has a diameter equal to the outer diameter of two *optical fibers* to be *spliced,* containing a *matched-index* epoxy, into which the two fibers may be inserted from opposite ends. The ends of the sleeve may be crimped to hold the fibers tightly while the epoxy cures. Also see *loose-tube splicer; tangential coupling*. See Figure P-11.

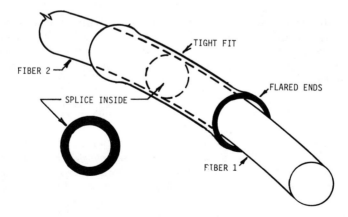

P-11. A precision sleeve splicer.

precombining. The *combining* of *multiplexed signals* prior to the *modulation* of the *carrier.* Synonymous with *premodulation combining.*

predetection combiner. A *circuit* or device that *combines* two or more *signals* prior to *demodulation* of any of the signals and prior to the demodulation of the *combined signal.* Also see *diversity combiner.*

predetection combining. A technique that is used to obtain an improved *signal* from multiple *radio receivers* that are involved in *diversity reception.* The process requires that all incoming *diversity transmission signals* be brought into approximate phase coincidence before being entered into a *diversity combiner.*

predetermined routing. In *message transmission,* a method of *routing messages* in which specific *instructions* for routing are used and applied to the *routing indicators* of *message headings* in order to assign relay responsibility and to prevent the need for specific routing instructions for each *message. Alternative routing* is also considered to be a form of predetermined routing.

prediction. See *frequency prediction.*

prediction publication. See *propagation prediction publication.*

prediction table. In *satellite communication systems,* a table that contains the longitude of *subsatellite points, node* times, and *orbit* inclinations at daily intervals for a particular *satellite* in order to allow pointing angles to be calculated for any point on the earth's surface that is within the satellite *earth coverage.* The table is used in conjunction with an acquisition table that is appropriate for the satellite's orbit in order to initiate *communications* via the satellite.

predictive coding. See *adaptive predictive coding (APC); linear predictive coding.*

pre-emphasis. In an *electromagentic wave* of many *frequencies* at the *input* of a *system,* a process that is designed to increase the magnitude of certain wave *components* with specific *frequencies* with respect to the magnitude of others in order to reduce adverse effects, such as *noise,* in other parts of the system. Also see *de-emphasis.*

pre-emphasis circuit. A modification in the *gain-frequency (frequency response)* characteristic of a *circuit,* normally by increasing the relative *amplitude* of the higher frequency *signal components* in conjunction with a separate, but corresponding decreasing of these amplitudes in a *de-emphasis* circuit to restore the original signal and thereby improve the *signal-to-noise ratio.* A de-emphasis of the lower *frequency components* and their restoration would have similar effects.

pre-emphasis improvement. The improvement in the *signal-to-noise ratio* of the *high-frequency* end of the *baseband* that results from passing the *modulating signal* at the *transmitter* through a *pre-emphasis network* that increases the *amplitude* of the higher *signal frequencies,* and then passing the *output* of a *discriminator* through a *de-emphasis network* to restore the original *signal power* distribution among the various frequencies.

pre-emphasis network. A *network* that is inserted into a *system* in order to increase the *amplitude* of *electromagnetic waves* or *signals,* with many different *frequencies,* in one range of frequencies with respect to the amplitudes of frequencies in another range of frequencies. Pre-emphasis is usually employed in *frequency modulation (FM)* or *phase modulation (PM) transmitters* in order to equalize the *modulating signal power* in terms of the *deviation ratio.* The *receiver demodulation* process includes a reciprocal network called a *de-emphasis network* that is used to restore the original *signal power* distribution among the various frequencies. Also see *de-emphasis network.*

preemption. 1. The *seizure,* usually automatic, of *communication system facilities* that are being used to serve lower *precedence traffic* in order to serve immediately higher precedence traffic. It is the act of seizing communication facilities for one group of *users* in preference to other users. 2. The reallocation of *communication services* and equipment from a lower *precedence* use to a higher precedence use. In some *systems, calls* and *transmissions* can be preempted while in progress, that is, during the *information transfer phase.* See *automatic preemption.*

preemption tone. In *telephone systems,* a distinctive tone that is used to indicate to connected *users* (customers, subscribers, parties) that their *call* has been preempted by a call of higher *precedence.* For example, a distinctive, steady, high-pitch tone heard for three seconds or until the preempted user hangs up.

prefix. One of the *parts* of the *heading* of a *message.* Its parts may include the *accounting information (prepaid, collect, service),* group count, and SVC, indicating that the message was a *service message.* In some *radiotelephone system messages,* the prefix is the part of the heading that consists only of the accounting information or the group count. See *amplifying prefix.*

prefix notation. A method of forming mathematical expressions in which each *operator* precedes its *operands.* The operator indicates the operation that is to be performed on the operands or on the intermediate results that follow it. For example, +AB indicates that the values of A and B are to be added, and ✕AB indicates that they are to be multiplied. Synonymous with *Lukasiewicz notation; Polish notation.* Also see *postfix notation.*

preform. See *optical-fiber preform.* See Figure P-12.

P-12. A *meter*-long glass **preform** (in the chuck) from which an *optical fiber* is being drawn for use in *lightwave communication systems* and *components*. (Courtesy of Bell Laboratories.)

pregroup combining. In *communication systems*, assembling a number of *narrow band channels*, such as 4-kHz wide *telephone channels*, into a specified *frequency band* in such a manner that after *pregroup translation*, they may be formed with other pregroups into a standard *group*, such as a *CCITT basic group*, by *frequency-division multiplexing*.

pregroup translation. In *communication systems*, the process of transposing in *frequency* a pregroup of *channels*, such as *telephone* or *data channels*, in such a manner that they may be formed into a standard *group*, such as a *CCITT basic group*, by *frequency-division multiplexing*. Also see *basic group*.

prelasing condition. The operating condition of a *laser* in which its *radiation* is primarily spontaneous and not *coherent*.

preliminary call. In *radio transmission,* a *call* that is designed to establish *communication* with a particular *station.* The preliminary call must include at least the *identification* of the *calling station* and the *called station.* It should also include a request to the called station to reply, although such can be implied by the recitation of the *call signs.*

preliminary call-up signal. In the schedule for an *area broadcast station* or a *coastal radio station,* one of the *calling signals,* such as the *collective call sign, transmitting station call sign,* schedule serial numbers, and other signals that immediately precede the *traffic list* of *messages* to be *transmitted.*

premodulation combining. See *precombining.*

Prentice's rule. A means of determining *prism power* at any point on a *lens.* Prism power equals *dioptric power* multiplied by the distance in centimeters from the *optical* center.

prepaid. In a *communication system,* a *prefix* in a *message* indicating that the charges for the message were paid at the *source,* usually prior to *transmission.* Also see *collect.*

preparation time. See *message preparation time.*

preselection filter. A *bandpass filter* for a *local oscillator* and for *frequency* rejection in the *signal path* prior to *down conversion* in a *receiver.* Synonymous with *preselector filter.*

preselector filter. See *preselection filter.*

presentation layer. In *open systems architecture,* the *layer* that provides the functions, procedures, services, and *protocol* that are selected by the *application layer.* For example, the functions may include data definition and control of *data* entry, data exchange, and data *display.* Also see *layer.*

preset conference. A *communication network* feature that permits the automatic *connection* of a fixed group of *users,* or a *closed user group with outgoing access,* by *keying* a single *directory number.*

preset jammer. A *jammer* in which the *frequency* of the *jamming transmitter* can be fixed before the transmitter is placed in *operation.* Preset jammers are most useful in airborne jamming operations where weight and space requirements may prohibit the use of operators or elaborate control equipment in flight. Preset jammers are often used in *barrage jamming* over a wide *band,* usually in an overlapping series of *frequency* bands.

press-to-talk operation. See *push-to-talk operation.*

press-to-type operation. See *push-to-type operation.*

press traffic. In a *communication system, messages* that contain text that is destined to be released to public *information* media, such as newspapers, magazines, *radio stations,* and *television stations.*

prevarication.   See *irrelevance.*

preventive maintenance.   Maintenance *operations,* including tests, measurements, adjustments, and parts replacement, that are performed specifically to prevent *faults* from occurring. Also see *corrective maintenance.*

primary.   In *high-level data link control (HDLC) procedures* that are used in *communication systems,* the part of a *data station* that supports the main *control functions* of the *data link,* and that generates *commands* for *transmission* and interprets *responses.*   Specific functions include initialization of *control signaling,* organization of *data* flow, and *error control* at the *data link level.*

primary aeronautical station.   A *station* in the *aeronautical mobile service,* that at any given instant has the right to select and to *transmit information* to a *secondary station,* and the responsibility to insure information *transfer.*   There is only one *primary station* on a *data link* or *radio net* at one time. It has control of the data link or radio net at a given instant. The assignment of primary status to a given station is temporary and is governed by standard control procedures. Primary status is normally conferred upon a station so that it may *transmit* a *message,* but a station need not have a message to transmit to be selected as the primary station. The primary station is selected by the *master net control station.*

primary axis.   In movable *antenna systems,* the axis that has the ground (earth) as a reference datum.   The secondary axis has the primary axis as a datum.   For example, the vertical axis about which an antenna may rotate.

primary channel.   1. The *channel* that is designated as a prime *transmission* channel and is the first choice when restoring high-*priority* (high-*precedence*) *circuits.* 2. In a *data communication network,* a transmission channel that has the highest *signaling rate* capability of all the channels that share a common *interface.*   A primary channel may support the *transfer* of *data* in one direction only, either direction alternately, or both directions simultaneously.   Also see *auxiliary channel; secondary channel.*

primary control.   See *central primary control.*

primary distribution system.   In *electric power networks,* a *system* of *alternating current (AC)* power distribution that supplies the primary windings of distribution *transformers* from the generating station or substation distribution *buses.*

primary frequency.   1. A *frequency* that is assigned for normal use on a particular *circuit.*   2. The *radiotelephone frequency* that is assigned to a *station, fixed* or *mobile,* as a first choice for *communication* in a *radiotelephone network.*

primary frequency standard.   A standard *frequency source* that meets national standards for *accuracy* and that can *operate* with no other frequency reference for calibration.   For example, a *cesium beam clock.*   Also see *frequency offset; standard time-frequency signal.*

primary guard.   In *aeronautical communications,* the principal responsibility for maintaining *communication* with an *aircraft station* during flight.

primary guard station. In *aeronautical communications,* the *station* that holds *primary guard* responsibility for a particular flight of an *aircraft station.*

primary power. In a *communication system,* a reliable *source* of *electric power.* It normally serves the *communication station* main *bus.* The source may be a government-owned generating plant or the public utility power system that serves the area in which the station is located. A Class A primary power source is one that provides an essentially continuous supply of electric power. Also see *auxiliary power.*

primary radar. *Radar* that uses only its own *reflection* from an object (target) and that does not depend on active *signals* that are *transmitted* by the object (target) that it finds or tracks. Also see *secondary radar.*

primary radiation source. A *source* that generates and *emits electromagnetic waves,* such as an energized *radio transmitter,* the sun, an energized *light* bulb, or an energized *LED.*

primary route. The predetermined path of a *message* from its *source* (sender or originating *station*) to a *message sink (receiver, addressee,* or destination *station).* *Routing* requires the selection of *routing indicators* for the *addressees.* In *telephone switchboard operation,* the primary route is the route that is to be attempted first by the *operators* or by the equipment when completing a *call.* *Alternative routing* is based on *network traffic* conditions and *supervisory* policy. Also see *alternative routing.*

primary ship-shore station. A shore-based *ship-shore station* that is responsible for providing the *guard* for any or all of the worldwide ship-shore *frequency* series that may be changed from time to time and that have direct access to *ship broadcast systems.* Also see *local ship-shore station; secondary ship-shore station.*

primary spectrum. The main, first, or the characteristic *chromatic aberration* of a *simple nonachromatized lens* or *prism.* Also see *secondary spectrum.*

primary station. In a *data communication network,* the *station* that is responsible for the *unbalanced* control of a *data link.* The primary station generates *commands* and interprets *responses.* It is responsible for initialization of *data* and *control information* interchange, organization and control of data flow, retransmission control, and all *recovery functions* at the *link level.*

primary substation. In *electric power networks,* equipment that *switches* or modifies *electric current, voltage, frequency,* or other characteristics of *primary power.*

prime focus feed. An *antenna feeder* arrangement in which the *radiating feed horn* is located at the *principal focus* point of the *main reflector.* Synonymous with *front-fed.* See *offset prime focus feed.*

prime number. A whole number, such as 17, that has no whole number divisors, except 1 and itself, that produce a whole number quotient, that is, with no remainder. The first few prime numbers are 1, 2, 3, 5, 7, 11, 13, 17, 19, and 23.

principal focus. See *focal point; principal focus point.*

principal focus point. The point to which *incident* parallel rays of *light* converge, or from which they diverge, when they have been acted upon by a *lens* or *mirror.* A lens has a single point of principal focus on each side of the lens. A mirror has but one principal focus. A lens or mirror has an infinite number of *image* points, *real* or *virtual,* one for each position of, or point on, the *object.* Synonymous with *principal focus.*

principal point. See *first principal point.*

principal ray. In the *object* space of an *optical system,* the *ray* directed at the first principal point, and hence in the *image* space the ray projected backward, intersecting the axis at the second principal point.

printed circuit. An *electrical circuit* that is formed on a *substrate* material with a metal clad surface that is coated with a photosensitive material. A *photographic* process is used to etch away the undesired metal to form *connections* between *circuit components* that are also mounted on the board. *Access* is by means of sliding surfaces and *connectors.*

printer. See *direct printer; Morse printer; page printer.*

printing perforator. A *perforator* that, when perforating tape, also prints on the tape the corresponding *character* or prints the *symbol* that represents each *control function.* For a *card punch,* the device that punches the cards and prints the corresponding *characters* on the card usually at the top of the corresponding column is called a card interpreter.

printing reperforator. A *reperforator* that, when reading and perforating tape, also prints on the tape the corresponding *character* or prints the *symbol* that represents each *control function.*

printing telegraphy. See *alphabetic telegraphy.*

printing-teletypewriter telegraphy (PTT). In *communication systems,* any method of manual *telegraph operation* in which *signals* are *transmitted* by means of a *keyboard* and are recorded by the *receiver* in the form of printed *characters.*

print position. The location on a *data medium* where a *graphic character* may be placed or formed.

print-through. A *transfer* of a recorded *signal* from one part of a *data medium* to another part of the recording medium when these parts are brought into physical contact. Print-through is normally undesired.

priority. See *frequency priority; restoration priority; with priority.*

priority facility. In *communication systems,* a *facility* that enables a *user* to exercise *precedence* over the other users of a communication system. The *priority* or *precedence designation* arrangements are handled by the system. The priority may be given to handling a *call,* a *packet transfer,* or to other services that are provided by the *network* or system.

priority precedence. The precedence designation that is reserved for calls and messages that require expeditious action by the addressees, that concern the conduct of operations in progress, and that relate to other important and urgent matters, and therefore require a precedence designation above that of routine precedence.

prism. A *transparent* body with at least two polished plane faces, inclined with respect to each other, from which *light* is *reflected* or through which light is *refracted.* When light is refracted by a prism whose *refractive index* exceeds that of the surrounding *medium,* it is deviated or bent toward the thicker part of the prism. See *penta prism.*

prism chromatic resolving power. When parallel *rays* of *light* are *incident* on a *prism,* the prism is oriented at the angle of minimum deviation at *wavelength L,* and the entire height of the prism is utilized, then the resolving power, *R,* deduced on the basis of Rayleigh's criterion, is:

$$R = L/\Delta L = B dn/dL$$

where *n* is the *refractive index* of the prism for the wavelength *L,* and *B* is the maximum thickness of prism traversed by the light rays. The quantities *dn/dL* and *B* are often called the *dispersion* and base-length of the prism, respectively.

prismograph. A graphic device for determining *prism power.*

privacy. 1. In *communication systems,* the *protection* that is afforded to *information transmitted* in a *communication system* or *network* in order to conceal it from persons within the system or network and outside the system or network. 2. The short-term *protection* that is afforded to those *messages* that require safeguarding, within existing laws, from unauthorized persons. For example, *radio communications* of law enforcement personnel. 3. The *protection* that is afforded by a *communication system* against unauthorized disclosure of the *information* in the system. The required protection may be accomplished by *communication security* measures, by directives to operating personnel, or by other means. 4. The right of a person's self-determination as to the degree to which the person is willing to share with others personal (private) *information* that is in the custody of others and that might be *compromised* by unauthorized exchange of such information. It is the right of persons and organizations to control the collection, *storage,* and dissemination by others of information about themselves. This right is above and beyond the professional ethics of doctors, lawyers, and clergymen to protect the personal information about their patients, clients, or congregation. Under the Information Privacy Act it is a legal right.

privacy code. A *code* that is used to protect the contents of a *message* from being understood when read by unauthorized persons but that does not afford any *security* or *protection* against organized *cryptanalysis.*

private aircraft station. An *aircraft station* that is on board an aircraft that is not operated by a commercial air carrier, a commercial airline, or a government-owned system. The aircraft is owned by a private person or a private organization.

private automatic branch exchange (PABX). A *private branch exchange (PBX)* in which the *connections* are made automatically and there is no *operator.*

private branch exchange (PBX). A *manually-operated telephone exchange* that is internal to and serves a single organization and usually has *connections* to another *telephone exchange* or *switching center.* The outside connection may be made via a *dial mode* or *dial service assistance switchboard.*

private branch exchange tie trunk. A direct *connection* between two *private branch exchanges (PBX's).*

private branch exchange trunk. A *trunk* that is used to interconnect a *private branch exchange (PBX)* with the *network switching center* that serves it.

private call. In *telephone system operation,* a *call* that is made on behalf of or in the interest of the *caller* rather than on behalf of the organization or in the interest of the organization to which the *telephone service* is being provided. Most organizations do not permit personal calls either to be made or received from organizational telephones. Synonymous with *personal call.*

private line. In *telephone systems,* an arrangement in which each *user* (customer, subscriber) *end-instrument,* particularly *telephones,* or set of end-instruments on the user's premises, is connected to a single and separate *local loop.* Thus, each instrument, or set of instruments, has a distinct *number* assigned only to the one user. There are no other user's end-instruments connected to that loop or assigned to that number. Privacy is complete, except perhaps for accidental *crosstalk* or *faulty connection.* Also see *party line.*

private operating agency. See *telecommunication private operating agency (TPOA).*

privilege. See *least privilege.*

probability. See *access-denial probability; added-block probability; block error probability; blocking probability; block loss probability; block misdelivery probability; disengagement-denial probability; outage probability; service probability.*

probability-analysis compaction. *Data compaction* in which an analytical formulation is used that is characterized by the expressions of a distribution of a set of measurements or *data* by certain numbers, such as only the median value and the standard deviation. Thus, only the median value and perhaps those values that exceed one, two, or three standard deviations need to be *transmitted* or stored rather than the entire set of measurements. This method of data compaction is based on the assumption that only the large deviations are significant and may require attention, action, interpretation, or analysis. All the other values that entered into the determination of the median and the standard deviation need not be stored or transmitted. See Figure P-13.

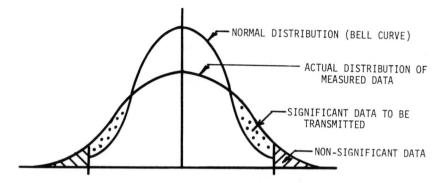

NORMAL DISTRIBUTION (BELL CURVE)

ACTUAL DISTRIBUTION OF
MEASURED DATA

SIGNIFICANT DATA TO BE
TRANSMITTED

NON-SIGNIFICANT DATA

P-13. In **probability analysis compaction,** only *data* outside of a normal distribution of values need be *stored* or *transmitted.* Extreme values may be ignored. Space, time, equipment, and cost may be saved.

probe.   See *fiber-optic probe.*

problem.   See *n-body problem; restricted circular three-body problem; three-body problem; two-body problem.*

problem-oriented language.   1. A *computer programming language* that is designed to express problems for *computer* solution in which the method of solution of the problems is not a primary factor.   2. See *application-oriented language.*

problem time.   In an *analog simulation,* the time during which the process that is being simulated actually takes place or is represented to take place. For example, in the ballistic trajectory of a missile, the time in *seconds* that corresponds to each coordinate position of the missile, though the missile is not actually being flown; or in the early days of the ENIAC (Electronic Numerical Integrator and Calculator) as the computer calculated the ordinate values of the trajectory of a simulated round of ammunition fired from a gun, one accumulator displayed the ordinate (altitude), another the abscissa (range) in meters, and a third accumulator expressed the time of flight since launching in seconds, namely the problem time. The calculation and the seconds displayed proceeded faster than the projectile actually took to fly, which is the real time. Also see *real-time operation.*

procedure.   In *communication system operation,* the actions that implement a *protocol.*   See *break-in procedure; call control procedure; circuit unavailability procedure; cross-band radiotelegraph procedure; data communication control procedure; flow control procedure; homing procedure; radiotelegraph procedure; radiotelephone procedure; ship-to-shore radiotelephone procedure; simplex radiotelegraph procedure.*

procedure-oriented language.   A *computer programming language* that is designed and used for expressing *algorithms* in a form suitable for *computer* solution and used primarily to facilitate the statement of *procedures.*

procedure word (PROWORD).   In *communication system operations,* such as in *voice radio* and *radiotelephone procedure,* a word that has an extended procedural meaning and is used relatively often when carrying on *communications*. For example ROGER, OVER, or OUT. The PROWORD in *voice systems* is used in place of the *prosign* in *telegraph* systems. It also provides for shorter and more meaningful communication system operation.

proceed-to-select. In *communication system operation*, pertaining to a *signal* or event in the *call access phase* of a *data call* that confirms the reception of a *call request signal* and advises the *calling data terminal equipment (DTE)* to proceed with the *transmission* of the *selection signals*. For example, pertaining to a *dial tone* in a *telephone system*.

proceed-to-select signal. In a *communication system,* a *signal* that indicates that the system is ready to receive a *selection signal.* For example, a *dial tone.*

process. See *axial vapor-phase oxidation process; double-crucible process; modified inside-vapor phase oxidation process; inside vapor-phase oxidation process; chemical vapor deposition (CVD) process; chemical vapor-phase oxidation process; modified chemical-vapor deposition process; molecular stuffing process; outside vapor-phase oxidation process; plasma-activated chemical vapor-deposition process; recovery process.*

process gain. In a *spread-spectrum communication system,* the *signal gain, signal-to-noise ratio,* signal shape, or other signal improvement obtained by *coherent band* spreading, remapping, and reconstitution of the desired signal.

processing. In *computers* and *communications,* the performing or causing of a sequence of events that are intended to accomplish a desired purpose or effect. For example, the performing of a sequence of *operations* on *data,* such as *storing, shifting, transmitting, receiving,* deleting, adding, changing, *translating, checking, converting,* distributing, or collecting data. See *automatic data processing (ADP); batch processing; data processing; distributed data processing; front-end processing; image processing; optical data processing; signal processing.*

processing equipment. See *automatic data processing equipment (ADPE).*

processing node. See *data processing node.*

processing station. See *data processing station.*

processing system. See *automatic data processing system (ADPS); distributed data processing system.*

processing terminal. See *data processing terminal.*

processing time. See *message processing time.*

processing unit. See *central processing unit (CPU).*

processor. In *computers* and *communication systems,* a *functional unit* that interprets *instructions* and executes them. When it is implemented in *hardware* and it does *data processing* it is called a data processor. When it is implemented in *software,* it is a *computer program* that performs the functions of a *compiler,* an *assembler,* a *translator,* or other software, in which case it uses specific *computer programming languages* to perform its functions. See *front-end processor; interface processor.*

processor unit. See *communication processor unit (CPU).*

process time. See *switching process time.*

product. See *bit-rate-length product; gain-bandwidth product; intermodulation product; modulation product.*

profile. See *communication security profile; graded-index profile; parabolic refractive-index profile; path profile; penetration profile; radial refractive index profile; step-index profile; uniform-index profile.*

profile fiber. See *uniform-index-profile fiber.*

profile mismatch loss. See *refractive-index profile mismatch loss.*

proforma message. A standard form of *message.* The nature of the successive elements that comprise the proforma message are usually understood by prearrangement among the *originator,* the *addressee,* and the *communication system operators.*

program. 1. To select a set of actions that is designed to achieve a specific result. For example, to prepare, design, write, and check a *computer program* by selecting a sequence of *instructions* and then testing the set to determine if in fact it accomplishes its intended purpose; or to select a sequence of *operations* in a *communication system.* 2. The product that results when a set of actions that is designed to achieve a specific result is selected. See *application program; computer program; diagnostic program.*

programmable logic. A set of *combinational logic elements* the interconnection of which can be changed by means of a *program,* that is, the logic elements are subject to program control. Usually a system of enabling and disabling of the logic elements *(logic circuits, logic gates)* is used. Synonymous with *variable logic.* Also see *fixed logic.*

programmable terminal. A *terminal* that can be *programmed* by the *user.* Synonymous with *programmable work station.*

programming. See *automatic programming; computer programming.*

programmer. 1. In a *digital system,* the part that has the function of controlling the timing and sequencing of *operations.* 2. A person who prepares sequences of *instructions* for execution, that is, one who *programs.* For example, a person who prepares a *computer program.*

program patch. See *computer program patch.*

progressive conference call.   A *conference call* in which the *operator* obtains each conferee on the conference *circuit* and either has the *originator* wait on the *line* or has the originator called back when all the conferees are on the line, depending on the time required to obtain all or most of the conferees on the line. Also see *meet-me conference call.*

progress signal.   See *call progress signal; waiting-in-progress signal.*

prompt.   1. In *interactive display systems,* to *display messages* in the *display space* on a *display surface* of a *display device* to help the *user* to plan and execute subsequent *operations.*   **2.** In *interactive display systems,* a *message displayed* on the *display surface* of a *display device* to help the *user* to plan and execute subsequent operations. Synonymous with *cue.*

propagation.   The movement or *transmission* of a *wave* in a *medium* or in *free space,* usually described in terms of *phase* or *group velocity.*   See *anomalous propagation; line-of-sight (LOS) propagation; scatter propagation; sporadic-E propagation.*

propagation constant.   In the *propagation* of an *electromagnetic wave* in a *waveguide,* such as an *optical fiber* or a metal pipe, the factor in the expression for the exponential variation characteristic of guided waves, namely:

$$e^{-pz} = e^{-ihz\ -az}$$

The term:

$$p = ih + a$$

includes both the *phase term, h,* and the *attenuation term, a,* governing the *propagation* characteristics of the *wave* in the guide.   *Dispersion* occurs because the propagation constant is a function of *frequency* and the materials of construction of the guide.   Also see *attenuation term; phase term.*

propagation ionospheric scatter.   See *backward propagation ionospheric scatter; forward propagation ionospheric scatter.*

propagation mode.   An allowable *electromagnetic field* condition that can exist in a *waveguide,* including *transverse electric* or *magnetic,* relative to the direction of *propagation* in the guide, each *mode* having a factor *(eigenvalue)* that defines the *propagation constant,* not the *attenuation factor,* for the discrete mode. The field can be described in terms of these modes, discontinuities and bends leading to mode conversion but not to *radiation.* In a *closed waveguide, standing waves* established in the transverse direction define the modes that propagate in the waveguide.   In an *open waveguide,* an *evanescent field* is established in the *transverse plane* and the mode is guided by the gradient of the *refractive index.*   **2.** The manner in which *electromagnetic signals* travel from a *transmitting antenna* to a *receiving antenna,* by *ground wave, sky wave, direct wave, ground reflection,* or *scatter.* Synonymous with *transmission mode.*   Also see *modal loss; mode volume.* See Figure P-14.

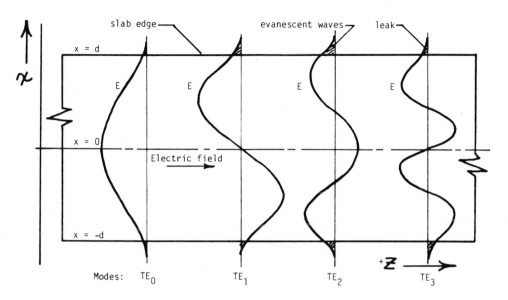

P-14. Lower order **propagation modes** in a *slab dielectric* (planar) *waveguide.*

propagation path obstruction. A man-made or natural physical feature that lies near enough to the *path* of an *electromagnetic wave* to cause a sensible effect on path *loss* exclusive of *reflection* effects. An obstruction may lie to the side, or even above the path, although usually it will lie below the path. Ridges, cliffs, buildings, and trees are examples of obstructions. If the clearance from the nearest point along the path, over the expected range of earth radius *K-factor,* exceeds 0.6 of the first *Fresnel zone* radius, the feature is not normally considered to be an obstruction. It will not have a significant effect on *propagation.* Also see *effective earth radius; Fresnel zone; K-factor; path clearance; path profile.*

propagation prediction publication. A publication that contains charts, guides, tables, and narrative *information* to enable *stations* to select optimum *frequencies* for *radio transmissions* given such factors as distance, time of day, season, area of earth, and *transmission power.*

propagation time delay. The time that a *signal* requires to travel from one point to another.

proportional vector. In *satellite communication systems,* that part of a *satellite command message* that indicates the magnitude or quantity of a function. For example, the number of degrees of angular movement of a steerable *antenna* or the number of thruster pulses required for an *orbital* or orientation adjustment.

proration. 1. In *communication systems,* the distribution or allocation of *parameters* such as *noise power* proportionally among a number of *tandem* connected items, such as equipment, *links,* or *trunks,* in order to balance the performance of *communication circuits.* 2. In a *telephone switching center,* the distribution or allocation of equipment or *components* proportionally among a number of functions in order to provide a requisite *service grade*.

prosign. One or more *characters,* such as letters, numerals, or *words,* that are used to represent complete statements that are frequently used in communications, such as SOS, AA to mean all after, or AB to mean all before, or in law enforcement *calls,* B&E to mean breaking and entry.

protected frequency. A *frequency* that is not to be deliberately *jammed* by one's own forces, particularly during a specified time period. Also see *guarded frequency; taboo frequency.*

protected information. *Information* that should not be disclosed to unauthorized persons. For example, information that is *security classified,* personal confidential, *private,* or proprietary. The protection is afforded by the steps that are taken to prevent unauthorized disclosure.

protected line. 1. In *optical* or wire *transmission systems,* a *line* that is safe from unauthorized physical access. 2. In *optical* or wire *transmission systems,* a line that cannot be damaged by normal environmental factors. Also see *secure line.*

protected net. See *ciphony-protected net.*

protected optical fiber distribution system. An *optical fiber distribution system* to which adequate *electrical, electromagnetic,* and *physical security* safeguards have been applied to permit its use for the *transmission* of unencrypted classified and sensitive national *security information.* The *system facilities* include all equipment and *lines* that are safeguarded. Major components are *transmission lines, user* (customer, subscriber) *end-instruments,* and *terminal equipment.* Also see *approved circuit.*

protected wireline distribution system. A *wireline distribution system* to which adequate *electrical, electromagnetic,* and *physical security* safeguards have been applied to permit its use for the *transmission* of unencrypted classified and sensitive national *security information.* The system *facilities* include all equipment and *lines* that are safeguarded. Major components are *transmission lines, user* (customer, subscriber) *end-instruments,* and *terminal equipment.* Also see *approved circuit.*

protection jamming. See *self-protection jamming.*

protection voice equipment. See *limited protection voice equipment.*

protective coating. See *optical protective coating.*

protective housing. See *laser protective housing.*

protocol. In *communication systems,* the rules for *communication system operation* that must be followed if *communication* is to be effected. Protocols may govern portions of a *network,* types of *service,* or administrative *procedures.* For example, a *data link protocol* is the specification of methods whereby *data com-*

munication over a data link is performed in terms of the particular *transmission mode, control procedures,* and *recovery procedures.* Protocols are designed to control the *layers* of a communication network or to control the exchange of *data* among *computers* in an *application network.* See *high-level protocol (HLP); layered protocol; layer protocol; link protocol; low-level protocol.*

protocol hierarchy. In *open systems architecture,* the distribution of *network protocol* among the various *layers* of the network. See Figure P-15.

PROTOCOL LAYER	FUNCTIONS
APPLICATION	COST ACCOUNTING, INFORMATION RETRIEVAL, TEXT EDITING
UTILITY	DATA TRANSFER, TERMINAL SUPPORT
USER	INTERPROCESS COMMUNICATION
ACCESS	NETWORK ACCESS SERVICES, SECURITY CONTROL
END TO END	TRAFFIC FLOW CONTROL
NODE TO NODE	CONGESTION CONTROL, ROUTING
LINK CONTROL	ERROR DETECTION, ERROR CORRECTION, INTEGRITY

P-15. **Protocol hierarchy** in a typical *open systems architecture* concept.

protocol translator. A collection of *hardware* and *software* that is required or used to *convert* the *high-level protocols* used in one *network* to those used in another network.

PROWORD. *Procedure word.*

proximity-fuze detonation. The detonation of a shell, bomb, missile, or other device that is equipped with a fuze that is activated by a *radio signal* that is *reflected* from an object, such as the ground or a target in space. The fuze *emits* an *electromagnetic wave* that is reflected from the target. The time that elapses between the launching of a signal and the receipt of the *echo* from the target is used to measure the distance from the target. The wave *propagation velocity* is known. The desired distance for detonation can be set. The time delay introduced by the fuze train is also known.

PRR. *Pulse repetition rate.*

psec. *Picosecond.*

pseudo-binary code. A three-*level signal code* in which a 0, or off *bit,* is represented by zero volts, but a 1, or on bit, is represented by either a positive or negative *pulse.* This group of codes includes *bipolar* and *duo-binary codes.* The representations for 0 or 1 may be reversed. Synonymous with *pseudo-ternary code.* Also see *duo-binary code.*

pseudo-flaw. In *security procedures,* an apparent *loophole* that is deliberately planted in *communication system operating procedures* or *computer programs* as a trap for intruders who are attempting a *penetration.* Also see *entrapment.*

pseudo-inverse filtering. An *image-restoration* technique that makes use of a type of *inverse filtering* in which a nonunique inverse-transformation function is used in lieu of a nonexistent exact unique transformation function. The technique is used to restore *images* to original form when the image-*distortion* function is known, can be derived, or can be produced and used even if it is nonunique. Ambiguity that may be produced can be removed using other specific criteria for selecting the appropriate *output* image, criteria that were not used in the inverse-transformation function.

pseudo-monopulse tracking system. In *radar systems,* a *signal tracking* device in which a *five-horn monopulse feed* is used and that produces *tracking error signals* that are analogous to *conical scan* difference patterns.

pseudorandom. Pertaining to a quality of randomness that can be defined by some arithmetic process and that is satisfactorily random for a given purpose by at least one of the standard statistical tests for randomness. A *signal* sequence of *binary didits* determined by a specific *algorithm* is not truly random however. It repeats itself after a period of time. It can be predicted by a *receiver* that is properly *coded* or controlled. Therefore, a pseudorandom sequence fails some test for randomness. It passes some tests for randomness. A binary pattern is only truly random when the next bit has a 0.50 probability of being a 0 or a 1 for all time. Having the property of being produced by a definite calculation process while simultaneously satisfying one or more of the standard tests for statistical randomness is the basic criterion for pseudorandomness.

pseudorandom binary sequence (PRBS). A sequence of *binary digits* that meets at least one of the conditions or criteria for randomness.

pseudorandom noise. *Noise* that satisfies one or more of the standard tests for statistical randomness. In most noise, there is a sequence of *pulses* that repeats itself, even after a long sequence of pulses. Most noise is *pseudorandom.* For example, *spread-spectrum modulated carrier transmissions* appear as pseudorandom noise to a *receiver* that is not locked to, or is incapable of correlating a locally-generated pseudorandom *code* with the received *signal.* Synonymous with *pseudonoise.*

pseudorandom number sequence. A sequence of numbers in which one or more of the standard tests for statistical randomness is satisfied. The sequence appears to lack any definite pattern, but there are one or more tests for randomness that it fails, such as the one that requires that the pattern not repeat itself, even after a long sequence of numbers. Sequences that are *pseudorandom* can be generated by *algorithms* that require a set of continuously executed arithmetic operations in which the *operand* for the next operation is the result of the previous set of operations, such as algorithms that generate the digits for the calculation of the value of π, the ratio of the circumference to the diameter of a circle; or of the value of e, the base of the natural logarithms.

pseudo-ternary code. See *pseudo-binary code.*

PSK. *Phase-shift keying.*

psophometer. An instrument that is arranged to give *visual* indication that corresponds to the *aural* effect of disturbing *electrical currents* and *voltages* of various *frequencies.* A psophometer usually incorporates a *weighting network,* the characteristics of which differ according to the type of *circuit* under consideration, such as high-fidelity music or commercial speech circuits.

psophometric electromotive force. The factor that permits the quantitative expression of the degree of *interference* that a disturbing *electromotive force (emf)* from outside *sources* would have on a *telephone* conversation. The psophometric emf is twice the psophometric *voltage* that would be measured across a *resistance* of 600 ohms closing the circuit at the point of measurement either directly or by means of an ideal *transformer* that *matches* the *impedance* of the circuit to 600 ohms, the sending end of the circuit being *terminated* by its *matched impedance.*

psophometric power. The *power* that is *absorbed* by a *resistance* of 600 ohms from a source of *psophometric electromotive force (emf).* The *psophometric power,* expressed in picowatts, that is, 10^{-12} watts, is given by the square of the psophometric emf, expressed in millivolts, divided by 0.0024.

psophometric voltage. The *circuit noise voltage* that is measured in a *line* with a *psophometer* that includes an *International Telecommunication Union* CCIF 1951 *weighting network.* The psophometric voltage is not the same as the *psophometric electromotive force (emf),* conceived as the emf in a generator (or line) with 600 ohms internal *resistance,* and hence, for practical purposes, numerically double the corresponding psophometric voltage. The situation is analagous to the fact that a battery (source of emf) with constant internal resistance delivers is maximum *power* to a *load* when the load *resistance* is equal to the internal resistance of the battery, in which case the power in the load is the same as the power consumed by the internal resistance of the battery, and the total power developed by the battery is twice that which is dissipated in the load. Psophometric voltage readings, in millivolts, are commonly converted to *dBm(psoph)* by the relation $dBm(psoph) = 20 \log_{10} v - 57.78,$ where v is the psophometric reading in millivolts. In a *telephone line,* the psophometric voltage is the *voltage* at a *frequency* of 800 Hz at a point in a telephone system, that, if it replaced the *disturbance voltage,* would produce the same degree of *interference* with a telephone conversation as the disturbance voltage.

psophometric weighting. The *noise weighting* that was established by the *International Telecommunication Union (ITU)* International Consultative Committee for Telephony (CCIF, now CCITT), designated as CCIF-1951 weighting, for use in a noise measuring set, that is, in a *psophometer.* It is a *telephone message* weighting characteristic that is based on the response of the human ear to differing *frequencies,* assuming perfect handset *transducers.* The shape of this characteristic is virtually identical to that of *F1A weighting.* The psophometer is, however, calibrated with a tone of 800 Hz, 0 dBm, so that the corresponding *voltage* across 600 ohms produces a reading of 0.775 V. This introduces a 1 dB adjustment in the formulas for conversion with dBa. Also see *dBm(psoph).*

psophometrically weighted dBm.   See *dBm(psoph); dBm0P.*

psychological warfare communication.   *Communication* methods, *systems,* or equipment that are used for the *transmission* of *messages* that contain psychological warfare *information.* It involves the use of *communication media* and the preparation and distribution of information. It is designed to bring information to bear on specified populations or to influence their attitudes and behaviors by means of disseminated information.

PTM.   *Pulse time modulation.*

PTT authority.   Post, *telegraph,* and *telephone* authority, usually the authority or organization in a country that provides *data transmission services* to the public.

publication.   See *communication publication; propagation prediction publication.*

public data network (PDN).   A *network* that is established and operated by a *recognized private operating agency (RPOA),* a *telecommunication administration,* a *communication administration,* or other administration or agency, for the specific purpose of providing *data transmission services* to the public. Also see Figure C-9.

public data transmission service.   A *data transmission service* that is established and operated by a *telecommunication administration,* a *recognized private operating agency (RPOA),* a *communication administration,* or other administration or agency. The services, including *circuit-switched, packet-switched,* and *leased circuit data transmission services,* are provided by means of a *public data network.*

public relations communication.   *Communication* methods, *systems,* or equipment that is used for the *transmission* of *messages* that are *addressed* to the public and that contain *information* about an organization and its *operations* deemed to be of interest to the public.

pull-down.   See *frame pitch.*

pulling machine.   See *fiber-pulling machine.*

pulsating direct current.   *Electric current* that is changing in value at regular or irregular intervals but flows in the same direction at all times. Also see *stationary direct current.*

pulse.   A temporal or spatial variation of the magnitude *(amplitude), phase, frequency,* or other parameter of a physical quantity, such as the *electric field intensity* of an *electromagnetic wave,* the variation being short relative to the time or space schedule of interest. It may be one of the elements of a repetitive *signal* that is characterized by the rise and decay in time of its magnitude, and is usually short in relation to the time span of interest. The final value is the same as the initial value. In *communications-electronics,* the pulse is usually a variation in the value of an electrical or acoustical quantity as a function of time such that the value departs from a given datum for a time interval and then returns to this datum for a much longer time interval than the length of the pulse. In *fiber optics,* the physical quantity is the *lightwave* intensity in an *optical fiber, bundle,* or *cable,* and the pulse is a sudden increase in amplitude, a sudden shift in phase, or a sudden shift in frequency, and a return to normal or other level in each case, of a modulated lightwave propagating in the fiber. See *earth-width pulse; electromagnetic pulse (EMP); Gaussian-shaped pulse; impulse; marking pulse; radio frequency pulse; teletype marking pulse.*

pulse-address multiple access (PAMA). The ability of a *communication satellite* to receive *signals* from several *earth stations* simultaneously and to *amplify, transfer, translate,* and *relay* the signals back to earth. Each earth station·is *addressed* by an assignment of a unique combination of *time* and *frequency slots.* This ability may be restricted by allowing only some of the earth stations to access the satellite at any given time. Thus, PAMA is an application of both *time-division multiple access* and *frequency-division multiple access.*

pulse amplitude. The magnitude of a *pulse.* For a specific designation an adjective should be used to indicate the nature of the amplitude, such as average, instantaneous, peak, and *root-mean-square.* Pulse amplitude is measured with respect to a specified reference value. Unless otherwise stated, it is usually the maximum deviation from the norm experienced by a physical quantity. For example, the maximum change that occurs in the intensity of a *lightwave* at a point in an *optical fiber* when a *pulse* propagates past the point, or in an *antenna,* the magnitude of a pulse could be expressed in terms of the *electric current* expressed in milliampters, the *voltage* expressed in volts, or the *field intensity* expressed in volts per meter, watts per square meter, or other equivalent units.

pulse-amplitude modulation (PAM). *Modulation* of a *pulse carrier* in which the *amplitude* of a continuous stream of equally-spaced *pulses* is varied according to instantaneous values of a *modulating signal.* In PAM, a pulse with an amplitude that is proportional to the signal amplitude at that moment is *transmitted* each time that the original signal is *sampled.* The pulses of the carrier are equally spaced but vary in amplitude. The minimum *bandwidth* that is required for this type of *modulation* is greater than that which is required for regular *double-sideband amplitude modulation (AM) transmission* by an amount that is equal to the ratio of the time interval between pulses. When pulses of this type are transmitted on an amplitude modulated basis, no *noise* advantage is gained over double-sideband AM with an *output* equal to the *average power* in the pulse transmission. However, PAM is readily adaptable to *time-division multiplexing.* Also see *pulse-frequency modulation.* Synonymous with *pulse height modulation.*

pulse carrier. A *carrier wave* that consists of a series of *pulses,* usually of constant *length,* constant *spacing,* constant *repetition rate,* and constant *amplitude,* when not *modulated. Pulse carriers* are usually used as *subcarriers.*

pulse code. In *data* representation schemes, the table or list of equivalences between the quantized value of a sample and the corresponding *signal, pulse* pattern, or *pulse train* that represents the corresponding *character, numeral,* or *word.*

pulse-code modulation (PCM). **1.** *Modulation* involving the *conversion* of a waveform from *analog* to *digital* form by means of *coding.* Synonymous with *pulse coding.* **2.** *Modulation* in which the *pulse amplitude, length,* or *position* has a definite code meaning. PCM requires definition of the type of modulation effected. The pulses may be light pulses *transmitted* in *optical fibers, bundles,* or *cables.* **3.** *Modulation* in which the modulation *signal* is *sampled* and the sample *quantized* and *coded* into a defined number of equal-duration *binary pulses;* i.e., each element of *information* consists of different kinds or numbers of pulses and *spaces.* PCM requires a large *bandwidth* because of the large number of pulses that must be transmitted. *Light* pulses have the *necessary bandwidths* at the *frequencies* involved. PCM as a *data quantization* and formatting technique is rather misnamed as such. The *modulating (baseband)* function is *sampled,* for example in terms of *amplitude,* and the observed *discrete* values are represented by a coded arrangement of equal-amplitude pulses, often a *binary* representation of the discrete value that is observed. The presence or absence of pulses, not their shape or amplitude, determine the intelligence that is conveyed. The *pulse train* is generally transmitted to a distant point by using another time-modualtion or keying technique on the data link. PCM is commonly used in *satellite* and industrial *telemetry,* and in large-capacity short distance *telephone circuits.* The number of possible signal amplitudes that can be represented depends upon the number of pulse *positions* in which the sample amplitude lies at the moment of sampling. At the *receiver,* each group is converted into a signal of the amplitude depicted by the *code.* The succession of signals thus created is passed through a smoothing network that reproduces an approximation of the original signal. In the reception of pulse signals, it is necessary only to determine whether or not a pulse is present in each of the time positions in a group of pulses. This can be done faithfully unless the *noise* peaks are strong enough to introduce a pulse where none should be, or to obliterate a pulse that is supposed to be there. To offset this in a long *link,* the pulses can be regenerated by *repeaters* along the link at intermediate points. PCM is subject to a unique type of noise that is caused by the small errors that are inherent in transmitting continuously varying signals as a series of discrete amplitude steps. This is known as granular or *quantizing noise.* To reduce this noise, additional amplitude steps can be used. However, additional steps require additional pulses in the pulse groups, and this increases the required bandwidth. Another way of reducing the granular noise is to compress the original signal before it is sampled and quantized, and then to expand it again in the receiver. This combination of compressing and expanding is called *companding.* The pulses for several different signals can be timed to permit *time-division multiplexing.* The fidelity of reproduction depends upon the number of pulses in the sampling group. The more amplitude samplings per pulse interval the closer the reconstructed signal will resemble the original signal that was sampled. PCM signals require a wide *frequency band* for transmission because of the large number of pulses that must be sent. However, they are not affected by circuit noise, unless the noise is so strong that its peaks are greater than one-half of the amplitude of the signal pulses. This is so because one-half of the pulse amplitude is usually chosen as the *threshold* for deciding whether there is a pulse at a *sample point* or there is no pulse at the sample point. If the sample is less than half, it is considered there is no pulse, if greater than half, it is considered that there is a pulse. Also see *balanced code; code conversion.* See *differential pulse code modulation (DPCM).*

pulse-code modulation (PCM) multiplexing. *Multiplexing* by deriving a single *digital signal* at a defined *digit* rate from two or more *analog channels* by a combination of *pulse-code modulation* and *time-division multiplexing.* The process is reversed for carrying out the inverse function, that is, for *demultiplexing.* When expressing PCM multiplexing values, the relevant equivalent *binary digit* rate should be stated, such as 2048 kbps PCM multiplexing.

pulse coding. See *pulse-code modulation.*

pulse compression. A reduction of the *pulse width.* It is an *impedance-matching filtering* technique that is used to *discriminate* against *signals* that do not correspond to the *transmitted signal.* See *optical-fiber pulse compression; radar pulse compression.*

pulse compression radar. *Radar* in which *transmitted signals* and *echoes* are passed through an *impedance-matched* narrow *bandpass filter* so as to reduce the pulse length.

pulse decay time. The time that is required for *pulse amplitude* to go from 90% to 10% of its peak value. Synonymous with *fall time.* Also see *pulse length; pulse rise time.*

pulsed frequency-modulated signal. In *spread-spectrum communication systems,* a *signal* in which a *pulsed carrier* is swept in *frequency* during the period of the pulse. On reception, a *matched filter* with a *pass-band* that varies in the same manner as the frequency of the *transmitted signal* carrier is needed in order to detect the signal. Synonymous with *chirp.*

pulse dispersion. The separation, distortion, or spreading of input *signals* propagating along the length of a *transmission line,* such as an *optical fiber.* This limits the useful transmission *bandwidth* of the line. The dispersion is expressed in time and distance as nanoseconds/kilometer. Three basic mechanisms for *dispersion* are the *material effect,* the *waveguide effect,* and the *multimode effect.* Specific causes include surface roughness, presence of *scattering* centers, bends in the guiding structure, deformation of the guide, and inhomogeneities of the guiding *medium.* Pulse dispersion is caused primarily by the fact that each of the frequencies that comprise a pulse is handled in a different manner; that is, the *attenuation* and the *propagation velocity* are different for each frequency. Synonymous with *pulse spreading.*

pulsed laser.   See *Q-switched repetitively-pulsed laser.*

pulse Doppler radar.   *Pulsed radar* in which the *Doppler effect* is used in order to obtain a direct measurement of the radial component of velocity of an object (target) relative to the *radar antenna.*

pulse duration.   See *pulse length.*

pulse-duration modualtion.   See *pulse-length modulation.*

pulse duty factor.   The ratio of average *pulse duration* to average pulse spacing, both expressed in the same units. Therefore a dimensionless quantity. The pulse spacing is the time between say the leading edges of pulses.

pulse-edge tracking.   *Tracking* on the edge of a *radar echo* rather than on the peak or the center of the echo. Pulse-edge tracking is used primarily to prevent capture of *tracking circuits* by fixed or slow moving objects, such as towers, mountains, or *chaff.* It maintains automatic range tracking to a minimum range, allowing closer approaches to objects (targets) for visual identification purposes. The effectiveness of this circuit is obtained by *operator* selection of the edge of the *signal pulse* for tracking control.

pulse-frequency modulation (PFM).   *Modulation* in which the *pulse repetition rate* of the *carrier* is varied in accordance with some characteristic of the *modulating signal.* It is a *bandwidth* expansion system for *digital data* in which the *carrier frequency* is made to vary linearly with the time across the *channel* bandwidth during each *data* period, that is, during the period that each *bit* of *information* is being *transmitted.* For example, *binary* states represented by 0 and 1 correspond to decreasing and increasing *frequencies,* respectively. The transmission method is that of *frequency modulation (FM).* The *modulating wave* form in the *time-frequency domain* is a succession of saw-tooth-shaped waves (slow rise, rapid fall or vice versa) with positive or negative slopes that correspond to the binary data. The system has advantages for *air-ground digital communication* and *geostationary satellite communication* with *marginal power budgets* because it combats *multipath reception* and *Doppler shifts.* In the *frequency code* method, *discrete* frequencies are used.

pulse height modulation.   See *pulse amplitude modulation.*

pulse interference suppression and blanking (PISAB).   In *radar systems,* a method of removing or *discriminating* against *interference* by *blanking* all *video signals* that are not *synchronous* with the *radar pulse repetition rate.* It is effective against *random pulse interference* and certain types of *jamming.*

pulse interval modulation.   A modified *pulse position modulation* scheme in which the interval between *carrier pulses* is changed in accordance with an intelligence-bearing variation in the *modulating signal.*

pulse-jet control. Control of thrusts that are applied to a *satellite* for *orbital* control, spin control, or orientation control. If the thrust of each pulse produces a fixed change in momentum, various values of momentum changes can be produced by changing the pulse-jet repetition rate. For example, thrusts for a spinning satellite may be applied once per revolution or a continuously applied thrust may have its amplitude changed in abrupt bursts of varying length.

pulse length. 1. The time interval or the spatial distance between the points on the leading and trailing edges of a *pulse* at which the instantaneous value bears a specified relation to the peak amplitude. A common figure for the relation is 10% of the peak amplitude. Another common figure is the time interval between the half-amplitude points on the *rise* and *decay* parts of the *pulse*. For pulses of odd shapes, the points on the pulse curves must be described as to their location with respect to some part of the pulse, otherwise the concept of pulse length has no meaning. 2. In *radar systems,* a measurement of *pulse transmission time* in *microseconds,* that is, the time that the *radar transmitter* is energized during each cycle. Synonymous with *pulse duration; pulse width.* Also see *pulse decay time; pulse rise time.* See *laser pulse length.*

pulse-length discrimination. The ability to distinguish variations in the *pulse length,* either the time duration or the spatial width, of each pulse in a sequence of pulses.

pulse-length discriminator. A device that measures the *pulse length* of *signals* and passes only those *pulses* that have a time duration that falls within a predetermined time interval specified by design tolerances. A pulse-length discriminator offers good discrimination aginst *long-pulse jamming,* most types of *low-frequency modulation,* and some forms of *interference.* It affords little or no protection against short pulses and *high-frequency modulation.*

pulse-length modulation. *Modulation* in which the *pulse length* (time duration or spatial width) of a *carrier pulse* is varied in accordance with an *attribute* of a modulating *signal.* The modulating signal may vary the time of occurrence of the leading edge or trailing edge of the carrier pulse, or both. 0's or 1's may be represented by a carrier wave that is on or off for longer or shorter periods of time. In pulse-length modulation, however, a pulse is transmitted for each *sampling* of the *signal.* The width (duration) of the pulse is proportional to the *amplitude* of the signal. Pulse-length modulation yields the same *signal-to-nosie* improvement as *pulse-position modulation* of the same peak power. However, the *average power* that is required is greater in pulse-length modulation because of the longer average duration of the pulses. Pulse-length modulation is rarely used for direct modulation of a *radio carrier,* but it has been applied in the intermediate processes of some *pulse-position modulation* receiving devices. The transformation is usually made by having the position of the short pulse control the starting time of the two longer pulses with a fixed terminating time. Synonymous with *pulse-duration modulation; pulse-telegraph modulation; pulse-width modulation.* See *suppressed-clock pulse-length modulation.*

pulse-link repeater. An arrangement of equipment that is used in *telephone signaling systems* for receiving *pulses* from one *E-and-M signaling circuit* and re-transmitting corresponding pulses into another E-and-M signaling circuit. Also see *E-and-M signaling.*

pulse modulation. **1.** *Modulation* of a *continuous-wave (CW) carrier* by a *pulse string.* **2.** *Modulation* of one or more characteristics of a *pulse carrier,* such as *modulation* of *pulse length, pulse position,* or *pulse amplitude.*

pulse-modulation radar jamming. *Jamming* that produces a confusing pattern on a *radar display device.* The pattern may vary from a number of apparent *echoes* often lying in radial lines to continuous spiral lines that are similar to running rabbits. The use of *circuits* with variable time constants may reduce the effects of *pulse-modulation radar jamming.*

pulse operation. See *coherent pulse operation.*

pulse-position modulation (PPM). **1.** In an *optical transmission system, modulation* that causes the arrival time of *pulses* at a *detector* to vary according to a *signal* impressed on a *pulsed* source, the detector output being a function of the arrival time with respect to a fixed time reference. **2.** *Modulation* in which *information* is conveyed by varying the time of occurrence of *pulses* in relation to a reference without varying their *length.* Normally, very narrow pulses deviate from uniformly-spaced reference positions by time intervals that are proportional to the instantaneous amplitudes of a *sampled input,* usually an *analog input.* In PPM, one pulse is sent out for each sampling of the *input signal.* The pulses are all of the same pulse *amplitude* and *length,* but the exact time of sending each pulse, that is, its position, varies within a range that depends on the amplitude of the same signal. When PPM is sent by *amplitude modulation (AM)* techniques it has a better *signal-to-noise ratio* than normal *double-sideband amplidude modulation (AM).* This improvement, in terms of *current* ratio is proportional to the *pulse shift* (in time) and to the *bandwidth* that is used. This requires a greater bandwidth, however, than double-sideband AM. The increase in bandwidth is proportional to the ratio of the maximum interval between pulses to the *pulse length.* Synonymous with *pulse-time modulation.*

pulse radar. *Radar* that makes use of *pulses,* that is, short bursts of *electromagnetic* energy. For example, 1-microsecond pulses, 5 microseconds apart, with a *radio frequency wave* of 10 MHz during the 1-μs pulse would have 10 cycles of RF energy in each pulse, each of these packets being 5 μs apart that is, 4 μs between pulses. The *pulse repetition rate* would be 200 *kpps.* Also see *pulse repetition rate.* See *complex-pulse radar.*

pulse radar jammer. See *locked-pulse radar jammer.*

pulse rate. See *maximum pulse rate.*

pulse regeneration. The process of restoring the *shape, amplitude,* and *positions* in time of *pulses* that have become *distorted* or *delayed* in *transmission.* Synonymous with *pulse reconstitution; pulse shaping.*

pulse-repetition frequency. See *pulse-repetition rate.*

pulse-repetition rate. The number of *pulses* that occur per unit time at a particular point in a *transmission medium* or free space, such as *pulses* per *second,* as used in *radar,* or pulses per minute, as in *satellite* thruster control. For example, in *radar systems,* the number of pulses that occur each second is the pulse repetition rate (PRR) which is not the *transmission frequency.* The transmission frequency is the frequency of the *high frequency* or *radio frequency* energy that is *transmitted* by the radar during the period of each pulse, that is, during the *length* of the pulse. Synonymous with *pulse repetition frequency.* Also see *pulse radar.* See *jittered-pulse repetition rate; staggered-pulse repetition rate.*

pulse rise time. The time that is required for a *pulse amplitude* instantaneous value to rise from one specified fraction of its peak value, say 10%, to another, say 90%. Also see *pulse decay time; pulse length.*

pulse shape. A characteristic of a *pulse,* such as its *amplitude, length,* or *position.* It is expressed usually as an *electrical current, voltage, power, field intensity,* or spatial distribution. It is often *displayed* as a function of *time, frequency, distance,* or other *parameter* or *domain.* For example, the figure that is produced by the outline of a pulse when it is viewed on a *cathode ray tube* as a *voltage* as a function of time.

pulse shaping. See *pulse regeneration.*

pulse spreading. See *pulse dispersion.*

pulse-spreading specification. A method of specifying or measuring the *pulse*-spreading or *pulse-dispersion* capability of a *transmission line* or *medium,* such as an *optical fiber.* For example, the 50% spreading time factor is given by:

$$\tau_{50} = (W_1 - W_2)^{1/2}/(L_1 - L_2)$$

where W_1 is the pulse width at 50% of the maximum *pulse amplitude* of a *test* specimen *output waveform,* W_2 is the pulse width at 50% of maximum pulse *amplitude* of a reference output waveform, L_1 is the length of the test specimen, and L_2 is the length of the reference.

pulse string. A series of *pulses* with similar *attributes.* The series may be in time as the pulses pass a point, or it may be in space in a *transmission medium,* such as a *transmission line.*

pulse stuffing. A process whereby *pulses* are inserted into a stream of pulses to achieve *synchronism* between two *digital communication systems.*

pulse test. See *shuttle-pulse test.*

pulse time modulation (PTM). *Modulation* in which the *time* of *occurrence* of a characteristic of a *pulse carrier* is varied with respect to a characteristic of the *modulating signal.* PTM includes *pulse-position modulation* and *pulse-length modulation.*

pulse train.   See *pulse string.*

pulse width.   See *pulse length.*

pulse-width discrimination.   See *pulse-length discrimination.*

pulse-width discriminator.   See *pulse-length discriminator.*

pulse-width modulation.   See *pulse-length modulation.*

pulsing.   See *key pulsing; multifrequency pulsing; wink pulsing.*

pumping.   In *electric circuits,* the action of an *oscillator* that provides cyclic changes to control a reaction device.   For example, the action that provides the sustaining power that results in *amplification* of a *signal* by a *parametric amplifier,* or the action that provides a *laser* with *input power* to sustain the *light-frequency emission.*   See Figure P-16.

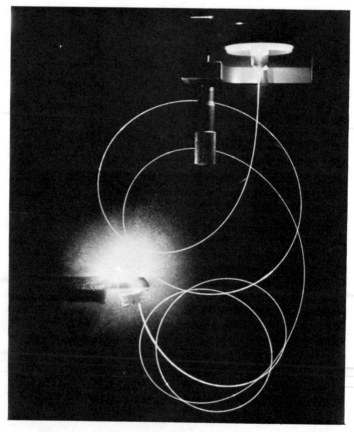

P-16.   *Laser* **pumping** provides *input* to a low-*loss optical fiber* for high *traffic-capacity lightwave communication systems.*   (Courtesy of Bell Laboratories.)

punch. See *card punch.*

punch card. A card in which a pattern of holes can be punched to represent *information.* The holes are the *data* that represent the information. Also see *Hollerith card.*

punch tape. A tape in which hole patterns can be punched to represent *information.* The holes are the *data* that represent the information.

pupil. See *artificial pupil; entrance pupil; exit pupil.*

pure binary numeration system. A fixed-*radix* positional numeration system that uses *numerals* with *binary digits,* a radix of 2, and descending powers of 2 from left to right, to indicate the weight that each digit contributes to the value being expressed by the entire numeral. The 1 digit usually indicates that the weight of the position that it is in is to be added to the total value, and the 0 usually indicates that the weight assigned to the position that it is in is not to be added to the total for the numeral. For example, the numeral 1101.01 is equivalent to the total value $1 \times 2^3 + 1 \times 2^2 + 0 \times 2^1 + 1 \times 2^0 + 0 \times 2^{-1} + 1 \times 2^{-2}$, which equals $8 + 4 + 0 + 1 + 0 + .25$, which sums to 13.25. Also see *binary notation.*

push button. See *virtual push button.*

push-button dialing. An alternative to rotary *dialing* on a *telephone* handset that provides faster *circuit selection* and reduced *telephone exchange* and line-holding time. Tone or *direct-current (DC) signals* are usually used for push-button dialing.

push-button signaling. See *push-button dialing.*

push-down. See *last-in-first-out (LIFO).*

push-to-talk operation. In *telephone* or two-way *voice radio systems, operation* of *communication* devices over a *speech circuit* in which *transmission* occurs from only one *station* at a time, the talker being required to keep a *switch* operated while talking and released while listening. Synonymous with *over-over operation; press-to-talk operation.* Also see *half-duplex circuit; half-duplex transmission.*

push-to-type operation. In *telegraph* or *data transmission systems, operation* of *communication* devices in which the *operator* must keep a *switch* operated in order to send *messages,* and the switch released in order to receive messages. It is usually used in *radio systems* in which the same *frequency* is employed for both *transmission* and *reception.* This is a derivative form of transmission and may be used in *simplex, half-duplex,* or *duplex operation.* Synonymous with *press-to-type operation.* Also see *half-duplex circuit; half-duplex transmission.*

push-up. See *first-in-first-out (FIFO).*

pW. Picowatt. A unit of power that is equal to 10^{-12} W. It is equivalent to −90 dBm. It is commonly used for both *weighted* and unweighted *noise* measurements. The context in which it is used must be carefully observed in order to fully appreciate its significance. Also see *pWp*.

pWp. A *pW, psophometrically weighted.* Also see *dBm(psoph); noise.*

pWp0. *Psophometrically weighted power* in *picowatts* referred to a *zero transmission level point (OTLP).*

pyrotechnic code. In *visual signaling systems,* a prearranged *code* in which meanings are assigned to the various *colors* and arrangements of *pyrotechnics.*

pyrotechnic distress signal. A *distress signal* that is *transmitted* by *pyrotechnic* means. For example, a single red *pyrotechnic light displayed* singly or in succession might indicate that the aircraft that launched it is in distress; or *pyrotechnic signals* of any *color* fired at short intervals might indicate that the ship that launched them is in distress.

pyrotechnic light. In *visual signaling systems,* a *signal* that consists of a temporary *source* of *light* produced by chemical reaction. Red, white, and green are among the standard *colors* that are used.

pyrotechnics. Devices that contain chemicals that produce a smoke or brilliant *light* when they are ignited and burned. They may be used for *signaling,* lighting dark areas, or obscuring vision. For example, fireworks, flares, rockets, Roman candles, or smoke bombs.

pyrotechnic signal. In *visual signaling systems,* a *signal* that is produced by a device that generates *light* or smoke by means of a chemical reaction, such as combustion or any other exothermal reaction.

pyrotechnic smoke. Smoke that is produced by means of an exothermal chemical reaction, such as combustion. The usual *colors* of *pyrotechnic* smoke are white, yellow, black, brown, orange, and red. Pyrotechnic smoke is used for *signaling, marking,* and to obscure vision.

pyrotechnic transmission. The transmission of *messages* by means of flares, rockets, fire, smoke, and other *pyrotechnics. Pyrotechnic communication* requires a great deal of emphasis on prearranged *coding* of *messages* for recognition, interpretation, and *decoding.*

PZT. *Piezoelectric transducer.*

Q

QA. *Quality assurance.*

Q-band. The *band* that is comprised of *frequencies* in the range form 36 GHz to 46 GHz. This band, now obsolete, was divided into 5 subranges of 2 GHz each. These were designated QA to QE. It also comprised frequencies in the range from 26 GHz to 40 GHz between the old K- and V-bands.

QC. *Quality control.*

Q-gain. An increase in the *output power* of an electrical device from obtaining *resonance* by *tuning* a *circuit*. The Q of a coil is given as $\omega L/R$, which is the ratio of the *inductive reactance* to the *resistance*. Q-gain is usually expressed in *decibels (dB)* or *nepers (N)*.

QPSK. *Quadrature phase-shift keying.*

QST. A standard operating *signal* that is used as a suffix to a *message* to indicate that the charge for the message immediately preceding it is to be ascertained.

Q-switch. A device that prohibits *pulsed laser emission* until energy increases to a certain level in the *active medium; pulse power* is increased by shortening pulse duration while keeping the pulse energy constant. The device provides shorter and more intense pulses at a higher *repetition rate* than could be achieved by pulsing the active medium.

Q-switched repetitively-pulsed laser. A *solid-state laser* whose continuous *emission* is converted into *pulses* by a *Q-switch*.

quad. A group of four wires that are composed of two *pairs* twisted together. The pairs have a long twist pitch and the quad has a short twist pitch.

quadded cable. A *cable* that is formed by taking four, or multiples of four, paired and separately *insulated cables* and twisting these together within an overall jacket. Also see *paired cable; spiral four cable*.

quadratic index profile. See *parabolic index profile*.

quadrature. The *phase* relationship between two *periodic* quantities varying with the same period, that is, with the same *frequency* or *repetition rate*, when the *phase difference* between them is one quarter of a period, that is, a spatial or *electrical* $90°$ or $\pi/2$ radians.

quadrature component. Either one of the two *orthogonal components* (right-angle components, Cartesian components) into which any *vector* quantity may be resolved. The *vector* sum of the two quadrature components, that is, the resultant, is the original vector from which they were resolved. The two components may vary in direction and magnitude, but they must sum to the original vector. For example, assuming that the vector is represented by the diameter of a circle, then the two quadrature components must be inscribed within either semicircle, and form a right triangle with the diameter as the hypotenuse. See Figure Q-1.

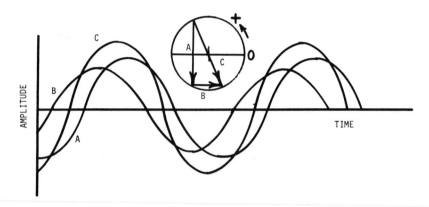

Q-1. For an arbitrary *wave* C, also represented by the *vector* C drawn as a diameter of a reference circle, the two **quadrature components** A and B shown as lagging and leading wave *components* respectively, also represented by the inscribed vectors A and B. Note that they are inscribed in a semicircle and therefore are at right angles. The sum of A and B waves equals C in magnitude at any instant.

quadrature phase-shift keying (QPSK). *Phase-shift keying* in which there are four *phase* states or *positions* in the *time* or *frequency domains* within a single period. Synonymous with *quadriphase keying; quaternary phase-shift keying.*

quadriphase keying. See *quadrature phase-shift keying.*

quadriphase modulation. *Modualtion* using *multiple phase-shift keying* in which four phase states of a *sinusoidal carrier wave* are used to convey four *digital data codes,* such as 00, 01, 10, and 11, one for each phase state or condition of the carrier. The members of each adjacent pair of the four phase states are in *quadrature* with each other.

quadriphase shift-keying. *Shift keying* in which 0's and 1's are represented by *phase shifts* of a *carrier wave* that occur at $0°$, $+90°$, $-90°$, and $180°$. Thus, four different *phase conditions* or *positions* are used in the *time domain* or the *frequency domain* within the period of a *sinusoidal carrier wave.* The *binary code* that is assigned to each of the phase conditions may vary, depending on the *sys-*

tem. Thus, 00, 01, 10, and 11 may be used with no *redundancy*. Other codes with redundancy may be used with improved *reliability*, resistance to *noise*, and reduction of *error*.

quadruple-diversity combining. The simultaneous *combining* of, or selection from, four independently *fading signals* and their *detection* through the use of *space, frequency, phase angle, time, modulation*, or *polarization* characteristics, or combinations of these. Also see *diversity order; diversity reception; dual-diversity combining*.

quadruplex system. A *telegraph system* that is arranged for the simultaneous independent *transmission* of two *messages* in each direction over a single *circuit*.

quality. See *image quality*.

quality assurance (QA). A planned and systematic pattern of actions necessary to provide adequate confidence that an item or product conforms to established technical performance specifications, standards, or requirements.

quality control (QC). A function in which control of quality of raw materials or produced material is exercised for the purpose of preventing the production of defective material and guaranteeing the production of material that meets performance specifications. See *circuit quality control*.

quantity. See *light quantity*.

quantization. The process of *digital encoding* or *coding* that involves the conversion of the exact instantaneous sample values of a continuous *signal* or *wave* to their nearest equivalent digital values selected from a finite set of *discrete* values. *Signal* quantization is a process in which the continuous range of values of a signal is divided into nonoverlapping, but not necessarily equal subranges. To each subrange a *discrete* value of the *output* is uniquely assigned. Whenever the signal value falls within a given subrange, the output has the corresponding discrete value. Thus, it is a process of converting the exact sample values of a signal to their nearest equivalent in a finite set of discrete values in order to permit *digital encoding* as a next possible step. Also see *quantization level; uniform encoding*.

quantization distortion. The *distortion* that results from a *quantization* process. The process introduces *errors* in the *output analog* and *digital signals*. Synonymous with *quantizing distortion*.

quantization level. A *discrete* value in a finite set of discrete values. For example, the discrete value of the *output* of a device that designates a particular subrange of the *input* in a *quantization* process.

quantization noise. An undesirable *random signal* that is caused by the *error* of approximation in a *quantization* process. It is solely dependent upon the particular quantization process that is used and the statistical characteristics of the quantized *signal*. Synonymous with *granular noise* and with *quantizing noise*.

quantizing distortion. See *quantization distortion*.

quantizing noise. See *quantization noise.*

quantized synchronization. See *amplitude quantized synchronization.*

quantum. A single smallest unit of *electromagnetic wave* energy equal in magnitude to:

$$Q.E. = hf$$

where *Q.E.* is the quantum energy, *h* is *Planck's constant,* and *f* is the *frequency* of the *electromagnetic radiation.* A quantum of energy is released when an electron in an excited or *radioactive* element moves from a higher to a lower *energy level.* A *photon* is a quantum of electromagnetic energy.

quantum efficiency. See *differential quantum efficiency; response quantum efficiency.*

quantum-limited operation. In the *operation* of a *photodetector,* the inability of the *detector* to measure *incident radiation* levels below a *threshold* level because of fluctuations in the *output current* that are not due to the incident radiation, i.e., not due to incident *photons.*

quantum noise. See *shot noise.*

quarter adder. A *binary adder* with two *inputs* that produces a *modulo-2 sum* and does not produce a carry *output digit.* It performs the function of an *EXCLUSIVE-OR gate.* Also see *binary half-adder.*

quarter-squares multiplier. An *analog multiplier,* that also may be *programmed* on a *digital computer,* whose *operation* is based on the identity $xy = [(x + y)^2 - (x - y)^2]/4$, where x and y are the *parameters* (factors) that are to be multiplied. The analog multiplier usually incorporates *inverters, analog* adders, and *square-law devices.*

quartet. A *byte* that is composed of four *binary digits.* For example, 1011.

quasianalog signal. A *digital signal* that has been *converted* to a form that is suitable for *transmission* over a specified *analog channel.* The specification of the analog channel should include *frequency* range, *frequency bandwidth, signal-to-noise (S/N),* and *envelope delay distortion* requirements. When this form of *signaling* is used to convey *message traffic* over *dial telephone systems,* it is often referred to as *voice-data.* A *modem* may be used for the conversion process. Synonymous with *voice-data signal.*

quasisynchronous. Pertaining to the state of being partially *synchronous,* nearly synchronous, or synchronous in a limited respect. For example, pertaining to a *satellite orbit* with a height that is nearly but not exactly that required for *geostationary synchronism* so that the apparent longitudinal motion, that is, the motion with respect to a meridian of longitude, of the satellite relative to its parent body is that of a slow drift in the *equatorial* plane.

quaternary. Pertaining to a number system with a *radix* of four. For exmaple, pertaining to an *n-ary code* in which n = 4, or an *n-ary digit* in which n = 4.

quaternary phase-shift keying. See *quadrature phase-shift keying.*

queue traffic. **1.** In a *store-and-forward switching center,* the outgoing *messages* that are awaiting *transmission* at the outgoing line position. **2.** In a *telephone system,* a series of *calls* that are waiting for *service.* Also see *buffer; called-party camp-on; calling-party camp-on; first-in-first-out (FIFO); last-in-first-out (LIFO); message switching.*

quick-engagement clip. In *visual signaling systems,* a clip that enables rapid attachment of *flags* and *pennants* to a *halyard* for quick hoisting of national and *signal flags* and *pennants.*

quintet. A *byte* that is composed of five *binary digits.* For example, 11001.

quotient. See *automatic recovery quotient (ARQ).*

R

rad. The basic unit of *radiation absorbed dose* that produces *ionization* of the material upon which it is *incident*. A dose of 1 rad is equivalent to the absorption of 100 ergs of radiation energy per gram of absorbing material. An erg is a dyne-centimeter. A dyne is 1/980th of a gram of force, and 10^7 ergs equal 1 joule.

radar. **1.** *Radio detection* and *ranging* (RADAR) equipment that is used to determine the distance to and the direction of objects (targets) by the *transmission* and *reflected return* of *electromagnetic energy*. It includes the methods and systems that use *beamed* and reflected electromagnetic energy for *detecting* and locating objects (targets); for measuring distance, velocity, altitude, and other characteristics of objects; and for various other purposes, such as navigation, homing, bombing, missile tracking, or mapping. **2.** A *radiodetermination system* that is based on the comparison of reference *signals* with *radio signals* that are *reflected* or *retransmitted* from the position to be determined. See *acquisition radar; airborne intercept radar; complex pulse radar; conical beam-split radar; continuous-wave radar; Doppler radar; early-warning radar; frequency agile radar; guidance radar; initial warning radar; long-range radar; metric radar; multiband radar; narrow-beam radar; primary radar; pulse-compression radar; pulse Doppler radar; pulse radar; search radar; secondary radar; side-loooking airborne radar; tracking radar; track-while-scan airborne intercept radar; variable-pulse recurrent-frequency radar; wide beam radar.*

radar altimetry area. A large and comparatively level terrain area that has a defined *elevation* that can be used in determining the altitude of airborne equipment by the use of *radar.*

radar beacon precipitation gage station. A *transponder station* that is in the *meteorological aids service.* *Emissions* are used for *telemetering* precipitation *data.*

radar beacon (RACON). **1.** A *radionavigation transponder* that is used to *transmit,* in *response* to a *received signal,* a *pulsed radio signal* with specific characteristics such that the *bearing* or *range* of the *transponder* from the interrogator may be determined. It may also be used to identify the transponder itself. **2.** A *radio beacon* in which *radar* is used to obtain *bearing* and distance to an object and to *transmit* this *information* by *radio* to another *station.* **3.** A *radionavigation system* that *transmits* automatically or in *response* to a predetermined *signal* that it receives. **4.** A *pulse radio signal* with specific characteristics.

radar beacon station. A *radionavigation land station* that employs a *radar beacon* (RACON). A RACON may be all or part of a *ship station* or an *aircraft station.*

radar blind range. The *range* that corresponds to the situation in which a *radar transmitter* is on and hence the *receiver* is off, so that the radar's *transmitted signal* does not saturate (blind) its own receiver. Thus, there is a time interval, namely the time interval between transmitted *pulses,* that might just correspond to the time interval for a pulse to travel to the object (target) and its *reflection* to travel back. This would cause an attempt to measure the range just as the radar transmitter is transmitting the next pulse. But the receiver is off, therefore this particular range cannot be measured. The width of the range value that can't be measured depends on the duration of the time interval that the radar receiver is off which depends on the length of the transmitted pulse. The return-time interval could be coincident with the very next radar transmitted pulse, that is, the first pulse following a transmitted pulse, or the second, or the third, and so on, giving rise to a succession of blind ranges. The blind ranges are given by $r_m = mc/2fn$, where r is the blind range, m is a positive *integer* that has the values $1, 2, 3, 4, \ldots$ and that indicates which of the blind ranges is being determined, c is the velocity of *electromagnetic wave propagation* in a vacuum (approximately 3×10^8 m/s), f is the *radar pulse repetition rate,* and n is the *absolute refractive index* of the *transmission medium* (nearly 1 for air).

radar blind speed. The magnitude of the radial component of velocity of an object (target) relative to a *radar* site, that cannot be measured by the radar unit. The *Doppler pulse repetition rate (PRR)* is the difference between the *transmitted pulses* PRR and the received pulses PRR. For example, when the object (target) is stationary with respect to the radar site, the reflected PRR is the same as the transmitted PRR and therefore a net zero signal is indicated for speed. If it happens that the Doppler PRR is the same as the transmitted (illuminating) PRR, or it is a multiple of the transmitted PRR, a zero signal is also obtained and hence the radar is considered blind to these speeds, one for each multiple of the radar transmitted (illuminating) pulse repetition rate. It is not the absolute magnitude of the speed of the object that is involved, but only the radial component of the velocity. The radial *components* of velocity blind speeds are given by $v_m = m\lambda f/102$, where v is the blind speed in knots; m is the multiple of the radar pulse repetition rate and the number of the blind speed, namely a positive integer, 1, 2, 3, 4, . . . , for the first, second, third, fourth, and so on, blind speed; λ is the *wavelength* of the illuminating radar in centimeters; and f is the *transmitter* pulse repetition rate in pps; and the 102 is a units conversion factor.

radar cross section. A measure of the extent to which an object (target) *reflects radar pulses.* The radar cross section of an aircraft can vary by a factor of over 1000, depending on the aspect angle of the aircraft to the radar. Radar reflection off the nose of the aircraft usually represents the smallest radar cross section, while a broadside presentation to the *signal* produces the greatest cross section. Shape, surface roughness, and reflective material, as well as orientation (size), also affect the radar cross section.

radar deception repeater. In *radar electronic warfare,* a *deception* device that samples an interrogating *radar signal,* instantaneously stores its *frequency,* and subsequently repeats the *signal* after changing one or more of its characteristics. The *repeater* may consist of a frequency memory device, a *wideband amplifier,* and a *pulse* programmer. Some repeaters deceive by repeating either a part or all of the received signal and creating false *signal* characteristics in order to deceive, mislead, or confuse a *computing system* or *operator.* Other repeaters deceive by amplifying and directly repeating all portions of a received signal without altering its characteristics. They may deceive by creating a fictitious reflective area that does not exist in terms of the size represented by the *transmitted* signal magnitude.

radar diplexing. A technique that permits the simultaneous *operation* of *radar* sets on at least two different *frequencies* while using a single (common) *antenna.*

radar display. A *graphic display* of a set of variables that are measured by means of *radar,* such as the *azimuth* of an object (target), the *range* to an object, or the *signal strength* received from an object, all usually in *real time.* The display also could be a delayed picture or a predicted picture of these variables. See *spot-barrage jamming radar display; spot-continuous-wave jamming radar display.*

radar echo. 1. In *radar systems,* the *electromagnetic* energy that is received by a *radar antenna* after *reflection* from an object. 2. The *deflection* or change in *intensity* of the *display element* on a *display surface,* such as a *cathode ray tube screen,* produced after the electromagnetic energy reflected from an object (target) is received by the *radar antenna,* and *amplified* and *processed* by the *radar receiver.*

radar height indicator. See *range-height indicator (RHI).*

radar homing beacon. A *beacon* in which *radar* is used to establish the *bearing* and distance from the beacon location to the *mobile station,* such as a *ship station* or *aircraft station,* that is being *tracked.* The *radar beacon* may be installed at any *fixed* or *mobile station,* such as a *land station,* aircraft station, or ship station.

radar horizon. The locus of points of tangency at which *rays* from a *radar antenna* are tangential to the earth's surface. On the open sea, this locus is to the horizon, that is, it is nearly horizontal, depending, say, on the height of the ships mast, but on land, the slope of the radar horizon line varies with the terrain in each different direction from the *antenna.* It could vary from a positive slope to a negative slope, depending on terrain features in a given direction. Also see *radio horizon range.*

radar information. See *raw radar information.*

radar jammer. See *airborne radar jammer; locked-pulse radar jammer.*

radar jamming. See *formation radar jamming; pulse-modualtion radar jamming.*

radar line-of-sight (LOS) equation.   An equation that expresses the *radar horizon range (RHR)* in terms of the radar *antenna* height, h, and the object (target) altitude, a, namely $RHR_s = (2h)^{1/2} + (2a)^{1/2} = 1.414(h^{1/2} + a^{1/2})$, where RHR_s is the radar horizon range in statute miles, and h and a are in feet.   The RHR is also given as $RHR_k = 4.12(h^{1/2} + a^{1/2})$, where RHR_k is the radar horizon range in kilometers, and h and a are in meters.   The *effective earth radius,* namely 4/3 times the actual earth radius is used in deriving these formulas.   Second order differentials are neglected.   They contribute less than 0.1 percent.   Also see *radio horizon range.*

radar masking.   The obliteration of *echoes* on a *radar display.*   For example, obliteration by *saturating* the receiving *antenna* with large-*amplitude wideband signals* that may be derived from *jamming, interference* from local *sources,* or low *signal-to-noise ratio.*   Wideband signals are produced by *white noise* generators operating over a wide range of *frequencies.*

radar mile.   The time that is required for a *radar pulse* to travel a distance of one mile to an object (target), reflect, and return to the receiver.   A radar statute mile is 10.8 *microseconds;* a radar *nautical mile* is 12.4 microseconds.   The time for any other unit distance is readily determined, such as the radar meter or the radar kilometer.

radar navigation.   The use of *radar* in navigation and pilotage.

radar netting.   The interconnection of several *radar systems* and their *connection* to a single center in order to provide *integrated operations,* maintain radar coverage of a large sector, exchange *raw radar information* among *systems,* and provide for centralized direction and control.   For example, if one radar system is experiencing technical difficulties or becomes otherwise nonoperational, other systems in the *net* can provide radar coverage of any resulting uncovered areas.

radar netting station.   A *station* that can receive *data* from *radar tracking stations* and exchange this *data* among other *radar tracking stations.*

radar picket.   A *radar system,* usually mounted in a vehicle, ship, or aircraft, that is stationed in relation to an area or group of mobile units for the purpose of increasing the *radar detection range* for radar protection of the area or group of mobile units.   For example, a radar system on board a ship to provide greater range in the direction of the area to be covered than can be achieved by a land-based radar.

radar planned-position indicator.   A *planned-position indicator* for a *radar system* that *displays* a map in polar coordinates of the area near or surrounding a *radar* installation.   Identified objects are dynamically displayed as *echoes* on the *display surface* at *screen coordinates* that correspond to their actual direction and *range* from the radar installation or from a specified origin.

radar pulse compression.   A technique that involves both stretching (expanding) the *transmitted radar pulse* and compressing the received *pulse (radar echo)* by using *matched-impedance filter* techniques. This permits an increase in the *average transmitted power* without an increase in *peak power* and with no loss in *range resolution.*

radar reflectivity.   The characteristic of an object (target) that causes it to *reflect electromagnetic waves,* such as *radar waves.*   The reflectivity is usually expressed in units of equivalent area of a flat *reflector* normal to the direction of *wave propagation,* that would produce the same *echo signal strength* as the object for a given *transmitted power.*

radar relay.   The *transmission* of *radar video signals* to a *display device.*

radar repeater.   A device that has several *display surfaces,* such as *cathode ray tube screens,* and is fitted with *facilities* that enable it to *display* selected *radar data* from locations that are normally remote from the *radar antenna.*

radar resolution cell.   The volume of space that is occupied by a *radar pulse.* The volume is determined by the *pulse length (PL)* and the horizontal and vertical *beamwidths* of the *transmitting radar.*   The radar cannot distinguish between two separate objects that lie within the same resolution cell.   The depth of the resolution cell (RCD) remains constant regardless of the distance from the transmitting antenna.   It does not increase with range.   The radar resolution cell depth (RCD) is obtained by multiplying the pulse length (PL) in microseconds by 150, that is, $RCD = 150\ PL.$ The height of the cell and the width of the cell do increase with range.   These are given by $W = HBW \times R/57$ and $H = VBW \times R/57,$ where W is the width of the cell, HBW is the horizontal beamwidth in degrees, R is the range, H is the height of the cell, and VBW is the vertical beamwidth in degrees.   The range, $R,$ is the distance from the radar antenna to the reflecting object (target).   The width and height will come out in the same units that the range is given.   For example, if the range is given in meters, the width and height of the radar resolution cell will be in meters.   The 57 merely converts degrees to radians.   If the beamwidths are given in radian measure, the 57 is simply omitted. Also see *range discrimination; range resolution.*

radar return.   A *signal* that has been *transmitted* by a *radar transmitter* and *reflected* back to the same or another radar's *receiver.*   Thus, an *echo* that is received by radar.

radar scan.   1. One complete revolution of a *search radar antenna.*   2. The area or angle that is covered by a *radar receiving antenna.*

radar scan-rate modulation deception.   A *radar deception* technique that is used against *tracking radars* and utilizes *modulation* of the *radar repeater* or *transponder output* at or near the *radar frequency.*   A particular form of this technique that is effective against *conical-scan, track-while-scan (TWS),* and *lobe-on-recieve only (LORO) tracking,* uses square wave (on-off) *gating* of the *output stage* of a repeater at a variable frequency that includes the scan frequency of the radar being countered.   As this modulation approaches the radar scan frequency, increasingly large *error signals* appear in the radar servo loops.   This causes rapid random gyration of the antenna system. Frequently these error signals thus introduced are sufficient to cause the radar to lose the object (target) completely. Since the scan *channel passbands* of conical-scan radars are quite narrow, typically one to four *hertz*, the modulation in the *countermeasure* must be swept slowly if a maximum effect is to be realized.

radarscope overlay. A transparent overlay for placing on a *radar screen* in order to identify and compare radar *echoes.*

radar screen. A *display surface* for a *radar system.*

radar sensitivity. 1. The *response* of a *radar receiver* to *signals* on its designed *frequency.* 2. A measure of the ability of a *receiver* to *amplify* and make usable very weak *signals.* Also see *minimum discernible signal.*

radar shadow. 1. The region that is obscured from the surveillance of a *radar* by obstructions, whether natural or artificial. 2. The region of low *intensity* or zero intensity *radar signal* that is produced behind an object by a *radar transmitter* that is in front of the object.

radar shift. The movement of the origin of a radial or *polar display* away from the center of the *display space* on the *display surface* of a *display device* such as a *cathode ray tube* or a *gas panel.*

radar signature. The detailed *wave shape* of the *radar echo* received by a *radar receiver.* *Signature analysis* permits aircraft identification, decoy versus missile with warhead *discrimination,* aircraft versus missile discrimination and other forms of object (target) identification. Also see *aircraft signature identification.*

radar silence. See *ship radar silence.*

radar spoking. In *radar systems,* periodic flashes of the rotating time-base on a radial display. Radar spoking is sometimes caused by *mutual interference.*

radar station. See *surveillance radar station.*

radar strobe. 1. An intensified spot in the sweep of a *deflection*-type indicator that is used as a reference mark for ranging or expanding a *display* (presentation). 2. An intensified sweep on a *plan-position indicator* or B-scope. Such a strobe may result from certain types of *interference,* or it may be purposely applied as a *bearing* or *heading* marker. 3. A *line* on a *console oscilloscope screen* that represents the *azimuth data* generated by a *radar.*

radar warning system. See *airborne radar warning system.*

radial distortion. An *aberration* of *lens systems* characterized by the *imaging* of an extra-axial straight line as a curved line without necessarily affecting the *resolving power* of the system. Unsymmetrical, or otherwise irregular, *distortions* of the *image* can also be caused by imperfect location of *optical* centers or irregularity of *optical surfaces.*

radially stratified fiber.   See *step-indexed fiber.*

radial refractive-index profile.   In an *optical fiber* with a circular cross section, the *refractive index* described as a function of the radial distance from the center. For example, the function:

$$n_r = n_o\, f(r)$$

where n_r is the *refractive index* at a radial distance r from the center, n_o is the refractive index at the center, and $f(r)$ is the function of r that expresses the index at the distance r from the center, usually independent of radial direction. See Figure R-1.

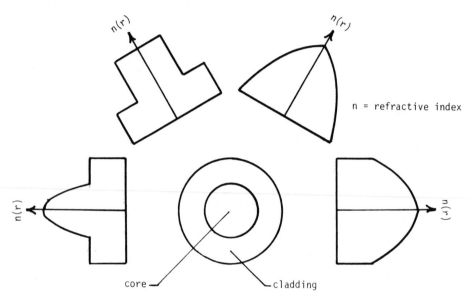

R-1. Typical *parabolic graded* and *stepped* **radial refractive index profiles** of *optical fibers.*

radiance.   The radiant *intensity* of *electromagnetic radiation* per unit projected area of a source or other area. It is the *radiant power* of electromagnetic radiation per *unit solid angle* and per unit surface area normal to the direction considered. The surface may be that of a *source* or a *detector* or it may be any other real or virtual surface intersecting the *flux.* The unit of measure is watts/steradian-square meter. The concept is usually applicable to the visible or near visible region of the electromagnetic *frequency spectrum.* Synonymous with *emittance.* See *spectral radiance.*

radiance conservation principle.   Passive *optical* peraphernalia cannot increase the *radiance* of a *source;* namely the radiance of an *image* cannot exceed that of the *object* when energy is not added to the *optical system.* Synonymous with *brightness conservation.*

radiant efficiency. The ratio of the forward *radiant flux* or *optical power* from a *source* to the total *power dissipation.*

radiant emittance. The *light flux radiated* per unit area of a *source.*

radiant energy. Energy *propagating* in the form of *electromagnetic waves;* normally measured in joules. Radiant energy does not involve the motion of material matter to achieve its propagation, in contrast to elastic or kinetic energy.

radiant exitance. The *radiant power emitted* into a full sphere (4π *steradians*) by a unit area of a *source.*

radiant flux. 1. The time rate of flow of *radiant energy.* It is measured in watts or in joules/second. 2. The *radiant energy* crossing or striking a surface per unit time, usually measured in watts.

radiant intensity. The *radiant power* per *unit solid angle* in the direction considered (i.e., the time rate of *transfer* of radiant energy per unit solid angle) or the *flux radiated* per unit solid angle about a specified direction. The unit of measure in watts/*steradian* or joules/(steradian-second). See *peak radiant intensity.*

radiant power. The time rate of flow of *electromagnetic energy.* It is measured in watts or joules/*second.*

radiant transmittance. The ratio of the *radiant flux transmitted* by an *object* to the *incident radiant flux.*

radiated power. See *effective isotropic radiated power; effective radiated power (ERP); equivalent isotropically-radiated power.*

radiated repeater. See *reradiating repeater.*

radiation. 1. In *radio communications,* the outward flow from a *source* of *radio frequency* energy in the form of *electromagnetic waves.* 2. Energy that flows in a *transmission medium* and that is in the form of *electromagnetic waves.* 3. The *electromagnetic waves* or photons that are *emitted* from a *source.* See *earth radiation; electromagnetic radiation; gamma radiation; infrared radiation; light amplification by stimulated emission of radiation; microwave amplification by stimulated emission of radiation; monochromatic radiation; polychromatic radiation; solar radiation; spurious radiation; thermal radiation.*

radiation absorbed dose. See *rad.*

radiation absorption factor. The ratio of the amount of absorbed heat energy to the energy of the total *luminous flux,* or *electromagnetic radiation* other than heat, *incident* upon a given surface area. For solar radiation, it is called the *solar absorption factor.*

radiation balance. See *earth radiation balance.*

radiation control. See *electromagnetic radiation control.*

radiation damage. See *optical fiber radiation damage.*

radiation device. See *incident radiation device.*

radiation effects on electronics. See *transient radiation effects on electronics (TREE).*

radiation efficiency. See *luminous radiation efficiency.*

radiation field. In *electromagnetic field theory,* the *field* in a region at that distance from an *antenna* or *source* of *electromagnetic radiation* at which the *electromagnetic field strength* varies inversely as the distance from the antenna or source. Other contributors to the field strength that vary inversely as the square and the cube of the distance are negligible. The radiation field occurs at distances greater than one-sixth of the *wavelength* from the source. The negligible components are the *induction field,* varying inversely as the square of the distance from the source, and the *electrostatic field,* varying inversely as the cube of the distance from the source. The differential tangential component of the *electric field vector* from an ideal *hertzian dipole antenna,* which most dipole antennas can be considered to be at the distance involved, is given by:

$$dE_\theta = (I \, dl \, \sin\theta / 4\pi\epsilon) \, [(-\omega \sin \omega t / r v^2) + (\cos \omega t / r^2 v) + (\sin \omega t / \omega r^3)]$$

radiation	induction	electrostatic
field	field	field

where I is the antenna *current,* dl is the elemental length of antenna bearing the current I, θ is the angle between the antenna direction of dl and the line from the dipole center to the point or measurement, ϵ is the *electric permittivity* of the intervening medium, ω is the angular *frequency* of the radiation, v is the *propagation* velocity equal to $(\mu\epsilon)^{-1}$, μ is the *magnetic permeability* of the medium, t is time, and r is the distance from the center of the dipole (antenna) to the point of measurement of dE_θ. The *radiation field* occupies a region in which the angular field distribution function is essentially independent of the distance from the *antenna.* If the antenna has a maximum overall dimension, D, that is large compared to the *wavelength,* the radiation field region is commonly taken to exist at distances greater than $2D^2/\lambda$ from the antenna, where λ is the wavelength. For an antenna that is focused at infinity, the radiation field region is referred to as the Fraunhofer region. Synonymous with *far field; far field region; far zone.* Also see *electrostatic field; induction field.*

radiation hazard. See *electromagnetic radiation hazard.*

radiation pattern. **1.** For an *antenna* or *light source,* a polar or spherical coordinate plot of the *electromagnetic radiant intensity* in each radial direction from the *antenna* or *light source.* The plot is usually a three-dimensional surface plotted in spherical coordinates in which the length of a radius *vector* from the origin at the source of the radiation pattern to the surface is proportional to the *radiant power density* or *electric field strength* in the direction in which the vector is drawn. The line of intersection of this surface with planes through the origin are usually displayed as antenna radiation patterns. The pattern is of the *radiation field* at considerable distance from the antenna, rather than the closer-in *induction* or *electrostatic fields.* For light sources, the *wavelength* is so short that there is only the radiation field, and only the *luminous intensity* is considered. 2. For an *optical fiber* or *fiber bundle,* the curve of the output *radiation intensity* plotted as a function of the angle between the *optical axis* of the fiber or bundle and a normal to the surface on which the radiation intensity is being measured, i.e., the output radiation versus direction of measurement relative to the optical axis. Typically, the radiation pattern for a light source or antenna is a graphical representation of power radiation of the antenna, that is usually shown for the two principal planes, namely azimuth and elevation. The radiation pattern of an antenna is usually measured in the *radiation field* (far field). This field is normally beyond the distance of $2D^2/\lambda$, where D is the radiating length of the antenna and λ is the *wavelength.* Synonymous with *antenna pattern.* Also see *directivity pattern; electromagnetic radiation; lobe; main lobe.*

radiation pattern plotter. A device that measures the *light intensity* in various directions from a *source* relative to a reference line or plane on the source, such as the front-*emitting surface* of an *LED* or *laser.* See Figure R-2.

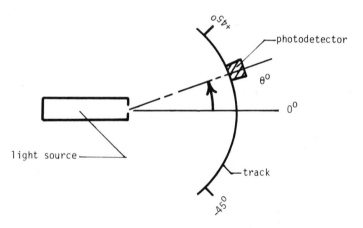

R-2. A **radiation pattern plotter** schematic.

radiation scattering. The diversion of *electromagnetic radiation* (thermal *(infrared), radio, video, microwave, gamma, x-ray radiation*) from its original path as a result of interactions or collisions with atoms, molecules, or large particles in the *atmosphere* or other *transmission media* between the source of radiation, such as a transmitting *antenna,* a *light source,* or a nuclear explosion, and a point that is some distance away. As a result of *scattering,* radiation, especially gamma rays, will be received at such a point from many directions instead of only from the direction of the source. Also see *electromagnetic radiation.*

radiation source. See *primary radiation source; secondary radiation source.*

radiation suppression. See *infrared radiation suppression.*

radiation temperature. See *total radiation temperature.*

radiation transfer index. In a *radiation transmission system,* the 1/10th root of the overall *transmission efficiency.* Thus, mathematically:

$$RTI = \alpha^{1/10}$$

where α is the ratio of the *radiation* flux, *power density, optical power,* or number of *photons* at the end, to the same unit at the beginning, of a transmission system for which the RTI is desired. Since db $= 10\log_{10}\alpha^{-1}$, it follows that:

$$RTI = 10^{-db/100}$$

and that $db = -100\log_{10} RTI$. *RTI*s are multiplied in a serial sequential system of components to obtain the overall *RTI* of the series combination.

radiative recombination. In an *electroluminescent diode* in which *electrons* and *holes* are injected into the p-type and n-type regions by application of a forward bias, the *recombination* of injected minority *carriers* with the majority carriers in such a manner that the energy released upon recombination results in the *emission* of *photons* of energy *hf,* which is approximately equal to the band-gap energy. *Radiative recombination* produces the *light* in an *LED* which can be *modulated* for *signaling* purposes using *optical fibers* for *transmission* or *integrated optical circuits* for *switching.* Also see *nonradiative recombination.*

radiator. A device that emits *radiation,* such as a *radio* or *television transmitting* antenna, a *light source,* or *radioactive* material. See *isotropic radiator.*

radii loss. See *mismatch-of-core-radii loss.*

radio. 1. A method of *communicating* over a distance by *modulating electromagnetic waves* by means of an intelligence-bearing *signal* and *radiating* these modulated waves by means of a *transmitter* and an *antenna.* **2.** A device, or pertaining to a device, that *transmits* or receives *electromagnetic waves* in the *frequency bands* that are between 10 kHz and 3000 GHz. See *combat-net radio; high-frequency radio; teleprinter-on-radio.*

radioactive atoms. An atom whose *electrons,* photons, or other atomic components are undergoing *energy band transitions* that result in *absorption* or *emission* of high-energy *quanta.*

radioactive particle. A particle of matter that is attached to *radioactive* atoms and therefore seems to be experiencing *radioactivity* itself.

radioactivity. The activity of *radioactive* atoms, such as the *emission* or *absorption* of *gamma radiation, x-rays,* or other high-energy *quanta.*

radio altimeter. A device that is used on board an aircraft and that makes use of the *reflection* of *radio waves* from the ground to determine the height of the aircraft above the ground. The equipment uses *beamed* and *reflected electromagnetic* energy to measure height above ground by means of a *phase* displacement between the *transmitted radio signal* and its *echo* reflected from the ground. The altitude in meters is 150 m/μs of phase displacement.

radio-and-wire integration (RWI). See *radio-wire integration*.

radio-approach aid. Equipment that makes use of *radio* to determine the position of an aircraft with considerable *accuracy* from the time it is in the vicinity of an airfield until it reaches a position from which landing can be carried out by direct visual means.

radio astronomy. Astronomy that is based on the *reception* of *radio waves* of *cosmic* origin.

radio astronomy service. A service that involves the use of *radio astronomy*.

radio astronomy station. A *station* in a *radio astronomy service*. A radio astronomy station is always a receiving station.

radio autocontrol. The control of an object by means of radio signals that are launched from the object and reflected back to the object from other objects. For example, control of the height above ground of an aircraft by ground reflection of signals originating from the aircraft.

radio baseband. The *baseband* of a *radio*. For example, the *frequency band* that is available for the *transmission* of all *calls* in the combined *radiotelephone* or other radio *signaling* or *data channels*.

radio baseband receive terminal. The point in the *baseband circuit* that is nearest to the *radio receiver* and from which *connection* is normally made to the *multiplex baseband receive terminal* or to an intermediate *facility*.

radio baseband send terminal. The point in the *baseband circuit* that is nearest to the *radio transmitter* and from which *connection* is normally made to the *multiplex baseband transmit terminal* or to an intermediate *facility*.

radio beacon. A *transmitter* that emits a distinctive or characteristic *electromagnetic signal* that is used for the determination of *bearings,* courses, or location in *radionavigation systems*. The electromagnetic signal, or the device that *transmits* the signal, is used to determine the bearing of the transmitter from a distant point using *direction-finding (DF)*. A radio beacon may also be used to determine the location of an object in space by *radar* and then to transmit bearing information by radio. Synonymous with *homing beacon*.

radio beacon station. A *station* in the *radionavigation service* that *emits* an *electromagnetic signal* that enables a *mobile station* to determine its *bearing* (direction) in relation to the radio beacon station. See *aeronautical radio beacon station; marine radio beacon station*.

radio beam. A *radiation pattern* from a *directional antenna* such that the energy of the *electromagnetic wave* that is *transmitted* is confined to a small angle in at least one dimension. The *beamwidth* is concentrated into a sector that is narrow in either *azimuth* or *elevation,* or both.

radio channel. An *assigned frequency band* of sufficient *width* and *frequency* for *radio communication.* The *bandwidth* of a *channel* depends upon the type of *transmission* and the frequency tolerance. Radio channel frequency is normally assigned for a particular *service,* a particular *modulation* scheme, and a specified *transmitter.* The particular service includes a specific *communication* function such as police, amateur, medical telemetry, aeronautical, broadcast, or military channel.

radio circuit. In *radiotelegraph communications,* a *circuit* between two *stations,* that has at least one *radio link,* that is, at least one segment of the connection path makes use of *electromagnetic waves* in *free space.*

radio communication. The use of *electromagnetic waves* in *free space* for *communication* purposes, that is, the use of *radio waves* that are not guided between the transmitting and receiving *antennas* by physical paths such as wire, *waveguides,* or *optical fibers.*

radio communication copy watch. To maintain a continuous *receiver watch* while keeping a complete *radio station log.* Also see *radio communication cover.*

radio communication cover. To maintain continuous *receiver watch* with a calibrated *transmitter* that is not necessarily available for immediate use. Maintenance of a complete *radio station log* is optional. Radio communication cover is a type of *radio communication copy watch.* Also see *guard watch; listening watch; radio communication copy watch.* Synonymous with *cover watch.*

radio communication guard. **1.** A *radio communication station* that is designated to listen for and record *transmissions* and to handle *traffic* on a designated *frequency* for certain other units or organizations. **2.** To maintain a continuous *receiver watch* with *transmitter* ready for immediate use. **3.** In *radio communications,* a *ship station, aircraft station,* or other *mobile station* that is designated to *copy, cover, guard,* or *listen* for *transmissions* and to handle *traffic* on a designated *frequency* for a number of other *mobile stations.* Also see *guard watch.*

radio control. The control of a mechanism or other apparatus by *electromagnetic waves,* such as the control of the movement of an aircraft, vehicle, missile, or other mobile unit, either manned or unmanned, from a *radio station* on the ground or in another mobile unit. Also see *radio telecontrol.*

radioconverter. See *telegraph radioconverter.*

radio coverage diagram. A diagram that shows the area within which a *radio station* is *broadcasting* an effective *signal strength* in relation to a given standard. For example, in each direction from the antenna, the *polar plot* of the distance from the *antenna* at which the signal strength is equal to a specified value, that is, it is the locus of all points at which the signal strength is equal to a specified value.

radio day. The scheduled period of time that a *radio station transmits,* usually during a single day. For example, the period from 6:00 AM to 9:00 PM each day that the station is actively *broadcasting.* Stations usually indicate the beginning and the end of their radio (broadcast) day.

radio deception. The employment of *radio transmission* to deceive the recipient of the *signals.* For example, the sending of false *messages* using deceptive *headings* and using misleading *call signs.* Also see *electronic warfare.*

radio detection. The *detection* of the presence of an object by *radio* without the precise determination of its position.

radio determination. The determination of the position, or the obtaining of *information* relating to position of an object, by means of the *propagation* of *radio waves.* Also see *radio goniometry; radio range finding.*

radio determination service. A service that makes use of *radio determination.*

radio determination station. A *station* in the *radio determination service.*

radio direction finding (RDF). *Radio determination* in which the reception of *radio waves* is used for the purpose of determining the direction of a *station* or object from a *transmitting station.* See *airborne radio direction finding.*

radio direction-finding equipment. Receiving equipment that is used to obtain the *bearings* of *transmitting stations,* in which the *receiver* is usually in the form of an automatic *direction finder* that automatically and continuously indicates the direction of a *transmitter* from itself *(receiver).*

radio direction-finding station. A *radio determination station* in which *radio direction finding* is used. The station is intended to determine only the direction of other stations by means of *transmission* from the latter.

radio Doppler. A method that is used for the determination of the radial component of the relative velocity between a *source* of *electromagnetic waves* and another object from a measurement of the difference in *frequency* that occurs between the *radio waves* that are *emitted* from the source and the waves that are *reflected* from the object. Also see *Doppler effect.*

radio equation. See *one-way radio equation.*

radio failure. The inability to *receive, transmit,* or both, by *radio.* Usually, in the event of radio *failure,* other means of *signaling* are used, such as wire or *optical fiber.* Aircraft experiencing radio failure fly a triangular pattern to the right if the *receiver* only is operating, to the left if the receiver and the *transmitter* are both inoperative, in an attempt to establish *radar* contact.

radio field intensity. See *field strength.*

radio fix. **1.** The location of a *radio transmitter* by finding the direction of the transmitter from two or more *receiver listening stations.* This is the method of *intersection.* **2.** The location of a *radio receiver* by determining the direction of two or more *transmitting stations,* the locations of which are known. This is the method of *resection.*

radio fixing aid. Equipment that makes use of *radio* to assist in the determination of the geographical position of *transmitting* or *receiving stations.*

radio frequency (RF). Those *frequencies* of the *electromagnetic spectrum* that are normally associated with *radio wave propagation.* The nomenclature of radio frequencies is as follows:

Frequency Subdivision	Frequency Range	Metric Subdivision
VLF	3–30 kHz	myriametric waves
LF	30–300 kHz	kilometric waves
MF	300–3000 kHz	hectometric waves
HF	3–30 MHz	decametric waves
VHF	30–300 MHz	metric waves
UHF	300–3000 MHz	decimetric waves
SHF	3–30 GHz	centimetric waves
EHF	30–300 GHz	millimetric waves
THF	300–3000 GHz	decimillimetric waves

Also see *frequency spectrum designation.*

radio frequency bandwidth. The difference between the highest and lowest values of the *emission frequencies* in the region of the *carrier frequency.* In single *channel* emission, it is the region of the carrier frequency beyond which the *amplitude* of any frequency, such as those that result from *modulation,* those that are *subcarrier frequencies,* or those that result from *distortion* products, is less than 5% (−26 dB) of the rated peak *output* amplitude of the carrier of a *single-tone sideband,* whichever is greater. For *multiplex* emission, the radio frequency *bandwidth* is the same, except that the 5% applies to the subcarrier or a single-tone sideband of the carrier, whichever is the greater. Synonymous with *RF bandwidth.* Also see *necessary bandwidth; nominal bandwidth; occupied bandwidth.*

radio frequency channel increment. The *frequency* separation between adjacent *channels* in a multichannel *transmission* system.

radio frequency combining. The *combining* of a number of multichannel *trunks* for *voice, digital data,* or other *transmissions* over a single *wideband facility* where the combining action occurs at *radio frequencies* as opposed to *video* or *audio frequencies.* Synonymous with *frequency-division multiplex combining.*

radio frequency interference (RFI). **1.** *Interference* that is generated or induced in electronic *circuits* and is in the *radio frequency range* of the *electromagnetic* *spectrum.* **2.** *Electromagnetic* phenomena that either directly or indirectly can contribute to a degradation in performance of a *receiver* or other *system.*

radio frequency intermodulation. A constituent of *nonlinear distortion* that consists of the occurrence of *harmonics* in the *response* of *electrical components.* The harmonics are caused by *intermodulation distortion* in the *radio frequency stages* of a *receiver.*

radio frequency power margin. An extra amount of *transmitter power* that may be specified by a designer because of uncertainties in the empirical design method, terrain characteristics, *atmospheric* variability, and variation in equipment *performance parameters* and characteristics. Synonymous with *design margin.* Also see *fade margin.*

radio frequency pulse. A *train, string,* or *packet* of *radio frequency waves* that have an *envelope* in the *shape* of a *pulse.* The number of *waves* in the RF pulse would be given by $n = ft$, where n is the number of waves (cycles) in the pulse, f is the radio frequency (RF) of the waves in the pulse, and t is the *pulse length.* For example, a 20 MHz RF wave with a 2 μs *pulse length* would have 40 wave cycles in each packet (pulse).

radio goniometry. The determination of the relative direction of a distant object by means of its *radio emissions,* whether the emissions are independent, reflected, or automatically retransmitted. Also see *radio determination; radio range finding.*

radiogram. A *telegram* that is *transmitted* via *radio.*

radio guard. A *radio station* that is designated to listen for, record, and handle *communication traffic* on a designated *frequency* for a certain other *station.*

radio horizon range (RHR). The distance at which a *direct radio wave* can reach a *receiving antenna* of given height from a *transmitting antenna* of given height. The radio horizon range in nautical miles, R, is given by the relation $R = 1.23(h_t^{1/2} + h_r^{1/2})$, where h_t and h_r are the heights of the transmitting and receiving antennas in feet. The radio horizon range, R, in nautical miles is also given by the relation $R = 2.23(h_t^{1/2} + h_r^{1/2})$, where h_t and h_r are the heights of the transmitting and receiving antennas in *meters.* The *effective earth radius,* 4/3 times the actual earth radius, is used in deriving the formulas. Second order differentials are neglected. They are of the order of 0.1%. Also see *radar horizon; radar line-of-sight equation.*

radio installation. All the equipment in a *radio station* that is required to make it fully operational for use, including *transducers, amplifiers, modulation equipment, transmitters, antennas,* and the vehicle, container, building or other structure in which it is housed.

radio landing aid. *Radio* equipment that is used to assist in the landing of an aircraft.

radio link. The *connection* of two points by *radio* in order to carry on *communication* between them.

radio location. *Radio determination* that is used for purposes other than those of *radionavigation.*

radio location land station. A *station* in the *radio location service* that is not intended to be used while in motion.

radio location mobile service. A *station* in the *radio location service* that is intended to be used while in motion or during temporary halts at unspecified points and while on board the vehicle.

radio location service. A *radiodetermination service* in which *radio location* is used to provide a *radionavigation service.*

radio location station. A station in a *radio location service.*

radio log. See *ship radio log.*

radiometer. An instrument designed to measure *electromagnetic radiant intensity.* See *fiber-optic visible-infrared spin-scan radiometer.*

radiometry. The science devoted to the measurement of *radiated electromagnetic power.* In *lightwave communications* and the use of *optical fibers,* the primary concern is for *radiometry* rather than *photometry.*

radionavigation. *Radio location* that is intended for the determination of position or for obstruction warning in navigation.

radionavigation aid. 1. A *radio facility* that is designed or usable for navigation. 2. Radio equipment that uses *electromagnetic waves,* normally between 10 kHz and 3000 GHz, for the purpose of assisting *aircraft stations* in air navigation and assisting *ship stations* in maritime navigation or pilotage.

radionavigation land station. A *station* in a *radionavigation service* that is not intended to be used while in motion.

radionavigation maintenance test land station. A *radionavigation land station* and maintenance test *facility* in an *aeronautical radionavigation service* that is used as a *radionavigation* calibration station for the *transmission* of essential *information* in connection with the testing and calibration of aircraft navigational aids. *Receivers, transmitters,* and *interrogators* that are used for maintenance and testing of aircraft *communication* equipment are installed at predetermined surface locations during testing operations.

radionavigation operational test land station. A *radionavigation land station* and operational test facility in the aeronautical *radionavigation service* that is used as a radionavigational calibration station for the *transmission* of essential *information* in connection with the testing and calibration of aircraft navigational aids, receiving equipment, and interrogators at predetermined surface locations.

The primary purpose of this *facility* is to permit a pilot to check a radionavigation system aboard the aircraft prior to takeoff.

radionavigation mobile station. A *station* in a *radionavigation service* that is intended to be used while in motion or during temporary halts at unspecified points and while on board the vehicle, ship, or aircraft.

radionavigaton satellite earth station. An *earth station* in a *radionavigation satellite service.*

radionavigation satellite service. A *service* in which *space stations* on *earth satellites* are used for the purpose of *radionavigation,* including the *transmission* or retransmission of supplementary *information* that may be necessary for the *operation* of the *radionavigation system.*

radionavigation satellite space station. A *space station* that is in a *radionavigation satellite service* and that is on an *earth satellite.*

radionavigation service. A *radio determination service* that is devoted to the provision of *radio aids* for aeronautical, maritime, and land mobile navigation. See *aeronautical radionavigation service; maritime radionavigation service.*

radionavigation station. A *station* that is in a *radionavigation service.*

radio net. An organization of *radio stations* that are capable of direct *communication* on a common *frequency.*

radio officer. See *senior ship radio officer.*

radio officer-of-the-watch. The *radio officer* who is responsible for a specified *radio watch* for specified time periods during the voyage of a ship.

radio operator. In *radio communication system operation,* a person who operates *radio transmission* or *receiving* equipment for the *transmission* and *reception* of *messages.*

radio organization. See *maritime air radio organization.*

radio organization chart. A chart that illustrates interrelated *fixed* and *mobile radio nets.*

radiophoto. A *facsimile transmission system* in which *electromagnetic waves* in the *radio frequency spectrum* are used for the *transmission* of *signals* that are generated by a *scanning transmitter* and a *recording receiver.*

radio positioning land station. A *station* in a *radio location service* that is not a *radionavigation station* and is not intended for *operation* while in motion.

radio positioning mobile station. A *station* in a *radio location service* that is not a *radionavigation station,* and that is intended for *operation* while in motion or during unspecified temporary halts while on board a vehicle.

radio position line determination. The determination of a position line by means of *radio location.*

radio range. A *radio aid* to air navigation that creates an infinite number of paths in space throughout a given sector or *azimuth* angle by various methods of *transmission* and *reception* of *electromagnetic waves.* See *omnidirectional radio range (omnirange); very-high frequency omnidirectional radio range; visual-aural radio range.*

radio range finding. *Radio location* in which the distance of an object is determined by means of its *radio emissions,* whether independent, *reflected,* or retransmitted on the same or other *wavelength.* Also see *radio determination; radio goniometry.*

radio range station. A *radionavigation land station* that is in an *aeronautical radionavigation service* and provides radial equisignal zones for location determination by a *receiver.* A radio range station may also be placed aboard a ship, aircraft, spacecraft, or land vehicle.

radio receiver. A *receiver* that is capable of accepting *radio frequency electromagnetic waves* and selectively converting them into an intelligible and useful form.

radio recognition. The *radio determination* of the character, individuality, or nature of a received *radio signal* and the drawing of conclusions concerning the *transmitting station* and its *operators* based on *signal analysis.*

radio recognition and identification. See *identification friend-or-foe (IFF).*

radio relay. 1. The reception and retransmission by a *radio station* of *signals* that are received either from another radio station or from a wire, *optical fiber, microwave, coaxial cable,* or other *line* portion of an *integrated line* and *radio communication system component.* 2. A terrestrial *point-to-point communication system,* such as a *microwave relay communication system* or a *satellite communication system.* The siting of *radio relay stations* and the *power* and *polar diagrams* of the *antenna patterns* are arranged for minimum *interference* with *satellite earth stations.* The *analog* and *digital baseband* arrangements are similar to satellite systems. Radio relay *links* may form part of the *connection* between an earth station and a *switching center.* See *down-the-hill radio relay.*

radio relay electronic counter-countermeasure. A measure that is used to counter deliberate efforts to introduce *interference (jamming)* into *radio relay circuits.*

radio relay plane. See *automatic radio relay plane.*

radio relay system. A *communication system* that is used to perform a *radio relay* function. For example, a *point-to-point radio transmission system* in which the *signals* are received, amplified, and retransmitted by one or more intermediate *radio stations.*

radio service. See *Armed Forces Radio Service.*

radio set. 1. An apparatus that consists of a *transmitter, receiver, antenna,* and related equipment and is used for the *transmission* and *reception* of *radio signals.* 2. A *radio transmitter* and *antenna.* 3. A *radio receiver* and *antenna.*

radio silence. A *radio communication system operating mode* or condition in which designated *transmitters* are not transmitting. During a radio silence period, all of certain specified radio equipment that is capable of *emitting electromagnetic radiation,* including certain *receivers,* are kept inoperative. *Radio transmissions* are not to be made. No electronic equipment is to be radiating. Radio silence may be required to reduce *interference* to *emergency traffic,* prevent confusion to navigational aids or *missile guidance,* or as a *radio communication electronic counter-countermeasure (ECCM),* to prevent the opportunity to gather intelligence through *interception* and *analysis* of *radio signals.* Also see *communication silence.* See *ship radio silence.*

radiosonde. An automatic *radio transmitter* in a *meteorological aids service* that is usually carried on an aircraft, free balloon, kite, or parachute, and that transmits meteorological *data.* The data is obtained by sensors, converted by *transducers,* and *telemetered* to the ground.

radiosonde station. A *station* that is in a *meteorological service* and uses *radiosonde* equipment.

radio station. An installation, assembly of equipment, location, or vehicle from which *radio signals* may be *transmitted* or *received.* The vehicle may be a *spacecraft,* aircraft, ship, or land vehicle. See *ship broadcast-area radio station; ship broadcast coastal radio station.*

radio telecontrol. The control of mechanisms, devices, equipment, *components,* and *systems* by *radio waves* sent to the items over greater distances than are involved in *radio control.* Also see *radio control.*

radiotelegraph communication. *Communication* in which *telegraph codes* are *transmitted* by *electromagnetic waves* in *guides* and *free space* rather than by *electric signals* in wires and *lightwaves* in *optical fibers.*

radiotelegraph distress frequency. The *international distress and calling frequency* for *radiotelegraphy,* such as 500 kHz, for use by *ship stations, aircraft stations,* or *survival craft stations,* for *distress calls, distress messages, urgency signals, safety signals,* and other *distress* and *urgency traffic.* Also see *calling frequency.*

radiotelegraph distress frequency. See *international radiotelegraph distress frequency.*

radiotelegraph lifecraft frequency. See *international radiotelegraph lifecraft frequency.*

radiotelegraph message format. The prescribed arrangement of the *parts* of a *message* that has been prepared for *radiotelegraph transmission.*

radiotelegraph operating method.   One of the three operating methods for passing *messages* from one *station* to another, namely the *receipt communication method,* the *broadcast communication method,* and the *intercept communication method.*   The operating method that is used in a particular situation is determined by the operational requirements.

radiotelegraph procedure.   A *procedure* that is used in *radiotelegraph communication systems.*   These procedures are designed to provide a concise and definite *language* whereby radiotelegraph communication may be conducted accurately, rapidly, and with the security that is obtainable on *radio circuits.*   Radiotelegraph procedures are used in *transmissions* over *radio* and *line circuits* that use the *international Morse code* as well as other codes.   When commercial messages are handled by noncommercial systems, the procedure is usually contained in the *message heading* or in the *calling* and *routing instructions.*   See *cross-band radiotelegraph procedure; simplex radiotelegraph procedure.*

radio telegraphy.   The *transmission* of *telegraph code messages* by means of *radio.*   Radio telegraphy is a *telecommunication* process that is concerned with reproduction at a distance of documentary matter such as written, printed, or pictorial matter, or the reproduction at a distance of any kind of *information.*

radiotelephone communication.   *Communication* in which *voice* or other *sound signals* are *transmitted* by *electromagnetic waves* in *guides* and *free space* rather than by *electric signals* in wires and *lightwaves* in *optical fibers.*

radiotelephone distress frequency.   An *international distress* and *calling frequency* for *mobile radiotelephone stations, survival craft,* and *emergency position-indicating radio beacons,* such as 2182 kHz.   See *international radio telephone distress frequency.*

radiotelephone frequency.   See *convoy radiotelephone frequency; maritime mobile radiotelephone frequency.*

radiotelephone numerals.   See *ship radiotelephone numerals.*

radiotelephone procedure.   Any *procedure* that is used in *radiotelephone communication systems,* such as a *calling party* identification procedure.   See *ship-to-shore radiotelephone procedure.*

radiotelephone system.   A *communication system* in which a *telephone* is used by the *calling* or *called party* and *radio links* are used in the *communication path* between them.

radiotelephone network.   A group of *radiotelephone aeronautical stations* that operate on, and *guard,* common *frequencies,* and support each other in a defined manner to ensure maximum dependability of *air-ground communications* for handling *air-ground traffic.*

radiotelephone voice system.   A *telecommunication system* for the *transmission* of speech or other sounds.

radiotelephony. The *transmission* of speech by means of *radio waves* that are *modulated* by a wave that is an electrical equivalent of a *sound wave.*

radio teleprinter. A *teleprinter* used in association with *radio circuits* and *networks.*

radio teletype (RATT or RTTY). The system of *communication* in which *teletypewriters (teleprinters)* are used to *communicate* over *radio circuits.* Also see *teletypewriter.*

radio teletypewriter. See *intership radio teletypewriter; ship-shore radio teletypewriter.*

radio transmission control. The control and limitation that is imposed upon *radio operation.* For example, the control that limits *transmissions* to the absolute minimum essential to carry on *communication traffic* or the control to insure that *transmission procedures* are precisely adhered to. See *port radio transmission control.*

radio transmission security. See *ship radio transmission security.*

radio transmitter. A device that may be used for the production, *modulation,* and amplification of *radio frequency* energy that may be *radiated* into *free space* by means of an *antenna* for the purpose of effecting *communication.* The *transmitter* energizes the antenna in order that the *radio waves* may be *coupled* to free space.

radiovoltaic. Pertaining to the production of a *voltage* that occurs when *ionizing* nuclear *alpha* and *beta particles* create *electron-hole* pairs in the crystal lattice of a *semiconductor* material. The effects of nuclear *radiation* on cadmium sulphide and cadmium telluride thin-film cells have been applied in this form of energy conversion for limited biomedical pusposes (typically 1 μw per cell). An alpha particle is a free helium nucleus and a beta particle is a free *electron.* Also see *photovoltaic.*

radio watch shift. See *area broadcast shift.*

radio wave. An *electromagnetic wave* with a *frequency* that is above 3 kHz and lower than 3000 GHz and that is *propagated* in *free space* or in material *transmission media.* Also see *Hertzian wave.*

radio-wire integration (RWI). The combination and interconnection of wire *circuits* and *radio facilities.* Synonymous with *radio and wire integration; wire-radio integration.*

radio-wire integration (RWI) device. An *interface* device that permits intercommunication between *wire circuits* and *radio facilities.* Also see *radio-wire interface.*

radio-wire interface (RWI). An *interface* between a single *channel radio net* and a *switched communication system.* Synonymous with *net radio interface; wire-radio interface.* Also see *radio-wire integration (RWI) device.*

radius. See *critical radius; effective earth radius.*

radix. The positive *integer* by which the weight of the *digit* place in a *numeral* of a given numeration system is multiplied to obtain the weight of the digit place with the next higher weight. For example, in the *decimal* numeration system, the radix of each digit place is 10 because the weight of a given digit place has to be multiplied by 10 to obtain the weight of the next higher place. Thus, the weight of the 1000's place is obtained by multiplying the weight of the 100's place by 10. In a *binary* numeration system, the radix is 2. In a *biquinary code* the radix of each 5's position is 2.

radome. A cover protecting an *antenna, light source,* or other radiating or *radiation receiver* from environmental damage. The radome must be designed to avoid *signal distortion,* although some *attenuation* is inevitable.

railings. The appearance of the *image* on a *radar screen* when *radar pulse jamming* at high *pulse repetition rates* (50 to 150 kHz) occurs. The jamming results in an image on the radar screen that resembles fence railings or a picket fence.

random. See *pseudorandom.*

random binary sequence. See *pseudorandom binary sequence.*

random bit-stream signaling. A method of *communication* that makes use of *bit*-intermittent *transmission* of *signals* on a *unit interval* basis without regard to the presence or absence of a *code* or *alphabet.* Synonymous with *intermittent-timing transmission.*

random conference. A conference that is established among *communication network users* (customers, subscribers) at their request to a *network operator.*

randomizer. 1. A device that is used to invert the sense (direction, polarity) of *pseudorandomly* selected *bits* of a *bit stream* to avoid long sequences of bits of the same sense. The same selection pattern must be used at the *receive terminal* in order to restore the original bit stream. 2. In *cryptographic equipment operations,* a *random bit* generator that starts all the *cryptoequipment* at the same point in the *key* stream.

randomly-phased orbit. An *orbit* in a system that consists of a group of *satellites* and in which the orbit or position of an individual satellite does not have a fixed or controlled time or spatial relationship to that of others in the same group. Also see *phased orbit.*

random noise. *Noise* that consists of *impulses* (disturbances) that occur at *random* in time. It consists of a large number of transient disturbances with a statistically random time distribution. *Thermal noise* is a random noise. See *triangular random noise.*

random scan. See *directed scan.*

random signal. A sequence of *pulses* such that each pulse does not have a fixed time relationship with any other pulse. Their individual *occurrence time* is unpredictable, although some rule of randomness may be broken. For example, they must occur within a fixed maximum time span from each other, or there may be a fixed number of *pulses* in a given time interval.

range. **1.** The maximum distance at which a *signal* from a *source* can be effectively received and used. **2.** In *radio communication,* the maximum distance between specified *radio stations* over which effective communication can be provided. **3.** In *radar,* the maximum distance at which an object (target) can be *detected* or *tracked.* Some of the factors that influence range are the *transmitted power,* the *antenna gain (directivity)* of the transmitting and receiving antennas, *receiver sensitivity, atmospheric* conditions, and, in the case of *radar,* the characteristics of the *reflecting* object (target). See *burn-through range; dynamic range; emission intercept range; frequency range; luminance range; maximum detection range; omnidirectional radio range (omnirange); optical range; orientation range; radar blind range; radio horizon range (RHR); radio range; slant range; very-high frequency omnidirectional radio range; visual-aural radio range.*

range advantage. In *radar,* the difference between the maximum range at which a *radar transmission* can be intercepted by a *search receiver* and the maximum *detection* range against the object using the search receiver. For example, the range advantage obtained by a small ship using *direction finding (DF) equipment* is greater than in the case of a large ship; a submarine has a greater range advantage than a frigate using similar equipment. Even if the range advantage is not great, DF equipment may still give earlier detection than would be gained by any other means.

range compression. See *luminance range compression.*

range discrimination. **1.** A measure of the *precision* with which *range* can be measured. A *radar* may have high range discrimination, that is, it can precisely measure range to a few *meters,* depending upon the depth of the *radar resolution cell.* It may have poor *bearing discrimination* and poor *elevation* discrimination depending upon the width and height of the radar resolution cell. A small *azimuth* or *elevation angle* corresponds to many *meters* at operating ranges. **2.** The ability of a *transmitter-receiver* to distinguish, separate, or identify, on the basis of *range,* a given *signal source* from all other *signals, noise,* or *interference.* For example, in *radar systems,* range discrimination is obtained from the width of the *range gate,* that is from the depth of the resolution cell. Also see *bearing discrimination; detection discrimination; radar resolution cell.*

range equation. See *self-screening range equation.*

range expansion. See *luminous range expansion.*

range finding. See *radio range finding.*

range gate. A *radar circuit* that measures the time interval between the instant a *pulse* from the *radar transmitter* is dispatched and the instant the *pulse echo* from an object is *detected* by the *radar receiver.* Both pulses can be *displayed* on a *screen,* the screen distance between them can be adjusted so that when they are made coincident, the range in convenient units, such as *meters, kilometers,* or *nautical miles,* can be read directly. It is the gate *time scale* that is adjusted until the pulses are coincident.

range-gate stealing. In *radar systems,* the process in which a *tracking radar* is caused to lose *range* tracking of an object (target). Range gate stealing operations against a *pulsed radar* causes the set to not hold lock. If the gate stealing cycle is fast, the radar may not appear to hold lock or to *break lock* quickly. Against a slower cycle, such as several seconds, distinct indications of *range gate capture* and *walkoff* may be evident. *Video* dims or *grass* recedes as the *jammer's retransmitted pulses* drive down the *radar's automatic gain control (AGC).* The radar overtake indication decreases or does not increase fully as range-gate walkoff occurs. The real object may become visible at shorter ranges. Breaklock occurs when the jammer completes its *transmission.*

range-gate walkoff. In a *radar system,* a continued increase in the *range* to an object (target) that is *displayed* as an *image* on a *radar* A-scope, B-scope, or other range display in which the *range gate* plays a role, in such a manner that the range to the object appears to increase to a maximum value. The range *pulse* gradually shifts out of the *display area* on the *display surface* of the *display device,* such as the *radar screen.*

range-height indicator (RHI). A device that *scans* an object (target) by *radar,* determines the *range,* or uses range *information* that is supplied by another *source,* measures the *elevation angle* or *depression angle,* computes the difference in elevation between the RHI installation and the object, and *displays* the range and height of the object. Synonymous with *radar height indicator; radio height indicator.*

range laser sonar. See *short-range laser sonar.*

range marker. In *radar systems,* a single calibration *pulse* (blip) that is fed to the time base of a *radar* radial *display (polar diagram).* The rotation of the time base shows the single pulses as a circle on the *plan position indicator screen.* It may be used to measure *range,* since it forms a range scale.

range-rate memory. A *radar circuit* that is used to reject spurious *signals,* such as from randomly dispensed *chaff,* that differ significantly from the *echo signal* obtained from the desired object (target), particularly in range closing rate. The circuit also provides range closing rate and tracking (lock-on) stability during momentary loss of *signal* because of *scintillation* effects.

range resolution. **1.** In *radar systems,* the ability of *radar equipment* to separate two *reflecting* objects (targets) on a similar *bearing* but at different *ranges* from the *antenna.* The range resolution is determined primarily by the *pulse length* that is used. The pulse length determines the depth of the *radar resolution cell.* The radar resolution cell depth, *RCD,* is given in *meters* by *RCD = 150PL,* where *PL* is the radar *pulse length* in *microseconds.* **2.** The *precision* and *accuracy* with which the *range* to a given or selected *signal source* can be measured or determined, that is, resolved. Range resolution precision may be expressed as a distance, percentage of range, or other expression of tolerance. Also see *detection resolution; radar resolution cell.*

range site. See *down-range site.*

range station. See *radio range station; omnidirectional range station.*

ranging. The process of establishing or measuring distance, usually from a known observation or reference point to an object. Some examples of different types of ranging methods or techniques include *echo,* intermittent, manual, navigational, explosive echo, *optical,* and *radar.* Synonymous with *spotting.* See *hybrid ranging; sound navigation and ranging (sonar).*

raster. A predetermined pattern of *scanning lines* that uniformly covers a *display space* on the *display surface* of a *display device.* The raster can be formed by a sweeping *light beam,* capable of (1) being modulated in *intensity* in order to draw or write a picture or (2) sensing the *reflectivity* or *luminance* of small areas or surfaces sequentially in order to read or sense an *image.* For example, a raster can be seen on a *television screen* when the *video signal* is suppressed (i.e., not received) by a television *receiver.*

raster count. The total number of *raster* scanning lines within a *display space* on a *display surface* of a *display device.* For example, the raster count could be the *raster density* times the height of the display space. In most *display systems* with rasters, the raster count is fixed, and the density changes with the vertical dimension of the display space, assuming the *scanning lines* are horizontal.

raster density. In *display systems,* the number of *scanning lines* per unit distance perpendicular to the scanning direction. The raster density times the vertical dimension of the *display space* equals the *raster count,* assuming that the scanning lines are horizontal.

raster display. The generation of a *display image* on the *display surface* of a *display device* that makes use of a *raster scan* to create the *image.*

raster scan. In *display systems,* a technique in which *display elements, display groups,* or *display images* are generated, recorded, or displayed by means of a line-by-line sweep across the *display space* of the *display surface* of the *display* *device.* For example, in a *coherent bundle* of *optical fibers* arranged in a Cartesian coordinate system, the *generation* of an *image* by energizing each fiber in sequence in a row, row-by-row from top to bottom with *wraparound,* as in the generation of a picture on a *television screen.* Although a raster scan is usually performed automatically by circuits built into the display device, it may also, like a *directed scan,* be directed by a *computer program.*

raster unit. The physical spatial distance between corresponding points on adjacent *scanning lines.* The unit should be constant over the *display space* to avoid distortion. The raster unit times the *raster count* usually gives the vertical dimension of the display space, assuming the scanning lines are horizontal.

rate. See *actual transfer rate; average error rate; average information rate; average transinformation rate; average transmission rate; binary serial signaling rate; bit error rate (BER); bit rate; block transfer rate; constant false alarm rate (CFAR); data signaling rate; data transfer rate; effective data transfer rate; effective transfer rate; error rate; interruption rate; jittered pulse repetition rate; maximum pulse rate; maximum stuffing rate; maximum user signaling rate; modulation rate; multiplex aggregate bit rate; Nyquist rate; pulse repetition rate; reading line rate; recording line rate; regeneration rate; repetition rate; residual error rate; sampling rate; scanning line rate; scan rate; staggered-pulse repetition rate.*

rated output power. The *power* that is available at a specified *output terminal* of a device under specified conditions of *operation.* This power may be further described regarding its nature. For example, maximum rated output power, average rated output power, instantaneous output power, real power, or reactive power.

rate efficiency. See *block rate efficiency.*

rate measuring equipment. See *error-rate measuring equipment.*

rate memory. See *range rate memory.*

rate transparency. See *data signaling rate transparency.*

rating. See *output rating; transmitter power output rating.*

ratio. See *access success ratio; aperture ratio; aspect ratio; blowback ratio; carrier-to-noise (C/N) ratio; carrier-to-noise power ratio; common-mode rejection ratio (CMRR); deviation ratio; disengagement-denial ratio; disengagement success ratio; E/N ratio; front-to-back ratio; inband noise power ratio; jamming-to-signal ratio; photodetector signal-to-noise ratio; post-detector signal/noise ratio; radiant power ratio; reduction ratio; reproduction ratio; signal-plus-noise to noise ratio (S+N)/N; signal-to-noise ratio (S/N); single-sideband noise power ratio; standing wave ratio (SWR); voltage standing wave ratio (VSWR).*

ratio-squared combiner. See *maximal-ratio combiner.*

ratio-square diversity combining method. See *maximal-ratio-square diversity combining method.*

RATT. See *radio teletype.*

RATTY. See *radio teletype.*

raw radar information. *Information* that is obtained directly from a *radar antenna,* from the *circuits* that control *displays,* or from *radar displays.*

ray. See *chief ray; direct ray; emergent ray; extraordinary ray; field ray; gamma ray; incident ray; light ray; meridional ray; optical ray; ordinary ray; paraxial ray; principal ray; reflected ray; skew ray.*

ray bundle. 1. A group of *ordinary rays,* in which the ordinary rays differ from one another in some detailed respect, such as *frequency (color)* or intensity, yet have one or more aspects in common, such as direction or velocity. For example, the *rays* of a *bundle* may be separated from each other by *dispersion* caused by a *prism,* in which case a multifrequency bundle of rays *incident* on the prism are separated into distinct ordinary rays of different color; in an *optical fiber,* dispersion will cause different frequencies to arrive at the end at different times, thus separating the frequencies of an *incident* bundle. 2. A group of *light rays* considered as such for some purpose or discussion. Synonymous with *bundle of rays.*

Rayleigh distribution. A mathematical statement of the *frequency* distribution of random variables for the case in which the variables have the same variance and are not correlated (not interdependent, not coherent).

Rayleigh fading. In *electromagnetic wave transmission, phase interference fading* that is due to *multipath* and that is approximated by the *Rayleigh distribution.* Also see *fading; fading distribution; multipath.*

Rayleigh scattering. *Scattering* of a *lightwave propagating* in a material *medium* due to the atomic or molecular structure of the material and variations in the structure as a function of distance. The *scattering losses* vary as the reciprocal of the fourth power of the *wavelength.* The distances between *scattering centers* are small compared to the wavelength. Rayleigh scattering sets a theoretical lower limit to be the *attenuation* of a propagating *lightwave* as a function of wavelength, ranging from 10 dB/km at 0.50 *micron* to 1 dB/km at 0.95 *micron.* Material scattering is caused primarily by Rayleigh scattering. Rayleigh scattering is also due to the variation in molecular density of intrinsic material; for example, the familiar light green *color* of pop bottles is due to Rayleigh scattering from distributed iron atoms. Also see *scattering.*

ray trajectory. The *path* or course taken by a *light ray* in a *transmission medium* or a vacuum. the trajectory at each point is perpendicular to the *wavefront* at that point. See Figure R-3. Also see Figures A-11 and H-1.

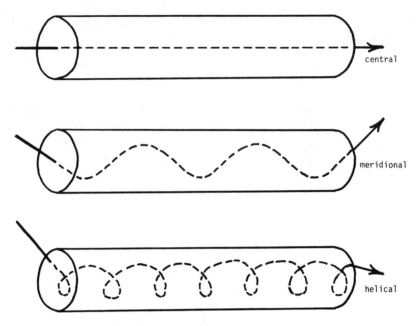

R-3. Typical **ray trajectories** in *graded-index fibers.*

RDF.   *Radio direction finding.*

reactance.   See *capacitive reactance; inductive reactance.*

reaction.   See *real time penetration reaction.*

reaction time.   See *switching reaction time.*

read.   **1.** To obtain *data* from a *storage* device, from a *data medium,* or from another *source.*   **2.** In *communications,* to understand a received *message.*   **3.** A *proword* that, when used interrogatively, means "Did you receive and understand the message that I just sent?"   When used in the declarative it means "I understand the message that I just received from you."

readability.   In *communication system operations,* the extent to which the content of a *message* is understood.   The readability of *signals* pertains to any means of *communication.*

readdressal.   See *message readdressal.*

reader.   See *coupled reperforator tape reader; microform reader; tape reader.*

reader-copier.   See *microform reader-copier.*

reading head.   See *tape reading head.*

reading line frequency.   See *reading line rate.*

reading line rate.   The scanning line rate during the reading (sensing) of an object (subject document, scene, picture). Synonymous with *reading line frequency.*

read-only memory (ROM).   See *fixed storage.*

ready condition.   In *communication system operations,* a *steady-state condition* at the *interface* between *data terminal equipment (DTE)* and *data circuit-terminating equipment (DCE)* that indicates that the DCE is ready to accept a *call request signal* or that the DTE is ready to accept an incoming *call.* See *not-ready condition.*

ready-for-data signal.   1. A *call control signal* that is *transmitted* by the *data circuit-terminating equipment (DCE)* to the *data terminal equipment (DTE)* to indicate that the *connection* is available for *data transfer* between both DTEs. 2. A condition that appears in the *backward direction* in the intere*xchange data channel* indicating that all the succeeding exchanges involved in the connection have been through connected, or a condition that appears in the *forward direction* in the interexchange data channel indicating that all the preceding exchanges involved in the connection have been through connected. This condition is sent by the *user terminal* and it corresponds to the ready-for-data state at the user *interface.*

ready signal.   See *controlled not-ready signal.*

real image.   An *image* represented by actual *rays* of *light* that, when *incident* upon a *reflecting* surface, can be seen or that, when incident upon a *transmitting medium,* can be transmitted a considerable distance. The *lightwave* in an *optical fiber* can convey a real image. Also see *virtual image.*

real time.   In *communication systems,* pertaining to the *transmission* or processing of *data* in connection with a process outside the system according to the time requirements imposed by the outisde system—such as observing pictures from an endoscope, *displaying telemetered* emergency medical *data* from a remote patient for immediate diagnosis and treatment, or transmitting live coverage of a news event.   It is the actual (calendar) time during which a physical process occurs. For example, it may pertain to the performance of a computation during the actual time that the related physical process occurs, in order that the results of the computation can be used in guiding the physical process. It may pertain to *systems* that operate in a *conversational* (interactive) *mode* and to processes that can be influenced by human action while they are in progress. In a communication system, it may pertain to the absence of significant time delay in the acquisition, transmission, and reception of information, such as in *radar tracking* of a moving object (target).

real-time operation.   1. A *mode* of *operation* of a *system* in which the occurrence of an event at the *input* is followed by the occurrence of a corresponding event at the *output* with no delay that is apparent to the system *user.* If the maximum absolute time delay appropriate to each application is specified and the maximum is not exceeded, the application is usually considered to be conducted in real time. 2. In *analog computing, operation* in the *compute mode* during which the *time scale factor* is 1. Also see *problem time.*

real-time penetration reaction. In *computer* and *communication security, a system response* to a *penetration attempt* that is *detected* and diagnosed in time to take action to prevent the penetration.

real-time transmission. *Transmission* of *data* with such little delay that the *information* is available in time to influence the process being monitored or controlled by the *data.*

real-world coordinate. In *display systems,* an actual physical coordinate of the *object* or part thereof or point within, whose *image* is *displayed* in the *display space* on the *display surface* of a *display device.* The *user* may select other more convenient coordinates for display or programming purposes (i.e., user coordinates), and of course the display device may have its own intrinsic coordinates inherent in the device (such as a 0-to-100 scale on a *plotter bed*) on a grid superimposed on a *CRT* screen (i.e., *screen coordinates*) or as numbered index markings on a *thumb wheel.* Also see *user coordinate; device coordinate.*

rebroadcast. A *radio relay system* in which a *simplex broadcast radio* at a *relay station* retransmits a received signal automatically or by manual operation of the equipment.

recall. See *camp-on-with-recall.*

recall signal. In *telephone switchboard operations,* the *signal* that is used to bring in an *operator* after a *call* has been established. For example, in some systems, the operator can be "flashed" by tapping on the hook or cradle switch of the *telephone instrument.*

recall response signal. In *telephone switchboard operations,* the *signal* that is sent to a *user* (customer, subscriber) *end-instrument* indicating that the user's *recall signal* has been *detected.*

receipt. In *communication system operations,* a *transmission* made by a receiving *station* to indicate that a *message* has been satisfactorily received.

receipt communication method. 1. A method of *communication system operation* in which the receiving *station* is required to send a receipt to the transmitting station for each *message* that is received. The receipt method of operation is used in an attempt to obtain certainty of reception. 2. A method of *communication* in which each *message* is receipted by each *addressee.* Also see *broadcast communication method; intercept communication method; relay communication method.*

receipt time. The date and time at which a *communication agency* completes reception of a *message* that is *transmitted* to it by another communication agency. For example, the time that a message is *received* from a *communication circuit* at a *telecommunication center.*

receive. To accept an entity, such as a *message, signal,* or *electromagnetic wave* that was *transmitted* from another place. Also see *transmit.*

receive-after-transmit time delay. The time interval from *keying off* the *local transmitter* (the stopping of transmission) until the *local receiver output* has increased to 90% of its *steady-state* value in *response* to a *signal* from a distant transmitter. This requires that the signal from a distant transmitter exists at the local receiver *input* prior to, or at the time of, keying off the local transmitter.

receive only. See *lobe-on-receive-only (LORO).*

receive-only teletypewriter. Pertaining to *teletypewriter* equipment that is arranged to *receive signals* and print *data,* without the capability to *transmit.* A receive-only machine is usually not provided with a *keyboard* or a *tape transmitter.* Also see *automatic send-and-receive (ASR) teletypewriter; keyboard send-receive (KSR) teletypewriter.*

received noise power. 1. The calculated or measured noise power at the receive end of a channel, link, or system within the bandwidth that is being used. 2. The absolute power of the noise that is measured or calculated at a receive point. The related bandwidth and the noise weighting must also be specified. 3. The value of noise power from all sources measured at the line terminals of a listening user's (customer's, subscriber's) telephone set. Either flat weighting or some other specific amplitude-frequency characteristic or noise weighting characteristic must be associated with the measurement.

received signal level. The value of a specified *bandwidth* of *signals* at the *receiver input terminals* relative to an established reference. The received *signal level* is often expressed in *decibels* with respect to 1 mW, or 0 dBm.

receiver. 1. In communication systems, a device that accepts *signals* from a *transmitter* or from a *transmission medium* (e.g., a *photodetector*) and usually extracts and furnishes their *information content.* 2. The portion of a *communication system* in which *electromagnetic waves* are *converted* into visible or audible *signals.* See *automatic receiver; continuous receiver; drum receiver; facsimile receiver; high-probability-of-intercept receiver; intercept receiver; jammer receiver; linear receiver; logarithmic receiver; low-probability-of-intercept receiver; optical receiver; optoelectronic receiver; panoramic receiver; radio receiver; search receiver; superheterodyne receiver; telephone receiver; warning receiver.* See Figure R-4. Also see Figures G-5 and S-2.

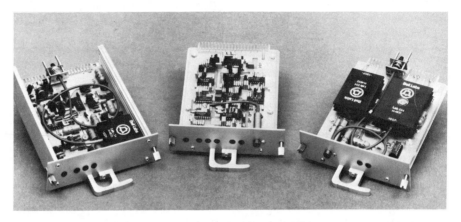

R-4. Developmental *lightwave* **receiver** *(optical detector)*, decision/timing *(frequency* and *phase* control), and *fiber-optic transmitter (optical source)* — 11 x 6 centimeter packages. (Courtesy of Bell Laboratories.)

receiver aperture. See *facsimile receiver aperture.*

receiver attack-time delay. The time interval from the instant of application of a step *input signal,* of a *level* (magnitude) equal to the *receiver sensitivity,* at the *receiver input* to the instant at which the *receiver output amplitude* reaches 90% of its *steady-state value.* This time delay includes the time for the receiver to cease squelching, if applicable.

receiver desensitization. The effect that occurs to a *radio* or *video receiver* when a high-*power carrier signal* of nearly the same operating *frequency* enters the receiver, *masks* its useful signal, and reduces its effective *sensitivity.*

receiver intermediate-frequency (IF) gain control. The control of the *intermediate frequency (IF) stage gain* in a *radio, video, microwave,* or *radar receiver.*

receiver location loss. In *satellite communications,* a single *parameter* that is used in *power balancing* calculations to account for the *path loss* variation with *earth station* location as a function of the *slant range* to the *satellite* and the reduction of satellite *antenna gain.* The antenna gain is measured from the on-axis maximum *signal* at the corresponding off-axis angle of the earth station. The *receiver* location loss can be computed for these variables as a function of each *station antenna elevation angle.* The loss can be used for the *down-link* design to establish the minimum signal *power* per *access* from the satellite for acceptable signal power above receiver *threshold.* It can also be used for the *up-link* design in calculating the minimum earth station *transmitter power* to achieve the minimum down-link *signal strength.*

receiver lockout system. See *lockout.*

receiver margin. See *synchronous receiver margin; telegraph receiver margin.*

receiver noise density.   See *carrier-to-receiver noise density.*

receiver release-time delay.   The time interval from removal of *electromagnetic* energy at the *receiver input* until the receiver *output* is *squelched.*

receiver threshold.   The minimum *input carrier-to-noise ratio* at a *receiver demodulator* for acceptable *signal-to-noise ratio* in the *baseband output.*

receiver weighting.   See *HA1-receiver weighting.*

receive teletypewriter.   See *automatic send-receive teletypewriter; keyboard send-receive teletypewriter.*

receive terminal.   See *multiplex baseband receive terminal; radio baseband receive terminal.*

receive time delay.   See *transmit-after-receive time delay.*

receiving element.   The accepting *terminus* of a junction of *optical* elements.

receiving system noise temperature.   The *temperature* that corresponds to the measured *noise voltage* due to thermal agitation of molecules and atoms in the *input circuit* of a *receiver. Noise temperature* is usually given in *kelvin,* such as 60 K. *Thermal noise* is caused by the motion of *conduction electrons* in materials (wires, resistors, semiconductors, inductors) due to their *temperature.* In fact, temperature is a measure of the average kinetic energy of moving molecules. From the statistical theory of thermodynamics, it can be shown that the *root-mean-square (RMS) noise voltage, E,* that is developed across a *resistance* is given by $E = (4RkT\Delta f)^{1/2}$, where R is the resistance in ohms, T is the *absolute temperature* in kelvin (kelvin = celsius + 273), k is *Boltzmann's constant* (k = 1.38 $\times$ 10^{-23} W-s/K), Δf is the *bandwidth* of the measuring system in *hertz,* and E is the developed *voltage* across the resistor in volts.

reception.   In *communication systems,* listening to, accepting, copying, collecting, recording, or viewing *received signals.* The received signals are usually *converted* into useful form by the receiving equipment. See *diversity reception; exhalted-carrier reception.*

reception congestion.   A *network congestion,* such as *contention, saturation,* or *delay,* that occurs at a *receiving station.* For example, the queue of *messages* or *calls* that may occur at a *switching center's data switching exchange (DSE).*

reception depth.   See *listening depth.*

reciprocal bearing.   1. The course-to-steer in order that a requesting *mobile station* may reach the *direction-finding (DF) station.* The course-to-steer is obtained by adding 180° to the true *bearing* of the requesting station from the DF station if the bearing is less than 180° and subtracting 180° if the bearing is greater than 180°. The course-to-steer is given without correction for wind or current. 2. The opposite direction to a given *bearing.* Also see *azimuth; back azimuth; reciprocal heading.*

reciprocal heading.   The opposite direction to a given *heading* (course). Also see *azimuth; back azimuth; reciprocal bearing.*

recirculating register.   A *register* that stores *data* by recirculating the data at a constant rate continuously.   Recirculating registers have been constructed of a string of *lumped capacitive* and *inductive* elements, and of *delay lines* that make use of the *piezoelectric* properties of fuzed quartz, or the *magnetostrictive* properties of ferrites or nickel wire.   If the data can be read out and statically retained at the same time the unit is said to provide nondestructive read-out. However, most recirculating registers are dynamic in the sense that the data is moving all the time and the read-out is simply a *gating* action.

reckoning.   See *dead reckoning.*

reckoning position.   See *dead-reckoning position.*

recognition.   The determination by any means of the character or individuality of persons; of objects, such as aircraft, ships, or tanks; or of phenomena such as *electromagnetic wave patterns* and *signals.*   See *character recognition; magnetic ink character recognition (MICR); optical character recognition (OCR); pattern recognition; radio recognition.*

recognition device.   See *pattern recognition device.*

recognized private operating agency (RPOA).   A *telecommunication private operating agency* that operates a *communication system* and that adheres to international communication conventions.   For example, the agencies that are obliged by their national governments to adhere to Article 19 of the International Telecommunication Convention and the Regulations that are annexed thereto.

recombination.   See *nonradiative recombination; radiative recombination.*

reconfiguration.   **1.** Rearrangement of the *connections* among the *components* of a *system.*   **2.** A repair strategy in which failed or failing components of a *system* are *switched* out of the system and replaced by other components.   For example, to switch out a *channel, trunk,* or *branch* in a *network* and switch in another in its place, in contrast to simply rerouting *traffic.*

reconnaissance.   See *electronic reconnaissance.*

reconstructed sample.   In *communication systems,* an *analog sample* that is generated at the *output* of a *decoder* when a specified *character signal* is applied at its *input.*   The *amplitude* of this sample is proportional to the value of the corresponding *encoded* sample.

record.   See *frequency record; local record.*

record communication facility.   **1.** The *communication facility* that is responsible for filing the original copy of a *transmitted message.*   Usually the facility that *files* the message is the facility that accepted the message for transmission.   **2.** A *communication facility* that handles *record traffic.*

recorded spot. In *facsimile transmission systems*, the *image* that is left by the *recording spot* on the *record sheet*.

recorded-spot x-dimension. In *facsimile systems*, the effective dimension of a *recorded spot* measured in the direction of the *recorded line*. The effective dimension is the largest center-to-center spacing between recorded spots that gives minimum peak-to-peak variation of density along the recorded line. The recorded-spot x-dimension applies to the type of equipment that responds to a constant density in the *image* copy by a succession of *discrete* spots. Also see *maximum keying frequency*,

recorded-spot y-dimension. In *facsimile systems*, the effective dimension of a *recorded spot* measured in the direction that is perpendicular the direction of the *recorded line*. The effective dimension is the largest center-to-center distance between recorded lines that gives minimum peak-to-peak variation of *density* across the recorded lines.

recorder. See *airborne direction-finding recorder; facsimile recorder; siphon recorder; traffic image recorder.*

recording. 1. In *facsimile systems*, the process of *converting* the *received electrical signal* to an *image* on the *record medium*. 2. The process of producing a *copy* of *data* on a *data medium*. For example, the storing of a *message* on *magnetic tape*. 3. The *data* that is stored on a *data medium*, such as a drum, disk, tape, or film. See *black recording; direct recording; electrochemical recording; electron-beam recording; electrolytic recording; electromechanical recording; electrostatic recording; electrothermal recording; fiberscope recording; ink vapor recording; NRZI magnetic recording; phase-encoded recording; photosensitive recording.* Also see Figure R-5 (p. 782)

recording area. See *film frame.*

recording line frequency. See *recording line rate.*

recording line rate. The *scanning line rate* during the recording (writing) of an *image*. Synonymous with *recording line frequency*.

recording medium. See *record medium.*

recording sheet. See *record sheet.*

recording signal. See *start-recording signal.*

recording spot. In *facsimile transmission*, the *source image* that is formed on the *record medium* by the *recorder*.

recording telegraphy. See *signal recording telegraphy.*

record medium. In *communication systems*, the physical *data medium* on which a recorder forms an image of the *object copy*. In *facsimile systems*, the record medium is called the *record sheet*. Synonymous with *recording medium*. Also see *record sheet*. See Figure R-5.

R-5. In a *record traffic integrated communication system,* a Marinefax® IV compact weather *recording* device with **record medium** for use in *fixed* and *mobile stations* where space is limited. (Courtesy of Alden Electronic and Impulse Recording Equipment Company, Inc.)

record sheet. In *facsimile transmission systems,* the *data medium* that is used to produce a visible *image* of the object copy in record form. It is the same as the *record medium* in other systems, such as *magnetic drum, tape,* and disk *storage* systems. Synonymous with *recording sheet.* Also see *record medium.*

record traffic. **1.** In *communication systems, traffic* that is recorded in permanent or semipermanent form by the *originator,* the *addressee,* or the *communication system.* **2.** In *communication systems, traffic* that is permanently or semipermanently recorded in *response* to administrative procedures or public law. **3.** *Messages* that have been electrically *transmitted* and that must be received by the *destination user* in such a form as to permit permanent or semipermanent *storage.*

recovery. See *off-line recovery; timing recovery.*

recovery process. **1.** In *data communications,* a *process* in which a *functional unit,* such as a *data station* or *switching exchange,* attempts to resolve conflicting or erroneous conditions that arise from the *transfer* of *data.* **2.** In *computer* and *communication system security,* the actions that are taken to restore a system's operational capability after a *failure* or *penetration.*

recovery quotient.   See *automatic recovery quotient (ARQ).*

recovery time.   The time that is required by a *receiver* to return to a zero *signal condition* after *receiving* an *input signal,* such as an overdrive signal or a *jamming pulse* of *saturation intensity.*

rectifier.   An electrical device that converts *alternating current (AC)* to *direct current (DC)* by presenting a high *resistance* in one direction and a low resistance in the opposite direction with the net result that the current only flows in one direction.   Vacuum tubes, crystal *diodes,* and certain *semiconductors* provide such a capability.   The resulting *wave shape,* though unidirectional, contains certain *frequencies* that may be easily filtered with a *low-pass filter,* such as a shunt *capacitor* or a series *inductor.*

recurrent-frequency radar.   See *variable-pulse recurrent-frequency radar.*

recursive filtering.   In *image restoration,* an *inverse-filtering* technique in which the function that operates upon the distorted *image,* to produce a less distorted image, is based upon a statistical estimation and smoothing technique involving recursive functions that make use of a linear combination of previous estimates. For example, if it is desired to estimate $f(x+1, y+1)$ as a function of its immediate upper-left neighbors and the value of the recorded image at those points, the estimate could be computed recursively in the form:

$$f(x+1, y+1) = a_1 f(x+1, y) + a_2 f(x, y+1) + a_3 f(x, y) + a_4 g(x, y)$$

where x and y are space coordinates in the two-dimensional image.

red-black concept.   In *secure communication systems,* the concept that *electrical circuits, components, systems,* and other equipment that handle *plain language security classified information* (red) should be separated from those that handle unclassified or *encrypted* security classified information (black).   Under this concept, red and black terminology is used to clarify specific criteria that relate to and differentiate between such circuits and the areas in which they are located.   Thus, the *circuits* can be given the protective marking and *protection* that are needed in accordance with the categories of *information* they carry.   For example, the red and black designations may change before and after *encryption* and before and after *decryption.*   Also see *black designation; compromising emanations; red designation.*

red designation.   In *secure communication systems,* a designation that is applied to all *lines,* such as *wire, coaxial cable, optical fiber,* and *waveguides,* within a *terminal* or *switching center* that carries *security classified plain language information.*   It applies to all lines that are between the *encrypted* side of the *online cryptoequipment* and the *user* (customer, subscriber) *end-instruments* or *terminal equipment,* to sets of equipment that terminate security classified or plain language processing equipment, and to areas that contain these lines, equipment, interconnections, and auxiliary facilities. Also see *black designation; red-black concept.*

remodulator. A *demodulator* that changes the form of *modulation* in a reverse manner from that of the conventional demodulator. For example, in *facsimile systems,* a *converter* that changes an *amplitude modulated signal* to an *audio frequency-shift modulated signal.*

redirected call. A *call* that had been connected but that had to be reconnected to another *party.*

redirected-call indicator. *Information* that is sent in the *forward direction* and that indicates that the *call* is a *redirected call.*

redirection. See *call redirection.*

redirection address. In *communication system operations, information* that is sent in the *backward direction,* consists of a number of *address signals,* and indicates the complete *address* to which a *call* is to be, or has been *directed.*

redirected-to-new-address signal. In *communication system operations,* a *signal* that is sent in the *backward direction* and indicates that a *call* has been *redirected* to an *address* other than the *destination address* selected by the *calling party.* Also see *redirect-to-new-address signal.*

redirect-to-new-address signal. In *communication system operations,* a *signal* that is sent in the *backward direction* and indicates that the *called party* has requested that the *call* be *redirected* to another *address.* Also see *redirected-to-new-address signal.*

reduced carrier. A *carrier wave* that is *transmitted* at a *power level* that is usually between 6 dB and 32 dB, preferably between 16 dB and 26 dB, below the *peak envelope power level.* A reduced carrier is usually transmitted in order to achieve *automatic frequency control* or *automatic gain control* at the *receiver.* Also see *full carrier; suppressed carrier.*

reduced carrier transmission. See *suppressed carrier transmission.*

reduction. 1. The relationship between the linear dimension of an *image* and the corresponding dimension of an *object* when the image is smaller than the object. For example, if an image is one-fourth the size of the original object, the reduction may be expressed as 4X, 1:4, 1/4, or 75% smaller. 2. In *display systems,* a reduced-size copy of a *display element; display group* or *display image.*

reduction ratio. The reciprocal of the number of times the linear dimensions of a *photograph, copy,* or *image* of an *object* would have to be enlarged in order to be as large as the object itself. Examples of reduction ratios are 1:16, 1:24, 1/16, 1/24, and 1 to 10.

redundancy. In *information theory,* the amount by which the *decision content* of a *message* or *data* exceeds the *entropy.* In mathematical notation, $R = H_o - H$, where R is the redundancy, H_o is the decision content, and H is the entropy. Usually, messages can be represented with fewer characters by using suitable codes. The redundancy may be considered as a measure of the decrease of the length of a message that may be accomplished by coding. See *relative redundancy*.

redundant code. A *code* in which more *signal elements* are used than are necessary to represent the intrinsic *information content* of a given amount of *text*, such as a *message*. For example, a 5-unit *code* in which all the *characters* of the *International Telegraph Alphabet Number 2 (ITA-2)* are used is not redundant. A 5-unit code that uses only the *digits* (numeric characters) and not the letters and other signs and *symbols* of the ITA-2 is redundant. A 7-unit code in which only the signals that have 4 *space* digits and 3 *mark* digits are used is redundant. An 8-unit code in which one of the bits is used for *parity* is redundant.

REED. *Restricted edge-emitting diode.*

reeling condition. The tensile, thermal, bending, torsional, compressive, and other stress or stimuli imposed on an *optical fiber, bundle,* or *cable* during the process of winding onto a spool or reel. See Figure R-6.

R-6. A 1-km spool of *optical waveguide fiber* ready for shipment, and cross-section of spool. **Reeling conditions** occur during winding. (Copyright 1979, Corning Glass Works. Reprinted by permission from Corning Glass Works, Telecommunication Products Department.)

reencryption. The process of *encrypting* again a *message* that has been previously *encrypted* and *transmitted,* without necessarily having a *decryption* process in between the two encryption *operations.*

reenlargement. 1. The restoration of an *image* of an *object* to a size that is larger than the size to which it was reduced. 2. The restoration of a *microimage* to a size that renders it legible to the normal unaided human eye. Synonymous with *blowback*.

reference antenna. An *antenna,* often theoretical, that has a *radiation pattern* that can be used as a basis of comparison for other antenna radiation patterns. For example, a *unit dipole antenna,* a *half-wave dipole antenna,* or an *isotropic* or *omnidirectional antenna.*

reference architecture. The structural features that describe the visibility points of *distributed systems.* For example, the *interfaces* and *protocols* that are necessary for the interconnection of the *components* of a *system.*

reference circuit. A theoretical *circuit* of specified length and configuration with a defined *transmission* characteristic, primarily used as a reference for measuring or defining the performance of other circuits and as a guide for planning, designing, developing, and operating circuits and *networks.* Normally, several types of reference circuits are defined, with different configurations, because there exists a wide range of distances over which *communications* are required.

reference clock. A *clock,* usually of high stability and *accuracy,* that is used to govern a *network* of mutually *synchronized* clocks of lower stability. The *failure* of the reference clock does not necessarily cause or result in the loss of *synchronism.* Also see *master clock.*

reference coupling. *Crosstalk coupling* that is necessary to produce a specified *signal level* in the *disturbed circuit* when a signal of specified magnitude is inserted into the *disturbing circuit.* For example, the crosstalk coupling that occurs when a 0 dBr signal is caused in the disturbed circuit when a test tone (signal) of 90 dBr is on the disturbing circuit. Both dBr values must be determined for the same *weighting* characteristic.

reference edge. The edge of a *data carrier* or *data medium* that is used to establish specifications or measurements for the layout of *data* on the carrier or medium. Synonymous with *guide edge.*

reference frequency. 1. A standard fixed *frequency* from which operational frequencies may be derived or with which they may be compared. The reference frequency may be used to specify an *assigned frequency* or to fix a *characteristic* or *carrier frequency.* 2. A *frequency* that has a fixed and specified position in the *frequency spectrum* with respect to the *assigned frequency* or another reference frequency. The displacement of the reference frequency from the assigned or other reference frequency has the same absolute value and sign as the displacement of the characteristic frequency from the center of the *frequency band* that is occupied by the *emission.* Also see *characteristic frequency.*

reference level. See *single-sideband reference level.*

reference modulation. A magnitude *(amplitude)* of a *modulating signal* that is used as a standard of comparison for measurement, indication, or application of various forms of *modulation.* For example, actual modulation amplitude can be expressed as a percentage of the reference modulation. If the reference modulation is 100% modulation, then the concept of 25%, 50%, 75%, or 90% modulation becomes useful. See *fixed-reference modulation.*

reference noise. The magnitude of *circuit noise* that will produce a *circuit* noise-meter *(psophometer)* reading that is equal to that produced by 10^{-12} watt (1 picowatt or –90 dBm) of *electrical power* at 1000 Hz for noise calibrated in *dBrn(144-line)* or *dBrnC*. For noise meters that are calibrated in *dBa(F1A)*, the reference noise is adjusted to –85 dBm.

reference system. In *communication systems,* any device, *component,* or *subsystem* that is used as a reference or basis of comparison. For example, a group or set of related *reference circuits, channels,* or *trunks.* See *worldwide geographic reference system.*

reference TLP. *Reference transmission level point.*

reference transmission level point. A point in a *transmission system* that is used as a reference point from which the *signal voltage, current,* or *power level* at other points may be measured or compared. The comparison is usually by *decibels,* though it may also be by *nepers,* ratio, or percentage. For example, the *zero transmission level point (OTLP);* or a *channel input terminal power level,* such that all *gains* and *losses* from that point may be expressed in dB with reference to that specified reference point power level. If the input terminal power level is 100 watts, and the output power at the end of the channel is 0.1 watt, the output power level is –30 dB, or down 30 dB from the reference transmission level point.

refile. In a *communication system,* the *conversion* of a *message* that is prepared for *transmission* in accordance with the *procedures* for one communication system into a message that is prepared for transmission in accordance with the procedures for another system. See *commercial refile.*

refile message. A *message* that is received at a *communication center* for *filing.* Since the message was filed at the originating communication center, the receiving center must refile it if it is to be dispatched over another communication system. The *filing time* for refile messages is the date and time that the message was received by the receiving communication center for refile. Also see *filing.*

reflectance. The ratio of the *reflected flux* to the *incident flux.* It applies to *radiant* and to *luminous flux.* Unless qualified, reflectance applies to *specular,* or regular, *reflection.* See *diffuse reflectance.*

reflectance loss. See *Fresnel reflection loss.*

reflected binary code. See *modified reflected binary code.*

reflected code. A *cyclic* (closed) *code* such that if the *code words (numerals)* are listed in a column, there is a line that can be considered as a *mirror,* above and below which the code words appear to be in reflected pairs if the most significant digits are ignored. The most significant digit is usually a 0 above the mirror and a 1 below the mirror. The resulting list looks as though the part below the mirror is a mirror image of the part above the mirror, except for the most significant digits. For example, a *gray code.*

reflected ray.   The *ray* of *electromagnetic radiation*, usually *light* leaving a *reflecting* surface. The ray indicates the *path* after reflection.

reflecting jammer.   In *radar system jamming,* a passive device or object that *reflects electromagnetic radiation* and that serves to confuse a *radar system.* For example, a large quantity of metallic or metallized strips or wires, such as window, *chaff,* or rope; or false target *reflectors,* such as corner-reflectors and Luneberg reflectors, that create a reflection similar to a large target. The jammer reflects electromagnetic radiation in such a manner as to obscure reflections from other objects to prevent their identification and to prevent successful *operation* of the radar system being *jammed.*

reflection.   When *electromagnetic waves,* more appropriately *light rays,* strike a smooth, polished surface, their return or bending back into the *medium* from whence they came. *Specular* or regular *reflection* from a polished surface, such as a *mirror,* will return a major portion of the light in a definite direction lying in the *plane* of the *incident ray* and the normal. After *specular reflection,* light can be made to form a sharp *image* of the original source. *Diffuse reflection* occurs when the surface is rough and the reflected light is *scattered* from each point in the surface. These diffuse rays cannot be made to form an image of the original source, but only of the diffusely reflecting surface itself. See *diffuse reflection; half-reflection; internal reflection; ionospheric reflection; specular reflection; total internal reflection.* Also see *Snell's law.*

reflection angle.   When a *ray* of *electromagnetic radiation* strikes a surface and is *reflected* in whole or in part by the surface, the angle between the normal to the reflecting surface and the reflected ray. Also see *critical angle.*

reflection coefficient.   1. The ratio of the *reflected field strength* to the *incident field strength* when an *electromagnetic wave* is *incident* upon an *interface* surface between *dielectric media* of different *refractive indices.* If, at oblique incidence, the *magnetic field* component of the incident wave is parallel to the interface, the reflection coefficient is given by:

$$R = (n_1 \cos A - n_2 \cos B)/(n_1 \cos A + n_2 \cos B)$$

where n_1 and n_2 are the reciprocals of the refractive indices of the incident and transmitted *mediums,* respectively, and A and B are the angles of *incidence* and *refraction* (with respect to normal), respectively. If, at oblique incidence, the electric field component of the incident wave is parallel to the interface, the reflection coefficient is given by:

$$R = (n_2 \cos A - n_1 \cos B)/(n_2 \cos A + n_1 \cos B)$$

These equations are known as the *Fresnel equations* for such cases. For large smooth surfaces, the reflection coefficient may be near unity, such as for highly polished mirrors. At near grazing incidence angles, that is nearly $90°$ from the normal to the surface, even rough surfaces may reflect relatively well. 2. At any specified point in a *transmission line* between a *power source* and a *power sink* (absorber), the vector ratio of the *electric field* associated with the reflected wave to that associated with the incident wave. The reflection coefficient, **RC**, is given by $RC = (Z_2 - Z_1)/(Z_2 + Z_1) = (SWR-1)/(SWR+1)$, where Z_1 is the *impedance* looking toward the source, Z_2 is the *impedance* looking toward the *load*, and **SWR** is the *standing wave ratio*. Also see *Fresnel reflection loss; transmission coefficient;* and Figure S-7.

reflection factor. The reciprocal of the scalar value of the *reflection loss.*

reflection image. An *image* formed by a reflecting surface. An unwanted *reflection image* is a *ghost image.* Also see *ghost image.*

reflection law. When a *ray* of *electromagnetic radiation* strikes a surface and is *reflected* in whole or in part by the surface, the *reflection angle* is equal to the *incidence angle,* the incident ray, reflected ray, and normal all being in the same plane.

reflection loss. In a *transmission line,* the ratio, usually *converted* to *decibels,* between the *incident wave* and the *reflected wave* at any discontinuity or *impedance* mismatch in the *line.* When the two impedances have opposite *phases* and appropriate magnitudes, a *reflection gain* may be obtained, that is, a negative loss. The reflection loss for a given *frequency* at the junction of a *power source* and a *power sink (load)* is given by $RL = -20 \log_{10} |(Z_1 + Z_2)/(4Z_1 Z_2)^{1/2}|$, where RL is the reflection loss in decibels, the vertical bars designate absolute magnitude, and Z_1 and Z_2 are the impedances of the power source and the load. It must be recognized that at any point in a transmission line, if power proceeds from say left to right, the impedance looking to the left is the source impedance and the impedance looking to the right is the load impedance, including any portions of line that may be between the point and the actual source and between the point and the actual load. The ratio, expressed in decibels, is the same as that of the scalar values of the volt-amperes delivered to the load to the volt-amperes that would be delivered to a load of the same impedance as the source. The reflection loss is equal to the number of decibels that correspond to the scalar value of the reciprocal of the *reflection factor.* See *Fresnel reflection loss.*

reflection loss. See *Fresnel reflection loss.*

reflective coating. See *highly-reflective coating.*

reflective jamming. *Jamming* in which *reflectors* are used to return false and confusing *signals* to the *radar receiver* that is being *jammed.* For example, jamming with a large quantity of metallic strips or wires, such as window, *chaff,* rope, or corner reflectors.

reflective sensor. See *fiber-optic reflective sensor.*

reflective star-coupler. An *optical-fiber coupling* device that enables *signals* in one or more fibers to be *transmitted* to one or more other fibers by entering the signals into one side of an optical cylinder, fiber, or other piece of material, with a *reflecting* back-surface in order to reflect the *diffused* signals back to the output *ports* on the same side of the material, for *conduction* away in one or more fibers. Also see *tee coupler; nonreflective star-coupler.*

reflectivity.   The *reflectance* of an *opaque* material (i.e., a material of such thickness so that further increases in thickness do not alter the reflectance). See *radar reflectivity; spectral reflectivity.*

reflectometer.   See *optical time-domain (OTD) reflectometer.*

reflector.   1. One or more *conductors* or conducting surfaces for *reflecting radiant* energy.   2. A surface *interface* with a high *reflection coefficient* at all *incidence angles.*   See *antenna reflector; subreflector; triple mirror.*

refracting crystal.   See *doubly-refracting crystal; multirefracting crystal.*

refraction.   The bending of oblique (non-normal) *incident electromagnetic waves* or *rays* as they pass from a *transmission medium* of one *refractive index* into a medium of a different refractive index, coupled with the changing of the *velocity* of *propagation* of the electromagnetic waves when passing from one medium to another with different refractive indices.   The waves or rays are usually changed in direction (i.e., bent) crossing the media *interface.*   Also see *refractive index; Snell's law.*   See *double refraction.*   Also see Figure S-8.

refraction angle.   When an *electromagnetic wave* strikes a surface of another *transmission medium* and is wholly or partially *transmitted* into the new medium, the acute angle between the normal to the surface at the point of *incidence* and the *refracted ray.*

refraction law.   See *Snell's law.*

refractive index.   1. The ratio of the *velocity* of *light* in a vacuum to the velocity of light in the *transmission medium* whose *refractive index* is desired; e.g., $n = 2.6$ for certain kinds of glass.   2. The ratio of the sines of the *incidence angle* and the *refraction angle* when light passes from one medium to another.   The index between two media is the relative index, while the index when the first medium is a vacuum is the absolute index of the second medium.   The refractive index expressed in tables is the absolute index, i.e., vacuum-to-substance at a certain *temperature,* with light of a certain *wavelength.*   Examples: vacuum, 1.000; air, 1.000292; water, 1.333; ordinary crown glass, 1.516.   Since the index of air is very close to that of vacuum, the two are often used interchangeably.   The refractive index of a substance is given as:

$$n = (\mu\epsilon/\mu_0\epsilon_0)^{1/2}$$

where μ is the *magnetic permeability* of the substance, ϵ is the *electric permittivity,* μ_0 is the *magnetic permeability* of a vacuum, and ϵ_0 is the *electric permittivity* of a vacuum, although nearly the same relative to air.   Synonymous with *absolute refractive index; index of refraction.*   Also see *relative refractive index.*   See *surface refractive index.*   See Figure R-7.

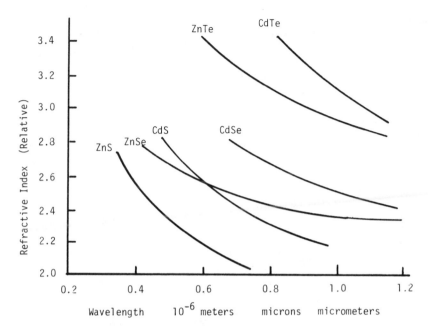

R-7. Refractive index as a function of *wavelength* for single-crystal films formed by solid-state diffusion for use in *integrated optical circuits.*

refractive index gradient. The rate of change of *refractive index* with respect to distance in a *transmission medium,* that is, the slope of the *refractive index profile.* For example, the difference between the *atmospheric refractive index* at two radial elevations divided by the difference in elevation. The refractive index gradient is a *vector.* At any point there is a maximum gradient in a specific direction. A *light ray* or *radio wave* that is *propagating* in the direction of the maximum gradient will not be *refracted.*

refractive-index profile. See *radial refractive-index profile.*

refractive-index-profile mismatch loss. A *loss* of *signal power* introduced by an *optical-fiber splice* of two optical fibers whose *graded refractive indices* are not the same.

reframing time. The time that elapses between the instant at which a valid *frame alignment signal* is available at the *receiving data terminal equipment (DTE)* and the instant at which *frame alignment* is established. The reframing time includes the time that is required for verification of the validity of the frame-alignment signal. Synonymous with *frame alignment recovery time.*

refresh rate. See *regeneration rate.*

regeneration. 1. The *gain* that results from *coupling* the *output* of an *amplifier* to its *input.* Synonymous with *positive feedback.* 2. The action of a *regenerative repeater* in which *digital signals* are amplified, reshaped, retimed, and retransmitted. 3. In a *storage* device whose stored data may deteriorate, the process of restoring the *data* to its latest undeteriorated state. 4. In *display systems,* the repeated production of *display elements, display groups,* or *display images* in the *display space* on the *display surface* of a *display device* so that they remain visible. For example, if regeneration is not accomplished on a *CRT* screen or on the *faceplate* of a *coherent bundle* of *optical fibers,* an initially-generated *image* will disappear when the energizing signal ceases or regeneration of the image ceases. See *pulse regeneration; signal regeneration.*

regeneration rate. The rate in times per unit at which a *display element, display group,* or *display image* is *regenerated* to either prevent loss of *data* in the continuous reading of the *image* by automated means, such as is accomplished in an *electrostatic storage* (Williams) *tube,* or to prevent flicker when viewed by the human eye, in which case the required regeneration rate will depend on the persistance of the screen or faceplate material and on the retentivity of the human retina. Synonymous with *refresh rate.*

regenerative repeater. A *repeater* in which *signals* are amplified, reshaped, retimed, reamplified, and retransmitted.

region. See *diffraction region; Fraunhofer region; International Telecommunication Union (ITU) world region.*

register. 1. A device that is capable of introducing the factor of time into a logic process. The register serves as a temporary *storage* for *characters* usually consisting of several *digits* each. 2. A *storage* device that has a specified storage capacity, such as a *bit,* a *byte,* or a *numeral (word),* and usually has a specific purpose. For example, in a *computer,* it may store the digits that form the *instruction word* that is currently being executed by the computer; or it may store the number of *call attempts* that did not result in *access success* or that resulted in *access failure* because of a *called party busy signal.* See *bounds register; feedback shift register; linear feedback shift register; Master International Frequency Register (MIFR); nonlinear feedback shift register; overflow register; peg count register; recirculating register; shift register; storage register; traffic usage register (TUR).*

register generator. See *shift-register generator.*

register length. The *storage* capacity of a *register.* For example, the length of a *register* that can store a 12-*digit decimal* number.

registration board. See *International Frequency Registration Board (IFRB).*

regular reflection. See *specular reflection.*

regular station. A *station* of a *communication network* that, under normal conditions is required to be in *communication* with a specified set of stations or is required to intercept communications from a specified set of stations. For example, a *fixed station* in an *aeronautical communication network* that is required to be in communication with *aircraft stations.*

regular transmission.   See *specular transmission.*

regulation.   See *two-pilot regulation.*

rejection gate.   See *NOR gate.*

rejection ratio.   See *common-mode rejection ratio (CMRR).*

relateral tell.   The *relaying* of *messages* between two *facilities* via a third facility not by design and particularly in a degraded *communication* environment or when a facility is in a *degraded service state.*

relations.   See *constitutive relations.*

relations communication.   See *public relations communication.*

relative bearing.   A *bearing* that is measured from some given reference direction or point, usually other than true north.

relative coordinate.   In *display systems*, a coordinate expressed in *relative coordinate data* that identifies an *addressable point* in the *display space* on the *display surface* of a *display device* or in *image storage space.*   The relative coordinate indicates the *displacement* between the given addressable point and some other addressable point in the particular coordinate system in which the points lie. Contrast with *absolute coordinate.*

relative coordinate data.   In *display systems*, such as computer *interactive display* terminals with *CRT* screens or *fiberscope faceplates* on the ends of *coherent bundles* of *optical fibers*, values that specify displacements from an actual coordinate, such as the displacement from a coordinate specified by *absolute coordinate data*, in a *display space* on the *display surface* of a *display device* or in an *image storage space.*   The coordinates specified by relative coordinate data may, for example, be contained in a *computer program*, stored in a *storage* unit (memory or buffer) within a display device, or recorded on a *hard-copy* document such as a sheet of paper.   In a coherent bundle of optical fibers, the coordinate of a particular fiber may be given relative to a given, fixed, or specified fiber in the bundle. Contrast with *absolute coordinate data.*   Synonymous with *absolute data.*

relative entropy.   In *information theory*, the ratio of the *absolute entropy* of a *message* or set of *data* to the *decision content* of the message or set of data. In mathematical notation, $H_r = H/H_o$, where H_r is the relative entropy, H is the absolute entropy, and H_o is the decision content of the given quantity of *information.*

relative level.   See *zero relative level.*

relative magnetic permeability.   The *incremental* or *absolute magnetic permeability*, μ, of a material *medium* compared with that of *free space*, μ_0. The *mag-*

netic permeability of free space in *SI* units, absolute or incremental, is $4\pi \times 10^{-7}$ (webers per square *meter*) per (ampere per meter), or webers per ampere-meter. Mathematically:

$$\mu_{\text{rel}} = \mu/\mu_0$$

For an *optical fiber*, the magnetic permeability is very nearly equal to that of free space. Thus, μ_{rel} for an optical fiber is very close to unity. Also see *absolute magnetic permeability; incremental magnetic permeability.*

relative order. In *display systems*, a *display command* in a *segment, display file,* or *computer program,* or the instruction repertory thereof, that can cause a *display device* to interpret the *data* following the order as *relative data* rather than *absolute data.* Contrast with *absolute order.*

relative phase telegraphy. *Telegraphy* in which *signal coding* is used that is dependent on the *phase* relation of an *input signal* to the previous *digit* rather than on its absolute value. Also see *differential encoding.*

relative redundancy. In *information theory,* the ratio of the *absolute redundancy* to the *decision content* of a quantity of *data,* such as a *message* or other set of data. In mathematical notation, $R_r = R/H_0 = (H_0-H)/H_0$, where R_r is the relative redundancy, R is the absolute redundancy, H_0 is the decision content, and H is the *entropy* of the given quantity of *data.*

relative transmission level. The *ratio* of the *signal power* at some point in a *transmission system* to the signal power at some other point chosen as the *reference.* The ratio is applicable during *operating* conditions. When performing a test, it is the ratio of the *test tone power* at any point in a *transmission system* to the test tone power at some point in the system chosen as the reference. The only difference in the test situation is that a test tone is used rather than the actual operating *signals.* The relative transmission level may be expressed as a ratio, a percentage, in *decibels,* or in *nepers.* Care must be taken to distinguish between *voltage, current,* and *power levels.*

relative refractive index. The *refractive index* of a substance relative to another substance; thus, if two glasses have refractive indices of $n_1 = 2.100$ and $n_2 = 1.781$, then the relative refractive index of substance 1 relative to substance 2 is $n_1/n_2 = 1.179$. Also see *refractive index.*

relative vector. In *display systems,* a *vector* that has a starting point specified by a vector, usually the last reached point of the immediately preceding *display element,* and an endpoint specified as a displacement from the starting point. Relative vectors are usually visually indicated on *display surfaces,* e.g., computer graphic *CRT* screens, *fiberscope faceplates,* and *LED* and *gas panels.* Synonymous with *incremental vector.* Contrast with *absolute vector.*

relay. 1. In *radio communication networks,* an arrangement in which *radio stations* communicate with one another via a third station. The purpose may be to increase the *range,* interconnect radio stations at different *frequencies,* or use different methods of *modulation*.   2. An electromechanical device in which a part that is connected in one *circuit* enables the control of *electrical currents* or *voltages* in other circuits. It usually consists of at leaat a *magnetic* coil connected to one circuit, that can control the movement of an armature fitted with contacts for opening and closing contacts in one or more other circuits. Using special arrangements of one or more coils and one or more spring-loaded armatures, the relay can be used to control high-power circuits with low-power *signals,* to serve as a *combinational logic gate,* or simply to open and close circuits. See *automatic tape relay; down-the-hill radio relay; message relay; neutral relay; polar relay; radar relay; radio relay; satellite relay; side stable relay; tape relay; telegraph relay; torn-tape relay; vibrating relay.*

relay communication method.   A method of *communication* in which a *station transmits* a *message* to another station that repeats the message, transmitting it to a third station that repeats it to a fourth, and so on, to the last station in the series or to the destination station. For example, the *radio relay* method, or the method of transmission that is used in a sequence of *microwave links.* Also see *broadcast communication method; intercept communication method; receipt communication method.*

relay configuration.   In *communication systems,* an operating arrangement in which a *circuit* is established between two stations via an intermediate relay station. Two *links* are utilized simultaneously and the *channel connections* at the relay station are accomplished completely within the station.

relay electronic counter-countermeasure.   See *radio relay electronic counter-countermeasure.*

relay equipment.   See *telegraph automatic relay equipment (TARE).*

relay net.   A *communication network* used for the *relaying* of *message traffic.*

relay pilot.   See *tape-relay pilot.*

relay plane.   See *automatic radio relay plane.*

relay satellite.   A *satellite* that has a *radio relay station* on board, that is, a *satellite station* that accepts *messages* and *retransmits* or *rebroadcasts* them.

relay station.   See *major relay station; minor relay station.*

relay switching.   See *semiautomatic continuous-tape relay switching.*

relay system.   See *automatic relay system (ARQ); manual relay system; radio relay system; semiautomatic relay system.*

relay working.   In *voice radio station operations,* a *mode* of operation in which the *operator* at a *radio relay station retransmits* a *message* by voice.

release.   1. In *communication systems,* to authorize the dispatch of a *message.* **2.** In *communication security,* to authorize the *transfer* of *security classified information* to another authority, organization, or nation. See *switching release.*

released acknowledgement signal. See *circuit-released acknowledgement signal.*

released signal. See *circuit-released signal.*

release time. **1.** In *communication systems,* the time after the end of an *enabling signal* during which suppression still continues, due to the time required for *terminals* to discharge, that is, due to *circuit time constants,* before remanent *inhibiting biases* are removed. The situation occurs in a *VOGAD system* and in *echo suppressors.* **2.** The time interval between de-energization of a *relay* coil and the beginning of contact opening (end of closure), or the time interval between de-energization of a relay coil and the beginning of closure (end of open), depending on the type of relay action, namely normally open or normally closed when not energized. See *call release time; message release time.*

release-time delay. See *receiver release-time delay; transmitter release-time delay.*

releasing officer. See *message releasing officer.*

reliability. **1.** The capability of a *functional unit* to perform a required function under stated conditions for a stated period of time. **2.** The probability that a *functional unit* will perform its intended function for a stated interval under stated conditions. For example, the probability that a *message* will arrive at its intended destination within a reasonable time and without undesired alteration of the *text* or loss of meaning. See *channel reliability; circuit reliability; communication reliability; hardware reliability; software reliability.*

relock. In *radar operations,* to reobtain *lock-on* on an object (target) on which the *tracking* was lost. Also see *lock-on; transfer lock.*

reluctance. See *magnetic reluctance.*

remanence. The *magnetization (polarization)* that remains in a *magnetized* material after an applied *magnetic field* has been removed.

remapping. In *spread-spectrum systems,* a process of *correlation* in which a spread-spectrum *signal* is converted into a coherent *narrow-band signal* and undesired signals are converted into wider *bandwidths.*

remodulation. A *transponder* that is usually in *satellite* or *line-of-sight radio relay links* and in which the incoming signal is first *down-converted* to an *intermediate frequency (IF), amplified,* and *demodulated* to obtain the *baseband.* The baseband is then used to *modulate* a *radio frequency (RF) carrier* that is *up-converted* for *transmission.*

remote access. Pertaining to *communication* with and among *data processing facilities* through the use of *data links.*

remote control. **1.** The control of a *functional unit* from a distant point by any means, such as by *electrical,* electronic, *electromagnetic,* sonic, or mechanical means. **2.** In *communication system operations, radio transmitter* control in which the control functions are performed electrically from a distance through the use of *wire, coaxial cable, optical fiber, microwave,* or *radio circuits.* For example, radio programs can originate downtown or from a *mobile unit* while the *transmitter* is at the foot of a tower with the *antenna* at the top; or a *receiver* in an aircraft and a *transmitter* on the ground can be used to control the flight of the aircraft.

remote control equipment. The equipment that may be used for the *monitoring, controlling, supervising,* and the performance of other functions of a *system* from a distance.

remote job entry. In *computer* and *communication system operations,* a *mode* of operation in which *computer programs, data,* or *control functions* may be entered into the system from a remote site and results obtained at the remote site through the use of *communication links.*

remote keying. In *cryptosystems,* the electrical distribution and insertion of *cryptographic key* variables into the key generator from a distant point, that is, through a *communication link.*

remotely-piloted vehicle. See *unretrievable remotely-piloted vehicle.*

remote master data circuit-terminating equipment. *Data circuit-terminating equipment (DCE)* that is capable of controlling other DCEs through the use of *communication links.*

remote operator signaling. *Signaling* between a *central office* and a remote *operator position* that allows a remote *operator* to process operator *calls* through the position.

remote orderwire. An extension of a local *engineering circuit* (orderwire) to a point that is more convenient for *operators* and maintenance personnel to perform required *monitoring* functions.

repair. See *mean-time-to-repair (MTTR).*

repairing circuit. See *self-repairing circuit.*

repeat. See *automatic-request repeat (ARQ).*

repeatability measure. A measure of the degree of spatial coincidence obtained when a specific *display element, display group,* or *display image* is desired to be repeatedly generated at the same *coordinate position.*

repeater. A device that processes its *input signal* for *retransmission.* In the case of *pulses,* it *amplifies, shapes,* retimes, or performs a combination of these and similar functions on an *input signal* for retransmission. In other cases, it may only *amplify* and *filter* an *analog signal,* or it may perform other *signal processing* or *image processing* and *restoration* functions. The repeater may handle one-way or two-way *transmission.* For example, the repeater may be situated along an extended rural *telephone line* or in a *submarine* (undersea) *cable;* or it may be a *transponder* in an *active satellite.* See *branching repeater; broadcast repeater;*

conference repeater; data conferencing repeater; deception repeater; drop repeater; four-wire repeater; heterodyne repeater; optical repeater; passive repeater; pulse-link repeater; radar deception repeater; radar repeater; regenerative repeater; reradiating repeater.

repeatered optical link. An *optical link* that has *optical repeaters* along its *cable* to reshape, time, and amplify the *lightwaves* or lightwave *pulses propagating* in its cable. A repeater spacing of 8 km is currently typical.

repeater jammer. A *receiver-transmitter* device that *amplifies,* multiplies, and *retransmits* the *signals* that it *receives,* for purposes of *deception* or *jamming.* See *coherent repeater jammer; swept-repeater jammer.*

repeater power. See *optical repeater power.*

repeating coil. A *voice-frequency transformer* that is characterized by a closed core, a pair of identical, *balanced primary (line)* windings, a pair of identical, but not necessarily *balanced secondary (drop)* windings, and a low *transmission loss* at *voice frequencies.* It permits the *transfer* of voice *electrical currents* from one winding to another by *magnetic* induction, the *matching* of line and drop *impedances,* and the longitudinal *isolation* of the line from the drop.

repeating ship. In *visual communication systems,* a ship that is equipped to *relay* a *message* manually or automatically, that elects to relay a message to facilitate *communications,* or through which a message is *routed.* See *light-repeating ship.*

reperforator. 1. A *receiver* that consists of a *perforator* that is controlled by *received signals,* that is, a receiver perforator. 2. In *teletypewriter systems,* a device that is used to punch a tape in accordance with arriving *signals,* permitting reproduction and *retransmission* of the signals, that is, a *retransmitting perforator.* Synonymous with *receiver-perforator; receiving perforator.* See *printing-reperforator.*

reperforator tape reader. See *coupled reperforator tape reader.*

reperforator-transmitter. A *teletypewriter* that consists of a *reperforator* and a *tape transmitter,* each independent of the other, and that is used as a *relaying* device. It is suitable for temporary *message-queueing* and for converting the *signaling rate* of incoming *data* to a different rate.

repertory dialer. A *telephone* set that stores a group of numbers that are frequently *called* by a *user* (customer, subscriber) and that *transmits* the *dialing information* to the *central office* by a single action.

repetition rate. 1. The number of *occurrences* of an event per unit of *time.* 2. In *telephone systems,* the number of times that *users* request a *connection* divided by the time interval during which the requests are made, that is, the number of *access attempts* per unit of time. The numbers are used to appraise the effectiveness of *transmission* over a *telephone line.* If the events are *pulses,* the *repetition rate* is the pulse rate. See *jittered-pulse repetition rate; pulse repetition rate; staggered-pulse repetition rate.*

repetitively-pulsed laser. See *Q-switched repetitively-pulsed laser.*

repetitive operation. In *analog systems,* the automatic repetition of the solution of a set of equations with fixed combinations of initial *conditions* and other *parameters.* Repetitive operation is often used to permit the *display* of an apparently steady solution. It is also used to permit manual adjustment or optimization of one or more parameters in order to obtain certain desired results in the solution.

reply. 1. A *message* to the *originator* of a previous message that contained a question. 2. The answer to a *challenge* in an *identification procedure.* 3. Any *response* to a *message* or *signal.* See *challenge and reply.*

reply authentication. See *challenge-and-reply authentication.*

report. See *interference report; jamming report; overdue report; situation report; weather report.*

reporting net. A *communication net* that is designed for the free and rapid interchange of *information* such as information that is normally associated with the maintenance of up to date plots, tactical situations, maps, picture coverage, *displays,* and related *data,* in contrast to command and control information. See *maritime patrol air reporting net.*

representation. See *analog representation; coded representation; numeric representation.*

reproducibility. In *information systems,* a measure of the ease with which an *object,* event, or *image* can be reproduced, or a known result can be obtained repetitively. It is essential that the *precision* of the reproudction or result be specified as a criterion for the determination of reproducibility.

reproduction ratio. The ratio of a linear dimension of a reproduced object, such as a document, to the corresponding dimension on the original *object.* For example, the ratio of the linear distance between two points on an object and the distance between the corresponding points on an *image* of the object.

reproduction speed. In *facsimile systems,* the area of the *record medium* that is covered per unit of time by the *receiver.*

request. See *access request; correction request; disengagement request; light request; statistics-on-request; tracer request.*

request data transfer. A *call control signal* that is sent by *data terminal equipment (DTE)* to *data circuit-terminating equipment (DCE)* to request the establishment of a *data connection.* Request data transfer *signals* are used in *switched* and *leased circuit service.*

request fix.   In *radiotelephone direction finding,* a request from a *mobile station* for a *determination* of *position* or direction by a *direction-finding station.*

request homing.   In *radiotelephone direction finding,* a request from a *mobile station* for course *information* to a *direction-finding station,* that will lead the requesting station to the direction-finding station.

request indicator.   See *called-line identification-request indicator; calling-line identification-request indicator.*

request-repeat.   See *error-detection and feedback; automatic request-repeat (ARQ).*

request-repeat (RQ) signal.   A *signal* from a *receiver* to a *transmitter* asking that a *message* be *transmitted* again.

request-repeat (RQ) system.   See *automatic request-repeat (ARQ).*

request separator character.   See *facility request separator character.*

request signal.   See *clear request signal; data terminal equipment (DTE) clear-request signal; data transfer request signal; facility request signal.*

request time.   See *call request time.*

request-to-send signal.   A *signal* that is generated by a *receiver* in order to *condition* a remote *transmitter* to commence *transmission.*   Also see *clear-to-send signal.*

reradiating repeater.   A *repeater* that *receives, amplifies, shapes,* and *radiates received signals* without *frequency translation.*

rering.   In *telephone system operations,* a *facility* that is provided on *trunk lines* for *recalling* a distant *operator* or for *ringing-off* where no *automatic signaling* is provided.

rerun.   1. In *communication systems,* the *retransmission* by the *transmitter* of a *received transmission.*   2. In *tape relay communication systems,* the *retransmission* by the *transmitter* of a *message* that was previously sent. The rerun message is usually stored on a *data medium* or in a *storage* device for subsequent comparison of the rerun message.   3. In *computing* and *automatic data processing,* a repeat of a *computer program run* from its beginning. The rerun may be necessary because of a false start, an interruption, a need to effect a required change, or for other reasons. Also see *retransmission.*

rescue beacon.   See *search-and-rescue beacon.*

rescue beacon frequency.   See *search-and-rescue beacon frequency.*

rescue communications.   1. *Scene-of-action communications* that occur at a rescue scene.   2. *Communications* that occur in connection with a rescue operation, including *stations* at the scene-of-action and at support or *message-relay* locations. See *search and rescue communications.*

rescue control channel. The *channel (frequency)* that is used at the scene of a rescue operation to control all activities in the area, such as evacuation, emergency medical operations, environmental control (fire, storm, cold), and actions intended to alleviate or remove the emergency conditions.

rescue frequency. See *scene-of-air-sea-rescue frequency.*

research earth station. See *space research earth station.*

research service. See *space research service.*

research space station. See *space research space station.*

research station. See *experimental research station.*

resection. *Position-finding triangulation* in which an unknown location of a single *receiver* can be determined by obtaining *bearings* from two sources of *radiation* whose locations are known. The intersection of the bearings through their locations determines the point on a map at which they cross, the point being the location of the receiver. Also see *intersection.* See Figure R-8.

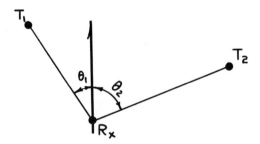

R-8. *Bearings (azimuths)* θ_1 and θ_2 are taken on two known *transmitters,* T_1 and T_2. *Back azimuths* (azimuths $\pm 180°$) through the location of the transmitters are used to obtain its location by the **resection** method of *triangulation.*

reset. In a *data processing system,* to cause a *counter* or *register* to take the state that corresponds to a previously specified value, such as the state of the initial value.

reset mode. See *initial condition mode.*

resettability. A measure of the ability to duplicate controllable conditions. For example, the ability to reset the *frequency* controls of *radio* equipment so as to obtain the exact same *frequency* of *transmission* or *tuning* as was previously obtained.

residual equalizer. See *line residual equalizer.*

residual error rate. The ratio of the number of *bits,* elements, *characters,* or *blocks* that are incorrectly *received* but undetected or uncorrected by the *error-*

control equipment, to the total number of bits, elements, characters, or blocks that were *transmitted.* Synonymous with *undetected error rate.*

residual magnetism. The *magnetization (polarization)* that remains in a magnetized material after all attempts to remove the magnetization have been made. For example, the magnetization remaining from *magnetic* recording of *data* after attempts at degaussing.

residual modulation. See *carrier noise level.*

resistance. A measure of the opposition to an *electric current* by a material or *free space* when a *potential difference (voltage)* or potential gradient is applied between two points. It is the value of *R* in the *Ohm's law* relation $I = V/R$, where *I* is the *electric current* and *V* is the potential difference that is applied across the resistive element (resistor). The *SI* unit of resistance is the ohm. It is also the reciprocal of the *conductance,* expressed in mhos, which is ohm spelled backward. The resistance of metallic *conductors* causes *attenuation* of required *electric signaling currents.* In *optical fibers,* the *propagation* of *electromagnetic waves* do not require the existence of electric currents, though there is some interaction between the *lightwaves* and *electrons,* which produces some losses in the form of heat and *scattering.* See *crosstalk resistance; EMI resistance; equivalent noise resistance; infrared detector dark resistance; load resistance; neutron bombardment resistance.*

resistance coupling. The *coupling* of *signals* or *noise* from one *conductor* to another by means of *resistance* or *conductance* between them.

resistance communication cable. See *intrusion-resistant communication cable.*

resistor. An *electric circuit* element that has the capability of providing *resistance* to the flow of *electric current* when a *potential difference* occurs across it.

resolution. In *display systems,* a measure of the capability of a device to distinguish between adjacent *objects* and *display* them as separate *images.* Thus, it is a measure of the sharpness of a *display image,* i.e., a measure of the degree to which *luminous intensity* discontinuities across the surface of the image match that of the actual object. Resolution is usually expressed as the number of points per unit of area or the number of lines per unit of length that are discernible as separate points or lines in the image. Also see *resolving power.* See *angular resolution; detection resolution; longitudinal resolution; range resolution; transverse resolution.*

resolution angle. See *limiting resolution angle.*

resolution cell. See *radar resolution cell.*

resolver. A device whose *input* variables are the polar coordinates of a point and whose output variables are the Cartesian coordinates of the same point, or vice versa. In mathematical notation, the device performs the coordinate conversion $x = \rho \cos\theta$ and $y = \rho \sin\theta$; or $\rho = (x^2 + y^2)^{1/2}$ and $\theta = \tan^{-1} y/x$.

resolving power. A measure of the ability of a *lens* or *optical system* to form separate and distinct *images* of two *objects* close together. Because of *diffraction* at the *aperture,* no optical system can form a perfect image of a point, but produces instead a small disk of *light* (airy disk) surrounded by alternately dark and bright concentric rings. When two object points are at that critical separation from which the first dark ring of one diffraction pattern falls upon the central disk of the other, the points are just resolved (i.e., distinguished as separated), and the points are said to be at the limit of *resolution.* See *bundle resolving power; chromatic resolving power; grating chromatic resolving power; prism chromatic resolving power; theoretical resolving power.*

resonance. The condition that exists in an *electrical circuit* when the *inductive reactance* and the *capacitive reactance* are of equal magnitude and energy oscillates between the *electric field* and the *magnetic field* of each. A collapsing magnetic field of the inductor stores its energy in the rising electric field of the capacitor. The discharging capacitor stores its energy in the magnetic field of the inductor, since the discharging capacitor is tantamount to an electric current. At resonance, the *series impedance* of the two elements is at a minimum and the *parallel impedance* is a maximum. Resonance is used for *tuning,* since resonance occurs at a particular frequency for given values of *inductance* and *capacitance.* At resonance, the *inductive reactance* and the *capacitive reactance* are equal, therefore $\omega L = 1/\omega C$ and $f = 1/2\pi(LC)^{1/2}$, where $\omega = 2\pi f$, in which f is the *frequency* in *hertz,* L is the *inductance* in henries, and C is the *capacity* in farads. Also see *resonant frequency.*

resonant cavity. A bounded region in a material *medium* (such as a free rectangular space in a *laser* crystal or a length of hollow tubing closed on both ends) or a region of such geometrical dimension (such as two parallel walls that are a multiple or submultiple of *wavelengths* apart) that a *standing wave* (*electromagnetic,* acoustic, or elastic) can be sustained and raised to high intensity by application of stimulation (applied energy of appropriate *frequency*) from outside or inside the cavity. Resonant cavities are used in some *lasers* in which they form part of the *laser head.*

resonant frequency. In an *electrical circuit,* the *frequency* at which *circuit inductive reactance* and *capacitive reactance* are equal, thus creating an oscillation or interchange of energy between the *magnetic* (inductive) *field* and the *electric* (capacitive) *field.* Also see *resonance.*

respond opportunity. See *response opportunity.*

response. 1. A *reply* to an inquiry (query). 2. In *data transmission,* the content of the *control field* of a *response frame* advising the *primary station* concerning the *processing* by the *secondary station* of one or more *command frames.* See *edge-response; electrooptic frequency response; impulse response; spectral response; spurious response; unnumbered response.*

response frame. 1. In *data transmission,* all *frames* that may be *transmitted* by a *secondary station.* 2. In *high-level data link control (HDLC) procedures,* all *frames* that may be *transmitted* by a *secondary station* or by a *combined station* that has the local or transmitting combined station *address.*

response message. A *message* that is sent in the *backward direction* and that contains an indication of the *called terminal line condition* or of a *network* condition, that contains *information* relating to *user* and *network facilities,* and, in the case of some user (customer, subscriber) facilities, that contains *addresses* or other identifying information.

response opportunity. In *data transmission,* the *link-level logical control condition* during which a given *secondary station* may *transmit* a *response.* Synonymous with *respond opportunity.*

response quantum efficiency. The ratio of the number of countable *output* events to the number of *incident photons* that occur when *electromagnetic energy* is incident upon a material, often measured as *electrons* emitted per incident photon. Response quantum efficiency is a measure of the efficiency of conversion or utilization of optical energy, being an indication of the number of events produced for each incident quantum for a *photodetector.* It is a measure of the probability that the photodetector triggers a measurable event when a photon is incident. Quantum efficiency is an intrinsic quality of materials, a function of *wavelength, incidence angle,* and *polarization* of the incident *electromagnetic field.* Normally, it is the number of electrons released or emitted, on the average, for each *incidence angle,* and *polarization* of the incident *electromagnetic field.* Electron-*hole* pairing by an incident photon is a complex probabilistic phenomenon that depends on the details of the *energy band* structure of the material.

response signal. See *partial response signal; recall response signal.*

response test. See *frequency-response test.*

response time. In a *data system,* the elapsed time between the end of *transmission* of an *enquiry message* and the beginning of the receipt of a *response message,* measured at the enquiry originating *station.*

responsibility. See *precedence responsibility.*

responsibility chain. See *visual responsibility chain.*

responsivity. 1. In a *photodetector,* the *electric current output* per unit of *optical power* input at a specified *wavelength* of *incident radiation;* e.g., 0.6 A/W at 0.900 *micron.* 2. The *optical power* output per unit of driving current input to a *light source,* such as an *LED* or a *laser;* e.g., 2 mW/μA at 0.810 *micron.* See *photodetector responsivity.*

restitution. In *communication systems,* a series of *significant conditions* that are determined by the decisions that are made according to the products of a *demodulation process.* Also see *demodulation; modulation; significant condition.* See *isochronous restitution; start-stop restitution.*

restoral. See *mean-time-to-service-restoral (MTTSR).*

restoration.   See *channel restoration; circuit restoration; image restoration.*

restoration circuit.   See *direct-current (DC) restoration circuit.*

restoration priority.   In *communication system operations,* the sequence in which *communication service* will be upgraded when *system capacity* becomes available after an extended *outage* or *degraded service state* period.   For example, certain *access lines* will usually have a high priority in obtaining improved service when capacity becomes available.   Other lines may have an intermediate or low priority.   Restoration priorities become highly significant in the event of extended *power* outages, natural disasters, and nuclear attack.

restricted area.   In *communication system security,* a physical space or area that is intended for use or access only by authorized persons.   Restricted areas are usually under special control and *security* measures to prevent unauthorized entry.   For example, aboard ship, the radio room is usually a restricted area.   It is usually locked when unattended, with keys in the possession of authorized persons only.   A *cryptoequipment* area in a *communication center* or *station* is usually in a restricted area.

restricted circular three-body problem.   A mathematical simplification of the *three-body problem* involving three-body orbital calculations in which one of the three bodies is assumed to have very small mass and is assumed to be under the attraction of two particles of very much larger mass that are moving in circular orbits about their common center of mass.   A problem of this kind is encountered, for example, in studies of the motion of an asteroid or comet under the influence of the attraction of the sun and jupiter.   The jovian orbit, to a first approximation, is considered to be circular.   The problem is also directly related to investigations of the motion of *spacecraft* and *satellites* in the earth-moon system.   No rigorous solution of the restricted circular three-body problem that is suitable for computing the coordinates of a moving body has yet been obtained on a fully analytical basis.   In *celestial mechanics,* approximate methods have been developed that enable a sufficiently exact solution of the problem for most purposes, such as *communication satellite orbital* calculations, including *geostationary earth satellites.*   Also see *n-body problem; three-body problem; two-body problem.*

restricted edge-emitting diode (REED).   An *edge-emitting LED;* i.e., a *light-emitting diode* in which *light* is emitted only over a small portion of an edge.   The restricted light-emitting region improves *coupling efficiency* with *optical fibers* and *integrated optical circuits.*

retention.   See *cable retention.*

reticle.   A scale, indicator, or pattern placed in one of the *focal planes* of an *optical* instrument that appears to the observer to be superimposed upon the field of view.   Reticles, in various patterns, are used to determine the center of the field or to assist in the gauging of distance, determining leads, or measurement.   A reticle may consist of fine wires, or *fibers,* mounted on a support at the ends, or may be etched on a clear, scrupulously polished and cleaned plane parallel plate of glass, in which case the entire piece of glass is the reticle.

retiming. In a *communication system,* the adjustment of the intervals between a pair of corresponding *significant instants* of *digital signals* in reference to a *timing signal.*

retransmission. 1. The *transmission* of the same *data* or *information* that was previously sent by a given *transmitter.* **2.** The *transmission* of received *data* or *information* by a *repeater* that had not transmitted that data or information before. **3.** The repetition of a *message, signal,* or other *transmission* that was previously *transmitted,* by the same or any other *mode* of transmission. Also see *rerun.* See *automatic retransmission.*

retransmit. To *transmit* the same set of *signals* that was *received,* either by the original *transmitter* or by a transmitter at the *receiver* location, whichever is specified.

retransmitter. See *automatic retransmitter; perforated-tape retransmitter.*

retrodirective reflector. See *triple mirror.*

return. See *carriage return; common return; ground return; radar return; sea return.*

return character. See *carriage return (CR) character.*

return circuit. See *ground-return circuit.*

return loss. The ratio, at the junction of a *transmission line* and a *terminating impedance,* of the *amplitude* of the *reflected wave* to the amplitude of the *incident wave,* expressed as a ratio, in *decibels,* in *nepers,* or as a percentage. The return loss is a measure of the dissimilarity between two *impedances.* It is equal to the number of decibels that corresponds to the scalar value of the reciprocal of the *reflection coefficient, RC,* and hence may be expressed as $RL = 1/RC = (Z_2 + Z_1)/(Z_2 - Z_1)$, where RL is the return loss, RC is the *reflection coefficient,* Z_1 is the impedance looking toward the *source* of a *signal,* and Z_2 is the impedance looking toward the *load,* or *sink.*

return-to-zero. See *non-return-to-zero (NRZ).*

return-to-zero (RZ) binary code. A *code* in which there are two *data* or *information* states that may be called 0 and 1 and in which there is a third state or *condition,* such as a neutral or rest condition, to which the *signal level* that is representing a *bit* returns during each *digit period.* Also see *non-return-to-zero (NRZ) binary code.*

return-to-zero change. See *non-return-to-zero change (NRZ-C).*

return-to-zero coding. *Coding* using *electrical* or *lightwave pulses* that return to a zero-level condition of *power, current, voltage, phase, luminous intensity, fre-*

quency, or other parameter between each on-condition. For example, the binary digits 111001 would be represented by three on-conditions each followed by an off-condition, followed by an off-condition for two time intervals, followed by on-condition for one time interval, and a return to the off-condition immediately following the last digit. There is a signal level corresponding to zero between each digit, regardless of whether the digit is a zero or a one.

return-to-zero level code. See *modified non-return-to-zero level code.*

return-to-zero mark. See *non-return-to-zero mark (NRZ-M).*

return-to-zero space. See *non-return-to-zero space (NRZ-S).*

reversal. See *partial tone reversal; phase flux reversal.*

reverse keying. See *phase-reverse keying.*

reverse-Polish notation. See *post-fix notation.*

reversible counter. A device with a finite number of states. Each state represents a number that can be increased or decreased by unity or by a given constant upon receipt of an appropriate *signal.* The device is usually capable of bringing the number that is represented to a specified value, such as zero.

reversible operation. See *one-way reversible operation.*

reverted. In *optical systems,* turned the opposite way so that right becomes left, and vice versa. For example, the effect produced by a *mirror* in *reflecting* an *image.*

reverted image. In an *optical system,* an *image,* the right side of which appears to be the left side, and vice versa.

RF. *Radio frequency.*

RF bandwidth. *Radio frequency bandwidth.*

RF equipment. See *industrial-scientific-medical RF equipment.*

RF heating equipment. See *industrial RF heating equipment.*

RFI. Radio *frequency interference.*

RF power margin. *Radio frequency power margin.*

RHI. *Range-height indicator.*

rhombic antenna. A *directional antenna* that is composed of long wire *radiators* comprising the sides of a rhombus. The two halves of the rhombus are fed equally in opposite *phase* at an apex. It is usually *terminated* and *unidirectional.* When it is unterminated, it is *bidirectional.* A rhombus is an equilateral parallelogram. It has the shape of a baseball diamond.

RHR. *Radio horizon range.*

ribbon. See *optical fiber ribbon.*

Richardson's law. The basic law of thermionic *emission*, expressed by the Richardson-Dushman equation, i.e., the current density (amperes/square *meter*) due to the thermal excitation in the cathode material is:

$$J = AT^2 e^{-bq/kT}$$

where T is the cathode *absolute temperature* (in *kelvin*), k is *Boltzmann's constant, A* is a material constant (in $Am^{-2}K^{-2}$), q is the electronic charge (in *coulombs*), and b is the work function (in joules/coulomb) for the cathode material. Note that this exponential function is quite steep.

right-angle adapter. A *connector* that allows an *optical fiber, bundle,* or *cable* to enter or leave an *optical transmitter* or *receiver* unit at right angles (90°) to the surface of the unit.

right-hand circular polarization. *Circular polarization* of an *electromagnetic wave* (e.g., a *lightwave* or a radio wave) in which the *electric field vector* rotates in a clockwise direction as seen by an observer looking in the direction of *propagation* of the wave. Synonymous with *right-circular polarization.*

right-hand helical polarization. *Polarization* of an *electromagnetic wave* (e.g., a *lightwave* or *radio wave*) in which the *electric field vector* rotates in a clockwise direction as it advances in the direction of *propagation* and as seen by an observer looking in the direction of propagation. The tip of the electric field vector advances like the thread of a right-hand screw when entering a fixed nut or tapped hole. Synonymous with *clockwise helical polarization.*

right-hand polarized electromagnetic wave. An *elliptically* or *circularly polarized electromagnetic wave* (e.g., a *lightwave* or a radio wave) in which the direction of rotation of the *electric vector* is clockwise as seen by an observer looking in the direction of *propagation* of the wave. Synonymous with *clockwise polarized electromagnetic wave.*

right-hand rule. See *Fleming's rule.*

right justify. **1.** To control the *printing positions* of *characters* on a *page* so that the right-hand margin of the printing is regular. **2.** To *shift* the contents of a *register*, if necessary, so that the *character* at the right-hand end of the *data* that have been *read* or *loaded* into the register is at a specified position in the register.

rights terminal. See *multiple-access-rights terminal.*

right through control. Control in a *switched communication network* in which the originating *nodal switching center (NSC)* determines the *route* of a *call* to the destination NSC and thus to the destination *terminal*. The control includes the setting up of the *connection* all the way through to the *called party* (customer, subscriber, destination user) *end-instrument.*

ring. In a *communication system,* a *signal* of specific duration and character that indicates to a *user* (customer, subscriber) that a *calling party* is engaged in an *access attempt.* See *guard ring; rering.*

ring around. In *communication network operations,* the improper *routing* of a *call* in which the route goes back through a *switching center* already involved in attempting to *complete* the same *call.*

ring back. 1. In *telephone switchboard operations,* to *ring* a *called party* using the *answering plug.* This is usually done after obtaining the *called party* (wanted *user,* customer, subscriber) in a *booked call.* The *calling plug* is connected to the *called party's line* and is therefore already in use. 2. The *signal* used to alert the *user* (customer, subscriber) who has placed a *call.*

ring connection. A method of connecting a set of *terminals* in which a single one-way ring *cable* goes from *station* to *station* in sequence, each terminal connected by a relatively short cable or *T-coupler* to the ring cable. Thus, the ring cable has no ends.

ring counter. A device that consists of a loop of interconnected *storage* elements, such as *flip-flops* (bistable circuits), only one of which can be in a specified state at any given time. Each successive applied *pulse* causes another element in the loop to *switch* to the specified state. The total count possible equals the number of *stages.* Also see *binary counter; modulus counter.*

ringdown. 1. In *telephone switching,* a method of *signaling* an *operator* in which a *ringing current* is sent over the *line* to operate a signaling device, such as a lamp or a drop of a self-locking *relay,* or both. The signal is intended to obtain the attention of the *operator.* 2. Pertaining to the type of *signaling* that is employed in manual *operation* of a *telephone system,* as opposed to *automatic dial signaling.* Ringdown signaling utilizes a continuous or pulsing *alternating-current (AC) signal* that is *transmitted* over the *line.* It can apply when no *switchboard* is involved, as well as between a switchboard and a *user* (customer, subscriber). The term ringdown originated in *magneto telephone operation,* in which cranking the magneto of a *user end-instrument* (telephone set) would ring its bell and cause a lever to fall down at the *central office switchboard.*

ringdown circuit. A *telephone circuit* on which the *signaling* is manually applied but not necessarily generated.

ringdown signaling. 1. The application of a *signal* to a *line* for the purpose of actuating a *line,* or *supervisory, signal indicator,* such as a signal lamp, bell, or buzzer to obtain the attention of an *operator* at a *switchboard.* 2. *Ringing* a *user's* end-instrument, by means of a manual generator or by actuating a *key* that connects a *signaling source* to the user's *line.*

ringer. See *optical fiber ringer.*

ringing signal. See *ringing tone.*

ring network. A *network configuration* in which each *node* is directly connected to two and only two *adjacent nodes.* Thus, one and only one *path* connects all nodes, there are no *endpoint nodes,* and there are no *ports* or *connections* to other *networks.* Also see *loop network.* See Figure R-9.

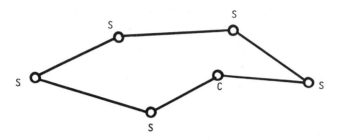

R-9. A six-*station* **ring network** that has one *control station.*

ring off. In *telephone switchboard operations,* to send a *clearing signal* to the *switchboard operator.* The *user* (customer, subscriber) uses the ring off to indicate to the *operator* that the *call* is *finished.*

ringing tone. In *telephone switchboard operation,* an audible indication that a *dialed* number is *ringing.* The ringing tone serves as a *status signal* to inform the *calling party* that the required *directory number* is being *called,* that it is not *busy,* that all *connections* to the number have been made, and that all that remains for the *call* to be *completed* is for the *called party* to remove the handset from the hook or lift it off its cradle switch to answer. Synonymous with *ringing signal.*

rings. See *Newton's rings.*

ring trip. In *telephone operations,* a *signal* that is sent to a *switchboard* by a *user's end-instrument* to indicate that the user has answered and to stop the *ringing tone (signal).* The ring trip is usually a *seize signal.* If the ring trip fails to function, it is possible that the ringing tone (signal) will *couple* to the *receiver* and ring in the *called party's* ear.

ripple voltage. The alternating *component* of the *unidirectional voltage* from a *rectifier* or generator that is used as a source of *direct-current (DC) power.* Ripple voltages are usually reduced to a minimum with *filters,* particularly to reduce *noise,* especially the 60 Hz ripple from a half-wave rectifier or the 120 Hz ripple from a full-wave rectifier.

riser. In *radar displays,* a *display element* that has appeared and suddenly disappeared from the *display surface.*

rise time. In *pulse circuits,* the time required for a pulse to reach a specified magnitude from a given level. For example, the time required for a voltage pulse to change from 0.1 to 0.9 of its maximum value. See *flux rise time.*

risk analysis. An analysis of *system* resources and their vulnerabilities to establish expected loss from certain events based on estimated or calculated probabilities of occurrence of those events.

RLC. *Resistance inductance capacitance.*

RMS. Root-mean-square. RMS is defined as the square root of the sum of the squares of the intensities or *amplitudes* of individual components of a function, such as the *frequency components* of a *signal* or of *electromagnetic radiation.* It is the square-root of the sum of the squares of the amplitudes of a set of variables. For example, if a set of three *sinusoidal voltages* occurred simultaneously in a *circuit,* their RMS value would be given by $V_{rms} = (V_a{}^2 + V_b{}^2 + V_c{}^2)^{1/2}$. The RMS value is the effective value for *power* calculations. It represents the total heating value of the individual voltages.

rod. See *optical mixing rod.*

rod coupler. See *fiber-optic rod coupler.*

rod multiplexer-filter. See *fiber-optic rod multiplexer-filter.*

rolling. In *display systems, scrolling* vertically—i.e., in a top-to-bottom, bottom-to-top, upward, or downward direction.

ROM. *Read-only memory.*

roof filter. See *roofing filter.*

roofing filter. A *low-pass filter* that is used to reduce the unwanted higher *frequencies.* Synonymous with *roof filter.*

room noise level. See *ambient noise level.*

root-mean-square. See *RMS.*

rotary dial. In *telephone systems,* a *call signaling* device that, when wound up and released, generates the *pulses* that are required for establishing a *connection* in the system.

rotary switching. In *telephone systems, switching* in which the selecting mechanism consists of a rotating element that utilizes groups of wipers, brushes, and contacts.

rotating. In *graphics* and *display systems,* turning a *display element, display group,* or *display image* about an axis perpendicular to the *display space* on the *display surface* of a *display device.* Contrast with *translating.* Also see *tumbling.*

rotating polarization. *Polarization* of an *electromagnetic wave* (e.g., a *lightwave* or a radio wave) such that the *polarization plane* rotates with an angular displacement or direction that is a function of the distance along the *ray* or *propagation* path.

rotation. See *antenna rotation; optical rotation.*

rotation period. See *antenna rotation period.*

rotator. See *image rotator.*

round trip. In *satellite communications,* the distance from an *originating station* through a *satellite* to a *receiving station* and back via the satellite to the originating station. This distance is used in computing the *round-trip delay time.*

round-trip delay time. In *satellite systems,* the time required for a *signal* to complete a round trip.

route. **1.** In *communication system operations,* the geographical *path* that is followed by a *call* or *message* over the *circuits* that are used in establishing any chain of *connections.* **2.** To determine the *path* that a *message* or *call* is to take in a *communication network.* **3.** To construct the *path* that a *call* or *message* is to take in a *communication network* in going from one *station* to another or from a *source user's end-instrument* to a *destination user's end-instrument.* See *primary route; virtual route.*

route dialing. The setting up of a *trunk call* over an automatically *switched communication network* in which the *source user* (customer, subscriber) or a *switchboard operator* is required to generate a *directory number* for each stage of the *route* to the *destination user.* For example, in route dialing in a *telephone system,* an *operator* would *dial* each *switching exchange* along the *route* as each *connection* is made.

route diversity. See *dispersion.*

route map. See *line-route map.*

route matrix. In a *communication network,* a record of the interconnections between pairs of *nodes* in the *network.* The status of these interconnections is used to produce direct *route,* alternate route, and available route tables from point to point.

routine. A sequence of *computer instructions* that is designed to accomplish a specific purpose or task or that has frequent use. Also see *computer program.* See *computer routine.*

routine meteorological broadcast. A *periodic* meteorological forecast of a general nature that is useful to all *stations* in a special weather *broadcast.* It usually is broadcast on *ship broadcast systems* by many nations. It is also broadcast on fleet and *merchant ship broadcast stations* by certain nations. Also see *emergency meteorological warning; special meteorological broadcast.*

routine precedence. The *precedence designation* that is used for all *messages* that require *transmission* by rapid (electrical) means but are not of sufficient urgency or importance to justify a higher precedence.

routing. The process of determining and prescribing the *path* or method to be used in forwarding *messages.* See *alternative routing; avoidance routing; collective routing; deterministic routing; diverse routing; predetermined routing; saturation routing.*

routing bulletin. See *routing directory.*

routing chart. In *telephone system operations, instructions* on *routing* that are in a diagrammatic or tabular form.

routing diagram. In a *communication system,* a diagram that shows all *connections* between all *switchboards, exchanges, switching centers,* or *stations* in a *system,* such as the connections between *primary relay, major relay, minor relay,* and *tributary stations* and supplementary *links.* The routing diagram is used to identify the stations and links, indicate *tape relay routes, transfer circuits, refile circuits, radio links, operational status, line conditions,* and other *network information* that is required for network *operations.*

routing directory. In *communication system operations,* an *alphabetical* listing of all *switchboards, exchanges, switching centers,* and *stations* in a *system.* It usually also indicates the first, or *primary route* for *communication traffic.* For example, in a *telephone network,* it may list primary route *switchboards* and also the *alternate route* switchboard adjacent to each primary board. Additional *information* may also be appended to the entries, such as *status,* hours of *operation,* or *outages.* Synonymous with *routing bulletin.*

routing indicator. In a *communication network,* a *station designator* or *address designator* that consists of a group of letters that identify a *station* or *addressee* within a *network.* It is used to facilitate the *routing* of *calls* and *messages.* It may also indicate the *status* of a station. The routing indicators are assigned to indicate the geographic location of a station; a fixed office of an organization, headquarters, command, activity, or unit; or the general location of a *tape relay* or *tributary station,* to facilitate the *routing* of *traffic* over the communication network, such as a *tape relay network* or a *telephone network.* See *alternative routing indicator; collective routing indicator; mobile unit routing indicator; special purpose routing indicator.*

routing indicator allocation. The *allocation* of a *block* of *routing indicators* to an organization for distribution among the elements of the organization. For example to allocate a block of 5-letter routing indicators all beginning with the letters AA to the First Field Army.

routing indicator assignment. The *assignment* of a *specific routing indicator,* from the *block* of *allocated routing indicators,* to a specific organizational element of the larger unit to which the block was allocated, or to specific geographical areas. For example, to assign the 5-letter routing indicator AABAA to the Headquarters of the Second Armored Division.

routing indicator delineation map. A map that shows the boundaries of each geographical area that has been assigned a letter for use in preparing *routing indicators* for *messages* for *destination users (addressees)* in those areas.

routing indicator delineation table. A table that shows preallocated worldwide *routing indicators.* They usually consist of from 4 to 7 *charactsrs,* each character designating a specific part of a *routing indicator,* such as a letter for each nation or geographical area, a letter for each *major relay station,* or a letter for *tributary stations.*

routing-line segregation. A method of *routing* in which the basic routing *line* of the *message heading* is altered as the message passes through each *relay station* involved in the *route.* Only those routing indicators that are pertinent to the onward *transmission* are left in the routing line of the standard *message format.* Also see *multiple-call messages.*

RTI. *Radiation transfer index.*

RTTY. *Radio teletype.*

rub. See *crush.*

rubber-banding. In *graphics* and *display systems,* a technique in which the ends of a set of straight *lines* are moved while the other ends remain fixed. For example, if several lines from the corners of the base of a projected *image* of a pyramid converge at the apex and the apex is moved, the ends of the lines will tend to follow the apex.

rub-out character. See *delete character.*

rule. See *Carson bandwidth rule; Fleming's rule; paging rule; Prentice's rule.*

run. 1. In *computers* and *automatic data processing,* a single execution of one or more jobs or a single, continuous execution of a *computer program* or *routine.* 2. In a *communication system,* the *transmission* of a complete *message* or the continuous transmission of a group of messages or *packets.* 3. In *systems* maintenance, a complete sequence of testing *operations.* Also see *rerun.* See *cable run.*

runner-cut. On the surfaces of glass and other ground or polished materials, a curved scratch, such as might be caused by a grinding or polishing wheel.

running fix. A method of determining the location of a *stationary signal source* by means of *direction finding (DF)* by one mobile DF unit from two or more locations at different times. If the *transmitter* that is being located is fixed, that is, is stationary, a running fix may be readily obtained. If it is moving slowly, a running fix may also be obtained to a reasonable *accuracy* if the DF station can move fast enough. If the mobile transmitter being located is fast moving, obtaining a running fix is difficult, since it can reduce to a simple chase. Also see *bearing intersection.*

runway-approach aid.   Any *system,* device, or marking that is used to assist pilots in the landing of aircraft.

RWI.   1. *Radio-wire integration.*   2. *Radio-wire interface.*

RZ coding.   *Return-to-zero coding.*

S

safe. See *fail safe.*

safety message. The *message* that follows the *safety signal.* It is sent at *distress frequencies* at certain times in certain world regions. For example, a few *seconds* before the 18th and 48th minutes after the hour in all *ITU* regions. The safety message contains warnings of hazards, such as ice, bad weather, earthquakes, wrecks, and fires.

safety service. A *radio communication service* that is used permanently or temporarily for the safeguarding of human life and property.

safety signal. A *signal* that is used to indicate that a *radio station* is about to *transmit* a *safety message,* such as a *message* concerning navigational safety, aeronautical safety, or public safety. *Stations* are requested not to make any *transmissions* that might interfere with the safety signal. For example, in *CW transmissions,* the safety signal TTT is sent three times. In voice, the word SECURITE, the French word for security, pronounced say-coor-ee-tay, is pronounced three times.

safety traffic. The totality of *messages* that regard safety, contain *emergency meteorological warnings,* or are deemed to be in the safety category of *emergency messages.* Safety messages usually take precedence over all traffic except *distress messages* and *urgent messages.*

sample. See *reconstructed sample; signal sample.*

sample-change compaction. *Data compaction* that is accomplished by specifying a constant level or easily definable varying level of a value of a *parameter* or variable, and also specifying the deviations in *discrete* or continuous values. For example, it is more compact, requires less *redundancy,* and is more efficient to store or *transmit* a numerical value and its *precision* values (tolerance) than to store or transmit the absolute values that express the limits of variation. Storing or transmitting 9021926+38 is more compact than transmitting 9021926 9021964.

sampling. See *center sampling; signal sampling.*

sampling frequency. See *sampling rate.*

sampling rate. In a *communication system,* the rate at which *signals* in a given *channel* are measured or *sampled* for subsequent *modulation, quantization, coding,* or conversion *(analog-digital).* The sampling rate is usually specified as the number of samples that are taken per unit of time. Synonymous with *sampling frequency.*

sampling signal.   1. The *signal* that is used to determine or measure the *signal level* of a given signal, that is, its instantaneous magnitude, at equally spaced instants of time.   The given signal may be somewhat satisfactorily reconstructed for most purposes from these samples, provided that at least two samples are taken during the period that corresponds to the highest frequency component of the signal being sampled.   2. The *signal* that is obtained from the process of sampling a given signal at equally spaced instants of time.   The reconstituted signal is the *envelope* of the signal that is obtained from the sampling process.   The envelope is obtained by a *detector* that usually consists of an *integrating circuit* with a *time constant* that is properly adjusted to the *sampling rate*.   Also see *sampling theorem*.   See Figure S-1.

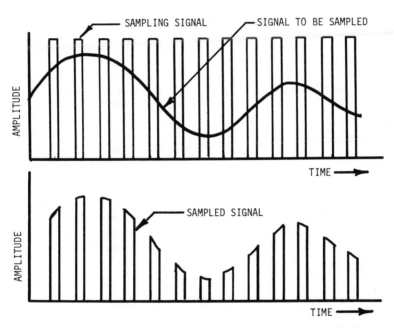

S-1.   If the **sampling signal** and the *signal* to be *sampled* are inserted into an *AND gate*, the *output* will be the *sampled signal*.   The output can be *digitized, transmitted, detected,* or otherwise processed.

sampling theorem.   In order for a waveform to be sampled and then effectively or satisfactorily reconstituted from the sampled *data*, it is necessary that the *sampling rate* be equal to or greater than twice the highest significant *frequency* component of the waveform.   Also see *sampling signal.*

sampling time.   The reciprocal of the *sampling rate*.   It is the time interval between corresponding points on two successive *sampling pulses* of the *sampling signal*.

sanitizing. In *computer, automatic data processing,* and *communication system security*, the degaussing or overwriting of sensitive *information* in *magnetic* or other *storage* media or *data media.* Synonymous with *scrubbing.*

SARAH. *Search-and-rescue-and-homing.*

SARBE. *Search-and-rescue beacon.*

saros. See *cycle of saros.*

satellite. An object or vehicle that is orbiting, or is intended to *orbit*, around the earth, moon, or other celestial body. For example, it may be a natural or artificial (man-made) body, which obeys Kepler's laws, in orbit around another body in space. Care must be taken when considering a body and its satellite, since in reality they are revolving about each other. Normally one considers the larger as the parent body and the smaller as the satellite. An important concept is that they are both revolving about their common center of gravity. For example, seen from the moon, the earth rises and sets once a month, giving the impression that the earth is revolving around the moon as a satellite to the moon, which, of course, it is. See *active communication satellite; communication satellite; earth satellite; geostationary satellite; nongeostationary satellite; passive communication satellite; relay satellite; synchronous earth satellite; synchronous satellite.*

satellite access. In *satellite communication systems,* establishment of contact with a *communication satellite space station.* For example, the moment at which an *earth station* commences to use a satellite space station as a *signal repeater,* that is, to use its *transponder.* Each *radio-frequency (RF) carrier* that is *relayed* by a satellite space station at any time is said to occupy an *access (channel).* Accesses (channels) are distinguished by *frequency, time,* or *code,* the selection depending on the *system configuration.* Also see *multiple access.*

satellite address. The identification *code* of the *communication satellite space station* for which a *message* or *transmission* is intended.

satellite antenna. See *global beam satellite antenna.*

satellite attitude. The angle between a *satellite* axis and a reference line. For example, the angle between an *antenna* axis and a line between the earth's center and the satellite's center.

satellite beacon. A *discrete radio-frequency (RF) signal* that is *radiated* by a *satellite* for *earth station antenna tracking.* It is *modulated* by an identifying *frequency* tone.

satellite channel mode. In *satellite communications,* one of four possible *connections* of *receive* and *transmit antennas,* namely *earth coverage* for both, earth coverage for *transmit* and *narrow beam* for *receive,* narrow beam for transmit and earth coverage for receive, and narrow beam for both.

satellite communication system. A *communication system* in which *messages* are *relayed* from *earth station* to earth station via *communication satellite space stations.* The *electromagnetic propagation path* includes an earth-orbiting *receiver-amplifier-transmitter* unit or a *reflector.* See Figure S-2. Also see Figures E-1 and S-12.

S-2. A ground *receiver* at an *earth station* in a **satellite communication system** for reception of weather pictures, *high-frequency (HF) radio facsimile broadcasts,* and *wireline* weather data. (Courtesy of Alden Electronic and Impulse Recording Equipment Company, Inc.)

satellite earth station. See *communication satellite earth station; meteorological satellite earth station; radionavigation satellite earth station.*

satellite earth terminal. That portion of a *satellite communication link* that is on the earth's surface and *receives, processes,* and *transmits messages* or *signals* between the earth and a *satellite.*

satellite hop-time.   See *transmit time.*

satellite link.   A *communication path* or *data link* that includes a *communication satellite space station* as part of its *signal path.*

satellite optical link.   A *lightwave beamed optical transmission channel,* usually consisting of a *laser source* and an *avalanche photodetector,* operating between the ground and an earth *satellite* or between earth satellites.

satellite point.   See *subsatellite point.*

satellite relay.   In a *communication satellite space station,* an *active* or *passive communication satellite repeater (transponder)* that *relays signals* between two *earth terminals (stations).*   For example, a *satellite orbiting* the earth, moon, or other celestial body with a *radio relay station* aboard.

satellite service.   See *communication satellite service; meteorological satellite service; radionavigation satellite service.*

satellite space station.   See *communication satellite space station; meteorological satellite space station; radionavigation satellite space station.*

satellite-switched time-division multiple-access (SS-TDMA).   In a *satellite communication system, multiple access* that is obtained by the use of *time-division multiplexing* with one or more of the *switching facilities* forming part of a *communication satellite space station.*

sat routing.   See *saturation routing.*

saturation.   In a *communication system,* the condition that exists in a system *component* when it cannot handle additional *communication traffic,* that is, it has reached its maximum *traffic capacity.*   The maximum *traffic intensity* for a given component is 1 *erlang.* When this occurs, the component is saturated.   See *communication system saturation.*

saturation jamming.   See *infrared saturation jamming.*

saturation routing.   In a *switched telephone network,* a *routing procedure* in which a *call* demand is extended forward from each *nodal switching center,* in turn, on a *broadcast* basis, over all the internodal *links* in a part of, or the whole of, a *network.*   The nodal switching center to which the *called party terminal* is connected acknowledges the call by means of a *signal* that is sent over the link on which the demand was first *received.*   This is repeated back progressively to the *calling party* nodal switching center so that the best available route between the centers can be selected for *routing* the call.   The same *procedure* can be used in *tape relay systems.*   Synonymous with *sat routing.*

saturation signaling.   In *communication systems, signaling* in which a *route* through a number of *switching* points to a *destination user* (customer, subscriber) is determined by simultaneously *interrogating* all switching points on a progressive basis through the *network* until the destination user's *end-instrument* is found and a *ringing signal* reaches it.

Savart law. See *Biot-Savart law.*

sawtooth keyboard. A manually-operated *keyboard* in which the energy that is required to move the *code* bars into the *positions* selected by the depression of a *key* is derived from the *operator.*

scalar. A *parameter,* variable, or quantity that possesses only magnitude *(amplitude)* and not direction. For example, speed (in contrast to velocity), mass, volume, or *signal-to-noise ratio.* In contrast, a *vector* possesses magnitude and direction. For example, velocity, *electric field,* displacement, or angular momentum. The magnitude of a vector is a scalar, but not vice versa. The gradient of a scalar, that is, its rate of change with respect to distance in a given direction, is a vector. The cross product of two vectors is another vector. It is also called the vector product. The dot product of two vectors is a scalar. It is also called the scalar product.

scalar feed horn. A corrugated *antenna feed horn* with a *radiation pattern* nearly axially symmetric and independent of *polarization.* Scalar feed horns are used in some shipborne *communication satellite earth stations.*

scale. In *display systems,* to enlarge or reduce the size of all or part of a *display element, display group,* or *display image* by multiplying the coordinates of the element, group, or image parts by a constant value that is greater than unity for enlargement and less than unity for reduction. Also see *enlargement; reduction.* See *coordinated time scale; gray scale; Kelvin temperature scale; time scale.*

scan. 1. The *path* that is followed by a moving *beam.* For example, the path that is periodically followed by an *electromagnetic wave* exploring *outer space,* an *electron beam* that is writing on a *cathode-ray tube screen,* or a single sweep of a *directional rotating antenna,* such as in a *searchlighting radar.* 2. In *electromagnetic* or *acoustic* search, one complete rotation of the *antenna.* The rotation establishes the time base for the scan. 3. To sweep (rotate) a *beam* about a point or about an axis or to pass over recorded data with a *reading head* or *light spot* as in a *facsimile transmitter.* See *circular scan; directed scan; flying-spot scan; radar scan; raster scan; sector scan.*

scan airborne intercept radar. See *track-while-scan airborne intercept radar.*

scanner. 1. A device that performs a *scanning operation.* 2. In *facsimile systems,* the part of the *transmitter* that systematically *translates* the densities of the *scanned* object (subject document) into a *signal* for *transmission.* 3. A device that examines a spatial pattern, one part after another, and generates *analog* or *digital signals* that correspond to the pattern. Scanners are often used in *mark sensing, pattern recognition,* or *character recognition* devices. 4. In *radar,* a ro-

tating directional antenna that *emits* a *beam* to search for possible objects (targets) in *space*. See *flying-spot scanner; optical scanner.*

scanning. 1. In *communication systems,* the process of determining, analyzing, or synthesizing the *light-intensity* values or equivalent *attributes* of parts of an *object, display image, picture element,* or graphic *character,* usually for purposes of *modulating* a *carrier* for *transmission.* In *television, facsimile,* or *picture transmission,* it is the process of analyzing or synthesizing successively, according to a predetermined method, the *light intensity* values or equivalent characteristics of the *elements* that constitute a *picture.* 2. In *radar,* the process of directing a *beam* of *radio frequency* energy successively over the elements of a given region, or the corresponding process in *reception.* Scanning involves the process of converting an *object* (scene, target) into *picture elements* that are then represented in succession by an *electrical signal.* It also involves the process of resolving the *image* from the *received signal.* See *conical scanning; dynamic scanning; electronic line scanning; frequency scanning; limited scanning; mark scanning; multiple-spot scanning; simple scanning.* Also see Figure S-12.

scanning density. In *facsimile systems,* the *line* advance in *scanning lines* per unit length, that is, the number of *scanning pitches* per unit length. It is the reciprocal of the scanning pitch.

scanning direction. In a *facsimile transmitter,* the direction obtained when *scanning* in the plane (developed in the case of a *drum transmitter*) of the *message* surface (subject document) along *lines* that run from right to left commencing at the top so that scanning commences at the top right-hand corner of the surface and finishes at the bottom left-hand corner of the surface. This is equivalent to scanning over a right-hand helix on a drum. The orientation of the *message* on the scanning plane is of no consequence. At the *receiver,* scanning takes place from right to left and top to bottom (in the above sense) for positive reception and from left to right and top to bottom (in the above sense) for negative reception. This is standard practice for *phototelegraphic transmission.*

scanning electron microscope (SEM). An *electron* microscope whose electron *beam* can scan an *object* field in a regular or controlled pattern. The SEM can be used to expose resist material in high-resolution *scanning* patterns in the fabrication of *integrated optical circuit* components.

scanning field. In *facsimile systems,* the total of the areas that are actually explored by the *scanning spot* during the *transmission* of a document or *message,* either at the *transmitter* or at the *receiver.*

scanning line. In *facsimile systems,* the area that is explored by the *scanning spot* in one *sweep* from one side of the *scanning field* to the other, either by a *transmitter* or by a *receiver.*

scanning line frequency.   See *scanning line rate.*

scanning line rate.   The number of *lines* that may be *scanned* per unit time for *reading* or *recording.*   For example, in *facsimile systems,* the number of times per minute that a fixed *line,* perpendicular to the direction of scanning, is crossed in one direction by a *scanning spot.*   In most conventional mechanical systems, this is equivalent to the *drum speed* in revolutions per unit of time.   In systems in which the *picture signal* is used while scanning in both directions, the scanning line rate is twice the above figure.   Synonymous with *scanning line frequency.*

scanning line length.   In *facsimile systems,* the length of a *scanning line.*   It is equal to the *spot speed* divided by the *scanning line rate.*   This is usually greater than the *available line length.*   See *total scanning line length.*

scanning line period.   In *facsimile systems,* the time interval between the *scanning* instants of two corresponding points in two consecutive *scanning lines* during *transmission* or *reception.*

scanning line usable length.   In *facsimile systems,* the maximum length of the *scanning line* that can be achieved with a particular set of *facsimile equipment.*

scanning period.   1. In *facsimile systems,* the time interval between two corresponding points on consecutive *scanning lines.*   It is the reciprocal of the *scanning line rate.*   2. In *radar,* the time taken by a *radar scanner* to complete a scan pattern and return to the starting point, or the time from any arbitrary point in the scanning pattern back to that same point.   Synonymous with *scan period.*

scanning pitch.   In *facsimile systems,* the distance between the corresponding edges of two *scanning lines.*   It is the reciprocal of the *scanning density.*

scanning rate.   See *scan rate.*

scanning shift.   See *negative scanning shift; positive scanning shift.*

scanning speed.   In *facsimile transmission systems,* the linear speed of the *scanning spot* in its movement over the *object* or document or over the *record medium.*

scanning spot.   1. In *facsimile transmission systems,* the portion of the area of the *object* or subject document to be *transmitted* that is *illuminated* at a given instant by the *reading head* when *scanning* the object or document.   2. In *facsimile reception systems,* the smallest area of the *record medium illuminated* by the *light source* to insure the synthesis of the *image* that was *transmitted.*   In the case of *phototelegraphy,* the scanning spot is the part of the *light-sensitive* area that is exposed at a given instant.   It is the part of the record medium that is in contact or subject to the influence of the scanning device. In *facsimile transmitters*, it is the area on the subject document that is viewed at any instant by the pickup system of the *scanner* of the *transmitter*.

scanning spot x-dimension. In *facsimile systems*, the effective *scanning spot* dimension measured in the direction of the *scanning line* on the *object* (subject document) that is being *transmitted*. The numerical value of the scanning spot x-dimension depends upon the type of system that is used.

scanning spot y-dimension. In *facsimile systems*, the effective *scanning spot* dimension measured perpendicular to the direction of the *scanning line* on the *object* (subject document) that is being *transmitted*. The numerical value of the scanning spot y-dimension depends upon the type of system that is used.

scan period. See *scanning period.*

scan rate. 1. The rate of *scanning* an *object* or *image*, usually expressed as distance per unit time, *characters* per unit time, *lines* or *display positions* per unit time, or area scanned per unit time. 2. In *facsimile systems*, the rate of linear *displacement* of the *scanning spot*. 3. In *radar systems*, the angular velocity of a *rotating antenna*, usually expressed in revolutions per minute. Synonymous with *scanning rate.*

scan rate modulation deception. See *radar scan rate modulation deception.*

scatter. The process in which the direction, *frequency*, or *polarization* of *sound* or *electromagnetic waves* is changed when the waves encounter one or more discontinuities in the *transmission medium* that have lengths of the order of a *wavelength*. Scattering usually implies a random or disordered change or distribution in the *incident* energy. See *backscatter; backward propagation ionospheric scatter; forward propagation ionospheric scatter; forward scatter; ionospheric scatter; tropospheric scatter.*

scattered seeds. *Seeds* that are usually spaced 5 or 10 cm, although occasionally they are spaced more closely or further apart. Scattered seeds are usually highly visible and coarse.

scattering. 1. The *deflection* of *electromagnetic waves* caused by synchronous movement of free and bound charges (e.g., *electrons*, protons, and *ions*) in a *transmission medium*, the scattered fields being created as a result of the movement. The scattered field and the *incident* field define the total field. 2. The *electromagnetic waves* consisting of *electromagnetic fields* that are set up by the synchronous movement of charges of molecular structural elements moving under the influence of the *incident radiation*. See *back scattering; Brillouin scattering; bulk material scattering; fiber scattering; radiation scattering; Rayleigh scattering.* See Figure S-3.

S-3. A *single optical fiber* showing *light* **scattering** through glass *cladding.* (Copyright 1979, Corning Glass Works. Reprinted by permission from Corning Glass Works, Telecommunication Products Department.)

scattering center. A site in the microstructure of a *transmission medium* at which *lightwaves* are *scattered;* e.g., a *vacancy defect,* an *interstitial defect,* an *inclusion* (such as a gas molecule, hydroxide *ion,* iron ion, or a trapped water molecule), or a *microcrack* or fracture. Scattering centers are frozen in the medium when it solidifies and may not necessarily cause *Rayleigh scattering,* which varies inversely as the fourth power of the *wavelength.* For example, there is a high *attenuation* band at 0.95 *micron* in glass due primarily to scattering and *absorption* by OH (hydroxide) ions. Iron selectively scatters green, giving rise to the green hue of certain soda pop bottles.

scattering coefficient In the *transmission* of *electromagnetic waves,* the part of the constant coefficient due to *scattering* in the exponent of the expression that describes *Bouger's law.* Absorption also contributes to the total coefficient. It is dependent upon the materials, such as impurities and intrinsic material, in which the waves are *propagating.*

scattering cross-section. The area on an *incident wavefront,* at a *reflecting* surface or *medium,* such as an *object* in space, through which will pass an amount of *power,* that, if *isotropically scattered* from that point, would produce the same power at a given *receiver* as is actually provided by the entire reflecting surface. Thus, when an electromagnetic wave is reflected from an object in space, and a portion of the reflected power reaches a receiving antenna, it is a simple matter to calculate the power of a hypothetical isotropic transmitter located at the object in space to produce the same power at the receiving antenna. Since the power per unit area of the original incident signal is known, it is again a simple matter to calculate the cross-sectional area at the object's location through which the same amount of power passes. This area is the scattering cross-section. Synonymous with *echo area*.

scattering loss. *Power loss* by an *electromagnetic wave* due to random *reflections* and *deflections* of the waves caused by the material elements in the *transmission medium* in which the waves are *propagating* as well as by impurities, imbedded particles and *inclusions*.

scatter propagation. In *electromagnetic wave propagation*, the propagation achieved by means of *scattering*, both *forward* and *backward*, caused by irregularities or discontinuities in the *ionization densities* of the *ionosphere* and the physical properties of the *troposphere*. Most of the irregularities and discontinuities are caused by turbulence.

scene-of-action communications. *Communication* methods, *systems,* or equipment used for *transmission* of *messages* to, from, or at a specific location for the purpose of reporting special events, controlling operations, or describing activities at the location, such as an air-sea rescue operation, an insurrection, a disaster area, or a sporting event.

scene-of-air-sea-rescue frequency. A *frequency* for *communication* between aircraft, surface vessels, and submarines in action at the scene of an air-sea rescue operation.

schedule. See *ship broadcast schedule; ship-to-shore schedule.*

scheduled time. The time period that a specified *functional unit* is intended to perform the function for which it was designed.

scientific-medical RF equipment. See *industrial-scientific-medical RF equipment.*

scintillation. 1. In *electromagnetic wave propagation*, a *random* fluctuation of a *received signal* about its mean value, the deviations usually being small compared to the *signal* magnitude. The effects of this phenomenon become more significant as the signal *frequency* increases. 2. In *radar systems,* the instability that occurs to a *displayed radar echo.* The instability may be due to many causes, such as variations in *propagation* conditions in the *transmission medium, phase* changes brought about by *chaff* elements, vibration of *tracked objects* (targets), and rapid fluctuations in the *amplitude* of the *received signal.* 3. In *satellite communication systems,* the rapid fluctuations of a *received signal amplitude* usually caused by *ionospheric turbulence.* These fluctuations occur at typical *communication satellite* frequencies of 4 GHz and 6 GHz. They are presumed to be due to very dense and thick irregular *layers* in the *F-layer,* although there is no *ionospheric absorption* in this part of the *frequency spectrum.* They usually exist only in the early part of the evening. The *scattering* irregularities *distort* the *phase* of the *wavefront* as the front moves along the *propagation path.* The *signal* received by the *satellite earth station* fluctuates with time. The fluctuations are greatest near the equator, but significant between 30°N and 30°S latitude. They show a very strong *diurnal* peak about one hour after local sunset and seasonal peaks near the *vernal* and *autumnal equinoxes.* The *amplitude* of the fluctuations are generally less than 4 dB with periods of 4 to 6 seconds between two successive *fades.*

scissoring.   1. In *display systems,* removing parts of *display elements, display groups,* or *display images,* in the *display space* on the *display surface* of a *display device* that lie outside a *window.*   **2.** In *display systems,* removing *display elements* from *display groups* or *display images,* or removing display elements or display groups from display images, that lie outside a *window.* Synonymous with *clipping.*

SCOI. *Standing communication operating instruction.*

scope. A device that *displays images* on a *screen* or on the retina of a person's eye, such as an *endoscope, fiberscope, oscilloscope, microscope, sniperscope,* or *telescope.* For example, in *radar systems,* the scope is usually a *cathode ray tube* or *gas panel* that *displays* the results of radar measurements. The word scope is usually an abbreviation. See *fiberscope.*

scramble.   1. In *telephony,* to make *plain text* or speech unintelligible to casual interpretation.   **2.** In *cryptography,* to mix *characters* in a *random* or *pseudo-random* fashion so as to render the text unintelligible until it is restored by a reverse process.

scrambler. A device that transposes, inverts, or substitutes *signals,* or otherwise *encodes* a *message* at the *transmitter* so as to make it unintelligible at a *receiver* that is not equipped with an appropriately set descrambling device. The scrambler produces an *output signal* sequence that is based on an *input* sequence and a transformation *algorithm* in such a manner that the output is unintelligible to those who do not have the knowledge concerning the nature of the algorithm. See *fiber-optic scrambler; speech scrambler.*

scrambling. In *communication security,* the process of altering, inverting, displacing, and substituting *signals,* such as *line, radio, video,* or *lightwave signals,* in order to make them unintelligible until they are unscrambled by properly set complementary *circuits.*

scratch. In *optics,* a marking or tearing of the surface that looks as though it had been caused by either a sharp or rough instrument. See *block reek; crush; runner-cut; sleek.*

screen. See *radar screen.*

screen coordinate. In *display systems,* a *device coordinate* consisting of the arbitrary coordinates placed on the *display surface* of a *display device.* For example, the coordinates placed on a grid ruled on a plastic material and placed on a *CRT* screen, on the *faceplate* of a *fiberscope,* or on an *LED* or *gas panel* screen.

screening range equation.   See *self-screening range equation.*

scrolling.   In *display systems,* the vertical (top-to-bottom) or horizontal (side-to-side) movement of all or part of a *display image* contained within a *window* or otherwise displayed in the *display space* on the *display surface* of a *display device* in such a manner that as new *data* appear at one edge of the window or display space, old data disappear at the opposite edge.

scrubbing.   See *sanitizing.*

SDM.   *Space division multiplex.*

SDMA.   *Space-division multiple access.*

search.   See *electronic search.*

search-and-lock jammer.   A *jammer* with a *transmitter* that is automatically controlled by a *receiver-transmitter tuning* device, which, when a *transmission* is *detected,* automatically tunes (locks) to that frequency and turns on the transmitter. After a certain period of time, it unlocks, ceases *jamming,* and recommences a search for a *frequency* to *jam.*

search-and-rescue beacon.   **1.** A *beacon* that is used by survivors of a distress situation to guide search and rescue units to the distress scene. **2.** A *beacon* that is used by search and rescue units as an aid in the conduct of search-and-rescue operations.

search-and-rescue beacon frequency.   A *frequency* used by *search-and-rescue beacons (SARBE).*   One frequency used for SARBE and for search-and-rescue-and homing (SARAH) systems is 243.5 MHz.

search-and-rescue communications.   *Communication* methods, *systems,* and equipment used for *transmission* of *messages* containing *information* about search-and-rescue *operations,* to or from search and rescue units or survivors. The messages are primarily used for the purpose of directing or coordinating search and rescue operations or used for the support of search-and-rescue operations.

search-and-rescue frequency.   A *radio frequency* that is specially designated for use by *mobile stations* during search-and-rescue operations. For example, 3023.5 kHz and 5680 kHz for *aeronautical mobile stations,* 8364 kHz for *survival craft,* 123.1 MHz for non-VHF equipped *stations.*

search jammer.   See *automatic search jammer.*

searchlighting.   In *radar systems,* a method of orienting a *radar beam* such that the beam is centered on the object (target) being tracked in order to provide greater concentrated power for increased *burn-through range.* This method will also provide a greater *data* rate from the object.

searchlight sonar. *Sonar* that develops a *sound wave (beam)* that resembles the beam produced by a *parabolic reflector* of a searchlight or torch. Synonymous with *single-pulse CW sonar.*

search radar. *Radar* that is specially designed to identify the existence of an object (target) rather than accurately determine its range or velocity.

search receiver. A *receiver* that can be tuned over a relatively wide *frequency band* in order to *detect*, identify, or measure *electromagnetic signals.*

sea rescue frequency. See *scene-of-air-sea-rescue frequency.*

sea return. In *radar system operations,* a *wave* or *echo* that is obtained by *reflection* from the sea.

sea surveillance system. A *system* for collecting, reporting, correlating, and presenting *information* that supports and is derived from the task of sea surveillance. Sea surveillance is performed primarily by *monitoring radio, video,* and other types of *transmission.*

second. A unit of time. One mean solar second is 1/31 556 925.9747 of the tropical year for 1900 January 0 at 1200 hours. The sidereal second is 1/86 400 of a sidereal day. The January 0 comes from the fact that the Julian day begins at noon, normally called 1200 hours, when the sun is at zenith. January 1 would imply the Gregorian calendar. December 31 would be the wrong day. In the International System of Units *(SI),* the time interval for one second is equal to 9 192 631 770 periods of the *radiation* that corresponds to the *transition* between the two hyperfine levels of the ground state of an atom of cesium 133. Synonymous with *cesium clock second.* See *bits per second; call-second; leap second; lumen-second.*

secondary. The part of a *data station* that executes *data link control functions* as required by the *primary.* In *high-level data link control (HDLC) procedures,* a secondary usually interprets received commands and generates responses for transmission.

secondary aeronautical station. A *land station, ship station,* or *mobile station,* other than a *net control, guard,* or *standby station,* in an *aeronautical mobile service net,* that provides a *communication service* with *aircraft stations.*

secondary axis. In movable *antenna systems,* the axis that has the *primary axis,* rather than the ground, as a datum.

secondary channel. A *data transmission channel* that has a lower *signaling rate* capability than the *primary channel* in a *system* in which two channels share a common *interface.* Also see *primary channel; auxiliary channel.*

secondary control point. In *high-level data link control (HDLC) procedures,* a point in a *data network* at which a *secondary* is located.

secondary frequency.   1. In a *radiotelephone network,* a *frequency* that is assigned to an *aircraft station* as a second choice for *air-ground communication.* 2. A *frequency* that is assigned for use on a particular *radio communication circuit* when the *primary frequency* becomes unusable.

secondary group.   See *supergroup.*

secondary radar.   *Radar* that uses active *signals* that are *transmitted* by an object and that does not rely on *reflection* of its own signals.   Also see *primary radar.*

secondary radiation source.   A source that *emits,* or appears to emit, *electromagnetic waves* but does not generate them.   For example, an *image* of a primary *source* in a *mirror,* an *illuminated parabolic reflector,* an illuminated *radar* target, or the moon.

secondary ship-shore station.   A shore-based *ship-shore station* that uses and *guards frequencies* other than those frequencies that are guarded by *primary stations* and that are designed to provide *communication* with *ship stations.*   Also see *local ship-shore station; primary ship-shore station.*

secondary spectrum.   The residual *chromatic aberration,* particularly the longitudinal chromatic aberration of an *achromatic lens.*   Unlike the *primary spectrum,* it causes the *image* formed in one particular *color* to lie nearest the *lens,* the images in all other *colors* being formed behind the first at distances that increase sharply toward both ends of the useful *wavelength* spectrum.   Also see *primary spectrum.*

secondary station.   1. In a *data communication network,* the *station* that is responsible for performing *unbalanced link-level operations,* as instructed by the *primary station.*   In *high-level data link control (HDLC) operations,* a secondary station interprets received *commands* and generates *responses.*   2. In an *aeronautical air-ground communication system,* a *station* that is destined or planned to serve as the next *guard station* during a particular flight of an *aircraft station.* For a particular flight, all stations other than the *primary guard station* and the secondary station are considered as *standby stations.*   Synonymous with *enroute guard station.*

secondary status.   In *high-level data link control (HDLC) operations,* the current condition of a *secondary station* with respect to processing the series of *commands* that are received from the *primary station.*

SECORD.   *Secure voice cord board.*

sector.   See *dead sector.*

sectorial harmonic function.   A *spherical harmonic function* in which the sign is consistent along lines of constant longitude but the magnitudes change with latitude.

sector scan.   A *scan* by a moving *antenna* in which the antenna oscillates through a specific angle.

sector sweep. To *scan* a specific solid angle vertically or horizontally with a *transmitting* or *receiving antenna.* For example, to conduct a *radar* or *direction-finding (DF)* search in a small angle only, so as to prevent *interference,* conserve *power,* and save time.

secure. Pertaining to the prevention of unauthorized use, *access, operation,* or interpretation. For example, a secure *message* cannot be interpreted or understood by unauthorized persons. Secured gear or equipment has been fastened, stored, or turned off to prevent access, use, damage, or alteration by unauthorized persons or natural forces. A secure *call sign* cannot be linked by unauthorized persons to the *plain language address designator.* The *information* that is *transmitted* in a secure *circuit* or *network* cannot be obtained by unauthorized persons. A *channel,* circuit, or net is secured by the provision of *online crypto-equipment* for *telegraph, data, facsimile,* or *voice operation* as appropriate. A circuit can be secured by closing it down. An area can be secured by closing and locking all doors and hatches leading to it.

secure communications. *Communications* that, by the use of *cryptographic* devices or physical protection, are protected from unauthorized *interception, traffic analysis,* or imitative *deception.*

secure line. In *optical* or wire *transmission systems,* a *line* carrying intelligence-bearing *signals,* that is *coded* in such a manner that the signals cannot be interpreted except by persons having knowledge of the code, and that is protected from unauthorized physical access and from damage by environmental factors. Also see *protected line.*

secure traffic. **1.** *Communication traffic* following or including an *encryption* process. **2.** *Communication traffic* that is handled by *secure communication systems.*

secure transmission. **1.** *Transmission* of *data* that can only be interpreted by the *addressee.* **2.** In *spread-spectrum systems,* the *transmission* of *binary coded* sequences that represent *information* that can only be recovered by persons or *systems* that have the proper *key* for the *spread-spectrum code-sequence generator,* that is, have a *synchronized* generator that is identical to that used for *transmission.*

secure voice. See *encrypted voice.*

secure voice communication system. See *AUTOSEVOCOM system.*

security. In *communications,* the condition that results when measures are taken that protect *information,* personnel, *systems, components,* and equipment from unauthorized persons, acts, or influences. See *add-on security; administrative security; communication security; data security; electronic emission security; electronic security (ELSEC); emanation security (EMSEC); environmental security; information security; long-term security; personnel security; physical security; ship radio transmission security; short-term security; signal security; tele-*

phone circuit security; teleprocessing security; traffic flow security; transmission security.

secure voice cord board (SECORD).   A desk-mounted *patch panel* that provides the capability for connecting a group of *lines* and *trunks,* such as 16 *wideband* (50 kb/s) or *narrowband* (2400 b/s) *user* (customer, subscriber) lines and five narrowband trunks, to *AUTOVON* or other narrowband facilities.

security audit.   In *computing, automatic data processing,* and *communication systems,* an audit that is designed to examine *data security procedures* for the purpose of evaluating their adequacy and compliance with established policy. See *external security audit; internal security audit.*

security classified.   Pertaining to *information* that must be handled according to specific rules in order to prevent *compromise* (unauthorized disclosure). For example, pertaining to confidential, secret, or top-secret information.

security custodian.   In *communication security,* the person who is responsible for the custody, accounting, handling, safeguarding, and required destruction of *communication security material* that is received from an issuing authority and is required to be kept on hand for use.

security equipment.   See *communication security equipment.*

security filter.   In *communication systems,* the *hardware, firmware,* or *software* used to prevent access to specified *data* by unauthorized persons or systems, such as by preventing *transmission,* preventing forwarding messages over unprotected lines or circuits, or requiring special codes for access to read-only files.

security information.   See *communication security information.*

security kernel.   In *computer* and *communication security,* the central part of a *computer* or *communication system software* or *hardware* that implements the basic security *procedures* for controlling *access* to *system* resources.

security material.   See *communication security material.*

security optical fiber.   See *optical-fiber trap.*

security policy.   See *communication security policy.*

security profile.   See *communication security profile.*

seed.   A gaseous *inclusion,* having an extremely small diameter, in glass or other *transparent medium.* See *scattered seed.*

seeding.   See *heavy seeding.*

seepage.   In *computer* and *communication security,* the gradual, piecemeal flow of *data,* presumed to be controlled by *security* measures, to unauthorized persons.

segment. In *interactive display systems,* a basic sequence of *display commands* or *instructions* in a *display file* that (1) enables the *transmission* and *display* of *display elements, display groups,* or *display images* in the *display space* on the *display surface* of a *display device,* and (2) enables their manipulation through the performance of *operations* upon the elements, groups, or images. See *ground segment; space segment.*

segmented encoding. *Encoding* in which an approximation to a smooth wave is obtained by a number of linear segments. Synonymous with *piece-wise linear encoding.* Also see *encoding law.*

segregation. See *routing-line segregation.*

seized condition. See *trunk-seized condition.*

seizure. See *line seizure.*

seizure signal. In *communication systems,* a *signal* that is used by the calling end of a *trunk* or *line* to indicate a *service* or *access request.* Seizure may occur in *telephone, facsimile, telegraph, tape-relay,* and other systems.

select. See *fast select.*

selecting. In a *communication system,* the process of requesting one or more *data stations* to *receive data.* Usually the stations are connected by a *multipoint connection* or are in a *net.*

selection. 1. In *telegraph receiver operation,* the primary *operation* of *telegraph translation* in which the *control character* or the *data character* to be printed is chosen manually or automatically by the interpretation of the *received signal.* For example, the use of a received set of *binary digits* to select a letter from an *alphabet;* or a person *(operator)* selecting a letter from an alphabet or a word from a vocabulary upon hearing a *Morse code* sequence. 2. The choosing of a *line* or *circuit,* or set of lines or circuits, the choice being based on the satisfaction of certain conditions or criteria. See *packet length selection.*

selection character. See *end-of-selection (EOS) character.*

selection position. See *decision instant.*

selection signal. A *signal,* usually consisting of the *electrical* representation of a set of *characters,* that indicates (represents) all the *information* needed to establish a *call.* The selection signal often consists of the *facility* request, the *address,* or both. The facility request usually precedes the address. There may be several facility requests and several addresses in a selection signal.

selection signal code. See *network multiple selection signal code.*

selection time. See *call selection time; post-selection time.*

selective absorption. The act or process by which a substance *absorbs* all the *frequencies* or *colors* contained in a *beam* of *electromagnetic radiation* such as *white light,* except those that it reflects or *transmits.* Some substances are *transparent* to *waves* of certain frequencies, allowing them to be transmitted, while absorbing waves of other frequencies. Some *reflecting* surfaces will absorb light of certain frequencies and reflect others. The color of a *transparent object* is the color it *transmits,* and the color of an *opaque object* is the color it *reflects.* Also see *selective transmission.*

selective cavity. A *radio frequency (RF) resonant cavity* that *filters* all but a *narrowband* of *frequencies.* Usually the length of the cavity is adjustable to obtain maximum selectivity for a specific frequency. The minimum length is 1/4 *wavelength* of the operating frequency.

selective combiner. A *circuit* or device that is used for selecting one of two or more *diversity signals,* in which only the signal that has the most desirable characteristics is selected and used. The selection process may be designed to operate on *signal amplitude, signal-to-noise ratio, transition* characteristics, or other signal characteristics. Also see *diversity combiner; maximal-ratio combiner.*

selective fading. *Fading* of a *transmitted signal* such that the various *frequency components* of the transmitted signal fluctuate or diminish independently of each other, such as by *selective absorptance, transmission,* or *transmittance.*

selective transmission. The act or process by which a substance *conducts* or *transmits* all the *colors* or *frequencies* in a *beam* of *light,* except those that it *reflects* or *absorbs.* Some substances transmit only certain colors and absorb or reflect all others. The color of a *tranparent object* is the color it transmits. The color of an *opaque object* is the color it reflects. Absorbed colors are not seen. Also see *selective absorption.*

selective transmittance. The property of variation of *transmittance* with the *wavelength* of *light transmitted* through a substance.

selective waveguide. See *frequency-selective waveguide.*

selectivity. In *communication systems,* the characteristic of a *receiver* that determines its ability to *discriminate* between a specific desired *signal* of a given *frequency* and many other coexistent undesired signals at other frequencies at a given location. See *adjacent channel selectivity; high selectivity.*

selector. In an *automatic telephone exchange,* a device that establishes a request for one or more *data stations* to *receive data.* See *group selector.*

selector pen. See *light pen.*

self-authentication. A *procedure* in which a *transmitting (calling) station* establishes its own validity without the participation of the *receiving (called) station.* The calling station establishes its own authenticity and the called station is not required to challenge the calling station. Self-authentication is usually used only when one-time (check-off) *authentication systems* are used to derive the authentication.

self-checking code. See *error-detecting code.*

self-demarcating code. A *code* in which the *symbols* are so selected and arranged that the occurrence of false combinations by interaction of segments
from two successive *code groups* is prevented. Thus, *data delimiters,* that is,
separators between code groups are not needed, though *redundancy* is increased.

self-evident code. A *code,* such as a *brevity code* or a *mnemonic code,* in which
the entries in the table of correspondences for *encoding* and *decoding* are fairly
obvious in a particular *language.*

SEL fiber. An *optical fiber* produced by Standard Electric Lorenz.

self-focusing optical fiber. An *optical fiber* that is capable of *focusing* its *wave
propagation* and *output* by precision-control of geometry, *refractive indices, light
wavelength,* and other *parameters.* The fiber is *frequency-selective.*

SELFOC fiber. *Self-focusing optical fiber* produced by Nippon Electric Company and Nihon Sheet Glass Company.

self-protection jamming. *Jamming* in which the equipment with a jamming capability is carried in the vehicle, aircraft, or ship that is being protected against
jamming *signals.* Also see *support jamming.*

self-repairing circuit. A *circuit* that can ameliorate the effects of a *failure* in itself, by itself, that is, without intervention by a person or another piece of
equipment. For example, self-repairing by automatic reconfiguration or connection to an installed spare part.

self-screening range equation. An equation that combines the *two-way radar
equation* and the *one-way radio equation* to obtain an expression for the maximum *detection* range at which a *reflected signal (echo)* that is present at a *radar
receiving antenna* can be *masked* by a signal that is *transmitted* from a remote location. Synonymous with *burn-through range equation.* Also see *burn-through
range; one-way radio equation; two-way radar equation.*

self-testing circuit. A *circuit* that can use the *data* it is *transmitting* to perform
tests on itself to insure that it is transmitting properly, that is, that all circuit
components are functioning properly.

SEM. *Scanning electron microscope.*

semanteme. An element of *language* that expresses a definite *image* or idea,
such as a *word* or a part of a word. For example, a *data element, data item,* or
code to which meaning has been assigned. Difficulties occur in *communication*
due to ambiguities among semantemes. If English were a ruly language, there
would be one and only one meaning for each semanteme. The story is told of a
misunderstanding in World War II in the Pacific. A supply depot commander reported that the ammunition he had received was *faulty.* He was instructed to
refuse the entire lot, so he sent it back to the mainland with great loss of life and

property. The original instruction meant that he should change the fuze assemblies. In those days refuse meaning to reject and refuse meaning to replace the fuses was the same word. Thus, the new spellings fuze and refuze were introduced. Also see *morpheme*.

semantics. The relationships between *characters* or groups of characters and their meanings, independent of the manner of their interpretation and use.

semaphore signaling. *Visual signaling* in which the positions of the hands each holding a *flag* are used to represent the letters of the *alphabet, numerals,* punctuation, and certain *procedure words* and *prosigns* that are used for the *transmission* of *messages*. Also see *Morse flag signaling; wigwag signaling*.

semiactive homing. A missile-to-target *guidance system* in which the missile tracks *radiation* that is *reflected* from the target but is originated by the missile-tracking ground or airborne *radar*. Also see *active homing; passive homing*.

semiautomatic continuous-tape relay switching. *Message switching* in which incoming *messages* at a *station* are *received* on continuous printed or perforated tape and given onward electrical *transmission* according to *routing* requirements or instructions *(routing indicators)* through a *pushbutton panel connection* of a *transmitter-distributor* into the appropriate *output channels*. Also see *semiautomatic relay system; torn-tape relay*.

semiautomatic relay system. A *tape relay communication system* in which *operator* intervention is required at a *tape relay station* to physically handle the *message* tapes without r*ekeying* any of the messages, in order to *route* them to other stations according to established *routing procedure* or according to the *routing indicators* in the messages. Also see *automatic relay system; semiautomatic continuous-tape relay switching; torn-tape relay*.

semiconductor. A material—such as diamond, silicon, germanium, gray tin, tellurium, and selenium—that has a filled *valence*-electron *energy band* separated by a finite *band-gap energy* from a higher-energy *conduction band*. Thus, semiconductors are neither *insulators,* with large band gaps and small electronic mobilities, nor metallic *conductors* with extremely high *conductivities*. Semiconductors possess covalent bonding wherein *electron* pairs are held tightly in the region between adjacent atoms or ions. The band-gap energy is the energy required to break an electron out of one of these bonds. Semiconductors are often grown in single crystals and sliced or cut, to form *diodes* or *transistors,* thus preserving an ordered crystal lattice structure suitable for accepting positive or negative *dopants*.

semiconductor laser. A *laser* in which *lasing* ocurs at the *junction* of N-type and P-type *semiconductor* materials. Synonymous with *diode laser; injection laser*.

semiduplex. Pertaining to the *operation* of a *communication circuit* in which one end is *duplex* and the other end is *simplex*. *Semiduplex operation* is sometimes used with *mobile stations*. The *base station* is operated as a duplex system and the mobile station as a simplex system.

semielectronic switch.   A *switch* that is composed of *electromechanical relays* and electronic *control circuits.* Also see *electronic switching system.*

semiotics.   The branch of science and technology that is devoted to the use of *symbols.* Semiotics is often subdivided into *syntax, semantics,* and *pragmatics.*

sending-end crossfire.   In *wire communication systems,* such as *teletype* and *facsimile systems,* the interfering *electrical current* in a *channel* that is caused when one or more *adjacent channels transmits* from the same end at which the *interference* is measured.

send-receive teletypewriter.   See *automatic send-receive teletypewriter; keyboard send-receive teletypewriter.*

send signal.   See *clear-to-send signal; request-to-send signal.*

send terminal.   See *multiplex baseband send terminal; radio baseband send terminal.*

senior ship radio officer.   The officer who is responsible for all matters pertaining to *communications* aboard a ship, including reporting to communication authorities before sailing.   Responsibilities include establishing *radio watch,* securing radio equipment, insuring that communication equipment is in operating condition, informing the ship's master concerning *broadcast schedules,* establishing *radio guard,* maintaining the *radio log,* arranging for *emergency communications,* and insuring radio operational discipline.

sense.   See *heading sense.*

sensing.   See *mark sensing.*

sensitive detector-demodulator.   See *phase-sensitive detector-demodulator.*

sensitive information.   In *computer* and *communication security, information* that requires a degree of protection and that should not be made available to anyone except authorized persons.   For example, *private* (personal) *information,* proprietary information, and defense *security information.*

sensitivity.   1. In a *radio receiver* or similar device, the minimum *input signal level* that is required to produce a specified *output* signal level that has a specified *signal-to-noise ratio.*   The input signal level may be expressed in *power* units, such as watts or dBm, or as *field strength,* such as *microvolts* per *meter,* or other *compatible* units. If voltage or current levels are specified, the input *impedance* must also be specified. 2. The extent of a *response* to an *input* stimulus.   See *high sensitivity; radar sensitivity.*

sensitivity-time control.   In *radar,* control that is performed by a *circuit* that reduces the *receiver sensitivity* for the first few thousand *meters* of each *scan* and then gradually restores the sensitivity to normal.

sensitized medium.   A medium that has been treated or coated with a substance that responds to a stimulus (such as pressure, heat, *light,* or other form of energy) so as to produce an *image* or a *copy*. For example, *photographic* paper, pressure-sensitive paper, or roll photofilm.

sensitized paper. Paper that has been treated or coated with a chemical substance that responds to a stimulus, such as pressure, heat, *light,* or other form of energy so as to produce an *image* or a *copy,* thus serving as a *data medium.*

sensor. A device or means to extend the natural senses. For example, equipment that detects or indicates terrain configuration or that detects the presence of objects or their motion by means of energy that is *emitted* or *reflected* by the objects; equipment that detects physical variables, such as *temperature,* pressure, humidity, weight, vibration, or acceleration; equipment that detects the presence or *intensity* of *illumination, radio waves, ionization density, electric fields,* or *magnetic fields;* or equipment that detects the presence of chemicals, such as pollutants and irritants; or the presence of *radioactivity.* Most *detectors* are in fact *transducers,* since they convert energy to another form and *amplify* it. They are usually designed to measure variations in the quantities that they are sensing. For example, an *optical* sensor of a *facsimile transmitter* measures the variation of *reflected light intensity* over the surface of the document being transmitted as the *light spot scans* the document *line* by line. See *fiber-optic reflective sensor; optical-fiber acoustic sensor; photo-conductive infrared sensor; sun sensor.*

sentinel. See *flag.*

separate-channel signaling. *Signaling* that utilizes the whole or part of a *channel frequency band* or *time slot* in a multichannel *system* in order to provide for *supervisory* and *control signals* for all the *traffic* channels in the multichannel system. The same time slots or frequency bands that are used for the *signaling* are not used for the *message traffic (mission traffic).*

separating character. See *information separator.*

separative sign. In *visual communication systems,* the *semaphore flag* positions that are used as a special *character* to separate *words.* One separative character is made by sending the characters ii as one group.

separator. See *address separator; information separator.*

separator character. See *facility request separator character.*

septet. A *byte* that is composed of seven *binary digits.*

sequence. See *flag sequence; frame check sequence; pseudorandom binary sequence; pseudorandom number sequence.*

sequence code. See *linear sequence code.*

sequence generator. See *Mersenne code-sequence generator; spread-spectrum code-sequence generator.*

sequence independence. See *bit-sequence independence.*

sequence modulation. See *direct sequence modulation.*

sequencing. See *packet sequencing.*

sequential. Pertaining to the occurrence of events in time sequence, with no simultaneity, overlap, or concurrence. For example, a serial sequence of *electrical pulses* that occur at a point as a function of time. See *bit sequential.*

sequential circuit. A *logic* device whose *output* values at any given instant depend on a set of *input* values and the internal state at that instant, and whose internal state depends on the immediately preceding input values and the preceding internal state. *Storage* is required to recall the previous state and input values. Since a sequential circuit can only assume a finite number of internal states, it may be regarded as a finite automaton. Also see *combinational circuit.* Synonymous with *sequential logic element.* Also see Figure L-7.

sequential connection. See *automatic sequential connection.*

sequential jamming. *Jamming* in which specific *frequencies,* or *frequency bands,* are jammed in succession until all frequencies have been jammed during a given time interval. At the end of the time interval, the jamming sequence is repeated.

sequential lobing. In *radar echo signal* sensing, the *sampling* of received energy at fixed points located symmetrically about the *antenna* axis in the *focal plane* of the *echo* by sequentially *switching* to the fixed points to obtain one angular coordinate.   The *error signal* is determined by comparing the *amplitude* of the signals in opposite *antenna feeds.*   *Lobing* permits optimizing the echo signal while *tracking* in order to remain on target and at the same time determine the precise radar angle. Also see *conical scanning; paired lobing.*

sequential logic element. See *sequential circuit.*

sequential operation. A *processing mode* in which two or more *operations* are performed one after the other in time sequence rather than in spatial sequence. For example, when a *source user* to *destination user connection* is *completed* in a *communication network,* the connections are serial. *Pulses emitted* from one end of the connection may then be emitted sequentially, that is, in time sequence while the connection remains established.

sequential transmission. See *serial transmission.*

serial. Pertaining to the performance of two or more activities in a device or system one after the other in either a spatial sequence or a time sequence. For example, the pulses in a *train* of *pulses* in transit in a *delay line* are in a serial relationship, or the pulses in a *pulse packet* in transit to a *communication satellite space station* are in a serial relationship. As the pulses arrive at a *terminal* point, they arrive sequentially, that is in time sequence at that point. To further illustrate, the links of a given chain are serial with respect to one another, though when moving over a sprocket, the links move sequentially with respect to the sprocket hub.

serial access. 1. Pertaining to the *sequential* or consecutive *transmission* of *data* to or from *storage*. 2. A process in which *data* are obtained from a *storage* device or are entered into a storage device in such a way that the process depends on the location of the data and on a reference to data that was previously *accessed*.

serial data stream. *Signals* that are sent either one after the other without interruption, or separately, but not simultaneously. *Digital messages* may be either *serial* by *signal element* and serial by *character*, in which each *character* is sent element by element, such as *bit* by bit; or *parallel* by *signal element* and serial by character, in which all the signal elements of a given character, such as all the bits of a given character, are sent at the same time on *parallel channels*, but the characters are sent one after the other.

serializer. See *parallel-to-serial converter*.

serial signaling rate. See *binary serial signaling rate*.

serial-to-parallel converter. A device that accepts a single time sequence of *signal elements* and converts them into a spatial distribution among multiple *parallel transmission output channels*. Each of the parallel output signal sequences requires a separate channel. Also see *parallel-to-serial converter*.

serial transmission. *Transmission* at successive time intervals of the individual *signal elements* that constitute the same *data* or *telegraph signal*. The *characters* are *transmitted* in a time sequence over a single *line*. The *serial* signal elements may be *transmitted* with or without interruption, provided that they are not transmitted simultaneously. Thus, the transmission of a group of bits that constitute a single character, or other entity of data, over a data *circuit*, one element at a time constitutes serial transmission.

series. See *frequency series; Galvanic series*.

service. See *absent subscriber service; aerodrome control service; aeronautical fixed service; aeronautical mobile service (AMS); aeronautical multicom service; aeronautical radionavigation service; amateur service; approach control service; Armed Forces Radio Service; broadcasting service; circuit-switched data transmission service; commercial communication service; common-user communication service; common-user service; communication satellite service; communication service; courier service; datagram service; data service; data transmission service; dedicated communication service; direction-finding service; directory service; facsimile service; fixed service; four-wire subset user service; general-purpose user service; graphic service; land mobile service; leased-circuit data transmission service; maritime radio navigation service; meteorological aids service; meteorological-satellite service; multiaddress service; off-hook service; on-call service; packet-switched data transmission service; public data transmission service; radio astronomy service; radio determination service; radio location service; radionavigation satellite service; radionavigation service; safety service; space research service; space service; special-grade service; special-network service; standard frequency service; telecommunication service; teleprinter exchange service; teletypewriter* *service; terrestrial service; trunk-grade service; user service; user-to-user service; voice-data service; voice service.*

serviceability. 1. The operational state of a *functional unit* or *system.* 2. In *communication systems,* a measure or the degree of the achievement of the best technical performance of a *communication service* together with the capability of rapid restoration of the service in the event of an interruption of the service.

service assistance switchboard. See *dial service assistance (DSA) switchboard.*

service bit. An *overhead bit,* such as a *bit* that is used for a request for repetition of a *message,* for a numbering system, or for some other assigned service function, but that is not a *check bit.* Also see *check bit; overhead bit.*

service channel. See *engineering channel.*

service circuit. See *engineering circuit.*

service class. A *designation* that indicates the type of *service* and privileges that are given to a particular *user,* or *user group,* by a communication system, usually via a user's *end-instrument.* Also see *classmarks.* See *telephone service class; user service class.*

service connection. See *laser service connection.*

service grade. 1. The quality specification of a *communication channel* or *system.* It may be stated in terms of *signal-to-noise ratio, bit error rate, message throughput rate, call blocking probability,* or other *performance parameter.* 2. In *communication systems,* a measure of the *traffic* handling capability of a *network* from the point of view of sufficiency of equipment and *trunking* throughout a multiplicity of *nodes.* 3. The probability of a *call* being *blocked* or delayed more than a specified interval, expressed as a decimal fraction, that is, in parts per unit. For example, the grade P-03 could denote a service grade in which three calls of each 100 *access attempts* will fail to *complete,* that is, will result in *access failure.* The service grade may be applied to the *busy-hour* or to some other specified period or set of *traffic* conditions. Service grade may be viewed independently from either end of the *trunk.* It may not necessarily be equal in each direction. 4. A subjective rating of *telephone* or other *communication* quality in which *users* (customers, subscribers) judge a *transmission* as excellent, good, fair, poor, or unsatisfactory. Synonymous with *grade of service.*

service information. In a *digital data transmission system, information* that is added to a *user message* to enable the equipment associated with the message to function correctly, and possibly to provide ancillary *facilities.*

service message. In *communication systems,* a brief, concise *message* between operating, supervisory, maintenance, administrative, or management personnel at *communication centers* or *relay stations* that pertains to any aspect of *traffic* handling, status of *facilities, circuit* conditions, or other matters that affect communication system operation, including *circuit continuity checks, tracer actions,* and *error corrections.*

service period. See *operational service period.*

service probability. The probability of obtaining a specified *service grade* or better during a specified period of time.

service restoral. See *mean-time-to-service-restoral (MTTSR).*

service signal. A *signal* that enables *data communication* equipment to function correctly, and possibly to provide ancillary *facilities.* For example, an equipment-not-in-service signal; or a *signal* that is *transmitted* automatically by a *communication network* to the *calling station,* indicating that an *access failure* was due to a certain cause. Synonymous with *housekeeping signal.*

service speed. 1. From the point of view of the *communication system user* (customer, subscriber), the time that elapses from the *release* of a *message* by an *originator* to its receipt by the *addressee,* that is the originator-to-recipient service speed. 2. From the point of view of the *communication system operator,* the time that elapses from the entry of a *message* into a *communication system (filing time)* until its receipt at the *destination addressee's communication facility (message-available-for-delivery time).* For example, in *communication systems* that handle direct *(real-time) traffic,* the service speed might be the interval between the time at which the *control signaling,* such as *address* and *precedence,* is inserted into the *system* and the time at which the *destination addressee's end-instrument* is either *seized* or found *busy.* In those systems that handle indirect *(store-and-forward) traffic,* the service speed might be the interval between the time at which the complete *message* is inserted into the system and the time at which the addressee's end-instrument is seized. In most instances, it is always essential to describe the conditions under which the service speed is determined. Synonymous with *speed of service.*

service state. See *operational service state.*

service time interval. In *communication system operations,* a *performance measurement period,* or a succession of performance measurement periods, during which a *communication service* is scheduled to perform its normal function, including *operation* time and *outage* time. For example, 0600 to 2200 hours, GMT, daily except Sunday 1200 to 2200 hours.

session. In *communication system operations,* a period of time, a grouping of equipment, or a set of actions. For example, (1) a *connection* between two *functional units,* such as two *terminals, stations,* or *computers,* that allows them to *communicate* for a period of time, (2) a logical association that is established and maintained between two functional units that allows them to communicate, (3) the period of time during which two functional units may communicate, or (4) the time or the actions that occur between *log-on* and *log-off* of a remote terminal.

session layer. In *open systems architecture,* the *layer* that provides the functions and services that may be used to establish and maintain *connections* among elements of a session, to maintain a dialog of requests and responses between the elements of a session, and to terminate the session. Also see *layer.*

set. In *communication* and *data processing systems,* to place a *functional unit* in a specified state. For example, to cause a counter to take the state that corresponds to a specified number, or to force a *flip-flop* (bistable circuit) into a specified state. See *alphabetic character set; alphabetic coded character set; alphanumeric character set; alphanumeric coded character set; character set; coded character set; code set; data set; engineering circuit multiplex set; four-wire terminating set; hybrid set; numeric character set; numeric coded character set; radio set; telegraph set; television set; tone wedge set; user set.*

set mode. The *operating mode* of an *analog computer* during which the coefficients of the equations, terms, or *parameters,* are entered. For example, *potentiometers* are set for division, gains are set for multiplying factors, and *summers* are set for constants of *integration.*

settling time. In *spread-spectrum frequency-shift keying, wavelength-modulated optical transmission systems,* or other systems requiring changes to different *frequencies,* the time required for the *frequency* of a multiple-frequency device to change to, and stabilize at, a new operating frequency.

set-up. See *call set-up.*

set-up time. See *call set-up time.*

sextet. A *byte* that is composed of six *binary digits.*

SF signaling. *Single-frequency (SF) signaling.*

SF signaling system. *Single-frequency (SF) signaling system.*

SF signal unit. See *single-frequency (SF) signaling system.*

shading. In *display systems,* to change the tone, *color,* shade of color, intensity, composition, or other attribute of a specific area or part of a *display element, display group,* or *display image* in the *display space* on the *display surface* of a *display device.*

shadow. See *radar shadow.*

shadow area. See *blind area.*

shannon. A unit of logarithmic measure of *information content* equal to the *decision content* of a set of two mutually exclusive events expressed as a logarithm to base two. For example, the decision content of a *character set* of eight *characters* equals 3 shannons, that is, $\log_2 8 = 3$. Synonymous with *information content binary unit.* Also see *decision content.*

shape.   See *pulse shape; wave shape.*

shaped pulse.   See *Gaussian-shaped pulse.*

shaped-reflector Cassegrain.   See *uniform-illumination Cassegrain.*

shape factor.   In a *filter,* a measure of how rapidly the filter *frequency response curve* falls or rises as a function of *frequency.* It is usually expressed in such units as *decibels* per *hertz,* decibels per *kilohertz,* or percent per kilohertz.

shaping.   See *signal shaping.*

shaping network.   An *electrical circuit* or *component* that is inserted into a *communication circuit* for improving or modifying the *wave shape* of *signals.* For example, a *pulse shaping circuit.*

shared disk.   In *communication* and *data processing systems,* a *magnetic disk* that may be used for *information storage* by two or more *systems* at the same time.

sharing.   See *frequency geographical sharing; frequency sharing; frequency time-sharing; geographical frequency-sharing; power sharing; time sharing.*

sharpening.   See *image sharpening.*

sheet.   See *record sheet.*

Sheffer-stroke gate.   See *NAND gate.*

SHF.   *Super-high frequency.*

shield.   See *ferrous shield.*

shielded enclosure.   An area, room, or box that is capable of preventing, usually by *attenuation* or *reflection,* the entry or exit of *electromagnetic fields, sound waves,* or both, that originate inside or outside of the enclosed volume. Necessary openings in the shielded enclosures, such as doors, air vents, and electrical feedthroughs, are especially designed to maintain the shielding. Electromagnetic shielding material is usually sheet metal. Soundproofing material is usually honeycombed, fibrous, nonelastic, nonmetallic material such as pressed straw or styrofoam.

shift.   **1.** In *communication systems,* a *machine function* that controls the positioning of certain *components* of *teletypewriter-teleprinter* equipment to permit the printing of upper case or lower case *characters* as required, that is, to permit a *case shift.* The movement from upper to lower case is accomplished by use of the *letters key* and from lower to upper case is accomplished by use of the *figures key,* or by the use of correspondingly coded tape perforations. **2.** In *radio communications* for merchant ships, the process that a convoy or independent *ship station* uses to change its *radio watch* from one *ship broadcast area* or subarea to the next. **3.** To move the *characters (digits)* in a *register* to the left or to the right. **4.** To change the *frequency* or the *phase* of a *signal.* See *area broad-*

cast shift; carrier shift; case shift; circular shift; compensating phase shift; data shift; Doppler shift; facsimile frequency shift; figures shift; frequency shift; Goos-Haenchen shift; letter shift; negative scanning shift; phase shift; positive scanning shift; radar shift; signal frequency shift; subcarrier frequency shift.

shift frequency-shift keying. See *narrow-shift frequency-shift keying.*

shift-in (SI) character. A *code extension character* that is used to terminate a series of *characters* that has been introduced by the *shift-out character.* For example, it makes effective again the characters of the *character set* that was in effect before the shift-out character occurred, usually a return to the normal or standard set. The shift-in character might cause the return to Roman font after the shift-out introduced italics. The terms "out" and "in" are usually with reference to the most prevalent set.

shift keying. See *differentially-coherent phase-shift keying (DCPSK); differential phase-shift keying (DPSK); double frequency-shift keying (DFSK); frequency-shift keying (FSK); multiple-frequency-shift keying (MFSK); multiple-phase-shift keying (MPSK); narrow-shift frequency-shift keying; phase-shift keying (PSK); quadrature-phase-shift keying (QPSK); wide-shift frequency-shift keying.*

shift-out (SO) character. A *code extension character* that introduces another or alternate *character set.* For example, a *character* that introduces the use of italics in lieu of Roman font in automatic type setting until the *shift-in (SI) character* occurs at which point there is a return to the regular font. The term "out" versus "in" is with reference to a designated set of characters, usually the more prevalent set.

shift register. A *storage* device in which a serially-ordered set of *data* may be moved, as a unit, a *discrete* number of storage locations. Shift registers may be constructed so that the stored data may be moved in more than one direction, such as right or left. Shift registers may also be constructed so that data may be entered (stored) from a multiplicity of *inputs.* They may be grouped in arrays of two or three dimensions in order to perform more complex data *operations.* Also see *storage register.* See *nonlinear feedback shift register; linear feedback shift register.* See Figure S-4 (p. 846)

shift-register generator. See *spread-spectrum code-sequence generator.*

shift signal. See *letter-shift signal.*

ship. See *constant-watch ship; guard ship; light-repeating ship; repeating ship.*

ship-air net. A *communication net* that is used to *transmit messages* from *ship stations* to *aircraft stations* and aircraft stations to ship stations. Also see *ship-to-air net.*

ship alarm signal. A *signal* that is automatically *transmitted* by *radio* in the event of a ship distress or emergency. For example, a standard alarm signal for merchant ships is an audio alarm that is activated by 12 four-second dashes with

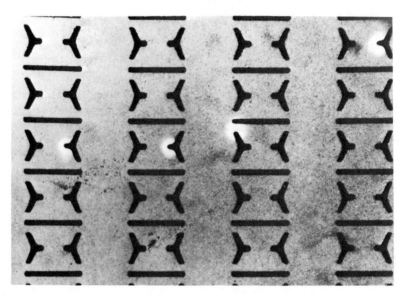

S-4. A **shift register** showing magnified *magnetic* bubbles (light circles) moving through a *circuit* pattern formed on a thin epitaxial film of unaxial garnet. An elongated bubble is in transition from one pole to the next. Bubbles are 0.003 in. in diameter. (Courtesy of Bell Laboratories.)

one-second intervals, transmitted at 500 kHz; or an alarm at 2182 kHz consisting of 2 audio tones of different pitch transmitting for a period of 30 to 60 seconds.

ship broadcast-area radio station.   A shore *radio station* that *transmits messages* to *ship stations* in a given long-range *broadcast area.*   Also see *ship broadcast coastal radio station.*

ship broadcast coastal radio station.   A shore *radio station* that *transmits messages* to *ship stations* in local coastal waters.   Usually local coastal stations do not *transmit* at times and *frequencies* that long range *ship broadcast-area radio stations* schedule their *transmissions.*   Also see *ship broadcast-area radio station.*

ship broadcast schedule.   The schedule of *transmissions* by a *ship broadcast-area radio station* or a *ship broadcast coastal radio station.*   The schedule normally consists of the *call tape,* the *preliminary call up,* the *traffic list,* the *messages* on the list, and the *sign-off transmission* after the last message.

ship broadcast service.   See *merchant ship broadcast service.*

ship call sign.   A *radio call sign* that is assigned to a ship.   The ship *signal letters* are used as the *ship international call sign.*   Ships that are assigned a call sign include merchant ships, miscellaneous government-owned ships, and private personally owned ships.

ship collective call sign. A *call sign* that is used by or assigned to a group of ships. For example, a call sign that is assigned to all the ships registered in Panama or all the ships in a specific convoy.

ship communications. *Communication* methods, *systems,* or equipment used for the *transmission* of *messages* that contain *information* about ship *operations,* including messages that are sent to or from ships or shore *communication facilities* for the purpose of coordinating ship movements, defining shipping routes, providing escort, handling distress and rescue operations, and handling other matters relating to maritime operations.

ship deck log. A log of significant events that are usually not of a classified nature and that occur on board a ship during a voyage. Also see *ship radio log.*

ship-fitting communication standard plan. A table of standard *communication* equipment and *components* that are recommended as minimum fit for ships of various classes and functions.

ship international call sign. The unencrypted *call sign* that is assigned to each ship. The call sign is equivalent to the name of the ship. See *military ship international call sign.*

ship net. See *ship-to-ship net.*

ship radar silence. A restriction against the use of a ship's *radar.* The silence may be maintained for such purposes as the reduction of *interference,* avoidance of confusion of launched missiles, prevention of *homing* of missiles on *radar transmissions,* and prevention of ship identification or discovery from *radar signal analysis (radar signature analysis).*

ship radio log. A record of events, important *messages,* and other matters that pertain to *communication operations* in a *ship station* during a voyage. Ship radio log entries may include on and off *watch operator's* signatures, dates, *ship call sign, schedules copied (received), date-time group* of messages transmitted, *frequencies* used, *data* on *messages received, radio silence* periods, *distress signals received, alarm signals* used, and other significant events concerning ship *safety traffic.* Also see *ship deck log.*

ship radio officer. See *senior ship radio officer.*

ship radio silence. A restriction against the use of a ship's radio equipment. The silence may be maintained for such purposes as the reduction of *interference,* avoidance of confusion of launched missiles, prevention of *homing* of missiles on *radio transmissions,* and prevention of ship identification or discovery from *radio signal analysis (radio signature analysis).*

ship radiotelephone numeral. **1.** One of the special pronunciations of the *decimal numerals* that are used over *maritime mobile voice radiotelephones* for international understanding. The numerals are unaone, bissotwo, terrathree, kartefour, pantafive, soxisix, setteseven, oktoeight, novenine, and nadazero. **2.** A ship *radiotelephone directory number* for *routing telephone calls* to a specific ship.

ship radio transmission security. *Communication security* measures that are taken to insure *operation* of a *ship station* in accordance with the rules and *procedures* prescribed in *security* regulations.

ship-shore communication net. See *maritime ship-shore communication net.*

ship-shore communications. *Communication* methods, *procedures,* or equipment that are used for the *transmission* of *messages* that contain *information* about ship-shore operations. The messages may be directed from shore *(land stations)* to *ship stations* and from ship stations to *shore stations.* Ship-shore (bidirectional) communications are primarily used for the purpose of coordinating, directing, or conducting operations that involve sea, ground, and air units, including *fixed* and *mobile stations.*

ship-shore net. A *radio net* that is used to send *messages* from *ship stations* to *shore stations (land stations)* and from land stations to ship stations. Also see *ship-to-shore net.*

ship-shore radio teletypewriter. A *teletypewriter (teleprinter)* that is used for sending and receiving messages in *ship-to-shore, shore-to-ship,* and *ship-shore radio nets.*

ship-shore station. See *local ship-shore station; primary ship-shore station; secondary ship-shore station.*

ship signaling. See *flashing-light ship signaling.*

ship station. **1.** A *mobile station* in the *maritime mobile service* that is located aboard a vessel, other than a *survival craft,* that is not permanently moored. **2.** The assigned spatial position of a ship in a convoy. **3.** An assigned duty position, location, or function aboard a ship. For example, a *communication station* or a pilot station. See *one-operator ship station.*

ship-to-air net. A *communication net* that is used to *transmit messages* from *ship stations* to *aircraft stations.* Also see *ship-air net.*

ship-to-ship net. A *communication net* that is used to *transmit* and *receive messages* among individual ships or ships in a convoy.

ship-to-shore net. A *communication net* that is used by *ship stations* for passing *messages* to *shore stations (land stations)* for onward *relay* or distribution. Also see *ship-shore net.*

ship-to-shore radiotelephone procedure. The *procedure* used to place *telephone calls* from ships to shore *telephone systems.* These procedures are described in Article 33, *International Telecommunication Union (ITU)* regulations.

ship-to-shore schedule. A list of the *call signs, answering frequencies, watch hours,* and *calling frequencies* for each *ship-to-shore station* in a *maritime communication system.* For example, for the *ship-to-shore station (radio)* Halifax, Nova Scotia, the call sign is VCS. One answering frequency is 4293.5 kHz, 0000–1000 GMT and the *calling band* is 4177 to 4187 kHz.

shock excitation. See *impulse excitation.*

shock test. See *thermal shock test.*

SHORAN. *Short-range aid to navigation.*

shore communications. See *ship-shore communications.*

shore net. A *radio net* that consists of *stations* on land but is used to handle *messages* that are destined for *ship stations* at sea. See *ship-shore net; ship-to-shore net.*

shore radiotelephone procedure. See *ship-to-shore radiotelephone procedure.*

shore radio teletypewriter. See *ship-shore radio teletypewriter.*

shore station. See *local ship-shore station; primary ship-shore station; secondary ship-shore station.*

short address. See *abbreviated address.*

short-range aid to navigation (SHORAN). A *short-range radionavigation system* that is used for obtaining precise *fixes* for *mobile receivers* and that consists of a *pulse transmitter* and *receiver,* and two *transponder beacons* at fixed points. A receiving station properly equipped can obtain a fix based on directions and *phase* relationships of received *signals,* with the assistance of appropriate charts and tables. Synonymous with *short range navigation; short-range radionavigation.*

short-range laser sonar. A *sonar* device for short *ranges* in which a controlled *laser beam* is used to produce separate identifiable *beams* and thus produce *code pulses* of a *carrier wave.*

short-range navigation. See *short-range aid to navigation.*

short-range radionavigation. See *short-range aid to navigation (SHORAN).*

short-term ionospheric forecast. A one-week or less forecast of *ionospheric* conditions that is distributed in *broadcast* or wire-*message* form. Sudden, very short duration ionospheric disturbances cause immediate *fading* and are unpredictable.

Certain ionospheric storms can be forecast. Also see *long-term ionospheric forecast.*

short-term security. The *protection* that is obtained from using a *cryptosystem* that will protect *communication traffic encrypted* with it from successful *cryptanalysis* for up to approximately one month. The length of time varies with each cryptoysystem, depending on the *cryptomaterials* used, the type of *cryptokey,* the principle employed, and the *encrypted communication traffic volume.*

short title. 1. An abbreviated form of a proper name. For example, CINCPAC for Commander-in-Chief Pacific Command or SUNOCO for Sun Oil Company. 2. An identifying combination of letters and numerals that is assigned to *communication security* material for brevity purposes. Synonymous with *abbreviated title.*

short wave. Pertaining to *electromagnetic waves* with a *frequency* that is above the *medium frequency (MF) range,* that is, above 3 MHz. This corresponds to *wavelengths* that are less than 100 m.

short-wave radio. See *high-frequency radio.*

shot noise. 1. In a *photodetector,* the *noise* caused by *current* fluctuations due to the *discrete* nature of charge *carriers* and random *emission* of charged particles from an emitter. The mean square shot noise current is:

$$MSSNC = 2qIb$$

where b is *bandwidth,* I is the average *photocurrent,* and q is the electronic charge of each charged particle. In the photodetector, I contains contributions due to the *signal* current, background-*radiation*-induced photocurrent, and *dark current.* This mean square shot noise current (amp square) is converted to *noise power* (watts) in the equivalent *resistance* of the photodetector and its *output circuit.* Shot noise current would reduce to zero if the magnitude of an individual charge tended to zero. This fact reflects the underlying cause of shot noise: The *discrete* nature of the charge. If there were no dark current and background radiation on the detector, so that the only contribution to average photocurrent was due to the *optical signal,* the resulting shot noise current density would produce noise which is the lower limit on detector noise; this leads to *quantum-noise*-limited sensitivity. The *quantum* limit to *optical* sensitivity is due to the granularity, or particle nature, of *light.* Thus, the minimum energy increment of an *electromagnetic* (optical) *wave* is hf, i.e., the energy of a *photon.* 2. The *noise* of *photocurrent* due to an *optical signal.* Thus, shot noise is the *quantum noise* given by the relation:

$$QN = hfb$$

in the limit, when photocurrent is due only to the optical signal, where h is *Planck's constant,* f is the frequency, and b is the *bandwidth.* Synonymous with *quantum noise.*

shutter. See *fallen clearing indicator shutter.*

shuttle-pulse test. A method of obtaining and viewing *pulse* shapes that would occur at regular intervals in a long-length *optical fiber,* in which a short length of fiber is equipped with a *reflector* at both ends, a pulse is launched through one *reflector,* and the pulse at the far end is sampled after each (2*N* − 1) transits, where *N* is an *integral* number of transits. Thus, *mode coupling, dispersion,* and other properties can be measured in short-lengths of *test* fibers.

SI. The abbreviation for International System of Units from the French "Système Internationale d'Unités," a coherent system of units based on the *meter,* kilogram, *second,* coulomb, and dependent units upon which international agreement has been reached by the General Conference on Weights and Measures.

SI character. See *shift-in (SI) character.*

side. See *equipment side; line side; local side.*

sideband. 1. The *frequency band,* above or below the *carrier,* that is produced by the process of *modulation.* 2. The *spectral* energy distributed above and below a *carrier frequency* of a *modulated electromagnetic wave.* Also see *single-sideband suppressed carrier.* See *double sideband; independent sideband; lower sideband; single sideband; upper sideband; vestigial sideband.*

sideband carrier. See *two independent-sideband carrier.*

sideband noise power ratio. See *single-sideband noise power ratio.*

sideband reference level. See *single-sideband reference level.*

sideband suppressed-carrier. See *double-sideband suppressed carrier.*

sideband suppressed-carrier transmission. See *single-sideband suppressed-carrier (SSB-SC) transmission.*

sideband transmission. A method of *transmission* in which the *frequencies* of *electromagnetic waves* that are produced by *amplitude modulation* occur above and below the *carrier frequency.* The waves with frequencies that are above the carrier are the *upper sideband* waves and those with frequencies below the carrier are the *lower sideband* waves. The two sidebands may carry the same or different *information.* The carrier itself may be suppressed and either of the sidebands may also be independently suppressed. In conventional *amplitude modulation (AM),* both sidebands carry the same information and the carrier is present. See *compatible sideband transmission; double-sideband transmission; independent sideband transmission; single-sideband transmission; two independent-sideband transmission; vestigial sideband transmission.*

sideband voice. See *single-sideband voice.*

side circuit. Either of the two *circuits* that are used for the derivation of a *phantom circuit.*

side lobe. 1. In an *antenna* or *light*-source *radiation* pattern, a portion of the radiated *beam* from the antenna or radiation source other than the *main beam* and usually smaller.   The side lobe is usually adjacent to the *main lobe* or another side lobe. Side lobes usually have much less *power density* than the main lobe at a given range, although at a different direction. In *laser* and *LED* emissions, as much of the energy as possible is confined to the main lobe. **2.** In a *directional antenna radiation pattern,* a *radiation lobe* in any direction other than that of the *main lobe* and other than that opposite to the main lobe. Also see *main lobe.*

side-lobe blanking.   A technique in *radar operation* in which the *signal strengths* between an *omnidirectional antenna* and a normal radar *antenna* are compared. The omnidirectional antenna, plus *receiver,* has slightly more *gain* than the *side lobes* of the normal antenna but less gain than the *main beam.* In ECCM, this technique is effective in removing *off-azimuth jamming* and *deception.* It has the disadvantages of turning off *receivers* where there could be objects of interest. Side-lobe blanking is used to remove *spoof jamming signals* at false *azimuths.*

side-lobe cancellation.   An anti-*interference,* anti*jamming* technique used in *radar systems,* in which the same *antenna* and *receiver* configuration is used as in *side-lobe blanking* except that a *gain* matching and cancelling process takes place. Extraneous *signals* that enter the *side lobe* of the main antenna are cancelled while the main *signals* from the object (target), that is, the *echoes,* remain uncancelled. This system exhibits cancellation on the order of 20 dB against a single *noise jammer* and also reduces the *radar system sensitivity* by the same amount.

side-lobe jamming.   *Jamming* through a *side lobe* of the *receiving antenna.* In this form of *radar jamming,* an attempt is made to obliterate the desired *signal* that is *received* through the *main lobe* of the receiving antenna. The technique can confuse the *operator* as to the real *azimuth* of the *jammer* because of the injection of multiple signals *(strobes).*

side-looking airborne radar.   High-*resolution* airborne *radar* in which the *radar beam* is directed at right angles to the direction of flight, or at right angles to the axis of the airframe. A presentation of terrain or moving longitudinal objects is produced.

sidereal day.   The actual mean period of one earth rotation, that is, 86 164 *seconds* (23h 56m 4.095s). It is the time interval between two successive *transits* of a fixed star past a given meridian on earth. Because of the star distance, the earth-star line can be considered as a fixed line in space for a period as short as one day. Also see *synodic period.*

side stable relay.   A *polar relay* that remains in the last *signaled* contact position.

sidetone.   The *transmission* and reproduction of sounds through a local path from the *transmitter* to the *receiver* of the same *user end-instrument.* See *telephone sidetone.*

Siecor cable.   An *optical cable* produced by Siecor Optical Cable, Inc. Typical cables currently are 1, 2, 4, 6, 8, and 10 *fibers* per *cable,* with 6 or 10 db/km *attenuation* at a *wavelength* of 0.820 *micron* at lengths up to several kilometers.

sight. See *line-of-sight (LOS)*.

sight equation. See *radar line-of-sight equation*.

sighting. An actual visual contact with an *object* by a person, rather than by means of an instrument such as *radar, sonar, sound, echo, reflection,* or *radio*.

sight link. See *line-of-sight link*.

sight propagation. See *line-of-sight (LOS) propagation*.

SIGINT. *Signal intelligence*.

sigma. In *telephone communications,* a group of *telephone* wires, usually the majority or all of the wires that constitute a *line* or *local loop,* that are treated as a unit in the computation of *noise,* or in the arrangement of *connections* for the measurement of noise or *electrical current balance*.

sigma modulation. See *delta sigma modulation*.

sign. See *aircraft call sign; answering sign; attention sign; call sign; collective call sign; front sign; indefinite call sign; individual call sign; international call sign; military call sign; military ship international call sign; net call sign; numeral sign; permanent voice call sign; personal sign; separative sign; ship call sign; ship collective call sign; ship international call sign; special panel signaling sign; visual call sign*.

signal. 1. A usually time-dependent value attached to a transient physical phenomenon used to convey *data;* e.g., the variation of *light intensity* at a point in an *optical waveguide* to represent a *binary digit,* the light level change *propagating* as a *pulse* along the guide. 2. An *impulse,* either electrical, as in a wire; acoustic, as used in *sonar;* or a short burst of *light* energy, as generated by a *laser* and *coupled* to an *optical fiber* for guidance and *transmission* and for conversion back to an electrical *pulse* at the far end of the fiber. 3. A visual or mechanical action to which meaning is assigned, such as puffs of smoke, *displays,* motion of flags or *pennants,* or motion of a cable, wire, or rope. 4. The intelligence, *message,* or *control function* that is to be conveyed over a *communication system*. 5. A *message,* the *text* of which consists of one or more letters, *words, characters, flags, visual displays,* hand positions, sounds, or other means, with prearranged meanings, and which is conveyed or *transmitted* by *visual, acoustical,* or *electrical means*. Also see *message*. See *access-barred signal; acknowledgement signal; address signal; alarm signal; alternate mark inversion (AMI) signal; analog signal; backward signal; baseband signal; black signal; bunched frame-alignment signal; busy signal; call-accepted signal; call-control signal; called-line identification signal; call-failure signal; calling line identification signal; calling signal; call-not-accepted signal; call progress signal; call-up signal; camp-on-busy signal; character signal; circuit-released-acknowledgement signal; circuit-released signal; clear confirmation signal; clear-forward signal; clear-request signal; clear-to-send signal; composite two-tone test signal; connection in-progress-signal; continuity-failure signal; controlled not-ready signal; data circuit-terminating equipment*

(DCE) clear signal; data circuit-terminating equipment (DCE) waiting signal; data terminal equipment (DTE) clear-request signal; data terminal equipment (DTE) waiting signal; data transfer request signal; digital signal; disabling signal; disjoint signal; distress signal; distributed frame-alignment signal; duobinary signal; duress signal; electronic signal; emergency signal; enabling signal; erasure signal; facility request signal; facsimile picture signal; figure-shift signal; forward signal; frame-alignment signal; function signal; ground-to-air visual body signal; identification-not-provided signal; inhibiting signal; international congestion signal; jamming signal; letter shift signal; maneuvering signal; marking signal; mark signal; minimum discernible signal; multiframe alignment signal; n-ary digital signal; narrowband signal; national circuit group congestion signal; national switching equipment congestion signal; octet timing signal; off-hook signal; on-hook signal; operating signal; out-of-order signal; partial response signal; phasing signal; preliminary call-up signal; proceed-to-select signal; pulsed frequency modulated signal; pyrotechnic distress signal; pyrotechnic signal; quasianalog signal; random signal; ready-for-data signal; recall signal; response signal; redirected-to-new-address signal; redirect-to-new-address signal; request-to-send signal; safety signal; sampling signal; seizure signal; selection signal; service signal; ship alarm signal; space signal; standard test signal; standard time-frequency signal; start-recording signal; stop-recording signal; start signal; stop signal; supervisory signal; symmetric signal; synchronization correction signal; synchronizing signal; system blocking signal; telegraph signal; terminal-engaged signal; ternary signal; test signal; timing signal; two-level optical signal; visual paulin signal; visual signal; waiting-in-progress signal; white signal; wideband signal.

signal alarm.   See *emergency signal alarm.*

signal amplitude.   The *electromagnetic signal strength,* measured as the *electric field intensity;* the *magnetic field intensity;* the maximum gradient, such as volts per meter; the *Poynting vector* intensity; or the *power* or energy density, such as watts or joules per cubic meter or watts per square meter; at a point in space and time at specified *frequencies* or *frequency bands.*

signal analysis.   The study of *received electromagnetic radiation (signals)* in order to determine their technical characteristics, their tactical or strategic use, or the character or nature of their *sources.*

signal center.   A combination of *signal communication facilities,* that may be operated in the field, on a ship, on an organization's premises, or in a building, and that usually consists of a *communication center,* a *telephone switching center,* and other appropriate means of *signal communication.*   Also see *communication center.*

signal code.   See *international signal code; international visual signal code; network multiple selection signal code.*

signal communication axis.   1. The line or route on which lies the starting position and probable future location of the command post of a military unit. 2. The main route along which *messages* are relayed or sent to and from tactical and service units during a military situation or exercise. Synonymous with *axis of signal communication.*

signal communication center. An agency that is responsible for the receipt, *transmission,* and delivery of *messages.* It may include a *message center* and *transmitting* and *receiving facilities.* Transmitting, receiving, and *relay stations* are not necessarily located in a *communication center,* nor are they necessarily signal communication centers in themselves, but facilities for their remote control may terminate in a signal communication center.

signal communications. The means that are used to convey *information* from one person, place, or machine to another, except by direct, unassisted conversation or by written correspondence through the mails.

signal contrast. A ratio or difference between any two specified *signals.* For example, in *facsimile systems,* the ratio between a *signal* that corresponds to a scanned white area on a document and a signal that corresponds to a black area on the document. The signals must be expressed in the same units, such as volts or watts *(amplitude), hertz (frequency),* or *electrical degrees (phase).* The ratio may be expressed as a fraction, a percentage, in *decibels,* or in *nepers.* See *facsimile signal contrast.*

signal conversion equipment. See *modem.*

signal converter. A device in which the *input* and *output signals* are formed according to the same *code,* but not necessarily according to the same type of *electrical modulation.*

signal delay. See *absolute signal delay.*

signal distance. **1.** A count of the number of *digit positions* in which the corresponding digits are different for two equal-length *binary* numerals; e.g., the signal distance between 011011 and 010110 is 3, since the digits differ in three places. **2.** The number of *digit positions* in which the corresponding digits of two *numerals* of the same length in any *radix* are different. For example, the signal distance between 106242370 and 140224270 is 5. Synonymous with *Hamming distance.* Also see *unit-distance code.*

signal distortion. See *teletypewriter signal distortion.*

signal element. A part of a *signal.* For example, a part of a *telegraph signal,* a single *pulse* in a group of pulses, a *bit* in a *binary numeral,* or a single *transition* from one *signal level* to another (a *voltage* change, a *phase shift,* or a *frequency* change). Parts are distinguished by their nature, magnitude, duration, and relative position, or by some combination of these features. Also see *significant instant; unit interval.*

signal frequency shift. In a *facsimile system,* the numerical difference between the *frequencies* that correspond to a *white signal* and a *black signal* at any point in the system.

signal generator. An instrument that produces *electrical voltages* or *currents, electromagnetic waves,* or other forms of *signals,* of known characteristics, such as *amplitude, wave shape, frequency,* and *timing* for any purpose, such as *transmission, modulation,* testing, or measurement.

signal group. A group of *characters* used for a specific *signaling* purpose. For example, a *call sign,* a *prosign,* a *basic group,* or an *address designator.*

signal imitation.   1. The process or practice of *detection, recognition,* and *identification* of *signals* and the duplication and *transmission* of them. 2. The false *operation* of a *receiver* by elements of speech or code patterns that occur in *communication traffic.*

signaling. 1. The use of *signals* for *communication.*   2. A method of conveying *signals* over a *circuit.*   3. The interchange of *signals* for the purpose of operating, controlling, managing, supervising, or maintaining a *communication system,* in contrast to the *user communication traffic,* that is, in contrast to the *user information transfer* for which the communication system was established. 4. The function of supplying and interpreting the *control* and *supervisory functions* that are required to establish suitable *transmission paths* in a *communication system.*   See *binary signaling; biphase signaling; channel-associated signaling; common-battery signaling; common-channel signaling; composite signaling; confirmation signaling; control signaling; dial signaling; digital carrier-interrupt signaling; digital mark-space signaling; digital signaling; direct current (DC) signaling; double-current signaling; dual-tone multifrequency signaling (DTMF); E-and-M lead signaling; flaghoist signaling; flashing-light ship signaling; free-line signaling; frequency-change signaling; frequency exchange signaling; inband signaling; low-level signaling; Morse flag signaling; multifrequency signaling; n-ary signaling; out-of-band signaling; panel signaling; random bit-stream signaling; remote operator signaling; ringdown signaling; saturation signaling; semaphore signaling; separate-channel signaling; simplex signaling; single-current signaling; single-frequency (SF) signaling; sound signaling; speech-plus signaling; status signaling; supervisory signaling; telephone circuit signaling; visual engaged signaling; wigwag signaling.*

signaling data link. A *data link* that is used only for *signaling* purposes and that is not used for the *transfer* of *user information.* It usually consists of a combination of two *data channels* that operate together in a single signaling *system.* The data channels operate in opposite directions and at the same *data signaling rate.*

signaling exchange. See *common-battery signaling exchange.*

signaling indicator. See *panel signaling indicator.*

signaling information. In a *communication system, information* that is used by the *system,* including its *operators,* to maintain control of the *calls, messages,* and other *transmissions* while they are being handled by the *system.* For example, *transmission control signals, call control signals, synchronizing signals,* and *address designators.*

signaling information content. The *information content* of a *message* that is related to a *call control procedure,* a management function, or other message-related or *user*-related action. Although it is part of the message, it is not entirely user information. For example, *address designators* and *routing information* are often a *signaling* function not provided by the user. However, *message alignment, synchronizing,* and *service signals* are not part of the *signaling information content* of a message. They are not in a message. They are required for proper system functioning for every message.

signaling information field. The fixed-length field of a *signal unit* in which *signaling information* is placed. This field does not necessarily exist in all signal units. The signaling information field usually may comprise a fixed number of *bits* in a given *system,* such as 40 bits in some systems. It may contain signaling information that pertains to the whole or a part of a *message.*

signaling lamp. A *light source* that can be easily flashed for *signaling* and that can be changed in *intensity,* angle of coverage, or direction when required.

signaling link. A *functional unit,* within a *signaling system,* that consists of one *signaling data link* and its associated *control functions.* See *functional signaling link.*

signaling panel code. A code that enables *numerals,* letters, and special signs to be *transmitted* by means of *panel signaling.* For example, a *panel code* that corresponds to *Morse code,* in that a *dot* is represented by a *panel* with its long axis at right angles to the line of code, and a *dash* is represented by a panel that is placed parallel to the line of code. The *Morse code indicator* and the *index flash* should be used to indicate the orientation of the *character* and therefore the direction of reading. Some Morse code characters become different characters when read in reverse. Other letters are symmetrical and therefore the same regardless of their orientation. Also see *panel signal indicator.*

signaling path. In a *transmission system,* a *path* provided for handling system *signals* used for *control, synchronization, checking, ringing, service,* and other system management functions rather than for the *data, messages,* or *calls* for which the system was established. The signaling path may also carry *power* for performing the signaling functions, such as *ringing* power, *repeater power,* and control power. Also see *optical repeater power.*

signaling power. In a *transmission system,* the power used to obtain attention at a *receiving station* for purposes of control or for indicating that a *connection* is desired. Signaling power may be obtained from an *optical-fiber* voice *lightwave carrier* and used to drive an *optoacoustic transducer* to produce a *signaling* tone.

signaling rate. See *binary serial signaling rate; data signaling rate; maximum user signaling rate.*

signaling rate transparency. See *data signaling rate transparency.*

signaling sign. See *special panel signaling sign.*

signaling system. See *directional signaling system; omnidirectional signaling system; single-frequency (SF) signaling system.*

signaling time slot. A *time slot* that starts at a particular *phase* or *significant instant* in each *frame* and is allocated to the *transmission* of *supervisory* and *control function data.*

signaling unit. See *DX signaling unit.*

signaling vocabulary. See *panel signaling vocabulary.*

signal intelligence (SIGINT). *Electronic intelligence (ELINT)* and *communication intelligence (COMINT)* combined. SIGINT is a form of intelligence activity that is carried out by using *communication-electronic systems* at the national or strategic level, though it may also be carried out at the tactical level when appropriate. Also see *electronic intelligence (ELINT); communication intelligence (COMINT).*

signal letters. The letters of an *international call sign* that are used in *visual signaling.*

signal level. The magnitude of a *signal parameter* or element, such as the *amplitude* of the *electric field intensity, voltage,* or *current,* or the magnitude of the *phase shift* or the *frequency.* Signal level may be expressed in absolute or relative quantities, such as *decibels,* percent, *millivolts, hertz,* volts per *meter, microamperes,* oersteds, *electrical degrees,* watts, watts per square meter, or *lumens* per square meter. See *facsimile signal level; peak signal level; received signal level.*

signal message. An assembly of *signaling information* that pertains to a *call* or *message* and is transferred via the *message transfer part.* The signal message includes the associated *message alignment indicators* and *service information.* Also see *message alignment indicator.*

signal/noise ratio. See *postdetector signal/noise ratio; signal-to-noise-ratio.*

signal operating instruction. See *signal operation instruction.*

signal operation instruction (SOI). A series of orders that are issued for the technical control and coordination of *signal communication* activities of an organization. The *instructions* are usually detailed and usually cover day-to-day *operations* that are related to *communications.* The SOI may also contain instructions for the regular changing of *encryption codes (cryptokeys)* and *cryptoprocedures.* Synonymous with *communication operation instruction (COI); signal operating instruction (SOI).*

signal parameter. Any of the characteristics that may be attributed to a *signal.* For example, the *intensity, color,* duration, and sequence for *visual signals;* and the *frequency, pulse length, pulse amplitude, polarization, modulation,* and *strength* for *electromagnetic* and *electrical signals.* Also see Figure N-4.

signal-plus-noise to noise ratio ((S+N)/N). The ratio of the *amplitude* (magnitude) of the useful or desired signal plus the accompanying *noise* to the amplitude (magnitude) of the noise at a given point in a *communication, computer,* or other *electrical* or electronic *system.*

signal processing. The transformation of an *input signal* (i.e., a specific *wave shape*) into some desirable form or other wave shape, usually by means of particular electronic *circuits, lens* systems, *waveguides, antennae,* or other circuit elements, such as *detectors, rectifiers, pulse compressors, pulse expanders, pulse generators,* nonlinear circuits, or *gates.* It includes the *detection, shaping, converting, coding,* or time *positioning* of an *electrical, electromagnetic,* or *acoustic signal.* Also see *automatic error detection; signal regeneration.* See Figure S-5.

S-5. A *digital* **signal processing** *chip* for performing *real-time data processing* tasks in *speech synthesis, voice recognition, filtering, tone detection,* and *line balancing* in *digital communication systems* at the rate of over a million *operations* per *second.* (Courtesy of Bell Laboratories.)

signal recording telegraphy. *Telegraphy* in which the *received signal elements* are recorded automatically for subsequent *translation* by an *operator.*

signal regeneration. The *transformation* or *restoration* of a *signal* to an original or predetermined configuration, shape, or position in time or space. For example, *signal* regeneration may include *amplifying, clipping, clamping, differentiating, integrating, clocking,* or other operations. Also see *signal processing.*

signals. See *asynchronous signals; coherent signals; orthogonal signals; synchronous signals.*

signal sample. The value of a specific *parameter* (characteristic), such as the *amplitude, frequency, phase,* or direction, of a *signal* at a chosen instant. For example, if a relatively wide *voltage pulse* and an extremely narrow *clock pulse* are both entered into a two-*input AND gate,* the *output* can be arranged to be the amplitude of the voltage pulse at the instant of the clock pulse, that is, the output will be an instantaneous sample of the input pulse. Also see *signal sampling.*

signal sampling. The process of taking samples of a particular *parameter* (characteristic) of a *signal.* Samples are usually taken at equal time intervals. Also see *signal sample.*

signal security. *Communication security (COMSEC)* and *electronic security (ELSEC)* combined. COMSEC and ELSEC include the *protection* that results from all measures that are designed to deny unauthorized persons *information* of value that might be derived from *interception* and *analysis* of *radiation* or *emission* from any *electrical,* electronic, or *electromagnetic systems, components,* or equipment or from related documentation. Also see *communication security (COMSEC); electronic security (ELSEC).*

signal support. The provision of personnel and equipment to organizations, or the provision of services, for the establishment of *communication systems* required by the organization. Signal support may be provided as an *integral* part of the organization being supported, or *communication services* may be furnished by a separate unit on an as required or on demand basis.

signal-to-noise ratio. 1. The ratio of the *signal* power to the *noise* power at a given point in a given system. 2. The ratio of the *amplitude* of the desired *signal* to the amplitude of noise, usually their *RMS* values, at a given point and at a given time. The *signal-to-noise ratio* is usually expressed in *decibels (dB),* in terms of peak values for *impulse noise* and RMS for *random noise.* Both the signal and the noise should be defined to avoid ambiguity. 3. The ratio of *signal power* at a selected point in a *circuit* to total circuit *noise power.* Synonymous with *signal/noise ratio.* See *photodetector signal-to-noise ratio.*

signal transformation. See *signal shaping.*

signal transition. The change from one *signaling condition* (level, magnitude) to another. For example, the change from the *signal level* that represents *mark* to the signal level that represents *space,* or from the level that represents 1 to the level that represents 0. The transition might be a change in *amplitude,* such as *voltage* level, a change in *frequency,* a change in *phase (phase shift),* or a change in any other *signal parameter.* The transition usually occurs in such a short period of time that it is considered as an instantaneous transition, although a finite time, such as the *time constant* for a voltage or *electric current* transition, is always required for a transition to take place.

signal unit (SU). The group of *bits* or *pulses* that are encompassed by a single *error* check process or covered by a specified set of *error-checking bits.* The signal unit includes the *check bits.* In most *communication systems,* all the *information* that is *transferred* by a system is *formatted* in signal units.

signal unit indicator. The field within a *signal unit* that is used to identify or distinguish different signal units.

signature. 1. In *communications-electronics,* the complete, usually *analog, signal* that is received from a *source,* such as from a heat *(infrared) source,* a *radio transmitter,* or a *radar transmitter* or target. Signatures may be analyzed to indicate the nature of the source and assist in its recognition and identification. 2. The *attributes* of an *electromagnetic wave* that has been *reflected* from or *transmitted* through an *object* and that contains *information* indicative of attributes of the object. See *electromagnetic signature; penetration signature; radar signature; spectrum signature; target signature.*

signature analysis. A *procedure* that is designed to yield *information* concerning a *radiation source* or a *reflector* of *radiation.* The procedure is based on the measured characteristics of a *received electrical, electromagnetic,* or *acoustic signal.* The analysis is directed toward the *frequency* composition, *amplitude, phase,* direction, *polarization, distortion, shape,* and other features and characteristics of the *received* signal.

signature identification. See *aircraft signature identification.*

significant backlog. In a *communication system,* a *communication traffic* backlog of such volume that *messages* are delayed at any point in the *system.* A backlog point may be a *receiver,* a *transmitter,* a *message processing* unit, a service section, a *cryptographic* section, a *store-and-forward switching center,* a *booked call position,* a *transceiver,* or any other point in a communication system or in a communication *facility.* Insufficient *circuit capacity,* personnel, or *processing* equipment may cause a backlog, as may an excessive *communication traffic volume. Communication system saturation* limits overload and creates a backlog.

significant condition. In *communication systems,* a condition of a *signal element* that represents the meaning of that signal element in accordance with a specified *code.* For example, a significant condition may be the state or condition of a device or signal that corresponds to a quantized value of a characteristic chosen for *modulation.* A *voltage level* of 8 mV might represent a *digit* value that corresponds to 1 and a voltage level of 0 might represent a digit value of 0, both conditions thus serving to represent *numerals* in the *pure binary numeration system.* The significant conditions of a signal could be specific *frequencies,* used in some *telephone* and *facsimile systems* to represent voice or *light intensity* levels. A significant condition could be one of two *phase positions* of a *carrier,* the two phase positions being used to represent *binary information.* Usually significant conditions are *discrete* values. Other values, of say *amplitude, frequency,* or *phase,* that occur in the *transition* from one significant condition to another, such as from one voltage level to another, are not significant conditions and are usually of no interest. In *digital data systems,* the significant conditions for representation of *quantized* values must be specified usually with a specified tolerance. Very often half-values are considered as *thresholds* for tolerance. In the example of the 8 mV given above, any level above 4 mV would be considered as the significant condition for the 1, and any level below 4 mV would be considered or interpreted as a 0. Also see *significant instant*. See *modulation significant condition*.

significant condition number. In a *telegraph* or other *signaling system,* the number of *significant conditions* that are employed in *modulation, restitution, quantization,* or other *coding* form to characterize a *signal* in the system. For example, 3 in the *alternate mark inversion signal* and in the *bipolar coding signal,* 2 in the *binary non-return-to-zero signal,* and 4 in the *quadriphase modulation signal.*

significant instant. During *modulation* or *restitution* of a *signal,* one of the instants at which one of the successive *significant conditions* of the *signal* begins, or in some cases, ends. The significant instants are usually the instant of *transition* from one significant condition to another. For example, the instant at which a *voltage level, phase position* of a *carrier wave,* or a *frequency,* changes from one level or value to another, such as from the level or value that denotes 1 to the level or value that denotes 0. The significant conditions and significant instants are those that are recognized by an appropriate device. Each of the significant instants is determined at the moment the appropriate device assumes a condition or state that is usable for performing a specific function, such as recording a *binary digit,* processing a *machine function,* modulating a *carrier,* or *gating* a *signal.* Also see *decision instant; signal element; significant condition; unit interval.*

significant instant distortion. In *modulation, demodulation,* or *transmission,* the ratio of the maximum time or distance displacement, expressed algebraically, of the actual *significant instant* from the ideal or desired significant instant, to the *unit interval.* The distortion is considered to be positive when the actual significant instant occurs in time or space after the ideal instant. The degree of significant instant distortion is usually expressed as a percentage of the unit interval.

significant interval. The time interval between two consecutive *significant instants.*

significant interval theoretical duration. The exact duration that is prescribed or desired for a *significant interval* in a *signal,* such as a *telegraph code, digital data code,* or *modulated wave.*

significance. See *weight.*

silence. See *communication silence; cone-of-silence; electronic silence; listening silence; radio silence; ship radar silence; ship radio silence.*

silence zone. See *skip zone.*

silica cladded fiber. See *doped-silica cladded fiber.*

silica fiber. See *low-loss FEP-clad silica fiber; plastic-clad silica fiber.*

silica graded fiber. See *doped-silica graded fiber.*

simple microscope. See *magnifier.*

simple scanning. In *facsimile transmission, scanning* in which only one *spot* at a time is used.

simplex circuit. **1.** A *transmission path* or *circuit* capable of transmitting *data* or *information* in both directions but only in one direction at a time. The circuit may be a single wire with *ground return,* or may be derived from the center of a *balanced two-wire circuit* and ground return. **2.** A *circuit* that provides *transmission* in one direction only. Also see *phantom circuit; simplexed circuit.*

simplex communication. See *two-way alternate communication.*

simplexed circuit. A *two-wire circuit* from which a *simplex circuit* is derived. The two-wire circuit and the simplex circuit may be used simultaneously. Also see *simplex circuit; phantom circuit.*

simplex operation. See *two-way alternate communication.*

simplex radiotelegraph procedure. A *radiotelegraph network operational procedure* in which a *calling station,* such as a *ship station, calls* another station, such as a *shore station, transmits* its *message,* and the *called station* answers, all on the same *frequency.* Also see *cross-band radiotelegraph procedure.*

simplex signaling. *Signaling* in which two *conductors* are used for a single *channel.* A center-tapped coil, or its equivalent, can be used at both ends for this purpose. The arrangement may be a one-way signaling scheme suitable for intraoffice use, or the *simplex* legs may be connected to (full) *duplex signaling circuits.* These can function like simplex signaling with *E-and-M lead signaling.* Also see *phantom circuit.*

simplex transmission. See *two-way-alternate communication.*

SIMSCRIPT. A *computer programming language* that is used primarily for *digital simulation.*

simulate. To represent the features, characteristics, *parameters,* or behavior of a physical or abstract *system* by the behavior of another system. For example, to represent a physical phenomenon by means of *operations* performed by a *computer,* or to represent the operations of a computer by those of another computer.

simulation. The representation of the features, characteristics, *parameters,* or behavior of a physical or abstract system by the behavior of another system. For example, the representation of a physical phenomenon by means of *operations* performed by a computer, or the representation of a computer by those of another computer. Also see *emulator; simulator.* See *computer simulation.*

simulator. A *functional unit* that can imitate the behavior of the *hardware* or *software* of a physical or abstract system. For example, a *programmed computer* that can *simulate* a *communication network,* the economy or ecology of a country, or a set of war games. Also see *computer simulation; emulator.*

simultaneous.   Pertaining to the *occurrence time* of two or more events that occur at the same instant.

simultaneous communication.   See *two-way-simultaneous communication.*

simultaneous direction finding.   A *direction-finding (DF) procedure* in which a *control station* of a *net* requests *addresses* to obtain *information* on an identified *transmission* at a precise instant and to report the information in a *formatted message.*   The *stations* in the net report to the control station in *alphabetical* order of their *call signs.*

sine condition.   The property of a *lens* in which the sine of the maximum angular opening of the *axial bundle* of *refracted rays* is no longer inversely proportional to the *f*-number for a given *refractive index.*   Also see *aperture ratio; aplanatic lens.*

sine-junction gate.   See *A-AND-NOT-B gate.*

sine wave.   A *wave* that has instantaneous values that correspond to the mathematical function $A \sin\theta = A \sin\omega t$, where A is the peak (maximum) *amplitude,* θ is a displacement angle, ω is the angular velocity, that is, $\omega = 2\pi f$, where f is the *frequency* and t is time.   The sine wave has smooth *transitions* from peak positive to peak negative values and vice versa.   Unless specially contrived, *electrical oscillators* tend to generate sine waves.   A sine wave may be constructed graphically by plotting the magnitude of the projection on a diameter of a circle of the radius of the circle drawn to a point on the circle from the origin as the point moves around the circle with the angular displacement of the radius vector as the independent variable and the length of the projection as the dependent variable.   Also see *Fourier analysis.*

sine wave object.   An *object* having a sinusoidal variation of *luminance,* having the advantage that the *image* will have a sinusoidal variation of illuminance and the only effect of degeneration by a *lens system* will be to decrease the *modulation* in the image relative to that in the object.

sine wave response.   See *modulation transfer function.*

singing.   An undesired self-sustaining *audio-frequency* oscillation of *electrical currents* in a *circuit,* usually caused by excessive *gain,* excessive *positive feedback* at a *frequency* in or above the *passband,* or unbalance of a hybrid *termination.*   When singing occurs in *very low frequency circuits,* it is called *motor boating.*

singing device.   See *antisinging device.*

singing margin.   The difference in *signal level* between the *singing point* and the operating *gain* of a *system* or *component.*

singing point.   The *threshold* at which additional *gain* in a *system* will cause self-oscillations.

single-band.   Pertaining to *communication* equipment, such as *radio transmitters* and *receivers,* that can operate in only one *frequency band.*

single-bundle cable.   See *single-channel single-bundle cable.*

single call.   In *radiotelegraph transmission,* a *call* in which only one *call sign* precedes the call sign of the *calling station.*

single-call message.   A *message* that will not require reprocessing, such as *routing line segregation,* at any *relay station.*

single-call-sign calling.   A method of establishing and conducting *radiotelegraph* and *radiotelephone communication* in which subordinate-*station call signs* are used exclusively.   The single call-sign calling *procedure* may be used when prior agreement has been reached by participating organizations, *stations, networks,* or countries.

single-channel single-bundle cable.   A *bundle* of *optical fibers* with a protective covering.

single-channel single-fiber cable.   A single *optical conductor* usually with a protective covering.

single clear.   In *telephone switchboard operation,* a single steady *supervisory signal* that may be *received* during *double-supervisory working* and that indicates that a *user* (customer, subscriber) or *operator* has *cleared* at one end of a *circuit* but not at the other end.

single-current signaling.   *Direct-current (DC) telegraphy,* with on-off working, in which the *battery voltage* is applied to the *line* in the *mark condition* and *electrical current* flows to operate the *receive relay.*   No voltage or current is applied in the *space condition.*   Both *transmitter* and *receiver* are biased to the off condition by mechanical or electrical means.   *Operation* is restricted to slow *signaling speeds* as the line takes time to charge and discharge.   *Noise* and *interference* affect the receiver during the space condition.   Bias of the receive relay needs frequent adjustment to balance varying line conditions and since the line current must overcome this bias, the relay *sensitivity* is low.   This type of *telegraph transmission* if effected by means of *unidirectional currents.*   Synonymous with *neutral telegraphy; neutral transmission; single-current telegraphy; single-current transmission; unipolar telegraphy; unipolar transmission.*

single-current system.   See *neutral direct-current telegraph system.*

single-current telegraphy.   See *single-current signaling.*

single-current transmission.   See *single-current signaling.*

single-current transmission system.   See *neutral direct-current telegraph system.*

single-domain network. A *network* that has one and only one *host processor.*

single-ended control. See *single-ended synchronization.*

single-ended synchronization. A *synchronization* control method that is used between two locations in which *phase error signals* that are used to control the *clock* at a location are derived from a comparison of the phase of the incoming signals and the phase of the *internal clock* at the same location. Synonymous with *single-ended control.*

single fiber. A *discrete conductor* of *lightwaves*—usually a single filament of glass, plastic, or both—the central *core* being of higher *refractive index* than the *cladding.* Single fibers may be combined into *bundles* and *cables.* Also see Figures F-4, S-3, T-11 and W-2.

single-fiber cable. See *multichannel single-fiber cable; single-channel single-fiber cable.*

single-fiber light guide. See *optical fiber.*

single-frequency interference. *Interference* that is caused by a single-*frequency source.* For example, interference in a *data transmission line,* that is induced by a 60 Hz *power source.*

single-frequency translation. A single *stage* of *up-converter* or *down-converter frequency translation.* Synonymous with *single-frequency conversion.*

single-frequency (SF) signaling. In *telephone communications,* a method of conveying *dialing signals* or *supervisory signals,* or both, with one or more specified single *frequencies.* The *signals* are normally used in *inband signaling* for *longhaul communications.*

single-frequency (SF) signaling system. In *telephone communications,* a *system* in which *single-frequency signaling* is used. For example, a system could *transmit direct-current (DC) signaling pulses* or *supervisory signals,* or both, over *carrier channels* or *cable pairs* on a 4-wire basis using a 2600 Hz *signal tone.* The conversion of *pulses* into tones, or vice versa, is done by single-frequency signal units. Synonymous with *SF signal unit.*

single harmonic. 1. One of the *harmonics* of a *fundamental frequency.* 2. A *sinusoidal wave* of only one *frequency.* For example, $v = v_m sin\omega t$, where v is the instantaneous value of the single harmonic wave, v_m is the maximum (peak) *amplitude* of the wave, $\omega = 2\pi f$ is the angular velocity of the wave, f is the frequency, and t is time.

single-harmonic distortion. The *signal distortion* that is caused by the presence of a given *harmonic* of a *fundamental frequency.* It is measured as the ratio of the *power* of any one *harmonic frequency* in a *signal* to the power of the fundamental frequency of the signal. This ratio is measured at the *output* of a device under specified conditions and may be expressed in dB. Also see *total harmonic distortion.*

single heterojunction. In a *laser diode,* a single *junction* involving two *energy level* shifts and two *refractive index* shifts, used to provide increased confinement of *radiation* direction, improved control of *radiative recombination,* and reduced *nonradiative* (thermal) *recombination.* Synonymous with *close-confinement junction.*

single lens. A *lens* composed of only one piece of glass or other *optical* material. Contrast with *compound lens.*

single-mode fiber. A *fiber waveguide* that supports the *propagation* of only one *mode.* Usually a low-loss *optical waveguide* with a very small *core* (2 to 8 *microns*). It requires a *laser source* for the *input signals* because of the very small *entrance aperture (acceptance cone).* The small core radius approaches the *wavelength* of the source; consequently, only a single mode is propagated.

single-mode launching. The insertion of a single *propagation mode* into a *waveguide* such as by controlling the *incidence angle, beam width,* skew angle, and *prism*-to-*fiber* gap when *light* from a *source* is passed through a prism into the side of a *fiber.*

single Morse system. See *neutral direct-current telegraph.*

single-node network. A *communication network* in which all *users* (customers, subscribers) are interconnected through one *node.* Also see *star network.*

single-operator period watch. A *communication watch* for a period of time that is based on the availability of only one *operator* at a *station.* If there are several stations in contact, the watch can be rotated among them. *Messages* that are intended for a given station can be held by the other stations when the operator of the given station is off duty. They can then be *relayed* when the operator is on duty. Also see *continuous communication watch; one operator ship; two-operator period watch.*

single-position magneto switchboard. A *magneto switchboard* that is operated by one *operator* without a *supervisor.*

single-precedence message. A *message* in which the same *precedence* is applicable to all *addressees,* that is, to both *action addressees* and *information addressees.* In single-precedence messages, only one *precedence designator* is needed. Also see *dual precedence message.*

single-pulse CW sonar. See *searchlight sonar.*

single sideband (SS or SSB). Pertaining to an *amplitude modulation* technique that is primarily used in *carrier telephony* and *high-frequency (HF) radio* to increase the *transmission* efficiency *(power)* and also to increase *electromagnetic spectrum* utilization in terms of the total number of *channels* available in a given *bandwidth.* Only one *sideband* is *transmitted* while the other sideband and the *carrier* are suppressed. Although proposed for the *uplink* and the *downlink* of *satellite systems,* its use in this field has been limited.

single-sideband reference level. The *power* of one of two equal tones that, when used together to *modulate* a *transmitter,* cause it to develop its *peak power output* or its *full rated output power.*

single-sideband noise power ratio. The ratio of the *power* measured at the *output,* in the *notch bandwidth,* with the *notch filter* in, to the power in the notch bandwidth with the notch filter out, again measured at the output. The notch filter is applied to an *input* sufficient to maintain the total *system mean noise power output* constant.

single-sideband suppressed-carrier (SSB-SC) transmission. *Single-sideband transmission* in which the *carrier* is suppressed. Thus, it pertains to *transmission* in which one of the two *sidebands* and the carrier are suppressed.

single-sideband transmission. *Transmission* in which one *sideband* is *transmitted* and the other is suppressed. The *carrier* may be *suppressed* or transmitted.

single-sideband voice. A *mode* of *voice radio transmission* in which one *sideband* is *transmitted,* while the *carrier* and the second sideband are *suppressed.*

single-simplex communication. See *two-way alternate communication.*

single-simplex operation. See *two-way alternate communication.*

single-tone interference. An undesired single *discrete frequency (single harmonic)* appearing in a *single channel.*

sink. 1. A device that accepts energy. For example, a device that accepts *data* from a *transmission medium* or *transmitter;* a device that collects energy from several sources; or a *power*-consuming device, such as a *resistive* or *capacitive* (for reactive power) *load* on a *circuit.* 2. In *communications,* the part of a *communication system* in which *messages* are considered to be *received.* Also see *source.* See *communication sink; data sink.*

sink user. See *destination user.*

sinusoidal function. A mathematical function that expresses the *amplitude* of the projected line segment formed on a diameter by a point that is moving in a circle, or if the speed is constant, the *amplitude* of the projection on a diameter as a function of time of the uniformly rotating radius *vector.* For example, $v = v_m sin\omega t$, where v is the instantaneous value of the sinusoidal function, v_m is the maximum amplitude, that is, the radius of the circle, ω is the angular velocity of the radius vector, and t is time. A function of such functions is also a sinusoidal function. *Electromagnetic waves* and *alternating currents (AC)* are usually sinusoidal functions, or at least can be represented as a summation of such functions. Also see *Fourier analysis.*

siphon recorder. A recorder in which the recording *stylus* is fed with ink via a fine siphon.

site. See *down-range site.*

site link. See *cross-site link.*

situation report. A report or *message* that is used to describe an existing or ongoing situation, incident, or action.

SI units. See *metric system.*

size. See *increment size; plotter step size; spot size.*

skew. In *facsimile systems,* angular deviation from rectangularity of the received *frame* due to *asynchronism* between *scanner* and *recorder.* It is a defect in reproduction in which *lines* that should be at right angles to the *scanning* direction are inclined to it, owing to a difference between the scanning speeds at *transmission* and *reception.* Skew is expressed numerically as the tangent of the angle of deviation.

skew ray. In a circular *optical fiber,* a *light ray* that is not confined to a plane, does not pass through the *optical axis,* is not parallel to the optical axis, and yet is *totally internally reflected,* thus taking a zig-zag path. In certain *graded index fibers,* the skew ray travels in a *helical path* along the fiber never intersecting the optical axis, particularly as long as the fiber is straight. It is not confined to the *meridian plane* or any other plane, nor is it a *meridional ray.* Also see *meridional ray.*

skim. In *optical* elements, streaks of dense *seeds* with accompanying small bubbles or *inclusions.*

skin effect. The tendency of *alternating current (AC)* to flow near the surface of a *conductor.* The current is thus restricted to a small part of the total cross-sectional area. The effect is to increase the *resistance* to the flow of current. The effect is caused by the *inductance* of the conductor, which causes an increase in the *inductive reactance* at high frequencies. The inner filaments experience an inductive reactance with all the surrounding filaments, their reactance thus being higher than the outer filaments. Thus, the current tends toward the lower reactance (outside) filaments. At *high frequencies,* the circumference is a better measure of resistance than the cross-sectional area. The depth of penetration of current can be very small compared to a diameter.

skip distance. The minimum distance between a *transmitting station* and the point of return to the earth of the *transmitted wave* that is *reflected* from the *ionosphere.* Also see *hop; skip zone.*

skip zone. A ring-shaped region, within the *transmission range,* in which *signals* from a *transmitter* are not *received.* It is the area between the farthest points reached by the *ground wave* and nearest points at which the *reflected sky waves* come back to the earth. Synonymous with *silence zone.* Also see *hop; skip distance.*

sky noise. The total *noise* that is *received* by an *antenna* from *sources* that are outside the earth, that is, from nonterrestrial *sources.* Noise from *satellites,* missiles, *spacecraft,* and other man-made sources, though outside the earth, are not considered as sky noise.

skywave.   1. An *electromagnetic wave* that travels upward in space from the *antenna* and that may or may not be returned to earth by *ionospheric refraction or reflection.*   2. A *wave* that descends upon the *earth* from a high elevation angle. Also see *surface wave.*

slab dielectric optical waveguide.   An *optical waveguide* consisting of rectangular layers or ribbons of materials of differing *refractive indices* that support one or more *lightwave transmission modes,* with the energy of the *transmitted waves* confined primarily to the layer of highest refractive index, the lower indexed *medium* serving as *cladding, jacketing,* or surrounding medium.   Slab dielectric optical waveguides are used in *integrated optical circuits* for geometrical convenience, in contrast to *optical fibers* in *cables* used for long-distance *transmission.*

slab dielectric waveguide.   An *electromagnetic waveguide* consisting of a *dielectric transmission medium* of rectangular cross section.   The width and thickness of the guide may be controlled to support specific *propagation modes;* it may be *cladded, protected, distributed,* and *electronically controllable;* and it may be mounted on *integrated optical circuit substrate.*   See *doubly-cladded slab dielectric waveguide.*   See Figure S-6.   Also see Figure E-2.

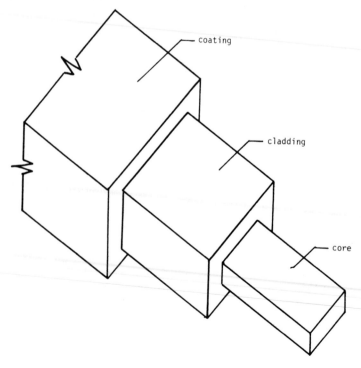

coating

cladding

core

S-6. **A slab dielectric waveguide,** perhaps of *micron* dimensions on *integrated optical-circuit chips.*

slant range. The *line-of-sight* distance between two points that are usually not at the same elevation. For example, the line-of-sight (direct) distance from a *transmitting antenna* to a specified object, such as a target or a *receiving antenna*.

slave station. **1.** In a *data communication network,* the *station* that is selected and controlled by a *master station.* The slave station can usually only *call,* or be called by, a *master station.* **2.** In *basic mode link control operations* of a *communication system* or *network,* the *station* that is selected by a *master station* to *receive data,* that is, to receive a *call.*

slave timing system. See *master-slave timing system.*

SLD. *Superluminescent diode.*

sleek. In *optical* elements, a polishing *scratch* without visible conchoidal fracturing of the edges.

sleeve splicer. See *precision-sleeve splicer.*

slew. See *clock phase slew.*

slewing. **1.** Rotating a *directional antenna* or *transducer* rapidly, usually in a horizontal or vertical direction, or both. **2.** Changing the *frequency* or *pulse repetition rate* of a *signal source.* **3.** Changing the *tuning* of a *receiver,* usually by *sweeping* through all *frequencies.*

slip. See *digital slip.*

slope. See *line slope.*

slope equalizer. A device or *circuit* that is used to achieve a specified *line slope.*

slope-keypoint compaction. A *data compaction* method that employs the statement of a specific point of departure and a direction or slope of departure, until the deviation from a prescribed condition exceeds a specific value, whereupon a new keypoint and a new slope are specified. The *storage* requirement and the *transmission time* and *space* requirements are reduced from the requirements when storing or transmitting uncompacted absolute values of a large number of points.

slope station. See *glide path-slope station.*

slot. See *channel time slot; digit time slot; frame-alignment time slot; signaling time slot; time slot.*

slot antenna. A *radiator* that is formed by a slot in a conducting surface or in the wall of a *waveguide.*

slow-sweep noise-modulated jamming. *Jamming* in which the *radar screen displays* bright "walking" *strobes* that vary a few degrees in *azimuth* and fluctuate in *intensity.*

Smith chart. A chart that is used to establish a set of real and complex coordinates for the *transmission line* generalized *voltage reflection coefficient* and can be used as an aid in transmission line performance analysis. For example, it can be used to determine *impedance, phase,* and *frequency* values at various fractions of a *wavelength* toward a *sinusoidal source* of *power* from a *load* of given *impedance* connected to a *uniform line* of given *characteristic impedance.* See Figure S-7.

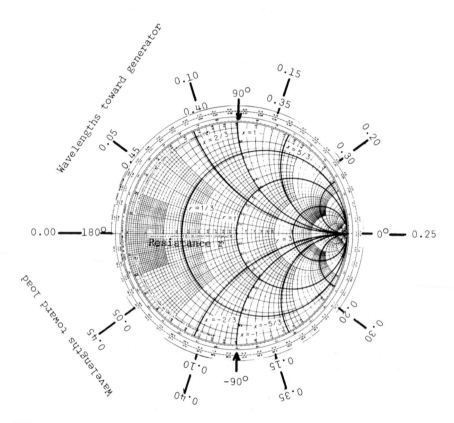

S-7. The *Smith Chart* coordinates for *transmission line* analysis. (From P. H. Smith, Transmission Line Calculator, *Electronics,* vol 12, pp 29–31, January 1939.)

smoke. See *pyrotechnic smoke.*

smooth earth. An idealized earth surface, such as water or very level terrain, that has *radio horizons* that are not formed by prominent ridges or mountains but are determined solely as a function of *antenna* height above ground and the *effective earth radius.* Also see *antenna height above average terrain; path profile.*

Snell's law. When *electromagnetic waves,* such as *light,* pass from a given *transmission medium* to a denser medium, its path is deviated toward the normal. When passing into a less dense medium, its path is deviated away from the normal. Often called the law of *refraction,* Snell's law defines this phenomenon by describing the relation between the *incidence angle* and the *refraction angle* as follows:

$$\sin\theta_0/\sin\theta_1 = n_1/n_0$$

where θ_0 is the incidence angle, θ_1 is the refraction angle, n_1 is the *refractive index* of the medium containing the *refracted ray,* and n_0 is the refractive index of the medium containing the *incident ray.* Stated in another way, both laws, that of *reflection* and of *refraction,* are attributed to Snell, namely, when the incident ray, the normal to the surface at the point of incidence of the ray on the surface, the reflected ray, and the refracted ray all lie in a single plane, the angle between the incident ray and the normal is equal in magnitude to the angle between the reflected ray and the normal. The ratio of the sine of the angle between the normal and the incident ray, to the sine of the angle between the normal and the refracted ray, is a constant. Also see *refraction.* See Figure S-8.

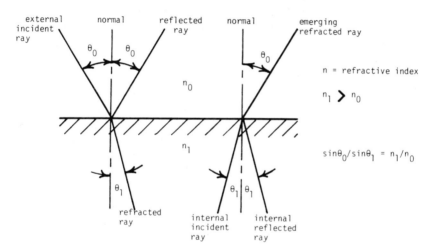

S-8. *Reflection* and *refraction* in accordance with **Snell's laws,** where the *incidence* and *reflection* angles are equal but the sines of the incidence and refraction angles are inversely as the *refractive indices* of the transmitting media.

(S+N)/N. *Signal-plus-noise to noise ratio.*

SNOBOL. A *computer programming language* that is used primarily for *string* handling.

snow. 1. In *video display systems, noise* that is uniformly distributed in a spotty or mottled fashion on a *screen,* such as a *radar* or *television screen.* The speckled background is caused by *random noise* on an *intensity-modulated cathode-ray tube display.* 2. The effect on a *radio* or *radar screen* that is caused by *sweep jamming* and that has a uniformly crosshatched or speckled appearance.

SNR. See *signal-to-noise ratio.*

SO character. See *shift-out character.*

soft. See *fail soft.*

soft copy. A *display element, display group,* or *display image* that is not permanent, not separable from the *display space* on the *display surface* of a *display device,* and usually not readily transportable in a physical sense except when the display device itself is transported or except in the sense that the elements, groups, or images can be *transmitted* as *signals* inside the display device or transmitted as signals over *communication lines,* in which case they are still soft copy. Examples of soft copy include *images* on *CRT* screens, *LED panels,* and *gas panels.* Usually soft copy is volatile in the sense that the copy, or image, is lost when *power* is removed from the display device. Contrast with *hard copy.*

soft limiting. A *limiting* action with appreciable variation in *output signal* in the *range* where the *amplitude, power,* or other *parameter* (characteristic) of the *output* is limited (controlled) when subjected to a fairly wide variation of *input signal.*

software. 1. *Computer programs, routines, compilers, assemblers, translators, procedures,* associated rules, and related documentation (such as operating manuals, wiring diagrams, and *logic diagrams*) that pertain to the *operation* of a *data processing system, communication system,* or other *system. Display systems,* particularly *interactive systems,* usually require accompanying software to support their *operation.* Contrast with *hardware* and with *firmware.* 2. In a *display system,* those *segments, display files, computer programs,* documents, and similar items required for *operation* of the *display system.* Contrast with *hardware* and with *firmware.*

software engineering. The branch of science and technology that is devoted to the design, development, and use of *software.* Design criteria include accuracy, efficiency, flexibility, comprehensibility, maintainability, time, and cost.

software reliability. 1. A measure of the extent to which *software* can be proven to be correct or to yield correct results. 2. The probability that *software* does not result in *system failure* or produce erroneous results. Also see *hardware reliability.*

SOH. The *start-of-heading transmission control character.*

SOI. 1. *Signal operating instruction.* 2. *Signal operation instruction.*

solar absorption factor. The *radiation absorption factor* for solar *radiation.*

solar array. An assembly of solar cells used for the production of *electrical power* by the *photovoltaic effect.* For example, a group of solar cells that cover most of the external surface of a *satellite* to provide electrical power for control and *communication.*

solar day. See *true solar day.*

solar eclipse. An *eclipse* of the sun by the moon as the moon moves between observer *(photodetector)* and the sun.

solar flare. A powerful eruption of *radiation* from the sun, associated with sunspots, and lasting 15 to 20 minutes. In rare instances a solar flare can last up to a few hours. Intense radiation reaches the earth some 26 hours after the eruption.

solar noise. *Electromagnetic radiation noise* received from the sun. Such noise can interfere with *radio, television, microwave,* and *lightwave communication.* All solar radiation is *electromagnetic;* the *infrared* and *visible wavelengths* are perhaps the most beneficial; the higher *frequencies* perhaps cause genetic changes. Solar noise is by far the most prominent *radio noise source.* At 1 GHz the solar noise *temperature* is approximately 2.8×10^5 K. This decreases in nearly logarithmic manner to 6×10^3 K at 30 GHz. When the *antenna beamwidth* is less than $0.5°$ (the angle subtended by the sun from the earth), the following empirical relationship may be used; $T_{sn} = (1.96/f) \times 10^{14}$. This relationship is obtained from $T_{sn}/290 = (675/f) \times 10^9$, where T_{sn} is the solar noise temperature in *kelvin* and f is the *frequency* in *hertz.* Also see *standard noise temperature.*

solar radiation. The totality of *electromagnetic radiation* from the sun. The range is from *low frequency* to the *frequency* of *cosmic rays* of the highest known frequency. The majority of the energy of solar radiation is in the *infrared, visible,* and *ultraviolet* regions of the *frequency spectrum.*

sole user. Pertaining to a *communication system* in which specific communication *facilities* or *components* within the system are provided for use by one or a relatively small number of *users* rather than for use by essentially all of the users in the area in which the system is located.

sole user circuit. An *exclusive user circuit* that is set up between a *user* (customer, subscriber) and one or more other users on a full-time basis for a defined period and is provided with automatic *restoration* of *connection* in the event of *failure.* Also see *exclusive-user circuit; switched hotline circuit.*

solid angle. See *unit solid angle.*

solid-state laser. A *laser* whose *active medium* is a solid material, such as glass, crystal, or *semiconductor material,* rather than gas or liquid.

sonar. *Sound navigation and ranging.* See *active sonar; laser sonar; long-range laser sonar; passive sonar; searchlight sonar; short-range laser sonar.*

sone. A unit used to define the *intensity* of loudness sensation. One sone corresponds to a loudness level of 40 *phons.* For loudness levels of 40 phons or greater, the relationship between loudness level, L, in phons and loudness level, S, in sones, is given by $log\ S = 0.0301(L-40)$. This relation is derived from the relation $S = 2^{(L-40)/10}$.

sonic equipment. See *ultrasonic equipment.*

sonic pen. A *stylus,* such as might be used to provide *coordinate data* in the *display space* on the *display surface* of a *display device,* that uses an *acoustic (sound) wave* to *couple* energy to the display surface to indicate position. The acoustic wave is highly directive for accurate positioning, thus enabling a specific location to be identified when energized.

sonobuoy. A *sonar* device that is used to detect submerged submarines and that, when activated, *relays information* by *radio.* It may be active or passive, and directional or nondirectional.

soot. The *dopant* material (e.g., germanium tetrachloride or titanium tetrachloride) deposited on a glass *substrate,* pattern, plug, or slug, followed by heating, oxidation, and *drawing* processes for forming an *optical fiber* with a controlled *stepped* or *graded refractive index* in its cross section. Also see *chemical vapor phase oxidation process.*

soot process. See *chemical vapor phase oxidation process.*

SOS. The *distress signal* when using *Morse code, CW,* or *radiotelegraph communication systems.*

SOSIC. Silicon-on-sapphire *integrated circuit.*

SOSTEL. *Solid-state electronic logic.*

sound. *voiced sound; unvoiced sound.*

sound communications. The use of *sound waves* to *transmit messages,* such as when transmitting *signals* by whistle, siren, horn, or other devices in which the duration of the sound signal can be controlled. *International Morse code* is used. Special meanings can be assigned to other sound formations. Percussion devices can be used for Morse code by using one stroke for a dot and two rapid strokes for a dash. Also see *sound signaling.*

sounder. A *telegraph receiving* instrument in which *Morse code signals* are *translated* into *sound signals* determined by intervals between two diverse sounds, by two different *audio frequencies,* or by audio frequency *dots* and *dashes.* See *echo sounder.*

sounding. See *air sounding; oblique-incidence sounding.*

sound navigation and ranging (sonar). A sonic device that is used primarily for the *detection* and location of underwater objects by *reflecting sound waves* from the objects or by *interception* of sound from an underwater, surface, or above-surface *sound source.* Sonar operates with sound waves in the same way that *radar* and *radio direction-finding* equipment operate with *electromagnetic waves,* including use of the *Doppler effect,* radial component of velocity measurement, and *triangulation.*

sound powered. Pertaining to a device, such as a *microphone* or *telephone,* that derives *power* by converting *acoustic* energy into *electrical power* without the aid of additional external power. It operates using the power that it converts.

sound-powered telephone. A *telephone* in which the operating *power* is derived from the *speech input.* No other *source* of power is used, except perhaps a *magneto* for *signaling,* that is, for operating attention devices, such as a bell or a buzzer. Also see *electrically-powered telephone.*

sound signaling. A means of *communication* in which *sound waves* are used for *transmission* of *signals* between a *transmitter* and a *receiver.* For example, whistles, sirens, bells, and other signal devices are used to *transmit messages* of signals or *codes* consisting of *modulated* sound waves. Sound waves may be used for *communication* using *international Morse code. Modulation* may consist of interrupting the sound wave or sound source to form *dots* and *dashes.* Also see *sound communication.*

sound wave. A longitudinal *wave* that consists of a sequence of pressure *pulses* or elastic displacements of air or other material, whether solid, liquid, or gas. For gases, the sound wave is a sequence of condensations (dense air) and rarifactions (less dense air) that travels through the gas. In solid matter, the sound wave is a traveling sequence of *elastic* compression and expansion *waves.* In liquids, the sound wave is a traveling sequence of combined elastic deformation and compression waves. The *propagation rate* (speed) in a *medium* is determined by the *temperature,* pressure, and elastic properties of the medium. Sound in air propagates at 1087 ft/s or 332 m/s at $0°$C. Its speed increases about 2 ft/s or 0.6 m/s for each Celsius degree rise in *temperature.* Synonymous with *acoustic wave.* Also see *elastic wave.*

source. In *communications,* that part of a *system* from which *signals* or *messages* are considered to originate. Also see *sink.* See *communication source; data source; lambertian source; light source; message source; optical fiber source; point source; primary radiation source; secondary radiation source; standard source; stationary message source; video optical source; virtual source; YAG/ LED source.*

source chirp. The *signal* from a *source* that *emits* a varying *frequency,* usually from shorter to longer *wavelengths* (i.e., higher to lower frequency) during a *pulse* time. The phenomenon results in *pulse compression* in *optical fibers* since the longer wavelengths of light emitted later will catch up with the shorter wavelengths emitted earlier. The frequency emitted sounds similar to a bird's chirp; thus the term *chirp.*

source-coupler loss. In an *optical data link, optical communication system,* or *optical fiber* system, the *loss,* usually expressed in decibels between the *light* source and the device or material that *couples* the light-source energy from the *source* to the *fiber cable.*

source-coupling efficiency. The maximum *luminous intensity* or *power-density* efficiency with which a *lambertian source,* such as an *LED* source, is *coupled* to a *graded refractive index optical fiber* is given by:

$$\eta_{sc} = A_f (N.A)^2 / 2A_s n_o^2$$

where A_f is the cross-sectional area of the fiber *core; N.A.* is the *numerical aperture,* which is the sine of one-half of the total *acceptance angle* and dependent upon the *refractive indices* of the core and the *cladding; A_s* is the cross-sectional area of the *source-emitted light beam;* and n_o is the refractive index of the *transmission medium* between the *light source* and the optical-fiber face.

source-fiber coupling. In *fiber-optic transmission systems,* the *transfer* of *optical signal power emitted* by a *light source* into an *optical fiber,* such *coupling* being dependent upon many factors, including geometry and fiber characteristics. Many optical fiber sources have an *optical fiber pigtail* for *connection* by means of a *splice* or a *connector* to a *transmission fiber.*

source flash detector. See *infrared point-source flash detector.*

source-to-fiber coupled power. The *optical power* that is actually *coupled* from a *light source* into the interior of an *optical fiber,* given by:

$$P_c = P_o (\Theta_a / \Theta_e) T$$

where P_o is the source optical power *output;* Θ_a is the *acceptance* solid *angle,* or angle of collection of the fiber; Θ_e is the *emission* solid angle, or *beam divergence,* of the light source; and T is the *transmission coefficient* of the optical system, i.e., of the source-to-fiber *interface.* In cases of *misalignment,* the Θ_a and the Θ_e must be replaced by the source and fiber cross-sectional areas.

source-to-fiber loss. In an *optical fiber, signal power loss* caused by the distance of separation between a signal *source* and the *conducting fiber.*

source user. The *user* providing the *information* that is to be *transferred* to a *destination user* during a particular *information transfer transaction.* Synonymous with *information source; message source.* Also see *destination user.*

space. 1. In *display systems,* any reference system in which a *display element, display group,* or *display image* can be described, located, defined, *displayed,* or operated upon. For example, a coordinate system. 2. A *machine function* that is used to control the horizontal movement of the carriage of a *teletypewriter (teleprinter)* and is required to advance the paper laterally without printing a *character* on the *page.* This movement is obtained by the use of the *space* bar, corresponding perforation, or *space signal.* 3. In *Morse code,* the designation given to one of the two *significant conditions* in the code, the other condition being designated the *mark* condition. 4. In *binary modulation,* the *significant condition* of *modulation* that is not specified as the *mark.* 5. The time interval between *characters* and *words* in *Morse code.* The space is a *signal element* of a given *condition* and a duration of two *unit intervals* between characters and six unit intervals between *words.* The space may occur between code elements, characters, or groups of characters. The space between signal elements may be one unit interval, that is, the interval of one *dot*. Between characters the space may also be three units; between groups, seven units. **6.** In *communication display devices* and *computer display devices,* a reference *system* in which a *display* can be defined. Synonymous with *spacing pulse; spacing signal.* Also see *mark.* See *display space; dead space; deep space; free space; image storage space; non-return-to-zero space (NRZ-S); outer space; unshift-on-space; virtual space.*

space active. Pertaining to a *telegraph signal* in which a *space* is represented by a *pulse,* such as a *direct-current (DC) condition* or a *constant-frequency signal* (tone), and a *mark* is represented by an *open circuit,* that is, by a *no-current condition.*

space character. A *character* that is usually represented by a blank site in a series of *graphics.* The space character, though not a *control character,* has a function equivalent to that of a *format effector* that causes the *print* or *display position* to move one position forward without producing the printing or displaying of any *graphic character.* Similarly, the space character may have a function that is equivalent to that of an *information separator (data delimiter).* Also see *horizontal tabulation character.*

space coding. See *biphase space coding.*

space-coherent light. *Light,* incident on a given area, in which the *amplitude, phase,* and time variation are predictable and correlated. The area is usually in a plane perpendicular to the direction of *propagation.* Spatial noncoherence refers to a random and unpredictable state of the *phase* over an area normal to the direction of propagation. Also see *coherent light, time-coherent light.*

space communications. See *free-space optical communications.*

space communication system. A group of cooperating *earth stations* and *space stations* that provides a given *space service* and that may use objects *(satellites, spacecraft)* in space for the *reflection* or *retransmission (relaying)* of *radio* or *video signals.*

spacecraft. **1.** Any type of space vehicle, including *earth satellites* or *deep space* probes, whether manned or unmanned. **2.** An artificial body that is capable of traveling beyond the earth's atmosphere but is not captured in orbit around a parent body. For example, a deep space probe. In the United States, the words spacecraft and satellite are used differently than defined above. In the US, *satellite* is the term for an artificial orbiting body without any control to maneuver while in orbit. In contrast, the word spacecraft is applied to a body that does have maneuver control, whether it is controlled from the ground or from an onboard crew or computer. In the US, a spacecraft can be fully or partially captured by a parent body. For example, the Skynet, NATO, and DSCS 2 satellites are all called spacecraft by the US control authorities.

spaced aerial diversity. See *spaced antenna diversity.*

spaced antenna diversity.   **1.** A method of *signal transmission* employing *antennas* or *sources* that are spatially separated. **2.** A method of *signal* reception employing *antennas* or *detectors* that are spatially separated, both are used for *transmitting* the same *information*.   It is a method of *transmission* or *reception,* or both, that is used to minimize the effects of fading by the simultaneous use of two or more antennas that are spaced a number of *wavelengths* apart.   It includes the use of two or more separate and independent *transmission media* for transmitting the same information and *combining* the *signals* from the separate paths to overcome the effects of *fading, transmission loss, delay, interference,* and other signal degradation effects.   Thus, it is diversity accomplished by the use of spatial separation.   Spaced antenna diversity transmission tends to minimize the effects of *flat* or *selective fading* by making use of common *polarization* and spatial separation of two or more transmitting or receiving antennas.   Their signals may be combined at *intermediate frequency (IF)* or *audio frequency (AF) stages* to yield a single *output signal.* This technique makes use of the fact that fading is often a very localized phenomenon.   The spacing of the antennas is usually about 2 or 3 wavelengths for *high-frequency (HF) systems.*   They may be 50 wavelengths apart for transmission systems that are designed to overcome the effects of *tropospheric scatter* or that make use of tropospheric scatter for *propagation* purposes. Synonymous with *spaced aerial diversity.*

space diversity.   The use of two or more separate and independent *transmission media* for *transmitting* the same *information* and then *combining* the *signals* from the *separate media.*   This method of *transmission* overcomes the effects of *fading, transmission loss,* delay, *interference,* and other effects that tend to degrade a *signal.*   Thus, it is diversity that is accomplished through the use of spatial separation.

space division.   In *communications,* the use of space to obtain *channel* separation.   For example, a *telegraph* or *telephone switching system* in which every *connection* requires an individual line through the *switching center.* This limits the number of connections between *stations* to the number of physical lines between them.   Also see *frequency division; time division.*

space-division multiple-access (SDMA).   In *satellite communication systems,* the division of *satellite communication traffic capacity* into *spot beam* areas in which all of the available *frequency band* is allocated for use on a spatial separation basis.   *Communication operations* in which SDMA is used may involve complex *routing* and *switching* within the *communication satellite* itself.

space-division multiplex.   A method of obtaining separate *channels* by means of spatial separation of *conductors* or *waveguides.*   For example, in *fiber optics,* a method of obtaining separate *channels* in a *cable* by using a separate *bundle* or individual *fiber* for each channel.   Each such space-division multiplexed channel may be *time-division* or *wavelength (frequency) division multiplexed.*

space-division multiplexing.   The use of spatial separation or *insulation* between *beams, conductors, optical fibers* or other *transmission media* in order to obtain *channel isolation.*   For example, the combining of several independent and isolated *fibers* or wires in a single *bundle* or *cable* in order to use each fiber (or bundle) as a separate *communication* path, *channel,* or set of channels. A typical arrangement for multiplexing might be to use *time-division multiplexing* on each space-division multiplexed fiber pair in an *optical cable.*   See *optical space-division multiplexing.*   See Figure S-9.

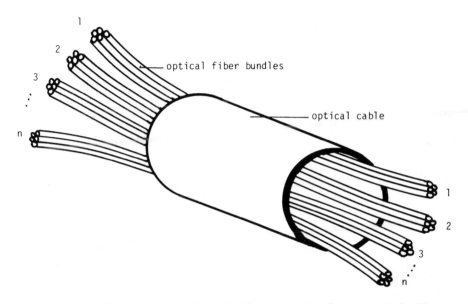

S-9. **Space-division multiplexing** by maintaining separate *bundles* in an *optical cable.*

space-division switching.   1. *Switching* in which the interconnections of *input* and *output terminations* are established and maintained with *electrical* or *optical* continuity. *Channels* are thus physically separated during *transmission.* **2.** A method of *transmission* in which *path routing* determination is accomplished in a *switch* that makes use of a set of physically separated matrix contacts or crosspoints.

space ground-link subsystem.   In *satellite communication systems,* an *integrated* set of *satellite tracking, telemetry,* and *command* equipment consisting of *communication functional units* in *satellites, space probes,* and *spacecraft.*

space hold.   A *telegraph no-traffic transmission condition* in which a steady *space* is *transmitted.*   Also see *mark hold.*

space intersection.   A geometric method that is used in geodetic and *satellite* ephemeris calculations. The method includes *triangulation* and *trilateration.*

space loss.   See *free space loss; isotropic space loss.*

space optical communications.   See *free-space optical communications.*

space research earth station.   An *earth station* in the *space research service.*

space research service.   A *space service* in which *spacecraft* or other objects in space are used for scientific or technological research purposes.

space research space station.   A *space station* in the *space research service.*

space segment.   In a *satellite communication system,* those parts of the *system* that are used for the launch and maintenance of *communication satellites,* including *tracking, telemetry,* and *command communications.* This is distinguished from the terrestrial systems that are concerned with the payload or primary function of the communication system and the *mission* of the communication satellite.   Thus, in satellite communications, the space segment is involved in satellite control.   The communication earth stations and traffic handling equipment constitute the *ground segment.*   Also see *ground segment.*

space service.   A *radiocommunication service* between *earth stations* and *space stations,* between space stations, or between earth stations when the signals are *retransmitted* by space stations. Transmission by *reflection* from objects in space is included as a space service function.   Reflection or *scattering* by the *ionosphere* or *transmission* within the earth's *atmosphere* is not included as a space service function.

space signal.   **1.** In *telegraph* and *teleprinter operations,* the *signal* that initiates the active condition in a *teletypewriter (teleprinter).*   Normally the space signal is used as the *signaling condition* that precedes the production of a *start signal* when using the *International Telegraph Alphabet Number 2 (ITA-2).*   **2.** In *telegraph* or *teleprinter operations,* the *signal* that corresponds to the *code* combination that causes the *printing position* to be advanced by one *character* pitch and that does not cause the printing of a *graphic character.*   **3.** The *signal* that corresponds to an *off-key* or non-*transmit* condition.   Contrast with *mark signal.*

space signaling.   See *digital mark-space signaling.*

space station.   A *station* in the *space service* located on an object that is beyond the major portion of the earth's *atmosphere.*   For example, it may be on a *satellite* that is in *orbit,* on a powered *spacecraft* probing a planet, or on a ballistic missile in flight, but not on an aircraft.   See *communication-satellite space station; meteorological satellite space station; radionavigation-satellite space station; space research space station; space telecommand space station; space telemetering space station; space tracking space station.*

space telecommand.   The use of *radiocommunication* for the *transmission* of *signals* to a *space station* to initiate, modify, or terminate functions of the equipment on a space object, including the space station itself.   It includes the transmission of *instructions (commands)* via space stations.

space telecommand earth station.   An *earth station* that *transmits messages* and *instructions* for *telecommand* purposes.

space telecommand space station. A *space station* that receives *messages (signals)* that are used for *space telecommand* purposes.

space telemetering. The use of *telemetering* equipment for the *transmission* of *messages (signals)* from a *space station.* The messages contain the results of measurements that are made in a *spacecraft,* including measurements that relate to the functioning of the spacecraft that contains the space station.

space telemetering earth station. An *earth station* that receives *messages (signals)* that are used for *telemetering.*

space telemetering space station. A *space station* that is used for *space telemetering* of *data* and *messages.*

space tracking. Determination of the *orbit,* velocity, or instantaneous position of an object in space by means of *radiodetermination,* excluding *primary radar,* for the purpose of establishing the precise movement or path of the object through space.

space tracking earth station. An *earth station* that *transmits* or *receives messages (signals)* for *space tracking.*

space tracking space station. A *space station* that *transmits,* or *receives* and *retransmits, messages (signals)* that are used for *space tracking.*

spacing bias. The uniform lengthening of the *pulse duration* of the *space pulses* at the expense of the *pulse duration* of the *mark pulses.*

spacing pulse. See *space.*

spacing signal. See *space.*

spar. See *Iceland spar.*

spare signal group. A *signal group,* such as a *basic group,* an *indefinite call sign,* a *collective call sign,* a *radio distinguishing group,* a *suffix* to a radio distinguishing group, or a *key* list for *encryption* of a *call sign,* to be used as a spare by a *ship station* for the duration of a voyage, a *land station* for a specified period, or an *aircraft station* for the duration of a flight.

spatial degree. A unit of measure of a plane angle in space, of such magnitude that 360 spatial degrees constitute a full plane rotation of a line about a point on the line. Also see *electrical degree.*

spatter. Small chunks of material that fly from the hot crucible onto the glass surface, and adhere there, in evaporative *coatings* of *optical* elements such as *lenses, prisms,* and *mirrors.*

speaker channel. See *engineering channel.*

speaker circuit. See *engineering circuit.*

special character. A *graphic character* in a *character set* that is not a letter, not a *digit,* and not a *space character.* For example, a hyphen, a comma, a slash, a question mark, or an equal sign.

special flag. In a *visual communication system,* a square *flag* on which a specific pattern of colors is used to represent a specific *word.*

special-grade access line. An *access line* especially *conditioned,* usually by providing *amplitude* and *delay equalization,* to give it characteristics suitable for handling special services, such as lower-speed *data signaling rates* of 600 to 2400 *bits* per *second.*

special-grade service. A *communication service* in which specially *conditioned trunks* between *switches* are used, and in which specially conditioned *access lines* are used to provide the required *transmission* capability for *secure voice, data,* and *facsimile transmission.*

special-grade user. A *telephone user* (subscriber, customer) provided with *special-grade service.*

special-grade trunk. A *telephone trunk* that has special qualities, such as *interference* free, uninterrupted, *dedicated connection service* for *voice transmission, data transmission,* or *facsimile transmission* capability, above those required for ordinary *voice transmission.*

special-handling designator. A repeated letter, usually repeated 5 times, that follows the classification letter as a *designator* for *messages* that require special handling.

special-meteorological broadcast. Complete meteorological *information* that is placed on a special *broadcast* or *facsimile broadcast* and copied by stations that are concerned. Also see *emergency meteorological warning; routine meteorological broadcast.*

special-network service. A type of *communication service* in which a special *network* is provided that affords *privacy* of service within a specified community of interest by denying all such network *users* (customers, subscribers) *access* to any of the general-network users (customers, subscribers). Also see *closed-user group.*

special optical cable. An *optical cable* with one or more design features intended to meet a particular performance requirement or environmental condition not found in standard or regular general-purpose quantity-produced optical cables. For example, a cable with a flat cross section, a heavy armor covering, an abnormally high tensile strength, or an extremely small or large diameter *optical fiber.* See Figure S-10.

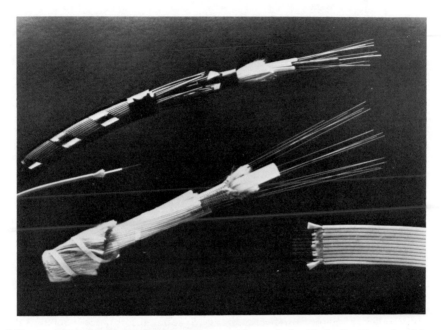

S-10. An armored *cable (top left)*, a miniature cable, a tubed cable for liquids, and a *ribbon* cable *(bottom right)* — all are Siecor **special optical cables.** (Courtesy of Siecor Optical Cables, Inc.)

special panel signaling sign. A special *panel display* that is used to indicate special prearranged *messages* from *ground stations* to *air stations.* For example, a *panel* with specified patterns or colors could be displayed on the ground to indicate special prearranged messages, such as "land in this direction," "pick up message here," "message drop not recovered," "unable to proceed," or "you may not proceed."

special pennant. In a *visual communication system,* a *pennant* of specified shape with a specified color pattern that is used to represent a particular *word* or to represent a *special panel signaling sign.*

special-purpose language. A *language* that can be used for *programming* the solution of a given class of problems, or for a given class of *applications,* such as engineering design, *communication network* control, *simulation,* or numerical control of machines or machine tools.

special purpose routing indicator. A *message routing indicator* designed and used to accomplish a special purpose. For example, a routing indicator that is used to indicate an emergency relocation site, an alternate command post, or an alternate *control station.*

specification. A description, usually intended primarily for use in provisioning and procurement, of the essential technical requirements for items, materials, or services, including the procedures (tests) needed to determine whether or not the requirements have been met. Specifications for items and materials should contain preservation, packaging, packing, and marking requirements for shipping, storage, distribution, and use. They should also include assembly, operating, repair, maintenance, and salvage instructions. See *pulse-spreading specification.*

speckle effect. A mottling effect produced by *color* distortion due to *interference* in *light transmission* caused by the *transmission medium,* such as an *optical fiber.*

speckle interferometer. An *interferometer* in which a *laser illuminates* a *diffusely reflecting* surface that is viewed through the interferometer, the *optical system* forming easily visible speckle patterns on the surface of the *image. Interference* with a reference *beam* causes the *light* and dark speckles to reverse shade when the *object* moves one-fourth of the *wavelength* along the *optical axis.* If the object is vibrated in the direction of the optical axis, the image washes out at vibrating places and remains intact at the vibrational nodes, i.e., where the vibrational amplitude is zero.

spectral absorptance. The *absorptance* of *electromagnetic radiation* by a material evaluated at one or more *wavelengths.* Spectral absorptance is numerically the same for *radiant* and *luminous flux.*

spectral absorption coefficient. In the *propagation* of *electromagnetic radiation,* through a *transmission medium,* the *attenuation coefficient, a,* in the expression:

$$I = I_o e^{-ax}$$

where I is the intensity of *radiation* at point x, and I_o is the initial intensity at the point from which x is measured, when the *attenuation* is due only to *absorption,* and not *scattering, dispersion, diffusion,* or *divergence.* The attenuation coefficient is a function of *frequency.* Also see *Bouger's law.*

spectral bandwidth. The *wavelength* interval in which a *radiated* spectral quantity is a specified fraction of its maximum value. The fraction is usually taken as 0.50 of the maximum *power level,* or 0.707 of the maximum (3 dB) *current* or *voltage level.* If the *electromagnetic radiation* is *light,* it is the *radiant intensity half-power points* that are used to bound the spectral bandwidth.

spectral density. The *power density* of *electromagnetic radiation* consisting of a continuous *spectrum* of *frequencies,* expressed in watts per hertz, taken over a finite *bandwidth.*

spectral emittance. The *radiant emittance* plotted as a function of *wavelength.*

spectral irradiance. The *irradiance* per unit *wavelength* intervals, normally measured in units of (watts per square *meter*) per *micron* of wavelength.

spectral order. See *diffraction grating spectral order.*

spectral power. See *peak spectral power.*

spectral radiance. *Radiance* per unit *wavelength* interval, usually measured in (watts per *steradian*)/(square *meter*) per *micron* of *wavelength.*

spectral reflectivity. The *reflectivity* of a surface evaluated as a function of wavelength.

spectral response. 1. The *responsivity* of a *photodetector* to various *wavelengths* of *incident electromagnetic radiation,* usually indicated as the *electrical current* or *power output* as a function of *incident* power *input,* such as amperes/watt, amperes/(lumen-second), or *coulombs*/lumen. 2. The *optical power output* of a *light source* as a function of driving current or driving power input, usually indicated as watts/ampere, *lumens*/(ampere-*second*), or lumens/*coulomb*. See Figure S-11. Also see Figure A-10.

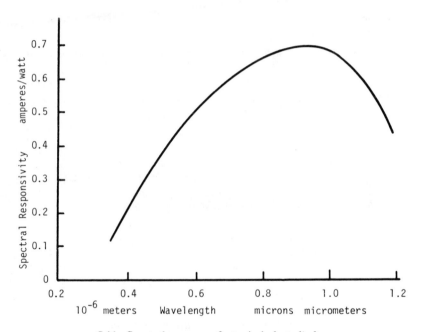

S-11. **Spectral response** of a typical *photodiode.*

spectral transmittance. *Transmittance* evaluated at one or more *wavelengths,* being numerically the same for *radiant* and *luminous flux.*

spectral wavelength. See *peak spectral wavelength.*

spectrometer. A *spectroscope* provided with an angle scale capable of measuring the angular deviation of *radiation* of different *wavelengths.* The spectrometer may also be used to measure angles between surfaces of *optical elements.*

spectroscope. An instrument capable of dispersing *radiation* into its *component wavelengths* and observing, or measuring, the resultant *spectrum*.

spectrum. A continuous range of *frequencies* of waves that have something in common; e.g., all frequencies that comprise a string of similar, equally spaced, rectangular *pulses;* all the frequencies that comprise *visible light;* or a group of radio frequencies. See *continuous spectrum; electromagnetic spectrum; frequency spectrum; frequency spectrum designation; primary spectrum; secondary spectrum; spread spectrum; visible spectrum; visual spectrum.*

spectrum analysis. An analysis that shows the distribution of energy or energy density contained in a set of *electromagnetic waves* of more than one *frequency,* as a function of frequency.

spectrum analyzer. See *integrated optical spectrum analyzer.*

spectrum code-sequence generator. See *spread-spectrum code-sequence generator.*

spectrum designation of frequency. See *frequency spectrum designation.*

spectrum signature. **1.** A collection of the *spectral* characteristics of *communication-electronic (C-E) equipment.* These characteristics may be either measured, computed, or estimated. Spectrum signatures may be obtained from *radio* and *radar transmitters* and *receivers, antennas, direction-finding (DF)* equipment, and other *(C-E) equipment.* Some of the *electromagnetic* characteristics that may be evident in a spectrum signature are *bandwidth, power output, sensitivity, selectivity, modulation, spurious radiation* and *responses, intermodulation, cross modulation, antenna beam pattern,* and *dynamic range.* **2.** The *electromagnetic wave* that is obtained as an *echo reflected* from an object in space. The *wave shape* contains *information* or evidence concerning the nature of the object. For example, the echo may be analyzed into the *amplitudes* of its *frequency components* as a function of time and used to identify the nature or motion of the *reflector* when this information is coupled with other information from other sources. The pattern of *frequencies, amplitudes,* and *phases* of components of an *electromagnetic wave* characterizes the output of a particular device thus enabling it to be distinguished from other devices.

specular reflection. *Reflection* from a smooth surface, curved or straight, so that there is negligible *diffusion* as *Snell's laws* of reflection and *refraction* are macroscopically obeyed over a uniformly directed surface. Thus, clear images that are sharp are obtained in specular *reflection.* Synonymous with *regular reflection.* Contrast with *diffuse reflection.* Also see *reflection.*

specular transmission. The *propagation* of *lightwaves* in a *transmission medium* such that *diffusion attenuation* is negligible and smooth changes in *refractive indices* result in the *refraction* of *rays* at the macroscopic level and the preservation of clear *images* during *propagation*. Specular transmission is desired in *optical waveguides* such as *optical fibers, bundles,* and *cables.* Contrast with *diffuse transmission.* Synonymous with *regular transmission.*

speech. See *coded speech.*

speech interpolation. See *analog speech interpolation; digital speech interpolation.*

speech-plus. Pertaining to a *circuit* that was designed and used for speech *transmission,* but to which other uses, such as *digital data transmission, facsimile transmission, telegraph,* or *signaling* superimposed on the speech signals, have been added by means of *multiplexing.*

speech-plus-duplex operation. *Communication system operation* in which speech and *telegraphy (duplex or simplex)* are *transmitted* simultaneously over the same *circuit. Mutual interference* is prevented by the use of *filters.* The circuit is normally used for the transmission of *voice signals.* Also see *composited circuit; duplex operation.*

speech-plus signaling. An arrangement of equipment that permits the use of part of a speech *band (voice frequency)* for the *transmission* of *signals* that are used for *signaling* (control) purposes. Also see *composited circuit.*

speech-plus telegraph. An arrangement of equipment that permits the use of a speech band *(voice frequency)* for *transmission* of *telegraph signals* for *data transmission.*

speech power unit. See *volume unit (VU).*

speech scrambler. A device in which speech *signals* are converted into unintelligible form before *transmission* to be restored to intelligible form at *reception.* The speech scrambler is used to obtain some measure of *privacy* in the event that *interception* by unauthorized persons should occur, such as by casual overhearing by unauthorized persons.

speech-spectrum truncation. See *voice-frequency truncation.*

speech synthesizer. A device that is capable of accepting *digital* or *analog data* and developing intelligible speech sounds that correspond to the *input data,* without resorting to recorded sounds or without simply being a *speech scrambler* operating in reverse. See Figure S-12.

S-12. Adjusting the pitch in a **speech synthesizer** to study the effects of speech rate and pitch on speech perception. (Courtesy of Bell Laboratories.)

speed.   See *drum speed; effective transmission speed; instantaneous transmission speed; lens speed; optical speed; radar blind speed; reproduction speed; scanning speed; service speed; spot speed; transmission speed.*

speed buffer.   See *data buffer.*

speed Morse.   See *high-speed Morse.*

speed of service.   See *service speed.*

speed-up tone.   See *camp-on-busy signal.*

spelling table.   See *syllabary.*

sphere.   See *celestial sphere.*

spherical harmonic function.   An *orthogonal* mathematical function in a spherical coordinate system, such as is used in defining the shape of the earth and points on its surface.   Its use is analogous to a *Fourier series* in a rectilinear coordinate system.   It is used to describe the *frequency components* of *electromagnetic waves* as a function of time and distance when *propagating* over the surface of the earth.   There are three classes of spherical harmonic functions. *Zonal harmonics* have values that are constant along parallels of latitude. *Sectorial harmonics* have values of consistent sign along lines of constant longitude but with magnitudes that change with latitude. *Tesseral harmonics* maintain a consistent sign within a *tessera* but change sign and magnitude as functions of both latitude and longitude.

spherical intensity. See *mean spherical intensity*.

spheroid. See *oblate spheroid*.

spherometer. An instrument for the precise measurement of the radius of curvature of surfaces.

spike. **1.** An extremely short *pulse* plotted in the *time domain*. **2.** An extremely *narrow band* plotted in the *frequency domain*. **3.** A bright spot that represents an object in space and that appears on a *radar planned position indicator (PPI) screen*. Synonymous with *pip*.

spill forward. In *automatic switching systems*, the *transfer* of full *control* of a *call* to the succeeding office by sending forward the complete *telephone address* of the *called party*.

spill-forward feature. In a *communication network*, a feature in the *operation* of an *intermediate central office* that assumes *routing control* of a *call* from the *originating office* by acting on incoming *trunk service routing indicators*. This increases the chances of a *completed call* by offering the call to more *trunk groups* than are available in or from the originating office.

spillover. **1.** In *antenna feed applications*, the part of the *radiated energy* from the *feed* that does not impinge on the *reflectors* and hence is spilled into the *back* and *side lobes*. **2.** In *alternating-current (AC) signaling* on *multilink connections*, the part of a signal that passes from one *link* section to another before the *connection* between the sections is broken.

spin-scan radiometer. See *fiber-optic visible-infrared spin-scan radiometer*.

spin stabilization. A form of control of a free body in which the attitude of the *satellite* missile, or other moving body is stabilized in space by its spinning about its axis of maximum moment of inertia in order to provide gyroscopic stability (rigidity). Forces tending to change the moment of inertia *vector* will be resisted.

spiral-four cable. A *quadded cable* with only four *conductors*. Synonymous with *star quadded cable*. Also see *quadded cable*.

splice. See *fiber-optic splice*.

splicer. See *loose-tube splicer; precision-sleeve splicer*.

splicing. See *field splicing; fusion splicing*.

splicing loss. An *insertion loss* caused by a *splice* in an *optical fiber* due primarily to an *axial misalignment* or axial *displacement* of the fibers, lateral eccentricity, or radial misalignment, differences in *core* diameter, *Fresnel reflection* at the *interface* or interfaces, *refractive index mismatch,* and other causes. Splicing losses can range from a fraction of a *decibel* to several decibels.

split homing. The *connection* of a *communication network terminal facility* to more than one *switching center* by separate *access lines,* each having separate *directory numbers.* Split homing is a *survivability* feature of a *communication system.*

spoiling. The process in which a suitably-sited *transmitter,* operating in a *synchronized* group, mutually adds to the service area of coverage of a *radio network,* but reduces or nullifys the value of the system as a *direction-finding (DF) radionavigation aid.*

spoking. See *radar spoking.*

spontaneous emission. In a *laser,* the *emission* of *light* that does not bear an *amplitude, phase,* or time relationship with an applied *signal* and is therefore a random noiselike form of *radiation.*

spoof. To deliberately induce a *user* of a *system,* such as a *communication system* or a *computer system,* to act incorrectly in relation to the system, or to deliberately cause a *component* of a system to perform incorrectly. For example, in *radar systems electronic countermeasures (ECM),* to cause an *operator* to believe that there is a target or targets at a particular location when they are in fact somewhere else, or to cause the operator to believe that there are many objects (targets) when there are in fact not more than two.

spoof jamming. The *radiation* of a *signal* that will appear, or be *received,* as a *radar echo signal* when there is no object from which the received signal could have *reflected* from.

sporadic E propagation. *Electromagnetic wave propagation* by means of *returns* from irregular *ionization layers* that appear at heights of about 90 km to 120 km. The maximum frequency that is returned from this *ionospheric layer* can be much greater than that from the normal *E layer.* Close to the equator it is essentially a daytime phenomenon, but in the *auroral zone* it is most prevalent at night. The effect causes *electromagnetic waves* to *forward-scatter* more readily, thus increasing the *range* of *very-high frequency (VHF) communication* due to increased *ionization (ion density)* of the *E-layer* of the *ionosphere.* It is more common in summer during daylight and early evening than in winter.

spot. See *recorded spot; recording spot; scanning spot; sun spot.*

spot-barrage jamming radar display. A *radar screen display* that consists of a bright *strobe* or wedge appearing at *jammer azimuth* at low *jam power, noise* patterns, bright strobes at other *azimuths,* and a dark wedge at jammer azimuth at high jam power.

spot beam. In *satellite communication systems,* a narrow, pencil-like *beam* from a *satellite station antenna* that *illuminates,* with high *power density,* a limited area of the earth. It usually uses *parabolic reflectors* rather than *omnidirectional antennas* or *earth-coverage antennas.* See Figure S-13.

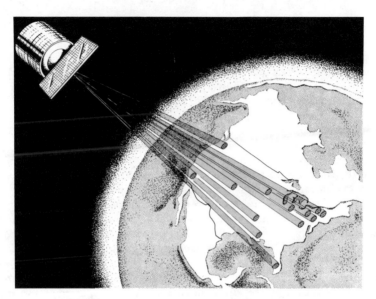

S-13. A *scanning* and **spot beam** *satellite narrow-beam focused microwave satellite communication system.* The beam would sweep across the U.S., be broken into *pulses* lasting a fraction of a second that would *poll* the numerous *earth stations,* each *transmitting* and *receiving information* within an allotted *time slot.* (Courtesy of Bell Laboratories.)

spot continuous-wave jamming radar display. A *radar screen display* that consists of a bright *strobe* or wedge appearing at *jammer azimuth* at low *jam power,* a dark wedge at jammer azimuth, and bright strobes at other azimuths at high jam power.

spot jammer. A *jammer* that directs its *jamming* energy against a single *narrow bandwidth* of *frequency,* thereby enhancing the chance of *saturating* a specific *receiver.* Although the jammer *transmits* a jamming *signal* over a narrow bandwidth, it may be *tunable* over a *wide frequency band.* It concentrates all of its power in a *narrow spectrum,* usually jamming only one *transmission* at a time. It usually *tunes* accurately, employs a tunable *directional antenna,* and is thus less likely to cause *interference* with other transmissions than a *barrage jammer.* See *automatic spot jammer; manual spot jammer.*

spot jamming. *Jamming* in which all the energy of a *jammer* is concentrated at a specific *channel* or *frequency.* Spot jamming offers the advantage of maximum *jamming power* on the selected *frequencies, channels,* or *transmitters* to be *jammed.* However, the large number of *emitters* at diverse *frequencies* in modern *communication-electronic (C-E) systems* tend to make its use difficult. Nevertheless, this is the most common form of jamming, primarily because it causes minimum *interference* with other C-E systems.

spot noise. *Noise* that is confined to a specific, usually narrow, portion of the *electromagnetic frequency spectrum.*

spot noise factor. The available *output noise power* per unit *bandwidth* divided by the portion of output noise power that is due to a *matched input termination* at the *standard noise temperature* of 290 K.

spot noise jamming. *Jamming* in which a single *radar* is *jammed* using a noise *bandwidth* that is slightly greater than the bandwidth of the radar that is being jammed. This could be the most effective form of jamming. Spot noise jamming is effective if one spot noise jammer is assigned to each radar to be jammed. However, care must be taken in how this is accomplished. For example, if the jammers are in separated aircraft the effect would be to give each radar to be jammed a clear view of one jamming aircraft. This would negate the jamming effectiveness quickly. This example is simple and unlikely, but the problem of a multiplicity of radars to be jammed is likely and its solution is not simple.

spot number. A number allocated to a *frequency.* Spot numbers are allocated throughout the *frequency spectrum* in *communication operations* in order to quickly identify *transmitters* or frequencies for each reference.

spot off-frequency jamming. *Jamming* in which the jamming *frequency* is near, but not at, the frequency that is being *jammed.* The effect is to reduce the effectiveness of an attempt to evade the jamming by moving off the frequency being jammed.

spot scanning. See *multiple-spot scanning.*

spot size. 1. The size of the *electron spot* on the face of a *cathode-ray tube.* The spot size is larger than the diameter of the electron *beam* because of the spill-over of electrons into adjacent areas of the *screen* near the spot. The spot size is a function of the ability of the tube to focus the electron beam, as well as of the electron gun *aperture.* 2. In *facsimile systems,* the diameter of the *scanning spot* or the *recording spot.*

spot speed. In *facsimile systems,* the speed of the *scanning spot* or the *recording spot* along the *available line.* The spot speed is generally measured on the *object* (document) or on the *record sheet.*

spotting.   See *ranging.*

spot x-dimension.   See *recorded spot x-dimension; scanning spot x-dimension.*

spot y-dimension.   See *recorded spot y-dimension; scanning spot y-dimension.*

spread.   See *irrelevance; multimode group-delay spread.*

spreading.   See *geometric spreading; pulse dispersion.*

spreading specification.   See *pulse-spreading specification.*

spread spectrum.   1. A *communication* technique in which the *information-modulated signal* is *transmitted* in a *bandwidth* that is considerably greater than the *frequency* content of the original *information.*   This technique affords the advantages of *interference* avoidance and *multiple access.*   **2.** Pertaining to any *signal* that has a large time-bandwidth product.   In communications, spread spectrum techniques may be employed as an anti*noise* signal-gain processing tool.   Spread spectrum *pulses* can be used for pulse *addressing systems.*   Other types of spread spectrum schemes are *wide-deviation frequency modulation (FM) phase-lock loops, frequency compressive feedback demodulation,* and *frequency hopping.*   **3.** Pertaining to a *signal* coding and *transmission* method in which a sequence of different *electromagnetic wave frequencies* are used in a pseudorandom sequence to transmit a given signal, the instantaneous frequencies being selected by a pseudorandom *pulse* generator that *gates* the available frequencies.   The system requires the use of a large *bandwidth* to accommodate all the frequencies.   A *signal-to-noise ratio* improvement is obtained as well as some antijamming capability and signal *security,* since the *receiver* must possess the same synchronized pseudorandom pulse generator to unscramble the received signal.   Also see *pseudorandom number sequence; spread-spectrum code-sequence generator;* Figure S-14.

spread-spectrum code-sequence generator.   A generator that produces a sequence of *binary pulses* (i.e., a pseudorandom sequence of zeros and ones) consisting of a *register* made of a bank of series-connected *flip-flops,* each of whose *outputs* are connected to the next flip-flop in the series, and a selection of individual flip-flop outputs *gated* back to the *input* of the first flip-flop, the final output sequence of binary pulses consisting of the states experienced by the last flip-flop. Synonymous with *shift-register generator.*   Also see *feedback shift register; frequency-hopping generator.*   See *modular spread-spectrum code-sequence generator.*   See Figure S-14.

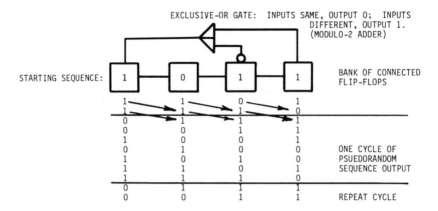

S-14. The *output* of the **spread-spectrum code-sequence generator** are the states of the *flip-flops*. These are used to *gate* different *frequencies*. The horizontal rows of *digits* are subsequent states. Each vertical column is derived from the column on its left as the *register* is stepped to the right. The left-most column is determined by the *output* of the *EXCLUSIVE-OR gate*. Its output is determined by the outputs of the right-most flip-flop and the second flip-flop from the right that has the *feedback tap*. The starting sequence, the feedback tap locations, and the number of flip-flops can be changed to obtain other *pseudorandom* number sequences for frequency control.

spread-spectrum multiple-access (SSMA). In *satellite communications, code-division multiple-access (CDMA)* in which all *carriers* that are *radiated* from *earth stations* occupy the entire *bandwidth* of the *satellite transponder,* not specific *frequencies* within the bandwidth. A special *code* is inserted into each carrier that enables it to be identified by the *addressed ground terminal.* Some of the coding methods that are commonly used are *phase modulation, frequency hopping,* and *phase-shift keying.* Also see *bandspreading techniques; maximal code sequence.*

spurious emission. *Electromagnetic radiation* that is produced by a *source* but is not used for *transmitting information* and is usually suppressed; e.g., *harmonic emission, sidebands, parasitic emission,* and *intermodulation products.* It includes any electromagnetic *emission* on a *frequency* or frequencies outside the emission *necessary bandwidth.* Their level may be reduced without affecting the *transmission* of *information.* Emissions that are in the immediate vicinity of the necessary bandwidth and that result from the *modulation* process for the transmission of information are not considered as spurious emissions.

spurious radiation. 1. Any unintentional *radiation,* that is, *spurious emission.* 2. In *telecommunications,* any *emission* at *frequencies* outside the intended *communication bandwidth.*

spurious response. 1. Any undesired *response* to *frequencies* outside the intended *communication bandwidth* of a device. 2. Any *response* other than the desired response of a device, especially of a *transducer.*

square law. See *inverse-square law.*

square-law device. A nonlinear device whose *output signal* values are proportional to the square of the *input signal* values.

square-law index profile. See *parabolic index profile.*

squares multiplier. See *quarter-squares multiplier.*

square-tube splicer. See *loose-tube splicer.*

square wave. A *wave* that has two-levels of *amplitude* that change from one level to the other in a relatively short time compared to the *wavelength.* When the instantaneous amplitude is plotted versus time or distance, the pulses appear to be rectangular in shape. When a square wave is *differentiated,* alternate polarity *spikes* are produced. When a square wave is integrated, a triangular *wave shape* is produced.

squaring loop. A *Costas loop* that includes a *square-law device* or *circuit.*

squelching. The reducing or eliminating of the *noise* in a *radio receiver* when no *carrier signal* is present.

squelch circuit. A *circuit* that reduces *background noise* in the absence of desired *input signals.* Also see *noise suppression.*

SS. *Single sideband.*

SSB. *Single sideband.*

SSB-SC transmission. *Single-sideband suppressed-carrier (SSB-SC) transmission.*

SSMA. *Spread-spectrum multiple-access.*

SS-TDMA. *Satellite-switched time-division multiple-access.*

stability. See *carrier frequency stability; clock stability; dimensional stability; fiber dimensional stability; frequency stability; frequency standard stability.*

stabilized local oscillator. A *local oscillator* with a fixed, constant (nondrifting) *output frequency.* For example, a stable *radio frequency* oscillator used as a local oscillator in the *superheterodyne radar receiver* in a moving object (target) *tracking* system.

stabilization. See *spin stabilization.*

stable relay. See *side stable relay.*

stage. See *junction stage.*

stagger. In *facsimile systems,* a *periodic error* in the *position* of the *recorded spot* along the *recorded line.*

staggered pulse repetition rate. The variation of the time interval between *radar pulses* in a predetermined fashion. This technique may eliminate *blind speeds* associated with fixed *pulse repetition rate (PRR) systems* and may also counter *repeater deception* as an *electronic counter-countermeasure (ECCM)*.

standard. See *data encryption standard; federal telecommunication standard (FTS); frequency standard; primary frequency standard; system standard; time standard.*

standard accuracy. See *frequency standard accuracy.*

standard-frequency broadcast. See *time-signal standard-frequency broadcast.*

standard frequency service. A *radio communication service* for the *transmission* of *electromagnetic waves* of specified *standard frequencies* of known high *accuracy* and *precision* intended for general use. The service is primarily intended for scientific and technical purposes that require a high degree of *frequency stability.*

standard frequency station. A *station* in the *standard frequency service.*

standard frequency-time signal. See *standard time-frequency signal.*

standard noise temperature. Approximately room *temperature,* 290 K. The standard noise temperature is used as a reference for *noise* measurements and for comparison of noise levels in electronic *components,* particularly in *circuits* with high *gain* and in low *signal-to-noise ratio* situations. Also see *solar noise.*

standard plan. See *aircraft communication standard plan; ship-fitting communication standard plan.*

standard precision. See *frequency standard precision.*

standard source. A reference *optical-power* source to which emitting and detecting devices may be compared for calibration purposes.

standard stability. See *frequency standard stability.*

standard telegraph level (STL). The *power* per individual *telegraph channel* that is required to yield the standard composite *data* level (operating *signal level*). For example, for a composite data level of -13 *dBm* at 0 dBm *transmission level point (TLP),* the STL would be -25 dBm for a 16 channel *voice frequency carrier telegraph (VFCT) terminal* from the relation $STL = -13 - 10 \log_{10} n = -(13 + 10 \log_{10} n)$, where n is the number of telegraph channels and the STL is in dBm. In this example, $n = 16$.

standard test signal. A single-*frequency sinusoidal wave* with a specified standardized *power* level that is used for testing *peak power transmission* capability; for measuring the *total harmonic distortion* of *circuits* or parts of circuits; for level adjustment and alignment of single and *tandem links;* and for other purposes. For example, a standard test signal is designed for use at the 600-Ω audio portions of a circuit. Generally it has a power level of 1 mW at a frequency of

1 kHz and is applied at the *zero level transmission reference point (OTLP)*. If 1 mW exceeds the limiting or linear signal range of the circuit under test, a power of −10 dBm at 0 dB level may be used to measure *gain* or *loss*. A corresponding decrease in test power at the *receiver* must be allowed to indicate the true gain or loss and hence the true level. Synonymous with *standard test tone*.

standard test tone.   See *standard test signal*.

standard time-frequency signal.   **1.** A time-controlled *radio signal* that is *broadcast* at scheduled intervals on a number of different *frequencies* by government-operated radio *stations* in the United States and other countries.   **2.** A *carrier frequency* and *time signal* that is emitted in allocated bands in conformity with the CCIR recommendations of the *International Telecommunication Union (ITU)*. In the United States, standard time and frequency signals are *broadcast* by the US Naval Observatory and the National Bureau of Standards. Synonymous with *standard frequency-time signal*. Also see *primary frequency standard*.

standby.   In *computer* and *communication system operations,* a· power-saving condition or status of operation of equipment. For example, a *radio station* operating condition in which the *operator* can *receive* but not *transmit*.

standby station.   **1.** A *station* in a *standby* status.   **2.** An *aircraft station, ship station,* or *land station* that is not designated as the *primary guard station,* or as the *secondary station,* for another station. The station generally remains in a standby status until called-upon to assume the role of a *guard station* or a *secondary station*.

standing communication operating instruction (SCOI).   An *instruction* that pertains to the *operation* of a *communication system*. Certain instructions in the SCOI, such as those that pertain to *cryptographic communication* and *crypto-keying material,* are changed as required to maintain *security*.

standing wave.   **1.** In contrast to a *propagating wave,* a wave that exists in a spatial dimension, such as on the length of a *transmission line*, in a *resonant cavity,* or on a *vibrating string* with fixed ends, but does not propagate. For example, a crest of a standing wave simply increases, decreases, and reverses direction while remaining at the same point on the line, in the cavity, or on the string. However, the amplitude has maxima and minima along a spatial dimension, the distance between the maxima, or any other corresponding point, usually being one-half of the *wavelength* in absolute terms or a whole wavelength when polarity is taken into account.   **2.** A distribution of *current, voltage,* or *field intensity* on a *transmission line* or *waveguide* formed by two sets of *waves propagating* in opposite directions, characterized by the presence of a number of successive maxima and minima. The *reflected* wave can occur as a result of *impedance* mismatch. Contrast with *traveling wave*. Synonymous with *stationary wave*.

standing wave ratio (SWR).   The ratio of the *amplitude* of a *standing wave* at an *antinode* to the amplitude at a *node*. The standing wave ratio, *SWR,* in a *uniform transmission line* or *waveguide* is $SWR = (1+RC)/(1-RC)$, where RC is the reflection coefficient.   Also see *antinode; node.*   See *voltage standing wave ratio (VSWR).*

stand-off jamming. *Jamming* that is accomplished from an *aircraft station, ship station,* or *land station* that is close enough to a group being protected, or to the *transmitters* being *jammed,* to accomplish effective jamming, but that does not accompany the group that is being protected.

star. See *D-star.*

star connection. A method of connecting a set of *terminals* in which each terminal is individually connected by a separate *cable* all the way to a *central distribution box* or *star coupler.*   See *nonreflective star-coupler; reflective star-coupler.*

stark effect. The splitting of *spectral* lines of *electromagnetic radiation* by an applied *electric field.*

star network. A *network configuration* in which there is one and only one *node* from which there is only one *path* to each *endpoint node* of the *network.* Synonymous with *centralized network.*   Also see *single-node network.*   See Figure S-15.

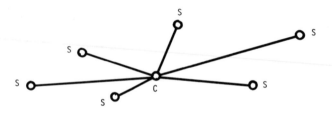

S-15. A **star network** with a *control station.*

star quadded cable. See *spiral four cable.*

start code. See *transmitter start code.*

starting powder. **1.** A raw glass powder for producing *optical fibers.*   The first step in the process of producing optical fibers is to purify the powder. **2.** Pure glass powder used for making *preforms.*

start message. See *go-ahead notice.*

start notice. See *go-ahead notice.*

start-of-heading (SOH) character. A *transmission control character* that is used as the first *character* of a *message heading.*

start-of-message indicator. An *indicator* that is used to activate *automatic message switching equipment.*   It is required on *messages* that pass into or through automatic switching systems to indicate the start of a message. For example, the

four-letter group ZCZC that is used in some *tape-relay communication systems.*
Synonymous with *start-of-transmission indicator.*

start-of-text (STX) character. A *transmission control character* that precedes
the *text* of a *message* and may be used to terminate the *message heading.*

start-of-transmission indicator. See *start-of-message indicator.*

start-recording signal. In *facsimile systems,* a *signal* that is used for starting the
process of *converting* the received *electrical signal* to an *image* on the *record
sheet.*

start signal. In a *start-stop transmission system,* a *signal* that precedes each *character, block,* or other set of *data* and that prepares the receiving device for the
reception of the *code elements* of the character, block, or other set of data. The
start signal is usually one *signal element.* It has the duration (length) of one *unit
interval.* Also see *stop signal.*

start-stop character. A *character* that includes a *start signal* at the beginning of
the *character* and one or two *stop signals* at the end of the character.

start-stop distortion. **1.** The ratio of the maximum difference, irrespective of
sign, between the actual and theoretical intervals that separate any *significant instant* of *modulation* (or of *demodulation*) from the significant instant of the *start
element* immediately preceding it, to the *unit interval.* **2.** The highest absolute
value of individual *distortion* affecting the *significant instants* of a *start-stop
modulation.* The degree of distortion of a start-stop modulation (or demodulation) is usually expressed as a percentage. Distinction can be made between the
degree of *late* (positive) *distortion* and the degree of *early* (negative) *distortion.*

start-stop equipment. Equipment that is used in a *telegraph system* in which
start-stop modulation is used.

start-stop margin. In *start-stop modulation,* the maximum amount of overall
start-stop distortion that is *compatible* with the correct *translation* by the start-
stop equipment of all the *character signals* that appear singly, that appear at the
maximum allowable speed, or that appear at the standard modulation rate.

start-stop modulation. *Modulation* that results from the *synchronous modulation* of the *signal elements* that constitute a *character* or *block* of characters,
with an undefined *significant interval* between the consecutive characters or
blocks of characters. Thus, start-stop modulation permits *transmission* of single
characters, or groups of characters, that are separated by time intervals of random length. The *start signals* prepare the receiving equipment to receive the
character or group of characters immediately following, and the *stop signals* place
the equipment in a rest condition so as to prepare it for the receipt and interpretation of the next start signal.

start-stop restitution. A characteristic that results from *isochronous restitution*
of the *signal elements* that constitute a *character, block,* or other set of *data* that

has an undefined *significant interval* between consecutive characters, blocks, or other sets of data.

start-stop transmission. *Asynchronous data transmission* in which each group of *signals* that represents a *character, block,* or other set of *data* is preceded by a *start signal* and is followed by a *stop signal.*

start-stop transmission system. An *asynchronous data transmission system* in which each group of signals that represents a *character, block,* or other set of *data* is preceded by a *start signal* and is followed by a *stop signal.* Also see *asynchronous communication system.* See *stepped start-stop transmission system.*

start-stop TTY distortion. See *teletypewriter signal distortion.*

state. See *degraded service state; excited state; ground state; idle state; operational service state; outage state.*

static. In *communication systems,* the *interference* caused by natural electrical disturbances in the *atmosphere* or by other *electromagnetic* phenomena. For example, the *noise* that is heard from a *radio receiver* and that is caused by *lightning* or *northern lights.* Also see *interference.* See *precipitation static.*

static data. *Data,* in a *storage* device, that remains stored and fixed in time and space, does not have to be regenerated to be retained, and does not have to be moved in order to be read or removed. For example, data in a *register* consisting of a group of storage devices, such as *flip-flops* or *magnetic cores,* used to store a number of *bits.* The bits usually may be entered into or removed from the storage devices in parallel or in series. The data stored in cathode-ray storage tubes or data stored on *magnetic tape,* drums, disks, or *cards* are not considered as static data because of their volatility or because the data media have to be moved relative to a reading head for the data to be read. Also see *staticizer.*

static electricity. An accumulation of positive or negative electric charges on a body that has the *capacity* to store or hold them. The accumulation of charge causes the build up of an *electrical potential difference (voltage)* with respect to other bodies. The accumulation of charges is discharged as soon as the voltage is high enough for a given path that can occur under the proper conditions. The discharge is equivalent to an *electric current.* The current and voltage can produce surges of *electromagnetic* energy causing *interference.* Static electricity can damage electronic circuitry, detonate explosives, set fires, harm living tissue, and cause equipment to malfunction. The harmful effects may be caused by electric polarization (high *electric fields*) or by *pulses* and induced currents (high *magnetic fields*) during discharging. Effective *grounding* of equipment is essential in order to reduce the effects of static electricity. Also see *electromagnetic radiation hazard; lightning.*

staticmagnetic field. See *magnetostatic field.*

staticizer. A device that *converts* a time sequence of states that represent *data* into a corresponding space distribution of simultaneous states that represent the same data. Also see *static data*.

static test mode. In *analog computing,* that *mode* of *operation* of an *analog computer* during which special initial conditions are set in order to check the connection of *components* and consequently the proper operation of all the components except the *integrators.* The setup and *patching* is tested in the static test mode.

station. 1. In *communications,* an assembly that comprises *data terminal equipment, data circuit-terminating equipment,* and the *interface* between them. 2. In *high-level data link control (HDLC) operation,* a *primary station, secondary station,* or *combined station.* 3. In *radio communications,* a separate *transmitter, receiver,* or *combination* of *transmitters* and *receivers,* and the accessory equipment that is required for the conduct of *radio communication services.* See *aeronautical advisory station; aeronautical broadcasting station; aeronautical fixed station; aeronautical marker beacon station; aeronautical multicom land station; aeronautical multicom mobile station; aeronautical radio beacon station; aeronautical station; aeronautical telemetering land station; aeronautical telemetering mobile station; aeronautical utility land station; aeronautical utility mobile station; aircraft station; altimeter station; area broadcast station; aviation instructional station; balanced station; base station; broadcasting station; called station; calling station; coast station; combined station; communication-satellite earth station; communication-satellite space station; configurable station; constant-watch station; control station; data input station; data processing station; data station; directly connected station; dual-access tributary station; earth station; experimental contract developmental station; experimental developmental station; experimental export station; experimental research station; experimental station; experimental testing station; fixed earth station; fixed station; flight telemetering land station; flight telemetering mobile station; flight test station; glide path-slope station; hydrological and meteorological fixed station; hydrological and meteorological land station; hydrological and meteorological mobile station; inquiry station; international broadcasting station; land station; localizer station; local ship-shore station; logical station; major relay station; marine broadcast station; marine radio beacon station; master net control station (MNCS); master station; meteorological-satellite earth station; meteorological-satellite space station; minor relay station; mobile earth station; mobile station; net control station; omnidirectional range station; one-operator ship station; operator-period station; out station; passive station; primary aeronautical station; primary guard station; primary ship-shore station; primary station; primary substation; private aircraft station; radar beam precipitation gage station; radar beacon station; radar netting station; radio astronomy station; radio beacon station; radio determination station; radio direction-finding station; radio location land station; radio location station; radionavigation land station; radionavigation maintenance test land station; radionavigation mobile station; radionavigation operational test land station; radionavigation satellite earth station; radionavigation satellite space station; radionav-*

igation station; radio positioning land station; radio positioning mobile station; radio range station; radiosonde station; regular station; secondary aeronautical station; secondary ship-shore station; secondary station; ship broadcast-area radio station; ship broadcast coastal radio station; ship station; slave station; space research space station; space station; space telecommand earth station; space telecommand space station; space telemetering earth station; space telemetering space station; space tracking earth station; space tracking space station; standard frequency station; standby station; surface station; surveillance radar station; survivalcraft station; telemetry-command station; telemetering fixed station; telemetering land station; telemetering mobile station; terminal station; terrestrial station; tracking-telemetry-command station; transport station; tributary station.

stationary direct current.   *Direct current (DC)* that does not vary in magnitude, that is, is steady rather than pulsating. Also see *pulsating direct current.*

stationary information source.   See *stationary message source.*

stationary message source.   A *message source* that *transmits messages* each of which has a probability of occurrence independent of its *occurrence time.* Synonymous with *stationary information source.*

stationary satellite.   See *geostationary satellite.*

stationary wave.   See *standing wave.*

station battery.   A separate battery *power source* within a *facility* that provides all *direct-current (DC) input power* requirements associated with the facility. Such a capability is often centrally located. The batteries may power *radio* and *telephone* equipment as well as provide controls for equipment and emergency lighting.

station call.   See *station-to-station call.*

station clock.   A *clock* that controls all *station* equipment requiring time control. A station clock may also be used to provide *timing* or *frequency signals* for other equipment.

station designator.   See *address designator.*

station keeping.   **1.** In *satellite communication systems,* the process of controlling a *satellite* to insure that it maintains a desired *orbit.* For example, maintaining a nominally *geostationary satellite* within a given region relative to the earth, or employing *data relays* from satellites to control the relative position of other satellites. **2.** The maintaining of an assigned position of a ship relative to other ships in a convoy. For example, each station (position) in a convoy could be assigned an *internal convoy call sign* that is relinquished to any ship that is assigned to occupy that position (station) in the convoy.

station load.   The total collective *power* requirement of all the equipment and *facilities* in a *station.*

station log. A chronological record of significant events that occur at a *station,* such as operating schedules, *message traffic* conditions, *outages,* message handling difficulties, delays, and names of operators.

station master log. See *aeronautical station master log.*

station side. See *equipment side.*

station symbol. A letter group that is used to indicate a class or type of *transmitting station.* For example, the letters BCI might be used to designate an *international broadcasting station.*

station-to-station call. In an *automatically switched telephone network,* a *long distance call* in which the *calling party* enters the *called party's number* and obtains the called party through the use of automatic equipment and hence without the assistance of a human *operator.* At least two *exchanges* (calling and called exchanges) are involved. Also see *local call; number call; person-to-person call.*

statistical multiplexing. *Multiplexing* in which *channels* are established on a statistical basis. For example, *connections* are made according to probability of need.

statistical time-division multiplexing. *Time-division multiplexing* in which *connections* to *communication circuits* are made on a statistical basis.

statistics-on-request. Upon the request of a *user* (customer, subscriber), certain *data* concerning the distribution of *calls* that are made under defined headings. For example, international calls, national calls, calls to certain *users* (customers, subscribers), total calls, and other related statistical information are furnished. *Information* concerning the nature or content of the subject matter of the calls is not furnished.

status. See *basic status; secondary status.*

status channel. A *channel* that is used to indicate whether a group of *bits* is for *data* exchange between *users* or for *communication system* or *transmission control* purposes.

status signaling. *Signaling* that is used to determine the progress of a *call.* Status signals could include *dial tone, ringing tone, busy signal,* and *number-unobtainable tone.*

statute mile. A unit of distance equal to 1.609 km, 0.869 nmi, or 5,280 ft. In some countries, these distances may be written as 1,609 km, 0,869 nmi, or 5 280 ft. Care must be taken, however, in the use of the comma as a decimal point.

steady-state condition. 1. In a *communication circuit,* a condition in which some specified characteristic of a condition, such as value, rate, *periodicity,* or *amplitude* of a *signal,* exhibits only negligible change over an arbitrarily long period of time. **2.** In an *electrical circuit,* a condition that occurs after all initial transients or fluctuating conditions have been *damped* out and in which *electrical currents, voltages,* or *fields* remain essentially constant or oscillate uniformly without changes in such characteristics as *amplitude, frequency,* or *wave shape.*

stealing. See *velocity gate stealing; range-gate stealing.*

steer. See *vector.*

step-index fiber. A *fiber* in which there is an abrupt change in *refractive index* between the *core* and *cladding* along a *fiber diameter,* with the core refractive index higher than the cladding refractive index. There may be more then one layer, each layer with a different refractive index that is uniform throughout the layer, with decreasing indices in the outside layer. Synonymous with *radially stratified fiber.*

step-index profile. The condition of having the *refractive index* of a material used in a *transmission medium* change abruptly from one value to another. For example, an abrupt change in refractive index at the *core-cladding interface* of an *optical fiber.*

stepped. See *bit stepped; character stepped.*

stepped start-stop transmission system. A *start-stop transmission system* in which the *start signals* occur at regular intervals. Also see *asynchronous communication.*

step size. See *plotter step size.*

stepwise variable optical attenuator. A device that *attenuates* the *intensity* of *lightwaves* when inserted into an *optical waveguide link* in *discrete* steps, each of which is selectable by some means, such as by changing sets of cells. For example, if fixed attenuation cells of 0, 3, 7, and 17 dB are used three at a time, attenuations of 3, 6, 10, 13, 20, 23, and 27 dB attenuations are achievable. Also see *optical attenuator.*

steradian (sr). A unit of *solid angular* measure, being the subtended surface area of a sphere-divided by the square of the sphere radius. There are 4π steradians in a sphere. The solid angle subtended by a cone of half-angle A is

$$SA = 2\pi(1 - \cos A).$$

See *unit solid angle.*

stick. See *joystick.*

stimulated emission. In a *laser,* the *emission* of *light* caused by a *signal* applied to the laser such that the *response* is directly proportional to, and in *phase* coherence with, the *electromagnetic field* of the stimulating signal. This *coherency* between applied signal and response is the key to the usefulness of the laser. Also see *spontaneous emission.*

stimulated emission of radiation. See *light amplification by stimulated emission of radiation; microwave amplification by stimulated emission of radiation.*

stimulator. See *fiber-optic myocardium stimulator.*

STL. *Standard telegraph level.*

stone. Small, solid, trapped *opaque* particles that occur in the glass and plastic used in *optical systems.* Stones cause *deflection, dispersion, diffusion, reflection, scattering,* and *absorption* in *optical elements* such as *lenses* and *optical fibers.*

stop. See *aperture stop; field stop; T-stop.*

stop-band. The *frequency band* of *electromagnetic waves* that a *filter* does not allow to pass. All other *frequencies* outside the stop-band are allowed to pass. Also see *pass-band.*

stop character. See *start-stop character.*

stop distortion. See *start-stop distortion.*

stop element. A *stop signal* that consists of one *signal element* and that has a duration (length) equal to or greater than a specified minimum value.

stop filter. See *bandstop filter.*

stop notice. In a *tape relay communication system,* a *service message* to a *relay* or to a *tributary station* requesting that the *operator* stop *transmitting* over a specified *channel* or channels. Synonymous with *stop message.* Also see *go-ahead notice.*

stop-recording signal. In *facsimile systems,* a *signal* that is used for stopping the process of *converting* the *received electrical signal* to an *image* on the *record sheet.*

stop restitution. See *start-stop restitution.*

stop signal. In a *start-stop transmission system,* a *signal* that follows each *character block,* or other set of *data* and prepares the *receiving* device for the *reception* of a subsequent character, block, or set of data. It may simply restore the receiving device to a quiescent or resting state. It may consist of one or more *bits* or *pulses* that terminate each transmitted character. However, the stop signal is usually limited to one *signal element* of duration (length) equal to or greater than one *unit interval.* Also see *start signal.*

stop transmission. See *start-stop transmission.*

stop transmission system. See *start-stop transmission system; stepped start-stop transmission system.*

storage. **1.** The retention of *data* in a device that holds the data. **2.** The action of placing data into a device that holds the data. A *functional unit* into which data can be placed, in which the data can be retained, and from which the data can be retrieved. The means of storing the data, or representing the data in *stor-*

age, may be chemical, electrical, mechanical, *magnetic,* or other means. The data in storage may be static or dynamic, or volatile or nonvolatile. Synonymous with *memory; store.*   See *buffer storage; core storage; fixed storage; intercept tape storage; permanent storage.* See Figure S-16.

S-16. A *magnetic* bubble **storage** device (in the metal container immediately above right end of ruler) that stores a 12-second voice *(analog) message* in *data bit (digital)* form. Steps in production from garnet *boule* to finished package are shown. (Courtesy of Bell Laboratories.)

storage compaction. Increasing the efficiency of utilization of the *storage capacity* of a storage device, such as by increasing the ratio of data stored to the storage capacity. For example, by relocating fragmented data or *programs* that are scattered in storage into contiguous areas thus filling in unused spaces.

storage bounds checking. Testing the results of a *computer program* that is designed to determine whether or not there is *access* to *storage* outside of the authorized limits. The technique is used to insure that unauthorized access to specified storage areas do not occur. Synonymous with *memory bounds checking*.

storage capacity. The amount of *data* that can be contained in a *storage* device. The capacity is usually measured or specified in *binary digits, bytes, characters, words,* or other application-related units of data.

storage center. In a *communication system,* a centralized *storage* unit for a *store-and-forward data transmission system.*

storage keyboard. A *keyboard* in which the *code* combination that is set up or connected by the depression of a given *key* does not directly or immediately control the *transmitter* but is *transferred* to one or more sets of *storage* units for subsequent control of the transmitter.

storage register. A *register* into which *data* can be inserted and retained, and from which they can be retrieved. Also see *shift register.*

storage space. See *image storage space.*

storage tube. A *CRT* that is capable of retaining a *display image* on its screen for an extended period of time. The *image* usually can be *scanned, amplified,* and recorded or *transmitted* by radio, wire, *optical fiber,* or other *transmission medium,* sequentially or simultaneously, such as when a picture is transmitted as a whole image over a *coherent bundle* of *optical fibers* and displayed on the *faceplate* of a *fiberscope* at the receiving end. The image on the storage tube screen is retained longer than is required for a *regeneration* cycle.

store. See *storage.*

store-and-forward. Pertaining to *data transmission* in which *data* or *messages* that are destined for other *switching centers* or for *users* connected to a given switching center, are temporarily stored until forwarded to their ultimate destination.

store-and-forward data transmission. **1.** *Data transmission* in which *data* and *messages* are temporarily stored at one or more intermediate points in a *route* prior to their delivery to the next point in the route or to the ultimate destination. The method is applied to the *relay* of *traffic* where a message or *packet* is sent from a *terminal station* of a *network* via a computer-controlled *switching center.* The switching center computer accepts, analyzes, stores, and retransmits each received message in accordance with *procedures* contained in the *computer programs.* Messages that are to be *transmitted* are assembled into a special *format* and stored ready for transmission at a suitable time. Disadvantages are the cost of *storage* and the delay in transmission. Two methods that may use *store-and-forward data transmission* are *message switching* and *packet switching.* Store-and-forward methods always increase *transmission time* owing to the added *addresses* and the *storage* time. An advantage is in *error control.* Packet switching offers a better overall performance for long messages than does normal *circuit switching.* The *handshake* method is normally employed for error control. **2.** The recording, by a *communication network* at a *user's* (customer's subscriber's) request, of a message for subsequent automatic forwarding to the designated *address.*

store-and-forward switching center.   A *message switching center* in which a *message* is accepted from the *originator* (sender) when it is offered, is held in *storage,* and is forwarded to the *destination user* in accordance with the *priority* or *precedence* that is placed upon the message by the originator (sender, source user). Also see *message switching.*

straggler message.   A *message* that has inadvertently passed through one or more *relay stations,* either trailing or attached to a preceding message, without being assigned a *station* or *channel* serial number and without the discrepancy being noticed immediately.

strain.   See *fiber strain.*

strap.   A *connection* or *jumper* wire between *terminals* on the same *block* of a *distribution frame.* Also see *cross connect.*

strapping.   See *cross strapping.*

strategic military communication system.   A *communication system* that is generally global in nature and is operated on either a common-user or a special purpose basis. While a strategic communication system may be confined to a specified area, or may be limited to a particular type of *traffic,* the configuration is usually such that interoperation with other strategic systems is possible when desired or required. Equipment and procedural *compatibility* among strategic systems is essential to facilitate efficient communication traffic interchange. A worldwide *routing* plan is a prerequisite to operating strategic communication systems.

stratosphere.   The portion of the earth's *atmosphere* between the *troposphere* and the *ionosphere.* The *temperature* of the stratosphere is practically constant in a vertical direction, that is, it is an isothermal region. The stratosphere is free from clouds, except for occasional dust clouds, and free from strong vertical air currents, that is, free from active convection. The height of its base varies in regular fashion with latitude and with the seasons over the earth as a whole and fluctuates irregularly from day to day over any particular place on earth. It extends in height from 10–13 km (6–8 mi) to about 50 km (30 mi). Synonymous with *isothermal region.* Also see *atmosphere; ionosphere; tropopause; troposphere.*

stray current.   *Electrical current* through *circuits* or *paths* other than the intended circuits or paths.

stream.   See *bit stream; data stream; mission bit stream; serial data stream.*

street address.   The *address* used for the physical geographic location of an organization. For example, the street address of the *International Organization for Standardization* is 1, Rue de Varembe, Genève, Suisse, that is, 1 Varembe Street, Geneva, Switzerland.

strength. See *field strength; optical-fiber tensile strength; twist strength.*

strength-member optical cable. See *central strength-member optical cable; peripheral strength-member optical cable.* Also see Figure F-3.

stria. A defect in *optical* materials consisting of a sharply defined streak of material having a slightly different *refractive index* than the main body of the material. Striae usually cause wavelike *distortions* in *objects* seen through the material, exclusive of similar distortions due to variations in thickness or curvature. Striae are usually caused by *temperature* variation, or poor mixing of ingredients, causing the density (refractive index) to vary in different places.

string. A linear series of entities, such as *bits, characters,* or other items. See *alphabetic string; bit string; null string; pulse string; symbol string; unit string.*

strip. See *bunching strip.*

stripe laser diode. A *laser diode* usually fabricated as a multiheterostructured monolithic element with deposited metallic stripes for *electrical conductors* to create necessary excitation, *fields,* and contacts.

strip-loaded diffused optical waveguide. A three-dimensional *optical waveguide,* constructed from a two-dimensional *diffused optical waveguide,* upon the surface of which a *dielectric* strip of a lower *refractive index* material has been deposited, thus confining the *electromagnetic fields* of the *propagating mode* to the vicinity of the strip and hence achieving a three-dimensional guide.

stripper. See *cladding-mode stripper.*

strobe. See *noise strobe; radar strobe.*

strobe triangulation. *Triangulation* in which a *jammer* is located by plotting the *azimuths* of the *jammed* sectors *(strobes)* of two or more remotely located *radars* that are jammed simultaneously by the *jammer.*

stroke character generator. A *character* generator that generates characters composed of adjacent or connected strokes for presentation in the *display space* on the *display surface* of a *display device,* usually as *alphanumeric* characters. Contrast with *dot-matrix character generator.*

stroke speed. See *scanning line rate.*

structure. See *frame multiplex structure; hierarchical structure.*

stuffer. A device that appends *redundant bits* to an *asynchronous bit stream* to bring the *bit rate* up to a standard constant value that may be subsequently handled by *synchronous* equipment or equipment with a different *transmission speed.* For example, a *time-division multiplexer* that assembles a number of *asynchronous channels* into a single stream. Also see *padding; stuffing character.*

stuffing. 1. The material in an *optical cable* used for such functions as mechanical spacing, *core wrap,* and *fiber buffer.* 2. The addition of *data items,* elements, or *codes* to a given set of *data* for the purpose of creating a specified amount of data rather than for the purpose of adding *information.* See *bit stuffing; destuffing; pulse stuffing.*

stuffing character. A *character* that is used on *isochronous transmission* and is added to *transmitted data* to bring the *character* rate up to a standard constant value that may be subsequently handled by synchronous equipment or equipment with a different *transmission speed.* For example, a character that is used to take account of differences in *clock frequencies.* Also see *stuffer.*

stuffing process. See *molecular stuffing process (MS).*

stuffing rate. See *maximum stuffing rate.*

stunt box. A device that controls the performance of certain *operations.* For example, in *data transmission,* a device that controls the nonprinting functions of a printer.

STX character. The *start-of-text transmission control character.*

stylus. A *pointer* that provides *coordinate data* when a *cursor* is positioned in the *display space* on the *display surface* of a *display device.* The coordinate data may control operations such as the movement of *display elements, display groups,* or *display images;* enter coordinate data; make selections from a *menu;* indicate *display positions;* or perform other such functions. Examples of styli include *light-pens,* sonic pens, *tablet styli,* and voltage pencils.

SU. *Signal unit.*

subband. A subdivision of a given *frequency band.* For example, a subdivision of the speech *frequency spectrum* into *channels* of differing *bandwidth* such that each subdivision makes an equal contribution to speech intelligibility. This example has a particular application in *vocoders.*

subcarrier. A *carrier wave* used as a *modulating* wave to modulate another carrier wave.

subcarrier frequency shift. The conveying of *information* by *shifting* an *audio frequency carrier* that is then used to *modulate* a *radio frequency carrier* for *radio transmission.* When only two *discrete* steps of *subcarrier frequency shift* are used it is known as *two-tone keying.*

SUB character. *Substitute character.*

subjunction gate. See *A-AND-NOT-B gate.*

submarine cable. See *submerged cable.*

submerged cable. An *electrical conductor* or *optical cable* specially designed to convey *messages* while immersed in a body of water. For example, a *coaxial ca-*

ble properly *insulated* laid across the bottom of a lake, harbor, river, strait, or ocean. Synonymous with *submarine cable*. See Figure S-17. Also see Figure L-4.

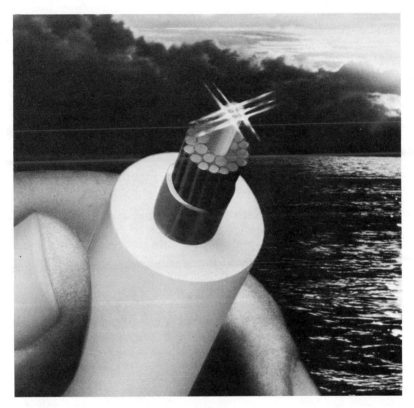

S-17. A glass *optical fiber cable* especially designed for installation as a **submerged cable** on the ocean floor. (Courtesy of Bell Laboratories.)

subreflector. An intermediate *antenna reflector* that forms part of the *propagation path* to and from other or main reflectors of an antenna. It is used to produce a desired *directive gain*.

subsatellite point. At any given time, the point where the earth's surface is intersected by a line from a *satellite* to the earth's center. To an observer at the subsatellite point, the satellite is at *zenith,* that is, directly overhead.

subscriber. **1.** The ultimate *user* (customer) of a *communication service*. **2.** The position, function, office, or unit that is associated with a *system directory* entry. **3.** An individual, activity, or organization that has access to a *communication* *system terminal* and is approved by the proper authority. **4.** In *telephone switchboard operation,* a person who is provided with or uses an *end-instrument,* such as a *telephone* or remote *terminal,* that is connected to an *exchange* or *central office.*

subscriber identification. See *user identification.*

subscriber line. See *line loop.*

subscriber service. See *absent subscriber service.*

subscriber set. See *user set.*

subscriber terminal equipment. See *data subscriber terminal equipment (DSTE).*

subscriber trunk dialing. See *direct distance dialing.*

subset. See *alphabetic character subset; alphanumeric character subset; character subset; numeric character subset.*

subsidence. **1.** In meteorology, a descending motion of air in the *atmosphere,* usually over a broad area. Air subsidence occurs most often in the upper atmosphere and is often revealed by cloud layers. **2.** In mining engineering, a sinking down of a part of the earth's crust due to underground excavations, underground water removal, rock shifts, erosion, cave collapse, or settling.

substation. See *distribution substation; primary substation.*

substitute character. A *control character* that is used in the place of a character that is recognized to be invalid, that is in *error,* or that cannot be represented on a given device, such as an underscored e that is used in place of ϵ (epsilon).

substrate. A material used to support or serve as a foundation, vehicle, or carrier for other material that has the required characteristics for specific application but does not have the proper physical strength to support itself; e.g., a block of material upon which *active materials* may be deposited by evaporative techniques or on which active materials may be bonded by cementing or etching techniques. The substrate is usually inert or *passive* relative to the active material mounted upon it.

subsystem. See *communication subsystem; space-ground-link subsystem.*

subtractor. A device that is capable of forming the algebraic or arithmetic difference between two quantities that are presented as *inputs.* Also see *comparator.*

success. See *access success; block transfer success; disengagement success.*

successful block delivery. The *transfer* of a nonduplicate *user information block* between the *source user* and the intended *destination user.* Successfully delivered blocks include *incorrect blocks* in addition to *successfully transferred* (correct) *blocks.*

successful block transfer. The transfer of only *correct,* nonduplicate, *user infor- mation blocks* between a *source user* and an intended *destination user.* Sucess- ful block transfer occurs at the moment when the last *bit* of the transferred block crosses the functional *interface* between the *telecommunication system* and the destination user's *end-instrument.* Successful block transfer can only occur within a defined *maximum block transfer time* after initiation of a *block transfer attempt.*

successful disengagement. The termination of *user information transfer* between a *source user* and a *destination user* in *response* to a *disengagement request.* Suc- cessful disengagement occurs at the earliest moment at which either user is able to initiate a new *information transfer transaction.* Also see *disengagement at- tempt; disengagement failure; disengagement phase; disengagement request; dis- engagement success; information transfer phase.*

success ratio. See *access success ratio; disengagement success ratio.*

sudden ionospheric disturbance. Abnormally high *ionization densities* in the *D- region* of the *ionosphere* caused by an occasional sudden outburst of *ultraviolet light* from the sun, that is, a *solar flare.* This results in a sudden increase in *radio- wave absorption* that is most severe in the upper *medium frequency (MF)* and lower *high frequency (HF) bands.* Also see *ionospheric disturbance.*

suffix. See *amplifying suffix.*

suffix notation. See *postfix notation.*

sum. See *logical sum.*

summer. In *analog systems,* a device that has an *output analog signal (variable)* that is equal to the sum, or a weighted sum, of two or more *input analog signals (variables).* Synonymous with *analog adder.*

summing integrator. In *analog systems,* a device that has an *output analog signal (variable)* that is the *integral* or a weighted sum of *input analog signals (variables)* with respect to time or with respect to another input analog signal (variable).

sun sensor. In a *satellite communication system,* a *satellite component* that is capable of sensing the time or *incidence angle* of *solar radiation* and providing an *electrical signal* that may be used to compute the satellite attitude or position.

sunspot. **1.** A dark marking in the photosphere (disk) of the sun when viewing it. The spots lie between $30°$ N and $30°$ S latitude on the sun's disk. They have a *temperature* that is about 2000 K lower than the surrounding photosphere. A spot lasts from a few hours to several months, depending on size. Sunspot size varies from a few hundred miles wide to several times the size of the earth. The sunspot cycle is periodic. There are approximately 11 years between successive maxima and minima. Maximum spots are associated with intense solar activity and *interference* with radio and video communications. Investigation of sunspot activity continues.   **2.** A *focused* spot of *light* that is an *image* of the sun and that often reaches kindling *temperature*.   **3.** A *focused* spot of *light* from a large incandescent lamp that is provided with a *filter* in order to imitate the light from the sun in color cinematography.

sunspot activity.   1. The *electromagnetic* effects that are produced by *sunspots.* The effects cause *interference,* disturbances, and anomalies in *radio* and *video transmission.*   **2.** The occurrence of *sunspots,* their growth, their disappearance, and the degradation of *ionospheric propagation* caused by the *magnetic* storms they induce.

sunspot cycle.   A cycle of about 11 years in which *sunspot activity* increases and decreases, the peak activity being marked by intense *magnetic fields* and magnetic storms on earth.   The *high frequencies (HF)* are *propagated* almost entirely by *ionospheric reflection* that is seriously degraded during severe sunspot activity every 11 years.   A disturbance of the solar surface appears as a relatively dark center (umbra) surrounded by a less dark area (penumbra).   Spots generally occur in groups, are relatively short lived, and, with few exceptions, are found in regions between 30° N and 30° S latitude of the sun's disk.

superencryption.   A further *encryption* of *encrypted text* for increased *security* or higher level of *privacy* of *messages.*

supergroup.   1. In *frequency-division multiplexing,* a grouping of *basic groups.* A supergroup is normally 60 *voice channels* or 5 basic groups of 12 voice channels each, occupying the *frequency band* from 312 kHz to 552 kHz.   Each group is the *lower sideband* of actual or *virtual carrier frequencies* of 420, 468, 516, and 612 kHz.   **2.** In *carrier telephony,* an assembly of a specified number of groups, such as 5 *basic groups* comprising 60 *channels,* in adjacent positions in a *frequency spectrum* that is outside the 312 kHz to 552 kHz basic group frequency range.   The CCITT standard *mastergroup* contains 5 supergroups.   United States' *commercial carriers* use 10 supergroups.   The terms *supermastergroup* and *jumbogroup* are sometimes used for 6 mastergroups.   Synonymous with *secondary group.*   See *channel supergroup; through supergroup.*

supergroup distribution frame (SGDF).   In *frequency-division modulation (FDM),* the *distribution frame* that provides *termination* and *connection facilities* for *group modulator output,* group *demodulator input, supergroup modulator input,* and supergroup *demodulator output circuits* of the supergroup *frequency spectrum* of 312 kHz to 552 kHz.

supergroup equipment.   See *through supergroup equipment.*

superheterodyne receiver.   A *receiver* that operates on the principle of mixing the *received signal* with a *local oscillator output signal* in order to improve *selectivity* and *amplification.*

superhigh frequency (SHF).   A *frequency* in the range from 3 GHz to 30 GHz (*wavelengths* from 1 to 10 cm).   The *alphabetic* designator of the range is SHF.

The numeric designator of the range is 10. Also see *frequency spectrum designation.*

superior position flaghoist. In *visual communication systems,* a *flaghoist signaling message* that is to be read ahead of others. It is usually placed higher or more forward than an *inferior position flaghoist message.* Also see *flaghoist signaling.*

superluminescent diode (SLD). A *light-emitting diode (LED)* with narrow *spectral* width and high-*radiance* and *stimulated emission.* The SLD serves as a source for *optical-fiber transmission systems.*

supermastergroup. See *jumbogroup.*

supervise. In *telephone switchboard operations,* the action of an *operator* in putting a *receiver* across a *line* to ascertain whether *communication* has been established satisfactorily or whether a *call* is *finished.*

supervision. See *backward supervision.*

supervisor. In *telephone switchboard operations,* an assistant to the *chief supervisor* who performs some of the duties of the chief supervisor and who directs, assists, and instructs the *operators* in the performance of their duties. The senior supervisor takes charge of the exchange in the absence of the chief supervisor. See *chief supervisor.*

supervisor position. The place, at a *communication station* or *center,* such as a *telephone exchange,* occupied by the *supervisor* of communication *operations* and at which is located special equipment for performing supervisory functions.

supervisory signaling. *Signaling* concerned with the initiation of a *call* and its termination by a *user* (customer, subscriber) or by a *switching center.* Supervisory signals include *off-hook, clear,* and *recall.*

supervisory signal. A *signal* used to indicate and control the various operating states of the *circuit* combinations involved in a particular *connection.* The signals show the state or progress of a *call.* Supervisory signals include *off-hook, clear,* and *recall.*

supervisory working. See *double supervisory working.*

supplement. See *network supplement.*

supplementary heading. In the readdressing of *messages,* a *heading* placed in front of the *preamble* to the message that is being readdressed. The supplementary heading for readdressed messages usually includes all procedural lines as required. All parts of the original message heading that precede the preamble are usually omitted.

support. See *signal support.*

support jamming. *Jamming* in which the equipment with a jamming capability is carried in a vehicle, aircraft, or ship that is not part of the group that is being protected. The equipment may also be land based and may be either in a *stand-off jamming* role or in an *escort jamming* role. Also see *self-protection jamming*.

suppressed carrier. A *carrier wave transmitted* at a *power level* more than 32 dB below the *peak envelope power* and preferably 40 dB or more below the peak envelope power. Also see *full carrier; reduced carrier.* See *double-sideband suppressed carrier; single-sideband suppressed carrier.*

suppressed-carrier transmission. *Transmission* in which the *carrier wave* is *suppressed* either partially or to the maximum extent possible. One or both of the *sidebands* may be *transmitted.* Synonymous with *reduced-carrier transmission.* See *double-sideband suppressed-carrier transmission; single-sideband suppressed-carrier (SSB-SC) transmission.*

suppressed-carrier transmission system. See *double-sideband suppressed-carrier transmission system.*

suppressed-clock pulse-length modulation. *Modulation* similar to *pulse-length modulation,* except that *clock information* is removed, thus reducing the required *bandwidth.*

suppression. See *infrared radiation suppression; noise suppression; zero suppression.*

suppression and blanking. See *pulse interference, suppression, and blanking.*

suppressor. See *echo suppressor; half-echo suppressor.*

surface. See *display surface; emitting surface; interface surface; optical surface.*

surface code. See *panel code.*

surface detection equipment. See *airport surface detection equipment.*

surface-emitting LED. A *light-emitting diode* with a *spectral output* that emanates from the surfaces of the layers. The surface-emitting LED has a lower output *intensity* and lower *coupling efficiency,* to an *optical fiber* or *integrated optical circuit,* than the *edge-emitting LEDs* and the *injection lasers.* Surface- and edge-emitting LEDs provide several milliwatts of *power* in the 0.8- to 1.2-*micron spectral range* at drive *currents* of 100 to 200 mA. Diode lasers at these currents provide tens of milliwatts. Synonymous with *front-emitting LED; Burrus LED.* Also see *edge-emitting LED.*

surface mirror. See *back-surface mirror; front-surface mirror.*

surface refractive index. The value of the *refractive index* of the *atmosphere* calculated from observations of pressure, *temperature,* and humidity at specific points near the earth's surface. The surface refractive index gradient is the difference between the refractive index at a given elevation and the index at the surface, divided by the difference in elevation. Synonymous with *surface refractivity.*

surface refractivity. See *surface refractive index.*

surface station. A *station* on or near the surface of the earth, such as a *land station, ship station, mobile* vehicular *station,* or *fixed station.* In *satellite communications,* an *aircraft station* is also considered as a surface station since it operates in the earth's atmosphere and relatively close to the surface of the earth compared to a *satellite orbit* or *deep space.*

surface-to-air communications. One-way *communication* from *surface stations,* such as *ship,* submarine, *land,* or *fixed stations,* to *aircraft stations.*

surface wave. 1. An *electromagnetic wave* that *propagates* along an *interface* between two different *transmission media* without *radiating* away from the *interface surface,* such as is obtained in an *optical fiber;* i.e., there is no energy converted from the surface wave field to some other form of energy nor is it *propagated* normal to the surface. 2. An *electromagnetic wave* that *propagates* relatively close to the earth's surface, which serves as the *interface* between two different media, namely, the ground (a conductor) and the air above the ground. Surface waves include *direct waves, indirect waves,* and *ground waves,* but not *skywaves.* Also see *skywave.*

surveillance. See *air surveilllance; electromagnetic surveillance; electronic surveillance; exploratory electromagnetic surveillance.*

surveillance radar. See *acquisition radar.*

surveillance radar station. A *radionavigation land station* in the *aeronautical radionavigation service* that employs *radar* to *display* the presence of objects within its range. A surveillance radar station may be a *ship station.*

survey. See *path survey.*

survivability. In *communications,* the capability of a *communication system* to resist any interruption or disturbance of service, particularly by warfare, fire, earthquake, *harmful radiation* or other physical or natural catastrophe rather than by *electromagnetic interference* or *crosstalk.* See *communication survivability; electromagnetic survivability.*

survivalcraft station. A *mobile station,* in the *maritime* or *aeronautical mobile service* that is intended solely for survival purposes and is located on board any lifeboat, liferaft, or other survival equipment to be used in an emergency or for search-and-rescue operations.

survivability. See *electromagnetic survivability.*

susceptibility. 1. The degree to which a device, equipment, or *system* is open to effective *degradation* due to one or more inherent weaknesses. For example, the degree to which a *communication system* is susceptible to *interference* from *sunspot activity.* 2. In *electronic warfare,* the degree to which electronic equipment is adversely affected by *radiated electromagnetic energy,* such as by *radiation* from *jammers.*

susceptiveness. In *telephone systems,* the tendency of *circuits* to pick up *noise* and low *frequency* induction from *power systems.* Susceptiveness to such induction depends on many factors, such as *telephone circuit balance, transpositions, conductor* spacing, and *isolation* from *ground.*

sweep.   1. In *electronic systems,* the pattern of *light* or marking on the face of a *cathode-ray tube* that is caused by the predetermined *deflection* and *modulation* of the *electron beam.* For example, the voltage-versus-time *deflection voltage* that is placed on one of the pairs of deflecting plates or one of the deflecting coils of the cathode-ray tube to enable a *display* of the voltage applied to the other pair of plates or to the other deflecting coil. The sweep voltage has the *waveshape* of a sawtooth, that is, it has a slow linear rise and a sudden drop. When only the sweep is applied, a single straight line will appear as a time baseline. If *magnetic* deflection is used, the same principles apply to the deflecting *currents.*   **2.** To vary the *frequency* of a *transmitter* continuously over a wide *frequency* range.   **3.** To *tune* a *receiver* continuously over a wide *frequency* range. See *antenna sweep; sector sweep.*

sweep jammer. A *jammer* that electronically *sweeps* a *narrow frequency band* of *jamming* energy over a *wide band.* The *transmitter emits* a jamming *signal* that consists of a *carrier wave, modulated* or unmodulated, the *frequency* of which is continuously varied within a given *bandwidth.*

sweep jamming. *Jamming* in which the *frequency* of the *jamming signal* is continuously varied within a specific *bandwidth.* A *narrow frequency band* of jamming energy is repeatedly swept over a relatively *wide frequency band.* Sweep jamming combines the advantages of both *spot* and *barrage jamming* by rapidly electronically *sweeping* a *narrowband* of jamming signals over a broad *frequency spectrum.* Ideally, the sweep rate is such as to be on any given *frequency* only long enough to accomplish its jamming task, returning to that frequency again before the expiration of the *jammed circuit recovery time.* The disadvantage of sweep jamming is in its high susceptibility to *electronic counter-countermeasures (ECCM).*

sweep noise-modulated jamming. See *slow-sweep noise-modulated jamming.*

swept jammer. A *jammer* whose *frequency* is varied continuously over specific *frequency bands.* The bands are usually just above and below the frequencies to be jammed.

swept-repeater jammer. A *sweep jammer* that *transmits* only on those *frequencies* that are within its *bandwidth* and that are specifically selected because they are in use by the *systems* that are being *jammed.*

swim. Relatively slow, undesired but graceful movement of *display elements, display groups,* or *display images* about their mean or normal positions in the *display space* on the *display surface* of a *display device.* For example, the slow movement of the display image on the surface of the *faceplate* of a *fiberscope* that might be caused when the image source at the opposite end of the attached *coherent bundle* of *optical fibers* is moved slowly relative to the bundle, or the slow movement of the display image on the screen of a *CRT* when the deflection-plate *bias voltage* fluctuates slowly. Swim is the same as *jitter,* except that swim is usually slower and of larger *amplitude* than jitter. Contrast with *jitter.*

switch. **1.** To transfer connection, contact, or *signal* continuity from one *circuit* or *channel* to another. **2.** A mechanical, electromechanical, or electronic device for making, breaking, or changing the *connections* in *circuits.* **3.** A *switching center.* See *analog switch; crossbar switch; digital switch; disconnect switch; ferrite switch; fuse disconnecting switch; horn gap switch; interrupt switch; laser frequency switch; mechanical optical switch; optical switch; packet switch; Q-switch; semielectronic switch; tandem switch; thin-film optical switch; trunk switch; waveguide switch.*

switchboard. A manually operated set of equipment at a *telephone exchange* on which the various *circuits* from *users* (subscribers, customers) and from other exchanges are terminated to enable *operators* to establish *communication* either between two users (subscribers, customers) on the same exchange, or between users on different exchanges. See *cordless switchboard; dial service assistance (DSA) switchboard; field switchboard; intermediate switchboard; magneto switchboard; monocord switchboard; multiposition switchboard; single-position magneto switchboard.*

switch busy hour. The *busy hour* for a single *switch.* Also see *group busy hour; network busy hour.*

switched. See *failure-fraction-automatically-switched.*

switched circuit. A *circuit* that may be temporarily established at the request of one or more *stations.*

switched connection. See *circuit-switched connection.*

switched data transmission service. See *circuit-switched data transmission service; packet-switched data transmission service.*

switched hot-line circuit. An *exclusive-user preprogrammed circuit* set up as required between a *user* (customer, subscriber) and one or more other users, in which the user action is limited to going *off-hook* to establish a *connection* within a short fixed time. Also see *exclusive-user circuit; sole user circuit.*

switched network. **1.** A *communication network* that has *switching facilities* or centers that perform the function of *message switching, packet switching,* or *circuit switching.* **2.** A *network* that provides *switched communication service.*

switched repetitively-pulsed laser. See *Q-switched repetitively-pulsed laser.*

switched time-division multiple-access. See *satellite-switched time-division multiple-access (SS-TDMA).*

switchgear. See *low-voltage enclosed air-circuit-breaker switchgear; metal clad switchgear.*

switching. The control or *routing* of *signals* in *circuits* to execute logical or arithmetic *operations* or to *transmit data* between specific points in a *network*. Switching may be accomplished in *optical fiber (lightwave) communication* circuits and in *optical integrated circuits.* See *analog switching; automatic message switching; automatic switching; beam lobe switching; circuit switching; digital data switching; digital switching; message switching; packet switching; rotary switching; semiautomatic continuous-tape relay switching; space-division switching; tactical automatic digital switching (TADS); time-division switching.*

switching and message distribution center. In a *communication system,* an installation in which *switching equipment* is used to connect *communication* equipment for *routing messages* or *packets* toward their ultimate *(addressee)* destinations and that also distributes messages to addressees in the local area served by the center.

switching center. 1. In a *communication system,* an installation in which *switching equipment* is used to connect *communication circuits* on a *message, packet,* or *circuit switching* basis. Synonymous with *central office; switching exchange; switching facility.* 2. In *telephone systems,* an *exchange* that is used primarily as a *switching* point for *traffic* between other exchanges. Synonymous with *central office.* 3. In *satellite communication systems,* the *interface* with existing terrestrial communication systems. 4. A center of an *integrated telegraph* and *telephone network* in which *store-and-forward message switching* is used. It contains message *switching equipment* capable of *terminating dedicated point-to-point circuits* and setting up *connections* via *nodal switching centers* of *communication system switched telegraph* and *telephone networks.* See *circuit switching center; gateway switching center; nodal switching center; store-and-forward switching center.*

switching circuit. A *circuit,* usually consisting of interconnected *gates* (such as *AND, OR,* and *NEGATION gates*) that can be used to perform arithmetic and *logic operations.* Switching circuits are used in *optical integrated circuits.*

switching equipment. *Communication* equipment used to effect the onward *transmission* of *information* through *connections* of *circuits, loops, channels,* or *trunks.* See *automatic switching equipment.*

switching equipment congestion signal. See *national switching equipment congestion signal.*

switching exchange. See *switching center; data switching exchange (DSE).*

switching facility. See *switching center.*

switching matrix. In *telephone systems,* the *connection* matrix that lies between incoming and outgoing *circuits* in an *automatic switching exchange.* The matrix may consist of *relays* connected to *crossbars* or *solid-state circuits* connected to cross-*buses.*

switching process time. The time from the first instant at which a *switching center* receives the *called party's address (number)* until the *ringing tone* or *busy signal* from the called party's *end-instrument* commences.

switching reaction time. In *telephone systems,* the time delay between the establishment of a *condition* and the receipt of a *signal* that indicates that condition.

switching release. In *telephone systems,* a *signal* sent to a *switchboard* to be used for disconnecting *circuits* and restoring them to the *idle state.*

switching system. Any mechanical, electrical, electromechanical, or electronic *system* that processes an *input signal* and delivers an *output signal.* For example, a *digital* system that processes an *input call* to an *output port.* Also see *circuit switching; message switching; packet switching.* See *electronic switching system.*

switching trunk. See *toll switching trunk.*

switching unit. See *circuit switching unit (CSU).*

switching variable. A variable that may assume only a finite number of possible values or states. For example, an unspecified *character* of a character set, such as a character set consisting of 0 and 1. Synonymous with *logic variable.*

switch message. A *message* that contains *information* obtained by listening to *radio broadcasts,* information such as the *frequency, call sign,* and *output power level* of a detected *transmitter.* See *amplifying switch message.*

switch-modulator. See *integrated-optical circuit filter-coupler-switch-modulator.*

switchroom. In *telephone switchboard operation,* a room in which a *switchboard,* as distinct from other equipment in an *exchange,* is situated.

SWR. *Standing wave ratio.*

syllabary. In a *code book,* a list of individual letters, combinations of letters, or syllables, that are accompanied by their equivalent *code groups* and are used for spelling out *words* or proper names that are not present in the vocabulary of a *code.* Synonymous with *spelling table.*

syllabic companding. The action of a *compandor* that is just fast enough to correct the *power level* of individual syllables of speech. During a syllable, the *gain* of the *expander* and the loss of the *compressor* are proportional to the *mean power talker.*

symbol. A representation of a concept, usually one upon which agreement has been reached as to the concept that is being represented. For example, a small circle of *light* on a *radar screen* used to represent an object (target) in space, a letter of an *alphabet* that is used, together with others, to form *words* to which meaning has been assigned, or a *flag* to represent a nation or country. See *accounting symbol; aiming symbol; station symbol; tracking symbol.*

symbolic language. A *computer programming language* that has an *instruction* repertory with instructions expressed in *symbols* that are convenient for use by persons rather than machines. For example, a language that has instructions like ADD for addition, SUB for subtraction, and MPY for multiplication, rather than X for addition, Y for subtraction, and Z for multiplication, which may be perfectly "convenient" to a machine.

symbol string. A *string* that consists only of *symbols.*

symmetrical binary code. A *code* that is derived from a *binary code* in which the sign of the *quantized* value, positive or negative, is represented by one *digit* and in which the remaining digits constitute a *binary number* that represents the magnitude. In any particular symmetrical binary code, the weight of each digit and the use that is made of the symbols 0 and 1 in the various digit positions must be specified.

symmetrical channel. A *channel* in which the *transmit* and *receive* directions *(forward direction* and *backward direction)* of *transmission* have the same *data signaling rate.*

symmetrical double-heterojunction diode. See *four-heterojunction diode.*

symmetrical pair cable. A *balanced transmission line* in a *multipaired cable* that has equal *conductor resistances* per unit length, equal *impedances* from each conductor to *ground (earth),* and equal *impedances* to other *lines.*

symmetric binary channel. A *channel* that is designed to *transfer messages* that consist of *binary characters* and that has the characteristic that the conditional probability of inadvertently (wrongly) changing any one *character* to the other character is equal for both characters.

symmetric-difference gate. See *EXCLUSIVE-OR gate.*

symmetric fiber. See *circularly symmetric fiber.*

symmetric signal. **1.** A *signal* that has a quality of symmetry with regard to some reference. For example, a signal in which, when represented with its *amplitude* on the vertical axis and time on the horizontal axis, the portion to the left of the origin is the mirror image of the portion to the right of the origin (vertical axis), whether direct or inverted. Thus, a symmetric signal may have one or more of many kinds of symmetry, such as x-axis symmetry, y-axis symmetry, zero-point (origin) symmetry, or arbitrary line symmetry. **2.** A *signal* that has both negative and positive polarities over a long period of time in such a manner that the net positive flow of *current* equals the net negative flow of current thus preventing long-term accumulation of charges and hence drifting *voltages* and baselines.

SYN. The *synchronous idle (SYN) transmission control character.*

SYN character. *Synchronous idle (SYN) character.*

synchronism. The simultaneous occurrence of two or more events on the same *date* (instant) of the same *coordinated time scale.* If the events are repetitive, a *significant instant* of one event bears a fixed time relation with a corresponding instant in the other events with which synchronism is maintained.

synchronization. In *communication systems,* the process of adjusting corresponding *significant instants* of two *signals* to obtain a desired fixed relationship between the instants. For example, in *facsimile transmission,* the establishment of equal *scanning line frequencies* at the *transmitter* and the *receiver;* in *spread-spectrum systems,* the obtaining of timing agreement between a transmitter and a receiver so that, coupled with the same *spread spectrum binary sequence generator,* the *information content* of the *received signal* can be recovered. See *amplitude quantized synchronization; analog synchronization; bilateral synchronization; double-ended synchronization; frame synchronization; linear analog synchronization; single-ended synchronization.*

synchronization acquisition time. The time required for a *receiving circuit* to acquire *bit synchronism* after application of the first *digital signal pulse* to the *circuit terminals.*

synchronization bit. A *binary digit* used for *character synchronization* in a *transmission system.*

synchronization correction signal. A *signal* used for correcting or recovering *synchronization* in a *synchronous system* after *synchronism* has been lost.

synchronization pattern. See *frame synchronization pattern.*

synchronization system. See *unilateral synchronization system.*

synchronized clock. A *clock* whose *output* is *synchronized* by another clock, that is, they are both synchronized to the same *timing signal* reference *source.* Also see *independent clock.*

synchronized network. See *democratically synchronized network; despotically synchronized network; hierarchically synchronized network; mutually synchronized network; oligarchically synchronized network.*

synchronized transmitter group. Two or more *transmitters* whose *transmitted signals* are *synchronized,* usually with the same *modulation* or *keying* from a single *signal source* and operating on exactly the same *frequency,* but not necessarily in the same *phase.* They may be used to completely *mask* another transmitter or to direct a signal in a specific direction by adjusting the phase relation between the transmitters.

synchronizing. The process of achieving *synchronization.* For example, in *facsimile systems,* the maintenance of predetermined speed relations between the *scanning spot* and the *recording spot* within each *scanning line.*

synchronizing pilot. In *frequency-division multiplexing (FDM),* a *reference frequency* that is used for maintaining the *synchronization* of the *oscillators* of a *carrier system* or for comparing the *frequencies* or *phases* of the *electric currents* or *voltages* generated by those oscillators.

synchronizing signal. A *signal* that is used for achieving and maintaining *synchronization.* For example, in *facsimile systems,* the signal that maintains predetermined speed relations between the *scanning spot* and the *recording spot* within each *facsimile scanning line;* in *digital data synchronous transmission systems,* the signal that is used to maintain *synchronism* between the *transmitter* and the *receiver* during *data transfer;* or in a synchronized *transmitter* group, the signal that is used to maintain synchronism among the transmitters of the group.

synchronous. 1. Pertaining to events that occur at the same time or at the same rate. For example, pertaining to processes that depend on the occurrence of specific events such as common timing *signals (clock pulses).* 2. Pertaining to events that occur with a regular or predictable time relationship among them. See *quasisynchronous.*

synchronous correction. The correction of the *phase* relationship between a *signal* in one device, such as a *receiver,* and a signal in another device, such as a *transmitter,* in a *synchronous system.* The *synchronism* is maintained by the use of a phase signal proportional to the phase difference between the two signals whose phase relation is being maintained. This signal is used to cause the device with advanced phase to slow up or shift back, or cause the delayed or lagging phase to speed up or shift forward, thus correcting the phase difference to the desired value, perhaps zero. If there is a continuous slippage in phase, that is, the *frequencies* are different, another signal is developed to cause one of the frequencies to either increase or decrease until the frequencies are the same and the *phase-lock circuit* can take over.

synchronous counter. A counter in which all stages of the counter are simultaneously moved to their next state. Thus, in a synchronous counter, the clock or input pulse being counted initiates all the changes simultaneously and the total time taken to count one pulse is much less than that of an equivalent asynchronous counter, in which the output state of each stage is dependent on the previous stages having changed, that is, the flip-flops do not all change state synchronously since it takes a finite time for changes to propagate through the counter.

synchronous cryptooperation. *Online cryptooperation* in which *terminal cryptoequipment* have timing *systems* to keep them in step. *Synchronism* of the system is independent of the *traffic* passing on the system *channels.*

synchronous data-link control. Control of *synchronous transmission* over *data links* in a *data network.*

synchronous data network. A *data network* in which *synchronization* is maintained between *data circuit-terminating equipment (DCE)* and a *data switching exchange (DSE),* and between DSEs. The *data signaling rates* are controlled by timing equipment within the *network.*

synchronous data transmission channel. A *data channel* in which *timing signals* are *transferred* with the *traffic* between the *data terminal equipment (DTE)* and the *data circuit-terminating equipment (DCE).*

synchronous demodulation. A form of *phase-sensitive angle demodulation* in which the *local oscillator* is *synchronized* (locked) in *frequency* and *phase* to the distant *transmitter,* after allowing for *Doppler shifts* in *frequency* due to any radial component of relative velocity between the transmitter and the *receiver* and after allowing for *phase delays* during *transmission,* that is, for *transit time.*

synchronous digital computer. A *digital computer* in which the execution of each *instruction* of a *program* is initiated by selected equally-spaced *signals* from a *master clock.* Also see *asynchronous digital computer.*

synchronous earth satellite. A *satellite* that *orbits* about the center of the earth in a circle in exact *synchronism* with the rotation of the earth, though not necessarily in the equatorial plane. If the satellite is at the proper height (altitude) and speed in the equatorial plane, it will always remain at a fixed point above the equator and hence is a *geostationary satellite.* Otherwise, the synchronous earth satellite will maintain a fixed longitude but oscillate back and forth in the sky. Three geostationary synchronous earth satellites can provide full *earth coverage* except in the polar regions because of the low *elevation angles* of the satellite when viewed from those regions. The satellite appears stationary but it is barely above the horizon.

synchronous equatorial satellite height. See *geostationary satellite height.*

synchronous height. The *orbital* height (altitude) of a *satellite* at which the period equals that of the parent body. The synchronous height for an earth *geostationary satellite* is 19 200 nmi, or 35 558.4 km, above the equator. (1 nmi = 1.852 km).

synchronous idle (SYN) character. A *transmission control character* that is used by *synchronous data transmission systems* as a *signal* for maintaining *synchronism* or for achieving synchronism between sets of *data terminal equipment (DTE)* particularly when no other character is being *transmitted.*

synchronous jamming. *Jamming* in which *signals* are used that are *modulated* at an exact multiple of the basic *pulse repetition rate* of the equipment, such as *radar systems* or *communication systems,* that is being *jammed.*

synchronous margin. In a *start-stop system,* the maximum value of the *margin* that is obtained by adjusting the *modulation rate* of the *input signals* to the most favorable value with respect to the timing characteristics of a *receiver.*

synchronous network. A *network* in which the *clocks* are controlled so as to run at identical rates, or at the same mean rate with limited relative *phase* displacement among them. Ideally the clocks are *synchronous,* but they may be *mesochronous* in practice. Mesochronous networks are frequently described as synchronous.

synchronous operation. See *asynchronous operation; bit-synchronous operation.*

synchronous orbit. An *orbit* in which a satellite has an orbital angular velocity that is synchronized with the rotational angular velocity of the earth or other parent body. If the orbital plane is also an equatorial plane the satellite will remain directly above a fixed point on the parent body surface at the equator. Thus, the *subsatellite point* is fixed. For the earth this occurs at an altitude of approximately 19,200 nmi above the equator. (1 nmi = 1.852 km.) This would be a *geostationary satellite.* If the satellite's orbital motion is *synchronized* with the rotation of the earth but not necessarily in the equatorial plane, the satellite remains at a fixed longitude but not above a fixed point.

synchronous receiver margin. The margin of a *synchronous receiver.* It is determined by the extent of *isochronous distortion.*

synchronous satellite. A *satellite* in a *synchronous orbit.*

synchronous signals. A set of *signals* such that between any two *significant instants* there is an *integral number* of *unit intervals,* as when keeping in step with a *clock* or a trigger signal. Also see *asynchronous signals.*

synchronous system. A *system* in which the component parts have *signals* in them that are in *synchronism* with each other. For example, a system in which a *transmitter* and a *receiver* are operating with a fixed time relationship with each other, a *telegraph* or *data system* in which *isochronous modulation* or *restitution* is used and in which the *transmitting* and *receiving* instruments operate continuously with a constant *phase* relationship, or an *alphabetic telegraphy system* in which *synchronous transmission* is used.

synchronous time-division multiplexing. *Multiplexing* in which *timing signals* are obtained from a *clock* that in turn controls both the *multiplexer* and the *data source.* Also see *asynchronous time-division multiplexing (ATDM).*

synchronous transmission. **1.** *Data transmission* in which the *occurrence time* of a specified *significant instant* in each *byte, character, word, block,* or other unit of *data,* such as the leading edge of a start *signal,* occurs in a specified time relationship with a preceding signal on the *channel,* in accordance with a specified *timing pulse,* or in accordance with a specified *time frame. Lightwave communication systems* may be operated both in synchronous transmission or *asynchronous transmission* modes. **2.** A *transmission process* such that between any two *significant instants* in the overall *bit stream* there is always an *integral number* of *unit intervals.* Also see *asynchronous transmission* and Figure D-10.

syncopated code. In *spread spectrum systems,* a *spread-spectrum binary code-sequence generator output* with *asynchronous bit timing.* The *pulses* in the *code* do not occur at regular or fixed *periodic* intervals.

synodic period. The time of revolution of any *satellite,* including the earth, with reference to the sun. The average *sidereal day* period of the moon about the earth is 27 and 1/3 days. This is compared to the average synodic period, or lunar month, of 29 and 1/2 days. Also see *sidereal day.*

syntax. The structure and relationships among expressions in a *language,* or the rules that govern the structure. Syntax includes the relationship within or among groups of *characters* independent of their specific meanings, interpretation, and use. It permits the determination of allowable or nonallowable expressions in a language, rather than being concerned with the specific meanings that are assigned to words and expressions. Examples of syntax rules include the syntactical rule of English that the letter q cannot begin a word unless it is followed by the letter u, a syntactical rule of mathematics is that a + sign or a − sign must always be followed by or be associated with a number or a *symbol* that can be evaluated as a number. Thus, a language can be completely described by listing the symbols, their uses, and the syntax that establishes their permissible arrangements. If the rules are never violated and nothing is permitted unless explicitly allowed by the rules, the language is said to be ruly. *Artificial languages* tend to be ruly, since syntax is seldom if ever violated. *Natural languages* tend to be unruly, since syntax is often violated.

synthesizer. See *speech synthesizer.*

synthesizing. See *frequency synthesizing.*

system. In *computers, information processing,* and *communications,* a group of persons, machines, and methods organized to accomplish a set of specific functions. A *communication system* includes all the *facilities* and equipment required to insure its proper maintenance and operation. See *active detection system; airborne radar warning system; aircraft control-warning system; air defense communication system; air-ground worldwide communication system; asynchronous communication system; authentication system; automatic data processing system (ADPS); automatic error detection and correction system; automatic relay system (ARQ); automatic telephone system; beacon navigation system; beam-riding guidance system; cipher system; ciphony communication system; code-dependent system; code-independent system; command and control system; command guidance system; common control system; communication subsystem; communication system; continuous time system; crossbar system; data system; directional signaling system; discrete-time filtering system; discrete-time system; display system; distributed data processing system; diversity system; Doppler system; double-sideband suppressed-carrier transmission system; electronic switching system; error-correcting system; error-detecting system; facsimile system; Federal Telecommunication System (FTS); fiber-optic transmission system; five-horn feed system; flashing-light communication system; four-horn feed system; frequency-and-amplitude (FRENA) system; ground controlled approach (GCA) system; guidance system; Hell system; high-grade cryptosystem; homing guidance system; hybrid communication system; hyperbolic navigation system; imaging system; inertial guidance system; instrument landing system (ILS); integrated communication system; integrated optical fiber system; interactive display system; Joint Uniform Telephone Communication Precedence System (JUTCPS); layered system; laser fiber-optic transmission system; lens system; local distribution system; long-distance direct-current (LDDC) dialing system; loop-disconnect system; loop-disconnect pulsing system; man-machine system; manual relay system; master-slave timing system; merchant ship broadcast system (MERCAST); metric system; monopulse antenna feed system; neutral direct-current telegraph system; nonin-*

ertial guidance system; omnidirectional signaling system; optical communication system; optical system; passive detection system; polarential telegraph system; precedence telephone system; primary distribution system; protected optical fiber distribution system; protected wireline distribution system; pseudomonopulse tracking system; pure binary numeration system; quadruplex system; radio relay system; radiotelephone system; radiotelephone voice system; reference system; satellite communication system; sea surveillance system; semi-automatic relay system; single-frequency (SF) signaling system; space-ground-link subsystem; start-stop transmission system; stepped start-stop transmission system; strategic military communication system; switching system; synchronous system; tactical communication system; teleautography system; telecommunication system; telephone system; terminal-guidance navigation system; terrain avoidance system; terrestrial system; threat warning system; unilateral synchronization system; visual communication system; Wheatstone automatic system; wideband communication system; wideband system; worldwide geographic reference system.

system abbreviations.   See *aeronautical communication system abbreviations.*

system blocking.   See *access denial.*

system blocking signal.   A control *(overhead) message* that is generated within a *communication system* to indicate the temporary unavailability of system resources that are required to complete an *access request.*   Also see *access denial; access failure; blocking.*

system budget.   See *power budget.*

system consolidation.   See *communication system consolidation.*

system controller.   1. In a *communication system,* a person at a *technical control facility* who is responsible for maintaining quality control of *switching functions* that are performed by *communication* equipment. 2. Equipment at a *technical control facility* that controls the functioning of switching and supporting equipment.

system down time.   The time interval during which a *user* (customer, subscriber) operating in a realistic environment would, due to a *system component malfunction,* either receive no *response* or an incorrect response from a system if the user attempted to request service from the system.

Système Internationale d'Unités.   International System of Units. See *SI.*

system environmental file.   A compilation of *information* concerning the location, height above ground, identity, *frequency assignment,* operational characteristics, and major equipment characteristics of surrounding *radiating communication-electronic* equipment that may be potentially important to *compatibility* studies for *communication system* design, development, and operation.

system integrity.   The assurance that a *computer, data processing system,* or *communication system* is logically designed, correctly operating, reliable, complete, and adequately protected in all *hardware* and *software* aspects. System integrity includes *data integrity*.

system loading. In a *frequency-division multiplexed (FDM) transmission system,* the *absolute power level,* referred to a *zero transmission level point (OTLP),* of the *composite signal,* including *speech, data,* and *signaling,* that is *transmitted* in one direction.

system management. See *communication system management.*

system noise temperature. See *receiving-system noise temperature.*

system of units. See *SI.*

system operating time. The time interval during which a *system* is capable of being operated and is producing accurate results in accordance with system standards.

system operator. See *telecommunication system operator.*

system overhead information. In a *communication system message,* the part of *overhead information* that is added by the system and is not delivered to the *destination user* or *addressee.* For example, *check characters, routing instructions,* or other *address groups.* Also see *user overhead.*

systems. See *heterogeneous computer systems; homogeneous computer systems.*

systems architecture. See *open systems architecture.*

system saturation. See *communication system saturation.*

system standard. 1. In *communication systems,* a minimum required electrical performance characteristic of *communication circuits* that is based on measured performance of developed *circuits* under the various operating conditions for which the circuits were designed. 2. A specific characteristic that is not dictated by electrical performance requirements, but is necessary in order to permit interoperation of *systems* and *components.* For example, the standards for operating *frequencies* or for *test tones.* Also see *design objective.*

system test time. The part of the *system* operating time during which the system is tested for proper *operation.*

T

table. See *garble table; look-up table; permutation table; prediction table; routing indicator delineation table; teletypewriter garble table.*

tablet. A flat surface over which a drawing or graph may be placed such that, when used with a *stylus* or *mouse, coordinate data* can be generated. The data correspond to the position of the stylus or mouse on the surface.

taboo frequency. A *frequency* on which *jamming* or other intentional *interference* is prohibited. A taboo frequency is of such importance that it must never be deliberately *jammed* or interfered with. Examples are *communication frequencies* that are identified for intelligence purposes and certain missile control frequencies. Such frequencies are used for *early-warning* air defense, intelligence purposes, command and control, and search and rescue operations. They are thus too important to be jammed. Also see *protected frequency; guarded frequency.*

tabulation character. See *horizontal tabulation character; vertical tabulation character.*

tack. In *flaghoist signaling,* the voice equivalent for the *tackline,* a two-*meter* length of *halyard* that is used as a *separator* between *flags* or *pennants* that, if not separated, would convey a different meaning.

tackline. In *visual communication systems,* a length of *halyard* about two *meters* long that is used in *flaghoist signaling* as a *separator* between *flags* or *pennants* that, if not separated, would convey a different meaning. The voice *prosign* for the *displayed* tackline is TACK.

tactical air operations communication net. See *maritime tactical air operations communication net.*

tactical automatic digital switching (TADS). In *military communication systems,* a *transportable store-and-forward message switching system* designed for rapid deployment in support of tactical forces.

tactical communications. In *military communication systems,* a method or means of conveying *information* of any kind, especially orders and decisions from one command, person, or place to another within the tactical forces, normally by means of electronic equipment, including *communication security* equipment that is organic to the tactical forces. Excluded are communication capabilities that are provided to tactical forces by nontactical military commands and to tactical forces by civil organizations.

tactical communication system.   A system, configured by various types of fixed-size self-contained assemblies and *components*, such as *radio repeaters* and *terminals; switching, transmission,* and *terminal equipment;* interconnect and control *facilities;* and related equipment; that are organic to tactical forces and that are designed to meet the requirements of changing tactical situations.   The tactical communication system may provide *secure voice* and *data communication* among *mobile users* to facilitate command and control functions within, and support of, tactical forces.   Based on different requirements of the multichannel *trunking networks,* a distinction is made between (1) tactical communication systems that require extremely short installation times, such as a few minutes or hours, necessitated by relocation requirements that are sometimes frequent, and (2) tactical communication systems for which longer time periods are available for installation and commencement of *operation.*   Tactical communication systems are generally composed of *mobile* or *transportable communication equipment* and *components* that are assigned as unit equipment in the hands of the personnel of the tactical unit.

tactical digital information link (TADIL).   A class of *data links* that have rigidly controlled *protocol* and are used for providing *communication* support to tactical units.

tactical load.   In *communication systems,* the part of the *operational load* that is required for weapons, detection, command and control systems, and related tactical functions.

TADIL.   *Tactical digital information link.*

TADS.   *Tactical automatic digital switching.*

tag.   See *flag.*

tagging.   See *aperture tagging.*

takeoff angle.   See *departure angle.*

tailing.   In *transmission systems,* the excessive prolongation of the decay of a *signal* when it is not desired.   It is due to a defect in a *transmission system* in which the *transition* to a new *signal level* is delayed.   For example, in *facsimile systems,* it is a defect in the reproduction of a signal in which a sudden variation in *luminance,* such as from black to white on the original (subject) document, is shifted irregularly in the *scanning* direction on the *record sheet.*   The same effect can occur on *video displays* and in *pulse transmission systems.*   Tailing does not apply to the reproduction of details that are smaller than the *picture element* and that may in some cases be deliberately prolonged at the *transmitter.*   Synonymous with *hangover.*

talbot.   In the meter-kilogram-second system of units, a unit of *luminous energy* equal to 10-million *lumergs* and also equal to 1 *lumen*-second.

talk. See *crosstalk.*

talker. See *mean power talker; medium power talker.*

talker volume distribution. See *mean-power-of-the-talker volume distribution.*

tandem. 1. The *connection* of the *output terminals* of one *network, circuit,* or *link* directly to the *input terminals* of another network, circuit, or link. For example, links that are employed in *microwave relays.* 2. The *connection* of a group of entities in series, as in a chain. Synonymous with *concantenation; catenation; chain.* Also see *cascading.*

tandem center. In a *communication system,* an installation in which *switching equipment* connects *trunks* to trunks, but does not connect any *local loops.*

tandem data circuit. A *data circuit* that contains more than two sets of *data circuit-terminating equipment (DCE)* in series, that is, in *tandem.*

tandem exchange. See *tandem switch.*

tandem switch. A manual or automatic *switch* that connects the *output terminals* of the *circuits* of one *trunk* to the *input terminals* of the circuits of another trunk, thereby connecting both trunks in series, that is, in *tandem.* Synonymous with *tandem exchange.*

tangent. 1. In a right triangle, the ratio of the side opposite a given acute angle to the side that is the shorter side of the given acute angle. The ratio is the tangent of the given angle. The hypotenuse is not involved in the ratio directly. 2. A line from a point outside a circle or a sphere touching the circle or sphere in only one point even though the line is extended to infinity. Tangents may also be drawn to other surfaces and curves. The only requirement is that the line is drawn so as to touch the curve or surface at only one point, even though the line is infinitely long.

tangential coupling. The *coupling* of one *optical fiber* to another by placing or fusing the *core* of the fiber containing a *signal* in close proximity for a short distance to another fiber core, to allow some of the signal to leak or spill over to the attached fiber, by subverting the original signal-bearing fiber from keeping all its light to itself. The degree of *coupling* is determined by the core-to-core spacing and the fused length. This method of coupling also makes use of the *evanescent waves* that are coupled to the waves in the *guide* but are traveling on the outside of the *optical waveguide.* Synonymous with *pick-off coupling.* Contrast with *butt coupling.* Also see *evanescent field coupling; loose-tube splicer; butt coupling.*

tap. To monitor, with or without authorization, the *information* that is being *transmitted* in a *communication circuit,* that is, to draw energy from a circuit. See *feedback tap.*

tape.   See *call tape; chadless tape; chad tape; computer tape; magnetic tape; punch tape; Wheatstone tape.*

tape leader.   See *magnetic tape leader.*

tape mark.   See *beginning-of-tape mark; end-of-tape mark.*

tape perforator.   A device that records *signals* on a paper tape by creating patterns of holes that are punched in accordance with a predetermined *code.*

taper.   See *optical taper.*

tape reader.   A device with a *tape reading head* that is capable of sensing hole patterns or cuts on a *perforated tape* and producing corresponding *electrical signals* in accordance with a predetermined *code.* See *coupled reperforator tape reader.*

tape reading head.   A device in an *automatic transmitter* that explores a tape and produces *electrical signals* that correspond to the hole patterns that are punched in the tape in accordance with a predetermined *code.*

tapered lens.   A *lens* whose cross section shows a greater edge thickness on one side than on the other.

tapered-plug connector.   A single *optical-fiber connector* that uses a *refractive-index matching material* between the fiber ends to eliminate *fiber interface loss.*

tape relay.   A method of *relaying messages* in which *message traffic* is *retransmitted* from one *channel* to another in such a manner that messages arriving on an incoming channel are recorded on *perforated tape,* this tape then being either fed directly and automatically into an *output channel* reader, or manually transferred to a *position* with an automatic *transmitter* on an output channel. The *reception* and retransmission of messages in tape form in *teletype-teleprinter systems* may be accomplished via manual, semiautomatic, or fully-automatic *relay stations.* See *automatic tape relay; torn-tape relay.*

tape relay pilot.   *Instructions* that are placed in a *message,* such as on format line 1 of a standard message, and that pertain to the *transmission* or handling of the message.

tape relay switching.   See *semiautomatic continuous-tape relay switching.*

tape retransmitter.   See *perforated-tape retransmitter.*

tape trailer.   See *magnetic tape trailer.*

tapoff.   See *optical tapoff.*

TARE.   *Telegraph automatic relay equipment.*

target indicator. See *coherent moving target indicator; moving target indicator (MTI).*

target signature. The characteristic pattern of a target (object) that is *displayed* or recorded by *detection* and *identification* equipment. Target signatures are usually *electromagnetic* or *sonic reflection* patterns. They may be subjected to *signature analysis.*

TASI. *Time-assignment speech interpolation.*

tau jitter. See *dither.*

Tbps. *Terabits/second,* i.e., 10^{12} bits/second.

TC. *Thermocouple.*

TCF. *Technical control facility.*

TDMA. *Time-division multiple access.*

TDTG. *True date-time group.*

TDM. *Time-division multiplexing.*

tea laser. See *transverse-electric atmosphere laser.*

technical control facility (TCF). In *communication systems,* a physical plant, or a designated and special configuration of a part thereof, that contains the necessary *distribution frames* and associated *panels, jacks,* and *switches;* monitoring, test, and processing equipment; and *engineering circuit* (orderwire) communication components to enable system control personnel to exercise essential operational control over communication *paths* and facilities. The facility permits them to make quality analyses of communication *channels;* monitor operations and maintenance functions; recognize and correct degraded conditions; restore disrupted communications; provide requested *communication service;* and otherwise take or direct such actions as may be required and practicable to ensure fast, reliable, and secure communication services.

technical control hubbing repeater. See *data conferencing repeater.*

technical load. In a *communication system,* the portion of the *operational load* that is required for conducting communication operations, including tactical operations if any, ancillary equipment, and lighting, air conditioning, or ventilation required for full continuity of communications. Also see *nontechnical load.* See *critical technical load; noncritical technical load.*

technical monitoring.   The monitoring of *signals* at selected points in a *communication system*.   For example, in *satellite communication systems*, the monitoring of *transmitted* and *received signals* at various points throughout an *earth station*.

technique.   See *bandspreading technique; coherent optical adaptive technique.*

tee coupler.   In an *optical fiber*, a *reflective* surface placed inside the fiber, at 45° to the direction of *wave propagation*.   The reflective surface allows a part of the *signal power* to be *reflected* from one side of the surface out of the fiber at right angles in one direction, and an *input* signal from the other side of the fiber to be reflected from the other side of the 45° reflective surface so as to propagate in the fiber longitudinally, in the same direction as the original signal to which the input signal is being added and the *output* signal is being taken.   Two T-couplers can be combined in a single unit for input and output of signals in both directions of propagation.   In addition to an *optical* component used to interconnect a number of terminals through optical *waveguides* by using partial reflections at *dielectric interfaces* or metallic surfaces, *coupling* can be accomplished simply by splitting the *waveguide bundle* so that fractions can *diverge* in different directions.   Also see *reflective star-coupler; nonreflective star-coupler.*   Synonymous with *bifurcation connector.*

technological penetration.   In *computer, data processing,* and *communication system security,* a *penetration* that is effected by circumventing or nullifying *hardware* or *software access* controls rather than by subverting *operators, users,* maintenance personnel, or other persons.

teleautography system.   A *telegraph system,* intended primarily for the immediate *transmission* and reproduction of handwritten *messages,* in which the *transmitted signals* represent the positions of the succession of points along each of the lines to be marked on a document and reproduced by the *receiver.*   Synonymous with *telewriting system.*   See Figure T-1 (p. 938).

telecommand.   See *space telecommand.*

telecommand earth station.   See *space telecommand earth station.*

telecommand space station.   See *space telecommand space station.*

telecommunication.   *Communication* over relatively large distances by any *transmission, emission,* or *reception* of *signals,* signs, writing, *images,* and sounds, or intelligence of any nature by *wire, radio, visual,* or other *electrical, electromagnetic, optical, acoustic,* or mechanical means.   The process enables one or more *users* to pass to one or more other users *information* of any nature delivered in any usable form, such as written or printed matter, fixed or moving pictures, *words,* music, visible or audible *signals,* or signals that can control the functioning of equipment or mechanisms.   See Figure T-2.   Also see Figure C-7.

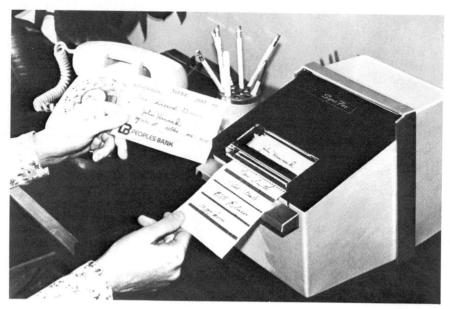

T-1. A Signafax® used as a **teleautography system** for high-speed *facsimile transmission* of signatures from a central file to *remote terminals*. (Courtesy of Alden Electronic and Impulse Recording Company, Inc.)

T-2. An occasional-use page-size tele*facsimile system* that provides a **telecommunication** capability. (Courtesy of Alden Electronic and Impulse Recording Equipment Company, Inc.)

telecommunication cable. See *fiber-optic telecommunication cable.*

telecommunication carrier. An organization that provides *telecommunication services.* The *carrier* may be a private organization, such as the Teletypewriter Exchange Service (TWX) or the International Teleprinter Network (TELEX), or a government agency. It may serve the general public, such as a *common carrier,* or it may serve only a select set of *users* (customers, subscribers), such as the *AUTOVON network* of the US Department of Defense.

telecommunication center. A *communication facility* that generally serves more than one organization or *terminal* and is responsible for *transmission,* receipt, acceptance, *processing,* and distribution of incoming and outgoing *messages* and for the performance of other *telecommunication services* and functions.

telecommunication circuit. A means of both-way *communication* between two points, comprising go and return *channels,* each with a *forward* and *backward direction* capability.

telecommunication conference. A conference between persons who are remote from one another but are linked by a *telecommunication system.* For example, a conference that makes use of a *conference call* or of *closed-circuit television.* Synonymous with *teleconference.*

telecommunication laser. A *laser* used as a *carrier wave source* whose *output* can be *modulated* to *transmit data* over long distances, such as between towers on mountains or between the earth and *satellites.*

telecommunication laser beam. A *laser beam* of *fixed frequency* that can be used as a *carrier wave. Modulation* of the beam enables the *transmission* of *information* between its *source station* and a *detector-receiver.*

telecommunication log. See *aeronautical telecommunication log.*

telecommunication network. See *civil telecommunication network; military telecommunication network.*

telecommunication organization. See *maritime air telecommunication organization.*

telecommunication private operating agency (TPOA). A private agency that operates a *telecommunication service, facility, network,* or *system* and that generates *signals* that interfere with the *operation* of systems operated by other agencies.

telecommunication security. *Communication security* applied to *telecommunication systems* and *components.*

telecommunication service. A specified set of *information transfer* capabilities that are provided to a group of *users* by a *telecommunication system.* The telecommunication service *user* (customer, subscriber) is responsible for the *information content* of *messages.* The telecommunication service has the responsibility for the acceptance, *transmission,* and delivery of messages.

telecommunication standard. See *Federal telecommunication standard (FTS).*

telecommunication system. A *system* that is used for *telecommunication.* A telecommunication system is delimited (bounded) by a set of functional *interfaces* that distinguish the system from its *users.* It performs the basic functions of acceptance or engagement, *transmission,* and delivery or disengagement of *messages* and *calls* for its *users* (customers, subscribers). See *Federal Telecommunications System (FTS).*

telecommunication system operator. The organization or person responsible for providing *telecommunication services* to *users* (customers, subscribers).

telecommunication union. See *International Telecommunication Union (ITU).*

telecommunication union world region. See *International Telecommunication Union (ITU) world region.*

teleconference. See *telecommunication conference.*

telecontrol. See *radio telecontrol.*

telegram. 1. Documented *information* in written, printed, or pictorial form that is given to a *telegraph service* for *transmission* by *telegraphy* and delivery to the *addressee.* Radio telegrams, that is, *radiograms,* are included in the concept of a telegram. 2. The document or the spoken *message* containing the *information* that was sent, *transmitted,* received, and delivered by a *telegraph service,* and any reproduction of the message made in the course of *transmission* or delivery to the *addressee.*

telegraph. A *system* of *communication* in which *coded signals* are used. See *multichannel voice frequency telegraph; speech-plus-telegraph; voice-frequency telegraph (VFTG or VFT).*

telegraph alphabet. A convention that indicates the correspondences between *telegraph characters* and the *coded signals* that represent them.

telegraph alphabet number 1. See *International Telegraph Alphabet Number 1.*

telegraph alphabet number 2. See *International Telegraph Alphabet Number 2.*

telegraph alphabet number 3. See *International Telegraph Alphabet Number 3.*

telegraph alphabet number 4.   See *International Telegraph Alphabet Number 4.*

telegraph alphabet number 5.   See *International Telegraph Alphabet Number 5.*

telegraph automatic relay equipment (TARE).   In a *telegraph communication network,* a *store-and-forward* device that has *connections* with *telegraph terminals* or with other TARE that are fixed, that is, are connected permanently on a *point-to-point* basis.

telegraph channel.   A *channel* that allows one-way *transmission* of *telegraph signals.*

telegraph circuit.   A pair of *telegraph channels* that permit two-way simultaneous *transmission* between two points.

telegraph code.   1. A group of rules and conventions according to which *telegraph signals* that are used to represent a *message* are formed, *transmitted,* and *translated* in a given *system.*   2. The *signals* that result from the application of the rules and conventions established to describe how a *message* should be formed, *transmitted,* and *translated* in a given *system.*

telegraph concentrator.   *Switching equipment* that enables *connections* to be established and disestablished as required between existing *circuits* and *telegraph sets.*   The number of circuit *terminations* always exceeds the number of telegraph sets, hence the need for the concentrator.

telegraph conversation.   An exchange, in *real time,* of *messages* between two *telegraph users* or *operators.*

telegraph demodulator.   A *demodulator* that processes a *telegraph signal* upon *reception* for subsequent use as an *audio signal, tape perforator input signal,* printer input signal, or other signal.

telegraph discriminator.   A *discriminator* for *converting frequency-shift telegraph transmission signals* into *direct-current (DC) telegraph transmission signals.*

telegraph distortion.   *Distortion* of *telegraph signals,* either during *modulation* or *demodulation (restitution),* that is usually caused when *significant intervals* do not have their exact theoretical duration (width or length).

telegraph distress frequency.   See *international radio telegraph distress frequency.*

telegraph error-rate measuring equipment.   *Test* equipment that can be used to conduct *local loop* tests in a *telegraph data transmission system* by substituting the test equipment for the normal *telegraph transmit* and *receive* equipment at the loop *terminals.*   Telegraph error-rate measuring (TERM) equipment generates telegraph test signals for transmission and compares them with the restored *output* from the local loop to measure the *data error rate.*

telegraph keyboard. A device that consists of an assembly of *keys* that can be used to control the *operation* of a *telegraph transmitter* or other *data source.* Each key, when actuated, causes the *transmission* of a different *graphic character, space character,* or *transmission control character.*

telegraph level. See *standard telegraph level (STL).*

telegraph lifecraft frequency. See *international radio telegraph lifecraft frequency.*

telegraph message format. See *radio telegraph message format.*

telegraph modulation. Succession in time of *significant conditions* that correspond to a *transmitted telegraph signal.* For example, a *high-frequency carrier wave* that is modulated by an *audio frequency signal,* and both the *carrier* and the signal are interrupted to form the *dots* and *dashes* of a *Morse code.*

telegraph modulator. A *modulator* that is controlled by a *telegraph signal,* such as an interrupted *direct-current (DC)* signal that represents the *dots* and *dashes* of the *Morse code* or the code of the *International Telegraph Alphabet Number 2,* or that represents the *binary pulse* patterns of the *International Telegraph Alphabet Number 5,* that is, the *ASCII seven-bit code strings.*

telegraph radioconverter. A device that accepts *audio* or *intermediate frequency telegraph signals* and *converts (translates)* them into *rectangular pulses* of constant *amplitude* that are capable of operating a *telegraph receiver* or *recorder.* Synonymous with *telegraph recording unit.*

telegraph receiver margin. The maximum value of *signal distortion* that is *compatible* with correct *translation (restitution, conversion, demodulation)* by a *teleprinter receiver, tape perforator,* or other *end-instrument.* The margin is determined when the signal arrives at the receiving end-instrument under the most unfavorable conditions of composition and *distortion.*

telegraph recording unit. See *telegraph radio recorder.*

telegraph relay. 1. A form of *store-and-forward telegraph transmission.* It is a process in which *messages* are first stored and then *transmitted* when the *destination addressee* or the next *storage* point in the *network* is available to receive them. 2. An electromagnet with a moving spring-loaded armature, a *circuit* making and breaking contact, and four *terminals,* two to the electromagnet coil and two to the circuit contact. It is designed to *transfer signals* in one circuit, to which the coil is connected, to another circuit, to which the contact is connected. It is used primarily for repeating *telegraph signals.*

telegraph set. The set of equipment and parts that constitute a *telegraph transmitter* and a *telegraph receiver,* both normally to be used at one *station.*

telegraph signal. A *signal* that is used to represent all or part of one or more *telegraph messages.* The signal could range from a single *dot, dash,* or *bit* to an entire sequence of *binary digits* that represent the *characters* of a complete message.

telegraph system. See *neutral direct-current telegraph system; polarential telegraph system.*

telegraph transmitter. A device for generating and *transmitting telegraph signals* over a *telegraph channel.*

telegraph word. A group of contiguous *signals* that represent a group of *characters* that are separated from other groups of characters by more *spaces* than are used to separate the characters in the group. Nominally, a telegraph word is considered to consist of six characters, that is, five actual characters and a *space character.* This is about the average length of words in English and *encrypted text* is usually divided into groups of five characters each and a space between the groups. *Telegraph traffic capacity* is usually given in words per minute.

telegraphy. A *system* of *transmission* used for the *communication* of *information* that is represented by *symbols,* such as letters and *numerals.* The symbols are represented by a preestablished set of *signals* in the form of a *code.* It is used primarily for *record communication* though it can also be used on a nonrecorded basis between *operators,* such as when the *Morse code* is used. Telegraphy includes any and all processes that provide for the transmission and reproduction at a distance of documentary matter. Thus, a telegraph system is a *telecommunication system.* Telegraphy does not include *pulse-code modulated (PCM) telephony.* See *alphabetic telegraphy; automatic telegraphy; document facsimile telegraphy; facsimile telegraphy; four-frequency diplex telegraphy; frequency-shift telegraphy; manual telegraphy; Morse telegraphy; mosaic telegraphy; picture facsimile telegraphy; printing-teletypewriter telegraphy (PTT); radio telegraphy; signal recording telegraphy; two-condition telegraphy.*

telemetering. The use of *telecommunication* facilities for automatically *transmitting, displaying,* and *recording data* at a distance from the point at which the data was sensed or measured. Usually, telemetering is accomplished by automatic *radio communication* in a *fixed* or *mobile service.* See *space telemetering; space telemetering earth station.*

telemetering fixed station. A *fixed station* used for *telemetering information* from a *source* of *information* to a *receiving station.*

telemetering land station. A *land station* the *emissions* of which are used for *telemetering.* See *aeronautical telemetering land station; flight telemetering land station.*

telemetering mobile station. A *mobile station,* the *emissions* of which are used for *telemetering information* from a *source* of *information* to a *receiver.* See *aeronautical telemetering mobile station; flight telemetering mobile station.*

telemetering space station. See *space telemetering space station.*

telemetry. The branch of science and technology devoted to the process of measuring the values of variables, such as pressure, *temperature,* humidity, blood flow, *radiation levels,* or *sound levels; transmitting* the results of the measurements by some means to a distant station; and interpreting, indicating, displaying, recording, or using the *information* that is obtained.

telemetry command. An *instruction* or *control function* sent from one point to another by means of *telemetered signals.* For example, in *satellite communication systems,* a *command* that is sent from an *earth station satellite control facility* to a *satellite* to adjust its *orbit,* or a command that is sent from a satellite to an earth station for *relaying* to another satellite.

telemetry-command station. An *earth station* used to *receive telemetered data* from *satellites* and to *transmit instructions (commands)* to satellites. Telemetry-command stations are separate from *communication stations.* They operate on a different *frequency* and perform a different function. They *track* and maintain satellites in *orbit* and set up *access channels.* Several telemetry-command stations may be controlled from a central station, usually one that has extensive *computer facilities.* See *tracking-telemetry-command station.*

telephone. 1. Pertaining to a *communication system* or device that makes use of *sound* and the *electrical* or *electromagnetic* representation of sound to *transmit messages,* that is, *calls.* 2. A *user* (subscriber, customer) *end-instrument* used to *transmit* and *receive voice* or *tone-coded messages* via an interconnecting *network.* A *telephone* end-instrument usually consists of a *transmitter* for converting *sound waves* into electrical signals, a *receiver* for converting *electrical signals* into sound waves, a *dialing* or *selection circuit,* and *signaling circuits.* Synonymous with *phone.* See *analog telephone; electrically-powered telephone; sound-powered telephone; underwater telephone.* Also see Figure D-2.

telephone circuit security. *Communication security* that is applied to a *telephone circuit.* It is a measure of the extent to which a telephone circuit is immune from unauthorized *monitoring (tapping)* by unauthorized persons or equipment on an effective basis. Thus, maximum telephone circuit security implies nonsusceptibility to unauthorized monitoring of *calls.*

telephone circuit signaling. In a *telephone system, signaling* that provides the *information* necessary to promote the orderly *transfer* of *call traffic* and that informs *users* (customers, subscribers) and equipment of the progress of a *call*. There are three categories of signaling involved in the *processing* and progress of a call, namely *supervisory, control,* and *status signaling*.

telephone cord circuit. A device that consists of one or more *plugs* and their associated flexible *conducting cords* for enabling the *connection* of *telephone circuits,* that is, enabling the connection of *local loops* to each other, local loops to *trunk circuits,* and trunk circuits to each other.

telephone directory. An *alphabetical* listing of the names of *users* (persons, processes, equipment, places, organizations, or services) of a *telephone system*. Each name in the list is followed by a *telephone number* and perhaps an *address*. Also see *inverted directory*.

telephone distress frequency. See *international radio telephone distress frequency; radiotelephone distress frequency*.

telephone exchange director. A *telephone exchange register* and *translator* that accepts all or part of a *called party's* (customer's, subscriber's) number in the form of *strings* of *dialed pulses*. It controls the *setting-up* of a *call* by *transmitting* the *strings* of *pulses* used for the code, tandem, numerical, and final *selectors* in succession for establishing a *connection* to a *telephone circuit* or *trunk*.

telephone number. The number that is assigned to a *telephone user* (customer, subscriber) for *routing telephone calls*. For example, the telephone number for the *International Organization for Standardization (ISO)* in Geneva, Switzerland, is (022) 34 12 40.

telephone patch. 1. A temporary *connection* between *circuits* or *systems*. 2. A *connection* between the *air-ground communication link* and the *local* or *long distance telephone system*. The connection is usually made at a specific *radiotelephone station*. Synonymous with *phone patch*.

telephone receiver. The part of a *telephone* instrument that serves as a *receiver* of *electrical signals* and *converts* them into *sound signals*. A *user* (customer, subscriber) listens to the *output* of the telephone receiver by placing it near the ear, or after *amplification,* listens to the sound from a *loudspeaker*.

telephone service class. A type of *telephone service* in which certain classes of *users* (customers, subscribers) are authorized to conduct certain types of business and are allowed *access* to certain *networks*. The class of user, the type of business, and the networks that are accessed determine the service class.

telephone sidetone. The *transmission* and reproduction of undesirable sounds through a local path from the *transmitting transducer* to the *receiving transducer* of the same *telephone* end-instrument while a person is talking or while other tones are entered into the *transmitter.*

telephone system.   A *communication system* set up for the *transmission* of speech and other sounds.   See *automatic telephone system; precedence telephone system.*

telephone traffic metering device.   A device that may be connected to *telephone circuits* and *switches* and is used to automatically record or count the occurrence or frequency of specific events, such as circuit uses, *access attempts,* and contacts to *busy lines.*

telephone transmitter.   The part of a *telephone* instrument that serves as a *transmitter* of *electrical signals* and *converts* the *sound signals* it receives into the electrical signals that it *transmits.*   The user speaks into the transmitter or allows other tones or *sound waves* to enter the transmitter. It is a form of *microphone.*

telephony.   A system of *telecommunications* in which voice or other *data* originally in the form of sounds are *transmitted* over long distances. The sounds are *converted* to *electrical currents* in *wires; electromagnetic, microwave,* or *radio signals; lightwaves* in *optical fibers;* or other forms.   It includes the science and practice of transmitting speech or other sounds, such as tones that represent *digits* or *signaling information,* over relatively long distances, and rendering the sounds audible upon receipt.   The distances involved are generally greater than earshot range.   See *radio telephony; voice telephony.*

telephoto.   Pertaining to pictures taken from a long distance from the object. See *wirephoto.*

telephoto lens.   An *objective lens system* consisting of a *positive* and a *negative component* separated from each other, having such *powers* and separation that the back *focal length* of the entire system is small in comparison with the equivalent focal length.   Such lenses are used for producing large *images* of distant *objects* without the necessity of a cumbersome length of the instrument.

teleprinter.   1. A *receive*-only device, similar to a typewriter without a *keyboard,* that is capable of accepting *signals* and printing *characters* that correspond to the signals.   **2.** A device that consists of a *keyboard transmitter* together with a printing *receiver* and operates in accordance with a *start-stop system,* the *start-stop elements* defining the beginning and the end of each *character.*   The teleprinter is a printing *telegraph* instrument that has a *signal*-actuated mechanism for automatically printing messages that are received in the form of electrical signals. The teleprinter keyboard is similar to that of a typewriter and is used to send messages. Also see *teletypewriter.*   See *radio teleprinter.*

teleprinter code.   See *International Telegraph Alphabet Number 2.*

teleprinter exchange service. A commercial service that provides *teleprinter communication services* on the same basis as *telephone service.* It operates through a *central switchboard* to various *stations* within the same city or other cities, or, via worldwide *networks,* to other countries. This service is limited to specific *users* (subscribers, customers) of the telephone service. It enables users to *communicate* directly and temporarily among themselves by means of *start-stop system* equipment that make use of the *public data transmission services* or *public data networks.* For example, the Teletypewriter Exchange Service (TWX) or the International Teleprinter Network (TELEX). Synonymous with *teletypewriter exchange service.*

teleprinter-on multiplex. A *teleprinter* connected to *multiplexed circuits.* Originally the teleprinter-on-multiplex involved the *conversion* of the 5-unit (level) teleprinter code, that is, *International Telegraph Alphabet Number 2,* into a 7-unit (level) code, that is, *International Telegraph Alphabet Number 5,* thus permitting *automatic error detection* at the *receiving* end by using the extra *bits* for automatic recovery.

teleprinter-on-radio. A *teleprinter* connected to *radiotelegraph circuits.* Originally the teleprinter-on-radio involved the *conversion* of the 5-unit (level) teleprinter code, that is *International Telegraph Alphabet Number 2,* into a 7-unit (level) code, that is, *International Telegraph Alphabet Number 5,* thus permitting *automatic error detection* at the *receiving* end by using the extra *bits* for automatic recovery.

teleprinting. The *transmission* and *reception* of *signals* that use *teleprinters* and associated equipment. It usually includes the use of *perforated tape, manual keyboards,* and printed *pages.* Teleprinting signals may be sent by *radio,* wire, or *optical fiber.* Synonymous with *teletypewriting.*

teleprocessing. 1. Pertaining to the overall function of an *information processing* and *data transmission system* that combines *telecommunications, automatic data processing,* and man-machine *interface* equipment as an *integrated* whole. 2. *Data processing* and *data transmission* by means of a combination of *computers* and *data communication facilities.* 3. *Data processing* by means of a combination of *computers* and sets of *data terminal equipment* connected by *telecommunication facilities.* For example, *distributed data processing* using *communication systems.* 4. Remote access *data processing* in which certain *input-output* functions at different locations are connected by *communication facilities.*

telescopic aerial. See *telescopic antenna.*

telescopic antenna. An *antenna* that can be extended or retracted (lengthened or shortened) by being constructed in the form of overlapping concentric cylinders that are able to slide inside of each other in order to adjust the length. Submarines are usually fitted with telescopic *high-frequency (HF)* and *very-high frequency (VHF)* antennas that allow the *transmission* and *reception* of *signals* at periscope depth by raising the antenna above the surface. Synonymous with *telescopic aerial.*

Teletype. Pertaining to *teletypewriting equipment.* Teletype is the trademark of The Teletype Corporation. The term has been adopted to apply to the general class of *transmitting* and *receiving* equipment that is used in *telegraph systems,* particularly *keyboard,* printing, and tape perforating and reading equipment. The common abbreviation for Teletype is TTY. See *radioteletype (RATT or RATTY).*

teletype marking pulse. That *significant condition* of *modulation* that results in an active *selective operation* in a *teletypewriter receiver.*

teletypewriter exchange service. See *teleprinter exchange service.*

teletypewriter position. The physical space and the *electrical connection* or *terminals* that are used by a *teletypewriter* or a *teleprinter* at a *station* in a *network* for *point-to-point* or *ground-air operations.*

teletypewriter (TTY). A printing *telegraph* instrument that has a *signal*-actuated mechanism for automatically printing received *strings* of *characters* in the form of *messages* and that usually has a *keyboard* similar to that of a typewriter for sending messages by manually depressing the *keys* or by using a *perforated tape transmitter.* A *teleprinter* is a receive-only unit that has no keyboard. *Radio circuits* that are used to carry TTY traffic are sometimes referred to as RTTY or RATT. Teletype is a trademark of The Teletype Corporation. Also see *radioteletype; teleprinter.* See *automatic send-receive teletypewriter; intership radio teletypewriter; keyboard send-receive teletypewriter; radio teletypewriter; receive-only teletypewriter; ship-shore radio teletypewriter.*

teletypewriter code. See *International Telegraph Alphabet Number 2.*

teletypewriter communication. *Communication* in which *teletypewriters,* teletypewriter *circuits, radioteletypewriters,* and related communication equipment is used. RATT is used to designate teletypewriter communications over a radio link. TTY designates teletypewriter communications over other than radio links, such as wire, *optical fiber, coaxial cable,* and *microwave links.*

teletypewriter control unit. A device that serves as the control, coordination, and *interface* unit between *teletypewriter* equipment and other *communication* equipment such as communication *channels* and *switching centers.*

teletypewriter exchange service. See *teleprinter exchange service.*

teletypewriter garble table. A table consisting of a matrix of *characters* that may be used as an aid in the interpretation of *garbled text* that may result from *gains* or *losses* of holes in tape or from picked up or *dropped pulses* on *circuits* that are connected to a *teletypewriter.*

teletypewriter network. A *communication network* consisting of a group of interconnected *teletypewriter stations.*

teletypewriter service. A *communication service* that provides a *network* that permits *users* to *communicate* with one another using *teletypewriters* or *tele-printers* as *end-instruments.* For example, The Bell System, the Teletypewriter Exchange Service (TWX), and the International Teleprinter Network (TELEX).

teletypewriter signal distortion. In a *teletypewriter communication system,* the *shifting* of the *phase* and *transition* points of *pulses* from their proper positions and points *(significant instants)* relative to the beginning of the *start pulse.* The magnitude of the *distortion* is expressed in percent of a perfect unit pulse length. Synonymous with *start-stop-TTY distortion.*

teletypewriter telegraphy. See *printing-teletypewriter telegraphy (PTT).*

teletypewriting. See *teleprinting.*

television. A *system* or *mode* of *telecommunication* in which a picture, scene, *display image* or other *object* is *scanned* to produce an *analog signal* that has an instantaneous value that corresponds to the *light intensity* at a scanned *spot* on the image. The signal is used to *modulate* a *carrier; control signals* such as *syn-chronizing signals* are superimposed; and *audio signals* are added. The *modulated carrier* is transmitted to a *receiver* that uses the signal to modulate and control a *display device* that reconstructs the scanned image on a *screen.* The screen may be part of a *cathode-ray tube, gas panel, LED panel, fiberscope,* or similar device. The *scanning rate* is sufficiently rapid so as to enable the *transmission* and *reception* of signals that represent changing pictures, scenes, display images, or objects in *real time* and *online.* *Television systems* use *electromagnetic waves* in *free space,* in *cables,* and in *fibers* and they make use of *satellites* for live coverage on a worldwide basis.

television set. A device that *displays* dynamic pictures generated by received *video signals* consisting of *modulated electromagnetic waves* that arrive at the *receiver antenna* via *free space* or *coaxial cable (waveguide).* A *television* camera generates the video signal by *scanning* an *image* of the scene that is to be *trans-mitted.* Primary transmission is by *broadcast.* Secondary transmission is via *cable.* Synonymous with *TV set.*

telewriter. The equipment that is used in *teleautography* in which the manually controlled movements of a *stylus* (pen) over a plane surface electrically control similar movements of a writing pen at the receiving end. The telewriter is used primarily for *point-to-point* rapid *transmission* of *messages* and sketches, such as between a machine shop and a design office or between two laboratories.

telewriting system. See *teleautography system.*

TELEX. The International Teleprinter Network. Also see *Teletypewriter exchange service. Teleprinter exchange service.*

tell. See *back tell; forward tell; lateral tell; overlap tell; relateral tell.*

telling. See *track telling.*

TE mode. A *mode* of *electromagnetic wave propagation* in a *waveguide* in which the *wave* is a *transverse electric wave.* Also see *TM mode.*

temperature. A measure of the average kinetic energy of the moving molecules or atoms of a substance, in which absolute zero temperature occurs when all molecular or atomic motion is zero. In common terms, a measure of the hotness or coldness of a substance using a defined scale. The *SI* unit of temperature is the *kelvin,* which is one-hundredth of the difference between the temperature of the freezing point and boiling point of water at sea level, with absolute zero at about -273.16 K. If the aforementioned points are 0 and 100, respectively, the scale is called Celsius or centigrade. Also see *Kelvin temperature scale.* See *ambient temperature; antenna gain-to-noise temperature (G/T); antenna noise temperature; color temperature; effective input noise temperature; equivalent noise temperature; front-end noise temperature; luminance temperature; receiving-system noise temperature; standard noise temperature; total radiation temperature.*

temperature scale. See *Kelvin temperature scale.*

temperature-compensating equalizer. See *line temperature-compensating equalizer.*

TEMPEST. A reference to investigations and studies of *compromising emanations.* Of primary interest are emanations from electronic *computer, communication,* command, and control equipment, that is, *radiation* or *emission* of *electromagnetic waves* or *conducted currents* that may cause unauthorized disclosure of *information.* The full *spectrum* of *communication-electronic (C-E)* equipment is included. The term is sometimes used synonymously to mean compromising emanations, as in *TEMPEST tests, TEMPEST inspections,* and TEMPEST proof. Also see *compromising emanations.*

TEMPEST inspection. An inspection designed to provide the means for conducting *facility* evaluations of *emanations* from *communication-electronic* equipment to determine the adequacy of *TEMPEST* control measures. For example, an installation engineering survey of *radiation levels.*

TEMPEST test. A laboratory *test* or an on site (field) test to determine the nature and extent of *conducted* or *radiated signals* that contain *compromising information,* that is, information that should not be disclosed without authorization, from *communication-electronic (C-E)* equipment. A test normally includes *detection* and measurement of these *signals*. Analyses are made to determine the correlation between the detected signals, their *strength,* and the extent to which they could be detected by unauthorized persons with specialized detection equipment.

temporally-coherent light. See *time-coherent light.*

temporary circuit. A *circuit* required for a limited, usually short period, such as a few hours or days. A temporary circuit is usually kept in *operation* for a period longer than required for a single *call* or *message transmission,* such as occurs in a *switched connection.* It is not kept in operation as long as a *permanent circuit* or connection.

TEM wave. *Transverse electromagnetic wave.*

tensile load test. In an *optical fiber, bundle,* or *cable,* a test to determine the breaking point or *transmission parameter* change, such as *attenuation, dispersion,* or elongation, under elevated tensile stresses. See Figure T-3.

T-3. *Optical cable* in a **tensile load test.** (Copyright 1979 Corning Glass Works. Reprinted by permission from Corning Glass Works, Telecommunication Products Department.)

tensile strength. See *optical-fiber tensile strength.*

tensiometer. A gauge, usually a direct-readout strain gauge, used to measure tension, such as might be encountered when laying, paying out, or *threading* a *cable.*

terabits/second (Tbps). A *signaling rate* of 10^{12} bits per second, i.e., one-million million bits per second.

terahertz. A *frequency,* cycle, or repetition rate of 10^{12} Hz, i.e., cycles per second. *Light* frequencies are approximately 10^{12} Hz, for a *wavelength* of 300 nm in a vacuum, the region of *ultraviolet light.*

term. See *attenuation term; phase term.*

terminal. 1. *Communication facilities* that constitute a point of origin or *termination* of a *circuit* or *channel.* 2. A collection of *hardware* and *software* that enables contact with, entry into, or exit from a *system,* such as a *computer, data processing,* or *communication system* or *network.* 3. A point, such as a jaw, post, screw, or joint at which an *electrical connection* can be made. See *computer terminal; data processing terminal; intelligent terminal; multiple-access-rights terminal; multiplex baseband receive terminal; multiplex baseband send terminal; packet mode terminal; radio baseband receive terminal; radio baseband send terminal; satellite earth terminal; user terminal.*

terminal automatic identification. Automatic identification in which the *answerback code* is provided by the *receiving terminal* itself.

terminal-engaged signal. A *signal* that is sent in the *backward direction* and that indicates that a *call* cannot be *completed* because the *called terminal* connecting the user *end-instrument* is engaged in another call. Also see *busy signal.*

terminal equipment. 1. An assembly of *communication* equipment required to *transmit* or *receive* a *signal* on a *channel* or *circuit* whether it be for immediate or delayed delivery. 2. In *radio relay systems,* equipment used at points where intelligence is inserted or derived, as distinct from equipment used to *relay* a reconstituted *signal.* 3. *Telephone* and *teletypewriter (telegraph) switchboards* and other centrally located equipment at which *wire* and *optical fiber circuits* are *terminated.* Terminal equipment provides centralized interconnections for *lines.* It includes *switchboards, patchboards, carrier converters, signal amplifiers,* and *repeaters.* 4. *Communication* equipment at each end of a *circuit,* used to permit the *stations* involved to accomplish the *mission* for which the circuit was established. 5. In a *communication network,* the *facilities* at a *station.* 6. The equipment that constitutes a point of origin or *termination* of a *line, circuit, channel,* or *data link.* See *data subscriber terminal equipment (DSTE); data terminal equipment (DTE).* See Figure T-4.

T-4. *Laser*-driven *optical fiber light-pulse* short-*trunk* **terminal equipment** exemplified by the MX3 *Lightwave Terminating Multiplex* Assembly.® (Courtesy of Bell Laboratories.)

terminal exchange.   In *telephone switchboard operations*, the *exchange* or *switchboard* to which a *called party (user)* is directly connected. For example, in a set of exchanges connected in *tandem*, the last exchange (switchboard) through which a *call* passes before reaching the *called party (destination user) end-instrument*.

terminal-guidance navigation system.   A navigation *system* that employs a device that seeks, points to, or homes on a *source* of *electromagnetic*, sound, or other energy, thus establishing the direction from its present position to the source of *radiation*. The seeking, pointing, or homing device may then be used to automatically steer in any desired direction with reference to the direction toward the source. For example, the device may be on board a missile. It may receive *infrared radiation* from the exhaust of an aircraft, establish a reference direction toward the infrared source, and direct the missile to fly on a course that will intercept the source.

terminal impedance. 1. The *impedance* measured at the unloaded *output terminals* of a device, *component,* or *circuit* such as a *transmission line* that is in normal operating condition. Thus, it is the internal impedance. 2. The ratio of *voltage* to *current* at the *output terminals* of a device including the *connected load.* 3. The *impedance* connected across the *output terminals* of a device, that is, the *load impedance.* The impedance is always the complex impedance. Also see *termination.*

terminal instrument. A *telecommunication* device that provides a point of origin or *termination* of a *circuit* or *channel.* For example, a *user's end-instrument,* such as a *telephone, teletypewriter, telegraph transmitter, telegraph receiver, facsimile transmitter, facsimile receiver,* or *fiberscope.*

terminal port. In a *data network,* the *functional unit* at a *node* through which *data* can enter or leave the network. For example, the port may be located at a node common to two or more networks, or it may be a designated *station* of one network connected to a designated station in another network for the purpose of *transferring traffic* between the networks. Synonymous with *transfer station.* Also see *gateway.*

terminal station. 1. *Receiving* equipment and associated *multiplex* equipment that are used at the ends of a *communication link.* 2. The last *station* in a sequence of *relay stations* involved in *routing* a *message* from the *originator* to the *addressee.* Thus, a given message is not routed beyond the terminal station for that message.

terminal switchboard. See *terminal exchange.*

terminating block. See *horizontal terminating block; vertical terminating block.*

terminating equipment. See *data circuit-terminating equipment (DCE).*

terminating set. See *four-wire terminating set.*

termination. 1. The *load* connected to a *transmission line* or other *circuit* or device. For a transmission line, if the termination *impedance* is equal to the *characteristic impedance* of the *line, wave reflections* from the end of the line will be avoided. 2. In *waveguides,* the point at which energy flowing along a waveguide continues in a nonwaveguide *propagation mode* into a *load.* Also see *terminal impedance.* See *idle-line termination.* Also see Figure F-6 and T-4.

termination efficiency test. In an *optical fiber, bundle,* or *cable,* a test designed to measure or evaluate the loss in *transmitted power* by a specified *termination* technique.

terminus. See *fiber-optic terminus.*

ternary signal. A *signal* that can assume one of three conditions of *power level, phase position, pulse length, frequency* value, or other *parameter* at any given instant. For example, a *pulse* that can have a positive, zero, or negative *voltage* value at any given instant, a sine wave that can assume *phase positions* of $0°$, $120°$, or $240°$ of *electrical position* with reference to a *clock pulse,* or a *carrier wave* that can assume any one of three different *frequencies* depending on a *modulation signal condition.* Also see *three-condition coding.*

terrain. See *antenna height above average terrain.*

terrain avoidance system. An electronic *system* that will provide a continuous indication of the relative distance or height of an aircraft from the terrain in front of and directly beneath the aircraft. The system is used to assist the pilot or autopilot in taking a proper course. The system operates similar to *radar.*

terrestrial latitude. The angle that lies between the *line* from a given point to the earth's center and the line from the equator, at the same longitude as the given point, to the earth's center. It is the central angle, at the earth's center, measured from the equatorial plane to a line from the earth's center through the point on the earth's surface whose latitude is desired. The latitude may be measured north or south from the equator in a longitudinal (meridian) plane. The latitude is designated as $0°$ at the equator and $90°$ at the poles.

terrestrial longitude. The angle measured from the Greenwich, England meridian along the earth's equator, or in a plane parallel to the equatorial plane and along a parallel of constant latitude, east or west, to the meridian through the given point whose longitude is desired. East longitudes from Greenwich are taken as positive and west as negative, the values of longitude thus never being greater than $180°$. The longitude is usually expressed in degrees, minutes, and seconds east or west. It may also be expressed in hours, minutes, and seconds, that is, in hour angles. Since the angular velocity of the earth's rotation is a constant, time and angular displacement are interchangeable.

terrestrial service. A *radio service* other than a *space service* or the *radio astronomy service.*

terrestrial station. A station in the *terrestrial service.*

terrestrial system. In *telecommunications,* a ground-based *communication system* as distinguished from a *satellite system.* For example, a system that is based on or makes use of cables, land-lines, tower-to-tower *microwave relays (line-of-sight),* or *radio land stations. Aircraft stations* are considered as part of terrestrial communication systems.

tessera. A curvilinear rectangle. For example, an area on the surface of the earth bounded by lines of constant longitude and latitude.

tesseral harmonic function. A *spherical harmonic (trigonometric) function* that has values that maintain a consistent sign within a *tessera* but change sign and magnitude as functions of both latitude and longitude.

test. **1.** A set of measurements of the performance of a *functional unit* that are made to establish conformity with specifications or design objectives. **2.** Physical measurements that are taken to verify conclusions obtained from mathematical modeling and analysis, or that are taken for the purpose of developing mathematical models. The test usually includes validation of the results. See *attenuation test; communication test; engaged test; Foucalt knife-edge test; frequency response test; hot-bend test; impact test; loop test; marginal test; penetration test; shuttle-pulse test; tempest test; tensile load test; termination efficiency test; thermal shock test; vibration test.* See Figure T-5.

T-5. *Optical fiber* rotating capstan **test.** (Copyright 1979, Corning Glass Works. Reprinted by permission from Corning Glass Works, Telecommunication Products Department.)

test antenna. An *antenna* of known performance characteristics that is used in determining performance characteristics of *transmission* equipment and associated *propagation paths.*

test chart. See *test pattern.*

test facility.   See *patch and test facility.*

testing station.   See *experimental testing station.*

test land station.   See *radionavigation maintenance test land station; radionavigation operational test land station.*

test loop.   In a *communication system,* a *loop (circuit)* formed by temporarily linking complementary sections of *modulator-demodulator, transmitter-receiver,* or other *input-output* devices. Thus, certain parts of a communication system, perhaps remote parts, may be isolated while local units are being tested. Placing equipment to be tested in a test loop enables testing to take place without actually going to remote sites or distant locations with the *test* equipment.

test loop translator.   A unit that is fed with a sample of a *transmitted signal* that it *translates* to another *frequency.* The new frequency is then fed to a *receiver* that is being *tested.* The receiver that is being tested also receives the originally transmitted frequency in a *test loop* configuration, thus enabling analysis of the performance of the *transmitter* and receiver. Also see *turn-around mixer.*

test mode.   See *static test mode.*

test pattern.   In *display systems,* a conventional or standard drawing with precise characteristics, usually with lines at various angles and spacings, used as a reference for evaluating the quality of *images,* the *resolving power* of *imaging systems,* or the distortion introduced by *optical* or other means of *image processing* such as by *spherical aberration, inverse filtering,* or *recursive filtering.* Synonymous with *test chart.*

test point.   A *terminal* that is within *electrical* equipment and provides *access* to *signals* for *fault detection,* fault isolation, *system test,* and troubleshooting purposes.

test signal.   A *signal* used for the purpose of *testing* the ability of equipment to effectively or properly handle the signal. For example, in *radiotelegraph communication systems,* a signal that is *transmitted* for testing *transmitters* and *receivers.* One standard test signal consists of not more than three groups of three V's followed by the transmitter *call sign* and terminated by the letters AR. See *composite two-tone test signal; standard test signal.*

test station.   See *flight test station.*

test time.   See *system test time.*

test tone.   A *tone* that is *transmitted* at a predetermined *power level* and *frequency* through a *transmission system* to facilitate the alignment of *gains* and *losses* of devices that are connected in series or in parallel in the *transmission line, circuit, channel,* or *path.* See *standard test tone.*

TE wave.   *Transverse electric wave.*

text.   In a *message,* the *words* that are used to describe the thought or idea that is desired to be *communicated* by the *originator* to the *addressees.* It consists of a sequence of *characters, words,* phrases, and sentences. In a *radiotelephone system message,* for example, the text may be preceded and followed by the word "break." In a *radiotelegraph* and *tape relay system message,* the text may be preceded and followed by the *prosign* BT. See *cipher text; message text; plain text.*

text character.   See *end-of-text (ETX) character; start-of-text (STX) character.*

theater-area command.   A military organization that is usually operated and controlled by national authorities and is normally designed and organized so that it may be transferred to an international organization at the appropriate time. *Communication* functions and *activities* are subject to the authority of the commander of the theater-area command. For example, the *theater director of communications-electronics* is responsible to the commander of the theater-area command.

theater director of communications-electronics.   An officer who is appointed by the *theater-area command* and is responsible for coordinating *communication-electronic (C-E) activities* in the theater or area.

The International System of Units.   See *SI.*

theorem.   See *four-color theorem; Parseval's theorem; sampling theorem.*

theoretical duration.   See *significant interval theoretical duration.*

theoretical margin.   The *margin* calculated from the design objectives, specifications, or construction data of a device such as a *telegraph receiver* or a *radio transmitter.* The assumption is made that the device is operating under ideal conditions.

theoretical resolving power.   The maximum possible *resolving power* determined by *diffraction,* frequently measured as an *angular resolution* determined from:

$$A = 1.22B/D$$

where A is the limiting resolution angle in radians, B is the *wavelength* of *light* at which the resolution is determined, and D is the effective diameter of the *aperture.*

theory.   See *electromagnetic theory; information theory.*

thermal blanket.   In *satellite communication systems,* and for *satellites* in general, an *insulating* material that is used in the construction of a satellite and is placed on the outside surface or around internal equipment for protection of the *satellite* and onboard equipment against environmental conditions.

thermal noise.   A fluctuating *voltage* or *source* of *currents* produced within an electrical *circuit* by thermal agitation of electrons, atoms, and molecules, the *noise level* being a function of *temperature.*   Thermal noise was first described by Nyquist in 1928.   The thermal noise *power, P,* is given by $P = kT\Delta f$, where P is the thermal noise *power* in watts, k is *Boltzmann's constant* (1.3804×10^{-23} joules/kelvin), T is the *conductor temperature* in *kelvin* and Δf is the *bandwidth* in *hertz.*   Thermal noise power is distributed equally throughout the *frequency spectrum.*   Synonymous with *Nyquist noise; Johnson noise.*

thermal noise-limited operation.   The operation of a *photodetector* wherein the minimum detectable *signal* is limited by the *thermal noise* of the *detector,* the *load resistance,* and the amplifier *noise.*

thermal radiation.   **1.** The process of *electromagnetic emission* in which the radiated energy is extracted from the thermal excitation of atoms or molecules. **2.** *Electromagnetic radiation* in the *infrared* region of the *frequency spectrum.* *Incident thermal radiation* in the infrared region of the frequency spectrum is sensed by living organisms as heat.   Excess exposure to infrared radiation can cause dehydration and severe damage to tissues even though a slow burn is involved.   Thermal radiation from heat sources such as industrial chimneys and aircraft exhaust can be used as a *homing source* of radiation. The infrared portion of the electromagnetic frequency spectrum is just below the *visible spectrum.*

thermal shock test.   In an *optical fiber, bundle,* or *cable,* a test of changes in parameters, such as *attenuation, pulse dispersion,* and *tensile strength,* with sudden and large changes in *temperature.*

thermocouple.   A loop made of two *thermojunctions* connected together, the resultant *current* in the loop being a function of the *temperature* difference between the two junctions.   If the current is calibrated, the temperature difference between the two junctions can be measured using the calibrated thermocouple.

thermoelectric effect.   The effect produced in a *conducting circuit* constructed of two wires of different metal fused to each other at the ends in such a manner that if a *temperature* difference is maintained between the junctions, an electrical current will flow in the circuit.

thermojunction.   A *junction* consisting of two dissimilar metals bonded together thereby forming an *interface* across which a voltage is developed when the junction is heated.   If two such junctions are held at different *temperatures* and are connected by electrical conductors, thus forming a *thermocouple,* current will be maintained in the loop and will be somewhat proportional to the temperature.

thermoneutral. Pertaining to a chemical reaction in which there is no overall energy change. The reaction is neither endothermal nor exothernal, that is the reaction neither requires heat to occur nor produces heat when it occurs.

thermoplastic. Pertaining to the property of a material that softens, melts, or fuses when heated and that rehardens when cooled. *Optical* glass and *optical fibers* are usually thermoplastic, except special glasses or ceramics of a refractory type. Contrast with *thermosetting.*

thermoplastic cement. An adhesive whose viscosity decreases as the *temperature* is raised. Canada balsam, resin, and pitch are common thermoplastic *optical cements.*

thermosetting. Pertaining to the property of a material that does not soften, melt, or fuse when heated, but often becomes even harder. Contrast with *thermoplastic.*

thermosetting cement. An adhesive that permanently sets or hardens at a certain high *temperature.* Methacrylate is a common thermosetting *optical cement.*

THF. *Tremendously high frequency.*

thick lens. A *lens* whose axial thickness is so large that the *principal points* and the *optical* center cannot be considered as coinciding at a single point on its *optical axis.*

thin film. See *optical thin film.*

thin-film circuit. A *circuit* constructed by creating thin films of material on an inert material substrate. The thin films may be on the order of 10^{-9} m thick. Circuit elements are created by control of geometry and material composition. They may be formed by evaporative deposition, etching, doping (fusion), or other methods. *Solid-state* semiconducting crystals are also used in their construction. If the film is of *magnetic material* the thin films can be used for *data storage* as well as for control purposes. Many *integrated circuits* consist of thin films. The circuits are used primarily to perform *combinational logic operations* such as those performed by *logic gates.* The circuits have an extremely high circuit element packing density, for example, 10 000 *logic elements* or *storage* elements per square inch. Also see Figure P-3.

thin-film laser element. In an *integrated optical circuit,* a *laser* constructed by thin-film techniques on the *substrate* for use in the *circuit* as a *light-source* to drive *optical slab dielectric waveguides* or *fibers.*

thin-film optical modulator. A device made of multilayered films of material of different *optical* characteristics capable of *modulating transmitted light* by using *electrooptic, electroacoustic,* or *magnetooptic* effects to obtain *signal* modulation.

Thin-film optical modulators are used as *component* parts of *integrated optical circuits.*

thin-film optical multiplexer.   A *multiplexer* consisting of layered *optical* materials that make use of *electrooptic, electroacoustic,* or *magnetooptic* effects to accomplish the multiplexing. Thin-film optical multiplexers may be *component* parts of *integrated optical circuits.*

thin-film optical switch.   A *switching* device for performing logic operations using *lightwaves* in thin films that usually support only one *propagation mode.* The films use *electrooptic, electroacoustic,* or *magnetooptic effects* to perform switching functions, such as are performed by *semiconductor* gates (AND, OR, NEGATION). Thin-film optical switches may be component parts of *integrated optical circuits.*

thin-film optical waveguide.   An *optical waveguide* consisting of thin laminar layers of materials with differing *refractive indices.* Lower indexed material is on the outside or serves as a *substrate.* Thin films usually support a single *electromagnetic wave propagation mode* and operate from *laser* sources. *Thin-film waveguide lasers, modulators, switches, directional couplers, filters,* and related *components* need to be *coupled* from *integrated optical circuits* to optical waveguide *transmission media,* such as *optical fibers* and *slab dielectric waveguides.*

thin-film waveguide.   See *periodically-distributed thin-film waveguide.*

thin lens.   A *lens* whose axial thickness is sufficiently small so that the *principal points,* the *optical* center, and the vertices of its two surfaces can be considered as coinciding at the same point on its *optical axis.*

third cosmic velocity.   The minimum radial velocity that an object must acquire at the earth's surface in order to overcome the attraction of the earth, the moon, and the sun, and thus to just leave the solar system with negligible velocity. The speed of the third cosmic velocity is approximately 16.7 km/s.

threading.   Pulling a *cable* in, around, over, under, and through various obstacles in order to use a single piece of cable from one distant point to another without *splicing.* For example, a *distribution frame* to and end *termination* in a different building.

threat warning system.   A *system* designed to provide warning of the existence of a potential or actual threat. For example, an electronic system installed aboard an aircraft for warning against ground, sea, and air threats. Threat warning systems include *radar, infrared, electrooptical, sonar,* and *visual systems.* Threats include storms, hurricanes, and military threats.

three-body problem. 1. The problem in *celestial mechanics* that concerns the motion of a small body, usually but not necessarily of negligible mass, relative to, and under the gravitational influence of, two other finite point masses that are also moving. 2. The motion of three bodies that are free to move under the attractive forces of each other according to Newton's law of universal gravitation. No other forces are involved. The three bodies are regarded as material particles with large distances between them compared to their size, that is, there are no collisions. Most often when dealing with the three-body problem it is necessary to determine the motion of two bodies relative to the third. The motion of all three bodies is encountered when studying the motion of the moon or other earth *satellites*, such as *communication satellites*, under the influence of the earth and the sun or when studying the motion of stars in three-star systems. Also see *two-body problem; restricted circular three-body problem; n-body problem.*

three-condition coding. Pertaining to a *telegraph, data transmission,* or other *signaling system code* or *signal* in which the number of *significant conditions,* such as *voltage level, frequency,* or *phase position,* is 3. Also see *ternary signal.*

threshold. 1. The minimum value of a *level,* state, or condition, such as that of a *signal,* that can be *detected* by a sensor in a *system* under consideration. For example, it may be a value used to denote predetermined levels pertaining to the volume of *message storage* utilized in a *message switching system,* or it may be the minimum value of a *parameter* used or needed to activate a device. 2. The limiting values between which a *parameter* value is to be constrained. See *absolute luminance threshold; FM improvement threshold; hearing threshold; outage threshold; pain threshold; receiver threshold.*

threshold extension. A change in the value of a *threshold.* For example, in a *receiver* the process of lowering the *noise* threshold by decreasing the receiver *bandwidth.* In an *angle modulation* receiver, this enables *signals* to be recovered from *input* that contains a large amount of noise.

threshold power. See *link threshold power.*

through. See *dial through.*

through control. See *right-through control.*

through group. A group of 12 *voice frequency (VF) channels* that goes through a *repeater* as a unit, without *frequency translation.*

through-group equipment. In *carrier telephone transmission,* equipment that accepts a *signal* from the *group receiver output* and *attenuates* it to the proper *signal level* for insertion at the *input* of a *group transmitter.* This is usually accomplished without *frequency translation.*

throughput. The number of *bits, bytes, characters, words, blocks, messages, calls,* or other units of *data* that pass through all or part of a *communication system* when the system is working at optimum *capacity,* usually when the system is working at *saturation.* Throughput is usually expressed in *data units* per unit of time, such as blocks per second or messages per day. Also see *efficiency factor; effective transmission speed; instantaneous transmission speed.*

through supergroup. A group of 60 *voice frequency (VF) channels* that goes through a *repeater* as a unit, without *frequency translation.*

through-supergroup equipment. In *carrier telephone transmission,* equipment that accepts the *multiplexed signal* from a *supergroup recevier output, amplifies* it, and provides the proper *signal level* to the *input* of a *supergroup transmitter.* This is usually accomplished without *frequency translation.*

thumb wheels. In *display systems,* a set of captive wheels, often mounted in the surface panel of a *display console,* used for manipulating a *cursor,* a set of cross-hairs, or a plotter *stylus* on the *display surface* of a *display device.* The radial angle through which the wheels are rotated corresponds to changes in *coordinate data.*

tick. See *time tick.*

ticket. See *call ticket.*

ticketed call. A *call* for which a record is made of certain facts concerning the call, such as the time it was placed, the duration, the *called* and *calling party* numbers, and the *operator's* initials.

tie trunk. A *telephone line* that directly connects either two *private branch exchanges (PBX)* or two private exchanges. See *private branch exchange tie trunk.*

tilt. See *beam tilt.*

time. See *access-denial time; access time; active time; acquisition time; attack time; block transfer time; call filing time; call release time; call request time; call selection time; call set-up time; chip time; computer time; data transfer time; disengagement time; down time; environmental loss time; filing time; flux rise time; Greenwich mean time (GMT); group delay time; guard time; holding time; lost time; maximum access time; maximum block transfer time; maximum disengagement time; message file time; message preparation time; message release time; occurrence time; out-of-frame alignment time; post-selection time; precise time; problem time; pulse decay time; pulse rise time; real time; receipt time; recovery time; reframing time; release time; response time; rise time; round-trip delay time; sampling time; scheduled time; settling time; system down time; system operating time; system test time; switching process time; switching reaction time; synchronization acquisition time; transmission time; transit time; variable time (VT).*

time-assignment speech interpolation (TASI). A technique used on certain *frequency-division multiplexed (FDM)* long *links* to improve utilization of *voice channels* by *switching* an additional *user* onto a momentarily *idle channel* when the original user has stopped speaking. When the first user resumes speaking any other momentarily idle channel will be used by that speaker, and so on.

time availability. See *circuit reliability*.

time between failures. See *mean time between failures (MTBF)*.

time between outages. See *mean time between outages (MTBO)*.

time block. In *communications*, an arbitrary grouping of several consecutive hours of a day, usually for a particular season, during which it is assumed that *propagation data* are statistically homogeneous and therefore somewhat predictable during the several hours.

time chart. See *time conversion chart*.

time code. A time *format* used for the *transmission* and identification of *timing signals*.

time-coherent light. *Light* of which at any point in time, the *amplitude, phase,* and time variation are predictable, the prediction being based on the amplitude, phase, and time variation at a previous time. Synonymous with *temporally-coherent light*. Also see *coherent-light; space-coherent light*.

time constant. A constant, usually expressed in *seconds,* whose value is indicative of the time required for a *system* or *circuit* to change from one state or *condition* to another. It is based on the exponential function:

$$x = e^{-t/a}$$

where x is the value of the state, a is the time constant, and t is the time, usually in seconds. Thus when $t = a$, $x = 1/e$, or about 0.37, and the system has changed about 63% toward its new value in one time constant. A system is considered to have changed its state 95% after the elapse of three time constants; e.g., an *electrical capacitor, C,* is considered discharged 95% through a *resistor, R,* after the elapse of $3RC$ seconds, when R is in ohms and C is in farads. See *fast time constant; logarithmic fast time constant (logFTC)*.

time control. See *sensitivity time control*.

time conversion chart. A table that enables time expressed in one *mode* at one location to be expressed in the same or another mode at another location and that enables the determination of time differences between locations. Time around the world is usually identified by a longitude time-zone letter suffix. Synonymous with *time chart*.

time delay.   See *propagation time delay; receive-after-transit time delay; receiver attack-time delay; receiver release-time delay; transmit-after-receive time delay; transmitter attack-time delay; transmitter release-time delay.*

time-delay distortion.   See *delay distortion.*

time-derived channel.   A *channel* obtained by *time-division multiplexing* a *line, circuit,* or another *channel.* Also see *frequency-derived channel.*

time diversity.   **1.** Pertaining to a method of *transmission* in which a *signal* is sent through the same *channel* more than once.   **2.** Any method of *transmission* and *reception* in which the same *information,* though it may be represented by different *signals,* is *transmitted* and *received* at the same *frequency* more than once, but not simultaneously.

time division.   In *communications,* the use of time to obtain separation between *channels.* For example, each channel is assigned a *time slot* on the same *circuit.* Thus, many *messages* are interleaved on a time basis. Also see *frequency division; space division.*

time-division duplexing.   *Duplexing* that is accomplished by the simultaneous *transmission* and *reception* of two *signals* each representing different *information* over a common *path* by using different time intervals for each signal.

time-division multiple access (TDMA).   In *satellite communications,* the use of time interleaving to provide multiple, and apparently simultaneous *transmission,* in a single *transponder* with a minimum of *interference.* This method of *time sharing* can be applied to other *systems* and *components.* See *satellite-switched time-division multiple access (SS–TDMA).*

time-division multiplex equipment.   *Communication equipment* that allows several (slow) *messages* to be *transmitted* through one *channel.* At the distant end, the *signal* may be *demultiplexed* by complementary equipment to obtain the individual messages. Also, the complete multiplexed signal may be fed to a *matched computer* for *demultiplexing.* Three general types of *channel time sharing* are used, namely, (1) *scanning (sampling),* in which each possible *input* is connected in turn until all have been scanned and the sequence is then repeated; (2) *polling,* in which a *code* is used to ask for a *message* that is ready to be transmitted now, and the one unit that is ready is connected and sends its *address* to the *communication center (exchange)* and if two or more units are ready at the same time a priority is arranged; and (3) addressing the remote device that then sends back a ready signal or a not-ready signal.

time-division multiplexing (TDM).   *Multiplexing* in which separate *channels* are established by connecting one *circuit* automatically to many *signal* sources sequentially in time. The signals from the several sources share the time of the circuit by using the circuit in successive *time slots.* Each *discrete* time interval is assigned to a particular signal *source*. *Synchronizing pulses* are used to assist in *demultiplexing* at the distant end of the circuit. Thus, the time of an *optical fiber* can be divided among many signal sources, by allowing two or more *signal* sources to use the channel at different times. The channel may be shared by automatically *switching* to the several sources and connecting each one to the channel during the specific time period allocated to that source. For example, if each source is assigned to a given channel for 1μsec out of each millisecond, 1 000 sources can be accommodated (i.e., multiplexed) to the channel. During a given time interval the entire *available frequency spectrum* can be used by the *channel* to which it is assigned. In general, time division-multiplexed systems use *pulse transmission*. The multiplexed *pulse string* may be considered to be the interleaved pulse strings of the individual *channels*. The individual channel pulses may be *modulated* in either an *analog* or *digital* manner. Also see *time sharing*. See *asynchronous time-division multiplexing (ATDM); synchronous time-division multiplexing*. See Figure T-6.

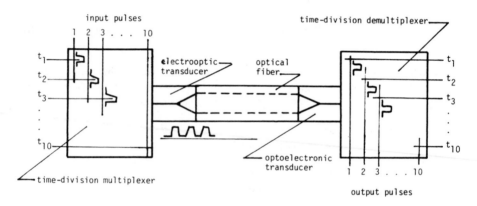

T-6. **Time-division multiplexing** on an *optical link*.

time-division switching. In a *switching system*, an arrangement in which the various *connections* share a common *path*, but are separated in time. This is accomplished by permitting each connection to use the common path in sequence for a short period of time. It is a switching technique in which the interconnections of *input* and *output terminations* are established repetitively for short time intervals such that the elements of the *switching matrix* may be time-shared by a number of terminations.

time-domain reflectometer. See *optical time-domain (OTD) reflectometer*.

time fill. See *interframe time fill*.

time filtering system. See *discrete-time filtering system*.

time frame. A specified period of time, based on two or more events or *significant instants,* using time as a basis of measurement or reference.

time-frequency signal. See *standard time-frequency signal.*

time group. See *date-time group; true date-time group (TDTG).*

time guard band. A time interval left vacant on a *channel* to provide a *margin* of safety against *intersymbol interference* in the *time domain* between *sequential operations,* such as *detection, integration, differentiation, transmission, encoding, decoding,* or *switching.* Also see *frequency guard band.*

time hopping. The *shifting* of the *occurrence time* of a *pulse* in accordance with a given *signal,* such as from a *code-sequence generator.*

time indication. See *automatic date-and-time indication.*

time interval. See *service time interval.*

time jitter. The short-term variation or instability in the duration of a specified interval or in the *occurrence time* of a specific event, such as a *signal transition* from one *significant condition* to another. When viewed with reference to a fixed *time frame,* the signal transition moves back and forth on the time axis.

time modulation. See *pulse time modulation.*

time objective. See *message time objective.*

time of arrival. See *estimated time of arrival (ETA).*

time of file (TOF). See *message file time.*

time operator. See *real-time operator.*

time-out. 1. A *network parameter* related to an enforced event that is designed to occur at the conclusion of a predetermined elapsed period of time. 2. A specified period of time that will be allowed to elapse in a *system* before a specified event is to take place, unless another specified event occurs first. In either case, the period is terminated when either event takes place. A time-out condition can be cancelled by the receipt of an appropriate time-out cancellation signal. For example, the 20 seconds that a *ringing signal* might be allowed to occur before automatic *disconnect* commences.

time scale. An arbitrary time-measuring *system* defined to relate events that occur with the passage of time. Time scales are usually graduated in *seconds,* multiples of a second (minute, hour, day, year), and submultiples of a second (millisecond, microsecond, nanosecond, picosecond).   See *coordinated time scale.*

time scale factor.   In *analog computers,* a number used as a *multiplier* to transform *problem time* to *computer time.*

time sharing.   1. A *mode* of *operation* that allows for the *interleaving* of two or more independent processes on one *functional unit.* 2. Pertaining to the inter- leaved use of time on a *computing system* that enables two or more *users* to exe- cute *computer programs* concurrently. 3. A *mode* of *operation* of a device or *system* that provides for its use by two or more entities at different times, though there is the appearance of simultaneous operation. For example, the distribution of the time of a single *communication channel* or *line* among a group of *users,* such as in *time-division multiplexing.* 4. A distribution of time of *operation* of equipment that would prevent unacceptable *interference* if two or more pieces of equipment were operated at the same time, such as two *radio stations* operating at the same *frequency* in close geographical proximity. Also see *frequency sharing.* See *frequency time sharing.*

time-signal standard-frequency broadcast.   A *radio, video,* or other *broadcast* that furnishes *information* about standard time in specified areas, that furnishes information about standard *frequencies,* and issues *timing signals* and standard frequency signals for the *synchronization* and calibration of equipment.

time slot.   Any time interval that can be recognized and uniquely defined. For example, the time interval between every 64th pulse from a *clock pulse* generator. See *channel time slot; digit time slot; frame-alignment time slot; signaling time slot.*

time standard.   A stable device that *emits signals* at exactly equal intervals such that their count can be used as a *precision clock.* It can be used to emit time and *frequency signals* for the calibration of other devices, such as *oscillators,* clocks, and other generators.

time system.   See *continuous time system; discrete time system.*

time tick.   A timing *mark output* of a *clock system.*

time to repair.   See *mean time to repair (MTTR).*

time to service restoral.   See *mean time to service restoral (MTTSR).*

time transmission.   See *real-time transmission.*

time zone.   An adopted relation of local time to *Greenwich mean time (GMT)* for a particular geographical area. A time zone is generally an *integral* number of hours ahead or behind GMT as far as clock time is concerned. Each time zone is assigned an identifying letter. The GMT at Greenwich, England, is identified by the letter Z (ZULU). In many *international communication networks,* ZULU time (GMT) is used on all *messages* rather than local standard or daylight saving time. A time zone is about 1 000 miles wide at the equator, though this varies according to land mass distributions around the world and according to natural boundaries and national borders.

timing extraction. See *timing recovery.*

timing recovery. The derivation of a *timing signal* from a *received signal.* Synonymous with *timing extraction.*

timing signal. 1. The *output* of a *clock.* 2. A *signal* that is used to *synchronize* interconnected equipment. Also see *clock; master-slave timing system.* See *octet timing signal.*

timing system. See *master-slave timing system.*

timing tracking accuracy. A measure of the ability of a timing *synchronization system* to minimize the *frequency* difference between a *master clock* and any slaved clock.

title. See *short title.*

TLP. Transmission *level (reference) point.*

TM mode. A *mode* of *electromagnetic wave propagation* in a *waveguide* in which the *wave* is a *transverse magnetic wave.* Also see *TE mode.*

TM wave. *Transverse magnetic wave.*

T-number. The equivalent *f-number* of a fictitious *lens* that has a circular opening and 100% *transmittance,* and that gives the same central *illumination* as the actual lens being considered. Mathematically:

$$T\text{-}number = EFL/Diameter\text{-}of\text{-}T\text{-}stop$$

or:

$$T\text{-}number = (EFL/2)(\pi/AT)^{1/2}$$

where *EFL* is the equivalent *focal length,* *A* is the area of the *entrance pupil,* *T* is the transmittance of the *lens system,* and $\pi = 3.1416$.

toggle. See *flip-flop.*

tolerance. See *frequency tolerance.*

tolerance-band compaction. See *fixed-tolerance-band compaction; variable tolerance band compaction.*

toll call. 1. In *telephone switchboard operation,* a *call* for which a specific monetary charge is incurred. The amount of the charge is usually based on the cost of service. This depends on the distance, call duration, time of day, specific day, taxes, adjustments, or other fixed or variable factors. 2. In *telephone switchboard operation,* a *call* between two *users* (customers, subscribers) both situated within areas between which a toll service is operated.

toll switching trunk. A *trunk* that connects one or more *terminal exchanges* (end offices) to a toll center as the first state of concentration of *toll call traffic.* Handling *operator*-assisted calls or providing operator assistance or operator participation may be optional functions. For example, in the United States, *common carrier telephony service* uses a toll center designated as 'Class 4C'. It is an office in which assistance in completing incoming calls is provided in addition to providing assistance in handling other traffic. A toll center that is designated as Class 4P is an office in which operators handle only outbound calls, or in which *switching* is performed without operator assistance.

tone. See *dial tone; disabling tone; engaged tone; number unobtainable tone; preemption tone; ringing tone; sidetone; test tone.*

tone-control aperture. In photographic receiving systems, such as *fiber-optic, facsimile,* or *Wirephoto,* an *aperture* designed to permit controlled variations in the amount of *light* reaching the light-sensitive recording material in relation to the magnitude of the received *signals* and the attributes of the material.

tone diversity. A method of *voice frequency telegraph (VFTG) transmission* in which two *channels* of a 16-channel VFTG carry the same *information.* This is commonly achieved by pairing the channels of a 16-channel VFTG to provide 8 channels with *dual diversity.* Also see *diversity reception.*

tone interference. See *single-tone interference.*

tone keying. See *two-tone keying.*

tone multifrequency signaling. See *dual-tone multifrequency signaling (DTMF).*

tone reversal. See *partial tone reversal.*

tone test signal. See *composite two-tone test signal.*

tone wedge. A wedge-shaped *optical element* that is made of material with a specific *absorptive* and *diffusive* capability and with specific *optical density* and that can serve as a member of a *tone wedge set.*

tone wedge set. A set of wedge-shaped *optical elements,* each with a slightly different *absorptive* and *diffusive* capability or *optical density* ranging in small steps from *transparent* to *opaque*, that can be inserted into an *optical system* to control tone or *intensity* from black to white through all shades of gray.

tool. See *fiber-cutting tool.*

topology. See *network topology.*

torn-tape relay. A *tape relay system* in which the *perforated tape* is manually *transferred* by an *operator* to the appropriate outgoing *transmitter position.* It is a method of *teletypewriter (teleprinter) operation* in which incoming *messages* are received on printed or perforated tape and are separated by tearing the tape so that individual messages may be processed and hand-carried to the appropriate outgoing *channel* in accordance with *routing instructions* and requirements. Also see *semiautomatic continuous-tape relay switching; semiautomatic relay system.*

total acceptance angle. Two times the *acceptance angle.* Also see *acceptance cone.*

total channel noise. The sum of *random noise, intermodulation noise, crosstalk,* and other *interference.* *Impulse noise* is usually not included in total channel noise because different techniques are required for its measurement.

total diffuse reflectance. See *diffuse reflectance.*

total emissivity. The ratio of the *radiation intensity* of a given surface to that of an ideal *blackbody* at the same *temperature.*

total harmonic distortion. The ratio of the sum of the *electrical powers* of all *harmonic frequencies* in a *signal,* other than the electrical power of the *fundamental frequency,* to the electrical power of the fundamental frequency in the signal. This ratio is measured at the *output* of a device under specified conditions and is usually expressed in *decibels* or in *nepers,* though it may also be expressed as a ratio, fraction, or percentage.

total internal reflection. The *reflection* that occurs within a substance because the *incidence angle* of *light* striking the boundary surface is greater than the *critical angle.* Also see *critical angle* and Figures C-13, E-5, and O-2.

total internal reflection angle. See *critical angle.*

total radiation temperature. The *temperature* at which a *blackbody radiates* a total amount of *electromagnetic radiation flux* equal to that radiated by the body whose total radiation temperature is being considered.

total scanning line length. In *facsimile systems,* the product of the *scanning speed* and the *scanning line period.* The total scanning line length is also equal to the sum of the *available line length* plus the product of the *scanning speed* times the *lost time.*

tower.   See *control tower.*

TPOA.   See *telecommunication private operating agency (TPOA).*

trace.   A visible reference line or a one-time *signal line* that appears in the *display space* on the *display surface* of a *cathode-ray tube, LED panel, gas panel, faceplate* of a *fiberscope,* or other display device.   It is usually caused either by a signal or a *sweep oscillator.*

tracer action.   In *communication systems,* particularly *telephone* and *telegraph* systems, the effort made by operating personnel at one *station* to determine the cause, source, or nature of errors introduced into *messages* or *operations* by personnel or equipment at other stations.   For example, an investigation to determine the reason for delay in delivery or for nondelivery of a message, or to determine the *number* of a *calling party's line* or *end-instrument.*

tracer request.   A request from a *user* or an *operator* of a *communication system* to conduct a *tracer action.*   For example, a request to determine the reason for the delay or nondelivery of a message, the source of an incoming call, or the charges for a *finished call.*

tracing.   See *call tracing; on-demand call tracing.*

track.   1. The *path,* or one of the set of paths, parallel to the reference edge, on a *data medium,* associated with a *signal* reading or writing *component* as the data medium is moved past the component.   A track may consist of a line of positions on a data medium that are influenced by, or that influence, a single writing or reading component.   For example, the ring-shaped portion of the surface of a magnetic drum associated with one head, or the line of positions on a *perforated tape, magnetic tape, magnetic card,* or magnetic disk that can be read by one head. 2. To maintain contact with a moving object, such as to maintain *radar* contact with a moving target or to maintain *direction-finding (DF)* contact with a moving *aircraft station.*   See *clock track.*

track-and-hold unit.   In *analog systems,* a device whose *output analog variable* is either the *input* variable or a sample of the input variable sampled by the action of an external *signal.*   When *tracking,* the device follows the input analog variable. When *holding,* the device holds the value of the input analog variable at the instant of *switching.*   Synonymous with *track-and-store unit.*

track-and-store unit.   See *track-and-hold unit.*

track ball.   See *control ball.*

track correlation. In *radar systems,* the *correlation* of *radar tracking data* for identification purposes, using all available data.

tracker. See *infrared angle tracker.*

tracking. In *display systems,* the process of following or determining the position of a moving *display writer,* using (1) a *stylus,* such as a *light pen, tablet stylus,* or voltage pencil, or (2) a *pointer,* such as a *control ball, joystick, mouse,* or *digitizer* moving a *cursor, aiming circle* or other *tracking symbol.* See *aided tracking; passive tracking; pulse-edge tracking; space tracking.*

tracking accuracy. See *timing tracking accuracy.*

tracking earth station. See *space tracking earth station.*

tracking radar. *Radar* that *tracks* objects by means of *lock-on.* Tracking radar usually receives *information* from *scanning radar* that is normally located in *ship stations, aircraft stations,* and *land stations.* The information enables the tracking radar to obtain a lock on the moving object. The tracking radar in a weapon system provides the information needed for target intercept guidance.

tracking space station. See *space tracking space station.*

tracking symbol. A symbol that is visible in the *display space* on the *display surface* of a *display device* and that can be moved and used to indicate the position of a *pointer.* The pointer may be a *stylus, joystick, control ball,* or *mouse.* It may be any device capable of generating *coordinate data.* Examples of display surfaces are *CRT* screens, *fiberscope faceplates, LED* or *gas panels,* or *plotter beds.*

tracking system. See *pseudo-monopulse tracking system.*

tracking-telemetry-command station. An *earth station* that determines *satellite* position and provides *telemetry* and *command facilities.*

track telling. In command, control, and *communications,* the process of communicating *radar* air surveillance *data* between *command and control systems* and *facilities.* Telling may be subdivided into *back tell, lateral tell, forward tell, overlap tell,* and *relateral tell.*

track-while-scan airborne intercept radar. An *airborne intercept radar* that can *track* an object (target) while it also *scans* for others. The track-while-scan radar can *search* and *track* in the same *mode.* The *signal* does not intermittently *illuminate* a *jamming* aircraft during search and constantly illuminate during *lock-on.* The signal at all times appears to be searching or intermittently illuminating.

traffic. In *communication systems,* the system control and *user information* that is moved in the form of *data* or *signals* over a *communication path. Traffic* includes the spatial totality of all the *messages* in a *communication system* or *network* and the flow rate of messages at a point in a network, *channel, trunk,* or other *path* or group of paths. It also includes the message intelligence, such as voice, *telegraph,* or other data for which the communication system was established. Routine and special messages between *system operator* and maintenance staff personnel also are part of the system traffic even though they are usually carried in channels separate from the channels that carry *user information,* that is, information for which the system was established. See *clear traffic; communication traffic; distress traffic; mission traffic; narrative traffic; press traffic; queue traffic; record traffic; safety traffic; secure traffic; urgency traffic; welfare traffic.*

traffic analysis.   **1.** In a *communication system,* the analysis of *traffic* rates, *volumes, densities, capacities,* and patterns for the express purpose of system performance inprovement.   **2.** The analysis of the external characteristics of *tactical* and *strategic information* and *communication systems* and *components* for the purpose of obtaining useful *information* of an intelligence value. This information can be used as a basis for drawing inferences of intelligence value, as an aid to *cryptoanalysis,* as a guide to efficient intercept operations, and as a basis for *communication deception.*   **3.** The analysis of the *communication-electronic* environment for use in the design, development, and operation of new communication systems.

traffic capacity.   The maximum *traffic* per unit time that a specified *communication system, subsystem,* or device can carry under specified conditions. See also *traffic load.*

traffic control communications.   See *air traffic control communications.*

traffic coordinator.   See *line traffic coordinator (LTC).*

traffic engineering.   In a *communication system,* the determination of the numbers and kinds of *circuits* and the quantity of related *terminating* and *switching* equipment required to meet anticipated *traffic loads* throughout the system.

traffic flow security.   In *communication system security,* the *protection* that results from the features that are inherent in some *cryptoequipment* and that conceal the presence of valid *messages* on a *communication circuit.* For example, traffic flow security can be partially achieved by causing a circuit to appear *busy* at all times or by *encrypting* the *source* and *destination* addresses of valid messages.

traffic frequency.   See *optimum traffic frequency (OTF).*

traffic intensity.   A measure of the average occupancy of a *facility* during a period of time, normally a *busy hour,* measured in *traffic units (erlangs)* and defined as the ratio of the time during which a facility is occupied continuously or cumulatively to the time that the facility is ready and available for occupancy. A traffic intensity of one traffic unit (one erlang) means the continuous occupancy of a facility during the time period under consideration or the time period of measurement, regardless of whether or not *information* is actually *transmitted*. For example, if a *telephone connection* is established between two *user's end-instruments*, and the connection remains for two hours, then even if the users are not talking, for that period the traffic intensity for those telephones is 1 erlang. If over a period of two hours, the phones were connected for only half an hour, then the traffic intensity for the period is 0.25 erlang. Also see *busy hour; call-second; erlang; traffic load.*

traffic list. A serial number followed by the appropriate *call sign* and *date-time group* of each *message* to be *transmitted*. For example, a *station* may transmit the *traffic list* prior to the *transmission* of messages in the order in which they are indentified on the traffic list. A broadcast serial number might consist of letters or figures followed by a serial number assigned consecutively to each message transmitted by an *area broadcast station* during a month.

traffic load. The total traffic carried by a *trunk* or *trunk group* during a specified time interval. Also see *busy hour; erlang; group busy hour; network busy hour; switch busy hour; traffic capacity; traffic intensity;* and Figure B-9.

traffic metering device. See *telephone traffic metering device.*

traffic overload protection. See *automatic traffic overload protection.*

traffic unit. See *erlang.*

traffic usage recorder. A device used for measuring the amount of *telephone traffic* carried by a group or several groups of *switches, trunks, lines, channels,* or other *communication system components.*

traffic usage register. A device used to indicate or record the usage time of *system components,* such as the total cumulative time of usage over an extended period for *communication lines, circuits, trunks, switches,* and other components, particularly for *telephone, telegraph, and facsimile equipment.* Usage time is recorded in convenient units, such as *hundred-call-second (CCS)* units.

traffic volume. See *communication traffic volume.*

trail. See *audit trail.*

trailer. See *magnetic tape trailer.*

trajectory. See *ray trajectory.*

transaction. See *information transfer transaction; interactive data transaction.*

transceiver. The combination of *transmitting* and *receiving* equipment in a common housing, usually for *portable* or *mobile* use, employing common *circuit components* for both transmitting and receiving. It is a device that is designed for *simplex operation*. See *home optical transceiver*. See Figure T-7. Also see Figures F-2, F-6, and M-5.

T-7.   A desktop *digital facsimile* **transceiver** for *communication* with *analog* and *digital* machines for *transmitting* a standard business letter worldwide in about a minute. (Courtesy of 3M Business Communication Products Division.)

transducer. A device capable of transforming energy from one form to another, usually with such fidelity that if the original energy represents *information,* the transformed energy can represent the same information, or its time derivative. For example, a *microphone* that *converts* a *sound wave* to a corresponding *electrical current,* a *modulated laser* that converts electrical currents to *modulated lightwaves,* a *photodetector* that converts modulated lightwaves to electrical currents, or a *piezoelectric* crystal that produces a *voltage* proportional to the time derivative of the pressure wave that impinges upon it. See *optoacoustic transducer.*

transfer. In *communications,* to move a data unit in its entirety from one location to another. See *call transfer; information transfer; successful block transfer.*

transfer attempt.   See *block transfer attempt.*

transfer characteristic.   An intrinsic *parameter* of a *system, subsystem,* or *component* that, when applied to the *input* of the system, subsystem, or component will partially describe its *output.* If all the transfer characteristics and the input are known, the output will be fully described. Also see *transfer function.*

transfer circuit.   **1.** A *circuit* provided for the *transfer* of *message traffic* from a *system* that is operated by one nation or group of nations into a system that is operated by another nation or group of nations.   **2.** A *circuit* used to *transfer* a *message* from one *network* to another via a *terminal port.* For example, a circuit used to transfer a message from a network that serves the *originator (source user)* to a network that serves an *addressee (destination user),* perhaps via intermediate networks.

transfer failure.   See *block transfer failure.*

transfer function.   The function that produces the *output* of a device or produces the result of an *operation* based on a given *input.* Since the output is obtained when the transfer function operates upon the input, given any two of these entities, the third can be determined. For example, in a negative (stable) *feedback system,* the transfer function, T, is given by $T = e_o/e_i = G/(1+GH)$, where e_o is the output, e_i is the input, G is the forward gain, and H is the backward gain. It is the *operator* that, when applied to an input, will describe the output. *Voltage gain, reflection coefficients, transmission coefficients,* and efficiency ratios are simple transfer functions. *Envelope delay distortion* is a more complex transfer function. Also see *feedback factor; transfer characteristic.* See *complex transfer function; fiber bundle transfer function; modulation transfer function; optical fiber transfer function.* See Figure T-8.

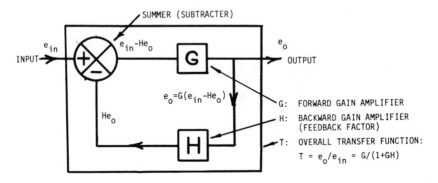

T-8. The overall **transfer function** for the above equipment is $G/(1 + GH)$, where G and H are the *forward* and *backward gains.*

transfer index.   See *radiation transfer index.*

transfer lock.   To change *lock-on* from one object (target) to another when a *tracking* device, such as a *radar, sonar, optical tracker,* or *direction finder,* is tracking an object. Also see *lock-on; relock.*

transfer part.   See *message transfer part.*

transfer phase.   See *data transfer phase.*

transfer rate.   See *actual transfer rate; block transfer rate; data transfer rate; effective data-transfer rate; effective transfer rate.*

transferred information content.   See *transinformation content.*

transfer request signal.   See *data transfer request signal.*

transfer station.   See *terminal port.*

transfer success.   See *block transfer success.*

transfer time.   See *block transfer time; data transfer time; maximum block transfer time.*

transfer transaction.   See *information transfer transaction.*

transinformation content.   See *mean transinformation content.*

transformer.   An *electrical* device that can convert a *voltage, current,* or *impedance* to either a higher or a lower level. See Figure T-9.

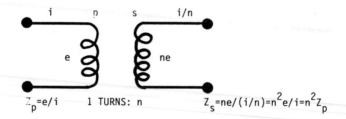

T-9. In this simple **transformer,** the primary, P, to secondary, S, turns ratio is 1:n. Thus, the voltage, e, ratio is n; the current, i, ratio is $1/n$; and the impedance, Z, ratio is n^2 (all primary-to-secondary ratios).

transient. See *dynamic variation.*

transient radiation effects on electronics (TREE). Temporal effects that are produced by *electromagnetic radiation incident* upon electronic *components,* particularly on active *circuit* elements, such as *transistors* and *integrated circuits.* For example, changing the circuit *parameters* of a transistor or *combinational logic circuit* so as to cause temporary or permanent shifts in their operating points and thus produce undesirable *voltage, power,* or *current* fluctuations or operating points. The net effect is to produce *noise, interference,* erroneous results, or *system failure.*

transimpedance. See *optical transimpedance.*

transinformation content. The difference between the *information content* that can be conveyed by the occurrence of an event and the conditional information content that can be conveyed by the occurrence of the same event but given the occurrence of another event. Synonymous with *mutual information content; transferred information content; transmitted information content.* See *character mean transinformation content.*

transinformation rate. See *average transinformation rate.*

transistor. A *semiconducting* material (e.g., germanium or silicon) with two *junctions,* three regions, alternately doped positive-negative-positive (pnp) or negative-positive-negative (npn), one outer region serving as the emitter, or source of charge *carriers,* the other as the collector, and the intervening layers as the base, operating in such a manner that a large reverse *bias* is placed on the base-collector junction. Small *signals* applied between the base and emitter controls larger *currents* and *power* in the base collector circuit, thus serving as a *power signal amplifier,* the power being supplied by the power *source* in the collector circuit. Thus, the transistor is a solid-state *active device.* The transistor is capable of amplifying *electric signals* such as *voltages, currents,* and *power;* mixing *signals;* performing *modulation* and *demodulation;* performing *gating, buffering, storing, shifting,* and *shaping* functions, and performing many other functions. A transistor can operate at *high frequencies* and perform most of the functions of vacuum tubes. It has a low *power* dissipation *loss,* is highly reliable, and serves well as a *logic device* for performing the Boolean functions of *AND, OR, NOR, NAND,* and others. It is particulary suited as a *switching device* for *computer* and *communication systems,* particularly in the areas of *transmission, multiplexing,* and *signal processing.* Transistors may be packaged as individual plug-in units, mounted on *printed circuit* boards, or be fabricated as integrated circuits by such processes as etching and evaporation to form *large-scale integrated (LSI) chips.* See *phototransistor.*

transistor-transistor logic (TTL). *Combinational circuits* that perform *logic operations,* such as *gating operations,* and that consist of *transistors* that are connected directly to each other in such a manner that the *output* of one or more transistors is used as the *input* to one or more other transistors with little or no intervening *circuit* elements. The circuits are used to a large extent in *large-scale integrated circuits (LSI).*

transit.   An *eclipse* of the sun by a planet as the planet moves between an observer or *photodetector* and the sun.

transition.   In *signaling,* the changing from one *significant* condition to another, such as the changing from one *voltage level* to another in a *square-wave telegraph signal,* the *shifting* from one *phase position* to another, or the *translation* from one *frequency* to another. See *signal transition.*

transition fiber.   An *optical element* of such geometric shape at *input* and *output* ends that it enables *coupling* between an element in an *integrated optical circuit* and an *optical fiber;* e.g., one with a rectangular cross section at input and a circular cross section at ouput with a smooth transition between the input and output geometric shapes.

transition frequency.   The *frequency* associated with two discrete *energy levels* in an atomic system. The transition frequency associated with energy levels E_2 and E_1 when E_2 is greater than E_1 is:

$$F_{2,1} = (E_2 - E_1)/h$$

where E_2 and E_1 are the energy levels, h is *Planck's constant,* and $F_{2,1}$ is the frequency associated with the two levels. If a transition from E_2 to E_1 occurs, a *photon* with frequency $F_{2,1}$ is likely to be *emitted.*

transition zone.   The zone between the end of the *electrostatic field* (near field) region of an *antenna* and the beginning of the *radiation field* (far field) region. The *transition* from one field to another is gradual. The transition zone (field) owes its existence primarily to the moving charges (*electric currents*) in the antenna. Also see *induction field.*

transit time.   In a *satellite communication system,* the time taken for a *signal* to *propagate* from one *earth station* to another via a *satellite link,* approximately 1/3 of a second for *geostationary earth satellites.*   Synonymous with *satellite hop-time; transmit time.*

translating.   In *graphics* and *display systems,* moving a *display element, display group,* or *display image* from one *coordinate position* to another without rotating the element, group, or image about a point within them or relative to a point in the coordinate system in the *display space* on the *display surface* of the *display device.* Contrast with *rotating.* Also see *tumbling.*

translation. **1.** In *communications,* the process of changing *frequency* without altering the *baseband data* or type of *modulation.* For example, *up-converters* and *down-converters* are used to translate *communication signals* in *satellites* and in *earth stations.* **2.** In *telegraph systems,* the function of a *telegraph receiver* in reestablishing the *text* of a *message* from the *received signal.* This function includes the recording of the text. **3.** The process of *converting text* from one *language* to another. **4.** In *computers* and *data processing,* the conversion of a *program* in one *computer programming language* to another program that will produce the same results when executed but is in another language, such as a *machine language* or another *common language.* The translation takes place from the source language to the object (or target) language. Also see *transliteration.* See *displacement; frequency translation; pregroup translation; single-frequency translation.*

translation equipment. See *channel translation equipment.*

translator. **1.** In *communication systems,* a device that is capable of changing the *frequency* of a *signal* without altering the *baseband data* or the type of *modulation.* **2.** A *computer program* that *translates* a *computer program* (source program) written in one *language* to a program (object program) written in another language, the object program being capable of producing the same results as the source program when executed. See *test loop translator.*

transliteration. The letter-by-letter or letter-by-letter-group conversion of *text* from the letters of one *alphabet* to the corresponding letters of another alphabet without changing the meaning but perhaps changing the pronunciation. For example, exchanging letters of the Roman alphabet for letters of the Greek alphabet, or Cyrillic or Hebrew letters for Roman letters. Transliteration includes changing the *binary code* patterns that are assigned to letters of a given alphabet, such as changing from the *extended binary coded decimal interchange code (EBCDIC)* to the American standard code for information interchange (*ASCII*). Synonymous with *alphabet translation.* Also see *translation.*

transmission. **1.** The process of *conducting radiant* energy through a *transmission medium.* **2.** The *propagation* of a *signal, message,* or other form of intelligence by any means, such as *radio, optical fiber, wire,* or *visual* means. **3.** The *transfer* of *electrical power* from one location to another over *electrical conductors,* such as high-*voltage* cross-country *transmission lines.* Also see *message.* See *analog transmission; anisochronous transmission; asynchronous transmission; biternary transmission; bit-stream transmission; black facsimile transmission; blind transmission; bursty transmission; colored-light transmission; compatible sideband transmission; data transmission; diffuse transmission; digital voice transmission; directional transmission; diversity transmission; double-current transmission; double-sideband transmission; duplex transmission; electrical transmission; flag-hoist transmission; flashing-light transmission; full-carrier transmission; half-duplex transmission; hand-flag transmission; independent-sideband transmission;*

infrared transmission; isochronous burst transmission; isochronous transmission; low-detectability electromagnetic wave transmission; parallel transmission; point-to-point transmission; pyrotechnic transmission; real-time transmission; secure transmission; selective transmission; serial transmission; sideband transmission; single-sideband suppressed-carrier (SSB-SC) transmission; single-sideband transmission; selective transmission; start-stop transmission; store-and-forward data transmission; suppressed-carrier transmission; synchronous transmission; two independent-sideband transmission; unidirectional transmission; vestigial sideband transmission; victim transmission; white facsimile transmission; white transmission; wireline transmission. See Figure T-10.

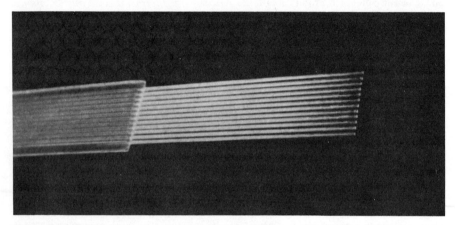

T-10. *Optical fibers* drawn from low-*loss* glass *preforms* assembled in a protective sheath for *fiber optic* **transmission** *systems.* (Reproduced with permission of AT&T Co.)

transmission authentication.   The establishment of the authority of the *originator* or source of *transmission.* It includes *self-authentication, station authentication,* and *message authentication.* Transmission authentication *procedures* enable *stations* to establish the authenticity of their own transmission.

transmission-block character.   See *end-of-transmission-block (ETB) character.*

transmission channel.   In a *communication network,* all of the *transmission facilities* between the *input* of an initiating *node* in a communication network and the *output* of a terminating node of the network. A transmission channel plus two *local loops* constitutes a *circuit.* Transmission channels may be of various *bandwidths,* such as nominal 3 kHz, nominal 4 kHz, or nominal 48 kHz (group). Also see *channel; circuit.* See *data transmission channel; nonsynchronous data transmission channel; synchronous data transmission channel.*

transmission character.   See *end-of-transmission (EOT) character.*

transmission circuit.   See *data transmission circuit.*

transmission coefficient.   1. The ratio of the *transmitted field strength* to the *incident* field strength when an *electromagnetic wave* is incident upon an *interface* surface between *dielectric media* of different *refractive indices*.   If, at oblique incidence, the *electric field* component of the incident wave is parallel to the interface, the transmission coefficient is given by:

$$T = 2n_2 \cos\!A/(n_2 \cos\!A + n_1 \cos\!B)$$

where n_1 and n_2 are the reciprocals of the *refractive indices* of the incident and transmitted media, respectively, and A and B are the *incidence angle* and *refraction angle* (with respect to the normal to the interface surface), respectively.   If, at oblique incidence, the *magnetic field* component of the incident wave is parallel to the interface surface, the transmission coefficient is given by:

$$T = 2n_2 \cos\!A/(n_1 \cos\!A + n_2 \cos\!B)$$

These equations are known as the *Fresnel equations* for these cases.   **2.** A number that indicates the probable performance of a portion of a *transmission channel, circuit, line, link,* or *trunk*.   The value of the transmission coefficient is inversely related to the quality of the channel, circuit, line, link, or trunk.   Also see *Fresnel reflection loss; reflection coefficient.*

transmission control.   See *radio transmission control.*

transmission control character.   A *character* used to control or facilitate the *transmission* of *data* over *communication networks*.   For example, the data *communication control characters ACK, DLE, ENQ, EOT, ETB, ETX, NAK, SOH, STX,* and *SYN*.   These data communication control characters are transmission control characters that facilitate the transmission of data over a *data link* between *data terminal equipment* at two separate *stations*.   Synonymous with *communication control character; data communication control character; data transmission control character.*   Also see *control character.*

transmission efficiency.   1. The ratio of *power* at the output of a device, system, *transmission line,* or other *functional unit* to the power at the input.   **2.** The number of good or correct *bits, bytes, characters, words,* or other *data units received* at a point divided by the total number of the same units that were *transmitted* to the point.

transmission ending.   In *radiotelegraph* and *radiotelephone transmission,* a *sign* or *symbol* used to indicate the end of a *message* or *transmission*.   For example, the *prosign* K, invitation to *transmit,* or the prosign AR, *end of transmission,* in a *radio* or *tape relay data transmission system.*

transmission factor.   See *internal optical density.*

transmission frequency.   In *radar,* the *radio* or *video frequency* of the cycles that are repeated within a *transmitted pulse length*.   The transmission frequency is not the *pulse repetition rate*.   The pulse repetition rate is the number of radar pulses that occur each second. Each individual pulse is transmitted for its entire length using a certain *frequency* or frequencies.

transmission function.   See *end-of-transmission function.*

transmission group.   See *digital transmission group.*

transmission identification.   An identification required in the *heading* of each *message* to provide a means of maintaining continuity of *traffic.*   For example, for *stations* that *transmit* directly into fully automatic *relay stations,* the transmission identification may consist of a *start-of-message indicator, station* and *channel* letters, a *figures shift, numeral characters,* and a *letters shift.*   The combination of letters and figures is used to identify a transmission on a channel between two stations.   It may consist of only a *station designator* and a *channel designator.*

transmission instruction.   In *radio telegraph communication,* an *instruction,* usually consisting of *prosigns, call signs, address designators,* and *operating signals,* that concerns the *routing, relaying,* and delivery of *messages.*   Direct communication between *stations* may preclude the necessity for transmission instructions.

transmission interface.   See *data transmission interface.*

transmission layer.   In a *layered system,* the set of functions and *protocols* that pertain to the *transfer* of *data* between geographically distinct locations.

transmission level.   1. The *signal power* at a given point in a *transmission system* relative to the signal power at an arbitrary selected or specified point, such as at the beginning of a *transmission line,* indicated in *decibels,* or relative to an arbitrarily selected *power level* such as 1W or 1mW, indicated as *dBW* or *dBm.* 2. At any point in a *transmission system,* the *power,* usually expressed in *dBm,* that should be measured at that point when a *standard test signal,* considered at 0 dBm, 1000 Hz, is transmitted at some point chosen as a reference point.   A point where a reading of −16 dBm is expected would be considered as a −16 *transmission level point,* sometimes abbreviated as −16 TLP.   The transmission level of a point is a function of the *system* design and is a measure of the design or nominal *gain* at 1000 Hz of the system between the chosen reference point, known as the *zero transmission level point (OTLP)* and the *test* point.   Absolute measurements of the *power* of *test signals* at any point are influenced by the actual level as well as by any deviations of the system from its desired gain.   See *relative transmission level.*

transmission level point (TLP).   A point in a *transmission system* at which the ratio, usually expressed in *decibels,* of the *power* of a *test signal* at that point to the power of the test signal at a reference point, is specified.   For example, a *zero transmission level point (OTLP)* is an arbitrarily established point in a *communication circuit* to which all relative levels at other points in the circuit are referred. Very often the measured *power level* at a point, usually expressed in *decibels* relative to a reference, is so closely associated with the point (place) in the circuit that the terms power level and point are used interchangeably. See *zero transmission level point.*

transmission level reference point.   See *reference transmission level point.*

transmission line.   The material *medium* or structure that forms all or part of a *path* from one place to another for directing the *transmission* of *electric, magnetic,* acoustic, elastic, *electromagnetic,* or other waves; such as a *dielectric slab, optical fiber, coaxial cable,* rectangular *waveguide,* or a *wire.* See *artificial transmission line; uniform transmission line.* See Figure T-11.

T-11. A coil of glass *fiber* for *long-haul optical link* **transmission lines.** (Courtesy of Bell Laboratories.)

transmission loss.   In *communications,* the decrease in the *power* of a *signal* during *transmission* from one point to another. The loss is usually expressed in *decibels.* This implies that the loss must first be expressed as a ratio between the *power level* at one point and a power level at another, the decrease being one of a ratio rather than of a difference.

transmission loss distance.   The distance in which a specified *power loss* or *attenuation* occurs to a *signal* of specified *wavelength propagating* in a *transmission medium.*   For example, the *lightwave* transmission loss distances for a 5-db loss at a wavelength of 0.850 *micron* are 1, 5, and 1 km for window glass or water, *optical glass,* and *low-loss optical fibers,* respectively.

transmission medium.   Any material substance that can be or is used for the *propagation* of *signals,* usually in the form of *modulated* radio, *light,* or acoustic waves, from one point to another, such as an *optical fiber, cable,* or *bundle;* a *wire;* a *dielectric* slab; water; or air.   By extension, *free space* can also be considered as a transmission medium for *electromagnetic waves.*   Contrast with *data medium.*

transmission mode.   See *propagation mode.*

transmission rate.   See *average transmission rate; effective transmission speed.*

transmission security.   **1.** The protection of *information* to prevent its unauthorized disclosure during *transmission.*   **2.** The result obtained from the *protection* given to prevent the unauthorized disclosure of *information* during *transmission.*   **3.** The *component* of *communication security* that results from the application of all measures that are designed to protect *transmissions* from *interception* and exploitation by means other than *cryptanalysis.*   See *ship radio transmission security.*

transmission service.   See *circuit-switched data transmission service; data transmission service; leased-circuit data transmission service; packet-switched data transmission service; public data transmission service.*

transmission speed.   The time rate at which *data, messages, signals,* or any other *information units* are sent from the *originator (source)* to the *addressee (sink).*   For example, *transmission speeds* may be measured or expressed in *bits* per *second* (b/s), *characters* per minute (c/m), *words* per minute (w/m or wpm), or other convenient units, such as *messages* per day.   Also see *transmission time.*   See *effective transmission speed; instantaneous transmission speed.*

transmission system.   See *double-sideband suppressed-carrier transmission system; fiber optic transmission system; laser fiber optic transmission system; start-stop transmission system; stepped start-stop transmission system.*

transmission time.   **1.** The time required for a *message* to pass a point in a *transmission system.*   This time is a function of the length of the message and the *signaling speed.*   **2.** The time that elapses between the start of *transmission* of a *message* at the *message source (originating station)* and the receipt of the end of the message at the *message sink (destination station).*   Also see *transmission speed.*

transmissivity. The *internal transmittance* per unit thickness of a nondiffusing substance, such as clear glass, plastic, or crystal.

transmit. To move an entity from one place to another. For example, to *broadcast radio waves,* to dispatch *data* via a *transmission medium,* or to *transfer* data from one set of *data circuit-terminating equipment (DCE)* to another via a *line.* It does not include *reception* and therefore is not *communication.* It is similar to dispatch and to *emit.* Also see *receive.*

transmit-after-receive time delay. The time interval from the removal of *radio frequency (RF)* energy at the local *receiver input* until the local *transmitter* is automatically *keyed-on* and the transmitted *power (RF signal amplitude)* has increased to 90% of its steady-state value. *High frequency (HF) transceiver* equipment is normally not designed with an interlock between receiver *squelch* and transmitter on-off *key.* The transmitter can be keyed-on at any time, independent of whether or not a signal is being received at the receiver input. Also see *transmitter attack-time delay; transmitter release-time delay.*

transmit flow control. In *data transmission procedure,* a control of the rate at which *data* may be *transmitted* from one point (*terminal*) so that it is equal to the rate at which it can be *received* or *buffered* at another point (terminal). This procedure may apply between *data terminal equipment (DTE)* and the adjacent *data switching exchange (DSE)* or between two DTEs. The *data signaling rate* may be controlled due to *network,* remote DTE, or other requirements. This procedure can be followed independently in the two directions of data *transfer,* thus permitting different data signaling rates in both directions of *transmission.*

transmittance. The ratio of the *flux* that is *transmitted* through an *object,* to the *incident radiant* or *luminous flux.* Unless qualified, the term is applied to regular, (i.e., *specular*) transmission. See *collimated transmittance; diffuse transmittance; internal transmittance; luminous transmittance; radiant transmittance; selective transmittance; spectral transmittance.*

transmittancy. The ratio of the *transmittance* of a solution to that of an equal thickness of the solvent alone.

transmitted information content. See *transinformation content.*

transmitted power. The energy per unit time (i.e., the power usually expressed in watts) *propagated* through a specified area (such as a *fiber cable* or other *waveguide*) or a specified cross-sectional area perpendicular to the direction of propagation (such as in a specified *solid angle*) or through a fictitious sphere completely surrounding the *transmitter.* Since instantaneous transmitted power can vary with time and the specified cross-sectional area can change, the power can assume various forms of measurement—such as the *peak envelope power,* the power in a given direction, the power averaged over time, the power averaged over an area or solid angle, the total *carrier* power delivered to an *antenna,* the total power *radiated* and integrated over all directions—or it may be the power limited to a specified portion of a *frequency spectrum* or *bandwidth.*

transmitter.   A device capable of generating, *modulating,* and sending a *signal* for *communication,* control, or other purpose.   For example, a *microphone, amplifier, modulator,* and *antenna* for sending *electromagnetic waves;* the mouthpiece, microphone, and *wire* in a *telephone* instrument; or a modulated *laser.* See *automatic numbering transmitter; automatic telegraph transmitter; drum transmitter; electrooptic transmitter; facsimile transmitter; flat-bed transmitter; jammer transmitter; optical transmitter; radio transmitter; reperforator-transmitter; telegraph transmitter; telephone transmitter; tunable transmitter.* See Figure T-12.

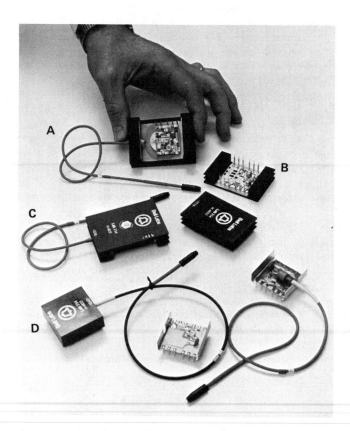

T-12.   a, b.   *laser* **transmitter** and *receiver* experimental packages, including transmitter. Package a contains the *laser chip* a fraction of a millimeter in size, attached to a *single-fiber light waveguide* in a protective sheath.   c.   The same two packages with covers.   d. The two sections of the *receiver* that is shown assembled with cover at left.   (Courtesy of Bell Laboratories.)

transmitter attack-time delay. The time interval from the instant of *keying-on* (turning on) of a *transmitter* to the instant at which the transmitted *radio frequency (RF) signal amplitude* has increased to 90% of its steady-state value. This delay excludes any necessary time for automatic *antenna tuning.* Also see *transmit-after-receive time delay; transmitter release-time delay.*

transmitter calibration factor. In a *satellite communication system,* a *parameter* used in *up-link power balancing* calculations to determine the minimum *earth station transmitter power* required on each *communication satellite link* in order to achieve the minimum *down-link signal strength* for *reception.* All system variables that influence *power levels* are taken into account in the calculations. The *output* power of an *earth station* is usually chosen as a *reference transmission level point.*

transmitter group. See *synchronized transmitter group.*

transmitter power output rating. A specified *output power* capability of a *radio transmitter.* Power ratings are usually specified as *peak envelope power (PEP), mean power (MP or PM),* or *carrier power (CP or PC).*

transmitter-receiver. See *home optical transceiver.*

transmitter release-time delay. The time interval from the instant of *keying-off* a *transmitter* until the *transmitted radio frequency (RF) signal amplitude* has decreased to 10% of its *keyed-on* steady-state value. Also see *transmit-after-receive time delay; transmitter attack-time delay.*

transmitter start code. A *code* that is sent by a *switching center* and is used for *polling* all *stations.* If a polled station has no *message* to *transmit,* it responds with an *answer-back code.* Also see *call-directory code.*

transmit time. See *transit time.*

transmit time delay. See *receive-after-transit time delay.*

transmitting element. The *radiating terminus* at an *optical junction.*

transmitting star-coupler. See *nonreflective star-coupler.*

transparency. 1. In *communication systems,* the property that allows the *transmission* of *signals* without changing their *electrical* characteristics or *coding* beyond the specified limits of *system* design. 2. An *image* fixed on a clear base by means of a *photographic* printing, chemical, or other process, especially designed for viewing by *transmitted light.* 3. That quality of a *data communication system* or device in which a *bit*-oriented *link protocol* is used that does not depend on the bit sequence structure used by the *data source.* 4. The quality of material that allows it to *conduct lightwaves* with minimal or no *absorption.* Also see *commonality.* See *data circuit transparency; data signaling rate transparency.*

transparent. 1. Pertaining to the property of a material in which *electromagnetic waves,* usually in the visible region of the *spectrum,* are *propagated* without *attenuation,* except for attentuation due to *divergence,* and thus pertaining to a material with an *extinction coefficient* of zero. Most *lenses, prisms, optical fibers,* and other *optical elements* are intended to be transparent. 2. Pertaining to *transparency.* Also see *Bouger's law.* See *code-independent.*

transparent interface. An *interface* that allows the interconnected equipment on both sides of the interface to operate without modification of input, output, circuitry, or operational procedures (i.e., protocol) after installation of the interface. Also see *commonality.*

transparent network. A *network* that has the property of *transparency* in regard to the *transmission* of *signals* and the nondependence on *bit* sequence structure.

transponder. A *radio* or *radar transmitter-receiver* that is capable of retransmitting *signals* automatically when the proper signals are received. The transponder depends on some *frequency* memory or timing procedure to effect on-frequency retransmissions. It is usually capable of accepting the electronic challenge of an *interrogator* and automatically transmitting an appropriate reply. In a *satellite communication system,* the transponder may consist of *receiver* and *transmitter signal relay* equipment. The *output* usually is of increased *power* and may be of different frequency and direction. It can serve as a *deception* device that receives a signal and returns another signal of a predetermined nature. For example, a transponder may create high-amplitude signals to create multiple false targets on a *radar screen.*

transportable. Pertaining to equipment that is designed to be carried or moved from location to location but is usually not operated while it is being moved.

transportable communication equipment. *Fixed* (stationary) *communication stations* or equipment specifically designed for ease of transportation and rapid assembly and disassembly for operation in a changing, field, moving, or tactical situation.

transport layer. In *open systems architecture,* the *layer* that directly provides functions for the actual movement of *data* among *network* elements. Also see *layer.* See *end-to-end transport layer.*

transport station. In *distributed systems,* the *protocols, procedures, processes,* and mechanisms that carry out the *data transfer protocols* of the *transport layer.*

transposition. 1. In *data transmission,* a transmission defect in which, during one *character* period, one or more *signal elements* are changed from one *significant condition* to the other, and an equal number of elements are changed in the opposite sense.   2. In *outside plant* construction, an interchange of positions of the several *conductors* of a *circuit* between successive lengths of *wire, optical fiber, cable,* or other conductors to achieve *electrical balance* and reduce *inductive interference,* since interference induced in one section in one direction will be induced in the opposite direction in another section.

transverse electric wave (TE wave).   An *electromagnetic wave propagating* or standing in *free space* or in a *transmission medium* but in such a manner that: (1) the *electric field vector* is transverse (i.e., perpendicular to the direction of propagation of the wave along the guide); (2) there is no electric field vector component in the direction of propagation along the guide; and (3) there is a *magnetic field vector component* in the direction of propagation.   Thus, the electric field vector is entirely transverse and does not have a longitudinal component but the magnetic field does have a longitudinal component.   The transmission medium is usually a *waveguide* of uniform cross section in the longitudinal direction, and the waves are usually *light* or radio waves.

transverse electromagnetic wave (TEM wave).   An *electromagnetic wave* whose *electric* and *magnetic field vectors,* although varying in time at every point in the space occupied by the wave, either in *free space* or in *transmission media,* are contained in a local plane, at the point, the orientation of which is independent of time.   Thus, in general, the orientation of the local planes is different for different points in the space or material medium, the exception being the special case of a *uniform plane-polarized electromagnetic wave.*

transverse-excited atmosphere laser (TEA).   A carbon-dioxide or other *gas laser* in which the *electric field* excitation of the *active medium* is transverse (across) to the flow of the active medium.   This type of *laser* operates in a gas pressure range higher than that required for *longitudinal excitation.*   Contrast with *longitudinally-excited atmosphere laser (LEA).*

transverse jitter.   In *facsimile transmission systems,* an effect due to the irregularity of the *scanning pitch* that results in concurrent overlap and underlap in the reproduced *image.*

transverse magnetic wave (TM wave).   An *electromagnetic wave propagating* or standing in *free space* or in a *transmission medium* in such a manner that (1) the *magnetic field vector* is transverse (i.e., perpendicular to the direction of propagation of the wave along the guide); (2) there is no magnetic field vector component in the direction of propagation of the wave along the guide; and (3) there is an *electric field vector* component in the direction of propagation. Thus, the magnetic field is entirely transverse and does not have a longitudinal component, but the *electric field* does have a longitudinal component. The transmission medium is usually a *waveguide* of uniform cross section in the longitudinal direction, and the waves are usually *light* or *radio waves.*

transverse resolution.   **1.** In a *facsimile receiver,* the dimension that is perpendicular to a *scanning line* and is the smallest recognizable detail of the *image* produced by the shortest *signal* capable of actuating the facsimile receiver under specified conditions.   **2.** In *phototelegraphy,* the dimension that is perpendicular to the *scanning line* and defines the finest detail of the *image* produced. It corresponds to the transverse dimension of the *picture element.* The transverse resolution is equal to the width of the *scanning pitch.* It includes the dimensions and the *luminance* of the finest detail that can be handled by the *system.* The *contrast* of the finest detail must be represented by a signal that corresponds to a *nominal black* or a *nominal white* in *digital systems* in which only two *signal levels* are used.

trap.   See *optical fiber trap; wave trap.*

trap door.   In *computer, data processing,* and *communication security,* a breach that is created intentionally in a *system* for the purpose of collecting, delaying, or destroying *data* and that is done so for unauthorized purposes.

trapped electromagnetic wave.   An *electromagnetic wave* that enters a layer of material that is surrounded on both sides by a layer of material of a lesser *refractive index* such that, if the wave is traveling parallel or nearly parallel to the surfaces of the layers and hence the *incident angles* with the surfaces are greater than the *critical angle,* (i.e., the angles are grazing with the surface) *total internal reflection* will occur on both sides and hence trap the wave. A *dielectric* slab or an *optical fiber* can serve as a wave trap, thus confining the wave to a desired direction of *propagation.* Also see *ducting.*

traveling wave.   A *wave propagating* in a *transmission medium* such that a particular point on the wave, such as a crest, has a velocity determined by the physical properties of the medium. The traveling wave is not reduced to a *standing wave* by *reflections* from a distant boundary. *Modulated lightwaves* in *optical fibers, bundles,* and *cables* are traveling waves. Contrast with *standing wave.*

traveling-wave tube (TWT).   An electron tube, or valve, in which an electron beam interacts with a guided *electromagnetic wave* resulting in amplification at ultra-high *frequencies.* The traveling-wave tube *amplifier* (TWTA) can be used as the final *power* amplifier of a typical *transmitter* in both *communication satellite* and *earth stations.*

tray.   A relatively flat usually rectangular container for housing or mounting *electrical* or *lightwave circuit components* and their interconnecting *cables,* wires, or *fibers.*

TREE.   *Transient radiation effects on electronics.*

tree network.   A *network* configuration in which there is one and only one *path* between any two *nodes.* See Figure T-13.

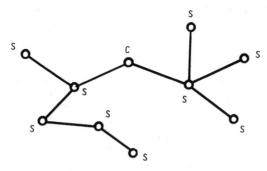

T-13. A **tree network** with a *control station.*

tremendously high frequency (THF). A *frequency* that lies in the range from 300 GHz to 3000 GHz. The *alphabetic* designator of the range is THF. The numeric designator of the range is 12. Also see *frequency spectrum designation.*

triad. A group of three *binary digits* that can be operated on or treated as a single entity by electronic circuits.

trials. See *acceptance trials.*

triangular-cored optical fiber. An *optical fiber* consisting of a *core* whose cross section is shaped like a triangle with bowed convex sides placed in a hollow *jacket* or *cladding* tube such that only the vertices of the core touch the inner walls of the jacket or cladding, with air surrounding the core. See Figure T-14.

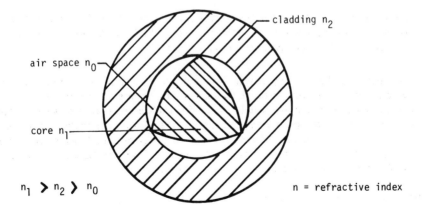

T-14. A **triangular-cored optical fiber** with airspace between *core* and *cladding.*

triangular random noise. *Random noise* that has a *spectral frequency* distribution in which the *noise power* per unit *bandwidth* is proportional to the square of the frequency.

triangulation. 1. *Direction finding* by either *intersection* or *resection*. 2. The *procedure* used to obtain a *fix* on a *transmitter* by plotting the *bearings* of the transmitter on a map from the plotted positions of the *stations* that are taking and reporting the bearings and obtaining the location of the *intersection* of those bearings. Instead of a map, tables of longitude and latitude can be used or the intersection can be calculated using the known positions and the bearing angles. The intersection is an area that is common to two or more sectors that are defined by the bearings that are taken. 3. A survey process in which accurate surveying and mapping is obtained from systematic point-to-point angular and distance measurements from which triangles are constructed and checked for closure. In *satellite communication systems, earth station* pointing angles and the accurately measured distance between *fixed earth stations* may be used for obtaining *antenna azimuth* and *elevation angles.* Also see *trilateration.* See *strobe triangulation.*

triangulation net. A special *communication net* established for handling *triangulation information.* The net is required to report the *bearing* of a *source* of *radiation,* moving or fixed, from two or more *stations* so that the position of the source may be determined. The position of the *stations* in the net are all known or are reported if they are mobile. The times at which the bearings are taken are also reported for use in connection with moving sources. If the amount of *traffic* is likely to be large the triangulation net may be separate from other communication and *reporting nets.*

tributary station. In a *data network,* any *station* other than the *control station,* particularly in a *multipoint connection* in which *basic mode link control procedures* are used. See *dual access tributary station.*

trilateration. A land survey process in which accurate mapping is obtained from systematic point-to-point distance (range) measurements. A minimum of three different measurements are usually made for each point that is surveyed. The distances between the points have to match in the form of triangles. In *satellite communications,* a *satellite ranging transponder* may be used to assist in accomplishing the task of locating points by trilateration. Points on different continents can be surveyed by the method. Also see *triangulation.*

trip. See *ring trip; round trip.*

trip delay time. See *round-trip delay time.*

triple mirror. Three reflecting surfaces, mutually at right angles to each other, arranged like the inside corner of a cube. The triple mirror may be constructed of solid glass, in which case the *transmitting* face is normal to the diagonal of the cube, or it may consist of the three plane *mirrors* supported in a precisely constructed metal framework. The triple reflector has a constant deviation of 180° for all *angles of incidence;* hence, a *ray* of *light* incident from any angle is reflected back parallel to itself. Synonymous with *corner-cube reflector, corner reflector; retrodirective reflector.*

Trojan horse. In *computer* and *communication security,* a *computer program* that is apparently or actually useful and at the same time contains a *trap door.*

tropopause. The transition zone between the *stratosphere* and the *troposphere.* The tropopause usually occurs at an altitude of about 8 000 to 14 000 m in polar and temperate zones, and about 17 000 m in the tropics (torrid zone). Also see *atmosphere; ionosphere; stratosphere; troposphere.*

troposcatter. See *tropospheric scatter.*

troposphere. The *layer* of the earth's *atmosphere,* between the surface of the earth and the *stratosphere,* in which about 80% of the total air mass is concentrated and in which *temperature* normally decreases with altitude. The thickness of the troposphere varies with the season and with the latitude. It is usually 16 km to 18 km over tropical regions and 10 km or less over the poles. Also see *atmosphere; ionosphere; stratosphere; tropopause.*

tropospheric scatter. 1. *Electromagnetic (radio) wave scattering* caused by irregularities or discontinuities in the physical properties of the *troposphere,* thus resulting in the *propagation* of the waves over long distances. 2. A method of transhorizon *radio communication* in which *frequencies* from approximately 350 MHz to approximately 8 400 MHz are used. The propagation mechanism is still not fully understood, though it includes several distinguishable but changeable mechanisms, such as *propagation* by *random reflection, refraction,* and *scattering* from irregularities in the *dielectric (electric permittivity)* gradient and irregularities in the air density of the *troposphere; smooth-earth diffraction;* and *diffraction* over isolated obstacles (*knife-edge effect*). Synonymous with *troposcatter.*

tropospheric wave. A *radio wave* that is *propagated* by *reflection* or *refraction* from a place of abrupt change in the *electric permittivity (dielectric constant),* or its smooth gradient, in the *troposphere.* A *ground wave* may be so altered that new *components* appear to arise from reflection in regions of rapidly changing electric permittivity. When these wave components are distinguishable from the original wave components, they are called tropospheric waves.

trouble-desk facility. In an *automatically-switched telephone network, facilities* such as *test boards* and associated *circuit patch bays* that are used to perform *test operations,* including *busy, talking, listening, signaling, transmission,* and *noise tests.*

true date-time group (TDTG). The original date and time that is assigned to a *message* for identification purposes. The TDTG, though not necessarily the *date-time group* that appears in the message *external heading,* remains identified with a message regardless of the number of times it is *transmitted, encrypted,* or *addressed.*

true field. See *view field.*

true solar day. The interval between two successive *transits* of the sun across a meridian (longitude) on earth. The length of a true solar day varies with the earth's rotation speed and time of year as the earth moves in its orbit around the sun. The true solar day has a mean of 86 404 seconds. Also see *civil day.*

truncation. 1. In *data transmission,* the deliberate removal of intelligence *signal components* without loss of *message* intelligibility. For example, the loss of *digits* from *overflow* or *shift operations* on a *computer,* resulting in less *precise* representation; the loss of *signals* that are outside a limited *bandwidth* where *noise* or *distortion* renders them unreliable; an acceptable reduction in signal bandwidth to obtain a reduction in the *transmitted power* needed to achieve a required *signal-to-noise ratio;* and an acceptable reduction in signal bandwidth to avoid *band* crowding and consequent *interference* from signals in the adjacent *frequencies,* that is, extending the width of the *guard band.* 2. In *computers* and *data processing,* the removal of the ends of *words* and numbers. For example, the removal of the last two *digits* of the number 38.020926 so as to obtain 38.0209, or the removal of the last three letters of the word little so as to obtain lit. See *voice-frequency truncation.*

trunk. A *transmission channel,* or group of channels connected between two *stations* or *nodes* in a *communication system,* both of which are usually *switching* centers or distribution points. *Optical cables,* with associated *light* sources, *photodetectors,* and related equipment, are being used as *trunks.* For example, a connecting *circuit* between *selectors* of different *rank* in an *automatic switching exchange,* between two parts of a *manual exchange,* or between the exchange equipment of two *switching centers.* In a *satellite communication system,* a trunk may consist of a *baseband multiplexed radio link* between two switching centers. Also see *transmission channel.* See *cross-office trunk; interposition trunk; one-way trunk; optical-fiber video trunk; private branch exchange tie trunk; special-grade trunk; tie trunk; toll switching trunk.* See Figure T-15.

trunk call. See *junction call.*

trunk circuit. In *telephone switchboard operations,* a *circuit* that directly connects two *exchanges.*

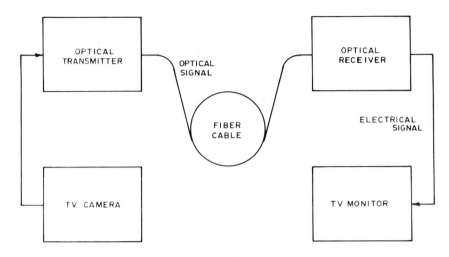

T-15. A **TV optical fiber link.** (Courtesy of the Belden Corp.)

trunk delay working. A *mode* of *telephone switchboard operation* in which all *calls* carried over specified *trunks* are *booked.*

trunk encryption device. A bulk *data encryption* device used to provide *secure communication* over a *wideband digital data transmission link.* It is usually located between the *output* of a *trunk group multiplexer* and a *wideband radio* or *cable facility.*

trunk exchange. In *telephone switchboard operation,* an *exchange* primarily devoted to handling *trunk calls.*

trunk-free condition. In *telephone system operations,* a condition represented by a *signal* sent in the *forward direction* in the interexchange *channel* when the *circuit* has been *released* by the sending *exchange,* that is, when the circuit is considered to be idle and available for a new *call,* or when waiting for release by the other exchange. This condition appears as *clearing signals* at the *user's* (customer's, subscriber's) *interface* or *end-instrument.*

trunk-grade service. The *communication service grade* provided by a *trunk network* under varying *communication traffic* conditions.

trunk group. 1. Two or more *trunks* of the same type between the same two points in a *network.* 2. A specified combination of *trunks* between a pair of *switching facilities.* See *high-usage trunk group.*

trunk group multiplexer. A *time-division multiplexer* that combines the *data* from individual *digital trunk groups* to obtain a higher *data signaling rate* in the *bit stream* for *transmission* over *wideband digital communication links.*

trunk line. See *common trunk line.*

trunk seized condition. In *telephone system operations,* a condition represented by a *signal* sent in the *forward direction* in the interexchange *channel* when a *circuit* is *seized* by a *user, operator,* or by *system* equipment. This condition appears as a *connection-in-progress signal* at the *destination user (called party,* customer, subscriber) *interface* or *end-instrument.*

trunk switch. In a *communication network,* a *switching exchange* that interconnects *trunk channels* in the *network.*

T-stop. The equivalent of a perfectly *transmitting,* circular opening of diameter D such that:

$$TA = \pi(D/2)^2 \text{ or } D = 2(TA/\pi)^{1/2}$$

where A is the area of the *entrance pupil* of the *objective,* T is the *transmittance* of the *lens system,* and $\pi = 3.1416$.

TTL. *Transistor-transistor logic.*

TTY. *Teletypewriter.*

tube. See *cathode-ray tube (CRT); dark-trace tube; storage tube; traveling-wave tube.*

tube photometer. See *photoemissive tube photometer.*

tube splicer. See *loose-tube splicer.*

tumbling. In *display systems,* modifying a two-dimensional *image* of an *object* so that the object appears as if it were turning about an axis that is not perpendicular to the *display surface.* Tumbling is usually performed on a two-dimensional representation of a three-dimensional object, enabling the viewer to obtain a better understanding of the object's form. If the object appears to be turning about an axis that is perpendicular to the display surface, the image is considered to be *rotating.* Also see *rotating.* Contrast with *translating.*

tunable laser. An organic dye or *optical parametric-oscillator laser* whose *emission* can be varied continuously across a broad *spectral* range. Sometimes the term is applied to carbon-dioxide or other *molecular lasers* whose emission can be *tuned* to one of several *wavelengths* (spectral lines).

tunable transmitter. A *radar* or *radio transmitter* in which the *operating frequency* can be altered, usually over a continuous range of frequencies but limited to a specific *bandwidth.* This capability enables frequency correction for possible undesirable frequency drifting, changing to other frequencies to improve *transmission* and *reception,* or changing to other frequencies to avoid *interference* or *jamming.*

tuning. The process of adjusting the *parameters* and *components* of a *circuit* so that it *resonates* at a particular *frequency* or so that the *current* or *voltage* is either maximized or minimized at a specific point in the circuit. Tuning is accomplished by adjusting the *capacitance* or the *inductance*, or both, of elements that are connected to or in the circuit. See *jammer out-tuning; local oscillator tuning.*

turbulence. See *ionospheric turbulence.*

turn-around mixer. In a *satellite communication system,* an *earth station component* that accepts a sample of an *up-link signal,* changes it in *frequency* by a frequency *translation* process, and then passes it through the *station receiver* for *test* purposes. Also see *test loop translator.*

turning flag. In *visual signaling systems,* a large-sized *flag* that may be flown to indicate that a moving ship convoy is about to execute a turn, that is, a change in course (direction). For example, a large-sized E-flag might be used to indicate a simultaneous turn by all ships at a 45° angle to the starboard and an I-flag for a similar turn to port. When the flag is hauled down, the turn is executed by all ships simultaneously in typical situations.

TV optical-fiber link. A *video signal link* that accepts an *electrical* video signal from a *television* camera, converts it into an *optical signal, transmits* it over an *optical cable,* and reconverts or reconstitutes it back to an electrical signal for use in a television monitor or set. See Figure T-16.

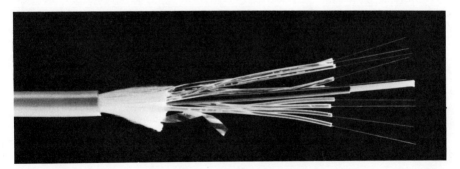

T-16. A Siecor 10-*fiber optical cable.* Each fiber is surrounded by a viscous polyurethane fiber *buffer* to insure that their mechanical and optical properties remain constant in a hostile environment. Each pair provides 672 voice *channels* at 44.7 Mbit/sec in a Fort Wayne, Indiana, installation for a *telephone* **trunk.** (Courtesy of Siecor Optical Cables, Inc.)

TV set. *Television set.*

twin cable. A *cable* composed of two *insulated conductors* that are laid parallel to each other and that are either attached to each other by insulation or are bound together with a common covering.

twinplex telegraphy. See *four-frequency diplex telegraphy.*

twin-sideband transmission. See *independent-sideband transmission.*

twisted ring counter. See *feedback shift register.*

twist strength. The ability of an *optical fiber, bundle,* or *cable* to withstand alternate torsional flexing without breaking fibers or reducing *transmission* capability.

two-adder. See *modulo-two adder.*

two addition. See *modulo-two addition.*

two-body problem. The problem in *celestial mechanics* that is concerned with the relative motion of two point masses that are influenced only by their mutual gravitational attraction and their inital velocities relative to each other or relative to a fixed frame of reference. For example, the undisturbed motion of a parent body and its satellite. The motion is normally an elliptical motion with one body at one of the foci of the ellipse. This situation is nearly reproduced in the solar system for solar orbits. The motion occurs in conic sections (circle, ellipse, parabola, hyperbola, or straight line) according to Kepler's and Newton's laws of motion. In the two-body problem, deviations caused by the attraction of other bodies are called perturbations. Also see *three-body problem; n-body problem; restricted circular three-body problem.*

two-condition telegraphy. *Telegraphy* or *data transmission* in which only two *significant conditions* are used in forming the *transmitted signals.* For example, telegraphy in which a simple on and off *signal* is used, that is, *electric current* and no-current conditions, two different *frequencies* are used to indicate *binary digits,* or positive and negative currents are used with zero-current condition not permitted.

two-frequency half-duplex. Pertaining to a *communication circuit* with a two-way simultaneous *traffic capacity* in which different *frequencies* are used for the two directions of *transmission.* Synonymous with *two-frequency simplex.*

two-frequency simplex. See *two-frequency half-duplex.*

two independent-sideband carrier. A *carrier wave* that has two *sidebands* each of which is independent of each other even though they are sidebands of the same carrier.

two independent-sideband transmission. *Transmission* in which a *carrier* is used that has two *sidebands* that are independent of each other even though they are sidebands of the same carrier. The center frequency of the independent sidebands may not be the same as the carrier frequency.

two-level optical signal. A *modulated lightwave carrier* that is at either one of two different *intensities* or *power-density* levels at any given instant. For example, a carrier that is either on or off depending on whether a 1 or a 0 is being *transmitted.*

two-operator period watch. A *communication watch* for a period of time that is based on the availability of two *operators* at the *station.* Also see *continuous communication watch; single-operator period watch.*

two-pilot regulation. In *frequency-division multiplexed (FDM) systems,* the use of two *pilot frequencies* within a *transmitted frequency band* so that the change in *attenuation* due to the twisting of *conductor pairs* can be detected and compensated.

two-source frequency keying. See *frequency exchange signaling.*

two-tone keying. 1. In *telegraph systems, keying* in which a *transmission path* is used that is composed of two *channels* in the same direction, one for *transmitting* the 0 or *space* for *binary modulation* and the other for transmitting the 1 or *mark* for the same modulation. 2. *Keying* in which the *modulating wave* causes the *carrier* to be *modulated* with one single tone for the *mark condition* and modulated with a different single tone for the *space condition.* Synonymous with *two-tone telegraph.* Also see *frequency shift keying; voice-frequency telegraph.*

two-tone telegraph. See *two-tone keying.*

two-tone test signal. See *composite two-tone test signal.*

two-way alternate communication. A *mode* of *operation* of a *communication system* in which *data* or *information* may be *transferred* in both directions, such as from *source* to *sink* and vice versa, one direction at a time. Two-way alternate communication *traffic* is usually handled on a *half-duplex* or two-way *simplex* link. Thus, one in which one user or subscriber claims the *channel* in order to *transmit* and the other subscriber cannot interrupt and transmit until the first has switched over. Lightweight mobile equipment sometimes consists of a *transmitter-receiver* in which some *circuits* are used for both transmitting and receiving, requiring the use of a push-to-talk *switch.* In *radio telegraph* or *data transmission systems,* two-way alternate communication may consist either of the use of a single *frequency, time slot,* or *code address* for *transmission,* and another frequency, time slot, or code address for *reception,* or the use of the same frequency, time slot, or code address for both transmission and reception. In *wire telegraph systems, simplex operation* may be used over either a *half-duplex circuit* or over a *neutral direct-current circuit.* Synonymous with *either-way communication; over-over communication; over-over mode; simplex communication; simplex operation; simplex transmission; single-simplex operation.*

two-way alternate operation. See *half-duplex operation.*

two-way radar equation.   An equation that expresses the *peak* or *average power signal* that is returned to a *radar antenna terminal* upon *reflection* from an object (target) as a function of *circuit* and *transmission medium parameters, transmitted power, antenna gain, wavelength*, object area, and *range*.   Also see *one-way radio equation; self-screening range equation*.

two-way simultaneous communication.   A mode of operation of a *communication system* in which *data* or *information* may be transferred in both directions (i.e., between *source* and *sink*) at the same time.   Synonymous with *both-way communication; duplex communication; duplex operation*.

two-way simultaneous operation.   See *duplex operation*.

two-wire circuit.   1. A *circuit* formed by two metallic *conductors* that are *insulated* from each other.   This is in contrast to a *four-wire circuit*.   2. A *circuit* in which one *line* or *channel* is used for *communication* in both directions.

TWT.   *Traveling-wave tube*.

TWX.   *Teletypewriter Exchange Service*.

Twyman-Green interferometer.   An *interferometer* in which the observer or *user* sees a contour map of the emergent *electromagnetic wavefront* in terms of the *wavelength* of the *light* used by or entering the *system*.

U

UHF. *Ultrahigh frequency.*

U-link bay. A rack or *panel* of *connectors* at which it is possible to connect to or break into any *signal line* that enters or leaves a *station.* It is used for *test* purposes.

ultrafiche. *Microfiche* that contains *images* that have an extremely small *reduction ratio,* such as less than 1:50. A high *blowback ratio* is required to render the images legible to the unaided eye.

ultrahigh frequency (UHF). A *frequency* that lies in the range from 300 MHz to 3 GHz. The *alphabetic* designator of the range is UHF. The numeric designator of the range is 9. Also see *frequency spectrum designation.*

ultrasonic equipment. Equipment used to generate *radio frequency* energy and to use that energy to excite or drive an electromechanical *transducer* for the production of high-frequency *sound waves* for industrial, scientific, medical, *communication,* or other purposes.

ultraviolet fiber optics. *Fiber optics* involving the use of *ultraviolet (UV) light-conducting components* designed to *transmit electromagnetic waves* shorter in *wavelength* than the waves in the visible region of the spectrum. Primary applications include medical technology, medicine, physics, materials testing, photochemistry, genetics, and many other fields. *Optical fibers* with high UV *transmittance* have been developed and are being used.

ultraviolet light. Rays of *electromagnetic radiant energy* immediately beyond the violet end of the *visible spectrum* and in the order of 390 to 100 nm in *wavelength.*

ultraviolet light guide. Special *optical* materials in various geometric shapes that have the special capability of transmitting *light* in the *ultraviolet* (UV) region of the *spectrum,* i.e., with a *wavelength* of 200 to 300 nm which is less than the wavelength of the *visible spectrum* used in *fiber optics,* about 0.9 to 1.0 *micron.* UV *light guides* are primarily used in medicine, biochemistry, microscopy, physiology, and medical engineering.

unaligned bundle. See *incoherent bundle.*

unavailability. A measure of the degree to which a *system, subsystem,* or *component* is not operable and is not in a committable or usable state at the start of a *mission,* particularly when the mission is called for at an unknown or *random* instant of time. The conditions that determine the operability and committability must be specified. Also see *availability.*

1003

unavailability procedure. See *circuit unavailability procedure.*

unbalanced line. A *transmission line* in which the magnitudes of the *signal voltages* on the two *conductors* are not equal with respect to ground. For example, a *coaxial cable,* since the inner conductor is shielded by the outer conductor they both cannot be equal with respect to *ground,* unless they are both grounded, in which case they cannot be used for *signals* except as ground returns.

unbalanced modulator. A *modulator* in which the *modulation factor* is different for the alternate half-cycles of the *carrier wave.* Synonymous with *asymmetrical modulator.* Also see *modulation factor.*

unbalanced wire circuit. A *circuit* with two sides (forward and return) that are inherently *electrically* unlike. For example, a *coaxial cable,* a single wire and a *ground return,* two wires of different size or material, or a circuit in which two identical sides take different *paths.*

uncoordinated bearing. A *bearing* determined by a single *direction-finding station.*

undercompensated optical fiber. An *optical fiber* whose *refractive-index profile* is adjusted so that the higher-order *propagation modes* arrive after the lower-order modes, as in the case of uncompensated fiber. The higher-order modes have higher *eigenvalues* in the solution of the *wave equations.* Also see *compensated optical fiber* and *overcompensated optical fiber.*

underlap. In *facsimile systems,* a defect in reproduction when the width of the *scanning line* is less than the *scanning pitch.*

underwater telephone. A *telephone* that can be used by one or more parties to *communicate* underwater, using either *sound, electric,* or *electromagnetic transmission.* Underwater telephones usually use *frequency-modulated (FM) carriers.*

undetected error rate. See *residual error rate.*

undisturbed day. A day in which *sunspot activities* or *ionospheric disturbances* do not interrupt *radio communication.*

undulator. A *receiver* used in *Morse telegraph systems* in which a two-position *stylus* feeds ink to a continuously moving paper tape in conformity with a two *significant-condition* incoming *signal,* thus creating a legible record. The instrument records *high-speed Morse* signals as a continuous ink line on a paper tape driven at constant speed. The pen moves side to side across the tape for *mark* and *space* signals and the long and short undulations can be converted to *text* by trained *operators.*

unidirectional antenna. An *antenna* that is intended to *radiate* a *wave* in one direction only at any given moment. To change the direction the antenna must be rotated or reoriented.

unidirectional channel.   See *one-way-only channel.*

unidirectional coupler.   A *directional coupler* that has *terminals* for sampling *waves* in only one direction in a *transmission line.*

unidirectional operation.   A method of operating a *transmission system* in one direction only between *terminals* or *stations,* one of which is a *transmitter* and the other a *receiver.*

unidirectional transmission.   A method of *transmission* between *terminals,* one of which can only serve as a *transmitter* and the other only as a *receiver.*

uniform density lens.   A layered *lens,* or blank, of which one layer is clear and the other is of *absorptive*-type glass; the clear portion is surfaced to the desired curvature, while the thickness of the tinted layer remains constant, which results in a lens with the same shade (i.e., *transmittance*) at the center as at the periphery.

uniform encoding.   An *analog-to-digital* conversion process in which all of the *quantization* subrange values are equal.   Synonymous with *uniform quantizing.* Also see *analog encoding; quantization; quantization level.*

uniform-illumination Cassegrain.   Pertaining to an *antenna reflector* shape in which the *field* pattern law is linear across the effective antenna area.   Synonymous with *shaped-reflector Cassegrain.*

uniform-index profile.   In materials used for *optical transmission,* a uniform linearly decreasing *refractive index* from the inside of the *transmission medium* radially toward the outside.

uniform-index-profile fiber.   A *graded-index optical fiber* in which the *refractive index* varies linearly from the center of the fiber radially to the outside surface, with a lower index at the outside surface.   Also see *graded-index fiber.*

uniform lambertian distribution.   A *lambertian distribution* that is uniform, or constant, over a specified surface.

uniformly distributed constant amplitude-frequency spectrum.   See *white noise.*

uniform plane-polarized electromagnetic wave.   A *plane-polarized electromagnetic wave* whose *electric* and *magnetic field vector* magnitudes *are independent* of the coordinate direction perpendicular to the direction of *propagation;* i.e., they are independent of the transverse coordinates but are dependent on the longitudinal coordinates in the direction of propagation.

uniform quantizing.   See *uniform encoding.*

uniform transmission line. A *transmission line* whose *electrical* properties (*resistance, inductance, capacitance*) for one segment of the line are the same as for any other segment of the same length along the line. Expressed mathematically, $dz/dl = a$, where dz is the elemental change in *impedance* over the elemental length dl and a is a constant. This must hold for all points along the line. For example, a *coaxial cable*, a *twisted pair* of *conductors*, or a single conductor at constant height above ground, without change in geometry, materials, or construction along their length. If a line has discontinuities in its electrical properties along its length, special provision can be made for preventing reflection of *waves* in the line, such as by *termination* in a *characteristic impedance* at points of discontinuity. In this case, the line will operate as, and appear to be, a uniform transmission line. Also see Figure C-10.

unilateral control system. See *unilateral synchronization system.*

unilateral synchronization system. A *synchronization* control system between two locations in which the *clock* at one location controls the clock at a second location, but the clock at the second location does not control the clock at the first location. Synonymous with *unilateral control system.*

unintelligible crosstalk. *Crosstalk* that gives rise to unintelligible sounds.

union. See *International Telecommunication Union (ITU).*

union gate. See *OR gate.*

unipolar. Pertaining to a method of *transmitting signals* with one polarity, that is, positive *voltage* or negative voltage signals, but not both. Usually, a *mark* is represented by an *electric current* in one direction, that is of one polarity, and a *space* is represented by the absence of current. The scheme is used in *single-current signaling.* Also see *bipolar.*

unipolar telegraphy. See *single-current signaling.*

unipolar transmission. See *single-current signaling.*

unit. See *airborne direction-finding unit; answer-back unit; central processing unit (CPU); circuit switching unit (CSU); communication processor unit (CPU); dead-zone unit; DX signaling unit; functional unit; input unit; noise measurement unit; output unit; raster unit; signal unit (SU); teletypewriter control unit; track-and-hold unit; volume unit (VU); X-unit (XU).*

unit code. See *n-unit code.*

unit code alphabet. See *n-unit code alphabet.*

unit disparity binary code. A *code* in which there is only a one *bit* difference between the quantity of bits that represent 1 and the quantity of bits that represent 0 in a *signal* sequence. This arangement minimizes the long-term *direct-current (DC) component* of the *signal* in the *line*.

unit-distance code. An unweighted *code* that changes by only one *bit* in one of the bit positions when going from one number to the next in a sequence of numbers. Use of one of the many unit-distance codes can minimize errors at *symbol* transition points when converting *analog* quantities into *digital* quantities. Also see *gray code; signal distance.*

unit element. In the representation of a *character*, a *signal element* that has a duration (length) equal to the *unit interval.*

unit indicator. See *signal unit indicator.*

unit interval. In a *system* in which *isochronous modulation* is used, an interval of time such that the durations (lengths) of *significant intervals* of the *modulation code* are all whole multiples of this interval. It is the shortest interval between *significant instants.* Also see *signal element; significant instant.*

unit of information content. See *natural unit of information content (nat).*

unit routing indicator. See *mobile unit routing indicator.*

unit solid angle. A steradian, defined as the solid angle that intercepts $1/4\pi$ of the surface of a sphere that has the vertex (apex) of the solid angle as its center. Thus, 4π steradians of solid angle intercept the entire surrounding sphere. Solid angles are measured in terms of the fraction of the surface of the surrounding sphere intercepted by the sidewalls of the solid angle, in contrast to degrees or radians for plane angles, in which an angle of 2π radians intercepts a complete circle. Solid angles are of interest in *coupling* a *light beam* confined to a given solid angle, thus specifying the *divergence* of the *rays* of the beam, into an *optical fiber.* Also see *aperture ratio.*

unit string. A *string* that consists of only one entity, such as one *bit* or one letter.

universal receiver-transmitter. In *data communications,* a *circuit* or device that is used in *asynchronous, synchronous,* or synchronous-asychronous applications to provide the *logic* to enable the *reception* of *data* in *serial* fashion and the *transmission* of the same data in *parallel* fashion, or vice versa. It is usually a *full-duplex circuit.*

universal time. See *Greenwich mean time.*

unmodulated continuous-wave jamming. *Jamming* by means of an unmodulated *carrier wave (CW) signal.* It may be used for *radar, communication, direction-finding, guided missile control,* and other types of jamming. The signal can be used for *spot jamming* or *sweep jamming.* A CW signal has virtually no *bandwidth,* thus giving it an appearance similar to *spot noise* on a *radar screen.*

unnumbered command. In *data transmission,* a *command* that does not contain sequence numbers in the *control field.* Also see *unnumbered response.*

unnumbered response. In *data transmission,* a *response* that does not contain sequence numbers in the *control field.* Also see *unnumbered command.*

unobtainable tone. See *number-unobtainable tone.*

unrepeated loop. A *loop* that does not make use of *repeaters* to *amplify signals* that *propagate* within the loop.

unretrievable remotely piloted vehicle. In *communication systems,* a *mobile station* that is on board a vehicle that is controlled by *signals* from another *station.* The vehicle is not retrieved either to be used again or to retrieve any of the on board *data.* Data obtained by the station in the vehicle is *relayed, retransmitted,* or *telemetered.*

unshift-on-space. A means by which a *telegraph receiver,* on receiving the *space signal,* is caused to *shift* from the *figures case* to the *letters case* while the *printing position* is advanced by one *character pitch* but without printing.

unsuccessful call. An *access attempt* that does not result in the establishment of a *connection,* that is, it does not result in *access success.*

unvoiced sound. A sound created by that part of the human speech production organs where the sounds are generated by forcing air through a movable constriction of the vocal tract without adding a sound from a vibrating vocal cord. Also see *voiced sound.*

up-converter. A device that converts an *input signal* with a given *frequency* to an *output signal* with a higher frequency, usually without changing the type of *modulation* and without loss of the *information content* of the signal. It is the converse of a *down-converter.* For example, in *satellite communication systems,* a *satellite station* or *earth station* uses an up-converter to *translate* a number of *baseband trunks* to a higher *carrier* frequency usually without changing the *modulation* method or the *occupied bandwidth.*

uplink. The portion of a *communication link* that is used for the *transmission* of *signals* from an *earth station* to a *satellitte station* or airborne platform. The link from earth station to satellite station usually includes the earth station *transmitter* and *antenna,* the earth-satellite *propagation path,* and the satellite station antenna and *receiver.* It is the converse of a *downlink.*

upper case. See *figure case.*

upper sideband. The *sideband* that has a higher *frequency* than the *carrier frequency.* Also see *lower sideband.*

upright position. See *erect position.*

urgency signal. A *signal* used to indicate that the *calling station* has a *message* to *transmit* that concerns the safety of persons and equipment. Usually the urgency signal is transmitted by an *aircraft station,* a *ship station,* or other *mobile station.* The urgency signal has priority over all other *communication traffic* other than *distress traffic.* For example, a *carrier wave (CW)* urgency signal is XXX transmitted three times. In voice, an urgency signal is the word PAN transmitted three times. Also see *urgency traffic.*

urgency traffic. All *messages* that contain *information* concerning the safety of persons and the protection of equipment. For example, a message from a *mobile station* with persons on board who will be in need of medical assistance in the near future or a message to a mobile station warning of eminent danger. Urgency traffic takes *precedence* over all other traffic except *distress traffic.* Also see *urgency signal.*

usable frequency. See *lowest usable frequency.*

usable length. See *scanning line usable length.*

usage recorder. See *traffic usage recorder.*

usage register. See *traffic usage register.*

useful high frequency. See *lowest useful high-frequency (LUF).*

useful line. See *available line.*

user. **1.** A person, process, device, *program,* or *system* that makes use of another person, process, device, program, or system. For example, a person who uses an *application network* to process or exchange *data,* a *computer* that uses a *communication network* to transfer a program to another computer, the *transducer* of a *sensor* that uses a *radio link* to *telemeter data* to a *receiving station,* a *calling party,* or a *facsimile transmitter* that uses a communication *channel* to *transmit* the contents of a document. **2.** A person, organization, or other entity that uses the services provided by a *communication system* for the *transfer* of *information* to others. A user may serve as the *source* or final destination of *information,* or both. **3.** *Hardware, software,* or a person that uses an *application network* for *data processing* and *information* exchange. **4.** A *subsystem* that makes use of the *system* of which it is a part. See *AUTODIN user; AUTOVON user; called user; common user; destination user; orignating user; sole user; source user; special-grade user.* See Figure U-1.

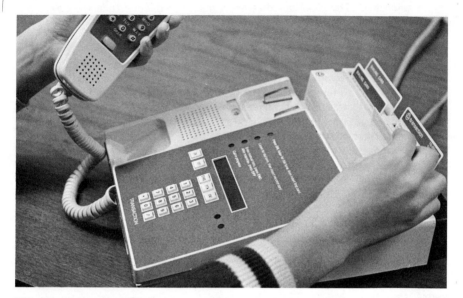

U-1. The Transaction II® *telephone,* a **user** *end-instrument* (for check verification, electronic fund transfer, and other *data transfers*) controlled by a *microprocessor.* (Courtesy of Bell Laboratories.)

user circuit. See *common-user circuit; exclusive-user circuit; sole-user circuit.*

user-class indicator. In a *communication system, information* that is sent in the *forward direction* and indicates the *user service class* of the *source user* (calling subscriber, *calling party,* originator, calling customer).

user communications. See *common-user communications.*

user coordinate. In *display systems,* a coordinate expressed in a coordinate system that is convenient for a *user* and independent of *device coordinates.* User coordinates are usually in a *virtual space* that is specified by the user, thus enabling *image* spatial manipulation *operations* to be performed, such as *translating, rotating, isolating, scaling, scissoring, scrolling, tumbling, mirroring, rubber-banding, rolling,* and *zooming.* Also see *device coordinate; real-world coordinate.*

user facility. In *communications,* a *facility* that is on a *user's* premises and is operated, leased, owned, or protected by the user. See *user service.* See Figure U-2.

user group. See *closed user group.*

user group with outgoing access. See *closed user group with outgoing access.*

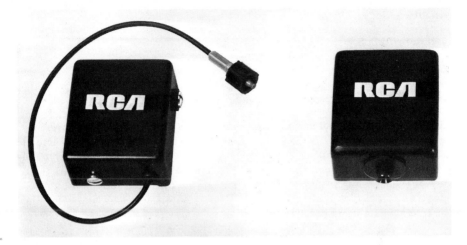

U-2.   *Transmitter* and *receiver modules* for a *fiber optic digital data link* user facility.
(Courtesy of RCA Electro-Optics and Devices.)

user identification.   In an *automatically-switched telephone network*, the number
used by the equipment to identify a *user's* (customer's, subscriber's) *end-instrument*.   For example, a three-*digit area code*, a three-digit exchange number, and a
four-digit *line* or *private branch exchange (PBX)* number, with perhaps an *extension* number for each end-instrument connected to the PBX.   Synonymous with
customer identification; subscriber identification.

user information.   *Information* that is *transferred* across the functional *interface*
from a *source user* to a *communication system* for the purpose of ultimate delivery
of the information to a *destination user.*   In *data communication systems,* the
user information includes *user overhead information.*

user information bit.   A *bit* that is *transferred* across the functional *interface*
from a *source user* to a *communication system* for the purpose of ultimate delivery
of the bit to a *destination user.*   User information bits do not include the *overhead
bits* that originate within, or have their primary functional effect within, the
communication system.   Bits that are introduced into a *message* by the user to
represent *user overhead information* are included.

user information block.   A *block* that contains at least one *user information bit.*

user language.   1. A *natural language* used by persons in a specific field, such as
engineering, medicine, law, or divine revelation, for developing or using another
special purpose language.   For example, an engineering language that is used to
develop a *computer programming language* such as *FORTRAN.* 2. In *communications,* a *language* that is used by a *user* of a *communication system.*

user line. See *line loop.*

user network. See *common-user network.*

user overhead. In a *communication system message,* the part of *overhead information,* such as the name and address of the addressee of the message, that is provided by the *source user.* Also see *system overhead.*

user part. A functional part of a *common-channel signaling system* that *transmits messages* to, and *receives* messages from, the *message transfer part.* There are different types or *user* parts for different systems. For example, in *telephone systems* and *data communication systems,* each user part is specific to a particular use of the signaling system. Thus, a user may be furnished a *dial tone,* a *called-party busy signal,* or a called-party *ringing tone,* but the user may not be furnished an intermediate-trunk-not-available signal or a *supervisory signal.* Also see *message transfer part.*

user service. A set of functions each of which is a part of a *data transmission service* or *facility* that is made available on demand to a *user.* They are provided to the user by a *system* or organization, such as a *communication system.* Some *communication facilities* may be available on a per *call* basis, and others may be assigned for an agreed period at the request of the *user.* Synonymous with *user facility.* See *common-user service; four-wire subset user service; general-purpose user service.*

user service class. A class (category) of *data transmission service* provided by a *communication system,* such as a *public data network,* in which the *data signaling rate,* the *terminal operating mode,* the *data code* structure, and other features, facilities, and services, are standardized.

user set. The *communication equipment,* exclusive of connecting *lines,* that is located on, used by, owned by, leased by, or protected by a *user.* For example, a *private branch exchange (PBX),* or an *end-instrument,* such as a *telephone, teletypewriter, television set,* or *radio set.* Synonymous with *customer set; subscriber set.*

user signaling rate. See *maximum user signaling rate.*

user terminal. An *input-output* device with which a *user* may *communicate* with another user via a *communication system.*

user-to-user service. In *communication systems,* a service in which two or more *users* (subscribers, customers) are mutually connected continuously over an extended period of time and in such a manner that it appears to the users that they are the only users of the communication system or *network* to which they are connected.

UTC. *Universal time coordinated.* See *coordinated time scale.*

utility land station. See *aeronautical utility land station.*

utility load. See nonoperational load.

utility mobile station. See *aeronautical utility mobile station.*

V

vacancy defect. In the somewhat ordered array of atoms and molecules in *optical-fiber* material, a site at which an atom or molecule is missing in the array. The defect can serve as a *scattering center,* causing *diffusion,* heating, *absorption,* and resultant *attenuation.* Also see *interstitial defect.* See Figure V-1.

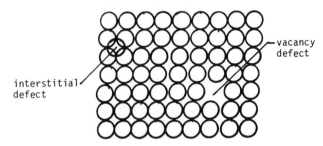

V-1. Molecular structure of glass for an *optical fiber* showing an interstitial and a **vacancy** defect.

valence band. In a *semiconductor,* the range of *electron* energy, lower than that of the *conduction band,* possessed by electrons that are held bound to an atom of the material, thus reducing *conductivity* for *electric currents* even under the influence of an applied *electric field.* When electron energies are raised (e.g., by thermal excitation or by *phonons*), electrons with the highest energy levels of the valence band are raised to the lower energy levels of the *conduction band,* thus leaving *holes* in the atoms whose electrons remain in the valence band. The valence band energy level is below the *conduction* band. In a conducting material (e.g., copper, aluminum, silver, gold, and lead), the valence band energy level is lower than in nonconductors, i.e., insulators, thus allowing the electrons to be more free to move as an *electric* current.

validation. The process of insuring that *test* results reach the proper level of *accuracy, precision,* and relevancy.

value. See *assumed value; peak-to-peak value.*

Van Allen belt. Two concentric *radiation-ionized* regions that are above the earth's equator and consist of *protons, electrons, ions,* and accompanying radiation at extremely high energy levels, that have been captured by the earth's *magnetic field.* The quantity, density, and energy level of the particles and radiation fluctuate with *solar activity.* The more energetic inner belt has a maximum radiation and particle density at about 3000 km above the equator and the outer belt has a maximum at about 16 000 km.

vapor deposition process. See *modified chemical vapor-deposition process; plasma-activated chemical-vapor deposition process.*

vapor-phase oxidation process. See *axial vapor phase oxidation process; chemical vapor-phase oxidation process; inside vapor-phase oxidation process; modified inside vapor-phase oxidation process; outside vapor-phase oxidation process.*

vapor recording. See *ink vapor recording.*

variable. See *analog variable; key variable; switching variable.*

variable function generator. In an *analog computing system,* a *function generator* in which the *function* that it generates may be set by the *user* before or during computation.

variable generator. See *key variable generator.*

variable logic. See *programmable logic.*

variable optical attenuator. See *continuous variable optical attenuator; stepwise variable optical attenuator.*

variable polarization. In an *electromagnetic wave, polarization* that can be varied at a given point in space and time by controlling the *source,* or by *operating* in the wave while it is *propagating,* such as by means of *electric* or *magnetic fields* or changing the *parameters* of the *transmission medium.*

variable precision coding compaction. *Data compaction* in which the *precision* required of a set of *data* can vary with the magnitude of an evaluated *function,* with time, with the value of the independent variable, or with some other *parameter.* The *coding* can be made to vary with requirements. For example, in the countdown of a rocket launch, *timing signals* every 15 minutes are sufficient several days or hours before a launch. As time passes and events become critical, intervals between timing signals must become shorter, until at launch fractions of a second become very significant. Thus, only a few signals need to be sent at certain times, enabling those to be compacted and thus reduce *storage* and *transmission* requirements.

variable-pulse recurrent-frequency radar. A *radar* that has a *pulse repetition rate (PRR)* that can be varied by a small amount about its nominal operating rate. This capability can be used to reduce *interference* from adjacent radars and other *sources* of *radiation,* to escape some forms of *jamming,* and to provide some protection against *deception* by using the variation as an *electronic counter-countermeasure (ECCM).* The PRR variation is normally about ±10%.

variable-slope delta modulation. See *continuously-variable-slope delta (CVSD) modulation.*

variable-spacing encryption. In the *operation* of certain *cryptoequipment*, *encryption* in which the normal spacing between *words* or *groups* is altered in a *random* manner during encryption.

variable time (VT). 1. Pertaining to an event, such as a *pulse,* that occurs in a time interval the duration (length) of which can be controlled or allowed to vary at *random.* 2. Pertaining to an event that occurs at a given instant and the *occurrence time* of which can be controlled.

variable-tolerance-band compaction. *Data compaction* in which several *discrete bands* are used to specify the operational limits of a quantity or *parameter.* For example, in the *transmission* of *data,* a prior arrangement can be made such that a specified variable can be assumed to be within a given range, and hence transmission of its value need not be made, unless the variable is greater or less than the band values, in which case a transmission is made for only as long as the variable remains outside the limits of the band. Thus, a transmission is made only when the value is abnormal, thus conserving transmission and *storage* requirements that would be necessary if the absolute value of the parameter were to be *transmitted* at regular intervals.

variation. See *dynamic variation; net loss variation.*

variation monitor. In a *communication system,* a device that is used for sensing deviations in *voltage, current, frequency, temperature,* or other *parameters* and is capable of initiating an action to restore the parameter to a nominal value, and perhaps also providing an alarm when the variation, that is, the departure from the nominal value, exceeds a specified value. For example, a device that *monitors* a *voltage source,* disconnects the source if the voltage level changes by a specified amount, reconnects the *load* to another voltage source, turns on a red light, and sounds a buzzer. Thus, power continuity is preserved within required levels and attendants are notified of the situation.

V-band. 1. An obsolete designation for a *band* of *frequencies* in the range from 46 GHz to 56 GHz. This band was divided into 5 subbands, designated VA to VE, each band being 2 GHz wide. 2. An obsolete designation for *frequencies* in the range from 40 GHz to 60 GHz between the old Q-band and the old O-band.

vector. 1. A *parameter* or variable that possesses both magnitude (*amplitude*) and direction, and that may or may not be a function of time. For example, velocity, *electric field,* displacement, or *refractive index gradient.* A *scalar* possesses only magnitude, for example, speed, mass, volume, or *signal-to-noise ratio.* 2. In *direction finding (DF), communication,* and navigation, to head or steer in a given direction. Synonymous with *course; steer.* See *absolute vector; electric vector; magnetic vector; Poynting vector; proportional vector; relative vector.*

vector generator. A *functional unit,* such as a *display device* or a *computer program,* that generates directed *line* segments. Short directed line segments connected in sequence may be used by a *curve generator* to generate curves for presentation as a *display element, display group,* or *display image* in the *display space* on the *display surface* of a *display device,* such as on a screen, a *fiberscope faceplate,* an *LED* or *gas panel,* or the surface of a *plotter.*

vee value. See *abbe constant.*

vehicle. See *unretrievable remotely piloted vehicle.*

vehicle harness. An assembly of interconnected equipment designed to control a *radio* and an *intercom system* on a vehicle and to provide other specified *communication facilities* on board the vehicle.

velocity. See *electromagnetic wave velocity; group velocity; phase-front velocity; phase velocity; third cosmic velocity.*

velocity gate stealing. In *radar systems,* the process in which the radial velocity *gate* in *Doppler radar* is caused to lose its ability to accurately determine the radial component of velocity of a tracked object (target).

velocity of light. The speed and direction (vector) of *monochromatic lightwaves,* i.e., the *phase velocity.* The velocity of light in a vacuum is 299,792.5 km/sec. In a vacuum, the velocity of all *frequencies* or *wavelengths* is the same. The phase velocity in a *medium* is given by:

$$v_p = c_0/n$$

where *n* is the *refractive index* of the medium and c_0 is the velocity of light in a vacuum, given above. Also see *group velocity.*

verified off-hook. In *telephone systems,* a *service* provided by a device inserted on each end of a *transmission circuit* for the purpose of verifying *supervisory signals* on the circuit. *Off-hook* service is a telephone service that establishes a *connection* from *calling party* to *called party* simply by removing the *phone* from its hook, cradle, pedestal, or switch and that *signals* the called party's *end-instrument* when it is removed.

verification. See *message verification.*

vernal equinox. The line of intersection of the celestial *equatorial plane* and the *ecliptic plane,* at which the sun passes from the southern hemisphere into the northern hemisphere. This intersection occurs about March 21, bringing spring to the northern hemisphere and autumn to the southern hemisphere.

vertex. In an *optical system,* the point of intersection of the *optical axis* with any *optical surface* in the system. See *node.*

vertical cover. The vertical angle (elevation) that an *electromagnetic wave emitter (antenna)* is capable of *scanning* or *illuminating.* Also see *horizontal cover.*

vertical coverage diagram. A *graphic* pattern that shows the distribution of *power* of a *radio* or *radar signal* in a vertical plane. The pattern is described in terms of altitude and range. If the *transmitter antenna* is considered to be at the origin or center of a polar coordinate system, then the length of a line from the origin to a perimeter of the pattern, that is, to any point on the pattern, is directly proportional to the *power* per *unit solid angle* in the direction in which the line is drawn. Thus, the pattern is usually drawn as the locus of the points where the energy density, that is the *power density,* is a constant or is one-half of the maximum value for the given range. The diagram may be drawn for any vertical plane. It is usually measured empirically. It may also be calculated from theoretical functions of known *parameters.*

vertically-polarized electromagnetic wave. A *uniform plane-polarized electromagnetic wave* in which the *electric field vector* is always and everywhere vertical, and hence the *polarization plane* is always vertical, the *magnetic field vector* is always horizontal, and the direction of *propagation* of the wave is determined by the direction of the magnetic field as determined by the *antenna.* Thus, a vertically polarized electromagnetic wave cannot have a propagation component in the vertical direction. Also see *horizontally-polarized electromagnetic wave.*

vertical polarization. See *fixed vertical polarization.*

vertical tabulation (VT) character. A *format effector* that causes the *print* or *display position* to move to the corresponding position on the next of a series of predetermined *lines.*

vertical terminating block. In *communication systems,* a group of *terminals* (points) at which contact can be made to permanent outside *lines* entering a *station.* Also see *combined distribution frame.*

very high frequency (VHF). A *frequency* that lies in the range from 30 MHz to 300 MHz. The *alphabetic* designator of the range is VHF. The numeric designator of the range is 8. Also see *frequency spectrum designation.*

very high frequency omnidirectional radio range. A *very high frequency (VHF) radio beacon* that operates between 108 MHz and 118 MHz as a *line-of-sight (LOS) system* and that operates over distances at which *signals* can be *received* that are a function of altitude as well as *transmitted power.* Two signals are transmitted, one fixed and one rotating. The *receiver* compares the *phase* of the signals and produces an indication of the *magnetic bearing* of the *radio range station.* Each radio range station identifies itself by transmitting a unique *code,* such as a three-letter code. Most VHF omnidirectional radio range stations are equipped with distance measuring equipment. It is a short range air navigation system that can provide a pilot with bearing information and left-right track signals from a selected *ground station*.

very low frequency (VLF). A *frequency* that lies in the *range* from 3 kHz to 30 kHz. The *alphabetic* designator of the range is VLF. The numeric designator of the range is 4. Also see *frequency spectrum designation*.

vestigial sideband. The small fraction of a *sideband* that is *transmitted* along with the whole or part of the *carrier* and the whole other sideband in an *amplitude modulated signal*. In this *mode* of *transmission*, part of the original carrier and a fraction of the other sideband is available at the *receiver* to assist in *demodulation*, thus making demodulation easier than in *single-sideband transmission*.

vestigial sideband transmission. *Double-sideband transmission* in which one *sideband*, the *carrier*, and only a portion of the other sideband are *transmitted*.

VF. *Voice frequency*.

VFT. *Voice frequency telegraph*. *Voice frequency transmission*.

VFTG. *Voice frequency telegraph*.

VHF. *Very high frequency*.

vibrating relay. A *telegraph relay* that has additional windings that are excited so as to produce a certain regular oscillation of the armature between its stops in the absence of line current in the main winding. The object is to increase the *sensitivity* of the *relay*.

vibration test. In an *optical fiber, bundle,* or *cable,* a *test* to measure *parameter* changes, such as breaking point, *attenuation, dither, dispersion,* and *modal* changes during and as a result of vibration at various *frequencies*.

victim emitter. A *source* of *electromagnetic* energy that is placed under electronic surveillance for, or is considered for, *monitoring, interception, deception, jamming, frequency* control, *net* discipline, electronic *emission control*, securing electronic intelligence, obtaining order of battle, obtaining target *information*, and other purposes. Thus, any *source* of *radiation* that is exploited for reasons other than its designed purpose.

victim frequency. 1. A *frequency* that is intended to be *jammed*. 2. A *frequency* that is undergoing *interference*. 3. The *frequency* of a *victim emitter*.

victim transmission. A *transmission* that is *intercepted* for intelligence purposes, that is selected for *electronic countermeasure (ECM)* action, or that is *transmitted* by a *victim emitter*.

video. Pertaining to *signals* or *frequencies* that are in the range from 100 kHz to several MHz and are generally used for *television transmission.*

video amplitude limiting. The preventing of a *video input signal* from driving *input circuits* above a fixed level of *amplitude.* For example, in *radar systems,* video amplitude limiting is used to prevent deterioration of *range-rate memory circuit* performance that is caused by a greater *amplitude* of *echo signals* from *chaff* when dispensed from an aircraft with a relatively small reflecting surface.

video discrimination circuit. A *circuit* that requires or forces a reduction in the *frequency band-pass* of the *video amplifier stage* in which it is used. For example, in *radar systems,* when *interference* is experienced, the video discrimination circuit will materially improve *reception.* A normal radar *signal* has a steep (sharp) *wavefront* that may be partially or totally deteriorated by certain types of *jamming.* This circuit may permit salvage of an otherwise lost signal if the signal is not completely deteriorated, that is, if the interference level is not equal to the desired signal.

video disk. See *optical video disk.*

video filter. A *filter* that will process, that is, either filter (remove) or pass, *frequencies* in the *bands* used in *video systems,* such as frequencies in the *very high (VHF)* and *ultrahigh frequency (VHF) ranges.*

video frequency. 1. The *frequency band* that extends from approximately 100 kHz to several MHz. 2. Pertaining to *frequencies* in the *very high frequency (VHF)* and *ultrahigh frequency (UHF) bands.* 3. The *frequency* that results from *television camera scanning,* ranging from 0 to 4 MHz.

video integrator feedback. A *radar signal reception* technique in which *received signals* are recirculated (fed back) through a *delay line* and in-*phase synchronous* signals are added. This recirculation reduces the *response* to *asynchronous* signals such as *noise, interference,* and *jamming.* The device usually is preceded by a *limiter.* It is particularly useful against *pulsed signals (spikes)* that result from noise or jamming.

video optical detector. In a *video-signal optical-fiber transmission system,* a device the *converts* a video *signal* in the fiber to an *electrical signal* in a *wire* or other *medium.* Also see *video optical source.*

video optical source. In a *video-signal optical-fiber transmission system,* a device that *converts* a video *electrical signal* in a wire or other medium to a *light signal* in an *optical fiber.*

videophone. A *telephone* that is *coupled* to an *imaging* device that enables the *called party* or the *calling party,* or both, to view one another as on *television,* if they so desire. See Figure V-2.

V-2. A **videophone** consisting of the AT&T Mod II Set® comprised of a picture *display* unit (containing the camera, picture tube, and *loudspeaker*), a control unit (containing control buttons, knobs, and *microphone*), a 12-button Touch-Tone^R *telephone,* and a service unit (containing the *power* supply, *logic circuits,* and *transmission equalizing circuits*). (Reproduced with permission of AT&T Co.)

video trunk. See *optical-fiber video trunk.*

view. In *satellite communication systems,* the ability of a *satellite station* to establish a *line-of-sight* relationship with an *earth station,* or vice versa, in such a manner that the satellite station is sufficiently above the horizon and clear of other *obstructions* so as to enable direct line-of-sight *communication.* Two earth stations have a satellite in mutual view when both earth stations have unobstructed line-of-sight contact with the satellite station.

viewer. See *infrared viewer.*

view field. The maximum cone or fan of *rays* passed through an *aperture* and measured at a given *vertex.* In an instrument, the view field is synonymous with "true field."

viewpoint. 1. In *display systems,* the origin from which angles and scales are used to map *real-world coordinates* of an *object* into the *user coordinates* or *device coordinates* of *display elements, display groups,* or *display images* in *image storage space* or in the *display space* on the *display surface* of a *display device.* 2. In *display systems,* the location from which *objects* are considered to be viewed for the purpose of creating *display elements, display groups,* or *display images* in *image storage space* or in the *display space* on the *display surface* of a *display device.*

viewport. See *window.*

vignetting. The loss of *light* through an *optical element* due to the entire *light ray bundle* not passing through a given area; i.e., a part of the bundle is blocked by *absorption, reflection,* or *deflection,* particularly due to a limitation in the size of the *pupil* or *aperture.*

violation. See *alternate mark (AMI) inversion violation.*

virgin medium. A *data medium* in or on which *data* can be recorded but have never been recorded. For example, an unmarked sheet of paper, paper tape with no holes or with only sprocket holes, or new *magnetic tape* on which data have never been recorded.

virtual call. A *call* in which use is made of a *virtual call capability.*

virtual call capability. A *user service* or *facility* in which a *call set-up procedure* and a *call clearing procedure* determine a period of *communication* between two sets of *data terminal equipment (DTEs)* in which *user's data* are *transferred* in the *network* in a *packet mode operation.* All the user's data are delivered from the network in the same order in which they were received by the network. Multiaccess DTEs may have several virtual calls underway at the same time. This facility usually requires end-to-end transfer control of *packets* within the network. Data may be delivered to the network before the *call set-up* has been *completed,* but it will not be delivered to the *destination user address* if the *call access attempt* is unsuccessful.

virtual call facility. A *user service* or *facility* that has a *virtual call capability.*

virtual carrier. The part of the *frequency spectrum* that a *carrier wave* would use if a carrier wave were present. Also see *permanent virtual circuit.*

virtual circuit. 1. A *communication* arrangement in which *data* from a *source user* may be *transferred* to a *destination user* over various real circuit configurations during a single period of communication. 2. In a *packet-switched network,* a *circuit* or *channel* that is established between *source* and *destination packet switches* and usually requires some form of setup prior to *data transfer.* The circuit as such may not be visible or obvious to a *user.* 3. In a *packet mode operation,* those *facilities* that are provided by a *network* for *transferring data* between *data terminals* and have the characteristics of the facilities that are provided by a physical connection. Synonymous with *virtual connection.* Also see *logical circuit; phantom circuit; physical circuit.* See *permanent virtual circuit.*

virtual connection. A *logical connection* that is made to a *virtual circuit.* Also see *virtual circuit.*

virtual image. The point from which a *divergent light ray bundle* appears to proceed when the rays have a given divergence but no real physical point of intersection. The distance of the virtual image is inversely proportional to the divergence of the rays. Since there is no physical intersection of rays, there is no *real image* that can be *focused* on a *screen.* The image of any real *object* produced by a *negative lens* or *convex mirror* is always virtual. The image produced by a *positive lens* of an object located within its *focal length* is also virtual. Also see *real image.*

virtual path. 1. In a *network,* a *path* between a *data source* and a *data sink* that uses one or more *virtual circuits.* 2. In a *network,* a *path* between a *data source* and a *data sink* that may be created by various physical circuit configurations without adding additional physical *facilities* to create the path that may be used for the *transmission* of *messages.* Synonymous with *logical route; virtual route.*

virtual push button. A *display element* or *display group* on the *display surface* of a *display device* used, in connection with a *stylus,* such as a *light-pen* or a *cursor,* as though it were a *function key.* Synonymous with *light button.*

virtual route. See *virtual path.*

virtual source. The apparent source of *electromagnetic waves* or the main *focal point* of an *antenna* or *light source,* that is an array or distribution of radiators. The *radiated* energy from the main *reflector* in a *compound antenna feed system* appears to radiate from the main reflector *focal point.*

virtual space. In *display systems,* a space in which *display elements, display groups,* and *display images* are defined in *user coordinates* that may be independent of *device coordinates* but may be related to *real-world coordinates.*

visibility. In *open systems architecture,* the extent to which the functions and *operations* in a *layer* below a given layer can be detected by the functions of the layer above, and vice versa. Normally layers mask each other, particularly when they are not adjacent.

visibility point. A *point* in a *system,* such as a *computing* or *communication system,* at which a contact or *connection* can be made. For example, the pins of a socket, a *plug,* a *connector,* or a binding post.

visible-infrared spin-scan radiometer. See *fiber-optic visible-infrared spin-scan radiometer.*

visible spectrum. The portion of the *electromagnetic frequency spectrum* to which the retina is sensitive and by which humans see. It extends from about 400 to about 750 nm in *wavelength.*

visual. See *audiovisual.*

visual-aural radio range. A *radionavigation aid* in an air or maritime navigation system that has four *radio range* legs, one pair of which provides a visual indication of range from the stations or a reference point, and the other pair of which provides an aural indication of range, at the *mobile station.*

visual body signal. See *ground-to-air visual body signal.*

visual call sign. A *communication system call sign transmitted* by a means visible to the eye. For example a call sign transmitted by *semaphore, flashing light, flaghoist, panel,* or *heliograph.* The eye may be aided with hand-held *optical instruments* such as *binoculars* and *telescopes.*

visual communication system. A *communication system* based on use of direct observation by the human eye, such as *systems* that involve the use of *heliographs,* sun flash, *semaphores, pennants,* arm and hand *signals,* smoke signals, *flares,* and *flags.* Contrast with *optical communication system.*

visual emergency. See *ground-air visual emergency.*

visual engaged signaling. In *telephone switchboard operation,* a visual indication that a *line* is no longer *busy.* When this *facility* is provided, it is not necessary for the *operator* to perform the *engaged test.*

visual paulin signal. In *visual signaling systems,* a *signal* that is sent by means of patterns made of folded tarpaulins or sails and is usually sent from surface to air, that is, from ground to air or from sea surface to air. In an emergency, the tarpaulins may be improvised with other materials. Its primary use is by survivors in distress situations. Synonymous with *visual sail signal; visual tarpaulin signal.*

visual responsibility chain. In *visual communication systems,* the sequence of *relaying* or *repeating stations* that have visual contact and along which *messages* can be sent.

visual sail signal. See *visual paulin signal.*

visual signal. A *signal* that can be seen by the unaided eye or by the eye aided with a hand-held *optical* instrument such as *binoculars* or *telescopes.* For example, a signal that is transmitted by the use of hands, *flags, panels,* smoke, *heliograph, semaphore,* or *wig-wag.*

visual signal code. See *international visual signal code.*

visual spectrum. The *band* of *color* produced by decomposing *white light* into its *components* by the process of *dispersion.* The rainbow is an example of a visual spectrum produced by the dispersion of white light by water droplets. Also see *electromagnetic spectrum.*

visual tarpaulin signal. See *visual paulin signal.*

VLF. *Very low frequency.*

vocabulary. See *panel signaling vocabulary.*

vocoder. A voice *coder* that consists of a *speech analyzer* and a *speech synthesizer* and is used to reduce the *bandwidth* requirement of speech signals. The analyzer circuitry converts the *input analog* speech *wave* into *narrowband digital signals.* The synthesizer converts the *encoded* digital signals received by the receive *component* into artificial speech sounds. For *communication security (COMSEC)* purposes, a vocoder may be used in conjunction with a *key* generator and a *modulator-demodulator (modem)* to *transmit digital encrypted* speech signals over normal narrowband voice *communication channels.* Synonymous with *voice-operated coder.* Also see *pattern-matching voice coder.*

VODAS. A voice-operated *antisinging* device used to prevent the overall *voice frequency* singing of a two-way *telephone circuit* by insuring that *transmission* can occur in only one direction at any given instant. The device is operated by sound that *attenuates* oscillations of any type or from any source, such as *resonance, interference, ringing, singing,* or *noise.*

VOGAD. A voice-operated *gain*-adjusting device that is used to give a substantially constant *output amplitude* for a wide range of *input* amplitudes. Synonymous with *voice-operated gain-adjusting device.* Also see *voice-grade circuit.*

voice. See *digitized voice; encrypted voice; single-sideband voice.*

voice call sign. See *permanent voice call sign.*

voice coder. See *pattern-matching voice coder.*

voice communication system. See *AUTOSEVOCOM system.*

voice cord board. See *secure voice cord board.*

voice-data service. A *communication system service* that handles *messages* in voice (*analog*) form and *data* (*digital*) form. Also see *data service.*

voice-data signal. See *quasianalog signal.*

voice-data tributary station. See *dual-access tributary station.*

voiced sound. Sound that is created by the speech organs in which sounds are generated by the vibration of vocal cords. Also see *unvoiced sound.*

voice encoder. See *channel voice encoder.*

voice equipment. See *limited-protection voice equipment.*

voice frequency (VF). A *frequency* that lies within the part of the *audio frequency range* that is used for the *transmission* of voiced sound. In most *communication systems* that handle voiced sounds, VF ranges from about 300 Hz to 3400 Hz. Also see *audio frequency.*

voice frequency carrier telegraph (VFCT). See *voice frequency telegraph (VFTG).*

voice frequency channel. A *channel* that is suitable for carrying *analog signals* and quasianalog signals and can handle *frequencies* in the *voice frequency (VF)* range, that is, from about 300 Hz to 3400 Hz.

voice frequency telegraph (VFTG or FVT). A *communication system* in which one or more *direct-current (DC) telegraph channels* are *multiplexed* into a *composite* nominal 4 kHz *voice frequency channel* for further *processing* through a *wire, optical fiber,* or *radio network.* It is a system of *telegraphy* in which one or more *carrier-frequency currents* are used that are within the voice frequency range. The *transmission* equipment conveys telegraph signals by voice frequency tones. Synonymous with *voice frequency carrier telegraph.* Also see *two-tone keying.* See *multichannel voice frequency telegraph.*

voice frequency truncation. The suppression of the higher *frequencies* of speech, that is, above about 3400 Hz, or the suppression of lower frequencies of speech, that is, below about 300 Hz, in speech *circuits* and audio circuits. Voice frequency truncation may occur as a consequence of circuit limitations or as an intended process to limit the *bandwidth* and eliminate *noise.* Synonymous with *speech spectrum truncation.*

voice-grade circuit. A *circuit* that has the *frequency response* and *attenuation* characteristics to effectively handle *voice frequency signals.* Also see *VOGAD; conditioned voice-grade circuit.*

voice-graphics tributary station. See *dual-access tributary station.*

voice intelligibility. In a *telephone communication system,* the capability of a voice of being understood without necessarily implying the ability to associate a particular voice with a particular person.

voice network. See *automatic voice network.*

voice-operated coder. See *vocoder.*

voice-operated device antisinging. See *VODAS.*

voice-operated gain-adjusting device. See *VOGAD.*

voice pipe. In *aural communication systems,* a hollow tube that is used to conduct voice *signals* from one place to another place, such as from the bridge to the engine room on a ship, from an entrance to a building to an apartment, or from a machine operator station to a supervisor's office.

voice-plus circuit. See *composite circuit.*

voice service. A *communication service* devoted to the *transmission* of *voiced sound,* that is, voiced calls such as in a *telephone system.* Unless *digitized voice* is indicated, voice service implies *analog signals* are involved.

voice system. See *radiotelephone voice system.*

voice telephony. Pertaining to a *communication system* established for the *transmission* of speech or other sounds.

voice transmission. See *digital voice transmission.*

voltage. See *common-mode voltage; common-return offset voltage; disturbance voltage; potential difference; psophometric voltage; ripple voltage.*

voltage drop. See *distribution voltage drop.*

voltage level. See *digital voltage level.*

voltage pencil. A *stylus* that can be used to identify *coordinate positions* in the *display space* on the *display surface* of a *display device;* it can be used to select *symbols* and operates from a *source* of *voltage;* and its presence can be detected at specific locations on the display surface.

voltage standing wave ratio (VSWR). The ratio of the maximum to the minimum *voltage* in the *standing wave pattern* that appears along a *transmission line.* It is used as a measure of the *match* or mismatch between the *transmission line* and its *load.* For an *antenna* transmission line, the VSWR is the ratio of the maximum to the minimum values of voltage or *current* in the standing wave pattern at the antenna *terminals.* A standing wave is produced when the antenna (load) *impedance* differs from the *characteristic impedance* of the transmission line.

voltaic. See *photovoltaic; radiovoltaic.*

volt-ohm-milliammeter. See *multimeter.*

volume. See *communication traffic volume; mode volume.*

volume distribution. See *mean-power-of-the-talker volume distribution.*

volume unit (VU). The unit of measurement for *electrical* speech *power* as measured by a VU meter in the prescribed manner. The VU meter is a volume indicator that is designed and constructed according to American National Standard C16.5-1942. It has a scale and specified dynamic and other characteristics that are used to obtain correlated readings of speech power that are necessitated by the rapid fluctuation in the level of voice *signals.* Zero VU equals zero *dBm,* that is, 1 mW, in measurements of *sinusoidal wave test tone power.* Synonymous with *speech power unit.*

VOX. A voice-operated *relay circuit* that permits the equivalent of *push-to-talk operation* of a *transmitter* by the *operator.*

VSWR. *Voltage standing wave ratio.*

VT. *Variable time.*

VU or **vu.** *Volume unit.*

v-value. See *normalized frequency.*

W

waiting-in-progress signal. In a *communication system,* a *signal* sent in the *backward direction* to indicate that the *called user* (*called party,* subscriber, customer) has the *connect-when-free facility* and is *busy* at the moment, and that the *call* has been placed in a *queue.*

waiting signal. See *data circuit-terminating equipment (DCE) waiting signal; data terminal equipment (DTE) waiting signal.*

walking code. A *binary code* that gives the appearance of walking *bit*-by-bit through a *register,* one bit for each number change. The code pattern is advanced by a count of one by *shifting* the number to the left (right). The bit that is shifted out is complemented and fed in at the right (left). Relatively simple counter circuits can be made to use this code. For example, a three-bit *unit-distance* walking code is 000, 001, 011, 111, 110, 100. Synonymous with *creeping code.*

warfare. See *electronic warfare.*

warfare communication. See *psychological warfare communication.*

warning. See *airborne early warning; emergency meteorological warning.*

warning net. A *communication network* used for the *transmission* of warnings of danger, such as natural disasters, approaching forces, bad weather, or *power* shortages. See *airborne early warning net.*

warning radar. See *early-warning radar; initial warning radar.*

warning receiver. A *receiver,* usually an *intercept* receiver, that has the primary function of altering the *user (operator)* to imminent danger.

warning system. See *airborne radar warning system; aircraft control-warning system; threat warning system.*

watch. See *communication watch; continuous communication watch; copy watch; guard watch; lens watch; listening watch; radio communication copy watch; single-operator period watch; two-operator period watch; world weather watch (WWW).*

watch ship. See *constant watch ship.*

watch station. See *constant watch station.*

wave. A movement to and fro or up and down, or an increase and decrease of a value or *parameter,* usually a physical parameter, such as *electric field, current, voltage, power,* energy, or material matter. A wave tends to *propagate,* though it can also be a *standing wave* that involves a variation in place, such as a voltage or current standing wave on a *transmission line.* It may be *periodic* or aperiodic, and it may be simply a single surge of a physical quantity such as a single *pulse.* In most instances a wave is considered to be a periodic, propagating phenomenon, such as a *radio wave.* See *audio-frequency wave; carrier wave; centimeter wave; complementary wave; decametric wave; decimetric wave; decimillimetric wave; direct wave; elastic wave; electromagnetic wave; evanescent wave; ground wave; hectometric wave; Hertzian wave; horizontally-polarized electromagnetic wave; indirect wave; interrupted continuous wave (ICW); leaky wave; metric wave; millimetric wave; Morse continuous-wave; myriametric wave; plane-polarized electromagnetic wave; radio wave; short wave; skywave; sound wave; standing wave; surface wave; transverse electric wave; transverse electromagnetic wave; transverse magnetic wave; trapped electromagnetic wave; traveling wave; tropospheric wave; uniform plane-polarized electromagnetic wave; vertically-polarized electromagnetic wave.*

wave analyzer.   A device capable of measuring the energy contained in specified or selected *bands* in an *electromagnetic wave frequency spectrum.*

wave equation.   The equation, based on *Maxwell's equations,* the *constitutive relations,* and the *vector* algebra, that relates the *electromagnetic field* of an *electromagnetic wave* time and space derivatives with the *transmission medium electrical permittivity* and *magnetic permeability* in a region without electrical charges or currents.   The solution of the wave equation yields the *electric* and *magnetic field* strengths everywhere.   The wave equation is given as either:

$$\nabla^2 H - \mu\epsilon\, \partial^2 H/\partial t^2 = 0$$

or

$$\nabla^2 E - \mu\epsilon\, \partial^2 E/\partial t^2 = 0$$

in a current- and charge-free *nonconducting medium,* where E is the *electric field intensity,* H is the *magnetic field intensity,* ϵ is the *electric permittivity,* and μ is the *magnetic permeability.* ∇ is the vector spatial derivative operator. The wave equation applies in *optical waveguides.*   Also see *eigenvalue.*

wave-form jamming.   See *periodic wave-form jamming.*

wavefront.   A surface normal to an *electromagnetic ray bundle* as it *propagates* from a source, the surface of the *wavefront* passing through those parts of the *waves* that are in the same *phase.*   For parallel *rays,* the wavefront is a plane. For rays diverging from or converging toward a point, the wavefront is spherical. The wavefront is perpendicular to the direction of *propagation* of the wave, and the *electric* and *magnetic field vectors* of the wave define a plane that is tangent to the wavefront surface at the point that the field vectors are determined.   The front is a three-dimensional surface of constant *optical path length* from the *source* and is orthogonal (i.e., perpendicular) to a *bundle* of rays.

wavefront compensation.   In *image restoration,* a method of *wavefront control* in which distortion of the original wavefront is removed by introduction of *coherent* compensatory *electromagnetic waves* by creating an error map of local deviation or tilt from ideal spherical waves and using these to correct the distortion.

wavefront control. The performing of operations in an *optical system* so as to manipulate the shape of the *wavefront* of an *electromagnetic wave,* usually in the *visible* and near visible region of the *frequency spectrum,* and usually with the intent of obtaining clear *images* of *illuminated objects* (i.e., of obtaining a spherical wavefront). Among the methods of wavefront control are *phase conjugation, aperture tagging, wavefront compensation,* and *image sharpening.*

waveguide. Any structure capable of confining and supporting the energy of an *electromagnetic wave* to a specific relatively narrow controllable *path* that is capable of being altered, such as a rectangular cross-section metal pipe, an *optical fiber* of circular cross section, or a *coaxial cable.* See *circular dielectric waveguide; closed waveguide; doubly-cladded slab dielectric waveguide; diffused optical waveguide; fiber-optical waveguide; frequency-selective waveguide; grooved waveguide; multimode waveguide; optical waveguide; periodically-distributed thin-film waveguide; planar diffused waveguide; slab-dielectric optical waveguide; slab dielectric waveguide; strip-loaded diffused heteroepitaxial optical waveguide; thin-film waveguide.* See Figure W-1.

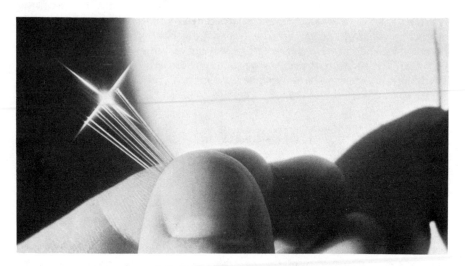

W-1. Twenty-four *optical-fiber light* **waveguides** arranged in two *ribbons* in one *cable* for voice and data traffic under Chicago. (Courtesy of Bell Laboratories.)

waveguide isolator. A *passive attenuator* in which *transmission losses* are much larger in one direction than in the other, thus causing *absorption* of end *reflections, backscatter,* and *noise.* Certain nonreciprocal properties can be obtained using ferrite materials.

waveguide delay distortion. In an *optical waveguide,* the *distortion* in received *signal* caused by the differences in *propagation* time for each *wavelength,* (i.e., the delay versus wavelength effect for each propagating *mode*), causing a *spreading* of the total *received* signal at the *detector.* Waveguide delay distortion contributes to *group-delay distortion,* along with *material dispersion* and *multimode group-delay spread.*

waveguide dispersion. The part of the total *dispersion* attributable to the dimensions of the *waveguide.* The cross-section dimensions are critical. They determine the *modes* that are allowed and not allowed to propagate. Waveguide dispersion increases as *frequency* decreases, due to the actual dimensions and their variation along the length of the guide.

waveguide mode. See *degenerate waveguide mode.*

waveguide switch. A mechanically or electrically controlled device that is capable of stopping or diverting the *propagation* of *electromagnetic* energy at a specific point in a *waveguide.*

wavelength. The length of a *wave* measured from any point on one wave to the corresponding point on the next wave, such as from crest to crest. Wavelength determines the nature of the various forms of *radiant energy* that comprise the *electromagnetic spectrum;* e.g., it determines the *color* of *light.* For a *sinusoidal wave,* the wavelength is the distance between points of corresponding phase of two consecutive cycles of the wave. The wavelength λ, is related to the *phase velocity v,* and the *frequency f,* by the relation $\lambda = v/f.$ Also see *light.* See *peak spectral wavelength; peak wavelength; zero material dispersion wavelength.*

wavelength-division multiplexing (WDM). In *optical communication systems,* the *multiplexing* of *lightwaves* in a single *transmission medium* such that each of the waves are of a different *wavelength* and are *modulated* separately before *insertion* into the medium. Usually, several *sources* are used, (such as a *laser,* or several lasers, or a *dispersed white light* source or sources), each having a distinctly different center wavelength. WDM is the same as *frequency-division multiplexing (FDM)* applied to *visible light* frequencies of the *electromagnetic spectrum.*

wave number. The reciprocal of the *wavelength* of a single-*frequency sinusoidal wave* such as a single-frequency *uniform plane-polarized electromagnetic wave* or *monochromatic lightwave.* The wave number is used for waves in or near the *visible spectrum,* since wavelength is more readily measured than frequency, but it is frequency, or wave number, that is directly related to energy. For example, photon energy is given by:

$$P.E. = hnc$$

where h is *Planck's constant,* n is the wave number, and c is the *velocity* of the *light.* The wave number is the number of *wavelengths* per unit distance in the direction of *propagation* that must be taken. Also see *wave parameter.*

wave object. See *sine wave object.*

wave parameter. A unit that is used in regard to *periodic waves,* such as *electromagnetic waves.* The wave parameter, p, is given by the relation $p = 2\pi/\lambda$, where λ is the *wavelength.* Also see *wave number.*

wave ratio. See *standing wave ratio (SWR); voltage standing wave ratio (VSWR).*

wave shape. In an *electromagnetic wave,* the wave-dependent *parameter,* such as *electric voltage, current, field intensity, power,* or *energy density,* specified as a function of time, *frequency,* spatial coordinates, or other independent parameters. For example, *wave shapes* may be *sinusoidal, rectangular,* triangular, sawtooth, *spiked, plane polarized, elliptically polarized,* or other arbitrary shape.

wave transmission. See *low-detectability electromagnetic wave transmission.*

wave trap. A device used to exclude unwanted *wave components* of a *signal,* such as unwanted *frequency* components, *noise,* or other *interference.* Traps are usually *tunable* to permit selection of unwanted or interfering signals.

wave velocity. See *electromagnetic wave velocity.*

WDM. *Wavelength-division multiplex.*

wear-out failure period. In a device with a large population of *components,* the third and final *failure period,* characterized by a rising *failure rate* above that of the *constant failure period.* It is caused by the increased rate at which deterioration causes components to reach the end of their designed useful lives. Also see *bathtub curve; component life.*

weather communications. *Communication* methods, *systems,* or equipment used for the *transmission* of *messages* that contain *information* about meteorological conditions. The messages are sent to and from weather forecasting services for the purpose of collecting and disseminating weather information.

weather report. A report that contains local weather *information* that is actually being experienced at the time the *message* is sent from a specific location. The weather report is usually contained in a specific *format,* such as the weather *code* form developed by the *World Meteorological Organization. Security measures* for the *transmission* of weather reports are adopted as required.

weather watch. See *World Weather Watch (WWW).*

wedge. See *tone wedge.*

wedge set. See *tone wedge set.*

weight. In the mathematics of numerical positional representation systems, the factor by which the value that is represented by a *character* in a *digit* place is multiplied in order to obtain its additive contribution to the value that is represented by a real number. For example, if the weights from a *straight binary number* are 8, 4, 2, 1, the additive contributions for the digits of the binary number 1101 are 8+4+0+1. This sum is equal to decimal 13, the equivalent of the binary number. In other numeration systems, the positions of a number have other weights.

weighting.   See *C-message weighting; flat weighting; F1A-line weighting; frequency weighting; HA1-receiver weighting; noise weighting; psophometric weighting; 144-line weighting; 144-receiver weighting.*

weighting network.   A *network (circuit)* that has a *loss* that varies with *frequency* of the *applied voltage* in a predetermined manner.   It is used for improving or correcting *transmission* characteristics and for *noise* measurements.   Also see *noise weighting.*

welfare traffic.   *Communication traffic* that consists of *messages* of a humanitarian nature, whether personal or official.

Wheatstone automatic system.   In *communications,* a *Morse system* in which *signals* are *transmitted* automatically and in which a previously prepared *perforated tape* is used for *transmission.*   A perforated tape for automatic printing or an *inked tape* for subsequent interpretation by an *operator* is used for *reception.*

Wheatstone tape.   A tape that is used for automatic *transmission* and *reception* of the *international Morse code.*   For transmission, the tape provides for a two-unit perforation, that is, two holes perforated transversely (vertically) form a *dot* and two holes perforated obliquely (diagonally) form a *dash.*   For *ink recording,* the tape is drawn through an ink recorder.   A pen draws a continuous ink line. Dots or dashes are indicated by fluctuations of the ink line.   The tape is read by a trained *operator.*   Synonymous with *Boehme tape.*

wheels.   See *thumb wheels.*

whisper facility.   A *telephone system facility* that enables whispered speech to be received at a *power level* nearly equal to that of normal speech.

white.   See *noisy white; nominal white; picture white.*

white facsimile transmission.   1. In an *amplitude-modulated facsimile system, transmission* in which the maximum *transmitted power* corresponds to the minimum *density* of the object copy or document being transmitted.   The minimum density area is an area designated as white, that is, all *colors* are *reflected* without selectivity.   2. In a *frequency-modulated facsimile system, transmission* in which the lowest *transmitted frequency* corresponds to the minimum *density* of the object copy or document being transmitted.   Also see *black facsimile transmission.*

white light.   *Electromagnetic waves* or *radiation* having a *spectral density* or energy distribution that produces the *color* sensation to the average human eye identical to that of average noon sunlight.   Also see *white noise.*

white noise.   *Electromagnetic waves* having a *spectral* or *power density* that is uniformly distributed throughout a broad *frequency spectrum* such as from 200 kHz to 10 MHz.   The actual frequency content depends on the method of generation of the *waves*. Thus, the spectral distribution of energy between specified frequency limits is such that the *noise power* per unit *bandwidth* is independent of frequency. It is noise that has a frequency spectrum that is continuous and uniform over a wide range of frequencies. Synonymous with *additive white Gaussian noise; uniformly distributed constant-amplitude frequency spectrum*. Also see *continuous spectrum; white light*.

white recording. 1. In *facsimile systems* in which *amplitude modulation* is used, recording in which the maximum received *power* corresponds to the minimum *density* (white) area of the *recording medium*. 2. In *facsimile systems* in which *frequency modulation* is used, recording in which the lowest frequency corresponds to the minimum density (white) area of the recording medium. Also see *black recording*.

white signal. In *facsimile systems*, the *signal* that results from the *scanning* of a minimum *density* (white) area of the *object* copy or document. The *signal* magnitude may correspond to signal *amplitude, frequency, phase-shift,* or other signal *parameter,* and white corresponds to the lowest values. Also see *black signal*.

who-are-you (WRU) character. A *transmission control character* used for (1) *switching* on an *answerback unit* in the *station* with which the *connection* has been established, or for (2) initiating a *response* that might include station identification, and indication of the type of equipment that is in service, and the status of the station. The *signal* corresponds to the *binary code* of 7 *bits* assigned to the WRU. When received by a station, the code triggers the receiving unit to *transmit* an *answerback code* to the *terminal* that transmitted the WRU signal. The *receiving unit* may be a *telegraph unit,* a *data terminal installation (DTE),* or other unit. Synonymous with *WRU signal*.

wicking. The amount of liquid, usually water, absorbed by one portion of an *optical cable* when an adjacent portion is immersed in water. Wicking is measured (1) by the weight of water absorbed in a specified time when a specified length is immersed vertically to a specified depth; (2) by the height to which a dye solution is raised vertically by capillary or soaking action when a specified length is immersed vertically to a specified depth in the dye solution; or (3) by other methods.

wideband. 1. Pertaining to a range of *frequencies* that is wide relative to the particular *frequency* or range of frequencies under consideration. For example, a range of 20 kHz to 80 kHz would be considered wideband since the *bandwidth* of 60 kHz is greater than 0.1% of the midband value of 50 kHz. 2. In *communication security systems,* pertaining to a *signal* that requires a bandwidth greater than 3 kHz. 3. In *telephone systems,* pertaining to the *transmission* of *signals* over a *frequency* range that is produced by a *modulated carrier* system, usually in the range from 60 kHz to 20 MHz. 4. Pertaining to a *circuit* having a wider *frequency response* than the normal type of *circuit* at the corresponding frequency. 5. Pertaining to *transmission facilities* that have a *bandwidth,* that is, a range of *frequencies* that they can handle, that is greater than that which is available on voice-grade facilities. 6. Pertaining to *data transmission facilities* that can send and receive *frequencies* that are greater than normal *voice-grade communication* frequencies of 4 kHz. Wideband facilities can carry many *voice* or *data channels* simultaneously and they can also be used for high-speed *digital data communication* at *data signaling rates* up to a million bps. **7.** Pertaining to *transmission facilities* that have a *frequency bandpass* capability of 20 kHz or greater. **8.** Pertaining to *electromagnetic waves* that occupy a relatively large portion of the *frequency spectrum*. The comparison may be made with equipment of comparable capability, with the portion of the frequency spectrum that is assigned to the particular use, or to the *bandwidth*-to-median-frequency ratio. The bandwidth is usually considered to be a maximum between the frequency limits where the *gain, response,* or *power* is reduced to one-half, or 3 db, from the maximum value. **9.** In *TEMPEST* applications, pertaining to *acoustic* or *electric signals* that have either a fast rise or a fast decay *(fast time constant)* in the energy *wave*. When interercepted by a detection system, such as a *radio receiver* and *oscilloscope,* these *signals* cannot be *tuned,* they cover a wide frequency range, and appear on the screen as a series of impulses. Lightning discharges, spark discharges, and certain commercially available *impulse* generators are examples of wideband signal sources. **10.** Pertaining to a system that uses or requires a *bandwidth* that is greater than 0.1% of its midband operating *frequency*. Synonymous with *broadband*.

wideband communication system. A *communication system* that is capable of handling, makes use of, or requires a wide range of *frequencies* and usually provides numerous *channels* of *communication* that use *frequency division multiplexing*. For example, *wideband systems* and *components* include multichannel *telephone cable, tropospheric scatter* communication systems, and multichannel *line-of-sight (LOS) microwave* systems. Since alternate channels are available in wideband systems, they possess increased *traffic capacity* but occupy a larger part of the *frequency spectrum* than *narrowband* systems.

wideband modem. **1.** A *modem* that has a *modulated output signal frequency spectrum* that is wider than that which can be wholly contained within, and faithfully *transmitted* through, a *voice channel* with a nominal 4 kHz *bandwidth*. **2.** A *modem* that has a *bandwidth* capability that is greater than a *narrowband modem,* which has a bandwidth less than 4 kHz. The 4 kHz is an arbitrary value. Other widths have been proposed as the limiting width between wideband and narrowband, such as 20 kHz.

wideband signal. **1.** A *voice frequency signal* that has a *spectral* content greater than 4 kHz wide. **2.** A *radio frequency signal* that occupies a *frequency band* greater than 0.1% of the midband frequency. Thus, at 10 MHz, a *signal* that has a *bandwidth* greater than 10 kHz would be a wideband signal. **3.** An *analog signal,* or an *analog* representation of a *digital signal,* whose essential *spectral* content is greater than that which can be contained within a *voice channel* of nominal 4 kHz *bandwidth*.

wideband system. **1.** A *system* in which a *bandwidth* greater than a specified bandwidth is used. For example, a group of *voice frequency channels* that use a bandwidth greater than 4 kHz or greater than 20 kHz. **2.** A *system* with a *multichannel bandwidth* greater than 0.1% of the midband *frequency* of *operation.* For example, an *ultrahigh frequency (UHF)* 2000 MHz transhorizon *tropospheric scatter transmission* system that uses a bandwidth greater than 2 MHz wide. Synonymous with *broadband system.* Also see *channel bank; channelization.*

wide-beam antenna.   An *antenna* that has a low *directive gain* and hence a broad *main lobe.* In *radar systems,* such an *antenna* is less difficult to *jam* than a *narrow-beam antenna* since the radar *display* will be more nearly saturated, but the radar will not be as accurate in *tracking* as a narrow beam antenna. Also, a large amount of energy is wasted in a wide beam when a specific object (target) is being tracked.

wide-beam radar.   A *radar* that *emits* a *signal* that has its energy spread over a large solid angle. The *radiation pattern* usually has relatively large *side lobes.* The wide beam may be likened to that of a flood light rather than that of a spot light. Each has its particular advantage for a specific application.

wide-shift frequency-shift keying.   In *radio telegraph communications, frequency-shift keying* in which a frequency shift of a large number of *hertz* is used. The frequency shift keying is used to distinguish *marks* from *spaces,* such as *dots* and *dashes* distinguished from spaces, or to distinguish tone from silence. For example, a frequency shift of +425 Hz could be used for the mark and a shift of −425 Hz could be used for the space, both with reference to the *assigned frequency.* Also see *narrow-shift frequency-shift keying.*

width.   See *laser pulse width; nominal line width; pulse width.*

Wiener filtering.   See *minimum mean square error restoration.*

wigwag signaling.   *Visual signaling* in which a *flag* is waved to the sender's right in a 90° arc to represent a *dot,* and a similar motion to the left represents a *dash,* in order to *transmit international Morse code.* Also see *Morse flag signaling; semaphore signaling.*

window.   1. In *display systems,* the particular part of all *free space* that can be represented by the *display space* of the *display surface* of a *display device.* For example, a particular area within a specified boundary on the *faceplate* of a *fiberscope* or *screen* of a *CRT.* 2. A defined, allocated, or dedicated part of space. Synonymous with *viewport.* See *glass window; noise window.*

wink.   In *telephone switching systems,* a single *supervisory pulse.*

wink pulsing.   In *telephone switching systems,* recurring *pulses* that are spaced and of such length (width, duration) that the off-period is very short compared to the on-period. For example, on *key telephone* equipment, the *hold* position (*condition*) of a *line* is often indicated by wink-pulsing a lamp at 120 *impulses* per minute with a 94% break, that is, the pulse is on for 470 ms and off for 30 ms.

wire.   A metallic *conductor* of *electric current,* usually long compared to its width or diameter. See *chicken wire; jumper wire; message; open wire.*

wire cable. A wrapped and sheathed bundle of separately *insulated wires,* usually copper, used to form many separate *channels* of *analog* and *digital signals.* See Figure W-2.

W-2. A monofilament cable (*single-fiber optical* cable) with a copper **wire cable.** (Copyright 1979, Corning Glass Works. Reprinted by permission from Corning Glass Works, Telecommunication Products Department.)

wire circuit. See *four-wire circuit; two-wire circuit; unbalanced wire circuit.*

wire-frame image. In *display systems,* an *image* of an *object,* presented in the *display space* on the *display surface* of a *display device,* showing all major lines, including *hidden lines,* as though the object itself was made only of *wires* that represent edges. Often, if hidden lines are not indicated as such, the view or orientation of the object, but not its shape, may be ambiguous.

wire integration. See *radio-wire integration.*

wire interface. See *radio-wire interface (RWI).*

wireline. Wirepaths that use metallic *conductors* to provide *electrical connections* between *components* of a system, such as a *communication system.*

wireline communications. The use of a physical *path* made of metallic *conductors* that are connected between *terminals* or other *components* of a *communication system.* Also see *optical fiber communications.*

wireline distribution system. See *protected wireline distribution system.*

wireline transmission. *Transmission* in which *telephone, telegraph, teletypewriter, facsimile, data, intercom, closed-circuit TV,* and other *signals* are *transmitted* in metallic *conductors.* The transmission is by means of *electric currents* that require the movement of electric charges (*electrons*) in order to build up *voltages.* Because of metallic presence and the dependence on high *conductivity, coaxial cables* and metallic hollow or *dielectric*-filled *waveguides* are considered as *wirelines.* However, *optical fibers,* the *atmosphere,* vacuum, *dielectrics, semiconductors,* and similar *transmission media* are not considered as wirelines.

wire-ored. 1. The *connection* of several *conductors* to a single point so that a *signal* on any conductor is *transmitted* to all other conductors and signals on all conductors are transmitted to any one conductor. 2. The *connection* of several conductors with incoming *signals* to a single point in such a manner that all signals are *transmitted* by a single *conductor* away from the point, whether or not arrangements are made to prevent signals on any incoming conductors from traveling on other incoming conductors.

wirephoto. A *facsimile transmission system* in which *wirelines* with *electrical currents* are used for the transmission of *signals* from a *scanning transmitter* to a *recording receiver.* Synonymous with *telephoto.*

wire-radio integration. See *radio-wire integration.*

wiretapping. See *active wiretapping; passive wiretapping.*

with priority. A *precedence designator* that is honored by commercial or *common carrier communication agencies,* or by nationalized *communication systems* and *recognized private operating agencies,* that indicates a degree of *precedence* to be provided to official *messages.*

WMO. *World Meteorological Organization.*

wooding. Pertaining to the undesirable obstruction of an *antenna beam* by other equipment, such as a ship's superstructure, a *radio* tower, or an aircraft frame.

word. A *string* of *characters, bytes, bits,* or other *symbols* that is considered, processed, or handled as a unit, that is, as a single entity. Usually meaning can be assigned to a word to represent *information.* In *telegraph communications,* six character intervals are considered as a word when computing *traffic capacity* in words per minute (wpm). The traffic capacity in wpm is computed by multiplying the *modulation rate* in *baud* by 10 and dividing the resulting product by the number of *unit intervals* per character. For example, if the modulation rate is 50 baud, that is, 50 unit intervals per second, and there are 5 unit intervals per character, the traffic capacity or traffic rate is $(50)(10)/5 = 100$ wpm at an implied 6 characters per word. The 50 unit intervals per second and the 5 unit intervals per character is equivalent to 10 characters per second, or 600 characters per minute (cpm), which is equivalent to 100 wpm at 6 characters per word as obtained before. See *alphabetic word; code word; computer word; inactive code word; numeric word; procedure word (proword); telegraph word.*

word length. The number of *characters, bytes, bits,* or other *data units* in a *word.*

work factor. In *computer* and *communication system security,* the effort or time that can be expected to be expended to overcome a protective measure and effect a *penetration* with specified expertise and resources.

working. See *delay working; direct working; double supervisory working; relay working; trunk delay working.*

working frequency. 1. A partcular *frequency* used during a given situation or operation, such as a search and rescue operation. For example, after contact is established on an *emergency (calling) frequency, stations* may shift to another (working) frequency during all or part of the emergency period. 2. The *frequency* that a *station* uses to *transmit* its *messages* to another station, particularly in *crossband radiotelegraph procedures.* Also see *answering frequency; calling frequency; crossband radiotelegraph procedure.*

working net. In *ship-shore communications,* the *communication net* that is usually used by *ship stations* for the *transmission* of *messages* to *shore stations.*

world coordinates. In *display systems,* device-independent coordinates that may be used to map *user coordinates.*

world region. See *International Telecommunication Union (ITU) world region.*

worldwide communication system. See *air-ground worldwide communication system.*

worldwide geographic reference system. A geographic location reference system in which the earth is divided into 24 $15°$ longitudinal zones, lettered A through Z, ommitting I and O, eastward from Greenwich, England; and 12 latitude zones of $15°$ each, lettered A through M omitting I, lettered northward from the south pole. Each resulting $15°$ zone is subdivided into $1°$ units, lettered eastward and northward from each southwest corner.

World Meteorological Organization (WMO). A specialized agency of the United Nations with headquarters in Geneva, Switzerland. It was founded in 1950. In 1951, it took over the International Meteorological Organization that was established in 1878. WMO seeks to promote, support, and encourage *stations* for meteorological and geophysical observations, including *meteorological satellite space stations.* Also see *world weather watch (WWW).*

world weather watch (WWW). An international world weather reporting system operated by the *World Meteorological Organization (WMO)* of the United Nations. The WWW also makes use of *meteorological satellite space stations.* Also see *World Meteorological Organization (WMO).*

worst hour. See *year worst hour.*

woven-fiber optics.   The application of textile-weaving and *fiber-optic* techniques for such purposes as production of reproducible-image guides, *image* dissectors, *color* image panels, and high-speed alphanumeric *display surfaces.*

wrap.   See *core wrap.*

wraparound.   In the use of *display systems,* the extension or continuation of an operation from a conceived last position in an *image* to a conceived first position in the *image.* For example, the continuation of a read *operation* or *cursor* move-ment from the last *character position* in a *display buffer storage* or *image storage space* to the first position in the buffer storage, or the automatic moving of a *cursor* from the lower right corner of a *display space* to the upper left corner.

wrapping.   In *open systems architecture,* the use of a *network* to connect two other networks, thus providing an increased interaction capability between the two connected networks.   Recurring application of wrapping results in a *hierar-chical structure.*

write.   To make a permanent or transient recording of *data* in a *storage* device or on a *data medium.*   For example, the *transfer* of a *block* of data from internal storage to external storage may mean writing from the point of view of the external storage and reading from the point of view of the internal storage. In its broadest sense, writing implies recording.

writer.   See *display writer.*

write-through.   In *display systems,* the capability of a *storage tube* to superimpose another *display image* on an *image* that has not yet disappeared after its *regenera-tion* has ceased.

writing bar.   In *facsimile transmission systems,* a part that is used in some *contin-uous receivers* in conjunction with a helix, comprising a rectilinear rib that deter-mines the position of the *scanning line* on the *record medium.* Synonymous with *chopper bar; writing edge.*

writing edge.   See *writing bar.*

WRU character.   *Who-are-you character.*

WRU signal.   See *who-are-you character.*

W-type fiber.   A *doubly-cladded optical fiber* with two layers of concentric *clad-ding,* in which the *core* usually has the largest *refractive index* and the inner clad-ding has the lowest refractive index. The W-type fiber has several advantages, such as reduced *bending losses,* over conventionally cladded fibers that have a *stepped* or *graded* decreasing refractive index all the way from the core axis to the out-side surface.

WWW.   *World weather watch.*

X

X-band. 1. *Frequencies* in the 10 GHz range used in surface *warning radar.* 2. *Frequencies* that are in the range from 5.2 to 10.9 GHz, between the old S- and K-*bands* and overlapping parts of the old C-, G-, J-, H-, and M-bands in the USA. This X-band was divided into 12 subbands, designated XA through XK. It also comprised frequencies in the range 8.2 to 12.4 GHz, between the old J- and P-bands, also in the USA. It comprised frequencies in the range from 7.0 to 12.0 GHz, overlapping part of the old C-band (Institution of Electrical and Electronic Engineers, UK).

x-dimension. See *recorded spot x-dimension; scanning spot x-dimension.*

x-ray. A *ray* of *electromagnetic waves* with *wavelengths* between 0.01 to 100 $\times$ 10^{-10} m and therefore a *frequency* of 0.03 to 300 $\times$ 10^{18} *Hz.* Since the energy of a *photon* is given as *Planck's constant* times the frequency, the energy is sufficient to deeply penetrate solids, ionize gases, and destroy or change molecular structures, such as those of living tissue. This energy can even penetrate directly through a substance with minimal or negligible *attenuation,* except for highly dense substances such as lead and gold; therefore, it must be used with great care for *communication* purposes, such as for producting x-ray photos.

XU. *X-unit.*

X-unit. A unit of *wavelength* for *x-rays* or *gamma rays.* 1 XU = 1.00202 angstroms, or approximately 10^{-10} m.

x-y mount. A variation of the basic *altitude-over-azimuth antenna mount,* with the primary axis parallel to the earth's surface for improved *zenith tracking,* such as might be used in *telescope* mounts and *satellite tracking* mounts.

Y

Yagi antenna. An *antenna* that consists of at least two elements, often three elements, namely a *radiator (dipole),* a *reflector* (mounted behind the dipole), and a director (mounted in front of the dipole), constructed to improve the *directional gain.*

YAG/LED source. A *laser light source* used for *optical-fiber transmission* consisting of neodymium (Nd) yttrium aluminum garnet (YAG) *crystal laser* usually pumped by a *light-emitting diode (LED).* A YAG/LED source emits a narrow *spectrum,* about 0.5 nm wide at a *wavelength* of 1064 nm (1.065 μm) at peak intensity; however, the source is inefficient and bulky. Synonymous with *aluminum garnet source.*

y-dimension. See *recorded spot y-dimension; scanning spot y-dimension.*

year worst hour. 1. In *electromagnetic transmission systems,* the hour of the year during which the median *noise* over any *radio path* is a maximum. 2. The hour of the year during which the greatest *transmission loss* occurs. Usually the greatest loss and the most noise occur at the same time.

y-mount. See *x-y mount.*

yttrium aluminum garnet source. See *YAG/LED source.*

<h1 style="text-align:center">Z</h1>

Zeeman effect. The splitting of *electromagnetic radiation* into its *component frequencies,* i.e., the splitting of *spectral wavelengths* (lines), by an applied *magnetic field.*

zenith. A point off the earth on a line from the center of the earth through the surface point of observation. This is in contrast to the *nadir,* a point on the earth's surface directly below an observer, below being defined as on a line between the observer and the center of the earth.

zero binary code. See *return-to-zero (RZ) binary code.*

zero-crossing counter. The number of times that a *radar input signal amplitude* (instantaneous value) exceeds (crosses) the *detection* level (*threshold*) that is established for detection. This *constant false alarm rate (CFAR)* technique uses a *wideband* limiting *intermediate frequency (IF) amplifier* followed by a zero-crossing counter that indicates an object (target) when the rate of crossing falls below a predetermined value. The limiting action of the wideband amplifier and the *random* nature of the *noise* permit the use of a fixed threshold detection level that is independent of the *power* or amplitude of the *input signal* and independent of total input noise power if the noise *spectrum* is *flat.* The false alarm rate is established in the absence of an object (target) by a counter at the output of the threshold circuit of the *detector.*

zerofill. To *character fill* with the representation (code) of the character that denotes zero. Also see *zeroize.*

zeroize. To restore a *storage* unit, or the contents of a storage unit, such as a *register,* to a condition in which all zeros are stored. Also see *zerofill.*

zero level code. See *modified non-return-to-zero-level code.*

zero-match gate. See *NOR gate.*

zero material dispersion wavelength. The *electromagnetic wavelength* at which there will be no *material dispersion.* The *wavelength* occurs at that point in the *frequency spectrum* at which the electronic *band edge absorption* and *ultraviolet* absorption cease and *infrared* absorption begins.

zero relative level. In *communication circuits,* the *voltage* and *impedance* reference point for *power* ratios. For example, in a *transmission line,* a voltage level of 0.775 V in 600 Ω is standard, that is, an absolute *power level* of 1 mW. Power is given as $P = V^2/R$, where V is voltage and R is resistance. Thus, $P = (0.775)^2/600$ = 1 mW. On the decibel scale, 1 mW is equivalent to 0 dBm, which may also be considered as 0 dBr.

zero transmission level point (OTLP).   An arbitrary point chosen in a *circuit* to which all *relative transmission levels* are referred.   The transmission level at the *transmitting switchboard* is frequently taken as the zero transmission level point. All other points are a number of dB above or below this point.   Points at a higher *power* level are given as +dBr and points at a lower power level are given as –dBr.

zero suppression.   In a *numeral,* the elimination of zeros that have no significance in the numeral.   Zeros that have no significance include those to the left of the left-most nonzero digit in the *integral* part of a numeral and those to the right of the right-most nonzero digit in the fractional part of the numeral.

ZIP code.   A *decimal-digit numeral* that is assigned to each post office in the United States.   It is used to expedite the transfer and forwarding of mail.   It is equivalent to the *address designator* and *address indicating group* that are used on *messages* for *electrical transmission.*   Though street names and house numbers are as significant as the name of the addressee on mail, the city, town, and state names are redundant when the ZIP code is given.   Current ZIP codes are 5 decimal digits.   An increase in the number of *characters* is planned.

Z-marker beacon.   A *beacon* that is identical with the *fan marker beacon* except that it is installed, as part of a four-course (leg) *radio range,* at the intersection of the four range legs.   It *radiates* vertically in order to indicate to *aircraft stations* exactly when they pass directly over the *range station,* or the extent to which they are on either side.   It is usually not *keyed* for identification.   It is so named because in conventional Cartesian coordinate systems, the z-axis is the vertical axis, while the x- and the y-axes are horizontal.   Also see *cone of silence.*

zonal harmonic function.   A *spherical harmonic* (trigonometric) *function* that has values that are constant along a parallel of latitude.

zone.   Any defined region or area in time or space, or any other *domain* such as *frequency, temperature,* velocity, pressure, or any other measureable or defined quantity.   For example, one of the world geographic reference system zones, a time zone, a landing area for aircraft or parachutists, the region of the *radiation field* of an *antenna,* or one of the *layers* of the *ionosphere.*   See *auroral zone; communication zone; control zone; drop zone; Fresnel zone; near zone; skip zone; time zone; transition zone.*

zone boundary limit marker.   See *drop-zone boundary limit marker.*

zone exchange.   In *telephone systems,* an *exchange* that is used as the main *switching center* for a certain number or group of exchange centers in a defined area.   Each zone exchange has access, directly or indirectly, to all other zone exchange centers.

zone impact point.   See *drop-zone impact point.*

zone indicator.   See *drop-zone indicator.*

zoom back.   In *display systems,* the act or process of creating a smaller *image* of an *object,* thus giving the appearance of moving away from the object. The *optical* angle of intercept required to place the image of the object on the retina is decreased. Contrast with *zoom in.*

zoom in.   In *display systems,* the act or process of creating a larger *image* of an *object,* thus giving the appearance of moving closer to the object. The *optical* angle of intercept required to place the image of the object on the retina is increased. Contrast with *zoom back.*

zooming.   In *display systems,* the *scaling* of that part of a *display element, display group,* or *display image* that lies within a *window* in such a manner as to give the appearance of movement toward or away from a point or an object of interest. Unless otherwise specified, to "zoom in" implies the appearance of moving closer to an object—i.e., to enlarge its image. To "zoom back" implies the reverse.

zoom lens.   An *optical system* that has *components* that move in such a way as to change the *focal length* while maintaining a fixed *image* position. Thus, the image size can be varied while the optical system is left in a fixed position. Synonymous with *pancratic lens.*

100% modulation.   **1.** The magnitude (*amplitude*) of a reference *modulation.* **2.** The magnitude (*amplitude*) that is selected to be the optimum, desired, or maximum magnitude (amplitude). **3.** The magnitude (amplitude) of a *modulating signal* that produces the full range of modulated signal variation, from zero to the maximum or reference value. For example, in an *amplitude modulated signal,* the situation that occurs when the *modulation envelope* just reaches the zero base line at one point in the cycle; or in a *phase modulated signal,* the situation that occurs when the modulation signal causes the *phase position* of the *modulated carrier* to just reach the zero *phase shift position.*

144-line weighting.   In *telephone systems,* a *noise weighting* that is used in a *noise* measuring set to measure noise on a *line* that would be terminated by an instrument with a Number 144-Receiver or similar instrument. The meter scale readings are in *dBrn(144-line).*

144-receiver weighting.   In *telephone systems,* a *noise weighting* that is used in a noise measuring set to measure noise across the *receiver* of an instrument that is equipped with a Number 144-Receiver. The meter scale readings are in *dBrn(144-receiver).*